# ALL · IN · ONE

# CISSP®

## EXAM GUIDE

## Third Edition

## ALL · IN · ONE

# CISSP®

## EXAM GUIDE

### Third Edition

## Shon Harris

**McGraw-Hill/Osborne**

New York • Chicago • San Francisco • Lisbon
London • Madrid • Mexico City • Milan • New Delhi
San Juan • Seoul • Singapore • Sydney • Toronto

The *McGraw·Hill* Companies

McGraw-Hill/Osborne
2100 Powell Street, 10th Floor
Emeryville, California 94608
U.S.A.

To arrange bulk purchase discounts for sales promotions, premiums, or fund-raisers, please contact McGraw-Hill/Osborne at the above address.

### CISSP® All-in-One Exam Guide, Third Edition

67890 DOC DOC 01987

Book p/n 0-07-225714-8 and CD p/n 0-07-225715-6
parts of
ISBN 0-07-225712-1

| **Acquisitions Editor** | **Proofreader** |
|---|---|
| Timothy Green | Pam Vevea |
| **Project Editor** | **Indexer** |
| Janet Walden | Claire Splan |
| **Acquisitions Coordinator** | **Composition** |
| Jennifer Housh | Apollo Publishing Services |
| **Technical Editor** | **Illustrator** |
| Clement Dupuis | Sue Albert |
| **Copy Editor** | **Series Design** |
| William McManus | Peter F. Hancik |

This book was composed with Adobe® InDesign®

*May more people in this world have the integrity
and the gentle loving strength of George Fairbairn, my grandpa.*

*I would also like to dedicate this book to my dog, Dallas, who we lost this year.
He made us better people just by being in our lives for the last eight years.*

# ABOUT THE AUTHOR

Shon Harris, CISSP, MCSE, is the president of Logical Security, a security consultant, a former engineer in the Air Force's Information Warfare unit, an instructor, and an author. She has authored two best-selling CISSP books, was a contributing author to *Hacker's Challenge: Test Your Incident Response Skills Using 20 Scenarios,* and a contributing author to *Gray Hat Hacking: The Ethical Hacker's Handbook* (both published by McGraw-Hill/ Osborne). Shon has taught computer and information security to a wide range of clients, some of which have included RSA, Department of Defense, Department of Energy, National Security Agency (NSA), Bank of America, Defense Information Systems Agency (DISA), BMC, and many more.

Shon was recognized as one of the top 25 women in the Information Security field by *Information Security Magazine.*

Shon is currently working on developing a full information security book series and practical hands-on exams that will be delivered through her company's virtual lab.

# CONTENTS AT A GLANCE

| | | |
|---|---|---|
| **Chapter 1** | Becoming a CISSP . . . . . . . . . . . . . . . . . . . . . . . . . . . . . . . . . . . . | 1 |
| **Chapter 2** | Security Trends . . . . . . . . . . . . . . . . . . . . . . . . . . . . . . . . . . . . . . . | 17 |
| **Chapter 3** | Information Security and Risk Management . . . . . . . . . . . . . . . . . . | 49 |
| **Chapter 4** | Access Controls . . . . . . . . . . . . . . . . . . . . . . . . . . . . . . . . . . . . . . | 123 |
| **Chapter 5** | Security Architecture and Design . . . . . . . . . . . . . . . . . . . . . . . . | 227 |
| **Chapter 6** | Physical and Environmental Security . . . . . . . . . . . . . . . . . . . . . . | 337 |
| **Chapter 7** | Telecommunications and Networking Security . . . . . . . . . . . . . . . | 415 |
| **Chapter 8** | Cryptography . . . . . . . . . . . . . . . . . . . . . . . . . . . . . . . . . . . . . . . . | 587 |
| **Chapter 9** | Business Continuity Planning . . . . . . . . . . . . . . . . . . . . . . . . . . . | 691 |
| **Chapter 10** | Regulations and Compliance . . . . . . . . . . . . . . . . . . . . . . . . . . . | 751 |
| **Chapter 11** | Applications Security . . . . . . . . . . . . . . . . . . . . . . . . . . . . . . . . . | 809 |
| **Chapter 12** | Operations Security . . . . . . . . . . . . . . . . . . . . . . . . . . . . . . . . . . | 899 |
| **Appendix A** | About the CD-ROM . . . . . . . . . . . . . . . . . . . . . . . . . . . . . . . . . | 945 |
| **Appendix B** | Who's Who? . . . . . . . . . . . . . . . . . . . . . . . . . . . . . . . . . . . . . . . . | 949 |
| **Glossary** | . . . . . . . . . . . . . . . . . . . . . . . . . . . . . . . . . . . . . . . . . . . . . . . . . | 953 |
| **Index** | . . . . . . . . . . . . . . . . . . . . . . . . . . . . . . . . . . . . . . . . . . . . . . . . . | 971 |

# CONTENTS

Foreword . . . . . . . . . . . . . . . . . . . . . . . . . . . . . . . . . . . . . . . . . xxiii

Acknowledgments . . . . . . . . . . . . . . . . . . . . . . . . . . . . . . . . . . xxv

Introduction . . . . . . . . . . . . . . . . . . . . . . . . . . . . . . . . . . . . . . xxvii

**Chapter 1    Becoming a CISSP** . . . . . . . . . . . . . . . . . . . . . . . . . . **1**

Why Become a CISSP? . . . . . . . . . . . . . . . . . . . . . . . . . . . . . 1

The CISSP Exam . . . . . . . . . . . . . . . . . . . . . . . . . . . . . . . . . . 2

CISSP: A Brief History . . . . . . . . . . . . . . . . . . . . . . . . . . . . . 7

How Do You Become a CISSP? . . . . . . . . . . . . . . . . . . . . . . . 7

Recertification Requirements . . . . . . . . . . . . . . . . . . . . . . . . 8

What Does This Book Cover? . . . . . . . . . . . . . . . . . . . . . . . . 9

Tips for Taking the CISSP Exam . . . . . . . . . . . . . . . . . . . . . 9

How to Use This Book . . . . . . . . . . . . . . . . . . . . . . . . . . . . . 11

    Questions . . . . . . . . . . . . . . . . . . . . . . . . . . . . . . . . . . 12

    Answers . . . . . . . . . . . . . . . . . . . . . . . . . . . . . . . . . . . . 15

**Chapter 2    Security Trends** . . . . . . . . . . . . . . . . . . . . . . . . . . . . **17**

How Security Became an Issue . . . . . . . . . . . . . . . . . . . . . . . 17

Areas of Security . . . . . . . . . . . . . . . . . . . . . . . . . . . . . . . . . 20

Information Warfare . . . . . . . . . . . . . . . . . . . . . . . . . . . . . . . 21

    Evidence of the Evolution of Hacking . . . . . . . . . . . . . . 22

    How Are Nations Affected? . . . . . . . . . . . . . . . . . . . . . . 24

    How Are Companies Affected? . . . . . . . . . . . . . . . . . . . 26

    The U.S. Government's Actions . . . . . . . . . . . . . . . . . . . 27

    So What Does This Mean to Us? . . . . . . . . . . . . . . . . . . 29

Hacking and Attacking . . . . . . . . . . . . . . . . . . . . . . . . . . . . . 29

Management . . . . . . . . . . . . . . . . . . . . . . . . . . . . . . . . . . . . . 30

Internet and Web Activities . . . . . . . . . . . . . . . . . . . . . . . . . 32

    Two-Tier Architecture . . . . . . . . . . . . . . . . . . . . . . . . . . 35

    Database Roles . . . . . . . . . . . . . . . . . . . . . . . . . . . . . . . . 37

A Layered Approach . . . . . . . . . . . . . . . . . . . . . . . . . . . . . . . 40

    Security at Different Layers . . . . . . . . . . . . . . . . . . . . . . 40

An Architectural View . . . . . . . . . . . . . . . . . . . . . . . . . . . . . 41

    A Layer Missed . . . . . . . . . . . . . . . . . . . . . . . . . . . . . . . 44

    Bringing the Layers Together . . . . . . . . . . . . . . . . . . . . . 44

Politics and Laws . . . . . . . . . . . . . . . . . . . . . . . . . . . . . . . . . 45

Education . . . . . . . . . . . . . . . . . . . . . . . . . . . . . . . . . . . . . . . 46

Summary . . . . . . . . . . . . . . . . . . . . . . . . . . . . . . . . . . . . . . . 47

**Chapter 3    Information Security and Risk Management** . . . . . . . . . . . **49**

Security Management . . . . . . . . . . . . . . . . . . . . . . . . . . . . . . 49

Security Management Responsibilities . . . . . . . . . . . . . . . . . 50

    The Top-Down Approach to Security . . . . . . . . . . . . . . . 51

Security Administration and Supporting Controls ............. 52
Fundamental Principles of Security ........................ 55
  Availability ........................................ 56
  Integrity ........................................... 56
  Confidentiality ..................................... 57
Security Definitions ..................................... 57
Organizational Security Model ........................... 60
  Security Program Components ........................ 61
  Business Requirements: Private Industry
    vs. Military Organizations ........................ 64
Information Risk Management ............................ 65
  Who Really Understands Risk Management? ............. 65
  Information Risk Management Policy .................. 66
  Risk Management Team .............................. 67
Risk Analysis ........................................... 68
  Risk Analysis Team ................................. 69
  Value of Information and Assets ..................... 70
  Costs That Make Up the Value ....................... 70
  Identifying Threats ................................. 71
  Quantitative Risk Analysis .......................... 73
  Qualitative Risk Analysis ........................... 78
  Quantitative vs. Qualitative ........................ 81
  Protection Mechanisms .............................. 82
  Putting It Together ................................. 85
  Total Risk vs. Residual Risk ........................ 86
  Handling Risk ...................................... 86
Policies, Standards, Baselines, Guidelines, and Procedures ...... 87
  Security Policy ..................................... 88
  Standards ......................................... 90
  Baselines .......................................... 91
  Guidelines ......................................... 92
  Procedures ........................................ 92
  Implementation .................................... 93
Information Classification .............................. 94
  Private Business vs. Military Classifications .......... 95
  Classification Controls ............................. 98
Layers of Responsibility ................................ 99
  Data Owner ....................................... 100
  Data Custodian .................................... 100
  System Owner ..................................... 101
  Security Administrator ............................. 101
  Security Analyst ................................... 101
  Application Owner ................................. 101
  Supervisor ........................................ 102
  Change Control Analyst ............................ 102

Data Analyst ..................................... 102
Process Owner ................................... 102
Solution Provider ................................ 103
User .......................................... 103
Product Line Manager ............................ 103
Why So Many Roles? ............................. 103
Personnel ...................................... 104
Structure ...................................... 104
Hiring Practices ................................. 105
Employee Controls .............................. 106
Termination .................................... 106
Security-Awareness Training ........................... 107
Different Types of Security-Awareness Training .......... 107
Evaluating the Program .......................... 109
Specialized Security Training ...................... 109
Summary ......................................... 110
Quick Tips ....................................... 111
Questions ...................................... 114
Answers ....................................... 118

**Chapter 4    Access Controls** ............................... **123**
Access Controls Overview ............................ 123
Security Principles ................................. 124
Availability .................................... 125
Integrity ...................................... 125
Confidentiality ................................. 126
Identification, Authentication, and Authorization ............. 126
Identification and Authentication ................... 129
Authorization .................................. 146
Access Control Models .............................. 161
Discretionary Access Control ...................... 162
Mandatory Access Control ........................ 163
Role-Based Access Control ........................ 165
Access Control Techniques and Technologies ............... 167
Rule-Based Access Control ........................ 167
Constrained User Interfaces ....................... 168
Access Control Matrix ........................... 169
Content-Dependent Access Control .................. 170
Context-Dependent Access Control .................. 171
Access Control Administration ........................ 171
Centralized Access Control Administration ............ 172
Decentralized Access Control Administration .......... 179
Access Control Methods ............................. 180
Access Control Layers ........................... 180
Administrative Controls .......................... 181

Physical Controls ............................... 183
Technical Controls .............................. 185
Access Control Types ............................... 188
Preventive: Administrative .......................... 190
Preventive: Physical ............................. 190
Preventive: Technical ............................ 190
Accountability ................................... 193
Review of Audit Information ...................... 194
Keystroke Monitoring ........................... 195
Protecting Audit Data and Log Information ............. 196
Access Control Practices ........................... 197
Unauthorized Disclosure of Information .............. 198
Access Control Monitoring .......................... 200
Intrusion Detection ............................. 200
Intrusion Prevention Systems ..................... 211
A Few Threats to Access Control ...................... 214
Dictionary Attack .............................. 214
Brute Force Attack ............................. 215
Spoofing at Logon ............................. 216
Summary ...................................... 217
Quick Tips .................................... 218
Questions .................................. 220
Answers ................................... 224

Chapter 5    Security Architecture and Design    .................... 227
Computer Architecture ............................. 229
Central Processing Unit ......................... 229
Operating System Architecture .................... 235
Process Activity ............................... 240
Memory Management ........................... 242
Memory Types ................................ 244
Virtual Memory ............................... 252
CPU Modes and Protection Rings ................... 253
Operating System Architecture .................... 256
Domains .................................... 258
Layering and Data Hiding ........................ 260
Virtual Machines .............................. 261
Additional Storage Devices ....................... 262
Input/Output Device Management ................... 263
System Architecture .............................. 266
Defined Subset of Subjects and Objects .............. 268
Trusted Computing Base ......................... 269
Security Perimeter ............................. 272
Reference Monitor and Security Kernel ............... 272

Security Policy ............................................... 274
Least Privilege ............................................... 275
Security Models ............................................... 275
State Machine Models ....................................... 277
Bell-LaPadula Model ........................................ 279
Biba Model ................................................ 282
Clark-Wilson Model ......................................... 284
Information Flow Model ..................................... 287
Noninterference Model ...................................... 290
Lattice Model .............................................. 291
Brewer and Nash Model ..................................... 293
Graham-Denning Model ..................................... 294
Security Modes of Operation .................................... 296
Dedicated Security Mode .................................... 297
System High-Security Mode .................................. 297
Compartmented Security Mode ............................... 297
Multilevel Security Mode .................................... 298
Trust and Assurance ........................................ 300
Systems Evaluation Methods .................................... 301
Why Put a Product Through Evaluation? ...................... 301
The Orange Book ........................................... 302
Rainbow Series ................................................ 306
Red Book .................................................. 307
Information Technology Security Evaluation Criteria ............. 309
Common Criteria ............................................... 312
Certification vs. Accreditation .................................. 314
Certification .............................................. 316
Accreditation ............................................. 316
Open vs. Closed Systems ....................................... 317
Open Systems ............................................. 317
Closed Systems ........................................... 318
A Few Threats to Security Models and Architectures ............. 318
Maintenance Hooks ........................................ 318
Time-of-Check/Time-of-Use Attack .......................... 319
Buffer Overflow ........................................... 321
Summary ..................................................... 325
Quick Tips .................................................... 325
Questions ................................................. 329
Answers .................................................. 333

Chapter 6    Physical and Environmental Security .................. 337
Introduction to Physical Security ............................... 337
Planning Process .............................................. 340
Crime Prevention Through Environmental Design ............. 344
Designing a Physical Security Program ....................... 349

Protecting Assets .................................... 362
Internal Support Systems .............................. 364
Electric Power .................................. 365
Environmental Issues ............................ 370
Ventilation .................................... 373
Fire Prevention, Detection, and Suppression ........... 373
Perimeter Security ................................... 380
Facility Access Control ........................... 381
Personnel Access Controls ........................ 387
External Boundary Protection Mechanisms ............ 388
Intrusion Detection Systems ....................... 397
Patrol Force and Guards .......................... 400
Auditing Physical Access ......................... 402
Summary ......................................... 402
Quick Tips ........................................ 403
Questions ..................................... 405
Answers ...................................... 410

**Chapter 7**    **Telecommunications and Networking Security**    ........    **415**
Open Systems Interconnection Reference Model .............. 417
Application Layer ............................... 420
Presentation Layer .............................. 421
Session Layer .................................. 422
Transport Layer ................................ 424
Network Layer ................................. 425
Data Link Layer ................................ 426
Physical Layer ................................. 428
Functions and Protocols in the OSI Model ............. 428
Tying the Layers Together ......................... 430
TCP/IP .......................................... 431
TCP .......................................... 432
IP Addressing ................................. 438
IPv6 ......................................... 439
Types of Transmission .............................. 439
Analog and Digital .............................. 439
Asynchronous and Synchronous ..................... 441
Broadband and Baseband .......................... 441
LAN Networking ................................... 442
Network Topology .............................. 443
LAN Media Access Technologies ..................... 446
Cabling ...................................... 453
Transmission Methods ........................... 458
Media Access Technologies ........................ 460
LAN Protocols ................................. 463
Routing Protocols .................................. 467

Networking Devices ................................... 470
    Repeaters ........................................ 470
    Bridges ......................................... 471
    Routers ......................................... 473
    Switches ........................................ 475
    Gateways ........................................ 479
    PBXs ............................................ 481
    Firewalls ....................................... 482
    Honeypot ........................................ 499
Networking Services and Protocols ..................... 500
    Network Operating Systems ....................... 501
    Domain Name Service ............................. 502
    Network Information System ...................... 505
    Directory Services .............................. 508
    Lightweight Directory Access Protocol ........... 509
    Network Address Translation ..................... 510
Intranets and Extranets ............................... 512
Metropolitan Area Network ............................. 514
Wide Area Network ..................................... 515
    Telecommunications Evolution .................... 516
    Dedicated Links ................................. 518
    WAN Technologies ................................ 520
Remote Access ......................................... 534
    Dial-Up and RAS ................................. 534
    ISDN ............................................ 535
    DSL ............................................. 537
    Cable Modem ..................................... 537
    VPN ............................................. 539
    Authentication Protocols ........................ 544
    Remote Access Guidelines ........................ 547
Wireless Technologies ................................. 548
    Wireless Communications ......................... 549
    WLAN Components ................................. 552
    Wireless Standards .............................. 554
    WAP ............................................. 565
    i-Mode .......................................... 566
    Mobile Phone Security ........................... 567
    War Driving for WLANs ........................... 568
    Satellites ...................................... 570
    3G Wireless Communication ....................... 570
Rootkits .............................................. 572
    Spyware and Adware .............................. 574
    Instant Messaging ............................... 574
Summary ............................................... 576

Quick Tips ........................................ 576
    Questions ..................................... 580
    Answers ...................................... 584

**Chapter 8**   **Cryptography** .................................. **587**
History of Cryptography ........................... 588
    Vigenere Cipher ............................... 590
Cryptography Definitions and Concepts .............. 593
    Kerckhoff's Principle ........................... 596
    Strength of the Cryptosystem .................... 596
    Services of Cryptosystems ....................... 597
    One-Time Pad ................................. 599
    Running and Concealment Ciphers ............... 601
    Steganography ................................ 602
Governments Involvement with Cryptography ......... 603
    Wassenaar Arrangement ........................ 603
Types of Ciphers ................................. 604
    Substitution Cipher ............................ 604
    Transposition Cipher ........................... 605
Methods of Encryption ............................ 607
    Symmetric vs. Asymmetric Algorithms ............ 607
    Block and Stream Ciphers ....................... 613
    Hybrid Encryption Methods ..................... 617
Types of Symmetric Systems ....................... 621
    Data Encryption Standard ....................... 621
    Triple-DES ................................... 629
    Advanced Encryption Standard ................... 629
    International Data Encryption Algorithm .......... 630
    Blowfish ..................................... 630
    RC4 ......................................... 631
    RC5 ......................................... 631
    RC6 ......................................... 631
Types of Asymmetric Systems ...................... 632
    Diffie-Hellman Algorithm ....................... 632
    RSA ......................................... 634
    El Gamal ..................................... 638
    Elliptic Curve Cryptosystem ..................... 638
    LUC ......................................... 638
    Knapsack .................................... 639
    Zero Knowledge Proof .......................... 639
Message Integrity ................................ 640
    One-Way Hash ................................ 640
    Various Hashing Algorithms ..................... 645
    Attack Against One-Way Hash Functions .......... 646
    Digital Signatures ............................. 648
    Digital Signature Standard ...................... 650

Public Key Infrastructure ............................... 651
    Certificate Authorities .......................... 652
    Certificates ....................................... 653
    Registration Authority ........................... 654
    PKI Steps ........................................ 655
Key Management ....................................... 657
    Key Management Principles ....................... 658
Link Encryption vs. End-to-End Encryption ............ 659
E-Mail Standards ...................................... 662
    Multipurpose Internet Mail Extension ............ 662
    Privacy-Enhanced Mail .......................... 663
    Message Security Protocol ....................... 664
    Pretty Good Privacy ............................. 664
Internet Security ...................................... 666
    Start with the Basics ............................ 666
Attacks ............................................... 675
    Ciphertext-Only Attack .......................... 676
    Known-Plaintext Attack ......................... 676
    Chosen-Plaintext Attack ......................... 676
    Chosen-Ciphertext Attack ........................ 676
    Differential Cryptanalysis ....................... 677
    Linear Cryptanalysis ............................ 677
    Side Channel Attacks ............................ 678
    Replay Attack ................................... 678
Summary ............................................. 679
Quick Tips ............................................ 680
    Questions ....................................... 683
    Answers ......................................... 687

Chapter 9    Business Continuity Planning ...................... 691
Business Continuity and Disaster Recovery ............. 692
    Business Continuity Steps ....................... 693
    Make BCP Part of the Security Policy and Program ........ 695
    Project Initiation ............................... 697
Business Continuity Planning Requirements ............ 699
    Business Impact Analysis ........................ 699
    Preventative Measures .......................... 706
    Recovery Strategies ............................. 707
    Business Process Recovery ....................... 708
    Facility Recovery ............................... 709
    Supply and Technology Recovery ................. 715
    End-User Environment ........................... 720
    Data Backup Alternatives ........................ 721
    Insurance ....................................... 728
    Recovery and Restoration ........................ 728
    Developing Goals for the Plans .................. 732

Implementing Strategies ......................... 733

Testing and Revising the Plan ...................... 734

Maintaining the Plan ............................. 739

Summary .............................................. 740

Quick Tips ............................................ 741

Questions ........................................ 743

Answers .......................................... 748

**Chapter 10    Regulations and Compliance** ...................... **751**

The Many Facets of Cyberlaw ......................... 752

Ethics ................................................ 752

Computer Ethics Institute ......................... 754

Internet Architecture Board ....................... 754

Generally Accepted Information Security Principles ....... 755

Motive, Opportunity, and Means .................... 756

Hackers and Crackers .................................. 757

Operations Security .............................. 757

Well-Known Computer Crimes .......................... 763

The Cuckoo's Egg ................................. 763

Kevin Mitnick .................................... 764

Chaos Computer Club .............................. 764

Cult of the Dead Cow ............................. 764

Phone Phreakers .................................. 765

Identification, Protection, and Prosecution .............. 766

Liability and Its Ramifications ...................... 767

Personal Information ............................. 770

Hacker Intrusion ................................. 771

Types of Laws ........................................ 772

Intellectual Property Laws ........................ 774

Equipment and Software Disposal Issues ................ 778

Computer Crime Investigations ......................... 778

Incident Response ................................ 778

Incident Handling ................................ 782

What Is Admissible in Court? ...................... 783

Surveillance, Search, and Seizure ................. 786

Interviewing and Interrogating .................... 787

Import and Export Laws ............................... 788

Transborder Information Flow ...................... 788

Privacy .............................................. 789

Laws, Directives, and Regulations .................... 791

Health Insurance Portability and Accountability Act ....... 792

Gramm-Leach-Bliley Act of 1999 ................... 792

Computer Fraud and Abuse Act ..................... 792

Federal Privacy Act of 1974 ...................... 793

European Union Principles on Privacy .............. 794

Computer Security Act of 1987 .................... 794

Security and Freedom Through Encryption Act ........... 794
Federal Sentencing Guidelines ....................... 795
Economic Espionage Act of 1996 .................... 795
International Cooperation Efforts ...................... 795
Group of Eight ................................... 795
Interpol ......................................... 796
European Commission ............................. 796
Summary .............................................. 796
Quick Tips ............................................. 797
Questions ........................................ 799
Answers .......................................... 804

Chapter 11    Applications Security ............................. 809
Software's Importance ................................... 809
Device vs. Software Security ............................. 810
Different Environments Demand Different Security ........... 812
Client/Server Model ............................... 812
Environment vs. Application Controls .................... 812
Complexity of Functionality ............................. 814
Data Types, Format, and Length ......................... 814
Implementation and Default Issues ...................... 815
Implementation ................................... 815
Failure States ......................................... 816
Database Management ................................... 816
Database Management Software ...................... 817
Database Models .................................. 818
Database Interface Languages ....................... 820
Relational Database Components .................... 821
Data Dictionary .................................. 821
Integrity ......................................... 824
Database Security Issues ........................... 826
Data Warehousing and Data Mining ................. 830
System Development .................................... 832
Management of Development ........................ 832
Life-Cycle Phases ................................. 833
Software Development Methods ..................... 845
Change Control ................................... 846
Capability Maturity Model .......................... 848
Software Escrow .................................. 849
Application Development Methodology .................... 850
Object-Oriented Concepts .......................... 850
Data Modeling ................................... 856
Software Architecture ............................. 857
Data Structures .................................. 857
ORBs and CORBA ................................ 859
Computer-Aided Software Engineering .............. 861

Prototyping ........................................ 862
COM and DCOM ................................. 863
Open Database Connectivity ...................... 863
Object Linking and Embedding ..................... 864
Dynamic Data Exchange .......................... 865
Distributed Computing Environment ................. 865
Mobile Code .................................... 866
Enterprise JavaBeans ............................. 867
Expert Systems and Knowledge-Based Systems .......... 867
Artificial Neural Networks ........................ 869
Java .......................................... 872
ActiveX ....................................... 873
Malicious Software (Malware) ...................... 874
Attacks ....................................... 878
Summary ........................................... 886
Quick Tips ......................................... 886
Questions ...................................... 890
Answers ....................................... 894

**Chapter 12   Operations Security** ........................... **899**
Role of the Operations Department ...................... 900
Administrative Management ........................ 900
Accountability .................................. 903
Security Operations and Product Evaluation ............ 904
Input and Output Controls ........................ 910
Network and Resource Availability ...................... 911
Single Points of Failure ........................... 911
RAID ......................................... 912
Clustering ..................................... 914
Backups ....................................... 914
E-Mail Security ..................................... 915
How E-Mail Works ............................... 916
Facsimile Security ............................... 920
Hack and Attack Methods ......................... 921
Penetration Testing .............................. 930
Operations Department ........................... 933
Summary ........................................... 934
Quick Tips ......................................... 935
Questions ...................................... 937
Answers ....................................... 941

**Appendix A   About the CD-ROM** ........................... **945**
Running the QuickTime Cryptography Video Sample .......... 946
Troubleshooting ................................. 947
Installing Total Seminars' Test Software .................. 947
Navigation ..................................... 947

Minimum System Requirements
for Total Seminars' Software . . . . . . . . . . . . . . . . . . . . . . . 948
Technical Support . . . . . . . . . . . . . . . . . . . . . . . . . . . . . . . 948

**Appendix B  Who's Who?** . . . . . . . . . . . . . . . . . . . . . . . . . . . . . . . . . . . **949**
NSA . . . . . . . . . . . . . . . . . . . . . . . . . . . . . . . . . . . . . . . . . . 949
NIST . . . . . . . . . . . . . . . . . . . . . . . . . . . . . . . . . . . . . . . . . 950
NCSC . . . . . . . . . . . . . . . . . . . . . . . . . . . . . . . . . . . . . . . . . 951
ISO . . . . . . . . . . . . . . . . . . . . . . . . . . . . . . . . . . . . . . . . . . . 951
ANSI . . . . . . . . . . . . . . . . . . . . . . . . . . . . . . . . . . . . . . . . . 952
IEEE . . . . . . . . . . . . . . . . . . . . . . . . . . . . . . . . . . . . . . . . . 952

**Glossary** . . . . . . . . . . . . . . . . . . . . . . . . . . . . . . . . . . . . . . . . . . . **953**

**Index** . . . . . . . . . . . . . . . . . . . . . . . . . . . . . . . . . . . . . . . . . . . **971**

# FOREWORD

As a teacher and practitioner of computer security, I am often asked the same two questions: How do I learn the basics of computer security to perform my job better, and how do I keep up-to-date with the latest security standards and practices?

The first recorded computer "incident" occurred in 1958. The first federally prosecuted crime identified as a computer crime involved modifying records at a bank in Minnesota in 1966. In the 1960s and 1970s, computer security was not taken seriously because it was not required as it is today. In 1976, the FBI established a four-week training course for its agents in the investigation of computer crime. Then, in 1977, Senator Ribicoff introduced the Federal Computer Systems Protection Act, which eventually became the Computer Fraud and Abuse Act of 1986. The publication *2600: The Hacker Quarterly* was started in 1984 (containing instructions on how to hack telecommunication systems and computers), and additional sources of computer security where illegal copies of software were made available to everyone (warez sites) were established around the world. Toward the end of the 1980s, new security products were being introduced into the marketplace and organizations were beginning to realize they needed a "security specialist" to help augment their traditional information technology departments.

I mention the FBI training course and the start of the *2600* publication because these two events were crucial to starting the process of capturing and codifying a set of guidelines relating to the security practitioner. If you look at the history of how computer security has evolved into what it is today, one thing stands out above all else—the control of information.

Nearly 20 years after the Morris worm wreaked havoc across the Internet, we still find ourselves struggling to patch systems, learn about the newest vendor vulnerabilities, and obtain information from our peers about potential trouble circulating through systems around the globe. For any IT professional, keeping up with new technologies, the associated business demands, and related security knowledge required to keep it all safe is a daunting task. The human element still remains the biggest single point of weakness when dealing with technological advancement and change.

The good news is that progress has been made in the area of providing information related to industry best practices and knowledge sharing. The National Security Agency has certified 59 colleges and universities as "Centers of Excellence" for teaching information assurance, with many more programs being developed and certified every year. Training organizations now include security topics along with other sources of IT and business training. Information Sharing and Analysis Centers (ISACs) have been established for all sectors of our nation's critical infrastructure. The National Institute of Standards and Technology (NIST) and other organizations are now publishing technical standards for security of the technologies that organizations rely upon to run their operations.

Shon Harris started this book in 2001 as a way of codifying a set of best practices that could also be used to satisfy the requirements for passing the CISSP exam. She has accomplished both tasks extremely well, and IT professionals are increasingly using this best-selling resource as a way of solidifying their security knowledge. I often use this book as an answer to the two questions I mentioned at the beginning, referring students to start with this book as a foundation upon which to build their security knowledge set. Obtaining the CISSP is a worthy objective, but absorbing the knowledge contained within this book will serve to make you a better security practitioner.

*–Jeff Recor*
Director, Walsh College Information Assurance Center
President, Olympus Security, Inc.

# ACKNOWLEDGMENTS

I would like to thank Sam Tomaino for attempting to explain to me many, many years ago how computers work; Dan Ferguson for never complaining about the barrage of questions I continually fling his way and for fostering my never-ceasing curiosity and quest for knowledge; and Joe Kowtko for the insight into the computing world and life in general that he continually provides me. Each one of these people has helped me write this book in more ways than they will ever know.

For my third edition, I would also like to thank the following individuals for taking their time to help me with some new topics:

- Dr. Burt Kaliski, vice president of research at RSA Security and chief scientist of its research center, RSA Laboratories.

- Dr. Dorothy Denning, professor in the Department of Defense Analysis at the Naval Postgraduate School.

- David Miller, whose work ethic, loyalty, and friendship I have found to be inspirational. I am truly grateful to have David as part of my life.

- Allen Harper, whose knowledge, impeccable character, and trustworthiness have made him a role model to many in this world—including myself.

- Clement Dupuis, who has a deep passion for sharing and helping others. Clement has proven to be a wonderful and irreplaceable mentor and friend to me.

- Tom and Kathy Conlon, my parents. Without their love and support, my life would be a lot different today.

And most especially, I would like to thank my husband, David Harris, for his continual support and love. Without his steadfast confidence in me, I would not be able to accomplish half the things I have taken on in this lifetime.

# INTRODUCTION

Over the last few years, the necessity for computer and information security has increased exponentially as web sites are being defaced, denial-of-service attacks are increasing, credit card information is being stolen, publicly available hacking tools are increasing in sophistication, and today's viruses and worms are causing more damage than ever before.

Companies have had to spend millions of dollars to clean up the effects of these issues and millions of dollars more to secure their perimeter and internal networks with equipment, software, consultants, and education. But after September 11, 2001, the necessity and urgency for this type of security has taken on a new paradigm. It has become apparent that governments, nations, and societies are vulnerable to many different types of attacks that can happen over the network wire and air waves. Societies depend heavily on all types of computing power and functionality, mostly provided by the public and private sectors. This means that although governments are responsible for protecting their citizens, citizens and their businesses must become more secure to protect the nation as a whole.

This type of protection can really only *begin* through proper education and understanding, and it must continue with a dedicated execution of this knowledge. The *CISSP All-in-One Exam Guide, Third Edition* is written to provide a foundation to the many different areas that make up effective security. We need to understand *all* of the threats and dangers we are vulnerable to and the steps that need to be taken to mitigate these vulnerabilities.

# Becoming a CISSP

This chapter presents the following:

- The reasons to become a CISSP
- What the CISSP exam entails
- What the Common Body of Knowledge contains
- The history of (ISC)$^2$ and the CISSP exam
- Recertification requirements
- An assessment test to gauge your current security knowledge

This book is intended to welcome you to the exciting world of security and start you on a new path toward obtaining your CISSP certification!

The Certified Information Systems Security Professional (CISSP) exam covers ten domains, each of which may be considered a full field of study in itself, with many individual books and papers written on just that subject. Thus, you may have the impression that to prepare properly for the CISSP exam you must read a stack of books. Without this third edition of *CISSP All-In-One Exam Guide* in hand, that impression may be true. However, the goal of this book is to provide in one resource all the information that you need to pass the CISSP exam. It also serves as a reference that you can use long after you achieve the CISSP certification.

## Why Become a CISSP?

Security is a hot issue, not only in the security and technology fields, but also in every organization, government agency, and military unit. *Computer and information security* used to be an obscure term known only by a few. Security expertise was considered of minimal importance because risks were low. Hacking required great skill and knowledge and thus was not a common practice. Today, however, most corporations and organizations are desperately searching for talented and experienced security professionals to help them protect the resources that keep their companies alive and competitive. The CISSP certification identifies you as a security professional who has successfully met a predefined standard of knowledge and experience that is well understood and respected throughout the industry at large. Keeping this certification current shows

1

that you have a serious interest in keeping abreast of security technologies and events relevant to practicing information security.

There are many reasons to achieve a CISSP certification:

- To meet a growing demand and thrive in an ever expanding field
- To broaden your current knowledge of security concepts and practices
- To bring security expertise to your current occupation
- To become more marketable in a competitive workforce
- To show a dedication to the security discipline
- To increase your salary and be eligible for more employment opportunities

The CISSP certification helps companies identify individuals who have the ability, knowledge, and experience to implement solid security practices, perform risk analysis, identify necessary countermeasures, and help the organization as a whole protect its facility, network, systems, and information. The CISSP certification also provides security professionals with the credential that represents the skill set they want to offer to employers. Today, a greater demand is put on security as an integral part of corporate success. This, in turn, increases the demand for highly skilled security professionals. The CISSP certification shows that a respected third-party organization has recognized an individual's technical and theoretical knowledge and expertise, and distinguishes that individual from those who lack the certification.

Understanding and implementing security practices is an essential part of being a good network administrator, programmer, or engineer. Job descriptions that do not specifically target security professionals often still require a potential candidate to have good understanding of security concepts and the ability to implement them. Many organizations cannot afford distinct network and security staffs. However, they understand that security has an important place in many aspects of technology and, therefore, often look to combine security knowledge with other technical knowledge in a single role. Having your CISSP designation can put you ahead of other individuals who do not possess this type of insight.

# The CISSP Exam

To meet the certification requirements of a CISSP, you are required to have one of the following:

- At least three years of experience in one (or more) of the ten domains and a college degree
- Four years of professional experience in one (or more) of the domains within the Common Body of Knowledge (CBK)
- Two years of experience plus a bachelor's degree or a master's degree in information security from a National Center of Excellence

Please visit **www.isc2.org** for a complete description of the requirements.

Because the CISSP exam covers the ten domains that make up the CISSP CBK, it is commonly described as "an inch deep and a mile wide"; meaning that the questions are not necessarily very detailed in nature and do not require you to be a super expert in each and every subject. However, the questions do require you to be familiar with many different subjects within the security arena.

The CISSP exam is made up of 250 multiple-choice questions, and you are given up to six hours to complete it. These questions are chosen from a large question bank to ensure that the exam is as unique as possible for each person. The exam bank constantly changes and evolves in order to reflect the real world of security. Exam questions are rotated and replaced in the bank as the need arises. Each question has four choices with only one correct answer. Only 225 questions are scored; the remaining 25 questions are included for research purposes only. These 25 questions are not distinguished from the questions that will be scored, so you will not know which questions are counted toward your overall grade. To pass the exam, you must obtain a minimum raw score of 700 points. Each question is weighted based on its level of difficulty, and not all questions are worth the same number of points. The exam is not product- or vendor-oriented. In other words, you will not be asked questions specific to Windows 2000, Unix, or Cisco, for example, but you will be tested on the security models and methodologies used by these types of systems. As of this writing, the exam fee is $499 for early registration, and $599 if registering within 16 days of the exam.

The International Information Systems Security Certification Consortium (ISC)[2] credential process changed in June 2002. Now to obtain this credential, you must have a sponsor who will vouch for your years of experience. Taking the exam is the first step, and obtaining certification is the second step. As noted earlier, to qualify to take the CISSP exam, you must have either four years of direct full-time security professional work experience in one or more of the ten domains that make up the CBK, or a combination of a college degree and three years of direct full-time security professional work experience in one or more of the ten domains. The experience does not have to be continuous, but rather can be spread out over some time. After passing the exam, you will be asked to supply documentation, supported by a sponsor, proving that you indeed have this type of experience. The sponsor will have to sign a document vouching for the security experience you are submitting. The sponsor can be either an existing CISSP in good standing or a manager that you report to or have reported to in the past.

The sponsorship requirement helps to ensure that someone who achieves the certification has real-world experience to offer companies. Book knowledge is extremely important for understanding theory, concepts, and standards and regulations, but it will never take the place of real, hands-on experience. The requirement to prove that you have practical experience upholds the value and relevance of the certification for both certificate holders and potential employers. A small sample group of individuals selected at random will be audited after passing the exam and supplying the experience information. The audit consists mainly of individuals from (ISC)[2] calling sponsors and other contacts supplied by the CISSP candidate to verify the experience provided is in fact real.

What makes this exam challenging is that most candidates, although they work in the security field, are not necessarily familiar with all ten CBK domains. If a security professional is considered an expert in vulnerability testing or application security, for example, she may not be familiar with physical security, cryptography, or security practices. Studying for this exam will stretch your boundaries of knowledge within the security field.

The exam questions address the ten CBK security domains, which are listed and described in Table 1-1.

| Domain | Description |
| --- | --- |
| Access Control Systems and Methodology | This domain examines mechanisms and methods used to enable administrators and managers to control what subjects can access, the extent of their capabilities after authorization and authentication, and the auditing and monitoring of these activities. Some of the topics covered include:<br>• Access control security models<br>• Identification and authentication technologies and techniques<br>• Access control administration<br>• Data ownership<br>• Attack methods |
| Telecommunications and Network Security | This domain examines internal, external, public, and private communication systems; networking structures; devices; protocols; and remote access and administration. Some of the topics covered include:<br>• OSI model and layers<br>• Local area network (LAN), metropolitan area network (MAN), and wide area network (WAN) technologies<br>• Internet, intranet, and extranet issues<br>• Virtual private networks (VPNs), firewalls, routers, bridges, and repeaters<br>• Network topologies and cabling<br>• Attack methods |
| Security Management Practices | This domain examines the identification of company assets, the proper way to determine the necessary level of protection required, and what type of budget to develop for security implementations with the goal of reducing threats and monetary loss. Some of the topics covered include:<br>• Data classification<br>• Policies, procedures, standards, and guidelines<br>• Risk assessment and management<br>• Personnel security, training, and awareness |

**Table 1-1**   Security Domains That Make Up the CISSP CBK

| Domain | Description |
|---|---|
| Applications and Systems Development Security | This domain examines the security components within operating systems and applications and how to best develop and measure their effectiveness. This domain looks at software life cycles, change control, and application security. Some of the other topics covered include:<br>• Data warehousing and data mining<br>• Various development practices and their risks<br>• System storage and processing components<br>• Malicious code |
| Cryptography | This domain examines methods and techniques for disguising data for protection purposes. This involves cryptography techniques, approaches, and technologies. Some of the topics covered include:<br>• Symmetric versus asymmetric algorithms and uses<br>• Public key infrastructure (PKI) and hashing functions<br>• Encryption protocols and implementation<br>• Attack methods |
| Security Architecture and Models | This domain examines concepts, principles, and standards for designing and implementing secure applications, operating systems, and systems. This covers international security measurement standards and their meaning for different types of platforms. Some of the topics covered include:<br>• Operating states, kernel functions, and memory mapping<br>• Security models, architectures, and evaluations<br>• Evaluation criteria: Trusted Computer Security Evaluation Criteria (TCSEC), Information Technology Security Evaluation Criteria (ITSEC), and Common Criteria<br>• Common flaws in applications and systems<br>• Certification and accreditation |
| Operations Security | This domain examines controls over personnel, hardware, systems, and auditing and monitoring techniques. This also covers possible abuse channels and how to recognize and address them. Some of the topics covered include:<br>• Administrative responsibilities pertaining to personnel and job functions<br>• Maintenance concepts of antivirus, training, auditing, and resource protection activities<br>• Preventive, detective, corrective, and recovery controls<br>• Standards, compliance, and due care concepts<br>• Security and fault tolerance technologies |
| Business Continuity Planning (BCP) and Disaster Recovery Planning (DRP) | This domain examines the preservation of business activities when faced with disruptions or disasters. This involves the identification of real risks, proper risk assessment, and countermeasure implementation. Some of the topics covered include:<br>• Business resource identification and value assignment<br>• Business impact analysis and prediction of possible losses<br>• Unit priorities and crisis management<br>• Plan development, implementation, and maintenance |

**Table 1-1** Security Domains That Make Up the CISSP CBK *(continued)*

| Domain | Description |
|---|---|
| Laws, Investigation, and Ethics | This domain examines computer crimes, laws, and regulations. This includes techniques in investigating a crime, gathering evidence, and handling procedures. It also covers how to develop and implement an incident-handling program. Some of the topics covered include:<br>• Types of laws, regulations, and crimes<br>• Licensing and software piracy<br>• Export and import laws and issues<br>• Evidence types and admissibility into court<br>• Incident handling |
| Physical Security | This domain examines threats, risks, and countermeasures to protect facilities, hardware, data, media, and personnel. This involves facility selection, authorized entry methods, and environmental and safety procedures. Some of the topics covered include:<br>• Restricted areas, authorization methods, and controls<br>• Motion detectors, sensors, and alarms<br>• Intrusion detection<br>• Fire detection, prevention, and suppression<br>• Fencing, security guards, and security badge types |

**Table 1-1** Security Domains That Make Up the CISSP CBK *(continued)*

(ISC)² attempts to keep up with the changes in technology and methodologies brought to the security field by adding a large number of new questions to the test question bank each year. These questions are based on current technologies, practices, approaches, and standards. For example, the CISSP exam given in 1998 did not have questions regarding wireless security, but present and future exams contain wireless security topics because of its evolution and most recent importance to the technology industry.

The test is based on internationally accepted information security standards and practices, and the same English-language version is given throughout the world. If you look at the (ISC)² web site for test dates and locations, you may find, for example, that the same test is offered this Tuesday in California and next Wednesday in Saudi Arabia.

If you do not pass the exam, you can retake it as soon as you would like. (ISC)² used to subject individuals to a waiting period before they could retake the exam, but this rule has been removed. (ISC)² now keeps track of which version of the exam you were provided on your first attempt and ensures that you will not have the same version for any retakes. (ISC)² provides a report to CISSP candidates who do not pass the exam, detailing the areas that were their weakest. Although you can take the exam again at any time, it would be wise to spend the time you need to properly study and go over the areas that you were weak in, but if you would like to give (ISC)² another $499 for the very next testing date, I am sure they will happily accept it.

# CISSP: A Brief History

Historically, computer security has not been a structured and disciplined profession; rather, it has lacked well-defined professional objectives and, consequently, has been misperceived.

In the mid-1980s, members of the computer security profession recognized that they needed a certification program that would give their profession structure and provide ways for computer security professionals to demonstrate competence and present evidence of their qualifications. Establishing such a program would help the credibility of the computer security profession as a whole and the individuals who make up the profession.

In November 1988, the Special Interest Group for Computer Security (SIG-CS) of the Data Processing Management Association (DPMA) brought together several organizations that were interested in forming a security certification program. The organizations included the Information Systems Security Association (ISSA), the Canadian Information Processing Society (CIPS), the Computer Security Institute (CSI), Idaho State University, and several U.S. and Canadian government agencies. As a voluntary joint effort, these organizations developed the necessary components to offer a full-fledged security certification for interested professionals. (ISC)² was formed in mid-1989 as a nonprofit corporation to develop a security certification program for information systems security practitioners. The certification was designed to measure professional competence and help companies in their selection of security professionals and personnel. (ISC)² was established in North America, but has quickly gained international acceptance and now offers training and testing capabilities all over the world.

Because security is a broad subject and covers many different areas within the technology and business worlds, the original consortium decided upon an information systems security CBK, which is made up of ten domains pertaining to every part of computer, network, business, and information security. In addition, because technology continues to change and evolve at a fast pace, staying current on security trends, technology, and business developments is a requirement to maintain the CISSP certification. The group developed a Code of Ethics, test specifications, a draft study guide, a training seminar, and the exam itself.

## How Do You Become a CISSP?

To become a CISSP, you must start at **www.isc2.org**. There you will find an exam registration form that you need to fill out and send to (ISC)². You will be asked to provide your security work history and documents for the necessary educational requirements. Graduating with a master's degree from one of the listed National Centers of Excellence and having two years of experience will also qualify you. These National Centers of Excellence are listed at **http://niatec.info/nsacoe2.htm**, and the list of colleges and universities is growing. You will also be asked to agree to read the (ISC)² Code of Ethics and sign a form indicating that you understand these requirements and promise to abide by them. You then provide payment along with the registration form, where you will also indicate your preference of exam location. The numerous testing sites and dates are listed at **www.isc2.org**.

Although two, three, or four cumulative years of related experience is required, it can be experience that was accrued over time. It does not need to be consecutive years of continuous experience; you can have gaps of time in between.

Some people feel as though they do not have the necessary experience to take this exam, but it is best to contact (ISC)² to see if you are actually qualified before throwing this chance away. Remember that the minimum requirement is experience in *one* of the ten domains, which could be physical security, networking, security management practices, or operations.

# Recertification Requirements

Once you successfully pass the CISSP exam and achieve certification, the certification is valid for three years. In order to recertify for an additional three years, you can opt to retake the CISSP exam (other certifications, such as Microsoft and Cisco certifications, require retaking the exam) or you can do what most CISSPs elect to do, earn continuing professional education (CPE) credits to qualify for exam-free recertification. Maintaining a CISSP certification this way requires earning 120 CPE credits over a three-year recertification period. So either you resit the exam or gain 120 CPE credits in the three-year period after taking the exam.

There are many types of activities that can qualify for CPE credits, and they are broken down into two main sections: activities directly related to information security, and educational activities that either enhance a security professional's skill and knowledge or enhance the knowledge of others through provision of training and education.

The following items can count as CPE credits to keep your CISSP certification current:

- Attending a vendor training course or presentation
- Attending a security conference
- Taking a university or college security course related to one of the CBK domains
- Publishing a security article or book
- Providing security training
- Serving on a board of a professional security organization or attending the meetings
- Engaging in self-study
- Reading a security book
- Working as a volunteer, such as proctoring (helping to monitor) a CISSP exam
- Creating and submitting questions for future exams

Other activities may be counted as CPE credits. Contact (ISC)² if you have questions on other items for which you would like to obtain credit.

CISSPs have up to 120 days after the end of the certificate holder's three-year recertification cycle to complete the necessary requirements. Any CPE credits exceeding the number required that were achieved during the last six months of the recertification cycle are carried forward for credit toward the next cycle.

Along with providing the necessary level of CPE credits, CISSPs are required to pay an annual maintenance fee, due each year on the anniversary of their successful CISSP certification.

There is substantial information regarding recertification on the (ISC)² web site, **www.isc2.org**.

# What Does This Book Cover?

This book covers everything you need to know to become an (ISC)²-certified CISSP. It teaches you how and why corporations develop and implement policies, procedures, guidelines, and standards. It goes over network, application, and system vulnerabilities, what exploits them, and how to counter these threats. The book explains physical security, operational security, and why systems implement the security mechanisms that they do. It also reviews U.S. and international security criteria and evaluations that are performed on systems for assurance ratings, what these criteria mean, and why they are used. This book also explains the legal and liability issues that surround computer systems and the data they hold, computer crimes, forensics, and what should be done to properly prepare computer evidence for court.

This book is meant to be a study guide for the CISSP exam, but it can also be used as a reference guide after you achieve your certification.

# Tips for Taking the CISSP Exam

The test is 250 questions and you are given up to six hours to take it. The exams are monitored by CISSP volunteer hosts and proctors. Depending on the facility that hosts the test, you may or may not be allowed to bring in food or drink, so plan ahead and eat a good breakfast full of protein and fructose for brainpower. Proctors who allow food and beverages typically require that they be in a closable container and generally do not allow you to place them on the desk or table where you could spill something on your exam paper. Some proctors allow you to keep your goodies in a bag next to you on the floor or at the front or back of the room. Proctors may inspect the contents of any and all articles entering the test room. Restroom breaks are usually limited to allowing only one person to leave at a time, so drinking 15 cups of coffee right before the exam might not be the best idea.

The exam questions are not long, which is good because the test has so many questions, but this also means you get less information about what the questions are really asking for. Make sure to read the question and the answers thoroughly instead of reading a few words and assuming you know what the question is asking right off the bat. Some of the answer choices may have only subtle differences, so be patient and give yourself the time to read through the question more than once.

Like most tests, it is best to go through the questions and answer the ones that you know immediately and then go back to the ones that are causing you more difficulty. The CISSP exam is not computerized, so you will have a piece of paper with bubbles to fill in, and one of several colored exam booklets with the questions in them. I know that you probably haven't seen this type of exam since the SAT, but it is back. The reason I bring this up is that if you scribble outside the lines on the answer sheet, the machine that reads your answers may count a correct answer as wrong. So, I suggest that you go through each question and mark the right answer in the booklet with the questions. Repeat this process until you have completed your selections. At that time, go through the questions again and fill in the bubbles. This approach leads to less erasing and fewer potential problems for the scoring machine. You are allowed to write and scribble on your question exam booklet in any which way that you choose. You will turn it in at the end of your exam, with your answer sheet, but only answers on the answer sheet will be counted, so make sure that you transfer your answers to all questions onto the answer sheet.

Other certification exams may be taking place at the same time, in the same room, such as exams for certification as an SSCP (Systems Security Certified Professional); ISSAP or ISSMP (Architecture and Management concentrations, respectively); or ISSEP (Engineering concentration), which is the (ISC)²/NSA government certification. These other exams vary in length and duration, so don't feel rushed if you see others leaving the room early, as they may be taking a shorter exam.

When you are finished, take an extra couple of minutes to make sure you answered each question and that you did not accidentally fill in two bubbles for one question. Unfortunately, you will not receive the results of your test right away. (ISC)² tells you that it can take up to six weeks, but the average is four days to two weeks to receive your results through e-mail, and in the mail.

If you passed the exam, the results sent to you will not contain your score; you will only know that you successfully passed. Candidates who do not pass the test are *always* provided with a score. They know exactly how close they got and which areas they need to focus more attention on for the next time. The domains are listed on this notification with a ranking of weakest to strongest. If you do not pass the exam, you likely will be very frustrated, but keep in mind that some very smart and talented security professionals did not pass on their first try, mainly because the test covers so many broad topics.

One of the most commonly heard complaints about this exam is the exam itself. The questions are not long-winded, like many Microsoft tests, but at times it is difficult to decipher between two answers that seem to say the same thing. Although (ISC)² has been removing the use of negatives, such as "not," "except for," etc., they do still appear in the exam. This is slowly being remedied and should become less and less of an issue over time.

Another complaint heard is that some test questions seem a bit subjective. For example, whereas it might be easy to answer objectively a technical question that asks for the exact mechanism used in Secure Sockets Layer (SSL) that protects against man-in-the-middle attacks, it's not quite as easy to answer objectively a question that asks if an eight-foot perimeter fence provides low, medium, or high security. This complaint is mentioned here not to criticize (ISC)$^2$ and the people who write the test, but rather to help you better prepare for the test.

This book covers all the necessary material for the test, as well as many questions and self-practice tests. Many of these questions are formatted in a way that is intended to better prepare you for what you will encounter on the actual test. So make sure to read all the material in the book, and pay close attention to the questions and their formats. Even if you know the subject quite well, you may still get some answers wrong—it is part of learning how to take tests in general.

Familiarize yourself with industry standards and expand your technical knowledge and methodology outside the boundaries of what you use today. I cannot stress enough that just because you are the top dog in your particular field, it does not ensure that you are properly prepared for each and every domain this exam covers. Take the assessment test in this chapter to gauge where you stand, and be ready to read a lot of material you have not read before.

# How to Use This Book

A lot of effort has gone into putting all the necessary information into this book; now it is up to you to put the effort into truly understanding this material and the necessary concepts. To best benefit from this book, you might want to use the following study method:

1. Study each chapter carefully and make sure you understand each concept presented. There are many concepts you need to fully understand, and glossing over a couple here and there could be detrimental in the end. There are over 300 individual topics in the CISSP CBK, so take the time you need to understand them.

2. Make sure to study and answer all of the questions at the end of the chapter and on the CD-ROM included with the book. If any of the questions confuse you, go back and study those sections again. Remember, some of the questions on the actual exam are a bit confusing because they do not seem straightforward. I have attempted to draft several questions in the same manner to prepare you for the exam. So do not ignore the confusing questions, thinking they're not worded well, but rather pay even closer attention to them because they are there for a very distinct purpose.

3. If you are not familiar with specific topics, such as firewalls, laws, physical security, or protocol functionality, use other sources of information (books, articles, and so on) to get more in-depth understanding of those subjects. Don't just rely on what you think you need to know to pass the CISSP exam.

4. After reading this book, study the questions and answers, and take the practice tests. Then review the (ISC)$^2$ study guide and make sure you are comfortable with each bullet item presented. If there are some items you are not comfortable with, revisit those chapters.

5. If you have taken other certification exams, such as Cisco, Novell, or Microsoft, you might be used to having to memorize details and configuration parameters. But remember, the CISSP test is "an inch deep and a mile wide," so make sure you understand the concepts of each of the subjects *before* trying to memorize the small, specific details.

## References

- (ISC)$^2$    www.isc2.org
- **CISSP.com web portal**    www.cissps.com
- **CISSP and SSCP Open Study Guides**    www.cccure.org

## Questions

To get a better feel for your level of expertise and your current level of readiness for the CISSP exam, run through the following questions:

1. What is derived from a passphrase?

    A. Personal password

    B. Virtual password

    C. User ID

    D. Valid password

2. Which access control method is user-directed?

    A. Nondiscretionary

    B. Mandatory

    C. Identity-based

    D. Discretionary

3. Which item is not part of a Kerberos authentication implementation?

    A. Message authentication code

    B. Ticket-granting ticket

    C. Authentication service

    D. Users, programs, and services

4. If a company has a high turnover rate, which access control structure is best?

    A. Role-based

    B. Decentralized

    C. Rule-based

    D. Discretionary

5. In discretionary access control, who/what has delegation authority to grant access to data?

   A. User

   B. Security officer

   C. Security policy

   D. Owner

6. Remote access security using a token one-time password generation is an example of which of the following?

   A. Something you have

   B. Something you know

   C. Something you are

   D. Two-factor authentication

7. What is a crossover error rate (CER)?

   A. Rating used to rank a biometric system

   B. The number of Type I errors

   C. The number of Type II errors

   D. The number reached when Type I errors exceed the number of Type II errors

8. What does a retina scan biometric system do?

   A. Examines the pattern, color, and shading of the area around the cornea

   B. Examines the patterns and records the similarities between an individual's eyes

   C. Examines the pattern of blood vessels at the back of the eye

   D. Examines the geometry of the eyeball

9. If you are using a synchronous token device, what does this mean?

   A. The device synchronizes with the authentication service by using internal time or events.

   B. The device synchronizes with the user's workstation to ensure that the credentials it sends to the authentication service are correct.

   C. The device synchronizes with the token to ensure that the timestamp is valid and correct.

   D. The device synchronizes by using a challenge-response method with the authentication service.

10. What is a clipping level?

    A. Threshold for an activity

    B. Size of control zone

    C. Explicit rules of authorization

    D. Physical security mechanism

11. Which intrusion detection system would monitor user and network behavior?

   A. Statistical

   B. Signature-based

   C. Static

   D. Host-based

12. When should a Class C fire extinguisher be used instead of Class A?

   A. When electrical equipment is on fire

   B. When wood and paper is on fire

   C. When a combustible liquid is on fire

   D. When the fire is in an open area

13. How does Halon suppress fires?

   A. It reduces the fire's fuel intake.

   B. It reduces the temperature of the area.

   C. It disrupts the chemical reactions of a fire.

   D. It reduces the oxygen in the area.

14. What is the problem with high humidity in a data processing environment?

   A. Corrosion

   B. Fault tolerance

   C. Static electricity

   D. Contaminants

15. What is the definition of a power fault?

   A. Prolonged loss of power

   B. Momentary low voltage

   C. Prolonged high voltage

   D. Momentary power outage

16. Who has the primary responsibility of determining the classification level for information?

   A. Functional manager

   B. Middle management

   C. Owner

   D. User

17. Which best describes the purpose of the ALE calculation?

   A. Quantifies the security level of the environment

   B. Estimates the loss potential from a threat

   C. Quantifies the cost/benefit result

   D. Estimates the loss potential from a threat in a one-year time span

18. How do you calculate residual risk?

    A. Threats × risks × asset value

    B. (Threats × asset value × vulnerability) × risks

    C. SLE × frequency = ALE

    D. (Threats × vulnerability × asset value) × control gap

19. What is the Delphi method?

    A. A way of calculating the cost/benefit ratio for safeguards

    B. A way of allowing individuals to express their opinions anonymously

    C. A way of allowing groups to discuss and collaborate on the best security approaches

    D. A way of performing a quantitative risk analysis

20. What are the necessary components of a smurf attack?

    A. Web server, attacker, and fragment offset

    B. Fragment offset, amplifying network, and victim

    C. Victim, amplifying network, and attacker

    D. DNS server, attacker, and web server

21. In phone phreaking, what is red boxing?

    A. Voltage manipulation

    B. Replaying the noise coins make when dropping into a pay phone

    C. Using a handheld device attached to a live phone wire to intercept calls

    D. Tone manipulation

22. What do the reference monitor and security kernel do in an operating system?

    A. Intercept and mediate subject attempting to access objects

    B. Point virtual memory addresses to real memory addresses

    C. House and protect the security kernel

    D. Monitor privileged memory usage by applications

## Answers

1. B

2. D

3. A

4. A

5. D

6. A
7. A
8. C
9. A
10. A
11. A
12. A
13. C
14. A
15. D
16. C
17. D
18. D
19. B
20. C
21. B
22. A

# Security Trends

This chapter presents the following:

- Evolution of computing and how it relates to security
- Different areas that fall under the security umbrella
- Information warfare
- Security exploits
- A layered approach to security
- Politics that affect security

Security is a fascinating topic because it covers so many different areas (physical, network, platform, application, and so on), each with its own risks, threats, and solutions. When information security is discussed, the theme is usually hackers and software vulnerabilities. Although these are big security concerns, they are only two components within the larger field of security issues. Hacking is foremost in people's minds with regard to security because that is what usually fascinates the media and thus makes the headlines. Hacking is considered flashy and newsworthy, whereas not much coverage is given to what is going on behind the scenes with corporations' global security issues and the Internet as a whole.

## How Security Became an Issue

It is interesting to pick up various computer books and see that there is usually a history section that sets the stage for where society is today pertaining to computing and data processing. Unlike histories that tell of times long past, the history of computing typically begins in the 1960s. A lot has happened in a short period of time, and computer security is just starting to reach its time in the limelight.

Roughly twenty-five years ago, the only computers were mainframes. They were few and far between and used for specialized tasks, usually running large batch jobs, one at a time, and carrying out complex computations. If users were connected to the mainframes, it was through "dumb" terminals that had limited functionality and were totally dependent on the mainframe for their operations and processing environment. This was a *closed environment* with little threat of security breaches or vulnerabilities being exploited. This does not mean that things were perfect, that security vulnerabilities did not exist, and that people were in a computing utopia. Instead, it meant there were a handful of people working in a "glass house" who knew how to operate the computer. They decided who could access the mainframe and when. This provided a much more secure environment, because of its simplicity, than what we see in today's distributed and interconnected world.

In the days of mainframes, web sites describing the steps of how to break into a specific application or operating system did not exist. The network stacks and protocols being used were understood by very few people relative to the vast number of people that understand stacks and protocols today. Point-and-click utilities that can overwhelm buffers or interrogate ports did not exist. This was a truly closed environment that only a select few understood.

If networks were connected, it was done in a crude fashion for specific tasks, and corporations did not totally depend on data processing as they do today. The operating systems of that time had problems, software bugs, and vulnerabilities, but not many people were interested in taking advantage of them. Computer operators were at the command line and if they encountered a software problem, they usually just went in and manually changed the programming code. All this was not that long ago, considering where we are today.

As companies became more dependent on the computing power of mainframes, the functionality of the systems grew and various applications were developed. It was clear that giving employees only small time slices of access to the mainframes was not as productive as it could be. Processing and computing power was brought closer to the employees, enabling them to run small jobs on their desktop computers while the big jobs still took place within the "glass house." This trend continued and individual computers became more independent and autonomous, only needing to access the mainframe for specific functionality.

As individual personal computers became more efficient, they continually took on more tasks and responsibilities. It was shown that several users accessing a mainframe was inefficient and that some major components needed to be more readily available so that users could perform their tasks in an efficient and effective way. This thinking led to the birth of the client/server model. Although many individual personal computers had the processing power to compute their own calculations and perform their own logic operations, it did not make sense that each computer held information that was needed by all other computers. Thus, programs and data were centralized on servers, with individual computers accessing them when necessary and accessing the mainframes less frequently, as shown in Figure 2-1.

With the increasing exposure to computing and processing, the individuals who used computers learned more about using the technology and getting the most out of it. However, the good things in life often have a darker side. Taking technology down from the pedestal of the mainframe and putting it into so many individuals' hands led to a lot of issues that never had to be dealt with in the mainframe days. Now there were thousands of people not versed and experienced in computing who had much more access to important data and processes. Barriers and protection mechanisms were not in place to protect employees and systems from mistakes, so important data got

**Figure 2-1**    The relationship between a mainframe, servers, and workstations

corrupted accidentally, and individual mistakes affected many other systems instead of just one.

Because so many more people were using systems, the software had to be made more "idiot-proof" so that a larger audience could use the same platform. Computer operators in the mainframe days understood what the systems expected, how to format input, and how to properly read output. When this power was put into individuals' desktops, all imaginable and unimaginable inputs were used, which corrupted information and mangled operating systems.

Companies soon realized that employees had to be protected from themselves and that the data had to be protected from mishaps and mistakes. The employees needed layers of software between them and the operating system components and data they could potentially destroy. Implementing these layers not only enhanced security, by separating users from the core of the operating systems and files, but also increased productivity as functionality continued to be inserted to make computers more useful to businesses and individuals.

As the computing world evolved, symbiotic relationships grew among the technological advances of hardware, circuitry, processing power, and software. Once a breakthrough was made that enabled a computer to contain more memory and hard drive space, new software was right on its heels to use it and demand more. When software hit a wall because it was not supplied with the necessary registers and control units, the hardware industry was Johnny-on-the-spot to develop and engineer the missing pieces to the equations. As the hardware end grew to provide a stable and rich platform for software, programmers developed software that provided functionality and possibilities not even conceived of a few years earlier. It has been a wonderful game of leapfrog that does not seem to have any end in sight.

Lovely story, but what does it mean to security?

In the beginning, the issues associated with bringing computing closer to individuals brought along many mistakes, technological hurdles, and operational issues not encountered in the workforce before. Computers are tools; just as a knife can be a useful tool to cut meat and vegetables, it can also be a dangerous tool if it is in the hands of someone with malicious intent. The vast capabilities and functionality that computers have brought to society have also brought complex and troubling methods of destruction, fraud, abuse, and insecurity.

Because computers are built on layers (hardware platform, chips, operating systems, kernels, network stacks, services, and applications), these complex issues have been interwoven throughout the stratum of computing environments. Plugging the holes, writing better software, and providing better perimeter security is often easier said than done because of the density of functionality within an infrastructure, interoperability issues, and the availability requirements of the necessary functionality.

Over a short period of time, people and businesses have come to depend greatly upon computer technology and automation in many different aspects of their lives. Computers run public utilities, military defense systems, financial institutions, and medical equipment, and are heavily used in every possible business sector. Almost every company relies on data processing for one reason or another. This level of dependence and the extent of integration that technology has attained in our lives have made security a much more necessary and essential discipline.

Computer security is a marathon to be run at a consistent and continual pace. It is not a short sprint, and it is not for those who lack dedication or discipline.

# Areas of Security

Security has a wide base that touches on several different areas. The developers of the CISSP exam had the vision to understand this and demand that an individual who claims to be a security expert and wants to achieve this certification must also show that his expertise does not just lie in one area of security. There are many areas of security that affect each other. Physical security is interrelated with information security, database security lies on top of operating system security, operations security affects how computer systems are used, disaster recovery deals with systems in emergency situations, and almost every instance has some type of legal or liability issue tied to it. Technology, hardware, people, and procedures are woven together as a security fabric, as illustrated in Figure 2-2. When it is time to identify and resolve a specific problem, several strands of the security fabric may need to be unraveled and scrutinized so that the best and most effective solution can be provided.

This chapter addresses some specific security issues regarding computers, information, and organizations. This is not an attempt to cover all relevant subjects, but rather to show specific instances to give you an idea of the vast area that security encompasses. The information in these sections is provided to set the stage for the deeper levels of coverage that will be addressed in the following chapters.

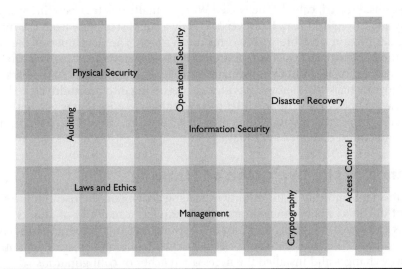

**Figure 2-2**   Technology, hardware, people, and procedures are woven together as a security fabric.

# Information Warfare

Computers and networks touch every facet of modern life. We are increasingly dependent on computer/network technology for communication, funds transfers, utility management, government services, military action, and maintaining confidential information. We use technology to provide energy, water supplies, emergency services, defense systems, electronic banking, and public health services. At the same time, this technology is being abused to perform illegal or malicious activities, such as steal credit card numbers, use the telephone systems fraudulently, illegally transmit trade secrets and intellectual property, deface web sites for political reasons, disrupt communications, reveal critical national secrets and strategies, and even commit extortion.

The term "information warfare" covers many different activities that pertain to individuals, organizations, and nations. *Information warfare* can be defined as any action to deny, exploit, corrupt, or destroy the enemy's information and its function, while at the same time protecting one's self against those same actions. Governments have used information warfare techniques to gather tactical information for years. Organizations have stolen competitors' trade secrets and plans for new products before they were released. Individuals have also used computers to steal money, access personal financial information, steal individual identification information, deface web sites, and cause destruction to draw attention to a particular cause.

Many of the hacking activities, viruses, and malware incidents documented thus far have been relatively benign. Most were carried out just so that the attacker could prove to himself and others that he is indeed clever enough to disrupt some businesses here and there, but not inflict the type of damage that is actually possible. Even though one of the worms released, called "The Naked Wife," actually deletes operating system files, it is only a lightweight threat. However, it is only a small step away from the more devastating destruction possible with worms and viruses. The developer of the worm is only getting self-satisfaction from the endeavor—the developer receives no money, trade secrets, or crucial military information and makes no political statements. But the trend of joyride hacking is showing evidence of evolving into profit-driven activities. As the old saying goes, "Why did the thief rob the bank? Because that is where the money was kept." Why are thieves attacking computers? Because that is where financial information and critical data are kept today.

## Evidence of the Evolution of Hacking

Several incidents indicate that not only is hacking activity on the rise, but the sophistication of the attacks is advancing rapidly. Alarmingly, a majority of attacks are using methods that have been understood for quite some time and for which fixes have been readily available. This proves that not enough network maintainers have kept up to date on security changes and installed the necessary patches or configurations.

It was discovered that a group of European hackers has been exploiting various computer vulnerabilities to steal millions of credit card numbers from U.S. computer systems associated with e-commerce and online banking. The FBI and Secret Service have been working with the National Infrastructure Protection Center (NIPC) to investigate this series of hacker attacks. The attackers actually contact the financial institutions and use extortion to increase the bounty from their misdeeds. They offer a "security service" to fix the systems, and if the institutions do not agree to pay, the attackers threaten more damage such as posting customers' credit card numbers on web sites available to the public. Many times this credit card information is sold to organized crime groups.

The public only hears about the viruses, worms, and hacks that make the news. Many other types of attacks are underway, and they will only become more prevalent. The main reason the public was being continually informed about the European hackers is that they were affecting so many financial institutions and customers. The FBI and Secret Service need the public to be aware and take the necessary steps to help stop this type of activity.

There have been many other financially motivated attacks. One involved a hacker who claimed to be 19 years old and from Russia. After he stole up to 300,000 credit card numbers from CD Universe customers in December 1999, he contacted the company, explained his actions, and then asked for a $100,000 ransom. When this money was not paid to him, he released thousands of the credit card numbers on the Internet. Another Russian hacker stole more than 55,000 credit card numbers from CreditCards .com. Again, a $100,000 ransom was requested and, after being ignored, 25,000 card numbers were posted on a web site.

In 2000, two hackers published a program that breaks the encryption mechanisms on older versions of IBM's e-commerce software. Using this tool and taking advantage of a server software flaw pertaining to address formatting made available the usernames and passwords of each and every account on a site using IBM's Net.Commerce and

WebSphere Commerce Suite software. The hackers reported that they knew of more than 330 web sites vulnerable to this type of attack.

In September 2000, Western Union shut down its web site for five days after hackers stole more than 15,000 customer credit card numbers. The intrusion may have happened when a firewall administrator brought the firewall down and left the web site open for 15 minutes, while performing routine software maintenance on it. Microsoft itself was attacked and the source code of a new product could have easily been manipulated or stolen.

Bibliofind, an online bookseller service, realized attackers had been accessing customer credit card information every month between October 2000 and February 2001. The credit card information of more than 98,000 customers was compromised. (Bibliofind is now owned by Amazon.com.)

In 2001, Egghead.com, based in California, had reports from some customers that their credit card numbers were stolen, and one person reported having a debit charge to a web site in Russia. Egghead.com delayed notifying customers about the intrusion into the customer database. Of course, such delays can affect the customers' faith and trust in their vendors and suppliers.

In April 2001, a large credit card company experienced a $20 million extortion attempt. In April 2002, the Bank of the State of California found out that 265,000 state employees had had their personal information stolen by a hacker. In August 2002, Daewoo Securities found out that $21.7 million in stock was illegally sold.

It has been reported that many financial institutions and brokerage firms have paid "hush money" to hackers who have carried out extortion acts. On October 29, 2002, a seminar sponsored by Cable & Wireless Internet Services addressed a 127-page study that details these issues along with others. The goal was to open others' eyes to the dependency of these types of institutions on public telecommunications systems, outsourcing services, and the growth of wireless technologies that open the door to these types of compromises.

In early 2004, BJ's Wholesale Club, Inc. experienced a break-in to their centralized database that holds credit card information for millions of customers. Because of this breach, Visa and MasterCard sent out warnings to their customers and advised them to watch their bills very carefully.

In early 2005, Choicepoint, a data gathering company, allowed individuals, who they thought were representing legitimate companies, access to 145,000 records within their database. The records held extensive private information on American citizens that could easily be used for identify theft. These individuals created several phony companies and used Choicepoint's information service to gather personal data. Each phony company collected the data over a period of time, so that the whole operation stayed under Choicepoint's radar. The individuals pieced together the information and compiled essentially full financial information on the victims, from credit reports to social security numbers. Only one person was arrested and received 16 months in jail.

In March 2005, hackers obtained 1.4 million credit card numbers by carrying out an attack on DSW Shoe Warehouse's database. In addition to obtaining credit card information, the attackers gained driver's license numbers and checking account numbers from 96,000 accounts.

In 2005, LexisNexis notified around 280,000 people that their passwords and IDs may have been accessed and stolen, and Bank of America lost their data backup tapes, which contained credit card account information for at least 1.2 million federal employees, many of whom worked at the Pentagon.

Examples of attempts to gain personal information are rampant. After discovering that fraudulent e-mail messages purporting to be from the Internal Revenue Service were being sent in an attempt to gain personal information, the IRS issued a notice that it does *not* use e-mail to contact taxpayers about issues related to their accounts. Yahoo .com issued warnings to its members to be careful about which web page they attempt to sign in on. Yahoo cautioned that the http://mail.yahoo.com/ address must include the trailing slash after the yahoo.com designation; otherwise, the address that shows up in the browser page could be bogus, an attempt to impersonate the official web site's sign-in page. Yahoo indicated that http://www.yahoo.com:login&mode=secure&i=b35 870c196e2fd4a&q=1@16909060 is a bogus URL.

The nonprofit organization Identity Theft Resource Center (**www.idtheftcenter .org**) issues notices about the latest scams and consumer alerts. It indicates that identity theft is the fastest growing crime in America today. Many of the compromises are coming from fraudulent e-mails (scams) and carelessly developed online shopping and online banking software. A variation of the scams includes the account verification schemes in which the thief attempts to obtain information from unsuspecting e-mail recipients by sending a mass e-mail message, purporting to be from eBay, PayPal, a bank, or some other legitimate organization, with an "Urgent" request for account verification and a warning that their account is about to expire. A link is provided that, when clicked, leads the victim to a web page that looks legitimate and asks for account information. These are known as *phisher* scams.

These examples represent only a small percentage of all the hacking activity that is going on. These attacks were identified and reported, but most are not. Many organizations do not report hacking activity because they are afraid of hurting their reputation, losing the faith of their customer base, and adversely affecting their shareholders and stock prices. Other attacks are not even realized or identified, and thus not reported. Computers and networks are great tools that have brought society much advancement, but like many other tools, they are also used for sinister purposes.

## How Are Nations Affected?

The art of war requires soldiers to outmaneuver the enemy and strike them down if necessary. In traditional warfare, the enemy was usually easily detectable. They were driving a tank, bombing from an airplane, attacking from a submarine, or shooting intercontinental missiles. Today, the enemy may be harder to find, some attacks are harder to track, and the objectives of the attacker are at times more nebulous. Many governments' military intelligence agencies have had to develop new methods of collecting information on potential foreign enemy movement, conducting surveillance, and proving guilt of criminal activities.

Although militaries still train most soldiers how to shoot, fight in combat, and practice evasive maneuvers, a new type of training is being incorporated. Because a majority of the military vehicles, weapons systems, and communication systems are controlled by technology, new soldiers need to know how to use these technological tools to achieve the same goal of the soldier of the past—to win in war. Today's soldiers need to know not only how to operate the new technology-driven weapons systems, but also how to defend these systems from attacks and possibly use them to attack the enemy's defense systems.

Disrupting communication has always been an important tactic in war because it impedes proper planning and warnings of imminent attacks. Knocking out communication lines is one of the first steps in the recipe of a successful attack. Today, most military communication is handled through computer-based systems, and the tools to disrupt communication of the enemy have changed. For example, the CIA reported to a U.S. congressional committee that foreign nations include information warfare in their military arsenal and provide defensive and offensive attack methods. These nations are devising documentation, strategic plans, and tools to carry out information warfare on other nations.

During the Persian Gulf War in 1991, it was reported that hackers from the Netherlands penetrated 34 American military sites that supported Operation Desert Storm activities. They extracted information about the exact location of military troops, weapon details, and movement of American warships. It could have been a different war if Saddam Hussein had actually bought this information when it was offered to him, but he did not—he thought it was a trick.

In another example, it was reported that the Irish Republican Army stole telephone bills to determine the addresses of potential targets in their political attacks. Authorities seized a batch of computer disks in Belfast and were able to decrypt the information after months of effort. This information was most likely gained by successfully hacking into the telephone company's database.

A report declassified in May 1995 stated that prior to the August 1991 coup attempt in the Soviet Union, the KGB had been writing and developing viruses to disrupt computer systems during times of war. Another report, by the U.S. Defense Intelligence Agency, indicated that Cuba had developed viruses to infect and damage U.S. civilian computers. There is no proof that these viruses were released and actually caused damage, but there is no proof that they weren't released, either. It has also been reported that during the 1999 Kosovo Air Campaign, false messages were injected into Yugoslavia's computer-integrated air defense systems to point the weapons at false targets. Examples such as these show that it is clear that military use of computer-based tools and attacks is growing in sophistication and utilization.

Almost every task in an individual's day interrelates with a technology that is controlled or monitored by a computer-based system. Turning on the lights, paying a gas bill, flying on a plane, talking on the telephone, and receiving medical treatment are all events that depend on large computer systems monitoring and providing the flow of service. Even sophisticated military defense systems rely on commercial power, communication, transportation, and monitoring capabilities, which are computer based. A country's strength relies on its privately owned critical infrastructures and industries. These private-sector infrastructures have already been victimized by computer attacks.

A concerted attack on any of these key economic sectors or governmental services could have widespread ramifications. Most governments have recognized this vulnerability and have started taking steps to evade these types of attacks and provide the necessary mechanisms to enable a quick and efficient recovery after an attack.

Enemy bullets used to come only from guns. Now different types of "bullets" come from laptops and personal computers. The next war could target a country's infrastructure with the new weapons—computer-generated attacks. Several factions of militaries are developing more robust and skilled information warfare units to act defensively and offensively in the best interest of their nation. There is a good reason. Future wars and power struggles may take place over computer lines instead of the more traditional battlefield.

**NOTE** The examples here are U.S.-centric, but the CISSP exam is not. The CISSP exam has evolved a greater international focus than in the past.

## How Are Companies Affected?

Many companies fail to understand how security implementations will help their bottom line: the profit margin. After all, business is done to make profit, and if there is not a direct correlation for an item that ties in neatly to the linear cost and profit concept, that item is often given low priority. However, today many companies are finding out how security affects their bottom line in ways they never expected.

If a company suffers a security breach, it will have to deal with a wide range of issues that it most likely is not prepared for. Several companies recently had their databases attacked and their customers' information compromised. Once customers find out that a company is not protecting their confidential and financial information properly, they will often take their business elsewhere. If the number of customers affected is in the range witnessed over the last year (10,000 to 1.4 million credit cards stolen at a time), and if the company loses a similar number of customers at one time, the company could go out of business. Of course, these events also affect the reputation of the company, its shareholders, and it stock price. In addition, the customers can sue the company, which could result in punitive damages and court fees. This would definitely impact the bottom line.

Organizations have had trade secrets and intellectual property stolen by employees who left to work for a competitor. In such instances, unless the original company has taken the proper steps to protect this data and inform its employees that this action is wrong, the company has no legal recourse. The company has to practice due care to protect its intellectual property from competitors inside and outside its walls. (For more information on legal issues, see Chapter 10.)

The industry is seeing more and more cases of employees being fired for improper use of computer systems. Many large companies have instituted policies of zero tolerance with respect to unauthorized or improper computer and Internet usage. However, if companies do not take the proper steps by having a comprehensive security policy in place and providing security awareness to the employees, they are often successfully sued for unfairly ending employment.

Another way a company can lose money and time is by its lack of readiness to react to a situation. If a network does not have properly configured security mechanisms, the company's IT staff usually spends unnecessary time and resources putting out fires. In addition, when they are racing in a chaotic manner to find a solution, they may be creating more open doors into the network without realizing it. Without proper security planning, a lot of money, staff productivity, and time are wasted that could be used for other tasks. As discussed in subsequent chapters in this book, companies that have a solid incident response plan or disaster recovery plan in place will know what to do in the event of a physical intrusion or cyber attack.

Many companies are covered by insurance in case of a natural disaster or a major security breach. However, to get a good insurance rate, companies must prove that they have a solid security program and that they are doing all that they can to protect their own investments. In some cases, insurance providers refused to pay for a company's loss because the company failed to have the correct security measures in place. A recent legal case involved a company which did not have a security policy, proper security mechanisms, and an updated disaster recovery plan in place. When a disaster struck, the insurance company refused to pay. The case went to court and the insurance company won; however, the greater loss to the company was not the court case.

Every business market is full of competition. If a company endures a security compromise that makes the press—which has been happening almost every month over the last year—it will have an even harder time attracting new business. A company wants to be in a position where all the customers come to it when another company suffers a security compromise, not the other way around.

## The U.S. Government's Actions

One of the U.S. government's responsibilities is to protect American resources, people, and their way of life. One complex task the government has been faced with recently is protecting several critical infrastructures from computer-based attacks. Because computer technology is relatively young and changing rapidly, and because security has only come into real focus over the last few years, all these core infrastructures contain their own vulnerabilities. If attackers disrupt these infrastructures, the ramifications may be far reaching. For example, if attackers were able to take down electrical grids, thus forcing the government to concentrate on that crisis, they could then launch militarily strikes on other fronts. This might sound like a John Grisham novel, but the U.S. government must consider such scenarios and devise defensive plans to respond. One of the biggest threats the United States faces is that terrorists or a hostile nation will attempt to inflict economic damage, disrupt business or productivity, and degrade our defense response by attacking the critical infrastructures.

On July 15, 1996, President Clinton approved the establishment of the President's Commission on Critical Infrastructure Protection (PCCIP). The responsibility of this commission was to investigate the types of attacks that were happening, extrapolate how attacks could evolve in the future, determine how they could affect the nation's computer infrastructures, and assess how vulnerable these structures were to such attacks at that time.

The PCCIP published its very sobering report, "Critical Foundations: Protecting America's Infrastructures," in 1997. The report outlined the current vulnerability level of critical U.S. infrastructures pertaining to criminal activity, natural disasters, international terrorists, hackers, foreign national intelligence, and information warfare. Long-standing security weaknesses, placing federal operations at serious risk, were identified and reported. In response to this report, President Clinton signed two orders, Presidential Decision Directives (PDDs) 62 and 63, to improve the nation's defenses against terrorism, other computer-based attacks, and information warfare activities. The focus of these directives was to address cyberattacks at a national level.

The report recognized that many of the nation's critical infrastructures were privately owned and operated. It was obvious that the government and the private sector had to work together to properly and successfully defend against cyberattacks. In fact, it was recognized that these government departments could *not* provide this level of protection without the help and sharing of information with the public sector. The position of National Coordinator was created within the Executive Office of the President to facilitate a partnership between the government and the private sector. The goal was for the government and the private sector to work together to strengthen the nation's defenses against cyberterrorism, theft, fraud, and other criminal activity. Out of this came the Critical Infrastructure Assurance Office (CIAO) under the Department of Commerce, Information Sharing and Analysis Centers (ISACs), and the NIPC under the sponsorship of the FBI.

ISACs provide a mechanism that enables information sharing among members of a particular industry sector. The information comes from public-sector organizations and government agencies, and is shared by both. Sources of information can be authenticated or anonymous, and the information can pertain to vulnerabilities, incidents, threats, and solutions. Submitted information is directed to the appropriate team members, who then investigate each submittal, quantify the seriousness of the vulnerability, and perform a trend analysis to identify the steps that might thwart this type of attack. The intent is to enhance the security of individual organizations and the entire nation one industry sector at a time.

In 2002, President Bush created the Office of Homeland Security in response to the attack on the United States on September 11, 2001. Departments of information technology and cybersecurity were included, and specific committees and roles were developed to protect against attacks that could negatively affect the nation's infrastructure. The bill was signed November 25, 2002, and allocated $2.12 billion for technology and cybersecurity.

These are just some of the changes that have been taking place, which shows the elevation of the importance of computer, business, architecture, personnel, and infrastructure security.

## So What Does This Mean to Us?

Evidence and trend analyses show that people, businesses, and countries are becoming increasingly dependent on computer/network technology for communication, funds transfers, utility management, government services, and military action. If any of these experienced a major disruption, millions of people could be affected. As our dependence grows, so should our protective measures.

Currently, the majority of computer attacks, hacks, and cracks are done for thrills and to measure one's own skills, and only a small percentage of attacks are motivated by financial gain. It is likely that this pattern will reverse in the future, and a majority of computer compromises and attacks will be for theft and fraud. At the same time, the laws will increase in severity so that computer joyriding will not be so joyful when one is caught snooping around or releasing a virus.

Militaries are quietly growing their information warfare units. This growth is a response to the computer-related military actions that have already occurred and reflects an awareness of the need to plan for the future. Computer networks, communication systems, and other resources not only are prime targets to reconfigure or destroy in the time of war or crisis, they are also good tools to use to watch other nations' movements and estimate their intentions during peacetime.

The antes are being raised, security issues are becoming more serious, and the effects are more detrimental. Take the necessary steps to protect yourself, your company, and your country.

# Hacking and Attacking

There has been a definite and distinct evolution of hacking, cracking, and attacking. At one time, it was a compliment to be called a hacker because it meant that you took the time to learn things about computers that many others did not know and had the discipline and desire to find out what makes a computer tick. These people did not perform malicious acts, but rather were the ones called upon when really tough problems left everyone else scratching their heads.

As computers became widespread as tools used in many environments, this definition started to change. The new hackers took on a profile of geeky young men who would rather spend their time pinging computers all over the Internet than looking for dates. Even this profile has evolved. Girls and women have joined this once all-male club and are just as knowledgeable and dangerous as the guys. Hacking is on the rise, and the profile of an attacker is changing. However, the real change in the profile is that the serious attackers are out for specific purposes with certain types of damage or fraud in mind.

The dangerous attacker is the one who is willing to do his homework. He will build a profile about the victim, find all the necessary information, and uncover many possible ways of getting into an environment before actually attempting it. The more an attacker knows about the environment, the more access points he has at his disposal. Attacks and hacks have involved information warfare, stealing money and credit cards, and defacing web sites for political reasons. These are usually groups of determined and knowledgeable individuals that are hard to stop.

Another dangerous evolutionary pattern is that the tools that are available to hackers these days are easy to use. It used to take a certain skill set to be able to enter a computer through a port, reconfigure system files, find the hidden data, and get out without being noticed. Today there are many tools with graphical user interface (GUI) front ends that only require a person to enter an IP address or range, and click the Start button. Some of these tools provide a quiet mode, which means the interrogations and exploit attempts will use methods and protocols that may not show up on intrusion detection systems (IDSs) or cause the user of that computer to recognize that something is going on. These tools enable people to carry out sophisticated attacks even if they do not understand the tool or the attack itself.

The proliferation of tools on the Internet, the ease of use of these tools, and the availability of web sites and books describing exactly how to exploit vulnerabilities have greatly increased the hacker population. So, some attack tools whose creation may have required in-depth knowledge of protocol behaviors or expert programming skills are now available to a wide range of people who have not necessarily ever heard of Transmission Control Protocol/Internet Protocol (TCP/IP).

As more vulnerabilities are uncovered every week, many more people are interested in trying out the exploits. Some just want to satisfy their curiosity, some want bragging rights over other hackers, and others have distinct destructive goals to accomplish.

There is another aspect of hacking and attacking, though. While it is natural to focus on the evil aspects, hacking can also be looked at as a continuous challenge to the computing society to come up with better products, practices, and procedures. If hackers were not continually trying to break products, the products would not necessarily continue to evolve in the way that they have. Sure, products would continue to grow in functionality, but not necessarily in security.

So maybe instead of looking at hackers as selfish individuals out to cause harm and destruction, they can be looked at as the thorn in the side of the computing society that keeps it on its toes and ensures that the next product will provide great functionality, but in a secure manner.

# Management

Security is a complex matter for many companies. Management usually feels that the IT department is responsible for choosing the correct technologies, installing and maintaining them, and keeping the environment secure. In general, management has never really been pulled inside the realm of computers and the issues that surround them. This distance and mentality hurts many companies when it comes to dealing with security effectively.

Historically, management has been responsible only for hitting its numbers— whether it be profit margins, sales goals, or productivity marks—and for managing people and projects. It has not had to think much about firewalls, hackers, and security breaches. However, this mindset is fading, and the new trend demands that management be much more involved in security and aware of how it affects the company as a whole.

It is management's responsibility to set the tone for what role security will play in the organization. Management must decide what data is valuable and needs to be protected, who is responsible for protecting it and to what extent, to what extent employees may access and use the data, and what the consequences are for noncompliance. However, as of this writing, few corporations see these issues in this light and instead bounce the responsibility for security back to the IT staff. The reason, usually, is not that management is trying to avoid blame for security lapses or shirk its responsibility, but rather that it lacks understanding of what information and enterprise security entails. Many organizations incorrectly assume that information security is a technical issue. It is not. Information security is a management issue that may require technical solutions. This is why information security professionals are so important. They must understand not only the goals and objectives of the organization, but also the technical issues involved in securing those assets that are most important.

Good security does not begin and end with erecting a firewall and installing antivirus software. Good security is planned, designed, implemented, maintained, and able to evolve. For security to be a good fit for a company, it has to be in line with the company's business goals and objectives. Management needs to understand security issues and how security affects the company and its customers, so that proper resources, time, and funding can be provided. In other words, information security should be applied in a top-down approach. Unfortunately, many times security is kept within the IT department, which can be overwhelmed with daily tasks and dealing with weekly disasters. In these cases, security is done in a reactionary, bottom-up approach, which drastically reduces its effectiveness. In addition, when the IT department requests funds for security purposes, it often falls on deaf ears.

It is too much responsibility to put the full brunt of the security of a whole company on the IT department. Security needs to be understood, supported, and funded from the top down. Management does not need to know the security mechanisms used, protocols in place, or configurations of components, but it does need to set the stage for everyone else to follow. Management should provide the framework and delegate who is to fill in the rest.

In February 2004, Wells Fargo Bank suffered its second theft of a laptop computer that contained confidential information from its customer database. The first laptop that was stolen, in November 2003, contained a database of 200,000 customer records. In the February 2004 incident, two Wells Fargo employees were in a St. Louis, Missouri gas station/convenience store, with their rental car parked outside. When they returned to their car, all the contents of the vehicle, including the laptop in the trunk, were gone. Wells Fargo waited more than a month before it notified the affected customers.

When a company is hacked and thousands of customers' credit cards are stolen, intellectual property is taken, confidential information is leaked, or the organization's reputation is damaged, it is the management staff that will be held accountable and expected to explain why due diligence and due care were not practiced in protecting the company and its resources. These explanations may be given to corporate offices, shareholders, judges, and customers. So it should be management who truly understands how security works within the organization and should be calling the shots from the beginning.

# Internet and Web Activities

The Internet was established so that universities and government organizations could communicate in a more instantaneous manner and share information easily. It not only provided a different communication path, it opened the door to the possibility of mass communication, as well as a new and exciting mechanism that could provide layers of functionality and potential for individuals and businesses all around the world.

Communication on the Internet consisted mainly of nongraphical e-mail, news groups, and File Transfer Protocol (FTP) sites to exchange files. When Hypertext Markup Language (HTML) came to life, people were able to make graphical representations of their concepts and ideas. These sites provided static pages with a small amount of capability to accept information from Internet users through forms and scripts. When entrepreneurs realized that the Internet was a new money-making forum for advertising and selling, sites became more abundant, web pages became more complex, and more products and services were offered. Companies started integrating this new communication mechanism into their business model.

A game of leapfrog began between telecommunication capabilities, Internet protocols, hardware platforms, and supporting applications. As HTML became more dynamic, web server applications were developed to manage these web pages and the back-end processes. This increased the need for more hard drive space, processing power, and memory accessible to the applications. Protocols evolved and matured to create a more stable and meaningful experience on the Internet. These protocols enabled confidential information to stay secret and provided the necessary level of integrity for data being transmitted. Web servers became more powerful in processing as they offered more functionality to the users. As more sites connected to each other, the Internet led to the development of the World Wide Web.

The Web is actually a layer that operates on top of the Internet. The Internet provides the hardware, platforms, and communication mechanisms, whereas the Web provides the abundant software capabilities and functionality. Figure 2-3 illustrates this difference.

As companies connected their networks to the Internet and brought their services to the Web, they connected to the world in an entirely new way. It is a great marketing tool for a business to enable thousands or millions of people to view its product line, understand its business objectives, and learn about the services it offers. However, this also opens the doors to others who are interested in finding out more about the company's network topology and applications being used, accessing confidential information, and maybe causing some mayhem here and there in the process.

**Figure 2-3**  There is a difference between the Internet and the World Wide Web. The Web is a layer that exists on top of the Internet.

Offering services through the Internet is not the same as offering just another service to a customer base. It can be a powerful and useful move for a company, but if done haphazardly or in a manner that is not clearly thought out, implemented, and maintained, it could end up hurting a company or destroying it.

The decisions regarding which software to use, which hardware configurations to make, and which security measures to take to establish a presence on the Web depend on the company, its infrastructure, and the type of data it needs to protect. In the beginning, a web server was just another server on the Internet with a connection outside of the network. Static pages were used, and no real information came from the Internet to the company through this channel. As forms and Common Gateway Interface (CGI) scripts were developed to accept customer information, and as the Internet as a whole became more used and well known, web servers were slowly moved to demilitarized zones (DMZs), the name given to perimeter networks (see Figure 2-4). Unfortunately, many web servers today still live inside of networks, exposing companies to a lot of vulnerabilities.

As the web servers and applications evolved from just showing customers a home page and basic services to providing complete catalogs of products and accepting orders via the Internet, databases had to be brought into the picture. Web servers and databases lived on the same system, or two systems within the DMZ, and provided information to (and accepted information from) the world. This setup worked until more customers were able to access back-end data (within the database) and corrupt it accidentally or intentionally. Companies eventually realized that there were not enough

DMZ with web servers          Internal network

**Figure 2-4** Web servers were eventually moved from the internal network to the DMZ.

layers and protection mechanisms between the users on the Internet and the companies' important data. Over time this has been improved upon by adding more layers of protective software and adding more physical layers, mainly through the use of firewalls.

This quickly brings us to where we are today. More and more companies are going online and connecting their once closed (or semiclosed) environments to the Internet, which exposes them to threats, vulnerabilities, and problems that they have not dealt with before. If a company has static web pages, its web servers and back-end needs are not half as complicated as the companies that accept payments and offer services or hold confidential customer information. The companies that take credit card numbers, allow customers to view their bank account information, and offer products and services over the Web can work in a two-tier (see Figure 2-5) or three-tier configuration.

Internet user

Database

Web server

**Figure 2-5** Attackers have easy access if databases are directly connected to web servers with no protection mechanisms.

## Two-Tier Architecture

A two-tier architecture includes a line of web servers that provide customers with a web-based interface and a back-end line of servers or databases that hold data and process the requests. Either the two tiers are within a DMZ or the back-end database is protected by another firewall. Figure 2-6 shows a two-tier architecture.

This architecture is fine for some environments, but for companies that hold bank or credit card information or other sensitive information, a three-tier architecture is usually more appropriate. In the three-tier architecture, the first line consists of a server farm that presents web pages to customers and accepts requests. The farm is usually clustered and redundant, to enable it to handle a heavy load of connections and balance that load between servers.

The back-end tier is basically the same as in the two-tier setup, which has database(s) or host systems. This is where sensitive customer information is held and maintained. The middle tier, absent in the two-tier setup, provides the most interesting functionality. In many cases, this is where the business logic lives and the actual processing of data and requests happens. Figure 2-7 shows the three-tier architecture.

The middle tier comprises application servers running some type of middleware, which either communicates with the Web (presentation tier) and can be customized for proprietary purposes and needs, or acts basically as another layer of server farms with off-the-shelf products. This layer takes the heavy processing tasks off the front-line servers and provides a layer of protection between the users on the Internet and the sensitive data held in the databases. The middleware is usually made up of components built with object-oriented languages. The objects are the entities that work as binary black boxes by taking in a request, retrieving the necessary information from the back-end servers, processing the data, and presenting it back to the requesting entity. Figure 2-8 illustrates how a component works as a black box.

**Figure 2-6**   A two-tier architecture consists of a server farm band back-end databases.

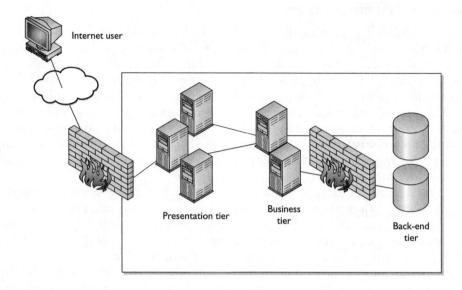

**Figure 2-7** A three-tier architecture comprises a front-end server farm, middle servers running middleware software, and back-end databases.

The three-tier architecture offers a lot of advantages. Security can be supplied in a more granular fashion if it is applied at different places in the tiers. The first firewall supports a particular security policy and provides the first line of defense. The first tier of web servers accepts only specific requests, can authorize individuals before accepting certain types of requests, and can dictate who gets to make requests to the next tiers. The middle tier can provide security at the component level, which can be very detail-oriented and specific in nature. No requests should be made from the Internet directly to the back-end databases. Several middlemen should have to pass the request, each

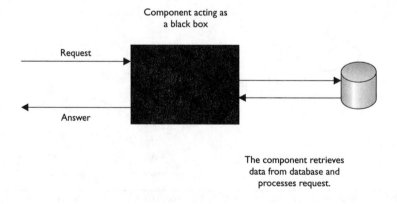

**Figure 2-8** Components take requests, pass them on, and process the answer.

looking out for specific security vulnerabilities and threats. The back-end databases are then acted upon by the components in the middle tier, not the users themselves.

The second firewall should support a different security policy. If an attacker gets through the first firewall, it makes no sense for the second firewall to have the same configurations and settings that were just defeated. This firewall should have different settings that are more restrictive, to attempt to stop a successful intruder at that particular stage.

## Database Roles

Many times, databases are configured to accept requests only from predefined roles, which ensures that if an intruder makes it all the way through the middleware and to the place that holds the goods, the intruder cannot make a request because she is not a member of one of the predefined roles. This scenario is shown in Figure 2-9.

All access attempts are first checked to make sure the requester is a member of a predefined and acceptable group. This means that individuals cannot make direct requests to the database, and it is highly unlikely that an attacker would be able to figure out the name of the group whose members are permitted to make requests to the database, much less add herself to the group. This is an example of another possible layer of protection available in a tiered approach of web-based operations.

 **CAUTION**   If group names are obvious or have not been changed from the defaults, extrapolating the group information from a network and making assumptions based on their names may be only a trivial task.

The discussion of Internet and web activities thus far has focused on architectural issues, giving you a broad overview of the network and how large components are

**Figure 2-9**   This database accepts requests only from members of the operators, accounting, and administrators roles. Other paths are restricted.

configured to secure the network. However, security vulnerabilities usually are found in smaller components and configuration details that are easier to overlook. A great three-tier architecture can be set up by strategically placing firewalls, web servers, and databases to maximize their layers of functionality and security, but an attack can still take place at the protocol, component, or service level of an operating system or application. The types of attacks cover a wide range, from denial-of-service (DoS) attacks, spoofing, and buffer overflows to using an application's own functionality against itself. By way of example, we will take a quick look at just one type of attack that has been used to steal millions of credit card numbers over the Internet.

## Microsoft Data Access Components

Many companies use Microsoft Internet Information Services (IIS) for their web server software. Without the proper patches installed, IIS has some specific vulnerabilities that can give attackers access to data on the back-end servers in a privileged mode, which enables them to capture or modify information. These vulnerabilities have been known for quite a while, but financial institutions are still falling victim to them because their IT staffs are not installing the necessary security patches and making the corresponding configuration changes.

Microsoft Data Access Components (MDACs), which are used in IIS and Windows platforms, have many functions and services. One of the services, Remote Data Service, enables web-based clients to issue Structured Query Language (SQL) queries to remote resources using HTTP. When an Internet user makes a request to the IIS server, the user executes the command at her browser, and the msadcs.dll on the IIS server facilitates this request and employs the Data Factory Object. The Data Factory Object enables requests to be sent to and received from the back-end database.

The problem lies in Microsoft's database engine, which enables embedded arguments to be passed within SQL query strings, as shown in Figure 2-10. This means that attackers can embed commands within a request made to the database, which in turn can execute shell commands, tunnel Open Database Connectivity (ODBC) requests to the

**Figure 2-10** Weaknesses in the components of IIS running on Windows enable attackers to access confidential information in back-end databases.

back-end database, and access secured, unpublished files. What makes this even more devastating is that IIS lets these ODBC commands run with system_local privileges.

In other words, the company could set up the right infrastructure, configure the necessary firewalls, disable unnecessary ports and services, and run the IDSs properly, yet still lose control of thousands or millions of credit card numbers to attackers because it failed to update the security patches.

This example shows that vulnerabilities can lie at a code level that many network administrators and security professionals are not necessarily aware of. There are usually two main camps in the computer world: infrastructure and programming. Security vulnerabilities lie in each camp and affect the other, so it's wise to have a full understanding of an environment and how security breaches can take place through infrastructure and code-based means.

So where do the vulnerabilities lie in web-based activities?

- Incorrect configurations at the firewall
- Web servers that are not hardened or locked down and are open to attacks to the operating system or applications
- Middle-tier servers that do not provide the right combination and detailed security necessary to access back-end databases in a controlled manner
- Databases and back-end servers that accept requests from any source
- Databases and back-end servers that are not protected by another layer of firewalls
- Failure to run IDSs to watch for suspicious activity
- Failure to disable unnecessary protocols and services on computers
- Failure to keep the computers patched and up to date

The list is endless, but one last item is important to touch on that is not approached as much as it should be in security: application and programming security. Security is usually thought of in terms of firewalls, IDSs, and port scanners. However, the vulnerabilities that are exploited are within the code of the operating systems and applications. If these problems did not exist in the programming code in the first place, there would be nothing to exploit and no real reason to have firewalls and IDSs.

Programming has usually been approached only in terms of how it can provide more functionality to the user, not in how it can protect the system it is installed upon or the data that it holds and processes. Attacks and exploits that are taking place today were not even in the minds of the programmers while they were coding their programs a couple of years ago; thus, they most likely did not think of coding differently and testing for these specific weaknesses.

The real security problems that companies are dealing with are embedded within the products they purchase and install. Only recently have vendors started to take these issues seriously and think about how programming should be done differently. However, proper techniques and extensive testing add a lot of expense and delay to developing a product, and most vendors are not willing to take on those extra expenses and delays without seeing more profit in the end. They have developed the mindset that it is more profitable to get the product to market quickly and worry about patching problems later, and consumers for the most part have acquiesced to this system. It is really up to the consumer market to demand more-secure products and to buy only the products that have the necessary embedded protection mechanisms and methods. Until then, administrators will spend their days patching systems and applications and adjusting firewall and IDS configurations to thwart new vulnerabilities. They will need to continually update attack signatures, and the rat race of trying to outrun hackers will continue.

# A Layered Approach

Networks have advanced in functionality and complexity. Because vulnerabilities can take place at different layers of an infrastructure, it has been necessary for vendors, developers, administrators, and security professionals to understand these layers and how each should be protected.

Often, you hear about a "layered approach" to security. You are supposed to implement different layers of protection to protect networks from different types of attacks. But what does a layered approach really mean? How do you know if you are applying a layered approach?

These are excellent questions that should be explored in depth if you are serious about protecting your interior and exterior networks from all of the possible security compromises and breaches. To protect an environment, you must truly understand the environment, the fixes that are to be applied, the differences between the numerous vendor applications and hardware variations, and how attacks are actually performed. The road to a secure environment is a winding one, with some bumps, sharp turns, and attacks that lunge out from the dark. However, the most important thing when navigating this road to security is to understand the facets of the adventure and that the road never ends.

## Security at Different Layers

The description of a layered approach to security can be an abstract and nebulous topic because theory has to be represented and implemented in reality. Many times, a layered approach means to implement solutions at different spectrums of the network. The spectrums can range from the programming code, the protocols that are being used, the operating system, and the application configurations, through to user activity and the security program that is supposed to govern all of these issues. A layered approach presents layers of barriers that an attacker must go through and compromise to get to the sought-after resource. Running antivirus software only on workstations is not a layered approach in battling viruses. Running antivirus software on each workstation, file server, and mail server and applying content filtering via a proxy server is considered a layered approach toward combating viruses. This is just one example of what has to take place.

How is file access protection provided in a layered approach? If an administrator puts all users in specific groups and dictates what those groups can and cannot do with the company's files, this is only one layer in the approach. To properly protect file access, the administrator must do the following:

- Configure application, file, and registry access control lists (ACLs) to provide more granularity to users' and groups' file permissions

- Configure the system default user rights (in a Windows environment) to give certain types of users certain types of rights

- Consider the physical security of the environment and the computers, and apply restraints where required

- Place users into groups that have implicit permissions necessary to perform their duties and no more

- Draft and enforce a strict logon credential policy so that not all users are logging on as the same user

- Implement monitoring and auditing of file access and actions to identify any suspicious activity

Sound like overkill? It really isn't. If an administrator makes all users log in using different accounts, applies file and registry ACLs, configures groups, and monitors audit logs but does not consider physical security, a user could use a floppy disk with a simple program to get around all other security barriers. All of these components must work in a synergistic manner to provide a blanket of security that individual security mechanisms could not fulfill on their own.

# An Architectural View

Once we look at different types of vulnerabilities, attacks, and threats, we find that they exist at different layers within a network. This digs into more of the technology of an environment and the complexity of each of these technologies at each layer. This applies to the various protocols, applications, hardware, and security mechanisms that work at one or more of the seven layers of the OSI model. (The OSI model is fully described in Chapter 7.) IP spoofing is an attack at the network layer, ARP attacks happen at the data link layer, traffic sniffing happens at several layers, and viruses enter through the application layer. If an organization just employs strict password rules and a firewall, this leaves many layers vulnerable to other types of attacks.

Organizations often put too much faith in their new shiny firewalls, IDSs, or antivirus software. Once one or more of these solutions are implemented, a false sense of security may lull the IT staff and travel up to management. It is more important to look at the flow of data in and out of a network and how the applications and devices work together. This is an architectural view, versus a device or application view.

Taking an architectural view, you must look at the data flow in and out of the environment, how this data is being accessed, modified, and monitored at different points, and how all the security solutions relate to each other in different situations. The firewall, for instance, is only part of the overall architecture. It is the architecture itself that needs to have an adequate level of security, not just the firewall. A network could either perform as a well-tuned orchestra or as several pieces that play wonderfully by themselves but give you a headache when they are all brought into the same room. Each individual security component could be doing its job by protecting its piece of the network, but the security function may be lost when it is time to interrelate or communicate with another security component.

Each environment is dissimilar because of the many variations in installed hardware, software, technologies, and configurations. However, the main differences between environments are the goals each is trying to achieve. A local area network (LAN) provides authentication, resources to its users, and an overall controlled inner atmosphere. A wide area network (WAN) provides connections between users at remote sites through protocol tunneling and access control. An e-commerce arrangement provides a web interface to Internet users, connection to data held on back-end servers, access control, and a different type of authentication from what LANs and WANs use. These diverse goals require different architectures, but can use the same basic security concepts.

Because there are particular levels within an environment, as shown in Figure 2-11, different types of attacks can happen at these levels. (Four of the seven layers of the OSI

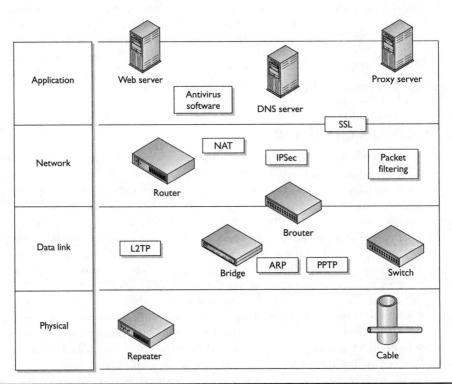

**Figure 2-11** A graphical representation of devices and protocols and where they appear within the OSI model

model are shown in Figure 2-11.) The following is a short list of countermeasures, the layers they work at, and the vulnerabilities they protect against:

- The firewall has packet filtering configured, which provides protection at the network layer. This combats a range of attacks, including some DoS and fragmentation hacks.

- Proxy software configurations protect at the application layer. These combat a range of attacks, including unauthorized access and packet spoofing.

- Network address translation (NAT) works at the network layer. This hides LAN IP addresses and topology.

- Shielded twisted pair (STP) cabling works at the physical layer. This helps protect against network eavesdropping and signal interference.

- A network intrusion detection sensor monitors network traffic at the network layer for known attack signatures. This identifies known attacks and resets TCP connections if necessary.

- IP Security (IPSec), which works at the network layer, is configured for virtual private network (VPN) connections into the perimeter network. This protects against masquerading, data manipulation, and unauthorized access to confidential information via encryption.

- Web server configuration provides protection within the application by using different sites for public versus confidential information. This protects against directory hopping and unauthorized access.

- Only necessary services and ports are enabled on all perimeter devices, which work at the network and transport layers. This reduces entry points into the network and DoS attacks.

- The mail server uses a store-and-forward method of messaging and runs antivirus software. This protects against viruses and DoS attacks.

- Secure Sockets Layer (SSL), which works at the transport layer, is configured at the web sites when customers need to access personal confidential information. This provides confidentiality and data integrity, and protects against masquerading.

- A network scanner runs a weekly probe on all perimeter network server ports at the network layer to identify new vulnerabilities. This protects against new vulnerabilities resulting from configuration changes or additional technologies being added.

- A web server uses embedded cryptography within Extensible Markup Language (XML) code and Distributed Component Object Model (DCOM) security. This provides confidentiality of information and restricts components from performing risky actions.

- Web servers require valid digital signatures from each other for proper communication. These protect against session hijacking and masquerading.

This list shows a small percentage of the activity that happens at different points of the OSI model and the company's network. If one or more of the devices or software had incorrect configurations or if the environment were missing one of these components, this could leave an open portal for an attacker to gain entry into the network.

## A Layer Missed

Many environments do not contain all the devices and components in the previous list of security vulnerabilities and solutions. The following example shows how employing several security mechanisms can seemingly provide a fully secured environment yet leave a small doorway of opportunity available for the clever attacker to take advantage of.

A network that has a firewall with packet filtering, a proxy server with content filtering, public and private DNS records clearly separated, SSL for Internet users, IPSec for VPN connections, public key infrastructure (PKI), and restricted service and port configuration may seem like a fortified environment, and a network administrator most likely implemented these mechanisms with the best intentions. However, one problem is that it is fortified only for a moment in time. Without a scanning device that probes the environment on a scheduled basis or an IDS that looks out for suspicious activity, the environment could be vulnerable even after the company has spent thousands of dollars to protect it. Technology and business drivers continually change, and so do networks and environments. When you configure a new application, apply a patch, or install a device, the change to the environment could have unpredictable consequences (not to mention the new ways hackers have found to circumvent the original security mechanisms).

## Bringing the Layers Together

It is not always necessary to purchase the newest security solutions on the market or pay top dollar for the hardware solution instead of buying the cheaper software solution. It *is* necessary to be aware of where threats can develop and take steps to make sure all the bases are covered. That's what is meant by a layered approach.

In the computer and network world, the complexity of the levels can be a bit overwhelming at times. The most important first step is to understand the environment that needs to be protected. Many times, new IT members enter an environment that was established years ago by another group of people. The environment is continually added on to; it is never stagnant. Usually, there is not an up-to-date network diagram because IT's current daily tasks are time consuming, there is a lack of useful documentation, and no one person understands how the entire network works. This means that when something goes wrong, 80 percent of the effort and time is spent in a chaotic scramble for a solution. It does not need to work this way, and there would be fewer security compromises if this scene were not so common.

Instead of looking at updating that old network diagram (or creating a first one) as a boring task, you could approach it as a fact-finding mission for crucial information.

Instead of putting down the IT staff after a successful hacker attack, you could change your attitude and think of what new practices need to be employed. New software, patches, and devices should be clearly tested prior to implementation for any unforeseen events. An IDS should be established in potentially vulnerable segments of the network, if not all segments. Security scans to seek out new vulnerabilities should take place regularly, not just when an audit is around the corner. In addition, every network administrator should stay up to date on the recent security compromises, be aware of how changes to the network could open a door to clever attackers, and keep those intrusion detection and antivirus signatures current.

Keeping up to date on network, software, configurations, and education can be overwhelming, but most of us in this line of work love to learn. Being effective in managing security means we will never stop learning.

# Politics and Laws

George W. Bush appointed a cybersecurity czar for the first time in 2001. This is a strong message that the U.S. government realizes the importance of security, both in the government and in the private sectors. Governments all over the world have started to look at computing, and the security issues that surround it, more seriously over the last few years. There is continual dialog about transborder issues pertaining to cryptography, what can be encrypted, at what strength, and by whom. There are also broader issues that come into play when an attack comes from another country that does not regulate such activity or does not consider it be illegal behavior. Different countries' legal systems are meeting many unprecedented challenges with regard to computer security.

As the Internet brings the world closer together, governments are beginning to reach agreements upon matters pertaining to computers, security, boundaries, and acceptable behavior. One sign of countries attempting to get in step with each other is the acceptance of the Common Criteria (which is discussed at length in Chapter 5). Most countries have their own way of evaluating and testing the security and assurance of a system or device. For instance, the United States has used the Trusted Computer System Evaluation Criteria (TCSEC), which is referred to as the Orange Book. The Canadians have the Canadian Trusted Computer Product Evaluation Criteria (CTCPEC), the Europeans have the Information Technology Security Evaluation Criteria (ITSEC), and other countries have developed their own criteria on how to determine the level of trust to place in the security of particular products and systems. The Common Criteria is an attempt to take the best of all of these methods and provide the world with one way of determining a product's security and protection level. In other words, it is an attempt to harmonize and standardize using one common tool to measure trust in products and systems.

Other than different countries viewing computer security differently, another barrier to proper security is how investigators deal with computer crimes. The courts have been running a continual game of catch-up. The legal system cannot keep ahead of (or even in step with) technology, which it must do if it is going to regulate it effectively and determine who is guilty or innocent. It is hard for a judge or jury to declare who is guilty or innocent in a computer crime because they are not educated on these types of crimes. Investigators have a hard time collecting usable evidence to present in court, and defense lawyers have few cases to cite as precedent where similar acts took place, because not many cases exist yet.

In addition, these difficulties start with law enforcement, who have a lack of personnel skilled in computer technology and computer forensics. If a person is accused of a cybercrime, law officers must search for evidence. But what do they search for? Law enforcement personnel do not necessarily know how to dump data from memory into a file or find remnants of data after the criminal has formatted the drive, nor do they necessarily understand how computer crimes take place so that they can look for the right clues. Law enforcement has to know how to remove evidence from computer systems and drives in a way that does not corrupt the data and that preserves its integrity so that it is admissible in court. They must gain much more computer knowledge and skills to be able to deal with computer crimes.

Computers are used in many types of crimes and provide many types of barriers that law enforcement and the courts are not used to dealing with. Data and communication may be encrypted, and there are jurisdiction issues if a crime took place in Europe but originated in North America. Also, much of the communication is spoofed, so law enforcement must know how to track down criminals through binary, hexadecimal, and packet header means.

These barriers and issues help criminals who are computer savvy. If they do get caught, many of them are not prosecuted to the extent they would be if they had committed a crime that the courts were used to dealing with.

Even though law enforcement has been lagging behind with the problem of cybercrime, there are initiatives at many levels to try to deal with the problem. Many international organizations, such as the G8, the United Nations, and the European Union, are trying to promote cooperation and harmonization in dealing with global computer crime.

These are tough issues for local police forces, Interpol, international judicial systems, the FBI, the CIA, and other organizations. However, with change comes growth. Governments are developing laws and procedures to effectively deal with computer crimes. Crime-fighting agencies are increasing personnel to include people with technology skills and are requiring computer security in many parts of these organizations.

# Education

Generally, if a person is considered a security specialist, he has to have the interest and discipline to teach himself security issues, go to seminars and conferences all over the world, read stacks of books, and have a wide range of experience in different environments. There has not been a uniform, standardized way of teaching security in vocational schools or universities. Some educational institutions offer security classes in their CIS or MIS programs, and some offer master's degrees or doctorates in computer security. However, such programs are few and far between.

Networking, programming, and engineering are widely taught. Security may be sprinkled in as an elective or not even offered, because there has not been a high demand or need for this type of knowledge in the job market. However, computer and information security is gaining in importance, need, and demand. This has caused a handful of schools to offer security classes and programs, and they will probably become more available as the job market demands more individuals with this skill set.

Not only do more security courses and programs need to be offered, business, networking, programming, and engineering classes need to integrate security training into them. Security should not be looked upon as an extra component or an option to be added later. It should be interwoven into the code as a program is being developed, and interwoven into the education of our new professionals. It should be an important piece of architecture and engineering. And it should be understood and practiced when networks are being built, added upon, and maintained.

Most governments have recognized that education is an important part of protecting their country's critical infrastructure. Countries have set up criteria for schools to follow, with government grants and subsidiaries awarded as incentives for schools who meet the criteria. If countries want to protect themselves and their resources from computer attacks and cyberattacks, they must provide their citizens with the necessary education.

# Summary

This chapter has touched on only a few of the exciting things that are happening within computer security and presented the types of damages that can be experienced if security is not taken seriously. It has been recognized for quite some time that computers, data processing capabilities, and the Internet are extremely important tools for a vast array of reasons. It has only recently been recognized that securing these items is an important task.

This chapter is intended to prepare you for the chapters that follow. Some chapters, or sections within chapters, might seem more interesting than others, but the CISSP certification was developed to ensure that you broaden your horizon when looking at and dealing with security issues. Information security would not be as effective if it were not provided with strong physical security; thus, it is important to know how each part works, and how they overlap and integrate. No part of security would be totally effective if it were not enforced by regulations, laws, and liability responsibilities. The courts and law enforcement agencies are becoming more involved in many issues of computer security, and understanding these issues can help you determine what is acceptable and what is illegal, and how to deal with the issues that fall in between.

Each chapter hereafter ends with a section called "Quick Tips." This section provides a clear-cut bulleted list of items that outlines what is important in the chapter for the CISSP exam. The same is true for the questions at the end of the chapter and on the accompanying CD-ROM; they help you zero in on some of the most critical concepts in the chapter. As stated before, these questions are presented in a way to prepare you for the exam. Each type of exam has its own way of asking questions. Novell and Microsoft may give simulations and long-winded, scenario-based questions. Cisco gives short questions that get right to the point. (ISC)$^2$ asks short, cognitive questions. Knowing how the exam is structured will help you achieve the CISSP certification.

# Information Security and Risk Management

This chapter presents the following:

- Security management responsibilities
- Difference between administrative, technical, and physical controls
- Three main security principles
- Risk management and risk analysis
- Security policies
- Information classification
- Security-awareness training

We hear about viruses causing millions of dollars in damages, hackers from other countries capturing credit card information from financial institutions, web sites of large corporations and governments being defaced for political reasons, and hackers being caught and sent to jail. These are the more exciting aspects of computer security, but realistically these activities are not what the average corporation or security professional usually has to deal with when it comes to daily or monthly security tasks. Although viruses and hacking get all the headlines, security management is the core of a company's business and information security structure.

## Security Management

Security management includes risk management, information security policies, procedures, standards, guidelines, baselines, information classification, security organization, and security education. These core components serve as the foundation of a corporation's security program. The objective of security, and a security program, is to protect the company and its assets. A risk analysis identifies these assets, discovers the threats that put them at risk, and estimates the possible damage and potential loss a company could endure if any of these threats become real. The results of the risk analysis help management construct a budget with the necessary funds to protect the recognized assets from their identified threats and develop applicable security policies that provide direction for security activities. Security education takes this information to each and every employee within the company so that everyone is properly informed and can more easily work toward the same security goals.

Security management has changed over the years because networked environments, computers, and the applications that hold information have changed. Information used to be held in a mainframe, which is a more centralized network structure. The mainframe and management consoles that were used to access and configure the mainframe were placed in a centralized area instead of the distributed networks we see today. Only certain people were allowed access and only a small set of people knew how the mainframe worked, which drastically reduced security risks. Users were able to access information on the mainframe through dumb terminals (they were called this because they had little or no logic built into them). This also drastically reduced the need for strict security controls to be put into place. However, the computing society did not stay in this type of architecture. Now, most networks are filled with personal computers that have advanced logic and processing power, users know enough about the systems to be dangerous, and the information is not centralized within one "glass house." Instead, the information lives on servers, workstations, and other networks. Information passes over wires and airways at a rate that was not even conceived of 10 to 15 years ago.

The Internet, extranets (business partner networks), and intranets not only make security much more complex, they make security even more critical. The core network architecture has changed from being a localized, stand-alone computing environment to a distributed computing environment that has increased exponentially with complexity. Although connecting a network to the Internet adds more functionality and services for the users and expands the company's visibility to the Internet world, it opens the floodgates to potential security risks.

Today, a majority of organizations could not function if they were to lose their computers and computing capabilities. Computers have been integrated into the business and individual daily fabric, and their sudden unavailability would cause great pain and disruption. Many of the larger corporations already realize that their *data* is as much an asset to be protected as their physical buildings, factory equipment, and other physical assets. As networks and environments have changed, so has the need for security. Security is more than just a firewall and a router with an access list; these systems have to be managed, and a big part of security is managing the actions of users and the procedures they follow. This brings us to security management practices, which focus on the continuous protection of company assets.

# Security Management Responsibilities

*Okay, who is in charge and why?*

In the world of security, management's functions involve determining objectives, scope, policies, priorities, standards, and strategies. Management needs to define a clear scope and, before 100 people run off in different directions trying to secure the environment, determine actual goals that are expected to be accomplished from a security program. Management also needs to evaluate business objectives, security risks, user productivity, and functionality requirements and objectives. Finally, management must define steps to ensure that all of these issues are accounted for and properly addressed.

Many companies look at the business and productivity elements of the equation only and figure that information and computer security fall within the IT administrator's responsibilities. In these situations, management is not taking computer and information security seriously, the consequence of which is that security will most likely remain underdeveloped, unsupported, underfunded, and unsuccessful. Security needs to be addressed at the highest levels of management. The IT administrator can consult with management on the subject, but the security of a company should not be delegated entirely to the IT administrator.

Security management relies on properly identifying and valuing a company's assets, and then implementing security policies, procedures, standards, and guidelines to provide integrity, confidentiality, and availability for those assets. Various management tools are used to classify data and perform risk analysis and assessments. These tools identify vulnerabilities and exposure rates and rank the severity of identified vulnerabilities so that effective countermeasures can be implemented to mitigate risk in a cost-effective manner. Management's responsibility is to provide protection for the resources it is responsible for and the company overall. These resources come in human, capital, hardware, and informational forms. Management must concern itself with ensuring that a security program is set up that recognizes the threats that can affect these resources and be assured that the necessary protective measures are put into effect.

The necessary resources and funding need to be available and strategic representatives need to be ready to participate in the security program. Management must assign responsibility and identify the roles necessary to get the security program off the ground and keep it thriving and evolving as the environment changes. Management must also integrate the program into the current business environment and monitor its accomplishments. Management's support is one of the most important pieces of a security program. A simple nod and a wink will not provide the amount of support required.

## The Top-Down Approach to Security

*I will be making the rules around here. Response: You are nowhere near the top—thank goodness!*

When a house is built, the workers start with a blueprint of the structure, then pour the foundation, and then erect the frame. As the building of the house continues, the workers know what the end result is supposed to be, so they add the right materials, insert doors and windows as specified in the blueprints, erect support beams, provide sturdy ceilings and floors, and add the plaster and carpet and smaller details until the house is complete. Then inspectors come in to ensure that the structure of the house and the components that were used to make it are acceptable. If this process did not start with a blueprint and a realized goal, the house could end up with an unstable foundation and doors and windows that don't shut properly. This house would not pass inspection; thus, a lot of time and money would have been wasted.

Building a security program is analogous to building a house. When designing and implementing a security program, the project managers need to determine the functionality and realize the end result expected. Many times, companies just start locking down computers and installing firewalls without taking the time to understand the overall security requirements, goals, and assurance levels they expect from security as a whole within their environment. The team involved in the process should start from the top with very broad ideas and terms and work its way down to detailed configuration settings and system parameters. At each step, the team needs to keep in mind the overall security goals so that each piece that it adds is sure to provide more granularity to the intended goal; this helps the team to avoid splintering the main objectives by running in 15 different directions at once.

The security policy works as a blueprint for a company's security program and provides the necessary foundation to build upon. This policy needs to be taken seriously from the beginning and developed with the idea that it will continually be reviewed to ensure that all security components stay in step and work to accomplish the same objectives and business goals.

The next step is to develop and implement procedures, standards, and guidelines that support the security policy and identify the security countermeasures and methods that need to be put into place. Once these items are developed, the security program increases in granularity by developing baselines and configurations for the chosen security controls and methods.

If security starts with a solid foundation and develops over time with understood goals and objectives, a company does not need to make drastic changes midstream. The process can be methodical, requiring less time, funds, and resources, and provide a proper balance between functionality and protection. This is not the norm, but with your insight, maybe you can help your company approach security in a more controlled manner. You could provide the necessary vision and understanding of how security should be properly planned, implemented, and evolved in an organized manner, thereby helping the company to avoid a result that is a giant heap of security products that are disjointed and full of flaws.

A security program should use a *top-down approach*, meaning that the initiation, support, and direction come from top management and work their way through middle management and then to staff members. In contrast, a *bottom-up approach* refers to a situation in which the IT department tries to develop a security program without getting proper management support and direction. A bottom-up approach is usually less effective, not broad enough, and doomed to fail. A top-down approach makes sure that the people actually responsible for protecting the company's assets (senior management) are driving the program.

# Security Administration and Supporting Controls

If there is not a current security administration role, one should be established by management. The security administration role is directly responsible for monitoring a majority of the facets of a security program. Depending on the organization, security needs, and size of the environment, the security administration may consist of one person or a group of individuals who work in a central or decentralized manner. Whatever its size, the security administration requires a clear reporting structure, understanding of responsibilities, and testing and monitoring capabilities, to make sure that compromises do not slip in because of a lack of communication or comprehension.

Information owners should dictate which users can access their resources and what those users can do with those resources after they access them. The security administration's job is to make sure that these objectives are implemented. The following controls should be utilized to achieve the management's security directives:

- **Administrative controls**  Include the developing and publishing of policies, standards, procedures, and guidelines; the screening of personnel; conducting security-awareness training; and implementing change control procedures.

- **Technical controls (also called logical controls)**  Consist of implementing and maintaining access control mechanisms, password and resource management, identification and authentication methods, security devices, and configuration of the infrastructure.

- **Physical controls**  Entail controlling individual access into the facility and different departments, locking systems and removing unnecessary floppy or CD-ROM drives, protecting the perimeter of the facility, monitoring for intrusion, and environmental controls.

Figure 3-1 illustrates how the administrative, technical, and physical controls work together to provide the necessary level of protection.

The *information owner* is usually a senior executive within the management group of the company, or head of a specific department. The information owner has the

**Figure 3-1**  Administrative, technical, and physical controls should work in a synergistic manner to protect a company's assets.

corporate responsibility for data protection and would be the one held liable for any negligence when it comes to protecting the company's information assets. The person who holds this role is responsible for assigning classifications to information and dictating how the data should be protected. If the information owner does not lay out the foundation of data protection and ensure that the directives are being enforced, she would be violating the due care concept.

 **NOTE** *Due care* is a legal term and concept used to help determine liability in a court of law. If someone is practicing due care, then they are acting responsibly and will have a lower probability of being found negligent and liable if something bad takes place.

By having a security administration group, a company ensures that it does not lose focus on security and that it has a hierarchical structure of responsibility in place. The security officer's job is to ensure that management's security directives are fulfilled, not to construct those directives in the first place. There should be a clear communication path between the security administration group and senior management to ensure that the security program receives the proper support and that management makes the decisions. Too often, senior management is extremely disconnected from security issues, despite the fact that when a serious security breach takes place, senior management has to explain the reasons to business partners, shareholders, and the public. After this humbling experience, the opposite problem tends to arise—senior management becomes too involved. A healthy relationship between the security administration group

## Example of Security Management

Anyone who has been involved with a security initiative understands that it involves a balancing act between securing an environment and still allowing the necessary level of functionality so that productivity is not affected. A common scenario that occurs at the start of many security projects is that the individuals in charge of the project know the end result they want to achieve and have lofty ideas of how quick and efficient their security rollout will be, but they fail to consult the users regarding what restrictions will be placed upon them. The users, upon finding out about the restrictions, then inform the project managers that they will not be able to fulfill certain parts of their job if the security rollout actually takes place as planned. This usually causes the project to screech to a halt. The project managers then have to initialize the proper assessments, evaluations, and planning to see how the environment can be slowly secured and how to ease users and tasks delicately into new restrictions or ways of doing business. Failing to consult users during the planning phase causes a lot of headaches and wastes time and money. Individuals who are responsible for security management activities must realize that they need to understand the environment and plan properly before they try to kick off the implementation phase of a security program.

and senior management should be developed from the beginning and communication should easily flow in both directions.

Inadequate management can undermine the entire security effort in a company. Among the possible reasons for inadequate management are that management does not fully understand the necessity of security; security is in competition with other management goals; management views security as expensive and unnecessary; or management applies lip service instead of real support to security. Powerful and useful technologies, devices, software packages, procedures, and methodologies are available to provide the exact level of security required, but without proper security management and management support, none of this really matters.

# Fundamental Principles of Security

*Now, what are we trying to accomplish again?*

There are several small and large objectives of a security program, but the main three principles in all programs are availability, integrity, and confidentiality. These are referred to as the *AIC triad*. The level of security required to accomplish these principles differs per company, because each has its own unique combination of business and security goals and requirements. All security controls, mechanisms, and safeguards are implemented to provide one or more of these principles, and all risks, threats, and vulnerabilities are measured for their potential capability to compromise one or all of the AIC principles. Figure 3-2 illustrates the AIC triad. Some documentation on this topic may reverse the acronym order, and call it the *CIA triad*. It still refers to the same concepts shown in Figure 3-2.

**Figure 3-2**
The AIC triad

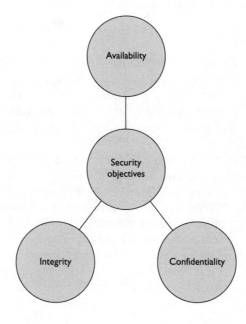

## Availability

*Emergency! I can't get to my data! Response: Turn the computer on!*

The systems and networks should provide adequate capacity in order to perform in a predictable manner with an acceptable level of performance. They should be able to recover from disruptions in a secure and quick manner so that productivity is not negatively affected. Single points of failure should be avoided, backup measures should be taken, redundancy mechanisms should be in place when necessary, and the negative effects from environmental components should be prevented. Necessary protection mechanisms need to be in place to protect against inside and outside threats that could affect the availability and productivity of the network, systems, and information. *Availability* ensures reliability and timely access to data and resources to authorized individuals.

System availability can be affected by device or software failure. Backup devices should be used and available to quickly replace critical systems, and employees should be skilled and available to make the necessary adjustments to bring the system back online. Environmental issues like heat, cold, humidity, static electricity, and contaminants can also affect system availability. These issues are addressed in detail in Chapter 6. Systems should be protected from these elements, properly grounded electrically, and closely monitored.

Denial-of-service (DoS) attacks are popular methods for hackers to disrupt a company's system availability and productivity. These attacks are mounted to reduce the ability of users to access system resources and information. To protect against these attacks, only the necessary services and ports should be available on systems, and intrusion detection systems (IDS) should monitor the network traffic and host activities. Certain firewall and router configurations can also reduce the threat of DoS attacks and possibly stop them from occurring.

## Integrity

*Integrity* is upheld when the assurance of accuracy and reliability of information and systems is provided, and unauthorized modification is prevented. Hardware, software, and communication mechanisms must work in a concerted manner to maintain and process data correctly and move data to intended destinations without unexpected alteration. The systems and network should be protected from outside interference and contamination.

Environments that enforce and provide this attribute of security ensure that attackers, or mistakes by users, do not compromise the integrity of systems or data. When an attacker inserts a virus, logic bomb, or back door into a system, the system's integrity is compromised. This can, in turn, negatively affect the integrity of information held on the system by corruption, malicious modification, or replacement of data with incorrect data. Strict access controls, intrusion detection, and hashing can combat these threats.

Users usually affect a system or its data's integrity by mistake (although internal users may also commit malicious deeds). For example, a user with a full hard drive may unwittingly delete configuration files under the mistaken assumption that deleting a boot.ini file must be okay because they don't remember ever using it. Or, for example, a user may insert incorrect values into a data processing application that ends up charging a customer $3,000,000 instead of $300. Incorrectly modifying data kept in databases is another common way that users accidentally corrupt data, a mistake that can have lasting effects.

Security should streamline the users' capabilities and give them only certain choices and functionality so that errors become less common and less devastating. System-critical files should be restricted from the users' view and access. Applications should provide mechanisms that check for valid and reasonable input values. Databases should let only authorized individuals modify data, and data in transit should be protected by encryption or other mechanisms.

## Confidentiality

*Confidentiality* ensures that the necessary level of secrecy is enforced at each junction of data processing and prevents unauthorized disclosure. This level of confidentiality should prevail while data resides on systems and devices within the network, as it is transmitted, and once it reaches its destination.

Attackers can thwart confidentiality mechanisms by network monitoring, shoulder surfing, stealing password files, and social engineering. These topics will be addressed in more depth in later chapters, but briefly, *shoulder surfing* is when a person looks over another person's shoulder and watches their keystrokes or views data as it appears on a computer screen. *Social engineering* is when one person tricks another person into sharing confidential information by posing as someone authorized to have access to that information.

Users can intentionally or accidentally disclose sensitive information by not encrypting it before sending it to another person, by falling prey to a social engineering attack, by sharing a company's trade secrets, or by not using extra care to protect confidential information when processing it.

Confidentiality can be provided by encrypting data as it is stored and transmitted, by using network traffic padding, strict access control, and data classification, and by training personnel on the proper procedures.

Availability, integrity, and confidentiality are critical principles of security. You should understand their meaning, how they are provided by different mechanisms, and how their absence can negatively affect an environment, all of which help you to best identify problems and provide proper solutions.

# Security Definitions

*I am vulnerable and see you as a threat. Response: Good.*

The words "vulnerability," "threat," "risk," and "exposure" often are used to represent the same thing even though they have different meanings and relationships to each other. It is important to understand each word's definition, but more important to understand its relationship to the other concepts.

A *vulnerability* is a software, hardware, or procedural weakness that may provide an attacker the open door he is looking for to enter a computer or network and have unauthorized access to resources within the environment. A vulnerability characterizes the absence or weakness of a safeguard that could be exploited. This vulnerability may be a service running on a server, unpatched applications or operating system software, unrestricted modem dial-in access, an open port on a firewall, lax physical security that allows anyone to enter a server room, or nonenforced password management on servers and workstations.

A *threat* is any potential danger to information or systems. The threat is that someone, or something, will identify a specific vulnerability and use it against the company or individual. The entity that takes advantage of a vulnerability is referred to as a *threat agent*. A threat agent could be an intruder accessing the network through a port on the firewall, a process accessing data in a way that violates the security policy, a tornado wiping out a facility, or an employee making an unintentional mistake that could expose confidential information or destroy a file's integrity.

A *risk* is the likelihood of a threat agent taking advantage of a vulnerability and the corresponding business impact. If a firewall has several ports open, there is a higher likelihood that an intruder will use one to access the network in an unauthorized method. If users are not educated on processes and procedures, there is a higher likelihood that an employee will make an intentional or unintentional mistake that may destroy data. If an IDS is not implemented on a network, there is a higher likelihood that an attack will go unnoticed until it is too late. Risk ties the vulnerability, threat, and likelihood of exploitation to the resulting business impact.

An *exposure* is an instance of being exposed to losses from a threat agent. A vulnerability exposes an organization to possible damages. If password management is lax and password rules are not enforced, the company is exposed to the possibility of having users' passwords captured and used in an unauthorized manner. If a company does not have its wiring inspected and does not put proactive fire prevention steps into place, it exposes itself to potentially devastating fires.

A *countermeasure*, or *safeguard*, is put into place to mitigate the potential risk. A countermeasure may be a software configuration, a hardware device, or procedure that eliminates a vulnerability or reduces the likelihood that a threat agent will be able to exploit a vulnerability. Examples of countermeasures include strong password management, a security guard, access control mechanisms within an operating system, the implementation of basic input/output system (BIOS) passwords, and security-awareness training.

If a company has antivirus software but does not keep the virus signatures up-to-date, this is a vulnerability. The company is vulnerable to virus attacks. The threat is that a virus will show up in the environment and disrupt productivity. The likelihood of a virus showing up in the environment and causing damage is the risk. If a virus infiltrates the company's environment, then a vulnerability has been exploited and the company is exposed to loss. The countermeasures in this situation are to update the signatures and install the antivirus software on all computers. The relationships among risks, vulnerabilities, threats, and countermeasures are shown in Figure 3-3.

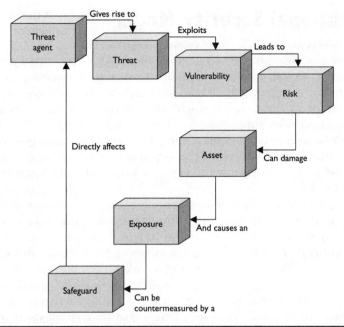

**Figure 3-3** The relationships among the different security components

Applying the right countermeasure can eliminate the vulnerability and exposure and reduce the risk. The company cannot eliminate the threat agent, but it can protect itself and prevent this threat agent from exploiting vulnerabilities within the environment.

## References

- **NIST Computer Security Resource Center**   csrc.ncsl.nist.gov
- **CISSP and SSCP Open Study Guides**   www.cccure.org
- **CISSP.com**   www.cissps.com

---

**Order of Concepts**

The proper order in which to evaluate these concepts as they apply to your own network is threat, exposure, vulnerability, countermeasures, and finally risk. This is because there can be a threat (new SQL attack) but unless your company has the corresponding vulnerability (SQL server with the necessary configuration), then the company is not exposed and it is not a vulnerability. If the vulnerability does reside in the environment, then a countermeasure is applied to reduce the risk.

# Organizational Security Model

*My security model is shaped like a pile of oatmeal. Response: Lovely.*

An organizational security model is a framework made up of many entities, protection mechanisms, logical, administrative, and physical components, procedures, business processes, and configurations that all work together in a synergistic way to provide a security level for an environment. Each model is different, but all models work in layers: one layer provides support for the layer above it and protection for the layer below it. Because a security model is a framework, companies are free to plug in different types of technologies, methods, and procedures to accomplish the necessary protection level for their environment. Figure 3-4 illustrates the pieces that can make up a security model.

Effective security requires a balanced approach and application of all security components and procedures. Some security components are technical (access control lists and encryption) and some are nontechnical (physical and administrative, such as developing a security policy and enforcing compliance), but each has an important place within the framework, and if one is missing or incomplete, the whole framework may be affected.

A security model has various layers, but it also has different types of goals to accomplish in different timeframes. You might have a goal for yourself today to brush your teeth, run three miles, finish the project you have been working on, and spend time with your kids. These are daily goals, or *operational goals*. You might have midterm goals to complete your master's degree, write a book, and get promoted. These take

**Figure 3-4** A comprehensive and effective security model has many integrated pieces.

more time and effort and are referred to as *tactical goals*. Your long-term goals may be to retire at age 55, save enough money to live comfortably, and live on a houseboat. These goals are *strategic goals* because they look farther into the future.

The same thing happens in security planning. Daily goals, or operational goals, focus on productivity and task-oriented activities to ensure that the company functions in a smooth and predictable manner. A midterm goal, or tactical goal, could be to integrate all workstations and resources into one domain so that more central control can be achieved. Long-term goals, or strategic goals, could be to move all the branches from dedicated communication lines to frame relay, implement IPSec virtual private networks (VPNs) for all remote users, and integrate wireless technology with the necessary security measures into the environment.

This approach to planning is called the *planning horizon*. A company usually cannot implement all changes at once, and some changes are larger than others. Many times, certain changes cannot happen until other changes take place. If a company wants to implement its own certificate authority and implement a full public key infrastructure (PKI) enterprise-wide, this cannot happen in a week if the company currently works in decentralized workgroups with no domain structure. So, its operational goals would be to keep production running smoothly and make small steps toward readying the environment for a domain structure. Its tactical goal would be to put all workstations and resources into a domain structure, and centralize access control and authentication. Its strategic goal would be to have all workstations, servers, and devices within the enterprise use the PKI to provide authentication, encryption, and more secure communication channels.

Security works best if the company's operational, tactical, and strategic goals are defined and work to support each other, which can be much harder than it sounds.

## Security Program Components

*I have a security policy, so I must have a security program. Response: You have just begun, my friend.*

Today, organizations, corporations, government agencies, and individuals are more involved in information security than ever before. With more regulations being promulgated by governments, continuing increases in both the number of attacks and the cost of fighting hackers and malware, and increasing dependence upon computing technology, concerns about information security are expanding from IT departments to the board rooms.

Most security professionals welcome this shift because it means that the decision makers are finally involved and more progress can be made enterprise-wide. Experienced security professionals have always known that technology is just a small portion of overall organizational security. Business people, who are now becoming more responsible and liable for security, are not so thrilled about this shift.

The common scenario in businesses and organizations is as follows: A CEO and board members eventually are forced to look at information security because of new regulations, because the costs of viruses and attacks have reached a threshold, or because a civil suit has been filed regarding a security breach. The company typically hires a consultant, who tells the CEO and board that they need a security policy and a network assessment. The company usually pays for both to be done and, with that accomplished, believes that the company is secure. However, this is a false sense of security, because the company still has no security program.

The company then hires a security officer (typically called either Corporate Security Officer [CSO] or Corporate Information Security Officer [CISO]). Senior management hires this person so that it can delegate all security activities and responsibilities, and get security off of their desk, but fails to give this person any real authority or budget. Then, when security compromises take place, the CSO becomes the sacrificial lamb—because we always need someone to blame.

Now, as security professionals, we have three choices for dealing with this common scenario:

- Stick our heads in the sand and hope all of this just goes away.
- Continue to be frustrated and confused, develop ulcers, and shake our fists at the unfriendly security gods in the sky.
- Understand that we, as a society, are in the first basic steps of our evolution in information security and therefore must be committed to learn and practice the industry's already developed best practices.

## Confusion and Security

Today, many business-oriented people who are not security professionals are responsible for rolling out security programs and solutions. Without proper education and training on these matters, companies end up wasting a lot of time and money.

"Implement port authentication, an IPSec VPN, a trusted front end, and intrusion prevention."

"To prevent a trusted front end we need to use IPSec to protect against port authentication."

Developing and rolling out a security program is not as difficult as many organizations make it, but it is new to them and new things are usually scary and confusing. This is why they should turn to standards and industry best practices, which provide the guidance and recipe for how to set up and implement a full security program.

The most commonly used standard is ISO 17799, which was derived from the de facto standard British Standard 7799 (BS 7799). It is an internationally recognized Information Security Management Standard that provides high-level, conceptual recommendations on enterprise security. It consists of two parts. Part 1 is an implementation guide with guidelines on how to build a comprehensive information security infrastructure. Part 2 is an auditing guide based on requirements that must be met for an organization to be deemed compliant with ISO 17799.

While there has been planty of controversy regarding the benefits and drawbacks of ISO 17799, it is the agreed upon mechanism to describe security processes and is the benchmark we use to indicate a "correct infrastructure." It is made up of ten domains, which are very close to the CISSP Common Body of Knowledge (CBK).

The ISO 17799 domains are as follows:

- **Information security policy for the organization**  Map of business objectives to security, management's support, security goals, and responsibilities.

- **Creation of information security infrastructure**  Create and maintain an organizational security structure through the use of security forum, security officer, defining security responsibilities, authorization process, outsourcing, and independent review.

- **Asset classification and control**  Develop a security infrastructure to protect organizational assets through accountability and inventory, classification, and handling procedures.

- **Personnel security**  Reduce risks that are inherent in human interaction by screening employees, defining roles and responsibilities, training employees properly, and documenting the ramifications of not meeting expectations.

- **Physical and environmental security**  Protect the organization's assets by properly choosing a facility location, erecting and maintaining a security perimeter, implementing access control, and protecting equipment.

- **Communications and operations management**  Carry out operations security through operational procedures, proper change control, incident handling, separation of duties, capacity planning, network management, and media handling.

- **Access control**  Control access to assets based on business requirements, user management, authentication methods, and monitoring.

- **System development and maintenance**  Implement security in all phases of a system's lifetime through development of security requirements, cryptography, integrity, and software development procedures.

- **Business continuity management**   Counter disruptions of normal operations by using continuity planning and testing.

- **Compliance**   Comply with regulatory, contractual, and statutory requirements by using technical controls, system audits, and legal awareness.

The ISO 17799 outlines the components that should make up each and every security program implemented today. Since companies and organizations are different, the emphasis on specific components may vary from one security program to the next, but each security program should be made up of these core elements.

## References

- **The ISO 17799 Service & Software Directory**   www.iso17799software.com
- **The ISO 17799 Directory**   www.iso-17799.com
- **The ISO 17799 Community Portal**   www.17799.com

## Business Requirements: Private Industry vs. Military Organizations

Which security model an organization should choose depends on its critical missions and business requirements. Private industry usually has much different missions and requirements than those of the military. Private industry thrives by beating the competition, which is done through marketing and sales, solid management decisions, understanding the target audience, and understanding the flow and ebb of the market. A private-sector business has a better chance of being successful if its data is readily available, so processing order requests and fulfilling service orders can happen quickly and painlessly for the customer. The data also needs to be accurate to satisfy the customers' needs. Out of the three security services (availability, integrity, and confidentiality), data integrity and availability usually rank higher than confidentiality to most private-sector businesses when compared to military requirements.

The military also thrives by beating its competition (other countries or its enemies), which requires proper training, readiness, intelligence, and deployment. Although the private industry does need a degree of secrecy and ensured confidentiality, confidentiality does not play as important of a role as it does with a military organization. The military has more critical information that must not fall into the wrong hands; therefore, out of the three main security services, confidentiality is the most important to the military sector. Thus, a military installation must implement a security model that emphasizes confidentiality and is stricter than a private-sector organization's security model.

# Information Risk Management

*Life is full of risk.*

Risk is the possibility of damage happening and the ramifications of such damage should it occur. *Information risk management (IRM)* is the *process* of identifying and assessing risk, reducing it to an acceptable level, and implementing the right mechanisms to maintain that level. There is no such thing as a 100 percent secure environment. Every environment has vulnerabilities and threats to a certain degree. The skill is in identifying these threats, assessing the probability of them actually occurring and the damage they could cause, and then taking the right steps to reduce the overall level of risk in the environment to what the organization identifies as acceptable.

Risks to a company come in different forms, and they are not all computer related. When a company purchases another company, it takes on a lot of risk in the hope that this move will increase its market base, productivity, and profitability. If a company increases its product line, this can add overhead, increase the need for personnel and storage facilities, require more funding for different materials, and maybe increase insurance premiums and the expense of marketing campaigns. The risk is that this added overhead might not be matched in sales; thus, profitability will be reduced or not accomplished.

When we look at information security, there are several types of risk a corporation needs to be aware of and address properly. The following items touch on the major categories:

- **Physical damage**   Fire, water, vandalism, power loss, and natural disasters
- **Human interaction**   Accidental or intentional action or inaction that can disrupt productivity
- **Equipment malfunction**   Failure of systems and peripheral devices
- **Inside and outside attacks**   Hacking, cracking, and attacking
- **Misuse of data**   Sharing trade secrets, fraud, espionage, and theft
- **Loss of data**   Intentional or unintentional loss of information through destructive means
- **Application error**   Computation errors, input errors, and buffer overflows

The threats need to be identified, classified by category, and evaluated to calculate their actual magnitude of potential loss. Real risk is hard to measure, but prioritizing the potential risks in order of which risk needs to be addressed first is attainable.

## Who Really Understands Risk Management?

Unfortunately, the answer to this question is that not enough people inside or outside of the security profession really understand risk management. Even though information security is "big business" today, the focus is more on applications, devices, protocols, viruses, and hacking. Although these items all need to be considered and weighed in risk management processes, they should be considered small pieces of the overall security puzzle, not the main focus of risk management.

Security is now a business issue, but businesses operate to make money, not to just be secure. A business is concerned with security only if it threatens its bottom line, which it can in many ways: loss of reputation and customer base after a database of credit card numbers is compromised; loss of thousands of dollars in operational expenses from a new computer worm; loss of proprietary information as a result of successful company espionage attempts; loss of confidential information from a successful social engineering attack; and so on. It is critical that security professionals understand these individual threats, but it is more important that they understand how to calculate the risk of these threats and map them to business drivers.

Knowing the difference between the definitions of "vulnerability," "threat," and "risk" may seem trivial to you, but it is more critical than most people truly understand. A vulnerability scanner can identify dangerous services that are running, unnecessary accounts, and unpatched systems. That is the easy part. But if you have a security budget of only $120,000 and you have a long list of vulnerabilities that need attention, do you have the proper skill to know which ones should be dealt with first? Since you have a finite amount of money and an almost infinite number of vulnerabilities, how do you properly rank the most critical vulnerabilities to ensure that your company is addressing the most critical issues *and* providing the most return on investment of funds?

This is what risk management is all about, and to organizations, corporations, and businesses across the world, it is more important than IDS, ethical hacking, malware, and firewalls. But risk management is not as "sexy" and therefore does not get its necessary attention or implementation.

## Information Risk Management Policy

*How do I put all of these risk management pieces together? Response: Let's check out the policy.*

Proper risk management requires a strong commitment from senior management, a documented process that supports the organization's mission, an IRM policy, and a delegated IRM team.

The IRM policy should be a subset of the organization's overall risk management policy (*risks to a company include more than just information security issues*) and should be mapped to the organizational security policies. The IRM policy should address the following items:

- Objectives of IRM team
- Level of risk the company will accept and what is considered an acceptable risk
- Formal processes of risk identification
- Connection between the IRM policy and the organization's strategic planning processes
- Responsibilities that fall under IRM and the roles that are to fulfill them

- Mapping of risk to internal controls
- Approach for changing staff behaviors and resource allocation in response to risk analysis
- Mapping of risks to performance targets and budgets
- Key indicators to monitor the effectiveness of controls

The IRM policy provides the infrastructure for the organization's risk management processes and procedures and should address all issues of information security, from personnel screening and the insider threat to physical security and firewalls. It should provide direction on how the IRM team relates information on company risks to senior management and how to properly execute management's decisions on risk mitigation tasks.

## Risk Management Team

Each organization is different in its size, security posture requirements, and security budget. One organization may have one individual responsible for IRM (poor soul) or a team that works in a coordinated manner. The overall goal of the team is to ensure that the company is protected in the most cost-effective manner. This goal can be accomplished only if the following components are in place:

- An established risk acceptance level provided by senior management
- Documented risk assessment processes and procedures
- Procedures for identifying and mitigating risks
- Appropriate resource and fund allocation from senior management
- Contingency plans where assessments indicate that they are necessary
- Security-awareness training for all staff members associated with information assets
- Ability to establish improvement (or risk mitigation) teams in specific areas when necessary
- Mapping of legal and regulation compliancy requirements to control and implement requirements
- Development of metrics and performance indicators to be able to measure and manage various types of risks
- Ability to identify and assess new risks as the environment and company changes
- Integration of IRM and the organization's change control process to ensure that changes do not introduce new vulnerabilities

Obviously, this list is a lot more than just buying a new shiny firewall and calling the company safe.

The IRM team, in most cases, is not made up of employees with the dedicated task of risk management. It consists of people who already have a full-time job in the company and are now tasked with something else. Thus, senior management support is necessary, so that proper resource allocation can take place.

Of course, all teams need a leader, and IRM is no different. One individual should be singled out to run this rodeo and, in larger organizations, this person should be spending 50 to 70 percent of their time in this role. Management needs to dedicate funds for this person to have the necessary training and risk analysis tools to ensure that it is a successful endeavor.

# Risk Analysis

*I have determined that our greatest risk is this paperclip. Response: Nice work.*

**Risk analysis**, which is really a tool for risk management, is a method of identifying vulnerabilities and threats and assessing the possible damage to determine where to implement security safeguards. Risk analysis is used to ensure that security is cost effective, relevant, timely, and responsive to threats. Security can be quite complex, even for well-versed security professionals, and it is easy to apply too much security, not enough security, or the wrong security components, and spend too much money in the process without attaining the necessary objectives. Risk analysis helps companies prioritize their risks and shows management the amount of money that should be applied to protecting against those risks in a sensible manner.

A risk analysis has four main goals:

- Identify assets and their values
- Identify vulnerabilities and threats
- Quantify the probability and business impact of these potential threats
- Provide an economic balance between the impact of the threat and the cost of the countermeasure

Risk analysis provides a *cost/benefit comparison*, which compares the annualized cost of safeguards to the potential cost of loss. A safeguard, in most cases, should not be implemented unless the annualized cost of loss exceeds the annualized cost of the safeguard itself. This means that if a facility is worth $100,000, it does not make sense to spend $150,000 trying to protect it.

It is important to figure out what you are *supposed* to be doing before you dig right in and start working. Anyone who has worked on a project without a properly defined scope can attest to this statement. Before an assessment and analysis is started, the team needs to carry out **project sizing** to understand what assets and threats are to be evaluated. Most assessments are focused on physical security, technology security, or personnel security. Trying to assess all of them at the same time can be quite an undertaking.

One of the team's tasks is to create a report that details the asset valuations. Senior management needs to review and accept the lists, and make them the scope of the IRM project. If management determines at this early stage that some assets are not important, the risk assessment team will not spend further time or resources to evaluate those assets. During discussions with management, everyone involved needs to have a firm understanding of the value of the security ACI triad—availability, confidentiality, and integrity—and how it directly relates to business needs.

Management should outline the scope, which most likely will be dictated by regulations and funds. Many projects have run out of funds, and consequently stopped, because proper project sizing was not conducted at the onset of the project. Don't let it happen to you.

A risk analysis helps integrate the security program objectives with the company's business objectives and requirements. The more the business and security objectives are in alignment, the more successful the two will be. The analysis also helps the company draft a proper budget for a security program and its constituent security components. Once a company knows how much its assets are worth and the possible threats they are exposed to, it can make intelligent decisions on how much money to spend on protecting those assets.

A risk analysis needs to be supported and directed by senior management if it is going to be successful. Management needs to define the purpose and scope of the analysis, appoint a team to carry out the assessment, and allocate the necessary time and funds to conduct the analysis. It is essential for senior management to review the outcome of the risk assessment and analysis and act on its findings. What good is it to go through all the trouble of a risk assessment and not react to its findings? Surprisingly, this does happen.

## Risk Analysis Team

Each organization has different departments. Each department has its own functionality, resources, tasks, and quirks. For the most effective risk analysis, an organization needs to build a risk analysis team that includes individuals from many or all departments, to ensure that all of the threats are identified and addressed. The team members may be part of management, application programmers, IT staff, systems integrators, and operational managers—indeed, any key personnel from key areas of the organization. This mix is necessary because if the risk analysis team comprises only individuals from the IT department, it may not understand, for example, the types of threats the accounting department faces with data integrity issues, or how the company as a whole would be affected if the accounting department's data files were wiped out by an accidental or intentional act. Or, as another example, the IT staff may not understand all the risks the employees in the warehouse would face if a natural disaster were to hit, or what it would mean to their productivity and how it would affect the organization overall. If the risk analysis team is unable to include members from various departments, it should, at the very least, make sure to interview people in each department so that it fully understands and can quantify all threats.

The risk analysis team also needs to include people who understand the processes that are part of their individual departments, meaning individuals who are at the right levels of each department. This is a difficult task, since managers tend to delegate any sort of risk analysis task to lower levels within the department. However, these lower levels may not have adequate knowledge and understanding of the processes that the risk analysis team may need to deal with.

When looking at risk, there are several questions that are helpful to keep in mind. Raising these questions helps to ensure that the risk analysis team and senior management know what is important. Team members need to ask the following: What event could occur (threat event)? What could be the potential impact (risk)? How often could it happen (frequency)? What level of confidence do we have in the answers to the first three questions (certainty)?

Viewing threats with these questions in mind helps the team to focus on the tasks at hand and assists in making the decisions more accurate and relevant.

## Value of Information and Assets

*If information does not have any value, then who cares about protecting it?*

The value placed on information is relative to the parties involved, what work was required to develop it, how much it costs to maintain, what damage would result if it were lost or destroyed, and what benefit another party would gain if it were to obtain the data. If a company does not know the value of the information and the other assets it is trying to protect, it does not know how much money and time it should spend on protecting them. If you were in charge of making sure that Russia does not know the encryption algorithms used when transmitting information to and from U.S. spy satellites, you would use more extreme (and expensive) security measures than you would use to protect your peanut butter and banana sandwich recipe from your next-door neighbor. The value of the information supports security measure decisions.

The previous examples refer to assessing the value of *information* and protecting it, but this logic applies toward an organization's facilities, systems, and resources. The value of the company's facilities needs to be assessed, along with all printers, workstations, servers, peripheral devices, supplies, and employees. You do not know how much is in danger of being lost if you don't know what you have and what it is worth in the first place.

## Costs That Make Up the Value

An asset can have both quantitative and qualitative measurements assigned to it, but these measurements need to be derived. The actual value of an asset is determined by the cost it takes to acquire, develop, and maintain it. The value is determined by the importance it has to the owners, authorized users, and unauthorized users. Some information is important enough to a company to go through the steps of making it a trade secret.

The value of an asset should reflect all identifiable costs that would arise if there were an actual impairment of the asset. If a server cost $4000 to purchase, this value should not be input as the value of the asset in a risk assessment. Rather, the cost of replacing or repairing it, the loss of productivity, and the value of any data that may be corrupted or lost need to be accounted for to properly capture the amount the company would lose if the server were to fail for one reason or another.

The following issues should be considered when assigning values to assets:

- Cost to acquire or develop the asset
- Cost to maintain and protect the asset
- Value of the asset to owners and users
- Value of the asset to adversaries
- Value of intellectual property that went into developing the information
- Price others are willing to pay for the asset
- Cost to replace the asset if lost
- Operational and production activities that are affected if the asset is unavailable
- Liability issues if the asset is compromised
- Usefulness and role of the asset in the organization

Understanding the value of an asset is the first step to understanding what security mechanisms should be put in place and what funds should go toward protecting it. A very important question is how much it could cost the company to *not* protect the asset.

Determining the value of assets may be useful to a company for a variety of reasons, including the following:

- To perform effective cost/benefit analyses
- To select specific countermeasures and safeguards
- To determine the level of insurance coverage to purchase
- To understand what exactly is at risk
- To conform to due care and comply with legal and regulatory requirements

Assets may be tangible (computers, facilities, supplies) or intangible (reputation, data, intellectual property). It is usually harder to quantify the values of intangible assets, which may change over time. How do you put a monetary value on a company's reputation? That's harder to solve than the Rubik's Cube.

## Identifying Threats

*Okay, what should we be afraid of?*

Earlier it was stated that the definition of a risk is the probability of a threat agent exploiting a vulnerability to cause harm to a computer, network, or company and the resulting business impact. There are many types of threat agents that can take advantage of several types of vulnerabilities, resulting in a variety of specific threats, as outlined in Table 3-1, which represents only a sampling of the risks that many organizations would have to address in their risk management programs.

There are other types of threats that can happen within a computerized environment that are much harder to identify than those listed in Table 3-1. These other threats

| Threat Agent | Can Exploit This Vulnerability | Resulting in This Threat |
|---|---|---|
| Virus | Lack of antivirus software | Virus infection |
| Hacker | Powerful services running on a server | Unauthorized access to confidential information |
| Users | Misconfigured parameter in the operating system | System malfunction |
| Fire | Lack of fire extinguishers | Facility and computer damage, and possibly loss of life |
| Employee | Lack of training or standards enforcement | Sharing mission-critical information |
| | Lack of auditing | Altering data inputs and outputs from data processing applications |
| Contractor | Lax access control mechanisms | Stealing trade secrets |
| Attacker | Poorly written application | Conducting a buffer overflow |
| | Lack of stringent firewall settings | Conducting a denial-of-service attack |
| Intruder | Lack of security guard | Breaking windows and stealing computers and devices |

**Table 3-1**   Relationship of Threats and Vulnerabilities

have to do with application and user errors. If an application uses several complex equations to produce results, the threat can be difficult to discover and isolate if these equations are incorrect or if the application is using inputted data incorrectly. This can result in *illogical processing* and *cascading errors* as invalid results are passed on to another process. These types of problems can lie within applications' code and are very hard to identify.

User errors, intentional or accidental, are easier to identify, by monitoring and auditing user activities. Audits and reviews need to be conducted to discover if employees are inputting values incorrectly into programs, misusing technology, or modifying data in an inappropriate manner.

Once the vulnerabilities and associated threats are identified, the ramifications of these vulnerabilities being exploited need to be investigated. Risks have *loss potential*, meaning what the company would lose if a threat agent were actually to exploit a vulnerability. The loss may be corrupted data, destruction of systems and/or the facility, unauthorized disclosure of confidential information, a reduction in employee productivity, and so on. When performing a risk analysis, the team also needs to look at *delayed loss* when assessing the damages that can occur. Delayed loss has negative effects on a company after a vulnerability is initially exploited. The time period can be anywhere from 15 minutes to years after the exploitation. Delayed loss may include reduced productivity over a period of time, reduced income to the company, accrued late penalties, extra expense to get the environment back to proper working conditions, delayed collection of funds from customers, and so forth.

For example, if a company's web servers are attacked and taken offline, the immediate damage could be data corruption, the man-hours necessary to place the servers back online, and the replacement of any code or components that may be required. The company could lose productivity if it usually accepts orders and payments via its web site. If it takes a full day to get the web servers fixed and back online, the company could lose a lot more sales and profits. If it takes a full week to get the web servers fixed and back online, the company could lose enough sales and profits to not be able to pay other bills and expenses. This would be a delayed loss. If the company's customers lose confidence in it because of this activity, it could lose business for months or years. This is a more extreme case of delayed loss.

These types of issues make more complex the process of properly quantifying losses that specific threats could cause, but they need to be taken into consideration to ensure that reality is represented in this type of analysis.

So, up to now, we have secured management's support of the risk analysis, constructed our team so that it represents different departments in the company, placed a value on each of the company's assets, and identified all the possible threats that could affect the assets. We have also taken into consideration all potential and delayed losses the company may endure per asset per threat. The next step is to use qualitative or quantitative methods to calculate the actual risk the company faces.

## Quantitative Risk Analysis

As previously mentioned, there are two types of approaches to risk analysis: quantitative and qualitative. *Quantitative risk analysis* attempts to assign real and meaningful numbers to all elements of the risk analysis process. These elements may include safeguard costs, asset value, business impact, threat frequency, safeguard effectiveness, exploit probabilities, and so on. When all of these are quantified, the process is said to be quantitative. Quantitative risk analysis also provides concrete probability percentages when determining the likelihood of threats. Each element within the analysis (asset value, threat frequency, severity of vulnerability, impact damage, safeguard costs, safeguard effectiveness, uncertainty, and probability items) is quantified and entered into equations to determine total and residual risks.

Purely quantitative risk analysis is not possible, because the method attempts to quantify qualitative items, and there are always uncertainties in quantitative values. If a severity level is high and a threat frequency is low, it is hard to assign corresponding numbers to these ratings and come up with a useful outcome.

Quantitative and qualitative approaches have their own pros and cons, and each applies more appropriately to some situations than others. Company management and the risk analysis team, and the tools they decide to use, will determine which approach is best.

**NOTE** Quantitative analysis uses risk calculations that attempt to predict the level of monetary losses and the percentage of chance for each type of threat. Qualitative analysis does not use calculations, but is more situation and scenario based.

## Automated Risk Analysis Methods

Collecting all the necessary data that needs to be plugged into risk analysis equations and properly interpreting the results can be overwhelming if done manually. There are several automated risk analysis tools on the market that can make this task much less painful and, hopefully, more accurate. The gathered data can be reused, greatly reducing the time required to perform subsequent analyses. The risk analysis team can also print out reports and comprehensive graphs to be presented to the management.

**NOTE** Vulnerability assessment and risk analysis tools are available in freeware and commercial versions. Obtaining serious results often requires taking a serious approach to finding the tools that best serve the accuracy of the project.

The objective of these tools is to reduce the manual effort of these tasks, perform calculations quickly, estimate future expected losses, and determine the effectiveness and benefits of the security countermeasures chosen. Most automatic risk analysis products port information into a database and run several types of scenarios with different parameters to give a panoramic view of what the outcome will be if different threats come to bear. For example, after such a tool has all the necessary information inputted, it can be rerun several times with different parameters to compute the potential outcome if a large fire were to take place; the potential losses if a virus were to damage 40 percent of the data on the main file server; how much the company would lose if an attacker were to steal all the customer credit card information held in three databases; and so on. Running through the different risk possibilities gives a company a more detailed understanding of which risks are more critical than others, and thus which ones to address first. Figure 3-5 shows a simple example of this process.

## Steps of a Risk Analysis

There are many methods and equations that could be used when performing a quantitative risk analysis, and many different variables that can be inserted into the process. This section covers some of the main steps that should take place in every risk analysis.

**Step 1: Assign Value to Assets**   For each asset, answer the following questions to determine its value:

- What is the value of this asset to the company?
- How much does it cost to maintain?
- How much does it make in profits for the company?
- How much would it be worth to the competition?

**Figure 3-5**
A simplistic example
showing the severity
of current threats
verses the probability
of them occurring

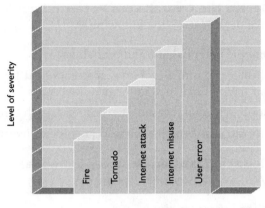

Level of severity

Fire  Tornado  Internet attack  Internet misuse  User error

Level of probability

- How much would it cost to re-create or recover?
- How much did it cost to acquire or develop?
- How much liability are you under pertaining to the protection of this asset?

**Step 2: Estimate Potential Loss per Threat**  To estimate potential losses posed by threats, answer the following questions:

- What physical damage could the threat cause and how much would that cost?
- How much loss of productivity could the threat cause and how much would that cost?
- What is the value lost if confidential information is disclosed?
- What is the cost of recovering from this threat?
- What is the value lost if critical devices were to fail?
- What is the single loss expectancy (SLE) for each asset, and each threat?

This is just a small sample of questions that should be answered. The specific questions will depend upon the types of threats the team uncovers.

**Step 3: Perform a Threat Analysis**  Take the following steps to perform a threat analysis:

- Gather information about the likelihood of each threat taking place from people in each department, past records, and official security resources that provide this type of data.
- Calculate the annualized rate of occurrence (ARO), which is how many times the threat can take place in a 12-month period.

**Step 4: Derive the Overall Loss Potential per Threat**   To derive the overall loss potential per threat, do the following:

- Combine potential loss and probability.
- Calculate the annualized loss expectancy (ALE) per threat by using the information calculated in the first three steps.
- Choose remedial measures to counteract each threat.
- Carry out cost/benefit analysis on the identified countermeasures.

**Step 5: Reduce, Transfer, or Accept the Risk**   For each risk, you can choose whether to reduce, transfer, or accept the risk:

- **Risk reduction methods**
  - Install security controls and components.
  - Improve procedures.
  - Alter environment.
  - Provide early detection methods to catch the threat as it's happening and reduce the possible damage it can cause.
  - Produce a contingency plan of how business can continue if a specific threat takes place, reducing further damages of the threat.
  - Erect barriers to the threat.
  - Carry out security-awareness training.
- **Risk transfer**   Buy insurance to transfer some of the risk, for example.
- **Risk acceptance**   Live with the risks and spend no more money toward protection.

Because we are stepping through a quantitative risk analysis, real numbers are used and calculations are necessary. *Single loss expectancy (SLE)* and *annualized loss expectancy (ALE)* were mentioned in the previous analysis steps. The SLE is a dollar amount that is assigned to a single event that represents the company's potential loss amount if a specific threat were to take place:

asset value × exposure factor (EF) = SLE

The *exposure factor (EF)* represents the percentage of loss a realized threat could have on a certain asset. So, for example, if a data warehouse has the asset value of $150,000, it might be estimated that if a fire were to occur, 25 percent of the warehouse would be damaged (and not more, because of a sprinkler system and other fire controls, proximity of a firehouse, etc.), in which case the SLE would be $37,500. This figure is derived to be inserted into the ALE equation:

SLE × annualized rate of occurrence (ARO) = ALE

## Accepting Risk

When a company decides to accept a risk, the decision should be based on cost (countermeasure costs more than potential loss) and an acceptable level of pain (company can live with the vulnerability and threat). But the company must also understand that this is a visibility decision, insofar as accepting a specific risk may impact its industry reputation.

The *annualized rate of occurrence (ARO)* is the value that represents the estimated frequency of a specific threat taking place within a one-year timeframe. The range can be from 0.0 (never) to 1.0 (at least once a year) to greater than one (several times a year) and anywhere in between. For example, if the probability of a flood taking place in Mesa, Arizona is once in 1000 years, the ARO value is 0.001.

So, if a fire taking place within a company's data warehouse facility can cause $37,500 in damages and the frequency, or ARO, of a fire taking place has an ARO value of 0.1 (indicating once in ten years), then the ALE value is $3750 ($37,500 × 0.1 = $3750).

The ALE value tells the company that if it wants to put in controls or safeguards to protect the asset from this threat, it can sensibly spend $3750 or less per year to provide the necessary level of protection. Knowing the real possibility of a threat and how much damage, in monetary terms, that the threat can cause is important to determining how much should be spent to try to protect against that threat in the first place. It would not make good business sense for the company to spend more than $3750 per year to protect itself from this threat.

Now that we have all these numbers, what do we do with them? Let's look at the example in Table 3-2, which shows the outcome of a risk analysis. With this data, the company can make intelligent decisions on what threats need to be addressed first because of the severity of the threat, the likelihood of it happening, and how much could be lost if the threat were realized. The company now also knows how much money it should spend to protect against each threat. This will result in good business decisions, instead of just buying protection here and there without a clear understanding of the big picture. Because the company has a risk of losing up to $6500 if data is corrupted by virus infiltration, up to this amount of funds can be earmarked toward providing antivirus software and methods to ensure that a virus attack will not happen.

| Asset | Threat | Single Loss Expectancy (SLE) | Annualized Rate of Occurrence (ARO) | Annual Loss Expectancy (ALE) |
|---|---|---|---|---|
| Facility | Fire | $230,000 | .1 | $23,000 |
| Trade secret | Stolen | $40,000 | .01 | $400 |
| File server | Failed | $11,500 | .1 | $1150 |
| Data | Virus | $6500 | 1.0 | $6500 |
| Customer credit card info | Stolen | $300,000 | 3.0 | $900,000 |

**Table 3-2** Breaking Down How SLE and ALE Values Are Used

We have just explored the ways of performing risk analysis through quantitative means. This method tries to measure the loss in monetary value and assign numeric sums to each component within the analysis. As stated previously, however, a pure quantitative analysis is not achievable because it is impossible to assign the exact figures to each component and loss values. Although we can look at past events, do our best to assess the value of the assets, and contact agencies that provide frequency estimates of disasters happening in our area, we still cannot say for a fact that we have a 10 percent chance of a fire happening in a year and that it will cause exactly $230,000 in damage. In quantitative risk analysis, we can do our best to provide all the correct information, and by doing so we will come close to the risk values, but we cannot predict the future and how much the future will cost us or the company.

## Results of a Risk Analysis

The risk analysis team should have clearly defined goals that it is seeking. The following is a short list of what generally is expected from the results of a risk analysis:

- Monetary values assigned to assets
- Comprehensive list of all possible and significant threats
- Probability of the occurrence rate of each threat
- Loss potential the company can endure per threat in a 12-month time span
- Recommended safeguards, countermeasures, and actions

Although this list looks short, there is usually an incredible amount of detail under each bullet item. This report will be presented to senior management, which will be concerned with possible monetary losses and the necessary costs to mitigate these risks. Although the reports should be as detailed as possible, there should be executive abstracts so that senior management may quickly understand the overall findings of the analysis.

## Qualitative Risk Analysis

*I think we are secure. Response: Great! Let's all go home.*

Another method of risk analysis is *qualitative*, which does not assign numbers and monetary values to components and losses. Instead, qualitative methods walk through different scenarios of risk possibilities and rank the seriousness of the threats and the validity of the different possible countermeasures. Qualitative analysis techniques

### Uncertainty

In risk analysis, *uncertainty* refers to the degree to which you lack confidence in an estimate. This is expressed as a percentage, from 0 percent to 100 percent. If you have a 30 percent confidence level in something, then it could be said that you have a 70 percent uncertainty level. Capturing the degree of uncertainty when carrying out a risk analysis is important, because it indicates the level of confidence the team and management should have in the resulting figures.

include judgment, best practices, intuition, and experience. Examples of qualitative techniques are Delphi, brainstorming, storyboarding, focus groups, surveys, questionnaires, checklists, one-on-one meetings, and interviews. The risk analysis team will determine the best technique for the threats that need to be assessed and the culture of the company and individuals involved with the analysis.

The team that is performing the risk analysis gathers personnel who have experience and education on the threats being evaluated. When this group is presented with a scenario that describes threats and loss potential, each member responds with their gut feeling and experience on the likelihood of the threat and the extent of damage that may result.

A scenario approximately one page in length is written for each major threat. The "expert," who is most familiar with this type of threat, should review the scenario to ensure that it reflects how an actual threat would be carried out. Safeguards that would diminish the damage of this threat are then evaluated, and the scenario is played out for each safeguard. The exposure possibility and loss possibility can be ranked as high, medium, or low on a scale of 1 to 5 or 1 to 10. Once the selected personnel rank the possibility of a threat happening, the loss potential, and the advantages of each safeguard, this information is compiled into a report and presented to management to help it make better decisions on how best to implement safeguards into the environment. The benefits of this type of analysis are that communication has to happen among the team members to rank the risks, safeguard strengths and weaknesses are identified, and the people who know these subjects the best provide their opinions to management.

Let's look at a *simple* example of a qualitative risk analysis.

The risk analysis team writes a one-page scenario explaining the threat of a hacker accessing confidential information held on the five file servers within the company. The risk analysis team then distributes the one-page scenario to a team of five people (the IT manager, database administrator, application programmer, system operator, and operational manager), who are also given a sheet to rank the threat's severity, loss potential, and each safeguard's effectiveness, with a rating of 1 to 5, 1 being the least severe, effective, or probable. Table 3-3 shows the results.

This data is compiled and inserted into a report and presented to management. When management is presented with this information, it will see that its staff (or a chosen set of security professionals) feels that purchasing a firewall will protect the company from this threat more than purchasing an intrusion detection system, or setting up a honeypot system.

---

### Delphi Methods

In this text we are describing the consensus Delphi method, where experts help to identify the highest-priority security issues and corresponding countermeasures. Another Delphi method, Modified Delphi technique, is a silent form of brainstorming. Participants develop ideas individually and silently with no group interaction. The ideas are submitted to a group of decision makers for consideration and action.

| Threat = Hacker Accessing Confidential Information | Severity of Threat | Probability of Threat Taking Place | Potential Loss to the Company | Effective-ness of Firewall | Effectiveness of Intrusion Detection System | Effective-ness of Honeypot |
|---|---|---|---|---|---|---|
| IT manager | 4 | 2 | 4 | 4 | 3 | 2 |
| Database administrator | 4 | 4 | 4 | 3 | 4 | 1 |
| Application programmer | 2 | 3 | 3 | 4 | 2 | 1 |
| System operator | 3 | 4 | 3 | 4 | 2 | 1 |
| Operational manager | 5 | 4 | 4 | 4 | 4 | 2 |
| Results | 3.6 | 3.4 | 3.6 | 3.8 | 3 | 1.4 |

**Table 3-3** Example of a Qualitative Analysis

This is the result of looking at only one threat, and the management will view the severity, probability, and loss potential of each threat so that it knows which threats cause the greatest risk and should be addressed first.

## Delphi Technique

The Delphi technique is a group decision method used to ensure that each member gives an honest opinion of what he or she thinks the result to a particular threat will be. This avoids a group of individuals feeling pressured to go along with others' thought processes and enables them to participate in an independent and anonymous way. Each member of the group writes down his or her opinion of a certain threat on a piece of paper and turns it into the team that is performing the analysis. The results are compiled and distributed to the group members, who then write down their comments anonymously and return them back to the analysis group. The comments are compiled and redistributed for more comments until a consensus is formed. This method is used to obtain an agreement on cost, loss values, and probabilities of occurrence without individuals having to agree verbally.

## Quantitative vs. Qualitative

*So which method should we use?*

Each method has its advantages and disadvantages, some of which are outlined in Table 3-4 for purposes of comparison.

The risk analysis team, management, risk analysis tools, and culture of the company will dictate which approach, quantitative or qualitative, will be used. The goal of either method is to estimate a company's real risk and rank the severity of the threats so that the correct countermeasures can be put into place within a practical budget.

| Attribute | Quantitative | Qualitative |
|---|---|---|
| Requires simple calculations | | X |
| Requires more complex calculations | X | |
| Involves high degree of guesswork | | X |
| Provides general areas and indications of risk | | X |
| Is easier to automate and evaluate | X | |
| Used in risk management performance tracking | X | |
| Provides credible cost/benefit analysis | X | |
| Uses independently verifiable and objective metrics | X | |
| Provides the opinions of the individuals who know the processes best | | X |
| Shows clear-cut losses that can be accrued within one year's time | X | |

**Table 3-4** Quantitative vs. Qualitative Characteristics

Table 3-4 refers to some of the positive aspects of the qualitative and quantitative approaches. But, not everything is always easy. In deciding to use either a qualitative or quantitative approach, the following points might need to be considered:

**Qualitative Cons:**

- The assessments and results are basically subjective.
- Usually eliminates the opportunity to create a dollar value for cost/benefit discussions.
- Difficult to track risk management objectives with subjective measures.
- Standards are not available. Each vendor has its own way of interpreting the processes and their results.

**Quantitative Cons:**

- Calculations are more complex. Can management understand how these values were derived?
- Without automated tools, this process is extremely laborious.
- Big need to gather detailed information about environment.
- Standards are not available. Each vendor has its own way of interpreting the processes and their results.

## Protection Mechanisms

*Okay, so we know we are at risk, we know the probability of it happening, now what do we do?*

The next step is to identify the current security mechanisms and evaluate their effectiveness.

Because a company has such a wide range of threats, not just computer viruses and attackers, each threat type needs to be addressed and planned for individually. Access control mechanisms used as security safeguards are discussed in Chapter 4. Software applications and data malfunction considerations are covered in Chapter 5. Site location, fire protection, site construction, power loss, and equipment malfunctions are examined in detail in Chapter 6. Telecommunication and networking issues are analyzed and presented in Chapter 7. Business continuity and disaster recovery concepts are addressed in Chapter 9. All of these subjects have their own associated risks and planning requirements.

This section addresses identifying and choosing the right countermeasures for computer systems. It gives the best attributes to look for and the different cost scenarios to investigate when comparing different types of countermeasures. The end product of the analysis of choices should demonstrate why the selected control is the most advantageous to the company.

## Countermeasure Selection

A security *countermeasure*, sometimes called a *safeguard*, must make good business sense, meaning that it is cost-effective and that its benefit outweighs its cost. This requires another type of analysis: a *cost/benefit analysis*. A commonly used cost/benefit calculation for a given safeguard is

(ALE before implementing safeguard) – (ALE after implementing safeguard) – (annual cost of safeguard) = value of safeguard to the company

For example, if the ALE of the threat of a hacker bringing down a web server is $12,000 prior to implementing the suggested safeguard, and the ALE is $3000 after implementing the safeguard, and the annual cost of maintenance and operation of the safeguard is $650, then the value of this safeguard to the company is $8350 each year.

The cost of a countermeasure is more than just the amount that is filled out on the purchase order. The following items need to be considered and evaluated when deriving the full cost of a countermeasure:

- Product costs
- Design/planning costs
- Implementation costs
- Environment modifications
- Compatibility with other countermeasures
- Maintenance requirements
- Testing requirements
- Repair, replacement, or update costs
- Operating and support costs
- Effects on productivity

Consider an example. Company A decides that to protect many of its resources, purchasing an IDS is warranted. So, the company pays $5500 for an IDS. Is that the total cost? Nope. This software should be tested in an environment that is segmented from the production environment to uncover any unexpected activity. After this testing is complete and the IT group feels that it is safe to insert the IDS into its production environment, the IT group must install the monitoring management software, install the sensors, and properly direct the communication paths from the sensors to the management console. The IT group may also need to reconfigure the routers to redirect traffic flow, and definitely needs to ensure that users cannot access the IDS management console. Finally, the IT group needs to configure a database to hold all attack signatures, and then run simulations.

Anyone who has worked in an IT group knows that some adverse reaction almost always takes place in this type of scenario. Network performance can take an unacceptable hit after installing this product, if it is an inline or proactive product. Users may no longer be able to access the Unix server for some mysterious reason. The IDS vendor may not have explained that two more service patches are necessary for the whole thing to work correctly. Staff time will need to be allocated for training, and to respond to all of the correct and incorrect alerts the new IDS sends out.

So, for example, the cost of this countermeasure could be $5500 for the product, $2500 for training, $3400 for the lab and testing time, $2600 for the loss in user productivity once the product was introduced into production, and $4000 in labor for router reconfiguration, product installation, troubleshooting, and installation of the two service patches. The real cost of this countermeasure is $18,000. If our total potential loss was calculated at $9000, we went over budget by 100 percent when applying this countermeasure for the identified risk. Some of these costs may be hard or impossible to identify before they are incurred, but an experienced risk analyst would account for many of these possibilities.

## Functionality and Effectiveness of Countermeasures

*The countermeasure doesn't work, but it's pretty. Response: Good enough.*

The risk analysis team will need to evaluate the safeguard's functionality and effectiveness. When selecting a safeguard, some attributes are more favorable than others. Table 3-5 lists and describes attributes that should be considered *before* purchasing and committing to a security protection mechanism.

| Characteristic | Description |
|---|---|
| Modular in nature | It can be installed or removed from an environment without adversely affecting other mechanisms. |
| Provides uniform protection | A security level is applied to all mechanisms it is designed to protect in a standardized method. |
| Provides override functionality | An administrator can override the restriction if necessary. |
| Defaults to least privilege | When installed, it defaults to a lack of permissions and rights instead of installing with everyone having full control. |
| Independence of safeguard and the asset it is protecting | The safeguard can be used to protect different assets, and different assets can be protected by different safeguards. |
| Flexibility and security | The more security the safeguard provides, the better. This functionality should come with flexibility, which enables you to choose different functions instead of all or none. |
| Clear distinction between user and administrator | A user should have fewer permissions when it comes to configuring or disabling the protection mechanism. |
| Minimum human intervention | When humans have to configure or modify controls, this opens the door to errors. The safeguard should require the least amount of input from humans as possible. |
| Easily upgraded | Software continues to evolve, and updates should be able to happen painlessly. |
| Auditing functionality | There should be a mechanism that is part of the safeguard that provides minimum and/or verbose auditing. |
| Minimizes dependence on other components | The safeguard should be flexible and not have strict requirements about the environment into which it will be installed. |
| Easily useable, acceptable, and tolerated by personnel | If the safeguards provide barriers to productivity or add extra steps to simple tasks, users will not tolerate it. |
| Must produce output in usable and understandable format | Important information should be presented in a format easy for humans to understand and use for trend analysis. |
| Must be able to reset safeguard | The mechanism should be able to be reset and returned to original configurations and settings without affecting the system or asset it is protecting. |

**Table 3-5**  Characteristics to Seek When Obtaining Safeguards

| Characteristic | Description |
|---|---|
| Testable | The safeguard should be able to be tested in different environments under different situations. |
| Does not introduce other compromises | The safeguard should not provide any covert channels or back doors. |
| System and user performance | System and user performance should not be greatly affected. |
| Proper alerting | Thresholds should be able to be set as to when to alert personnel of a security breach, and this type of alert should be acceptable. |
| Does not affect assets | The assets in the environment should not be adversely affected by the safeguard. |

**Table 3-5** Characteristics to Seek When Obtaining Safeguards *(continued)*

Safeguards can provide deterrence attributes if they are highly visible. This tells potential evildoers that adequate protection is in place and that they should move on to an easier target. Although the safeguard may be highly visible, evildoers should not be able to attain the way that it works, enabling them to attempt to modify the safeguard, or know how to get around the reaches of the protection mechanism. If users know how to disable the antivirus program that is taking up CPU cycles or know how to bypass a proxy server to get to the Internet without restrictions, they will do it.

## Putting It Together

To perform a risk analysis, a company first decides what assets need to be protected and to what extent. It also indicates the amount of money that can go toward protecting specific assets. Next, it needs to evaluate the functionality of the available safeguards and determine which ones would be most beneficial for the environment. Finally, the company needs to appraise and compare the costs of the safeguards. These steps and the resulting information enable management to make the most intelligent and informed decisions about selecting and purchasing countermeasures. Figure 3-6 illustrates these steps.

### We Are Never Done

Only by reassessing the risks, on a periodic basis, can a statement of safeguard performance be trusted. If the risk has not changed, and the safeguards implemented are functioning in good order, then it can be said that the risk is being properly mitigated. Regular IRM monitoring will support the information security risk ratings.

Vulnerability analysis and continued asset identification and valuation are also important tasks of risk management monitoring and performance. The cycle of continued risk analysis is a very important part of determining whether the safeguard controls that have been put in place are appropriate and necessary to safeguard the assets and environment.

Figure 3-6
The main three steps
in risk analysis

## Total Risk vs. Residual Risk

The reason that a company implements countermeasures is to reduce its overall risk to an acceptable level. As stated earlier, no system or environment is 100 percent secure, which means there is always some risk left over to deal with. This is called *residual risk*.

Residual risk is different from *total risk*, which is the risk a company faces if it chooses not to implement any type of safeguard. A company may choose to take on total risk if the cost/benefit analysis results indicate that this is the best course of action. For example, if there is a small likelihood that a company's web servers can be compromised and the necessary safeguards to provide a higher level of protection cost more than the potential loss in the first place, the company will choose not to implement the safeguard, choosing to deal with the total risk.

There is an important difference between total risk and residual risk and which type of risk a company is willing to accept. The following are conceptual formulas:

threats × vulnerability × asset value = total risk

(threats × vulnerability × asset value) × controls gap = residual risk

During a risk assessment, the threats and vulnerabilities are identified. The possibility of a vulnerability being exploited is multiplied by the value of the assets that are being assessed, which results in the total risk. Once the controls gap (protection the control cannot provide) is factored in, the result is the residual risk. Implementing countermeasures is a way of mitigating risks. Because no company can remove all threats, there will always be some residual risk. The question is what level of risk the company is willing to accept.

## Handling Risk

*Now that we know about the risk, what do we do with it?*

Once a company knows the amount of total and residual risk it is faced with, it must decide how to handle it. There are four basic ways of dealing with risk: transfer it, reject it, reduce it, or accept it.

Many types of insurance are available to companies to protect their assets. If a company decides that the total or residual risk is too high to gamble with, it can purchase insurance, which would *transfer the risk* to the insurance company.

If the company implements countermeasures, this *reduces the risk*. If a company is in denial about its risk or ignores it, it is *rejecting the risk*, which can be very dangerous and is unadvisable. The last approach is to *accept the risk*, which means the company understands the level of risk it is faced with and the potential cost of damage and decides to just live with it and not implement the countermeasure. Many companies will accept risk when the cost/benefit ratio indicates that the cost of the countermeasure outweighs the potential loss value.

## References

- *Risk Management Guide for Information Technology Systems, Recommendations of the National Institute of Standards and Technology*   http://csrc.nist.gov/publications/nistpubs/800-30/sp800-30.pdf
- **Carnegie Mellon Software Engineering Institute**   www.sei.cmu.edu/organization/programs/sepm/risk/
- *Handbook of Information Security Management*, **Domain 3, "Risk Management and Business Continuity Planning," Micki Krause and Harold F. Tipton, Editors (CRC Press LLC)**   www.cccure.org/Documents/HISM/223-228.html
- *Security Metrics Guide for Information Technology Systems*   http://csrc.nist.gov/publications/nistpubs/800-55/sp800-55.pdf
- *Threat and Risk Assessment Working Guide* **(Government of Canada, 1999)** www.cse-cst.gc.ca/en/documents/publications/gov_pubs/itsg/itsg04.pdf

# Policies, Standards, Baselines, Guidelines, and Procedures

*The risk assessment is done. Let's call it a day. Response: Nope, there's more.*

Computers and the information that is processed on them usually have a direct relationship with a company's critical missions and objectives. Because of this level of importance, senior management should make protecting these items a high priority and provide the necessary support, funds, time, and resources to ensure that systems, networks, and information are protected in the most logical and cost-effective manner possible. A comprehensive management approach needs to be developed to accomplish these goals successfully.

For a company's security plan to be successful, it needs to start at the top level and be useful and functional at every single level within the organization. Senior management needs to define the scope of security and identify and decide what needs to be protected and to what extent. Management must understand the regulations, laws, and liability issues that it is responsible for complying with regarding security and ensure that the company as a whole fulfills its obligations. Senior management also needs to determine what is to be expected from employees and what the consequences of noncompliance will be. These decisions should be made by the individuals who will be held ultimately responsible if something goes wrong.

A security program contains all the pieces necessary to provide overall protection to a corporation and sets forth a long-term security strategy. A security program should have security policies, procedures, standards, guidelines, baselines, security-awareness training, an incident response plan, and a compliance program. The human resources and legal departments need to be involved in the development and enforcement of some of these elements.

The language, level of detail, formality of the policy, and supporting mechanisms should be examined by the policy developers. Security policies, standards, guidelines, and procedures must be developed with a realistic view to be most effective. Highly structured organizations usually follow guidelines in a more uniform way. Less structured organizations may need more explanation and emphasis to promote compliance. The more detailed the rules are, the easier it is to know when one has been violated. However, overly detailed documentation and rules can prove to be more burdensome than helpful. On the other hand, many times, the more formal the rules, the easier they are to enforce. The business type, its culture, and its goals need to be evaluated to make sure the proper language is used when writing security documentation.

## Security Policy

*Oh look, this paper tells us what we need to do. I am going to put smiley face stickers all over it.*

A *security policy* is an overall general statement produced by senior management (or a selected policy board or committee) that dictates what role security plays within the organization. A security policy can be an organizational policy, issue-specific policy, or system-specific policy. In an *organizational security policy*, management establishes how a security program will be set up, lays out the program's goals, assigns responsibilities, shows the strategic and tactical value of security, and outlines how enforcement should be carried out. This policy must address relative laws, regulations, and liability issues and how they are to be satisfied. The organizational security policy provides scope and direction for all future security activities within the organization. It also describes the amount of risk senior management is willing to accept.

The organizational security policy has several important characteristics that need to be understood and implemented:

- Business objectives should drive the policy's creation, implementation, and enforcement. The policy should not dictate business objectives.

- It should be an easily understood document that is used as a reference point for all employees and management.

- It should be developed and used to integrate security into all business functions and processes.

- It should be derived from and support all legislation and regulation applicable to the company.

- It should be reviewed and modified as a company changes, such as through adoption of a new business model, merger with another company, or change of ownership.

- Each iteration of the policy should be dated and under version control.

- The units and individuals who are governed by the policy must have access to the applicable portions and not be expected to have to read all policy material to find direction and answers.

An *issue-specific policy*, also called a functional implementing policy, addresses specific security issues that management feels need more detailed explanation and attention to make sure a comprehensive structure is built and all employees understand how they are to comply with these security issues. For example, an organization may choose to have an e-mail security policy that outlines what management can and cannot do with employees' e-mail messages for monitoring purposes, specifies which e-mail functionality employees can or cannot use, and addresses specific privacy issues.

As a more specific example, an e-mail policy might state that management can read any employee's e-mail messages that reside on the mail server, but not when they reside on the user's workstation. The e-mail policy might also state that employees cannot use e-mail to share confidential information or to pass inappropriate material, and may be subject to monitoring of these actions. Before they use their e-mail clients, employees should be asked to confirm that they have read and understand the e-mail policy, either by signing a confirmation document or clicking Yes in a confirmation dialog box. The policy provides direction and structure for the staff by indicating what they can and cannot do. It informs the users of the expectations of their actions, and it provides liability protection in case an employee cries "foul" for any reason dealing with e-mail use.

**NOTE** A policy needs to be technology- and solution-independent. It needs to outline the goals and missions, but not tie the organization to specific ways of accomplishing them.

A *system-specific policy* presents the management's decisions that are specific to the actual computers, networks, applications, and data. This type of policy may provide an approved software list, which contains a list of applications that may be installed on individual workstations. This policy may describe how databases are to be used and protected, how computers are to be locked down, and how firewalls, IDSs, and scanners are to be employed.

Policies are written in broad terms to cover many subjects in a general fashion. Much more granularity is needed to actually support the policy, and this happens with the use of procedures, standards, and guidelines. The policy provides the foundation. The procedures, standards, and guidelines provide the security framework. And the necessary security components, implementations, and mechanisms are used to fill in the framework to provide a full security program and secure infrastructure.

## Types of Policies

Policies generally fall into one of the following categories:

- **Regulatory**  This type of policy ensures that the organization is following standards set by specific industry regulations. This policy type is very detailed and specific to a type of industry. This is used in financial institutions, health care facilities, public utilities, and other government-regulated industries.

- **Advisory**  This type of policy strongly advises employees regarding which types of behaviors and activities should and should not take place within the organization. It also outlines possible ramifications if employees do not comply with the established behaviors and activities. This policy type can be used, for example, to describe how to handle medical information, handle financial transactions, or process confidential information.

- **Informative**  This type of policy informs employees of certain topics. It is not an enforceable policy, but rather one to teach individuals about specific issues relevant to the company. It could explain how the company interacts with partners, the company's goals and mission, and a general reporting structure in different situations.

## Standards

*Some things you just gotta do.*

*Standards* refer to mandatory activities, actions, rules, or regulations. Standards can give a policy its support and reinforcement in direction. Standards could be internal, or externally mandated (government laws and regulations).

Organizational security standards may specify how hardware and software products are to be used. They can also be used to indicate expected user behavior. They provide a means to ensure that specific technologies, applications, parameters, and procedures are implemented in a uniform manner across the organization. An organizational standard may require all employees to have their company identification badges on their person at all times, to challenge unknown individuals about their identity and purpose for being in a specific area, or to encrypt confidential information. These rules are usually compulsory within a company, and if they are going to be effective, they need to be enforced.

As stated in an earlier section, there is a difference between tactical and strategic goals. A strategic goal can be viewed as the ultimate endpoint; the tactical goals are the steps to achieve it. As shown in Figure 3-7, standards, guidelines, and procedures are the tactical tools used to achieve and support the directives in the security policy, which is considered the strategic goal.

**Figure 3-7**
Policy establishes the strategic plans, and the lower elements provide the tactical support.

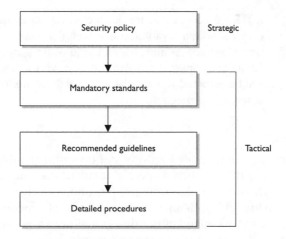

## Baselines

There are a couple of definitions for *baseline*. A baseline can refer to a point in time that is used as a comparison for future changes. Once risks have been mitigated, and security put in place, a baseline is formally reviewed and agreed upon, after which all further comparisons and development are measured against it. A baseline results in a consistent reference point.

Let's say that your doctor has told you that you are 400 pounds because of your diet of donuts, pizza, and soda. (This is very frustrating to you because the TV commercial said you could eat whatever you wanted and just take their very expensive pills each day and lose weight.) The doctor tells you that you need to exercise each day and get your heart rate double its normal rate for 30 minutes twice a day. How do you know when you are at double your heart rate? You find out your baseline (regular heart rate) by using one of those arm thingies with a little ball attached. So you start at your baseline and continue to exercise until you have doubled it or die, whichever comes first.

Baselines are also used to define the minimum level of protection that is required. In security, specific baselines can be defined per system type, which indicates the necessary settings and the level of protection that is being provided. For example, a company may stipulate that all accounting systems must meet an Evaluation Assurance Level (EAL) 4 baseline. This means that only systems that have gone through the Common Criteria process and achieved this rating can be used in this department evaluation. Once the systems are properly configured, this is the necessary baseline. When new software is installed, when patches or upgrades are applied to existing software, or when other changes take place to the system, there is a good chance that the system may no longer be providing its necessary minimum level of protection (its baseline). Security personnel must assess the systems as changes take place and ensure that the baseline level of security is always being met. If a technician installs a patch on a system and does not assess its new baseline, there could be new vulnerabilities introduced into the system that will allow evildoers easy access into the network.

**NOTE** Baselines that are not technology-oriented should be created and enforced within organizations as well. For example, a company can mandate that all employees must have a badge with a picture ID in view while in the facility at all times. It can also state that visitors must sign in at a front desk and be escorted while in the facility. If these are followed, then this creates a baseline of protection.

## Guidelines

*Guidelines* are recommended actions and operational guides to users, IT staff, operations staff, and others when a specific standard does not apply. Guidelines can deal with the methodologies of technology, personnel, or physical security. There are always gray areas in life, and guidelines can be used as a reference during those times. Whereas standards are specific mandatory rules, guidelines are general approaches that provide the necessary flexibility for unforeseen circumstances.

A policy might state that access to confidential data must be audited. A supporting guideline could further explain that audits should contain sufficient information to allow for reconciliation with prior reviews. Supporting procedures would outline the necessary steps to configure, implement, and maintain this type of auditing.

## Procedures

*Procedures* are detailed step-by-step tasks that should be performed to achieve a certain goal. The steps can apply to users, IT staff, operations staff, security members, and others who may need to carry out specific tasks. Many organizations have written procedures on how to install operating systems, configure security mechanisms, implement access control lists, set up new user accounts, assign computer privileges, audit activities, destroy material, report incidents, and much more.

Procedures are considered the lowest level in the policy chain because they are closest to the computers and users (compared to policies) and provide detailed steps for configuration and installation issues.

Procedures spell out how the policy, standards, and guidelines will actually be implemented in an operating environment. If a policy states that all individuals who ac-

### Modular Elements

Standards, guidelines, and baselines should not be in one large document. Each has a specific purpose and a different audience. A document describing how to be in compliance with a specific regulation may go to the management staff, whereas a detailed procedure on how to properly secure a specific operating system would be directed toward an IT member. Keeping standards, guidelines, and baselines separate and modular in nature helps for proper distribution and updating when necessary.

cess confidential information must be properly authenticated, the supporting procedures will explain the steps for this to happen by defining the access criteria for authorization, how access control mechanisms are implemented and configured, and how access activities are audited. If a standard states that backups should be performed, then the procedures will define the detailed steps necessary to perform the backup, the timelines of backups, the storage of backup media, and so on. Procedures should be detailed enough to be both understandable and useful to a diverse group of individuals.

To tie these items together, let's walk through an example. A corporation's security policy indicates that confidential information should be properly protected. It states the issue in very broad and general terms. A supporting standard mandates that all customer information held in databases must be encrypted with the Advanced Encryption Standard (AES) algorithm while it is stored and that it cannot be transmitted over the Internet unless IPSec encryption technology is used. The standard indicates what type of protection is required and provides another level of granularity and explanation. The supporting procedures explain exactly how to implement the AES and IPSec technologies, and the guidelines cover how to handle cases when data is accidentally corrupted or compromised during transmission. All of these work together to provide a company with a security structure.

## Implementation

*Where are the policies that we spent $100,000 to develop? Response: What is a policy again?*

Unfortunately, security policies, standards, procedures, baselines, and guidelines often are written because an auditor instructed a company to document these items, but then they live on a file server and are not shared, explained, or used. To be useful, they need to be put into action. No one is going to follow the rules if people don't know that the rules exist. Security policies and the items that support them not only have to be developed, but also have to be implemented and enforced.

To be effective, employees need to know about security issues within these documents; therefore, the policies and their supporting counterparts need visibility. Awareness training, manuals, presentations, newsletters, and legal banners can achieve this visibility. It needs to be clear that the directives came from senior management and that the full management staff supports these policies. Employees need to understand what is expected of them in their actions, behaviors, accountability, and performance.

Implementing security policies and the items that support them shows due care by the company and its management staff. Informing employees of what is expected of them and the consequences of noncompliance can come down to a liability issue. If a company fires an employee because he was downloading pornographic material to the company's computer, the employee may take the company to court and win if the employee can prove that he was not properly informed of what was considered acceptable and unacceptable use of company property and what the consequences were. Security-awareness training is covered in later sections, but understand that companies that do not supply this to their employees are not practicing due care and can be held negligent and liable in the eyes of the law.

## Due Care and Due Diligence

Due care and due diligence are terms that are used throughout this book. *Due diligence* is the act of investigating and understanding the risks the company faces. A company practices *due care* by developing and implementing security policies, procedures, and standards. Due care shows that a company has taken responsibility for the activities that take place within the corporation and has taken the necessary steps to help protect the company, its resources, and employees from possible threats. So, due diligence is understanding the current threats and risks and due care is implementing countermeasures to provide protection from those threats. If a company does not practice due care and due diligence pertaining to the security of its assets, it can be legally charged with negligence and held accountable for any ramifications of that negligence.

## References

- **NCSA Security Policies and Procedures** www.ncsa.uiuc.edu/UserInfo/Security/policy/
- **SANS Institute Security Policy Project** www.sans.org/resources/policies
- **Information Security Policy World** www.information-security-policies-and-standards.com

# Information Classification

*My love letter to my dog is top secret. Response: As it should be.*

Earlier, this chapter touched upon the importance of recognizing what information is critical to a company and assigning a value to it. The rationale behind assigning values to different types of data is that it enables a company to gauge the amount of funds and resources that should go toward protecting each type of data, because not all data has the same value to a company. After the exercise of identifying important information, it should then be properly classified. A company has a lot of information that is created and maintained. The reason to classify data is to organize it according to its sensitivity to loss, disclosure, or unavailability. Once data is segmented according to its sensitivity level, the company can decide what security controls are necessary to protect different types of data. This ensures that information assets receive the appropriate level of protection, and classifications indicate the priority of that security protection. The primary purpose of data classification is to indicate the level of confidentiality, integrity, and availability protection that is required for each type of data set.

Data classification helps ensure that the data is protected in the most cost-effective manner. Protecting and maintaining data costs money, but it is important to spend this money for the information that actually requires protection. Going back to our very sophisticated example of U.S. spy satellites and the peanut butter and banana sandwich recipe, a company in charge of encryption algorithms used to transmit data to and from U.S. spy satellites would classify this data as top secret and apply complex and highly technical security controls and procedures to ensure that it is not accessed in an unauthorized method and disclosed. On the other hand, the sandwich recipe would have a lower classification, and your only means of protecting it might be to not talk about it.

Each classification should have separate handling requirements and procedures pertaining to how that data is accessed, used, and destroyed. For example, in a corporation, confidential information may be accessed only by senior management and a select few others throughout the company. Accessing the information may require two or more people to enter their access codes. Auditing could be very detailed and monitored daily, and paper copies of the information may be kept in a vault. To properly erase this data from the media, degaussing or zeroization procedures may be required. Other information in this company may be classified as sensitive, allowing a slightly larger group of people to view it. Access control on the information classified as sensitive may require only one set of credentials. Auditing happens but is only reviewed weekly, paper copies are kept in locked file cabinets, and the data can be deleted using regular measures when it is time to do so. Then, the rest of the information is marked public. All employees can access it, and no special auditing or destruction methods are required.

## Private Business vs. Military Classifications

Earlier we touched on how organizations choose different security models, depending upon the type of organization, its goals, and its objectives. Military organizations are more concerned than most private-sector businesses about not disclosing confidential information. Private-sector businesses are usually more concerned with the integrity and availability of data. These different perspectives affect data classification also.

To properly implement data classifications, a company must first decide upon the sensitivity scheme its is going to use. One company may choose to use only two layers of classifications, while another company may choose to use more. Table 3-6 explains the types of classifications available. Note that some classifications are used for commercial businesses, whereas others are military classifications.

The following shows the levels of sensitivity from the highest to the lowest for commercial business:

- Confidential
- Private
- Sensitive
- Public

The following shows the levels of sensitivity from the highest to the lowest for the military:

- Top secret
- Secret
- Confidential
- Sensitive but unclassified
- Unclassified

| Classification | Definition | Examples | Organization That Would Use This |
|---|---|---|---|
| Public | • Disclosure is not welcome, but it would not cause an adverse impact to company or personnel. | • How many people are working on a specific project<br>• Upcoming projects | Commercial business |
| Sensitive | • Requires special precautions to ensure the integrity and confidentiality of the data by protecting it from unauthorized modification or deletion.<br>• Requires higher than normal assurance of accuracy and completeness. | • Financial information<br>• Details of projects<br>• Profit earnings and forecasts | Commercial business |
| Private | • Personal information for use within a company.<br>• Unauthorized disclosure could adversely affect personnel. or company | • Work history<br>• Human resources information<br>• Medical information | Commercial business |
| Confidential | • For use within the company only.<br>• Data that is exempt from disclosure under the Freedom of Information Act or other laws and regulations.<br>• Unauthorized disclosure could seriously affect a company. | • Trade secrets<br>• Health care information<br>• Programming code<br>• Information that keeps a company competitive | Commercial business / Military |
| Unclassified | • Data is not sensitive or classified. | • Computer manual and warranty information<br>• Recruiting information | Military |
| Sensitive but unclassified (SBU) | • Minor secret.<br>• If disclosed, it could cause serious damage. | • Medical data<br>• Answers to test scores | Military |
| Secret | • If disclosed, it could cause serious damage to national security. | • Deployment plans for troops<br>• Nuclear bomb placement | Military |
| Top secret | • If disclosed, it could cause grave damage to national security. | • Blueprints of new wartime weapons<br>• Spy satellite information<br>• Espionage data | Military |

**Table 3-6** Commercial Business and Military Data Classification

It is important to not go overboard and come up with a long list of classifications, which will only cause confusion and frustration for the individuals who are going to use the system. The classifications should not be too restrictive and detailed-oriented, either, because many types of data may need to be classified.

Each classification should be unique and separate from the others and not have any overlapping effects. The classification process should also outline how information and applications are controlled and handled through their life cycles (from creation to termination).

Once the scheme is decided upon, the company or government agency needs to develop the criteria it is going to use to decide what information goes into which classification. The following list shows some criteria parameters that an organization may use to determine the sensitivity of data:

- Usefulness of data
- Value of data
- Age of data
- The level of damage that could be caused if the data were disclosed
- The level of damage that could be caused if the data were modified or corrupted
- Legal, regulatory, or contractual responsibility to protect the data
- Effects the data has on national security
- Who should be able to access the data
- Who should maintain the data
- Where the data should be kept
- Who should be able to reproduce the data
- What data requires labels and special marking
- Whether encryption is required for the data
- Whether separation of duties is required

Data is not the only thing that needs to be classified. Applications and sometimes whole systems need to be classified. The applications that hold and process classified information need to be evaluated for the level of protection that they provide. You do not want a program filled with security vulnerabilities to process and "protect" your most sensitive information. The application classifications should be based on the assurance (confidence level) the company has in the software and the type of information it can store and process.

**NOTE**   An organization needs to make sure that whoever is backing up classified data—and whoever has access to backed-up data—has the necessary clearance level. A large security risk can be introduced if low-end technicians with no security clearance can have access to this information during their tasks.

## Data Classification Procedures

The following outlines the necessary steps for a proper classification program:

1. Define classification levels.

2. Specify the criteria that will determine how data is classified.

3. Have the data owner indicate the classification of the data she is responsible for.

4. Identify the data custodian who will be responsible for maintaining data and its security level.

5. Indicate the security controls, or protection mechanisms, that are required for each classification level.

6. Document any exceptions to the previous classification issues.

7. Indicate the methods that can be used to transfer custody of the information to a different data owner.

8. Create a procedure to periodically review the classification and ownership. Communicate any changes to the data custodian.

9. Indicate termination procedures for declassifying the data.

10. Integrate these issues into the security-awareness program so that all employees understand how to handle data at different classification levels.

Now that we have chosen a sensitivity scheme, the next step is to specify how each classification should be dealt with. We need to specify provisions for access control, identification, and labeling along with how data in specific classifications is stored, maintained, transmitted, and destroyed. We also need to iron out auditing, monitoring, and compliance issues. Each classification requires a different degree of security and, therefore, different requirements from each of the mentioned items.

## Classification Controls

As mentioned earlier, which types of controls are implemented per classification depends upon the level of protection that management and the security team have determined is needed. The numerous types of controls available are discussed throughout this whole book. But some considerations pertaining to sensitive data and applications are common across most organizations:

- Strict and granular access control for all levels of sensitive data and programs (see Chapter 4 for coverage of access controls, along with file system permissions that should be understood)

- Encryption of data while stored and while in transmission (see Chapter 8 for coverage of all types of encryption technologies)

- Auditing and monitoring (determine what level of auditing is required and how long logs are to be retained)

- Separation of duties (determine whether two or more people need to be involved in accessing sensitive information to protect against fraudulent activities; if so, define and document procedures)

- Periodic reviews (review classification levels, and the data and programs that adhere to them, to ensure that they are still in alignment with business needs; data or applications may also need to be reclassified or declassified, depending upon the situation)

- Backup and recovery procedures (define and document)

- Change control procedures (define and document)

- File and file system access permissions (define and document)

## References

- *Guide for Mapping Types of Information and Information Systems to Security Categories, Volume 1*   http://csrc.nist.gov/publications/nistpubs/800-60/SP800-60V1-final.pdf

- *Handbook of Information Security Management*, **Domain 4, Chapter 4-1-1, "Information Classification: A Corporate Implementation Guide," by Jim Appleyard (CRC Press LLC)**   www.cccure.org/Documents/HISM/303-308.html

# Layers of Responsibility

Senior management and other levels of management understand the vision of the company, the business goals, and the objectives. The next layer down is the functional management, whose members understand how their individual departments work, what roles individuals play within the company, and how security affects their department directly. The next layers are operational managers and staff. These layers are closer to the actual operations of the company. They know detailed information about the technical and procedural requirements, the systems, and how the systems are used. The employees at these layers understand how security mechanisms integrate into systems, how to configure them, and how they affect daily productivity. Each layer has a different insight into what type of role security plays within an organization. Each layer should have input into the best security practices, procedures, and chosen controls to ensure that the agreed upon security level provides the necessary level of protection without negatively affecting the company's productivity.

Although each layer is important to the overall security of an organization, there are specific roles that must be clearly defined. Individuals who work in smaller environments (where everyone has to wear several hats) may get overwhelmed with the number of roles that are presented next. Many commercial businesses do not have this level of structure in their security teams, but many government agencies and military units do.

What you need to understand are the responsibilities that need to be assigned, and whether they are assigned to just a few people or to a large security team. These roles are the data owner, data custodian, system owner, security administrator, security analyst, application owner, supervisor (user manager), change control analyst, data analyst, process owner, solution provider, user, product line manager, and the guy who gets everyone coffee.

## Data Owner

The *data owner* (information owner) is usually a member of management, in charge of a specific business unit, and is ultimately responsible for the protection and use of a specific subset of information. The data owner has due care responsibilities and thus will be held responsible for any negligent act that results in the corruption or disclosure of the data. The data owner decides upon the classification of the data that he is responsible for and alters that classification if the business needs arise. This person is also responsible for ensuring that the necessary security controls are in place, ensuring that proper access rights are being used, defining security requirements per classification and backup requirements, approving any disclosure activities, and defining user access criteria. The data owner approves access requests or may choose to delegate this function to business unit managers. And it is the data owner who will deal with security violations pertaining to the data he is responsible for protecting. The data owner, who obviously has enough on his plate, delegates responsibility of the day-to-day maintenance of the data protection mechanisms to the data custodian.

## Data Custodian

*Hey you, custodian, clean up my mess! Response: Wrong type of custodian.*

The *data custodian* (information custodian) is responsible for maintaining and protecting the data. This role is usually filled by the IT department, and the duties include performing regular backups of the data, periodically validating the integrity of the data, restoring data from backup media, retaining records of activity, and fulfilling the requirements specified in the company's security policy, standards, and guidelines that pertain to information security and data protection.

---

### Data Owner Issues

Each business unit should have a data owner, to protect the unit's most critical information. The company's policies need to give the data owners the necessary authority to carry out their tasks.

This is not a technical role, but rather a business role that must understand the relationship between the unit's success and the protection of this critical asset. Not all business people understand this role, so they need to be provided with the necessary training.

## System Owner

*I am god over this system! Response: You are responsible for a printer? Your mother must be proud.*

The system owner is responsible for one or more systems, each of which may hold and process data owned by different data owners. A system owner is responsible for integrating security considerations into application and system purchasing decisions and development projects. The system owner is responsible for ensuring that adequate security is being provided by the necessary controls, password management, remote access controls, operating system configurations, and so on. This role needs to ensure that the systems are properly assessed for vulnerabilities and must report any to the incident response team and data owner.

## Security Administrator

*Hey, I have administrator rights! Response: Great, you're a security administrator. I quit.*

Anyone who has a root account on Unix or Linux systems or an administrator account on Windows or Macintosh systems actually has security administrator rights. (Unfortunately, too many people have these accounts in most environments.) This means that they can give and take away permissions, set security configurations, and mess everything up if they are having a bad day.

However, just because a person has a root or administrator account does not mean that they are fulfilling the security administrator role. A security administrator's tasks are many, and include creating new system user accounts, implementing new security software, testing security patches and components, and issuing new passwords. (The security administrator should not actually approve new system user accounts; this is a responsibility of the supervisor.) The security administrator role needs to make sure that access rights that are given to users support the policies and data owner directives.

## Security Analyst

*I have analyzed your security and you have it all wrong. Response: What a surprise.*

This role works at a higher, more strategic level than the previously described roles and helps to develop policies, standards, and guidelines and set various baselines. Whereas the previous roles are "in the weeds" and focusing on their pieces and parts of the security program, a security analyst helps define the security program elements and follows through to ensure that the elements are being carried out and practiced properly. This person works more at a design level than at an implementation level.

## Application Owner

Some applications are specific to individual business units; for example, the accounting department has accounting software, R&D has software for testing and development, and quality assurance uses some type of automated system. The application owners, usually the business unit managers, are responsible for dictating who can and cannot access their applications (subject to staying in compliance with the company's security policies, of course).

Since each unit claims ownership of its specific applications, the application owner for each unit is responsible for the security of the unit's applications. This includes testing, patching, performing change control on the programs, and making sure that the right controls are in place to provide the necessary level of protection.

## Supervisor

This role, also called user manager, is ultimately responsible for all user activity and any assets created and owned by these users. For example, suppose that Kathy is the supervisor of ten employees. Her responsibilities would include ensuring that these employees understand their responsibilities with respect to security, distributing initial passwords, making sure that the employees' account information is up-to-date, and informing the security administrator when an employee is fired, suspended, or transferred. Any change that pertains to an employee's role within the company usually affects what access rights they should and should not have, so the user manager needs to inform the security administrator of these changes immediately.

## Change Control Analyst

*I am in charge of change control and I order you to change your socks!*

As some wise people somewhere say, the only thing that is constant is change. So, when change needs to take place someone needs to make sure it is safe. The change control analyst is responsible for approving or rejecting requests to make changes to the network, systems, or software. This role needs to make sure that the change will not introduce any vulnerabilities, that it has been properly tested, and that it is properly rolled out. The change control analyst needs to understand how various changes can affect security, interoperability, performance, and productivity. Or a company can choose to just roll out the change and see what happens.

## Data Analyst

Having proper data structures, definitions, and organization is very important to a company. The data analyst is responsible for ensuring that data is stored in a way that makes the most sense to the company and the individuals who need to access and work with it. For example, payroll information should not be mixed with inventory information, the purchasing department needs to have a lot of its values in monetary terms, and the inventory system needs to follow a standardized naming scheme. The data analyst role may be responsible for architecting a new system that will hold company information or advising in the purchase of a product that will do this.

The data analyst works with the data owners to help ensure that the structures that are set up coincide with and support the company's business objectives.

## Process Owner

Have you heard the now common mantra, "Security is not a product, it's a process"? This is very true. Security should be considered and treated like just another business process, not as its own island, nor treated like a redheaded step child that has cooties. *(Author is a redheaded step child, but currently has no cooties.)*

All organizations have a lot of processes; how to take orders from customers, how to make widgets to fulfill these orders, how to ship the widgets to the customers, and how to collect from customers when they don't pay their bills. An organization could not function properly without well-defined processes.

The process owner is responsible for properly defining, improving upon, and monitoring these processes. A process owner is not necessarily tied to one business unit or application. Complex processes involve a lot of variables that can span across different departments, technologies, and data types.

## Solution Provider

*I came up with the solution to world peace, but then I forgot it. Response: Write it down on this napkin next time.*

Every vendor you will ever talk to will tell you that *they* are the right solution provider for whatever ails you. In truth, there are several different types of solution providers, because the world is full of different problems. This role is called upon when a business has a problem or requires that a process be improved upon. For example, if company A needs a solution that supports digitally signed e-mails and an authentication framework for employees, it would turn to a public key infrastructure (PKI) solution provider. A solution provider works with the business unit managers, data owners, and senior management to develop and deploy a solution to reduce the company's pain points.

## User

The *user* is any individual who routinely uses the data for work-related tasks. The user must have the necessary level of access to the data to perform the duties within their position and is responsible for following operational security procedures to ensure the data's confidentiality, integrity, and availability to others.

## Product Line Manager

Who's the guy responsible for explaining business requirements to vendors and wading through their rhetoric to see if the product is right for the company? Who is the guy responsible for ensuring compliance to license agreements? Who is the guy translating business requirements into objectives and specifications for the developer of a product or solution? Who is the guy who decides if his company *really* needs to upgrade their operating system version every time Microsoft wants to make more money? That would be the product line manager.

This role must understand business drivers, business processes, and the technology that is required to support them. The product line manager evaluates different products in the market, works with vendors, understands different options a company can take, and advises management and business units on the proper solutions that are needed to meet their goals.

## Why So Many Roles?

A decision maker is not the proper role for the data custodian or system administrator in protecting system resources. They may have the technical knowledge of how security mechanisms should be implemented and configured, but they should not be put into a position of deciding how the company approaches security and what security measures should be implemented. Too many times companies handle security at the administrator level. In these situations, security is not viewed in broad enough terms. Proper risk analysis is usually not performed. Senior management is not fully aware of the risks the company faces. Not enough funds are available for security, and when a security breach takes place, there is not an efficient way of dealing with it. As stated previously, security should work in a top-down fashion to be ultimately successful.

A company's security is not tied only to the type of firewall installed and the timeliness of security patches being applied. A company is an environment filled with various resources, activities, people, and practices. The security of the environment needs to be approached in a holistic way, with each part of security addressed in a serious and responsible manner. Although most environments will not contain all of the roles outlined previously, all of these responsibilities still need to be carried out.

## References

- **Security School for CISSP Training: Domain Spotlight on Security Management Practices**   http://searchsecurity.techtarget.com/content/0,290959,sid14_gci1010840,00.html
- *NIST Administrative Manual*, Subchapter 11.02, "Information Technology Security"   www.nist.gov/admin/mo/adman/1102.HTM
- *Information Security Management Handbook*, Domain 3, Chapter 3-5-3, "Information Protection: Organization, Roles, and Separation of Duties," by Rebecca Herold (CRC Press LLC, 2003)   www.delcreo.com/delcreo/free/docs/Information%20Protection.pdf

## Personnel

There are many facets of personnel responsibilities that fall under management's umbrella, and several of these facets have a direct correlation to the overall security of the environment.

Although society has evolved to be extremely dependent upon technology in the work area, people are still the key ingredient to a successful company. Within security, people are often the weakest link. Either accidentally through mistakes or lack of training or intentionally through fraud and malicious intent, personnel cause more security issues than hacker attacks, outside espionage, or equipment failure. Although the future actions of individuals cannot be predicted, it is possible to minimize the risks by implementing preventive measures. These include hiring the most qualified individuals, performing background checks, using detailed job descriptions, providing necessary training, enforcing strict access controls, and terminating individuals in a way that protects all parties involved.

## Structure

If a company wants to have effective employee safety, management needs to put in place a certain structure and actually follow it. This structure includes clear definitions of responsibilities, lines of authority, and acceptable reprimands for specific activities.

A clear-cut structure takes the mystery out of who does what, and how things are handled in different situations.

There are several items that can be put into place to reduce the possibilities of fraud, sabotage, misuse of information, theft, and other security compromises. *Separation of duties* makes sure that one individual cannot complete a critical task by herself. In the movies, when a submarine captain needs to launch a nuclear torpedo to blow up the enemy and save civilization as we know it, the launch usually requires three codes to be entered into the launching mechanism by three different senior crewmembers. This is an example of separation of duties, and it ensures that the captain cannot complete such an important and terrifying task all by herself.

 **NOTE**  Separation of duties may also reduce errors. If one person makes a mistake, there is a high probability that another person will catch and correct it.

In an organization that practices separation of duties, collusion must take place for fraud to be committed. *Collusion* means that at least two people are working together to cause some type of destruction or fraud.

In a software development environment, there should be clear distinctions between programmers, testing environments, libraries, operations, and production. Programmers should be able to work on their code and test it as needed. Once the programmer is finished with her tasks, she turns the code over to quality assurance, who in turn run their own tests in another environment that mirrors the production environment. Once the code passes all the necessary tests, it should be stored in a software library.

When it is necessary for the code to go into production, it moves from the library to the production environment. Code should not go from the programmer directly to production without testing and checking it into the library. The test environment should be clearly differentiated from the production environment to ensure that untested code does not accidentally go into production. And the programmer should not tinker with the software once it is in production. These clear-cut methods make sure that no steps are skipped in the phases of software development and that changes are not made in unstructured and dangerous ways.

## Hiring Practices

*I like your hat. You're hired!*

Depending on the position that needs to be filled, a level of screening should be done by human resources to ensure that the company hires the right individual for the right job. Skills should be tested and evaluated, and the caliber and character of the individual should be examined. Joe might be the best programmer in the state, but if someone looks into his past and finds out that he served prison time because he hacked into banks and stole money, the hiring manager might not be so eager to bring Joe into the organization.

*Nondisclosure agreements* need to be developed and signed by new employees to protect the company and its sensitive information. Any conflicts of interests need to be addressed, and there should be different agreements and precautions taken with temporary and contract employees.

References should be checked, military records reviewed, education verified, and if necessary, a drug test should be administered. Many times, important personal behaviors can be concealed, and that is why hiring practices now include scenario questions, personality tests, and observations of the individual, instead of just looking at a person's work history. When a person is hired, he is bringing in his business skills and whatever other baggage he carries. A company can reduce its heartache pertaining to personnel by first conducting useful and carefully carried-out hiring practices.

## Employee Controls

A management structure must be in place to make sure that everyone has someone to report to and that the responsibility for another person's actions is spread equally and intelligently. Consequences for noncompliance or unacceptable behavior must be communicated before an event takes place. Proper supervisory skills need to be acquired and used to ensure that operations go smoothly and any out-of-the-ordinary activities can be taken care of before they get out of control.

*Rotation of duties* (rotation of assignments) is an important control to keep each department a healthy and productive part of the company. No one person should stay in one position for a long period of time because they may end up having too much control over a segment of the business. Such total control could result in fraud, data modification, and misuse of resources. Employees in sensitive areas should be forced to take their vacations, which is known as a *mandatory vacation* policy. While they are on vacation, other individuals fill their positions and thus can usually detect any fraudulent errors or activities. Two of the many ways to detect fraud or inappropriate activities would be a discovery of activity from someone's user account, while they're supposed to be away on vacation, or if a specific problem stopped while someone is away and not active on the network. These anomalies are worthy of investigation.

Two variations of separation of duties and control are *split knowledge* and *dual control*. In both cases, two or more individuals are authorized and required to perform a duty or task. In the case of split knowledge, no one person knows or has all the details to perform a task. For example, two managers might be required to open a bank vault, with each only knowing part of the combination. In the case of dual control, two individuals are again authorized to perform a task, but both must be available and active in their participation to complete the task or mission. For example, two officers must perform an identical key-turn in a nuclear missile submarine, each out of reach of the other, to launch a missile. The control here is that no one person has the capability of launching a missile, because they cannot reach to turn both keys at the same time.

## Termination

Because terminations can happen for a variety of different reasons and terminated people will have different reactions, companies should have a specific set of procedures to follow with each and every termination. For example:

- The employee must leave the facility immediately under the supervision of a manager or security guard.

- The employee must surrender any identification badges or keys, complete an exit interview, and return company supplies.

- That user's accounts and passwords should be disabled or changed immediately.

It seems harsh and cold when this actually takes place, but too many companies have been hurt by vengeful employees who have lashed out at the company when their positions were revoked for one reason or another. If an employee is disgruntled in any way or the termination is unfriendly, that employee's accounts should be disabled right away and all passwords on all systems changed.

# Security-Awareness Training

The management's directives pertaining to security are captured in the security policy, and the standards, procedures, and guidelines are developed to support these directives. However, these directives will not be effective if no one knows about them and how the company expects them to be implemented. For security to be successful and effective, senior management on down to the rest of the staff need to be fully aware of the importance of enterprise and information security. All employees should understand the underlying significance of security and the specific security-related requirements expected of them.

The controls and procedures of a security program should reflect the nature of the data being processed. A company that sells baseball cards would not need the level of structured controls and security procedures that may be required of a company that develops heat-seeking missiles. These different types of companies would also have very different cultures. For a security-awareness program to be effective, these considerations must be understood. The program should be developed in a fashion that makes sense for that environment.

For an organization to achieve the desired results of its security program, it must communicate the what, how, and why of security to its employees. Security-awareness training should be comprehensive, tailored for specific groups, and organization-wide. The goal is that each employee understands the importance of security to the company as a whole and to each individual. Expected responsibilities and acceptable behaviors need to be clarified, and noncompliance repercussions, which could range from a warning to dismissal, need to be explained before being invoked.

## Different Types of Security-Awareness Training

*I want my training to have a lot of pictures and pop-up books.*

There are usually at least three separate audiences for a security-awareness program: management, staff, and technical employees. Each type of awareness training needs to be geared toward the individual audience to ensure that each group understands its particular responsibilities, liabilities, and expectations. If technical security training were given to senior management, their eyes would glaze over as soon as protocols and firewalls were mentioned. On the flip side, if legal ramifications, company liability issues pertaining to protecting data, and shareholders' expectations were discussed with the IT group, they would quickly start a game of hangman or tic-tac-toe with their neighbor.

Members of management would benefit the most from a short, focused security-awareness orientation that discusses corporate assets and financial gains and losses pertaining to security. They need to know how stock prices can be negatively affected by compromises, about possible threats and their outcomes, and why security needs to be integrated into the environment in the same way as other business processes. Because members of management must lead the rest of the company in support of security, they must gain the right mindset about its importance.

Mid-management would benefit from a more detailed explanation of the policies, procedures, standards, and guidelines and how they map to the individual departments for which they are responsible. Middle managers should be taught why their support for their specific departments is critical and what their level of responsibility is for ensuring that employees practice safe computing activities. They should also be shown how the consequences of noncompliance by individuals who report to them can affect the company as a whole and how they, as managers, may have to answer for such indiscretions.

The technical departments must receive a different presentation that aligns more to their daily tasks. They should receive a more in-depth training to discuss technical configurations, incident handling, and indications of different types of security compromises so they can be properly recognized.

Each group needs to know to whom it should report suspicious activity and how to handle these situations. Employees should not try to combat an attacker or address fraudulent activities by themselves. Each employee should be told to report these issues to upper management, and upper management should determine how to handle the situation.

The presentation given to staff members needs to demonstrate why security is important to the company and to them individually. The better they understand how insecure activities can negatively affect them, the more willing they will be to participate in preventing such activities. This presentation should have many examples of acceptable and unacceptable activities. Examples of these activities can include questioning an unknown individual in a restricted portion of the facility, appropriate usage of Internet and e-mail, not removing company-owned material, and intellectual property issues. The employees should fully understand what is expected of them and what could happen if they do not follow these guidelines. It is usually best to have each employee sign a document indicating that they have heard and understand all the security topics discussed and understand the ramifications of noncompliance. This reinforces the importance to the employee and also provides evidence down the road if the employee claims that they were never told about these expectations.

Security training should happen periodically and continually. We learn mostly by repetition, and this training should take place at least once a year. The goal is to get individuals to understand not only how security works in their environment, but also why it is important. The main reason to perform security-awareness training is to modify employees' behavior and attitude toward security.

## Evaluating the Program

Security-awareness training is a type of control, and just like any other control it should be monitored and evaluated for its effectiveness. There is no reason to spend money on something that is not working, and there is no reason not to improve something if it needs improvement. Therefore, after employees attend awareness training, a company may give them questionnaires and surveys to gauge their retention level and to get their feedback about the training, to evaluate the program's effectiveness. Unfortunately, some people will be resistant and negative because they feel as though they are being forced to do something that they do not want to do, or are being talked down to. Just expect this attitude here and there and use your wonderful wit, charm, and communication skills with them.

A good indication of the effectiveness of the program can be captured by comparing the number of reports of security incidents that were made before and after the training. If the reports increased after the training, this means that people were listening and followed through on the information that was provided to them.

 **NOTE**   For online training, capture individuals' names and what training modules have or have not been completed within a specific time period. This can then be integrated into their job performance documentation.

Security-awareness training must repeat the most important messages in different formats, be kept up-to-date, be entertaining, positive, and humorous, be simple to understand, and—most important—be supported by senior management. Management needs to allocate the resources for this activity and enforce its attendance within the organization.

## Specialized Security Training

Companies today spend a lot of money on security devices and technologies, but they commonly overlook the fact that individuals need to be trained to use these devices and technologies. Without such training, the money invested toward reducing threats is wasted and the company is still insecure. Many individuals seem to agree that people are the weakest link in security, but not enough effort goes into educating these people so that a long laundry list of threats is reduced.

Different roles require different types of training (firewall administration, risk management, policy development, IDSs, and so on). A skilled staff is one of the most critical components to the security of a company, and not enough companies are spending the funds and energy necessary to give their staffs proper levels of security education.

## References

- CISSP and SSCP Open Study Guides   www.cccure.org
- *Information Technology Security Training Requirements: A Role- and Performance-Based Model,* by Dorothea de Zafra et al., NIST Special Publication 800-16 (April 1998)   http://csrc.nist.gov/publications/nistpubs/800-16/800-16.pdf
- CSRC Awareness, Training, and Education links   http://csrc.nist.gov/ATE/

# Summary

A security program should address issues from a strategic, tactical, and operational view, as shown in Figure 3-8. Security management embodies the administrative and procedural activities necessary to support and protect information and company assets throughout the enterprise. It includes development and enforcement of security policies

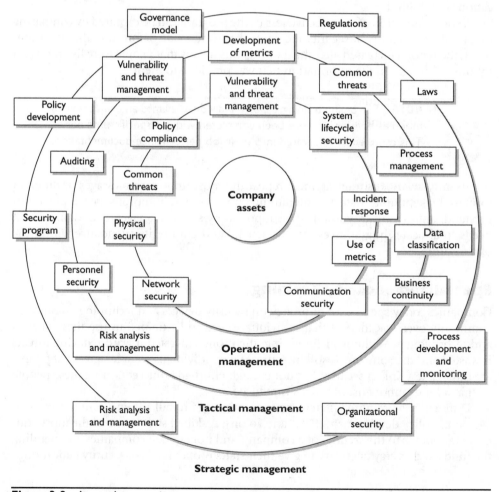

**Figure 3-8**   A complete security program contains many items.

and their supporting mechanisms: procedures, standards, baselines, and guidelines. It encompasses risk management, security-awareness training, and proper countermeasure selection and implementation. Personnel (hiring, terminating, training, and management structure) and operational (job rotation and separation of duties) activities must also be conducted properly to ensure a secure environment. Management must understand the legal and ethical responsibilities it is required to respect and uphold.

Security is a business issue and should be treated as such. It needs to be properly integrated into the company's overall business goals and objectives because security issues can negatively affect the resources the company depends upon. More and more corporations are finding out the price that has to be paid when security is not given the proper attention, support, and funds. This is a wonderful world to live in, but bad things can happen. The ones who realize this notion not only survive, but also thrive.

## Quick Tips

- A vulnerability is the absence of a safeguard or a weakness that could be exploited.
- A threat is the possibility that someone would exploit a vulnerability.
- A risk is the probability of a threat agent exploiting a vulnerability and the loss potential from that action.
- Reducing vulnerabilities and/or threats reduces the risk.
- An exposure is an instance of being exposed to losses from a threat.
- A countermeasure, also called a safeguard, mitigates the risk.
- A countermeasure can be an application, software configuration, hardware, or procedure.
- If someone is practicing due care, they are acting responsibly and will have a lower probability of being found negligent and liable if a security breach takes place.
- Security management has become more important over the years because networks have evolved from centralized environments to distributed environments.
- The objectives of security are to provide availability, integrity, and confidentiality protection to data and resources.
- Strategic planning is long term, tactical planning is midterm, and operational planning is day to day. They make up a planning horizon.
- ISO 17799 is a comprehensive set of controls comprising best practices in information security and provides guidelines on how to set up and maintain security programs.
- Security components can be technical (firewalls, encryption, and access control lists) or nontechnical (security policy, procedures, and compliance enforcement).

- Asset identification should include tangible assets (facilities, hardware) and intangible assets (corporate data, reputation).

- Project sizing, which means to understand and document the scope of the project, needs to be done before a risk analysis is performed.

- Assurance is a degree of confidence that a certain security level is being provided.

- Security management should work from the top down, from senior management down to the staff.

- Which security model a company should choose depends on the type of business, its critical missions, and its objectives.

- Risk can be transferred, rejected (ignored), reduced, or accepted.

- An example of risk transference is when a company buys insurance.

- Ways to reduce risk include improving security procedures and implementing safeguards.

- If a company is rejecting risk, it is choosing to ignore it, which can be dangerous.

- Threats $\times$ vulnerability $\times$ asset value = total risk

- (Threats $\times$ vulnerability $\times$ asset value) $\times$ controls gap = residual risk

- The main goals of risk analysis are the following: identify assets and assign values to them, identify vulnerabilities and threats, quantify the impact of potential threats, and provide an economic balance between the impact of the risk and the cost of the safeguards.

- Information risk management (IRM) is the *process* of identifying, assessing, and reducing risk to an acceptable level and implementing the right mechanisms to maintain that level of risk.

- A quantitative risk analysis attempts to assign monetary values to components within the analysis.

- A purely quantitative risk analysis is not possible because qualitative items cannot be quantified with precision.

- Capturing the degree of uncertainty when carrying out a risk analysis is important, because it indicates the level of confidence the team and management should have in the resulting figures.

- When determining the value of information, the following issues need to be considered: the cost to acquire and develop data; the cost to maintain and protect data; the value of the data to owners, users, and adversaries; the cost of replacement if the data is lost; the price others are willing to pay for the data; and the usefulness of the data.

- Automated risk analysis tools reduce the amount of manual work involved in the analysis. They can be used to estimate future expected losses and calculate the benefits of different security measures.

- Single loss expectancy (SLE) is the amount that could be lost if a specific threat agent were to exploit a vulnerability.

- Single loss expectancy × frequency per year = annualized loss expectancy (SLE × ARO = ALE)

- Qualitative risk analysis uses judgment and intuition instead of numbers.

- Qualitative risk analysis involves people with the requisite experience and education evaluating threat scenarios and rating the probability, potential loss, and severity of each threat based on their personal experience.

- The Delphi technique is a group decision method where each group member can vote anonymously.

- When choosing the right safeguard to reduce a specific risk, the cost, functionality, and effectiveness need to be evaluated and a cost/benefit analysis needs to be performed.

- A security policy is a statement by management dictating the role security plays in the organization.

- Procedures are detailed, step-by-step actions that should be followed to achieve a certain task.

- A standard specifies how hardware and software are to be used. Standards are compulsory.

- A baseline is a minimum level of security.

- Guidelines are recommendations and general approaches that provide advice and flexibility.

- Job rotation is a control to detect fraud.

- Mandatory vacations is a control type that can help detect fraudulent activities.

- Separation of duties ensures that no single person has total control over an activity or task.

- Split knowledge and dual control are two aspects of separation of duties.

- Data is classified to assign priorities to data and ensure that the appropriate level of protection is provided.

- Data owners specify the classification of data.

- Security has functional requirements, which define the expected behavior from a product or system, and assurance requirements, which establish confidence in the implemented products or systems overall.

- The security program should be integrated with current business objectives and goals.

- Management needs to define the scope and purpose of security management, provide support, appoint a security team, delegate responsibility, and review the team's findings.

- The security team should include individuals from different departments within the organization and not just technical personnel.

- A risk can have delayed loss and/or delayed damages, meaning that losses can be experienced over a period of time or damages can be experienced at a later date.

- A qualitative rating would be expressed in high, medium, or low, or on a scale of 1 to 5 or 1 to 10. A quantitative result would be expressed in dollar amounts and percentages.

- Safeguards should default to least privilege, have fail-safe defaults, and have override capabilities.

- Safeguards should be imposed uniformly so everyone has the same restrictions and functionality.

- A key element during the initial security planning process is to define reporting relationships.

- The data custodian (information custodian) is responsible for maintaining and protecting the data.

- A security analyst works at a strategic level and helps to develop policies, standards, and guidelines and set various baselines.

- Application owners are responsible for dictating who can and cannot access their applications, and for the level of protection these applications provide for the data they process and the company.

## Questions

Please remember that these questions are formatted and asked in a certain way for a reason. You must remember that the CISSP exam is asking questions at a conceptual level. Questions may not always have the perfect answer, and the candidate is advised against always looking for the perfect answer. The candidate should look for the best answer in the list.

1. Who has the primary responsibility of determining the classification level for information?

   A. Functional manager

   B. Senior management

   C. Owner

   D. User

2. Which group causes the most risk of fraud and computer compromises?

   A. Employees

   B. Hackers

C. Attackers

D. Contractors

3. If different user groups with different security access levels need to access the same information, which of the following actions should management take?

  A. Decrease the security level on the information to ensure accessibility and usability of the information.

  B. Require specific written approval each time an individual needs to access the information.

  C. Increase the security controls on the information.

  D. Decrease the classification label on the information.

4. What does management need to consider the most when classifying data?

  A. Type of employees, contractors, and customers who will be accessing the data.

  B. Availability, integrity, and confidentiality.

  C. First assess the risk level and disable countermeasures.

  D. The access controls that will be protecting the data.

5. Who is ultimately responsible for making sure data is classified and protected?

  A. Data owners

  B. Users

  C. Administrators

  D. Management

6. What is a procedure?

  A. Rules on how software and hardware must be used within the environment

  B. Step-by-step directions on how to accomplish a task

  C. Guidelines on how to approach security situations that are not covered by standards

  D. Compulsory actions

7. Which factor is the most important item when it comes to ensuring that security is successful in an organization?

  A. Senior management support

  B. Effective controls and implementation methods

  C. Updated and relevant security policies and procedures

  D. Security awareness by all employees

8. When is it acceptable to not take action on an identified risk?

    A. Never. Good security addresses and reduces all risks.

    B. When political issues prevent this type of risk from being addressed.

    C. When the necessary countermeasure is complex.

    D. When the cost of the countermeasure outweighs the value of the asset and potential loss.

9. What are security policies?

    A. Step-by-step directions on how to accomplish security tasks

    B. General guidelines used to accomplish a specific security level

    C. Broad, high-level statements from the management

    D. Detailed documents explaining how security incidents should be handled

10. Which is the most valuable technique when determining if a specific security control should be implemented?

    A. Risk analysis

    B. Cost/benefit analysis

    C. ALE results

    D. Identifying the vulnerabilities and threats causing the risk

11. Which best describes the purpose of the ALE calculation?

    A. Quantifies the security level of the environment

    B. Estimates the loss possible for a countermeasure

    C. Quantifies the cost/benefit result

    D. Estimates the loss potential of a threat in a span of a year

12. Tactical planning is:

    A. Midterm

    B. Long term

    C. Day-to-day

    D. Six months

13. What is the definition of a security exposure?

    A. An instance of being exposed to losses from a threat

    B. Any potential danger to information or systems

    C. An information security absence or weakness

    D. A loss potential of a threat

14. An effective security program requires a balanced application of:

    A. Technical and nontechnical methods

    B. Countermeasures and safeguards

    C. Physical security and technical controls

    D. Procedural security and encryption

15. The security functionality defines the expected activities of a security mechanism, and assurance defines:

    A. The controls the security mechanism will enforce

    B. The data classification after the security mechanism has been implemented

    C. The confidence of the security the mechanism is providing

    D. Cost/benefit relationship

16. Which statement is true when looking at security objectives in the private business sector versus the military sector?

    A. Only the military has true security.

    B. Businesses usually care more about data integrity and availability, whereas the military is more concerned with confidentiality.

    C. The military requires higher levels of security because the risks are so much higher.

    D. The business sector usually cares most about data availability and confidentiality, whereas the military is most concerned about integrity.

17. How do you calculate residual risk?

    A. Threats $\times$ risks $\times$ asset value

    B. (Threats $\times$ asset value $\times$ vulnerability) $\times$ risks

    C. SLE $\times$ frequency = ALE

    D. (Threats $\times$ vulnerability $\times$ asset value) $\times$ controls gap

18. Which of the following is not a purpose of doing a risk analysis?

    A. Delegate responsibility

    B. Quantify impact of potential threats

    C. Identify risks

    D. Define the balance between the impact of a risk and the cost of the necessary countermeasure

19. Which of the following is not a management role in the process of implementing and maintaining security?

    A. Support

    B. Perform risk analysis

    C. Define purpose and scope

    D. Delegate responsibility

20. Why should the team that is going to perform and review the risk analysis information be made up of people in different departments?

    A. To make sure the process is fair and that no one is left out.

    B. It shouldn't. It should be a small group brought in from outside the organization because otherwise the analysis is biased and unusable.

    C. Because people in different departments understand the risks of their department and it ensures that the data going into the analysis is as close to reality as possible.

    D. Because the people in the different departments are the ones causing the risks, so they should be the ones held accountable.

21. Which best describes a quantitative risk analysis?

    A. Scenario-based analysis to research different security threats

    B. A method used to apply severity levels to potential loss, probability of loss, and risks

    C. A method that assigns monetary values to components in the risk assessment

    D. A method that is based on gut feelings and opinions

22. Why is a truly quantitative risk analysis not possible to achieve?

    A. It is possible, which is why it is used.

    B. It assigns severity levels. Thus, it is hard to translate into monetary values.

    C. It is dealing with purely quantitative elements.

    D. Quantitative measures must be applied to qualitative elements.

23. If there are automated tools for risk analysis, why does it take so much time to complete?

    A. A lot of data has to be gathered to be inputted into the automated tool.

    B. Management has to approve it and then a team has to be built.

    C. Risk analysis cannot be automated because of the nature of the assessment.

    D. Many people have to agree on the same data.

24. Which of the following is a legal term that pertains to a company or individual taking reasonable actions and is used to determine liability?

    A. Standards

    B. Due process

    C. Due care

    D. Downstream liabilities

## Answers

1. C. A company can have one specific data owner or different data owners who have been delegated the responsibility of protecting specific sets of data. One of the responsibilities that goes into protecting this information is properly classifying it.

2. **A.** It is commonly stated that internal threats comprise 70–80 percent of the overall threat to a company. This is because employees already have privileged access to a wide range of company assets. The outsider who wants to cause damage must obtain this level of access before she can carry out the type of damage that internal personnel can carry out. A lot of the damages that are caused by internal employees are brought about by mistakes and system misconfigurations.

3. **C.** If data is going to be available to a wide range of people, more granular security should be implemented to ensure that only the necessary people access the data and that the operations they carry out are controlled. The security implemented can come in the form of authentication and authorization technologies, encryption, and specific access control mechanisms.

4. **B.** The best answer to this question is B because, to properly classify data, the data owner needs to evaluate the availability, integrity, and confidentiality requirements of the data. Once this evaluation is done, it will dictate which employees, contractors, and users can access the data, which is expressed in answer A. This assessment will also help determine the controls that should be put into place.

5. **D.** The key to this question is the use of the word "ultimately." Management is ultimately responsible for everything that takes place within a company. It needs to make sure on an ongoing basis that data and resources are being properly protected. Management can delegate tasks to others, but it is ultimately responsible.

6. **B.** Standards are rules that must be followed, thus they are compulsory. Guidelines are recommendations. Procedures are step-by-step instructions.

7. **A.** Without senior management's support, a security program will not receive the necessary attention, funds, resources, and enforcement capabilities.

8. **D.** Companies may decide to live with specific risks they are faced with if the cost of trying to protect themselves would be greater than the potential loss if the threat were to become real. Countermeasures are usually complex to a degree, and there are almost always political issues surrounding different risks, but these are not reasons to not implement a countermeasure.

9. **C.** A security policy captures senior management's perspectives and directives on what role security should play within the company. Security policies are usually general and use broad terms so that they can cover a wide range of items.

10. **B.** Although the other answers may seem correct, B is the best answer here. This is because a risk analysis is performed to identify risks and come up with suggested countermeasures. The ALE tells the company how much it could lose if a specific threat became real. The ALE value will go into the cost/benefit analysis, but the ALE does not address the cost of the countermeasure and the benefit of a countermeasure. All the data captured in answers A, C, and D is inserted into a cost/benefit analysis.

11. **D.** The ALE calculation estimates the potential loss that can affect one asset from a specific threat within a one-year time span. This value is used to figure out the amount of money that should be earmarked to protect this asset from this threat.

12. **A.** There are three types of goals that make up the planning horizon: operational, tactical, and strategic. The tactical goals are midterm goals that must be accomplished before the overall strategic goal is accomplished.

13. **A.** An exposure is an instance of being exposed to losses from a threat agent. A vulnerability can cause an organization to be exposed to possible damages. For example, if password management is lax and password rules are not enforced, the company can be exposed to the possibility of having users' passwords captured and used in an unauthorized manner.

14. **A.** Security is not defined by a firewall, an access control mechanism, a security policy, company procedures, employee conduct, or authentication technologies. It is defined by all of these and how they integrate together within an environment. Security is neither purely technical nor purely procedural, but rather a mix of the two.

15. **C.** The functionality describes how a mechanism will work and behave. This may have nothing to do with the actual protection it provides. Assurance is the level of confidence in the protection level a mechanism will provide. When systems and mechanisms are evaluated, their functionality and assurance should be examined and tested individually.

16. **B.** Although answer C may seem correct to you, it is a subjective answer. Businesses will see their threats and risks as being more important than another organization's threats and risks. The military has a rich history of having to keep its secrets secret. This is usually not as important in the commercial sector relative to the military.

17. **D.** The equation is more conceptual than practical. It is hard to assign a number to a vulnerability and a threat individually. This equation enables you to look at the potential loss of a specific asset and look at the controls gap (what the specific countermeasure cannot protect against). What is left is the residual risk. Residual risk is what is left over after a countermeasure is implemented.

18. **A.** The other three answers are the main reasons to carry out a risk analysis. An analysis is not carried out to delegate responsibilities. Management will take on this responsibility once the results of the analysis are reported to it and it understands what actually needs to be carried out.

19. **B.** The number one ingredient management needs to provide when it comes to security is support. Management needs to define the role and scope of security and allocate the funds and resources. Management also delegates who does what pertaining to security. It does not carry out the analysis, but rather

is responsible for making sure one is done and that management acts on the results it provides.

20. **C.** An analysis is only as good as the data that goes into it. Data pertaining to risks the company faces should be extracted from the people who understand best the business functions and environment of the company. Each department understands its own threats and resources, and may have possible solutions to specific threats that affect its part of the company.

21. **C.** A quantitative risk analysis assigns monetary values and percentages to the different components within the assessment. A qualitative analysis uses opinions of individuals and a rating system to gauge the severity level of different threats and the benefits of specific countermeasures.

22. **D.** During a risk analysis, the team is trying to properly predict the future and all the risks that future may bring. It is somewhat of a subjective exercise and requires educated guessing. It is very hard to properly predict that a flood will take place once in ten years and cost a company up to $40,000 in damages, but this is what a quantitative analysis tries to accomplish.

23. **A.** An analysis usually takes a long time to complete because of all the data that must be properly gathered. There are generally a lot of different sources for this type of data, and properly extracting it is extremely time consuming. In most situations, it involves setting up meetings with specific personnel and going through a question-and-answer process.

24. **C.** A company's or individual's actions can be judged by the "Prudent Person Rule," which looks at how a prudent or reasonable person would react in similar situations. Due care means to take these necessary actions to protect the company and its assets, customers, and employees. Computer security has many aspects pertaining to practicing due care. If management does not ensure that these things are in place, it can be found negligent.

# Access Controls

This chapter presents the following:
- Identification methods and technologies
- Authentication methods, models, and technologies
- Discretionary, mandatory, and nondiscretionary models
- Accountability, monitoring, and auditing practices
- Emanation security and technologies
- Intrusion detection systems
- Possible threats to access control practices and technologies

A cornerstone in the foundation of information security is to control how resources are accessed so that they can be protected from unauthorized modification or disclosure. The controls that enforce access control can be technical, physical, or administrative in nature.

## Access Controls Overview

*Access controls* are security features that control how users and systems communicate and interact with other systems and resources. They protect the systems and resources from unauthorized access and can be a component that participates in determining the level of authorization after an authentication procedure has successfully completed. Although we usually think of a user as the entity that requires access to a network resource or information, there are many other types of entities that require access to other network entities and resources that are subject to access control. It is important to understand the definition of a subject and an object when working in the context of access control.

*Access* is the flow of information between a subject and an object. A *subject* is an active entity that requests access to an object or the data within an object. A subject can be a user, program, or process that accesses an object to accomplish a task. When a program accesses a file, the program is the subject and the file is the object. An *object* is a passive entity that contains information. An object can be a computer, database, file, computer program, directory, or field contained in a table within a database. When you look up information in a database, you are the active subject and the database is the passive object. Figure 4-1 illustrates subjects and objects.

Access control is a broad term that covers several different types of mechanisms that enforce access control features on computer systems, networks, and information. Access control is extremely important because it is one of the first lines of defense used to fight against unauthorized access to systems and network resources. When a user is prompted for a username and password to be able to use a computer, this is access control. Once the user logs in and later attempts to access a file, that file may have a list of users and groups that have the right to access it. If the user is not on this list, the user is denied. This is another form of access control. The users' permissions and rights may be based on their identity, clearance, and/or group membership. Access controls give organizations the ability to control, restrict, monitor, and protect resource availability, integrity, and confidentiality.

## Security Principles

The three main security principles for any type of security control are

- Availability
- Integrity
- Confidentiality

These principles, which were touched upon in Chapter 3, will be a running theme throughout this book because each core subject of each chapter approaches these prin-

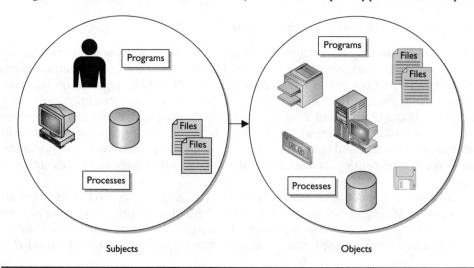

**Figure 4-1**   Subjects are active entities that access objects; objects are passive entities.

ciples in a unique way. In Chapter 3, you read that security management procedures include identifying threats that can negatively affect the availability, integrity, and confidentiality of the company's assets and finding cost-effective countermeasures that will protect them. This chapter looks at the ways that the three principles can be affected and protected through access control methodologies and technologies.

Every control that is used in computer and information security provides at least one of these security principles. It is critical that security professionals understand all of the possible ways that these principles can be provided and circumvented.

## Availability

*Hey, I'm available. Response: But no one wants you.*

Information, systems, and resources need to be available to users in a timely manner so productivity will not be affected. Most information needs to be accessible and available to users when it is requested so that they can carry out tasks and fulfill their responsibilities. Accessing information does not seem that important until it is inaccessible. Administrators experience this when a file server goes offline or a highly used database is out of service for one reason or another. Fault tolerance and recovery mechanisms are put into place to ensure the continuity of the *availability* of resources. User productivity can be greatly affected if requested data is not readily available.

Information has various attributes, such as accuracy, relevance, timeliness, and privacy. It may be extremely important for a stockbroker to have information that is accurate and timely, so that he can buy and sell stocks at the right times at the right prices. The stockbroker may not necessarily care about the privacy of this information, only that it is readily available. A soft drink company that depends on its soda pop recipe would care about the privacy of this trade secret, and the security mechanisms in place need to ensure this secrecy.

## Integrity

Information must be accurate, complete, and protected from unauthorized modification. When a security mechanism provides *integrity*, it protects data, or a resource, from being altered in an unauthorized fashion. If some type of illegitimate modification does occur, the security mechanism must alert the user in some fashion. One example is when a user sends a request to her online bank account to pay her $24.56 water utility bill. The bank needs to be sure that the integrity of that transaction was not altered during transmission, so the user does not end up paying the utility company $240.56 instead. Integrity of data is very important. What if a confidential e-mail was sent from the Secretary of State to the President of the United States and was intercepted and altered without a security mechanism in place that disallows this or alerts the President that this message has been altered? Instead of receiving a message reading, "We would love for you and your wife to stop by for drinks tonight," the message could be altered to say, "We have just bombed Libya." Big difference.

## Confidentiality

*This is my secret and you can't have it. Response: I don't want it.*

*Confidentiality* is the assurance that information is not disclosed to unauthorized individuals, programs, or processes. Some information is more sensitive than other information and requires a higher level of confidentiality. Control mechanisms need to be in place to dictate who can access data and what the subject can do with it once they have accessed it. These activities need to be controlled, audited, and monitored. Examples of information that could be considered confidential are health records, financial account information, criminal records, source code, trade secrets, and military tactical plans. Some security mechanisms that would provide confidentiality are encryption, logical and physical access controls, transmission protocols, database views, and controlled traffic flow.

It is important for a company to identify the data that needs to be classified, so that the company can ensure that a top priority of security protects this information and keeps it confidential. If this information is not singled out, too much time and money can be spent on implementing the same level of security for critical and mundane information alike. It may be necessary to configure virtual private networks (VPNs) between organizations and use the IPSec encryption protocol to encrypt all messages passed when communicating about trade secrets, sharing customer information, or making financial transactions. This takes a certain amount of hardware, labor, funds, and overhead. The same security precautions are not necessary when communicating that today's special in the cafeteria is liver and onions with a roll on the side. So, the first step in protecting data's confidentiality is to identify which information is sensitive and to what degree, and then implement security mechanisms to protect it properly.

Different security mechanisms can supply different degrees of availability, integrity, and confidentiality. The environment, the classification of the data that is to be protected, and the security goals need to be evaluated to ensure that the proper security mechanisms are bought and put into place. Many corporations have wasted a lot of time and money not following these steps and instead buying the new "gee whiz" product that recently hit the market.

# Identification, Authentication, and Authorization

For a user to be able to access a resource, he first must prove that he is who he claims to be, has the necessary credentials, and has been given the necessary rights or privileges to perform the actions he is requesting. Once these steps are completed successfully, the user can access and use network resources; however, it is necessary to track the user's activities and enforce accountability for his actions. *Identification* describes a method of ensuring that a subject (user, program, or process) is the entity it claims to be. Identification can be provided with the use of a username or account number. To be properly *authenticated*, the subject is usually required to provide a second piece to the credential set. This piece could be a password, passphrase, cryptographic key, personal identification number (PIN), anatomical attribute, or token. These two credential items are com-

## Race Condition

A race condition is possible when two or more processes use a shared resource, as in data within a variable. It is important that the processes carry out their functionality in the correct sequence. If process 2 carried out its task on the data before process 1, the result will be much different than if process 1 carried out its tasks on the data before process 2. A race condition is when processes carry out their tasks on a shared resource in an incorrect order.

In software, when the authentication and authorization steps are split into two functions, there is a possibility that an attacker could use a race condition to force the authorization step to be completed *before* the authentication step. This would be a flaw in the software that the attacker has figured out how to exploit. A *race condition* is when two or more processes use the same resource and the sequences of steps within software can be carried out in improper order, which can drastically affect the output. So, an attacker can force the authorization step to take place before the authentication step and gain unauthorized access to a resource.

pared to information that has been previously stored for this subject. If these credentials match the stored information, the subject is authenticated. But we are not done yet.

Once the subject provides its credentials and is properly identified, the system it is trying to access needs to determine if this subject has been given the necessary rights and privileges to carry out the requested actions. The system will look at some type of access control matrix or compare security labels to verify that this subject may indeed access the requested resource and perform the actions it is attempting. If the system determines that the subject may access the resource, it *authorizes* the subject.

Although identification, authentication, and authorization have close and complementary definitions, each has distinct functions that fulfill a specific requirement in the process of access control. A user may be properly identified and authenticated to the network, but he may not have the authorization to access the files on the file server. On the other hand, a user may be authorized to access the files on the file server, but until she is properly identified and authenticated, those resources are out of reach. Figure 4-2 illustrates the three steps that must happen for a subject to access an object.

The subject needs to be held accountable for the actions taken within a system or domain. The only way to ensure accountability is if the subject is uniquely identified and the subject's actions are recorded.

*Logical access controls* are tools used for identification, authentication, authorization, and accountability. They are software components that enforce access control measures for systems, programs, processes, and information. The logical access controls can be embedded within operating systems, applications, add-on security packages, or database and telecommunication management systems. It can be challenging to synchronize all access controls and ensure that all vulnerabilities are covered without producing overlaps of functionality. However, if it were easy, security professionals would not be getting paid the big bucks!

**Figure 4-2**
There are three steps that must happen for a subject to access an object: identification, authentication, and authorization.

NOTE   The words "logical" and "technical" can be used interchangeably in this context. It is conceivable that the CISSP exam would refer to logical and technical controls interchangeably.

An individual's identity needs to be verified during the authentication process. Authentication usually involves a two-step process: entering public information (a username, employee number, account number, or department ID) and then entering private information (a static password, smart token, cognitive password, one-time password, PIN, or digital signature). Entering public information is the identification step and entering private information is the authentication step of the two-step process. Each technique used for identification and authentication has its pros and cons. Each should be properly evaluated to determine the right mechanism for the correct environment.

NOTE   A cognitive password is based on a user's opinion or life experience. The password could be a mother's maiden name, a favorite color, or a dog's name.

## References

- **Secure programmer: Prevent race conditions**   www-128.ibm.com/developerworks/library-combined/l-sprace.html

- **"What Are Race Conditions and Deadlocks?" Microsoft Knowledge Base Article 317723**   http://support.microsoft.com/default.aspx?scid=kb;en-us;Q317723

# Identification and Authentication

*Now, who are you again?*

Once a person has been identified, through the user ID or a similar value, she must be authenticated, which means she must prove she is who she says she is. There are three general factors that can be used for authentication: something a person knows, something a person has, and something a person is.

Something a person knows can be, for example, a password, PIN, mother's maiden name, or combination to a lock. Authenticating a person by something that she knows is usually the least expensive to implement. The downside to this method is that another person may aquire this knowledge and gain unauthorized access to a system or facility.

Something a person has can be a key, swipe card, access card, or badge. This method is common for accessing facilities, but could also be used to access sensitive areas or to authenticate systems. A downside to this method is that the item can be lost or stolen, which could result in unauthorized access.

Something specific to a person becomes a bit more interesting. This is not based on if the person is a Republican, a martian, or a moron—it is based on a physical attribute. Authenticating a person's identity based on a unique physical attribute is referred to as biometrics. (For more information, see the upcoming section, "Biometrics.")

*Strong authentication* contains two out of these three methods: something a person knows, has, or is. Using a biometric system by itself does not provide strong authentication because it provides only one out of the three methods. Biometrics supplies what a person is, not what a person knows or has. For a strong authentication process to be in place, a biometric system needs to be coupled with a mechanism that checks for one of the other two methods. For example, many times the person has to type a PIN number into a keypad before the biometric scan is performed. This satisfies the "what the person knows" category. Conversely, the person could be required to swipe a magnetic card through a reader prior to the biometric scan. This would satisfy the "what the person has" category. Whatever identification system is used, for strong authentication to be in the process, it must include two out of the three categories. This is also referred to as *two-factor authentication*.

## Identification Component Requirements

When issuing identification values to users, the following should be in place:

- Each value should be unique, for user accountability.
- A standard naming scheme should be followed.
- The value should be nondescriptive of the user's position or tasks.
- The value should not be shared between users.

## Identity Management

*There are too many of you who want to access too much stuff. Everyone just go away!*

*Identity management* is a broad term that encompasses the use of different products to identify, authenticate, and authorize users through automated means. Selling identity management products is now a flourishing market that focuses on reducing administrative costs, increasing security, and improving upon service levels throughout enterprises. The continual increase in complexity and diversity of networked environments only increases the complexity of keeping track of who can access what and when. Users usually access several different types of systems throughout their daily tasks, which makes controlling access and providing the necessary level of protection on different data types difficult and full of obstacles. This complexity usually results in unforeseen and unidentified holes in asset protection, overlapping and contradictory controls, and policy and regulation noncompliance. It is the goal of identity management technologies to simplify the administration of these tasks and bring sanity to chaos.

The following are many of the common problems that enterprises deal with today in controlling access to assets:

- **Various types of users need different levels of access**   Internal users, contractors, outsiders, partners, etc.

- **Resources have different classification levels**   Confidential, internal use only, private, public, etc.

- **Diverse identity data must be kept on different types of users**   Credentials, personal data, contact information, work-related data, digital certificates, cognitive passwords, etc.

- **The corporate environment is continually changing**   Business environment needs, resource access needs, employee roles, actual employees, etc.

Despite all of these challenges, access control is expected to be consistent, efficient, transparent, reliable, and secure. (Sigh…)

The traditional identity management process has been manual, using directory services with permissions and profiles. This approach has proven incapable of keeping up with complex demands and thus has been replaced with the use of newly arrived automated applications that are rich in functionality, including enterprise-wide products and single sign-on solutions. The following are some of the services that these types of products supply:

- User provisioning
- Password synchronization and resetting
- Self service for users on specific types of activities
- Delegation of administrative tasks
- Centralized auditing and reporting
- Integrated workflow and increase in business productivity

- Decrease in network access points
- Regulatory compliance

The following sections explain the various types of authentication methods commonly used and integrated in many identity management processes and products today.

## References

- **"Securing Identity: Part 3 – Infrastructure Versus Management," by META Group (March 13, 2003)**   www.entrust.com/resources/pdf/metagroupreport.pdf
- **"Identity Management in the Real World," by Deborah Radcliff, CSOonline .com (Nov. 2004)**   www.csoonline.com/read/110104/idmgmt.html

## Biometrics

*I would like to prove who I am. Please look at the blood vessels at the back of my eyeball. Response: Gross.*

*Biometrics* verifies an individual's identity by analyzing a unique personal attribute or behavior, which is one of the most effective and accurate methods of verifying identification. Biometrics is a very sophisticated technology; thus, it is much more expensive and complex than the other types of identity verification processes. A biometric system can make authentication decisions based on an individual's behavior, as in signature dynamics, but these can change over time and possibly be forged. Biometric systems that base authentication decisions on physical attributes (iris, retina, fingerprint) provide more accuracy, because physical attributes typically don't change, absent some disfiguring injury, and are harder to impersonate.

A biometric system scans an attribute or behavior of a person and compares it to a record that was created in an earlier enrollment process. Because this system inspects the grooves of a person's fingerprint, the pattern of someone's retina, or the pitches of someone's voice, it has to be extremely sensitive. The system must perform accurate and repeatable measurements of anatomical or physiological characteristics. This type of sensitivity can easily cause false positives or false negatives. The system must be calibrated so that these false positives and false negatives occur infrequently and the results are as accurate as possible.

When a biometric system rejects an authorized individual, it is called a *Type I error* (false rejection rate). When the system accepts impostors who should be rejected, it is called a *Type II error* (false acceptance rate). The goal is to obtain low numbers for each type of error, but Type II errors are the most dangerous and thus the most important to avoid.

When comparing different biometric systems, many different variables are used, but one of the most important metrics is the *crossover error rate (CER)*. This rating is stated as a percentage and represents the point at which the false rejection rate equals the false acceptance rate. This rating is the most important measurement when determining the system's accuracy. A biometric system that delivers a CER of 3 will be more accurate than a system that delivers a CER of 4.

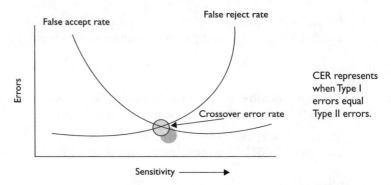

NOTE  Crossover error rate (CER) is also called equal error rate (EER).

What is the purpose of this CER value anyway? Using the CER as an impartial judgment of a biometric system helps to create standards by which products from different vendors can be fairly judged and evaluated. If you are going to buy a biometric system, you need a way to compare the accuracy between different systems. You can just go by the different vendors' marketing material (they all say they are the best), or you can compare the different CER values of the products to see which one really is more accurate than the others. It is also a way to keep the vendors honest. One vendor may tell you, "We have absolutely no Type II errors." This would mean that their product would not allow any imposters to be improperly authenticated. But what if you asked the vendor how many Type I errors their product had and she sheepishly replied, "We average around 90 percent of Type I errors." That would mean that 90 percent of the authentication attempts would be rejected, which would negatively affect your employees' productivity. So you can ask about their CER value, which represents when the Type I and Type II errors are equal, to give you a better understanding of the product's overall accuracy.

Individual environments have specific security level requirements, which will dictate how many Type I and Type II errors are acceptable. For example, a military institution that is very concerned about confidentiality would be prepared to accept a certain number of Type I errors, but would absolutely not accept any false accepts (Type II errors). Because all biometric systems can be calibrated, if you lower the Type II error rate by adjusting the system's sensitivity, it will result in an increase in Type I errors. The military institution would obviously calibrate the biometric system to lower the Type II errors to zero, but that would mean that it would have to accept a higher rate of Type I errors.

Biometrics is the most expensive method of verifying a person's identity, and it faces other barriers to becoming widely acceptable. These include user acceptance, enrollment timeframe, and throughput. Many times people are reluctant to let a machine read the pattern of their retina or scan the geometry of their hand. This lack of enthusiasm has slowed down the widespread use of biometric systems within our society. The enrollment phase requires an action to be performed several times to capture a clear and distinctive reference record. People are not particularly fond of expending this time and energy when they are used to just picking a password and quickly typing it into their console. When a person attempts to be authenticated by a biometric system, sometimes the system will request an action to be completed several times. If the system was unable to get a clear reading of an iris scan or could not capture a full voice verification print, the individual may have to repeat the action. This causes low throughput, stretches the individual's patience, and reduces acceptability.

There are many types of biometric systems that examine different personal characteristics. With each type of system, the individual must go through an enrollment process, which captures the biometric data and stores it in a reference file. This reference file is used later when the person attempts to be authenticated.

The following is an overview of the different types of biometric systems and the physiological characteristics they examine.

**Fingerprint**   Fingerprints are made up of ridge endings and bifurcations exhibited by the friction ridges and other detailed characteristics that are called *minutiae*. It is the distinctiveness of these minutiae that gives each individual a unique fingerprint. An individual places his finger on a device that reads the details of the fingerprint and compares this to a reference file. If the two match, the individual's identity has been verified.

**NOTE**   Fingerprint systems store the full fingerprint, which is actually a lot of information that takes up hard drive space and resources. The finger-scan technology extracts specific features from the fingerprint and stores just that information, which takes up less hard drive space and allows for quicker database lookups and comparisons.

**Palm Scan**   The palm holds a wealth of information, and has many aspects that are used to identify an individual. The palm has creases, ridges, and grooves throughout that are unique to a specific person. The palm scan also includes the fingerprints of each finger. An individual places his hand on the biometric device, which scans and captures this information. This information is compared to a reference file and the identity is either verified or rejected.

**Hand Geometry** The shape of a person's hand (the length and width of the hand and fingers) defines hand geometry. This trait differs significantly between people and is used in some biometric systems to verify identity. A person places her hand on a device that has grooves for each finger. The system compares the geometry of each finger, and the hand as a whole, to the information in a reference file to verify that person's identity.

**Retina Scan** A system that reads a person's retina scans the blood-vessel pattern of the retina on the backside of the eyeball. This pattern has shown to be extremely unique between different people. A camera is used to project a beam inside the eye and capture the pattern and compare it to a reference file recorded previously.

**Iris Scan** The iris is the colored portion of the eye that surrounds the pupil. The iris has unique patterns, rifts, colors, rings, coronas, and furrows. The uniqueness of each of these characteristics within the iris is captured by a camera and compared with the information gathered during the enrollment phase.

**NOTE** When using an iris pattern biometric system, the optical unit must be positioned so that the sun does not shine into the aperture; thus, when implemented, it must have proper placement within the facility.

**Signature Dynamics** When a person signs a signature, usually they do so in the same manner and speed each time. Signing a signature produces electrical signals that can be captured by a biometric system. The physical motions performed when someone is signing a document create these electrical signals. The signals provide unique characteristics that can be used to distinguish one individual from another. Signature dynamics provides more information than a static signature, so there are more variables to verify when confirming an individual's identity and more assurance that this person is who he claims to be.

Signature dynamics is different from a digitized signature. A digitized signature is just an electronic copy of someone's signature and is not a biometric system that captures the speed of signing, the way the person holds the pen, and the pressure the signer exerts to generate the signature.

**Keyboard Dynamics** Whereas signature dynamics is a method that captures the electrical signals when a person signs a name, keyboard dynamics captures electrical signals when a person types a certain phrase. As a person types a specified phrase, the biometric system captures the speed and motions of this action. Each individual has a certain style and speed, which translate into unique signals. This type of authentication is more effective than typing in a password, because a password is easily obtainable. It is much harder to repeat a person's typing style than it is to acquire a password.

**Voice Print** There are many subtle distinguishing differences in people's speech sounds and patterns. A biometric system that is programmed to capture a voice print and compare it to the information captured in a reference file can differentiate one individual from another. During the enrollment process, an individual is asked to say several different words. Later, when this individual needs to be authenticated, the biometric system jumbles these words and presents them to the individual. The individual then repeats the sequence of words given. This is used as a deterrent so that others will not attempt to record the session and play it back in hopes of obtaining unauthorized access.

**Facial Scan** A system that scans a person's face takes many attributes and characteristics into account. People have different bone structures, nose ridges, eye widths, forehead sizes, and chin shapes. These are all captured during a facial scan and compared to an earlier captured scan held within a reference record. If the information is a match, the person is positively identified.

**Hand Topography** Whereas hand geometry looks at the size and width of an individual's hand and fingers, hand topology looks at the different peaks and valleys of the hand, along with its overall shape and curvature. When an individual wants to be authenticated, she places her hand on the system. Off to one side of the system, a camera snaps a side-view picture of the hand from a different view and angle than that of systems that target hand geometry, and thus captures different data. This attribute is not unique enough to authenticate individuals by itself and is commonly used in conjunction with hand geometry.

## References

- **Michigan State University Biometrics Research web site** biometrics.cse.msu.edu
- **The Biometric Consortium home page** www.biometrics.org

## Passwords

User identification coupled with a reusable password is the most common form of system identification and authorization mechanisms. A password is a protected string of characters that is used to authenticate an individual. As stated previously, authentication factors are based on what a person knows, has, or is. A password is something the user knows.

Passwords are one of the most used authentication mechanisms employed today. It is important that the passwords are strong and properly managed.

**Password Management** Although passwords are the most commonly used authentication mechanisms, they are also considered one of the weakest security mechanisms available. Why? Users usually choose passwords that are easily guessed (spouse's name, user's birth date, or dog's name), tell others their passwords, and many times write the passwords down on a sticky note and cleverly hide it under the keyboard. To most users, security is usually not the most important or interesting part of using their computers—except when someone hacks into their computer and steals confidential information. Then security is all the rage.

This is where password management steps in. If passwords are properly generated, updated, and kept secret, they can provide effective security. Password generators can be used to create passwords for users. This ensures that a user will not be using "Bob" or "Spot" for a password, but if the generator spits out "kdjasijew284802h," the user will surely scribble it down on a piece of paper and safely stick it to the monitor, which defeats the whole purpose. If a password generator is going to be used, the tools should create uncomplicated, pronounceable, non-dictionary words to help users remember them so that they aren't tempted to write them down.

If the users can choose their own passwords, the operating system should enforce certain password requirements. The operating system can require that a password contain a certain number of characters, unrelated to the user ID, include special characters, include upper- and lowercase letters, and not be easily guessable. The operating system can keep track of the passwords a specific user generates, to ensure that no passwords are reused. The users should also be forced to change their passwords periodically. All of these factors make it harder for an attacker to guess or obtain passwords within the environment.

If an attacker is after a password, she can try a few different techniques:

- **Electronic monitoring** Listening to network traffic to capture information, especially when a user is sending her password to an authentication server. The password can be copied and reused by the attacker at another time, which is called a *replay attack.*

- **Access the password file** Usually done on the authentication server. The password file contains many users' passwords and, if compromised, can be the source of a lot of damage. This file should be protected with access control mechanisms and encryption.

- **Brute force attacks** Performed with tools that cycle through many possible character, number, and symbol combinations to uncover a password.

- **Dictionary attacks** Files of thousands of words are used to compare to the user's password until a match is found.

- **Social engineering** An attacker falsely convinces an individual that she has the necessary authorization to access specific resources.

There are techniques that can be implemented to provide another layer of security for passwords and their use. After each successful logon, a message can be presented to a user indicating the date and time of the last successful logon, the location of this logon, and if there were any unsuccessful logon attempts. This alerts the user if suspicious activity has been going on, and if anyone has attempted to log on using his credentials. An administrator can set operating parameters that allow a certain number of failed logon attempts to be accepted before a user is locked out; this is a type of *clipping level.* The user can be locked out for five minutes or a full day after the threshold (or clipping level) has been exceeded. It depends on how the administrator configures this mechanism. An audit trail can also be used to track password usage and successful and unsuccessful logon attempts. This audit information should include the date, time, user ID, and workstation the user logged on from.

A password's lifetime should be short but practical. Forcing a user to change a password on a more frequent basis provides more assurance that the password will not be guessed by an intruder. If the lifetime is too short, however, it causes unnecessary management overhead and users may forget which password is active. A balance between protection and practicality needs to be decided upon and enforced.

As with many things in life, education is the key. Password requirements, protection, and generation should be addressed in security-awareness programs so that users understand what is expected of them, why they should protect their passwords, and how passwords can be stolen. Users should be an extension to a security team, not the opposition.

**Password Checkers**   Several organizations test user-chosen passwords using tools that perform dictionary and/or brute force attacks to detect the weak passwords. This helps make the environment as a whole less susceptible to dictionary and exhaustive attacks that are used to discover users' passwords. Many times the same tools used to attempt to crack a password are used by a network administrator to make sure the password is strong enough. Most security tools have this dual nature. They are used by security professionals and IT staff to test for vulnerabilities within their environment in the hope of uncovering them and fixing them before an attacker finds the vulnerabilities. An attacker uses the same tools to uncover vulnerabilities to exploit before the security professional can fix them. It is the never-ending cat-and-mouse game.

If a tool is called a *password checker*, it is a tool used by a security professional to test the strength of a password. If a tool is called a *password cracker*, it is usually used by a hacker; however, most of the time, these tools are one and the same.

You need to obtain management's approval before attempting to test (break) employees' passwords with the intent of identifying weak passwords. Explaining that you are trying to help the situation, not hurt it, *after* you have uncovered the CEO's password is not a good situation to be in.

**Password Hashing and Encryption**   In most situations, if an attacker sniffs your password from the network wire, she still has some work to do before she actually knows your password value, because most systems hash the password with a hashing algorithm, commonly MD4 or MD5, to ensure that passwords are not sent in cleartext.

 **NOTE**   The hashing process and hashing algorithms will be covered in Chapter 8.

In a Windows environment the passwords are stored in a Security Accounts Management (SAM) database in their hashed version. For extra protection, administrators can use a Syskey utility, which encrypts the database that stores the passwords with a locally stored system key. Syskey can work in three modes, each increasing in the protection provided:

- **Mode 1**  System key is generated, encrypted, and stored locally. Computer can restart and work normally with no user interaction.

- **Mode 2**  System key is generated, encrypted, and stored locally but is password protected. When the computer restarts, the administrator must enter the password to "unlock Syskey," and this password is not stored locally.

- **Mode 3**  System key is generated, encrypted, and stored on a floppy disk or CD-ROM. The computer cannot start up properly without a user providing the floppy disk.

Although some people think the world is run by Microsoft, there are also other types of operating systems out there, such as Unix and Linux. These systems do not use registries and SAM databases, but contain their user passwords in a file cleverly called passwd. Now, this passwd file does not contain passwords in cleartext; instead, your password is used to encrypt a block of bits with a one-way function and the resulting value is stored in this file. Unix-type systems zest things up by using salts in this process. *Salts* are random values that are added to the encryption process to add more complexity. The more randomness entered into the encryption process, the harder it is for the bad guy to decrypt and uncover your password. The use of a salt means that the same password can be encrypted into 4096 different formats, which makes it much more difficult for an attacker to uncover the *right* format for your system.

**Password Aging**  Many systems enable administrators to set expiration dates for passwords, forcing users to change them at regular intervals. The system may also keep a list of the last five to ten passwords (password history) and not let the users revert back to previously used passwords.

**Limit Logon Attempts**  A threshold can be set to allow only a certain number of unsuccessful logon attempts. After the threshold is met, the user's account can be locked for a period of time or indefinitely, which requires an administrator to manually unlock the account. This protects against dictionary and other exhaustive attacks that continually submit credentials until the right combination of username and password is discovered.

## Cognitive Passwords

*What is your mother's name? Response: Shucks, I don't remember. I have it written down somewhere.*

*Cognitive passwords* are fact- or opinion-based information used to verify an individual's identity. A user is enrolled by answering several questions based on her life experiences. Passwords can be hard for people to remember, but that same person will not likely forget her mother's maiden name, favorite color, dog's name, or the school she graduated from. After the enrollment process, the user can answer the questions asked of her to be authenticated, instead of having to remember a password. This authentication process is best for a service the user does not use on a daily basis because it takes longer than other authentication mechanisms. This can work well for help-desk services. The user can be authenticated via cognitive means. This way, the person at the help desk can be sure he is talking to the right person, and the user in need of help does not need to remember a password that may be used once every three months.

## One-Time Passwords

A *one-time password* is also called a dynamic password. It is used for authentication purposes and is only good once. After the password is used, it is no longer valid; thus, if a hacker obtained this password, it could not be reused. This type of authentication mechanism is used in environments that require a higher level of security than static passwords provide. There are two general types of one-time password generating tokens: synchronous and asynchronous. The token device generates the one-time password for the user to submit to an authentication server. The following sections explain these concepts.

### SecureID

SecureID, from RSA Security, Inc., is one of the most widely used time-based tokens. One version of the product generates the one-time password by using a mathematical function on the time, date, and ID of the token card. Another version of the product requires a PIN to be entered into the token device.

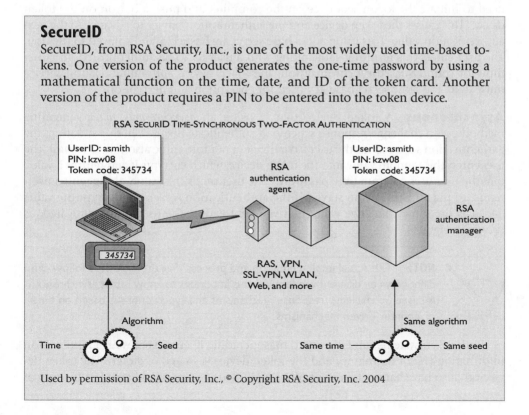

RSA SECURID TIME-SYNCHRONOUS TWO-FACTOR AUTHENTICATION

Used by permission of RSA Security, Inc., © Copyright RSA Security, Inc. 2004

**Token Device**   The *token device,* or password generator, is usually a handheld device that has an LCD display and possibly a keypad. This hardware is separate from the computer the user is attempting to access. The token device and authentication service need to be synchronized in some manner to be able to authenticate a user. The token device presents the user with a list of characters to be entered as a password when logging onto a computer. Only the token device and authentication service know the meaning of these characters. Because the two are synchronized, the token device will present the exact password the authentication service is expecting. This is a one-time password, also called a token, and is no longer valid after initial use.

**Synchronous**   A *synchronous token device* synchronizes with the authentication service by using time or a counter as the core piece of the authentication process. If the synchronization is *time based,* the token device and the authentication service must hold the same time within their internal clocks. The time value on the token device and a secret key are used to create the one-time password, which is displayed to the user. The user enters this value and a user ID into the computer, which then passes them to the server running the authentication service. The authentication service decrypts this value and compares it to the value that it expected. If the two match, the user is authenticated and allowed to use the computer and resources.

If the token device and authentication service use *counter-synchronization,* the user will need to initiate the logon sequence on the computer and push a button on the token device. This causes the token device and the authentication service to advance to the next authentication value. This value and a base secret are hashed and displayed to the user. The user enters this resulting value along with a user ID to be authenticated. In either time- or counter-based synchronization, the token device and authentication service must share the same secret base key used for encryption and decryption.

**Asynchronous**   A token device that is using an *asynchronous token*-generating method uses a challenge/response scheme to authenticate the user. In this situation, the authentication server sends the user a challenge, a random value also called a *nonce.* The user enters this random value into the token device, which encrypts it and returns a value that the user uses as a one-time password. The user sends this value, along with a username, to the authentication server. If the authentication server can decrypt the value and it is the same challenge value that was sent earlier, the user is authenticated, as shown in Figure 4-3.

---

 **NOTE**   The actual implementation and process that these devices follow can differ between different vendors. What is important to know is that asynchronous is based on challenge/response mechanisms and synchronous is based on time- or counter-driven mechanisms.

---

Both token systems can fall prey to masquerading if a user shares his identification information (ID or username) and the token device is shared or stolen. The token device can also have battery failure or other malfunctions that would stand in the way of

**Figure 4-3**
Authentication using an asynchronous token device includes a workstation, token device, and authentication service.

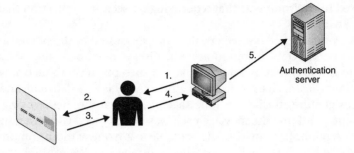

1. Challenge value displayed on workstation.
2. User enters challenge value and PIN into token device.
3. Token device presents a different value to the user.
4. User enters new value into the workstation.
5. Value sent to authentication service on server.
6. Authentication service is expecting a specific value.
7. User is authenticated and allowed access to workstation.

a successful authentication. However, this type of system is not vulnerable to electronic eavesdropping, sniffing, or password guessing.

If the user has to enter a password or PIN into the token device before it provides a one-time password, then strong authentication is in effect because it is using two factors—something the user knows (PIN) and something the user has (the token device).

**NOTE**  One-time passwords can also be generated in software, in which case a piece of hardware such as a token device is not required. These are referred to as *soft tokens* and require that the authentication service and application contain the same base secrets, which are used to generate the one-time passwords.

## References

- "A One-Time Password System," by N. Haller, et al., IETF Network Working Group (Feb. 1998)  www.ietf.org/rfc/rfc2289.txt

- RSA SecurID Authentication home page  www.rsasecurity.com/node .asp?id=1156

- "A Token of Our Esteem," by Timothy O'Shea (Sept. 1999) www.networkcomputing.com/1018/1018f1.html

## Cryptographic Keys

Another way to prove one's identity is to use a private key or generate a digital signature. A private key or digital signature could be used in place of using a password. Passwords are the weakest form of authentication and can be easily sniffed as they travel over a network. Private keys and digital signatures are forms of authentication used in environments that require higher security protection than what is provided by passwords.

A private key is a secret value that should be in the possession of one person, and one person only. It should never be disclosed to an outside party. A digital signature is a technology that uses a private key to encrypt a hash value (message digest). The act of encrypting this hash value with a private key is called *digitally signing* a message. A digital signature attached to a message proves that the message originated from a specific source, and that the message itself was not changed while in transit.

A public key can be made available to anyone without compromising the associated private key; this is why it is called a public key. We explore private keys, public keys, digital signatures, and public key infrastructure (PKI) in Chapter 8, but for now, understand that a private key and digital signatures are other mechanisms that can be used to authenticate an individual.

## Passphrase

A *passphrase* is a sequence of characters that is longer than a password (thus a "phrase") and, in some cases, takes the place of a password during an authentication process. The user enters this phrase into an application and the application transforms the value into a *virtual password*, making the passphrase the length and format that is required by the application. (For example, an application may require your virtual password to be 64 bits to be used as a key with the AES algorithm.) If a user wants to authenticate to an application, such as Pretty Good Privacy (PGP), he types in a passphrase, let's say StickWithMeKidAndYouWillWearDiamonds. The application converts this phrase into a virtual password that is used for the actual authentication. The user usually generates the passphrase in the same way that a user creates a password the first time he logs onto a computer. A passphrase is more secure than a password because it is longer, and thus harder to obtain by an attacker. In many cases the user is more likely to remember a passphrase than a password.

## Memory Cards

The main difference between memory cards and smart cards is their capacity to process information. A *memory card* holds information but cannot process information. A *smart card* holds information and has the necessary hardware and software to actually process that information. A memory card can hold a user's authentication information, so that the user only needs to type in a user ID or PIN and present the memory card, and if the data that the user entered matches the data on the memory card, the user is successfully authenticated. If the user presents a PIN value, then this is an example of two-factor authentication—something the user knows, and something the user has. A memory card can also hold identification data that is pulled from the memory card by a reader. It travels with the PIN to a back-end authentication server. An example of a memory card is a swipe card that must be used for an individual to be able to enter a building. The user enters a PIN and swipes the memory card through a card reader. If this is the correct combination, the reader flashes green and the individual can open the door and enter the building. Another example is an ATM card. If Buffy wants to withdraw $40 from her checking account, she needs to enter the correct PIN and slide the ATM card (or memory card) through the reader.

Memory cards can be used with computers, but they require a reader to process the information. The reader adds cost to the process, especially when one is needed per computer, and card generation adds additional cost and effort to the whole authentication process. Using a memory card provides a more secure authentication method than using a password because the attacker would need to obtain the card and know the correct PIN. Administrators and management need to weigh the costs and benefits of a memory token-based card implementation to determine if it is the right authentication mechanism for their environment.

## Smart Card

*My smart card is smarter than your memory card.*

A smart card has the capability of processing information because it has a microprocessor and integrated circuits incorporated into the card itself. Memory cards do not have this type of hardware and lack this type of functionality. The only function they can perform is simple storage. A smart card, which adds the capability to process information that is stored on it, can also provide a two-factor authentication method because the user may have to enter a PIN to unlock the smart card. This means the user must provide something she knows (PIN) and something she has (smart card).

Two general categories of smart cards are the contact and the contactless types. The *contact* smart card has a gold seal on the face of the card. When this card is fully inserted into a card reader, electrical fingers wipe against the card, in the exact position that the chip contacts are located. This will supply power and data I/O to the chip for authentication purposes. The *contactless* smart card has an antenna wire that surrounds the perimeter of the card. When this card comes within an electromagnetic field of the reader, the antenna within the card generates enough energy to power the internal chip. Now, the results of the smart card processing can be broadcast through the same antenna, and the conversation of authentication can take place. The authentication can be completed by using a one-time password, by using a challenge/response value, or by providing the user's private key if it is used within a PKI environment.

Contact and contactless smart card architectures

**NOTE** There are two types of contactless smart cards: hybrid and combi. The hybrid card has two chips, with the capability of utilizing both the contact and contactless formats. A combi card has one microprocessor chip that can communicate to contact or contactless readers.

The information held within the memory of a smart card is not readable until the correct PIN is entered. This fact and the complexity of the smart token make these cards resistant to reverse-engineering and tampering methods. If George loses the smart card he uses to authenticate to the domain at work, the person who finds the card would need to know his PIN to be able to do any real damage. The smart card can also be programmed to store information in an encrypted fashion, as well as detect any tampering with the card itself. In the event that tampering is detected, the information stored on the smart card can be automatically wiped.

The drawbacks to using a smart card are the extra cost of the readers and the overhead of card generation, as with memory cards, although this cost is decreasing. The smart cards themselves are more expensive than memory cards because of the extra integrated circuits and microprocessor.

**Smart Card Attacks**   Smart cards are more tamperproof than memory cards, but where there is sensitive data there are individuals who are motivated to circumvent any countermeasure that the industry throws at them.

Over the years people have become very inventive in the development of various ways to attack smart cards. For example, individuals have introduced computational errors into smart cards with the goal of uncovering the encryption keys that are being used and stored on the cards. These "errors" are introduced by manipulating some environmental component of the card (changing input voltage, clock rate, temperature fluctuations). The attacker reviews the result of an encryption function after introducing an error to the card and also reviews the correct result, which the card performs when no errors are introduced. Analysis of these different results allows an attacker to reverse-engineer the encryption process, with the hopes of uncovering the encryption key. This type of attack is referred to as *fault generation*.

*Side-channel attacks* are nonintrusive and are used to uncover sensitive information about how a component works without trying to compromise any type of flaw or weakness. As an analogy, suppose that you want to figure out what your boss does each day at lunch time but you feel too uncomfortable to ask her. So you follow her, and you see that she enters a building holding a small black bag and exits exactly 45 minutes later with the same bag and her hair not looking as great as when she went in. You keep doing this day after day and come to the conclusion that she must be working out. Now you could have just read the sign on the building that said "Gym," but we will give you the benefit of the doubt here but not call you for any further private investigator work.

So a noninvasive attack is one in which the attacker watches how something works and how it reacts in different situations instead of trying to "invade" it with more intrusive measures. Some examples of side channel attacks that have been carried out on smart cards are *differential power analysis* (examining the power emissions that are released

## Interoperability

An ISO/IEC standard, 14443, outlines the following items for smart card standardization:

- **ISO/IEC 14443-1**   Physical characteristics
- **ISO/IEC 14443-2**   Radio frequency power and signal interface
- **ISO/IEC 14443-3**   Initialization and anticollision
- **ISO/IEC 14443-4**   Transmission protocol

In the industry today, lack of interoperability is a big problem. Although vendors claim to be "compliant with ISO/IEC 14443," many have developed technologies and methods in a more proprietary fashion. The lack of true standardization has caused some large problems because smart cards are being used for so many different applications. In the United States, the DoD is rolling out smart cards across all of their agencies, and NIST is developing a framework and conformance testing programs specifically for interoperability issues.

during processing), *electromagnetic analysis* (examining the frequencies that are emitted), and timing (how long a specific process takes to complete).

*Software attacks* are also considered noninvasive attacks. A smart card has software just like any other device that does data processing, and anywhere there is software there is the possibility of software flaws that can be exploited. The main goal of this type of attack is to input instructions into the card that will allow for the attacker to extract account information, which he can use to make fraudulent purchases. Many of these types of attacks can be disguised by using equipment that looks just like the legitimate reader.

If you would like to be more intrusive in your smart card attack, you could give *microprobing* a try. Microprobing uses needles to remove the outer protective material on the card's circuits, by using ultrasonic vibration. Once this is completed, then data can be accessed and manipulated by directly tapping into the card's ROM chips.

## References

- **NIST Smart Card Standards and Research web page**   http://smartcard .nist.gov/
- **Smart Card Alliance home page**   www.smartcardalliance.org
- **"Smart Cards: A Primer," by Rinaldo Di Giorgio, *JavaWorld* (Dec. 1997)**   www.javaworld.com/javaworld/jw-12-1997/jw-12-javadev.html
- **"What Is a Smart Card," HowStuffWorks.com**   http://electronics .howstuffworks.com/question332.htm

- *Securing Java: Getting Down to Business with Mobile Code,* Chapter 8, Section 5, "How Secure Are Smart Cards?" by Edward Felten and Gary McGraw (Wiley, 1999)   www.securingjava.com/chapter-eight/chapter-eight-5.html

## Authorization

*Now that I know who you are, let's see if I will let you do what you want.*

Although authentication and authorization are quite different, together they comprise a two-step process that determines whether an individual is allowed to access a particular resource. In the first step, authentication, the individual must prove to the system that he is who he claims to be—a permitted system user. After successful authentication, the system must establish whether the user is authorized to access the particular resource and what actions he is permitted to perform on that resource.

Authorization is a core component of every operating system, but applications, security add-on packages, and resources themselves can also provide this functionality. For example, suppose that Marge has been authenticated through the authentication server and now wants to view a spreadsheet that resides on a file server. When she finds this spreadsheet and double-clicks on the icon, she will see an hourglass instead of a mouse pointer. At this stage, the file server is seeing if Marge has the rights and permissions to view the requested spreadsheet. It also checks to see if Marge can modify, delete, move, or copy the file. Once the file server searches through an access matrix and finds that Marge does indeed have the necessary rights to view this file, the file opens up on Marge's desktop. The decision of whether or not to allow Marge to see this file was based on access criteria. Access criteria is the crux of authentication.

## Access Criteria

*You can perform that action only because we like you, and you wear a funny hat.*

We have gone over the basics of access control. This subject can get very granular in its level of detail when it comes to dictating what a subject can or cannot do to an object or resource. This is a good thing for network administrators and security professionals, because they want to have as much control as possible over the resources they have been put in charge of protecting, and a fine level of detail enables them to give individuals just the precise level of access that they need. It would be frustrating if access control permissions were based only on full control or no access. These choices are very limiting, and an administrator would end up giving everyone full control, which would provide no protection. Instead, there are different ways of limiting access to resources and, if they are understood and used properly, they can give just the right level of access desired.

Granting access rights to subjects should be based on the level of trust a company has in a subject and the subject's need to know. Just because a company completely trusts Joyce with its files and resources does not mean she fulfills the need-to-know criteria to access the company's tax returns and profit margins. If Maynard fulfills the need-to-know criteria to access employees' work histories, it does not mean that the company trusts him to access all of the company's other files. These issues need to be identified and integrated into the access criteria. The different access criteria can be broken up into roles, groups, location, time, and transaction types.

Using *roles* is an efficient way to assign rights to a type of user who performs a certain task. This role is based on a job assignment or function. If there is a position within a company for a person to audit transactions and audit logs, the role that this person would fill would only need a read function to those types of files. This role would not need full control, modify, or delete privileges.

Using *groups* is another effective way of assigning access control rights. If several users require the same type of access to information and resources, putting them into a group and then assigning rights and permissions to that group is easier to manage than assigning rights and permissions to each and every individual separately. If a specific printer is available only to the accounting group, when a user attempts to print to it, the group membership of the user will be checked to see if she is indeed in the accounting group. This is one way that access control is enforced through a logical access control mechanism.

*Physical or logical location* can also be used to restrict access to resources. Some files may be available only to users who can log on interactively to a computer. This means the user must be physically at the computer and enter the credentials locally versus logging on remotely from another computer. This restriction is implemented on several server configurations to restrict unauthorized individuals from being able to get in and reconfigure the server remotely.

Logical location restrictions are usually done through network address restrictions. If a network administrator wants to ensure that status requests of an intrusion detection management console are accepted only from certain computers on the network, the network administrator can configure this within the software.

*Time of day*, or temporal isolation, is another access control mechanism that can be used. If a security professional wants to ensure that no one is accessing payroll files between the hours of 8:00 P.M. and 4:00 A.M., that configuration can be implemented to ensure that access at these times is restricted. If the same security professional wants to ensure that no bank account transactions happen during days on which the bank is not open, she can indicate in the logical access control mechanism that this type of action is prohibited on Sundays.

*Transaction-type* restrictions can be used to control what data is accessed during certain types of functions and what commands can be carried out on the data. An online banking program may allow a customer to view his account balance, but may not allow the customer to transfer money until he has a certain security level or access right. A bank teller may be able to cash checks up to $2000, but would need a supervisor's access code to retrieve more funds for a customer. A database administrator may be able to build a database for the human resources department, but may not be able to read certain confidential files within that database. These are all examples of transaction-type restrictions to control access to data and resources.

> ## Authorization Creep
>
> As employees work at a company over time and move from one department to another, they often are assigned more and more access rights and permissions. This is commonly referred to as *authorization creep*. It can be a large risk for a company, because too many users have too much privileged access to company assets. Users' access needs and rights should be periodically reviewed to ensure that the principle of least privilege is being properly enforced.

## Default to No Access

*If you're unsure, just say no.*

Access control mechanisms should default to no access, to provide the necessary level of security and ensure that no security holes go unnoticed. A wide range of access levels is available to assign to individuals and groups, depending on the application and/or operating system. A user can have read, change, delete, full control, or no access permissions. The statement that security mechanisms should default to no access means that if nothing has been specifically configured for an individual or the group she belongs to, that user should not be able to access that resource. If access is not explicitly allowed, it should be implicitly denied. Security is all about being safe, and this is the safest approach to practice when dealing with access control methods and mechanisms. In other words, all access controls should be based on the concept of starting with zero access, and building on top of that. Instead of giving access to everything, and then taking away privileges based on need to know, the better approach is to start with nothing and add privileges based on need to know.

Most access control lists (ACLs) that work on routers and packet-filtering firewalls default to no access. Figure 4-4 shows that traffic from Subnet A is allowed to access Subnet B, traffic from Subnet D is not allowed to access Subnet A, and Subnet B is allowed to talk to Subnet A. All other traffic transmission paths not listed here are not allowed by default. Subnet D cannot talk to Subnet B because such access is not explicitly indicated in the router's ACL.

## Need to Know

*If you need to know, I will tell you. If you don't need to know, leave me alone.*

The *need-to-know* principle is similar to the **least-privilege** principle. It is based on the concept that individuals should be given access only to the information that they absolutely require in order to perform their job duties. Giving any more rights to a user just asks for headaches and the possibility of that user abusing the permissions assigned to him. An administrator wants to give a user the least amount of privileges she can, but just enough for that user to be productive when carrying out tasks. Management will decide what a user needs to know, or what access rights are necessary, and the administrator will configure the access control mechanisms to allow this user to have that level of access and no more, and thus the least privilege.

For example, if management has decided that Dan the copy boy needs to know where the files that he needs to copy are located and needs to know how to print them, this fulfills Dan's need-to-know criteria. Now, an administrator could give Dan full

Access Control List

- Subnet A can access Subnet B.
- Subnet D cannot access Subnet A.
- Subnet B can access Subnet A.

**Figure 4-4** What is not explicitly allowed should be implicitly denied.

control of all the files he needs to copy, but that would not be practicing the least-privilege principle. The administrator should restrict Dan's rights and permissions to only allow him to read and print the necessary files, and no more. Besides, if Dan accidentally deletes all the files on the whole file server, whom do you think management will hold ultimately responsible? Yep, the administrator.

It is important to understand that it is management's job to determine the security requirements of individuals and how access is authorized. The security administrator configures the security mechanisms to fulfill these requirements, but it is not her job to determine security requirements of users. Those should be left to the owners. If there is a security breach, management will ultimately be held responsible, so it should make these decisions in the first place.

## Single Sign-On

*I only want to have to remember one username and one password for everything in the world!*

Many times employees need to access many different computers, servers, databases, and other resources in the course of a day to complete their tasks. This often requires the employees to remember multiple user IDs and passwords for these different computers. In a utopia, a user would need to enter only one user ID and one password to be able to access all resources in all the networks this user is working in. In the real world, this is hard to accomplish for all system types.

Because of the proliferation of client/server technologies, networks have migrated from centrally controlled networks to heterogeneous, distributed environments. The propagation of open systems and the increased diversity of applications, platforms, and operating systems have caused the end user to have to remember several user IDs and passwords just to be able to access and use the different resources within his own network. Although the different IDs and passwords are supposed to provide a greater level of security, they often end up compromising security (because users write them down) and causing more effort and overhead for the staff that manages and maintains the network.

As any network staff member or administrator can attest to, too much time is devoted to resetting passwords for users who have forgotten them. More than one employee's productivity is affected when forgotten passwords have to be reassigned. The network staff member who has to reset the password could be working on other tasks, and the user who forgot the password cannot complete his task until the network staff member is finished resetting the password. Many help-desk employees report that a majority of their time is spent on users forgetting their passwords. System administrators have to manage multiple user accounts on different platforms, which all need to be coordinated in a manner that maintains the integrity of the security policy. At times the complexity can be overwhelming, which results in poor access control management and the generation of many security vulnerabilities because the user IDs and passwords are usually written down and posted on the side of the monitor or underneath the user's keyboard. This fact defeats the purpose of using passwords in the first place. A lot of time is spent on multiple passwords, and in the end, they do not provide us with more security.

The increased cost of managing a diverse environment, security concerns, and user habits, coupled with the users' overwhelming desire to remember one set of credentials, has brought about the idea of *single sign-on (SSO)* capabilities. These capabilities would allow a user to enter credentials one time and be able to access all resources in primary and secondary network domains. This reduces the amount of time users spend authenticating to resources and it enables the administrator to streamline user accounts and better control access rights. It improves security by reducing the probability that users will write down passwords and reduces the administrator's time spent on adding and removing user accounts and modifying access permissions. If an administrator needs to disable or suspend a specific account, she can do it uniformly instead of having to alter configurations on each and every platform.

So that is our utopia: log on once and you are good to go. What bursts this bubble? Mainly interoperability issues. For SSO to actually work, every platform, application, and resource needs to accept the same type of credentials, in the same format, and interpret their meanings the same. When Steve logs onto his Windows NT 4.0 workstation and gets authenticated by a mixed-mode Windows 2000 domain controller, it needs to authenticate him to the resources he needs to access on the Apple computer, the Unix server running VisionFS, the mainframe host server, the MICR print server, and the Windows XP computer in the secondary domain that has the plotter connected to it. Nice idea, until reality hits.

Single sign-on technology enables a user to enter credentials one time to be able to access all preauthorized resources within the domain.

There is also a security issue to consider in an SSO environment. Once an individual is in, he is in. If an attacker was able to uncover one credential set, he would have access to every resource within the environment that the compromised account has access to.

There are different types of SSO technologies. Each has its own advantages and disadvantages, shortcomings, and quality features. It is rare to see a real SSO environment; rather, you will see a cluster of computers and resources that accept the same credentials, whereas other resources still require more work on the administrator or user side to access the systems. The SSO technologies that may be addressed in the CISSP exam are described in the next sections.

## Kerberos

*Sam, there is a three-headed dog in front of the server!*

*Kerberos* is the name of a three-headed dog that guards the entrance to the underworld in Greek mythology. This is a great name for a security technology that provides authentication functionality, with the purpose of protecting a company's assets. Kerberos is an authentication protocol and was designed in the mid-1980s as part of MIT's Project Athena. It works in a client/server model and is based on symmetric key cryptography. The protocol has been used for years in Unix systems and is currently the default authentication method for Windows 2000 and 2003 operating systems.

Commercial products supporting Kerberos are becoming more frequent, so this one might be a keeper.

Kerberos is an example of a single sign-on system for distributed environments, and is a de facto standard for heterogeneous networks. Kerberos incorporates a wide range of security technologies, which gives companies much more flexibility and scalability when they need to provide an encompassing security architecture. However, this open architecture also invites interoperability issues. When vendors have a lot of freedom to customize a protocol, it usually means that no two vendors will customize it in the same fashion. This creates interoperability and incompatibility issues.

Kerberos uses symmetric key cryptography and provides end-to-end security. Although it allows the use of passwords for authentication, it was designed specifically to eliminate the need to transmit passwords over the network. Most Kerberos implementations work with shared secret keys.

**Main Components in Kerberos**    The *Key Distribution Center (KDC)* is the most important component within a Kerberos environment. The KDC holds all users' and services' secret keys. It provides an authentication service, as well as key distribution functionality. The clients and services trust the integrity of the KDC, and this trust is the foundation of Kerberos security.

The KDC provides security services to *principals*, which can be users, applications, or network services. The KDC must have an account for, and share a secret key with, each principal. For users, a password is transformed into a secret key value. The secret key is used to send sensitive data back and forth between the principal and the KDC, and is used for user authentication purposes.

A *ticket* is generated by the KDC and given to a principal when that principal, let's say a user, needs to authenticate to another principal, let's say a print server. The ticket enables one principal to authenticate to another principal. If Emily needs to use the print server, she needs to prove to the print server she is who she claims to be and that she is authorized to use the printing service. So Emily requests a ticket from the KDC. The KDC gives Emily the ticket, and in turn, Emily passes this ticket on to the print server. If the print server approves of this ticket, Emily is allowed to use the print service.

A KDC provides security services for a set of principals. This set is called a *realm* in Kerberos. The KDC is the trusted authentication server for all users, applications, and services within a realm. One KDC can be responsible for one realm or several realms. Realms are used to allow an administrator to logically group resources and users.

So far, we know that principals (users and services) require the KDC's services to authenticate to each other; that the KDC has a database filled with information about each and every principal within its realm; that the KDC holds and delivers cryptographic keys and tickets; and that tickets are used for principals to authenticate to each other. So how does this process work?

**Kerberos Authentication Process**    The user and the KDC share a secret key; the service and the KDC share a different secret key. The user and the requested service do not share a symmetric key in the beginning. The user trusts the KDC because they share a secret key. They can encrypt and decrypt data they pass between each other, and thus have a protected communication path. Once the user authenticates to the service, they too will share a symmetric key (session key) that will enable them to encrypt and decrypt the information they need to pass to each other. This is how Kerberos provides data transmission protection.

Here are the exact steps:

1. Emily comes in to work and enters her username and password into her workstation at 8 A.M.

2. The Kerberos software on Emily's computer sends the username to the authentication service (AS) on the KDC, which in turn sends Emily a ticket granting ticket (TGT) that is encrypted with Emily's password (secret key).

3. If Emily has entered her correct password, then this TGT is decrypted and Emily gains access to her local workstation desktop.

4. When Emily needs to send a print job to the print server, her system sends the TGT to the ticket granting service (TGS), which runs on the KDC. (This allows Emily to prove that she has been authenticated and allows her to request access to the print server.)

5. The TGS creates and sends a second ticket to Emily, which she will use to authenticate to the print server. This second ticket contains two instances of the same session key, one encrypted with Emily's secret key and the other encrypted with the print server's secret key. The second ticket also contains an *authenticator*, which contains identification information on Emily, her system's IP address, and a timestamp.

6. Emily's system receives the second ticket, decrypts and extracts the session key, adds a second authenticator set of identification information to the ticket, and sends the ticket onto the print server.

7. The print server receives the ticket, decrypts and extracts the session key, and decrypts and extracts the two authenticators in the ticket. If the printer server can decrypt and extract the session key, it knows that the KDC created the ticket, because only the KDC has the secret key that was used to encrypt the session key. If the authenticator information that the KDC and the user put into the ticket matches, then the print server knows that it received the ticket from the correct principal.

8. Once this is completed, it means that Emily has been properly authenticated to the print server and the server prints her document.

This is an extremely simplistic overview of what is going on in any Kerberos exchange, but it gives you an idea of the dance that is taking place behind the scenes whenever you interact with any network service in an environment that uses Kerberos. Figure 4-5 provides a simplistic view of this process.

The authentication service is the part of the KDC that authenticates a principal, and the TGS is the part of the KDC that makes the tickets and hands them out to the principals. TGTs are used so that the user does not have to enter his password each time he needs to communicate with another principal. After the user enters his password, it is

1. User authenticates to AS.
2. AS sends initial ticket to user.
3. User requests to access file server.
4. TGS creates new ticket with session keys.
5. User extracts one session key and sends ticket to file server.

**Figure 4-5**  The user needs to receive a ticket from the KDC before being able to use the requested resource.

temporarily stored on his system, and any time the user needs to communicate with another principal, he just reuses the TGT.

Be sure you understand that a session key is different from a secret key. A secret key is shared between the KDC and a principal and is static in nature. A session key is shared between two principals and is generated when needed and destroyed after the session is completed.

If a Kerberos implementation is configured to use an *authenticator*, the user sends to the printer server her identification information and a timestamp encrypted with the session key they share. The printer server decrypts this information and compares it with the identification data the KDC sent to it about this requesting user. If the data is the same, the printer server allows the user to send print jobs. The timestamp is used to help fight against replay attacks. The printer server compares the sent timestamp with its own internal time, which helps to determine if the ticket has been sniffed and copied by an attacker and submitted at a later time in hope of impersonating the legitimate user and gaining unauthorized access.

The primary reason to use Kerberos is that the principals do not trust each other enough to communicate directly. In our example, the print server will not print anyone's print job without that entity authenticating itself. So none of the principals trust each other directly; they only trust the KDC. The KDC creates tickets to vouch for the individual principals when they need to communicate. Suppose that I need to communicate directly with you, but you do not trust me enough to listen and accept what I am saying. If I first give you a ticket from something you do trust (KDC), this basically says, "Look, the KDC says I am a trustworthy person. The KDC asked me to give this ticket to you to prove it." Once that happens, *then* you will communicate directly with me.

The same type of trust model is used in PKI environments. (More information on PKI is presented in Chapter 8.) In a PKI environment, users do not trust each other directly, but they all trust the certificate authority (CA). The CA vouches for the individuals' identities by using digital certificates, the same as the KDC vouches for the individuals' identities by using tickets.

So why are we talking about Kerberos? Because it is one example of a single sign-on technology. The user enters a user ID and password one time and one time only. The tickets have time limits on them that administrators can configure. Many times, the lifetime of a TGT is eight to ten hours, so when the user comes in the next day, he will have to present his credentials again.

**Weaknesses of Kerberos**   Kerberos is an authentication protocol that can provide confidentiality of the sensitive data being passed back and forth over a network. The following are some of the potential weaknesses of Kerberos:

- The KDC can be a single point of failure. If the KDC goes down, no one can access needed resources. Redundancy is necessary for the KDC.

- The KDC must be able to handle the number of requests it receives in a timely manner. It must be scalable.

- Secret keys are temporarily stored on the users' workstations, which means it is possible for an intruder to obtain these cryptographic keys.

- Session keys are decrypted and reside on the users' workstations, either in a cache or in a key table. Again, an intruder can capture these keys.

- Kerberos is vulnerable to password guessing. The KDC does not know if a dictionary attack is taking place.

- Network traffic is not protected by Kerberos if encryption is not enabled.

Kerberos needs to be transparent (work in the background without the user needing to understand it), scalable (work in large, heterogeneous environments), reliable (distributed server architecture to ensure that there is no single point of failure), and secure (provide authentication and confidentiality).

## Kerberos and Password-Guessing Attacks

Just because an environment uses Kerberos does not mean that the systems are vulnerable to password-guessing attacks. The operating system itself will (should) provide the protection of tracking failed login attempts. The Kerberos protocol does not have this type of functionality, so another component must be in place to counter these types of attacks. No need to start ripping Kerberos out of your network environment after reading this section; your operating system provides the protection mechanism for this type of attack.

## References

- **Kerberos FAQ**   www.nrl.navy.mil/CCS/people/kenh/kerberos-faq.html
- **MIT Kerberos Papers and Documentation web page**   www.mit.edu/afs/ athena.mit.edu/astaff/project/kerberos/www/papers.html

## SESAME

The *Secure European System for Applications in a Multi-vendor Environment (SESAME)* project is a single sign-on technology that was developed to extend Kerberos functionality and improve upon its weaknesses. SESAME uses symmetric and asymmetric cryptographic techniques to protect exchanges of data and to authenticate subjects to network resources.

**NOTE**   Kerberos is a strictly symmetric key–based technology, whereas SESAME is based on both asymmetric and symmetric key cryptography.

Kerberos uses tickets to authenticate subjects to objects, whereas SESAME uses Privileged Attribute Certificates (PACs), which contain the subject's identity, access capabilities for the object, access time period, and lifetime of the PAC. The PAC is digitally signed so that the object can validate that it came from the trusted authentication server, which is referred to as the Privileged Attribute Server (PAS). The PAS holds a similar role to that of the KDC within Kerberos. After a user successfully authenticates to the authentication service (AS), he is presented with a token to give to the PAS. The PAS then creates a PAC for the user to present to the resource he is trying to access. Figure 4-6 shows a basic overview of the SESAME process.

**NOTE**   Kerberos and SESAME can be accessed through the Generic Security Services Application Programming Interface (GSS-API), which is a generic API for client-to-server authentication. Using standard APIs enables vendors to communicate with and use each other's functionality and security. Kerberos Version 5 and SESAME implementations allow any application to use their authentication functionality as long as the application knows how to communicate via GSS-API.

## References

- **SESAME in a Nutshell**   www.cosic.esat.kuleuven.ac.be/sesame/html/sesame_ what.html
- **SESAME links**   www.cosic.esat.kuleuven.ac.be/sesame/html/sesame_links.html

1. User sends credentials.
2. AS sends token to use to communicate with the PAS.
3. User requests to access resource and sends token to PAS.
4. PAS creates and sends a PAC to user.
5. User sends PAC to authenticate to the resource.

**Figure 4-6** SESAME is very similar to Kerberos.

## Security Domains

*I am highly trusted and have access to many resources. Response: So what.*

The term "domain" has been around a lot longer than Microsoft, but when people hear this term, they often think of a set of computers and devices on a network segment being controlled by a server that runs Microsoft software, referred to as a domain controller. A domain is really just a set of resources that is available to a subject. Remember that a subject can be a user, process, or application. Within an operating system, a process has a domain, which is the set of system resources that is available to the process to carry out its tasks. These resources can be memory segments, hard drive space, operating system services, and other processes. In a physical network environment, a domain is a set of physical and logical resources that is available, which can include routers, file servers, FTP service, web servers, and so forth.

The term *security domain* just builds upon the definition of domain by adding the fact that resources within this logical structure (domain) are working under the same security policy and managed by the same group. So, a network administrator may put all of the accounting personnel, computers, and network resources in Domain 1 and all of the management personnel, computers, and network resources in Domain 2. These items fall into these individual containers because they not only carry out similar types of business functions, but also, and more importantly, have the same type of trust level. It is this common trust level that allows entities to be managed by one single security policy.

The different domains are separated by logical boundaries, such as firewalls with ACLs, directory services making access decisions, and objects that have their own ACLs indicating which individuals and groups can carry out operations on them. All of these security mechanisms are examples of components that enforce the security policy for each domain.

Domains can be architected in a hierarchical manner that dictates the relationship between the different domains and the ways in which subjects within the different domains can communicate. Subjects can access resources in domains of equal or lower trust levels. Figure 4-7 shows an example of hierarchical network domains. Their communication channels are controlled by security agents (firewalls, router ACLs, directory services), and the individual domains are isolated by using specific subnet mask addresses.

Remember that a domain does not necessarily pertain only to network devices and segmentations, but can also apply to users and processes. Figure 4-8 illustrates how users

**Figure 4-7** Network domains that are used to separate different network segments

and processes can have more granular domains assigned to them individually based on their trust level. Group 1 has a high trust level and can access both a domain of its own trust level (Domain 1) and a domain of a lower trust level (Domain 2). User 1, who has a lower trust level, can access only the domain at his trust level and nothing higher. The system enforces these domains with access privileges and rights provided by the file system and operating system security kernel.

So why are domains in the "Single Sign-On" section? Because several different types of technologies are available today that are used to define and enforce these domains and security policies that are mapped to them: domain controllers in a Windows environment, enterprise resource management (ERM) products, Microsoft Passport, and the various products that provide SSO functionality. The goal of each of them is to allow a user (subject) to sign in one time and be able to access the different domains that are available to them without having to reenter any other credentials.

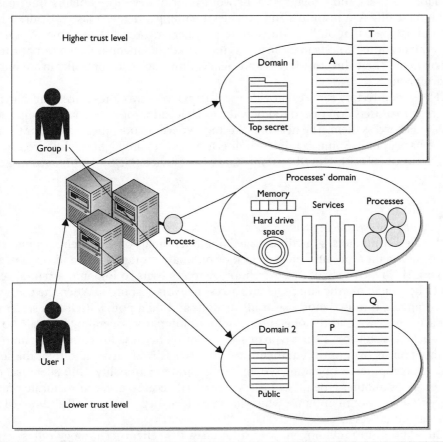

**Figure 4-8** Subjects can access specific domains based on their trust levels.

## References

- *Underlining Technical Models for Information Technology Security, Recommendations of the National Institute of Standards and Technology,* by Gary Stoneburner, NIST Special Publication 800-33 (Dec. 2001) http://csrc.nist.gov/publications/nistpubs/800-33/sp800-33.pdf
- "New Thinking About Information Technology Security," by Marshall Abrams, PhD and Michael Joyce (first published in *Computers & Security,* Vol. 14, No. 1, pp. 57–68)  www.acsac.org/secshelf/papers/new_thinking.pdf

## Directory Services

A network service is a mechanism that identifies resources (printers, file servers, domain controllers, and peripheral devices) on a network and provides a way to make them available to users and programs. A network directory service contains information about these different resources and provides a naming scheme. It also provides a hierarchical database that outlines the resources' characteristics, such as name, logical and physical location, subjects that can access them, and the operations that can be carried out on them. These directory services are held within a domain controller in a Windows environment.

Network directory services provide users access to network resources transparently, meaning that users don't need to know the exact location of the resources or the steps required to access them. The network directory services handle these issues for the user in the background. Some examples of directory services are Lightweight Directory Access Protocol (LDAP), Novell NetWare Directory Service (NDS), and Microsoft Active Directory.

## Thin Clients

*Hey, where's my operating system? Response: You don't deserve one.*

Diskless computers, sometimes called dumb terminals or thin clients, cannot store much information because of their lack of on-board storage space and necessary resources. This type of client/server technology forces users to log onto a central server just to be able to use the computer and access network resources. When the user starts the computer, it runs a short list of instructions and then points itself to a server that will actually download the operating system, or interactive operating software, to the terminal. This enforces a strict type of access control, because the computer cannot do anything on its own until it authenticates to a centralized server, and then the server gives the computer its operating system, profile, and functionality. Thin-client technology provides another type of SSO access for users, because users authenticate only to the central server or mainframe, which then provides them access to all authorized and necessary resources.

In addition to providing an SSO solution, a thin-client technology offers several other advantages. A company can save money by purchasing thin clients instead of powerful and expensive PCs. The central server handles all application execution, pro-

## Examples of Single Sign-On Technologies

- **Kerberos**  Authentication protocol that uses a KDC and tickets, and is based on symmetric key cryptography

- **SESAME**  Authentication protocol that uses a PAS and PACs, and is based on symmetric and asymmetric cryptography

- **Security domains**  Resources working under the same security policy and managed by the same group

- **Thin clients**  Terminals that rely upon a central server for access control, processing, and storage

cessing, and data storage. The thin client displays the graphical representation and sends mouse clicks and keystroke inputs to the central server. Having all of the software in one location, instead of distributed throughout the environment, allows for easier administration, centralized access control, easier updates, and standardized configurations. It is also easier to control malware infestations and the theft of confidential data because the thin clients often do not have CD-ROM, DVD, or floppy drives.

# Access Control Models

An *access control model* is a framework that dictates how subjects access objects. It uses access control technologies and security mechanisms to enforce the rules and objectives of the model. There are three main types of access control models: discretionary, mandatory, and nondiscretionary (also called role-based). Each model type uses different methods to control how subjects access objects, and each has its own merits and limitations. The business and security goals of an organization will help prescribe what access control model it should use, along with the culture of the company and the habits of conducting business. Some companies use one model exclusively, whereas others combine them to be able to provide the necessary level of protection.

These models are built into the core or the kernel of the different operating systems and possibly their supporting applications. Every operating system has a security kernel that enforces a reference monitor concept, which differs depending upon the type of access control model that has been embedded into the system. For every access attempt, before a subject can communicate with an object, the security kernel reviews the rules of the access control model to determine whether the request is allowed.

The following sections explain these different models, their supporting technologies, and where they should be implemented.

## Discretionary Access Control

*It is up to me to allow you to access my files. Response: Mother, may I?*

If a user creates a file, he is the owner of that file. An identifier for this user is placed in the file header. Ownership might also be granted to a specific individual. For example, a manager for a certain department might be made the owner of the files and resources within her domain. A system that uses *discretionary access control (DAC)* enables the owner of the resource to specify which subjects can access specific resources. This model is called discretionary because the control of access is based on the discretion of the owner.

In a DAC model, access is restricted based on the authorization granted to the users. This means that users are allowed to specify what type of access can occur to the objects they own. If an organization is using a DAC model, the network administrator can allow resource owners to control who has access to their files. The most common implementation of DAC is through ACLs, which are dictated and set by the owners and enforced by the operating system. This does not lend itself to a centrally controlled environment and can make a user's ability to access information dynamic versus the more static role of mandatory access control (MAC).

Most of the operating systems that you may be used to dealing with are based on DAC models, such as all Windows, Linux, and Macintosh systems and most flavors of Unix. When you look at the properties of a file or directory and you see the choices that allow you to control which users can have access to this resource and to what degree, you are witnessing an instance of ACLs enforcing a DAC model.

DACs can be applied to both the directory tree structure and the files it contains. The PC world has access permissions of No Access, Read (r), Write (w), Execute (x), Delete (d), Change (c), and Full Control. The Read attribute allows you to read the file but not make changes. The Change attribute allows you to read, write, execute, and delete the file but does not allow you to change the ACLs or the owner of the files. Obviously, the attribute of Full Control allows you to make any changes to the file and its permissions and ownership.

It is through the discretionary model that Sam can share his D: drive with David so that David can copy all of Sam's MP3s. Sam can also block access to his D: drive from his manager so that his manager does not know that Sam is wasting valuable time and resources by downloading MP3s and sharing them with friends.

## References

- *Security in Open Systems,* Node 25, "Discretionary Access Control," by Robert Bagwell, et al., NIST Special Publication 800-7 (July 1994) http://csrc.nist.gov/publications/nistpubs/800-7/node25.html
- *Wikipedia* definition of access control   http://en.wikipedia.org/wiki/Access_control

### Identity-Based Access Control

DAC systems grant or deny access based on the identity of the subject. The identity can be a user identity or group membership. So, for example, a data owner can choose to allow Bob (user identity) and the Accounting group (group membership identity) to access his file.

## Mandatory Access Control

In a *mandatory access control (MAC)* model, users and data owners do not have as much freedom to determine who can access files. The operating system makes the final decision and can override the users' wishes. This model is much more structured and strict and is based on a security label system. Users are given a security clearance (secret, top secret, confidential, and so on), and data is classified in the same way. The clearance and classification data is stored in the security labels, which are bound to the specific subjects and objects. When the system makes a decision about fulfilling a request to access an object, it is based on the clearance of the subject, the classification of the object, and the security policy of the system. The rules for how subjects access objects are made by the security officer, configured by the administrator, enforced by the operating system, and supported by security technologies.

Security labels are attached to all objects; thus, every file, directory, and device has its own security label with its classification information. A user may have a security clearance of secret, and the data that he requests may have a security label with the classification of top secret. In this case, the user will be denied because his clearance is not equivalent or does not dominate (equal or higher than) the classification of the object.

 **NOTE**   The terms "security labels" and "sensitivity labels" can be used interchangeably.

Each subject and object must have an associated label with attributes at all times, because this is part of the operating system's access-decision criteria. Each subject and object does not require a physically unique label, but can be logically associated. For example, all subjects and objects on Server 1 can share the same label of secret clearance and classification.

This type of model is used in environments where information classification and confidentiality is of utmost importance, such as a military institution. Special types of Unix systems are developed based on the MAC model. A company cannot simply choose to turn on either DAC or MAC. It has to purchase an operating system that has been specifically designed to enforce MAC rules. DAC systems do not understand security labels, classifications, or clearances, and thus cannot be used in institutions that require this type of structure for access control. The most recently released MAC system is SE Linux, developed by the NSA and Secure Computing. Trusted Solaris is a product based on the MAC model that most people are familiar with (relative to other MAC products).

## References

- *Security in Open Systems,* Node 36, "Determining MAC Access," by Robert Bagwell, et al., NIST Special Publication 800-7 (July 1994)   http://csrc.nist.gov/publications/nistpubs/800-7/node36.html

- *Integrating Flexible Support for Security Policies into the Linux Operating System,* Node 2, "Security Architecture," by Peter Loscocco and Stephen Smalley, National Security Agency research paper (2001)   www.nsa.gov/selinux/papers/freenix01/node2.html

- **Access Control**   www.list.gmu.edu/infs762/infs762su04ng/l1-access-control.ppt

## Sensitivity Labels

*I am very sensitive. Can I have a label? Response: Nope.*

When the MAC model is being used, every subject and object must have a sensitivity label, also called a security label. It contains a classification and different categories. The classification indicates the sensitivity level, and the categories enforce need-to-know rules. Figure 4-9 illustrates a sensitivity label.

The classifications follow a hierarchical structure, one level being more trusted than another. However, the categories do not follow a hierarchical scheme, because they represent compartments of information within a system. The categories can correspond to departments (UN, Information Warfare, Treasury), projects (CRM, AirportSecurity, 2003Budget), or management levels. In a military environment, the classifications could be top secret, secret, confidential, and unclassified. Each classification is more trusted than the one below it. A commercial organization might use confidential, proprietary, corporate, and sensitive. The definition of the classification is up to the organization and should make sense for the environment in which it is used.

The categories portion of the label enforces need-to-know rules. Just because someone has a top-secret clearance does not mean that she now has access to all top-secret information. She must also have a need to know. As shown in Figure 4-9, if Cheryl has a top-secret clearance but does not have a need to know that is sufficient to access any of the listed categories (Dallas, Max, Cricket), she cannot look at this object.

**Figure 4-9**
A sensitivity label is made up of a classification and categories.

**NOTE** In MAC implementations, the system makes access decisions by comparing the subject's clearance and need-to-know level to that of the security label. In DAC, the system compares the subject's identity to the ACL on the resource.

## Role-Based Access Control

*I am in charge of chalk, thus I need full control of all servers! Response: Good try.*

A *role-based access control (RBAC)* model, also called *nondiscretionary access control*, uses a centrally administered set of controls to determine how subjects and objects interact. This type of model allows access to resources to be based on the role the user holds within the company. It is referred to as nondiscretionary because assigning a user to a role is unavoidably imposed. This means that if you are assigned only to the Contractor role in a company, there is nothing you can do about it. You don't have the discretion to determine what role you will be assigned.

The more traditional access control administration is based on just the DAC model, where access control is specified at the object level with ACLs. This approach is more complex because the administrator has to translate organizational authorization policy into permission when configuring ACLs. As the number of objects and users grows within an environment, users are bound to be granted unnecessary access to some objects, thus violating the least-privilege rule and increasing the risk to the company. The RBAC approach simplifies access control administration by allowing permissions to be managed in terms of user job roles.

In an RBAC model, a role is defined in terms of the operations and tasks that the role will need to carry out, whereas a DAC model outlines which subjects can access what objects.

Let's say we need a research and development analyst role. We develop this role not only to allow an individual to have access to all product and testing data, but also, and more importantly, to outline the tasks and operations that the individual can carry out on this data. When the analyst role makes a request to access the new testing results on the file server, in the background the operating system reviews the role's access levels before allowing this operation to take place.

**NOTE** Introducing roles also introduces the difference between rights being assigned explicitly and implicitly. If rights and permissions are assigned explicitly, it indicates that they are assigned directly to a specific individual. If they are assigned implicitly, it indicates that they are assigned to a role or group and the user inherits those attributes.

An RBAC model is the best system for a company that has high employee turnover. If John, who is mapped to the contractor role, leaves the company, then Chrissy, his replacement, can be easily mapped to this role. That way, the administrator does not need to continually change the ACLs on the individual objects. He only needs to create a role (contractor), assign permissions to this role, and map the new user to this role.

## RBAC, MAC, DAC

A lot of confusion exists regarding whether RBAC is a type of DAC model or type of MAC model. Different sources claim different things, but in fact it is a model in its own right. In the 1960s and 1970s, the U.S. military and NSA did a lot of research on the MAC model. DAC, which also sprang to life in the '60s and '70s, has its roots in the academic and commercial research laboratories. The RBAC model, which started to gain popularity in the 1990s, can be used in combination with MAC and DAC systems. For the most up-to-date information on the RBAC model, go to **http://csrc.nist.gov/rbac**, which has documents that describe an RBAC standard and independent model, with the goal of clearing up this continual confusion.

## References

- Role Based Access Control   http://hissa.nist.gov/project/rbac.html
- Role Based Access Control Case Studies   http://csrc.nist.gov/rbac
- "Proposed Standard for Role Based Access Control," by David Ferraiolo, et al. (first published in *ACM Transactions on Information and System Security*, Vol. 4, No. 3, Aug. 2001, pp. 224–274)   http://csrc.nist.gov/rbac/rbacSTD-ACM.pdf
- "Role-Based Access Control for the Web," by John Barkley, et al., CALS Expo International & 21st Century Commerce 1998: Global Business Solutions for the New Millennium (1998)   http://hissa.ncsl.nist.gov/rbac/cals-paper.html
- "A Role-Based Access Control Model and Reference Implementation Within a Corporate Intranet," by John Barkley, D. Richard Kuhn, and David Ferraiolo (first published in *ACM Transactions on Information and System Security*, Vol. 2, No. 1, Feb. 1999, pp. 34–64)   www.ecs.syr.edu/faculty/chin/cse774/readings/rbac/p34-ferraiolo.pdf

## Access Control Models

The main characteristics of the three different access control models are important to understand.

- DAC   Data owners decide who has access to resources, and ACLs are used to enforce the security policy
- MAC   Operating systems enforce the system's security policy through the use of security labels
- RBAC   Access decisions are based on each subject's role and/or functional position

# Access Control Techniques and Technologies

Once an organization determines what type of access control model it is going to use, it needs to identify and refine its technologies and techniques to support the model. The following sections describe the different access controls and technologies available to support different access control models.

## Rule-Based Access Control

*Everyone will adhere to my rules. Response: Who are you again?*

*Rule-based access control* uses specific rules that indicate what can and cannot happen between a subject and an object. It is based on the simple concept of "if X then Y" programming rules, which can be used to provided finer-grained access control to resources. Before a subject can access an object in a certain circumstance, it must meet a set of predefined rules. This can be simple and straightforward, as in "if the user's ID matches the unique user ID value that is in the provided digital certificate, then the user can gain access." Or there could be a set of complex rules that must be met before a subject can access an object. For example, "if the user is accessing the system between Monday and Friday and between 8 A.M. and 5 P.M., and if the user's security clearance equals or dominates the object's classification, and if the user has the necessary need to know, then the user can access the object."

Rule-based access control is not necessarily identity-based. The DAC model is identity-based. For example, an identity-based control would stipulate that Tom Jones can read File1 and modify File2. So when Tom attempts to access one of these files, the operating system will check his identity and compare it to the values within an ACL to see if Tom can carry out the operations he is attempting. In contrast, here is a rule-based example: a company may have a policy that dictates that e-mail attachments can only be 5MB or smaller. This rule affects all users. If rule-based was identity-based, it would mean that Sue can accept attachments of 10MB and smaller, Bob can accept attachments 2MB and smaller, and Don can only accept attachments 1MB and smaller. This would be a mess and too confusing. Rule-based access controls simplify this by setting a rule that will affect all users across the board—no matter what their identity is.

Rule-based access allows a developer to define specific and detailed situations in which a subject can or cannot access an object, and what that subject can do once access is granted. Traditionally, rule-based access control has been used in MAC systems as an enforcement mechanism of the complex rules of access that MAC systems provide; today, rule-based access is used in other types of systems and applications, as well.

Many routers and firewalls use rules to determine which types of packets are allowed into a network and which are rejected. Rule-based access control is a type of compulsory control, because the administrator sets the rules and the users cannot modify these controls.

## References

- "Creating a Policy-Aware Web: Discretionary, Rule-based Access for the World Wide Web," Tim Berners-Lee, et al.   www.w3.org/2004/09/Policy-Aware-Web-acl.pdf

- "Roles or Rules: The Access Control Debate," by John Desmond, *eSecurityPlanet* Security Advisors article (July 29, 2003) www.esecurityplanet.com/views/article.php/2241671

## Constrained User Interfaces

Constrained user interfaces restrict users' access abilities by not allowing them to request certain functions or information, or to have access to specific system resources. There are three major types of restricted interfaces: menus and shells, database views, and physically constrained interfaces.

When menu and shell restrictions are used, the options that users are given are the commands that they can execute. For example, if an administrator wants users to be able to execute only one program, that program would be the only choice available on the menu. This limits the users' functionality. A *shell* is a type of virtual environment within a system; it is the user's interface to the operating system and works as a command interpreter. If restricted shells were used, the shell would contain only the commands the administrator wants the users to be able to execute.

Many times, a database administrator will configure a database so that users cannot see fields that require a level of confidentiality. *Database views* are mechanisms used to restrict user access to data that is contained in databases. If the database administrator wants managers to be able to view their employees' work records but not their salary information, then the salary fields would not be available to these types of users. Similarly, when payroll employees look at the same database, they will be able to view the salary information but not the work history information. This example is illustrated in Figure 4-10.

Physically constraining a user interface can be implemented by providing only certain keys on a keypad or certain touch buttons on a screen. You see this when you

**Figure 4-10**
Different database views of the same tables

| Harris, D | $45,000 | 8am-5pm |
|---|---|---|
| Torkelson, T | $60,000 | 6pm-2am |
| Kowtko, J | $45,000 | 8am-5pm |
| Swenson, J | $65,000 | 6pm-2am |

Payroll database view

| Harris, D | Work history | 8am-5pm |
|---|---|---|
| Torkelson, T | Work history | 6pm-2am |
| Kowtko, J | Work history | 8am-5pm |
| Swenson, J | Work history | 6pm-2am |

Manager database view

get money from an ATM machine. This device has a type of operating system that can accept all kinds of commands and configuration changes, but you are physically constrained from being able to carry out these functions. You are presented with buttons that only enable you to withdrawal, view your balance, or deposit funds. Period.

## Access Control Matrix

*The matrix—let's see, should I take the red pill or the blue pill?*

An *access control matrix* is a table of subjects and objects indicating what actions individual subjects can take upon individual objects. Matrices are data structures that programmers implement as table lookups that will be used and enforced by the operating system. Table 4-1 provides an example of an access control matrix.

This type of access control is usually an attribute of DAC models. The access rights can be assigned directly to the subjects (capabilities) or to the objects (ACLs).

## Capability Tables

A *capability table* specifies the access rights a certain subject possesses pertaining to specific objects. A capability table is different from an ACL because the subject is bound to the capability table, whereas the object is bound to the ACL.

The capability corresponds to the subject's row in the access control matrix. In Table 4-1, Diane's capabilities are File1: read and execute; File2: read, write, and execute; File3: no access. This outlines what Diane is capable of doing to each resource. An example of a capability-based system is Kerberos. In this environment, the user is given a ticket, which is his capability table. This ticket is bound to the user and dictates what objects that user can access and to what extent. The access control is based on this ticket, or capability table, not on an ACL bound to the object, although ACLs and capability tables can be used together. Figure 4-11 shows the difference between a capability table and an ACL.

A capability can be in the form of a token, ticket, or key. When a subject presents a capability component, the operating system (or application) will review the access rights and operations that are outlined in the capability component and allow the subject to carry out just those functions. A capability component is a data structure that contains a unique object identifier and access rights the subject has to that object. The object may be a file, array, memory segment, or port. Each user, process, and application in a capability system has a list of capabilities.

| User | File1 | File2 | File3 |
|------|-------|-------|-------|
| Diane | Read and execute | Read, write, and execute | No access |
| Katie | Read and execute | Read | No access |
| Chrissy | Read, write, and execute | Read and execute | Read |
| John | Read and execute | No access | Read and write |

**Table 4-1**  Example of an Access Control Matrix

**Figure 4-11**
A capability table is
bound to a subject,
whereas an ACL is
bound to an object.

Capability Table

Plotter—Print
Printer1—Print
Printer2—No access
Accountng.xls—Full control
Accounting.doc—Read, write
Payroll.xls—No access
Clipart—Full control

Access Control List

Tom Harris—Print
Joni Swenson—Full control
Maynard Harris—No access
Evelyn Seaton—Print
Iqqi Hammond—Full control
David Arnold—Print

## Access Control Lists

*Access control lists (ACLs)* are used in several operating systems, applications, and router configurations. They are lists of subjects that are authorized to access a specific object and they define what level of authorization is granted. Authorization can be specified to an individual or group.

ACLs map values from the access control matrix to the object. Whereas a capability corresponds to a row in the access control matrix, the ACL corresponds to a column of the matrix. The ACL for File1 in Table 4-1 is shown in Table 4-2.

## Content-Dependent Access Control

As the name suggests, with *content-dependent access control*, access to objects is determined by the content within the object. This often is used in databases. The earlier example pertaining to database views showed how content-dependent access control can work. The content of the database fields dictates which users can see specific information within the database tables.

Let's say we give department managers access to the payroll database, but specific managers would be given access only to the records that display those employees who actually work for them. That would require the access control system to look at the contents of the data in order to decide whether to give access or not. Therefore, that would be considered content-dependent access control.

Content-dependent filtering is used when corporations employ e-mail filters that look for specific strings, such as "confidential", "social security number", "top secret", and any other types of words that the company deems unacceptable. Corporations also

**Table 4-2**
The ACL
for File1

| User | File1 |
|---|---|
| Diane | Read and execute |
| Katie | Read and execute |
| Chrissy | Read, write, and execute |
| John | Read and execute |

have this in place to control web surfing, where filtering is done to look for specific words, to try to figure out whether employees are gambling or looking at pornography.

## Context-Dependent Access Control

*First you kissed a parrot, then you threw your shoe, and then you did a jig. That's the right sequence, you are allowed access.*

Context-dependent access control differs from content-dependent access control in that it makes access decisions based on the context of a collection of information rather than on the sensitivity of the data. A system that is using context-dependent access control "reviews the situation" and then makes a decision. For example, firewalls make context-based access decisions when they collect state information on a packet before allowing it into the network. A stateful firewall understands the necessary steps of communication for specific protocols. For example, in a TCP connection, the sender sends an SYN packet, the receiver sends an SYN/ACK, and then the sender acknowledges that packet with an ACK packet. A stateful firewall understands these different steps and will not allow packets to go through that do not follow this sequence. So, if a stateful firewall receives a SYN/ACK and there was not a previous SYN packet that correlates with this connection, the firewall understands that this is not right and disregards the packet. This is what stateful means—something that understands the necessary steps of a dialog session. And this is an example of context-dependent access control, where the firewall understands the *context* of what is going on and includes that as part of its access decision.

# Access Control Administration

Once an organization develops a security policy, supporting procedures, standards, and guidelines (described in Chapter 3), it must choose the type of access control model: DAC, MAC, or role-based. After choosing a model, the organization needs to select and implement different access control technologies and techniques. Access control matrices, restricted interfaces, and content-dependent, context-dependent, and rule-based controls are just a few of the choices.

If the environment does not require a high level of security, the organization will choose discretionary and/or role-based. The DAC model enables data owners to allow other users to access their resources, so an organization should choose the DAC model only if it is fully aware of what it entails. If an organization has a high turnover rate and/or requires a more centralized access control method, the role-based model is more appropriate. If the environment requires a higher security level and only the administrator should be able to grant access to resources, then a MAC model is the best choice.

What is left to work out is how the organization will administer the access control model. Access control administration comes in two basic flavors: centralized and decentralized. The decision makers should understand both approaches so that they choose and implement the proper one to achieve the level of protection required.

## Access Control Techniques

Access control techniques are used to support the access control models.

- **Access control matrix**   Table of subjects and objects that outlines their access relationships
- **ACL**   Bound to an object and indicates what subjects can access it
- **Capability table**   Bound to a subject and indicates what objects that subject can access
- **Content-based access**   Bases access decisions on the sensitivity of the data, not solely on subject identity
- **Context-based access**   Bases access decisions on the state of the situation, not solely on identity or content sensitivity
- **Restricted interface**   Limits the user's environment within the system, thus limiting access to objects
- **Rule-based**   Restricts subjects' access attempts by predefined rules

## Centralized Access Control Administration

*I control who can touch the carrots and who can touch the peas. Response: Could you leave now?*

A *centralized access control administration* method is basically what it sounds like: one entity (department or individual) is responsible for overseeing access to all corporate resources. This entity (security administrator) configures the mechanisms that enforce access control, processes any changes that are needed to a user's access control profile, disables access when necessary, and completely removes these rights when a user is terminated, leaves the company, or moves to a different position. This type of administration provides a consistent and uniform method of controlling users' access rights. It supplies strict control over data because only one entity (department or individual) has the necessary rights to change access control profiles and permissions. Although this provides for a more consistent and reliable environment, it can be a slow one, because all changes must be processed by one entity.

The following sections present some examples of centralized remote access control technologies. Each of these authentication protocols is referred to as an AAA protocol, which stands for authentication, authorization, and auditing. (Some resources have the last *A* stand for accounting, but it is the same functionality—just a different name.)

Depending upon the protocol, there are different ways to authenticate a user in this client/server architecture. The traditional authentication protocols are Password Authentication Protocol (PAP), Challenge Handshake Authentication Protocol (CHAP), and a newer method referred to as Extensible Authentication Protocol (EAP). Each of these authentication protocols is discussed at length in Chapter 7.

## RADIUS

*So, I have to run across half of a circle to be authenticated? Response: Don't know. Give it a try.*

Remote Authentication Dial-In User Service (RADIUS) is a client/server authentication protocol that authenticates and authorizes remote users. A network may have access servers, a modem pool, DSL, ISDN, or T1 line dedicated for remote users to communicate through. The access server requests the remote user's logon credentials and passes them back to a RADIUS server, which houses the usernames and password values. The remote user is a client to the access server, and the access server is a client to the RADIUS server.

Most ISPs today use RADIUS to authenticate customers before they are allowed access to the Internet. The access server and customer's software negotiate, through a handshake procedure, and agree upon an authentication protocol (PAP, CHAP, or EAP). The customer provides to the access server a username and password. This communication takes place over a PPP connection. The access server and RADIUS server communicate over the RADIUS protocol. Once the authentication is completed properly, the customer's system is given an IP address and connection parameters, and is allowed access to the Internet. The access server notifies the RADIUS server when the session starts and stops, for billing purposes.

RADIUS is also used within corporate environments to provide road warriors and home users access to network resources. RADIUS allows companies to maintain user profiles in a central database. When a user dials in and is properly authenticated, a preconfigured profile is assigned to him to control what resources he can and cannot access. This technology allows companies to have a single administered entry point, which provides standardization in security and a simplistic way to track usage and network statistics.

RADIUS was developed by Livingston Enterprises for its network access server product series, but was then published as RFC 2138 and RFC 2139. This means that it is an open protocol that any vendor can use and manipulate to be able to work within its individual products. Because RADIUS is an open protocol, it can be used in different types of implementations. The format of configurations and user credentials can be held in LDAP servers, various databases, or text files. Figure 4-12 shows some examples of possible RADIUS implementations.

## TACACS

*Terminal Access Controller Access Control System (TACACS)* has a very funny name. Not funny ha-ha, but funny "huh?" TACACS has been through three generations: TACACS, Extended TACACS (XTACACS), and TACACS+. TACACS combines its authentication and authorization processes, XTACACS separates authentication, authorization, and auditing processes, and TACACS+ is XTACACS with extended two-factor user authentication. TACACS uses fixed passwords for authentication and TACACS+ allows users to use dynamic (one-time) passwords, which provides more protection.

**Figure 4-12** Environments can implement various different RADIUS infrastructures.

 **NOTE** TACACS+ is really not a new generation of TACACS and XTACACS; it is a brand new protocol that provides similar functionality and shares the same naming scheme. Because it is a totally different protocol, it is not backward compatible with TACACS or XTACACS.

TACACS+ provides basically the same functionality as RADIUS with a few differences in some of its characteristics. First, TACACS+ uses TCP as its transport protocol, while RADIUS uses UDP. "So what?" you may be thinking. Well, any software that is developed to use UDP as its transport protocol has to be "fatter" with intelligent code that will look out for the items that UDP will not catch. Since UDP is a connectionless protocol, it will not detect or correct transmission errors. So RADIUS has to have the necessary code to detect packet corruption, long timeouts, or dropped packets. Since the developers of TACACS+ choose to use TCP, the TACACS+ software does not have to have the extra code to look for and deal with these transmission problems. TCP is a connection-oriented protocol, and that is its job and responsibility.

RADIUS encrypts the user's password only as it is being transmitted from the RADIUS client to the RADIUS server. Other information, as in the username, accounting, and authorized services, is passed in cleartext. This is an open invitation for attackers to capture session information for replay attacks. Vendors who integrate RADIUS into their products need to understand these weaknesses and integrate other security mechanisms to protect against these types of attacks.

TACACS+ encrypts all of this data and thus does not have the vulnerabilities that are inherent in the RADIUS protocol.

The RADIUS protocol combines the authentication and authorization functionality. TACACS+ uses a true AAA architecture, which separates the authentication, authorization, and accounting functionalities. This gives a network administrator more flexibility in how remote users are authenticated. For example, if Tom is a network administrator and has been assigned the task of setting up remote access for users, he will have to decide between RADIUS and TACACS+. If the current environment already authenticates all of the local users through a domain controller using Kerberos, then Tom can configure the remote users to be authenticated in this same manner, as shown in Figure 4-13. Instead of having to maintain a remote access server database of remote user credentials and a database within Active Directory for local users, Tom can just configure and maintain one database. The separation of authentication, authorization, and accounting functionality provides this capability. TACACS+ also enables the network administrator to define more granular user profiles, which can control the actual commands that users can carry out.

Remember that RADIUS and TACACS+ are both protocols, and protocols are just agreed-upon ways of communication. When a RADIUS client communicates with a RADIUS server, it does so through the RADIUS protocol, which is really just a set of defined fields that will accept certain values. These fields are referred to as attribute-value pairs (AVPs). As an analogy, suppose that I send you a piece of paper that has several different boxes drawn on it. Each box has a headline associated with it: first name, last name, hair color, shoe size. You fill in these boxes with your values and send it back to me. This is basically how protocols work; the sending system just fills in the boxes (fields) with the necessary information for the receiving system to extract and process.

Since TACACS+ allows for more granular control on what users can and cannot do, TACACS+ has more AVPs, which allows the network administrator to define ACLs, filters, user privileges, and much more.

## Watchdog

Watchdog timers are commonly used to detect software faults, such as a process ending abnormally or hanging. The watchdog functionality sends out a type of "heartbeat" packet to determine whether a service is responding; if it is not, the process can be terminated or reset. This guards against software deadlocks, infinite loops, and process prioritization problems. This functionality can be used in AAA protocols to determine whether packets need to be resent and whether connections that are experiencing problems need to be closed and reopened.

**Figure 4-13** TACACS+ works in a client/server model.

So, RADIUS is the appropriate protocol when simplistic username/password authentication can take place and users only need an Accept or Deny for obtaining access, as in ISPs. TACACS+ is the better choice for environments that require more sophisticated authentication steps and tighter control over more complex authorization activities, as in corporate networks.

## Diameter

*If we create our own technology, we get to name it any goofy thing we want! Response: I like Snizzernoodle.*

**Diameter** is a protocol that has been developed to build upon the functionality of RADIUS and overcome many of its limitations. The creators of this protocol decided to call it Diameter as a play on the term RADIUS, as in *the diameter is twice the radius.*

Diameter is another AAA protocol that provides the same type of functionality as RADIUS and TACACS+ but also provides more flexibility and capabilities to meet the

## Mobile IP

This technology allows a user to move from one network to another and still use the same IP address. It is an improvement upon the IP protocol because it allows a user to have a *home IP address*, associated with his home network, and a *care-of address*. The care-of address changes as he moves from one network to the other. All traffic that is addressed to his home IP address is forwarded to his care-of address.

new demands of today's complex and diverse networks. At one time, all remote communication took place over PPP and SLIP connections and users authenticated themselves through PAP or CHAP. Those were simpler, happier times when our parents had to walk uphill both ways to school wearing no shoes. As with life, technology has become much more complicated and there are more devices and protocols to choose from than ever before. Today, we want our wireless devices and smart phones to be able to authenticate themselves to our networks and we use roaming protocols, Mobile IP, Ethernet over PPP, and other crazy stuff that the traditional AAA protocols cannot keep up with. So in came the smart people with a new AAA protocol, Diameter, that can deal with these issues and many more.

Up until the conception of Diameter, IETF has had individual working groups who defined how Voice over IP (VoIP), Fax over IP (FoIP), Mobile IP, and remote authentication protocols work. Defining and implementing them individually in any network can easily result in too much confusion and interoperability. It requires customers to roll out and configure several different policy servers and increases the cost with each new added service. Diameter provides a base protocol, which defines header formats, security options, commands, and AVPs. This base protocol allows for extensions to tie in other services, such as VoIP, FoIP, Mobile IP, wireless, and cell phone authentication. So Diameter can be used as an AAA protocol for all of these different uses.

As an analogy, consider a scenario in which ten people all need to get to the same hospital, which is where they all work. They all have different jobs (doctor, lab technician, nurse, janitor, and so on), but they all need to end up at the same location. So, they can either all take their own cars and their own routes to the hospital, which takes up more hospital parking space and requires the gate guard to authenticate each and every car, or they can take a bus. The bus is the common element (base protocol) to get the individuals (different services) to the same location (networked environment). Diameter provides the common AAA and security framework that different services can work within, as illustrated in Figure 4-14.

 **NOTE** Roaming Operations (ROAMOPS) allows PPP users to gain access to the Internet without the need of dialing into their home service provider. The individual service providers, who have roaming agreements, carry out cross-authentication for their customers, so users can dial into any service provider's point of presence and gain Internet access.

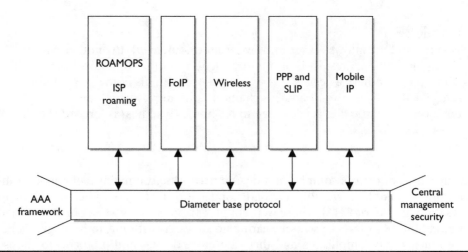

**Figure 4-14** Diameter provides an AAA architecture for several services.

RADIUS and TACACS+ are client/server protocols, which means that the server portion cannot send unsolicited commands to the client portion. The server portion can only speak when spoken to. Diameter is a peer-based protocol that allows either end to initiate communication. This functionality allows the Diameter server to send a message to the access server to request the user to provide another authentication credential if she is attempting to access a secure resource. This functionality also allows the Diameter server to disconnect the user if necessary for one reason or another.

Diameter is backward compatible with RADIUS, uses UDP and AVPs, and provides proxy server support. It has better error detection and correction functionality and fail-over properties than RADIUS, thus provides better network resilience. Diameter also provides end-to-end security through the use of IPSec or TLS, which is not available in RADIUS.

Diameter has the functionality and ability to provide the AAA functionality for other protocols and services because it has a large AVP set. RADIUS has $2^8$ (256) AVPs and Diameter has $2^{32}$ (a whole bunch). Recall from earlier in the chapter that AVPs are like boxes drawn on a piece of paper that outline how two entities can communicate back and forth. So, more AVPs allow for more functionality and services to exist and communicate between systems. Diameter provides the following AAA functionality:

- **Authentication**
  - PAP, CHAP, EAP
  - End-to-end protection of authentication information
  - Replay attack protection
- **Authorization**
  - Redirects, secure proxies, relays, and brokers
  - State reconciliation

- Unsolicited disconnect
- Reauthorization on demand
- **Accounting**
  - Reporting, ROAMOPS accounting, event monitoring

You may not be familiar with Diameter, because it is relatively new. It probably won't be taking over the world tomorrow, but it will be used by ISPs that need to provide the type of services that are being demanded of them, and then slowly seep down into corporate networks as more products are available. RADIUS has been around for a long time and has served its purpose well, so don't expect it to exit the stage any time soon.

## References

- **RFC 3588 – Diameter Base Protocol**  www.faqs.org/rfcs/rfc3588.html
- **RFC 2869 – RADIUS Extensions**  www.faqs.org/rfcs/rfc2869.html
- **RFC 2865 – Remote Authentication Dial In User Service (RADIUS)** www.faqs.org/rfcs/rfc2865.html
- **RFC 2975 – Introduction to Accounting Management**  www.faqs.org/rfcs/ rfc2975.html

## Decentralized Access Control Administration

*Okay, everyone just do whatever you want.*

A *decentralized access control administration* method gives control of access to the people closer to the resources—the people who may better understand who should and should not have access to certain files, data, and resources. In this approach, it is often the functional manager who assigns access control rights to employees. An organization may choose to use a decentralized model if its managers have better judgment regarding which users should be able to access different resources, and there is no business requirement that dictates that strict control through a centralized body is necessary.

Changes can happen faster through this type of administration because not just one entity is making changes for the whole organization. However, there is a possibility that conflicts of interest could arise that may not benefit the organization. Because no single entity controls access as a whole, different managers and departments can practice security and access control in different ways. This does not provide uniformity and fairness across the organization. One manager could be too busy with daily tasks and decide that it is easier to let everyone have full control over all the systems in the department. Another department may practice a more strict and detail-oriented method of control by giving employees only the level of permissions needed to fulfill their tasks.

Also, certain controls can overlap, in which case actions may not be properly proscribed or restricted. If Mike is part of the accounting group and recently has been under suspicion for altering personnel account information, the accounting manager may restrict his access to these files to read-only access. However, the accounting manager does not realize that Mike still has full-control access under the network group he is also a member of. This type of administration does not provide methods for consistent control, as a centralized method would. Another issue that comes up with decentralized administration is lack of proper consistency pertaining to the company's protection. For example, when Sean is fired for looking at pornography on his computer, some of the groups Sean is a member of may not disable his account. So, Sean may still have access after he is terminated, which could cause the company heartache if Sean is vindictive.

# Access Control Methods

Access controls can be implemented at various layers of a network and individual systems. Some controls are core components of operating systems or embedded into applications and devices, and some security controls require third-party add-on packages. Although different controls provide different functionality, they should all work together to keep the bad guys out and the good guys in, and to provide the necessary quality of protection.

Most companies do not want people to be able to walk into their building arbitrarily, sit down at an employee's computer, and access network resources. Companies also don't want every employee to be able to access all information within the company, as in human resource records, payroll information, and trade secrets. Companies want to have some assurance that employees who can access confidential information will have some restrictions put upon them so that a disgruntled employee does not have the ability to delete financial statements, tax information, and top-secret data that would put the company at risk. There are several types of access controls that prevent these things from happening, as discussed in the sections that follow.

## Access Control Layers

There are three broad categories of access control: administrative, technical, and physical. Each category has different access control mechanisms that can be carried out manually or automatically. All of these access control mechanisms should work in concert with each other to protect an infrastructure and its data.

Each category of access control has several components that fall within it, as shown here:

- **Administrative Controls**
  - Policy and procedures
  - Personnel controls
  - Supervisory structure
  - Security-awareness training
  - Testing

- **Physical Controls**
  - Network segregation
  - Perimeter security
  - Computer controls
  - Work area separation
  - Data backups
  - Cabling
  - Control zone
- **Technical Controls**
  - System access
  - Network architecture
  - Network access
  - Encryption and protocols
  - Auditing

The following sections explain each of these categories and components and how it relates to access control.

## Administrative Controls

Senior management must decide what role security will play in the organization, including the security goals and objectives. These directives will dictate how all the supporting mechanisms will fall into place. Basically, senior management provides the skeleton of a security infrastructure and then appoints the proper entities to fill in the rest.

The first piece to building a security foundation within an organization is a security policy. It is management's responsibility to construct a security policy and delegate the development of the supporting procedures, standards, and guidelines, indicate which personnel controls should be used, and specify how testing should be carried out to ensure that all pieces fulfill the company's security goals. These items are *administrative controls* and work at the top layer of a hierarchical access control model. (Administrative controls are examined in detail in Chapter 3, but are mentioned here briefly to show the relationship to logical and physical controls pertaining to access control.)

## Policy and Procedures

*Now, what's our overall plan?*

A *security policy* is a high-level plan that states management's intent pertaining to how security should be practiced within an organization, what actions are acceptable, and what level of risk the company is willing to accept. This policy is derived from the laws, regulations, and business objectives that shape and restrict the company. The security policy provides direction for each employee and department regarding how security should be implemented and followed, and the repercussions for noncompliance.

Procedures, guidelines, and standards provide the details that support and enforce the company's security policy.

## Personnel Controls

Personnel controls indicate how employees are expected to interact with security mechanisms, and address noncompliance issues pertaining to these expectations. These controls indicate what security actions should be taken when an employee is hired, terminated, suspended, moved into another department, or promoted. Specific procedures need to be developed for each situation, and many times the human resources and legal departments are involved with making these decisions.

The separation of duties and rotation of duties are also personnel controls that need to be dictated by management. The *separation of duties* should be enforced so that no one individual can carry out a critical task alone that could prove to be detrimental to the company. A bank teller who has to get supervisory approval to cash checks over $2000 is an example of separation of duties. For a security breach to occur, it would require *collusion*, which means that more than one person would need to commit fraud, and their efforts would need to be concerted. The use of separation of duties drastically reduces the probability of security breaches and fraud.

*Rotation of duties* means that people rotate jobs so that they know how to fulfill the obligations of more than one position. In many companies, only one person knows how to work that big important machine that keeps the company in business. If this person gets hit by a bus or finds a better job, the company's productivity can drop while it frantically trains the new person. If there were a practice of rotation of duties within this company, other employees would be able to cover the duties while a replacement is being trained.

Another benefit of rotation of duties is that if an individual attempts to commit fraud within his position, detection is more likely to happen if there is another employee who knows what tasks should be performed in that position and how they should be performed.

## Supervisory Structure

Management must construct a supervisory structure in which each employee has a superior to report to, and that superior is responsible for that employee's actions. This forces management members to be responsible for employees and take a vested interest in their activities. If an employee is caught hacking into a server that holds customer credit card information, that employee *and* her supervisor will face the consequences. This is an administrative control that aids in fighting fraud and enforcing proper control.

## Security-Awareness Training

*How do you know they know what they are supposed to know?*

In many organizations, management has a hard time spending money and allocating resources for items that do not seem to affect the bottom line: profitability. This is why training traditionally has been given low priority, but as computer security becomes more and more of an issue to companies, they are starting to recognize the value of security-awareness training.

A company's security depends upon technology and people, and people are usually the weakest link and cause the most security breaches and compromises. If users understand how to properly access resources, why access controls are in place, and the ramifications for not using the access controls properly, a company can reduce many of the types of security incidents that take place.

## Testing

All security controls, mechanisms, and procedures need to be tested on a periodic basis to ensure that they properly support the security policy, goals, and objectives set for them. This testing can be a drill to test reactions to a physical attack or disruption of the network, a penetration test of the firewalls and perimeter network to uncover vulnerabilities, a query to employees to gauge their knowledge, or a review of the procedures and standards to make sure they still align with business or technology changes that have been implemented. Because change is constant and environments continually evolve, security procedures and practices should be continually tested to ensure that they align with management's expectations and stay up to date with each addition to the infrastructure. It is management's responsibility to make sure these tests take place.

## Physical Controls

We will go much further into physical security in Chapter 6, but it is important to understand that there are physical controls that must support and work with administrative and technical (logical) controls to supply the right degree of access control. Examples of physical controls include having a security guard verify individuals' identities prior to entering a facility, erecting fences around the exterior of the facility, making sure server rooms and wiring closets are locked and protected from environmental elements (humidity, heat, and cold), and allowing only certain individuals to access work areas that contain confidential information. Some physical controls are introduced next, but again, these and more physical mechanisms are explored in depth in Chapter 6.

## Network Segregation

*I have used my LEGO set to outline the physical boundaries between you and me. Response: Can you make the walls a little higher please?*

Network segregation can be carried out through physical and logical means. A network might be physically designed to have all AS400 computers and databases in a certain area. This area may have doors with security swipe cards that allow only individuals who have a specific clearance to access this section and these computers. Another section of the network may contain web servers, routers, and switches, and yet another network portion may have employee workstations. Each area would have the necessary physical controls to ensure that only the permitted individuals have access into and out of those sections.

## Perimeter Security

How perimeter security is implemented depends upon the company and the security requirements of that environment. One environment may require employees to be authorized by a security guard by showing a security badge that contains picture identification before being allowed to enter a section. Another environment may require no authentication process and let anyone and everyone into different sections. Perimeter security can also encompass closed-circuit TVs that scan the parking lots and waiting areas, fences surrounding a building, lighting of walkways and parking areas, motion detectors, sensors, alarms, and the location and visual appearance of a building. These are examples of perimeter security mechanisms that provide physical access control by providing protection for individuals, facilities, and the components within facilities.

## Computer Controls

Each computer can have physical controls installed and configured, such as locks on the cover so that the internal parts cannot be stolen, the removal of the floppy and CD-ROM drives to prevent copying of confidential information, or implementation of a protection device that reduces the electrical emissions to thwart attempts to gather information through airwaves.

## Work Area Separation

Some environments might dictate that only particular individuals can access certain areas of the facility. For example, research companies might not want office personnel to be able to enter laboratories, so that they can't disrupt experiments or access test data. Most network administrators allow only network staff in the server rooms and wiring closets, to reduce the possibilities of errors or sabotage attempts. In financial institutions, only certain employees can enter the vaults or other restricted areas. These examples of work area separation are physical controls that are used to support access control and the overall security policy of the company.

## Data Backups

Backing up data is a physical control to ensure that information can still be accessed after an emergency or a disruption of the network or a system. When a network administrator of a bank backs up that day's transaction records, account histories, and financial information, it is stored on a type of physical media (tape, drive, or CD-ROM) and usually kept in a fireproof safe or copied and transported to an offsite facility. This provides physical protection of this data and a way to recover this information in case the original data is lost.

## Cabling

There are different types of cabling that can be used to carry information throughout a network. Some cable types have sheaths that protect the data from being affected by the electrical interference of other devices that emit electrical signals. Some types of cable have protection material around each individual wire to ensure that there is no cross-talk between the different wires. All cables need to be routed throughout the facility in a manner that is not in people's way or that could be exposed to any danger of being cut, burnt, crimped, or eavesdropped upon.

## Technical Controls

Technical controls, also called logical controls, are the software tools used to restrict subjects' access to objects. They are core components of operating systems, add-on security packages, applications, network hardware devices, protocols, encryption mechanisms, and access control matrixes. These controls work at different layers within a network or system and need to maintain a synergistic relationship to ensure that there is no unauthorized access to resources and that the resources' availability, integrity, and confidentiality are guaranteed. Technical controls protect the integrity and availability of resources by limiting the number of subjects that can access them and protect the confidentiality of resources by preventing disclosure to unauthorized subjects. The following sections explain how some technical controls work and where they are implemented within an environment.

## System Access

Different types of controls and security mechanisms control how a computer is accessed. If an organization is using a MAC architecture, the clearance of a user is identified and compared to the resource's classification level to verify that this user can access the requested object. If an organization is using a DAC architecture, the operating system checks to see if a user has been granted permission to access this resource. The sensitivity of data, clearance level of users, and users' rights and permissions are used as logical controls to control access to a resource.

There are many types of technical controls that enable a user to access a system and the resources within that system. A technical control may be a username and password combination, a Kerberos implementation, biometrics, public key infrastructure (PKI), RADIUS, TACACS, or authentication using a smart card through a reader connected to a system. These technologies verify that the user is who he says he is by using different types of authentication methods. Once a user is properly authenticated, he can be authorized and allowed access to network resources. These technologies are addressed in further detail in future chapters, but for now understand that system access is a type of technical control that can enforce access control objectives.

## Network Architecture

The architecture of a network can be constructed and enforced through several logical controls to provide segregation and protection of an environment. Whereas a network can be segregated physically by walls and location, it can also be segregated logically through IP address ranges and subnets and by controlling the communication flow between the segments. Often, it is important to control how one segment of a network communicates with another segment.

Figure 4-15 is an example of how an organization may segregate its network and determine how network segments can communicate. This example shows that the organization does not want the internal network and the demilitarized zone (DMZ) to

**Figure 4-15** Technical network segmentation controls how different network segments communicate.

have open and unrestricted communication paths. There is usually no reason for internal users to have direct access to the systems in the DMZ, and cutting off this type of communication reduces the possibilities of internal attacks on those systems. Also, if an attack comes from the Internet and successfully compromises a system on the DMZ, the attacker must not be able to easily access the internal network, which this type of logical segregation protects against.

This example also shows how the management segment can communicate with all other network segments, but those segments cannot communicate in return. The segmentation is implemented because the management consoles that control the firewalls and IDSs reside in the management segment, and there is no reason for users, other than the administrator, to have access to these computers.

A network can be segregated physically and logically. This type of segregation and restriction is accomplished through logical controls.

## Network Access

Systems have logical controls that dictate who can and cannot access them and what those individuals can do once they are authenticated. This is also true for networks. Routers, switches, firewalls, and bridges all work as technical controls to enforce access restriction into and out of a network, and access to the different segments within the network. If an attacker from the Internet wants to gain access to a specific computer, chances are that she will have to hack through a firewall, router, and a switch just to be able to start an attack on a specific computer that resides within the internal network. Each device has its own logical controls that make decisions about what entities can access them and what type of actions they can carry out.

Access to different network segments should be granular in nature. Routers and firewalls can be used to ensure that only certain types of traffic get through to each segment.

## Encryption and Protocols

Encryption and protocols work as technical controls to protect information as it passes throughout a network and resides on computers. They ensure that the information is received by the correct entity, and that it is not modified during transmission. These logical controls can preserve the confidentiality and integrity of data and enforce specific paths for communication to take place. (Chapter 8 is dedicated to cryptography and encryption mechanisms.)

## Control Zone

*I will ensure that no signal escapes this room by using my incredible mental abilities. Response: How about using a control zone instead?*

A *control zone* is physical control. It is a specific area that surrounds and protects network devices that emit electrical signals. These electrical signals can travel a certain distance and can be contained by a specially made material, which is used to construct the control zone. Some companies use extra metallic material in their building walls to zone off areas that have computers that deal with top-secret information. The control zone is used to resist penetration attempts and disallow sensitive information to "escape" through the airwaves. We will address how information can be captured from emitted electrical waves in the "Emanation Security" section of this chapter, but for now understand that a control zone is used as a physical control to ensure that confidential information is contained and to hinder intruders from accessing information through the airwaves. Figure 4-16 depicts a control zone. Companies that have very sensitive information would likely protect that information by creating control zones around the systems that are processing that information.

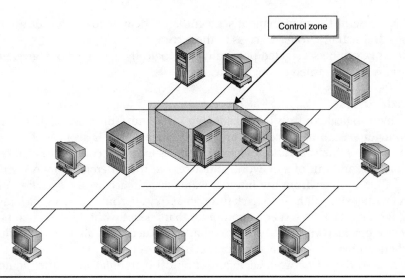

**Figure 4-16** Companies can implement control zones, which control the amount of electrical signals that are emitted from sections of the facility.

## Auditing

Auditing tools are technical controls that track activity within a network, on a network device, or on a specific computer. Even though auditing is not an activity that will deny an entity access to a network or computer, it will track activities so that a network administrator can understand the types of access that took place, identify a security breach, or warn the administrator of suspicious activity. This information can be used to point out weaknesses of other technical controls and help the administrator understand where changes need to be made to preserve the necessary security level within the environment.

**NOTE** Many of the subjects touched on in these sections will be fully addressed and explained in later chapters. What is important to understand is that there are administrative, technical, and physical controls that work toward providing access control, and you should know several examples of each for the exam.

# Access Control Types

As previously stated, access control types (administrative, physical, and technical) work at different levels, but different levels of what? They work together at different levels within their own categories. A security guard is a type of control used to scare off evil-doers and ensure that only authorized personnel enter a building. If an intruder gets around the security guard in some manner, he could be faced with motion detectors, locks on doors, and alarms. These layers are depicted in Figure 4-17.

**Figure 4-17**
Security should
be implemented
in layers, which
provides several
barriers to attackers.

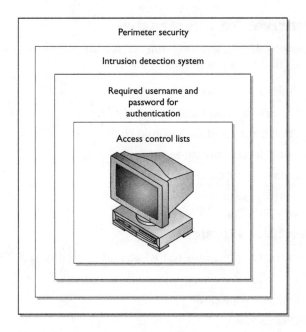

Perimeter security

Intrusion detection system

Required username and
password for
authentication

Access control lists

Each control works at a different level of granularity, but it can also perform different functionalities. The different functionalities of access controls are *preventive, detective, corrective, deterrent, recovery,* and *compensative.* When looking at a security structure
of an environment, it is most productive to use a preventive model and then use detective, recovery, and corrective mechanisms to help support this model. Basically, you
want to stop any trouble before it starts, but you need to be able to quickly react and
combat trouble if it does find you. All security controls should be built on the concept
of preventive security. However, it is not feasible to prevent everything; therefore, what
you cannot prevent, you should be able to quickly detect. That's why preventive and
detective controls should always be implemented together and should complement
each other. To take this concept further, what you can't prevent, you should be able to
detect, and if you detect something, it means that you weren't able to prevent it, and
therefore you should take corrective action to make sure that it is indeed prevented the
next time around. Therefore, all three types work together, preventive, detective, and
corrective.

The control types described next (administrative, physical, and technical) are preventive in nature. These are important to understand when developing a security access
control model and when taking the CISSP exam.

### Preventive: Administrative

The following are the *soft* mechanisms that are put into place to enforce access control and protection for the company as a whole:

- Policies and procedures
- Effective hiring practices
- Pre-employment background checks
- Controlled termination processes
- Data classification and labeling
- Security awareness

### Preventive: Physical

The following can physically restrict access to a facility, specific work areas, or computer systems:

- Badges, swipe cards
- Guards, dogs
- Fences, locks, mantraps

### Preventive: Technical

The following are logical controls that are part of operating systems, third-party application add-ons, or hardware units:

- Passwords, biometrics, smart cards
- Encryption, protocols, call-back systems, database views, constrained user interfaces
- Antivirus software, ACLs, firewalls, routers, clipping levels

Table 4-3 shows how these categories of access control mechanisms perform different security functions. However, Table 4-3 does not necessarily cover all the possibilities. For example, a fence can provide preventive and deterrent measures by making it harder for intruders to access a facility, but it could also be a compensative control. If a company cannot afford a security guard, it might erect a fence to act as the compensative physical control. Each control is able to meet more requirements than what is listed in the table. Table 4-3 is only an example to show the relationship among the different controls and the security attributes they could provide.

---

 **NOTE** Locks are usually considered delay mechanisms because they only delay a determined intruder. The goal is to delay access long enough to allow law enforcement or the security guard to respond to the situation.

| Type of Control: | Preventive | Detective | Corrective | Deterrent | Recovery | Compensative |
|---|---|---|---|---|---|---|
| | Avoid undesirable events from occurring | Identify undesirable events that have occurred | Correct undesirable events that have occurred | Discourage security violations | Restore resources and capabilities | Provide alternatives to other controls |
| **Category of Control:** | | | | | | |
| **Physical** | | | | | | |
| Fences | X | | | X | | |
| Locks | X | | | X | | |
| Badge system | X | | | X | | |
| Security guard | X | X | | X | | |
| Biometric system | X | | | | | |
| Mantrap doors | X | | | X | | |
| Lighting | X | | | | | |
| Motion detectors | | X | | | | |
| Closed-circuit TVs | | X | | X | | |
| Alarms | X | X | | X | | |
| Backups | | | | | X | |
| **Administrative** | | | | | | |
| Security policy | X | | | | | |
| Monitoring and supervising | X | X | | X | | X |
| Separation of duties | X | | | | | |
| Job rotation | | X | | | | |

**Table 4-3** Services That Security Controls Provide

| Type of Control: | Preventive | Detective | Corrective | Deterrent | Recovery | Compensative |
|---|---|---|---|---|---|---|
| Information classification | X | | | | | |
| Personnel procedures | X | | | X | | X |
| Investigations | | X | | | | |
| Testing | X | | | | | |
| Security-awareness training | X | | | X | | |
| **Technical** | | | | | | |
| ACLs | X | | | | | |
| Routers | X | | | | | |
| Encryption | X | | | | | |
| Audit logs | | X | | | | |
| IDS | | X | | | | |
| Antivirus software | X | X | X | | X | |
| Firewalls | X | | | X | | |
| Smart cards | X | | | | | |
| Dial-up call-back systems | X | | | | | |
| Alarms and alerts | | X | | | | |

**Table 4-3** Services That Security Controls Provide *(continued)*

There are several types of security mechanisms, and they all need to work together. The complexity of the controls and of the environment they are in can cause the controls to contradict each other or leave gaps in security. This can introduce unforeseen holes in the company's protection that are not fully understood by the implementers. A company may have very strict technical access controls in place and all the necessary administrative controls up to snuff, but if any person is allowed to physically access any system in the facility, then clear security dangers are present within the environment. Together these controls should work in harmony to provide a healthy, safe, and productive environment.

# Accountability

Auditing capabilities ensure that users are accountable for their actions, verify that the security policies are enforced, and can be used as investigation tools. There are several reasons why network administrators and security professionals want to make sure accountability mechanisms are in place and configured properly: to be able to track bad deeds back to individuals, detect intrusions, reconstruct events and system conditions, provide legal recourse material, and produce problem reports. Audit documentation and log files hold a mountain of information—the trick is usually deciphering it and presenting it in a useful and understandable format.

Accountability is tracked by recording user, system, and application activities. This recording is done through auditing functions and mechanisms within an operating system or application. Audit trails contain information about operating system activities, application events, and user actions. Audit trails can be used to verify the health of a system by checking out performance information or certain types of errors and conditions. After a system crashes, a network administrator often will review audit logs to try and piece together the status of the system and attempt to understand what events could be attributed to the disruption.

An administrator configures what actions and events are to be audited and logged. In a high-security environment, the administrator would configure more activities to be captured and set the threshold of those activities to be more sensitive. The events can be reviewed to identify where breaches of security occurred and if the security policy had been violated. If the environment does not require such level of security, the events analyzed would be fewer with less demanding thresholds.

Items and actions to be audited can become an endless list. A security professional should be able to assess an environment and its security goals, know what actions should be audited, and know what is to be done with that information after it is captured—without wasting too much disk space, CPU power, and staff time. The following gives a broad overview of the items and actions that can be audited and logged:

- **System-level events**
  - System performance
  - Logon attempts (successful and unsuccessful)

- Logon ID
- Date and time of each logon attempt
- Lockouts of users and terminals
- Use of administration utilities
- Devices used
- Functions performed
- Requests to alter configuration files
- **Application-level events**
  - Error messages
  - Files opened and closed
  - Modifications of files
  - Security violations within application
- **User-level events**
  - Identification and authentication attempts
  - Files, services, and resources used
  - Commands initiated
  - Security violations

The threshold (clipping level) and parameters for each of these items needs to be configured. For example, an administrator can audit each logon attempt or just each failed logon attempt. System performance can look only at the amount of memory used within an eight-hour period, or the memory, CPU, and hard drive space used within an hour.

Intrusion detection systems (IDSs) continually scan audit logs for suspicious activity. If an intrusion or harmful event takes place, audit logs are usually kept to be used later to prove guilt and prosecute if necessary. If severe security events take place, many times the IDS will alert the administrator or staff member so that they can take proper actions to end the destructive activity. If a dangerous virus is identified, administrators may take the mail server offline. If an attacker is accessing confidential information within the database, this computer may be temporarily disconnected from the network or Internet. If an attack is in progress, the administrator may want to watch the actions taking place so that she can track down the intruder. IDSs can watch for this type of activity during real time and/or scan audit logs and watch for specific patterns or behaviors.

## Review of Audit Information

*It does no good to collect it if you don't look at it.*

Audit trails can be reviewed manually or through automated means—either way, they must be reviewed and interpreted. If an organization reviews audit trails manually, it needs to establish a system of how, when, and why they are viewed. Usually audit logs are very popular items right after a security breach, unexplained system action, or system disruption. An administrator or staff member rapidly tries to piece together the activities that led up to the event. This type of audit review is event-oriented. Audit trails can also be viewed periodically to watch for unusual behavior of users or systems, and to help understand the baseline and health of a system. Then there is a real-time, or near real-time, audit analysis that can use an automated tool to review audit information as it is created. Administrators should have a scheduled task of reviewing audit data. The audit material usually needs to be parsed and saved to another location for a certain time period. This information should be stated in the company's security policy and procedures.

Reviewing audit information manually can be overwhelming. There are applications and audit trail analysis tools that reduce the volume of audit logs to review and improve the efficiency of manual review procedures. A majority of the time, audit logs contain information that is unnecessary, so these tools parse out specific events and present them in a useful format. There are three main types of audit trail analysis tools: audit reduction, variance detection, and attack signature detection.

An *audit-reduction tool* does just what its name suggests—reduces the amount of information within an audit log. This tool discards mundane task information and records system performance, security, and user functionality information that can be useful to a security professional or administrator. A *variance-detection* tool can monitor computer and resource usage trends and detect variations. If an employee works from 8:00 A.M. to 5:00 P.M., which is the normal time his computer is used and resources are accessed, and recently this computer has been used at 2:00 A.M. and on the weekend, the variance-detection tool can capture this information and alert the administrator of unusual activity. If an *attack signature–detection* tool is used, the application will have a database of information that has been known to indicate specific attacks. This type of tool parses audit logs in search of certain patterns. If a pattern matches a pattern or signature held within its database, the tool indicates that an attack has taken place or is in progress.

## Keystroke Monitoring

*Oh, you typed an L; let me write that down. Oh, and a P, and a T, and an S…hey, slow down!*

*Keystroke monitoring* is a type of auditing that can review and record keystrokes entered by a user during an active session. The person using this type of monitoring can have the characters written to an audit log to be reviewed at a later time. This type of auditing is usually done only for special cases and only for a specific amount of time, because the amount of information captured can be overwhelming. If a security professional or administrator is suspicious of an individual and his activities, she may invoke this type of monitoring. In some authorized investigative stages, a keyboard dongle may be unobtrusively inserted between the keyboard and the computer to capture all the keystrokes entered, including power-on passwords.

A hacker can also use this type of monitoring. If an attacker can successfully install a Trojan horse on a computer, the Trojan horse can install an application that captures data as it is typed into the keyboard. Most of the time these programs are most interested in user credentials and can alert the attacker when credentials have been successfully captured.

There are privacy issues with this type of monitoring, and administrators could be subject to criminal and civil liabilities if it is done without proper notification to the employees and authorization from management. If a company wants to be able to use this type of auditing, it should state so in the security policy, address the issue in security-awareness training, and present a banner notice to the user warning that the activities at that computer may be monitored in this fashion. These steps should be taken to protect the company from violating an individual's privacy, and they should inform the users where their privacy boundaries start and stop pertaining to computer use.

## Protecting Audit Data and Log Information

If an intruder breaks into your house, he will do his best to cover his tracks by not leaving fingerprints or any other clues that can be used to tie him to the criminal activity. The same is true in computer fraud and illegal activity. The intruder will work to cover his tracks. Attackers often delete audit logs that hold this incriminating information. (Deleting specific incriminating data within audit logs is called *scrubbing*.) Deleting this information can cause the administrator to not be alerted or aware of the security breach, and can destroy valuable data. Therefore, audit logs should be protected by strict access control.

Only certain individuals (the administrator and security personnel) should be able to view, modify, and delete audit trail information. No other individuals should be able to view this data, much less modify or delete it. The integrity of the data can be ensured with the use of digital signatures, message digest tools, and strong access controls. Its confidentiality can be protected with encryption and access controls, if necessary, and it can be stored on **write-once media** (CD-ROM) to prevent loss or modification of the data. Unauthorized access attempts to audit logs should be captured and reported.

Audit logs may be used in a trial to prove an individual's guilt, demonstrate how an attack was carried out, or corroborate a story. The integrity and confidentiality of these logs will be under scrutiny. Proper steps need to be taken to ensure that the confidentiality and integrity of the audit information is not compromised in any way.

## References

- **Authentication, Authorization, and Accounting (AAA) Charter** www.ietf .org/html.charters/aaa-charter.html
- **Google authentication categories** http://directory.google.com/Top/ Computers/Security/Authentication
- *Security in Open Systems,* **NIST Special Publication 800-7 (July 1994)** http://csrc.nist.gov/publications/nistpubs/800-7/node2.html

# Access Control Practices

*The fewest number of doors open allows the fewest number of flies in.*

We have gone over how users are identified, authenticated, and authorized, and how their actions are audited. These are necessary parts of a healthy and safe network environment. You also want to take steps to ensure that there are no unnecessary open doors and that the environment stays at the same security level you have worked so hard to achieve. This means that you need to implement good access control practices. Not keeping up with daily or monthly tasks usually causes the most vulnerabilities in an environment. It is hard to put out all the network fires, fight the political battles, fulfill all the users' needs, and still keep up with small maintenance tasks. However, many companies have found that not doing these small tasks caused them the greatest heartache of all.

The following is a list of tasks that need to be accomplished on a regular basis to ensure that security stays at a satisfactory level:

- Deny access to systems by undefined users or anonymous accounts.
- Limit and monitor the usage of administrator and other powerful accounts.
- Suspend or delay access capability after a specific number of unsuccessful logon attempts.
- Remove obsolete user accounts as soon as the user leaves the company.
- Suspend inactive accounts after 30 to 60 days.
- Enforce strict access criteria.
- Enforce the need-to-know and least-privilege practices.
- Disable unneeded system features, services, and ports.
- Replace default password settings on accounts.
- Limit and monitor global access rules.
- Ensure that logon IDs are nondescriptive of job function.
- Remove redundant resource rules from accounts and group memberships.
- Remove redundant user IDs, accounts, and role-based accounts from resource access lists.
- Enforce password rotation.
- Enforce password requirements (length, contents, lifetime, distribution, storage, and transmission).
- Audit system and user events and actions and review reports periodically.
- Protect audit logs.

Even if all of these countermeasures are in place and properly monitored, there are ways that data can be lost in an unauthorized manner. The next section looks at these issues and their corresponding countermeasures.

## Unauthorized Disclosure of Information

There are several ways that information can become available to others for whom it is not intended, which can bring about unfavorable results. Sometimes this is done intentionally, but it can be done unintentionally as well. Information can be disclosed unintentionally when one falls prey to attacks that specialize in causing this disclosure. These attacks are social engineering, covert channels, malicious code, and electrical airwave sniffing. Information can be disclosed accidentally through object reuse methods, which are explained next. (Social engineering was discussed in Chapter 3; covert channels are discussed in Chapter 5.)

## Object Reuse

*Can I borrow this floppy? Response: Let me destroy it first.*

*Object reuse* issues pertain to reassigning to a subject media that previously contained one or more objects. Huh? This means before someone uses a hard drive, floppy disk, or tape, it should be cleared of any residual information that was on it previously. This concept also applies to objects that are reused by computer processes, such as memory locations, variables, and registers. The sensitive information that may be left by a process should be securely cleared before allowing another process the opportunity to access the object. This ensures that information not intended for this individual or any other subject is not disclosed. Many times, floppy disks are exchanged casually in a work environment. What if a supervisor lent a floppy to an employee without erasing it and it contained confidential employee performance reports and salary raises forecasted for the next year? This could prove to be a bad decision and maybe turn into a morale issue if the information was passed around. Formatting a disk or deleting files only removes the pointers to the files; it does not remove the actual files. This information will still be on the disk and available until the operating system needs that space and overwrites those files. So, for media that holds confidential information, more extreme methods should be taken to ensure that the files are actually gone, not just their pointers.

Sensitive data should be classified (secret, top secret, confidential, unclassified, and so on) by the data owners. How the data is stored and accessed should also be strictly controlled and audited by software controls. However, it does not end there; before allowing one subject to use media that was previously used, the media should be erased or degaussed. (This responsibility usually falls on the operations department.) If media holds sensitive information and cannot be purged, there should be steps on how to properly destroy it so that there is no way for others to obtain this information.

 **NOTE** Sometimes hackers actually configure a sector on a hard drive so that it is marked as bad and unusable to an operating system, but this sector is actually fine and may hold malicious data. The operating system will not write information to this sector because it thinks it is corrupted. This is a form of *data hiding*. Some boot-sector virus routines are capable of putting the main part of their code (payload) into a specific sector of the hard drive, overwriting any data that may have been there, and then protecting it as a bad block.

# Emanation Security

*Quick, cover your computer and your head in tinfoil!*

All electronic devices emit electrical signals. These signals can hold important information, and if an attacker buys the right equipment and positions himself in the right place, he could capture this information from the airwaves and access data transmissions as if he had a tap directly on the network wire.

There have been several incidents in which intruders have purchased inexpensive equipment and used it to intercept electrical emissions as they radiated from a computer. This equipment can reproduce data streams and display the data on the intruder's monitor, enabling the intruders to learn of covert operations, find out military strategies, and uncover and exploit confidential information. This is not just stuff found in spy novels; it really happens, so the proper countermeasures have been devised.

**Tempest**    *Tempest* started out as a study carried out by the DoD and then turned into a standard that outlines how to develop countermeasures that control spurious electrical signals that are emitted by electrical equipment. There is special shielding that is used on equipment to suppress the signals as they are radiated from devices. Tempest equipment is implemented to prevent intruders from picking up information through the airwaves with listening devices. There are specific standards that this type of equipment must meet to be rated as providing Tempest shielding protection. Tempest refers to standardized technology that suppresses signal emanations with shielding material. Vendors who manufacture this type of equipment must be certified to this standard.

The devices (monitors, computers, printers, and so on) have an outer metal coating, referred to as a *Faraday cage*. This is made of metal with the necessary depth to ensure that only a certain amount of radiation is released. In devices that are Tempest rated, other components are also modified, especially the power supply, to help reduce the amount of electricity that is used.

There are allowable limits of emission levels that can radiate and still be considered safe. The approved products must ensure that only this level of emissions is allowed to escape the devices. This type of protection is usually needed only in military institutions, although other highly secured environments do utilize this type of safeguard.

Many military organizations are concerned with stray radio frequencies emitted by computers and other electronic equipment because an attacker may be able to pick them up, reconstruct them, and give away some secrets that were meant to stay secret.

Tempest technology is complex, cumbersome, and expensive, and therefore only used in highly sensitive areas that really need this high level of protection.

Two alternatives to Tempest exist: use white noise or use a control zone concept, both of which are explained next.

**NOTE** Tempest is the name of a program, and now a standard, that was developed in the late 1950s by the U.S. and British governments. It was developed to deal with electrical and electromagnetic radiation emitted from electrical equipment, mainly computers. This type of equipment is usually used by intelligence, military, government, and law enforcement agencies, and the selling of this type of equipment is under constant scrutiny.

**White Noise**   A countermeasure used to combat intruders from extracting information from electrical transmissions is white noise. *White noise* is a uniform spectrum of random electrical signals. It is distributed over the full spectrum so that the bandwidth is constant and an intruder is not able to decipher real information from random noise or random information.

**Control Zone**   Another alternative to using Tempest equipment is to use the zone concept, which was addressed earlier in this chapter. Some facilities use material in their walls to contain electrical signals. This prevents intruders from being able to access information that is emitted via electrical signals from network devices. This control zone creates a type of security perimeter and is constructed to protect against unauthorized access to data or compromise of sensitive information.

# Access Control Monitoring

Access control monitoring is a method of keeping track of who attempts to access specific network resources. It is an important detective mechanism, and there are different technologies that can fulfill this need. It is not enough to invest in antivirus and firewall solutions. Companies are finding that monitoring their own internal network has become a way of life.

## Intrusion Detection

*Intrusion detection systems (IDSs)* are different from traditional firewall products because they are designed to detect a security breach. *Intrusion detection* is the process of detecting an unauthorized use of, or attack upon, a computer, network, or telecommunications infrastructure. IDSs are designed to aid in mitigating the damage that can be caused by hacking, or breaking into sensitive computer and network systems. The basic intent of the IDS tool is to spot something suspicious happening on the network and sound an alarm by flashing a message on a network manager's screen, or possibly sending a page or even reconfiguring a firewall's ACL setting. The IDS tools can look for sequences of data bits that might indicate a questionable action or event, or monitor system log and activity recording files. The event does not need to be an intrusion to sound the alarm; any kind of "non-normal" behavior will do the trick.

Although there are different types of IDS products, they all have three common components: sensors, analyzers, and administrator interfaces. The sensors collect traffic and user activity data and send it to an analyzer, which looks for suspicious activity. If the analyzer detects an activity that it is programmed to deem as fishy, it sends an alert to the administrator's interface.

There are two main types of IDS: *network-based*, which monitor network communications, and *host-based*, which can analyze the activity within a particular computer system.

IDSs can be configured to watch for attacks, parse audit logs, terminate a connection, alert an administrator as attacks are happening, protect system files, expose a hacker's techniques, illustrate which vulnerabilities need to be addressed, and possibly help track down individual hackers.

## Network-Based IDS

*All the sailors love NIDS, because it is always in promiscuous mode.*

A network-based IDS (NIDS) uses sensors, which are either host computers with the necessary software installed or dedicated appliances—each with its network interface card (NIC) in promiscuous mode. NICs watch for traffic that has the address of its host system, broadcasts, and sometimes multicast addresses. The NIC driver copies the data from the transmission medium and sends it up the network protocol stack for processing. When a NIC is put into promiscuous mode, the NIC driver captures all traffic and passes it to an analyzer to look for specific types of patterns.

A NIDS monitors network traffic and cannot "see" the activity going on inside a computer itself. To monitor the activities within a computer system, a company would need to implement a host-based IDS.

## Host-Based IDS

A *host-based IDS (HIDS)* can be installed on individual workstations and/or servers and watch for inappropriate or anomalous activity. HIDSs are usually used to make sure users do not delete system files, reconfigure important settings, or put the system at risk in any other way. So, whereas the NIDS understands and monitors the network traffic, a HIDS's universe is limited to the computer itself. A HIDS does not understand or review network traffic, and a NIDS does not "look in" and monitor a system's activity. Each has its own job and stays out of the other's way.

In most environments, HIDS products are installed only on critical servers, not on every system on the network, because of the resource overhead and the administration nightmare that such an installation would cause.

Just to make life a little more confusing, HIDS and NIDS can be one of the following types:

- Signature based
- Statistical anomaly based

- Protocol anomaly based
- Traffic anomaly based
- Rule based
  - Stateful matching
  - Model based

## Knowledge- or Signature-Based Intrusion Detection

Knowledge is accumulated by the IDS vendors about specific attacks and how they are carried out. Models of how the attacks are carried out are developed and called *signatures*. Each identified attack has a signature, which is used to detect an attack in progress or determine if one has occurred within the network. Any action that is not recognized as an attack is considered acceptable.

An example of a signature is a packet that has the same source and destination IP address. All packets should have a different source and destination IP address, and if they have the same address, this means a Land attack is under way. In a Land attack, a hacker modifies the packet header so that when a receiving system responds to the packet, it is responding to its own address. Now that seems as though it should be benign enough, but vulnerable systems just do not have the programming code to know what to do in this situation, so they freeze or reboot. Once this type of attack was discovered, the signature-based IDS vendors wrote a signature that looks specifically for packets that contain the same source and destination address.

Signature-based IDS are the most popular IDS products today, and their effectiveness depends upon regularly updating the software with new signatures, as with antivirus software. This type of IDS is weak against new types of attacks because it can recognize only the ones that have been previously identified and have had signatures written for them. Attacks or viruses that have been discovered in production environments are referred to as being "in the wild." Attacks and viruses that exist but have not been released are referred to as being "in the zoo." No joke.

## Statistical Anomaly–Based Intrusion Detection

*Through statistical analysis I have determined that I am an anomaly in nature. Response: You have my vote.*

*Statistical anomaly–based IDS* is a behavioral-based system. Behavioral-based IDS products do not use predefined signatures, but rather are put in a learning mode to build a profile of an environment's "normal" activities. This profile is built by continually sampling the environment's activities. The longer the IDS is put in a learning mode, in most instances, the more accurate a profile it will build and the better protection it will provide. After this profile is built, all future traffic and activities are compared to it. The same type of sampling that was used to build the profile takes place, so the same type of data is being compared. Anything that does not match the profile is seen as an attack, in response to which the IDS sends an alert. With the use of complex statistical algorithms, the IDS looks for anomalies in the network traffic or user activity. Each packet is given an anomaly score, which indicates its degree of irregularity. If the score is higher than the established threshold of "normal" behavior, then the preconfigured action will take place.

The benefit of using a statistical anomaly–based IDS is that it can react to new attacks. It can detect "0 day" attacks, which means that an attack is new to the world and no signature or fix has been developed yet. These products are also capable of detecting the "low and slow" attacks, in which the attacker is trying to stay beneath the radar by sending a few packets at a time over a longer period of time. The IDS should be able to detect these types of attacks because they are different enough from the contrasted profile.

Now for the bad news. Since the only thing that is "normal" about a network is that it is constantly changing, developing the correct profile that will not provide an overwhelming number of false positives can be difficult. Many IT staff members know all too well this dance of chasing down alerts that end up being benign traffic or activity. In fact, some environments end up turning off their IDS because of the amount of time these activities take up. (Proper education on tuning and configuration will reduce the number of false positives.)

If an attacker detects that there is an IDS on a network, she will then try to detect the type of IDS it is so that she can properly circumvent it. With a behavioral-based IDS, the attacker could attempt to integrate her activities into the behavior pattern of the network traffic. That way, her activities are seen as "normal" by the IDS and thus go undetected. It is a good idea to ensure that there is no current attack activity that is under way while the IDS is in learning mode. If this takes place, the IDS will never alert you of this type of attack in the future because it sees this traffic as typical of the environment.

If a corporation decides to use a statistical anomaly–based IDS, it needs to ensure that the staff members who are implementing and maintaining it understand protocols and packet analysis. Because this type of an IDS sends generic alerts, compared to other types of IDSs, it is up to the network engineer to figure out what the actual issue

## Attack Techniques

It is common for hackers to first identify whether an IDS is present on the network that they are preparing to attack. If one is present, that attacker may first attack the IDS to bring it off line by a denial-of-service. Another tactic is to send the IDS incorrect data, which will make the IDS send off specific alerts indicating that a certain attack is under way, when in truth it is not. The goal of these activities is either to disable the IDS or to distract the network and security individuals so that they will be busy chasing the wrong packets, while the real attack takes place.

> ## What's in a Name?
> Signature-based IDSs are also known as misuse-detection systems, and behavioral-based IDSs are also known as profile-based systems.

is. For example, a signature-based IDS reports the type of attack that has been identified, and a rule-based IDS identifies the actual rule that the packet does not comply with. In a statistical anomaly–based IDS, all the product really understands is that something "abnormal" has happened, which just means that the event does not match the profile.

Determining the proper thresholds for statistically significant deviations is really the key for the successful use of a behavioral-based IDS. If the threshold is set too low, nonintrusive activities are considered attacks (false positives). If the threshold is set too high, then malicious activities are not identified (false negatives).

Once an IDS discovers an attack, several things can take place, depending upon the capabilities of the IDS and the policy that has been assigned to it. The IDS can send an alert to a console to tell the right individuals that an attack is being carried out; send an e-mail or page to the individual who has been delegated to respond to such activities; kill the connection of the detected attack; or reconfigure a router or firewall to try to stop any further similar attacks. A modifiable response condition might include anything from blocking a specific IP address to redirecting or blocking a certain type of activity.

**Protocol Anomaly–Based IDS**   A statistical anomaly–based IDS can use protocol anomaly–based filters. These types of IDSs have specific knowledge of each protocol that they will be monitoring. A protocol anomaly pertains to the format and behavior of a protocol. The IDS builds a model (or profile) of each protocol's "normal" usage. Keep in mind, however, that protocols have *theoretical* usage, as outlined in their corresponding RFCs, and *real-world* usage, which refers to the fact that vendors seem to always "color outside the lines" and not strictly follow the RFCs in their protocol development and implementation. So, most profiles of individual protocols are a mix between the official and real-world versions of the protocol and its usage. When the IDS is activated, it looks for anomalies that do not match the profiles built for the individual protocols.

Although there are several vulnerabilities within operating systems and applications that are available to be exploited, many more successful attacks take place by exploiting vulnerabilities in the protocols themselves. At the OSI data link layer, the Address Resolution Protocol (ARP) does not have any protection against ARP attacks where bogus data is inserted into its table. At the network layer, the Internet Control Message Protocol (ICMP) can be used in a Loki attack to move data from one place to another, when this protocol was designed to only be used to send status information—

not user data. IP headers can be easily modified for spoofed attacks. At the transport layer, TCP packets can be injected into the connection between two systems for a session hijacking attack.

---

 **NOTE** When an attacker compromises a computer and loads a backdoor on the system, he will need to have a way to communicate to this computer through this backdoor and stay "under the radar" of the network firewall and IDS. Hackers have figured out that a small amount of code can be inserted into an ICMP packet, which is then interpreted by the backdoor software loaded on a compromised system. Security devices are usually not configured to monitor this type of traffic because ICMP is a protocol that is supposed to be used just to send status information—not commands to a compromised system.

---

Because every packet formation and delivery involves many protocols, and because more attack vectors exist in the protocols than in the software itself, it is a good idea to integrate protocol-anomaly filters in any network behavioral-based IDS.

**Traffic Anomaly–Based IDS** Most behavioral-based IDSs have traffic-anomaly filters, which detect changes in traffic patterns as in DoS attacks or a new service that appears on the network. Once there is a profile that is built that captures the baselines of an environment's ordinary traffic, all future traffic patterns are compared to that profile. As with all filters, the thresholds are tunable to adjust the sensitivity, to reduce the number of false positives and false negatives. Since this is a type of statistical anomaly–based IDS, it can detect unknown attacks.

## Rule-Based Intrusion Detection

A rule-based IDS takes a different approach than a signature-based or statistical anomaly–based system. A signature-based IDS is very straightforward. For example, if a signature-based IDS detects a packet that has all of its TCP header flags with the bit value of 1, it knows that an xmas attack is under way—so it sends an alert. A statistical anomaly–based IDS is also straightforward. For example, if Bob has logged onto his computer at 6 A.M. and the profile indicates that this is abnormal, the IDS sends an alert, because this is seen as an activity that needs to be investigated. Rule-based intrusion detection gets a little bit more tricky, depending upon the complexity of the rules that are used.

Rule-based intrusion detection is commonly associated with the use of an expert system. An expert system is made up of a knowledge base, inference engine, and rule-based programming. Knowledge is represented as rules, and the data that is to be analyzed is referred to as facts. The knowledge of the system is written in rule-based programming (IF *situation* THEN *action*). These rules are applied to the facts, the data that comes in from a sensor, or a system that is being monitored. For example, in scenario 1 the IDS pulls data from a system's audit log and stores it temporarily in its fact database, as illustrated in Figure 4-18. Then, the preconfigured rules are applied to

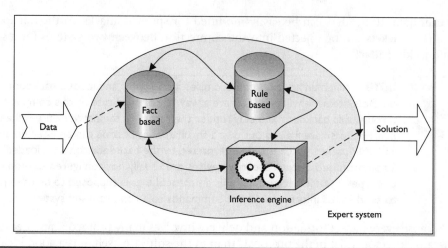

**Figure 4-18** Rule-based IDS and expert system components

this data to indicate whether anything suspicious is taking place. In our scenario, the rule states "IF *a root user creates File1* AND *creates File2* SUCH THAT *they are in the same directory* THEN *there is a call to AdministrativeTool1* TRIGGER *send alert.*" This rule has been defined such that if a root user creates two files in the same directory and then makes a call to a specific administrative tool, an alert should be sent.

It is the inference engine that provides some artificial intelligence into this process. An inference engine can infer new information from provided data by using inference rules. To understand what inferring means in the first place, let's look at the following;

Socrates is a man.
All men are mortals.

Then we can infer that Socrates is mortal. If you are asking "What does this have to do with a hill of beans?" just hold on to your hat—here we go.

Regular programming languages deal with the "black and white" of life. The answer is either yes or no, not maybe this or maybe that. Although computers can carry out complex computations at a much faster rate than humans, they have a harder time guessing, or inferring, answers because they are very structured. The fifth-generation programming languages (artificial intelligence languages) are capable of dealing with the grayer areas of life and can attempt to infer the right solution from the provided data.

So, in a rule-based IDS that is based on an expert system, the IDS gathers data from a sensor or log, and the inference engine uses its preprogrammed rules on it; if the characteristics of the rules are met, then an alert or solution is provided, as illustrated in Figure 4-18.

There are two basic types of rule-based IDSs that you need to understand: state-based IDSs and model-based IDSs.

**State-Based IDS** Before you can get too deep into understanding how a state-based IDS works, you need to understand what the state of a system or application actually is. Every change that an operating system experiences (user logs on, user opens application, application communicates to another application, user inputs data, and so on) is considered a state transition. In a very technical sense, all operating systems and applications are just lines and lines of instructions that are written to carry out functions on data. The instructions have empty variables, which is where the data is held. So when you use the calculator program and you type in 5, there is an empty variable that has just been populated with this value. By entering that value, you change the state of that application. When applications communicate with each other, they populate empty variables that are provided in each application's instruction set. So, a state transition is when a variable's value changes, which usually happens continuously within every system.

There are specific state changes (activities) that take place for specific types of attacks. If an attacker is going to carry out a remote buffer overflow, then the following state changes will take place:

1. The remote user connects to the system.
2. The remote user sends data to an application (the data exceeds the allocated buffer for this empty variable).
3. The data is executed and overwrites the buffer and possibly other memory segments.
4. Malicious code executes.

So, *state* is a snapshot of an operating system's values in volatile, semipermanent, and permanent memory locations. In a state-based IDS, the initial state is the state prior to the execution of an attack, and the compromised state is the state after successful penetration. The IDS has rules that outline what state transition sequences should sound an alarm. The activity that takes place between the initial and compromised state is what the state-based IDS looks for, and it sends an alert if any of the state-transition sequences match its preconfigured rules.

This type of IDS scans for attack signatures in the context of a stream of activity instead of just looking at individual packets. It can only identify known attacks and requires frequent updates of its signatures.

**Model-Based IDS** In a model-based IDS, the product has several scenario models that represent how specific attacks and intrusions take place. The models outline how the system would behave if it were under attack, the different steps that would be carried out by the attacker, and the evidence that would be available for analysis if specific intrusions took place.

The IDS takes in the audit log data and compares it to the different models that have been developed, to see if the data meets any of the models' specifications. If the IDS finds data in an audit log that matches the characteristics in a specific model, it sends an alert.

As analogy, suppose that we have a model that states the following: if it looks like a duck, sounds like a duck, and walks like a duck—it's a duck. So, we do our in-depth analysis upon the creature in front of us. We compare each characteristic in the model and find that each matches, so we conclude that the creature is a duck.

## IDS Types

It is important to understand the characteristics that make the different types of IDS technologies distinct. Here is a summary:

- **Signature based**
  - Pattern matching, similar to antivirus software
  - Signatures must be continuously updated
  - Cannot identify new attacks
- **Statistical anomaly based**
  - Behavioral-based system that learns the "normal" activities of an environment
  - Can detect new attacks
  - Two types:
    **Protocol anomaly based**   Unusual format or behavior of protocols
    **Traffic anomaly based**   Unusual format of traffic patterns
- **Rule based**
  - Use of IF/THEN rule-based programming within expert systems
  - Use of expert system allows for artificial intelligence characteristics
  - The more complex the rules, the more demands on software and hardware processing requirements
  - Cannot detect new attacks
  - Two types:
    **Stateful matching**   Tracking system state changes that indicate an attack is under way
    **Model based**   Models of attack scenarios are built and then captured data is compared to the models to uncover malicious activities

## References

- "The Science of IDS Attack Identification" (Cisco Systems white paper) www.cisco.com/en/US/products/sw/secursw/ps976/products_white_ paper09186a0080092334.shtml

- "Intrusion Detection Terminology (Part Two)," by Andy Cuff (SecurityFocus Infocus Archive, last updated Sept. 24, 2003) www.securityfocus.com/infocus/1733

- Honeypots.net IDS Software links page   www.honeypots.net/ids/products

- "State of the Practice of Intrusion Detection Technologies," by Julia Allen, et al., Software Engineering Institute, Carnegie Mellon University (Jan. 1999) www.sei.cmu.edu/publications/documents/99.reports/99tr028/ 99tr028abstract.html

## IDS Sensors

Network-based IDSs use sensors for monitoring purposes. A sensor, which works as an analysis engine, is placed on the network segment the IDS is responsible for monitoring. The sensor receives raw data from an event generator, as shown in Figure 4-19, and compares it to a signature database, profile, or model, depending upon the type of IDS. If there is some type of a match, which indicates suspicious activity, the sensor works with the response module to determine what type of activity needs to take place (alerting through instant messaging, page, e-mail, or carry out firewall reconfiguration, and so on). The sensor's role is to filter received data, discard irrelevant information, and detect suspicious activity.

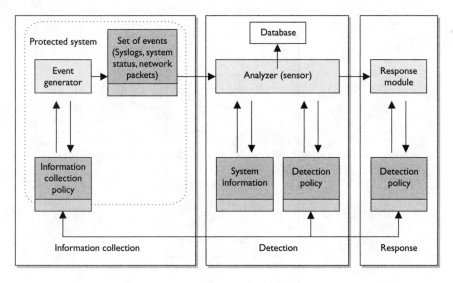

**Figure 4-19**   Basic architecture of an NDIS

## Switched Environments

NIDSs have a harder time working on a switched network, when compared to traditional nonswitched environments, because data is transferred through independent virtual circuits and not broadcasted, as in nonswitched environments. The IDS sensor acts as a sniffer and does not have access to all the traffic in these individual circuits. So, we have to take all the data on each individual virtual private connection, make a copy of it, and put the copies of the data on one port (spanning port) where the sensor is located. This allows the sensor to have access to all the data going back and forth on a switched network.

A monitoring console monitors all sensors and supplies the network staff with an overview of the activities of all the sensors in the network. A difficulty arises in a switched environment, where traffic is forwarded through a virtual private connection and is not rebroadcast to all the ports. The switch should have a management port, enabling all traffic on that switch to be mirrored to one port, where the sensor is placed. (This is also referred to as a *spanning port*, where all traffic from all ports can be mirrored to one port.)

These are the components that enable network-based intrusion detection to actually work. Sensor placement is a critical part of configuring an effective IDS. An organization can place a sensor outside of the firewall to detect attacks and place a sensor inside the firewall (in the perimeter network) to detect actual intrusions. Sensors should also be placed in highly sensitive areas, DMZs, and on extranets. Figure 4-20 shows the sensors reporting their findings to the central console.

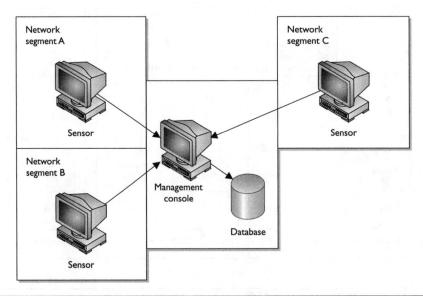

**Figure 4-20**   Sensors need to be placed in each network segment that is to be monitored by the IDS.

The IDS can be centralized, as firewall products that have IDS functionality integrated within them, or distributed, with multiple sensors throughout the network.

## Network Traffic

If the network traffic volume exceeds the IDS system's threshold, attacks may go unnoticed. Each vendor's IDS product has its own threshold, and you should know and understand that threshold before it you purchase and implement the IDS.

In very high-traffic environments, multiple sensors should be in place to ensure that all packets are investigated. If necessary to optimize network bandwidth and speed, different sensors can be set up to analyze each packet for different signatures. That way, the analysis load can be broken up over different points.

## Intrusion Prevention Systems

*An ounce of prevention does something good. Response: Yeah, causes a single point of failure.*

In the industry, there is constant frustration with the inability of existing products to stop the bad guys from accessing and manipulating corporate assets. This has created a market demand for vendors to get creative and come up with new, innovative technologies and new products for companies to purchase, implement, and still be frustrated with.

The next "big thing" in the IDS arena is the intrusion prevention system (IPS). The traditional IDS only detects that something bad may be taking place and sends an alert. The goal of an IPS is to detect this activity and not allow the traffic to gain access to the target in the first place, as shown in Figure 4-21. So, an IPS is a preventative and proactive technology, whereas an IDS is a detective and after-the-fact technology.

As of this writing, the industry is debating what the real definition of IPS is, and many vendors are attempting to be the king of the hill in this market. But the general concept of the definition is agreed upon, which is a focus on prevention rather than detection. The goal is to combine into one product the "stop the packets in their tracks" functionality that firewalls provide with the in-depth packet analysis that an IDS provides. As within the IDS arena, there are host-based IPS products and network-based IPS products. A majority of the network-based IPS products are inline devices, which means that all traffic must go through and be monitored by the IPS before going any

## Intrusion Responses

Most IDSs are capable of several types of response to a triggered event. An IDS can send out a special signal to drop or kill the packet connections, at both the source and destinations. This effectively disconnects the communication, and does not allow it to be transmitted. An IDS might block a user from accessing a resource on a host system, if the threshold is set to trigger this response. An IDS can send alerts of an event trigger to other hosts, IDS monitors, and administrators. And, finally, some IDSs can reconfigure themselves to perform some predefined action.

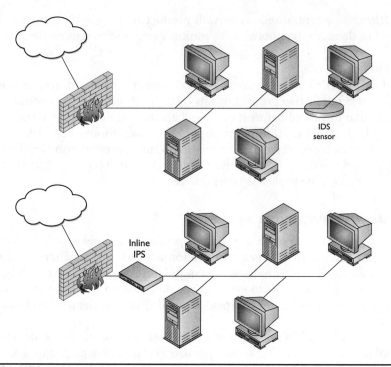

**Figure 4-21** IDS vs. IPS architecture

further down its path. This is a concern for many companies because any inline device can be a traffic bottleneck, reduce performance, and pose a single point of failure. (Vendors are working hard to provide technologies to deal with each of these issues.)

Most NIPSs have two NICs, external and internal facing. Traffic arrives on the external NIC and is analyzed by the engine. If the packets are deemed safe, they go on their way out the internal-facing NIC. If the packets are deemed malicious, then the packet is discarded.

Only time will tell whether IPS products will replace IDS products. Some people feel as though it is just a new term for marketing purposes, whereas others feel as though it is the next step in our evolution of information and computer security technology advances. The rest of us should just get some popcorn and watch how this play unfolds.

## References

- **"Intrusion Prevention Versus Intrusion Detection," by Markus DeShon (SecureWorks white paper)** www.secureworks.com/en/html/printer/internet/techResourceCenter/Intrusion-prevention-versus-intrusion-detection.html

- "Intrusion Prevention Systems: The Next Step in the Evolution of IDS," by Neil Desai (SecurityFocus Infocus Archive, last updated Feb. 27, 2003) www.securityfocus.com/infocus/1670

- "Intrusion Prevention Systems (IPS), Part 1: Deciphering the inline Intrusion Prevention hype, and working toward a real-world, proactive security solution" (Secure Computing white paper, 2003)   www.securecomputing .com/pdf/Intru-Preven-WP1-Aug03-vF.pdf

- "Rule-Based Intrusion Detection," from the Software Engineering Institute (SEI) Software Technology Roadmap   www.sei.cmu.edu/str/descriptions/ rbid.html

## Honeypot

*Hey, curious, ill-willed, and destructive attackers, look at this shiny new vulnerable computer.*

A *honeypot* is a computer set up as a sacrificial lamb on the network. The system is not locked down and has open ports and services enabled. This is to entice a would-be attacker to this computer instead of attacking authentic production systems on a network. The honeypot contains no real company information, and thus will not be at risk if and when it is attacked.

This enables the administrator to know when certain types of attacks are happening so that he can fortify the environment and perhaps track down the attacker. The longer the hacker stays at the honeypot, the more information that will be disclosed about her techniques.

It is important to draw a line between *enticement* and *entrapment* when implementing a honeypot system. There are legal and liability issues around each. If the system only has open ports and services that an attacker might want to take advantage of, this would be an example of enticement. If the system has a web page indicating that the user can download files, and once the user does this the administrator charges this user with trespassing, it would be entrapment. Entrapment is where the intruder is induced or tricked into commiting a crime. Entrapment is illegal and cannot be used when charging an individual with hacking or unauthorized activity.

## References

- **The Honeynet Project**   http://project.honeynet.org
- **"What Is a Honeypot?" by Loras Even, SANS (July 12, 2000)**   www.sans .org/resources/idfaq/honeypot3.php

## Network Sniffers

*I think I smell a packet! Response: Nope. It's my feet.*

A packet or network *sniffer* is a general term for programs or devices that are able to examine traffic on a LAN segment. Traffic that is being transferred over a network medium is transmitted as electrical signals, encoded in binary representation. The sniffer has to have a protocol-analysis capability to recognize the different protocol values to properly interpret their meaning.

The sniffer has to have access to a network adapter that works in promiscuous mode and a driver that captures the data. This data can be overwhelming, so it must be properly filtered. The filtered data is stored in a buffer, and this information is displayed to a user and/or captured in logs. Some utilities have sniffer and packet-modification capabilities, which is how some types of spoofing and man-in-the-middle attacks are carried out.

Network sniffers are used by the people in the white hats (administrators and security professionals) usually to try to track down a recent problem with the network. But the guys in the black hats (attackers and crackers) can use them to learn about what type of data is passed over a specific network segment and to modify data in an unauthorized manner. Black hats usually use sniffers to obtain credentials as they pass over the network medium.

 **NOTE** Sniffers are dangerous because they are very hard to detect and their activities are difficult to audit.

# A Few Threats to Access Control

As a majority of security professionals know, there is more risk and a higher probability of an attacker causing mayhem from within an organization than from outside the organization. However, many people within organizations do not know this fact, because they only hear stories about the outside attackers who defaced a web server or circumvented a firewall to access confidential information.

An attacker from the outside can enter through remote dial-in entry points, enter through firewalls and web servers, physically break in, or exploit a partner communication path (extranet, vendor connection, and so on). An insider has legitimate reasons for using the systems and resources, but can misuse his privileges and launch an actual attack also. The danger of insiders is that they have already been given a wide range of access that a hacker would have to work to obtain, they probably have intimate knowledge of the environment, and generally they are trusted. We have discussed many different types of access control mechanisms that work to keep the outsiders outside and restrict the insiders' abilities to a minimum and audit their actions. Now we will look at some specific attacks that are commonly carried out in environments today by insiders or outsiders.

## Dictionary Attack

There are several programs that enable an attacker (or proactive administrator) to identify user credentials. This type of program is fed lists (dictionaries) of commonly used words or combinations of characters, and then compares these values to capture passwords. In other words, the program hashes the dictionary words and compares the resulting message digest with the system password file that also stores its passwords in one-way hashed format. If the hashed values match, it means that a password has just been uncovered. Once the right combination of characters is identified, the attacker can use this password to authenticate herself as a legitimate user. Because many systems have a threshold that dictates how many failed logon attempts are acceptable, the same type of activity can happen to a captured password file. The dictionary-attack program encrypts the combination of characters and compares it to the encrypted entries in the password file. If a match is found, the program has uncovered a password.

The dictionaries come with the password cracking programs, and extra dictionaries can be found on several sites on the Internet.

**NOTE** Passwords should never be transmitted or stored in cleartext. Most operating systems and applications put the passwords through hashing algorithms, which result in hash values, also referred to as message digest values.

## Countermeasures

To properly protect an environment against dictionary and other password attacks, the following practices should be followed:

- Do not allow passwords to be sent in cleartext.
- Encrypt the passwords with encryption algorithms or hashing functions.
- Employ one-time password tokens.
- Use hard-to-guess passwords.
- Rotate passwords frequently.
- Employ an IDS to detect suspicious behavior.
- Use dictionary cracking tools to find weak passwords chosen by users.
- Use special characters, numbers, and upper- and lowercase letters within the password.
- Protect password files.

## Brute Force Attack

*I will try over and over until you are defeated. Response: Okay, wake me when you are done.*

There are several types of **brute force attacks**, but overall they are attacks that continually try different inputs to achieve a predefined goal. Brute force is defined as "trying every possible combination until the correct one is identified." So in a brute force password attack, the software tool will see if the first letter is an "a" and continue through the alphabet until that single value is uncovered. Then the tool moves on to the second value and so on.

The most effective way to uncover passwords is through a hybrid attack, which combines a dictionary attack and a brute force attack. If a dictionary tool has found that a user's password starts with Dallas, then the brute force tool will try Dallas1, Dallas01,

Dallasa1, and so on until a successful logon credential is uncovered. (A brute force attack is also known as an exhaustive attack.)

These attacks are also used in *wardialing* efforts, in which the wardialer inserts a long list of phone numbers into a wardialing program in hopes of finding a modem that can be exploited to gain unauthorized access. A program is used to dial many phone numbers and weed out the numbers that are used for voice calls and fax machine services. The attacker usually ends up with a handful of numbers he can now try to exploit to gain access into a system or network.

So, a brute force attack perpetuates a specific activity with different input parameters until the goal is achieved.

## Countermeasures

For phone brute force attacks, auditing and monitoring of this type of activity should be in place to uncover patterns that could indicate a wardialing attack:

- Perform brute force attacks to find weaknesses and hanging modems.
- Make sure only necessary phone numbers are made public.
- Provide stringent access control methods that would make brute force attacks less successful.
- Monitor and audit for such activity.
- Employ an IDS to watch for suspicious activity.
- Set lockout thresholds.

## Spoofing at Logon

*So, what are your credentials again?*

An attacker can use a program that presents to the user a fake logon screen, which often tricks the user into attempting to log on. The user is asked for a username and password, which are stored for the attacker to access at a later time. The user does not know this is not his usual logon screen because they look exactly the same. A fake error message can appear, indicating that the user mistyped his credentials. At this point, the fake logon program exits and hands control over to the operating system, which

---

### Phishing Attacks

Phishing attacks usually take place through e-mail schemes that request users to disclose personal or financial information. The e-mail usually appears to come from a legitimate corporation (financial institutions, PayPal, eBay, credit card companies, service providers, and so on) asking the person to update their account information or threatening to terminate accounts. The e-mail contains a link that takes the user to a web site that looks like the official site. It is at this site where the user is asked to enter their credentials, account numbers, and possibly credit card information.

prompts the user for a username and password. The user assumes he mistyped his information and doesn't give it a second thought, but an attacker now knows the user's credentials.

This has become a common attack on the Internet in phishing attacks and identity theft attempts. Hackers have created web sites that look just like www.amazon.com, www.ebay.com, and many of the other popular sites people use today in e-commerce transactions.

### Countermeasures

An operating system can be configured to display the number of failed logon attempts. If the first logon attempt seemed to have failed, but was really the attacker's program capturing the entered credentials, and it was not reported at the second attempt and the user could get suspicious as to what just took place.

A guaranteed *trusted path* can be provided by the operating system. A trusted path is a communication link between the user and the kernel that cannot be circumvented as described in the scenario of a fake logon screen. Windows 2000 uses a sequence of CTRL-ALT-DEL to invoke the operating system's logon screen. (However, some sneaky fake programs can set themselves to be called upon by this combination of keys also.)

For countermeasures to phishing attacks, the following are common best practices:

- Be skeptical of e-mails indicating that you need to make changes to your accounts or warnings indicating that accounts will be terminated without you doing some type of activity online.
- Call the legitimate company to find out if this is a fraudulent message.
- Review the address bar to see if the domain name is correct.
- When submitting any type of financial information or credential data, an SSL connection should be set up, which is indicated in the address bar (https://) and a closed-padlock icon in the browser at the bottom-right corner.
- Do not click on an HTML link within an e-mail. Type the URL out manually instead.
- Do not accept e-mail in HTML format.

## Summary

Access controls are security features that are usually considered the first line of defense in asset protection. They are used to dictate how subjects access objects, and their main goal is to protect the objects from unauthorized access. These controls can be administrative, physical, or technical in nature and can supply preventive, detective, deterrent, recovery, compensative, and corrective services.

Access control defines how users should be identified, authenticated, and authorized. These issues are carried out differently in different access control models and technologies, and it is up to the organization to determine which best fits its business and security needs.

# Quick Tips

- Access is a flow of information between a subject and an object.
- A subject is an active entity that requests access to an object, which is a passive entity.
- A subject can be a user, program, or process.
- Confidentiality is the assurance that information is not disclosed to unauthorized subjects.
- Some security mechanisms that provide confidentiality are encryption, logical and physical access control, transmission protocols, database views, and controlled traffic flow.
- There are three main access control models: discretionary, mandatory, and nondiscretionary.
- Discretionary access control (DAC) enables data owners to dictate what subjects have access to the files and resources they own.
- Mandatory access control (MAC) uses a security label system. Users have clearances, and resources have security labels that contain data classifications. MAC compares these two attributes to determine access control capabilities.
- Nondiscretionary access control uses a role-based method to determine access rights and permissions.
- Role-based access control is based on the user's role and responsibilities within the company.
- There are three main types of restricted interface measurements: menus and shells, database views, and physically constrained interfaces.
- Access control lists are bound to objects and indicate what subjects can use them.
- A capability table is bound to a subject and lists what objects it can access.
- There are two main ways of administrating access control: centralized and decentralized.
- Some examples of centralized administration technologies are RADIUS, TACACS+, and Diameter.
- A decentralized administration example is a peer-to-peer working group.
- Examples of administrative controls are a security policy, personnel controls, supervisory structure, security-awareness training, and testing.
- Examples of physical controls are network segregation, perimeter security, computer controls, work area separation, data backups, and cable.
- Examples of technical controls are system access, network architecture, network access, encryption and protocols, and auditing.

- Access control mechanisms provide one or more of the following functionalities: preventive, detective, corrective, deterrent, recovery, or compensative.

- For a subject to be able to access a resource, it must be identified, authenticated, authorized, and should be held accountable for its actions.

- Authentication can be accomplished by biometrics, a password, a passphrase, a cognitive password, a one-time password, or a token.

- A Type I error in biometrics means the system rejected an authorized individual, and a Type II error means an imposter was authenticated.

- A memory card cannot process information, but a smart card can.

- Access controls should default to no access.

- Least-privilege and need-to-know principles limit users' rights to only what is needed to perform tasks of their job.

- Single sign-on requires a user to be authenticated to the network only one time.

- Single sign-on can be accomplished through Kerberos, SESAME, domains, and thin clients.

- In Kerberos, a user receives a ticket from the KDC to be able to authenticate to a service.

- The Kerberos user receives a ticket granting ticket (TGT), which allows him to request access to resources through the ticket granting service (TGS). The TGS generates a new ticket with the session keys.

- Types of access control attacks include denial of service, spoofing, dictionary, brute force, and wardialing.

- Audit logs can track user activities, application events, and system events.

- Keystroke monitoring is a type of auditing that tracks each keystroke made by a user.

- Audit logs should be protected and reviewed.

- Object reuse can unintentionally disclose information.

- Just removing pointers to files is not always enough protection for proper object reuse.

- Information can be obtained via electrical signals in airwaves. The ways to combat this type of intrusion are Tempest, white noise, and control zones.

- User authentication is accomplished by what someone knows, is, or has.

- One-time password-generating token devices can use synchronous or asynchronous methods.

- Strong authentication requires two of the three user authentication attributes (what someone knows, is, or has).

- Kerberos addresses privacy and integrity but not availability.

- The following are weaknesses of Kerberos: the KDC is a single point of failure; it is susceptible to password guessing; session and secret keys are locally stored; KDC needs to always be available; and there must be management of secret keys.

- IDSs can be statistical (monitors behavior) or signature based (watches for known attacks).

- Degaussing is a safeguard against disclosure of confidential information because it returns media back to its original state.

- Two types of statistical anomaly–based IDS are protocol anomaly based and traffic anomaly based.

- Two types of rule-based IDS are stateful and model-based IDS.

## Questions

Please remember that these questions are formatted and asked in a certain way for a reason. You must remember that the CISSP exam is asking questions at a conceptual level. Questions may not always have the perfect answer, and the candidate is advised against always looking for the perfect answer. The candidate should look for the best answer in the list.

1. Which of the following statements correctly describes biometric methods?

   A. They are the least expensive and provide the most protection.

   B. They are the most expensive and provide the least protection.

   C. They are the least expensive and provide the least protection.

   D. They are the most expensive and provide the most protection.

2. What is derived from a passphrase?

   A. Personal password

   B. Virtual password

   C. User ID

   D. Valid password

3. Which of the following statements correctly describes passwords?

   A. They are the least expensive and most secure.

   B. They are the most expensive and least secure.

   C. They are the least expensive and least secure.

   D. They are the most expensive and most secure.

4. What is the reason for enforcing the separation of duties?

   A. No one person can complete all the steps of a critical activity.

   B. It induces an atmosphere for collusion.

C. It increases dependence on individuals.

D. It makes critical tasks easier to accomplish.

5. Which of the following is not a logical access control?

A. Encryption

B. Network architecture

C. ID badge

D. Access control matrix

6. An access control model should be applied in a _____ manner.

A. Detective

B. Recovery

C. Corrective

D. Preventive

7. Which access control policy is enforced when an environment uses a nondiscretionary model?

A. Rule based

B. Role based

C. Identity based

D. Mandatory

8. How is a challenge/response protocol utilized with token device implementations?

A. This protocol is not used; cryptography is used.

B. An authentication service generates a challenge, and the smart token generates a response based on the challenge.

C. The token challenges the user for a username and password.

D. The token challenges the user's password against a database of stored credentials.

9. Which access control method is user-directed?

A. Nondiscretionary

B. Mandatory

C. Identity based

D. Discretionary

10. Which provides the best authentication?

A. What a person knows

B. What a person is

C. What a person has

D. What a person has and knows

11. Which item is not part of a Kerberos authentication implementation?

    A. Message authentication code

    B. Ticket granting service

    C. Authentication service

    D. Users, programs, and services

12. Which model implements access control matrices to control how subjects interact with objects?

    A. Mandatory

    B. Centralized

    C. Decentralized

    D. Discretionary

13. What does authentication mean?

    A. Registering a user

    B. Identifying a user

    C. Validating a user

    D. Authorizing a user

14. If a company has a high turnover rate, which access control structure is best?

    A. Role based

    B. Decentralized

    C. Rule based

    D. Discretionary

15. A password is mainly used for what function?

    A. Identity

    B. Registration

    C. Authentication

    D. Authorization

16. The process of mutual authentication involves _____.

    A. A user authenticating to a system and the system authenticating to the user

    B. A user authenticating to two systems at the same time

    C. A user authenticating to a server and then to a process

    D. A user authenticating, receiving a ticket, and then authenticating to a service

17. Reviewing audit logs is an example of which security function?

    A. Preventive

    B. Detective

   C. Deterrence

   D. Corrective

18. In discretionary access control security, who has delegation authority to grant access to data?

   A. User

   B. Security office

   C. Security policy

   D. Owner

19. Which could be considered a single point of failure within a single sign-on implementation?

   A. Authentication server

   B. User's workstation

   C. Logon credentials

   D. RADIUS

20. What role does biometrics play in access control?

   A. Authorization

   B. Authenticity

   C. Authentication

   D. Accountability

21. What determines if an organization is going to operate under a discretionary, mandatory, or nondiscretionary access control model?

   A. Administrator

   B. Security policy

   C. Culture

   D. Security levels

22. What type of attack attempts all possible solutions?

   A. Dictionary

   B. Brute force

   C. Man-in-the-middle

   D. Spoofing

23. Spoofing can be described as which of the following?

   A. Eavesdropping on a communication link

   B. Working through a list of words

   C. Session hijacking

   D. Pretending to be someone or something else

24. Which of the following is not an advantage of a centralized access control administration?

A. Flexibility

B. Standardization

C. Higher level of security

D. No need for different interpretations of a necessary security level

25. Which of the following best describes what role-based access control offers companies in reducing administrative burdens?

A. It allows entities closer to the resources to make decisions about who can and cannot access resources.

B. It provides a centralized approach for access control, which frees up department managers.

C. User membership in roles can be easily revoked and new ones established as job assignments dictate.

D. It enforces an enterprise-wide security policy, standards, and guidelines.

## Answers

1. **D.** Compared to the other available authentication mechanisms, biometric methods provide the highest level of protection and are the most expensive.

2. **B.** Most systems do not use the actual passphrase or password the user enters. Instead, they put this value through some type of encryption or hashing function to come up with another format of that value, referred to as a virtual password.

3. **C.** Passwords provide the least amount of protection, but are the cheapest because they do not require extra readers (as with smart cards and memory cards), do not require devices (as do biometrics), and do not require a lot of overhead in processing (as in cryptography). Passwords are the most common type of authentication method used today.

4. **A.** Separation of duties is put into place to ensure that one entity cannot carry out a task that could be damaging or risky to the company. It requires two or more people to come together to do their individual tasks to accomplish the overall task. If a person wanted to commit fraud and separation of duties was in place, they would need to participate in collusion.

5. **C.** A logical control is the same thing as a technical control. All of the answers were logical in nature except an ID badge. Badges are used for physical security and are considered physical controls.

6. **D.** The best approach to security is to try to prevent bad things from taking place by putting the necessary controls and mechanisms in place. Detective

controls should also be put in place, but a security model should not work from a purely detective approach.

7. **B.** Roles work as containers for users. The administrator or security professional creates the roles and assigns rights to them and then assigns users to the container. The users then inherit the permissions and rights from the containers (roles), which is how implicit permissions are obtained.

8. **B.** An asynchronous token device is based on challenge/response mechanisms. The authentication service sends the user a challenge value, which the user enters into the token. The token encrypts or hashes this value, and the user uses this as her one-time password.

9. **D.** The DAC model allows users, or data owners, the discretion of allowing other users access to their resources. DAC is implemented by ACLs, which the data owner can configure.

10. **D.** This is considered a strong authentication approach because it is two-factor— it uses two out of the possible three authentication techniques (something a person knows, is, or has).

11. **A.** Message authentication code (MAC) is a cryptographic function and is not a key component of Kerberos. Kerberos is made up of a KDC, a realm of principals (users, services, applications, devices), an authentication service, tickets, and a ticket granting service.

12. **D.** DAC is implemented and enforced through the use of access control lists (ACLs), which are held in a matrix. MAC is implemented and enforced through the use of security labels.

13. **C.** Authentication means to validate the identity of a user. In most systems, the user must submit some type of public information (username, account number) and a second credential to prove this identity. The second piece of the credential set is private and should not be shared.

14. **A.** It is easier on the administrator if she only has to create one role, assign all of the necessary rights and permissions to that role, and plug a user into that role when needed. Otherwise, she would need to assign and extract permissions and rights as each individual came and left the company.

15. **C.** As stated in a previous question, passwords are the most common authentication mechanism used today. They are used to validate a user's identity.

16. **A.** Mutual authentication means that it is happening in both directions. Instead of just the user having to authenticate to the server, the server also has to authenticate to the user.

17. **B.** Reviewing audit logs takes place after the fact, after some type of incident happens. It is detective in nature because the security professional is trying to figure out what exactly happened, how to correct it, and possibly who is responsible.

18. **D.** This question may seem a little confusing if you were stuck between user and owner. Only the data owner can decide who can access the resources she owns. She may be a user and she may not. A user is not necessarily the owner of the resource. Only the actual owner of the resource can dictate what subjects can actually access the resource.

19. **A.** In a single sign-on technology, all users are authenticating to one source. If that source goes down, authentication requests cannot be processed.

20. **C.** Biometrics is a technology that validates an individual's identity by reading a physical attribute.

21. **B.** The security policy sets the tone for the whole security program. It dictates the level of risk the management and company are willing to accept. This in turn dictates the type of controls and mechanisms that are to be put into place to ensure that this level of risk is not exceeded.

22. **B.** A brute force attack tries a combination of values in an attempt to discover the correct sequence that represents the captured password or whatever the goal of the task is. It is an exhaustive attack, meaning the attacker will try over and over again until she is successful.

23. **D.** Spoofing is the process of pretending to be another person or process with the goal of obtaining unauthorized access. Spoofing is usually done by using a bogus IP address, but it could be done by using someone else's authentication credentials.

24. **A.** A centralized approach does not provide as much flexibility as a decentralized access control administration, because one entity is making all the decisions instead of several entities that are closer to the resources. A centralized approach is more structured in nature, which means that there is less flexibility.

25. **C.** An administrator does not need to revoke and reassign permissions to individual users as they change jobs. Instead, the administrator assigns permissions and rights to a role, and users are plugged into those roles.

# Security Architecture and Design

This chapter presents the following:

- Computer hardware architecture
- Operating system architectures
- Trusted computing base and security mechanisms
- Protection mechanisms within an operating system
- Various security models
- Assurance evaluation criteria and ratings
- Certification and accreditation processes
- Attack types

Computer and information security covers many areas within an enterprise. Each area has security vulnerabilities and, hopefully, some corresponding countermeasures that raise the security level and provide better protection. Not understanding the different areas and security levels of network devices, operating systems, hardware, protocols, and applications can cause security vulnerabilities that can affect the environment as a whole.

Two fundamental concepts in computer and information security are the security model, which outlines how security is to be implemented—a "blueprint" essentially— and the architecture of a computer and operating system, which fulfills this blueprint.

A *security policy* is a statement that outlines how entities access each other, what operations different entities can carry out, what level of protection is required for a system or software product, and what actions should be taken when these requirements are not met. The policy outlines the expectations that the hardware and software must meet to be considered in compliance. A *security model* outlines the requirements necessary to properly support and implement a certain security policy. If a security policy dictates that all users must be identified, authenticated, and authorized before accessing network resources, the security model might lay out an access control matrix that should be constructed so that it fulfills the requirements of the security policy. If a security policy states that no one from a lower security level should be able to view or modify information at a higher security level, the supporting security model will outline the necessary logic and rules that need to be implemented to ensure that under no circumstance can a lower-level subject access a higher-level object in an unauthorized manner. A security model provides a deeper explanation of how a computer operating system should be developed to properly support a specific security policy.

**NOTE** Individual systems and devices can have their own security policies. These are not the organizational security policies that contain management's directives. The systems' security policies, and the models they use, should enforce the higher-level organizational security policy that is in place. A system policy dictates the level of security that should be provided by the individual device or operating system.

*Computer security* can be a slippery term because it means different things to different people. There are many aspects of a system that can be secured, and security can happen at various levels and to varying degrees. As stated in previous chapters, information security consists of the following main attributes:

- **Availability**   Prevention of loss of access to resources and data
- **Integrity**   Prevention of unauthorized modification of data and resources
- **Confidentiality**   Prevention of unauthorized disclosure of data and resources

These main attributes branch off into more granular security attributes, such as authenticity, accountability, nonrepudiation, and dependability. How does a company know which of these it needs, to what degree they are needed, and whether the operating systems and applications they use actually provide these features and protection? These questions get much more complex as one looks deeper into the questions and products themselves. Companies are not just concerned about e-mail messages being encrypted as they pass through the Internet. They are also concerned about the confidential data stored in their databases, the security of their web farms that are connected directly to the Internet, the integrity of data-entry values going into applications that process business-oriented information, internal users sharing trade secrets, external attackers bringing down servers and affecting productivity, viruses spreading, the internal consistency of data warehouses, and much more.

These issues not only affect productivity and profitability, but also raise legal and liability issues with regard to securing data. Companies, and the management that runs them, can be held accountable if any one of the many issues previously mentioned goes wrong. So it is, or at least it should be, very important for companies to know what security they need and how to be properly assured that the protection is actually being provided by the products they purchase.

Many of these security issues must be thought through before and during the design and architectural phase for a product. Security is best if it is designed and built into the foundation of operating systems and applications and not added on as an afterthought. Once security is integrated as an important part of the design, it has to be engineered, implemented, tested, audited, evaluated, certified, and accredited. The security that a product provides has to be rated on the availability, integrity, and confidentiality it claims to provide. Consumers then use these ratings to determine if specific products provide the level of security they require. This is a long road, with many entities involved with different responsibilities.

This chapter takes you from the steps that are necessary before actually developing an operating system to how these systems are evaluated and rated by governments and other agencies, and what these ratings actually mean. However, before we dive into these concepts, it is important to understand how the basic elements of a computer system work. These elements are the pieces that make up any computer's architecture.

# Computer Architecture

*Put the processor over there by the plant, the memory by the window, and the secondary storage upstairs.*

Computer architecture encompasses all of the parts of a computer system that are necessary for it to function, including the operating system, memory chips, logic circuits, storage devices, input and output devices, security components, buses, and networking components. The interrelationships and internal working of all of these parts can be quite complex, and making them work together in a secure fashion consists of complicated methods and mechanisms. Thank goodness for the smart people who figured this stuff out! Now it is up to us to learn how they did it and why.

The more you understand how these different pieces work and process data, the more you will understand how vulnerabilities actually occur and how countermeasures work to impede and hinder vulnerabilities from being introduced, found, and exploited.

 **NOTE** This chapter interweaves the hardware and operating system architectures and their components to show you how they work together.

## Central Processing Unit

*The CPU seems complex. How does it work? Response: Black magic. It uses eye of bat, tongue of goat, and some transistors.*

The *central processing unit (CPU)* is the brain of a computer. In the most general description possible, it fetches instructions from memory and executes them. Although a CPU is a piece of hardware, it has its own instruction sets (provided by the operating system) that are necessary to carry out its tasks. Each CPU type has a specific architecture and set of instructions that it can carry out. The operating system has to be designed to be able to work within this CPU architecture. This is why one operating system may be able to work on a Pentium processor but not a SPARC processor.

**NOTE** Scalable Processor Architecture (SPARC) is a type of Reduced Instruction Set Computing (RISC) chip developed by Sun Microsystems. SunOS, Solaris, and some Unix operating systems have been developed to work on this type of processor.

The chips within the CPU cover only a couple of square inches, but contain over 40 million transistors. All operations within the CPU are performed by electrical signals at different voltages in different combinations, and each transistor holds this voltage, which represents 0s and 1s to the computer. The CPU contains registers that point to memory locations that contain the next instructions to be executed and that enable the CPU to keep status information of the data that needs to be processed. A *register* is a temporary storage location. Accessing memory to get information on what instructions and data need to be executed is a much slower process than accessing a register, which is a component of the CPU itself. So when the CPU is done with one task, it asks the registers, "Okay, what do I have to do now?" And the registers hold the information that tells the CPU what its next job is.

The actual execution of the instructions is done by the *arithmetic logic unit (ALU)*. The ALU performs mathematical functions and logical operations on data. The ALU can be thought of as the brain of the CPU and the CPU as the brain of the computer.

Software holds its instructions and data in memory. When action needs to take place on the data, the instructions and data memory addresses are passed to the CPU registers, as shown in Figure 5-1. When the control unit indicates that the CPU can process them, the instructions and data memory addresses are passed to the CPU for actual processing, number crunching, and data manipulation. The results are sent back to the requesting process's memory address.

An operating system and applications are really just made up of lines and lines of instructions. These instructions contain empty variables, which are populated at run

**Figure 5-1** Instruction and data addresses are passed to the CPU for processing.

time. The empty variables hold the actual data. There is a difference between instructions and data. The instructions have been written to carry out some type of functionality on the data. For example, let's say that you open a Calculator application. In reality, this program is just lines of instructions that allow you to carry out addition, subtraction, division, and other types of mathematical functions that will be executed on the data that you provide. So, you type in 3 + 5. The 3 and the 5 are the data values. Once you click the = button, the Calculator program tells the CPU that it needs to take the instructions on how to carry out addition and apply these instructions to the two data values 3 and 5. The ALU carries out this instruction and returns the result of 8 to the requesting program. This is when you see the value 8 in the Calculator's field. To users, it seems as though the Calculator program is doing all of this on its own, but it is incapable of this. It depends upon the CPU and other components of the system to carry out this type of activity.

The *control unit* manages and synchronizes the system while different applications' code and operating system instructions are being executed. The control unit is the component that fetches the code, interprets the code, and oversees the execution of the different instruction sets. It determines what application instructions get processed and in what priority and time slice. It controls when instructions are executed, and this execution enables applications to process data. The control unit does not actually process the data; it is like the traffic cop telling traffic when to stop and start again, as illustrated in Figure 5-2. The CPU's time has to be sliced up into individual units and assigned to processes. It is this time slicing that fools the applications and users into thinking that the system is actually carrying out several different functions at one time. While the operating system can carry out several different functions at one time (multitasking), in reality the CPU is executing the instructions in a serial fashion (one at a time).

A CPU has several different types of registers, containing information about the instruction set and data that needs to be executed. *General registers* are used to hold variables and temporary results as the ALU works through its execution steps. The

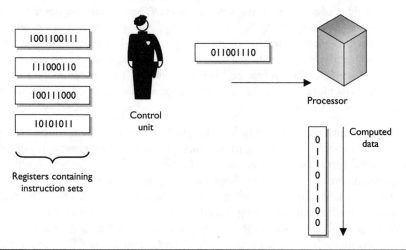

**Figure 5-2** The control unit works as a traffic cop, indicating when instructions are sent to the processor.

general registers are like the ALU's scratch pad to use while it is working. *Special registers* (dedicated registers) hold information such as the program counter, stack pointer, and program status word (PSW). The *program counter* register contains the memory address of the next instruction that needs to be fetched. After that instruction is executed, the program counter is updated with the memory address of the next instruction set that needs to be processed. It is similar to a boss and secretary relationship. The secretary keeps the boss on schedule and points her to the necessary tasks that she needs to carry out. This allows the boss to just concentrate on carrying out the tasks instead of having to worry about the "busy work" that is being done in the background.

Before we get into what a stack pointer is, we first need to know what a stack is. Each process has its own *stack*, which is a memory segment that the process can read from and write to. Let's say that you and I need to communicate through a stack. What I do is put all of the things that I need to say to you in a stack of papers. The first paper tells you how you can respond to me when you need to, which is called a return pointer. The next paper has some instructions that I need you to carry out. The next piece of paper has the data that I need you to use when you carry out these instructions. So, I write down on individual pieces of paper all that I need you to do for me and *stack* them up. When I am done, I signal to you that I need you to read my stack of papers. You take the first page off of my stack and carry out my request. Then you take the second page and carry out that request. You continue to do this until you are at the bottom of my stack, which contains my return pointer. You look at this return pointer (which is my memory address) to know where to send the results of all the instructions I asked you to carry out. This is how processes communicate to other processes and to the CPU. One process stacks up its information that it needs to communicate to the CPU. The CPU has to keep track of where it is in the stack, which is the purpose of the stack pointer. Once the first item on the stack is executed, then the *stack pointer* moves down to direct the CPU where the next piece of data is located.

**NOTE** The traditional way of explaining how a stack works is to use the analogy of stacking up trays in a cafeteria. When people are done eating, they place their trays on a stack of other trays, and when the cafeteria employees need to get the trays for cleaning, they take the last tray that was put on top and work down the stack. This analogy is used to explain how a stack works in the mode of "last in first off." The process that is being communicated to takes the last piece of data the requesting process laid down off the top of the stack and works down the stack.

The *program status word (PSW)* holds different condition bits. One of the bits indicates whether the CPU should be working in *user mode* (also called *problem state*) or *privileged mode* (also called *kernel* or *supervisor mode*). The crux of this chapter is to teach you how operating systems protect themselves. They need to protect themselves from applications, utilities, and user activities if they are going to provide a stable and safe environment. One of these protection mechanisms is implemented through the use of these different execution modes. When an *application* needs the CPU to carry out its instructions, the CPU works in user mode. This mode has a lower privilege level and many of the CPU's instructions and functions are not available to the requesting application. The reason for the extra caution is that the developers of the operating system do not know who developed the application or how it is going to react, so the CPU works in a lower privileged mode when executing these types of instructions. By analogy, if you are expecting visitors who are bringing their two-year-old boy, you move all of the breakables that someone under three feet can reach. No one is ever sure what a two-year-old toddler is going to do, but it usually has to do with breaking something. An operating system and CPU are not sure what applications are going to attempt, which is why this code is executed in a lower priviledge.

If the PSW has a bit value that indicates that the instructions that need to be executed are to be carried out in privileged mode, this means that a trusted process (an operating system process) made the request and can have access to the functionality that is not available in user mode. An example would be if the operating system needed to communicate with a peripheral device. This is a privileged activity that applications cannot carry out. When these types of instructions are passed to the CPU, the PSW is basically telling the CPU, "The process that made this request is an alright guy. We can trust him. Go ahead and carry out this task for him."

Memory addresses of the instructions and data that need to be processed are held in registers until needed by the CPU. The CPU is connected to an *address bus*, which is a hard-wired connection to the RAM chips in the system and the individual input/output (I/O) devices. Memory is cut up into sections that have individual addresses that are associated with them. I/O devices (CD-ROM, USB device, hard drive, floppy drive, and so on) are also allocated specific unique addresses. If the CPU needs to access some data, either from memory or from an I/O device, it sends down the address of where the needed data is located. The circuitry associated with the memory or I/O device recognizes the address that the CPU sent down the address bus and instructs the memory or device to read the requested data and put it on the *data bus*. So the address bus is used by the CPU to indicate the location of the instructions that need to be processed, and the memory or I/O device responds by sending the data that resides at that memory location through the data bus. This process is illustrated in Figure 5-3.

**Figure 5-3**
Address and data buses are separate and have specific functionality.

Once the CPU is done with its computation, it needs to return the results to the requesting program's memory. So, the CPU sends the requesting program's address down the address bus and sends the new results down the data bus with the command `write`. This new data is then written to the requesting program's memory space.

The address and data buses can be 8, 16, 32, or 64 bits wide. Most systems today use a 32-bit address bus, which means that the system can have a large address space ($2^{32}$). Systems can also have a 32-bit data bus, which means that the system can move data in parallel back and forth between memory, I/O devices, and the CPU. (A *32-bit data bus* means that the size of the chunks of data that a CPU can request at a time is 32 bits.)

## Multiprocessing

Some specialized computers have more than one CPU, for increased performance. An operating system must be developed specifically to be able to understand and work with more than one processor. If the computer system is configured to work in *symmet-*

### Processor Evolution

The following table provides the different characteristics of the various processors that have been used over the years.

| Name | Date | Transistors | Microns | Clock Speed | Data Width | MIPS |
|------|------|-------------|---------|-------------|------------|------|
| 8080 | 1974 | 6000 | 6 | 2 MHz | 8 bits | 0.64 |
| 80286 | 1982 | 134,000 | 1.5 | 6 MHz | 16 bits | 1 |
| Pentium | 1993 | 3,100,000 | 0.8 | 60 MHz | 32 bits, 64-bit bus | 100 |
| Pentium 4 | 2000 | 42,000,000 | 0.18 | 1.5 GHz | 32 bits, 64-bit bus | 1700 |

The following list defines the terms of measure used in the preceding table:

- **Microns**  Indicates the width of the smallest wire on the CPU chip (a human hair is 100 microns thick).

- **Data width**  Indicates how much data the ALU can accept and process; 64-bit bus refers to the size of the data bus. So, modern systems fetch 64 bits of data at a time, but the ALU works only on instruction sets in 32-bit sizes.

- **MIPS**  Millions of instructions per second, which is a basic indication of how fast a CPU can work (but other factors are involved, such as clock speed).

- **Clock speed**  Indicates the speed at which the processor can execute instructions. An internal clock is used to regulate the rate of execution, which is broken down into cycles. A system that runs at 100 MHz means that there are 100 million clock cycles per second. Processors working at 4 GHz are now available, which means that the CPU can execute 4 thousand million cycles per second.

*ric mode*, this means that the processors are handed work as needed. It is like a load-balancing environment. When a process needs instructions to be executed, a scheduler determines which processor is ready for more work and sends it on. If the system is configured to work in *asymmetric mode*, this usually means that the computer has some type of time-sensitive application that needs its own personal processor. So, the system scheduler will send instructions from the time-sensitive application to CPU 1 and send all the other instructions (from the operating system and other applications) to CPU 2.

## Operating System Architecture

An operating system provides an environment for applications and users to work within. Every operating system is a complex beast, made up of various layers and modules of functionality. It has the responsibility of managing the underlying hardware components, memory management, I/O operations, file system, process management, and providing system services. We next look at each of these responsibilities of every operating system, but you must realize that whole books are written on just these individual topics, so the discussion here is only topical.

## Process Management

*Well just look at all of these processes squirming around like little worms. We need some real organization here!*

Operating systems, utilities, and applications in reality are just lines and lines of instructions. They are static lines of code that are brought to life when they are initialized and put into memory. Applications work as individual units, called processes, and the operating system has several different processes carrying out various types of functionality. A *process* is the set of instructions actually running. A program is not considered a process until it is loaded into memory and activated by the operating system. When a process is created, the operating system assigns resources to it, such as a memory segment, CPU time slot (interrupt), access to system application programming interfaces (APIs), and files to interact with. The *collection* of the instructions and the assigned resources is referred to as a process.

The operating system has many processes, which are used to provide and maintain the environment for applications and users to work within. Some examples of the functionality that individual processes provide include displaying data onscreen, spooling print jobs, and saving data to temporary files. Today's operating systems provide *multiprogramming*, which means that more than one program (or process) can be loaded into memory at the same time. This is what allows you to run your antivirus software, word processor, personal firewall, and e-mail client all at the same time. Each of these applications runs as one or more processes.

---

 **NOTE** Many resources state that today's operating systems provide multiprogramming and multitasking. This is true, in that multiprogramming just means that more than one application can be loaded into memory at the same time. But in reality, multiprogramming was replaced by multitasking, which means that more than one application can be in memory at the same time *and* the operating system can deal with requests from these different applications *simultaneously*.

Earlier operating systems wasted their most precious resource—CPU time. For example, when a word processor would request to open a file on a floppy drive, the CPU would send the request to the floppy drive and then wait for the floppy drive to initialize, for the head to find the right track and sector, and finally for the floppy drive to send the data via the data bus to the CPU for processing. To avoid this waste of CPU time, multitasking was developed, which enabled more than one program to be loaded into memory at one time. Instead of sitting idle waiting for activity from one process, the CPU could execute instructions for other processes, thereby speeding up the necessary processing required for all the different processes.

As an analogy, if you (CPU) put bread in a toaster (process) and just stand there waiting for the toaster to finish its job, you are wasting time. On the other hand, if you put bread in the toaster and then, while it's toasting, feed the dog, make coffee, and come up with a solution for world peace, you are being more productive and not wasting time.

Operating systems started out as cooperative and then evolved into preemptive multitasking. *Cooperative multitasking*, used in Windows 3.1 and early Macintosh systems, required the processes to voluntarily release resources that they were using. This was not necessarily a stable environment, because if a programmer did not write his code properly to release a resource when his application was done using it, the resource would be committed indefinitely to his application and thus unavailable to other processes. With *preemptive multitasking*, used in Windows 9x, NT, 2000, XP, and in Unix systems, the operating system controls how long a process can use a resource. The system can suspend a process that is using the CPU and allow another process access to it through the use of *time sharing*. So, in operating systems that used cooperative multitasking, the processes had too much control over resource release, and when an application hung, it usually affected all the other applications and sometimes the operating system itself. Operating systems that use preemptive multitasking run the show, and one application does not negatively affect another application as easily.

Different operating system types work within different process models. For example, Unix and Linux systems allow their processes to create new children processes, which is referred to as *forking*. Let's say that you are working within a shell of a Linux system. That shell is the command interpreter and an interface that enables the user to interact with the operating system. The shell runs as a process. When you type in a shell the command `cat file1 file2 | grep stuff`, you are telling the operating system to concatenate (`cat`) the two files and then search (`grep`) for the lines that have the value of `stuff` in them. When you press the ENTER key, the shell forks two children processes—one for the `cat` command and one for the `grep` command. Each of these children processes takes on the characteristics of the parent process, but has its own memory space, stack, and program counter values.

A process can run in *running state* (CPU is executing its instructions and data), *ready state* (waiting to send instructions to the CPU), or *blocked state* (waiting for input data, such as keystrokes from a user). These different states are illustrated in Figure 5-4. When a process is blocked, it is waiting for some type of data to be sent to it. In the preceding example of typing the command `cat file1 file2 | grep stuff`, the `grep` process cannot actually carry out its functionality of searching until the first pro-

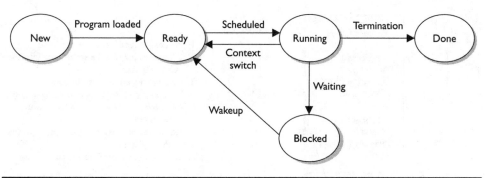

**Figure 5-4** Processes enter and exit different states.

cess (`cat`) is done combining the two files. The `grep` process will put itself to *sleep* and will be in the blocked state until the `cat` process is done and sends the `grep` process the input it needs to work with.

**NOTE** Not all operating systems create and work in the process hierarchy as do Unix and Linux systems. Windows systems do not fork new children processes, but instead creates new processes that work independently. This is deeper than what you need to know for the CISSP exam, but life is not just about this exam—right?

The operating system is responsible for creating new processes, assigning them resources, synchronizing their communication, and making sure that nothing insecure is taking place. The operating system keeps a *process table*, which has one entry per process. The table contains each individual process's state, stack pointer, memory allocation, program counter, and status of open files in use. The reason the operating system documents all of this status information is that the CPU needs all of it loaded into its registers when it needs to interact with, for example, process 1. When process 1's CPU time slice is over, all of the current status information on process 1 is stored in the process table so that when its time slice is open again, all of this status information can be put back into the CPU registers. So, when it is process 2's time with the CPU, its status information is transferred from the process table to the CPU registers, and transferred back again when the time slice is over. These steps are shown in Figure 5-5.

How does a process know when it can communicate with the CPU? This is taken care of by using *interrupts*. An operating system fools us, and applications, into thinking that it and the CPU are carrying out all tasks (operating system, applications, memory, I/O, and user activities) simultaneously. In fact, this is impossible. Most CPUs can do only one thing at a time. So the system has hardware and software interrupts. When a device needs to communicate with the CPU, it has to wait for its interrupt to be called upon. The same thing happens in software. Each process has an interrupt assigned to it.

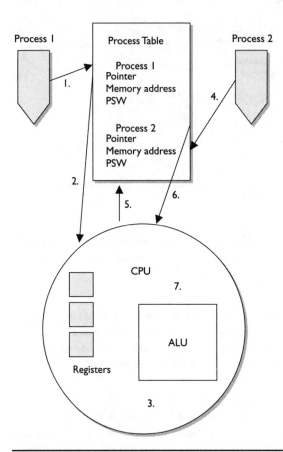

**Figure 5-5** A process table contains process status data that the CPU requires.

It is like pulling a number at a customer service department in a store. You can't go up to the counter until your number has been called out.

When a process is interacting with the CPU and an interrupt takes place (another process has requested access to the CPU), the current process's information is stored in the process table, and the next process gets its time to interact with the CPU.

 **NOTE** Some critical processes cannot afford to have their functionality interrupted by another process. The operating system is responsible for setting the priorities for the different processes. When one process needs to interrupt another process, the operating system compares the priority levels of the two processes to determine if this interruption should be allowed.

## Thread Management

*What are all of these hair-like things hanging off of my processes? Response: Threads.*

As described earlier, a process is a program in memory; more precisely, a process is the program's instructions and all the resources that are assigned to the process by the operating system. It is just easier to group all of these instructions and resources together and control it as one entity, which is a process. When a process needs to send something to the CPU for processing, it generates a thread. A *thread* is made up of an individual instruction set and the data that needs to be worked on by the CPU.

Process

Threads of code

Most applications have several different functions. Word processors can open files, save files, open other programs (such as an e-mail client), and print documents. Each one of these functions requires a thread (instruction set) to be dynamically generated. So, for example, if Tom chooses to print his document, the word processor process generates a thread that contains the instructions of how this document should be printed (font, colors, text, margins, and so on). If he chooses to send a document via e-mail through this program, another thread is created that tells the e-mail client to open and what file needs to be sent. Threads are dynamically created and destroyed as needed. Once Tom is done printing his document, the thread that was generated for this functionality is destroyed.

A program that has been developed to carry out several different tasks at one time (display, print, interact with other programs) is capable of running several different threads simultaneously. An application with this capability is referred to as a *multithreaded* application. An operating system that can understand and deal with the requests of several different threads, through the use of interrupts, is a multithreading system.

**NOTE** Each thread shares the same resources of the process that created it. So, all the threads created by a word processor work in the same memory space and have access to all the same files and system resources.

## Definitions

The concepts of how computer operating systems work can be overwhelming at times. For test purposes make sure that you understand the following definitions:

- **Multiprogramming** An operating system can load more than one program in memory at one time.

- **Multitasking** An operating system can handle requests from several different processes loaded into memory at the same time.

- **Multithreading** An application has the ability to run multiple threads simultaneously. An operating system can handle requests from several different threads at the same time.

- **Multiprocessing** The computer has more than one CPU.

## Process Scheduling

Scheduling and synchronizing various processes and their activities is part of process management, which is a responsibility of the operating system. Several components need to be considered during the development of an operating system, which will dictate how process scheduling will take place. A scheduling policy is created to govern how threads will interact with other threads. Different operating systems can use different schedulers, which are basically algorithms that control the timesharing of the CPU. As stated earlier, the different processes are assigned different priority levels (interrupts), which dictate which processes overrule other processes when CPU time allocation is required. The operating system creates and deletes processes as needed, and oversees them changing state (ready, blocked, running). The operating system is also responsible for controlling deadlocks between processes that are attempting to use the same resources.

When a process makes a request for a resource (memory allocation, printer, secondary storage devices, disk space, etc.), the operating system creates certain data structures and dedicates the necessary processes for the activity to be completed. Once the action takes place (a document is printed, a file is saved, or data is retrieved from the drive), the process needs to tear down these built structures and release the resources back to the resource pool so that they are available for other processes. If this does not happen properly, a *deadlock* situation may occur or a computer may not have enough resources to process other requests (resulting in a denial of service). A deadlock situation may occur when each process in a set of processes is waiting for an event to take place and that event can only be caused by another process in the set. Because each process is waiting for its required event, none of the processes will carry out their events—so the processes just sit there staring at each other.

One example of a deadlock situation is when process A commits resource 1 and needs to use resource 2 to properly complete its task, but process B has committed resource 2 and needs resource 1 to finish its job. So both processes are in deadlock because they do not have the resources they need to finish the function they are trying to carry out. This situation does not take place as often as it used to, as a result of better programming. Also, operating systems now have the intelligence to detect this activity and either release committed resources or control allocation of resources so that they are properly shared between processes.

Operating systems have different methods of dealing with resource requests and releases and solving deadlock situations. In some systems, if a requested resource is unavailable for a certain period of time, the operating system kills the process that is "holding on to" that resource. This action releases the resource from the process that had committed it and restarts the process so that it is "clean" and available to be used by other applications. Other operating systems might require a program to request all the resources it needs *before* it actually starts executing instructions, or require a program to release its currently committed resources before it may acquire more.

## Process Activity

*Process 1, go into your room and play with your toys. Process 2, go into your room and play with your set of toys. No intermingling and no fighting!*

Computers can run different applications and processes at the same time. The processes have to share resources and play nice with each other to ensure a stable and safe computing environment that maintains its integrity. Some memory, data files, and variables are actually shared between different processes. It is critical that more than one process does not attempt to read and write to these items at the same time. The operating system is the master program that prevents this type of action from taking place and ensures that programs do not corrupt each other's data held in memory. The operating system works with the CPU to provide time slicing through the use of interrupts to ensure that processes are provided with adequate access to the CPU. This also ensures that critical system functions are not negatively affected by rogue applications.

To protect processes from each other, operating systems can implement process isolation. *Process isolation* is necessary to ensure that processes do not "step on each other's toes," communicate in an insecure manner, or negatively affect each other's productivity. Older operating systems did not enforce process isolation as well as systems do today. This is why in earlier operating systems, when one of your programs hung, all other programs, and sometimes the operating system itself, hung. With process isolation, if one process hangs for some reason, it will not affect the other software running. (Process isolation is required for preemptive multitasking.) There are different methods for carrying out process isolation:

- Encapsulation of objects
- Time multiplexing of shared resources
- Naming distinctions
- Virtual mapping

When a process is *encapsulated*, no other process understands or interacts with its internal programming code. When process A needs to communicate with process B, process A just needs to know how to communicate with process B's interface. An interface defines how communication must take place between two processes. As an analogy, think back to how you had to communicate with your third-grade teacher. You had to call her Mrs. SoandSo, say please and thank you, and speak respectfully to get whatever it was you needed. The same thing is true for software components that need to communicate with each other. They have to know *how* to communicate properly with each other's interfaces. The interfaces dictate the type of requests that a process will accept and the type of output that will be provided. So, two processes can communicate with each other, even if they are written in different programming languages, as long as they know how to communicate with each other's interface. Encapsulation provides *data hiding*, which means that outside software components will not know how a process works and will not be able to manipulate the process's internal code. This is an integrity mechanism and enforces modularity in programming code.

Time multiplexing was already discussed, although we did not use this term. *Time multiplexing* is a technology that allows processes to use the same resources. As stated earlier, a CPU has to be shared between many processes. Although it seems as though all applications are running (executing their instructions) simultaneously, the operating system is splitting up time shares between each process. Multiplexing means that there are several data sources and the individual data pieces are piped into one communication channel. In this instance, the operating system is coordinating the different requests from the different processes and piping them through the one shared CPU. An operating system has to provide proper time multiplexing (resource sharing) to ensure that a stable working environment exists for software and users.

*Naming distinctions* just means that the different processes have their own name or identification value. Processes are usually assigned process identification (PID) values, which the operating system and other processes use to call upon them. If each process is isolated, that means that each process has its own unique PID value.

*Virtual mapping* is different from physical mapping of memory. An application is written such that basically it thinks that it is the only program running on an operating system. When an application needs memory to work with, it tells the operating system's memory manager how much memory it needs. The operating system carves out that amount of memory and assigns it to the requesting application. The application uses its own address scheme, which usually starts at 0, but in reality, the application does not work in the *physical* address space that it thinks it is working in. Rather, it works in the address space that the memory manager assigns to it. The physical memory is the RAM chips in the system. The operating system chops up this memory and assigns portions of it to the requesting processes. Once the process is assigned its own memory space, then it can address this portion however it needs to, which is called virtual address mapping. Virtual address mapping allows the different processes to have their own memory space; the memory manager ensures that no processes improperly interact with another process's memory. This provides integrity and confidentiality.

## Memory Management

To provide a safe and stable environment, an operating system must exercise proper memory management, which is one of the most important tasks that it carries out, because basically everything happens in memory. It is similar to how we are dependent upon oxygen and gravity to work. If either is not properly managed by nature, we are in trouble.

The goals of memory management are to

- Provide an abstraction level for programmers
- Maximize performance with the limited amount of memory available
- Protect the operating system and applications loaded into memory

*Abstraction* means that the details of something are hidden. Developers of applications do not know the amount or type of memory that will be available in each and every system their code will be loaded on. If a developer had to be concerned with this type of detail, then her application would be able to work only on the one system that maps to all of her specifications. To allow for portability, the memory manager hides all of the memory issues and just provides the application with a memory segment.

Every computer has a memory hierarchy. There are small amounts of memory that are very fast and expensive (registers, cache) and larger amounts of memory that are slower and less expensive (RAM, hard drive). The portion of the operating system that keeps track of how these different types of memory are used is lovingly called the memory manager. Its jobs are to allocate and deallocate different memory segments, enforce access control to ensure that processes are interacting only with their own memory segments, and swap memory contents from RAM to the hard drive.

The memory manager has five basic responsibilities:

- **Relocation**
    - Swap contents from RAM to the hard drive as needed (explained later in the "Virtual Memory" section)
    - Provide pointers for applications if their instructions and memory segment have been moved to a different location in main memory
- **Protection**
    - Limit processes to interact only with the memory segments that are assigned to them
    - Provide access control to memory segments
- **Sharing**
    - Use complex controls to ensure integrity and confidentiality when processes need to use the same shared memory segments
    - Allow many users with different levels of access to interact with the same application running in one memory segment
- **Logical organization**
    - Allow for the sharing of specific software modules, such as dynamic link library (DLL) procedures
- **Physical organization**
    - Segment the physical memory space for application and operating system processes

 **NOTE**  A dynamic link library (DLL) is a set of functions that applications can call upon to carry out different types of procedures. For example, the Windows operating system has a crypt32.dll that is used by the operating system and applications for cryptographic functions. Windows has a set of DLLs, which is just a library of functions to be called upon.

How can an operating system make sure that a process only interacts with its memory segment? When a process creates a thread, because it needs some instructions and data processed, there are two registers used by the CPU. A *base register* contains the beginning address that was assigned to the process and a *limit register* contains the ending address, as illustrated in Figure 5-6. The thread contains an address of where the instruction and data reside that need to be processed. The CPU compares this address to the base and limit registers to make sure that the thread is not trying to access a memory segment outside of its bounds. So, the base register makes it impossible for a thread to reference a memory address below its allocated memory segment, and the limit register makes it impossible for a thread to reference a memory address above this segment.

**Figure 5-6**
Base and limit registers are used to contain a process in its own memory segment.

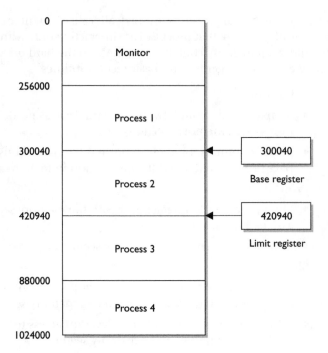

Memory is also protected through the use of user and privileged modes of execution, as previously mentioned, and covered in more detail later in the "CPU Modes and Protection Rings" section.

## Memory Types

The operating system instructions, applications, and data are held in memory, but so are the basic input/output system (BIOS), device controller instructions, and firmware. They do not all reside in the same memory location or even the same type of memory. The different types of memory, what they are used for, and how each is accessed can get a bit confusing because the CPU deals with several different types for different reasons.

The following sections outline the different types of memory that can be used within computer systems.

### Random Access Memory

*Random access memory (RAM)* is a type of temporary storage facility where data and program instructions can temporarily be held and altered. It is used for read/write ac-

---

### Hardware Segmentation

Systems of a higher trust level may need to implement *hardware segmentation* of the memory used by different processes. This means that memory is separated physically instead of just logically. This adds another layer of protection to ensure that a lower-privileged process does not access and modify a higher-level process's memory space.

tivities by the operating system and applications. It is described as *volatile* because if the computer's power supply is terminated, then all information within this type of memory is lost.

RAM is an integrated circuit made up of millions of transistors and capacitors. The capacitor is where the actual charge is stored, which represents a 1 or 0 to the system. The transistor acts like a gate or a switch. A capacitor that is storing a binary value of 1 has several electrons stored in it, which have a negative charge, whereas a capacitor that is storing a 0 value is empty. When the operating system writes over a 1 bit with a 0 bit, in reality it is just emptying out the electrons from that specific capacitor.

One problem is that these capacitors cannot keep their charge for long. Therefore, a memory controller has to "recharge" the values in the capacitors, which just means that it continually reads and writes the same values to the capacitors. If the memory controller does not "refresh" the value of 1, the capacitor will start losing its electrons and become a 0 or a corrupted value. This explains how *dynamic RAM (DRAM)* works. The data being held in the RAM memory cells has to be continually and dynamically refreshed, so that your bits do not magically disappear. This activity of constantly refreshing takes time, which is why DRAM is slower than static RAM.

 **NOTE** When we are dealing with memory activities, we use a time metric of nanoseconds (ns), which is a billionth of a second. So if you look at your RAM chip and it states 70 ns, this means that it takes 70 nanoseconds to read and refresh each memory cell.

*Static RAM (SRAM)* does not require this continuous-refreshing nonsense; it uses a different technology, by holding bits in its memory cells without the use of capacitors, but it *does* require more transistors than DRAM. Since SRAM does not need to be refreshed, it is faster than DRAM, but since SRAM requires more transistors, it takes up more space on the RAM chip. Manufacturers cannot fit as many SRAM memory cells on a memory chip as they can DRAM memory cells, which is why SRAM is more expensive. So, DRAM is cheaper and slower, and SRAM is more expensive and faster. It always seems to go that way. SRAM has been used in cache, and DRAM is commonly used in RAM chips.

Because life is not confusing enough, we have many other types of RAM. The main reason for the continual evolution of RAM types is that it directly affects the speed of the computer itself. Many people, mistakenly, think that just because you have a fast processor, your computer will be fast. However, memory type and size and bus sizes are also critical components. Think of memory as pieces of paper used by the system to hold instructions. If the system had small pieces of papers (small amount of memory) to read and write from, it would spend most of its time looking for these pieces and lining them up properly. When a computer spends more time moving data from one small portion of memory to another than actually processing the data it is referred to as *thrashing*. This causes the system to crawl in speed and your frustration level to increase.

The size of the data bus also makes a difference in system speed. You can think of a data bus as a highway that connects different portions of the computer. If a ton of data needs to go from memory to the CPU and can only travel over a 4-lane highway, compared to a 64-lane highway, there will be delays in processing. So the processor, memory type and amount, and bus speeds are critical components to system performance.

The following are additional types of RAM that you need to understand:

- **Synchronous DRAM (SDRAM)** Synchronizes itself with the system's CPU and synchronizes signal input and output on the RAM chip. It coordinates its activities with the CPU clock so that the timing of the CPU and the timing of the memory activities are synchronized. This increases the speed of transmitting and executing data.

- **Extended data out DRAM (EDO DRAM)** Is faster than DRAM because DRAM can access only one block of data at a time, whereas EDO DRAM can capture the next block of data while the first block is being sent to the CPU for processing. It has a type of "look ahead" feature that speeds up memory access.

- **Burst EDO DRAM (BEDO DRAM)** Works like (and builds upon) EDO DRAM in that it can transmit data to the CPU as it carries out a read option, but it can send more data at once (burst). It reads and sends up to four memory addresses in a small number of clock cycles.

- **Double data rate SDRAM (DDR SDRAM)** Carries out read operations on the rising and falling cycles of a clock pulse. So instead of carrying out one operation per clock cycle, it carries out two and thus can deliver twice the throughput of SDRAM. Basically, it doubles the speed of memory activities, when compared to SDRAM, with a smaller number of clock cycles. Pretty groovy.

 **NOTE** These different RAM types require different controller chips to interface with them; therefore, the motherboards that these memory types are used on often are very specific in nature.

Well, that's enough about RAM for now. Let's look at other types of memory that are used in basically every computer in the world.

## Read-Only Memory

*Read-only memory (ROM)* is a *nonvolatile* memory type, meaning that when a computer's power is turned off, the data is still held within the memory chips. When data is inserted into ROM memory chips, it cannot be altered. Individual ROM chips are manufactured with the stored program or routines designed into it. The software that is stored within ROM is called *firmware.*

*Programmable read-only memory (PROM)* is a form of ROM that can be modified after it has been manufactured. PROM can be programmed only one time because the voltage that is used to write bits into the memory cells actually burns out the fuses that connect the individual memory cells. The instructions are "burned into" PROM using a specialized PROM programmer device.

*Erasable and programmable read-only memory (EPROM)* can be erased, modified, and upgraded. EPROM holds data that can be electrically erased or written to. To erase the data on the memory chip, you need your handy-dandy ultraviolet (UV) light device that provides just the right level of energy. The EPROM chip has a quartz window, which is where you point the UV light. Although playing with UV light devices can be fun for the whole family, we have moved on to another type of ROM technology that does not require this type of activity.

To erase an EPROM chip, you must remove the chip from the computer and wave your magic UV wand, which erases *all* of the data on the chip—not just portions of it. So someone invented *electrically erasable programmable read-only memory (EEPROM)*, and we all put our UV light wands away for good.

EEPROM is similar to EPROM, but its data storage can be erased and modified electrically by onboard programming circuitry and signals. This activity erases only one byte at a time, which is slow. And because we are an impatient society, yet another technology was developed that is very similar, but works more quickly.

*Flash memory* is a special type of memory that is used in digital cameras, BIOS chips, memory cards for laptops, and video game consoles. It is a solid-state technology, meaning that it does not have moving parts and is used more as a type of hard drive than memory.

Flash memory basically moves around different levels of voltages to indicate that a 1 or 0 needs to be held in a specific address. It acts as a ROM technology rather than a RAM technology. (For example, you do not lose pictures stored on your memory stick in your digital camera just because your camera loses power. RAM is volatile and ROM is nonvolatile.) When Flash memory needs to be erased and turned back to its original state, a program initiates the internal circuits to apply an electric field. The erasing function takes place in blocks or on the entire chip instead of erasing one byte at a time.

Flash memory is used as a small disk drive in most implementations. Its benefits over a regular hard drive are that it is smaller, faster, and lighter. So let's deploy Flash memory everywhere and replace our hard drives! Maybe one day. Today it is relatively expensive compared to regular hard drives.

## References

- **Unix/Linux Internals Course and Links**  www.softpanorama.org/Internals
- **Linux Knowledge Base and Tutorial**  www.linux-tutorial.info/ modules.php?name=Tutorial&pageid=117
- **Fast, Smart RAM, Peter Wayner, Byte.com (June 1995)**  www.byte.com/art/ 9506/sec10/art2.htm

## Cache Memory

*I am going to need this later, so I will just stick it into cache for now.*

*Cache memory* is a type of memory that is used for high-speed writing and reading activities. When the system assumes (through its programmatic logic) that it will need to access specific information many times throughout its processing activities, it will store the information in cache memory so that it is easily and quickly accessible. Data in cache can be accessed much more quickly than data stored in real memory. Therefore, any information needed by the CPU very quickly, and very often, is usually stored in cache memory, thereby improving the overall speed of the computer system.

An analogy is how the brain stores information that it uses often. If one of Marge's primary functions at her job is to order parts, which requires telling vendors the company's address, Marge stores this address information in a portion of her brain from which she can easily and quickly access it. This information is held in a type of cache. If Marge was asked to recall her third-grade teacher's name, this information would not necessarily be held in cache memory, but in a more long-term storage facility within her noggin. The long-term storage within her brain is comparable to a system's hard drive. It takes more time to track down and return information from a hard drive than from specialized cache memory.

**NOTE** Different motherboards have different types of cache. Level 1 (L1) is faster than Level 2 (L2), and L2 is faster than L3. Some processors and device controllers have cache memory built into them. L1 and L2 are usually built into the processors and the controllers themselves.

## Memory Mapping

*Okay, here is your memory, here is my memory, and here is Bob's memory. No one use each other's memory!*

Because there are different types of memory holding different types of data, a computer system does not want to let every user, process, and application access all types of memory anytime they want to. Access to memory needs to be controlled to ensure that data does not get corrupted and that sensitive information is not available to unauthorized processes. This type of control takes place through memory mapping and addressing.

The CPU is one of the most trusted components within a system, and therefore it can access memory directly. It uses physical addresses instead of pointers (logical addresses) to memory segments. The CPU has physical wires connecting it to the memory chips within the computer. Because physical wires connect the two types of components, physical addresses are used to represent the intersection between the wires and the transistors on a memory chip. Software does not use physical addresses; instead, it uses logical memory addresses. Accessing memory indirectly provides an access control layer between the software and the memory, which is done for protection and efficiency. Figure 5-7 illustrates how the CPU can access memory directly using physical addresses and how software must use memory indirectly through a memory mapper.

Let's look at an analogy. You would like to talk to Mr. Marshall about possibly buying some acreage in Iowa. You don't know Mr. Marshall personally, and you do not want to give out your physical address and have him show up at your doorstep. Instead, you would like to use a more abstract and controlled way of communicating, so you give Mr. Marshall your phone number so that you can talk to him about the land and determine whether you want to meet him in person. The same type of thing happens in computers. When a computer runs software, it does not want to expose itself unnecessarily to software written by good and bad programmers. Computers enable software to access memory

**Figure 5-7**   The CPU and applications access memory differently.

indirectly by using index tables and pointers, instead of giving them the right to access the memory directly. This is one way the computer system protects itself.

When a program attempts to access memory, its access rights are verified and then instructions and commands are carried out in a way to ensure that badly written code does not affect other programs or the system itself. Applications, and their processes, can only access the memory allocated to them, as shown in Figure 5-8. This type of memory architecture provides protection and efficiency.

The physical memory addresses that the CPU uses are called *absolute addresses*. The indexed memory addresses that software uses are referred to as *logical addresses*. And *relative addresses* are based on a known address with an offset value applied. As explained previously, an application does not "know" that it is sharing memory with other applications. When the program needs a memory segment to work with, it tells the memory manager how much memory it needs. The memory manager allocates this much physical memory, which could have the physical addressing of 34,000 to 39,000, for example. But the application is not written to call upon addresses in this numbering scheme. It is most likely developed to call upon addresses starting with 0 and extending to, let's say, 5000. So the memory manager allows the application to use its own addressing scheme—the logical addresses. When the application makes a call to one of these "phantom" logical addresses, the memory manager must map this address to the actual physical address. (It's like two people using their own naming scheme. When Bob asks Diane for a ball, Diane knows he really means a stapler. Don't judge Bob and Diane, it works for them.)

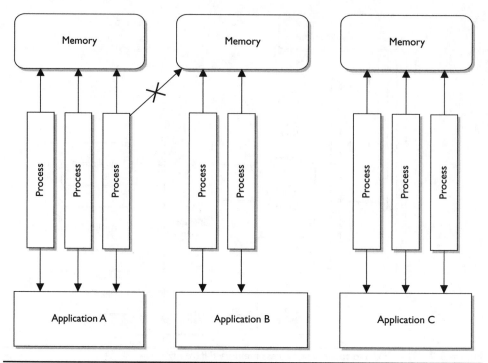

**Figure 5-8** Applications, and the processes they use, access their own memory segments only.

The mapping process is illustrated in Figure 5-9. When an application needs its instructions and data to be processed by the CPU, the physical addresses are loaded into the base and limit registers. When a thread indicates the instruction that needs to be processed, it provides a logical address. The memory manager maps the logical address to the physical address, so the CPU knows where the instruction is located. The thread will actually be using a relative address, because the application uses the address space of 0 to 5000. When the thread indicates that it needs the instruction at the memory address 3400 to be executed, the memory manager has to work from its mapping of logical address 0 to the actual physical address and then figure out the physical address for the logical address 3400. So the logical address 3400 is relative to the starting address 0.

As an analogy, if I know that you use a different number system than everyone else in the world, and you tell me that you need 14 cookies, I would need to know where to start in *your* number scheme to figure out how many cookies to really give you. So, if you inform me that in "your world" your numbering scheme starts at 5, I would map 5 to 0 and know that the offset is a value of 5. So when you tell me you want 14 cookies (the relative number), I take the offset value into consideration. I know that you start at the value 5, so I map your logical address of 14 to the physical number of 8. (But I would not give you 8 cookies, because you made me work too hard to figure all of this out. I will just eat them myself.)

So the application is working in its "own world" using its "own addresses," and the memory manager has to map these values to reality, which means the absolute address values.

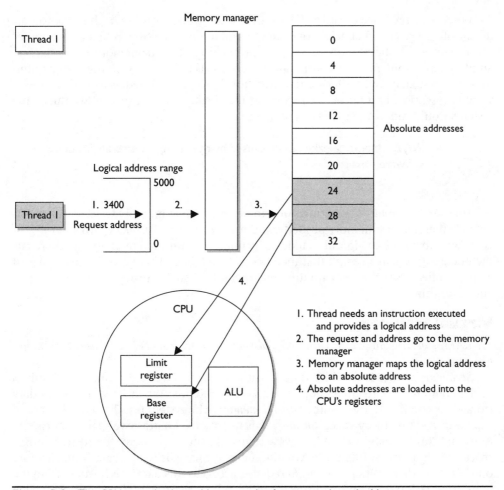

**Figure 5-9** The CPU uses absolute addresses and software uses logical addresses.

## Memory Leaks

*Oh great, the memory leaked all over me. Does someone have a mop?*

When an application makes a request for a memory segment, it is allocated a specific memory amount by the operating system. When the application is done with the memory, it is supposed to tell the operating system to release the memory so that it is available to other applications. This is only fair. But some applications are written poorly and do not indicate to the system that this memory is no longer in use. If this happens enough times, the operating system could become "starved" for memory, which would drastically affect the system's performance.

When a memory leak is identified in the hacker world, this opens the door to new denial-of-service (DoS) attacks. For example, when it was uncovered that a Unix application and a specific version of a Telnet protocol contained memory leaks, hackers amplified the problem. They continually sent requests to systems with these vulnerabilities. The systems would allocate resources for these network requests, which in turn would cause more and more memory to be allocated and not returned. Eventually the systems would run out of memory and freeze.

 **NOTE** Memory leaks can be caused by operating systems, applications, and software drivers.

There are two main countermeasures to protect against memory leaks: develop better code that releases memory properly, and use a *garbage collector*. A garbage collector is software that runs an algorithm to identify unused committed memory and then tells the operating system to mark that memory as "available." There are different types of garbage collectors that work with different operating systems, programming languages, and algorithms.

## Virtual Memory

*My RAM is overflowing! Can I use some of your hard drive space? Response: No, I don't like you.*

*Secondary storage* is considered nonvolatile storage media and includes such things as the computer's hard drive, floppy disks, or CD-ROMs. When RAM and secondary storage are combined, the result is *virtual memory*. The system uses hard drive space to extend its RAM memory space. *Swap space* is the reserved hard drive space that is used to extend RAM capabilities. Windows systems use the pagefile.sys file to reserve this space. When a system fills up its volatile memory space, it writes data from memory onto the hard drive. When a program requests access to this data, it is brought from the hard drive back into memory in specific units, called *page frames*. This process is called *paging*. Accessing data that is kept in pages on the hard drive takes more time than accessing data kept in memory because physical disk read/write access has to take place. There are internal control blocks, maintained by the operating system, to keep track of what page frames are residing in RAM, and what is available "offline," ready to be called into RAM for execution or processing, if needed. The payoff is that it seems as though the system can hold an incredible amount of information and program instructions in memory, as shown in Figure 5-10.

A security issue with using virtual swap space is that when the system is shut down, or processes that were using the swap space are terminated, the pointers to the pages are reset to "available" even though the actual data that was written to disk is still physically there. This data could conceivably be compromised and captured. On a very secure operating system, there are routines to wipe the swap spaces after a process is done with it, before it is used again. The routines should also erase this data before a system shutdown, at which time the operating system would no longer be able to maintain any control over what happens on the hard drive surface.

**Figure 5-10**  Data from RAM is moved to the hard drive in page frames.

 **NOTE**  If a program, file, or data is encrypted and saved on the hard drive, it will be decrypted when it is used by the controlling program. While this unencrypted data is sitting in RAM, the system could write out that data to the swap space on the hard drive, in its unencrypted state. Attackers have figured out how to gain access to this space in unauthorized manners.

## References

- "Introduction to Virtual Memory," by Tuncay Basar, Kyung Kim, and Bill Lemley   www.cne.gmu.edu/itcore/virtualmemory/vmintro.html
- **Memory Hierarchy**   http://courses.ece.uiuc.edu/ece411/lectures/ LecturesSpring05/Lectures_2.07.pdf
- "Virtual Memory," by Prof. Bruce Jacob, University of Maryland at College Park (2001)   www.ee.umd.edu/~blj/papers/CS-chapter.pdf
- **LabMice.net links to articles on memory leaks**   http://labmice.techtarget .com/troubleshooting/memoryleaks.htm

## CPU Modes and Protection Rings

*If I am corrupted, very bad things can happen. Response: Then you need to go into ring 0.*

If an operating system is going to be stable, it must be able to protect itself from its users and their applications. This requires the capability to distinguish between operations performed on behalf of the operating system itself and operations performed on behalf of the users or applications. This can be complex because the operating system software may be accessing memory segments, sending instructions to the CPU for processing, and accessing secondary storage devices at the same time. Each user application (e-mail client, antivirus program, web browser, word processor, personal firewall, and so on) may also be attempting the same types of activities at the same time. The operating system must keep track of all of these events and ensure that none of them violates the system's overall security policy.

The operating system has several protection mechanisms to ensure that processes do not negatively affect each other or the critical components of the system itself. One has already been mentioned: memory protection. Another security mechanism that the system uses is *protection rings*. These rings provide strict boundaries and definitions for what the processes that work within each ring can access and what operations they can successfully execute. The processes that operate within the inner rings have more privileges than the processes operating in the outer rings, because the inner rings only permit the most trusted components and processes to operate within them. Although operating systems may vary in the number of protection rings they use, processes that execute within the inner rings are usually referred to as existing in privileged, or supervisor, mode. The processes working in the outer rings are said to execute in user mode.

 **NOTE** The actual ring architecture that is used by a system is dictated by the processor and the operating system. The hardware chip (processor) is constructed to provide a certain number of rings, and the operating system must be developed to also work in this ring structure. This is one reason why an operating system platform may work with an Intel chip but not an Alpha chip, for example. They have different architectures and ways to interpret instruction sets.

Operating system components operate in a ring that gives them the most access to memory locations, peripheral devices, system drivers, and sensitive configuration parameters. Because this ring provides much more dangerous access to critical resources, it is the most protected. Applications usually operate in ring 3, which limits the type of memory, peripheral device, and driver access activity and is controlled through the operating system services or system calls. The different rings are illustrated in Figure 5-11. The type of commands and instructions that are sent to the CPU from applications in the outer rings are more restrictive in nature. If an application tries to send instructions to the CPU that fall outside of its permission level, the CPU treats this violation as an exception and may show a general protection fault or exception error and attempt to shut down the offending application.

Protection rings support the availability, integrity, and confidentiality requirements of multitasking operating systems. The most commonly used architecture provides four protection rings:

- **Ring 0**   Operating system kernel
- **Ring 1**   Remaining parts of the operating system
- **Ring 2**   I/O drivers and utilities
- **Ring 3**   Applications and user activity

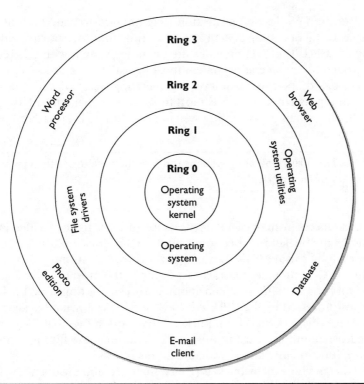

**Figure 5-11** More trusted processes operate within lower-numbered rings.

These protection rings provide an intermediate layer between subjects and objects, and are used for access control when a subject tries to access an object. The ring determines the access level to sensitive system resources. The lower the number, the greater the amount of privilege that is given to the process that runs within that ring. Each subject and object is logically assigned a number (0 through 3) depending upon the level of trust the operating system assigns it. A subject in ring 3 cannot directly access an object in ring 1, but subjects in ring 1 can directly access an object in ring 3. Entities can only access objects within their own ring and cannot directly communicate with objects in higher rings. When an application needs access to components in rings that it is not allowed to directly access, it makes a request of the operating system to perform the necessary tasks. This is handled through system calls, where the operating system executes instructions that are not allowed in user mode. The request is passed off to an operating system service, which works at a higher privilege level and can carry out the more sensitive tasks.

When the operating system executes instructions for processes in rings 0 and 1, it operates in supervisor mode or privileged mode. When the operating system executes instructions for applications and processes in ring 3, it operates in user mode. User mode provides a much more restrictive environment for the application to work in, which in turn protects the system from misbehaving programs.

If CPU execution modes and protection rings are new to you, think of protection rings as buckets. The operating system has to work within the structure and confines provided by the CPU. The CPU provides the operating system with different buckets, labeled 0 through 3. The operating system must logically place processes into the different buckets, based upon the trust level the operating system has in those processes. Since the operating system kernel is the most trusted component, it and its processes go into bucket 0. The remaining operating system processes go into bucket 1 and all user applications go into bucket 3.

**NOTE**  Many operating systems today do not use the second protection ring very often, if at all.

So, when a process from bucket 0 needs its instructions to be executed by the CPU, the CPU checks the bucket number (ring number) and flips a bit indicating that this process can be fully trusted. This means that this process can interact with all of the functionality the CPU provides to processes. Some of the most privileged activities are I/O and memory access attempts. When another process, this time from bucket 3, needs its instructions processed by the CPU, the CPU first looks at what bucket this process came from. Since this process is from bucket 3, the CPU knows that the operating system has the least amount of trust in this process and therefore flips a bit that restricts the amount of functionality that is available to this process.

The CPU dictates how many buckets (rings) there are, and the operating system will be developed to use either two or all of them.

## Operating System Architecture

*You can't see me and you don't know that I exist, so you can't talk to me. Response: Fine by me.*

Operating systems can be developed by using several types of architecture. The architecture is the framework that dictates how the operating system's services and functions are placed and how they interact. This section looks at the monolithic, layered, and client/server structures.

A *monolithic operating system architecture* is commonly referred to as "The Big Mess" because of its lack of structure. The operating system is mainly made up of various procedures that can call upon each other in a haphazard manner. Figure 5-12 illustrates a monolithic architecture. In these types of systems, modules of code can call upon each other as needed. The communication between the different modules is not as structured and controlled as in a layered architecture, and data hiding is not provided. MS-DOS is an example of a monolithic operating system.

A *layered operating system* architecture separates system functionality into hierarchical layers. For example, a system that followed a layered architecture was strangely enough called THE. THE had five layers of functionality. Layer 0 controlled access to the processor and provided multiprogramming functionality; layer 1 carried out memory management; layer 2 provided interprocess communication; layer 3 dealt with I/O devices; and layer 4 was where the applications resided. The processes at the different layers each had interfaces to be used by processes in layers below and above them.

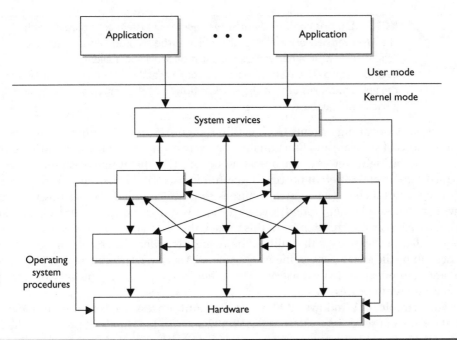

**Figure 5-12**  A monolithic architecture does not provide much structure.

This is different from a monolithic architecture, in which the different modules can communicate with any other module. Layered operating systems provide *data hiding*, which means that instructions and data (packaged up as procedures) at the various layers do not have direct access to the instructions and data at any other layers. Each procedure at each layer has access only to its own data and a set of functions that it requires to carry out its own tasks. If a procedure can access more procedures than it really needs, this opens the door for more successful compromises. For example, if an attacker is able to compromise and gain control of one procedure, and this procedure has direct access to all other procedures, the attacker could compromise a more privileged procedure and carry out more devastating activities.

A monolithic operating system provides only one layer of security. In a layered system, each layer should provide its own security and access control. If one layer contains the necessary security mechanisms to make security decisions for all the other layers, then that one layer knows too much about (and has access to) too many objects at the different layers. This directly violates the data-hiding concept. Modularizing software and its code increases the assurance level of the system, because if one module is compromised, it does not mean that all other modules are now vulnerable. Examples of layered operating systems are THE, VAX/VMS, Multics, Unix (although THE and Multics are no longer in use).

**NOTE** Do not confuse client/server *operating system* architecture with client/server *network* architecture, which is the traditional association for "client/server." In a network, an application works in a client/server model because it provides distributed computing capabilities. The client portion of the application resides on the workstations and the server portion is usually a back-end database or server.

Windows operating systems work within a client/server architecture, which means that portions of software and functionality that were previously in the monolithic kernel are now at the higher levels of the operating system. The operating system functions are divided into several different processes that run in user mode, instead of kernel mode.

The goal of a client/server architecture is to move as much code as possible from having to work in kernel mode (privileged mode) so that the system has a leaner kernel, referred to as the *microkernel*. In this model, the requesting process is referred to as the client, and the process that fulfills the request is called the server. The server processes can be file system server, memory server, I/O server, or process server. These servers are commonly called *subsystems*. The client is either a user process or another operating system process.

For example, in Windows 2000, when the Paint process needs to display a graphic on the screen, it sends its request to the Win32 subsystem. The Paint process is the client and the Win32 subsystem is the server. The microkernel just controls client-to-server communication, instead of providing the functionality to the requesting processes itself. The microkernel is the "traffic cop," directing communication, ensuring that it is safe, and dealing with problems as they come up. The Windows operating system architecture is illustrated in Figure 5-13.

## Domains

*Okay, here are all the marbles you can play with. We will call that your domain of resources.*

A *domain* is defined as a set of objects that a subject is able to access. This domain can be all the resources a user can access, all the files available to a program, the memory segments available to a process, or the services and processes available to an application. A subject needs to be able to access and use objects (resources) to perform tasks, and the domain defines which objects are available to the subject and which objects are untouchable and therefore unusable by the subject.

**NOTE** Remember that a thread is a portion of a process. When the thread is generated it shares the same domain (resources) as its process.

These domains have to be identified, separated, and strictly enforced. An operating system and CPU may work in privileged mode and user mode. The reason to even use these different modes, which are dictated by the protection ring, is to define different domains. When a process's instructions are being executed in privileged mode, the process has a much larger domain to work with (or more resources to access); thus, it can carry out more activities. When an operating system process works in privileged mode,

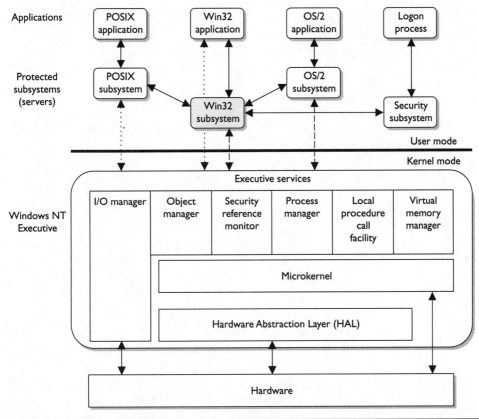

**Figure 5-13** Subsystems fulfill the requests of the client processes.

it can access more memory segments, transfer data from an unprotected domain to a protected domain, and directly access and communicate with hardware devices. An application that functions in user mode cannot access memory directly and has a more limited amount of resources available to it. Only a certain segment of memory is available to this application, and that segment must be accessed in an indirect and controlled fashion.

A process that resides in a privileged domain needs to be able to execute its instructions and process its data with the assurance that programs in a different domain cannot negatively affect its environment. This is referred to as an *execution domain*. Because processes in a privileged domain have access to sensitive resources, the environment needs to be protected from rogue program code or unexpected activities resulting from programs in other domains. Some systems may only have distinct user and privilege areas, whereas other systems may have complex architectures that contain up to ten execution domains.

An execution domain has a direct correlation to the protection ring that a subject or object is assigned to. The lower the protection ring number, the higher the privilege and the larger the domain. This concept is depicted in Figure 5-14.

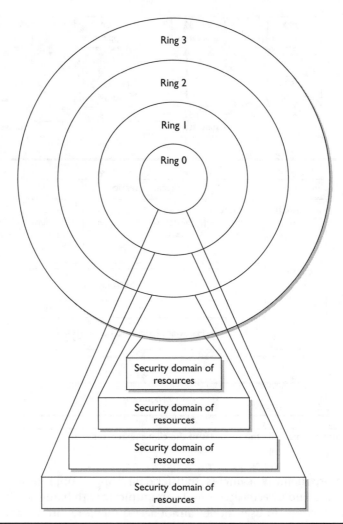

**Figure 5-14** The higher the level of trust, the larger the number of available resources.

## Layering and Data Hiding

Although, academically, there are three main types of architectures for operating systems, the terms *layering* and *data hiding* are commonly used when talking about protection mechanisms for operating systems—even ones that follow the client/server architecture, because it also uses layering and data hiding to protect itself.

A layered operating system architecture *mainly* addresses how functionality is laid out and is available to the users and programs. It provides its functionality in a hierarchy, whereas a client/server architecture provides functionality in more of a linear fashion. A request does not have to go through various layers in a client/server architecture. The request just goes to the necessary subsystem. But in terms of security, both architectures use layer and data hiding to protect the operating system itself.

It is almost too bad that we have so many terms—execution domains, protection rings, layering, data hiding, protection domains, CPU modes, etc.—because in reality they all are different ways to describe the same thing that takes place within every operating system today. When people are first learning these topics, many of these concepts seem discreet and totally unrelated. But in reality, these concepts have to work together in a very orchestrated manner for the whole operating system to work and provide the level of protection that it does.

As previously discussed, the operating system and CPU work within the same architecture, which provides protection rings. A process's protection domain (execution domain) is determined by the protection ring that it resides within. When a process needs the CPU to execute instructions, the CPU works in a specific mode (user or privileged) depending upon what protection ring the process is in. Layering and data hiding are provided by placing the different processes in different protection rings and controlling how communication takes place from the less trusted and the more trusted processes.

So, layering is a way to provide buffers between the more trusted and less trusted processes. The less trusted processes cannot directly communicate with the more trusted processes, but rather must submit their requests to an operating system service. This service acts as a broker or a bouncer that makes sure that nothing gains unauthorized access to the more trusted processes. This architecture protects the operating system overall, including all the applications and user activities that are going on within it.

## Virtual Machines

*I would like my own simulated environment so that I can have my own world. Response: No problem. Just slip on this straightjacket first.*

If you have been into computers for a while, you might remember computer games that did not have the complex, life-like graphics of today's games. Pong and Asteroids were what we had to play with when we were younger. In those simpler times, the games were 16-bit and were written to work in a 16-bit MS-DOS environment. When our Windows operating systems moved from 16-bit to 32-bit, the 32-bit operating systems were written to be backward compatible, so someone could still load and play a 16-bit game in an environment that the game did not understand. The continuation of this little life pleasure was available to users because the operating systems created *virtual machines* for the games to run in.

A virtual machine is a simulated environment. When a 16-bit application needs to interact with the operating system, it has been developed to make system calls and interact with the computer's memory in a way that would only work within a 16-bit operating system—not a 32-bit system. So, the virtual machine simulates a 16-bit operating system, and when the application makes a request, the operating system converts the 16-bit request into a 32-bit request (this is called *thunking*) and reacts to the request appropriately. When the system sends a reply to this request, it changes the 32-bit reply into a 16-bit reply so that the application understands it.

Although not many people run 16-bit games anymore, we do use virtual machines for other purposes. The product VMWare creates individual virtual machines so that a user can run multiple operating systems on one computer at the same time. The Java

Virtual Machine (JVM), used by basically every web browser today, creates virtual machines (called sandboxes) in which Java applets run. This is a protection mechanism, because the sandbox contains the applet and does not allow it to interact with the operating system and file system directly. The activities that the applet attempts to carry out are screened by the JVM to see if they are safe requests. If the JVM determines that an activity is safe, then the JVM carries out the request on behalf of the applet.

**NOTE** Malware has been written that escapes the "walls of the sandbox" so that it can carry out its deeds without being under control of the JVM. These compromises, as well as Java and the JVM, will be covered in more detail in Chapter 11.

## References

- **Operating Systems – OS System Architectures, by Arno Jacobsen, University of Toronto** www.eecg.toronto.edu/~jacobsen/os/week7-os-architecture.pdf
- *The Design of PARAS Microkernel*, **Chapter 2, "Operating System Models," by Rajkumar Buyya (1998)** www.gridbus.org/~raj/microkernel/chap2.pdf
- **Chapter 12, "Windows NT/2000," by M.I. Vuskovic** http://medusa.sdsu .edu/cs570/Lectures/chapter12.pdf
- **Answers.com definitions of** *virtual machine* www.answers.com/topic/ virtual-machine

## Additional Storage Devices

Besides the memory environment discussed previously, there are many types of physical storage devices that need to be discussed, along with the ramifications of security compromises that could affect them. Many, if not all, of the various storage devices used today enable the theft or compromise of data in an organization. As their sizes have become smaller, their capacities have grown larger. Floppy disks, while small in relative storage capacity (about 1.44MB of data), have long been known to be a source of viruses and data theft. A thief who has physical access to a computer with an insecure operating system can use a basic floppy disk to boot the system.

Many PCs and Unix workstations have a BIOS that allows the machine to be booted from devices other than the floppy disk, such as a CD-ROM or even a USB thumb drive. Possible ways to harden the environment include password-protecting the BIOS, so that a nonapproved medium cannot take over the machine, and controlling access to the physical environment of the computer equipment.

There have been many instances in which removable storage units have come up missing. Two noteworthy incidents occurred in July 2004, at which time both Los Alamos National Laboratory and Sandia National Laboratories reported missing storage media containing classified information. This raised enough of a concern at Los Alamos that the military research facility was totally shut down, with no employees allowed to enter, while a thorough search and investigation was performed. Sandia National Laboratories reported it was missing a computer floppy disk marked classified, which it later located.

Rewritable CD/DVDs, mini-disks, optical disks—virtually any portable storage medium—can be used to compromise security. Current technology headaches for the security professional include USB thumb drives and USB-attachable MP3 players that are capable of storing multiple gigabytes of data. The first step in prevention is to update existing security policies (or implement new ones) to include the new technologies. Even cellular phones can be connected to computer ports for data, sound, image, and video transmission that could be out of bounds of an outdated security policy. Technologies such as Bluetooth, FireWire, and Blackberry all have to be taken into account when addressing security concerns and vulnerabilities.

## Input/Output Device Management

*Some things come in, some things go out. Response: We took a vote and would like you to go out.*

We have covered a lot of operating system responsibilities up to now, and we are not stopping yet. An operating system also has to control all input/output devices. It sends commands to them, accepts their interrupts when they need to communicate with the CPU, and provides an interface between the devices and the applications.

I/O devices are usually considered block or character devices. A block device works with data in fixed-size blocks, each block with its own unique address. A disk drive is an example of a block device. A character device, such as a printer, network interface card, or mouse, works with streams of characters, without using any fixed sizes. This type of data is not addressable.

When a user chooses to print a document, open a stored file on a word processor, or save files to a jump drive, these requests go from the application the user is working in, through the operating system, and to the device requested. The operating system uses a device driver to communicate with a device controller, which may be a circuit card that fits into an expansion slot. The controller is an electrical component with its own software that provides a communication path that enables the device and operating system to exchange data. The operating system sends commands to the device controller's registers and the controller then writes data to the peripheral device or extracts data to be processed by the CPU, depending on the given commands. If the command is to extract data from the hard drive, the controller takes the bits and puts them into the necessary block size and carries out a checksum activity to verify the integrity of the data. If the integrity is successfully verified, then the data is put into memory for the CPU to interact with.

Operating systems need to access and release devices and computer resources properly. Different operating systems handle accessing devices and resources differently. For example, Windows NT is considered a more stable and safer data processing environment than Windows 9x because applications in Windows NT cannot make direct requests to hardware devices. Windows NT and Windows 2000 have a much more controlled method of accessing devices than Windows 9x. This method helps to protect the system from badly written code that does not properly request and release resources. This level of protection helps to ensure the resources' integrity and availability.

> ## Why Does My Video Card Need to Have Its Own RAM?
> The RAM on a video card is really just a type of buffer. The application or operating system writes the pixel values into this RAM space instead of writing to the system's RAM. The pixel values are then displayed to the user on the monitor screen. Graphic-intensive games work better with video cards with a lot of RAM, because storing this display information on the system's RAM takes too long for the read and write procedures. This results in delayed reactions between the user's interaction commands and what is displayed on the screen. We never seemed to have these problems when we all played Pong.

## Interrupts

When an I/O device has completed whatever task that was asked of it, it needs to inform the CPU that the necessary data is now in memory for processing. The device's controller sends a signal down a bus, which is detected by the interrupt controller. (This is what it means to use an interrupt. The device signals the interrupt controller and is basically saying, "I am done and need attention now.") If the CPU is busy *and* the device's interrupt is not a higher priority than whatever job is being processed, then the device has to wait. The interrupt controller sends a message to the CPU, indicating what device needs attention. The operating system has a table (called the interrupt vector) of all the I/O devices connected to it. The CPU compares the received number with the values within the interrupt vector so that it knows which I/O device needs its services. The table has the memory addresses of the different I/O devices. So when the CPU understands that the hard drive needs attention, it looks in the table to find the correct memory address. This is the new program counter value, which is the initial address of where the CPU should start reading from.

One of the main goals of the operating system software that controls I/O activity is to be device independent. This means that a developer can write an application to read (open a file) or write (save a file) to any device (floppy disk, jump drive, hard drive, CD-ROM drive). This level of abstraction frees application developers from having to write different procedures to interact with the various I/O devices. If a developer had to write an individual procedure of how to write to a CD-ROM drive, *and* how to write to a floppy disk, *and* how to write to a jump drive, *and* how to write to a hard disk, and so on, each time a new type of I/O device was developed, all of the applications would have to be patched or upgraded.

There are different ways that operating systems can carry out software I/O procedures. We will look at the following methods:

- Programmed I/O
- Interrupt-driven I/O
- I/O using DMA

- Premapped I/O
- Fully mapped I/O

**Programmable I/O**   If an operating system is using *programmable I/O*, this means that the CPU sends data to an I/O device and polls the device to see if it is ready to accept more data. If the device is not ready to accept more data, the CPU wastes time by waiting for the device to become ready. For example, the CPU would send a byte of data (a character) to the printer and then ask the printer if it is ready for another byte. The CPU sends the text to be printed one byte at a time. This is a very slow way of working and wastes precious CPU time. So the smart people figured out a better way: interrupt-driven I/O.

**Interrupt-Driven I/O**   If an operating system is using *interrupt-driven I/O*, this means that the CPU sends a character over to the printer and then goes and works on another process's request. When the printer is done printing the first character, it sends an interrupt to the CPU. The CPU stops what it is doing, sends another character to the printer, and moves to another job. This process (send character—go do something else—interrupt—send another character) continues until the whole text is printed. Although the CPU is not waiting for each byte to be printed, this method does waste a lot of time dealing with all the interrupts. So we excused those smart people and brought in some smarter people, who came up with I/O using DMA.

**I/O Using DMA**   *Direct memory access (DMA)* is a way of transferring data between I/O devices and the system's memory without using the CPU. This speeds up data transfer rates significantly. When used in I/O activities, the DMA controller feeds the characters to the printer without bothering the CPU. This method is sometimes referred to as *unmapped I/O*.

**Premapped I/O**   *Premapped I/O* and fully mapped I/O (described next) does not pertain to performance, as do the earlier methods, but provides two approaches that can directly affect security. In a premapped I/O system, the CPU sends the physical memory address of the requesting process to the I/O device, and the I/O device is trusted enough to interact with the contents of memory directly. So the CPU does not control the interactions between the I/O device and memory. The operating system trusts the device to behave properly. Scary.

**Fully Mapped I/O**   Under *fully mapped I/O*, the operating system does not fully trust the I/O device. The physical address is not given to the I/O device. Instead, the device works purely with logical addresses and works on behalf (under the security context) of the requesting process. So the operating system does not trust the device to interact with memory directly. The operating system does not trust the process or device and acts as the broker to control how they communicate with each other.

## Beam Me Up, Scotty!

A cofounder of Intel, Gordon Moore, came up with Moore's Law, which states that the number of electronic components (transistors, capacitors, diodes) will double every 18 months. No one really paid attention to this until it came to be true every 18 months or so. Now he is right up there with Nostradamus.

So chip makers have continually put an amazing amount of stuff on one tiny piece of silicon, but we will soon hit the wall and have to look for other types of technologies. Today, people are looking at quantum physics to make up tomorrow's processor. In quantum physics, particles are not restricted to holding just two states (1 or 0), but instead can hold these states simultaneously and other states in between. Freaky.

And other individuals are looking to our own personal DNA, which holds the instructions for our bodies. There have already been experiments in which DNA was used for computation processes. It can carry out complex computations in parallel instead of serially like today's processors. But it sounds kind of gross.

You won't find a quantum or DNA computer at Best Buy any time soon, but one day maybe.

## References

- Chapter 12, "I/O Management and Disk Scheduling," by Joseph Kee-Yin
  www.comp.hkbu.edu.hk/~jng/comp2320/2320-C11.ppt
- I/O Management, by Sotirios Terzis (1/12/2000)   www.cs.tcd.ie/Sotirios
  .Terzis/3BA3/L9/
- Introduction to Operating Systems, by B. Ramamurthy (1/25/2002)
  www.cse.buffalo.edu/faculty/bina/cse421/spring02/jan25.pdf

# System Architecture

Designing a system from the ground up is a complicated task that has many intricate and abstract goals that have to be achieved through mathematics, logic, design, programming code, and implementation. Fundamental design decisions need to be made when constructing a system. Security is only one of the goals of a system, but it is the goal security professionals are most concerned about.

Availability, integrity, and confidentiality can be enforced at different places within an enterprise. For example, a company may store customer credit card information in a database that many users can access. This information, obviously, requires protection to ensure that it is not accessed or modified in an unauthorized manner. We should start with general questions and gradually drill down into the details. Where should this protection be placed? Should there be access controls that screen users when they log in and assign them their rights at that point dictating what data they can and cannot access? Should the data files holding the credit card information be protected at the file system level? Should protection be provided by restricting users' operations and activities? Or should there be a combination of all of these? The first and most general question is, "Where should the protection take place: at the user's end, where the data is stored, or by restricting user activities within the environment?" This is illustrated in Figure 5-15.

The same type of questions have to be answered when building an operating system. Once these general questions have been answered, the placement of the mechanisms needs to be addressed. Security mechanisms can be placed at the hardware, kernel, operating system, services, or program layers. At which layer(s) should security mechanisms be implemented? If protection is implemented at the hardware layer, then a broad level of protection is provided, because it provides a baseline of security for all the components that work on top of the hardware layer. If the protection mechanisms are closer to the user (in the higher levels of the operating system architecture), the security is more detail oriented and focused than mechanisms that work at the lower levels of the architecture.

No matter where the security mechanism is placed within the operating system architecture, the more complex the security mechanism becomes, the less assurance it usually provides. The reason is that greater complexity of the mechanism demands more technical understanding from the individuals who install, test, maintain, and use it. The more complex the security mechanism, the harder it is to fully test it under all possible conditions. On the other hand, simplistic mechanisms may not be able to provide the desired richness of functionality and options, although they are easier to install, maintain, use, and test. So the trade-offs between functionality and assurance need to be fully understood to make the right security mechanism choices when designing a system.

Once the designers have an idea of what the security mechanisms should focus on (users, operations, or data), what layer(s) the mechanisms should be placed at (hardware, kernel, operating system, services, or program), and how complex each mechanism is, they need to build and integrate the mechanisms in such a way that they have a proper relationship with other parts of the system.

First, the design team needs to decide what system mechanisms to trust and place in protection ring 0. Then, the team needs to specify how these modules of code can interact in a secure manner. Although it might seem that you would want to trust all the components within the system, this would cause too much overhead, complexity, and performance bottlenecks. For a mechanism to be trusted, it must perform in a predictable and secure manner and not adversely affect other trusted or untrusted mechanisms. In return, these trusted components have access to more privileged services, have

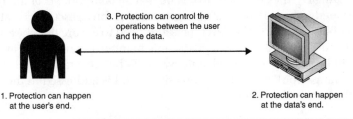

3. Protection can control the operations between the user and the data.

1. Protection can happen at the user's end.

2. Protection can happen at the data's end.

**Figure 5-15** Security can take place in three main areas.

> ## Security Architecture
>
> The security architecture is one component of a product's overall architecture and is developed to provide guidance during the design of the product. It should outline the level of assurance that is required and potential impacts that this level of security could have during the development stages and on the product overall. As the software development project moves from architecture, to design, to specifications, and then code development, the security architecture and requirements become more granular with each step.

direct access to memory, usually have higher priority when requesting CPU processing time, and have more control over system resources. So the trusted subjects and objects need to be identified and distinguished from the untrusted ones and placed into defined subsets.

## Defined Subset of Subjects and Objects

*I totally trust you. You can do whatever you want. Response: I want to leave.*

As stated previously, not all components need to be trusted and therefore not all components fall within the *trusted computing base (TCB)*. The TCB is defined as the total combination of protection mechanisms within a computer system. The TCB includes hardware, software, and firmware. These are part of the TCB because the system is sure that these components will enforce the security policy and not violate it.

The components that do fall within the TCB need to be identified and their accepted capabilities need to be defined. For example, a system that does not require a high level of trust may permit all authenticated users to access and modify all files on the computer. This subset of subjects and objects is large and the relationship between them is loose and relaxed. A system that requires a higher level of trust may permit only two subjects to access all files on a computer system, and permit only one of those subjects to actually modify all the files. This subset is much smaller and the rules being enforced are more stringent and detailed.

If developers want to develop a system that achieves an Orange Book assurance rating of D (very low), then what makes up the TCB is not much of an issue because the system will not be expected to provide a very high level of security. However, if the developers want to develop a system with an Orange Book rating of B2 or B1 (much higher than rating D), they will need to ensure that all components of the TCB carry out their tasks properly. These TCB components need to enforce strict rules that dictate how subjects and objects interact. The developers also need to ensure that these components are identified, audited, and react in a predictable manner, because these are the components that will be scrutinized, tested, and evaluated before a rating of B2 or B1 can be given. (The Orange Book is an evaluation criteria and is addressed in the section "The Orange Book" later in the chapter.)

# Trusted Computing Base

The term "trusted computing base," which originated from the Orange Book, does not address the level of security that a system provides, but rather the level of trust that a system provides, albeit from a security sense. This is because no computer system can be totally secure. The types of attacks and vulnerabilities change and evolve over time, and with enough time and resources, most attacks become successful. However, if a system meets a certain criteria, it is looked upon as providing a certain level of trust, meaning that it will react predictably in different types of situations.

The TCB does not address *only* operating system components, because a computer system is not made up of *only* an operating system. The TCB addresses hardware, software components, and firmware. Each can affect the computer's environment in a negative or positive manner, and each has a responsibility to support and enforce the security policy of that particular system. Some components and mechanisms have direct responsibilities in supporting the security policy, such as firmware that will not let a user boot a computer from a floppy disk, or the memory manager that will not let processes overwrite other processes' data. Then there are components that do not enforce the security policy but must behave properly and not violate the trust of a system. Examples of the ways in which a component could violate the system's security policy include an application that attempts to make a direct call to a piece of hardware instead of using the proper system calls through the operating system, a program that attempts to read data outside of its approved memory space, or a piece of software that does not properly release resources after use.

A TCB is usually a very abstract concept for people who are not system designers, and many books or papers do not make it any easier to fully understand what this term means. If an operating system is using a TCB, this means that the system has a hardened kernel that compartmentalizes system processes. The kernel is made up of hardware, software, and firmware, so in a sense the kernel is the TCB. But the TCB can include other components, such as trusted commands, programs, and configuration files that can directly interact with the kernel. For example, when installing a Unix system, the administrator can choose to install the TCB during the setup procedure. If the TCB is enabled, then the system has a trusted path, a trusted shell, and system integrity–checking capabilities. A *trusted path* is a communication channel between the user, or program, and the kernel. The TCB provides protection resources to ensure that this channel cannot be compromised in any way. A *trusted shell* means that someone who is working in that shell cannot "bust out of it" and other processes cannot "bust into" it.

There are several Unix commands that are part of the TCB, such as `setuid` (set process ID) and `setguid` (set process group ID). Only a privileged user, as in root, should be able to change process ID information.

Earlier operating systems (MS-DOS, Windows 3.11, and Novell Netware release 3, for example) did not have TCBs. Windows 95 has a TCB, but it can be used only while working in 32-bit mode. Windows NT was the first version of Windows that truly incorporated the idea of a TCB. As of this writing, Microsoft is using the words "Trustworthy Computing" a lot, but this is not just a Microsoft concept. Several vendors came together to develop a better TCB by agreeing to improve methods on how to protect software from being compromised. Microsoft is just the first vendor to implement it, in its Windows 2003 product. Microsoft is basically building upon its current TCB and calling it the Next-Generation Secure Computing Base (NGSCB). (It must be better, it has a longer name!) And Microsoft renamed its security kernel "nexus." How NGSCB actually works is beyond the scope of this book and the exam, but basically the operating system is doing what it is supposed to be doing, only better—better isolation between trusted and untrusted processes, better memory management, more secure I/O operations, and better software authentication mechanisms. So we are all one step closer to more secure systems and world peace.

Every operating system has specific components that would cause the system grave danger if they were compromised. The TCB provides extra layers of protection around these mechanisms to help ensure that they are *not* compromised, so that the system will always run in a safe and predictable manner.

## How Does the TCB Do Its Magic?

The processes within the TCB are the components that protect the system overall. So the developers of the operating system must make sure that these processes have their own *execution domain*. This means that they reside in ring 0, their instructions are executed in privileged state, and no less trusted processes can directly interact with them. The developers need to ensure that the operating system maintains an isolated execution domain, so that their processes cannot be compromised or tampered with. The resources that the TCB processes use must also be isolated, so that tight access control can be provided and all access requests and operations can be properly audited. So basically, the operating system tells all the other processes that they cannot play with the TCB processes and that they cannot play with the TCB's resources.

The four basic functions of the TCB are process activation, execution domain switching, memory protection, and I/O operations. We·have really covered all of these things already throughout previous sections without using this exact terminology, so here's a recap. *Process activation* deals with the activities that have to take place when a process is going to have its instructions and data processed by the CPU. As described earlier, the CPU fills its registers with information about the requesting process (program counter, base and limit addresses, user or privileged mode, etc.). A process is "activated" when its interrupt is called upon, enabling it to interact with the CPU. A process is "deactivated" when its instructions are completely executed by the CPU or when another process with a higher priority calls upon the CPU. When a process is deactivated, the CPU's registers have to be filled with new information about the new requesting process. The data that is getting switched in and out of the registers may be sensitive in nature, so the TCB components must make sure all of this is taking place securely.

For an analogy, suppose that five people all want to ask your advice at the same time. There is only one of you, so each person has a certain amount of time that they can spend with you. Person 1 gives you her papers, so that you can read through them and figure out her problem so that you can give her a proper answer. As you are reading Person 1's papers, Person 2 comes barging into the room claiming that he has an emergency. So you put Person 1's papers down on your desk and start reading Person 2's papers to figure out his problem. Eventually you have five people around you, and you can only spend five seconds with each of them at a time. As you talk to one individual, you must grab the right file from your desk. These files have sensitive information, so you have to make sure to keep all the files straight and make sure that the people cannot read one another's files. This is what the TCB and the CPU are doing as they are dealing with several different process requests at one time. Instead of reading stacks of paper, the CPU reads instructions and data on a memory segment stack.

*Execution domain switching* takes place when a process needs to call upon a process in a higher protection ring. As explained earlier, less trusted processes run in user mode and cannot carry out activities such as communicating with hardware or directly sending requests to the kernel. Therefore, a process running in user mode (ring 3) must make a request to an operating system service, which works in ring 1. The less trusted process will have its information loaded into the CPU's registers and then when the CPU sees that an operating system service has been called it switches domains and security context. This means that the information of the operating system service process is loaded into the CPU's registers and the CPU carries out those instructions in privileged mode. So, execution domain switching refers to when the CPU has to go from executing instructions in user mode to privileged mode and back. All of this has to happen properly or a less trusted process might be executed in privileged mode and have direct access to system resources.

Memory protection and I/O operations have been discussed in previous sections, so just realize that these operations are the responsibility of the components within the TCB.

The TCB is responsible for carrying out the TCB memory protection and I/O operations securely. It does this by compartmentalizing into discreet units, which are the processes that make up the kernel. This ensures that if a kernel process is compromised, it does not mean that all the processes are now under the control of the attacker.

Not every part of a system needs to be trusted. Part of evaluating the trust level of a system is to identify the architecture, security services, and assurance mechanisms that make up the TCB. During the evaluation process, the tests must show how the TCB is protected from accidental or intentional tampering and compromising activity. For systems to achieve a higher trust level rating, they must meet well-defined TCB requirements, and the details of their operational states, developing stages, testing procedures, and documentation will be reviewed with more granularity than systems that are attempting to achieve a lower trust rating.

By using specific security criteria, trust can be built into a system, evaluated, and certified. This approach can provide a measurement system for customers to use when comparing one product to another. It also gives vendors guidelines on what expectations are put upon their systems and provides a common assurance rating metric so that when one group talks about a C2 rating, everyone else understands what that term means.

The Orange Book is one of these evaluation criteria. It defines a trusted system as hardware and software that utilize measures to protect the integrity of unclassified or classified data for a range of users without violating access rights and the security policy. It looks at all protection mechanisms within a system that enforce the security policy and provide an environment that will behave in a manner expected of it. This means that each layer of the system must trust the underlying layer to perform the expected functions, provide the expected level of protection, and operate in an expected manner under many different situations. When the operating system makes calls to hardware, it anticipates that data will be returned in a specific data format and behave in a consistent and predictable manner. Applications that run on top of the operating system expect to be able to make certain system calls, receive the required data in return, and operate in a reliable and dependable environment. Users expect the hardware, operating system, and applications to perform in particular fashions and provide a certain level of functionality. For all of these actions to behave in such predicable manners, the requirements of a system must be addressed in the planning stages of development, not afterwards.

## Security Perimeter

*Now, whom do we trust? Response: Anyone inside the security perimeter.*

As stated previously, not every process and resource falls within the TCB, so some of these components fall outside of an imaginary boundary referred to as the *security perimeter*. A security perimeter is a boundary that divides the trusted from the untrusted. For the system to stay in a secure and trusted state, precise communication standards must be developed to ensure that when a component within the TCB needs to communicate with a component outside the TCB, the communication cannot expose the system to unexpected security compromises. This type of communication is handled and controlled through interfaces.

For example, a resource that is within the boundary of the TCB, or security perimeter, must not allow less trusted components access to critical system resources. The processes within the TCB must also be careful about the commands and information they accept from less trusted resources. These limitations and restrictions are built into the interfaces that permit this type of communication to take place and are the mechanisms that enforce the security perimeter. Communication between trusted components and untrusted components needs to be controlled to ensure that the system stays stable and safe.

---

 **NOTE** The TCB and security perimeter are not physical entities, but conceptual constructs used by the operating system developers to delineate between trusted and untrusted components.

---

## Reference Monitor and Security Kernel

Up to now, our computer system architecture developers have accomplished many things in developing their system. They have defined where the security mechanisms will be located (hardware, kernel, operating system, services, or programs), the processes that are within the TCB, and how the security mechanisms and processes will interact with each other. They have defined the security perimeter that separates the trusted and untrusted components. They have developed proper interfaces for these entities to communicate securely. Now they need to develop and implement a mechanism that ensures that the subjects that access objects have been given the necessary permissions to do so. This means the developers need to develop and implement a reference monitor and security kernel.

The *reference monitor* is an abstract machine that mediates all access subjects have to objects, both to ensure that the subjects have the necessary access rights and to protect the objects from unauthorized access and destructive modification. For a system to achieve a higher level of trust, it must require subjects (programs, users, or processes) to be fully authorized prior to accessing an object (file, program, or resource). A subject must not be allowed to use a requested resource until the subject has proven that it has been granted access privileges to use the requested object. The reference monitor is an access control concept, not an actual physical component, which is why it is normally referred to as the "reference monitor concept" or an "abstract machine."

The *security kernel* is made up of hardware, software, and firmware components that fall within the TCB and implements and enforces the reference monitor concept. The security kernel mediates all access and functions between subjects and objects. The security kernel is the core of the TCB and is the most commonly used approach to building trusted computing systems. There are three main requirements of the security kernel:

- It must provide isolation for the processes carrying out the reference monitor concept, and the processes must be tamperproof.

- It must be invoked for every access attempt and must be impossible to circumvent. Thus, the security kernel must be implemented in a complete and foolproof way.

- It must be small enough to be able to be tested and verified in a complete and comprehensive manner.

These are the requirements of the reference monitor; therefore, they are the requirements of the components that provide and enforce the reference monitor concept—the security kernel.

These issues work in the abstract but are implemented in the physical world of hardware devices and software code. The assurance that the components are enforcing the abstract idea of the reference monitor is proved through testing and functionality.

 **NOTE** The reference monitor is a concept in which an abstract machine mediates all access to objects by subjects. The security kernel is the hardware, firmware, and software of a TCB that implements this concept. The TCB is the totality of protection mechanisms within a computer system that work together to enforce a security policy. The TCB contains the security kernel and all other security protection mechanisms.

The following is a quick analogy to show you the relationship between the processes that make up the kernel, the kernel itself, and the reference monitor concept. Individuals make up a society. The individuals represent the processes, and the society represents the kernel. For a society to have a certain standard of living, its members need to interact in specific ways, which is why we have laws. The laws represent the reference monitor, which enforces proper activity. Each individual is expected to stay within the bounds of the laws and act in specific ways so that society as a whole is not adversely affected and the standard of living is not threatened. The components within a system must stay within the bounds of the reference monitor's laws so that they will not adversely affect other components and threaten the security of the system.

### References

- **"Rationale Behind the Evaluation Classes"** www.kernel.org/pub/linux/libs/ security/Orange-Linux/refs/Orange/OrangeI-II-6.html
- **The Reference Monitor Concept** http://citeseer.ist.psu.edu/299300.html
- **Implementing Complete Mediation** www.cs.cornell.edu/html/cs513-sp99/ NL05.html

### Security Policy

As previously stated, the TCB contains components that directly enforce the security policy, but what is a security policy? A security policy is a set of rules and practices that dictates how sensitive information and resources are managed, protected, and distributed. A security policy expresses exactly what the security level should be by setting the goals of what the security mechanisms are supposed to accomplish. This is an important element that has a major role in defining the design of the system. The security policy is a foundation for the specifications of a system and provides the baseline for evaluating a system.

Chapter 3 examined security policies in depth, but those policies were directed toward the company itself. The security policies being addressed here are for operating systems, devices, and applications. The different policies are similar but have different targets: an organization as opposed to an individual computer system.

A system provides trust by fulfilling and enforcing the security policy and oversees the communication between subjects and objects. The policy must indicate which subjects can access individual objects, and which actions are acceptable and unacceptable. The security policy provides the framework for the system's security architecture.

For a system to provide an acceptable level of trust, it must be based on an architecture that provides the capabilities to protect itself from untrusted processes, intentional or accidental compromises, and attacks at different layers of the system. A majority of the trust ratings obtained through formal evaluations require a defined subset of subjects and objects, explicit domains, and the isolation of processes so that their access can be controlled and the activities performed on them can be audited.

Let's regroup. We know that a system's trust is defined by how it enforces its own security policy. When a system is tested against a specific criteria, a rating is assigned to the system and this rating is used by customers, vendors, and the computing society as a whole. The criteria will determine if the security policy is being properly supported and enforced. The security policy lays out the rules and practices pertaining to how a system will manage, protect, and allow access to sensitive resources. The reference monitor is a concept that says all subjects must have proper authorization to access objects, and this concept is implemented by the security kernel. The security kernel comprises all the resources that supervise system activity in accordance with the system's security policy and is part of the operating system that controls access to system resources. For the security kernel to work correctly, the individual processes need to be isolated from each other and domains need to be defined to dictate which objects are available to which subjects.

Security policies that prevent information from flowing from a high security level to a lower security level are called *multilevel security policies*. These types of policies permit a subject to access an object only if the subject's security level is higher than or equal to the object's classification.

As previously stated, the concepts covered in the previous sections are abstract ideas that will be manifested in physical hardware components, firmware, software code, and activities through designing, building, and implementing a system. These ideas are like abstract goals and dreams we would like to accomplish, which are obtained by our physical hard work and discipline.

## Least Privilege

Once resources and processes are isolated properly, *least privilege* needs to be enforced. This means that a process has no more privileges than necessary to be able to fulfill its functions. Only processes that *need* to carry out critical system functions should be allowed to, and other, less privileged processes should call upon the more privileged processes to carry out these types of activities when necessary. This type of indirect activity protects the system from poorly written or misbehaving code. Processes should possess a level of privilege only as long as they really need it. If a process needs to have its status elevated so that it can interact directly with a system resource, as soon as its tasks are complete, the process's status should be dropped to a lower privilege to ensure that another mechanism cannot use it to adversely affect the system. Only processes that need complete system privileges are located in the kernel; other, less privileged processes call upon them to process sensitive or delicate operations.

As an example of least privilege access control, the system backup program may have read access on the files, but it does not need to be able to modify the files. Similarly, the restore program would be allowed to write files to the disk, but not to read them.

# Security Models

An important concept in the design and analysis of secure systems is the security model, because it incorporates the security policy that should be enforced in the system. A model is a symbolic representation of a policy. It maps the desires of the policymakers into a set of rules that a computer system must follow.

The reason this chapter has repeatedly mentioned the security policy and its importance is that it is an abstract term that represents the objectives and goals a system must meet and accomplish to be deemed secure and acceptable. How do we get from an abstract security policy to the point at which an administrator is able to uncheck a box

> ### Relationship Between a Security Policy and a Security Model
>
> If someone tells you to live a healthy and responsible life, this is a very broad, vague, and abstract notion. So when you ask this person how this is accomplished, they outline the things you should and should not do (do not harm others, do not lie, eat your vegetables, and brush your teeth). The security policy provides the abstract goals, and the security model provides the dos and don'ts necessary to fulfill these goals.

on the GUI to disallow David from accessing configuration files on his system? There are many complex steps in between that take place during the system's design and development.

A security model maps the abstract goals of the policy to information system terms by specifying explicit data structures and techniques that are necessary to enforce the security policy. A security model is usually represented in mathematics and analytical ideas, which are then mapped to system specifications, and then developed by programmers through programming code. So we have a policy that encompasses security goals like "each subject must be authorized to access each object." The security model takes this requirement and provides the necessary mathematical formulas, relationships, and structure to be followed to accomplish this goal. From there, specifications are developed per operating system type (Unix, Windows, Macintosh, and so on), and individual vendors can decide how they are going to implement mechanisms that meet these necessary specifications.

So in a very general and simplistic example, if a security policy states that subjects need to be authorized to access objects, the security model would provide the mathematical relationships and formulas explaining how $x$ can access $y$ only through the outlined specific methods. Specifications are then developed to provide a bridge to what this means in a computing environment and how it maps to components and mechanisms that need to be coded and developed. The developers then write the program code to produce the mechanisms that provide a way for a system to use ACLs and give administrators some degree of control. This mechanism presents the network administrator with a GUI that enables the administrator to choose (via check boxes, for example) which subjects can access what objects, to be able to set this configuration within the operating system. This is a rudimentary example, because security models can be very complex, but it is used to demonstrate the relationship between the security policy and the security model.

Some security models, such as the Bell-LaPadula model, enforce rules to provide confidentiality protection. Other models, such as the Biba model, enforce rules to provide integrity protection. Formal security models, such as Bell-LaPadula and Biba, are used to provide high assurance in security. Informal models, such as Clark-Wilson, are used more as a framework to describe how security policies should be expressed and executed.

A security policy outlines goals without regard to how they will be accomplished. A model is a framework that gives the policy form and solves security access problems for particular situations. Several security models have been developed to enforce security policies. The following sections provide overviews of each model.

## Formal Models

Using models in software development has not become as popular as once imagined, primarily because vendors are under pressure to get products to market as soon as possible. Using formal models takes more time during the architectural phase of development, extra time that many vendors feel they cannot afford. Formal models are definitely used in the development of systems that cannot allow errors or security breaches, such as air traffic control systems, spacecraft software, railway signaling systems, military classified systems, and medical control systems. This does not mean that these models, or portions of them, are not used in industry products, but rather that industry vendors do not always follow these models in the purely formal and mathematical way that the models were designed for.

## State Machine Models

*No matter what state I am in, I am always safe.*

In *state machine models*, to verify the security of a system, the state is used, which means that all current permissions and all current instances of subjects accessing objects must be captured. Maintaining the state of a system deals with each subject's association with objects. If the subjects can access objects only by means that are concurrent with the security policy, the system is secure. State machines have provided a basis for important security models. A state of a system is a snapshot of a system at one moment of time. There are many activities that can alter this state, which are referred to as *state transitions*. The developers of an operating system that will implement the state machine model need to look at all the different state transitions that are possible and assess whether a system that starts up in a secure state can be put into an insecure state by any of these events. If all of the activities that are allowed to happen in the system do not compromise the system and put it into an insecure state, then the system executes a secure state machine model.

The state machine model is used to describe the behavior of a system to different inputs. It provides mathematical constructs that represent sets (subjects and objects) and sequences. When an object accepts an input, this modifies a state variable. A simplistic example of a state variable is (Name, Value), as shown in Figure 5-16. This variable is part of the operating system's instruction set. When this variable is called upon to be used, it can be populated with (Color, Red) from the input of a user or program. Let's say that the user enters a different value, so now the variable is (Color, Blue). This is a simplistic example of a state transition. Some state transitions are this simplistic, but the complexity comes in when the system has to decide if this transition should be allowed. To allow this transition, the object's security attributes and the access rights of the subject must be reviewed and allowed by the operating system.

Developers who implement the state machine model must identify all the initial states (default variable values) and outline how these values can be changed (inputs that will be accepted) so that the various number of final states (resulting values) still ensure that the system is safe. The outline of how these values can be changed are often implemented through condition statements: "if *condition* then *update*."

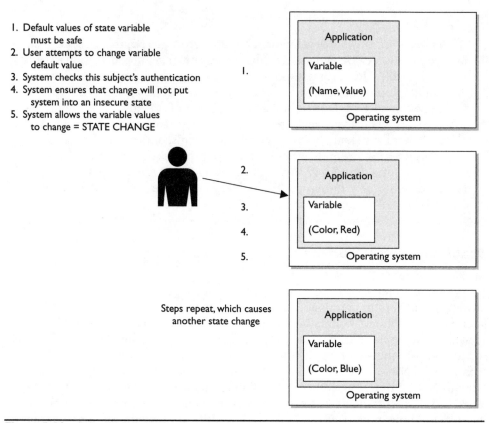

1. Default values of state variable
   must be safe
2. User attempts to change variable
   default value
3. System checks this subject's authentication
4. System ensures that change will not put
   system into an insecure state
5. System allows the variable values
   to change = STATE CHANGE

1.

2.

3.

4.

5.

Steps repeat, which causes
another state change

Application

Variable

(Name, Value)

Operating system

Application

Variable

(Color, Red)

Operating system

Application

Variable

(Color, Blue)

Operating system

**Figure 5-16** A simplistic example of a state change.

A system that has employed a state machine model will be in a secure state in each and every instance of its existence. It will boot up into a secure state, execute commands and transactions securely, allow subjects to access resources only in secure states, and shut down and fail in a secure state. Failing in a secure state is extremely important. It is imperative that if anything unsafe takes place, the system must be able to "save itself" and not make itself vulnerable. When an operating system displays an error message to the user or reboots or freezes, it is executing a safety measure. The operating system has experienced something that is deemed illegal and it cannot take care of the situation itself, so to make sure it does not stay in this insecure state, it reacts in one of these fashions. So if an application or system freezes on you, know that it is simply the system trying to protect itself and your data.

There are several points to consider when developing a product that uses a state machine model. Initially, the developer must define what and where the state variables are. In a computer environment, all data variables could independently be considered state variables, and an inappropriate change to one could conceivably change or corrupt the system or another process's activities. Next, the developer must define a secure state for each state variable. The next step is to define and identify the allowable state transition functions. These functions will describe the allowable changes that can be made to the state variables.

After the state transition functions are defined, they must be tested to verify that the overall machine state will not be compromised and that these transition functions will keep the integrity of the system (computer, data, program, or process) intact at all times.

## Bell-LaPadula Model

*I don't want anyone to know my secrets. Response: We need Mr. Bell and Mr. LaPadula in here then.*

In the 1970s, the U.S. military used time-sharing mainframe systems and was concerned about the security of these systems and leakage of classified information. The *Bell-LaPadula model* was developed to address these concerns. It was the first mathematical model of a multilevel security policy used to define the concept of a secure state machine and modes of access and outlined rules of access. Its development was funded by the U.S. government to provide a framework for computer systems that would be used to store and process sensitive information. The model's main goal is to prevent secret information from being accessed in an unauthorized manner.

A system that employs the Bell-LaPadula model is called a *multilevel security system* because users with different clearances use the system, and the system processes data with different classifications. The level at which information is classified determines the handling procedures that should be used. The Bell-LaPadula model is a state machine model that enforces the *confidentiality* aspects of access control. A matrix and security levels are used to determine if subjects can access different objects. The subject's clearance is compared to the object's classification and then specific rules are applied to control how subject-to-object interactions can take place.

This model uses subjects, objects, access operations (read, write, and read/write), and security levels. Subjects and objects can reside at different security levels and will have relationships and rules dictating the acceptable activities between them. This model, when properly implemented and enforced, has been mathematically proven to provide a very secure and effective operating system. It is an information-flow security model also, which means that information does not flow in an insecure manner.

The Bell-LaPadula model is a subject-to-object model. An example would be how you (subject) could read a data element (object) from a specific database and write data into that database. The Bell-LaPadula model focuses on ensuring that subjects are properly authenticated—by having the necessary security clearance, need to know, and formal access approval—before accessing an object.

Three main rules are used and enforced in the Bell-LaPadula model: the simple security rule, the *-property (star property) rule, and the strong star property rule. The *simple security rule* states that a subject at a given security level cannot *read* data that resides at a higher security level. For example, if Bob is given the security clearance of secret, this rule states that he cannot read data classified as top secret. If the organization wanted Bob to be able to read top-secret data, it would have given him that clearance in the first place.

The *\*-property rule* (star property rule) states that a subject in a given security level cannot *write* information to a lower security level. The simple security rule is referred to as the "no read up" rule, and the \*-property rule is referred to the as the "no write down" rule, as shown in Figure 5-17. The third rule, the *strong star property rule*, states that a subject that has read and write capabilities can only perform those functions at the same security level, nothing higher and nothing lower. So, for a subject to be able to read and write to an object, the clearance and classification must be equal.

These three rules indicate what states the system can go into. Remember that a state is the values of the variables in the software at a snapshot in time. If a subject has performed a read operation on an object at a lower security level, the subject now has a variable that is populated with the data that was read, or copied into its variable. If a subject has written to an object at a higher security level, the subject has modified a variable within that object's domain.

 **NOTE** In access control terms, the word *dominate* means to be higher than or equal to. So if you see a statement such as "A subject can only perform a read operation if the access class of the subject dominates the access class of an object," this just means that the subject must have a clearance that is higher than or equal to the object.

The state of a system changes as different operations take place. The Bell-LaPadula model defines a secure state, meaning a secure computing environment and the allowed actions, which are security-preserving operations. This means that the model provides a secure state and only permits operations that will keep the system within a secure state and not let it enter into an insecure state. So if 100 people access 2000 objects in a day using this one system, this system is put through a lot of work and several complex activities have to take place. However, at the end of the day, the system is just as secure as it was at the beginning of the day. This is the definition of the *Basic Secu-*

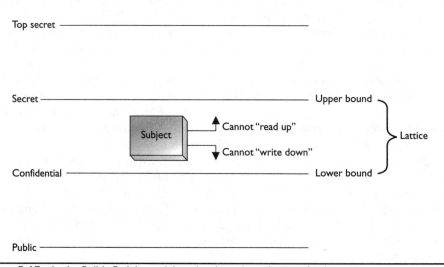

**Figure 5-17** In the Bell-LaPadula model, each subject has a lattice of rights.

*rity Theorem* used in computer science, which states that if a system initializes in a secure state and all allowed state transitions are secure, then every subsequent state will be secure no matter what inputs occur.

**NOTE** The *tranquility principle*, which is also used in this model, means that subjects and objects cannot change their security levels once they have been instantiated (created).

An important thing to note is that the Bell-LaPadula model was developed to make sure secrets stay secret; thus, it provides and addresses confidentiality only. This model does not address integrity of the data the system maintains—only who can and cannot access the data and what operations can be carried out.

**NOTE** Ensuring that information does not flow from a higher security level to a lower level is referred to as *controlling unauthorized downgrading of information*, which would take place through a "write down" operation. An actual compromise occurs if and when a user at a lower security level reads this data.

## So What Does This Mean and Why?

Chapter 4 discussed mandatory access control (MAC) systems versus discretionary access control (DAC) systems. All MAC systems are based on the Bell-LaPadula model, because it allows for multilevel security to be integrated into the code. Subjects and objects are assigned labels. The subject's label contains its clearance label (top secret, secret, or confidential) and the object's label contains its classification label (top secret, secret, or confidential). When a subject attempts to access an object, the system compares the subject's clearance label and the object's classification label and looks at a matrix to see if this is a legal and secure activity. In our scenario, it is a perfectly fine activity, and the subject is given access to the object. Now, if the subject's clearance label is top secret and the object's classification label is secret, the subject cannot write to this object, because of the *-property rule, which makes sure that subjects cannot accidentally or intentionally share confidential information by writing to an object at a lower

---

### Rules to Know

The main rules of the Bell-LaPadula model that you need to understand are

- **Simple security rule** A subject cannot read data within an object that resides at a higher security level ("No read up" rule).

- ***- property rule** A subject cannot write to an object at a lower security level ("No write down" rule).

- **Strong star property rule** For a subject to be able to read and write to an object, the subject's clearance and the object's classification must be equal.

security level. As an example, suppose that a busy and clumsy general (who has top secret clearance) in the army opens up a briefing letter (which has a secret classification) that will go to all clerks at all bases around the world. He attempts to write that the United States is attacking Cuba. The Bell-LaPadula model will come into action and not permit this general to write this information to this type of file because his clearance is higher than that of the memo.

Likewise, if a nosey military staff clerk tried to read a memo that was available only to generals and above, the Bell-LaPadula model would stop this activity. The clerk's clearance is lower than that of the object, the memo, and this violates the simple security rule of the model. It is all about keeping secrets secret.

 **NOTE** It is important that MAC operating systems and MAC databases follow these rules. In Chapter 11, we will look at how databases can follow these rules by the use of polyinstantiation.

## Biba Model

The *Biba model* was developed after the Bell-LaPadula model. It is a state machine model and is very similar to the Bell-LaPadula model. Biba addresses the *integrity* of data within applications. The Bell-LaPadula model uses a lattice of security levels (top secret, secret, sensitive, and so on). These security levels were developed mainly to ensure that sensitive data was only available to authorized individuals. The Biba model is not concerned with security levels and confidentiality, so it does not base access decisions upon this type of lattice. The Biba model uses a lattice of integrity levels.

If implemented and enforced properly, the Biba model prevents data from any *integrity* level from flowing to a higher integrity level. Biba has two main rules to provide this type of protection:

- **\*-integrity axiom**   A subject cannot write data to an object at a higher integrity level (referred to as "no write up").
- **Simple integrity axiom**   A subject cannot read data from a lower integrity level (referred to as "no read down").

The name "simple integrity axiom" might sound a little goofy, but this rule protects the subject and data at a higher integrity level from being corrupted by data at a lower integrity level. This is all about trusting the source of the information. Another way to look at it is that trusted data is "clean" data and untrusted data (from a lower integrity level) is "dirty" data. Dirty data should not be mixed with clean data, because that could ruin the integrity of the clean data.

The simple integrity axiom applies not only to subjects creating the data, but also to processes. A process of lower integrity should not be writing to trusted data of a higher integrity level. The areas of the different integrity levels are compartmentalized within the application that is based on the Biba model.

An analogy would be if you were writing an article for *The New York Times* about the security trends over the last year, the amount of money businesses lost, and the cost/benefit ratio of implementing firewalls, IDSs, and vulnerability scanners. You do not want to get your data and numbers from any old web site without knowing how those figures were calculated and the sources of the information. Your article (data at a higher integrity level) can be compromised if mixed with unfounded information from a bad source (data at a lower integrity level).

When you are first learning about the Bell-LaPadula and Biba models, they may seem very similar, and the reasons for their differences may be somewhat confusing. The Bell-LaPadula model was written for the U.S. government, and the government is very paranoid about leakage of its secret information. In its model, a user cannot write to a lower level because that user might let out some secrets. Similarly, a user at a lower level cannot read anything at a higher level because that user might learn some secrets. However, not everyone is so worried about confidentiality and has such big, important secrets to protect. The commercial industry is more concerned about the *integrity* of its data. An accounting firm is more worried about keeping its numbers straight and making sure decimal points are not dropped or extra zeros are not added in a process carried out by an application. The accounting firm is more concerned about the integrity of this data and is usually under little threat of someone trying to steal these numbers, so the firm would use software that employs the Biba model. Of course, the accounting firm does not look for the name Biba on the back of a product or make sure it is in the design of its application. Which model to use is something that was decided upon and implemented when the application was being designed. The assurance ratings are what consumers use to determine if a system is right for them. So, even if the accountants are using an application that uses the Biba model, they would not necessarily know (and we're not going to tell them).

If you don't have enough rules to understand so far, here's another one. The *invocation property* in the Biba model states that a subject cannot invoke (call upon) a subject at a higher integrity level. Well, how is this different from the other two Biba rules? The *-integrity axiom (no write up) dictates how subjects can *modify* objects. The simple integrity axiom (no read down) dictates how subjects can *read* objects. The invocation property dictates how one subject can communicate with and initialize other subjects at run time. An example of a subject invoking another subject is when a process sends a request to a procedure to carry out some type of task. So the rules may seem similar, but they really lay down the parameters for different types of activities that can take place within an application.

## Bell-LaPadula vs. Biba

The Bell-LaPadula model is used to provide *confidentiality*. The Biba model is used to provide *integrity*. The Bell-LaPadula and Biba models are informational flow models because they are most concerned about data flowing from one level to another. Bell-LaPadula uses security levels and Biba uses integrity levels. It is important for CISSP test takers to know the rules of Biba and Bell-LaPadula. Their rules sound very similar, simple and *rules—one writing one way and one reading another way. A tip for how to remember them is that if the word "simple" is used, the rule is talking about reading. If the rule uses * or "star," it is talking about writing. So now you just need to remember the reading and writing directions per model.

## References

- Module 5, "Security Policies and Security Models"   www.radium.ncsc.mil/ tpep/library/ramp-modules/mod_05.pdf
- **Security Models**   www.iwar.org.uk/comsec/resources/security-lecture/ showb1a7.html
- **Course study materials for Introduction to Security, University of Cambridge, Dr. Markus Kuhn, principle lecturer (academic year 2003–2004)**   www.cl.cam.ac.uk/Teaching/2003/IntroSecurity/slides.pdf
- **Chapter 3.3, "Models of OS Protection," by Fred Cohen**   www.all.net/ books/ip/Chap3-3.html

## Clark-Wilson Model

The *Clark-Wilson model* was developed after Biba and takes some different approaches to protecting the integrity of information. This model uses the following elements:

- **Users**   Active agents
- **Transformation procedures (TPs)**   Programmed abstract operations, such as read, write, and modify
- **Constrained data items (CDIs)**   Can be manipulated only by TPs
- **Unconstrained data items (UDIs)**   Can be manipulated by users via primitive read and write operations
- **Integrity verification procedures (IVPs)**   Run periodically to check the consistency of CDIs with external reality

Although this list may look overwhelming, it is really quite straightforward. When an application uses the Clark-Wilson model, it separates data into one subset that needs to be highly protected, which is referred to as a constrained data item (CDI) and another subset that does not require a high level of protection, which is called an unconstrained data item (UDI). Users cannot modify critical data (CDI) directly. Instead, the subject (user) must be authenticated to a piece of software, and the software procedures (TPs) will carry out the operations on behalf of the user. For example, when Kathy needs to update information held within her company's database, she will not be allowed to do so without a piece of software controlling these activities. First, Kathy must authenticate to a program, which is acting as a front end for the database, and then the program will control what Kathy can and cannot do to the information in the database. This is referred to as *access triple*: subject (user), program (TP), and object (CDI). A user cannot modify CDI without using a TP.

So, Kathy is going to input data, which is supposed to overwrite some original data in the database. The software (TP) has to make sure that this type of activity is secure and will carry out the write procedures for Kathy. Kathy (and any type of subject) is not trusted enough to manipulate objects directly.

The CDI must have its integrity protected by the TPs. The UDI does not require such a high level of protection. For example, if Kathy did her banking online, the data on her bank's servers and databases would be split into UDI and CDI categories. The CDI category would contain her banking account information, which needs to be highly protected. The UDI data could be her customer profile, which she can update as needed. TPs would not be required when Kathy needed to update her UDI information.

In some cases, a system may need to change UDI data into CDI data. For example, when Kathy updates her customer profile via the web site to show her new correct address, this information will need to be moved into the banking software that is responsible for mailing out bank account information. The bank would not want Kathy to interact directly with that banking software, so a piece of software (TP) is responsible for copying that data and updating this customer's mailing address. At this stage, the TP is changing the state of the UDI data to CDI. These concepts are shown in Figure 5-18.

Remember that this is an integrity model, so it must have something that ensures that specific integrity rules are being carried out. This is the job of the IVP. The IVP ensures that all critical data (CDI) follows the application's defined integrity rules. What usually turns people's minds into spaghetti when they are first learning about models is that models are theoretical and abstract. Thus, when they ask the common question, "What are these defined integrity rules that the CDI must comply with?" they are told, "Whatever the vendor chooses them to be."

A model is made up of constructs, mathematical formulas, and other PhD kinds of stuff. The model provides the framework that can be used to build a certain characteristic into software (confidentiality, integrity, and so on). So the model does not stipulate what integrity rules the IVP must enforce; it just provides the framework, and the

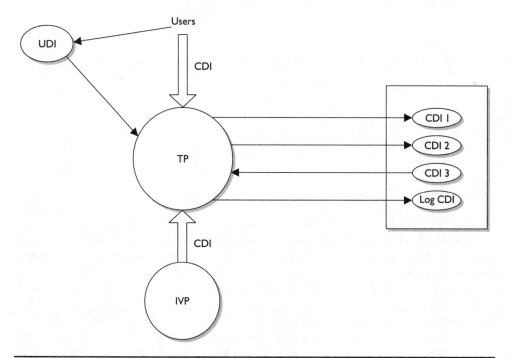

**Figure 5-18**   Subjects cannot modify CDI without using TP.

vendor chooses the integrity rules. The vendor implements integrity rules that its customer base needs the most. So if a vendor is developing an application for a financial institution, the UDI could be customer profiles that they are allowed to update and the CDI could be the bank account information, usually held on a mainframe. The UDI data does not need to be as highly protected and can be located on the same system or another system. A user can have access to UDI data without the use of a TP, but when the user needs to access CDI, they must use TP. So the vendor who develops the product will determine what type of data is considered UDI and what type of data is CDI and develop the TPs to control and orchestrate how the software enforces the integrity of the CDI values.

In a banking application, the IVP would ensure that the CDI represents the correct value. For example, if Kathy has $2000 in her account and then deposits $50, the CDI for her account should now have a value of $2050. The IVP ensures the consistency of the data. So after Kathy carries out this transaction and the IVP validates the integrity of the CDI (new bank account value is correct), then the CDI is considered to be in a *consistent state*. TPs are the only components that are allowed to modify the state of the CDIs. In our example, TPs would be software procedures that carry out deposit, withdraw, and transfer functionalities. Using TPs to modify CDIs is referred to as a **well-formed transaction**.

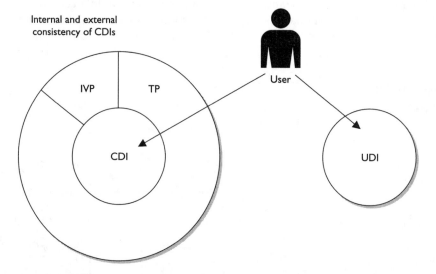

A well-formed transaction is a series of operations that are carried out to transfer the data from one consistent state to the other. If Kathy transfers money from her checking account to savings account, this transaction is made up of two operations: subtract money from one account and add it to a different account. By making sure that the new values in her checking and savings accounts are accurate and their integrity is intact, the IVP maintains internal and external consistency. The Clark-Wilson model also outlines how to incorporate **separation of duties** into the architecture of an application. If we follow our same example of banking software, if a customer needs to withdraw over $10,000, the application may require a supervisor to log in and authenticate this transaction. This is a countermeasure to potential fraudulent activities. The model provides the rules that the developers must follow to properly implement and enforce separation of duties through software procedures.

## Goals of Integrity Models

The following are the three main goals of integrity models:

- Prevent unauthorized users from making modifications

- Prevent authorized users from making improper modifications (separation of duties)

- Maintain internal and external consistency (well-formed transaction)

Clark-Wilson addresses each of these goals in its model. Biba only addresses the first goal.

Internal and external consistency is provided by the IVP, which ensures that what is stored in the system as CDI properly maps to the input value that modified its state. So if Kathy has $2500 in her account and she withdraws $2000, the resulting value in the CDI is $500.

To summarize, the Clark-Wilson model enforces the three goals of integrity by using access triple (subject, software [TP], object), separation of duties, and auditing. This model enforces integrity by using well-formed transactions (through access triple) and separation of user duties.

 **NOTE**   The access control matrix was covered in Chapter 4. This is another commonly used model in operating systems and applications.

## Information Flow Model

*Now, which way is the information flowing in this system? Response: Not to you.*

The Bell-LaPadula model focuses on preventing information from flowing from a high security level to a low security level. The Biba model focuses on preventing information from flowing from a low integrity level to a high integrity level. Both of these models were built upon the *information flow model.* Information flow models can deal with any kind of information flow, not only from one security (or integrity) level to another.

In the information flow model, data is thought of as being held in individual and discreet compartments. In the Bell-LaPadula model, these compartments are based on security levels. Remember that MAC systems (which you learned about in Chapter 4) are based on the Bell-LaPadula model. MAC systems use labels on each subject and object. The subject's label indicates the subject's clearance and need to know. The object's label indicates the object's classification and categories. If you are in the army and have a top-secret clearance, this does not mean that you can access all of the army's top-secret information. Information is *compartmentalized,* based on two factors—classification and need to know. Your clearance has to dominate the object's classification and your security profile must contain one of the categories listed in the object's label, which enforces need to know. So Bell-LaPadula is an information flow model that ensures that information cannot flow from one compartment to another in a way that threatens the confidentiality of the data. Biba compartmentalizes data based on integrity levels. It is an information flow model that controls information flow in a way that is intended to protect the integrity of the most trusted information.

How can information flow within a system? The answer is *many* ways. Subjects can access files. Processes can access memory segments. When data is moved from the hard drive's swap space into memory, information flows. Data is moved into and out of registers on a CPU. Data is moved into different cache memory storage devices. Data is written to the hard drive, thumb drive, CD-ROM drive, and so on. Properly controlling all of these ways of how information flows can be a very complex task. This is why the information flow model exists—to help architects and developers make sure that their software does not allow information to flow in a way that can put the system or data in danger. One way that the information flow model provides this type of protection is by ensuring that covert channels do not exist in the code.

## Covert Channels

*I have my decoder ring, cape, and pirate's hat on. I will communicate to my spy buddies with this tribal drum and a whistle.*

A *covert channel* is a way for an entity to receive information in an unauthorized manner. It is an information flow that is not controlled by a security mechanism. This type of information path was not developed for communication; thus, the system does not properly protect this path, because the developers never envisioned information being passed in this way. Receiving information in this manner clearly violates the system's security policy.

The channel to transfer this unauthorized data is the result of one of the following conditions:

- Oversight in the development of the product
- Improper implementation of access controls
- Existence of a shared resource between the two entities
- Installation of a Trojan horse

### Other Types of Covert Channels

Although we are looking at covert channels within programming code, covert channels can be used in the outside world as well. Let's say that you are going to attend one of my lectures. Before the lecture begins, you and I agree on a way of communicating that no one else in the audience will understand. I tell you that if I twiddle a pen between my fingers in my right hand, that means there will be a quiz at the end of class. If I twiddle a pen between my fingers in my left hand, there will be no quiz. It is a covert channel, because this is not a normal way of communicating and it is secretive. (In this scenario, I would twiddle the pen in both hands to confuse you and make you stay after class to take the quiz all by yourself. Shame on you for wanting to be forewarned about a quiz!)

There are two types of covert channels: timing and storage. In a *covert timing channel*, one process relays information to another by modulating its use of system resources. The modulation of system resources may entail accessing the hard drive or using excessive CPU cycles. For example, if one process writes to the hard drive 30 times within 30 seconds, this could mean something to another process that is programmed to look for this type of activity. The second process may watch for this "signal" and, once it receives it, carry out whatever evil activity it is programmed to do. You can think of it as a type of Morse code, but with the use of some type of system resource.

Covert channel

In a *covert storage channel*, one process writes data to a storage location and another process directly, or indirectly, reads it. The problem occurs when the processes are at different security levels and therefore are not supposed to be sharing sensitive data. For example, suppose that an attacker figures out that two processes with different trust levels can both view the pagefile.sys file. Process 1 writes some type of confidential information to the pagefile.sys file, and the attacker can make process 2 read it. This would go against the information flow rules of the system and directly negate the security policy.

Information flow models produce rules on how to ensure that covert channels do not exist. But there are many ways that information flows within a system, so identifying and rooting out covert channels is usually more difficult than one would think at first glance.

**NOTE** An overt channel is a channel of communication that was developed specifically for communication purposes. Processes should be communicating through overt channels, not covert channels.

**Countermeasures** Because all operating systems have some type of covert channels, it is not always feasible to get rid of them all. The number of acceptable covert channels usually depends on the assurance rating of a system. A system that has an Orange Book rating of B2 has fewer covert channels than a C1 system, because a B2 rating represents a higher assurance level of providing a particular protection level when compared to the C1 rating. There is not much a user can do to counteract these channels; instead, the channels must be addressed when the system is constructed and developed.

**NOTE** The Orange Book and its ratings are fully covered later in the section "The Orange Book."

In the Orange Book, covert channels in operating systems are not addressed until the security level B2 and above because these are the systems that would be holding data sensitive enough for others to go through all the necessary trouble to access data in this fashion.

## References

- "Secure Databases: An Analysis of Clark-Wilson Model in a Database Environment," by Xiaocheng Ge, Fiona Polack, and Régine Laleau www-users.cs.york.ac.uk/~fiona/PUBS/CAiSE04.pdf

- "Access Control: Theory and Practice"  www.cs.purdue.edu/homes/ninghui/courses/Fall03/lectures/lecture11_6.pdf

- "New Thinking About Information Technology Security," by Marshall D. Abrams, PhD and Michael V. Joyce (first published in *Computers & Security*, Vol. 14, No. 1, pp. 57–68)  www.acsac.org/secshelf/papers/new_thinking.pdf

### Noninterference Model

*Stop touching me. Stop touching me. You are interfering with me!*

Multilevel security properties can be expressed in many ways, one being *noninterference*. This concept is implemented to ensure that any actions that take place at a higher security level do not affect, or interfere with, actions that take place at a lower level. This type of model does not concern itself with the flow of data, but rather with what a subject knows about the state of the system. So if an entity at a higher security level performs an action, it cannot change the state for the entity at the lower level.

If a lower-level entity was aware of a certain activity that took place by an entity at a higher level and the state of the system changed for this lower-level entity, the entity might be able to deduce too much information about the activities of the higher state, which in turn is a way of leaking information.

Users at a lower security level should not be aware of the commands executed by users at a higher level and should not be affected by those commands in any way.

Let's say that Tom and Kathy are both working on a multilevel mainframe at the same time. Tom has the security clearance of secret and Kathy has the security clearance of top secret. Since this is a central mainframe, the terminal Tom is working at has the context of secret, and Kathy is working at her own terminal, which has a context of top secret. This model states that nothing that Kathy does at her terminal should directly or indirectly affect Tom's domain (available resources and working environment). So whatever commands she executes or whichever resources she interacts with should not affect Tom's experience of working with the mainframe in any way. This sounds simple enough, until you actually understand what this model is *really* saying.

It seems very logical and straightforward that when Kathy executes a command, it should not affect Tom's terminal. But the real intent of this model is to address covert channels and inference attacks. The model looks at the shared resources that the different users of a system will use and tries to identify how information can be passed from a process working at a higher security clearance to a process working at a lower security clearance. Since Tom and Kathy are working on the same system at the same time, they will most likely have to share some type of resources. So the model is made up of rules to ensure that Kathy cannot pass data to Tom through covert storage or timing channels.

The other security breach that this model addresses is the inference attack. An *inference attack* occurs when someone has access to some type of information and can infer (or guess) something that he does not have the clearance level or authority to know. For example, let's say that Tom is working on a file that contains information about supplies that are being sent to Russia. He closes out of that file and one hour later attempts to open the same file. During this time, this file's classification has been elevated to top secret, so when Tom attempts to access it, he is denied. Tom can infer that some type of top-secret mission is getting ready to take place with Russia. He does not have clearance to know this, thus it would be an inference attack or "leaking information." (Inference attacks are further explained in Chapter 11.)

## Lattice Model

A lattice is a mathematical construct that is built upon the notion of a group. The most common definition of the **lattice model** is "a structure consisting of a finite partially ordered set together with least upper and greatest lower bound operators on the set." Further explanation of this statement is usually shown in the following type of representation:

Let $S$ be a set and $\leq$ be a relation on $S$ that satisfies

- $\forall s \in S : s \leq s$ (reflexive)

- $\forall s, t \in S : (s \leq t) \wedge (t \leq s) \Rightarrow s = t$ (antisymmetric)

- $\forall s, t, u \in S : (s \leq t) \wedge (t \leq u) \Rightarrow s \leq u$ (transitivity)

- $\forall s, t \in S : \exists u \in S, u = lub\ (s, t)$ (least upper bound)

- $\forall s, t \in S : \exists w \in S, w = glb\ (s, t)$ (greatest lower bound)

There are two things wrong with this type of explanation. First, "a structure consisting of a finite partially ordered set together with least upper and greatest lower bound operators on the set" can only be understood by someone who understands the model in the first place. This is similar to the common definition of metadata: "data about data." Only *after* you really understand what metadata is does this definition make any sense to you. So this definition of lattice model is not overly helpful.

The problem with the mathematical explanation is that it is in weird alien writings that only people who obtain their master's or PhD degree in mathematics can understand. This model needs to be explained in everyday language, so that even Homer Simpson can understand it. So let's give it a try.

The MAC model was explained in Chapter 4 and then built upon in this chapter. In this model, the subjects and objects have labels. Each subject's label contains the clearance and need-to-know categories that this subject can access. Suppose that Kathy's security clearance is top secret and she has been formally granted access to the compartments named Iraq and Korea, based on her need to know. So Kathy's security label states the following: TS {Iraq, Korea}. Table 5-1 shows the different files on the system in this scenario. The system is based on the MAC model, which means that the operating system is making access decisions based on security label contents.

Kathy attempts to access File B; since her clearance is greater than File B's classification, she can read this file but not write to it. (Remember, under Bell-LaPadula, a higher-level subject can read down, but not write up). This is where the *"partially ordered set* together with *least upper* and *greatest lower bound* operators on the set" comes into play. A set is a subject (Kathy) and an object (file). It is a partially ordered set because all of the access controls are not completely equal. The system has to decide between read, write, full control, modify, and all the other types of access permissions used in this operating system. So, "partially ordered" means that the system has to apply the most restrictive access controls to this set, and "least upper bound" means that the system looks at one access control's statement (Kathy can read the file) and the other access control's statement (Kathy cannot write to the file) and takes the least *upper* bound value. Since no write is more restrictive than read, Kathy's *least upper bound* access to this file is read and her greatest lower bound is no write. Figure 5-19 illustrates the bounds of access. This is just a confusing way of saying, "The most that Kathy can do with this file is to read it. The least she can do is to *not* write to it."

Let's figure out the least upper bound and greatest lower bound access levels for Kathy and File C. Kathy's clearance equals File C's classification. Under the Bell-LaPadula model, this is when the strong star property would kick in. (Remember that the strong star property states that a subject can read and write to an object of the same security level.) So the least upper bound is write and the greatest lower bound is read.

If we look at File D's security label, we see that it has a category that Kathy does not have in her security label, which is Iran. This means that Kathy does not have the necessary need to know to be able to access this file. Kathy's least upper bound and greatest lower bound access permission is no access.

So why does this model state things in a very confusing way when in reality it describes pretty straightforward concepts? First, I am describing this model in the most simplistic and basic terms possible so that you can get the basic meaning of the purpose of the model. These seemingly straightforward concepts build in complexity when you think about all the subject-to-object communications that go on within an operating system during any one second. Also, this is a formal model, which means that it can be proven mathematically to provide a specific level of protection if all of its rules are followed properly. Learning these models is similar to learning the basics of chemistry. A student first learns about the components of an atom (protons, neutrons, and electrons) and how these elements interact with each other. This is the easy piece. Then the student gets into organic chemistry and has to understand how these components work

| Kathy's Security Label | File B's Security Label | File C's Security Label | File D's Security Label |
|---|---|---|---|
| Top Secret {Iraq, Korea} | Secret {Iraq} | Top Secret {Iraq, Korea} | Secret {Iraq, Korea, Iran} |

**Table 5-1**   Security Access Control Elements

**Figure 5-19**
Bounds of access
through the lattice
model

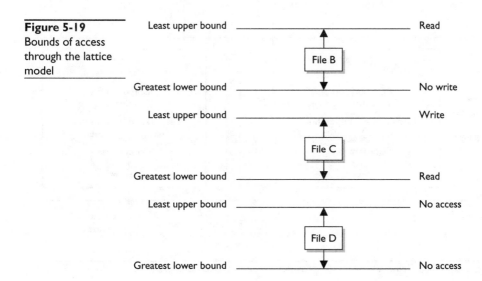

together in complex organic systems (weak and strong attractions, osmosis, and ionization). The student then goes to quantum physics to learn that the individual elements of an atom actually have several different subatomic particles (quarks, leptons, and mesons). In this book, you are just learning the basic components of the models. There is a lot more complexity once you start looking under the covers.

## Brewer and Nash Model

*A wall separates our stuff, so that you can't touch my stuff. Response: Your stuff is green and smells funny. I don't want to touch it.*

The **Brewer and Nash model**, also called the **Chinese Wall model**, was created to provide access controls that can change dynamically depending upon a user's previous actions. The main goal of the model is to protect against conflicts of interest by users' access attempts. For example, if a large marketing company provides marketing promotions and materials for two banks, an employee working on a project for Bank A should not look at the information the marketing company has on its other bank customer, Bank B. Such action could create a conflict of interest because the banks are competitors. If the marketing company's project manager for the Bank A project could view information on Bank B's new marketing campaign, he may try to trump its promotion to please his more direct customer. The marketing company would get a bad reputation if it allowed its internal employees to behave so irresponsibly.

This marketing company could implement a product that tracks the different marketing representatives' access activities and disallows certain access requests that would present this type of conflict of interest. In Figure 5-20, we see that when a representative accesses Bank A's information, the system automatically makes Bank B's information off limits. If the representative accessed Bank B's data, Bank A's information would be off limits. These access controls change dynamically depending upon the user's authorizations, activities, and previous access requests.

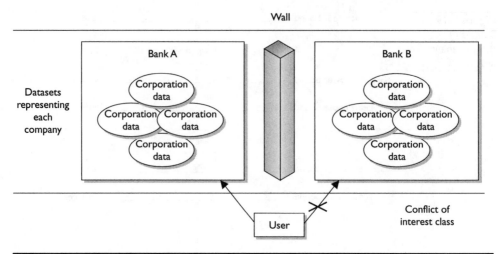

**Figure 5-20** The Chinese Wall model provides dynamic access controls.

The Chinese Wall model is also based on an information flow model. No information can flow between subjects and objects in a way that would result in a conflict of interest. The model states that a subject can write to an object if, and only if, the subject cannot read another object that is in a different dataset. So if we stay with our example, the project manager could not write to any objects within the Bank A dataset if he currently has read access to any objects in the Bank B data set.

This is only one example of how this model can be used. There are other industries that have their own possible conflicts of interest. If you were Martha's stockbroker, you should not be able to read a dataset that indicates that a stock's price is getting ready to go down *and* be able to write to Martha's account indicating that she should sell the stock she has.

## Graham-Denning Model

Remember that these are all models, thus they are not very specific in nature. Each individual vendor must decide upon how it is going to actually meet the rules outlined in the chosen model. Bell-LaPadula and Biba don't define how the security and integrity ratings are defined and modified, nor do they provide a way to delegate or transfer access rights. The *Graham-Denning model* addresses these issues and defines a set of basic rights in terms of commands that a specific subject can execute on an object. This model has eight primitive protection rights, or rules of how these types of functionalities should take place securely, which are outlined here:

- How to securely create an object
- How to securely create a subject
- How to securely delete an object
- How to securely delete a subject

- How to securely provide the read access right
- How to securely provide the grant access right
- How to securely provide the delete access right
- How to securely provide transfer access rights

These things may sound insignificant, but when we are talking about building a secure system they are very critical.

---

## Security Models Recap

All of these different models can get your head spinning. Most people are not familiar with all of them, which can make it all even harder to absorb. The following are the core concepts of the different models.

**Bell-LaPadula Model** This confidentiality model describes the allowable information flows and formalizes the military security policy. It is the first mathematical model of a multilevel security policy that defines the concept of a secure state and necessary modes of access.

- **Simple security rule** A subject cannot read data at a higher security level (no read up).
- **\*-property rule** A subject cannot write data to an object at a lower security level (no write down).
- **Strong star property rule** A subject can perform read and write functions only to the objects at its same security level.

**Biba Model** This model protects the integrity of the information within a system and the activities that take place. It addresses the first goal of integrity.

- **Simple integrity axiom** A subject cannot read data at a lower integrity level (no read down).
- **\*-integrity axiom** A subject cannot modify an object in a higher integrity level (no write up).

**Clark-Wilson Model** This integrity model is implemented to protect the integrity of data and to ensure that properly formatted transactions take place. It addresses all three goals of integrity.

- Subjects can access objects only through authorized programs (access triple).
- Separation of duties is enforced.
- Auditing is required.

**Access Control Matrix Model** This is a model in which access decisions are based on objects' ACLs and subjects' capability tables.

> **Information Flow Model** This is a model in which information is restricted in its flow to only go to and from entities in a way that does not negate the security policy.
>
> **Noninterference Model** This model states that commands and activities performed at one security level should not be seen by or affect subjects or objects at a different security level.
>
> **Brewer and Nash Model** This model allows for dynamically changing access controls that protect against conflicts of interest. Also known as the Chinese Wall model.
>
> **Graham-Denning Model** This model shows how subjects and objects should be created and deleted. It also addresses how to assign specific access rights.

### References

- **Various Papers on Models** http://citeseer.ist.psu.edu/context/20585/0
- **Module 8, "Mandatory Access Control and Labels"** www.radium.ncsc.mil/tpep/library/ramp-modules/mod_08.txt
- **"A Lattice Model of Secure Information Flow," by Dorothy E. Denning (first published in** *Communications of the ACM*, **Vol. 19, No. 5, pp. 236–243 (May 1976)** www.cs.georgetown.edu/~denning/infosec/lattice76.pdf
- **Course syllabus for Security, University of Cambridge, Dr. Ross Anderson, principle lecturer (Jan. 1999)** www.cl.cam.ac.uk/Teaching/1998/Security/
- **Access Control and Security Policy Models** http://www.tml.hut.fi/Opinnot/T-110.402/2003/Luennot/titu20031024.pdf

# Security Modes of Operation

A system can operate in different modes depending on the sensitivity of the data being processed, the clearance level of the users, and what those users are authorized to do. The mode of operation describes the security conditions under which the system actually functions.

These modes are used in MAC systems, which hold one or more classifications of data. Several things come into play when determining the mode that the operating system should be working in:

- The types of users who will be directly or indirectly connecting to the system
- The type of data (classification levels, compartments, and categories) that are processed on the system
- The clearance levels, need to know, and formal access approvals that the users will have

The following sections describe the different security modes that operating systems can be developed and configured to work in.

## Dedicated Security Mode

*Our system only holds secret data and we can all access it.*

A system is operating in a *dedicated security mode* if *all* users have a clearance for and a formal need to know about *all* data processed within the system. All users have been given formal access approval for *all* information on the system and have signed nondisclosure agreements (NDAs) pertaining to this information. The system can handle a single classification level of information.

Many military systems have been designed to handle only one level of security, which works in dedicated security mode. This requires everyone who uses the system to have the highest level of clearance required by any and all data on the system. If a system holds top-secret data, only users with that clearance can use the system. Other military systems work with multiple security levels, which is done by compartmentalizing the data. These types of systems can support users with high and low clearances simultaneously.

## System High-Security Mode

*Our system only holds secret data, but only some of us can access all of it.*

A system is operating in *system high-security mode* when all users have a security clearance to access the information but not necessarily a need to know for all the information processed on the system. So, unlike in the dedicated security mode, in which all users have a need to know pertaining to *all* data on the system, in system high-security mode, all users have a need to know pertaining to *some* of the data.

This mode also requires all users to have the highest level of clearance required by any and all data on the system. However, even though a user has the necessary security level to access an object, the user may still be restricted if they do not have a need to know pertaining to that specific object.

## Compartmented Security Mode

*Our system has various classifications of data, and each individual has the clearance to access all of the data, but not necessarily the need to know.*

A system is operating in *compartmented security mode* when all users have the clearance to access all the information processed by the system in a system high-security configuration, but might not have the need to know and formal access approval. This means that if the system is holding secret and top-secret data, all users must have at least a top-secret clearance to gain access to this system. This is how compartmented and multilevel security modes are different. Both modes require the user to have a valid need to know, NDA, and formal approval, but compartmented security mode requires the user to have a clearance that dominates (above or equal to) any and all data on the system, whereas multilevel security mode just requires the user to have clearance to access the data she will be working with.

In compartmented security mode, users are restricted from accessing some information because they do not need to access it to perform the functions of their jobs and they have not been given formal approval to access it. This would be enforced by having on all objects security labels that reflect the sensitivity (classification level, classification category, and handling procedures) of the information. In this mode, users can access a compartment, of data only, enforced by mandatory access controls.

The objective is to ensure that the minimum possible number of people learn of information at each level. Compartments are categories of data with limited number of subjects cleared to access data at each level. *Compartmented mode workstations (CMWs)* enable users to process multiple compartments of data at the same time, if they have the necessary clearance.

## Multilevel Security Mode

*Our system has various classifications of data, and each individual has the clearance and need to know to access only individual pieces of data.*

A system is operating in *multilevel security mode* when it permits two or more classification levels of information to be processed at the same time when not all of the users have the clearance or formal approval to access all the information being processed by the system. So all users must have formal approval, NDA, need to know, and the necessary clearance to access the data that they need to carry out their jobs. In this mode, the user cannot access all of the data on the system, only what she is cleared to access.

The Bell-LaPadula model is an example of a multilevel security model because it handles multiple information classifications at a number of different security levels within one system simultaneously.

## Guards

Software and hardware guards allow the exchange of data between trusted (high assurance) and less trusted (low assurance) systems and environments. Let's say that you are working on a MAC system (working in dedicated security mode of secret) and you need the system to communicate with a MAC database (working in multilevel security mode, which goes up to top secret). These two systems provide different levels of protection. As previously stated, if a system with lower assurance could directly communicate with a system of higher assurance, then security vulnerabilities and compromises could be introduced. So, a software guard can be implemented, which is really just a front-end product that allows interconnectivity between systems working at different security levels. (There are different types of guards, and they can carry out filtering, processing requests, data blocking, and data sanitization.) Or a hardware guard can be implemented, which is a system with two NICs connecting the two systems that need to communicate. The guard is an add-on piece that provides a level of strict access control between different systems.

The guard accepts requests from the system of lower assurance, reviews the request to make sure it is allowed, and then submits the request to the system of higher assurance. The goal is to ensure that information does not flow from a high security level to a low security level in an unauthorized manner.

Guards can be used to connect different MAC systems working in different security modes and to connect different networks working at different security levels. In many cases, the less trusted system can send messages to the more trusted system but can only receive acknowledgments in return. This is common when e-mail messages need to go from less trusted systems to more trusted classified systems.

## Security Modes Recap

Many times it is easier to understand these different modes when they are laid out in a clear and simplistic format. Pay attention to the italic words, because they emphasis the differences between the various modes.

**Dedicated Security Mode**   All users must have...

- Proper clearance for all information on the system
- Formal access approval for all information on the system
- Signed NDA for all information on the system
- Valid need to know for *all* information on the system

All users can access all data.

**System High-Security Mode**   All users must have...

- Proper clearance for all information on the system
- Formal access approval for all information on the system
- Signed NDA for all information on the system
- Valid need to know for *some* information on the system

All users can access some data, based on their need to know.

**Compartmented Security Mode**   All users must have...

- Proper clearance for the highest level of data classification on the system
- Formal access approval for all information they will access on the system
- Signed NDA for all information they will access on the system
- Valid need to know for *some* of the information on the system

All users can access some data, based on their need to know and formal access approval.

**Multilevel Security Mode**   All users must have...

- Proper clearance for all information they will access on the system
- Formal access approval for all information they will access on the system
- Signed NDA for all information they will access on the system
- Valid need to know for *some* of the information on the system

All users can access some data, based on their need to know, clearance, and formal access approval.

## References

- "Data Protection Measures"   www.tpub.com/ans/51.htm
- "Personal Computer Security"   www.cs.nps.navy.mil/curricula/tracks/ security/notes/chap02_17.html
- "Physical Model of Operations"   chacs.nrl.navy.mil/publications/ CHACS/1997/jifi_web/node24.html
- Chapter 8, "Automated Information System Security"   www.dss.mil/isec/ chapter8.htm
- *National Industrial Security Program Operating Manual (NISPOM)*, U.S. Department of Defense   www.tscm.com/Nispom.html

## Trust and Assurance

*I trust that you will act properly, thus I have a high level of assurance in you. Response: You are such a fool.*

As discussed earlier in the section "Trusted Computing Base," no system is really secure because, with enough resources, attackers can compromise almost any system in one way or another; however, systems can provide levels of trust. The trust level tells the customer how much protection he can expect out of this system and the *assurance* that the system will act in a correct and predictable manner in each and every computing situation.

The TCB comprises all the protection mechanisms within a system (software, hardware, firmware). All of these mechanisms need to work in an orchestrated way to enforce all the requirements of a security policy. When evaluated, these mechanisms are tested, their designs are inspected, and their supporting documentation is reviewed and evaluated. How the system is developed, maintained, and even delivered to the customer are all under review when the trust for a system is being gauged. All of these different components are put through an evaluation process and assigned an assurance rating, which represents the level of trust and assurance that the testing team has in the product. Customers then use this rating to determine which system best fits their security needs.

Assurance and trust are similar in nature, but slightly different with regard to product ratings. In a trusted system, all protection mechanisms work together to process sensitive data for many types of uses, and will provide the necessary level of protection per classification level. Assurance looks at the same issues but in more depth and detail. Systems that provide higher levels of assurance have been tested extensively and have had their designs thoroughly inspected, their development stages reviewed, and their technical specifications and test plans evaluated. You can buy a car and you can trust it, but you have a much deeper sense of assurance of that trust if you know how the car was built, what it was built with, who built it, what tests it was put through, and how it performed in many different situations.

In the Trusted Computer Security Evaluation Criteria (TCSEC), commonly known as the Orange Book (addressed shortly), the lower assurance level ratings look at a system's protection mechanisms and testing results to produce an assurance rating, but the higher assurance level ratings look more at the system design, specifications, development procedures, supporting documentation, and testing results. The protection mechanisms in the higher assurance level systems may not necessarily be much different from those in the lower assurance level systems, but the way they were designed and built is under much more scrutiny. With this extra scrutiny comes higher levels of assurance of the trust that can be put into a system.

# Systems Evaluation Methods

A *security evaluation* examines the security-relevant parts of a system, meaning the TCB, access control mechanisms, reference monitor, kernel, and protection mechanisms. The relationship and interaction between these components are also evaluated. There are different methods of evaluating and assigning assurance levels to systems. Two reasons explain why more than one type of assurance evaluation process exist: methods and ideologies have evolved over time, and various parts of the world look at computer security differently and rate some aspects of security differently. Each method will be explained and compared.

## Why Put a Product Through Evaluation?

Submitting a product to be evaluated against the Orange Book, Information Technology Security Evaluation Criteria, or Common Criteria is no walk in the park for a vendor. In fact, it is a really painful and long process, and no one wakes up in the morning thinking, "Yippee! I have to complete all of the paperwork that the National Computer Security Center requires so that my product can be evaluated!" So, before we go through these different criteria, let's look at *why* anyone would even put themselves through this process.

If you were going shopping to buy a firewall, how would you know what level of protection each provides and which is the best product for your environment? You could listen to the vendor's marketing hype and believe the salesperson who informs you that a particular product will solve all of your life problems in one week. Or you could listen to the advice of an independent third party who has fully tested the product and does not have any bias toward the product. If you choose the second option, then you join a world of people who work within the realm of assurance ratings in one form or another.

In the United States, the National Computer Security Center (NCSC) is an organization within the National Security Agency (NSA) that is responsible for evaluating computer systems and products. It has a group, Trusted Product Evaluation Program (TPEP), which oversees the testing by approved evaluation entities of commercial products against a specific set of criteria.

So, a vendor creates a product and submits it to an approved evaluation entity that is compliant with the TPEP guidelines. The evaluation entity has groups of testers who will follow a set of criteria (for many years it was the Orange Book but now is moving toward the Common Criteria) to test the vendor's product. Once the testing is over, the product is assigned an assurance rating. So, instead of having to trust the marketing hype of the financially motivated vendor, you as a consumer can take the word of an objective third-party entity that fully tested the product.

This evaluation process is very time consuming and expensive for the vendor. Not every vendor puts its product through this process, because of the expense and delayed date to get it to market. Typically, a vendor would put its product through this process if its main customer base will be making purchasing decisions based on assurance ratings. In the United States, the Department of Defense *is* the largest customer, so major vendors put their main products through this process with the hope that the Department of Defense (and others) will purchase their products.

## The Orange Book

The U.S. Department of Defense developed the *Trusted Computer System Evaluation Criteria (TCSEC)*, which is used to evaluate operating systems, applications, and different products. This evaluation criteria is published in a book with an orange cover, which is called appropriately the *Orange Book*. (We like to keep things simple in security!) Customers use the assurance rating that the criteria presents as a metric when comparing different products. It also provides direction for manufactures so that they know what specifications to build to, and provides a one-stop evaluation process so customers do not need to have individual components within the systems evaluated.

The Orange Book is used to evaluate whether a product contains the security properties the vendor claims it does and whether the product is appropriate for a specific application or function. The Orange Book is used to review the functionality, effectiveness, and assurance of a product during its evaluation, and it uses classes that were devised to address typical patterns of security requirements.

TCSEC provides a classification system that is divided into hierarchical divisions of assurance levels:

- **A**   Verified protection
- **B**   Mandatory protection
- **C**   Discretionary protection
- **D**   Minimal security

Classification A represents the highest level of assurance and D represents the lowest level of assurance.

Each division can have one or more numbered classes with a corresponding set of requirements that must be met for a system to achieve that particular rating. The classes with higher numbers offer a greater degree of trust and assurance. So B2 would offer more trust than B1, and C2 would offer more trust than C1.

The criteria include four main topics—security policy, accountability, assurance, and documentation—but these actually break down into seven different areas:

- **Security policy**   The policy must be explicit and well defined and enforced by the mechanisms within the system.
- **Identification**   Individual subjects must be uniquely identified.
- **Labels**   Access control labels must be associated properly with objects.

- **Documentation**   Documentation must be provided, including test, design, and specification documents, user guides, and manuals.

- **Accountability**   Audit data must be captured and protected to enforce accountability.

- **Life cycle assurance**   Software, hardware, and firmware must be able to be tested individually to ensure that each enforces the security policy in an effective manner throughout their lifetimes.

- **Continuous protection**   The security mechanisms and the system as a whole must perform predictably and acceptably in different situations continuously.

These categories are evaluated independently, but the rating that is assigned at the end does not specify these different objectives individually. The rating is a sum total of these items.

Each division and class incorporates the requirements of the ones below it. This means that C2 must meet its criteria requirements and all of C1's requirements, and B3 has its requirements to fulfill along with those of C1, C2, B1, and B2. Each division or class ups the ante on security requirements and is expected to fulfill the requirements of all the classes and divisions below it.

So, when a vendor submits a product for evaluation, it submits it to the NCSC. The group that oversees the processes of evaluation is called the Trusted Products Evaluation Program (TPEP). Successfully evaluated products are placed on the Evaluated Products List (EPL) with their corresponding rating. When consumers are interested in certain products and systems, they can check the appropriate EPL to find out their assigned security levels.

### Isn't the Orange Book Dead?

We are moving from the Orange Book to the Common Criteria in the industry, so a common question is, "Why do I have to study this Orange Book stuff?" Just because we are going through this transition, does not make the Orange Book unimportant. It was the first evaluation criteria and was used for 20 years. Many of the basic terms and concepts that have carried through originated in the Orange Book. And we still have several products with these ratings that eventually will go through the Common Criteria evaluation process.

The CISSP exam is moving steadily from the Orange Book to the Common Criteria all the time, but don't count the Orange Book out yet.

As a follow-on observation, many people are new to the security field. It is a booming market, which means a flood of not-so-experienced people will be jumping in and attempting to charge forward without a real foundation of knowledge. To some readers, this book will just be a nice refresher and something that ties already known concepts together. To other readers, many of these concepts are new and more challenging. If a lot of this stuff is new to you—you are new to the market. That is okay, but knowing how we got where we are today is very beneficial because it broadens your view of *deep* understanding—instead of just memorizing for an exam.

## Division D: Minimal Protection

There is only one class in this division. It is reserved for systems that have been evaluated but fail to meet the criteria and requirements of the higher divisions.

## Division C: Discretionary Protection

The C rating category has two individual assurance ratings within it, which are described next. The higher the number of the assurance rating, the more protection that is provided.

**C1: Discretionary Security Protection**   Discretionary access control is based on individuals and/or groups. It requires a separation of users and information, and identification and authentication of individual entities. Some type of access control is necessary so that users can ensure that their data will not be accessed and corrupted by others. The system architecture must supply a protected execution domain so that privileged system processes are not adversely affected by lower-privileged processes. There must be specific ways of validating the system's operational integrity. The documentation requirements include design documentation, which shows that the system was built to include protection mechanisms, test documentation (test plan and results), a facility manual, so that companies know how to install and configure the system correctly, and user manuals.

The type of environment that would require this rating is one in which users are processing information at the same sensitivity level; thus, strict access control and auditing measures are not required. It would be a trusted environment with low security concerns.

**C2: Controlled Access Protection**   Users need to be identified individually to provide more precise access control and auditing functionality. Logical access control mechanisms are used to enforce authentication and the uniqueness of each individual's identification. Security-relevant events are audited, and these records must be protected from unauthorized modification. The architecture must provide resource, or object, isolation so that proper protection can be applied to the resource and actions taken upon it can be properly audited. The object reuse concept must also be invoked, meaning that any medium holding data must not contain any remnants of information after it is released for another subject to use. If a subject uses a segment of memory, that memory space must not hold any information after the subject is done using it. The same is true for storage media, objects being populated, temporary files being created—all data must be efficiently erased once the subject is done with that medium.

This class requires a more granular method of providing access control. The system must enforce strict logon procedures and provide decision-making capabilities when subjects request access to objects. A C2 system cannot guarantee that it will not be compromised, but it supplies a level of protection that would make attempts to compromise it harder to accomplish.

The type of environment that would require systems with a C2 rating is one in which users are trusted but a certain level of accountability is required. C2, overall, is regarded to be the most reasonable class for commercial applications, but the level of protection is still relatively weak.

## Division B: Mandatory Protection

Mandatory access control is enforced by the use of security labels. The architecture is based on the Bell-LaPadula security model, and evidence of reference monitor enforcement must be available.

**B1: Labeled Security**    Each data object must contain a classification label and each subject must have a clearance label. When a subject attempts to access an object, the system must compare the subject's and object's security labels to ensure that the requested actions are acceptable. Data leaving the system must also contain an accurate security label. The security policy is based on an informal statement, and the design specifications are reviewed and verified.

This security rating is intended for environments that require systems to handle classified data.

**NOTE**    Security labels are not required until security rating B; thus, C2 does not require security labels but B1 does.

**B2: Structured Protection**    The security policy is clearly defined and documented, and the system design and implementation are subjected to more thorough review and testing procedures. This class requires more stringent authentication mechanisms and well-defined interfaces among layers. Subjects and devices require labels, and the system must not allow covert channels. A trusted path for logon and authentication processes must be in place, which means that the subject communicates directly with the application or operating system, and no trapdoors exist. There is no way to circumvent or compromise this communication channel. There is a separation of operator and administration functions within the system to provide more trusted and protected operational functionality. Distinct address spaces must be provided to isolate processes, and a covert channel analysis is conducted. This class adds assurance by adding requirements to the design of the system.

The type of environment that would require B2 systems is one that processes sensitive data that requires a higher degree of security. This type of environment would require systems that are relatively resistant to penetration and compromise.

**B3: Security Domains**    In this class, more granularity is provided in each protection mechanism, and the programming code that is not necessary to support the security policy is excluded. The design and implementation should not provide too much complexity, because as the complexity of a system increases, so must the skill level of the individuals who need to test, maintain, and configure it; thus, the overall security can be threatened. The reference monitor components must be small enough to test properly and be tamperproof. The security administrator role is clearly defined, and the system must be able to recover from failures without its security level being compromised. When the system starts up and loads its operating system and components, it must be done in an initial secure state to ensure that any weakness of the system cannot be taken advantage of in this slice of time.

The type of environment that requires B3 systems is a highly secured environment that processes very sensitive information. It requires systems that are highly resistant to penetration.

### Division A: Verified Protection

Formal methods are used to ensure that all subjects and objects are controlled with the necessary discretionary and mandatory access controls. The design, development, implementation, and documentation are looked at in a formal and detailed way. The security mechanisms between B3 and A1 are not very different, but the way that the system was designed and developed is evaluated in a much more structured and stringent procedure.

**A1: Verified Design**   The architecture and protection features are not much different from systems that achieve a B3 rating, but the assurance of an A1 system is higher than a B3 system because of the formality in the way the A1 system was designed, the way the specifications were developed, and the level of detail in the verification techniques. Formal techniques are used to prove the equivalence between the TCB specifications and the security policy model. More stringent change configuration is put in place with the development of an A1 system, and the overall design can be verified. In many cases, even the way in which the system is delivered to the customer is under scrutiny to ensure that there is no way of compromising the system before it reaches its destination.

The type of environment that would require A1 systems is the most secure of secured environments. This type of environment deals with top-secret information and cannot adequately trust anyone using the systems without strict authentication, restrictions, and auditing.

 **NOTE**   TCSEC addresses confidentiality, but not integrity. Functionality of the security mechanisms and the assurance of those mechanisms are not evaluated separately, but rather are combined and rated as a whole.

### References

- Trusted Computer System Evaluation Criteria (Orange Book), U.S. Department of Defense (Dec. 26, 1985)   www.boran.com/security/tcsec.html
- Lecture notes for Cryptography and Network Security, Part 7, "Trusted Computer Systems," William Stallings, lecturer, Dr. Lawrie Brown, author   williamstallings.com/Extras/Security-Notes/lectures/trusted.html

# Rainbow Series

*Why are there so many colors in the rainbow? Response: Because there are so many product types that need to be evaluated.*

The Orange Book mainly addresses government and military requirements and expectations for their computer systems. Many people within the security field have pointed out several deficiencies in the Orange Book, particularly when it is being applied to systems that are to be used in commercial areas instead of government organizations. The following list summarizes a majority of the troubling issues that security practitioners have expressed about the Orange Book:

- It looks specifically at the operating system and not at other issues like networking, databases, and so on.

- It focuses mainly on one attribute of security, confidentiality, and not at integrity and availability.

- It works with government classifications and not the protection classifications that commercial industries use.

- It has a relatively small number of ratings, which means many different aspects of security are not evaluated and rated independently.

The Orange Book places great emphasis on controlling which users can access a system and virtually ignores controlling what those users do with the information once they are authorized. Authorized users can, and usually do, cause more damage to data than outside attackers. Commercial organizations have expressed more concern about the integrity of their data, whereas military organizations stress that their top concern is confidentiality. Because of these different goals, the Orange Book is a better evaluation tool for government and military systems.

Because the Orange Book focuses on the operating system, many other areas of security were left out. The Orange Book provides a broad framework for building and evaluating trusted systems, but it leaves many questions about topics other than operating systems unanswered. So, more books were written to extend the coverage of the Orange Book into other areas of security. These books provide detailed information and interpretations of certain Orange Book requirements and describe the evaluation processes. These books are collectively called the *Rainbow Series* because the cover of each is a different color.

For an explanation of each book and its usage, please refer to the following references.

## References

- **Rainbow Series**  csrc.ncsl.nist.gov/secpubs/rainbow/
- **Rainbow Series and related documents from the Federation of American Scientists**  www.fas.org/irp/nsa/rainbow.htm

## Red Book

The Orange Book addresses single-system security, but networks are a combination of systems, and each network needs to be secure without having to fully trust each and every system connected to it. The *Trusted Network Interpretation (TNI)*, also called the

*Red Book* because of the color of its cover, addresses security evaluation topics for networks and network components. It addresses isolated local area networks and wide area internetwork systems.

Like the Orange Book, the Red Book does not supply specific details about how to implement security mechanisms; instead, it provides a framework for securing different types of networks. A network has a security policy, architecture, and design, as does an operating system. Subjects accessing objects on the network need to be controlled, monitored, and audited. In a network, the subject could be a workstation and an object could be a network service on a server.

The Red Book rates confidentiality of data and operations that happen within a network and the network products. Data and labels need to be protected from unauthorized modification, and the integrity of information as it is transferred needs to be ensured. The source and destination mechanisms used for messages are evaluated and tested to ensure that modification is not allowed.

Encryption and protocols are components that provide a lot of the security within a network, and the Red Book measures their functionality, strength, and assurance.

The following is a brief overview of the security items addressed in the Red Book:

- **Communication integrity**
  - **Authentication**   Protects against masquerading and playback attacks. Mechanisms include digital signatures, encryption, timestamp, and passwords.
  - **Message integrity**   Protects the protocol header, routing information, and packet payload from being modified. Mechanisms include message authentication and encryption.
  - **Nonrepudiation**   Ensures that a sender cannot deny sending a message. Mechanisms include encryption, digital signatures, and notarization.
- **Denial-of-service prevention**
  - **Continuity of operations**   Ensures that the network is available even if attacked. Mechanisms include fault tolerant and redundant systems and the capability to reconfigure network parameters in case of an emergency.
  - **Network management**   Monitors network performance and identifies attacks and failures. Mechanisms include components that enable network administrators to monitor and restrict resource access.
- **Compromise protection**
  - **Data confidentiality**   Protects data from being accessed in an unauthorized method during transmission. Mechanisms include access controls, encryption, and physical protection of cables.
  - **Traffic flow confidentiality**   Ensures that unauthorized entities are not aware of routing information or frequency of communication via traffic analysis. Mechanisms include padding messages, sending noise, or sending false messages.

- **Selective routing**  Routes messages in a way to avoid specific threats. Mechanisms include network configuration and routing tables.

Assurance is derived by comparing how things actually work to a theory of how things should work. Assurance is also derived by testing configurations in many different scenarios, evaluating engineering practices, and validating and verifying security claims.

TCSEC was introduced in 1985 and retired in December 2000. It was the first methodical and logical set of standards developed to secure computer systems. It was greatly influential to several countries who based their evaluation standards on the TCSEC guidelines. TCSEC was finally replaced with the Common Criteria.

# Information Technology Security Evaluation Criteria

The *Information Technology Security Evaluation Criteria (ITSEC)* was the first attempt at establishing a single standard for evaluating security attributes of computer systems and products by many European countries. The United States looked to the Orange Book and Rainbow Series, and Europe employed ITSEC to evaluate and rate computer systems. (Today, everyone is migrating to the Common Criteria, explained in the next section.)

There are two main attributes of a system's protection mechanisms when they are evaluated under ITSEC: functionality and assurance. When the functionality of a system's protection mechanisms is being evaluated, the services that are provided to the subjects (access control mechanisms, auditing, authentication, and so on) are examined and measured. Protection mechanism functionality can be very diverse in nature because systems are developed differently just to provide different functionality to users. Nonetheless, when functionality is evaluated, it is tested to see if the system's protection mechanisms deliver what its vendor says they deliver. Assurance, on the other hand, is the degree of confidence in the protection mechanisms, and their effectiveness and capability to perform consistently. Assurance is generally tested by examining development practices, documentation, configuration management, and testing mechanisms.

It is possible for two systems' protection mechanisms to provide the same type of functionalities and have very different assurance levels. This is because the underlying mechanisms providing the functionality can be developed, engineered, and implemented differently. System A and System B may have protection mechanisms that provide the same type of functionality for authentication, in which case both products would get the same rating for functionality. But System A's developers could have been sloppy and careless when developing their authentication mechanism, in which case their product would receive a lower assurance rating. ITSEC actually separates these two attributes (functionality and assurance) and rates them separately, whereas TCSEC clumps them together and assigns them one rating (D through A1).

The following list shows the different types of functionalities and assurance items that are tested during an evaluation.

- **Security functional requirements**
  - Identification and authentication
  - Audit
  - Resource utilization
  - Trusted paths/channels
  - User data protection
  - Security management
  - Product access
  - Communications
  - Privacy
  - Protection of the product's security functions
  - Cryptographic support
- **Security assurance requirements**
  - Guidance documents and manuals
  - Configuration management
  - Vulnerability assessment
  - Delivery and operation
  - Life-cycle support
  - Assurance maintenance
  - Development
  - Testing

Consider again our example of two systems that provide the same functionality (pertaining to the protection mechanisms) but have very different assurance levels. Using the TCSEC approach, the difference in assurance levels will be hard to distinguish because the functionality and assurance level are rated together. Under the ITSEC approach, the functionality is rated separately from the assurance, so the difference in assurance levels will be more noticeable. In the ITSEC criteria, classes F1 to F10 rate the functionality of the security mechanisms, whereas E0 to E6 rate the assurance of those mechanisms.

So a difference between ITSEC and TCSEC is that TCSEC bundles functionality and assurance into one rating, whereas ITSEC evaluates these two attributes separately. The other differences are that ITSEC was developed to provide more flexibility than TCSEC, and ITSEC addresses integrity, availability, and confidentiality whereas TCSEC addresses only confidentiality. ITSEC also addresses networked systems, whereas TCSEC deals with stand-alone systems.

Table 5-2 is a general mapping of the two evaluation schemes to show you their relationship to each other.

| ITSEC | TCSEC |
|-------|-------|
| E0 | = D |
| F1 + E1 | = C1 |
| F2 + E2 | = C2 |
| F3 + E3 | = B1 |
| F4 + E4 | = B2 |
| F5 + E5 | = B3 |
| F5 + E6 | = A1 |
| F6 | = Systems that provide high integrity |
| F7 | = Systems that provide high availability |
| F8 | = Systems that provide data integrity during communication |
| F9 | = Systems that provide high confidentiality (like cryptographic devices) |
| F10 | = Networks with high demands on confidentiality and integrity |

**Table 5-2**  ITSEC and TCSEC Mapping

As you can see, a majority of the ITSEC ratings can be mapped to the Orange Book ratings, but then ITSEC took a step farther and added F6 through F10 for specific needs consumers might have that the Orange Book does not address.

ITSEC is criteria for operating systems and other products, which it refers to individually as the target of evaluation (TOE). So if you are reading literature discussing the ITSEC rating of a product and it states that the TOE has a rating of F1 and E5, you know that the TOE is the product that was evaluated and that it has a low functionality rating and a high assurance rating.

The ratings are based on effectiveness and correctness. Effectiveness means that the TOE meets the security claims that the vendor has specified. This analysis looks at the construction and operational vulnerabilities and the ease of use, to ensure that the proper security settings do not get in the way of productivity. Correctness deals with how the TOE was built and implementation issues. This type of analysis looks at the architectural design, how the security mechanisms enforce the policy, and the operational documentation and environment.

## References

- **Criteria and Methods of Evaluations of Information Systems**   www.cordis .lu/infosec/src/crit.htm
- **ITSEC home page**   www.iwar.org.uk/comsec/resources/standards/itsec.htm

# Common Criteria

*"TCSEC is too hard, ITSEC is too soft, but the Common Criteria is just right," said the baby bear.*

The Orange Book and the Rainbow Series provide evaluation schemes that are too rigid for the business world. ITSEC attempted to provide a more flexible approach by separating the functionality and assurance attributes and considering the evaluation of entire systems. However, this flexibility added complexity because evaluators could mix and match functionality and assurance ratings, which resulted in too many classifications to keep straight. Because we are a species that continues to try to get it right, the next attempt for an effective and usable evaluation criteria was the *Common Criteria*.

In 1990, the International Organization for Standardization (ISO) identified the need of international standard evaluation criteria to be used globally. The Common Criteria project started in 1993 when several organizations came together to combine and align existing and emerging evaluation criteria (TCSEC, ITSEC, Canadian Trusted Computer Product Evaluation Criteria [CTCPEC], and the Federal Criteria). The Common Criteria was developed through a collaboration among national security standards organizations within the United States, Canada, France, Germany, the United Kingdom, and the Netherlands.

The benefit of having a worldwide recognized and accepted set of criteria is that it helps consumers by reducing the complexity of the ratings and eliminating the need to understand the definition and meaning of different ratings within various evaluation schemes. This also helps manufacturers because now they can build to one specific set of requirements if they want to sell their products internationally, instead of having to meet several different ratings with varying rules and requirements.

The Orange Book evaluates all systems by how they compare to the Bell-LaPadula model. The Common Criteria provides more flexibility by evaluating a product against a protection profile, which is structured to address a real-world security need. So while the Orange Book says, "Everyone march in this direction in this form using this path," the Common Criteria asks, "Okay, what are the threats we are facing today and what are the best ways of battling them?"

Under the Common Criteria model, an evaluation is carried out on a product and is assigned an *Evaluation Assurance Level (EAL)*. The thorough and stringent testing increases in detailed-oriented tasks as the assurance levels increase. The Common Criteria has seven assurance levels. The range is from EAL1, where functionality testing takes place, to EAL7, where thorough testing is performed and the system design is verified. The different EAL packages are listed here:

- **EAL 1**   Functionally tested
- **EAL 2**   Structurally tested
- **EAL 3**   Methodically tested and checked
- **EAL 4**   Methodically designed, tested, and reviewed
- **EAL 5**   Semiformally designed and tested
- **EAL 6**   Semiformally verified design and tested
- **EAL 7**   Formally verified design and tested

**NOTE**  When a system is "formally verified" this means that it is based on a model that can be mathematically proven.

The Common Criteria uses *protection profiles* in its evaluation process. This is a mechanism that is used to describe a real-world need of a product that is not currently on the market. The protection profile contains the set of security requirements, their meaning and reasoning, and the corresponding EAL rating that the intended product will require. The protection profile describes the environmental assumptions, the objectives, and the functional and assurance level expectations. Each relevant threat is listed along with how it is to be controlled by specific objectives. The protection profile also justifies the assurance level and requirements for the strength of each protection mechanism.

The protection profile provides a means for a consumer, or others, to identify specific security needs; this is the security problem that is to be conquered. If someone identifies a security need that is not currently being addressed by any current product, that person can write a protection profile describing the product that would be a solution for this real-world problem. The protection profile goes on to provide the necessary goals and protection mechanisms to achieve the necessary level of security and a list of the things that can go wrong during this type of system development. This list is used by the engineers who develop the system, and then by the evaluators to make sure the engineers dotted every *i* and crossed every *t*.

The Common Criteria was developed to stick to evaluation classes but also to retain some degree of flexibility. Protection profiles were developed to describe the functionality, assurance, description, and rationale of the product requirements.

Like other evaluation criteria before it, the Common Criteria works to answer two basic questions about products being evaluated: what does its security mechanisms do (functionality), and how sure are you of that (assurance)? This system sets up a framework that enables consumers to clearly specify their security issues and problems; developers to specify their security solution to those problems; and evaluators to unequivocally determine what the product actually accomplishes.

A protection profile contains the following five sections:

- **Descriptive elements**  Provides the name of the profile and a description of the security problem that is to be solved.

- **Rationale**  Justifies the profile and gives a more detailed description of the real-world problem to be solved. The environment, usage assumptions, and threats are illustrated along with guidance on the security policies that can be supported by products and systems that conform to this profile.

- **Functional requirements**  Establishes a protection boundary, meaning the threats or compromises that are within this boundary to be countered. The product or system must enforce the boundary established in this section.

- **Development assurance requirements**  Identifies the specific requirements that the product or system must meet during the development phases, from design to implementation.

- **Evaluation assurance requirements**  Establishes the type and intensity of the evaluation.

The evaluation process is just one leg of determining the functionality and assurance of a product. Once a product achieves a specific rating, it only applies to that particular version and only to certain configurations of that product. So if a company buys a firewall product because it has a high assurance rating, the company has no guarantee that the next version of that software will have that rating. The next version will need to go though its own evaluation review. If this same company buys the firewall product and installs it with configurations that are not recommended, the level of security the company was hoping to achieve can easily go down the drain. So all of this rating stuff is a formalized method of reviewing a system being evaluated in a lab. When the product is implemented in a real environment, factors other than its rating need to be addressed and assessed to ensure that it is properly protecting resources and the environment.

 **NOTE** When a product is assigned an assurance rating, this means it has the *potential* of providing this level of protection. The customer has to properly configure the product to actually obtain this level of security. The vendor should provide the necessary configuration documentation, and it is up to the customer to keep the product properly configured at all times.

### References

- **Computer Security Resource Center (CSRC) Common Criteria for IT Security Evaluation** csrc.nist.gov/cc/
- **Common Criteria** www.radium.ncsc.mil/tpep/library/ccitse/index.html
- **Common Criteria overview, Rycombe Consulting** www.rycombe.com/cc.htm

# Certification vs. Accreditation

We have gone through the different types of evaluation criteria that a system can be appraised against to receive a specific rating. This is a very formalized process, following which the evaluated system or product will be placed on an EPL indicating what rating it achieved. Consumers can check this listing and compare the different products and systems to see how they rank against each other in the property of protection. However, once a consumer buys this product and sets it up in their environment, security is not guaranteed. Security is made up of system administration, physical security, installation, and configuration mechanisms within the environment, and other security issues. To fairly say a system is secure, all of these items need to be taken into account. The rating is just one piece in the puzzle of security.

## Different Components of the Common Criteria

The different components of the Common Criteria are shown and described here:

- **Protection profile**   Description of needed security solution.
- **Target of evaluation**   Product proposed to provide needed security solution.
- **Security target**   Vendor's written explanation of the security functionality and assurance mechanisms that meet the needed security solution; in other words, "This is what our product does and how it does it."
- **Packages—EALs**   Functional and assurance requirements are bundled into packages for reuse. This component describes what must be met to achieve specific EAL ratings.

## Certification

*How did you certify this product? Response: It came in a very pretty box. Let's keep it.*

**Certification** is the comprehensive technical evaluation of the security components and their compliance for the purpose of accreditation. A certification process may use safeguard evaluation, risk analysis, verification, testing, and auditing techniques to assess the appropriateness of a specific system. For example, suppose that Dan is the security officer for a company that just purchased new systems to be used to process its confidential data. He wants to know if these systems are appropriate for these tasks and if they are going to provide the necessary level of protection. He also wants to make sure that they are compatible with his current environment, do not reduce productivity, and do not open doors to new threats—basically he wants to know if these are the right products for his company. He could pay a company that specializes in these matters to perform the necessary procedures to certify the systems or it can be carried out internally. The evaluation team will perform tests on the software configurations, hardware, firmware, design, implementation, system procedures, and physical and communication controls.

The goal of a certification process is to ensure that a system, product, or network is right for the customer's purposes. Customers will rely upon a product for slightly different reasons, and environments will have various threat levels. So a particular product is not necessarily the best fit for every single customer out there. (Of course, vendors will try to convince you otherwise.) The product has to provide the right functionality and security for the individual customer, which is the whole purpose of a certification process.

The certification process and corresponding documentation will indicate the good, the bad, and the ugly about the product and how it works within the given environment. Dan will take these results and present them to his management for the accreditation process.

## Accreditation

*Accreditation* is the formal acceptance of the adequacy of a system's overall security and functionality by management. The certification information is presented to management, or the responsible body, and it is up to the management to ask questions, review the reports and findings, and decide whether to accept the product and whether any corrective action needs to take place. Once satisfied with the system's overall security as it is presented, management makes a formal accreditation statement. By doing this, management is stating that it understands the level of protection the system will provide in its current environment and understands the security risks associated with installing and maintaining this system.

**NOTE** Certification is a technical review that assesses the security mechanisms and evaluates their effectiveness. Accreditation is management's official acceptance of the information in the certification process findings.

Because software, systems, and environments continually change and evolve, the certification and accreditation should also continue to take place. Any major addition of software, change to the system, or modification of the environment should initiate a new certification and accreditation cycle.

# Open vs. Closed Systems

Computer systems can be developed to integrate easily with other systems and products (open systems) or can be developed to be more proprietary in nature and work with only a subset of other systems and products (closed systems). The following sections describe the difference between these approaches.

## Open Systems

*I want to be able to work and play well with others. Response: But, no one wants to play with you.*

Systems that are described as *open* are built upon standards, protocols, and interfaces that have published specifications, which enable third-party vendors to develop add-on components and devices. This type of architecture provides interoperability between products created by different vendors. This interoperability is provided by all the vendors involved who follow specific standards and provide interfaces that enable each system to easily communicate with other systems and allow add-ons to hook into the system easily.

A majority of the systems in use today are open systems. The reason that an administrator can have Windows NT 4.0, Windows 2000, Macintosh, and Unix computers communicating easily on the same network is because these platforms are open. If a software vendor creates a closed system, it is restricting its potential sales to proprietary environments.

**NOTE** In Chapter 11, we will look at the standards that support interoperability, including CORBA, DCOM, J2EE, and more.

## No More Pencil Whipping

Many organizations are taking the accreditation process more seriously than they did in the past. Unfortunately, sometimes when a certification process is completed and the documentation is sent to management for review and approval, management members just blindly sign the necessary documentation without really understanding what they are signing. Accreditation means that management is accepting the *risk* that is associated with allowing this new product to be introduced into the organization's environment. When large security compromises take place, the buck stops at the individual who signed off on the offending item. So as these management members are being held more accountable for what they sign off on and as more regulations make executives personally responsible for security, the pencil whipping of accreditation papers is decreasing, but has not stopped.

## Closed Systems

*I only want to play with you and him. Response: Just play with him.*

Systems that are referred to as *closed* use an architecture that does not follow industry standards. Interoperability and standard interfaces are not employed, to enable easy communication between different types of systems and add-on features. Closed systems are proprietary, meaning that the system can only communicate with like systems.

A closed architecture can provide more security to the system because it does not have as many doorways in, and it operates in a more secluded environment than open environments. Because a closed system is proprietary, there are not as many tools to thwart the security mechanisms and not as many people who understand its design, language, and security weaknesses to exploit. A majority of the systems today are built with open architecture to enable them to work with other types of systems, easily share information, and take advantage of the functionality that third-party add-ons bring. However, this opens the doors to more hacks, cracks, and attacks. You can't have your cake and eat it too it seems.

# A Few Threats to Security Models and Architectures

Now that we have talked about how everything is supposed to work, let's take a quick look at some of the things that can go wrong when designing a system.

Software almost always has bugs and vulnerabilities. The rich functionality demanded by users brings about deep complexity, which usually opens the doors to problems in the computer world. Also, vulnerabilities are always around because attackers continually find ways of using system operations and functionality in a negative and destructive way. Just like there will always be cops and robbers, there will always be attackers and security professionals. It is a game of trying to outwit each other and seeing who will put the necessary effort into winning the game.

---

 **NOTE** Carnegie Mellon University estimates that there are 5 to 15 bugs in every 1000 lines of code. Windows 2000 has 40–60 million lines of code.

## Maintenance Hooks

In the programming world, *maintenance hooks* are a type of backdoor. They are instructions within software that only the developer knows about and can invoke. They are placed in the software to give the developer easy access to the code. They allow the developer to view and edit the code without having to go through regular access controls. During the development phase of the software, these can be very useful, but if they are not removed before the software goes into production, they can cause major security issues.

The maintenance hook is usually initiated by a random sequence of keystrokes that provides access into the software without having to go through normal access control and security checks and mechanisms.

An application that has a maintenance hook enables the developer to execute commands by using a specific sequence of keystrokes. Once this is done successfully, the developer can be inside the application looking directly at the code or configuration files. She might do this to watch problem areas within the code, check variable population, export more code into the program, or fix problems that she sees taking place. Although this sounds nice and healthy, if an attacker finds out about this maintenance hook, he can take more sinister actions. So all maintenance hooks need to be removed from software before it goes into production.

 **NOTE** Many would think that since security is more in the minds of people today, that maintenance hooks would be a thing of the past. This is not true. Developers are still using maintenance hooks, because of their lack of understanding or care of security issues, and many maintenance hooks still reside in older software that organizations are using.

## Countermeasures

Because maintenance hooks are usually inserted by programmers, they are the ones who usually have to take them out before the programs go into production. Code reviews and unit and quality assurance testing should always be looking out for backdoors, in case the programmer overlooked extracting them. Because maintenance hooks are within the code of an application or system, there is not much a user can do to prevent their presence, but when a vendor finds out that a backdoor exists in its product, it usually develops and releases a patch to reduce this vulnerability. Because most vendors sell their software without including the associated source code, it may be very difficult for companies who have purchased software to identify backdoors. The following lists some preventative measures against backdoors:

- Use a host intrusion detection system to watch for an attacker using a backdoor into the system.
- Use file system encryption to protect sensitive information.
- Implement auditing to detect any type of backdoor use.

## Time-of-Check/Time-of-Use Attack

Specific attacks can take advantage of the way a system processes requests and performs tasks. A *time-of-check/time-of-use (TOC/TOU) attack* deals with the sequence of steps that a system uses to complete a task. This type of attack takes advantage of the dependency on the timing of events that take place in a multitasking operating system.

As stated previously, operating systems and applications are in reality just lines and lines of instructions. An operating system has to carry out instruction 1, then instruction 2, then instruction 3, and so on. This is how it is written. If an attacker can get in between instruction 2 and 3 and manipulate something, then she can control the result of these activities.

An example of a TOC/TOU attack is if process 1 validates the authorization of a user to open a noncritical text file and process 2 carries out the `open` command. If the attacker can change out this noncritical text file with a password file while process 1 is carrying out its task, she has just obtained access to this critical file. (It is a flaw within the code that allows this type of compromise to take place.)

 **NOTE** This type of attack is also referred to as an *asynchronous attack*. Asynchronous describes a process in which the timing of each step may vary. The attack gets in between these steps and modifies something. Race conditions are also considered TOC/TOU attacks by some in the industry.

A *race condition* is when two different processes need to carry out their tasks on one resource. The processes need to follow the correct sequence. Process 1 needs to carry out its work before process 2 accesses the same resource and carries out its tasks. If process 2 goes before process 1, the outcome could be very different. If an attacker can manipulate the processes so that process 2 does its task first, she can control the outcome of the processing procedure. Let's say that process 1's instructions are to add 3 to a value and process 2's instructions are to divide by 15. If process 2 carries out its tasks before process 1, the outcome would be different. So if an attacker can make process 2 do its work before process 1, she can control the result.

Looking at this issue from a security perspective, there are several types of race condition attacks that are quite concerning. If a system splits up the authentication and authorization steps, an attacker could be authorized before she is even authenticated. For example, in the normal sequence, process 1 verifies the authentication before allowing a user access to a resource, and process 2 authorizes the user to access the resource. If the attacker makes process 2 carry out its tasks before process 1, then she can access a resource without the system making sure she has been authenticated properly.

So although the terms "race condition" and "TOC/TOU attack" are sometimes used interchangeably, in reality they are two different things. A race condition is an attack in which an attacker makes processes execute out of sequence to control the result. A TOC/TOU attack is when an attacker jumps in between two tasks and modifies something to control the result.

## Countermeasures

It would take a dedicated attacker with great precision to perform these types of attacks, but it is possible and has been done. To protect against race condition attacks, it is best to *not* split up critical tasks that can have their sequence altered. This means that the system should use atomic operations where only one system call is used to check authentication and then grant access in one task. This would not give the processor the opportunity to switch to another process in between two tasks. Unfortunately, using these types of atomic operations is not always possible.

To avoid TOC/TOU attacks, it is best if the operating system can apply software locks to the items that it will use when it is carrying out its "checking" tasks. So if a user requests access to a file, while the system is validating this user's authorization, it should put a software lock on the file that is being requested. This ensures that the file cannot be deleted and replaced with another file. Applying locks can be carried out easily on files, but it is more challenging to apply locks to database components and table entries to provide this type of protection.

## Buffer Overflow

*My cup runneth over and so does my buffer.*

Today, many people know the term buffer overflow and the basic definition, but it is important for security professionals to understand what is going on beneath the covers.

A *buffer overflow* takes place when too much data is accepted as input to an application or operating system. A buffer is an allocated segment of memory. A buffer can be overflowed arbitrarily with too much data, but for it to be of any use to an attacker, the code that is inserted into the buffer must be of a specific length followed up by commands the attacker wants to be executed. So, the purpose of a buffer overflow may be either to make a mess, by shoving arbitrary data into various memory segments, or to accomplish a specific task, by pushing into the memory segment a carefully crafted set of data that will accomplish a specific task. This task could be to open a command shell with administrative privilege or execute malicious code.

Let's take a deeper look at how this is accomplished. Software may be written to accept data from a user, web site, database, or another application. The accepted data needs something to happen to it, because it has been inputted for some type of manipulation or calculation or to be used as a parameter to be passed to a procedure. A procedure is code that can carry out a specific type of function on the data and return the result to the requesting software, as shown in Figure 5-21.

When a programmer writes a piece of software that will accept data, this data will be stored in a variable. When this software calls upon a procedure to carry out some type of functionality, it stacks the necessary instructions and data in a memory segment for the procedure to read from. (Memory stacks were explained earlier in the chapter, but we will go over them again in this section.)

The data that is accepted from an outside entity is placed in a variable. This variable has to have a place to live in memory, which is called a buffer. A buffer is like a memory container for data. The buffer needs to be the right size to accept the inputted data. So if the input is supposed to be one character, the buffer should be one byte in size. If a programmer does not ensure that only one byte of data is being inserted into the software, then someone can input several characters at once and overflow that specific buffer.

The buffers hold data, which are placed on a memory stack. You can think of a buffer as a small bucket to hold water (data). We have several of these small buckets stacked on top of one another (memory stack), and if too much water is poured into the top bucket, it spills over into the buckets below it (buffer overflow) and overwrites the instructions and data on the memory stack.

## What Is a Stack and How Does It Work?

If you are interacting with an application that calculates mortgage rates, you have to put in the parameters that need to be calculated—years of loan, percentage of interest rate, and amount of loan. These parameters are passed into empty variables and put in a

**Figure 5-21** A memory stack has individual buffers to hold instructions and data.

linear construct (memory stack), which acts like a queue for the procedure to pull from when it carries out this calculation. The first thing your mortgage rate application lays down on the stack is its return pointer. This is a pointer to the requesting application's memory address that tells the procedure to return control to the requesting application after the procedure has worked through all the values on the stack. The mortgage rate application then places on top of the return pointer the rest of the data you have inputted and sends a request to the procedure to carry out the necessary calculation, as illustrated in Figure 5-21. The procedure takes the data off the stack starting at the top, so it is first in, last off (FILO). The procedure carries out its functions on all the data and returns the result and control back to the requesting mortgage rate application once it hits the return pointer in the stack.

So the stack is just a segment in memory that allows for communication between the requesting application and the procedure or subroutine. The potential for problems comes into play when the requesting application does not carry out proper *bounds checking* to ensure that the inputted data is of an acceptable length. Look at the following C code to see how this could happen:

```
#include <stdio.h>
    int main(int argc, char **argv) {
        char buf1 [5] = "1111";
        char buf2 [7] = "222222";
        strcpy (buf2, "3333333333");
        printf ("%s\n", buf2);
printf ("%s\n", buf1);
    return 0;}
```

 **CAUTION**   You do not need to know C programming for the CISSP exam. We are digging deep into this topic because buffer overflows are so common and have caused grave security breaches over the years. For the CISSP exam, you just need to understand the overall concept of a buffer overflow.

Here we are setting up a buffer (buf1) to hold four characters and a NULL value, and second buffer (buf2) to hold six characters and a NULL value. (The NULL values indicate the buffer's end place in memory.) If we viewed these buffers, we would see the following:

```
Buf2
\0 2 2 2 2 2 2
Buf1
\0 1 1 1 1
```

The application then accepts ten 3s into buf2, which can only hold six characters. So the six variables in buf2 are filled and then the four variables in buf1 are filled, over-writing the original contents of buf1. This took place because the `strcpy` command did not make sure that the buffer was large enough to hold that many values. So now if we looked at the two buffers, we would see the following:

```
Buf2
\0 3 3 3 3 3 3
Buf1
\0 3 3 3 3
```

But what gets even more interesting is when the actual return pointer is written over, as shown in Figure 5-22. In a carefully crafted buffer overflow attack, the stack is filled properly so that the return pointer can be overwritten and control is given to the malicious instructions that have been loaded onto the stack instead of back to the requesting application. This allows the malicious instructions to be executed in the security context of the requesting application. If this application is running in a privileged mode, then the attacker has more permissions and rights to carry out more damage.

The attacker must know the size of the buffer to overwrite and must know the addresses that have been assigned to the stack. Without knowing these addresses, she could not lay down a new return pointer to her malicious code. The attacker must also write this dangerous payload to be small enough so that it can be passed as input from one procedure to the next.

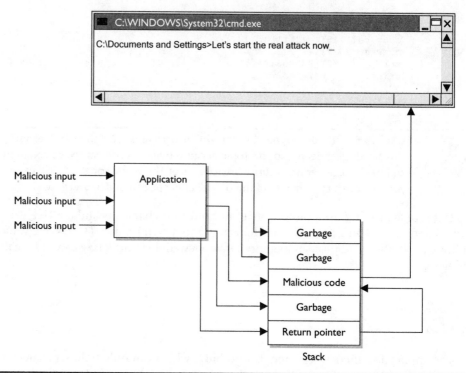

**Figure 5-22**   Illustration of a buffer overflow attack

Windows' core is written in the C language and has layers and layers of object-oriented code on top of it. When a procedure needs to call upon the operating system to carry out some type of task, it calls upon a system service via an API call. The API works like a doorway to the operating system's functionality.

The C language is susceptible to buffer overflow attacks because it allows for direct pointer manipulations to take place. Specific commands can provide access to low-level memory addresses without carrying out bounds checking. The C functions that do perform the necessary boundary checking include `sprintf( )`, `strcat( )`, `strcpy( )`, and `vsprintf( )`.

An operating system has to be written to work with specific CPU architectures. These architectures dictate system memory addressing, protection mechanisms, and modes of execution, and work with specific instruction sets. This means that a buffer overflow attack that works on an Intel chip will not necessarily work on a Motorola or a SPARC processor. These different processors set up the memory address of the stacks differently, so the attacker may have to craft different buffer overflow code for different platforms. This is usually not an obstacle since most of the time the code is already written and available via different hacking web sites.

## Countermeasures

Buffer overflows are in the source code of various applications and operating systems. They have been around since programmers started developing software. This means that it is very difficult for a user to identify and fix them. When a buffer overflow is identified, the vendor usually sends out a patch. So keeping systems current on updates, hotfixes, and patches is usually the best countermeasure. There are also some products that are installed on systems that can watch for input values that could result in buffer overflows. But the best countermeasure is proper programming. This means to use bounds checking. If an input value is only supposed to be nine characters, then the application should only accept nine characters and no more. Some languages are more susceptible to buffer overflows than others. So programmers should understand these issues, use the right languages for the right purposes, and carry out code review to identify buffer overflow vulnerabilities.

# Summary

The architecture of a computer system is very important and comprises many topics. The system has to ensure that memory is properly segregated and protected, ensure that only authorized subjects access objects, ensure that untrusted processes cannot perform activities that would put other processes at risk, control the flow of information, and define a domain of resources for each subject. It also must ensure that if the computer experiences any type of disruption, it will not result in an insecure state. Many of these issues are dealt with in the system's security policy, and the security model is built to support the requirements of this policy.

Once the security policy, model, and architecture have been developed, the computer operating system, or product, must be built, tested, evaluated, and rated. An evaluation is done by comparing the system to a predefined criteria. The rating that is assigned to the system depends upon how it fulfills the requirements of the criteria. Customers use this rating to understand what they are really buying and how much they can trust this new product. Once the customer buys the product, it must be tested within their own environment to make sure it meets their company's needs, which takes place through certification and accreditation processes.

# Quick Tips

- Two systems can have the exact same hardware, software components, and applications, but provide different levels of protection because of the different security policies and security models that the two systems were built upon.

- A CPU contains a control unit, which controls the timing of the execution of instructions and data, and an ALU, which performs mathematical functions and logical operations.

- Most systems use protection rings. The more privileged processes run in the lower-numbered rings and have access to all or most of the system resources. Applications run in higher-numbered rings and have access to a smaller amount of resources.

- Operating system processes are executed in privileged or supervisor mode, and applications are executed in user mode, also known as "problem state."

- Secondary storage is nonvolatile and can be a hard drive, CD-ROM drive, floppy drive, tape backup, or a jump drive.

- Virtual storage combines RAM and secondary storage so that the system seems to have a larger bank of memory.

- A deadlock situation occurs when two processes are trying to access the same resource at the same time or when a process commits a resource and does not release it.

- Security mechanisms can focus on different issues, work at different layers, and vary in complexity.

- The more complex a security mechanism is, the less amount of assurance it can usually provide.

- Not all system components fall under the trusted computing base (TCB), which includes only those system components that enforce the security policy directly and protect the system. These components are within the security perimeter.

- Components that make up the TCB are hardware, software, and firmware that provide some type of security protection.

- A security perimeter is an imaginary boundary that has trusted components within it (those that make up the TCB) and untrusted components outside it.

- The reference monitor concept is an abstract machine that ensures that all subjects have the necessary access rights before accessing objects. Therefore, it mediates all accesses to objects by subjects.

- The security kernel is the mechanism that actually enforces the rules of the reference monitor concept.

- The security kernel must isolate processes carrying out the reference monitor concept, must be tamperproof, must be invoked for each access attempt, and must be small enough to be properly tested.

- A security domain is all the objects available to a subject.

- Processes need to be isolated, which can be done through segmented memory addressing, encapsulation of objects, time multiplexing of shared resources, naming distinctions, and virtual mapping.

- A security policy is a set of rules that dictates how sensitive data is to be managed, protected, and distributed. It provides the security goals that the system must accomplish.

- The level of security a system provides depends upon how well it enforces the security policy.

- A multilevel security system processes data at different classifications (security levels), and users with different clearances (security levels) can use the system.

- Processes should be assigned least privilege so that they have just enough system privileges to fulfill their tasks and no more.

- Some systems provide security at different layers of their architectures, which is called layering. This separates the processes and provides more protection for them individually.

- Data hiding occurs when processes work at different layers and have layers of access control between them. Processes need to know how to communicate only with each other's interfaces.

- A security model maps the abstract goals of a security policy to computer system terms and concepts. It gives the security policy structure and provides a framework for the system.

- A closed system is often proprietary to the manufacturer or vendor, whereas the open system allows for more interoperability.

- The Bell-LaPadula model deals only with confidentiality, and the Biba and Clark-Wilson models deal only with integrity.

- A state machine model deals with the different states a system can enter. If a system starts in a secure state, all state transitions take place securely, and the system shuts down and fails securely, the system will never end up in an insecure state.

- A lattice model provides an upper bound and a lower bound of authorized access for subjects.

- An information flow security model does not permit data to flow to an object in an insecure manner.

- The Bell-LaPadula model has a simple security rule, which means that a subject cannot read data from a higher level (no read up). The *-property rule means that a subject cannot write to an object at a lower level (no write down). The strong star property rule dictates that a subject can read and write to objects at its own security level.

- The Biba model does not let subjects write to objects at a higher integrity level (no write up), and it does not let subjects read data at a lower integrity level (no read down). This is done to protect the integrity of the data.

- The Bell-LaPadula model is used mainly in military systems. The Biba and Clark-Wilson models are used in the commercial sector.

- The Clark-Wilson model dictates that subjects can only access objects through applications. This model also illustrates how to provide separation of duties, functionality, and auditing tasks within software.

- If a system is working in a dedicated security mode, it only deals with one level of data classification, and all users must have this level of clearance to be able to use the system.

- Compartmented and multilevel security modes enable the system to process data classified at different classification levels.

- Trust means that a system uses all of its protection mechanisms properly to process sensitive data for many types of users. Assurance is the level of confidence you have in this trust and that the protection mechanisms behave properly in all circumstances predictably.

- The Orange Book, also called Trusted Computer System Evaluation Criteria (TCSEC), was developed to evaluate systems built to be used mainly by the military. Its use was expanded to evaluate other types of products.

- In the Orange Book, D classification means that a system provides minimal protection and is used for systems that were evaluated but failed to meet the criteria of higher divisions.

- In the Orange Book, the C division deals with discretionary protection, and the B division deals with mandatory protection (security labels).

- In the Orange Book, the A classification means that the system's design and level of protection are verifiable and provide the highest level of assurance and trust.

- In the Orange Book, C2 requires object reuse protection and auditing.

- In the Orange Book, B1 is the first rating that requires security labels.

- In the Orange Book, B2 requires security labels for all subjects and devices, the existence of a trusted path, routine covert channel analysis, and provision of separate administrator functionality.

- The Orange Book deals mainly with stand-alone systems, so a range of books were written to cover many other topics in security. These books are called the Rainbow Series.

- ITSEC evaluates the assurance and functionality of a system's protection mechanisms separately, whereas TCSEC combines the two into one rating.

- The Common Criteria was developed to provide a globally recognized evaluation criteria and is in use today. It combines sections of TCSEC, ITSEC, CTCPEC, and the Federal Criteria.

- The Common Criteria uses protection profiles and ratings from EAL1 to EAL7.

- Certification is the technical evaluation of a system or product and its security components. Accreditation is management's formal approval and acceptance of the security provided by a system.

- A covert channel is an unintended communication path that transfers data in a way that violates the security policy. There are two types: timing and storage covert channels.

- A covert timing channel enables a process to relay information to another process by modulating its use of system resources.

- A covert storage channel enables a process to write data to a storage medium so that another process can read it.

- A maintenance hook is developed to let a programmer into the application quickly for maintenance. This should be removed before the application goes into production or it can cause a serious security risk.

- An execution domain is where instructions are executed by the CPU. The operating system's instructions are executed in a privileged mode, and applications' instructions are executed in user mode.

- Process isolation ensures that multiple processes can run concurrently and the processes will not interfere with each other or affect each other's memory segments.

- The only processes that need complete system privileges are located in the system's kernel.

- A single state machine processes data of a single security level. A multistate machine processes data at two or more security levels without risk of compromising the system's security.

- TOC/TOU stands for time-of-check/time-of-use. This is a class of asynchronous attacks.

- The Biba model addresses the first goal of integrity, which is to prevent unauthorized users from making modifications.

- The Clark-Wilson model addresses all three integrity goals: prevent unauthorized users from making modifications, prevent authorized users from making improper modifications, and maintain internal and external consistency.

- In the Clark-Wilson model, users can only access and manipulate objects through programs. It uses access triple, which is subject-program-object.

## Questions

Please remember that these questions are formatted and asked in a certain way for a reason. You must remember that the CISSP exam is asking questions at a conceptual level. Questions may not always have the perfect answer, and the candidate is advised against always looking for the perfect answer. The candidate should look for the best answer in the list.

1. What flaw creates buffer overflows?

    A. Application executing in privileged mode

    B. Inadequate memory segmentation

    C. Inadequate protection ring use

    D. Insufficient bounds checking

2. The operating system performs all except which of the following tasks?

    A. Memory allocation

    B. Input and output tasks

    C. Resource allocation

    D. User access to database views

3. If an operating system allows sequential use of an object without refreshing it, what security issue can arise?

   A. Disclosure of residual data

   B. Unauthorized access to privileged processes

   C. Data leakage through covert channels

   D. Compromise of the execution domain

4. What is the final step in authorizing a system for use in an environment?

   A. Certification

   B. Security evaluation and rating

   C. Accreditation

   D. Verification

5. What feature enables code to be executed without the usual security checks?

   A. Temporal isolation

   B. Maintenance hook

   C. Race conditions

   D. Process multiplexing

6. If a component fails, a system should be designed to do which of the following?

   A. Change to a protected execution domain

   B. Change to a problem state

   C. Change to a more secure state

   D. Release all data held in volatile memory

7. What security advantage does firmware have over software?

   A. Difficult to modify without physical access

   B. Requires a smaller memory segment

   C. Does not need to enforce the security policy

   D. Is easier to reprogram

8. Which is the first level of the Orange Book that requires classification labeling of data?

   A. B3

   B. B2

   C. B1

   D. C2

9. Which of the following best describes the security kernel?

   A. A software component that monitors activity and writes security events to an audit log

B. A software component that determines if a user is authorized to perform a requested operation

C. A software component that isolates processes and separates privileged and user modes

D. A software component that works in the center protection ring and provides interfaces between trusted and untrusted objects

10. The Information Technology Security Evaluation Criteria was developed for which of the following?

A. International use

B. U.S. use

C. European use

D. Global use

11. A security kernel contains which of the following?

A. Software, hardware, and firmware

B. Software, hardware, and system design

C. Security policy, protection mechanisms, and software

D. Security policy, protection mechanisms, and system design

12. What is the purpose of base and limit registers?

A. Countermeasure buffer overflows

B. Time sharing of system resources, mainly the CPU

C. Process isolation

D. TCB enforcement

13. A guard is commonly used with a classified system. What is the main purpose of implementing and using a guard?

A. Ensure that less trusted systems only receive acknowledgements and not messages

B. Ensure proper information flow

C. Ensure that less trusted and more trusted systems have open architectures and interoperability

D. Allow multilevel and dedicated mode systems to communicate

14. The trusted computing base (TCB) controls which of the following?

A. All trusted processes and software components

B. All trusted security policies and implementation mechanisms

C. All trusted software and design mechanisms

D. All trusted software and hardware components

15. What is the imaginary boundary that separates components that maintain security from components that are not security related?

    A. Reference monitor

    B. Security kernel

    C. Security perimeter

    D. Security policy

16. Which model deals only with confidentiality?

    A. Bell-LaPadula

    B. Clark-Wilson

    C. Biba

    D. Reference monitor

17. What is the best description of a security kernel from a security point of view?

    A. Reference monitor

    B. Resource manager

    C. Memory mapper

    D. Security perimeter

18. When is security of a system most effective and economical?

    A. If it is designed and implemented from the beginning of the development of the system

    B. If it is designed and implemented as a secure and trusted front end

    C. If it is customized to fight specific types of attacks

    D. If the system is optimized before security is added

19. In secure computing systems, why is there a logical form of separation used between processes?

    A. Processes are contained within their own security domains so that each does not make unauthorized accesses to other processes or their resources.

    B. Processes are contained within their own security perimeter so that they can only access protection levels above them.

    C. Processes are contained within their own security perimeter so that they can only access protection levels equal to them.

    D. The separation is hardware and not logical in nature.

20. What type of attack is taking place when a higher-level subject writes data to a storage area and a lower-level subject reads it?

    A. TOC/TOU

    B. Covert storage attack

    C. Covert timing attack

    D. Buffer overflow

21. What type of rating does the Common Criteria give to products?

    A. PP

    B. EPL

    C. EAL

    D. A–D

22. Which best describes the *-integrity axiom?

    A. No write up in the Biba model

    B. No read down in the Biba model

    C. No write down in the Bell-LaPadula model

    D. No read up in the Bell-LaPadula model

23. Which best describes the simple security rule?

    A. No write up in the Biba model

    B. No read down in the Biba model

    C. No write down in the Bell-LaPadula model

    D. No read up in the Bell-LaPadula model

24. Which of the following was the first mathematical model of a multilevel security policy used to define the concepts of a security state and mode of access, and to outline rules of access?

    A. Biba

    B. Bell-LaPadula

    C. Clark-Wilson

    D. State machine

25. Which of the following is a true statement pertaining to memory addressing?

    A. The CPU uses absolute addresses. Applications use logical addresses. Relative addresses are based on a known address and an offset value.

    B. The CPU uses logical addresses. Applications use absolute addresses. Relative addresses are based on a known address and an offset value.

    C. The CPU uses absolute addresses. Applications use relative addresses. Logical addresses are based on a known address and an offset value.

    D. The CPU uses absolute addresses. Applications use logical addresses. Absolute addresses are based on a known address and an offset value.

## Answers

1. **D.** A buffer overflow takes place when too much data is accepted as input. Programmers should implement the correct security controls to ensure that this does not take place. This means they need to perform bounds checking and parameter checking to ensure that only the allowed amount of data is actually accepted and processed by the system.

2. **D.** The operating system has a long list of responsibilities, but implementing database views is not one of them. This is the responsibility of the database management software.

3. **A.** If an object has confidential data and this data is not properly erased before another subject can access it, this leftover or residual data can be accessible. This can compromise the data and system's security by disclosing this confidential information. This is true of media (hard drives) and memory segments.

4. **C.** Certification is a technical review of a product, and accreditation is management's formal approval of the findings of the certification process. This question asked you which step was the final step of authorizing a system before it is to be used in an environment, and that is what accreditation is all about.

5. **B.** Maintenance hooks get around the system's or application's security and access control checks by allowing whoever knows the key sequence to access the application and most likely its code. Maintenance hooks should be removed from any code before it gets into production.

6. **C.** The state machine model dictates that a system should start up securely, carry out secure state transitions, and even fail securely. This means that if the system encounters something it deems unsafe, it should change to a more secure state for self-preservation and protection.

7. **A.** Firmware is a type of software that is held in a ROM or EROM chip. It is usually used to allow the computer to be able to communicate with some type of peripheral device. The system's BIOS instructions are also held in firmware on the motherboard. In most situations, firmware cannot be modified unless someone has physical access to the system. This is different from other types of software that may be modified remotely or through logical means.

8. **C.** These assurance ratings are from the Orange Book. B levels and on up require security labels to be used, but the question asks which is the first level to require this. B1 comes before B2 and B3, thus it is the correct answer.

9. **B.** A security kernel is the software component that enforces access control for the operating system. A reference monitor is the abstract machine that holds all of the rules of access for the system. The security kernel is the active entity that enforces the reference monitor's rules. They control the access attempts of any and all subjects; a user is just one example of a subject.

10. **C.** In ITSEC, the *I* does not stand for international, it stands for information. This is a criteria that was developed to be used by European countries to evaluate and rate their products.

11. **A.** The security kernel makes up the main component of the TCB, which is made up of software, hardware, and firmware. The security kernel performs a lot of different activities to protect the system; enforcing the reference monitor's access rules is just one of those activities.

12. **C.** The CPU has base and limit registers that hold the starting and ending memory addresses that a process is allowed to work within. This ensures that the process is isolated from other processes in that it cannot interact with another process's memory segment.

13. **B.** The guard accepts requests from the less trusted entity, reviews the request to make sure it is allowed, and then submits the request on behalf of the less trusted system. The goal is to ensure that information does not flow from a high security level to a low security level in an unauthorized manner.

14. **D.** The TCB contains and controls all protection mechanisms within the system, whether they are software, hardware, or firmware.

15. **C.** The security perimeter is a boundary between items that are within the TCB and items that are outside the TCB. It is just a mark of delineation between these two groups of items.

16. **A.** The Bell-LaPadula model was developed for the U.S. government with the main goal of keeping sensitive data unreachable to those who were not authorized to access and view it. This model was the first mathematical model of a multilevel security policy used to define the concepts of a security state and mode of access and to outline rules of access. The Biba and Clark-Wilson models do not deal with confidentiality, but with integrity instead.

17. **A.** The security kernel is a portion of the operating system's kernel and enforces the rules outlined in the reference monitor. It is the enforcer of the rules and is invoked each time a subject makes a request to access an object.

18. **A.** It is difficult to add useful and effective security at the end of developing a product or to add security as a front end to an existing product. Adding security at the end of a project is usually more expensive because it will break items and the team will need to go back to the drawing board and redesign and recode portions of the product.

19. **A.** Processes are assigned their own variables, system resources, and memory segments, which make up their domain. This is done so that they do not corrupt each other's data or processing activities.

20. **B.** A covert channel is being used when something is using a resource for communication purposes and that is not the reason this resource was created. A process can write to some type of shared media or storage place that another process will be able to access. The first process writes to this media and the second process reads it. This action goes against the security policy of the system.

21. **C.** The Common Criteria uses a different assurance rating system than the previously used criteria. It has packages of specifications that must be met for a product to obtain the corresponding rating. These ratings and packages are called Evaluation Assurance Levels (EALs). Once a product achieves any type of rating, customers can view this information on an Evaluated Products List (EPL).

22. **A.** The *-integrity axiom (or star integrity axiom) indicates that a subject of a lower integrity level cannot write to an object of a higher integrity level. This rule is put into place to protect the integrity of the data that resides at the higher level.

23. **D.** The simple security rule is implemented to ensure that any subject at a lower security level cannot view data that resides at a higher level. The reason this type of rule is put into place is to protect the confidentiality of the data that resides at the higher level. This rule is used in the Bell-LaPadula model. Remember that if you see "simple" in a rule it pertains to reading, and * or "star" pertains to writing.

24. **B.** This is a formal definition of the Bell-LaPadula model, which was created and implemented to protect government and military confidential information.

25. **A.** The physical memory addresses that the CPU uses are called absolute addresses. The indexed memory addresses that software uses are referred to as logical addresses. And relative addresses are based on a known address with an offset value applied.

# Physical and Environmental Security

This chapter presents the following:

- Administrative, technical, and physical controls
- Facility location, construction, and management
- Physical security risks, threats, and countermeasures
- Electric power issues and countermeasures
- Fire prevention, detection, and suppression
- Intrusion detection systems

Security is very important to organizations and their infrastructures, and physical security is no exception. Physical security encompasses a different set of threats, vulnerabilities, and risks than the other types of security that have been addressed so far. Physical security mechanisms include site design and layout, environmental components, emergency response readiness, training, access control, intrusion detection, and power and fire protection. Physical security mechanisms protect people, data, equipment, systems, facilities, and a long list of company assets.

## Introduction to Physical Security

Physical security of computers and their resources in the 1960s and 1970s was not as challenging as it is today, because computers were mostly mainframes that were locked away in server rooms, and only a handful of people knew what to do with them anyway. Today, there is a computer on almost every desk in every company, and access to devices and resources is spread throughout the environment. Companies have several wiring closets and server rooms, and remote and mobile users take computers and resources out of the facility. Properly protecting these computer systems, networks, facilities, and employees has become an overwhelming task to many companies.

Theft, fraud, sabotage, vandalism, and accidents are raising costs for many companies because environments are becoming more complex and dynamic. Security and complexity are at the opposite sides of a spectrum. As environments and technology become more complex more vulnerabilities are introduced that allow for compromises to take place. Most companies have had memory or processors stolen from workstations and some have had computers and laptops taken. Even worse, many companies have been victims of more dangerous crimes, such as robbery at gunpoint, a shooting rampage by a disgruntled employee, anthrax, bombs, and terrorist activities. Many companies may have implemented security guards, closed-circuit TV (CCTV) surveillance, intrusion detection systems (IDSs), and requirements for employees to maintain a higher level of awareness of security risks. These are only some of the items that fall within the physical security boundaries. If any one of these does not provide the necessary protection level, then it could be the weak link that causes potentially dangerous security breaches.

Most people in the information security field do not think as much about *physical* security as they do about *computer* security and the associated hackers, ports, viruses, and technology-oriented security countermeasures. But information security without proper physical security could be a waste of time.

Even people within the physical security market do not always have a holistic view of physical security; there are so many components and variables to understand, people have to specialize in specific fields, such as secure facility construction, risk assessment and analysis, secure data center implementation, fire protection, IDS and CCTV implementation, personnel emergency response and training, legal and regulatory aspects of physical security, and so on. Each has its own focus and skill set, but for an organization to have a solid physical security program, all of these areas need to be understood and addressed.

Just as most software is built with functionality as the number one goal, with security somewhere farther down the priority list, many facilities and physical environments are built with functionality and aesthetics in mind, with not as much concern for providing levels of protection. Many thefts and deaths could be prevented if all organizations were to implement physical security in an organized, mature, and holistic manner. Most people are not aware of many of the crimes that happen every day. Many people are also not aware of all the civil lawsuits that stem from organizations not practicing due diligence and due care pertaining to physical security. The following is a short list of some examples of things companies are sued for pertaining to improper physical security implementation and maintenance:

- An apartment complex does not respond to a report of a broken lock on a sliding glass door and subsequently a woman who lives in that apartment is raped by an intruder
- Bushes are growing too close to an ATM, allowing criminals to hide behind them and attack individuals as they withdraw money from their accounts
- A portion of an underground garage is unlit, which allows an attacker to sit and wait for an employee who works late
- A gas station's outside restroom has a broken lock, which allows an attacker to enter after a female customer and kill her
- A convenience store hangs too many advertising signs and posters on the exterior windows, prompting thieves to choose this store because the signs hide crime taking place inside the store from people driving or walking by

There are many examples like that taking place every day. These crimes might make it to our local news stations, but there are too many of them to be reported in national newspapers or on network news. It is important as a security professional to evaluate security from the standpoint of a potential criminal, to detect and remedy any points of vulnerability that could be exploited by criminals.

Physical security has a different set of vulnerabilities, threats, and countermeasures from that of computer and information security. The set for physical security has more to do with physical destruction, intruders, environmental issues, theft, and vandalism. When security professionals look at *information* security, they think about how someone can enter an environment in an unauthorized manner through a port, modem, or wireless access point. When security professionals look at *physical* security, they are concerned with how people can physically enter an environment and cause an array of damages.

The threats that an organization faces fall into many different categories:

- **Natural environmental threats**   Floods, earthquakes, storms and tornadoes, fires, extreme temperature conditions, and so forth

- **Supply system threats**   Power distribution outages, communications interruptions, and interruption to other natural energy resources such as water, steam, and gas, and so forth

- **Manmade threats**   Unauthorized access (both internal and external), explosions, damage by angry employees, employee errors and accidents, vandalism, fraud, theft, and so forth

- **Politically motivated threats**   Strikes, riots, civil disobedience, terrorist attacks and bombings, and so forth

In all situations, the primary consideration, above all else, is that nothing should impede *life safety* goals. When we discuss life safety, we're looking at how to protect human life above all else. Good planning helps to balance life safety concerns and other security measures. For example, baring a door to prevent unauthorized physical intrusion might prevent individuals from being able to escape in the event of a fire.

**NOTE**   Life safety goals should always take precedence all other types of goals.

A physical security program should comprise safety and security mechanisms. Safety deals with the protection of life and assets against fire, natural disasters, and devastating accidents. Security addresses vandalism, theft, and attacks by individuals. Many times there is an overlap between the two, but both types of threat categories need to be understood and properly planned for. This chapter addresses both safety and security mechanisms that every security professional should be aware of.

Physical security needs to be implemented based on a *layered defense model*, which means that physical controls should work together in a tiered architecture. The concept is that if one layer fails, other layers will protect the valuable asset. Layers would be implemented moving from the perimeter toward the asset. For example, you would have a fence, then your facility walls, then an access control card device, then a guard, then an IDS, and then locked computer cases and safes. This series of layers will protect the company's most sensitive assets, which would be placed in the innermost control zone of the environment. So if the bad guy were able to climb over your fence and outsmart the security guard, he would still have to circumvent several layers of controls before getting to your precious resources and systems.

Security needs to protect all the assets of the organization and enhance productivity by providing a secure and predictable environment. Good security enables employees to focus on their tasks at hand, and encourages evildoers to move on to a more vulnerable and easier target. This is the hope, anyway. Keeping in mind the AIC security triad that has been presented in previous chapters, we look at physical security that can affect the *availability* of company resources, the *integrity* of the assets and environment, and the *confidentiality* of the data and business processes.

# Planning Process

*Okay, so what are we doing and why? Response: We have no idea.*

A designer, or team of designers, needs to be identified to create or improve upon an organization's current physical security program. The team must work with management to define the objectives of the program, design the program, and develop performance-based metrics and evaluation processes to ensure that the objectives are continually being met.

The objectives of the physical security program depend upon the level of protection required for the various assets and the company as a whole. And this required level of protection, in turn, depends upon the organization's acceptable risk level. This acceptable risk level should be derived from the laws and regulations with which the organization must comply and from the threat profile of the organization overall. This requires identifying who and what could damage business assets, identifying the types of attacks and crimes that could take place, and understanding the business impact of these threats. The type of physical countermeasures required and their adequacy or inadequacy can only be measured against the organization's threat profile. A financial institution has a much different threat profile, and thus a much different acceptable risk level, when compared to a grocery store. The threat profile of a hospital is different from the threat profile of a military base or a government agency. The team needs to understand the types of adversaries that it must consider, the capabilities of these adversaries, and the resources and tactics that these individuals would use. (Review Chapter 3 for a discussion of acceptable risk level concepts.)

Physical security is a combination of people, processes, procedures, and equipment to protect resources. The design of a solid physical security program should be methodical and weigh the objectives of the program and the available resources. Although every organization is different, the approach to constructing and maintaining a physical security program is the same. The organization must first define the vulnerabilities, threats, threat agents, and targets.

**NOTE** Remember that a vulnerability is a weakness and a threat is the potential that someone will identify this weakness and use it against you. The threat agent is the person or mechanism that actually exploits this identified vulnerability.

Threats need to be broken down into different categories, such as internal and external threats. Inside threats may include misbehaving devices, fire hazards, or internal employees who aim to damage the company in some way. Internal employees have intimate knowledge of the company's facility and assets, which is usually required to carry out tasks and responsibilities—but this makes it easier for the insider to carry out damaging activity without being noticed. Unfortunately, a large threat to companies can be their own security guards, which is usually not realized until it is too late. These people have keys and access codes to all portions of a facility and usually work during employee off hours. This gives the guards ample windows of opportunity to carry out their crimes. It is critical for a company to carry out a background investigation, or pay a company to perform this service, before hiring a security guard. If you hire a wolf to guard the chicken coop, things can get ugly.

External threats come in many different forms as well. Government buildings are usually chosen targets for some types of political revenge. If a company performs abortions or conducts animal research, then activists are usually a large and constant threat. And, of course, banks and armored cars are tempting targets for organized crime members.

A threat that is even trickier to protect against is *collusion*, in which two or more people work together to carry out fraudulent activity. Many criminal cases have uncovered insiders working with outsiders to defraud or damage a company. The types of controls for this type of activity are procedural protection mechanisms, which were described at length in Chapter 3. This may include separation of duties, preemployment background checks, rotations of duties, and supervision.

## Commission on Critical Infrastructure Protection

In Chapter 2 we looked at the President's Commission on Critical Infrastructure Protection (PCCIP), which requires organizations that are part of the national critical infrastructure to have adequate protection mechanisms in place. Although this executive order deals with technical protection of systems and data, it also deals with physical protection of the facilities themselves. It outlines that power systems, emergency services, water supply systems, gas and oil transportation, and government services must be evaluated to ensure that proper physical security is implemented. It really does not make a lot of sense to ensure that hackers can't get to your server if you don't also ensure that someone can't just walk in and steal your server.

Legislation that has been passed over the last few years has increased the emphasis on protecting facilities that use or produce biological and chemical agents against terrorist acts.

As with any type of security, most attention and awareness surrounds the exciting and headline-grabbing tidbits about large crimes being carried out and criminals being captured. In information security, most people are aware of viruses and hackers but not the components that make up a corporate security program. The same is true for physical security. Many people talk about current robberies, murders, and other criminal activity at the water cooler but do not pay attention to the necessary framework that should be erected and maintained to reduce these types of activities. An organization's physical security program should address the following goals:

- **Crime and disruption prevention through deterrence**   Fences, security guards, warning signs, and so forth
- **Reduction of damage through the use of delaying mechanisms**   Layers of defenses that slow down the adversary, such as locks, security personnel, barriers
- **Crime or disruption detection**   Smoke detectors, motion detectors, CCTV, and so forth
- **Incident assessment**   Response of security guards to detected incidents and determination of damage level
- **Response procedures**   Fire suppression mechanisms, emergency response processes, law enforcement notification, consultation with outside security professionals

So, an organization should try to prevent crimes and disruptions from taking place, but must also plan to deal with these things when they do indeed happen. A criminal should be delayed in her activities by having to penetrate several layers of controls before gaining access to a resource. All types of crimes and disruptions should be able to be detected through components that make up the physical security program. Once an intrusion is detected, a security guard should be called upon to assess the situation. The security guard must then know how to properly respond to a large range of potentially dangerous activities. The emergency response activities could be carried out by the organization's internal security team or by outside experts.

This all sounds straightforward enough, until the team that is responsible for developing the physical security program looks at all the possible threats, the finite budget that the team has to work with, and the complexity of choosing the right combination of countermeasures and ensuring that they all work together in a manner that ensures no gaps of protection. All of these components must be understood in depth before the design of a physical security program can begin.

As with all security programs, you can determine how beneficial and effective your physical security program is only if it is monitored through a performance-based approach. This means that you should devise measurements and metrics to measure the effectiveness of the chosen countermeasures. This enables management to make informed business decisions when investing in the protection of the organization's physical security. The goal is to increase the performance of the physical security program and decrease the risk to the company in a cost-effective manner. You should establish a baseline of performance and thereafter continually evaluate performance to make sure that the company's protection objectives are being met. The following provides some examples of possible performance metrics:

- Number of successful crimes
- Number of successful disruptions
- Number of unsuccessful crimes or disruptions
- Time between detection, assessment, and recovery steps
- Business impact of disruptions
- Number of false-positive detection alerts
- Time it took for a criminal to defeat a control
- Time it took to restore the operational environment

Capturing and monitoring these types of metrics enables the organization to identify deficiencies, evaluate improvement measures, and perform cost/benefit analyses.

The physical security team needs to carry out a risk analysis, which will identify the organization's vulnerabilities, threats, and business impacts. The team should present these findings to management and work with management to define an acceptable risk level for the physical security program. From there, the team needs to develop baselines (minimum levels of security) and metrics to be able to evaluate and determine if the baselines are being met by the implemented countermeasures. Once the team identifies and implements the countermeasures, the performance of these countermeasures should be continually evaluated and expressed in the previously created metrics. These performance values are compared to the set baselines. If the baselines are continually maintained, then the security program is successful, because the company's acceptable risk level is not being exceeded. This is illustrated in Figure 6-1.

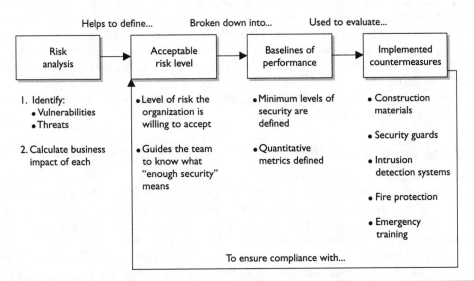

**Figure 6-1**   Relationships of risk, baselines, and countermeasures

So, before an effective physical security program can be rolled out, the following steps must be taken:

1. Identify a team of internal employees and/or external consultants who will build the physical security program through the following steps.

2. Carry out a risk analysis to identify the vulnerabilities and threats and calculate the business impact of each threat.

3. Work with management to define an acceptable risk level of the physical security program.

4. Derive the required performance baselines from the acceptable risk level.

5. Create countermeasure performance metrics.

6. Develop criteria from the results of the analysis, outlining the level of protection and performance required for the following categories of the security program:

   • Deterrence

   • Delaying

   • Detection

   • Assessment

   • Response

7. Identify and implement countermeasures for each program category.

8. Continuously evaluate countermeasures against the set baselines to ensure that the acceptable risk level is not exceeded.

Once these steps have taken place (or continue to take place, in the case of step 8), then the team is ready to move forward in its actual design phase. The design will incorporate the controls that are required for each category of the program; deterrence, delaying, detection, assessment, and response. We will dig deeper into these categories and their corresponding controls later in the chapter, in the "Designing a Physical Security Program" section.

One of the most commonly used approaches in physical security program development is described in the following section.

## Crime Prevention Through Environmental Design

*This place is so nice and pretty and welcoming. No one would want to carry out crimes here.*

**Crime Prevention Through Environmental Design (CPTED)** is a discipline that outlines how the proper design of a physical environment can reduce crime by directly affecting human behavior. It provides guidance in loss and crime prevention through proper facility construction and environmental components and procedures.

CPTED concepts were developed in the 1960s. They have been built upon and matured as our environments and crime types have evolved. CPTED has been used not just to develop corporate physical security programs, but also for large-scale activities such

## Similarities in Approaches

The risk analysis steps are very similar to the steps outlined in Chapter 3 for the development of an organizational security program and the steps outlined in Chapter 9 for a business impact analysis, because each of these processes (development of an information security program, a physical security program, or a business continuity plan) accomplishes goals that are similar to the goals of the other two processes, but with different focuses. Each process requires a team to carry out a risk analysis, to determine the company's threats and risks. An information security program looks at the internal and external threats to resources and data through business processes and technological means. Business continuity looks at how natural disasters and disruptions could damage the organization. And physical security looks at internal and external physical threats to the company resources.

Each requires a solid risk analysis process. Review Chapter 3 to understand the core components of every risk analysis.

as development of neighborhoods, towns, and cities. It addresses landscaping, entrances, facility and neighborhood layouts, lighting, road placement, and traffic circulation patterns. It looks at microenvironments, such as offices and restrooms, and macroenvironments, such as campuses and cities. The crux of CPTED is that the physical environment can be manipulated to create behavioral effects that will reduce crime and the fear of crime. It looks at the components that make up the relationship between humans and their environment. This encompasses the physical, social, and psychological needs of the users of different types of environments and predictable behaviors of these users and offenders.

CPTED provides guidelines on items that some of us might not consider. For example, hedges and planters around a facility should not be higher than 2.5 feet tall, so that they cannot be used to gain access to a window. A data center should be located at the center of a facility, so that the facility's walls will absorb any damages from external forces, instead of the data center. Street furnishings (benches and tables) encourage people to sit and watch what is going on around them, which discourages criminal activity. A corporation's landscape should not include wooded areas or other places where intruders can hide. Ensure that CCTV cameras are mounted in full view, so that criminals know that their activities will be captured and other people know that the environment is well monitored and thus safer.

CPTED and target hardening are two different approaches. *Target hardening* focuses on denying access through physical and artificial barriers (alarms, locks, fences, and so on). Traditional target hardening can lead to restrictions on the use, enjoyment, and aesthetics of an environment. Sure, we can implement hierarchies of fences, locks, and intimidating signs and barriers—but how pretty would that be? If your environment is a prison, then this look might be what you need. But if your environment is an office building, then you are not looking for a Fort Knox décor, but you still need to provide the necessary levels of protection. The protection mechanisms would need to be more subtle and unobtrusive.

Let's say that your organization's team needs to protect a door that is at the side of your facility. The traditional target-hardening approach would be to put locks, alarms, and cameras on the door, install an access control mechanism, such as a proximity reader, and instruct security guards to monitor this door. The CPTED approach would ensure that there is not a sidewalk leading to this door from the front of the building, if you don't want customers to use it. The CPTED approach would also ensure that there are not tall trees or bushes that block the ability to view someone using this door. Barriers such as trees and bushes may make intruders feel more comfortable in attempting to break in through a door if it is in a secluded area.

The best approach is usually to build an environment from a CPTED approach and then apply the target-hardening components on top of the design where needed.

If a parking garage was developed using the CPTED approach, the stair towers and elevators within the garage may have glass windows instead of metal walls, so that people feel safer and potential criminals will not carry out crimes in this more visible environment. Pedestrian walkways would be created such that people could look out across the rows of cars and see any suspicious activities. The different rows for cars to park in would be separated by low walls and structural pillars, instead of solid walls, to allow pedestrians to view activities within the garage.

CPTED provides three main strategies to bring together the physical environment and social behavior to increase overall protection: natural access control, natural surveillance, and territorial reinforcement.

## Natural Access Control

*Natural access control* is the guidance of people entering and leaving a space by the placement of doors, fences, lighting, and even landscaping. For example, an office building may have external bollards with lights in them, as shown in Figure 6-2. These bollards actually carry out different safety and security services. The bollards themselves protect the facility from physical destruction by preventing people from driving their cars into the building. The light emitted helps to ensure that criminals do not have a dark place to hide. And the lights and bollard placement guide people along the sidewalk to the entrance, instead of using signs or railings. As shown in Figure 6-2, the landscape, sidewalks, lighted bollards, and clear sight lines are used as natural access controls. They work together to give individuals a feeling of being in a safe environment and dissuade criminals by working as deterrents.

---

 **NOTE** Bollards are short posts that are commonly used to prevent vehicular access and to protect a building or people walking on a sidewalk from vehicles. They can also be used to direct foot traffic.

---

Clear lines of sight and transparency can be used to discourage potential offenders, because of the visible absence of places to hide or carry out criminal activities.

**Figure 6-2**
Sidewalks, lights, and landscaping can be used for protection.

The CPTED model shows how *security zones* can be created. An environment's space should be divided into zones with different security levels, depending upon who needs to be in that zone and the associated risk. The zones can be labeled as controlled, restricted, public, or sensitive. This is conceptually similar to data classification, as described in Chapter 3. In a data classification program, different classifications are created, along with data handling procedures and the level of protection that each classification requires. The same is true of physical zones. Each zone should have a specific protection level that is required of it, which will help dictate the types of controls that should be put into place.

Access control should be in place to control and restrict individuals from going from one security zone to the next. Access control should also be in place for all facility entrances and exits. The security program development team needs to consider other ways in which intruders can gain access to buildings, such as by climbing adjacent trees to access skylights, upper-story windows, and balconies. The following controls are commonly used for access controls within different organizations:

- Limit the number of entry points
- Force all guests to go to a front desk and sign in before entering the environment
- Reduce the number of entry points even further after hours or during the weekend when not as many employees are around
- Have a security guard validate a picture ID before allowing entrance
- Require guests to sign in and be escorted
- Encourage employees to question strangers

Access barriers can be naturally created (cliffs, rivers, hills), existing manmade elements (railroad tracks, highways), or artificial forms designed specifically to impede movement (fences, closing streets).

## Natural Surveillance

Surveillance can also take place through organized means (security guards), mechanical means (CCTV), and natural strategies (straight lines of sight, low landscaping, raised entrances). The goal of *natural surveillance* is to make criminals feel uncomfortable, by providing many ways that observers could potentially see them, and make all other people feel safe and comfortable, by providing an open and well-designed environment.

Natural surveillance is the use and placement of physical environmental features, personnel walkways, and activity areas in ways that maximize visibility. Figure 6-3 illustrates a stairway in a parking garage that was designed to be open to allow for easy observation.

## Territorial Reinforcement

The third CPTED strategy is *territorial reinforcement*, which creates physical designs that emphasize or extend the company's physical sphere of influence so that legitimate users feel a sense of ownership of that space. Territorial reinforcement can be implemented through the use of walls, fences, landscaping, light fixtures, flags, clearly marked addresses, and decorative sidewalks. The goal of territorial reinforcement is to create a sense of a dedicated community. Companies implement these elements so that employees feel proud of their environment and have a sense of belonging, which they will defend if required to do so. These elements are also implemented to give potential offenders the impression that they do not belong there, that their activities are at risk of being observed, and that their illegal activities will not be tolerated or ignored.

Most corporate environments use a mix of the CPTED and target-hardening approaches. CPTED deals mainly with the construction of the facility, its internal and

**Figure 6-3**
Open areas reduce
the likelihood of
criminal activity.

## Activity Support

CPTED also encourages activity support, which is planned activities for the areas that need to be protected. These activities are designed to get people to work together to increase the overall awareness of acceptable and unacceptable activities in the area. The activities could be neighborhood watch groups, company barbeques, block parties, or civic meetings. This strategy is sometimes the reason for particular placement of basketball courts, soccer fields, or baseball fields in open parks. The increased activity will hopefully keep the bad guys from milling around doing things the community does not welcome.

external designs, and exterior components such as landscaping and lighting. If the environment is built based on CPTED, then the target hardening is like the icing on top of the cake. The target-hardening approach applies more granular protection mechanisms, such as locks and motion detectors. The rest of the chapter looks at physical controls that can be used in both models.

## Designing a Physical Security Program

*Our security guards should wear pink uniforms and throw water balloons at intruders. Response: Very scary environment indeed!*

If a team is organized to assess the protection level of an existing facility, it needs to investigate the following:

- HVAC systems
- Construction materials of walls and ceilings
- Power distribution systems
- Communication paths and type (copper, telephone, fiber)
- Surrounding hazardous materials
- Exterior components:
  - Topography
  - Proximity to airports, highways, railroads
  - Potential electromagnetic interference from surrounding devices
  - Climate
  - Soil
- Existing fences, detection sensors, cameras, barriers
- Working hours of employees
- Operational activities that depend upon physical resources
- Vehicle activity
- Neighbors

To properly obtain this information, the team should do surveys and interview various employees. All of this collected data will help the team to evaluate the current controls, identify weaknesses, and ensure that operational productivity is not negatively affected by implementing new controls.

Although there are usually written policies and procedures on what *should* be taking place pertaining to physical security, policies and reality do not always match up. It is important for the team to observe how the facility is used, daily activities that could introduce vulnerabilities, and how the facility is protected. This information should be documented and compared to the information within the written policy and procedures. In most cases, there are gaps that must be addressed and fixed. Just writing out a policy does no one any good if it is not actually followed.

Every organization must comply with various regulations, whether they be safety and health regulations, fire codes, state and local building codes, Departments of Defense, Energy, or Labor requirements, or some other agency's regulations. The organization may also have to comply with requirements of the Occupational Safety and Health Administration (OSHA) and the Environmental Protection Agency (EPA), if it is operating in the United States, or with the requirements of equivalent organizations within another country. The physical security program development team must understand all the regulations that the organization must comply with and how to reach compliance through physical security and safety procedures.

Legal issues must be understood and addressed properly also. These issues may include access availability for the disabled, liability issues, failure to protect assets and people, excessive force used by security guards, and so on. There is a long laundry list of things that can get a company into legal trouble if it is not doing what it is supposed to. Occasionally, the legal trouble may take the form of a criminal case; for example, if doors default to being locked when power is lost and consequently employees are trapped and killed during a fire, criminal negligence may be alleged. Legal trouble can also come in the form of civil cases; for example, if a company does not remove the ice on its sidewalks and a pedestrian falls and breaks his ankle, the pedestrian may sue the company. The company may be found negligent and held liable for damages.

Every organization should have a *facility safety officer*, whose main job is to understand all the components that make up the facility and what the company needs to do to protect its assets and stay within compliance. This person should oversee facility management duties day in and day out, but should also be heavily involved with the team that has been organized to evaluate the organization's physical security program.

A physical security program is a collection of controls that are implemented and maintained to provide the protection levels necessary to be in compliance with the physical security policy. The policy should embody all the regulations and laws that must be adhered to and should set the risk level the company is willing to accept.

By this point, the team has carried out a risk analysis, which consisted of identifying the company's vulnerabilities, threats, and business impact pertaining to the identified threats. The program design phase should begin with a structured outline, which will evolve into a framework. This framework will then be fleshed out with the necessary controls and countermeasures. The outline should contain the program categories and the necessary countermeasures. The following is a simplistic example:

   I. Deterrence of criminal activity

      A. Fences

      B. Warning signs

      C. Security guards

      D. Dogs

   II. Delay of intruders to help ensure that they can be caught

      A. Locks

      B. Defense-in-depth measures

      C. Access controls

   III. Detection of intruders

      A. External intruder sensors

      B. Internal intruder sensors

   IV. Assessment of situations

      A. Security guard procedures

      B. Communication structure (calling tree)

   V. Response to intrusions and disruptions

      A. Response force

      B. Emergency response procedures

      C. Police, fire, medical personnel

The team can then start addressing each phase of the security program, usually starting with the facility.

## Facility

*I can't see the building. Response: That is the whole idea.*

When a company decides to erect a building, it should consider several factors before pouring the first batch of concrete. Of course, land prices, customer population, and marketing strategies are reviewed, but as security professionals, we are more interested in the confidence and protection that a specific location can provide. Some organizations that deal with top-secret or confidential information make their facilities unnoticeable so that they do not attract the attention of would-be attackers. The building may be hard to see from the surrounding roads, the company signs and logos may be small and not easily noticed, and the markings on the buildings may not give away any information that pertains to what is going on inside that building. It is a type of urban camouflage that makes it harder for the enemy to seek them out.

A company should evaluate how close the facility would be to a police station, fire station, and medical facilities. Many times, the proximity of these entities raises the real estate value of properties, but for good reason. If a chemical company that manufactures highly explosive materials needs to build a new facility, it may make good business sense to put it near a fire station. (Although the fire station might not be so happy.) If another company that builds and sells expensive electronic devices is expanding and needs to move operations into another facility, police reaction time may be looked at when choosing one facility location over another. Each of these issues—police station, fire station, and medical facility proximity—can also reduce insurance rates and must be looked at carefully. Remember that the ultimate goal of physical security is to ensure the safety of personnel. Always keep that in mind when implementing any sort of physical security control. Protect your fellow humans, be your brother's keeper, and *then* run.

Some buildings are placed in areas surrounded by hills or mountains to help prevent eavesdropping of electrical signals emitted by the facility's equipment. In some cases, the organization itself will build hills or use other landscaping techniques to guard against eavesdropping. Other facilities are built underground or right into the

## Issues with Selecting a Facility Site

When selecting a location for a facility, some of the following items are critical to the decision-making process:

- **Visibility**
  - Surrounding terrain
  - Building markings and signs
  - Types of neighbors
  - Population of the area
- **Surrounding area and external entities**
  - Crime rate, riots, terrorism attacks
  - Proximity to police, medical, and fire stations
  - Possible hazards from surrounding area
- **Accessibility**
  - Road access
  - Traffic
  - Proximity to airports, train stations, and highways
- **Natural disasters**
  - Likelihood of floods, tornadoes, earthquakes, or hurricanes
  - Hazardous terrain (mudslides, falling rock from mountains, or excessive snow or rain)

side of a mountain for concealment and disguise in the natural environment, and for protection from radar tools, spying activities, and aerial bomb attacks.

## Construction

*We need a little more than glue, tape, and a stapler.*

Physical construction materials and structure composition need to be evaluated for their appropriateness to the site environment, their protective characteristics, their utility, and their costs and benefits. Different building materials provide different levels of fire protection and have different rates of combustibility, which correlate with their fire ratings. When making structural decisions, the decision of what type of construction material to use (wood, concrete, or steel) needs to be considered in light of what the building is going to be used for. If an area is going to be used to store documents and old equipment, it has far different needs and legal requirements than if it is going to be used for employees to work in every day.

The *load* (how much weight that can be held) of a building's walls, floors, and ceilings needs to be estimated and projected to ensure that the building will not collapse in different situations. In most cases, this may be dictated by local building codes. The walls, ceilings, and floors must contain the necessary materials to meet the required fire rating and to protect against water damage. The windows (interior and exterior) may need to provide ultraviolet (UV) protection, may need to be shatterproof, or may need to be translucent or opaque, depending on the placement of the window and the contents of the building. The doors (exterior and interior) may need to have directional opening, have the same fire rating as the surrounding walls, prohibit forcible entries, display emergency egress markings, and, depending on placement, have monitoring and attached alarms. In most buildings, raised floors are used to hide and protect wires and pipes, but in turn these floors need to be electrically grounded because they are raised.

Building codes may regulate all of these issues, but there are still many options within each category that the physical security program development team should review for extra security protection. The right options should accomplish the company's security and functionality needs and still be cost effective.

### Ground

If you are holding a power cord that has two skinny metal pieces and one fatter, rounder metal piece, which all go into the outlet—what is that fatter, rounder piece for? It is a ground connector, which is supposed to act as the conduit for any excess current to ensure that people and devices are not negatively affected by a spike in electrical current. So, in the wiring of a building, where do you think this ground should be connected? Yep, to the ground. Old mother earth. But many buildings are not wired properly and the ground connector is connected to nothing. This can be very dangerous, since the extra current has nowhere to escape but into our equipment or ourselves.

When designing and building a facility, the following major items need to be addressed from a physical security point of view:

- **Walls**
  - Combustibility of material (wood, steel, concrete)
  - Fire rating
  - Reinforcements for secured areas
- **Doors**
  - Combustibility of material (wood, pressed board, aluminum)
  - Fire rating
  - Resistance to forcible entry
  - Emergency marking
  - Placement
  - Locked or controlled entrances
  - Alarms
  - Secure hinges
  - Directional opening
  - Electric door locks that revert to an unlocked state for safe evacuation in power outages
  - Type of glass—shatterproof or bulletproof glass requirements
- **Ceilings**
  - Combustibility of material (wood, steel, concrete)
  - Fire rating
  - Weight-bearing rating
  - Drop-ceiling considerations
- **Windows**
  - Translucent or opaque requirements
  - Shatterproof
  - Alarms
  - Placement
  - Accessibility to intruders
- **Flooring**
  - Weight-bearing rating
  - Combustibility of material (wood, steel, concrete)
  - Fire rating

- Raised flooring (electrical grounding)
- Nonconducting surface and material
- **Heating, ventilation, and air conditioning**
  - Positive air pressure
  - Protected intake vents
  - Dedicated power lines
  - Emergency shutoff valves and switches
  - Placement
- **Electric power supplies**
  - Backup and alternate power supplies
  - Clean and steady power source
  - Dedicated feeders to required areas
  - Placement and access to distribution panels and circuit breakers
- **Water and gas lines**
  - Shutoff valves—labeled and brightly painted for visibility
  - Positive flow (material flows out of building, not in)
  - Placement—properly located and labeled
- **Fire detection and suppression**
  - Placement of sensors and detectors
  - Placement of suppression systems
  - Type of detectors and suppression agents

The risk analysis results will help the team determine the type of construction material that should be used when constructing a new facility. There are several grades of building construction to choose from. For example, *light frame construction material* provides the least amount of protection against fire and forcible entry attempts. It is made up of untreated lumber that would be combustible during a fire. Light frame construction material is usually used to build homes, primarily because it is cheap but also because homes typically are not under the same types of fire and intrusion threats that office buildings might be.

*Heavy timber construction material* is commonly used for office buildings. Combustible lumber is still used in this type of construction, but there are requirements on the thickness and composition of the materials to provide more protection from fire. The construction materials must be at least four inches in thickness. More dense woods are used and are fastened with metal bolts and plates. Whereas light frame construction material has a fire survival rate of 30 minutes, the heavy timber construction material has a fire rate of one hour.

A building could be made up of *incombustible material* such as steel, which provides a higher level of fire protection than the previously mentioned materials but loses its strength under extreme temperatures, which may cause the building to collapse. So, although the steel will not burn, it may melt and weaken. If a building consists of *fire-resistant material*, the construction material is fire-retardant and has steel rods encased inside of concrete walls and support beams. This provides the most protection against fire and forced entry attempts.

The team should choose its construction material based on the identified threats of the organization and the fire codes that must be complied with. If a company is just going to have some office workers in a building and has no real adversaries that would attempt to destroy the facility, then the light frame or heavy timber construction material would be used. Facilities for government organizations, which are under threats of domestic and foreign terrorist acts, would be built with fire-resistant materials. A financial institution would also use fire-resistant and reinforcement material within its building. This is especially true for its exterior walls, through which thieves may attempt to drive vehicles to gain access to the vaults.

Calculations of approximate penetration times for different types of explosives and attacks are based on the thickness of the concrete walls and the gauge of rebar used. (*Rebar* refers to the steel rods that are encased within the concrete.) So even if the concrete can be damaged, it will take longer to actually cut or break through the rebar. Using thicker rebar and properly placing it within the concrete provides even more protection.

Reinforced walls, rebar, and the use of double walls can be used as delaying mechanisms. The idea is that it will take the bad guy longer to get through two reinforced walls, which gives the response force sufficient time to arrive at the scene and stop the attacker.

## Entry Points

Understanding the company needs and types of entry points for a specific building is critical. The various types of entry points may include doors, windows, roof access, fire escapes, chimneys, and service delivery access points. Second and third entry points must also be considered, such as internal doors that lead into other portions of the building and to exterior doors, elevators, and stairwells. Windows at the ground level should be fortified, because they could be easily broken. Fire escapes, stairwells to the roof, and chimneys are many times overlooked as potential entry points.

**NOTE** Ventilation ducts and utility tunnels can also be used by intruders and thus must be properly protected with sensors and access control mechanisms.

The weakest portion of the structure will most likely be attacked first. The weakest portion of a facility is usually its doors and windows. With regard to doors, the weaknesses usually lie within the frames, hinges, and door material. The bolts, frames, hinges, and material that make up the door should all provide the same level of strength and protection. For example, if a company implements a heavy, nonhollow steel door but uses weak hinges that could be easily extracted, the company is just wasting money. The attacker can just remove the hinges and remove this strong and heavy door.

The door and surrounding walls and ceilings should also provide the same level of strength. If another company has an extremely fortified and secure door but the surrounding wall materials are made out of regular light frame wood, then it is also wasting money on doors. There is no reason to spend a lot of money on one countermeasure that can be easily circumvented by breaking a weaker countermeasure in the same proximity.

**Doors** There are different door types for various functionalities:

- Vault doors
- Personnel doors
- Industrial doors
- Vehicle access doors
- Bullet-resistant doors

Doors can be hollow-core or solid-core. The team needs to understand the various entry types and the potential forced-entry threats, which will help them determine what type of door should be implemented. Hollow-core doors can be easily penetrated by kicking or cutting them; thus, they are usually used internally. The team also has a choice of solid-core doors, which are made up of various materials to provide different fire ratings and protection from forced entry. As stated previously, the fire rating and protection level of the door needs to match the fire rating and protection level of the surrounding walls.

Hinges and strike plates should be secure, especially on exterior doors or doors that are being used to protect sensitive areas. The hinges should have pins that cannot be removed. The door frames need to provide the same level of protection as the door itself.

Fire codes dictate the number and placement of doors with panic bars on them. These are the cross bars that release an internal lock to allow a locked door to open. Panic bars can be on regular entry doors and also emergency exit doors. Those are the ones that usually have the sign that indicates that the door is not an exit point and that an alarm will go off if opened. It might seem like fun and a bit tempting to see if the alarm will *really* go off or not—but don't try it. You are just asking for yelling and dirty looks from the facility management group.

Mantraps and turnstiles can be used so that unauthorized individuals entering a facility cannot get out if it is activated. A *mantrap* is a small room with two doors. The first door is locked; a person is identified and authenticated by a security guard, biometric system, smart card reader, or swipe card reader. Once the person is authenticated and access is authorized, the first door opens and allows the person into the mantrap. The first door locks and the person is trapped. The person must be authenticated again before the second door unlocks and allows him into the facility. Some mantraps use biometric systems that weigh the person who enters, to ensure that only one person at a time is entering the mantrap area. This is a control to counter piggybacking.

Doorways with automatic locks can be configured to be fail-secure or fail-safe. A *fail-safe* setting means that if a power disruption occurs that affects the automated locking system, the doors default to being unlocked. A *fail-secure* configuration means that the doors default to being locked if there are any problems with the power.

**Windows**  Windows should be properly placed (this is where security and aesthetics can come to blows) and should have frames of the proper strengths, the necessary glazing material, and possibly protective covering. The glazing material, which is applied to the windows as they are being made, may be standard, tempered, acrylic, wire, or laminated on glass. *Standard glass* windows are commonly used in residential homes and are easily broken. *Tempered glass* is made by heating the glass and then suddenly cooling it. This increases its mechanical strength, which means that it can handle more stress and is harder to break. It is usually five to seven times stronger than standard glass.

*Acrylic glass* can be made out of polycarbonate acrylic, which is stronger than standard glass but produces toxic fumes if burned. Polycarbonate acrylics are stronger than regular acrylics, but both are made out of a type of transparent plastic. Because of their combustibility, their use may be prohibited by fire codes. The strongest window material is glass-clad polycarbonate. It is resistant to a wide range of threats (fire, chemical, breakage), but of course is much more expensive. These types of windows would be used in areas that are under the greatest threat.

Some windows are made out of glass that has *embedded wires*. There are actually two sheets of glass, with the wiring in between. The wires help reduce the likelihood of the window being broken or shattering.

*Laminated glass* has two sheets of glass with a plastic film in between them. This added plastic makes it much more difficult to break the window. As with other types of glass, laminated glass can come in different depths. The greater the depth (more glass and plastic), the more difficult it is to break.

---

## Window Types

A security professional may be involved with the planning phase of building a facility, and each of these items comes into play when constructing a secure building and environment. The following sums up the types of windows that can be used:

- **Standard**  No extra protection. Cheapest and the lowest level of protection.

- **Tempered**  Glass is heated and then cooled suddenly to increase its integrity and strength.

- **Acrylic**  Type of plastic instead of glass. Polycarbonate acrylics are stronger than regular acrylics.

- **Wired**  Mesh of wire is embedded between two sheets of glass. This wire helps to prevent the glass from shattering.

- **Laminated**  Plastic layer between two outer glass layers. Plastic layer helps to increase the strength against breakage.

- **Solar window film**  Provides extra security by being tinted and extra strength through the film's material.

- **Security film**  Transparent film is applied to the glass to increase its strength.

A lot of window types have a film on them that provides efficiency in heating and cooling. They filter out UV rays and are usually tinted, which can make it harder for the bad guy to peep in and monitor internal activities. Some window types have a different type of film that is applied to make it more difficult to break in case of exploding bombs, storms, or adversaries tying to break it.

## Internal Compartments

Many components that make up a facility must be looked at from a security point of view. *Internal partitions* are used to create barriers between one area and another. These partitions can be used to segment separate work areas, but should never be used in protected areas that house sensitive systems and devices. Many buildings have dropped ceilings, meaning the interior partitions do not extend to the true ceiling—only to the dropped ceiling. An intruder can lift a ceiling panel and climb over the partition. This example of intrusion is shown in Figure 6-4. In many situations, this would not require forced entry, specialized tools, or much effort. (In some office buildings, this may even be possible from a common public-access hallway.) These types of internal partitions should not be relied upon to provide protection for sensitive areas.

## Computer and Equipment Rooms

It used to be necessary to have personnel within the computer rooms for proper maintenance and operations. Today, most servers, routers, bridges, mainframes, and other equipment that are housed in computer rooms can be controlled remotely. This enables computers to live in rooms that have fewer people milling around and spilling coffee. Because the computer rooms no longer have personnel sitting and working in them for long periods, the rooms can be constructed in a manner that is efficient for equipment instead of people.

Smaller systems can be stacked vertically to save space. They should be mounted on racks or placed inside equipment cabinets. The wiring should be close to the equipment to save on cable costs and to reduce tripping hazard.

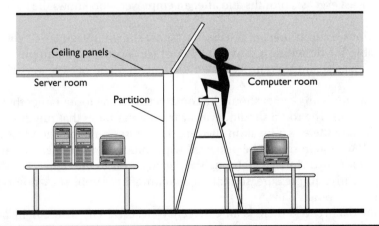

**Figure 6-4**  An intruder can lift ceiling panels and enter a secured area with little effort.

Data centers, server rooms, and wiring closets should be located in the core areas of a facility, near wiring distribution centers. Strict access control mechanisms and procedures should be implemented for these areas. The access control mechanisms may be smart card readers, biometric readers, or combination locks, as described in Chapter 4. These restricted areas should have only one *access* door, but fire code requirements typically dictate that there must be at least two doors to most data centers and server rooms. Only one door should be used for daily entry and exit and the other door should be used only in emergency situations. This second door should not be an access door, which means that people should not be able to come in through this door. It should be locked, but should have a panic bar that will release the lock if pressed.

These restricted areas ideally should not be directly accessible from public areas like stairways, corridors, loading docks, elevators, and restrooms. This helps to ensure that the people who are by the doors to secured areas have a specific purpose for being there, versus being on their way to the restroom or standing around in a common area talking with others.

Because data centers usually hold expensive equipment and the company's critical data, their protection should be thoroughly thought out before implementation. Data centers should not be located on the top floors because it would be more difficult for an emergency crew to access it in a timely fashion in case of a fire. By the same token, data centers should not be located in basements, so that flooding does not affect the systems. And if a facility is in a hilly area, the data center should be located well above ground level. Data centers should be located at the core of a building, to provide protection from natural disasters or bombs and to provide easier access to emergency crews if necessary.

Which access controls and security measures should be implemented for the data center depends upon the sensitivity of the data being processed and the protection level that is required. Alarms on the doors to the data processing center should be activated during off hours and there should be policies dictating how to carry out access control during normal business hours, after hours, and during emergencies. If a combination lock is used to enter the data processing center, the combination should be changed at least every six months and after an employee who knows the code leaves the company.

The various controls that are discussed next are shown in Figure 6-5. The team that is responsible for designing a new data center (or evaluating a current data center) should understand all the controls shown in Figure 6-5 and be able to choose what is needed.

The data processing center should be constructed as one room rather than different individual rooms. The room should be away from water pipes that run throughout the building, in case there is a break in the line that causes a flood. The vents and ducts from the HVAC system should be protected with some type of barrier bars and should be too small for anyone to crawl through and gain access to the center. The data center must have positive air pressure, so that no contaminants can be sucked into the room and into the computers' fans.

In many data centers there is an emergency electrical Off switch right next to the door so that someone can turn off the power if necessary. If there is a fire, someone should hit this emergency Off switch as they are leaving the room before the fire sup-

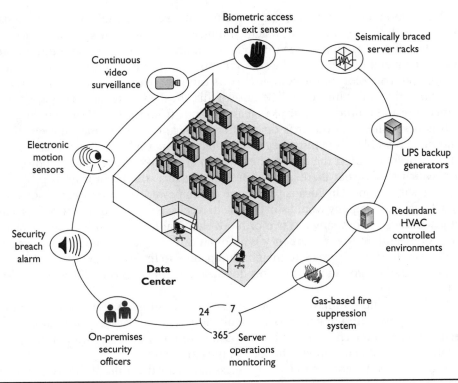

**Figure 6-5**  A data center should have many physical security controls.

pression agent is released. This is critical if the suppression agent that is being used is water, because water and electricity is not a good match—especially during a fire. A company can install a fire suppression system that is tied into this switch, so that when a fire is detected the electricity is automatically shut off right before the suppression material is released. (The suppression material could be a type of gas, such as halon or FM-200, or water. Gases are usually a better choice for environments that are filled with computers. We will cover different suppression agents in the "Fire Prevention, Detection, and Suppression" section later in the chapter.)

Portable fire extinguishers should be located close to the equipment and should be easy to see and access. Smoke detectors or fire sensors should be implemented, and water sensors should be placed under the raised floors. Since most of the wiring and cables run under the raised floors, it is important that water does not get to these places and, if it does, that an alarm sound if water is detected.

**NOTE**  If there is any type of water damage in a data center or facility, mold and mildew could easily become a problem. Instead of allowing things to "dry out on their own," many times it is better to use industry-strength dehumidifiers, water movers, and sanitizers to ensure that secondary damage does not occur.

It is important to maintain the proper temperature and humidity levels within data centers, which is why an HVAC system should be implemented specifically for this room. Too high of a temperature can cause components to overheat and turn off; too low of a temperature can cause the components to work more slowly. If the humidity is high, then corrosion of the computer parts can take place; if humidity is low, then static electricity can be introduced. Because of this, the data center needs to have its own temperature and humidity controls that are separate from the rest of the building.

It is best if the data center is on a different electrical system than the rest of the building, if possible. If anything negatively affects the main building's power, this will not carry over and affect the center. The data center may require redundant power supplies, which means that there are two or more feeders coming in from two or more electrical substations. The idea is that if one of the power company's substations were to go down, the company would still be able to receive electricity from the other feeder. But just because a company has two or more electrical feeders coming into its facility does not mean that true redundancy is automatically in place. Many companies have paid for two feeders to come into their building, only to find out that both feeders were coming from the same substation! This defeats the whole purpose of having two feeders in the first place.

Data centers need to have their own backup power supplies, either an uninterrupted power supply (UPS) or generators. The different types of backup power supplies are discussed later in the chapter, but it is important to know at this point that the power backup must be able to support the load of the data center.

Many companies choose to use large glass panes for the walls of the data center so that personnel within the center can be viewed at all times. This glass should be shatter-resistant since the window is acting as an exterior wall. The center's doors should not be hollow, but rather secure, solid-core doors. Doors should open out rather than in so that they don't damage equipment when opened. Best practices indicate that the door frame should be fixed to adjoining wall studs and that there should be at least three hinges per door. These characteristics would make the doors much more difficult to break down.

# Protecting Assets

The main threats that physical security components combat are theft, interruptions to services, physical damage, compromised system and environment integrity, and unauthorized access.

Real loss is determined by the cost to replace the stolen items, the negative effect on productivity, the negative effect on reputation and customer confidence, fees for consultants that may need to be brought in, and the cost to restore lost data and production levels. Many times, companies just perform an inventory of their hardware and provide value estimates that are plugged into risk analysis to determine what the cost to the company would be if the equipment were stolen or destroyed. However, the information held within the equipment may be much more valuable than the equipment itself, and proper recovery mechanisms and procedures also need to be plugged into the risk assessment for a more realistic and fair assessment of cost.

Laptop theft is increasing at incredible rates each year. Laptops have been stolen for years, but in the past they were stolen mainly to sell the hardware. Now laptops are also being stolen to gain sensitive data for identity theft crimes. The CSI/FBI 2003 Computer Crime and Security Survey indicates that U.S. companies lost around $6.8 million in laptop theft. Gartner Group estimates that a stolen laptop costs a company around $6000, which does not account for any data lost or potential exposure to secondary crimes. *Time* magazine estimated that 1600 laptops are stolen each day in the U.S. alone. These thefts take place in airports, hotels, from cars, and within office buildings. In August 2002, close to 2000 Internal Revenue Service laptops that may have contained taxpayers' confidential information went unaccounted for. In August 2002, five agencies under Justice Department jurisdiction reported 400 missing laptop computers. The classification level of 218 of the missing laptops was unknown, and the report noted, "It is possible that the missing laptop computers would have been used to process and store national security or sensitive law enforcement information that, if divulged, could harm the public."

In June 2004, GMAC Financial Services had two laptops stolen from an employee's car that exposed about 200,000 of its customers' personal data. In May 2005, MCI had a laptop stolen that contained around 16,500 current and former employees' personal information. This list could go on and on for hundreds of pages. What is important to understand is that this is a rampant and potentially very dangerous crime. Many people claim, "My whole life is on my laptop" or possibly their PDA. Since employees use laptops as they travel, they may have extremely sensitive company or customer data on their systems that can easily fall into the wrong hands. The following list provides many of the protection mechanisms that can be used to protect laptops and the data that they hold:

- Inventory all laptops, including serial numbers so that they can be properly identified if recovered.
- Harden the operating system.
- Password protect the BIOS.
- Register all laptops with the vendor and file a report when one is stolen. If a stolen laptop is sent in for repairs, it will be flagged by the vendor.
- Do not check a laptop as luggage when flying.
- Never leave a laptop unattended and carry it in a nondescriptive carrying case.
- Engrave the laptop with a symbol or number for proper identification.
- Use a slot lock with a cable to connect a laptop to a stationary object.
- Back up the data from the laptop and store it on a stationary PC or backup media.
- Use specialized safes if storing laptops in vehicles.
- Encrypt all sensitive data.

Tracing software can be installed so that your laptop can "phone home" if it is taken away from you. There are several products that provide this tracing capability. Once installed and configured, the software periodically sends in a signal to a tracking center.

If you report that your laptop has been stolen, the vendor of this software will work with service providers and law enforcement to track down and return your laptop.

A company may have a need for a safe. Safes are commonly used to store backup data tapes, original contracts, or other types of valuables. The safe should be penetration resistant and/or provide fire protection, depending upon the need. The types of safes that an organization can choose from are

- **Wall safe**   Embedded into the wall and easily hidden
- **Floor safe**   Embedded into the floor and easily hidden
- **Chests**   Stand-alone safes
- **Depositories**   Safes with slots, which allow the valuables to be easily slipped in
- **Vaults**   Safes that are large enough to provide walk-in access

If a safe has a combination lock, it should be changed periodically and only a small subset of people should have access to the combination or key. The safe should be in a visible location, so that anyone who is interacting with the safe can be seen. The goal is to uncover any unauthorized access attempts. Some safes have passive or thermal relocking functionality. If the safe has a *passive relocking* function, it can detect when someone attempts to tamper with the safe, in which case extra internal bolts will fall into place to ensure that it cannot be compromised. If a safe has a *thermal relocking* function, when a certain temperature is met (possibly from drilling), an extra lock is implemented to ensure that the valuables are properly protected.

# Internal Support Systems

*This place has no air conditioning or water. Who would want to break into it anyway?*

Having a fortified facility with secure compartmentalized areas and protected assets is nice, but having lights, air conditioning, and water within this facility is even better. Physical security needs to address these support services, because their malfunction or disruption could negatively affect the organization in many ways.

Although there are many incidents of various power losses here and there for different reasons (storms, hurricanes, California running out of electricity), one of the most notable power losses took place in August 2003 when eight East Coast states and portions of Canada lost power for several days. Although there were rumors about a worm causing this disruption, it was found to be a software bug in GE Energy's XA/21 system. This disaster left over 50 million people without power for days, caused four nuclear power plants to be shut down, and put a lot of companies in insecure and chaotic states. Security professionals need to be able to help organizations handle both the small bumps in the road, such as power surges or sags, and the gigantic sink holes in the road, such as what happened in the United States and Canada on August 14, 2003.

## Electric Power

*We don't need no stinkin' power supply. Just rub these two sticks together.*

Because computing and communication has become so essential in the corporate world, power failure is a much more devastating event than it was 10 to 15 years ago. The need for good plans to fall back on is crucial to provide the assurance that a business will not be drastically affected by storms, high winds, hardware failure, lightning, or other events that can stop or disrupt power supplies. A continuous supply of electricity assures the availability of company resources; thus, a security professional needs to be familiar with the threats to electric power and corresponding countermeasures.

There are several types of power backup capabilities. Before a company chooses one, it should calculate the total cost of anticipated downtime and its effects. This information can be gathered from past records and other businesses in the same area on the same power grid. The total cost per hour for backup power is derived by dividing the annual expenditures by the annual standard hours of use.

Large and small issues can cause power failure or fluctuations. The effects manifest in variations of voltage that can last a millisecond to days. A company can pay to have two different supplies of power to reduce its risks, but this approach can be costly. Other, less expensive mechanisms are to have generators or UPSs in place. Some generators have sensors to detect power failure and will start automatically upon failure. Depending on the type and size of the generator, it might provide power for hours or days. UPSs are usually short-term solutions compared to generators.

## Power Protection

There are three main methods of protecting against power problems: UPSs, power line conditioners, and backup sources. UPSs use battery packs that range in size and capacity. A UPS can be online or standby. *Online UPS systems* use AC line voltage to charge a bank of batteries. When in use, the UPS has an inverter that changes the DC output from the batteries into the required AC form and regulates the voltage as it powers computer devices. This conversion process is shown in Figure 6-6. Online UPS systems

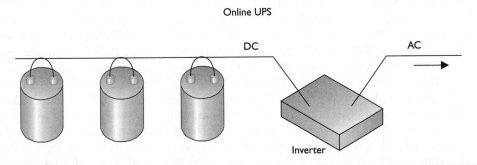

**Figure 6-6** A UPS device converts DC current from its internal or external batteries to usable AC by using an inverter.

have the normal primary power passing through them day in and day out. They constantly provide power from their own inverters, even when the electric power is in proper use. Since the environment's electricity passes through this type of UPS all the time, the UPS device is able to quickly detect when a power failure takes place. An on-line UPS can provide the necessary electricity and picks up the load after a power failure much more quickly than a standby UPS.

*Standby UPS* devices stay inactive until a power line fails. The system has sensors that detect a power failure, and the load is switched to the battery pack. The switch to the battery pack is what causes the small delay in electricity being provided. So an on-line UPS picks up the load much more quickly than a standby UPS, but costs more of course.

Backup power supplies are necessary when there is a power failure and the outage will last longer than a UPS can last. Backup supplies can be a redundant line from another electrical substation or from a motor generator and can be used to supply main power or charge the batteries in a UPS system.

A company should identify critical systems that need protection from interrupted power supplies, and then estimate how long secondary power would be needed and how much power is required per device. Some UPS devices provide just enough power to allow systems to shut down gracefully, whereas others allow the systems to run for a longer period. A company needs to determine whether systems should have only enough power supply to be shut down in a proper manner or actually need to be up and running to keep critical operations available.

Just having a generator in the closet should not give a company the warm fuzzy feeling of protection. The alternate power source should be tested periodically to make sure it works, and to the extent expected. It is never good to get all the way to an emergency only to find out that the generator does not work, or someone forgot to buy the gas necessary to keep the thing running.

## Electric Power Issues

Electric power enables us to be productive and functional in many different ways, but if it is not installed, monitored, and respected properly, it can do us great harm.

When *clean* power is being provided, the power supply contains no interference or voltage fluctuation. The possible types of interference (or *line noise*) are *electromagnetic interference (EMI)* or *radio frequency interference (RFI)*, which is disturbance to the flow of electric power while it travels across a power line, as shown in Figure 6-7. EMI can be created by the difference between three wires: hot, neutral, and ground, and the magnetic field that they create. Lightning and electrical motors can induce EMI, which could then interrupt the proper flow of electrical current as it travels over wires to, from, and within buildings. RFI can be caused by anything that creates radio waves. Fluorescent lighting is one of the main causes of RFI within buildings today, so does that mean we need to rip out all the fluorescent lighting? Well, that is one choice, but we could also just use shielded cabling where fluorescent lighting could cause a problem. If you would just take a break from reading, climb up into your office's dropped

**Figure 6-7**   RMI and EMI can cause line noise on power lines.

ceiling, and look around you would probably see wires bundled and tied up to the *true* ceiling. If your office is using fluorescent lighting, the power and data lines should not be running over or on top of the fluorescent lights. This is because the radio frequencies that are being given off can interfere with the data or power current as it travels through these wires. Now, get back down from the ceiling. We have work to do.

## Electric Power Definitions

The following list summarizes many of the electric power concepts so far:

- **Ground**   The pathway to the earth to enable excessive voltage to dissipate
- **Noise**   Electromagnetic or frequency interference that disrupts the power flow and can cause fluctuations
- **Transient noise**   Short duration of power line disruption
- **Inrush current**   The initial surge of current required when there is an increase in power demand
- **Clean power**   Electrical current that does not fluctuate
- **EMI**   Electromagnetic interference
- **RFI**   Radio frequency interference

Interference interrupts the flow of an electrical current, and fluctuations can actually deliver a different level of voltage than what was expected. Each fluctuation can be damaging to devices and people. The following explains the different types of voltage fluctuations that are possible with electric power:

- **Power excess**
  - **Spike**   Momentary high voltage
  - **Surge**   Prolonged high voltage
- **Power loss**
  - **Fault**   Momentary power outage
  - **Blackout**   Prolonged, complete loss of electric power
- **Power degradation**
  - **Sag/dip**   Momentary low voltage condition, from one cycle to a few seconds
  - **Brownout**   Prolonged power supply that is below normal voltage
  - **In-rush current**   Initial surge of current required to start a load

When an electrical device is turned on, it can draw a large amount of current, which is referred to as *in-rush current*. If the device sucks up enough current, it can cause a *sag* in the available power for the surrounding devices. This could negatively affect their performance. As stated earlier, it is a good idea to have the data processing center and devices on a different electrical wiring segment from that of the rest of the facility, if possible, so that the devices will not be affected by these issues. For example, if you are in a building or house without efficient wiring and you turn on a vacuum cleaner or microwave, you may physically see the lights quickly dim because of this in-rush current. The drain on the power supply caused by in-rush currents still happens in other environments when these types of electrical devices are used—you just might not be able to physically see the effects. Any type of device that would cause such a dramatic in-rush current should not be used on the same electrical segment as data processing systems.

**Surge**   A *surge* is a momentary rise in voltage from a power source. Surges can cause a lot of damage very quickly. A surge is one of the most common power problems and is controlled with surge protectors. These protectors use a device called a *metal oxide varistor*, which moves the excess voltage to ground when a surge occurs. Its source can be from a strong lightning strike, a power plant going online or offline, a shift in the commercial utility power grid, and electrical equipment within a business starting and stopping. Most computers have a built-in surge protector in their power supplies, but these are baby surge protectors and cannot provide protection against the damage that larger surges (as from storms) can cause. So, you need to ensure that all devices are properly plugged into larger surge protectors, whose only job is to absorb any extra current before it is passed to electrical devices.

**Blackout**   A *blackout* is when the voltage drops to zero. This can be caused by lightning, a car taking out a power line, storms, or failure to pay the power bill. It can last for seconds or days. This is when a backup power source is required for business continuity.

**Brownout**  When power companies are experiencing high demand, they frequently reduce the voltage in an electrical grid, which is referred to as a *brownout*. Constant-voltage transformers can be used to regulate this fluctuation of power. They can use different ranges of voltage and only release the expected 120 volts, alternating current, to devices.

**Noise**  Noise on power lines usually results from a transformer being hit by an automobile, lightning, and fluorescent lighting. Frequency ranges overlap, which can affect electrical device operations. Lightning sometimes produces voltage spikes on communications and power lines, which can destroy equipment or alter data that is being transmitted. When generators are switched on because power loads have increased, they too can cause voltage spikes that can be harmful and disruptive. Storms and intense cold or heat can put a heavier load on generators and cause a drop in voltage. Each of these instances is an example of how normal environmental behaviors can affect power voltage, eventually adversely affecting equipment, communications, or the transmission of data.

Because these and other occurrences are common, mechanisms should be in place to detect unwanted power fluctuations, to protect the integrity of the data processing environment. *Voltage regulators* and *line conditioners* can be used to ensure a clean and smooth distribution of power. The primary power runs through a regulator or conditioner. They have the capability to absorb extra current if there is a spike, and to store energy to add current to the line if there is a sag. The goal is to keep the current flowing at a nice, steady level so that neither motherboard components nor employees get fried.

Many data centers are constructed to take power-sensitive equipment into consideration. Because surges, sags, brownouts, blackouts, and voltage spikes frequently cause data corruption, the centers are built to provide a high level of protection against these events. Other types of environments usually are not built with these things in mind and do not provide this level of protection. Offices usually have different types of devices connected and plugged into the same outlets. Outlet strips are plugged into outlet strips, which are connected to extension cords. This causes more line noise and reduction of voltage to each device. Figure 6-8 depicts an environment that can cause line noise, voltage problems, and possibly a fire hazard.

## Preventive Measures and Good Practices

*Don't stand in a pool of water with a live electrical wire. Response: Hold on, I need to write that one down.*

When dealing with electric power issues, the following items can help protect devices and the environment:

- Plug in every device to a surge protector to protect from excessive current.
- Shut down devices in an orderly fashion to help avoid data loss or damage to devices due to voltage changes.
- Employ power line monitors to detect frequency and voltage amplitude changes.
- Use regulators to keep voltage steady and power clean.
- Protect distribution panels, master circuit breakers, and transformer cables with access controls.

**Figure 6-8** This configuration can cause a lot of line noise and poses a fire hazard.

- Provide protection from magnetic induction through shielded lines.
- Use shielded cabling for long cable runs.
- Do not run data or power lines directly over fluorescent lights.
- Use three-prong connections and adapters if using two-prong cables.
- Do not plug outlet strips and extension cords into each other.

## Environmental Issues

Improper environmental controls can cause damage to services, hardware, and lives. Interruption of some services can cause unpredicted and unfortunate results. Power, heating, ventilation, air-conditioning, and air-quality controls can be complex and contain many variables. They all need to be operating properly and be monitored regularly.

During facility construction, the physical security team needs to make certain that water, steam, and gas lines have proper shutoff valves, as shown in Figure 6-9, and *positive drains*, which means their contents flow out instead of in. If there is ever a break in a main water pipe, the valve to shut off water flow must be readily accessible. Similarly, in case of fire in a building, the valve to shut off the gas lines must be readily accessible. In case of a flood, a company wants to ensure that material cannot travel up

**Figure 6-9**  Water, steam, and gas lines should have emergency shutoff valves.

through the water pipes and into its water supply or facility. Facility, operations, and security personnel should know where these shutoff valves are, and there should be strict procedures to follow in these types of emergencies. This will help reduce the potential damage.

Most electronic equipment must operate in a climate-controlled atmosphere. Although it is important to keep the atmosphere at a proper working temperature, it is important to understand that the components within the equipment can suffer from overheating even in a climate-controlled atmosphere if the internal computer fans are not cleaned or are blocked. When devices are overheated, the components can expand and contract, which causes components to change their electronic characteristics, reducing their effectiveness or damaging the system overall.

 **NOTE**  The climate issues involved with a data processing environment is why it needs its own separate HVAC system. Maintenance procedures should be documented and properly followed. HVAC activities should be recorded and reviewed annually.

Maintaining appropriate temperature and humidity is important in any facility, especially facilities with computer systems. Improper levels of either can cause damage

## Preventive Steps Against Static Electricity
The following are some simple measures to prevent static electricity:

- Use antistatic flooring in data processing areas.
- Ensure proper humidity.
- Have proper grounding for wiring and outlets.
- Don't have carpeting in data centers, or have static-free carpets if necessary.
- Wear antistatic bands when working inside computer systems.

to computers and electrical devices. High humidity can cause corrosion, and low humidity can cause excessive static electricity. This static electricity can short out devices, cause the loss of information, or provide amusing entertainment for unsuspecting employees.

Lower temperatures can cause mechanisms to slow or stop, and higher temperatures can cause devices to use too much fan power and eventually shut down. Table 6-1 lists different components and their corresponding damaging temperature levels.

In drier climates, or during the winter, the air contains less moisture, which can cause static electricity when two dissimilar objects touch each other. This electricity usually travels through the body and produces a spark from a person's finger that can release several thousand volts. This can be more damaging than you would think. Usually the charge is released on a system casing and causes no damage, but sometimes it is released directly to an internal computer component and causes damage. People who work on the internal parts of a computer usually wear antistatic armbands to reduce the chance of this happening.

In more humid climates, or during the summer, more humidity is in the air, which can also affect components. Particles of silver can begin to move away from connectors onto copper circuits, which cement the connectors into their sockets. This can adversely affect the electrical efficiency of the connection. A *hygrometer* is usually used to monitor humidity. It can be manually read, or an automatic alarm can be set up to go off if the humidity passes a set threshold.

| Table 6-1 | Material or Component | Damaging Temperature |
|---|---|---|
| Components Affected by Specific Temperatures | Computer systems and peripheral devices | 175°F |
| | Magnetic storage devices | 100°F |
| | Paper products | 350°F |

## Ventilation

*Can I smoke in the server room? Response: Security!*

Air ventilation has several requirements that must be met to ensure a safe and comfortable environment. A closed-loop recirculating air-conditioning system should be installed to maintain air quality. "Closed-loop" means that the air within the building is reused after it has been properly filtered, instead of bringing outside air in. Positive pressurization and ventilation should also be implemented to control contamination. *Positive pressurization* means that when an employee opens a door, the air goes out, and outside air does not come in. If a facility were on fire, you would want the smoke to go out the doors instead of being pushed back in when people are fleeing.

The assessment team needs to understand the various types of contaminants, how they can enter an environment, the damage they could cause, and the steps to ensure that a facility is protected from dangerous substances or high levels of average contaminants. Airborne material and particle concentrations must be monitored for inappropriate levels. Dust can affect a device's functionality by clogging up the fan that is supposed to be cooling the device. Excessive concentrations of certain gases can accelerate corrosion and cause performance issues or failure of electronic devices. Although most disk drives are hermetically sealed, other storage devices can be affected by airborne contaminants. Air-quality devices and ventilation systems deal with these issues.

## Fire Prevention, Detection, and Suppression

*We can either try to prevent fires or have one really expensive weenie-roast.*

The subject of physical security would not be complete without a discussion about fire safety. A company must meet national and local standards pertaining to fire prevention, detection, and suppression methods. *Fire prevention* includes training employees on how to react properly when faced with a fire, supplying the right equipment and ensuring that it is in working order, making sure there is an easily reachable fire suppression supply, and storing combustible elements in the proper manner. Fire prevention may also include using proper noncombustible construction materials and designing the facility with containment measures that provide barriers to minimize the spread of fire and smoke. These thermal or fire barriers can be made up of different types of construction material that is noncombustible and has a fire-resistant coating applied to them.

*Fire detection* response systems come in many different forms. Manual detection response systems are the red pull boxes that you see on many walls in many buildings. Automatic detection response systems have sensors that react when they detect the presence of fire or smoke. We will review different types of detection systems in the next section.

*Fire suppression* is the use of a suppression agent to put out a fire. Fire suppression can take place manually through handheld portable exstinguishers, or automatically through automated systems such as sprinkler systems, or halon or $CO_2$ discharge systems. The upcoming "Fire Suppression" section reviews the different types of suppression agents and where they are best used. Automatic sprinkler systems are widely used and highly effective in protecting buildings and their contents. When deciding upon

## Fire Resistant Ratings

Fire resistant ratings are the result of tests that are carried out in laboratories using specific configurations of environmental settings. The American Society for Testing and Materials (ASTM) is the organization that creates the standards that dictate how these tests should be carried out and how to properly interpret the test results. ASTM accredited testing centers carry out the evaluations in accordance with these standards and assign fire resistant ratings that are then used in federal and state fire codes. The tests evaluate the fire resistance of different types of materials in various environmental configurations. Fire resistance represents the ability of a laboratory-constructed assembly to contain a fire for a specific period of time. For example, a 5/8-inch-thick drywall sheet installed on each side of a wood stud provides a one-hour rating. If the thickness of this drywall is doubled, then this would be given a two-hour rating. The rating system is used to classify different building components.

the type of fire suppression systems to install, a company needs to evaluate many factors, including an estimate of the occurrence rate of a possible fire, the amount of damage that could result, the types of fires that would most likely take place, and the types of suppression systems to choose from.

Fire protection processes should consist of implementing early smoke or fire detection devices and shutting down systems until the source of the heat is eliminated. A warning signal may be sounded by a smoke or fire detector before the suppression agent is released, so that if it is a false alarm or a small fire that can be handled without the automated suppression system, someone has time to shut down the suppression system.

## Types of Fire Detection

Fires present a dangerous security threat because they can damage hardware and data and risk human life. Smoke, high temperatures, and corrosive gases from a fire can cause devastating results. It is important to evaluate the fire safety measurements of a building and the different sections within it.

A fire begins because something ignited it. Ignition sources can be failure of an electrical device, improper storage of combustible materials, carelessly discarded cigarettes, malfunctioning heating devices, and arson. A fire needs fuel (paper, wood, liquid, and so on) and oxygen to continue to burn and grow. The more fuel per square meter, the more intense the fire will become. A facility should be built, maintained, and operated to minimize the accumulation of fuels that can feed fires.

There are four classes (A, B, C, and D) of fire, which are explained in the "Fire Suppression" section. You need to know the differences between the types of fire so that you know how to properly extinguish each type. Portable fire extinguishers have markings that indicate what type of fire they should be used on, as illustrated in Figure 6-10. The markings indicate what types of chemicals are within the canisters and what types of fires they have been approved to be used on. Portable extinguishers should be located within 50 feet of any electrical equipment and located near exits. The extinguishers should be marked clearly, with an unobstructed view. They should be easily reachable and operational by employees, and inspected quarterly.

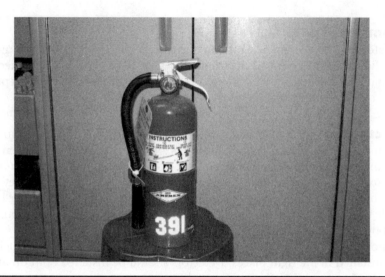

**Figure 6-10**   Portable extinguishers are marked to indicate what type of fire they should be used on.

A lot of computer systems are made of components that are not combustible but will melt or char if overheated. Most computer circuits use only two to five volts of direct current, which usually cannot start a fire. If a fire does happen in a computer room, it will most likely be an electrical fire caused by overheating of wire insulation or by overheating components igniting surrounding plastics. Prolonged smoke usually occurs before combustion.

There are several types of detectors, each of which works in a different way. The detector can be activated by smoke or heat.

**Smoke Activated**   Smoke-activated detectors are good for early-warning devices. They can be used to sound a warning alarm before the suppression system activates. A *photoelectric device*, also referred to as an optical detector, detects the variation in light intensity. The detector produces a beam of light across a protected area, and if the beam is obstructed, the alarm sounds. Figure 6-11 illustrates how a photoelectric device works. Another type of photoelectric device samples the surrounding air by drawing air into a pipe. If the light source is obscured, the alarm will sound.

**Figure 6-11**   A photoelectric device uses a light emitter and a receiver.

### Automatic Dial-Up Alarm

Fire detection systems can be configured to call the local fire station, and possibly the police station, to report a detected fire. The system plays a prerecorded message that gives the necessary information so that the officials can properly prepare for the stated emergency and arrive at the right location.

**Heat Activated**  Heat-activated detectors can be configured to sound an alarm either when a predefined temperature (fixed temperature) is reached or when the temperature increases over a period of time (rate-of-rise). *Rate-of-rise temperature sensors* usually provide a quicker warning than *fixed-temperature sensors* because they are more sensitive, but they can also cause more false alarms. The sensors can either be spaced uniformly throughout a facility, or implemented in a line type of installation, which is operated by a heat-sensitive cable.

It is not enough to have these fire and smoke detectors installed in a facility; they must be installed in the right places. Detectors should be installed both on and above suspended ceilings and below raised floors, because companies run many types of wires in both places that could start an electrical fire. No one would know about the fire until it broke through the floor or dropped ceiling if detectors were not placed in these areas. Detectors should also be located in enclosures and air ducts, because smoke can gather in these areas before entering other spaces. It is important that people are alerted about a fire as quickly as possible so that damage may be reduced, fire suppression activities may start quickly, and lives may be saved. Figure 6-12 illustrates the proper placement of smoke detectors.

**Figure 6-12**
Smoke detectors
should be located
above suspended
ceilings, below
raised floors, and
in air vents.

Suspended
ceiling

Air vent

Raised
floor

Smoke
detector

## Plenum Area

Wiring and cables are strung through *plenum areas,* such as the space above drop-down ceilings, the space in wall cavities, and the space under raised floors. Plenum areas should have fire detectors. Also, only plenum-rated cabling should be used in plenum areas, which is cabling that is made out of material that does not let off hazardous gases if it burns.

## Fire Suppression

*How about if I just spit on the fire? Response: I am sure that will work just fine.*

It is important to know the different types of fires and what should be done to properly suppress them. Each fire type has a rating that indicates what materials are burning. Table 6-2 shows the four types of fire and their suppression methods, which all employees should know.

There are several ways to suppress a fire, all of which require that certain precautions be taken. In many buildings, suppression agents located in different areas are designed to initiate after a specific trigger has been set off. Each agent has a zone of coverage, meaning an area that the agent supplier is responsible for. If a fire ignites within a certain zone, it is the responsibility of that suppression agent device to initiate, and then suppress that fire. There are different types of suppression agents: water, halon, foams, $CO_2$ and more. $CO_2$ is good for putting out fires but bad for many types of life forms. If an organization uses $CO_2$, the suppression releasing device should have a delay mechanism within it that makes sure that the agent does not start applying $CO_2$ to the area until after an audible alarm has sounded and people have been given time to evacuate. $CO_2$ is a colorless, odorless substance that is potentially lethal because it removes oxygen from the air. Gas masks do not provide protection against $CO_2$. This type of fire suppression mechanism is best used in unattended facilities and areas.

For Class B and C fires, specific types of dry powders can be used, which include sodium or potassium bicarbonate, calcium carbonate, or monoammonium phosphate. The first three powders interrupt the chemical combustion of a fire. Monoammonium phosphate melts at low temperatures and excludes oxygen from the fuel.

Foams are mainly water based and contain a foaming agent that allows them to float on top of a burning substance to exclude the oxygen.

| Fire Class | Type of Fire | Elements of Fire | Suppression Method |
|---|---|---|---|
| A | Common combustibles | Wood products, paper, and laminates | Water, foam |
| B | Liquid | Petroleum products and coolants | Gas, $CO_2$, foam, dry powders |
| C | Electrical | Electrical equipment and wires | Gas, $CO_2$, dry powders |
| D | Combustible metals | Magnesium, sodium, potassium | Dry powder |

**Table 6-2** Four Types of Fire and Their Suppression Methods

## Halon

Halon is a gas that was widely used in the past to suppress fires because it interferes with the chemical combustion of the elements within a fire. It mixes quickly with the air and does not cause harm to computer systems and other data processing devices. It was used mainly in data centers and server rooms.

It was discovered that halon has chemicals (chlorofluorocarbons) that deplete the ozone and that concentrations greater than 10 percent are dangerous to people. Halon used on extremely hot fires degrades into toxic chemicals, which is even more dangerous to humans.

Some really smart people figured that the ozone was important to keep around, which caused halon to be federally restricted, and no companies are allowed to purchase and install new halon extinguishers. Companies that still have halon systems have been instructed to replace them with nontoxic extinguishers.

The following are EPA-approved replacements for halon:

- FM-200
- NAF-S-III
- CEA-410
- FE-13
- Water
- Inergen
- Argon
- Argonite

 **NOTE** There is actually a Class K fire, for commercial kitchens. These fires should be put out with a wet chemical, which is usually a solution of potassium acetate. This chemical works best when putting out cooking oil fires.

A fire needs fuel, oxygen, and high temperatures. Table 6-3 shows how different suppression substances interfere with these elements of fire.

| Combustion Elements | Suppression Methods | How Suppression Works |
|---|---|---|
| Fuel | Soda acid | Removes fuel |
| Oxygen | $CO_2$ | Removes oxygen |
| Temperature | Water | Reduces temperature |
| Chemical combustion | Gas—halon or halon substitute | Interferes with the chemical reactions between elements |

**Table 6-3** How Different Substances Interfere with Elements of Fire

By law, companies that have halon extinguishers do not have to replace them, but the extinguishers cannot be refilled. So, companies that have halon extinguishers do not have to replace them right away, but when the extinguisher's lifetime runs out, FM-200 extinguishers or other EPA-approved chemicals should be used.

 **NOTE** Halon has not been manufactured since January 1, 1992, by international agreement. The Montreal Protocol banned halon in 1987, and countries were given until 1992 to comply with these directives. The most effective replacement for halon is FM-200, which is similar to halon but does not damage the ozone.

The HVAC system should be connected to the fire alarm and suppression system so that it properly shuts down if a fire is identified. A fire needs oxygen, and this type of system can feed oxygen to the fire. Plus, the HVAC can spread deadly smoke into all areas of the building. Many fire systems can configure the HVAC to shut down if a fire alarm is triggered.

## Water Sprinklers

*I'm hot. Go pull that red thingy on the wall. I need some water.*

Water sprinklers typically are simpler and less expensive than halon and FM-200 systems but can cause water damage. In an electrical fire, the water can increase the intensity of the fire, because it can work as conductor for electricity—only making the situation worse. If water is going to be used in any type of environment with electrical equipment, the electricity must be turned off before the water is released. Sensors should be used to shut down the electric power before water sprinklers activate. Each sprinkler head should activate individually to avoid wide-area damage, and there should be shutoff valves so that the water supply can be stopped if necessary.

A company needs to take great care in deciding which suppression agent and system is best for it. Four main types of water sprinkler systems are available: wet pipe, dry pipe, preaction, and deluge.

**Wet Pipe**   *Wet pipe systems* always contain water in the pipes and are usually discharged by temperature control level sensors. One disadvantage of wet pipe systems is that the water in the pipes may freeze in colder climates. Also, if there is a nozzle or pipe break, it can cause extensive water damage. These types of systems are also called *closed head systems.*

**Dry Pipe**   In *dry pipe systems,* the water is not actually held in the pipes. The water is contained in a "holding tank" until it is released. The pipes contain pressurized air, which is reduced when a fire or smoke alarm is activated, allowing the water valve to be opened by the water pressure.

Water is not allowed into the pipes that feed the sprinklers until an actual fire is detected. First, a heat or smoke sensor is activated; then, the water fills the pipes leading to the sprinkler heads, the fire alarm sounds, the electric power supply is disconnected, and finally water is allowed to flow from the sprinklers. These pipes are best used in colder climates because the pipes will not freeze. Figure 6-13 depicts a dry pipe system.

**Figure 6-13** Dry pipe systems do not hold water in the pipes.

**Preaction** *Preaction systems* are similar to dry pipe systems in that the water is not held in the pipes but is released when the pressurized air within the pipes is reduced. Once this happens, the pipes are filled with water, but it is not released right away. A thermal-fusible link on the sprinkler head has to melt before the water is released. The purpose of combining these two techniques is to give people more time to respond to false alarms or to small fires that can be handled by other means. Putting out a small fire with a handheld extinguisher is better than losing a lot of electrical equipment to water damage. These systems are usually used only in data processing environments rather than the whole building, because of the higher cost of these types of systems.

**Deluge** A *deluge system* has its sprinkler heads wide open to allow a larger volume of water to be released in a shorter period. Because the water being released is in such large volume, these systems are usually not used in data processing environments.

# Perimeter Security

*Halt! Who goes there?*

The first line of defense is perimeter control at the site location, to prevent unauthorized access to the facility. As mentioned earlier in this chapter, physical security should be implemented by using a layered defense approach. For example, before an intrude can get to the written recipe for your company's secret barbeque sauce, she will need to climb or cut a fence, slip by a security guard, pick a door lock, circumvent a biometric access control reader that protects access to an internal room, and then break into the safe that holds the recipe. The idea is that if an attacker breaks through one control layer, there will be others in her way before she can obtain the company's crown jewels.

 **NOTE** It is also important to have a diversity of controls. For example, if one key works on four different door locks, the intruder has to obtain only one key. Each entry should have its own individual key or authentication combination.

This defense model should work in two main modes: one mode during normal facility operations and another mode during the time the facility is closed. When the facility is closed, all doors should be locked with monitoring mechanisms in strategic positions to alert security personnel of suspicious activity. When the facility is in operation, security gets more complicated because authorized individuals need to be distinguished from unauthorized individuals. Perimeter security deals with facility and personnel access controls, external boundary protection mechanisms, intrusion detection, and corrective actions. The following sections describe the elements that make up these categories.

## Facility Access Control

Access control needs to be enforced through physical and technical components when it comes to physical security. Physical access controls use mechanisms to identify individuals who are attempting to enter a facility or area. They make sure that the right individuals get in and the wrong individuals stay out, and provide an audit trail of these actions. Having personnel within sensitive areas is one of the best security controls because they can personally detect suspicious behavior. However, they need to be trained on what activity is considered suspicious and how to report such activity.

Before a company can put into place the proper protection mechanisms, it needs to conduct a detailed review to identify which individuals should be allowed into what areas. Access control points can be identified and classified as external, main, and secondary entrances. Personnel should enter and exit through a specific entry, deliveries should be made to a different entry, and sensitive areas should be restricted. Figure 6-14 illustrates the different types of access control points into a facility. After a company has identified and classified the access control points, the next step is to determine how to protect them.

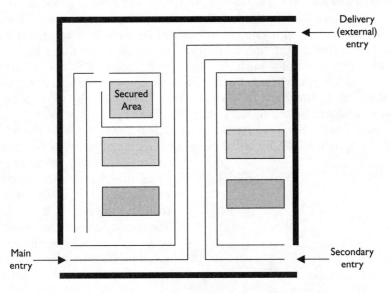

**Figure 6-14**   Access control points should be identified, marked, and monitored properly.

## Locks

Locks are inexpensive access control mechanisms that are widely accepted and used. Locks are considered delaying devices to intruders. The longer it takes to break or pick a lock, the longer a security guard or police officer has to arrive on the scene if the intruder has been detected. Almost any type of a door can be equipped with a lock, but keys can be easily lost and duplicated, and locks can be picked or broken. If a company depends solely on a lock-and-key mechanism for protection, an individual who has the key can come and go as he likes without control and can remove items from the premises without detection. Locks should be used as part of the protection scheme, but should not be the sole protection scheme.

Locks vary in functionality. Padlocks can be used on chained fences, preset locks are usually used on doors, and programmable locks (requiring a combination to unlock) are used on doors or vaults. Locks come in all types and sizes. It is important to have the right type of lock so that it provides the correct level of protection.

To the curious mind or a determined thief, a lock is considered a little puzzle to solve, not a deterrent. In other words, locks may be merely a challenge, not necessarily something to stand in the way of malicious activities. Thus, you need to make the challenge difficult, through the complexity, strength, and quality of the locking mechanisms.

 **NOTE** The delay time provided by the lock should match the penetration resistance of the surrounding components (door, door frame, hinges). A smart thief takes the path of least resistance, which may be to pick the lock, remove the pins from the hinges, or just kick down the door.

**Mechanical Locks** There are two main types of mechanical locks, the warded lock and the tumbler lock. The *warded lock* is the basic padlock, as shown in Figure 6-15. It has a spring-loaded bolt with a notch cut in it. The key fits into this notch and slides the bolt from the locked to the unlocked position. The lock has *wards* in it, which are metal projections around the keyhole, as shown in Figure 6-16. The correct key for a specific ward lock has notches in it that fit in these projections and a notch to slide the bolt back and forth. These are the cheapest locks, because of their lack of any real sophistication, and are also the easiest to pick.

The *tumbler lock* has more pieces and parts than a ward lock. As shown in Figure 6-17, the key fits into a cylinder, which raises the lock metal pieces to the correct height so that the bolt can slide to the locked or unlocked position. Once all of the metal pieces are at the correct level, then the internal bolt can be turned. The correct key has the correct size and sequences of notches to move these metal pieces into their correct position.

**Figure 6-15**
Warded lock

**Figure 6-16**
A key fits into a notch to turn the bolt to unlock the lock.

Locking bolt

Wards

The three types of tumbler locks are the pin tumbler, wafer tumbler, and lever tumbler. The *pin tumbler* lock, shown in Figure 6-17, is the most commonly used tumbler lock. The key has to have just the right grooves to put all the spring-loaded pins in the right position so that the lock can be locked or unlocked.

*Wafer tumbler* locks (also called disc tumbler locks) are the small, round locks that you usually see on file cabinets. They use flat discs (wafers) instead of pins inside the locks. They often are used as car and desk locks. This type of lock does not provide much protection because it can be easily circumvented.

**Figure 6-17**
Tumbler lock

Spring

Driver

Pin

Cylinder

Key

**NOTE** Some locks have interchangeable cores, which allow for the core of the lock to be taken out. You would use this type of lock if you wanted one key to open several locks. You would just replace all locks with the same core.

*Combination locks*, of course, require the correct combination of numbers to unlock them. These locks have internal wheels that have to line up properly before being unlocked. A user spins the lock interface left and right by so many clicks, which lines up the internal wheels. Once the correct turns have taken place, all the wheels are in the right position for the lock to release and open the door. The more wheels within the locks, the more protection that is provided. Newer combination locks do not use internal wheels, but rather have a keypad that allows a person to type in the combination instead of turning a knob with a combination faceplate. An example of an electronic combination lock is shown in Figure 6-18.

*Cipher locks,* also known as programmable locks, are keyless and use keypads to control access into an area or facility. The lock requires a specific combination to be entered into the keypad and possibly a swipe card. They cost more than traditional locks, but their combinations can be changed, specific combination sequence values can be locked out, and personnel who are in trouble or under duress can enter a specific code that will open the door and initiate a remote alarm at the same time. Thus, compared to traditional locks, cipher locks can provide a much higher level of security and control of who can access a facility.

The following are some functionalities commonly available on many cipher combination locks that improve the performance of access control and provide for increased security levels:

- **Door delay**   If a door is held open for a given time, an alarm will trigger to alert personnel of suspicious activity.

- **Key override**   A specific combination can be programmed to be used in emergency situations to override normal procedures or for supervisory overrides.

**Figure 6-18**
Electronic
combination lock

- **Master keying**  Enables supervisory personnel to change access codes and other features of the cipher lock.

- **Hostage alarm**  If an individual is under duress and/or held hostage, a combination he enters can communicate this situation to the guard station and/or police station.

If a door is accompanied by a cipher lock, it should have a corresponding visibility shield so that a bystander cannot see the combination as it is keyed in. Automated cipher locks must have a backup battery system and be set to unlock during a power failure so that personnel are not trapped inside during an emergency.

**NOTE**  It is important to change the combination of locks and use random combination sequences. Often, people do not change their combinations or clean the keypads, which allows an intruder to know what key values are used in the combination, because they are the dirty and worn keys. The intruder then just needs to figure out the right combination of these values.

Some cipher locks require all users to know and use the exact same combination, which does not allow for any individual accountability. Some of the more sophisticated cipher locks allow for specific codes to be assigned to unique individuals. This provides more accountability, because each individual is responsible for keeping his access code secret, and entry and exit activities can be logged and tracked. These are usually referred to as *smart locks*, because they are designed to only allow authorized individuals access at certain doors at certain times.

**NOTE**  Hotel key cards are also known as smart cards. They are programmed by the nice hotel guy or gal behind the counter. The access code on the card can allow access to a hotel room, workout area, business area, and better yet—the mini bar.

**Device Locks**  Unfortunately, hardware has a tendency to "walk away" from facilities; device locks are necessary to thwart these attempts. Cable locks consist of a vinyl-coated steel cable that can secure a computer or peripheral to a desk or other stationary components, as shown in Figure 6-19.

**Figure 6-19**
FMJ/PAD.LOCK's notebook security cable kit secures a notebook by enabling the user to attach the device to a stationary component within an area.

The following are some of the device locks available and their capabilities:

- **Switch controls**   Cover on/off power switches.
- **Slot locks**   Secure the system to a stationary component by the use of steel cable that is connected to a bracket that is mounted in a spare expansion slot.
- **Port controls**   Block access to disk drives or unused serial or parallel ports.
- **Peripheral switch controls**   Secure a keyboard by inserting an on/off switch between the system unit and the keyboard input slot.
- **Cable traps**   Prevent the removal of input/output devices by passing their cables through a lockable unit.

**Administrative Responsibilities**   It is important for a company to not only choose the right type of lock for the right purpose, but also to follow proper maintenance and procedures. Keys should be assigned by facility management, and this assignment should be documented. There should be written procedures that detail how keys are to be assigned, inventoried, and destroyed when necessary, and what should happen if and when keys are lost. There should be a role within the company's facility management team that is assigned the responsibility of overseeing key and combination maintenance.

Most organizations have master keys and submaster keys for the facility management staff. A master key opens all the locks within the facility, and the submaster keys open one or more locks. Each lock has its own individual, unique keys as well. So if a

---

## Lock Strengths

There are basically three grades of locks:

- **Grade 1**   Commercial and industrial use
- **Grade 2**   Heavy-duty residential/light duty commercial
- **Grade 3**   Residential/consumer expendable (i.e., "throw-away" locks)

The cylinders within the locks fall into three main categories:

- **Low security**   No pick or drill resistance provided
  - Can fall within any of the three grades of locks
- **Medium security**   A degree of pick resistance protection provided
  - Uses tighter and more complex keyways (notch combination)
  - Can fall within any of the three grades of locks
- **High security**   Pick resistance protection through many different mechanisms
  - Only used in grade 1 and 2 locks

facility has 100 offices, the occupant of each office can have her own key. A master key allows access to all offices for security personnel and for emergencies. If one security guard is responsible for monitoring half the facility, he can be assigned one of the submaster keys for just those offices.

Since these master and submaster keys are powerful, they must be properly guarded and not widely shared. A security policy should outline what portions of the facility and which device types need to be locked. As a security professional, you should understand what type of lock is most appropriate for each situation, the level of protection provided by various types of locks, and how these locks can be circumvented.

**Circumventing Locks**   Each lock type has corresponding tools that can be used to pick it (open it without the key). A *tension wrench* is a tool that is shaped like an *L* and is used to apply tension to the internal cylinder of a lock. The lock picker uses a lock pick to manipulate the individual pins to their proper placement. Once certain pins are "picked" (put in their correct place), the tension wrench holds these down while the lock picker figures out the correct settings for the other pins. Once the intruder figures out the proper pin placement, the wrench is used to then open the lock.

Intruders may carry out another technique, referred to as *raking*. To circumvent a pin tumbler lock, a lock pick is pushed to the back of the lock and quickly slid out while providing upward pressure. This movement makes many of the pins fall into place. A tension wrench was also put in to hold the pins that pop into the right place. If all the pins did not slide to the necessary height for the lock to open, the intruder holds the tension wrench and uses a thinner pick to move the rest of the pins into place.

Now, if this is all too much trouble for the intruder, she can just drill the lock, use bolt cutters, or attempt to break through the door, break through the door frame, or remove the hinges. There are just so many choices for the bad guys.

## Personnel Access Controls

Proper identification needs to verify if the person attempting to access a facility or area should actually be allowed in. Identification and authentication can be verified by matching an anatomical attribute (biometric system), by using smart or memory cards (swipe cards), by presenting a photo ID to a security guard, by using a key, or by providing a card and entering a password or PIN.

A common problem with controlling authorized access into a facility or area is called *piggybacking*. This occurs when an individual gains unauthorized access by using someone else's legitimate credentials or access rights. Usually an individual just follows another person closely through a door without providing any credentials. The best preventive measures against piggybacking are to have security guards at access points and to educate employees about good security practices.

If a company wants to use a card badge reader, it has several types of systems to choose from. Individuals usually have cards that have embedded magnetic strips that contain access information. The reader can just look for simple access information within the magnetic strip, or it can be connected to a more sophisticated system that scans the information, makes more complex access decisions, and logs badge IDs and access times.

If the card is a memory card, then the reader just pulls information from it and makes an access decision. If the card is a smart card, the individual may be required to enter a PIN or password, which the reader compares against the information held within the card or in an authentication server. (Memory and smart cards are covered in Chapter 4.)

These access cards can be used with *user-activated readers,* which just means the user actually has to do something—swipe the card or enter a PIN. *System sensing access control readers,* also called *proximity devices* or *transponders,* recognize the presence of an approaching object within a specific area. This type of system does not require the user to swipe the card through the reader. The reader sends out interrogating signals and obtains the access code from the card without the user having to do anything.

 **NOTE** *Electronic access control (EAC) tokens* is a generic term that is used to describe proximity authentication devices, which can be proximity readers, programmable locks, or biometric systems, which identify and authenticate users before allowing them entrance into physically controlled areas.

## External Boundary Protection Mechanisms

*Let's build a fort and let only the people who know the secret handshake inside!*

Proximity protection components are usually put into place to provide one or more of the following services:

- Control of pedestrian and vehicle traffic flows
- Various levels of protection for different security zones
- Buffers and delaying mechanisms to protect against forced entry attempts
- Limit and control entry points

These services can be provided by using the following control types:

- **Access control mechanisms**   Locks and keys, an electronic card access system, personnel awareness
- **Physical barriers**   Fences, gates, walls, doors, windows, protected vents, vehicular barriers
- **Intrusion detection**   Perimeter sensors, interior sensors, annunciation mechanisms
- **Assessment**   Guards, CCTV cameras
- **Response**   Guards, local law enforcement agencies
- **Deterrents**   Signs, lighting, environmental design

Several types of perimeter protection mechanisms and controls can be put into place to protect a company's facility, assets, and personnel. They can deter would-be intruders, detect intruders and unusual activities, and provide ways of dealing with these issues when they arise. Perimeter security controls can be natural (hills, rivers) or manmade (fencing, lighting, gates). Landscaping is a mix of the two. In the beginning of this chapter, we explored CPTED and how this approach is used to reduce the likelihood of crime. Landscaping is a tool used in the CPTED method. Sidewalks, bushes, and created paths can point people to the correct entry points, and trees and spiky bushes can be used as natural barriers. These bushes and trees should be placed such that they cannot be used as ladders or accessories to gain unauthorized access to unapproved entry points. Also, there should not be an overwhelming number of trees and bushes, which could provide intruders with places to hide. In the following sections, we look at the manmade components that can work within the landscaping design.

## Fencing

*I just want a little fence to keep out all the little mean people.*

Fencing can be quite an effective physical barrier. Although the presence of a fence may only delay dedicated intruders in their access attempts, it can work as a psychological deterrent by telling the world that your company is serious about protecting itself.

Fencing can provide crowd control and helps control access to entrances and facilities. However, fencing can be costly and unsightly. Many companies plant bushes or trees in front of the fence that surrounds their buildings for aesthetics and to make the building less noticeable. But this type of vegetation can damage the fencing over time or negatively affect its integrity. The fencing needs to be properly maintained, because if a company has a sagging, rusted, pathetic fence, it is equivalent to telling the world that the company is not truly serious and disciplined about protection. But a nice, shiny, intimidating fence can send a different message—especially if the fencing is topped with three rungs of barbed wire.

When deciding upon the type of fencing, there are several factors to consider. The gauge of the metal should correlate to the types of physical threats the company would most likely endure. After carrying out the risk analysis (covered earlier in the chapter), the physical security team should understand the probability of enemies attempting to cut the fencing, drive through it, or climb over or crawl under it. Understanding these threats will help the team determine the necessary gauge and mesh sizing of the fence wiring.

The risk analysis data will also help indicate what height of fencing the organization should implement. Fences come in varying heights, and each height provides a different level of security:

- Fences *three to four feet high* only deter casual trespassers.
- Fences *six to seven feet high* are considered too high to climb easily.
- Fences *eight feet high* (possibly with strands of barbed or razor wire at the top) means you are serious about protecting your property. They often deter the more determined intruder.

The barbed wire on top of fences can be tilted in or out, which also provides extra protection. If the organization is a prison, then it would have the barbed wire on top of

## Gauges and Mesh Sizes

The gauge of fence wiring is the thickness of the wires used within the fence mesh. The lower the gauge number, the larger the wire diameter:

- 11 gauge = 0.120-inch diameter
- 9 gauge = 0.148-inch diameter
- 6 gauge = 0.192-inch diameter

The mesh sizing is the minimum clear distance between the wires. Common mesh sizes are 2 inches, 1 inch, and 3/8 inch. It is more difficult to climb or cut fencing with smaller mesh sizes, and the heavier gauged wiring is harder to cut. The following list indicates the strength levels of the most common gauge and mesh sizes used in chain-link fencing today:

- **Extremely high security**   3/8-inch mesh, 11 gauge
- **Very high security**   1-inch mesh, 9 gauge
- **High security**   1-inch mesh, 11 gauge
- **Greater security**   2-inch mesh, 6 gauge
- **Normal industrial security**   2-inch mesh, 9 gauge

the fencing pointed in, which makes it harder for prisoners to climb and escape. If the organization is a military base, then the barbed wire would be tilted out, making it harder for someone to climb over the fence and gain access to the premises.

Critical areas should have fences at least eight feet high to provide the proper level of protection. The fencing should not sag in any areas and must be taut and securely connected to the posts. The fencing should not be easily circumvented by pulling up its posts. The posts should be buried sufficiently deep in the ground and should be secured with concrete, to ensure that the posts cannot be dug up or tied to vehicles and extracted. If the ground is soft or uneven, this might provide ways for intruders to slip or dig under the fence. In these situations, the fencing should actually extend into the dirt to thwart these types of attacks.

Fences work as "first line of defense" mechanisms. A few other controls can be used also. Strong and secure gates need to be implemented. It does no good to install a highly fortified and expensive fence and then have an unlocked or weenie gate that allows for easy access.

## PIDAS Fencing

Perimeter Intrusion Detection and Assessment System (PIDAS) is a type of fencing that has sensors on the wire mesh and at the base of the fence. It is used to detect if someone attempts to cut or climb the fence. It has a passive cable vibration sensor that sets off an alarm if an intrusion is detected. PIDAS is very sensitive and can cause many false alarms.

There are basically four distinct types of classification when it comes to gates:

- **Class I**   Residential usage.
- **Class II**   Commercial usage, where general public access is expected; examples include a public parking lot entrance, a gated community, or a self storage facility.
- **Class III**   Industrial usage, where limited access is expected; an example is a warehouse property entrance that is not intended to serve the general public.
- **Class IV**   Restricted access; this includes a prison entrance that is monitored either in person or via closed circuitry.

Each gate classification has its own long list of implementation and maintenance guidelines to ensure the necessary level of protection. These classifications and guidelines are developed by Underwriters Laboratory (UL), a nonprofit organization that tests, inspects, and classifies electronic devices, fire protection equipment, and specific construction materials. This is the group that certifies these different items to ensure that they are in compliance with national building codes. They have a specific code, UL-325, which deals with garage doors, drapery, gates, and louver and window operators and systems.

So, whereas in the information security world we look to NIST for our best practices and industry standards, in the physical security world, we look to UL for the same type of direction.

 **NOTE**   UL standards can be found at **www.ul.com**. A good introduction to the UL-325 standard, which deals with gates, can be found at **www.abrpaint .com/services/GatesFencing/ul325intro.htm**.

## Bollards

*Bollards* usually look like small concrete pillars outside a building. Sometimes companies try to dress them up by putting flowers or lights in them to soften the look of a protected building. They are placed by the sides of buildings that have the most immediate threat of someone driving a vehicle through the exterior wall. They are usually placed between the facility and a parking lot and/or between the facility and a road that runs close to an exterior wall. Within the United States after September 11, 2001, many military and government institutions, which did not have bollards, hauled in huge boulders to surround and protect sensitive buildings. They provided the same type of protection that bollards would provide. These were not overly attractive but provided the sense that the government was serious about protecting those facilities.

## Lighting

Many of the items mentioned in this chapter are things that people take for granted day in and day out during our usual busy lives. Lighting is certainly one of these items that you would probably not give much thought to, unless it was not there. Unlit (or improperly lit) parking lots and parking garages have invited many attackers to carry out criminal activity that they may not have engaged in otherwise if the proper lighting was in place. Breaking into cars, stealing cars, and attacking employees as they leave the office are the more common types of attacks that take place in these situations. Someone who is not a security professional may think, "This area should be better lit." But a security professional should understand that the right illumination needs to be in place, that no dead spots (unlit areas) should exist between the lights, and that all areas where individuals may walk should be properly lit. A security professional should also understand the various types of lighting that are available and where they should be used.

Wherever an array of lights is being used, each light covers its own zone or area. The zone that each light is able to cover depends upon the illumination of light that is being produced, which usually has a direct relationship to the wattage capacity of the bulbs. In most cases, the higher the wattage of the lamps, the more illumination that they produce. It is important that the zones of illumination coverage overlap. For example, if a company has an open parking lot, then light poles need to be implemented within the correct distance of each other to eliminate any dead spots. If the lamps that will be used provide a 30-foot radius of illumination, then the light poles should be erected less than 30 feet apart so that there is an overlap between the areas of illumination.

If an organization does not implement the right types of lights and ensure that they provide proper coverage, it increases the probability of criminal activity, accidents, and lawsuits.

Exterior lights that provide protection usually require less illumination intensity than interior working lighting, except for areas that require security personnel to inspect identification credentials for authorization. It is also important to have the correct lighting when using various types of surveillance equipment. The correct contrast between a potential intruder and background items needs to be provided, which only happens with the correct illumination and placement of lights. If the light is going to bounce off of dark, dirty, or darkly painted surfaces, then more illumination is required for the necessary contrast between people and the environment. If the area has clean concrete and light-colored painted surfaces, then not as much illumination is required. This is because when the same amount of light is falling on an object and the surrounding background, an observer has to depend upon the contrast to be able to tell them apart.

When lighting is installed, it should be directed toward areas where potential intruders would most likely be coming from and directed away from the security force posts. For example, lighting should be pointed at gates or exterior access points, and the guard locations should be more in the shadows, or under a lower amount of illumination. This is referred to as *glare protection* for the security force. If you are familiar with military operations, you might know that when you are approaching a military entry point, there is a fortified guard building with lights pointing toward the oncoming cars. A large sign instructs you to turn off your headlights, so that the guards are not temporarily blinded by your lights and have a clear view of anything coming their way.

Lights used within the organization's security perimeter should be directed outward, which keeps the security personnel in relative darkness and allows them to easily view intruders beyond the company's perimeter.

An array of lights that provides an even amount of illumination across an area is usually referred to as *continuous lighting*. Examples are the evenly spaced light poles in a parking lot, light fixtures that run across the outside of a building, or series of fluorescent lights used in parking garages. If the company's premises is relatively close to another company's property, a railway, an airport, or a highway, it may need to ensure that the lighting does not "bleed over" property lines in an obtrusive manner. So, the illumination needs to be *controlled*, which just means that an organization should erect lights and use illumination in such a way that does not blind its neighbors or any passing cars, trains, or planes.

You probably are familiar with the special home lighting gadgets that turn certain lights on and off at predetermined times, giving the illusion to potential burglars that a house is occupied even when the residents are away. Companies can use similar technology, which is referred to as *standby lighting*. The security personnel can configure the times that different lights turn on and off, so that potential intruders think that different areas of the facility are populated.

 **NOTE** Redundant or backup lights should be available in case of power failures or emergencies. Special care must be given to understand what type of lighting is needed in different parts of the facility in these types of situations. This lighting may run on generators or battery packs.

*Responsive area illumination* takes place when an IDS detects suspicious activities and turns on the lights within a specific area. When this type of technology is plugged into automated IDS products, there is a high likelihood of false alarms. Instead of continuously having to dispatch a security guard to check out these issues, a CCTV can be implemented to scan the area for intruders.

If intruders want to disrupt the security personnel or decrease the probability of being seen while attempting to enter a company's premises or building, they could attempt to turn off the lights or cut power to them. This is why lighting controls and switches should be in protected, locked, and centralized areas.

## Surveillance Devices

Usually, installing fences and lights does not provide the necessary level of protection a company needs to protect its facility, equipment, and employees. Areas need to be under surveillance so that improper actions are noticed and taken care of before damage occurs. Surveillance can happen through visual detection or through devices that use sophisticated means of detecting abnormal behavior or unwanted conditions. It is important that every organization have a proper mix of lighting, security personnel, IDSs, and surveillance technologies and techniques.

## Visual Recording Devices

Because surveillance is based on sensory perception, surveillance devices usually work in conjunction with guards and other monitoring mechanisms to extend their capabilities and range of perception. A *closed-circuit TV (CCTV)* is a commonly used monitoring device in most organizations, but before purchasing and implementing a CCTV, you need to consider several items:

- **Purpose of CCTV**   Detect, assess, and/or identify intruders
- **Type of environment the CCTV camera will work in**   Internal or external areas
- **Field of view that is required**   Large or small area that needs to be monitored
- **Amount of illumination of the environment**   Lit areas, unlit areas, areas affected by sunlight
- **Integration with other security controls**   Guards, IDSs, alarm systems

The reason that you need to consider these items before you purchase a CCTV product is that there are so many different types of cameras, lenses, and monitors that make up the different CCTV products. You need to understand what is expected of this physical security control, so that you purchase and implement the right type.

CCTVs are made up of cameras, transmitters, receivers, a recording system, and a monitor. The camera captures the data and transmits it to a receiver, which allows for the data to be displayed on a monitor. This data is recorded so that it can be reviewed at a later time if needed. Figure 6-20 shows how multiple cameras can be connected to one multiplexer, which allows for several different areas to be monitored at one time. The multiplexer accepts video feed from all the cameras and interleaves these transmissions over one line to the central monitor. This is more effective and efficient than the older systems that require the security guard to physically flip a switch from one environment to the next. In these older systems, the guard can view only one environment at a time, which of course makes it more likely that suspicious activities will be missed.

A CCTV sends the captured data from the camera's transmitter to the monitor's receiver, usually through a coaxial cable, instead of broadcasting the signals over a public network. This is where the term "closed-circuit" comes in. This circuit should be tamperproof, which means that an intruder cannot manipulate the video feed that the security guards are monitoring. The most common type of attack is to replay previous recordings without the security personnel knowing it. For example, if an attacker is able to compromise a company's CCTV and play the recording from the day before, the security guards would not know that an intruder is in the facility carrying out some type of crime. This is one reason why CCTVs should be used in conjunction with intruder detection controls, which we address in the next section.

 **NOTE**   CCTVs should have some type of recording system. Digital recorders save images to hard drives and allow for advanced search techniques that are not possible with videotape recorders. Digital recorders use advanced compression techniques, which drastically reduces the storage media requirements.

**Figure 6-20** Several cameras can be connected to a multiplexer.

Most of the CCTV cameras in use today use light-sensitive chips called *charged-coupled devices (CCDs)*. The CCD is an electrical circuit that receives input light from the lens and converts it into an electronic signal, which is then displayed on the monitor. Images are focused through a lens onto the CCD chip surface, which forms the electrical representation of the optical image. It is this technology that allows for the capture of extraordinary detail of objects and precise representation, because it has sensors that work in the infrared range, which extends beyond human perception. The CCD sensor picks up this extra "data" and integrates it into the images shown on the monitor, to allow for better granularity and quality in the video.

CCDs are also used in fax machines, photocopiers, bar code readers, and even telescopes. CCTVs that use CCDs allow for more granular information within an environment to be captured and shown on the monitor when compared to the older CCTV technology that relied upon cathode ray tubes (CRTs).

There are two main types of lenses used in CCTV: fixed focal length and zoom (varifocal). The *focal length* of a lens defines its effectiveness in viewing objects from a horizontal and vertical view. The focal length value relates to the angle of view that can be achieved. Short focal length lenses provide wider-angle views and long focal length lenses provide a narrower view. The size of the images that will be shown on a monitor along with the area that can be covered by one camera are defined by the focal length. For example, if a company implements a CCTV camera in a warehouse, the focal length lens values should be between 2.8 and 4.3 millimeters (mm), so that the whole area can be captured. If the company implements another CCTV camera that monitors an entrance, that lens value should be around 8mm, which allows for a smaller area to be monitored.

**NOTE** Fixed focal length lenses are available in various fields of views: wide, medium, and narrow. A lens that provides a "normal" focal length creates a picture that approximates the field of view of the human eye. A wide-angle lens has a short focal length and a telephoto lens has a long focal length. When a company selects a fixed focal length lens for a particular view of an environment, it should understand that if the field of view needs to be changed (wide to narrow), the lens must be changed.

So, if we need to monitor a large area, we use a lens with a smaller focal length value. Great, but what if a security guard hears a noise or thinks that he sees something suspicious? A fixed focal length lens is stationary, meaning the guard cannot move the camera from one point to the other and properly focus the lens automatically. The *zoom* lenses provide flexibility by allowing the viewer to change the field of view to different angles and distances. The security personnel usually have a remote-control component integrated within the centralized CCTV monitoring area that allows them to move the cameras and zoom in and out on objects as needed. When both wide scenes and close-up captures are needed, then a zoom lens is best. This type of lens allows for the focal length to change from wide angle to telephoto while maintaining the focus of the image.

To understand the next characteristic, depth of field, think about pictures that you might take while on vacation with your family. For example, if you want to take a picture of your spouse with the Grand Canyon in the background, the main object of the picture is your spouse. Your camera is going to zoom in and use a *shallow depth of focus*. This provides a softer backdrop, which will lead the viewers of the photograph to the foreground, which is your spouse. Now, let's say that you get tired of taking pictures of your spouse and want to get a scenic picture of just the Grand Canyon itself. The camera would use a *greater depth of focus*, so that there is not such a distinction between objects in the foreground and background.

The depth of field is necessary to understand when choosing the correct lenses and configurations for your company's CCTV. The **depth of field** refers to the portion of the environment that is in focus when shown on the monitor. The depth of field varies depending upon the size of the lens opening, the distance of the object being focused on, and the focal length of the lens. The depth of field increases as the size of the lens opening decreases, the subject distance increases, or the focal length of the lens decreases. So, if you want to cover a large area and not focus on specific items, it is best to use a wide-angle lens and a small lens opening.

CCTV lenses have *irises*, which control the amount of light that enters into the lens. *Manual iris lenses* have a ring around the CCTV lens that can be manually turned and controlled. A lens that has a manual iris would be used in areas that have fixed lighting, since the iris cannot self-adjust to changes of light. An *auto iris lens* should be used in environments where the light changes, as in an outdoor setting. As the environment brightens, this is sensed by the iris, which automatically adjusts itself. Security personnel will configure the CCTV to have a specific fixed exposure value, which the iris is responsible for maintaining. On a sunny day, the iris lens closes to reduce the amount of light that enters into the camera; at night, the iris opens to capture more light—just like our eyes.

When choosing the right CCTV for the right environment, you must determine the amount of light that is present in the environment. Different CCTV camera and lens products have specific illumination requirements to ensure the best quality of the images as possible. The illumination requirements are usually represented in the lux value, which is a metric used to represent illumination strengths. The illumination can be measured by using a light meter. The intensity of light (illumination) is measured and represented in measurement units of lux or footcandles. (The conversion between the two is one footcandle = 10.76 lux.) The illumination measurement is not something that can be accurately provided by the vendor of a light bulb, because there are things within the environment that can directly affect the illumination. This is why illumination strengths are most effectively measured where the light source is implemented.

Next, you need to consider the mounting requirements of the CCTV cameras. The cameras can be implemented in a *fixed mounting* or a mounting that allows the camera to move when necessary. A fixed camera cannot move in response to security personnel commands, whereas cameras that provide *PTZ capabilities* can pan, tilt, or zoom as necessary.

So, buying and implementing a CCTV system may not be as straightforward as it seems. As a security professional, you would need to understand the intended use of the CCTV, the environment that will be monitored, and the functionalities that will be required by the security staff who will use the CCTV on a daily basis. The different components that can make up a CCTV product are shown in Figure 6-21.

Great—your assessment team has done all of its research and bought and implemented the correct CCTV system; now it would be nice if someone actually watched the monitors for suspicious activities. Realizing that monitor watching is a mentally deadening activity may lead your team to implement a type of *annunciator system*. Different types of annunciator products are available that can either "listen" for noise and activate electrical devices, such as lights, sirens, or CCTV cameras, or detect movement. Instead of expecting a security guard to stare at a CCTV monitor for eight hours straight, the guard can carry out other activities and be alerted by an annunciator if movement is detected on a screen.

## Intrusion Detection Systems

Surveillance techniques are used to watch for unusual behaviors, whereas intrusion detection devices are used to sense changes that take place in an environment. Both are monitoring methods, but they use different devices and approaches. This section addresses the types of technologies that can be used to detect the presence of an intruder. An example of a perimeter scanning device is shown in Figure 6-22.

**Figure 6-21** A CCTV product can comprise several components.

IDSs are used to detect unauthorized entries and to alert a responsible entity to respond. These systems can monitor entries, doors, windows, devices, or removable coverings of equipment. Many work with magnetic contacts or vibration-detection devices that are sensitive to certain types of changes in the environment. When a change is detected, the IDS device sounds an alarm either in the local area, or in both the local area and to a remote police or guard station.

IDSs can be used to detect changes in the following:

- Beams of light
- Sounds and vibrations
- Motion
- Different types of fields (microwave, ultrasonic, electrostatic)
- Electrical circuit

**Figure 6-22**
Different perimeter
scanning devices
work by covering
a specific area.

IDSs can be used to detect intruders by using electro-mechanical systems (magnetic switches, metallic foil in windows, pressure mats) or volumetric systems. Volumetric systems are more sensitive because they detect changes in subtle environmental characteristics, such as vibration, microwaves, ultrasonic frequencies, infrared values, and photoelectric changes.

*Electro-mechanical systems* work by detecting a change or break in a circuit. The electrical circuits can be strips of foil embedded or connected to windows. If the window breaks, the foil strip breaks, which sounds an alarm. Vibration detectors can detect movement on walls, screens, ceilings, and floors when the fine wires embedded within the structure are broken. Magnetic contact switches can be installed on windows and doors. If the contacts are separated because the window or door is opened, an alarm will sound.

Another type of electro-mechanical detector is a pressure pad. This is placed underneath a rug or portion of the carpet and is activated after hours. If someone steps on the pad, an alarm initiates, because no one is supposed to be in this area during this time.

Types of volumetric IDSs are photoelectric, acoustical-seismic, ultrasonic, and microwave.

A *photoelectric system* (or *photometric system*) detects the change in a light beam and thus can be used only in windowless rooms. These systems work like photoelectric smoke detectors, which emit a beam that hits the receiver. If this beam of light is interrupted, an alarm sounds. The beams emitted by the photoelectric cell can be cross-sectional and can be invisible or visible beams. *Cross-sectional* means that one area can have several different light beams extending across it, which is usually carried out by using hidden mirrors to bounce the beam from one place to another until it hits the light receiver. These are the most commonly used systems in the movies. You probably have seen James Bond and other noteworthy movie spies or criminals using night-vision goggles to see the invisible beams and then stepping over them.

A *passive infrared system (PIR)* identifies the changes of heat waves in an area it is configured to monitor. If the particles' temperature within the air rise, it could be an indication of the presence of an intruder, so an alarm is sounded.

An *acoustical detection system* uses microphones that are installed on floors, walls, or ceilings. The goal is to detect any sound that is made during a forced entry. Although these systems are easily installed, they are very sensitive and cannot be used in areas that can be affected by the sounds of storms or traffic. *Vibration sensors* are very similar and are also implemented to detect forced entry. Financial institutions may choose to implement these types of sensors on exterior walls, where bank robbers may attempt to drive a vehicle through. They are also commonly used around the ceiling and flooring of vaults to detect someone trying to make an unauthorized bank withdrawal.

*Wave-pattern motion detectors* range in the frequency of waves that they monitor. The different frequencies are microwave, ultrasonic, and low frequency. All of these devices generate a wave pattern that is sent over a sensitive area and reflected back to a receiver. If the pattern is returned undisturbed, the device does nothing. If the pattern returns altered, because something in the room is moving, then an alarm sounds.

A *proximity detector*, or *capacitance detector*, emits a measurable magnetic field. The detector monitors this magnetic field, and an alarm sounds if the field is disrupted. These devices are usually used to protect specific objects (artwork, cabinets, or a safe) versus protecting a whole room or area. Capacitance change in an electrostatic field can be used to catch a bad guy, but first you need to understand what capacitance change means. An electrostatic IDS creates an electrostatic magnetic field, which is just an electric field associated with static electric charges. All objects have a static electric charge. All objects are made up of many subatomic particles, and when everything is stable and static, these particles make up one holistic electric charge. This means that there is a balance between the electric capacitance and inductance. Now if an intruder enters the area, his subatomic particles will mess up this lovely balance in the electrostatic field, causing a capacitance change, and an alarm will sound. So if you want to rob a company that uses these types of detectors, leave the subatomic particles that make up your body at home.

The type of motion detector that a company chooses to implement, its power capacity, and its configurations dictate the number of detectors needed to cover a sensitive area. Also, the size and shape of the room and the items within the room may cause barriers, in which case more detectors would be needed to provide the necessary level of coverage.

IDSs are support mechanisms that are intended to detect and announce an attempted intrusion. They will not prevent or apprehend intruders, so they should be seen as an aid to the organization's security forces.

## Patrol Force and Guards

One of the best security mechanisms is a security guard and/or a patrol force to monitor a facility's grounds. This type of security control is more flexible than other security mechanisms, provides good response to suspicious activities, and works as a great deterrent. However, it can be a costly endeavor, because it requires a salary, benefits, and time off. People sometimes are unreliable. Screening and bonding is an important part of selecting a security guard, but this only provides a certain level of assurance.

## Intrusion Detection Systems Characteristics

IDSs are very valuable controls to use in every physical security program, but several things need to be understood before their implementation.

- Expensive and requires human intervention to respond to the alarms
- Redundant power supply and emergency backup power are necessary
- Can be linked to a centralized security system
- Should have a fail-safe configuration, which means to default to "activated"
- Should detect, and be resistant to, tampering

IDSs and physical protection measures ultimately require human intervention. Security guards can be at a fixed post or can patrol specific areas. Different organizations will have different needs from security guards. They may be required to check individual credentials and enforce filling out a sign-in log. They may be responsible for monitoring IDSs and expected to respond to alarms. They may need to issue and recover visitor badges, respond to fire alarms, enforce rules established by the company within the building, and control what materials can come into or go out of the environment. The guard may need to verify that doors, windows, safes, and vaults are secured; report identified safety hazards; enforce restrictions of sensitive areas; and escort individuals throughout facilities.

The security guard should have clear and decisive tasks that she is expected to fulfill. The guard should be fully trained on the activities she is expected to perform and on the responses expected from her in different situations. The guard should have a central control point to check in to, two-way radios to ensure proper communication, and necessary access into the areas she is responsible for protecting.

The best security has a combination of security mechanisms and does not depend on just one component of security. A security guard should be accompanied by other surveillance and detection mechanisms.

## Dogs

Dogs have proven to be highly useful in detecting intruders and other unwanted conditions. Their hearing and sight outperform those of humans, and their intelligence and loyalty can be used for protection.

The best security dogs go through intensive training to respond to a wide range of commands and to perform many tasks. Dogs can be trained to hold an intruder at bay until security personnel arrive or to chase an intruder and attack. Some dogs are trained to smell smoke so that they can alert others to a fire.

Of course, dogs cannot always know the difference between an authorized person and an unauthorized person, so if someone goes into work after hours, she can have more on her hands than expected. Dogs can provide a good supplementary security mechanism, or a company can ask the security guard to bare his teeth at the sight of an unknown individual instead. Whatever works.

## Auditing Physical Access

Physical access control systems can use software and auditing features to produce audit trails pertaining to access attempts. The following information should be logged and reviewed:

- Date and time of access attempt
- Entry point in which access was attempted
- User ID used when access was attempted
- Unsuccessful access attempts, especially if during unauthorized hours

As with audit logs produced by computers, access logs are useless unless someone actually reviews them. A security guard may be required to review these logs, but a security professional or a facility manager should also review these logs periodically. Management needs to know where entry points into the facility exist and who attempts to use them.

Audit and access logs are detective, not preventive. They are used to piece together a situation after the fact instead of attempting to prevent an access attempt in the first place.

# Summary

Our distributed environments have put much more responsibility on the individual user, facility management, and administrative procedures and controls than in the old days. Physical security is not just the night guard who carries around a big flashlight. Now, security can be extremely technical, comes in many forms, and raises many liability and legal issues. Natural disasters, fires, floods, intruders, vandals, environmental issues, construction materials, and power supplies all need to be planned for and dealt with.

Every organization should develop, implement, and maintain a physical security program that contains the following control categories: deterrence, delay, detection, assessment, and response. It is up to the organization to determine its acceptable risk level and the specific controls that are required to fulfill the responsibility of each category.

Physical security is not often thought about when people think of organizational security and company asset protection, but real threats and risks need to be addressed and planned for. Who cares if a hacker can get through an open port on the web server if the building is burning down?

## References

- **International CPTED Association (ICA)**   www.cpted.net
- **Security.Org's reference links relating to locks, safes, and security**
  http://security.org/dial-80/links.htm
- **FIPS Publications series**   www.itl.nist.gov/fipspubs/by-num.htm

# Quick Tips

- Physical security is usually the first line of defense against environmental risks and unpredictable human behavior.

- Crime Prevention Through Environmental Design (CPTED) combines the physical environment and sociology issues that surround it to reduce crime rates and the fear of crime.

- The value of property within the facility and the value of the facility itself need to be ascertained to determine the proper budget for physical security so that security controls are cost effective.

- Automated environmental controls help minimize the resulting damage and speed the recovery process. Manual controls can be time consuming and error prone, and require constant attention.

- Physical construction materials and structure composition need to be evaluated for their protective characteristics, their utility, and their costs and benefits.

- Some physical security controls may conflict with the safety of people. These issues need to be addressed; human life is always more important than protecting a facility or the assets it contains.

- When looking at locations for a facility, consider local crime, natural disaster possibilities, and distance to hospitals, police and fire stations, airports, and railroads.

- HVAC should maintain the appropriate temperature and humidity levels, provide closed-loop recirculating air conditioning, and positive pressurization and ventilation.

- High humidity can cause corrosion, and low humidity can cause static electricity.

- Dust and other air contaminants may adversely affect computer hardware, and should be kept to acceptable levels.

- Administrative controls include drills and exercises of emergency procedures, simulation testing, documentation, inspections and reports, prescreening of employees, post-employment procedures, delegation of responsibility and rotation of duties, and security awareness training.

- Emergency procedure documentation should be readily available and periodically reviewed and updated.

- Proximity identification devices can be user activated (action needs to be taken by a user) or system sensing (no action needs to be taken by the user).

- A transponder is a proximity identification device that does not require action by the user. The reader transmits signals to the device, and the device responds with an access code.

- Exterior fencing can be costly and unsightly, but can provide crowd control and help control access to the facility.

- Interior partitions may not go all the way up to the ceiling; therefore, an intruder can remove a ceiling tile and climb over the partition into a critical portion of the facility.

- Intrusion detection devices include motion detectors, CCTVs, vibration sensors, and electro-mechanical devices.

- Intrusion detection devices can be penetrated, are expensive to install and monitor, require human response, and are subject to false alarms.

- CCTV enables one person to monitor a large area, but should be coupled with alerting functions to ensure proper response.

- Security guards are expensive but provide flexibility in response to security breaches and can deter intruders from attempting an attack.

- A cipher lock uses a keypad and is programmable.

- Company property should be marked as such, and security guards should be trained how to identify when these items leave the facility in an improper manner.

- Media should be protected from destruction, modification, theft, unauthorized copying, and disclosure.

- Floors, ceilings, and walls need to be able to hold the necessary load and provide the required fire rating.

- Water, steam, and gas lines need to have shutoff valves and positive drains (substance flows out instead of in).

- The threats to physical security are interruption of services, theft, physical damage, unauthorized disclosure, and loss of system integrity.

- The primary power source is what is used in day-to-day operations, and the alternate power source is a backup in case the primary source fails.

- Power companies usually plan and implement brownouts when they are experiencing high demand.

- Power noise is a disturbance of power and can be caused by electromagnetic interference (EMI) or radio frequency interference (RFI).

- EMI can be caused by lightning, motors, and the current difference between wires. RFI can be caused by electrical system mechanisms, fluorescent lighting, and electrical cables.

- Power transient noise is disturbance imposed on a power line that causes electrical interference.

- Power regulators condition the line to keep voltage steady and clean.

- UPS factors that should be reviewed are the size of the electrical load the UPS can support, the speed with which it can assume the load when the primary source fails, and the amount of time it can support the load.

- Shielded lines protect from electrical and magnetic induction, which causes interference to the power voltage.

- Perimeter protection is used to deter trespassing and to enable people to enter a facility through a few controlled entrances.

- Fire detectors should be located on and above suspended ceilings, below raised floors, and in air ducts to provide maximum fire detection.

- A fire needs high temperatures, oxygen, and fuel. To suppress it, one or more of those items needs to be reduced or eliminated.

- Gases, like halon, FM-200, and other halon substitutes, interfere with the chemical reaction of a fire.

- The HVAC should be turned off before activation of a fire suppressant to ensure that it stays in the needed area and smoke is not distributed to different areas of the facility.

- Portable fire extinguishers should be located within 50 feet of electrical equipment and should be inspected quarterly.

- $CO_2$ is a colorless, odorless, and potentially lethal substance because it removes the oxygen from the air to suppress fires.

- Piggybacking, when unauthorized access is achieved to a facility via another individual's legitimate access, is a common concern with physical security.

- Halon is no longer available because it depletes the ozone. FM-200 or other similar substances are used instead of halon.

- Proximity systems require human response, can cause false alarms, and depend on a constant power supply, so these protection systems should be backed up by other types of security systems.

- Dry pipe systems reduce the accidental discharge of water because the water does not enter the pipes until an automatic fire sensor indicates that there is an actual fire.

- In locations with freezing temperatures where broken pipes cause problems, dry pipes should be used.

- A preaction pipe delays water release.

- CCTVs are best used in conjunction with other monitoring and intrusion alert methods.

## Questions

Please remember that these questions are formatted and asked in a certain way for a reason. You must remember that the CISSP exam is asking questions at a conceptual level. Questions may not always have the perfect answer, and the candidate is advised against always looking for the perfect answer. The candidate should look for the best answer in the list.

1. What is the first step that should be taken when a fire has been detected?

    A. Turn off the HVAC system and activate fire door releases.

    B. Determine which type of fire it is.

    C. Advise individuals within the building to leave.

    D. Activate fire suppression system.

2. A company needs to implement a CCTV system that will monitor a large area outside the facility. Which of the following is the correct lens combination for this?

    A. A wide-angle lens and a small lens opening

    B. A wide-angle lens and a large lens opening

    C. A wide-angle lens and a large lens opening with a small focal length

    D. A wide-angle lens and a large lens opening with a large focal length

3. When should a Class C fire extinguisher be used instead of a Class A fire extinguisher?

    A. When electrical equipment is on fire

    B. When wood and paper are on fire

    C. When a combustible liquid is on fire

    D. When the fire is in an open area

4. Which of the following is not a true statement about CCTV lenses?

    A. Lenses that have a manual iris should be used in outside monitoring.

    B. Zoom lenses will carry out focus functionality automatically.

    C. Depth of field increases as the size of the lens opening decreases.

    D. Depth of field increases as the focal length of the lens decreases.

5. How does halon fight fires?

    A. Reduces the fire's fuel intake

    B. Reduces the temperature of the area and cools the fire out

    C. Disrupts the chemical reactions of a fire

    D. Reduces the oxygen in the area

6. What is a mantrap?

    A. A trusted security domain

    B. A logical access control mechanism

    C. A double-door facility used for physical access control

    D. A fire suppression device

7. What is true about a transponder?

    A. It is a card that can be read without sliding it through a card reader.

    B. It is a passive proximity device.

    C. It is a card that a user swipes through a card reader to gain access to a facility.

    D. It exchanges tokens with an authentication server.

8. When is a security guard the best choice for a physical access control mechanism?

    A. When discriminating judgment is required

    B. When intrusion detection is required

    C. When the security budget is low

    D. When access controls are in place

9. Which of the following is a not a characteristic of an electrostatic intrusion detection system?

    A. Creates an electrostatic field and monitors for a capacitance change

    B. Used as an intrusion detection system for large areas

    C. Produces a balance between the electric capacitance and inductance of an object

    D. Can detect if an intruder comes within a certain range of an object

10. What is a common problem with vibration-detection devices used for perimeter security?

    A. They can be defeated by emitting the right electrical signals in the protected area.

    B. The power source is easily disabled.

    C. They cause false alarms.

    D. They interfere with computing devices.

11. Which of the following is an example of glare protection?

    A. Using automated iris lenses with short focal lengths

    B. Using standby lighting, which is produced by a CCTV camera

    C. Directing light toward entry points and away from a security force post

    D. Ensuring that the lighting system uses positive pressure

12. Which of the following is not a main component of CPTED?

    A. Natural access control

    B. Natural surveillance

    C. Territorial reinforcement

    D. Target hardening

13. What are the problems that may be caused by humidity in an area with electrical devices?

    A. High humidity causes excess electricity, and low humidity causes corrosion.

    B. High humidity causes corrosion, and low humidity causes static electricity.

    C. High humidity causes power fluctuations, and low humidity causes static electricity.

    D. High humidity causes corrosion, and low humidity causes power fluctuations.

14. What does positive pressurization pertaining to ventilation mean?

    A. When a door opens, the air comes in.

    B. When a fire takes place, the power supply is disabled.

    C. When a fire takes place, the smoke is diverted to one room.

    D. When a door opens, the air goes out.

15. Which of the following answers contains a category of controls that does not belong in a physical security program?

    A. Deterrence and delaying

    B. Response and detection

    C. Assessment and detection

    D. Delaying and lighting

16. Which is not an administrative control pertaining to emergency procedures?

    A. Intrusion detection systems

    B. Awareness and training

    C. Drills and inspections

    D. Delegation of duties

17. If an access control has a fail-safe characteristic but not a fail-secure characteristic, what does that mean?

    A. It defaults to no access.

    B. It defaults to being unlocked.

    C. It defaults to being locked.

    D. It defaults to sounding a remote alarm instead of a local alarm.

18. Which of the following is not considered a delaying mechanism?

    A. Locks

    B. Defense-in-depth measures

    C. Warning signs

    D. Access controls

19. What are the two general types of proximity identification devices?

    A. Biometric devices and access control devices

    B. Swipe card devices and passive devices

    C. Preset code devices and wireless devices

    D. User-activated devices and system sensing devices

20. Which of the following answers best describes the relationship between a risk analysis, acceptable risk level, baselines, countermeasures, and metrics?

    A. The risk analysis output is used to determine the proper countermeasures that are required. Baselines are derived to measure these countermeasures. Metrics are used to track countermeasure performance to ensure that baselines are being met.

    B. The risk analysis output is used to help management understand and set an acceptable risk level. Baselines are derived from this level. Metrics are used to track countermeasure performance to ensure that baselines are being met.

    C. The risk analysis output is used to help management understand and set baselines. An acceptable risk level is derived from these baselines. Metrics are used to track countermeasure performance to ensure that baselines are being met.

    D. The risk analysis output is used to help management understand and set an acceptable risk level. Baselines are derived from the metrics. Metrics are used to track countermeasure performance to ensure that baselines are being met.

21. Most of today's CCTV systems use charged-coupled devices. Which of the following is not a characteristic of these devices?

    A. Receives input through the lenses and converts them into electronic signal

    B. Captures signals in the infrared range

    C. Provides better-quality images

    D. Records data on hard drives instead of tapes

22. Which is not a drawback to installing intrusion detection and monitoring systems?

    A. Expensive to install

    B. Cannot be penetrated

    C. Requires human response

    D. Subject to false alarms

23. What is a cipher lock?

    A. A lock that uses cryptographic keys

    B. A lock that uses a type of key that cannot be reproduced

    C. A lock that uses a token and perimeter reader

    D. A lock that uses a keypad

24. If a cipher lock has a door delay option, what does that mean?

    A. After a door is open for a specific period, the alarm goes off.

    B. It can only be opened during emergency situations.

      C. It has a hostage alarm capability.

      D. It has supervisory override capability.

25. Which of the following best describes the difference between a warded lock and a tumbler lock?

      A. A tumbler lock is more simplistic and easier to circumvent than a ward lock.

      B. A tumbler lock uses an internal bolt and a ward lock uses internal cylinders.

      C. A tumbler lock has more components than a ward lock.

      D. A ward lock is mainly used externally and a tumbler lock is used internally.

# Answers

1. **C.** Human life takes precedence. Although the other answers are important steps in this type of situation, the first step is to warn others, to save as many lives as possible.

2. **A.** The depth of field refers to the portion of the environment that is in focus when shown on the monitor. The depth of field varies depending upon the size of the lens opening, the distance of the object being focused on, and the focal length of the lens. The depth of field increases as the size of the lens opening decreases, the subject distance increases, or the focal length of the lens decreases. So if you want to cover a large area and not focus on specific items, it is best to use a wide-angle lens and a small lens opening.

3. **A.** A Class C fire is an electrical fire. Thus, an extinguisher with the proper suppression agent should be used. The following table shows the fire types, their attributes, and suppression methods:

| Fire Class | Type of Fire | Elements of Fire | Suppression Method |
|---|---|---|---|
| A | Common combustibles | Wood products, paper, and laminates | Water, foam |
| B | Liquid | Petroleum products and coolants | Gas, $CO_2$, foam, dry powders |
| C | Electrical | Electrical equipment and wires | Gas, $CO_2$, dry powders |
| D | Combustible metals | Magnesium, sodium, potassium | Dry powder |

4. **A.** Manual iris lenses have a ring around the CCTV lens that can be manually turned and controlled. A lens that has a manual iris would be used in an area that has fixed lighting, since the iris cannot self-adjust to changes of light. An auto iris lens should be used in environments where the light changes, such as an outdoor setting. As the environment brightens, this is sensed by the iris, which automatically adjusts itself. Security personnel will configure the CCTV

to have a specific fixed exposure value, which the iris is responsible for maintaining. The other answers are true.

5. **C.** Halon is a type of gas that is used to interfere with the chemical reactions between the elements of a fire. A fire requires fuel, oxygen, high temperatures, and chemical reactions to burn properly. Different suppressant agents have been developed to attack each aspect of a fire: $CO_2$ displaces the oxygen, water reduces the temperature, and soda acid removes the fuel.

6. **C.** A mantrap is a small room with two doors. The first door is locked; a person is identified and authenticated by a security guard, biometric system, smart card reader, or swipe card reader. Once the person is authenticated and access is authorized, the first door opens and allows the person into the mantrap. The first door locks and the person is trapped. The person must be authenticated again before the second door unlocks and allows him into the facility.

7. **A.** A transponder is a type of physical access control device that does not require the user to slide a card through a reader. The reader and card communicate directly. The card and reader have a receiver, transmitter, and battery. The reader sends signals to the card to request information. The card sends the reader an access code.

8. **A.** Although many effective physical security mechanisms are on the market today, none can look at a situation and make a judgment about it and make a decision on what the next step should be. A security guard is employed when a company needs to have a countermeasure that can think and make decisions in different scenarios.

9. **B.** An electrostatic IDS creates an electrostatic field, which is just an electric field associated with static electric charges. The IDS creates a balanced electrostatic field between itself and the object that is being monitored. If an intruder comes within a certain range of the object that is being monitored, then there is capacitance change. The IDS can detect this change and sound an alarm.

10. **C.** This type of system is sensitive to sounds and vibrations and detects the changes in the noise level of an area it is placed within. This level of sensitivity can cause many false alarms. These devices do not emit any waves; they only listen for sounds within an area and are considered passive devices.

11. **C.** When lighting is installed, it should be directed toward areas where potential intruders would most likely be coming from and away from the security force posts. For example, lighting should be pointed at gates or exterior access points, and the guard locations should be in the shadows, or under a lower amount of illumination. This is referred to as "glare protection" for the security force.

12. **D.** Natural access control is the use of the environment to control access to entry points, such as using landscaping and bollards. An example of natural surveillance is the construction of pedestrian walkways so that there is a clear line of sight of all the activities in the surroundings. Territorial reinforcement gives people a sense of ownership of a property so that they will tend to

protect it. These are all parts of CPTED. Target hardening has to do with implementing locks, security guards, and proximity devices.

13. **B.** High humidity can cause corrosion, and low humidity can cause excessive static electricity. Static electricity can short out devices or cause loss of information.

14. **D.** Positive pressurization means that when someone opens a door, the air goes out and outside air does not come in. If a facility were on fire and the doors were opened, positive pressure would cause the smoke to go out instead of being pushed back into the building.

15. **D.** The categories of controls that should make up any physical security program are deterrence, delaying, detection, assessment, and response. Lighting is a control itself, not a category of controls.

16. **A.** Awareness and training, drills and inspections, and delegation of duties are all items that have a direct correlation to proper emergency procedures. It is management's responsibility to ensure that these items are in place, properly tested, and carried out. Intrusion detection systems are technical controls.

17. **B.** A fail-safe setting means that if there were a power disruption that would affect the automated locking system, the doors would default to being unlocked. A fail-secure configuration means that a door would default to being locked if there were any problems with the power.

18. **C.** Every physical security program should have delaying mechanisms, which have the purpose of slowing down an intruder in his activities so that security personnel can be alerted and arrive at the scene. A warning sign is a deterrence control, not a delaying control.

19. **D.** A user-activated system requires the user to do something: swipe the card through the reader and/or enter a code. A system sensing device recognizes the presence of the card and communicates with it without the user needing to carry out any activity.

20. **B.** The physical security team needs to carry out a risk analysis, which will identify the organization's vulnerabilities, threats, and business impacts. The team should present these finding to management and work with management to define an acceptable risk level for the physical security program. From there the team needs to develop baselines (minimum levels of security) and develop metrics to be able to evaluate and determine if the baselines are being met by the implemented countermeasures. Once the team identifies and implements the countermeasures, the countermeasures' performance should be continually evaluated and expressed in the previously created metrics. These performance values are compared to the set baselines. If the baselines are continually maintained, then the security program is successful because the company's acceptable risk level is not being exceeded.

21. **D.** The CCD is an electrical circuit that receives input light from the lens and converts it into an electronic signal, which is then displayed on the monitor. Images are focused through a lens onto the CCD chip surface, which forms the electrical representation of the optical image. It is this technology that allows for the capture of extraordinary detail of objects and precise representation, because it has sensors that work in the infrared range, which extends beyond human perception. The CCD sensor picks up this extra "data" and integrates it into the images shown on the monitor, to allow for better granularity and quality in the video. CCD does not record data.

22. **B.** Monitoring and intrusion detection systems are expensive, require someone to respond when they set off an alarm, and, because of their level of sensitivity, can cause several false alarms. Like any other type of technology or device, they have their own vulnerabilities that can be exploited and penetrated.

23. **D.** Cipher locks, also known as programmable locks, use keypads to control access into an area or facility. The lock can require a specific combination to be entered into the keypad and a swipe card.

24. **A.** A security guard would want to be alerted when a door has been open for an extended period. It may be an indication that something is taking place other than a person entering or exiting the door. A security system can have a threshold set so that if the door is open past this period, an alarm sounds.

25. **C.** The tumbler lock has more pieces and parts than a ward lock. The key fits into a cylinder, which raises the lock metal pieces to the correct height so that the bolt can slide to the locked or unlocked position. A ward lock is easier to circumvent than a tumbler lock.

# Telecommunications and Networking Security

This chapter presents the following:
- OSI model
- TCP/IP and many other protocols
- LAN, WAN, MAN, intranet, and extranet technologies
- Cable types and data transmission types
- Network devices and services
- Communications security management
- Telecommunications devices
- Remote access methods and technologies
- Wireless technologies

Telecommunications and networking use various mechanisms, devices, software, and protocols that are interrelated and integrated. Networking is one of the more complex topics in the computer field, mainly because so many technologies and concepts are involved. A network administrator or engineer must know how to configure networking software, protocols and services, and devices; deal with interoperability issues; install, configure, and interface with telecommunications software and devices; and troubleshoot effectively. A security professional must understand these issues and be able to analyze them a few levels deeper to recognize fully where vulnerabilities can arise within networks. This can be an overwhelming and challenging task. However, if you are someone who enjoys challenges and appreciates the intricacies of technology, then maintaining security and networking infrastructures may be more fun than work.

As a security professional, you cannot advise others on how to secure an environment if you do not fully understand how to do so yourself. To secure an application that contains a buffer overflow, for example, you must understand what a buffer overflow is, what the outcome of the exploit is, how to identify a buffer overflow properly, and possibly how to write program code to remove this weakness from the program. To secure a network architecture, you must understand the various networking platforms involved, network devices, and how data flows through a network. You must understand how various protocols work, their purposes, their interactions with other protocols, how they may provide exploitable vulnerabilities, and how to choose and implement the appropriate types of protocols in a given environment. You must also understand the different types of firewalls, routers, switches, and bridges, when one is more appropriate than the other, where they are to be placed, their interactions with other devices, and the degree of security each provides.

The many different types of devices, protocols, and security mechanisms within an environment provide different functionality, but they also provide a layered approach to security. Layers within security are important, so that if an attacker is able to bypass one layer, another layer stands in the way to protect the internal network. Many networks have routers, firewalls, intrusion detection systems (IDSs), antivirus software, and more. Each specializes in a certain piece of security, but they all should work in concert to provide a layered approach to security.

Although networking and telecommunications are complicated topics to understand, it is that complexity that makes it the most fun for those who truly enjoy these fields. However, complexity can be the enemy of security. It is important to understand the components within an environment and their relationships to other components that make up the environment as a whole. This chapter addresses many of the telecommunications and networking aspects that are included in many networks.

*Telecommunications* is the electrical transmission of data among systems, whether through analog, digital, or wireless transmission types. The data can flow across copper wires, coaxial cable, fiber, or airwaves, the telephone company's public-switched telephone network (PSTN), or a service provider's fiber cables, switches, and routers. Definitive lines exist between the media used for transmission, the technologies, the protocols, and whose equipment is being used. However, the definitive lines get blurry when one follows how data that is created on a user's workstation flows within seconds through a complex path of Ethernet cables, to a router that divides the company's network and the rest of the world, through the Asynchronous Transfer Mode (ATM) switch provided by the service provider, to the many switches the packets transverse throughout the ATM cloud, on to another company's network, through its router, and to another user's workstation. Each piece is interesting, but when they all integrate and work together, it is awesome.

Telecommunications usually refers to telephone systems, service providers, and carrier services. Most telecommunications systems are regulated by governments and international organizations. In the United States, telecommunications systems are regulated by the Federal Communications Commission (FCC), which includes voice and data transmissions. In Canada, agreements are managed through Spectrum, Information Technologies and Telecommunications (SITT), Industry Canada. Globally, organizations develop policies, recommend standards, and work together to provide standardization and the capability for different technologies to properly interact.

The main standards organizations are the International Telecommunication Union (ITU) and the International Standards Organization (ISO). Their models and standards have shaped our technology today, and the technological issues governed by these organizations are addressed throughout this chapter.

**NOTE**   Do not get overwhelmed with the size of this chapter and the amount of information within it. This chapter, as well as the others, attempts to teach you the concepts and meanings behind the definitions and answers you will need for the CISSP exam. This book is not intended to give you one-liners to remember for the exam, but rather it teaches you the meaning behind the answers. The "Quick Tips" section at the end of the chapter and the questions help you zero in on the most important concepts for the exam itself.

# Open Systems Interconnection Reference Model

*I don't understand what all of these protocols are doing. Response: Okay, let's make a model to explain it then.*

ISO is a worldwide federation that works to provide international standards. In the early 1980s, ISO worked to develop a protocol set that would be used by all vendors throughout the world to allow the interconnection of network devices. This movement was fueled with the hopes of ensuring that all vendor products and technologies could communicate and interact across international and technical boundaries. The actual protocol set did not catch on as a standard, but the model of this protocol set, OSI model, was adopted and is used as an abstract framework to which most operating systems and protocols adhere.

Many people think that the OSI reference model arrived at the beginning of the computing age as we know it and helped shape and provide direction for many if not all networking technologies. However, this is not true. In fact, it was introduced in 1984, at which time the basics of the Internet had already been developed and implemented, and the basic Internet protocols had been in use for many years. The Transmission Control Protocol/Internet Protocol (TCP/IP) protocol suite actually has its own model that is often used today when examining and understanding networking issues. Figure 7-1 shows the differences between the OSI and TCP/IP networking models. In this chapter, we will focus more on the OSI model.

**NOTE**   The host-to-host layer is sometimes called the transport layer in the TCP/IP model.

## Protocol

A network *protocol* is a standard set of rules that determines how systems will communicate across networks. Two different systems that use the same protocol can communicate and understand each other despite their differences, similar to how two people can communicate and understand each other by using the same language.

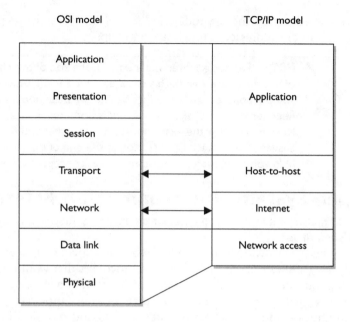

**Figure 7-1**
The OSI and TCP/IP
networking models

The OSI reference model, as described by ISO Standard 7498, provides important guidelines that are used by vendors, engineers, developers, and others. The model segments the networking tasks, protocols, and services into different layers. Each layer has its own responsibilities regarding how two computers communicate over a network. Each layer has certain functionalities, and the services and protocols that work within that layer fulfill them.

The OSI model's goal is to help others develop products that will work within an open network architecture. An *open network* architecture is one that no vendor owns, that is not proprietary, and that can easily integrate various technologies and vendor implementations of those technologies. Vendors have used the OSI model as a jumping-off point for developing their own networking frameworks. These vendors used the OSI model as a blueprint and developed their own protocols and interfaces to produce functionality that is different from or overlaps that of other vendors. However, because these vendors use the OSI model as their starting place, integration of other vendor products is an easier task, and the interoperability issues are less burdensome than if the vendors had developed their own networking framework from scratch.

Although computers communicate in a physical sense (electronic signals are passed from one computer over a wire to the other computer), they also communicate through logical channels. Each protocol at a specific OSI layer on one computer communicates with a corresponding protocol operating at the same OSI layer on another computer. This happens through *encapsulation*.

Logical data movement

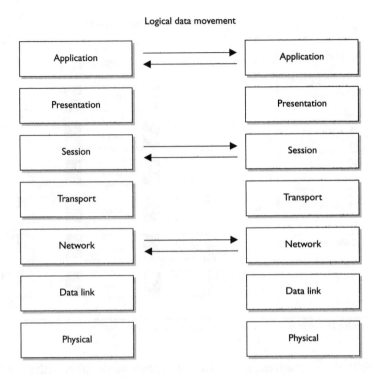

Here's how encapsulation works: A message is constructed within a program on one computer and then passed down through the protocol's stack. A protocol at each layer adds its own information to the message; thus, the message grows in size as it goes down the protocol stack. The message is then sent to the destination computer, and the encapsulation is reversed by taking the packet apart through the same steps used by the source computer that encapsulated it. At the data link layer, only the information pertaining to the data link layer is extracted, and the message is sent up to the next layer. Then at the network layer, only the network layer data is stripped and processed and the packet is again passed up to the next layer, and so on. This is how computers communicate logically. The information stripped off at the destination computer informs it how to interpret and process the packet properly. Data encapsulation is shown in Figure 7-2.

A protocol at each layer has specific responsibilities and control functions that it performs and data format syntaxes that it expects. Each layer has a special interface (connection point) that allows it to interact with three other layers; 1) communications from the interface of the layer above it, 2) communications to the interface of the layer below it, and 3) communications with the same layer in the interface of the target packet address. The control functions, added by the protocols at each layer, are in the form of headers and trailers of the packet.

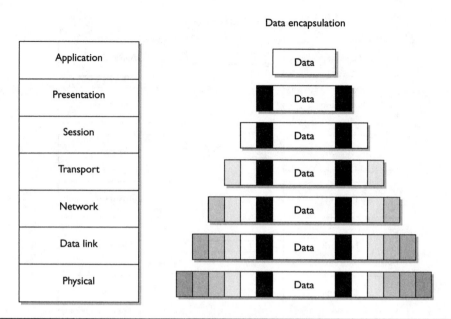

**Figure 7-2**  Each OSI layer adds its own information to the data packet.

The benefit of modularizing these layers, and the functionality within each layer, is that various technologies, protocols, and services can interact with each other and provide the proper interfaces to enable communications. This means that a computer can use an application protocol developed by Novell, a transport protocol developed by Apple, and a data link protocol developed by IBM to construct and send a message over the network. The protocols, technologies, and computers that operate within the OSI model are considered *open systems*. Open systems are capable of communicating with other open systems because they implement international standard protocols and interfaces. The specification for each layer's interface is very structured, while the actual code that makes up the internal part of the software layer is not defined. This makes it easy for vendors to write plug-in modularized layers to substitute, for the purposes of adding vendor-specific extensions and functions.

Understanding the functionalities that take place at each OSI layer and the corresponding protocols that work at those layers helps you to understand the overall communication process between computers. Once you understand this process, a more detailed look at each protocol will show you the full range of options each protocol provides and the security weaknesses embedded into each of those options.

## Application Layer

*Hand me your information. I will take it from here.*

The *application layer*, layer 7, works closest to the user and provides file transmissions, message exchanges, terminal sessions, and much more. This layer does not include the actual applications but includes the protocols that support the applications. When an application needs to send data over the network, it passes instructions and the data to the protocols that support it at the application layer. This layer processes and properly formats the data and passes it down to the next layer within the OSI model. This happens until the data that the application layer constructed contains the essential information from each layer necessary to transmit data over the network. The data is then put on the network cable and is transmitted until it arrives at the destination computer.

Some examples of the protocols working at this layer are the Simple Mail Transfer Protocol (SMTP), Hypertext Transfer Protocol (HTTP), Line Printer Daemon (LPD), File Transfer Protocol (FTP), Telnet, and Trivial File Transfer Protocol (TFTP). Figure 7-3 shows how applications communicate with the underlying protocols through APIs. If a user makes a request to send an e-mail message through her e-mail client Outlook, the e-mail client sends this information to SMTP. SMTP adds its information to the user's information and passes it down to the presentation layer.

 **NOTE**    The application layer in the TCP/IP architecture model is equivalent to a combination of the application, presentation, and session layers in the OSI model (refer to Figure 7-1).

## Presentation Layer

*You will now be transformed into something that everyone can understand.*

The *presentation layer*, layer 6, receives information from the application layer protocols and puts it in a format that all computers following the OSI model can understand. This layer provides a common means of representing data in a structure that can be properly processed by the end system. This means that when a user constructs a Word document and sends it out to several people, it does not matter whether the receiving computer has different word processing programs; each of these computers will be able to receive this file and understand and present it to its user as a document. It is the data representation processing that is done at the presentation layer that enables this to take place. For example, when a Windows XP computer receives a file from another computer system, information within the file's header explains what type of file it is. The Windows XP operating system has a list of file types it understands and a table

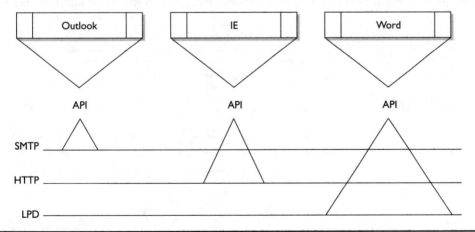

**Figure 7-3**    Applications send requests to an API, which is the interface to the supporting protocol.

describing what program should be used to open and manipulate each of these file types. For example, the sender could create a Word file in Word 2000, while the receiver uses Open Office. The receiver can open this file because the presentation layer on the sender's system converted the file to American Standard Code for Information Interchange (ASCII), and the receiver's computer knows that it opens these types of files with its word processor, Open Office.

The presentation layer is not concerned with the meaning of data, but with the syntax and format of that data. It works as a translator, translating the format an application is using to a standard format used for passing messages over a network. If a user uses a Corel application to save a graphic, for example, the graphic could be a Tagged Image File Format (TIFF), Graphic Interchange Format (GIF), or Joint Photographic Experts Group (JPEG) format. The presentation layer adds information to tell the destination computer the file type and how to process and present it. This way, if the user sends this graphic to another user who does not have the Corel application, the user's operating system can still present the graphic because it has been saved into a standard format. Figure 7-4 shows how the presentation layer can convert a file into different standard file types.

This layer also handles data compression and encryption issues. If a program requests a certain file to be compressed and encrypted before being transferred over the network, the presentation layer provides the necessary information for the destination computer. It includes instructions on the encryption or compression type that was used and how to properly present it to the user. Instructions are added to the data package that tell the receiving system how to decrypt or decompress the data properly.

## Session Layer

*I don't want to talk to a computer. I want to talk to an application.*

When two applications need to communicate, or transfer information, a connection session may need to be set up between them. The *session layer*, layer 5, is responsible for establishing a connection between the two applications, maintaining it during the transfer of data, and controlling the release of this connection. A good analogy for the functionality within this layer is a telephone conversation. When Kandy wants to

**Figure 7-4**
The presentation layer receives data from the application layer and puts it into a standard format.

call a friend, she uses the telephone. The telephone network circuitry and protocols set up the connection over the telephone lines and maintains that communication path, and when Kandy hangs up, it releases all the resources it was using to keep that connection open.

Similar to how telephone circuitry works, the session layer works in three phases: connection establishment, data transfer, and connection release. It provides session re-start and recovery if necessary and provides the overall maintenance of the session. When the conversation is over, this path is broken down and all parameters are set back to their original settings. This process is known as *dialog management.* Figure 7-5 depicts the three phases of a session. Some protocols that work at this layer are Network File System (NFS), Structured Query Language (SQL), NetBIOS, and remote procedure call (RPC).

The session layer protocol can enable communication between two applications to happen in three different modes:

- **Simplex**   Communication takes place in one direction.
- **Half-duplex**   Communication takes place in both directions, but only one application can send information at a time.
- **Full-duplex**   Communication takes place in both directions, and both applications can send information at the same time.

Many people have a hard time understanding the difference between what takes place at the session layer versus the transport layer, because their definitions sound similar. Session layer protocols control application-to-application communication,

**Figure 7-5**
The session layer sets up the connection, maintains it, and tears it down once communication is completed.

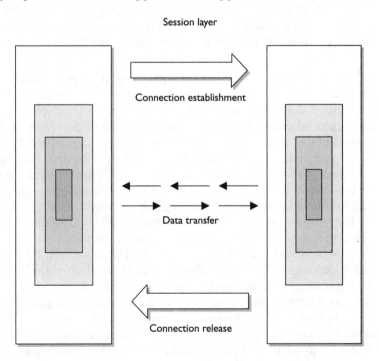

Session layer

Connection establishment

Data transfer

Connection release

whereas the transport layer protocols handle computer-to-computer communication. For example, if you are using a product that is working in a client/server model, in reality you have a small piece of the product on your computer (client portion) and the larger piece of the software product is running on a different computer (server portion). The communication between these two pieces of the same software product needs to be controlled, which is why session layer protocols even exist. Session layer protocols take on the functionality of middleware, which allows software on two different computers to communicate. The next section will dive into the functionality of the transport layer protocols.

## Transport Layer

*How do I know if I lose a piece of the message? Response: The transport layer will fix it for you.*

When two computers are going to communicate through a connection-oriented protocol, they will first agree on how much information each computer will send at a time, how to verify the integrity of the data once it is received, and how to determine whether a packet was lost along the way. The two computers agree on these parameters through a handshaking process at the *transport layer*, layer 4. The agreement on these issues before transferring data helps provide more reliable data transfer, error detection, correction, recovery, and flow control, and it optimizes the network services needed to perform these tasks. The transport layer provides end-to-end data transport services and establishes the logical connection between two communicating computers.

 **NOTE** Connection-oriented protocols, such as TCP, provide reliable data transmission when compared to connectionless protocols, such as UDP. This distinction is covered in more detail in the "TCP/IP" section, later in the chapter.

The functionality of the session and transport layers is similar insofar as they both set up some type of session or virtual connection for communication to take place. The difference is that protocols that work at the session layer set up connections between *applications*, whereas protocols that work at the transport layer set up connections between *computer systems*. For example, we can have three different applications on computer A communicating to three applications on computer B. The session layer protocols keep track of these different sessions. You can think of the transport layer protocol as the bus. It does not know or care what applications are communicating with each other; it just provides the mechanism to get the data from one system to another.

The transport layer receives data from many different applications and assembles the data into a stream so that it can be properly transmitted over the network. The main protocols that work at this layer are TCP, User Datagram Protocol (UDP), and Sequenced Packet Exchange (SPX). Information is passed down from different entities at higher layers to the transport layer, which must assemble the information into a stream, as shown in Figure 7-6. The stream is made up of the various data segments passed to it. Just like a bus can carry a variety of people, the transport layer protocol can carry a variety of types of application data. (The host-to-host, or transport, layer in the TCP/IP architecture model is equivalent to the transport layer in the OSI model; refer to Figure 7-1.)

**Figure 7-6**
TCP formats data
from applications
into a stream to
be prepared for
transmission.

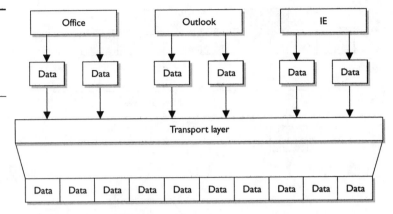

Assemble data into a stream

 **NOTE** Different references can place specific protocols at different layers.
For example, many references place the Secure Sockets Layer (SSL) protocol
in the session layer, while other references place it in the transport layer. It
is not that one is right or wrong. The OSI model tries to draw boxes around
reality, but some protocols straddle the different layers. SSL is made up of two
protocols—one works in the lower portion of the session layer and the other
works in the transport layer. For purposes of the CISSP exam, SSL resides in
the transport layer.

## Network Layer

*Many roads lead to Rome.*

The main responsibilities of the *network layer*, layer 3, are to insert information
into the packet's header so that it can be properly addressed and routed, and then to
actually route the packets to their proper destination. In a network, many routes can
lead to one destination. The protocols at the network layer must determine the best
path for the packet to take. Routing protocols build and maintain their routing tables
at this layer. These tables are maps of the network, and when a packet needs to be sent
from computer A to computer M, the protocols check the routing table, add the necessary information to the packet's header, and send it on its way.

The protocols that work at this layer do not ensure the delivery of the packets. They
depend on the protocols at the transport layer to catch any problems and resend packets if necessary. IP is a common protocol working at the network layer, although other
routing and routed protocols work there as well. Some of the other protocols are the
Internet Control Message Protocol (ICMP), Routing Information Protocol (RIP), Open
Shortest Path First (OSPF), Border Gateway Protocol (BGP), and Internet Group Management Protocol (IGMP). Figure 7-7 shows that a packet can take many routes and
that the network layer enters routing information into the header to help the packet
arrive at its destination. (The Internet layer in the TCP/IP architecture model is equivalent to the network layer in the OSI model; refer to Figure 7-1.)

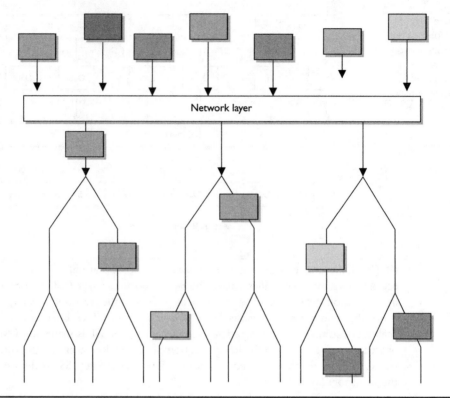

**Figure 7-7** The network layer determines the most efficient path for each packet to take.

## Data Link Layer

As we continue down the protocol stack, we are getting closer to the actual network wire over which all this data will travel. The outer format of the data packet changes slightly at each layer, and it comes to a point where it needs to be translated into local area network (LAN) or wide area network (WAN) technology binary format for proper line transmission. This happens at the *data link layer*.

 **NOTE** APSTNDP—To remember all the layers within the OSI model in the correct order, memorize "All People Seem To Need Data Processing." Remember that you are starting at layer 7, the application layer, at the top.

LAN and WAN technologies can use different protocols, network interface cards (NICs), cables, and transmission methods. Each of these technologies has different data format structures, and they interpret electricity voltages in different ways. The *data link layer*, layer 2, is where the network stack knows what format the data frame must be in to transmit properly over Token Ring, Ethernet, ATM, or Fiber Distributed Data

Interface (FDDI) networks. If the network is an Ethernet network, for example, all the computers will expect the header to be a certain length, the flags to be positioned in a certain place within the packet, and the trailer information to be in a certain place with specific fields. On a Token Ring network, the computers would expect most of these parameters to be in different places and the frames to have particular formats. The data link layer is responsible for proper communication within these technologies and for changing the data into the necessary format for the physical layer. It will also manage to reorder frames that are received out of sequence, and notify upper-layer protocols when there are transmission error conditions.

The data link layer is divided into two functional sublayers, the Logical Link Control (LLC) and the Media Access Control (MAC). The LLC, defined in the IEEE 802.2 specification, communicates with the protocol immediately above it, the network layer. The MAC will have the appropriately loaded protocols to interface with the protocol requirements of the physical layer. The IEEE MAC specification for Ethernet is 802.3, Token Ring is 802.5, wireless LAN is 802.11, etc. So when you see a reference to an IEEE standard, such as 802.11, 802.16, 802.3, and so on, it refers to the protocol that is working at the MAC sublayer of the data link layer of a protocol stack.

Some of the protocols that work at the data link layer are the Serial Line Internet Protocol (SLIP), Point-to-Point Protocol (PPP), Reverse Address Resolution Protocol (RARP), Layer 2 Forwarding (L2F), Layer 2 Tunneling Protocol (L2TP), FDDI, and Integrated Services Digital Network (ISDN). Figure 7-8 shows how the data link layer converts the information into bits and the physical layer converts those bits into electrical signals. (The network interface layer in the TCP/IP architecture model is equivalent to a combination of the data link and physical layers in the OSI model; refer to Figure 7-1.)

**Figure 7-8**
The data link layer converts the data into bits for the physical layer.

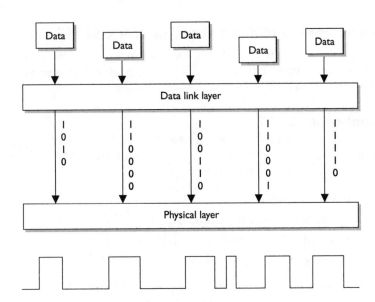

Each network technology (Ethernet, Token Ring, and so on) defines the compatible wire type (coaxial, twisted pair, or fiber) that is required to enable network communication. Each network technology also has defined electronic signaling and bit patterns. This means, for example, that a signal of 0.5 volts may represent a *0* on one technology and a *1* on another technology. The data link layer protocol specifies the proper bit patterns, and the physical layer protocol translates this information into electrical encoding and electricity state transitions. Network cards bridge the data link and physical layers. Information is passed down through the first six layers and reaches the network card driver at the data link layer. Depending on the network technology being used (Ethernet, Token Ring, FDDI, and so on), the network card driver encodes the bits at the data link layer, which are then turned into electricity states at the physical layer and placed onto the wire for transmission.

## Physical Layer

*Everything ends up as electrical signals anyway.*

The *physical layer*, layer 1, converts bits into voltage for transmission. Signals and voltage schemes have different meanings for different LAN and WAN technologies. If a user sends data through his dial-up software and out his modem onto a telephone line, the data format, electrical signals, and control functionality are much different than if that user sends data through the NIC and onto a unshielded twisted pair (UTP) wire for LAN communication. The mechanisms that control this data going onto the telephone line, or the UTP wire, work at the physical layer. This layer controls synchronization, data rates, line noise, and medium access. Specifications for the physical layer include the timing of voltage changes, voltage levels, and the physical connectors for electrical, optical, and mechanical transmission.

## Functions and Protocols in the OSI Model

For the exam, you will need to know the functionality that takes place at the different layers of the OSI model, along with specific protocols that work at each layer. Here is a quick overview of each layer and its components.

## Application

The protocols at the application layer handle file transfer, virtual terminals, network management, and fulfilling networking requests of applications. Here are a few of the protocols that work at this layer:

- File Transfer Protocol (FTP)
- Trivial File Transfer Protocol (TFTP)
- Simple Network Management Protocol (SNMP)
- Simple Mail Transfer Protocol (SMTP)
- Telnet
- Hypertext Transfer Protocol (HTTP)

## Presentation

The services of the presentation layer handle translation into standard formats, data compression and decompression, and data encryption and decryption. No protocols work at this layer, just services. Here are some of the presentation layer standards:

- American Standard Code for Information Interchange (ASCII)
- Extended Binary-Coded Decimal Interchange Mode (EBCDIC)
- Tagged Image File Format (TIFF)
- Joint Photographic Experts Group (JPEG)
- Motion Picture Experts Group (MPEG)
- Musical Instrument Digital Interface (MIDI)

## Session

The session layer protocols set up connections between applications; maintain dialog control; and negotiate, establish, maintain, and tear down the communication channel. Here are some of the protocols that work at this layer:

- Network File System (NFS)
- NetBIOS
- Structured Query Language (SQL)
- Remote procedure call (RPC)

## Transport

The protocols at the transport layer handle end-to-end transmission and segmentation into a data stream. The following protocols work at this layer:

- Transmission Control Protocol (TCP)
- User Datagram Protocol (UDP)
- Secure Sockets Layer (SSL)
- Sequenced Packet Exchange (SPX)

## Network

The responsibilities of the network layer protocols include internetworking service, addressing, and routing. Here are some of the protocols that work at this layer:

- Internet Protocol (IP)
- Internet Control Message Protocol (ICMP)
- Internet Group Management Protocol (IGMP)
- Routing Information Protocol (RIP)
- Open Shortest Path First (OSPF)
- Novel Internetwork Packet Exchange (IPX)

## Data Link

The protocols at the data link layer convert data into LAN or WAN frames for transmission, convert messages into bits, and define how a computer accesses a network. This layer is divided into the Logical Link Control (LLC) and the Media Access Control (MAC) sublayers. Here are some of the protocols that work at this layer:

- Address Resolution Protocol (ARP)
- Reverse Address Resolution Protocol (RARP)
- Point-to-Point Protocol (PPP)
- Serial Line Internet Protocol (SLIP)

## Physical

Network interface cards and drivers convert bits into electrical signals, and control the physical aspects of data transmission, including optical, electrical, and mechanical requirements. Here are some of the standard interfaces at this layer:

- High-Speed Serial Interface (HSSI)
- X.21
- EIA/TIA-232 and EIA/TIA-449

 **NOTE** The security services that are defined in the OSI security model include data integrity (protection from modification and destruction), data confidentiality (protection from disclosure), authentication (verification of identity of the communication source), and access control services (enable mechanisms to allow or restrict access).

## Tying the Layers Together

*Pick up all of these protocols from the floor and put them into a stack—a network stack.*

The OSI model is used as a framework for many products and many types of vendors. Various types of devices and protocols work at different parts of this seven-layer model. Whereas computers can interpret and process data at each of the seven layers, routers can understand information only up to the network layer, because a router's main function is to route packets, which does not require knowledge about any further information within the packet. A router peels back the header information until it reaches the network layer data, where the routing and IP address information is located. The router looks at this information to make its decisions on where the packet should be sent next. Bridges understand only up to the data link layer, and repeaters understand data only at the physical layer. Figure 7-9 shows what level of the OSI model each type of device understands.

## References

- **Protocols.com listing of data communications protocols**   www.protocols.com
- **Google listings of protocols**   http://directory.google.com/Top/Computers/ Internet/Protocols

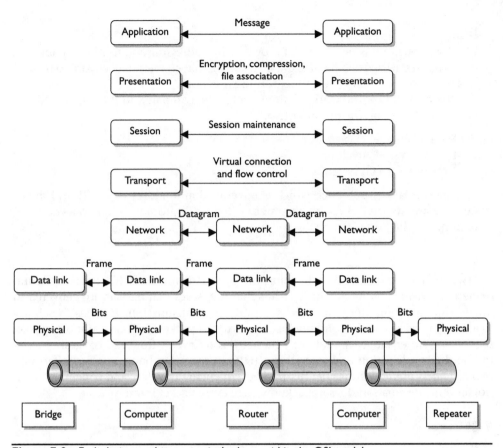

**Figure 7-9** Each device works at a particular layer within the OSI model.

- *Linktionary* **definition of OSI model**   www.linktionary.com/o/osi.html
- *Wikipedia* **entry for OSI model**   http://en.wikipedia.org/wiki/OSI_model

# TCP/IP

*Transmission Control Protocol/Internet Protocol (TCP/IP)* is a suite of protocols that governs the way that data travels from one device to another. Besides its eponymous two main protocols, TCP/IP includes other protocols as well. IP is a network layer protocol and provides datagram routing services. IP's main task is to support internetwork addressing and packet routing. It is a connectionless protocol that envelopes data passed to it from the transport layer. The IP protocol addresses the datagram with the source and destination IP addresses. The protocols within the TCP/IP suite work together to break down the data passed from the application layer into pieces that can be moved along a network. They work with other protocols to transmit the data to the destination computer and then to reassemble the data back into a form that the application layer can understand and process.

> ## IP
>
> IP is a connectionless protocol that provides the addressing and routing capabilities for each package of data. It is the mechanism that enables the network to read IP addresses and implement proper routing functions.
>
> The data, IP, and network relationship can be compared to the relationship between a letter and the postal system:
>
> Data = Letter
> IP = Addressed envelope
> Network = Postal system
>
> The message is the letter, which is enveloped and addressed by IP, and the network and its services enable the message to be sent from its origin to its destination, like the postal system.

Two main protocols work at the transport layer: TCP and UDP. *TCP* is a reliable and *connection-oriented protocol*, which means that it ensures that packets are delivered to the destination computer. If a packet is lost during transmission, TCP has the ability to identify this issue and resend the lost or corrupted packet. TCP also supports packet sequencing (to ensure each and every packet was received), flow and congestion control, and error detection and correction. *UDP*, on the other hand, is a *best-effort* and *connectionless protocol*. It has neither packet sequencing nor flow and congestion control, and the destination does not acknowledge every packet it receives.

## TCP

TCP is referred to as a connection-oriented protocol because, before any user data is actually sent, handshaking takes place between the two systems that want to communicate. Once the handshaking completes successfully, a virtual connection is set up between the two systems. UDP is considered a connectionless protocol because it does not go through these steps. Instead, UDP sends out messages without first contacting the destination computer and does not know if the packets were received properly or dropped. Figure 7-10 shows the difference between a connection-oriented and a connectionless protocol.

UDP and TCP sit together on the transport layer, and developers can choose which to use when they are coding applications. Many times, TCP is the transport protocol of choice because it provides reliability and ensures that the packets are delivered. For example, SMTP is used to transmit e-mail messages and uses TCP because it needs to make sure that the data is delivered. TCP provides a full-duplex, reliable communica-

Connection-oriented communication
performs handshaking, sets up a virtual
circuit, and verifies that each packet
reaches its destination.

Host A

Host B

Connectionless communication
just puts the packets
on the wire.

**Figure 7-10**  Connection-oriented vs. connectionless protocol functionality

tion mechanism, and if any packets are lost or damaged, they are re-sent; however, TCP requires a lot of system overhead.

If a programmer knows that data dropped during transmission is not detrimental to the application, he may choose to use UDP because it is faster and requires fewer resources. For example, UDP is a better choice than TCP when a server sends status information to all listening nodes on the network. A node will not be negatively affected if, by some chance, it did not receive this status information, because the information will be re-sent every 30 minutes.

UDP and TCP are transport protocols that applications use to get their data across a network. They both use ports to communicate with upper OSI layers and to keep track of various conversations that take place simultaneously. The ports are also the mechanism used to identify how other computers access services. When a TCP or UDP message is formed, a source and destination port are contained within the header information along with the source and destination addresses; this makes up a *socket*. This is how packets know where to go—by the address—and how to communicate with the right service or protocol on the other computer—by the port number. The IP address acts as the doorway to a computer, and the port acts as the doorway to the actual protocol or service. To communicate properly, the packet needs to know these doors. Figure 7-11 shows how packets communicate with applications and services through ports.

**Figure 7-11** The packet can communicate with upper-layer protocols and services through a port.

## Well-Known Ports

Port numbers up to 1023 (0–1023) are called *well-known ports*, and almost every computer in the world has the exact same protocol mapped to the exact same port number. That is why they are called *well known*—everyone follows this same standardized approach. This means that on almost every computer, port 25 is mapped to SMTP, port 21 is mapped to FTP, port 80 is mapped to HTTP, and so on. This mapping between lower-numbered ports and specific protocols is a *de facto standard,* which just means that we all do this and that we do not have a standards body telling us this is how it should be done. The fact that almost everyone follows this approach translates to more interoperability among systems all over the world.

**NOTE** Ports 0–1023 can be used only by privileged system or root processes.

Because this is a de facto standard and not a standard that absolutely has to be followed, administrators can map different protocols to different port numbers if that fits their purpose.

The following shows some of the most commonly used protocols and the ports to which they are usually mapped:

- Telnet port 23
- SMTP port 25
- HTTP port 80
- SNMP ports 161 and 162
- FTP ports 21 and 20

The difference between TCP and UDP can also be seen in the their message formats. Because TCP offers more services than UDP, it must contain much more information within its packet header format, as shown in Figure 7-12. Table 7-1 lists the major differences between TCP and UDP.

## TCP Handshake

*Every proper dialog begins with a polite handshake.*

TCP must set up a virtual connection between two hosts before any data is sent. This means that the two hosts must agree on certain parameters, data flow, windowing, error detection, and options. These issues are negotiated during the handshaking phase, as shown in Figure 7-13.

The host that initiates communication sends a synchronous (SYN) packet to the receiver. The receiver acknowledges this request by sending a SYN/ACK packet. This packet translates into, "I have received your request and am ready to communicate with you." The sending host acknowledges this with an acknowledgment (ACK) packet, which translates into, "I received your acknowledgment. Let's start transmitting our data." This completes the handshaking phase, after which a virtual connection is set up, and actual data can now be passed. The actual connection that has been set up at this point is considered *full duplex,* which means that transmission in both directions is possible using the same transmission line.

| Source port | Destination port |
|---|---|
| Sequence number | |
| Acknowledgment number | |

| Offset | Reserved | Flags | Window |
|---|---|---|---|

| Checksum | Urgent pointer |
|---|---|
| Options | Padding |
| Data | |

TCP format

| Source port | Destination port |
|---|---|
| Length | Checksum |
| Data | |

UDP format

**Figure 7-12** TCP carries a lot more information within its segment format because it offers more services than UDP.

## Data Structures

*What's in a name?*

As stated earlier, the message is usually formed and passed to the application layer from a program and sent down through the protocol stack. Each protocol at each layer adds its own information to the message and passes it down to the next level. This concept is usually referred to as *encapsulation*. As the message is passed down the stack, it

| Service | TCP | UDP |
|---|---|---|
| Reliability | Ensures that packets reach their destinations, returns ACKs when a packet is received, and is a reliable protocol. | Does not return ACKs and does not guarantee that a packet will reach its destination, and is an unreliable protocol. |
| Connection | Connection oriented, thus it performs handshaking and develops a virtual connection with destination computer. | Connectionless, thus it does no handshaking and does not set up a virtual connection. |
| Packet sequencing | Uses sequence numbers within headers to make sure that each packet within a transmission is received. | Does not use sequence numbers. |
| Congestion controls | The destination computer can tell the source if it is overwhelmed and to slow the transmission rate. | The destination computer does not communicate back to the source computer about flow control through UDP. |
| Usage | Used when reliable delivery is required. | Used when reliable delivery is not required, such as in streaming video and status broadcasts. |
| Speed and overhead | Uses a considerable amount of resources and is slower than UDP. | Uses fewer resources and is faster than TCP. |

**Table 7-1**   Major Differences Between TCP and UDP

**Figure 7-13**
TCP three-way
handshake

goes through a sort of evolution, and each stage has a specific name that indicates what is taking place. When an application formats data to be transmitted over the network, the data is called a *message*. The message is sent to the transport layer, where TCP does its magic on the data. The bundle of data is now a *segment*. The segment is sent to the network layer. The network layer adds routing and addressing, and now the bundle is called a *datagram*. The network layer passes off the datagram to the data link layer, which frames the datagram with a header and a trailer, and now it is called a *frame*. Figure 7-14 illustrates these stages.

Sometimes when an author refers to a datagram, she is specifying the stage in which the data is located within the protocol stack. If the literature is describing routers, which work at the network layer, the author might use the word *datagram*, because the data at this level has routing and addressing information attached. If an author is describing network traffic and flow control, she might use the word *frame*, because all data actually ends up in the frame format before it is put on the network wire. However, sometimes an author simply refers to all data packages as *packets*.

The important thing here is that you understand the various steps that a data package goes through when it moves up and down the protocol stack and that just because an author refers to data as a *packet* does not necessarily mean that she is indicating the data structure.

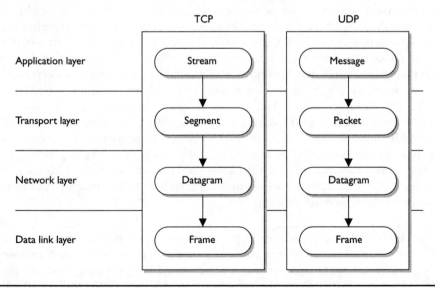

**Figure 7-14** The data goes through its own evolutionary stages as it passes through the layers within the network stack.

## IP Addressing

*Take a right at the router and a left at the access server. I live at 10.10.2.3.*

Each node on the same network must have a unique IP address. Today, the most commonly used version of IP is *IP version 4 (IPv4)*, but its addresses are so high in demand that their supply has started to run out. *IP version 6 (IPv6)* was created to address this shortage. (IPv6 also has many security features built into it that are not part of IPv4.)

IPv4 uses 32 bits for its addresses, whereas IPv6 uses 128 bits; thus, IPv6 provides more possible addresses to work with. Each address has a host portion and a network portion, and the addresses are grouped into *classes* and then into *subnets*. The subnet mask of the address differentiates the groups of addresses that define the subnets of a network. IPv4 address classes are listed here:

| | | |
|---|---|---|
| Class A | 0.0.0.0 to 127.255.255.255 | First byte is the network portion and the remaining three byes are the host portion |
| Class B | 128.0.0.0 to 191.255.255.255 | First two bytes are the network portion and the remaining two bytes are the host portion |
| Class C | 192.0.0.0 to 223.255.255.255 | First three bytes are the network portion and the remaining one byte is the host portion |
| Class D | 224.0.0.0 to 239.255.255.255 | Used for multicast addresses |
| Class E | 240.0.0.0 to 255.255.255.255 | Reserved for research |

If the traditional subnet masks are used, they are referred to as classful or classical IP addresses. If an organization needs to create subnets that do not follow these traditional sizes, then it would use classless IP addresses. This just means that a different subnet mask would be used to define the network and host portions of the addresses. After it became clear that available IP addresses were running out, as more individuals and corporations participated on the Internet, classless interdomain routing (CIDR) was created. A Class B address range is usually too large for most companies, and a class C address range is too small, so CIDR provides the flexibility to increase or decrease the class sizes as necessary. (Subnetting is beyond the scope of this book. If you need more information on this topic, please review the references in this section.)

Although each node has an IP address, people usually refer to their hostname rather than their IP address. Hostnames, such as **www.logicalsecurity.com**, are easier for humans to remember than IP addresses, such as 10.13.84.4. However, the use of these two nomenclatures requires mapping between the hostnames and IP addresses, because the computer understands only the numbering scheme. This process is addressed in the "Domain Name Service" section.

 **NOTE** IP provides addressing, packet fragmentation, and packet timeouts. To ensure that packets do not continually traverse a network forever, IP provides a Time to Live (TTL) value that is decremented every time the packet passes through a router. IP can also provide a Type of Service (ToS) capability, which means that it can prioritize different packets for time-sensitive functions.

## IPv6

*What happened to version 5? Response: It smelled funny.*

IPv6, also called IP next generation (IPng), not only has a larger address space than IPv4 to support more IP addresses, it has many other capabilities that IPv4 does not. The new functions within IPv6 are beyond the scope of this book, but we will look at a few of them, because IPv6 is the way of the future. IPv6 allows for scoped addresses, which enables an administrator to restrict specific addresses for file servers or file and print sharing. IPv6 has IPSec integrated into the protocol stack, which provides end-to-end secure transmission and authentication. The protocol offers for autoconfiguration, which makes administration much easier, and it does not require network address translation (NAT) to extend its address space. NAT was developed because IPv4 addresses were running out. Although the NAT technology is extremely useful, it has caused a lot of overhead and transmission problems because it breaks the client/server model that many applications use today. IPv6 has more flexibility and routing capabilities and allows for Quality of Service (QoS) priority values to be assigned to time-sensitive transmissions.

Although IPv6 provides many more benefits than IPv4, its rollout and industry acceptance have been slower than expected, mainly because of interoperability issues between IPv4 and IPv6. Another reason that the industry did not jump on the IPv6 bandwagon when it came out years ago is that NAT was developed, which reduced the speed at which IP addresses were being depleted. Although IPv6 has a lot of complications in its implementation process, the industry will most likely end up implementing it all over the world. It is currently most widely adopted and implemented in Asia and will soon be used in every country.

**NOTE**  NAT is covered in the "Network Address Translation" section.

# Types of Transmission

Data transmission can happen in different ways (analog or digital), can use different controlling schemes (synchronous or asynchronous), and can use either only one channel over a wire (baseband) or several different channels over one wire (broadband). These transmission types and their characteristics are described in the following sections.

## Analog and Digital

*Would you like your signals wavy or square?*

**Analog transmission signals** are continuously varying electromagnetic waves that can be carried over air, water, twisted-pair cable, coaxial cable, or fiber-optic cable. Through a process of *modulation*, data is combined with a carrier signal of a specific frequency. The modulation of a signal differs in *amplitude* (height of the signal) and *frequency* (number of waves in a defined period of time), as shown in Figure 7-15. This means that data is put on the back of a carrier signal. The carrier signals provide many radio stations, frequency ranges, and communication channels. Each radio station is given a certain carrier signal and frequency to use for its transmission. This is how three different country stations can exist on three different radio channels, for example.

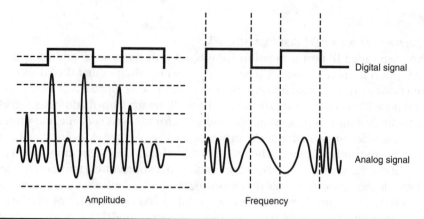

**Figure 7-15** Analog signals are measured in amplitude and frequency, whereas digital signals represent binary digits as electrical pulses.

Computers use digital signals when moving data from one component to another within the computer itself. When this computer is connected to a telephone line via a dial-up connection, a modem (for *modulate/dem*odulate) must transform this digital data into an analog signal, because this is what is expected and used on the telephone lines. The modem actually modulates the digital data into an analog signal. Once the data reaches the destination computer, it must be transformed back into a digital state so that the destination computer can understand it. **Digital signals** represent binary digits as electrical pulses. Each individual pulse is a signal element and represents either a 1 or a 0. **Bandwidth** refers to the number of electrical pulses that can be transmitted over a link within a second, and these electrical pulses carry individual *bits* of information.

Digital signals are more reliable than analog signals over a long distance and provide a clear-cut and efficient signaling method because the voltage is either *on* (1) or *not on* (0), compared to interpreting the waves of an analog signal. Digital signals can easily be extracted from noise and retransmitted. It is more difficult to extract analog signals from background noise because the amplitudes and frequency of the waves slowly lose form. This is because an analog signal could have an infinite number of values or states, whereas a digital signal exists in discrete states. A digital signal is a square wave, which does not have all of the possible values of the different amplitudes and frequencies of an analog signal. Digital systems are superior to analog systems in that they can transport more calls and data transmissions on the same line at higher quality over longer distances.

Voice and data transmissions used to be transmitted mainly via analog signals over telecommunications links, but today, most communication is digitized. Telephone companies digitize telephone calls, and many corporate telephone systems are digitized. Other than radio waves used by radio stations, ham radios, and the like, the only communication that is still analog is what goes from a residential house or business to the telephone company's central office. This section of the telecommunications network is referred to as the *local loop* or *last mile*.

## Asynchronous and Synchronous

*It's all in the timing.*

Two devices can communicate through asynchronous or synchronous means, depending on the type of communication and whether the two systems are synchronized in any way. *Asynchronous communication* is used when the two devices are not synchronized in any way. The sender can send data at any time, and the receiving end must always be ready. *Synchronous communication* takes place between two devices that are synchronized, usually via a clocking mechanism.

Usually, when two devices have a large amount of data to transfer, they use synchronous transmission; with a small amount of data, they use asynchronous transmission. This does not mean one device can decide, "Huh, this is a big heap of data. I better send it through my synchronous route instead of asynchronously." Instead, systems that usually transfer large amounts of data are developed and configured with synchronous communication mechanisms, and systems that transfer smaller amounts of data are developed with asynchronous means.

One example of asynchronous communication takes place between a terminal and a terminal server. If a user is using a system that has terminal-emulation software running, she uses the desktop that the terminal server wants her to use. She sees only her desktop on her computer, while all processing actually takes place on the terminal server. This means that every mouse click, keystroke, and command she initiates travels over the networking cable to the terminal server, where the server performs the actions that correspond with these commands. The results are transmitted back to the user's desktop so that it seems to her that her computer did the work—when in fact it was done on the terminal server, which could be on another floor or at another location altogether. This type of technology usually transmits a small amount of data at a time; thus, it uses asynchronous data transmission.

Modems also use asynchronous data transmission. Because the data can travel at any time and be any length, stop and start delimiters must be used to tell the receiving end when to start processing a request and when to stop. Each character, which is really just a string of 1s and 0s, has a start-of-character bit and a stop bit attached before and after the character byte. This produces a lot of overhead and extra bits, but it's necessary in asynchronous communication.

Synchronous communication, on the other hand, transfers data as a stream of bits instead of framing it in start and stop bits. The synchronization can happen between two systems using the same clocking mechanism, or a signal can be encoded into the data stream to let the receiver synchronize with the sender of the message. This synchronization needs to take place before the first message is sent. The sending system can transmit a digital clock pulse to the receiving system, which translates into, "We will start here and work in this type of synchronization scheme."

## Broadband and Baseband

*How many channels can you shove into this one wire?*

*Baseband* uses the entire communication channel for its transmission, whereas *broadband* divides the communication channel into individual and independent channels so that different types of data can be transmitted at the same time. Baseband permits only one signal to be transmitted at a time, whereas broadband carries several signals over different channels. For example, a coaxial cable TV (CATV) system is a broadband technology that delivers multiple television channels over the same cable. This system can also provide home users with Internet access, but this data is transmitted at a different frequency spectrum than the TV channels. Ethernet is a baseband technology that uses the entire wire for just one channel.

Broadband encompasses many different types of technologies, but one general rule is that it provides data transmissions higher than 56 Kbps, which is what a standard modem dial-up connection line provides. Broadband communications provide channels for data transmission and can be used by many users. The types of broadband communication systems available today are leased lines (T1, T3), Broadband ISDN, ATM, Digital Subscriber Line (DSL), broadband wireless, and CATV.

# LAN Networking

*We really need to connect all of these resources together.*

The following are the four main reasons to have a network:

- To allow communication between computers
- To share information
- To share resources
- To provide central administration

Most users on a network need to use the same type of resources, such as information, printers, file servers, plotters, fax machines, Internet connections, and so on. Why not just string all the computers together and have these resources available to all? Great idea, and we shall call it *networking*!

Networking has made amazing advances in just a short period of time. In the beginning of the computer age, mainframes were the name of the game. They were isolated powerhouses, and many had "dumb" terminals hanging off them. However, this was not true networking. In the late 1960s and early 1970s, some technical researchers came up with ways of connecting all the mainframes and Unix systems to enable them to communicate. This marked the Internet's baby steps.

Microcomputers evolved and were used in many offices and work areas. Slowly, dumb terminals got a little smarter and more powerful as users needed to share office resources. *Bam,* Ethernet was developed, which allowed for true networking. There was no turning back after this.

 **NOTE** Identification and authentication are a large part of networking and are covered extensively in Chapter 4. However, it is important to note that node authentication, by itself, should not be used to establish trustworthiness of a user within the network. Within a distributed network, knowing whom to trust is a major security issue.

## References

- IEEE Standards Working Groups   grouper.ieee.org/groups

- *Introduction to Networking and Data Communications,* by Eugene Blanchard (2001)   www.thelinuxreview.com/howto/intro_to_networking/

- "Ultimate Guide to Networking: Part One," by Michael Furdyk, HardwareCentral tutorial (June 3, 2005)   www.hardwarecentral.com/hardwarecentral/tutorials/158/1/

- "How Analog and Digital Recording Works: Analog Wave," by Marshall Brain, HowStuffWorks   http://electronics.howstuffworks.com/analog-digital2.htm

## Network Topology

*Okay, so where is everything?*

The physical arrangement of computers and devices is called a ***network topology***. Topology refers to the manner in which a network is *physically* connected and shows the layout of resources and systems. There is a difference between the physical network topology and the logical topology. A network can be configured as a physical star but work logically as a ring, as in the Token Ring technology.

Which type of topology is best for a particular network depends on such things as how nodes are supposed to interact, which protocols are used, the types of applications that are available, the reliability, expandability, and physical layout of a facility, existing wiring, and the technologies implemented. The wrong topology or combination of topologies can negatively affect the network's performance, productivity, and growth possibilities.

This section describes the basic types of network topologies. Most networks are much more complex and are usually implemented using a combination of topologies.

## Ring Topology

A ***ring topology*** has a series of devices connected by unidirectional transmission links, as shown in Figure 7-16. These links form a closed loop and do not connect to a central system, as in a star topology (discussed a little later). In a physical ring formation, each node is dependent upon the preceding nodes. In simple networks, if one system fails,

**Figure 7-16**
A ring topology forms a closed-loop connection.

all other systems could be negatively affected because of this interdependence. Today, most networks have redundancy in place or other mechanisms that will protect a whole network from being affected by just one workstation misbehaving, but one disadvantage of using a ring topology is that this possibility exists.

## Bus Topology

In a simple *bus topology*, a single cable runs the entire length of the network. Nodes are attached to the network through drop points on this cable. Data communications transmit the length of the medium, and each packet transmitted has the capability of being "looked at" by all nodes. Each node decides to accept or ignore the packet, depending upon the packet's destination address.

There are two main types of bus topologies: linear and tree. The *linear bus topology* has a single cable with nodes attached. A *tree topology* has branches from the single cable, and each branch can contain many nodes.

In simple implementations of a bus topology, if one workstation fails, other systems can be negatively affected because of the degree of interdependence. In addition, because all nodes are connected to one main cable, the cable itself becomes a potential single point of failure. Traditionally, Ethernet uses bus and star topologies.

## Star Topology

In a *star topology*, all nodes connect to a central device such as a switch. Each node has a dedicated link to the central device. The central device needs to provide enough throughput that it does not turn out to be a detrimental bottleneck for the network as a whole. Because a central device is required, it is a potential single point of failure, so redundancy may need to be implemented. Switches can be configured in flat or hierarchical implementations so that larger organizations can use them.

When one workstation fails on a star topology, it does not affect other systems, as in the ring or bus topologies. In a star topology, each system is not as dependent on others as it is dependent on the central connection device. This topology generally requires less cabling than other types of topologies; as a result, there is a lower chance of cut cables, and detecting cable problems is an easier task.

Not many networks use true linear bus and ring topologies anymore within LAN environments. A ring topology can be used for a backbone network, but most LANs are constructed in a star topology because it enables the network to be more resilient and not as affected if an individual node experiences a problem. Remember that there is a difference between media access methods and the physical topology. Even though a network is Token Ring or Ethernet, this describes only how each node accesses the media and deals with traffic. Although Token Ring is usually thought of as a ring and Ethernet is considered a bus implementation, these descriptions apply only to how they work logically, which takes place at the data link layer. They can be easily implemented physically as a star, and they usually are.

## Mesh Topology

*This network is a mess! Response: We like to call it a mesh.*

In a *mesh topology*, all systems and resources are connected to each other in a way that does not follow the uniformity of the previous topologies, as shown in Figure 7-17. This arrangement is usually a network of interconnected routers and switches that provides multiple paths to all the nodes on the network. In a full mesh topology, every node is directly connected to every other node, which provides a great degree of redundancy. In a partial mesh topology, every node is not directly connected. The Internet is an example of a partial mesh topology.

A summary of the different network topologies and their important characteristics is provided in Table 7-2.

No matter what topology is used, most LANs have a backbone in place, which is a cable and protocol combination that connects network segments together. The backbone works at a higher speed than the individual network segments, which allows data to quickly move from one network to the other. Whereas the network segments would most likely be using UTP and Ethernet, the backbone could be using 10Base5, FDDI, or Fast Ethernet. An analogy is a city's streets and highways. On the streets (network segments), cars (data) move more slowly, but the streets are connected to a highway (backbone), which enables cars to get from one location to another, distant location very quickly. Similarly, a backbone allows data to cover a larger distance very quickly.

 **NOTE** When using a ring or bus topology, all nodes between the source and destination systems have access to this data transmission. This means that it is easier for an attacker to gain access to a lot of potentially sensitive data.

**Figure 7-17**
In a mesh topology, each node is connected to all other nodes, which provides for redundant paths.

| Topology | Characteristics | Problems | Technologies That Usually Work |
|----------|-----------------|----------|--------------------------------|
| Bus | Uses a linear, single cable for all computers attached. All traffic travels the full cable and can be viewed by all other computers. | If one station experiences a problem, it can negatively affect surrounding computers on the same cable. | Ethernet |
| Ring | All computers are connected by a unidirectional transmission link, and the cable is in a closed loop. | If one station experiences a problem, it can negatively affect surrounding computers on the same ring. | FDDI |
| Star | All computers are connected to a central device, which provides more resilience for the network. | The central device is a single point of failure. | Logical bus (Ethernet) and ring topologies (Token Ring) |
| Tree | A bus topology that does not have one linear cable, but instead uses branches of cables. | | Ethernet |
| Mesh | Computers are connected to each other, which provides redundancy. | Requires more expense in cabling and extra effort to track down cable faults. | Internet |

Table 7-2   Summary of Network Topologies

## LAN Media Access Technologies

A *LAN* is a network that provides shared communication and resources in a relatively small area. What defines a LAN, as compared to a WAN, depends on the physical medium, encapsulation protocols, and functionality. For example, a LAN could use 10Base-T cabling, IPX/SPX protocols, and routing protocols, and it could enable users who are in the same local building to communicate. A WAN, on the other hand, could use fiber-optic cabling and the L2TP encapsulation protocol, and could enable users from one building to communicate with users in another building in another state (or country). A WAN connects LANs over great distances geographically. Most of the differences between these technologies are found at the data link layer.

---

### Q & A

**Question:** A LAN is said to cover a relatively small geographical area. When is a LAN no longer a LAN?

**Answer:** When two distinct LANs are connected by a router, the result is an *internetwork*, not a larger LAN. Each distinct LAN has its own addressing scheme, broadcast domain, and communication mechanisms. If two LANs are connected by a different data link layer technology, such as frame relay or X.25, they are considered a WAN.

The term *local* in the context of a LAN refers not so much to the geographical area as to the limitations of a LAN with regard to the shared medium, the number of devices and computers that can be connected to it, the transmission rates, the types of cable that can be used, and the devices that can be used. If a network administrator develops a very large LAN that would more appropriately be multiple LANs, too much traffic could result in a big performance hit, or the cabling could be too long, in which case *attenuation* (signal loss) becomes a factor. In environments where there are too many nodes, routers, bridges, and switches may be overwhelmed, and administration of this network could get complex, which opens the door for errors, collisions, and security holes. The network administrator should follow the specifications of the technology he is using, and once he has maxed out these numbers, he should consider implementing two or more LANs instead of one large LAN. LANs are defined by their physical topologies, data link layer technologies, protocols, and devices used. The following sections cover these topics and how they interrelate.

## References

- **IEEE LAN/MAN Standards Committee**   grouper.ieee.org/groups/802

- **"Introduction to Networking Protocols and Architecture," lecture by Raj Jain, The Ohio State University (March 31, 2000)**   www.cse.ohio-state.edu/~jain/ cis677-00/e_2int.htm

- *Internetworking Technology Handbook*, **Chapter 2, "Introduction to LAN Protocols," Cisco Systems, Inc.**   www.cisco.com/univercd/cc/td/doc/ cisintwk/ito_doc/introlan.htm

## Ethernet

*Ethernet* is a LAN-sharing technology that enables several devices to communicate on the same network. Ethernet usually uses a bus or star topology. If a linear bus topology is used, all devices connect to one cable. If a star topology is used, each device is connected to a cable that is connected to a centralized device, such as a switch. Ethernet was developed in the 1970s, became commercially available in 1980, and was named the IEEE 802.3 standard.

Ethernet has seen quite an evolution in its short history, from purely coaxial cable installations that worked at 10 Mbps to mostly Category 5 twisted-pair cable that works at speeds of 100 Mbps, 1000 Mbps (1 Gbps), and 10 Gbps.

Ethernet is defined by the following characteristics:

- Shares media (all devices must take turns using the same media, and collisions can take place)
- Uses broadcast and collision domains
- Uses the carrier sense multiple access with collision detection (CSMA/CD) access method
- Supports full duplex on twisted-pair implementations
- Can use coaxial or twisted-pair media
- Is defined by standard IEEE 802.3

Ethernet addresses how computers share a common network and how they deal with collisions, data integrity, communication mechanisms, and transmission controls. These are the common characteristics of Ethernet, but Ethernet does vary in the type of cabling schemes and transfer rates it can supply. There are several types of Ethernet implementations, as outlined in Table 7-3. The following sections discuss 10Base2, 10Base5, and 10Base-T, which are common implementations.

**10Base2**   10Base2, ThinNet, uses coaxial cable. It has a maximum cable length of 185 meters, provides 10-Mbps transmission rates, and requires British Naval Connectors (BNCs) to network devices.

**10Base5**   10Base5, ThickNet, uses a thicker coaxial cable that is not as flexible as ThinNet and is more difficult to work with. However, ThickNet can have longer cable segments than ThinNet and is often used as the network backbone. ThickNet is more resistant to electrical interference than ThinNet and is usually preferred when stringing wire through electrically noisy environments that contain heavy machinery and magnetic fields. ThickNet also requires BNCs because it uses coaxial cables.

**10Base-T**   10Base-T uses twisted-pair copper wiring instead of coaxial cabling. Twisted-pair wiring uses one wire to transmit data and the other to receive data. 10Base-T is usually implemented in a star topology, which provides easy network configuration. In a star topology, all systems are connected to centralized devices, which can be in a flat or hierarchical configuration.

10Base-T networks have RJ-45 connector faceplates to which the computer connects. The wires usually run behind a wall and connect the faceplate to a punchdown block within a wiring closet. The punchdown block is often connected to a 10Base-T hub that serves as a doorway to the network's backbone cable or to a central switch. This type of configuration is shown in Figure 7-18.

**Fast Ethernet: Ethernet in Overdrive**   Not surprisingly, 10 Mbps was considered heaven-sent when it first arrived on the networking scene, but soon many users were demanding more speed and power. The smart people had to gather into small rooms and hit the whiteboards with ideas, calculations, and new technologies. The result of these meetings, computations, engineering, and testing was Fast Ethernet.

*Fast Ethernet* is regular Ethernet, but it runs at 100 Mbps over twisted-pair wiring instead of at 10 Mbps. Around the same time that Fast Ethernet arrived, another 100-Mbps technology was developed: 100-VG-AnyLAN. This technology did not use Ethernet's traditional CSMA/CD and did not catch on like Fast Ethernet did.

| Ethernet Type | Cable Type | Speed |
|---|---|---|
| 10Base2, ThinNet | Coaxial | 10 Mbps |
| 10Base5, ThickNet | Coaxial | 10 Mbps |
| 10Base-T | UTP | 10 Mbps |
| 100Base-TX, Fast Ethernet | UTP | 100 Mbps |
| 1000Base-T, Gigabit Ethernet | UTP | 1000 Mbps |

**Table 7-3**   Types of Ethernet

**Figure 7-18** Ethernet hosts connect to a punchdown block within the wiring closet, which is connected to the backbone via a hub or switch.

Fast Ethernet uses the traditional CSMA/CD (explained in the "CSMA" section later in the chapter) and the original frame format of Ethernet. This is why it is used in many enterprise LAN environments today. One environment can run 10- and 100-Mbps network segments that can communicate via 10/100 hubs or switches.

Four main types of Fast Ethernet exist today; their differences pertain to the cabling and transmission distances. For more information on these four types, refer to the following references.

---

## Q & A

**Question:** Why does my NIC have two input connectors that are shaped differently?

**Answer:** Most NICs provide support for 10Base2 and 10Base-T. The round connector is used for 10Base2, which is the BNC used for coaxial wiring. The connector that looks like a phone connector supports 10Base-T, which is twisted-pair wiring.

## References

- **University of New Hampshire InterOperability Laboratory: Fast Ethernet Consortium**  www.iol.unh.edu/consortiums/fe
- **Dan Kegel's Links for Fast Ethernet documents**  http://alumni.caltech.edu/~dank/fe
- **Charles Spurgeon's Ethernet Web Site**  www.ethermanage.com/ethernet

## Token Ring

*Where's my magic token? I have something to say. Response: We aren't giving it to you.*

Like Ethernet, *Token Ring* is a LAN technology that enables the communication and sharing of networking resources. The Token Ring technology was originally developed by IBM and is now defined by the IEEE 802.5 standard. It uses a token-passing technology with a star-configured topology. The *ring* part of the name pertains to how the signals travel, which is in a logical ring. Each computer is connected to a central hub, called a *Multistation Access Unit (MAU)*. Physically, the topology can be a star, but the signals and transmissions are passed in a logical ring.

A *token-passing technology* is one in which a device cannot put data on the network wire without having possession of a *token,* a control frame that travels in a logical circle and is "picked up" when a system needs to communicate. This is different from Ethernet, in which all the devices attempt to communicate at the same time. This is why Ethernet is referred to as a "chatty protocol" and has collisions. Token Ring does not endure collisions, since only one system can communicate at a time, but this also means that communication takes place more slowly when compared to Ethernet.

At first, Token Ring technology had the ability to transmit data at 4 Mbps; later it was improved to transmit at 16 Mbps. When a frame is put on the wire, each computer looks at it to see whether the frame is addressed to it. If the frame does not have that specific computer's address, the computer puts the frame back on the wire, properly amplifies the message, and passes it to the next computer on the ring.

Token Ring employs a couple of mechanisms to deal with problems that can occur on this type of a network. The *active monitor* mechanism removes frames that are continually circulating on the network. This can occur if a computer locks up or is taken offline for one reason or another and cannot properly receive a token destined for it. With the *beaconing* mechanism, if a computer detects a problem with the network, it sends a beacon frame. This frame generates a failure domain, which is between the computer that issued the beacon and its neighbor downstream. The computers and devices within this failure domain will attempt to reconfigure certain settings to try to work around the detected fault. Figure 7-19 depicts a Token Ring network in a physical star configuration.

Token Ring networks were popular in the 1980s and 1990s, and although some are still around, Ethernet has become much more popular and has taken over the LAN networking market.

**Figure 7-19** Token Ring network

## References

- **Token Ring FAQ**   www.faqs.org/faqs/LANs/token-ring-faq
- *Token-Ring Technical Summary,* **TechFest**   www.techfest.com/networking/lan/token.htm

**Q & A**

**Question:** Where do the differences between Ethernet, Token Ring, and FDDI lie?

**Answer:** These technologies are data link layer technologies. The data link layer is actually made up of a MAC sublayer and an LLC sublayer. These technologies live at the MAC layer and have to interface to the LLC layer. These LAN technologies differ in how they communicate to the protocol stack and what type of functionalities they can provide.

## FDDI

*Fiber Distributed Data Interface (FDDI)* technology, developed by the American National Standards Institute (ANSI), is a high-speed token-passing media access technology. FDDI has a data transmission speed of up to 100 Mbps and is usually used as a backbone network using fiber-optic cabling. FDDI also provides fault tolerance by providing a second counter-rotating fiber ring. The primary ring has data traveling clockwise and is used for regular data transmission. The second ring transmits data in a counterclockwise fashion and is invoked only if the primary ring goes down. Sensors watch the primary ring and, if it goes down, invoke a ring *wrap* so that the data will be diverted to the second ring. Each node on the FDDI network has relays that are connected to both rings, so if a break in the ring occurs, the two rings can be joined.

When FDDI is used as a backbone network, it usually connects several different networks, as shown in Figure 7-20.

Before Fast Ethernet and Gigabit Ethernet hit the market, FDDI was used mainly as campus and service provider backbones. Because FDDI can be used for distances up to 100 kilometers, it was often used in metropolitan area networks (MANs). The benefit of FDDI is that it can work over long distances and at high speeds with minimal interference. It enables several tokens to be present on the ring at the same time, causing more communication to take place simultaneously, and it provides predictable delays that help connected networks and devices to know what to expect and when.

**Figure 7-20**   FDDI rings can be used as backbones to connect different LANs.

A version of FDDI, Copper Distributed Data Interface (CDDI), can work over UTP cabling. Whereas FDDI would be used more as a MAN, CDDI can be used within a LAN environment to connect network segments.

**NOTE** FDDI-2 provides fixed bandwidth that can be allocated for specific applications. This makes it work more like a broadband connection, which allows for voice, video, and data to travel over the same lines.

Table 7-4 sums up the important characteristics of the technologies described in the preceding sections.

## Cabling

*Why are cables so important? Response: Without them, our electrons would fall onto the floor.*

Network cabling and wiring are important when setting up a network or extending an existing one. Particular types of cables need to be used with specific data link layer technologies. Cable types vary in speeds, maximum lengths, and connectivity issues with NICs. In the 1970s and 1980s, coaxial cable was the way to go, but in the late 1980s, twisted-pair wiring hit the scene and today it is the most popular networking cable used.

Electrical signals travel as currents through cables and can be negatively affected by many factors within the environment, such as motors, fluorescent lighting, magnetic forces, and other electrical devices. These items can corrupt the data as it travels through the cable, which is why cable standards are used to indicate cable type, shielding, transmission rates, and cable distances.

| LAN Implementation | IEEE Standard | Characteristics |
|---|---|---|
| Ethernet | 802.3 | • Shared media—all devices must take turns using the same media and detect collisions<br>• Uses broadcast and collision domains<br>• Uses CSMA/CD access method<br>• Can use coaxial or twisted-pair media<br>• Transmission speeds of 10 Mbps–1 Gbps |
| Token Ring | 802.5 | • All devices connect to a central MAU<br>• Token-passing media access method<br>• Transmission speeds of 4–16 Mbps<br>• Uses an active monitor and beaconing |
| FDDI | 802.8 | • Token-passing media access method<br>• Dual counter-rotating rings for fault tolerance<br>• Transmission speeds of 100 Mbps<br>• Operates over long distances at high speeds and is therefore used as a backbone<br>• CDDI works over UTP |

**Table 7-4** LAN Media Access Methods

Cabling has bandwidth and data throughput rate values associated with it. Although these two terms are related, they are indeed different. The *bandwidth* of a cable indicates the highest frequency range that it uses; for instance, 10Base-T uses 10 MHz and 100Base-TX uses 80 MHz. This is different from the actual amount of data that can be pushed through a cable. The *data throughput rate* is the actual amount of data that goes through the wire after compression and encoding have been used. 10Base-T has a data rate of 10 Mbps and 100Base-TX has a data rate of 100 Mbps. The bandwidth can be thought of as the size of the pipe, and the data throughput rate is the actual amount of data that travels through that pipe.

## Coaxial Cable

*Coaxial cable* has a copper core that is surrounded by a shielding layer and grounding wire, as shown in Figure 7-21. This is all encased within a protective outer jacket. Compared to twisted-pair cable, coaxial cable is more resistant to electromagnetic interference (EMI), provides a higher bandwidth, and supports the use of longer cable lengths. So, why is twisted-pair cable more popular? Twisted-pair cable is cheaper and easier to work with, and the move to switched environments that provide hierarchical wiring schemes has overcome the cable-length issue of twisted-pair cable.

The two main types of coaxial cable used within LAN environments are 50-ohm cable (used for digital signaling) and 75-ohm cable (used for high-speed digital signaling and analog signaling). The coaxial cable types are 10Base2 (ThinNet) and 10Base5 (ThickNet). Coaxial cable can transmit using either a *baseband* method, whereby the cable carries only one channel, or a *broadband* method, whereby the cable carries several channels.

## Twisted-Pair Cable

*This cable is kind of flimsy. Why do we use it? Response: It's cheap and easy to work with.*

Twisted-pair cabling has insulated copper wires that are surrounded by an outer protective jacket. If the cable has an outer foil shielding, it is referred to as *shielded twisted pair (STP)*, which adds protection from radio frequency interference and electromagnetic interference. Another type of twisted-pair cabling does not have this extra outer shielding and is called *unshielded twisted pair (UTP)*.

The cable contains copper wires that twist around each other, as shown in Figure 7-22. This twisting of the wires protects the signals they carry from radio frequency and electromagnetic interference, as well as crosstalk. Each wire forms a balanced circuit, because the voltage in each pair uses the same amplitude, just with opposite phases.

**Figure 7-21**
Coaxial cable

Sheath    Insulation (PVC, Teflon)

Braided shielding    Conducting core

**Figure 7-22**
Twisted-pair cabling
uses copper wires.

Outer      Insulated     Copper wire
jacket        wires       conductor

The tighter the twisting of the wires, the more resistant the cable is to interference and attenuation. UTP has several categories of cabling, each of which has its own unique characteristics. The difference in the category ratings is based on how tightly wound the cables are.

The twisting of the wires, the type of insulation used, the quality of the conductive material, and the shielding of the wire determine the rate at which data can be transmitted. The UTP ratings indicate which of these components were used when the cables were manufactured. Some types are more suitable and effective for specific uses and environments. Table 7-5 lists the cable ratings.

Copper cable has been around for many years; it is inexpensive and easy to use. A majority of the telephone systems today use copper cabling with the rating of voice grade. Twisted-pair wiring is the preferred network cabling, but it also has its drawbacks. Copper actually resists the flow of electrons, which causes a signal to degrade

| UTP Category | Characteristics | Usage |
|---|---|---|
| Category 1 | Voice-grade telephone cable | Not recommended for network use, but modems can communicate over it |
| Category 2 | Data transmission up to 4 Mbps | Used in mainframe and minicomputer terminal connections, but not recommended for high-speed networking |
| Category 3 | 10 Mbps for Ethernet and 4 Mbps for Token Ring | Used in 10Base-T network installations |
| Category 4 | 16 Mbps | Used usually in Token Ring networks |
| Category 5 | 100 Mbps for 100Base-TX and CDDI networks; has high twisting, and thus low crosstalk | Used in 100Base-TX, CDDI, Ethernet, and ATM installations; most widely used for new network installations |
| Category 6 | 155 Mbps | Used in new network installations requiring high-speed transmission |
| Category 7 | 1 Gbps | Used in new network installations requiring higher-speed transmission |

**Table 7-5**   UTP Cable Ratings

after it has traveled a certain distance. This is why cable lengths are recommended for copper cables; if these recommendations are not followed, a network could experience signal loss and data corruption. Copper also radiates energy, which means that information can be monitored and captured by intruders. UTP is the least secure networking cable compared to coaxial and fiber. If a company requires higher speed, higher security, and cables to have longer runs than what is allowed in copper cabling, fiber-optic cable may be a better choice.

## Fiber-Optic Cable

*Hey, I can't tap into this fiber cable. Response: Exactly.*

Twisted-pair cable and coaxial cable use copper wires as their data transmission media, but fiber-optic cable uses a type of glass that carries light waves, which represent the data that is being transmitted. The glass core is surrounded by a protective cladding, which in turn is encased within an outer jacket.

Because it uses glass, fiber-optic cabling has higher transmission speeds that allow signals to travel over longer distances. Fiber cabling is not as affected by attenuation and EMI when compared to cabling that uses copper. It does not radiate signals, as does UTP cabling, and is difficult to eavesdrop on; therefore, fiber-optic cabling is much more secure than UTP, STP, or coaxial.

Using fiber-optic cable sounds like the way to go, so you might wonder why you would even bother with UTP, STP, or coaxial. Unfortunately, fiber-optic cable is extremely expensive and difficult to work with. Fiber-optic cable is usually used in backbone networks and environments that require high data transfer rates. Most networks use UTP and connect to a backbone that uses fiber.

## Cabling Problems

Cables are extremely important within networks, and when they experience problems, the whole network could experience problems. This section addresses some of the more common cabling issues many networks experience.

**Noise** *Noise* on a line is usually caused by surrounding devices or by characteristics of the wiring's environment. Noise can be caused by motors, computers, copy machines, florescent lighting, and microwave ovens, to name a few. This background noise

---

### Backbone

If a UTP cable is used and a cable segment is longer than 185 meters, attenuation may occur. Basically, the data is in the form of electrons, and these electrons have to "swim" through a copper wire. However, this is more like swimming upstream, because there is a lot of resistance on the electrons working in this media. After a certain distance, the electrons start to slow down and their encoding format loses form. If the form gets too degraded, the receiving system cannot interpret them any longer. This is why the standard stipulates a maximum of 185 meters. If a network administrator needs to run a cable longer than this, she needs to integrate a repeater or some type of device that will amplify the signal and ensure that it gets to its destination in the right encoding format.

can combine with the data being transmitted over the cable and distort the signal, as shown in Figure 7-23. The more noise that interacts with the cable, the more likely that the receiving end will not receive the data in the form that was originally transmitted. (How these issues affect power lines is discussed in Chapter 6.)

**Attenuation** *Attenuation* is the loss of signal strength as it travels. The longer a cable, the more attenuation that is introduced, which causes the signal that is carrying data to deteriorate. This is why standards include suggested cable run lengths; once data travels over a certain distance, the resistance of electron flow aggregates and destroys the integrity of the signal.

The effects of attenuation increase with higher frequencies; thus, 100Base-TX at 80 MHz has a higher attenuation rate than 10Base-T at 10 MHz. This means that cables used to transmit data at higher frequencies should have shorter cable runs to ensure that attenuation does not become an issue.

Attenuation can also be caused by cable breaks and malfunctions. This is why cables should be tested. If a cable is suspected of attenuation problems, cable testers can inject signals into the cable and read the results at the end of the cable.

**Crosstalk** As previously mentioned, UTP is susceptible to *crosstalk*, which occurs when electrical signals of one wire spill over to another wire. When the different electrical signals mix, their integrity degrades and data corruption can occur. UTP is much more vulnerable to crosstalk than STP or coaxial because it does not have extra layers of shielding to help protect against it.

As stated earlier, the two-wire pairs within twisted-pair cables form a balanced circuit because they both have the same amplitude, just with different phases. Crosstalk and background noise can throw off this balance, and the wire can actually start to act like an antenna, which means it will be more susceptible to picking up other noises in the environment.

## Fire Rating of Cables

*This cable smells funny when it's on fire.*

Just as buildings must meet certain fire codes, so must wiring schemes. A lot of companies string their network wires in drop ceilings—the space between the ceiling and the next floor—or under raised floors. This hides the cables and prevents people

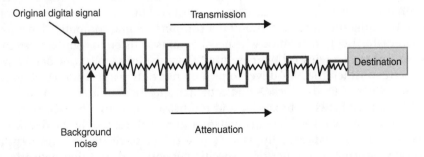

**Figure 7-23**  Background noise can merge with an electronic signal and alter the signal's integrity.

from tripping over them. However, when wires are strung in places like this, they are more likely to catch on fire without anyone knowing about it. Some cables produce hazardous gases when on fire that would spread throughout the building quickly. Network cabling that is placed in these types of areas, called *plenum space*, must meet a specific fire rating to ensure that it will not produce and release harmful chemicals in case of a fire. A building's ventilation system usually is located in this plenum space, so if toxic chemicals were to get into that area, they could be easily spread throughout the building in minutes.

*Nonplenum cables* usually have a polyvinyl chloride (PVC) jacket covering, whereas plenum-rated cables have jacket covers made of fluoropolymers. When setting up a network or extending an existing network, it is important that you know which wire types are required in which situation.

You must consider the following factors when choosing cabling for a network: the company's budget for the network, ease of handling, possible signal interference, distance of the cable run, necessary speed of transmission, security, and fire rating.

Cables should be installed in unexposed areas so that they are not easily tripped over, damaged, or eavesdropped upon. The cables should be strung behind walls and in the protected spaces between the ceiling and next floor. In some situations, wires are encapsulated within *pressurized conduits* so that if someone attempts to access a wire, the pressure of the conduit will change, causing an alarm to sound and a message to be sent to the administrator.

In environments where heavy machinery or other devices that create electromagnetic fields are used, STP or fiber-optic cable should be installed. If security is a top priority to a company, fiber-optic cable should be used.

## Transmission Methods

A packet may need to be sent to only one workstation, to a set of workstations, or to all workstations on a particular subnet. If a packet needs to go from the source computer to one particular system, a *unicast* transmission method is used. If the packet needs to go to a specific group of systems, the sending system uses the *multicast* method. If a system wants all computers on its subnet to receive a message, it will use the *broadcast* method.

Unicast is pretty simple because it has a source address and a destination address. The data goes from point A to Z, it is a one-to-one transmission, and everyone is happy. Multicast is a bit different in that it is a one-to-many transmission. Multicasting enables one computer to send data to a selective group of computers. A good example of multicasting is tuning into a radio station on a computer. Some computers have software that enables the user to determine whether she wants to listen to country western, pop, Christian, or head-banging rock, for example. Once the user selects one of these genres, the software must tell the NIC driver to pick up not only packets addressed to its specific MAC address, but also packets that contain a specific multicast address.

The difference between broadcast and multicast is that in a broadcast, one-to-all transmission, everyone gets the data, whereas in a multicast, only the few who have chosen to receive the data actually get it. So how does a server, three states away, multicast to one particular computer on a specific network and no other networks in between? Good question, glad you asked. The user who elects to receive a multicast actually has to tell her local router that she wants to get frames with this particular multicast address passed her way. The local router must tell the router upstream, and this process continues so that each router between the source and destination know where to pass this multicast data. This ensures that the user can get her head-banging rock music without other networks being bothered with this extra data. (The user does not actually need to tell her local router anything; the software on her computer communicates to a routing protocol to handle and pass along the information.)

IP multicast protocols use a Class D address, which is a special address space designed especially for multicasting. It can be used to send out information, multimedia data, and even real-time video and voice clips.

IGMP is used to report multicast group memberships to routers. When a user chooses to accept multicast traffic, she becomes a member of a particular multicast group. IGMP is the mechanism that allows her computer to inform the local routers that she is part of this group and to send traffic with a specific multicast address to her system.

## Reference

- *Internetworking Technology Handbook*, Chapter 43, "Internet Protocol Multicast," Cisco Systems, Inc. www.cisco.com/univercd/cc/td/doc/cisintwk/ito_doc/ipmulti.htm

---

### Transmission Definitions

The following is a summary of many of the concepts that we have addressed so far.

- **Digital signals**  Represent binary digits as discrete electrical pulses

- **Analog signals**  Continuous signals that vary by amplification and frequency

- **Asynchronous communication**  Transfers data sequentially, uses start and stop bits, and requires that communicating devices to communicate at the same speed

- **Synchronous communication**  High-speed transmission controlled by electronic clock timing signals

- **Baseband transmission**  Uses the full bandwidth for only one channel and has a low data transfer rate

- **Broadband transmission**  Divides the bandwidth into many channels, enabling different types of data to be transmitted, and provides a high data transfer rate

- **Unicast transmission**  Occurs when a packet is sent from one source computer to one destination computer

- **Multicast transmission**  Occurs when a packet is sent from one source computer to several specific computers

- **Broadcast transmission**  Occurs when a packet is sent from one source computer to all computers on a certain network segment

## Media Access Technologies

The physical topology of a network is the lower layer, or foundation, of a network. It determines what type of media will be used and how the media will be connected between different systems. Media access technologies deal with how these systems communicate over this media and are usually represented in protocols, NIC drivers, and interfaces. LAN access technologies set up the rules of how computers will communicate on a network, how errors are handled, what physical medium is to be used, the maximum transmission unit (MTU) size of frames, and much more. These rules enable all computers and devices to communicate and recover from problems, and enable users to be productive in accomplishing their networking tasks. Each participating entity needs to know how to communicate properly so that all other systems will understand the transmissions, instructions, and requests. This is taken care of by the LAN media access technology.

 **NOTE** An MTU is a parameter that indicates how much data a frame can carry on a specific network. Different types of network technologies may require different MTU sizes, which is why frames are sometimes fragmented.

## Token Passing

A *token* is a 24-bit control frame used to control which computers communicate at what intervals. The token is passed from computer to computer, and only the computer that has the token can actually put frames onto the wire. The token grants a computer the right to communicate. The token contains the data to be transmitted and source and destination address information. When a system has data that it needs to transmit, it has to wait to receive the token. The computer then connects its message to the token and puts it on the wire. Each computer checks this message to determine whether it is addressed to it, which continues until the destination computer receives the message. The destination computer makes a copy of the message and sets a bit to tell the source computer that it did indeed get its message. Once this gets back to the source computer, it removes the frames from the network. The destination computer makes a copy of the message, but only the originator of the message can remove the message from the token and network.

If a computer that receives the token does not have a message to transmit, it sends the token to the next computer on the network. An empty token has a header, data field, and trailer, but a token that has an actual message has a new header, destination address, source address, and a new trailer.

This type of network access method is used by Token Ring and FDDI technologies.

 **NOTE** Some applications and network protocol algorithms work better if they can communicate at determined intervals, instead of "whenever the data arrives." In token-passing technologies, traffic arrives in this type of deterministic nature because not all systems can communicate at one time; only the system that has control of the token can communicate.

## CSMA

Ethernet protocols define how nodes are to communicate, recover from errors, and access the shared network cable. Ethernet uses CSMA as an access method to the network cable. There are two distinct types of CSMA: CSMA/CD and CSMA/CA.

A transmission is called a *carrier*, so if a computer is transmitting frames, it is performing a carrier activity. When computers use the *carrier sense multiple access with collision detection (CSMA/CD)* protocol, they monitor the transmission activity, or carrier activity, on the wire so that they can determine when would be the best time to transmit data. Each node monitors the wire continuously and waits until the wire is free before it transmits its data. As an analogy, consider several people gathered in a group talking here and there about this and that. If a person wants to talk, she usually listens to the current conversation and waits for a break before she proceeds to talk. If she does not wait for the first person to stop talking, she will be speaking at the same time as the other person, and the people around them may not be able to understand fully what each is trying to say.

When using the CSMA/CD access method, computers listen for the absence of a carrier tone on the cable, which indicates that no one else is transmitting data. If two computers sense this absence and transmit data at the same time, contention and a collision can take place. *Contention* means that the nodes have to compete for the same shared medium. A *collision* happens when two or more frames collide, which most likely corrupts both frames. If a computer puts frames on the wire and its frames collide with another computer's frames, it will abort its transmission and alert all other stations that a collision just took place. All stations will execute a random collision timer to force a delay before they attempt to transmit data. This random collision timer is called the *back-off algorithm*. CSMA/CD is the access method used in the 802.3 Ethernet networking standard. (Collisions are usually reduced by dividing a network with bridges or switches.)

*Carrier sense multiple access with collision avoidance (CSMA/CA)* is an access method in which each computer signals its intent to transmit data before it actually does so. This tells all other computers on the network not to transmit data right now because doing so could cause a collision. Basically, a system listens to the shared medium to determine whether it is busy or free. Once the system identifies that the "coast is clear" and it can put its data on the wire, it sends out a broadcast to all other systems, telling them that it is going to transmit information. It is similar to saying, "Everyone shut up. I am going to talk now." Each system will wait a period of time before attempting to transmit data, to ensure that collisions do not take place. The wireless LAN technology, 802.11, uses CSMA/CA for its media access functionality.

**Collision Domains** As indicated in the preceding section, a collision occurs on Ethernet networks when two computers transmit data at the same time. Other computers on the network detect this collision because the overlapping signals of the collision increase the voltage of the signal above a specific threshold. The more devices on a contention-based network, the more likely collisions will occur, which increases

> ## Carrier-Sensing and Token-Passing Access Methods
>
> Overall, carrier-sensing access methods are faster than token-passing access methods, but the former do have the problem of collisions. A network segment with many devices can cause too many collisions and slow down the network's performance. Token-passing technologies do not have problems with collisions, but they do not perform at the speed of carrier-sensing technologies. Network switches can help significantly in isolating the network resources, for both the CSMA/CD and the token-passing methods, because they reduce contention.

network *latency* (data transmission delays). A *collision domain* is a group of computers that are contending, or competing, for the same shared communication medium.

An unacceptable amount of collisions can be caused by a highly populated network, a damaged cable or connector, too many repeaters, or cables that exceed the recommended length. If a cable is longer than what is recommended by the Ethernet specification, two computers on opposite ends of the cable may transmit data at the same time. Because the computers are so far away from each other, they may both transmit data, listen to ensure that a collision did not occur, determine that a collision did not occur, and then go merrily along with their business. If the cable is too long, the computers may not listen long enough for evidence of a collision. If the destination computers receive these corrupted frames, they then have to send a request to the source system to retransmit the message, causing even more traffic.

These types of problems are dealt with mainly by implementing collision domains. An Ethernet network can have broadcast and collision domains. One subnet will be on the same broadcast and collision domain if it is not separated by routers or bridges. If the same subnet is divided by bridges, the bridges can enable the broadcast traffic to pass between the different parts of a subnet, but not the collisions, as shown in Figure 7-24. This is how collision domains are formed. Isolating collision domains reduces the amount of collisions that take place on a network and increases its overall performance.

Another benefit of restricting and controlling broadcast and collision domains is that it makes sniffing the network and obtaining useful information more difficult for an intruder as he traverses the network. A useful tactic for attackers is to install a Trojan horse that sets up a network sniffer on the compromised computer. The sniffer is usually configured to look for a specific type of information, such as usernames and passwords. If broadcast and collision domains are in effect, the compromised system will have access only to the broadcast and collision traffic within its specific subnet or broadcast domain. The compromised system will not be able to listen to traffic on other broadcast and collision domains, and this can greatly reduce the amount of traffic and information available to an attacker.

## Polling

*Hi. Do you have anything you would like to say?*

The third type of LAN media access method is polling. In an environment where a *polling* LAN media access method is used, some systems are configured as primary stations and others are configured as secondary stations. At predefined intervals, the pri-

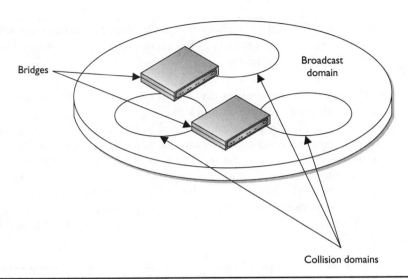

**Figure 7-24** Collision domains within one broadcast domain

mary station asks the secondary station if it has anything to transmit. This is the only time a secondary station can communicate.

Polling is a method of monitoring multiple devices and controlling network access transmission. If polling is used to monitor devices, the primary device communicates with each secondary device in an interval to check its status. The primary device then logs the response it receives and moves on to the next device. If polling is used for network access, the primary station asks each device if it has something to communicate to another device. Network access transmission polling is used mainly with mainframe environments.

## LAN Protocols

Some protocols, such as UDP, TCP, and IP, were addressed in earlier sections. Networks are made up of these and many other types of protocols that provide an array of functionality. Several of the most widely used TCP/IP protocols, ARP, RARP, and ICMP, are discussed in the following sections.

### Address Resolution Protocol

*This IP does me no good! I need a MAC!*

On a TCP/IP network, each computer and network device requires a unique IP address and a unique physical hardware address. Each NIC has a unique physical address that is programmed into the ROM chips on the card by the manufacturer. The physical address is also referred to as the *Media Access Control (MAC)* address. The network layer works with and understands IP addresses, and the data link layer works with and understands physical MAC addresses. So, how do these two types of addresses work together since they operate at different layers?

**NOTE** A MAC address is unique because the first 24 bits represent the manufacturer code and the last 24 bits represent the unique serial number assigned by the manufacturer.

When data comes from the application layer, it goes to the transport layer for sequence numbers, session establishment, and streaming. The data is then passed to the network layer, where routing information is added to the packet and the source and destination IP addresses are attached to the data bundle. Then it goes to the data link layer, which must find the MAC address and add it to the header portion of the frame. When a frame hits the wire, it only knows what MAC address it is heading toward. At this lower layer of the OSI model, the mechanisms do not even understand IP addresses. So if a computer cannot resolve the IP address passed down from the network layer to the corresponding MAC address, it cannot communicate with that destination computer.

 **NOTE** A frame is data that is fully encapsulated, with all of the necessary headers and trailers.

MAC and IP addresses must be properly mapped so that they can be correctly resolved. This happens through the *Address Resolution Protocol (ARP)*. When the data link layer receives a frame, the network layer has already attached the destination IP address to it, but the data link layer cannot understand the IP address and thus invokes ARP for help. ARP broadcasts a frame requesting the MAC address that corresponds with the destination IP address. Each computer on the subnet receives this broadcast frame, and all but the computer that has the requested IP address ignore it. The computer that has the destination IP address responds with its MAC address. Now ARP knows what hardware address corresponds with that specific IP address. The data link layer takes the frame, adds the hardware address to it, and passes it on to the physical layer, which enables the frame to hit the wire and go to the destination computer. ARP maps the hardware address and associated IP address and stores this mapping in its table for a predefined amount of time. This caching is done so that when another frame destined for the same IP address needs to hit the wire, ARP does not need to broadcast its request again; it just looks in its table for this information.

Sometimes attackers alter a system's ARP table so that it contains incorrect information; this is called *ARP table poisoning*. The attacker's goal is to receive packets that were intended for another computer. This is a type of *masquerading* attack. For example, if computer A has an IP address of 10.19.34.3 and a MAC address of *x* and computer B has this mapping in its ARP table, an attacker can alter the ARP table to indicate that IP address 10.19.34.3 is mapped to MAC address *y* (the attacker's MAC address), so that any packets computer B tries to send to computer A actually go to the attacker's computer.

## References

- Address Resolution Protocol (ARP), explanation by Gorry Fairhurst
  www.erg.abdn.ac.uk/users/gorry/course/inet-pages/arp.html
- *Connected: An Internet Encyclopedia*, "ARP Protocol Overview,"
  **Freesoft**   www.freesoft.org/CIE/Topics/61.htm

## Reverse Address Resolution Protocol

A computer can receive its IP addresses in a few different ways when it first boots up. If it has a statically assigned address, nothing needs to happen. If a computer depends upon a Dynamic Host Configuration Protocol (DHCP) server to assign it the correct IP address, it boots up and makes a request to the DHCP server. The DHCP server assigns the IP address, and everyone is happy. But what if the environment has diskless workstations, meaning they have no operating systems?

Diskless workstations have just enough code to know how to boot up and broadcast for an IP address, and they may have a pointer to the server that holds the operating system. The diskless workstation knows its hardware address, so it broadcasts this information so that a listening server can assign it the correct IP address. As with ARP, *Reverse Address Resolution Protocol (RARP)* frames go to all systems on the subnet, but only the RARP server responds. Once the RARP server receives this request, it looks in its table to see which IP address matches the broadcast hardware address. The server then sends a message that contains its IP address back to the requesting computer. The system now has an IP address and can function on the network.

The *Boot Protocol (BOOTP)* was created after RARP to enhance the functionality that RARP provides for diskless workstations. The diskless workstation can receive its IP address, the name server address for future name resolutions, and the default gateway address from the BOOTP server. BOOTP usually provides more functionality to diskless workstations than RARP.

The evolution of this protocol has gone as follows; RARP evolved into BOOTP, which evolved into DHCP.

## Internet Control Message Protocol

The *Internet Control Message Protocol (ICMP)* is basically IP's "messenger boy." ICMP delivers status messages, reports errors, replies to certain requests, reports routing information, and is used to test connectivity and troubleshoot problems on IP networks.

---

### The Difference Between ARP and RARP

ARP knows the IP address and broadcasts to find the matching hardware address, the MAC address. RARP knows the hardware address and broadcasts to find the IP address.

The most commonly understood use of ICMP is the *ping* utility. When a person wants to test connectivity to another system, he may ping it, which sends out ICMP ECHO REQUEST frames. The replies on his screen that are returned to the ping utility are called ICMP ECHO REPLY frames and are responding to the ECHO REQUEST frames. If a reply is not returned within a predefined time period, the ping utility sends more ECHO REQUEST frames. If there is still no reply, ping indicates that the host is unreachable.

ICMP also indicates when problems occur with a specific route on the network and tells surrounding routers about better routes to take based on the health and congestion of the various pathways. Routers use ICMP to send messages in response to datagrams that could not be delivered. The router selects the proper ICMP response, wraps it into an IP frame, and sends it back to the requesting host, indicating that problems were encountered with the transmission request.

ICMP is used by other connectionless protocols, not just IP, because connectionless protocols do not have any way of detecting and reacting to transmission errors, as do connection-oriented protocols. In these instances, the connectionless protocol may use ICMP to send error messages back to the sending system to indicate networking problems.

## References

- **RFC 792 – Internet Control Message Protocol**   http://www.ietf.org/rfc/rfc792.txt

- **"LOKI ICMP Tunneling Back Door," Internet Security Systems' X-Force Database**   http://xforce.iss.net/xforce/xfdb/1452

- **Securing Routers Against Hackers and DoS (PowerPoint Presentation)**   net-services.ufl.edu/~security/itsa/attacks-ronnau.ppt

### Loki Attack

The ICMP protocol was developed to send status messages, not to hold or transmit user data. But someone figured out how to insert some data inside of an ICMP packet, which can be used to communicate to an already compromised system. Loki is actually a client/server program that is used by hackers to set up back doors on systems. The attacker attacks a computer and installs the server portion of the Loki software. This server portion "listens" on a port, which is the backdoor that an attacker can use to access the system. To gain access and open a remote shell to this computer, an attacker sends commands inside of ICMP packets. This is usually successful, because most routers are configured to allow ICMP traffic to come and go out of the network, based on the assumption that this is safe because ICMP was developed to not hold any data or a payload.

# Routing Protocols

*I have protocols that will tell you where to go. Response: I would like to tell YOU where to go.*

Individual networks on the Internet are referred to as autonomous systems (ASs). These ASs are independently controlled by different corporations and organizations. An AS is made up of routers, which are administered by a single entity and use a common Interior Gateway Protocol (IGP). The boundaries of these ASs are delineated by border routers. These routers connect to the border routers of other ASs and run interior and exterior routing protocols. Internal routers connect to other routers within the same AS and run interior routing protocols. So, in reality, the Internet is just a network made up of ASs and routing protocols.

The architecture of the Internet that supports these various ASs is created so that no entity that needs to connect to a specific AS needs to know or understand the interior protocols that can be used. Instead, for ASs to communicate, they just have to be using the same exterior routing protocols (see Figure 7-25). As an analogy, suppose that you want to deliver a package to a friend who lives in another state. You give the package to your brother, who is going to take a train to the edge of the state and hand it to the postal system at that junction. So you know how your brother will arrive at the edge of the state—by train. You do not know how the postal system will then deliver your package to your friend's house (truck, car, bus), but that is not your concern. It will get to its

**Figure 7-25**  Autonomous systems

destination without your participation. Similarly, when one network communicates with another network, the first network puts the data packet (package) on an exterior protocol (train), and when the data packet gets to the border router (edge of the state), the data is transferred to whatever interior protocol is being used on the receiving network. The routing protocols are used by routers to identify a path between the source and destination systems.

Routing protocols can be dynamic or static. A *dynamic routing protocol* can discover routes and build a routing table. Routers use these tables to make decisions on the best route for the packets they receive. A dynamic routing protocol can change the entries in the routing table based on changes that take place to the different routes. When a router that is using a dynamic routing protocol finds out that a route has gone down or is congested, it sends an update message to the other routers around it. The other routers use this information to update their routing table, with the goal of providing efficient routing functionality. A *static routing protocol* requires the administrator to manually configure the router's routing table.

*Route flapping* refers to the constant changes in the availability of routes. If a router does not receive an update that a link has gone down, the router will continue to forward packets to that route, which is referred to as a "black hole."

There are two main types of routing protocols: distance-vector and link-state routing. *Distance-vector routing protocols* make their routing decisions based on the distance (or number of hops) and a vector (a direction). The protocol takes these variables and uses them with an algorithm to determine the best route for a packet. *Link-state routing protocols* build a more accurate routing table because they build a topology database of the network. These protocols look at more variables than just the number of hops between two destinations. They use packet size, link speed, delay, loading, and reliability as the variables in their algorithms to determine the best routes for packets to take.

So, a distance-vector routing protocol only looks at the number of hops between two destinations and considers each hop to be equal. A link-state routing protocol sees more pieces to the puzzle than just the number of hops, but understands the status of each of those hops and makes decisions based on these factors also. As you will see, RIP is an example of a distance-vector routing protocol and OSPF is an example of a link-state routing protocol. OSPF is preferred and is used in large networks. RIP is still around but should only be used in smaller networks.

De facto and proprietary interior protocols are being used today. The following are just a few of them:

- **Routing Information Protocol** RIP is a standard that outlines how routers exchange routing table data and is considered a distance-vector protocol, which means that it calculates the shortest distance between the source and destination. It is considered a legacy protocol, because of its slow performance and lack of functionality. It should only be used in small networks. RIP version 1 has no authentication and RIP version 2 sends passwords in cleartext or hashed with MD5.

- **Open Shortest Path First** OSPF uses link-state algorithms to send out routing table information. The use of these algorithms allows for smaller, more frequent routing table updates to take place. This provides a more stable network than RIP, but requires more memory and CPU resources to support this extra processing. OSPF allows for a hierarchical routing network that has a backbone link connecting all subnets together. OSPF has replaced RIP in many networks today. Authentication can take place with cleartext passwords or hashed passwords, or you can choose to configure no authentication on the routers using this protocol.

- **Interior Gateway Routing Protocol**   IGRP is a distance-vector routing protocol that was developed by and is proprietary to Cisco Systems. Whereas RIP uses one criterion to find the best path between the source and destination, IGRP uses five criteria to make a "best route" decision. A network administrator can set weights on these different metrics so that the protocol works best in that specific environment.

**NOTE**   Although most routing protocols have authentication functionality, most routers do not have this functionality enabled.

The exterior routing protocols used by routers connecting different ASs are generically referred to as exterior gateway protocols (EGPs). The *Border Gateway Protocol (BGP)* enables routers on different ASs to share routing information to ensure effective and efficient routing between the different networks. BGP is commonly used by Internet service providers to route data from one location to the next on the Internet.

**NOTE**   There is an exterior routing protocol called Exterior Gateway Protocol, but it has been widely replaced by BGP, and now the term "exterior gateway protocol" and the acronym EGP are used to refer generically to a type of protocol rather than to specify the outdated protocol.

BGP uses a combination of link-state and distance-vector routing algorithms. It creates a network topology by using its link-state functionality and transmits updates on a periodic basis instead of continuously, which is how distance-vector protocols work. Network administrators can apply weights to the different variables that are used by link-state routing protocols when determining the best routes. These configurations are collectively called the *routing policy.*

There are several types of attacks that can take place on routers through their routing protocols. A majority of the attacks have the goal of misdirecting traffic through the use of spoofed ICMP messages. An attacker can masquerade as another router and submit routing table information to the victim router. After the victim router integrates this new information, it may be sending traffic to the wrong subnets or computers, or even to a nonexistent address (black hole). These attacks are successful mainly when routing protocol authentication is not enabled. When authentication is not required, a router can accept routing updates without knowing whether or not the sender is a legitimate router. An attacker could divert a company's traffic to review confidential information or to just disrupt traffic, which would be considered a DoS attack.

> ## Wormhole Attack
>
> An attacker can capture a packet at one location in the network and tunnel it to another location in the network. In this type of attack, there are two attackers, one at each end of the tunnel (referred to as a *wormhole*). Attacker A could capture an authentication token that is being sent to an authentication server, and then send this token to the other attacker, who then uses it to gain unauthorized access to a resource. This can take place on a wired or wireless network, but it is easier to carry out on a wireless network because the attacker does not need to actually penetrate a physical wire.
>
> The countermeasure to this type of attack is to use a leash, which is just data that is put into a header of the individual packets. The leash restricts the packet's maximum allowed transmission distance. The leash can be either geographical, which ensures that a packet stays within a certain distance of the sender, or temporal, which limits the lifetime of the packet.
>
> It is like the idea of invisible fences that are used on animals. You put a collar (leash) on your dog (packet) and it restricts him from leaving your yard (network segment).

There are other types of DoS attacks, such as flooding a router port, buffer overflows, and SYN floods. Since there are many different types of attacks that can take place, there are just as many countermeasures to be aware of to thwart these types of attacks. Most of these countermeasures involve authentication and encryption of routing data as it is transmitted back and forth through the use of shared keys or IPSec. For a good description of how these attacks can take place and their corresponding countermeasures, take a look at the Cisco Systems white paper *SAFE: Best Practices for Securing Routing Protocols* (**www.cisco.com/warp/public/cc/so/neso/vpn/prodlit/sfblp_wp.pdf**).

# Networking Devices

Several types of devices are used in LANs, MANs, and WANs to provide intercommunication between computers and networks. The use of these devices varies according to their functionality, capabilities, intelligence, and network placement. We will look at the following devices:

- Repeaters
- Bridges
- Routers
- Switches

## Repeaters

A *repeater* provides the simplest type of connectivity, because it only repeats and amplifies electrical signals between cable segments, which enables it to extend a network.

Repeaters work at the physical layer and are add-on devices for extending a network connection over a greater distance. The device amplifies signals because signals attenuate the farther they have to travel.

Repeaters can also work as line conditioners by actually cleaning up the signals. This works much better when amplifying digital signals than when amplifying analog signals, because digital signals are discrete units, which makes extraction of background noise from them much easier for the amplifier. If the device is amplifying analog signals, any accompanying noise often is amplified as well, which may further distort the signal.

A *hub* is a multiport repeater. A hub is often referred to as a *concentrator* because it is the physical communication device that allows several computers and devices to communicate with each other. A hub does not understand or work with IP or MAC addresses. When one system sends a signal to go to another system that is connected to it, the signal is broadcast to all the ports, and thus to all the systems connected to the concentrator.

## Bridges

*Is this like a bridge over troubled waters? Response: You are not funny.*

A *bridge* is a LAN device that is used to connect LAN segments. It works at the data link layer and therefore works with MAC addresses. A repeater does not work with addresses; it just forwards all signals it receives. When a frame arrives at a bridge, the bridge determines whether or not the MAC address is on the local network segment. If the MAC address is not on the local network segment, the bridge forwards the frame to the necessary network segment.

A bridge is used to divide overburdened networks into smaller segments to ensure better use of bandwidth and traffic control. A bridge amplifies the electrical signal, as does a repeater, but it has more intelligence than a repeater and is used to extend a LAN and enable the administrator to filter frames so that she can control which frames go where.

When using bridges, you have to watch carefully for **broadcast storms**. Because bridges can forward all traffic, they forward all broadcast packets as well. This can overwhelm the network and result in a broadcast storm, which degrades the network bandwidth and performance.

Three main types of bridges are used: local, remote, and translation. A *local bridge* connects two or more LAN segments within a local area, which is usually a building. A *remote bridge* can connect two or more LAN segments over a MAN by using telecommunications links. A remote bridge is equipped with telecommunications ports, which enable it to connect two or more LANs that are separated by a long distance and can be brought together via telephone lines. A *translation bridge* is needed if the two LANs being connected are different types and use different standards and protocols. For example, consider a connection between a Token Ring network and an Ethernet network. The frames on each network type are different sizes, the fields contain different protocol information, and the two networks transmit at different speeds. If a regular bridge were put into place, Ethernet frames would go to the Token Ring network and vice versa, and neither would be able to understand messages that came from the other network segment. A translation bridge does what its name implies—it translates between the two network types.

The following list outlines the functions of a bridge:

- Segments a large network into smaller, more controllable pieces
- Uses filtering based on MAC addresses

- Joins different types of network links while retaining the same broadcast domain

- Isolates collision domains within the same broadcast domain

- Bridging functionality can take place locally within a LAN or remotely to connect two distant LANs.

- Can translate between protocol types

---

 **NOTE** Do not confuse routers and bridges. Routers work at the network layer and filter packets based on IP addresses. Bridges work at the data link layer and filter frames based on MAC addresses. Routers usually do not pass broadcast information. Bridges do pass broadcast information.

---

## Forwarding Tables

*You go that way. And you—you go this way!*

A bridge must know how to get a frame to its destination—that is, it must know to which port the frame must be sent and where the destination host is located. Years ago, network administrators had to type route paths into bridges so that the bridges had static paths indicating where to pass frames that were headed for different destinations. This was a tedious task and prone to errors. Today bridges use *transparent bridging*.

If transparent bridging is used, a bridge starts to learn about the network's environment as soon as it is powered on and as the network changes. It does this by examining frames and making entries in its forwarding tables. When a bridge receives a frame from a new source computer, the bridge associates this new source address and the port on which it arrived. It does this for all computers that send frames on the network. Eventually, the bridge knows the address of each computer on the various network segments and to which port each is connected. If the bridge receives a request to send a frame to a destination that is not in its forwarding table, it sends out a query frame on each network segment except for the source segment. The destination host is the only one that replies to this query. The bridge updates its table with this computer address and the port to which it is connected, and forwards the frame.

Many bridges use the *Spanning Tree Algorithm (STA)*, which adds more intelligence to the bridges. STA ensures that frames do not circle networks forever, provides redundant paths in case a bridge goes down, assigns unique identifiers to each bridge, assigns

---

### Q & A

**Question:** What is the difference between two LANs connected via a bridge versus two LANs connected via a router?

**Answer:** If two LANs are connected with a bridge, the LANs have been extended, because they are both in the same broadcast domain. A router can be configured not to forward broadcast information, so if two LANs are connected with a router, an internetwork results. An *internetwork* is a group of networks connected in a way that enables any node on any network to communicate with any other node. The Internet is an example of an internetwork.

priority values to these bridges, and calculates path costs. This creates much more efficient frame-forwarding processes by each bridge. STA also enables an administrator to indicate whether he wants traffic to travel certain paths instead of others.

If *source routing* is used instead of transparent bridging, the packets contain the necessary information within them to tell the bridge where they should go. The packets hold the forwarding information so that they can find their way to their destination without needing bridges and routers to dictate their paths. If the computer wants to dictate its forwarding information instead of depending on a bridge, how does it know the correct route to the destination computer? The source computer sends out explorer packets that arrive at the destination computer. These packets contain the route information the packets had to take to get to the destination, including what bridges they had to pass through. The destination computer then sends these packets back to the source computer, and the source computer strips out the routing information, inserts it into the packets, and sends them on to the destination.

 **NOTE**  External devices and border routers should not accept packets with source routing information within their headers, because that information will override what is laid out in the forwarding and routing tables configured on the intermediate devices. You want to control how traffic traverses your network; you don't want packets to have this type of control and be able to go wherever they want. Source routing can be used by attackers to get around certain bridge and router filtering rules.

## References

- **IETF Bridge MIB Charter**   www.ietf.org/html.charters/bridge-charter.html
- **Ethernet Bridges and Switches, explanation by Gorry Fairhurst**   www.erg. abdn.ac.uk/users/gorry/course/lan-pages/bridge.html

## Routers

We are going up the chain of the OSI layers while discussing various networking devices. Repeaters work at the physical layer, bridges work at the data link layer, and routers work at the network layer. As we go up each layer, each corresponding device has more intelligence and functionality because it can look deeper into the frame. A repeater looks at the electrical signal. The bridge can look at the MAC address within the header. The router can peel back the first header information and look farther into the frame and find out the IP address and other routing information. The farther a device can look into a frame, the more decisions it can make based on the information within the frame. We will see later that gateways can look all the way to the *core* of the frame, which contains the data that the user sent in the first place—not just addresses and routing information.

Routers are layer 3, or network layer, devices that are used to connect similar or different networks. (For example, they can connect two Ethernet LANs or an Ethernet LAN to a Token Ring LAN.) A router is a device that has two or more interfaces and a routing table so that it knows how to get packets to their destinations. It can filter traffic based on access control lists (ACLs), and it fragments packets when necessary. Because routers have more network level knowledge, they can perform higher-level functions such as calculating the shortest and most economical path between the sending and receiving hosts.

A router discovers information about routes and changes that take place in a network through its routing protocols (RIP, BGP, OSPF, and others). These protocols tell routers if a link has gone down, if a route is congested, and if another route is more economical; they also update routing tables and indicate if a router is having problems or has gone down.

A bridge uses the same network address for all of its ports, but a router assigns a new address per port, which enables it to connect more networks together.

The router may be a dedicated appliance or a computer running a networking operating system that is dual homed. When packets arrive at one of the interfaces, the router compares those packets to its ACLs. This list indicates what packets are allowed in and what packets are denied. Access decisions are based on source and destination IP addresses, protocol type, and source and destination ports. An administrator may block all packets coming from the 10.10.12.0 network, any FTP requests, or any packets headed toward a specific port on a specific host, for example. This type of control is provided by the ACLs, which the administrator must program and update as necessary.

What actually happens inside the router when it receives a packet? Let's follow the steps:

1. A frame is received on one of the interfaces of a router. The router views the routing data.

2. The router retrieves the destination IP network address from the datagram.

3. The router looks at its routing table to see which port matches the requested destination IP network address.

4. If the router does not have information in its table about the destination address, it sends out an ICMP error message to the sending computer indicating that the message could not reach its destination.

5. If the router does have a route in its routing table for this destination, it decrements the TTL value and sees whether the MTU is different for the destination network. If the destination network requires a smaller MTU, the router fragments the datagram.

6. The router changes header information in the frame so that the frame can go to the next correct router, or if the destination computer is on a connecting network, the changes made enable the frame to go directly to the destination computer.

7. The router sends the frame to its output queue for the necessary interface.

Table 7-6 provides a quick review of the differences between routers and bridges.

When is it best to use a repeater, bridge, or router? A repeater is used if an administrator needs to expand a network and amplify signals so that they do not weaken on longer cables. However, a repeater will forward collision and broadcast information because it does not have the intelligence to decipher among different types of traffic.

| Bridge | Router |
|--------|--------|
| Reads header information, but does not alter it | Creates a new header for each frame |
| Builds forwarding tables based on MAC addresses | Builds routing tables based on IP addresses |
| Uses the same network address for all ports | Assigns a different network address per port |
| Filters traffic based on MAC addresses | Filters traffic based on IP addresses |
| Forwards broadcast packets | Does not forward broadcast packets |
| Forwards traffic if a destination address is unknown to the bridge | Does not forward traffic that contains a destination address unknown to the router |

**Table 7-6** Main Differences Between Bridges and Routers

Bridges work at the data link layer and have a bit more intelligence than a repeater. Bridges can do simple filtering, and they separate collision domains, not broadcast domains. A bridge should be used when an administrator wants to divide a network into segments to reduce traffic congestion and excessive collisions.

A router splits up a network into collision domains and broadcast domains. A router gives more of a clear-cut division between network segments than repeaters or bridges. A router should be used if an administrator wants to have more defined control of where the traffic goes, because more sophisticated filtering is available with routers, and when a router is used to segment a network, the result is more controllable sections.

A router is used when an administrator wants to divide a network along the lines of departments, workgroups, or other business-oriented divisions. A bridge divides segments based more on the traffic type and load.

## References

- *Internetworking Technology Handbook*, **Chapter 5, "Routing Basics," Cisco Systems, Inc.** www.cisco.com/univercd/cc/td/doc/cisintwk/ito_doc/routing.htm

- **Active IETF Working Groups** www.ietf.org/html.charters/wg-dir.html

## Switches

*I want to talk to you privately. Let's talk through this switch.*

Switches combine the functionality of a repeater and the functionality of a bridge. A switch amplifies the electrical signal, like a repeater, and has the built-in circuitry and intelligence of a bridge. It is a multiport connection device that provides connections for individual computers or other hubs and switches. Any device connected to one port can communicate with a device connected to another port with its own virtual private link. How does this differ from the way in which devices communicate using a bridge or a hub? When a frame comes to a hub, the hub sends the frame out through all of its ports. When a frame comes to a bridge, the bridge sends the frame to the port to which the destination network segment is connected. When a frame comes to a switch, the switch sends the frame directly to the destination computer or network; a reduction of traffic results. Figure 7-26 illustrates a network configuration that has computers directly connected to their corresponding switches.

On Ethernet networks, computers have to compete for the same shared network medium. Each computer must listen for activity on the network and transmit its data when it thinks the coast is clear. This contention and the resulting collisions cause traffic delays and use up precious bandwidth. When switches are used, contention and collisions are not issues, which results in more efficient use of the network's bandwidth and decreased latency. Switches reduce or remove the sharing of the network medium and the problems that come with it.

A switch is a multiport bridging device, and each port provides dedicated bandwidth to the device attached to it. A port is bridged to another port so that the two devices have an end-to-end private link. The switch employs full-duplex communication so that one wire pair is used for sending and another pair is used for receiving. This ensures that the two connected devices do not compete for the same bandwidth.

Basic switches work at the data link layer and forward traffic based on MAC addresses. However, today's layer 3, layer 4, and other layer switches have more enhanced functionality than layer 2 switches. These higher-level switches offer routing functionality, packet inspection, traffic prioritization, and QoS functionality. These switches are referred to as *multilayered switches* because they combine data link layer, network layer, and other layer functionalities.

Multilayered switches use hardware-based processing power, which enables them to look deeper within the packet, to make more decisions based on the information found within the packet, and then to provide routing and traffic management tasks. Usually this amount of work creates a lot of overhead and traffic delay, but multilayered switches perform these activities within an application-specific integrated circuit (ASIC). This means that most of the functions of the switch are performed at the hardware and chip level rather than at the software level; this is a much quicker method.

**Figure 7-26**
Switches enable devices to communicate with each other via their own virtual link.

## Layer 3 and 4 Switches

*I want my switch to do everything, even make muffins.*

Layer 2 switches only have the intelligence to forward a frame based on its MAC address and do not have a higher understanding of the network as a whole. A layer 3 switch has the intelligence of a router; it not only can route packets based on their IP addresses, but also can choose routes based on availability and performance. A layer 3 switch is basically a router on steroids because it moves the route lookup functionality to the more efficient switching hardware level.

The basic distinction between layer 2, 3, and 4 switches is the header information the device looks at to make forwarding or routing decisions (data link, network, or transport OSI layers). But layer 3 and 4 switches can use tags, which are assigned to each destination network or subnet. When a packet reaches the switch, the switch compares the destination address with its Tag Information Base, which is a list of all the subnets and their corresponding tag numbers. The switch appends the tag to the packet and sends it to the next switch. All the switches in between this first switch and the destination host just review this tag information to determine which route it needs to take, instead of analyzing the full header. Once the packet reaches the last router or switch, this tag is removed and the packet is sent to the destination. This process increases the speed of routing of packets from one location to another.

The use of these types of tags, referred to as *Multiprotocol Label Switching (MPLS)*, not only allows for faster routing, but also addresses service requirements for the different packet types. Some time-sensitive traffic (such as video conferencing) requires a certain level of service (QoS) that guarantees a minimum rate of data delivery to meet the requirements of a user or application. When MPLS is used, different priority information is placed into the tags to help ensure that the time-sensitive traffic has a higher priority than less-sensitive traffic.

Many enterprises today use a switched network in which computers are connected to dedicated ports on Ethernet switches, Gigabit Ethernet switches, ATM switches, and more. This evolution of switches, added services, and the capability to incorporate repeater, bridge, and router functionality have made switches an important part of today's networking world.

Because security requires control over who can access specific resources, more intelligent devices can provide a higher level of protection, because they can make more detail-oriented decisions regarding who can access resources. When devices can look deeper into the packets, they can consider more information to make access decisions, which provides more granular access control.

As previously stated, switching makes it more difficult for intruders to sniff and monitor network traffic because no broadcast and collision information is continually traveling throughout the network. Switches provide a security service that the other devices cannot provide. *Virtual LANs (VLANs)* are also an important part of switching networks, because they enable administrators to have more control over their environment and they can isolate users and groups into logical and manageable entities. VLANs are described in the next section.

## References

- Enterasys Whitepapers   www.enterasys.com/products/whitepapers
- *Internetwork Design Guide*, Chapter 12, "Designing Switched LAN Internetworks," Cisco Systems, Inc.   www.cisco.com/univercd/cc/td/doc/cisintwk/idg4/nd2012.htm
- *Multiprotocol Label Switching (MPLS)*, International Engineering Consortium   www.iec.org/online/tutorials/mpls/

## VLANs

*What does the V stand for? Response: Varmint!*

The technology behind switches has introduced the capability to use virtual LANs (VLANs). VLANs enable administrators to separate and group computers logically based on resource requirements, security, or business needs instead of the standard physical location of the systems. When using repeaters, bridges, and routers, systems and resources are grouped in a manner that is dictated by their physical location. Figure 7-27 shows how computers that are physically located next to each other can be grouped logically into different VLANs. Administrators can form these groups based on the users' and company's needs instead of the physical location of systems and resources.

**Figure 7-27**
VLANs enable administrators to put systems into logical networks.

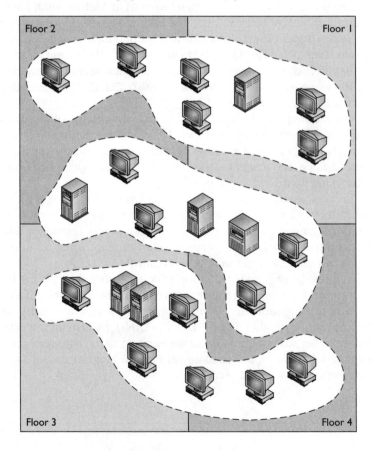

An administrator may want to place the computers of all users in the marketing department in the same VLAN network, for example, so that all users receive the same broadcast messages and can access the same types of resources. This arrangement could get tricky if a few of the users are located in another building or on another floor, but VLANs provide the administrator with this type of flexibility. VLANs also enable an administrator to apply particular security policies to respective logical groups. This way, if tighter security is required for the payroll department, for example, the administrator can develop a policy, add all payroll systems to a specific VLAN, and apply the security policy only to the payroll VLAN.

A VLAN exists on top of the physical network, as shown in Figure 7-28. If workstation P1 wants to communicate with workstation D1, the message has to be routed— even though the workstations are physically next to each other—because they are on different logical networks.

## Gateways

*Gateway* is a general term for software running on a device that connects two different environments and many times acts as a translator for them or somehow restricts their interactions. Usually a gateway is needed when one environment speaks a different language, meaning it uses a certain protocol that the other environment does not understand. The gateway can translate Internetwork Packet Exchange (IPX) protocol packets to IP packets, accept mail from one type of mail server and format it so that another type of mail server can accept and understand it, or connect and translate different data link technologies such as FDDI to Ethernet.

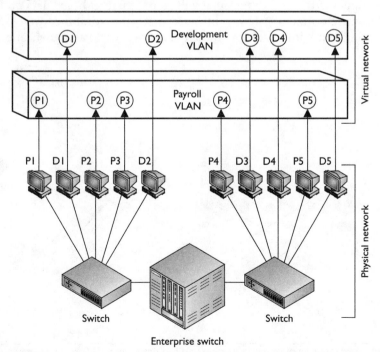

**Figure 7-28** VLANs exist on a higher level than the physical network and are not bound to it.

Gateways perform much more complex tasks than connection devices, such as routers and bridges. However, some people refer to routers as gateways when they connect two unlike networks (Token Ring and Ethernet) because the router has to translate between the data link technologies. Figure 7-29 shows how a network access server (NAS) functions as a gateway between telecommunications and network connections.

When networks connect to a backbone, a gateway can translate the different technologies and frame formats used on the backbone network versus the connecting LAN protocol frame formats. If a bridge were set up between an FDDI backbone and an Ethernet LAN, the computers on the LAN would not understand the FDDI protocols and frame formats. In this case, a LAN gateway would be needed to translate the protocols used between the different networks.

A popular type of gateway is an *electronic mail* gateway. Because several e-mail vendors have their own syntax, message format, and ways of dealing with message transmission, e-mail gateways are needed to convert messages between e-mail server software. For example, suppose that David, whose corporate network uses Sendmail, writes an e-mail message to Dan, whose corporate network uses Microsoft Exchange. The e-mail gateway will convert the message into a standard that all mail servers understand—usually X.400—and pass it on to Dan's mail server.

Another example of a gateway is a voice and media gateway. Recently, there has been a drive to combine voice and data networks. This provides for a lot of efficiency because the same media can be used for both types of data transfers. However, voice is a streaming technology, whereas data is usually transferred in packets. So, this shared media eventually has to communicate with two different types of networks: the telephone company's PSTN, and routers that will take the packet-based data off to the Internet. This means that a gateway must separate the combined voice and data information and put it into a form that each of the networks can understand.

NAS

**Figure 7-29**  Several types of gateways can be used in a network; a NAS is one example.

Table 7-7 lists the devices that have been covered in the "Networking Devices" section and points out their important characteristics.

## PBXs

*I have to dial a 9 to get an outside line. Does that mean that the CIA is watching me? Response: Yep.*

Telephone companies use switching technologies to transmit phone calls to their destinations. A telephone company's central office houses the switches that connect towns, cities, and metropolitan areas through the use of optical fiber rings. So, for example, when Dusty makes a phone call from his house, the call first hits the local central office of the telephone company that provides service to Dusty, and then the switch within that office decides whether it is a local or long-distance call and where it needs to go from there. A *Private Branch Exchange (PBX)* is a private telephone switch that is located on a company's property. This switch performs some of the same switching tasks that take place at the telephone company's central office. The PBX has a dedicated connection to its local telephone company's central office, where more intelligent switching takes place.

A PBX can interface with several types of devices and provides a number of telephone services. The data is multiplexed onto a dedicated line connected to the telephone company's central office. Figure 7-30 shows how data from different data sources can be placed on one line at the PBX and sent to the telephone company's switching facility.

PBXs use digital switching devices that can control analog and digital signals. Older PBXs may support only analog devices, but most PBXs have been updated to digital. This move to digital systems and signals has reduced a number of the PBX and telephone security vulnerabilities that used to exist. However, that in no way means that PBX fraud does not take place today. Many companies, for example, have modems hanging off their PBX to enable the vendor to dial in and perform maintenance to the system. These modems are usually unprotected doorways into a company's network. The modem should be activated only when a problem requires the vendor to dial in, and it should be disabled otherwise.

| Device | OSI Layer | Functionality |
|--------|-----------|---------------|
| Repeater | Physical | Amplifies signal and extends networks |
| Bridge | Data link | Forwards packets and filters based on MAC addresses; forwards broadcast traffic, but not collision traffic |
| Router | Network | Separates and connects LANs creating internetworks; routers filter based on IP addresses |
| Switch | Data link | Provides a private virtual link between communicating devices; allows for VLANs; reduces collisions; impedes network sniffing |
| Gateway | Application (although different types of gateways can work at other layers) | Connects different types of networks; performs protocol and format translations |

**Table 7-7** Comparison of the Devices and Their Functionality

**Figure 7-30** A PBX combines different types of data on the same lines.

In addition, many PBX systems have default system manager passwords that are hardly ever changed. These passwords are set by default; therefore, if 100 companies purchased and implemented 100 PBX systems from the PBX vendor ABC and they do not reset the password, a *phreaker* (a phone hacker) who knows this default password now has access to 100 PBX systems. Once a phreaker breaks into a PBX system, she can cause mayhem by rerouting calls, reconfiguring switches, or configuring the system to provide her and her friends with free long-distance calls. This type of fraud happens more often than most companies realize, because many companies do not closely watch their phone bills.

PBX systems are also vulnerable to brute force and other types of attacks, in which phreakers use scripts and dictionaries to guess the necessary credentials to gain access to the system. In some cases, phreakers have listened to and changed people's voice messages. So, for example, when people call to leave Bob a message, they might not hear his usual boring message, but a new message that is screaming obscenities and insults.

## Firewalls

*A wall that is on fire will stop anyone. Response: That's the idea.*

*Firewalls* are used to restrict access to one network from another network. Most companies use firewalls to restrict access to their networks from the Internet. They may also use firewalls to restrict one internal network segment from accessing another internal segment. For example, if the network administrator wants to make sure that employees cannot access the Research and Development network, he would place a firewall between this network and all other networks and configure the firewall to allow only the type of traffic he deems acceptable.

A firewall device supports and enforces the company's network security policy. An organizational security policy provides high-level instructions on acceptable and unacceptable actions as they pertain to security. The firewall has a more defined and granular security policy that dictates what services are allowed to be accessed, what IP addresses and ranges are to be restricted, and what ports can be accessed. The firewall is described as a "choke point" in the network, because all communication should flow through it, and this is where traffic is inspected and restricted.

A firewall is actually a type of gateway that may be a router, server, or specialized hardware device. It monitors packets coming into and out of the network it is protecting. It filters out the packets that do not meet the requirements of the security policy. It can discard these packets, repackage them, or redirect them, depending upon the firewall configuration and security policy. Packets are filtered based on their source and destination addresses and ports by service, packet type, protocol type, header information, sequence bits, and much more. Vendors can use specific functionality and parameters for identification and access restriction.

Many times, companies set up firewalls to construct a *demilitarized zone (DMZ)*, which is a network segment that is located between the protected and the unprotected networks. The DMZ provides a buffer zone between the dangerous Internet and the goodies within the internal network that the company is trying to protect. As shown in Figure 7-31, two firewalls are usually installed to form the DMZ. The DMZ usually contains web, mail, and DNS servers, which must be hardened systems because they would be the first in line for attacks. Many DMZs also have an IDS sensor that listens for malicious and suspicious behavior.

Many different types of firewalls are available, because each environment may have unique requirements and security goals. Firewalls have gone through an evolution of their own and have grown in sophistication and functionality. The following sections describe the various types of firewalls.

**Figure 7-31**   At least two firewalls, or firewall interfaces, are usually used to construct a DMZ.

The types of firewalls we will review are

- Packet filtering
- Stateful
- Proxy
- Dynamic packet filtering
- Kernel proxy

We will then dive into the three main firewall architectures, which are

- Screened host
- Dual-home
- Screened subnet

Then we will look at honeypots and their uses, so please return all seats to their upright position and lock your trays in front of you—we will be taking off shortly.

## Packet Filtering Firewalls

*I don't like this packet. Oh, but I like this packet. I don't like this packet. This other packet is okay.*

*Packet filtering* is a security method of controlling what data can flow into and out of a network. Packet filtering takes place by using ACLs, which are developed and applied to a device. ACLs are lines of text, called *rules*, that the device applies to each packet that it receives. The lines of text provide specific information pertaining to what packets can be accepted and what packets must be denied. For instance, an ACL may have one line that states that any packets coming from the IP range 172.168.0.0 must be denied; a second line that indicates that no packets using the Telnet service are allowed to enter the network; a third line indicating that no traffic headed toward port 443 is allowed; and a fourth line that indicates that all traffic on port 80 is acceptable and should be routed to a specific IP address, which is the web server. Each time the device receives a packet, it compares the information in the packet's header to each line in the ACL. If the packet indicates that it is using Telnet or requests to make a connection to port 443, it is discarded. If the packet header information indicates that it wants to communicate through port 80 using HTTP over TCP, the packet is accepted and redirected to the web server.

This filtering is based on network layer information, which means that the device cannot look too far into the packet itself. It can make decisions based on header information only, which is limited. Most routers use ACLs to act as a type of firewall and use a router table to carry out routing decisions, but they do not provide the level of protection provided by other types of firewalls, which look deeper into the packet. Because packet filtering looks only at the header information, it is not application dependent, as many proxy firewalls are. Packet-filtering firewalls also do not keep track of the state of a connection, which takes place in a stateful inspection firewall (discussed next). Packet filtering is the method used by the first-generation firewall—that is, it is the first type that was created and used, and other types that were developed subsequently fall into later generations.

> ## Pros and Cons of Packet Filtering
> Pros:
>
> - Scaleable
> - Provides high performance
> - Application independent
>
> Cons:
>
> - Does not look into the packet past the header information
> - Low security relative to other options
> - Does not keep track of the state of a connection

## Stateful Firewalls

*This packet came from Texas, so it is okay. Response: It's a different type of state.*

When packet filtering is used, a packet arrives at the router, and the router runs through its ACLs to determine whether this packet should be allowed or denied. If the packet is allowed, it is passed on to the destination host, or to another router, and the router forgets about the packet. This is different from stateful inspection filtering, which remembers and keeps track of what packets went where until each particular connection is closed.

Stateful filtering is like a nosy neighbor who gets into people's business and conversations. She keeps track of who said what and when. This can be annoying until your house is burglarized. Then you and the police will want to talk to the nosy neighbor, because she knows everything that is going on in the neighborhood and would be the most likely one to know that something unusual happened. A stateful inspection firewall is nosier than a regular filtering device, because it keeps track of what computers say to each other. This requires that the firewall maintain a *state table*, which is like a score sheet of who said what to whom.

Stateful inspection firewalls also make decisions on what packets to allow or disallow, but their functionality goes a step further. For example, a regular packet-filtering device may deny any UDP packets requesting service on port 25, and a stateful packet-filtering device may have a rule to allow UDP packets through only if they are responses to outgoing requests. So, for example, if Mitchell sends a request to a computer on a different network, this request is logged in the firewall's state table, to indicate that Mitchell's computer made a request and that packets should be coming back to Mitchell. When the computer on the Internet responds to Mitchell, these packets are compared to the data in the state table at the firewall. Because the state table has information about a previous request for these packets, the firewall allows the packets to pass through. If, on the other hand, Mitchell had not made any requests and packets were coming in from the Internet to him, the firewall would see that no previous request for this information was received and then would look at its ACLs to see if these packets should be allowed.

Regular packet filtering compares incoming packets to rules defined in the firewall's ACLs. When a stateful inspection firewall receives a packet, it first looks in its state table to see whether a connection has already been established and whether this data was requested. If there was no previous connection and the state table holds no information about the packet, the packet is compared to the device's ACLs. If the ACL allows this type of traffic, the packet is allowed to access the network. If that type of traffic is not allowed, the packet is dropped.

Most stateful inspection firewalls work at the network and transport layers. It depends upon the product, but many times when a connection begins, the firewall investigates all layers of the packet (all headers, payload, and trailers). Once the initial packets go through this in-depth inspection, the firewall then just reviews the network and transport header portions for the rest of the session. Scaling down the inspection in this manner is done to increase performance.

Although stateful inspection provides an extra step of protection, it also adds more complexity because this device must now keep a dynamic state table and remember connections. Stateful inspection firewalls unfortunately have been the victims of many types of denial-of-service (DoS) attacks. Several types of attacks are aimed at flooding the state table with bogus information. The state table is a resource, similar to a system's hard drive space, memory, and CPU. When the state table is stuffed full of bogus information, the device may either freeze or reboot. In addition, if this firewall has to be rebooted for some reason, it will lose its information on all recent connections; thus, it may deny legitimate packets.

## Proxy Firewalls

*Meet my proxy. He will be our middleman.*

A *proxy* is a middleman. A proxy intercepts and inspects messages before delivering them to the intended recipients. Suppose you need to give a box and a message to the president of the United States; you could not just walk up to the president and hand over these items. Instead, you would have to go through a middleman, likely the secret service, who would accept the box and message and thoroughly inspect the box to en-

---

### Stateful Inspection Firewall Characteristics

The following lists some important characteristics of stateful inspection firewalls:

- Maintains a state table that tracks each and every communication channel.
- Provides a high degree of security and does not introduce the performance hit that application proxy firewalls introduce.
- Scaleable and transparent to users.
- Provides data for tracking connectionless protocols such as UDP and ICMP.
- Stores and updates state and context of the data within the packets.
- Considered a third-generation firewall.

sure that nothing dangerous was inside. This is what a proxy firewall does—it accepts messages either entering or leaving a network, inspects them for malicious information, and, when it decides the messages are okay, passes the data on to the destination computer. Proxy firewalls are second-generation firewalls.

A proxy firewall stands between a trusted and untrusted network and makes the connection, each way, on behalf of the source. So, if a user on the Internet requests to send data to a computer on the internal protected network, the proxy firewall gets this request first and looks it over for suspicious information. The request does not automatically go to the destination computer—instead, the proxy firewall accepts the request on behalf of the computer it is protecting. If the proxy firewall decides the packet is safe, it sends it on to the destination computer. When the destination computer replies, the reply goes back to the proxy firewall, which repackages the packet to contain the source address of the proxy firewall, not the host system on the internal network. What is important is that a proxy firewall breaks the communication channel: there is no direct connection to internal computers.

This type of firewall makes a copy of each accepted packet before transmitting it. It repackages the packet to hide the packet's true origin. If an attacker attempts to scan or probe a company's network, he will receive only information that has been intercepted and repackaged by the proxy server. The returned packets will have only the IP address of the firewall, and the information released will be sparse; thus the internal network is protected and hidden.

The proxy firewall is the only machine that talks to the outside world. This ensures that no computer has direct access to internal computers. This also means that the proxy server is the only computer that needs a valid public IP address. The rest of the computers on the internal network can use private (nonroutable IP addresses on the Internet) addresses, because no computers on the outside will see their addresses anyway.

## Pros and Cons of Proxy Firewalls

Pros:

- Looks at the information within a packet, possibly all the way up to the application layer.
- Provides better security than packet filtering.
- Breaks the connection between trusted and untrusted systems.

Cons:

- Some proxy firewalls support only a limited number of applications.
- Degrades traffic performance.
- Application-based proxy firewalls may have scalability and performance issues.
- Breaks client/server model, which is good for security but sometimes bad for functionality.

Many firewalls are *multihomed*, meaning that they have more than two NICs. This allows the company to create several independent DMZs. One interface is connected to the untrusted network (usually the Internet), another interface is connected to the trusted network (internal company network), and the other interfaces segment different DMZs. One DMZ may have the company's web servers, while the other DMZ has the company's public mail and DNS server.

Other types of firewalls can reside and work on a dual-homed firewall; proxy firewalls being one of them. These firewall architectures are discussed in the "Firewall Architecture" section, later in the chapter.

Two types of proxy firewalls can be used—application-level and circuit-level, which are described next.

**Application- and Circuit-Level Proxies**   Proxies have been described as middlemen between untrusted external hosts and trusted internal hosts. However, there are more issues to understand when looking at the two different types of proxy firewalls available. *Application-level proxies* inspect the entire packet and make access decisions based on the content of the packet. They understand various services and protocols and the commands that are used by them. An application-level proxy can distinguish between an FTP GET command and an FTP PUT command, for example, and make access decisions based on this granular level of information; on the other hand, packet-filtering firewalls can allow or deny FTP requests only as a whole, not by the commands used within the FTP protocol.

An application-level proxy works for one service or protocol. A computer can have many types of services and protocols (FTP, NTP, SMTP, Telnet, and so on)—thus, one application-level proxy per service is required. This does not mean that one proxy firewall per service is required, but rather that one portion of the firewall product is dedicated to understanding how a specific protocol works and how to properly filter it for suspicious data.

A *circuit-level proxy* creates a circuit between the client computer and the server and provides protection at the session layer. It does not understand or care about the higher-level issues that an application-level proxy deals with. It knows the source and destination addresses and makes access decisions based on this type of header information.

Providing application-level proxy services can be a tricky undertaking. The proxy must totally understand how specific protocols work and what commands within that protocol are legitimate. This is a lot to know and look at during the transmission of data. As an analogy, picture a screening station at an airport that is made up of many employees, all with the job of interviewing people before they are allowed into the airport and onto an airplane. These employees have been trained to ask specific questions and detect suspicious answers and activities, and have the skill set and authority to detain suspicious individuals. Now, suppose that each of these employees speaks a different language, because the people that they interview come from different parts of the world. So, one employee who speaks German could not understand and identify suspicious answers of a person from Italy, because they do not speak the same language. This is the same for an application-level proxy firewall. Each proxy is a piece of software that has been designed to understand how a specific protocol "talks" and how to identify suspicious data within a transmission using that protocol.

**NOTE** Any type of proxy firewall deconstructs the packets that they receive. This means that they take the packet apart and analyze the pieces for suspicious activity.

If the application-level proxy firewall does not understand a certain protocol or service, it cannot protect this type of communication. In this scenario, a circuit-level proxy is useful, because it does not deal with such complex issues. An advantage of a circuit-level proxy is that it can handle a wider variety of protocols and services than an application-level proxy, but the downfall is that the circuit-level proxy cannot provide the degree of granular control that an application-level proxy provides. Life is just full of compromises.

A circuit-level proxy works similarly to a packet filter in that it makes access decisions based on address, port, and protocol type. It looks at the data within the packet header rather than the data within the payload of the packet. It does not know whether the contents within the packet are safe or unsafe.

An application-level proxy is dedicated to a particular protocol or service. At least one proxy is used per protocol because one proxy could not properly interpret all the commands of all the protocols coming its way. A circuit-level proxy works at a lower layer of the OSI model and does not require one proxy per protocol because it does not look at such detailed information.

*SOCKS* is an example of a circuit-level proxy gateway that provides a secure channel between two computers. When a SOCKS-enabled client sends a request to access a computer on the Internet, this request actually goes to the network's SOCKS proxy server, as shown in Figure 7-32 which inspects the packets for malicious information and checks its policy rules to see whether this type of connection is allowed. If the packet is acceptable and this type of connection is allowed, the SOCKS server sends the message to the destination computer on the Internet. When the computer on the Internet responds, it

## Application-Level vs. Circuit-Level Proxy Firewall Characteristics

Application-level proxy firewall:

- Different proxy required for each service allowed
- Provides more intricate control than circuit-level proxy firewalls
- Requires more processing per packet and thus is slower than a circuit-level proxy firewall

Circuit-level proxy firewall:

- Does not require a proxy for each and every service
- Does not provide the detailed access control that an application-level proxy firewall provides
- Provides security for a wider range of protocols

**Figure 7-32** The SOCKS server usually sits behind a router, and each SOCKS client must have SOCKS software installed.

sends its packets to the SOCKS server, which again inspects the data and then passes it on to the client computer.

The SOCKS server can screen, filter, audit, log, and control data flowing in and out of a protected network. Because of its popularity, many applications and protocols have been configured to work with SOCKS in a manner that takes less configuration on the administrator's part, and various firewall products have integrated SOCKS software to provide circuit-based protection.

Because SOCKS is a circuit-level proxy, it does not provide detailed, protocol-specific control. The SOCKS product includes the SOCKS server software, which can run on Unix servers; a SOCKS client library; SOCKS-ified versions of several applications and protocols; and SOCKS wrappers for utilities such as traceroute and ping.

## SOCKS Proxy Firewall Characteristics
The following are some important characteristics of a SOCKS firewall:

- Circuit-level proxy firewall
- Requires clients to be "SOCKS-ified" with SOCKS client software
- Can be resource intensive
- Provides authentication and encryption features similar to other VPN protocols, but is not considered a traditional VPN protocol

## Dynamic Packet Filtering

When an internal system needs to communicate to an entity outside of its trusted network, it has to choose a source port so that the receiving system knows how to respond properly. The receiving system requires an IP address and a port number so that its response can properly find its way to the sender's computer. Ports up to 1023 are called *well-known ports* and are reserved for server-side services. The sender must choose a dynamic port higher than 1023 when it sets up a connection with another entity. The dynamic packet-filtering firewall then creates an ACL that allows the external entity to communicate with the internal system via this high port. If this were not an available option for your dynamic packet-filtering firewall, you would have to allow "punch holes" in your firewalls for all ports above 1023, because the client side chooses these ports dynamically and the firewall would never know exactly on which port to allow or disallow traffic.

 **NOTE**   The standard port for HTTP is 80, which mean that a server will have a service listening on port 80 for HTTP traffic. HTTP (and most other protocols) works in a type of client/server model. The server portion uses the well-known ports (FTP uses 20 and 21, SMTP uses 25) so that everyone knows how to connect to those services. A client will not use one of these well-known ports.

An internal system could choose a source port of 11,111 for its message to the outside system. This frame goes to the dynamic packet-filtering firewall and builds an ACL, as illustrated in Figure 7-33, that indicates that a response from the destination computer to this internal system's IP address and port 11,111 is to be allowed. When the destination system sends a response, the firewall allows it. These ACLs are dynamic in nature, so once the connection is finished (either an FIN or RST packet is received), the ACL is removed from the list. On connectionless protocols, such as UDP, the connection times out and then the ACL is pulled.

The benefit of a dynamic packet-filtering firewall, which is a fourth-generation firewall, is that it gives you the option of allowing any type of traffic outbound and allowing only response traffic inbound.

## Kernel Proxy Firewalls

*This firewall is made out of kernels of corn. Response: Why are you here?*

A *kernel proxy firewall* is considered a fifth-generation firewall. It differs from all the previously discussed firewall technologies because it creates dynamic, customized TCP/IP stacks when a packet needs to be evaluated.

When a packet arrives at a kernel proxy firewall, a new virtual network stack is created, which is made up of only the protocol proxies that are necessary to examine this specific packet properly. If it is an FTP packet, only the FTP proxy is loaded in the stack. The packet is scrutinized at every layer of the stack, not just at the data payload. This means the data link header will be evaluated along with the network header, transport header, session layer information, and the application layer data. If anything is deemed unsafe at any one of these layers, the packet is discarded.

**Figure 7-33**
Dynamic packet
filtering adds ACLs
when connections
are created.

Server

1. Client makes
connection to
external entity.

3. External system
is allowed to reply
through router.

Internal system

Router

2. Router dynamically
adds a new ACL.

Kernel proxy firewalls are faster than application layer proxy firewalls because all of the inspection and processing takes place in the kernel and does not need to be passed up to a higher software layer in the operating system. It is still a proxy-based system, so the connection between the internal and external entity is broken by the proxy acting as a middleman, and it can perform NAT by changing the source address, as do the preceding proxy-based firewalls.

Table 7-8 lists the important concepts and characteristics of the firewall types discussed in the previous sections. Although various firewall products can provide a mix of these services and work at different layers of the OSI model, it is important that you understand the basic definitions and functionalities of these firewall types.

| Firewall Type | OSI Layer | Characteristics |
|---|---|---|
| Packet filtering | Network layer | Looks at destination and source addresses, ports, and services requested. Routers using ACLs dictate acceptable access to a network. |
| Application-level proxy | Application layer | Looks deep into packets and makes granular access control decisions. It requires one proxy per service. |
| Circuit-level proxy | Network layer | Looks only at the header packet information. It protects a wider range of protocols and services than does an application-level proxy, but does not provide the detailed level of control available to an application-level proxy. |
| Stateful | Network layer | Looks at the state and context of packets. Keeps track of each conversation using a state table. |
| Kernel proxy | Application layer | Faster because processing is done in the kernel. One network stack is created for each packet. |

**Table 7-8** Differences Between Firewalls

## Appliances

A firewall may take the form of either software that is installed on a regular computer using a regular operating system or a dedicated hardware appliance that has its own operating system. The second choice is usually more secure, because the vendor uses a stripped-down version of an operating system (usually Linux or BSD). Operating systems are full of code and functionality that is not necessary for a firewall. This extra complexity opens the doors for vulnerabilities. If a hacker can exploit and bring down a company's firewall, then the company is very exposed and in danger.

### Firewall Architecture

*Firewalls are great, but where do we put them?*

Firewalls can be placed in a number of areas on a network, to meet particular needs. They can protect an internal network from an external network and act as a choke point for all traffic. A firewall can be used to segment network sections and enforce access controls between two or more subnets. Firewalls can also be used to provide a DMZ between an internal network and an external network.

Firewall software should be installed on a locked-down system, which is called a bastion host.

**Bastion Host** *Bastion host* is just another name for a locked-down (or hardened) system. A bastion host is usually a highly exposed device, because it is the front line in a network's security and its existence is known on the Internet. This means that the device must be extremely secure—no unnecessary services should be running, unused subsystems must be disabled, vulnerabilities must be patched, unnecessary user accounts must be disabled, and ports that are not needed must be closed. A bastion host is not tied to firewall software and activities; it is just a system that is properly locked down. Any system that resides within the DMZ should be installed on a bastion host since it is closer to the Internet and most likely closer to those who would like to do it harm. If firewall software is not installed on a locked-down operating system, or bastion host, the firewall is vulnerable.

**Dual-Homed Firewall** *Dual-homed* refers to a device that has two interfaces: one facing the external network and the other facing the internal network. If firewall software is installed on a dual-homed device, and it usually is, the underlining operating system should have packet forwarding and routing turned off, for security reasons. If they are enabled, the computer will not apply the necessary ACLs, rules, or other restrictions required of a firewall. When a packet comes to the external NIC from the untrusted network on a dual-homed firewall, and the operating system has forwarding enabled, the operating system will forward the traffic instead of passing it up to the firewall software for inspection.

Many network devices today are *multihomed*, which just means that they have several NICs that are used to connect several different networks. Multihomed devices are commonly used to house firewall software, since the job of a firewall is to control the traffic as it goes from one network to another. A common multihomed firewall architecture allows a company to have several DMZs, as described earlier. One DMZ may hold devices that are shared between companies in an extranet, another DMZ may house the company's DNS and mail servers, and yet another DMZ may hold the company's web servers. Different DMZs are used for two reasons: to control the different traffic types (for example, make sure that HTTP traffic only goes toward the web servers and DNS requests go toward the DNS server) and to ensure that if one system on one DMZ is compromised, the other systems in the rest of the DMZs are not accessible to this attacker.

**Screened Host**   A *screened host* is a firewall that communicates directly with a perimeter router and the internal network. Figure 7-34 shows this type of architecture.

Traffic that is received from the Internet is first filtered via packet filtering on the outer router. The traffic that makes it past this phase is sent to the screened-host firewall, which applies more rules to the traffic and drops the denied packets. Then the traffic moves to the internal destination hosts. The screened host (the firewall) is the only device that receives traffic directly from the router. No traffic goes directly from the Internet, through the router, and to the internal network. The screened host is always part of this equation.

If the firewall is an application-based system, protection is provided at the network layer by the router and at the application layer by the proxy. This arrangement offers a high degree of security, because for an attacker to be successful, she would have to compromise two systems.

What does the word *screening* mean in this context? As shown in Figure 7-34, the router is a screening device and the firewall is the screened host. This just means that there is a layer that scans the traffic and gets rid of a lot of the "junk" before it is directed toward the firewall. A screened host is different from a screened subnet, which is described next.

Internal network

Screening
device

Screened
host

**Figure 7-34**   A screened host is a firewall that is screened by a router.

**Screened Subnet**  A *screened-subnet* architecture adds another layer of security to the screened-host architecture. The external router is similar to that shown in Figure 7-34. It applies packet filtering to data entering the network and ports the traffic to the firewall. However, instead of the firewall then redirecting the traffic to the internal network, an interior router also filters the traffic. The use of these two physical firewalls creates a DMZ.

In an environment with only a screened host, if an attacker successfully breaks through the firewall, nothing lies in her way to prevent her from having full access to the internal network. In an environment using a screened subnet, the attacker would have to hack through another router (or firewall) to gain access. In this layered approach to security, the more layers provided, the better the protection. Figure 7-35 shows a simple example of a screened subnet.

The examples shown in the figures are simple in nature. Often, more complex networks and DMZs are implemented in real-world systems. Figures 7-36 and 7-37 show some other possible architectures of screened subnets and their configurations.

The screened-subnet approach provides more protection than a stand-alone firewall or a screened-host firewall because three devices are working together and all three devices must be compromised before an attacker can gain access to the internal network. This architecture also sets up a DMZ between the two routers, which functions as a small network isolated among the trusted internal and untrusted external networks. The internal users usually have limited access to the servers within this area. Web, e-mail, and other public servers often are placed within the DMZ. Although this solution provides the highest security, it also is the most complex. Configuration and maintenance can prove to be difficult in this setup, and when new services need to be added, three systems may need to be reconfigured instead of just one.

The complexity and configuration of the DMZ, perimeter network, and screened hosts and subnets are dictated by the company security policy. The required level of security, and the services that need to be available to internal and external users, should be clearly outlined in this policy.

**Figure 7-35**   When using a screened subnet, two firewalls are used to create a DMZ.

**Figure 7-36** A screened subnet can have different networks within it and different firewalls that filter for specific vulnerabilities.

 **NOTE** Sometimes a screened-host architecture is referred to as a single-tiered configuration and a screened subnet is referred to as a two-tiered configuration. If there are three firewalls that create two separate DMZs, this may be called a three-tiered configuration.

## "Shoulds" of Firewalls

*Look both ways before crossing a street, and always floss. Response: Wrong rule set.*

The default action of any firewall should be to implicitly deny any packets not explicitly allowed. This means that if no rule states that the packet can be accepted, that packet should be denied, no questions asked. Any packets entering the network that have a source address of an internal host should be denied. *Masquerading*, or *spoofing*, is a popular attacking trick in which the attacker modifies a packet header to have the

**Figure 7-37** Some architectures have separate screened subnets with different server types in each.

source address of a host inside the network that she wants to attack. This packet is spoofed and illegitimate. There is no reason that a packet coming from the Internet should have an internal source network address, so the firewall should deny it. The same is true for outbound traffic. No traffic should be allowed to leave a network that does not have an internal source address. If this occurs, it means that someone, or some program, on the internal network is spoofing traffic. This is how *zombies* work—the agents used in distributed DoS (DDos) attacks. If packets are leaving a network with different source addresses, these packets are spoofed and the network is most likely being used as an accomplice in a DDoS attack.

When security is a top priority for a company, its firewalls should reassemble fragmented packets before sending them on to their destination. In some types of attacks, the hackers alter the packets and make them seem to be something they are not. When

## Firewall Architecture Characteristics

It is important to understand the following characteristics of these firewall architecture types.

**Dual-homed:**

- Single computer with separate NICs connected to each network
- Used to divide an internal trusted network from an external untrusted network
- Must disable computer's forwarding and routing functionality so the two networks are truly segregated

**Screened host:**

- Router filters (screens) traffic before it is passed to the firewall.

**Screened subnet:**

- External router filters (screens) traffic before it enters the subnet. Traffic headed toward the internal network then goes through the firewall and possibly another router.

a fragmented packet comes to a firewall, the firewall is seeing only part of the picture. It will make its best guess as to whether this piece of a packet is malicious or not. Because these fragments contain only a part of the full packet, the firewall is making a decision without having all the facts. Once all fragments are allowed through to a host computer, they can be reassembled into malicious packages that can cause a lot of damage. In environments that require higher security, the firewall should accept each fragment, assemble the fragments into a complete packet, and then make an access decision based on the whole packet. The drawback to this, however, is that firewalls that do reassemble packet fragments before allowing them to go on to their destination computer cause traffic delay and more overhead. It is up to the security officer and company to decide whether this configuration is necessary and whether the added traffic delay is acceptable.

Many companies choose to deny network entrance to packets that contain source routing information, which was mentioned earlier. *Source routing* means that the packet decides how to get to its destination, not the routers in between the source and destination computer. Source routing moves a packet throughout a network on a predetermined path. The sending computer must know about the topology of the network and how to route data properly. This is easier for the routers and connection mechanisms in between, because they do not need to make any decisions on how to route the packet. However, it can also pose a security risk. When a router receives a packet that contains source routing information, it figures the packet knows what needs to be done and passes it on. In some cases, not all filters may be applied to the packet, and a network administrator may want packets to be routed only through a certain path and not the route that a particular packet dictates. To make sure none of this misrouting happens, many firewalls are configured to check for source routing information within the packet and deny it if it is present.

Unfortunately, once a company erects a firewall, it may have a false sense of security. Firewalls are only one piece of the puzzle, and security has a lot of pieces.

The following list addresses some of the disadvantages of firewalls:

- Most of the time a distributed approach needs to be used to control all network access points, which cannot usually happen through the use of just one firewall.

- Firewalls can present a potential bottleneck to the flow of traffic.

- Firewalls can restrict desirable services that users may want to access. (This is a disadvantage to the users, but an advantage to the security professional.)

- Most firewalls do not provide protection from viruses being downloaded or passed through e-mail, and hooks to virus-detection techniques are needed.

- Border firewalls provide little protection against the inside attacker.

- Firewalls do not protect against rogue modems in listening mode.

- Firewalls do not protect against rogue wireless APs.

The role of firewalls is becoming more and more complex as they evolve and take on more functionality and responsibility. At times, this complexity works against the network administrator and security professional because it requires them to understand and properly implement additional functionality. Without understanding the different types of firewalls and architectures available, many more security holes can be introduced, which lays out the welcome mat for attackers.

## Honeypot

*Hey! Here is a vulnerable system to attack!*

A *honeypot* system is a computer that usually sits in the screened subnet, or DMZ, and attempts to lure attackers to it instead of to actual production computers. To make a honeypot system lure attackers, administrators may enable services and ports that are popular to exploit. However, the administrator must be careful to ensure that this box is isolated in such a way that, when it is attacked, the hacker is not successful at accessing other computers on the network. Some honeypot systems have services *emulated*, meaning the actual service is not running but software that acts like those services is available. In Chapter 10, honeypot systems are discussed in the context of *enticement versus entrapment*. A legal honeypot can entice attackers to access the computer and attempt to hack into it, but it cannot entrap them. The example given in Chapter 10 shows that having a banner on one system indicating that free MP3s are available to download on the honeypot system is entrapment, because this sets up the user to access the honeypot for reasons other than the intent to harm. If services are running, ports are open, and banners are available for viewing, this will be quite enough to entice, not entrap, attackers.

Some network administrators want to keep the attackers away from their other systems and set up honeypots as decoys. Other administrators want to go after those who hurt them. These administrators would keep detailed logs, enable auditing, and perform different degrees of forensics in the hopes of turning over the attackers to the authorities for prosecution.

### Network Segregation and Isolation

Chapter 6 covers network segregation and isolation in depth, but it is an important component that interrelates with the topics in this chapter and thus merits brief mention here. It is important that you segregate networks and subnets from each other. This usually means implementing routers that do not pass on broadcast and collision domain information and using different address schemes for different segments. Many networks today use Ethernet technology, which continually broadcasts information that can be useful to inside and outside attackers. Because data is so freely broadcasted in these environments, you must make sure that networks that house sensitive information are properly segmented from other network sections.

The architecture of a network should be clearly thought out, fully documented, and fully tested. A network administrator may not want everyone to be able to talk directly to a mainframe that holds critical information, for example. This traffic should be ported through one channel and filtered by a router or firewall. An administrator also may not want everyone on the network to be able to access the administrator's subnet, which holds the management consoles for all the routers, IDSs, logging servers, and auditing systems. The computers within this subnet need to talk to different systems throughout the network, but there is really no good reason that regular users should be able to access this subnet freely. This subnet needs to be isolated by ACLs enforced by surrounding routers (or firewalls) and properly segregated.

Also, it is one thing to document what one *thinks* the architecture of a network is, but just because it is on paper does not make it true. If the network schematic indicates that no one from subnet A can contact subnet B because of a specific firewall setting, this needs to be tested and penetration attacks should be launched to determine whether this is indeed true.

# Networking Services and Protocols

So far, we have touched on protocols, technologies, topologies, and devices that can be used within a LAN environment. These services are not used in LAN environments only, however; they are also used in MAN and WAN infrastructures. The purpose of splitting the discussion into LAN and WAN sections is to provide a clear-cut explanation of the differences between these networking concepts. As stated earlier in this chapter, a network is set up to enable users to communicate with each other, create central administration, and share resources. The resources usually come in the form of networking services, and the following sections address some of the most-used services in most LAN environments.

# Network Operating Systems

A *network operating system (NOS)* is special software designed to control network resource access and provide the necessary services to enable a computer to interact with the surrounding network. A NOS is different from a single-user operating system. A NOS is built to work in a client/server model, in which resources, files, and applications are centralized and all users access them on servers (rather than having individual copies of those resources stored on each and every workstation). A NOS manages the connections and links between systems and components.

A NOS also has built-in authentication mechanisms that are necessary for a network environment and auditing functionality. Single-user operating systems do not enforce strong authentication. Anyone who has worked on Windows 95 or 98 knows that you can click the OK or Cancel button when the OS requests a username and password, even if you don't type in any information. These operating systems do not require authentication. However, anyone who has worked on Windows NT or Windows 2000 systems knows that these systems will not let you access the user Desktop environment if you do not know the correct username and password.

Single-user operating systems can work in a peer-to-peer environment (a type of workgroup) and implement resource and file sharing. However, a peer-to-peer environment does not provide the level of security, centralized management, and access control necessary in most environments. Single-user operating systems also do not have the powerful directory services that NOSs provide. This is an important piece of most networks today.

The following is a short list of many of the services NOSs may provide that most single-user systems do not:

- Directory services
- Internetworking, routing, and WAN support
- Support for remote dial-up users
- Clustering functionality
- Strong authentication, authorization, access control, and auditing
- File and printing services, including backup and replication services
- Management and administration tools for remote clients
- Software distribution, and software and hardware inventory functionality
- Fault-tolerance capabilities

When a user of a computer running a NOS needs to access a resource on the network, the NOS software uses a *redirector*, which points the computer to the actual requested resource. Often, this redirector functionality works at a lower layer of processing than the higher-level requesting application. The application usually does not realize that the resource is not stored on the local computer. This reduces a lot of confusion and extra work for the programmers of the applications, because they do not need to figure out how to track down network resources themselves.

## References

- **Network World Research Center: Operating Systems** www.nwfusion.com/topics/nos.html
- **Google listings for operating systems** http://directory.google.com/Top/Computers/Software/Operating_Systems

## Domain Name Service

Imagine how hard it would be to use the Internet if we had to remember actual specific IP addresses. The *Domain Name Service (DNS)* is a method of resolving hostnames to IP addresses so that names can be used instead of IP addresses when referencing unique hosts on the Internet. Not too many years ago, when the Internet was made up of about 100 computers (versus over 1 million now), a list used to be kept that mapped every user's hostname to their IP address. This list was kept on an FTP server so that everyone could access it. It did not take long for the task of maintaining this list to become overwhelming, and the computing community looked to automate it.

A hierarchical system for domain names was developed, and in 1992 the National Science Foundation (NSF) awarded Network Solutions, Inc. (NSI) the contract to manage and maintain domain names and the registration process of those names. NSI handled the name registration and a hostname resolution directory of DNS servers. It also maintained the authoritative databases of the Internet, which are the root DNS servers. An authoritative root DNS server contained 13 files, one for each of the top-level domain servers.

Until 1999, the Internet Assigned Numbers Authority (IANA) maintained and coordinated the allocation of IP addresses. Large Internet service providers (ISPs) would apply to the registries for blocks of these IP addresses and allocate the blocks to smaller ISPs or individual users. However, after 1999, the Internet Corporation for Assigned Names and Numbers (ICANN) took over the responsibilities of IP address block allocation, DNS management, and root server system management. NSI still maintains the authoritative root databases.

Wonderful. We have had a history lesson, but how does DNS work and what is its place in a network?

When a user types in a uniform resource locator (URL) in his web browser, the URL is made up of words or letters that are in a sequence that makes sense to that user, such as **www.logicalsecurity.com**. However, these words are only for humans—computers work with IP addresses. So after the user enters this URL and presses ENTER, behind the scenes his computer is actually being directed to a DNS server that will resolve this URL, or hostname, into an IP address that the computer understands. Once the hostname has been resolved to an IP address, the computer knows how to get to the web server holding the requested web page.

Many companies have their own DNS servers to resolve their internal hostnames. These companies usually also use the DNS servers at their ISPs to resolve hostnames on the Internet. An internal DNS server can be used to resolve hostnames on the entire network, but usually more than one DNS server is used so that the load can be split up and so that redundancy and fault tolerance are in place.

Within DNS servers, networks are split up into *zones*. One zone may contain all hostnames for the marketing and accounting departments, and another zone may contain hostnames for the administration, research, and legal departments. The DNS server that holds the files for one of these zones is said to be the *authoritative* name server for that particular zone. A zone may contain one or more domains, and the DNS server holding those host records is the authoritative name server for those domains.

The DNS server contains records that map hostnames to IP addresses, which are referred to as *resource records*. When a user's computer needs to resolve a hostname to an IP address, it looks to its TCP/IP settings to find its DNS server. The computer then sends a request, containing the hostname, to the DNS server for resolution. The DNS server looks at its resource records and finds the record with this particular hostname, retrieves the address, and replies to the computer with the corresponding IP address.

It is recommended that a *primary* and a *secondary* DNS server be placed in each zone. The primary DNS server contains the actual resource records for a zone, and the secondary DNS server contains copies of those records. Users can use the secondary DNS server to resolve names, which takes a load off of the primary server. If the primary server goes down for any reason or is taken offline, users can still use the secondary server for name resolution. Having both a primary and secondary DNS server provides fault tolerance and redundancy to ensure that users can continue to work if something happens to one of these servers.

The primary and secondary DNS servers synchronize their information through a *zone transfer*. After changes take place to the primary DNS server, those changes need to be replicated to the secondary DNS server. It is important to configure the DNS server to allow zone transfers to take place only between the specific servers. For years now, attackers have been carrying out zone transfers to gather very useful network information from victims' DNS servers. Unauthorized zone transfers can take place if the DNS servers are not properly configured to restrict this type of activity.

## Internet DNS and Domains

Networks on the Internet are connected in a hierarchical structure, as are the different DNS servers, as shown in Figure 7-38. While performing routing tasks, if a router does not know the necessary path to the requested destination, that router passes the packet up to a router above it. The router above it knows about all the routers below it. This router has a broader view of the routing that takes place on the Internet and has a better chance of getting the packet to the correct destination. This holds true with DNS servers also. If one DNS server does not know which DNS server holds the necessary resource record to resolve a hostname, it can pass the request up to a DNS server above it.

The naming scheme of the Internet resembles an inverted tree with the root servers at the top. Lower branches of this tree are divided into top-level domains, with second-level domains under each. The most common top-level domains are listed here:

- **COM**   Commercial
- **EDU**   Education
- **MIL**   U.S. military organization
- **INT**   International treaty organization

- **GOV** Government
- **ORG** Organizational
- **NET** Networks

So how do all of these DNS servers play together in the Internet playground? When a user types in a URL to access a web site that sells computer books, for example, his computer asks its corporate authoritative DNS server if it can resolve this hostname to an IP address. Because this web site is most likely not on the corporate network, this particular DNS server will not usually know the necessary IP address of that web site. The DNS server does not just reject the user's request, but rather passes it on to another DNS on the Internet. The request for this hostname resolution continues through different DNS servers until it reaches one that knows the IP address. This information is reported back to the user's computer. The user's computer then attempts to access the web site using the IP address, and soon the user is buying computer books, happy as a clam.

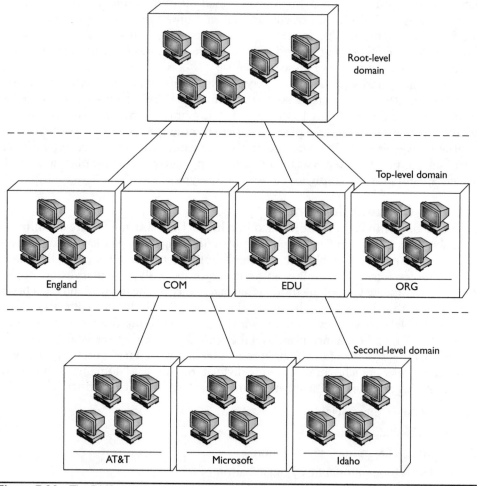

**Figure 7-38** The DNS naming hierarchy is similar to the routing hierarchy on the Internet.

DNS server and hostname resolution is extremely important in corporate networking and Internet use. Without it, users would have to remember and type in the IP address for each web site and individual system, instead of the name. That would be a mess.

## DNS Poisoning

There are several ways of carrying out a DNS poisoning attack. Every time we seem to fix one vulnerability that allows this type of attack to take place, attackers uncover new ways to accomplish this type of malicious behavior.

As stated earlier, not every DNS server knows the IP address of every hostname it is asked to resolve. When a request for a hostname-to-IP address mapping arrives at a DNS server (server A), the server reviews its resource records to see if it has the necessary information to fulfill this request. If the server does not have a resource record for this hostname, it forwards the request to another DNS server (server B), which in turn reviews its resource records and, if it has the mapping information, sends the information back to server A. Server A caches this hostname-to-IP address mapping in its memory (in case another client requests it) and sends the information on to the requesting client.

With the preceding information in mind, consider an example scenario. Andy the attacker wants to make sure that any time one of his competitor's customers tries to visit the competitor's web site, the customer is instead pointed to Andy's web site. So, Andy installs a tool that listens for requests that leave DNS server A asking other DNS servers if they know how to map the competitor's hostname to its IP address. Once Andy sees that server A sends out a request to server B to resolve the competitor's hostname, Andy quickly sends a message to server A indicating that the competitor's hostname resolves to Andy's web site's IP address. Server A's software accepts the first response that it gets, so server A caches this mapping information and sends it on to the requesting client. Now when the client tries to reach Andy's competitor's web site, she is instead pointed to Andy's web site. This will happen subsequently to any user who uses server A to resolve the competitor's hostname to an IP address, because this information is cached on server A.

Previous vulnerabilities that have allowed this type of activity to take place have been addressed, but this type of attack is still taking place because when server A receives a response to its request, it does not authenticate the sender. If *DNSSEC* (DNS security, which is part of the DNS Bind software) were enabled on server A, then server A would, upon receiving a response, validate the digital signature on the message before accepting the information, to make sure that the response is from an authorized DNS server. This sounds simple enough, but for DNSSEC to be rolled out properly, all of the DNS servers on the Internet would have to participate in a PKI to be able to validate digital signatures. (Digital signatures and PKI are covered in Chapter 8.) This would be an overwhelming task, which is why DNSSEC is rarely used today. So we have a fix to this problem...we just don't know how to roll it out properly.

## Network Information System

*Okay, who has my configuration files and who is going to resolve hostnames for me?*

*Network Information System (NIS)* works like a telephone book—which is why it was originally called YP (Yellow Pages)—for locating network resources. NIS enables users and applications to locate and access files and programs anywhere on the network through a central NIS server. NIS typically is used to "track down" password files, e-mail aliases, and host tables.

 **NOTE** A host table is a file that contains hostname-to-IP mappings. It is used in the same way that DNS is, but it is a file that computers can use to map a hostname to a specific IP address instead of a technology or a product. This is why NIS is sometimes compared to DNS, because they both provide the necessary mechanisms for computers to be able to uncover the IP address of a system.

In a Unix environment systems use certain system configuration files (passwords, network settings, user accounts) and in a network it is usually easier if all of the systems contain identical configuration files. Instead of maintaining these files individually for each computer, NIS is a way to have all of these configuration files stored and maintained centrally. When a computer boots up, instead of looking at its own local configuration file, it contacts the NIS server, which provides group files, password files, host tables, services and their port numbers, and information about the resources on the domain.

NIS works in a client/server architecture. The workstations run a client process (yp-bind) that identifies the NIS server process (ypserv) through a broadcast. This happens when the workstation boots or when an application is looking for specific information, such as how to locate the network's print server. This is similar to how the DHCP service works. Instead of relying upon local files or configurations for its IP address and network configuration, a computer, when it boots up, makes a request to the DHCP server. The DHCP server sends over the necessary configurations, which the system implements. This allows all of the systems to be configured in a uniform manner, which is necessary for network transmissions to take place transparently and seamlessly.

Just like every other protocol and technology that was developed in the '70s and '80s, NIS was developed specifically with functionality in mind—not security. For example, the encrypted password files are available to any requesting computer. Hackers have used this availability to capture the password file and brute-force it to gain unauthorized access. All information leaving the NIS server is in plaintext, allowing attackers to eavesdrop, and authentication is not enforced before critical files are handed over.

Another attack against NIS involves masquerading as an NIS server. Let's say that Valerie would like to gain access to Marc's computer, but she does not have an account or credentials to do so. So, Valerie first sends a broadcast to the NIS server to gather the current configuration files that everyone on the network uses. Then she modifies these files by adding her account and password. Then she listens for Marc's system to broadcast out to the NIS server. Once Marc's system makes this broadcast, Valerie sends her modified files to his system. Marc's system installs theses files, which set up an account for Valerie so that she can log on to his system whenever she wants to.

As more attackers took advantage of these weaknesses, it became clear that NIS needed an upgrade. So the smart people fixed a lot of these issues and added a plus sign to the name, NIS+. Pretty clever.

*NIS+* improved upon performance and security issues. The NIS namespace is flat, which works fine for smaller networks that do not require much scalability. NIS+ uses a hierarchical namespace, as DNS does. Using this type of namespace structure allows the service to adapt to a company's network and easily grow when necessary. NIS requires manual updates (from the master NIS server to all of the slave NIS servers), which could take hours to days because it has to be done through batch processes. NIS+ allows for automated updates that happen incrementally. NIS stores data in maps, whereas NIS+ stores this information in 16 predefined tables. Table 7-9 summarizes the differences between NIS and NIS+.

For security purposes, the developers really just added Secure Remote Procedure Call (S-RPC). RPC is a protocol that is discussed in detail in Chapter 11, but for now, you just need to know that it allows clients and servers to communicate in a client/ server model. When an NIS client needs to communicate with the NIS server, and vice versa, their communication takes place over the session layer RPC protocol. By using S-RPC, NIS+ has authentication, authorization, and encryption functionality. For example, when a user or computer needs to access the NIS+ server, the user's identity and S-RPC password are validated. The user is then placed into a class (owner, group, world, nobody), which dictates what the user can and can't do to the NIS+ objects. The communication between the NIS+ client and server is encrypted so that eavesdropping cannot take place.

NIS+ is backward compatible with NIS, which opens up a hole for hackers to exploit. If Valerie's system has NIS client software, and the NIS+ server is configured to be backward compatible, the NIS client can access files without first having to be authenticated and authorized. So, Valerie can get a hold of the password file and start cracking away. This type of vulnerability is usually available if the network administrator does not understand the difference between these two services and what this type of configuration can lead to.

And, of course, NIS+ can be attacked itself. If the Unix system that has the NIS+ server software installed is compromised, then a hacker can modify the setting, add himself as a user on all systems, and gain access to password files.

NIS+ can be configured to run in one of its three security modes:

- **Level 0**   No security. Any system or user has full access to NIS+ objects. Should be used for configuration and testing processes only.

- **Level 1**   Provides a low level of security, but does not require authentication. Should be used only for testing processes.

- **Level 2**   Default level that has authentication and authorization enabled. If someone makes a request with no credentials, she is put into the nobody class, which restricts all activities.

|  | **NIS** | **NIS+** |
|---|---|---|
| **Naming Structure** | Flat | Hierarchical |
| **Data Storage** | Stored in two-column maps | Stored in multicolumn tables |
| **Security** | No security | Authentication, authorization, and encryption |
| **Data Source** | Only choice | Client's choice: NIS, NIS+, DNS, or local /etc files |
| **Updates** | Updates through batch processes | Incremental updates propagated immediately |

**Table 7-9**   NIS and NIS+ Differences

## Directory Services

A *directory* **service** has a hierarchical database of users, computers, printers, resources, and attributes of each. The directory is mainly used for lookup operations, which enable users to track down resources and other users easily to facilitate access. Most directory service databases are built on the X.500 model and use the Lightweight Directory Access Protocol (LDAP) to access the directory database. (LDAP is discussed in the next section.)

Directory services are often compared to telephone white and yellow pages where, if you want to know how to contact someone, you can easily look though the white or yellow pages and find the necessary contact information. The same is true about directory services, although usually they contain much more than just phone numbers. (Actually, DNS is a type of directory service.)

The directory itself uses classes of objects and subclasses of those objects to provide organization to the directory repository, which is usually a database. Then, the administrator can apply policies to these objects in a centralized manner. The entities within objects may be users, their location, and peripheral information, resources, profiles, electronic commerce information, network services, and much more. The administrator can then develop access control, security, and auditing policies that dictate how and by whom these objects can be accessed, after which each of these actions can be audited. Policies can also be developed and applied to control bandwidth management, firewall filtering, VPN access, and QoS.

Many different directories are developed and maintained by the IT department. These directories can be based on business or security needs, and they can have different security policies, access controls, and profiles applied to them. When more than one directory is in use, the directories need a way to communicate with each other; this takes place through *metadirectories*. *Metadata* is data about data. Metadirectories hold top-level information about the directory itself, which enables a user in one directory to quickly locate an object he is looking for in a totally different directory.

Each directory follows a specific *schema*, like regular databases. The schema provides structure to the directory repository and defines how objects and their relationships are to be represented. Each directory service vendor has a baseline schema that enables administrators to define their own objects and corresponding attributes. However, like many other types of products, interoperability issues may occur between vendors' schemas, in which case they cannot easily communicate with each other. If one company buys another company and needs to merge their networks and combine their directory services, for example, this can turn into a tricky and hairy project.

Directory services offer rich services to users, administrators, and networks as a whole. They enable administrators to maintain and control all resources and users within an environment. The directory database acts as a holding place for almost all of the network's important information and enables users to track down needed services or resources easily and quickly. Two examples of directory services are Microsoft Active Directory and Novell Directory Services (NDS). Although both are based on the X.500 model, they do not easily communicate with each other.

Many services are made available to users within a network, which is a big reason for constructing a network in the first place. This section described NOS, DNS, and directory services, but a network offers much more—for example, many networks offer print services that enable many users to share local and remote printers. The administrators have centralized network management services that let them view the network as a whole from one graphical application, add and delete users, troubleshoot network issues, audit activities, add and remove services, control remote user access, and more. Some networks have terminal-emulation services, which enable users to have a lower-powered workstation that sees only the desktop. The operating system actually sits on a server somewhere else and does all the processor-intense activities.

Networks and networking are interesting, confusing, and rewarding constructs of today's computing world. However, networking complexity causes many errors, security holes, and vulnerabilities to occur, and this is what potential attackers are counting on. The more you know and understand about networking and how each component works with other components, the more efficiently you can apply security mechanisms and provide a higher level of protection.

## Lightweight Directory Access Protocol

*Lightweight Directory Access Protocol (LDAP)* is a client/server protocol used to access network directories such as Microsoft Active Directory or NDS. These directories follow the X.500 standard. The first iteration of this protocol, Directory Access Protocol (DAP), was created to be a front-end client for X.500 directory services. The idea was that it would be the interface for every service provided by a directory that followed the X.500 standard. Well, the X.500 standard ended up being too complex to actually fully implement, and DAP also was extremely complex and resource hungry. So today, our directory services follow a portion of the X.500 standard and we use a slimmed-down ("lightweight") version of DAP.

The LDAP specification works with directories that organize their database in a hierarchical tree structure. The tree has leaves (entries) with unique distinguished names (DNs). These names are hierarchical and describe the object's place within the tree. The entries can define network resources, computers, people, wireless devices, and more. Each entry has an attribute and a value. The attributes are like the columns in a relational database and provide descriptive information about the entry. For example, if the entry is a printer, then the attributes could be the IP address, name of the printer, MAC address, and a description. The values are the data items that fill in these fields. So the attribute provides the field, and when the field is populated with data, this is that attribute's value. Each company defines its own directory structure, attributes, and values so that they best meet the company's needs.

 **NOTE** The newest LDAP version, version 3, has an extensive security model embedded that supports Internet security standards such as transport layer security (TLS).

## References

- **IETF LDAP (v3) Revision Charter**  www.ietf.org/html.charters/ldapbis-charter.html

- **RFC 2256 – A Summary of the X.500(96) User Schema for Use with LDAPv3**  www.ietf.org/rfc/rfc2256.txt

- **ITtoolbox LDAP resources**  http://networking.ittoolbox.com/nav/t.asp?t=384&p=387&h1=384&h2=387

## Network Address Translation

*I have one address I would like to share with everyone!*

When computers need to communicate with each other, they need to use the same type of addressing scheme so that everyone understands how to find and talk to one another. The Internet uses the IP address scheme, and any computer or network that wants to communicate with other users on the network must conform to this scheme; otherwise, that computer will sit in a virtual room with only itself to talk to.

However, IP addresses have become scarce (until the full adoption of IPv6) and expensive. So some smart people came up with *network address translation (NAT)*, which enables a network that does not follow the Internet's addressing scheme to communicate over the Internet.

Private IP addresses have been reserved for internal LAN address use, as outlined in RFC 1918. These addresses can be used within the boundaries of a company, but they cannot be used on the Internet because they will not be properly routed. NAT enables a company to use these private addresses and still be able to communicate transparently with computers on the Internet.

The following lists current private IP address ranges:

- **10.0.0.0–10.255.255.255**   Class A network

- **172.16.0.0–172.31.255.255**   16 contiguous Class B networks

- **192.168.0.0–192.168.255.255**   256 contiguous Class C networks

NAT is a gateway that lies between a network and the Internet (or another network) that performs transparent routing and address translation. Because IP addresses were depleting fast, IPv6 was developed in 1999, which was intended to be the long-term fix to the address shortage problem. NAT was developed as the short-term fix to enable more companies to participate on the Internet. However, to date, IPv6 is slow in acceptance and implementation, while NAT has caught on like wildfire. Many firewall vendors have implemented NAT into their products, and it has been found that NAT actually provides a great security benefit. When attackers want to hack a network, they first do what they can to learn all about the network and its topology, services, and addresses. Attackers cannot easily find out a company's address scheme and its topology when NAT is in place, because NAT acts like a large nightclub bouncer by standing in front of the network and hiding the true IP scheme.

NAT hides internal addresses by centralizing them on one device, and any frames that leave that network have only the source address of that device, not of the actual computer that sends the message. So when a message comes from an internal computer with the address of 10.10.10.2, for example, the message is stopped at the device running NAT software, which happens to have the IP address of 1.2.3.4. NAT changes the header of the frame from the internal address, 10.10.10.2, to the valid IP address of the NAT device, 1.2.3.4. (Yes, I know 1.2.3.4 isn't valid, but I think you get the concept.) When a computer on the Internet replies to this message, it replies to the address 1.2.3.4. The NAT device changes the header on this reply message to 10.10.10.2 and puts it on the wire for the internal user to receive.

There are three basic types of NAT implementations that can be used:

- **Static mapping**  The NAT software has a pool of public IP addresses configured. Each private address is statically mapped to a specific public address. So computer A always receives the public address x, computer B always receives the public address y, and so on. This is usually used for servers that need to keep the same public address at all times.

- **Dynamic mapping**  The NAT software has a pool of IP addresses, but instead of statically mapping a public address to a specific private address, it works on a first come, first served basis. So if Bob needs to communicate over the Internet, his system makes a request to the NAT server. The NAT server takes the first IP on the list and maps it to Bob's private address. The balancing act is to estimate how many computers will most likely need to communicate outside the internal network at one time. This estimate is the number of public addresses that the company purchases, instead of purchasing one public address for each computer.

- **Port address translation (PAT)**  The company owns and uses only one public IP address for all systems that need to communicate outside the internal network. How in the world could all computers use the exact same IP address? Good question. Here's an example: The NAT device has an IP address of 127.50.41.3. When computer A needs to communicate with a system on the Internet, the NAT device documents this computer's private address and source port number (10.10.44.3 port 43,887). The NAT device changes the IP address in the computer's packet header to 127.50.41.3, with the source port 40,000. When computer B also needs to communicate with a system on the Internet, the NAT device documents the private address and source port number (10.10.44.15 port 23,398) and changes the header information to 127.50.41.3 with source port 40,001. So when a system responds to computer A, the packet first goes to the NAT device, which looks up the port number 40,000 and sees that it maps to computer A's real information. So the NAT device changes the header information to address 10.10.44.3 and port 43,887 and sends it to computer A for processing. A company can save a lot more money by using PAT, because the company needs to buy only a few public IP addresses, which are used by all systems in the network.

Most NAT implementations are *stateful*, meaning they keep track of a communication between the internal host and an external host until that session is ended. The NAT device needs to remember the internal IP address and port to send the reply messages back. This stateful characteristic is similar to stateful inspection firewalls, but NAT does not perform scans on the incoming packets to look for malicious characteristics. Instead, NAT is a service that is usually performed on routers or firewalls within a company's screened subnet.

Although NAT was developed to provide a quick fix for the depleting IP address problem, it has actually put the problem off for quite some time. The more companies that implement private address schemes, the less likely IP addresses will become scarce. This has been helpful to NAT and the vendors that implement this technology, but it has put the acceptance and implementation of IPv6 much farther down the road.

### References

- RFC 1631 – The IP Network Address Translator (NAT)  www.faqs.org/rfcs/ rfc1631.html
- *Daryl's TCP/IP Primer*, Chapter 11, "Network Address Translation (NAT)," by Daryl Banttari  www.tcpipprimer.com/nat.cfm
- "NAT Basics," HomeNetHelp  www.homenethelp.com/web/explain/ about-NAT.asp

# Intranets and Extranets

*We kind of trust you, but not really. We're going to put you on the extranet.*

Web technologies and their uses have exploded with functionality, capability, and popularity. Companies set up internal web sites for centralized business information such as employee phone numbers, policies, events, news, and operations instructions. Many companies have also implemented web-based terminals that enable employees to perform their daily tasks, access centralized databases, make transactions, collaborate on projects, access global calendars, use videoconferencing tools and whiteboard applications, and obtain often-used technical or marketing data.

Web-based clients are different from workstations that log into a network and have their own desktop. Web-based clients limit a user's ability to access the computer's system files, resources, and hard drive space, access back-end systems, and perform other tasks. The web-based client can be configured to provide a GUI with only the buttons, fields, and pages necessary for the users to perform tasks. This gives all users a standard universal interface with similar capabilities.

When a company uses the Internet and web-based technologies inside its networks, it is using an *intranet*, a "private" network that uses Internet technologies, such as TCP/IP. The company has web servers and client machines using web browsers, and it uses the TCP/IP protocol suite. The web pages are written in HTML or XML and are accessed via HTTP.

Using web-based technologies has many pluses. They have been around for quite some time, they are easy to implement, no major interoperability issues occur, and with just a click on a link, a user can be taken to the location of the requested resource. Web-based technologies are not platform-dependent, meaning that all web sites and pages may be maintained on a Unix server, and all different flavors of client workstations can access them—they only need a web browser.

An *extranet* extends outside the bounds of the company's network to enable two or more companies to share common information and resources. Business partners commonly set up extranets to accommodate business-to-business communication. An extranet enables business partners to work on projects together, share marketing information, communicate and work collaboratively on issues, post orders, and share catalogs, pricing structures, and information on upcoming events. Trading partners often use electronic data interchange (EDI), which provides structure and organization to electronic documents, orders, invoices, purchase orders, and a data flow. EDI has evolved into web-based technologies to provide easy access and easier methods of communication.

For many businesses, an extranet can create a weakness or hole in their security if the extranet is not implemented and maintained properly. Properly configured firewalls need to be in place to control who can use the extranet communication channels. Extranets used to be based mainly on dedicated links, which are more difficult for attackers to infiltrate, but today many extranets are set up over the Internet, which requires properly configured VPNs and security policies.

## Value-Added Networks

Many different types of companies use EDI for internal communication and for communication with other companies. A very common implementation is between a company and its supplier. For example, there are supplier companies that provide inventory to many different companies, such as Target, Wal-Mart, and Kmart. Many of these supplies are made in China and then shipped to a warehouse somewhere in the United States. When Wal-Mart needs to order more inventory, it sends its request through an EDI network, which is basically an electronic form of our paper-based world. Instead of using paper purchase orders, receipts, and forms, EDI provides all of this digitally. A *value-added network (VAN)* is an EDI infrastructure developed and maintained by one company (called a *service bureau*) for use by other companies.

A Wal-Mart store tracks its inventory by having employees scan bar codes on individual items. When the inventory of an item becomes low, a Wal-Mart employee sends a request for more of that specific item. This request goes to a mailbox at a VAN that Wal-Mart pays to use, and the request is then pushed out to a supplier that provides this type of inventory for Wal-Mart. Because Wal-Mart (and other stores) deals with thousands of suppliers, using a VAN simplifies the ordering process; instead of an employee having to track down the right supplier and submit a purchase order, this all happens in the background through an automated EDI network, which is managed by a VAN.

### References

- **Intranet Road Map (guide and tutorial)** www.intranetroadmap.com
- **CIO Intranet/Extranet Knowledge Management Resource Center** www.cio .com/forums/intranet
- *Intranet Journal* www.intranetjournal.com

# Metropolitan Area Network

*Behind every good man…. Response: Wrong MAN.*

A *metropolitan area network (MAN)* is usually a backbone that connects LANs to each other and LANs to WANs, the Internet, and telecommunications and cable networks. A majority of today's MANs are *Synchronous Optical Networks (SONET)* or FDDI rings provided by the telecommunications service providers. (FDDI technology was discussed earlier in the chapter.) These rings cover a large area, and businesses can connect to the rings via T1, fractional T1, and T3 lines. Figure 7-39 illustrates two companies connected via SONET ring and the devices that are usually necessary to make this type of communication possible. This is a simplified example of a MAN; in reality, several businesses are usually connected to one ring.

SONET is actually a standard for telecommunications transmissions over fiber-optic cables. Carriers and telephone companies have deployed SONET networks for North America, and if they follow the SONET standards properly, these various networks can communicate with little difficulty.

SONET is *self-healing,* meaning that if a break in the line occurs, it can use a backup redundant ring to ensure that transmission continues. All SONET lines and rings are fully redundant. The redundant line waits in the wings in case anything happens to the primary ring.

SONET networks can transmit voice, video, and data over optical networks. Slower-speed SONET networks often feed into larger, faster SONET networks, as shown in Figure 7-40. This enables businesses in different cities and regions to communicate.

**Figure 7-39** A MAN covers a large area and enables businesses to connect to each other, to the Internet, or to other WAN connections.

**Figure 7-40**  Smaller SONET rings connect to larger SONET rings to construct individual MANs.

## References

- **RFC 2615 – PPP over SONET/SDH**  www.faqs.org/rfcs/rfc2615.html
- **TechFest WAN links**  www.techfest.com/networking/wan.htm

# Wide Area Network

LAN technologies provide communication capabilities over a small geographic area, whereas *wide area network (WAN)* technologies are used when communication needs to travel over a larger geographical area. LAN technologies encompass how a computer puts its data onto a network cable, the rules and protocols of how that data is formatted and transmitted, how errors are handled, and how the destination computer picks up this data from the cable. When a computer on one network needs to communicate with a network on the other side of the country or in a different country altogether, WAN technologies kick in.

The network must have some avenue to other networks, which is most likely a router that communicates with the company's service provider's routers or telephone company facilities. Just as several types of technologies lie within the LAN arena, several technologies lie within the WAN arena. This section touches on many of these WAN technologies.

## LAN and WAN Protocols

Communication error rates are lower in LAN environments than in WAN environments, which makes sense when you compare the complexity of each environment. WAN traffic may have to travel hundreds or thousands of miles and pass through several different types of devices, cables, and protocols. Because of this difference, most LAN MAC protocols are connectionless and most WAN communication protocols are connection oriented. Connection-oriented protocols provide reliable transmission, because they have the capability of error detection and correction.

## Telecommunications Evolution

*On the eighth day, God created the telephone.*

Telephone systems have been around for about 100 years, and they started as copper-based analog systems. Central switching offices connected individual telephones manually (via human operators) at first, and later by using electronic switching equipment. After two telephones were connected, they had an end-to-end connection, or an end-to-end circuit. Multiple phone calls were divided up and placed on the same wire, which is called multiplexing. *Multiplexing* is a method of combining multiple channels of data over a single transmission path. The transmission is so fast and efficient that the ends do not realize that they are sharing a line with many other entities. They think they have the line all to themselves.

In the mid-1960s, digital phone systems emerged with T1 trunks, which carried 24 voice communication calls over two pairs of copper wires. This provided a 1.544-Mbps transmission rate, which brought quicker service but also the capability to put more multiplexed calls on one wire. When calls take place between switching offices, say local phone calls, they are multiplexed on T1 lines. When a longer-distance call needs to take place, the calls coming in on the T1 lines are multiplexed on T3 lines, which can carry up to 28 T1 lines. This is shown in Figure 7-41.

The next entity to join the telecommunications party was fiber optics, which enabled even more calls to be multiplexed on one trunk line over longer distances. Then came optical carrier technologies, SONET, which transmitted digitized voice signals in packets. SONET is a standard for telecommunications transmission over fiber-optic cables. This standard sets up the necessary parameters for transporting digital information over optical systems. Telecommunications carriers used this technology to multiplex lower-speed optical links into higher-speed links, similar to how lower-speed LANs connect to higher-speed WAN links today. Figure 7-42 shows an example of SONET rings connected together.

Figure 7-42 shows how telecommunications carriers can provide telephone and Internet access to companies and individuals in large areas. The SONET standard enables all carriers to interconnect.

The next evolutionary step in telecommunications history is Asynchronous Transfer Mode (ATM). ATM encapsulates data in fixed cells and can be used to deliver data over the SONET network. The analogy of a highway and cars is used to describe the SONET and ATM relationship. SONET is the highway that provides the foundation, or network, for the cars, ATM packets, to travel on.

**Figure 7-41** Local calls are multiplexed on T1 lines and longer-distance calls are moved from T1 lines to T3 multiplexed lines.

**Figure 7-42** SONET technology enables several optical communication loops to communicate.

ATM is a high-speed network technology that is used in LAN and WAN implementations by carriers, ISPs, and telephone companies. ATM uses a fixed cell size instead of the variable frame size used by earlier technologies. This fixed size provides better performance and a reduced overhead for error handling. (More information on ATM technology is provided in the "ATM" section a little later.)

Here is a quick snapshot of telecommunications history:

- Copper lines carry purely analog signals
- T1 lines carry up to 24 conversations
- T3 lines carry up to 28 T1 lines
- Fiber-optics and the SONET network used
- ATM over SONET used

SONET was developed in the United States to achieve a data rate around 50 Mbps to support the data flow from T1 lines (1.544 Mbps) and T3 lines (44.736 Mbps). Data travels over these T-carriers as electronic voltage to the edge of the SONET network. Then the voltage must be converted into light to run over the fiber-optic carrier lines, known as optical carrier (OC) lines. Each OC-1 frame runs at a signaling rate of 51.84 Mbps, with a throughput of 44.738 Mbps.

 **NOTE** Optical carry links can provide different bandwidth values: OC-1 = 51.84 Mbps, OC-3 = 155.52 Mbps, OC-12 = 622.08 Mbps, and so on.

The Europeans have a different infrastructure and chose to use Synchronous Digital Hierarchy (SDH), which supports E1 lines (2.048 Mbps) and E3 lines (34.368 Mbps). SONET is a standard for North America and SDH is a standard for the rest of the world. SDH and SONET are similar but just different enough to be incompatible. For communication to take place between SDH and SONET lines, a gateway needs to do the proper signaling translation.

You've had only a quick glimpse at an amazing, complex giant referred to as *telecommunications.* Many more technologies are being developed and implemented to increase the amount of data that can be efficiently delivered in a short period of time.

## Dedicated Links

A *dedicated link* is also called a *leased line* or *point-to-point* link. It is one single link that is pre-established for the purposes of WAN communications between two destinations. It is *dedicated,* meaning that only the destination points can communicate with each other. This link is not shared by any other entities at any time. This was the main way companies communicated in the past, because not as many choices were available as there are today. Establishing a dedicated link is a good idea for two locations that will communicate often and require fast transmission and a specific bandwidth, but it is expensive compared to other possible technologies that enable several companies to share the same bandwidth and also share the cost. This does not mean that dedicated lines are not in use; they definitely are used, but many other options are now available, including X.25, frame relay, and ATM technologies.

## T-Carriers

*T-carriers* are dedicated lines that can carry voice and data information over trunk lines. They were developed by AT&T and were initially implemented in the early 1960s to support pulse-code modulation (PCM) voice transmission. This was first used to digitize the voice over a dedicated, two-point, high-capacity connection line. The most commonly used T-carriers are T1 lines that provide up to 1.544 Mbps and T3 lines that provide up to 45 Mbps, as mentioned earlier. Both are digital circuits that multiplex several individual channels into a higher-speed channel.

These lines perform multiplex functionality through time-division multiplexing (TDM). What does this multiplexing stuff really mean? Consider a T1 line, which can multiplex up to 24 channels. If a company has a PBX connected to a T1 line, which in turn connects to the telephone company switching office, 24 calls can be chopped up and placed on the T1 line and transferred to the switching office. If this company did not use a T1 line, it would have to have 24 individual twisted pairs of wire to handle this many calls.

As shown in Figure 7-43, data is inputted into these 24 channels and transmitted. Each channel gets to insert up to 8 bits into its established time slot. Twenty-four of these 8-bit time slots make up a T1 frame. That does not sound like much information, but 8000 frames are built per second. Because this happens so quickly, the receiving end does not notice a delay and does not know that it is sharing its connection and bandwidth with up to 23 other devices.

Originally, T1 and T3 lines were used by the carrier companies, but they have been replaced mainly with optical lines. Now T1 and T3 lines feed data into these powerful and super-fast optical lines. The T1 and T3 lines are leased to companies and ISPs that need high-capacity transmission capability. Sometimes, T1 channels are split up between companies who do not really need the full bandwidth of 1.544 Mbps. These are called *fractional* T lines. The different carrier lines and their corresponding characteristics are listed in Table 7-10.

As mentioned earlier, dedicated lines have their drawbacks. They are expensive and inflexible. If a company moves to another location, a T1 line cannot easily follow it. A dedicated line is expensive because companies have to pay for a dedicated connection with a lot of bandwidth even when they do not use the bandwidth. Not many companies require this level of bandwidth 24 hours a day. Instead, they may have data to send out here and there, but not continuously.

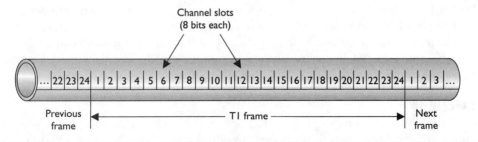

**Figure 7-43** Multiplexing puts several phone calls, or data transmissions, on the same wire.

| Carrier | # of T1s | # Voice Channels | Speed (Mbps) |
|---------|----------|------------------|--------------|
| Fractional | 1/24 | 1 | .064 |
| T1 | 1 | 24 | 1.544 |
| T2 | 4 | 96 | 6.312 |
| T3 | 28 | 672 | 44.736 |
| T4 | 168 | 4032 | 274.760 |

**Table 7-10** T1 Hierarchy Summary Chart

The cost of a dedicated line is determined by the distance to the destination. A T1 line run from one building to another building 2 miles away is much cheaper than a T1 line that covers 50 miles or a full state.

### Reference

- "All You Wanted to Know About T1 But Were Afraid to Ask," by Bob Wachtel, Data Comm for Business, Inc.   www.dcbnet.com/notes/9611t1.html

## WAN Technologies

*I can't throw my packets that far! Response: We have technology for that.*

WAN technologies, as I am sure you have guessed, are used to enable networks to communicate over long distances. Several varieties of WAN technologies are available to companies today. The information that a company evaluates to decide which is the most appropriate WAN technology for it usually includes functionality, bandwidth demands, service level agreements, required equipment, cost, and what is available from service providers. The following sections go over some of the WAN technologies available today.

## CSU/DSU

A *Channel Service Unit/Data Service Unit (CSU/DSU)* is required when digital equipment will be used to connect a LAN to a WAN. This connection can take place with T1 and T3 lines, as shown in Figure 7-44. A CSU/DSU is necessary because the signals and frames can vary between the LAN equipment and the WAN equipment used by service providers.

The DSU device converts digital signals from routers, bridges, and multiplexers into signals that can be transmitted over the telephone company's digital lines. The DSU device ensures that the voltage levels are correct and that information is not lost during the conversion. The CSU connects the network directly to the telephone company's line. The CSU/DSU is not always a separate device and can be part of a networking device.

The CSU/DSU provides a digital interface for Data Terminal Equipment (DTE), such as terminals, multiplexers, or routers, and an interface to the Data Circuit-Terminating Equipment (DCE) device, such as a carrier's switch. The CSU/DSU basically works as a translator and, at times, as a line conditioner.

## Switching

Dedicated links have one single path to traverse; thus, there is no complexity when it comes to determining how to get packets to different destinations. Only two points of reference are needed when a packet leaves one network and heads toward the other. It

**Figure 7-44** A CSU/DSU is required for digital equipment to be able to communicate with telecommunications lines.

gets much more complicated when thousands of networks are connected to each other, which is often when switching comes in to play.

Two main types of switching can be used: circuit switching and packet switching. *Circuit switching* sets up a virtual connection that acts like a dedicated link between two systems. ISDN and telephone calls are examples of circuit switching, which is shown in the lower half of Figure 7-45.

When the source system makes a connection with the destination system, they set up a communication channel. If the two systems are local to each other, fewer devices need to be involved with setting up this channel. The farther the two systems are from each other, the more the devices are required to be involved with setting up the channel and connecting the two systems.

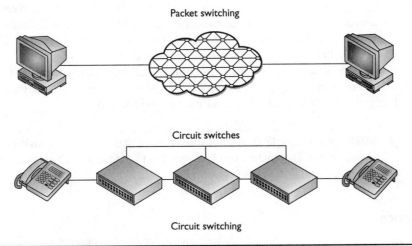

**Figure 7-45** Circuit switching provides one road for a communication path, whereas packet switching provides many different possible roads.

An example of how a circuit-switching system works is daily telephone use. When one person calls another, the same type of dedicated virtual communication link is set up. Once the connection is made, the devices supporting that communication channel do not dynamically move the call through different devices, which is what takes place in a packet-switching environment. The channel remains configured at the original devices until the call, or connection, is done and torn down.

*Packet switching*, on the other hand, does not set up a dedicated virtual link, and packets from one connection can pass through a number of different individual devices (see the top of Figure 7-45), instead of all of them following one another through the same devices. Some examples of packet-switching technologies are the Internet, X.25, and frame relay. The infrastructure that supports these methods is made up of routers and switches of different types. They provide multiple paths to the same destinations, which provides a high degree of redundancy.

In a packet-switching network, the data is broken up into packets containing frame check sequence numbers. These packets go through different devices, and their paths can be dynamically altered by a router or switch that determines a better route for a specific packet to take. Once the packets are received at the destination computer, all the packets are reassembled, according to their frame check sequence numbers, and interpreted.

**NOTE** Packet switching is based on statistical time-division multiplexing (STDM), which analyzes statistics on the various possible routes to make the decision on the best route for a packet.

Because the path that a packet will take on a packet-switching environment is not set in stone, there could be variable delays when compared to a circuit-switching technology. This is okay, because packet-switching networks usually carry data rather than voice. Because voice connections clearly detect these types of delays, in many situations a circuit-switching network is more appropriate for voice connections. Voice calls usually provide a steady stream of information, whereas a data connection is "burstier" in nature. When you talk on the phone, the conversation keeps a certain rhythm. You and your friend do not talk extremely fast and then take a few minutes in between conversations to stop talking and create a void with complete silence. However, this is usually how a data connection works. A lot of data is sent from one end to the other at one time, and then dead time occurs until it is time to send more data.

**NOTE** Voice over IP (VoIP) does move voice data over packet-switched environments. This technology is covered in the section "Multiservice Access Technologies," later in the chapter.

## Reference

- "Packet Switching Simulation," by Gilbert Ohana and Ohad Parush, RAD Data Communications   www.rad.com/networks/1998/packet/ps.htm

## Circuit Switching vs. Packet Switching

The following points provide a concise summary of the differences between circuit and packet switching technologies.

**Circuit switching:**

- Connection-oriented virtual links
- Traffic travels in a predictable and constant manner
- Fixed delays
- Usually carries voice-oriented data

**Packet switching:**

- Packets can use many different dynamic paths to get to the same destination
- Traffic is usually bursty in nature
- Variable delays
- Usually carries data-oriented data

## Frame Relay

*Why are there so many paths to choose from?*

For a long time, many companies used dedicated links to communicate with other companies. Company A had a pipeline to company B that provided a certain bandwidth 24 hours a day and was not used by any other entities. This was great because only the two companies could use the line, so a certain level of bandwidth was always available, but it was expensive and most companies did not use the full bandwidth each and every hour that this link was available. Thus, the companies spent a lot of money for a service that they did not use all the time. Today, instead of using dedicated lines, companies are turning to frame relay.

*Frame relay* is a WAN protocol that operates at the data link layer. It is a WAN solution that uses packet-switching technology that enables multiple companies and networks to share the same WAN media. Whereas direct point-to-point links have a cost based on the distance between the endpoints, the frame relay cost is based on the amount of bandwidth used. Because several companies and networks use the same media and devices (routers and switches), the cost can be greatly reduced per company compared to dedicated links.

If a company knows that it will usually require *x* amount of bandwidth each day, it can pay a certain fee to make sure that this amount of bandwidth is always available to it. If another company knows that it will not have a high bandwidth requirement, it can pay a lower fee that does not guarantee the higher bandwidth allocation. This second company will have the higher bandwidth available to it anyway—at least until that link gets busy, and then the bandwidth level will decrease. (Companies that pay more to ensure that a higher level of bandwidth will always be available pay a *committed information rate*, or *CIR*.)

Two main types of equipment are used in frame relay connections: Data Terminal Equipment (DTE) and Data Circuit-Terminating Equipment (DCE). The DTE is usually a customer-owned device, such as a router or switch, that provides connectivity between the company's own network and the frame relay network. DCE is the service provider's, or telecommunications company's, device that does the actual data transmission and switching in the frame relay cloud. So the DTE is a company's ramp onto the frame relay network, and the DCE devices actually do the work within the frame relay cloud.

The frame relay cloud is the collection of DCEs that provides switching and data communications functionality. Several service providers provide this type of service, and some providers use other providers' equipment—it can all get confusing because a packet can take so many different routes. This collection is called a *cloud* to differentiate it from other types of networks, and because when a packet hits this cloud, users do not usually know the route that their frames will take. The frames will be sent either through permanent or switched virtual circuits that are defined within the DCE or through carrier switches.

Frame relay is an any-to-any service that is shared by many users. As stated earlier, this is beneficial because the costs are much lower than those of dedicated leased lines. Because frame relay is shared, if one subscriber is not using its bandwidth, it is available for others to use. On the other hand, when traffic levels increase, the available bandwidth decreases. This is why subscribers who want to ensure that a certain bandwidth is always available to them pay a higher committed rate.

Figure 7-46 shows five sites being connected via dedicated lines versus five sites connected through the frame relay cloud. The first solution requires many dedicated lines that are expensive and not flexible. The second solution is cheaper and provides companies much more flexibility.

**Virtual Circuits** Frame relay (and X.25) forwards frames across virtual circuits. These circuits can be either permanent, meaning that they are programmed in advance,

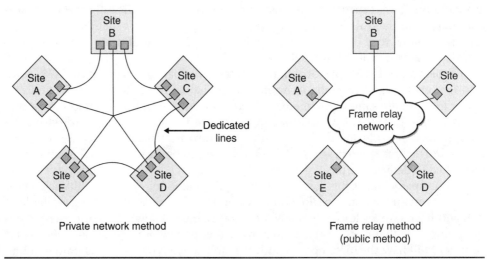

**Figure 7-46** A private network connection requires several expensive dedicated links. Frame relay enables users to share a public network.

or switched, meaning that the circuit is quickly built when it is needed and torn down when it is no longer needed. The *permanent virtual circuit (PVC)* works like a private line for a customer with an agreed-upon bandwidth availability. When a customer decides to pay for the committed rate, a PVC is programmed for that customer to ensure that it will always receive a certain amount of bandwidth.

Unlike PVCs, *switched virtual circuits (SVCs)* require steps similar to a dial-up and connection procedure. The difference is that a permanent path is set up for PVC frames, whereas when SVCs are used, a circuit needs to be built. It is similar to setting up a phone call over the public network. During the setup procedure, the required bandwidth is requested, the destination computer is contacted and must accept the call, a path is determined, and forwarding information is programmed into each switch along the SVC's path. SVCs are used for teleconferencing, establishing temporary connections to remote sites, data replication, and voice calls. Once the connection is no longer needed, the circuit is torn down and the switches forget that it ever existed.

Although a PVC provides a guaranteed level of bandwidth, it does not have the flexibility of an SVC. If a customer wants to use her PVC for a temporary connection, as mentioned earlier, the customer must call the carrier and have it set up, which can take hours.

## References

- **Frame Relay Forum**  www.mplsforum.org
- **Alliance Datacom Frame Relay Resource Center**  www.alliancedatacom.com/framerelay.asp

## X.25

*X.25* is an older WAN protocol that defines how devices and networks establish and maintain connections. Like frame relay, X.25 is a switching technology that uses carrier switches to provide connectivity for many different networks. It also provides an any-to-any connection, meaning that many users use the same service simultaneously. Subscribers are charged based on the amount of bandwidth they use, unlike dedicated links, for which a flat fee is charged.

Data is divided into 128 bytes and encapsulated in High-level Data Link Control (HDLC) frames. The frames are then addressed and forwarded across the carrier switches. Much of this sounds the same as frame relay—and it is, but frame relay is much more advanced and efficient when compared to X.25, because the X.25 protocol was developed and released in the 1970s. During this time, many of the devices that were connected to networks were dumb terminals and mainframes, the networks did not have built-in functionality and fault tolerance, and the Internet overall was not as foundationally stable and resistant to errors as it is today. When these characteristics were not part of the Internet, X.25 was required to compensate for these deficiencies and to provide many layers of error checking, error correcting, and fault tolerance. This made the protocol fat, which was required back then; but today it slows down data transmission and provides a lower performance rate than frame relay or ATM.

## ATM

*Asynchronous Transfer Mode (ATM)* is another switching technology, but instead of being a packet-switching method, it uses a cell-switching method. ATM is a high-speed networking technology used for LAN, MAN, WAN, and service provider connections. Like frame relay, it is a connection-oriented switching technology; it creates and uses a fixed channel. IP is an example of a connectionless technology. Within the TCP/IP protocol suite, IP is connectionless and TCP is connection oriented. This means that IP segments can be quickly and easily routed and switched without each router or switch in between having to worry about whether the data actually made it to its destination; that is TCP's job. TCP works at the source and destination ends to ensure that data was properly transmitted, and it resends data that ran into some type of problem and did not get delivered properly. When using ATM or frame relay, the devices in between the source and destination have to be more conscious of data and whether it gets to where it needs to go, unlike when a purely connectionless protocol is being used.

ATM is a cell-switching technology rather than a packet-switching technology. Data is segmented into fixed-size cells of 53 bytes, instead of variable-size packets. This provides for more efficient and faster use of the communication paths. ATM sets up virtual circuits, which act like dedicated paths between the source and destination. These virtual circuits can guarantee bandwidth and QoS. For these reasons, ATM is a good carrier for voice and video transmission.

ATM technology is used by carriers and service providers and makes up part of the core technology of the Internet, but ATM technology can also be used for a company's private use in backbones and connections to the service provider's networks.

Traditionally, companies used dedicated lines, usually T-carrier lines, to connect to the public networks. However, companies have also moved to implementing an ATM switch on their network, which connects them to the carrier infrastructure. Because the fee is based on bandwidth used instead of a continual connection, it can be much cheaper. Some companies have replaced their Fast Ethernet and FDDI backbones with ATM. When ATMs are used as private backbones, the companies have ATM switches that take the Ethernet, or whatever data link technology is being used, and frame them into the 53-byte ATM cells.

### Quality of Service

*Quality of Service (QoS)* is a capability that allows a protocol to distinguish between different classes of messages and assign priority levels. Some applications, such as video conferencing, are time sensitive, meaning that delays would cause unacceptable performance of the application. A technology that provides QoS allows an administrator to assign a priority level to time-sensitive traffic. The protocol then ensures that this type of traffic has a specific or minimum rate of delivery.

QoS allows a service provider to guarantee a level of service to its customers. QoS began with ATM and then was integrated into other technologies and protocols that are responsible for moving data from one place to another. There are four different types of ATM QoS services, listed next, that are available to customers. Each service maps to a specific type of data that will be transmitted.

- **Constant Bit Rate (CBR)**   Connection-oriented channel that provides a consistent data throughput for time-sensitive applications, such as voice and video applications. Customers specify the necessary bandwidth requirement at connection setup.

- **Variable Bit Rate (VBR)**   Connection-oriented channel that is best used for delay-insensitive applications because the data throughput flow is uneven. Customers specify their required peak and sustained rate of data throughput.

- **Unspecified Bit Rate (UBR)**   Connectionless channel that does not promise a specific data throughput rate. Customers cannot and do not need to control their traffic rate.

- **Available Bit Rate (ABR)**   Connection-oriented channel that allows for the bit rate to be adjusted. Customers are given the bandwidth that remains after a guaranteed service rate has been met.

ATM supports various interfaces to provide this type of flexibility and use. A DSU device is used to connect a LAN to the public ATM network. This architecture is used when a company's network is connected to the ATM network via a router or bridge. The DSU device is necessary to make sure that the digital signals are converted to a signal type the ATM network can understand.

ATM sets up a fixed channel for all data to transfer through during a transmission. The fixed channels are preprogrammed into the switches along that particular communication path.

ATM was the first protocol to provide true QoS, but as the computing society has increased its desire to send time-sensitive data throughout many types of networks, developers have integrated QoS into other technologies.

There are three basic levels of QoS:

- **Best-effort service**   No guarantee of throughput, delay, or delivery. Traffic that has priority classifications goes before traffic that has been assigned this classification. Most of the traffic that travels on the Internet has this classification.

- **Differentiated service**   Compared to best-effort service, traffic that is assigned this classification has more bandwidth, shorter delays, and fewer dropped frames.

- **Guaranteed service**   Ensures specific data throughput at guaranteed speed. Time-sensitive traffic (voice and video) is assigned this classification.

Administrators can set the classification priorities (or use a policy manager product) for the different traffic types, which the protocols and devices will then carry out.

## Reference

- **The ATM Forum**   www.atmforum.com

## SMDS

*Switched Multimegabit Data Service (SMDS)* is a high-speed packet-switched technology used to enable customers to extend their LANs across MANs and WANs. When a company has an office in one state that needs to communicate with an office in a different state, for example, the two LANs can use this packet-switching protocol to communicate across the already established public network. This protocol is connectionless and can provide bandwidth on demand.

Although some companies still use this technology, it has been greatly replaced with frame relay. Service providers usually maintain only the networks that currently use this technology instead of offering it to new customers.

## SDLC

*Synchronous Data Link Control (SDLC)* protocol is based on networks that use dedicated, leased lines with permanent physical connections. It is used mainly for communications with IBM hosts within a Systems Network Architecture (SNA). Developed by IBM in the 1970s, SDLC is a bit-oriented, synchronous protocol that has evolved into other communication protocols such as HDLC, Link Access Procedure (LAP), and Link Access Procedure-Balanced (LAPB).

SDLC was developed to enable mainframes to communicate with remote locations. The environments that use SDLC usually have primary systems that control secondary stations' communication. SDLC provides the polling media access technology, which is the mechanism that enables secondary stations to communicate on the network. Figure 7-47 shows the primary and secondary stations on an SDLC network.

## HDLC

*High-level Data Link Control (HDLC)* protocol is also a bit-oriented link layer protocol used for transmission over synchronous lines. HDLC is an extension of SDLC, which is mainly used in SNA environments. HDLC provides high throughput, because it supports full-duplex transmissions, and is used in point-to-point and multipoint connections.

Like SDLC, HDLC works with primary stations that contact secondary stations to establish data transmission. Vendors have developed their own parameters within their versions of HDLC, which has resulted in interoperability issues between vendors' HDLC implementations.

**Figure 7-47** SDLC is used mainly in mainframe environments within an SNA network.

## HSSI

*High-Speed Serial Interface (HSSI)* is an interface used to connect multiplexers and routers to high-speed communications services such as ATM and frame relay. It supports speeds up to 52 Mbps, as in T3 WAN connections, which are usually integrated with router and multiplex devices to provide serial interfaces to the WAN.

These interfaces define the electrical and physical interfaces to be used by DTE/DCE devices; thus, HSSI works at the physical layer. The interface was developed by Cisco and T3plus Networking.

## References

- *Internetworking Technology Handbook*, Chapter 12, "High-Speed Serial Interface," Cisco Systems, Inc.   www.cisco.com/univercd/cc/td/doc/cisintwk/ito_doc/hssi.htm

- "High-Speed Serial Interface (HSSI) Design Specification," by John T. Chapman (Cisco Systems, Inc.) and Mitri Halabi (T3plus Networking, Inc.)   http://cio.cisco.com/warp/public/459/8.html

## Multiservice Access Technologies

*Voice in a packet. What will they think of next?*

*Multiservice access technologies* combine several types of communication categories (data, voice, and video) over one transmission line. This provides for higher performance, reduced operational costs, and greater flexibility, integration, and control for the customers. The regular phone system is based on a circuit-switched, voice-centric network, referred to as the *public-switched telephone network (PSTN)*. The PSTN uses circuit switching instead of packet switching. When a phone call is made, the call is placed at the PSTN interface, which is the user's telephone. This PSTN is connected to the telephone company's local loop via copper wiring. Once the signals for this phone call reach the telephone company's central office (the end of the local loop), they are part of the telephone company's circuit-switching world. A connection is made between the source and the destination, and as long as the call is in session, the data flows through the same switches.

When a phone call is made, the connection has to be set up, signaling has to be controlled, and the session has to be torn down. This takes place through the Signaling System 7 protocol. When *Voice over IP (VoIP)* is used, its protocols must be properly transmitted so that the devices involved can understand this different signaling scheme.

The PSTN is being replaced by data-centric, packet-oriented networks that can support voice, data, and video. The new VoIP networks use different switches, protocols, and communication links. This means that VoIP has to go through a tricky transition stage that enables the old systems and infrastructures to communicate with the new systems until the old systems are dead and gone.

High-quality compression is used with VoIP technology, and the identification numbers (phone numbers) are IP addresses. This technology gets around some of the barriers that are present in the PSTN today. The interface devices (telephones) have embedded functions and logic that make it more difficult to implement different types of services that the network as a whole can support. In VoIP, the interface to the network can be a computer, server, PBX, or anything else that runs a telephone application. This provides more flexibility when it comes to adding new services and provides a lot more control and intelligence to the interfacing devices.

Because this is a packet-oriented switching technology, latency delays are possible. This manifests as longer delays within a conversation and a slight loss of synchronicity in the conversation. When someone using VoIP for a phone call experiences these types of lags in the conversation, it means that the packets holding the other person's voice message got queued somewhere within the network and are on their way. This is referred to as *jittering,* but protocols are being developed to help smooth out these issues and provide a more continuous telephone call experience.

 **NOTE** Applications that are time sensitive, such as voice and video signals, need to work over an isochronous network. This means that all of the components in the network that are responsible for providing the necessary uniform timing work with a common clock and are properly synchronized.

Four main components are needed for VoIP: IP telephony device, call-processing manager, voicemail system, and voice gateway. The *IP telephony device* is just a phone that has the necessary software that allows it to work as a network device. Traditional phone systems require a "smart network" and a "dumb phone." In VoIP, the phone must be "smart" by having the necessary software to take analog signals, digitize them, break them into packets, and create the necessary headers and trailers for the packets to find their destination. The *voicemail system* is a storage place for messages and provides user directory lookups and call-forwarding functionality. A *voice gateway* carries out packet routing and provides access to legacy voice systems and backup calling processes.

When a user makes a call, his "smart phone" sends a message to the *call-processing manager* to indicate that a call needs to be set up. When the person at the destination takes her phone off of the hook, this notifies the call-processing manager that the call has been accepted. The call-processing manager notifies both the sending and receiving phones that the channel is active, and voice data is sent back and forth over a traditional data network line.

Moving voice data through packets is more involved than moving regular data through packets. This is because data is usually sent in bursts, in which voice data is sent as a constant stream. A delay in data transmission is not noticed as much as is a delay in voice transmission. The VoIP technology, and its supporting protocols, has advanced to provide voice data transmission with improved bandwidth, variability in delay, round-trip delay, and packet loss issues.

Using VoIP means a company has to pay for and maintain only one network, instead of one network dedicated to data transmission and another network dedicated to voice transmission. This saves money and administration overhead, but there are security issues that need to be understood and dealt with.

Hackers can intercept incoming and outgoing calls, carry out DoS attacks, spoof phone calls, and eavesdrop on sensitive conversations. Many of the countermeasures to these types of attacks are the same types of countermeasures that are used on traditional data-oriented networks:

- Keep patches updated on each network device involved with VoIP transmissions
  - Call manager server
  - Voicemail server
  - Gateway server
- Identify unidentified or rogue telephony devices
- Implement authentication so that only authorized telephony devices are working on the network
- Install and maintain:
  - Stateful firewalls
  - VPN for sensitive voice data
  - Intrusion detection
- Filter unnecessary ports on routers, switches, PCs, and IP telephones

---

 **NOTE**   Voice data can travel over IP, frame relay, and ATM transmission protocols.

---

**H.323 Gateways**   The ITU-T recommendations cover a wide variety of multimedia communication services. H.323 is part of this family of recommendations, but it is also a standard that deals with video, real-time audio, and data packet–based transmissions where multiple users can be involved with the data exchange. An H.323 environment features terminals, which can be telephones or computers with telephony software, gateways that connect this environment to the PSTN, multipoint control units, and gatekeepers that manage calls and functionality.

Like any type of gateway, H.323 gateways connect different types of systems and devices and provide the necessary translation functionality. The H.323 terminals are connected to these gateways, which in turn can be connected to the PSTN. These gateways translate protocols used on the circuit-based telephone network and the packet-based VoIP network. The gateways also translate the circuits into packets and packets into circuits as required.

Today it is necessary also to implement the gateways that enable the new technology to communicate with the old, but soon the old PSTN may be a thing of the past and all communication may take place over packets instead of circuits.

The newer technology looks to provide transmission mechanisms that will involve much more than just voice. Although we have focused mainly on VoIP, other technologies support the combination of voice and data over the same network, such as Voice over ATM (VoATM) and Voice over Frame Relay (VoFR). ATM and frame relay are connection-oriented protocols and IP is connectionless. This means that frame relay and ATM provide better QoS and less jittering and latency.

The best of both worlds is to combine IP over ATM or frame relay. This allows for packet-oriented communication over a connection-oriented network that will provide an end-to-end connection. IP is at the network layer and is media independent—it can run over a variety of data link layer protocols and technologies.

Traditionally, a company has on its premises a PBX, which is a switch between the company and the PSTN, and T1 or T3 lines connect the PBX to the telephone company's central office, which houses switches that act as ramps onto the PSTN. When WAN technologies are used instead of accessing the PSTN through the central office switches, the data is transmitted over the frame relay, or ATM, cloud. An example of this configuration is shown in Figure 7-48.

Because frame relay and ATM utilize PVCs and SVCs, they both have the ability to use SVCs for telephone calls. Remember that a CIR is used when a company wants to ensure that it will always have a certain bandwidth available. When a company pays for this guaranteed bandwidth, it is paying for a PVC for which the switches and routers are programmed to control its connection and for that connection to be maintained. SVCs, on the other hand, are set up on demand and are temporary in nature. They are perfect for making telephone calls or transmitting video during videoconferencing.

## WAN Technology Summary

We have covered several WAN technologies in the previous sections. Table 7-11 provides a snapshot of the important characteristics for each.

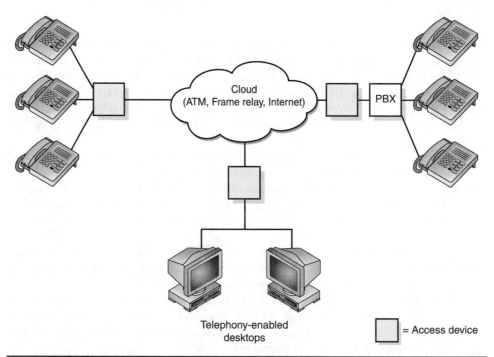

**Figure 7-48** Regular telephone calls connect phones to the PSTN. Voice over WAN technologies connect calls to the Internet cloud.

| WAN Technology | Characteristics |
|---|---|
| Dedicated line | • Dedicated, leased line that connects two locations<br>• Expensive compared to other WAN options<br>• Secure because only two locations are using the same media |
| Frame relay | • High-performance WAN protocol that uses packet-switching technology, which works over public networks<br>• Shared media among companies<br>• Uses SVCs and PVCs<br>• Fee based on bandwidth used |
| X.25 | • First packet-switching technology developed to work over public networks<br>• Shared media among companies<br>• Lower speed than frame relay because of its extra overhead<br>• International standard and used more in countries other than the U.S.<br>• Uses SVCs and PVCs |
| SMDS | • High-speed switching technology used over public network |
| ATM | • High-bandwidth switching and multiplexing technology that has a low delay<br>• Uses 53-byte fixed-size cells<br>• Very fast because of the low overhead |
| SDLC | • Enables mainframes to communicate with remote offices<br>• Provides polling mechanism to allow primary and secondary stations to communicate |
| HDLC | • New and improved SDLC protocol<br>• A data encapsulation method for synchronous serial links<br>• Point-to-point and multipoint communication |
| HSSI | • DTE/DCE interface to enable high-speed communication over WAN links |
| VoIP | • Combines voice and data over the same IP network media and protocol<br>• Reduces costs of implementing and maintaining two different networks |

**Table 7-11**  Characteristics of WAN Technologies

## References

- *Voice over IP Quick Start Guide,* Cisco Systems, Inc.   www.cisco.com/univercd/cc/td/doc/product/access/acs_mod/cis3600/voice/4936vqsg.htm
- **IETF IP Telephony Charter**   www.ietf.org/html.charters/iptel-charter.html
- **Frame Relay Forum**   www.mplsforum.org
- **The ATM Forum**   www.atmforum.com/aboutatm/2.html
- *Voice Telephony over Asynchronous Transfer Mode (VToA),* International Engineering Consortium   www.iec.org/online/tutorials/vtoa/

# Remote Access

*I need to talk to you, but I am way over here!*

Remote access covers several technologies that enable remote and home users to connect to networks that will grant them access to network resources that help them to perform their tasks. Most of the time, these users must first gain access to the Internet through an ISP, which sets up a connection to the destination network.

For many corporations, remote access is a necessity because it enables users to obtain up-to-date information, it reduces networking costs by using the Internet as the access media instead of expensive dedicated lines, and it extends the workplace for employees to their homes or on the road. Remote access can streamline access to resources and information through Internet connections and provides a competitive advantage by letting partners, suppliers, and customers have closely controlled links. The most common types of remote connectivity methods used are VPNs, dial-up connections, ISDN, cable modems, and DSL connections.

## Dial-Up and RAS

Remote access is usually gained by connecting to a network access server (NAS), which acts as a gateway and can be an endpoint to a PPP session. The NAS provides authentication and authorization.

Users dial into a *Remote Access Service (RAS)* server, which performs authentication by comparing the provided credentials with the database of credentials it maintains. A type of access authentication technology used in remote-connection situations is RADIUS, which is covered in Chapter 4. An administrator can set several configurations to dictate what actions take place when a remote user attempts to connect to the NAS. Usually a request for a username and password takes place, and the NAS may hang up the call to call the user back at a predefined phone number. This security activity is used to try to ensure that only authenticated users are given access to the network, and it reverses the long-distance charges back to the company. Even if an attacker finds out the logon credentials necessary to gain remote access, it is unlikely that the attacker will also be at the predefined phone number. However, this security measure can be compromised if someone implements call forwarding.

When attackers are trying to find an entry point into a network, they often target remote access methods. They realize that many companies who have a stack of modems (or other types of access points) to provide remote access to their network are under the false impression that their firewall that monitors Internet traffic somehow magically protects all access to their network. If such a company has not implemented any (or strong) access control over the RAS, attackers can easily walk into its network without ever having to bother with the firewall.

*Wardialing* is used by many attackers to identify remote access modems. Specially written program tools can be used to dial a large bank of phone numbers that is fed to them. The tools log valid data connections (modems used for data transmission) and attempt to identify the system on the other end of the phone line. Some of these tools have the option of performing a dictionary attack, which attempts many possible username and password combinations in the hopes of being authorized and allowed access to the network. Wardialing enables an attacker to find all the modems that provide remote access into a network. Once she finds a modem, she attempts to access the network through this entry point. If unprotected modems are used within an infrastructure, they are usually much easier to compromise than a firewall.

Companies often have modems hanging off of workstations here or there without much ado. Employees may install them or the IT staff may install them and then forget about them. Thus, it is important for companies to perform wardialing on their own network to make sure that no unaccounted for modems are attached. Some corporate PBX phone systems have the capability to detect modem signals on analog phone lines and audit/record their usage. This feature can be implemented to support the appropriate security policy of "no unauthorized devices are to be attached to the data and telephone network."

When you are looking at the security angle of remote access, the three most important rules to enforce are the following:

- All users on the remote access equipment must be fully authenticated to proceed with its use.

- No covert or inappropriate access to the communication circuits is allowed.

- After authentication, users shall have access to those authorized services to which they are entitled, and no more.

## ISDN

*Integrated Services Digital Network (ISDN)* is a communications protocol provided by telephone companies and ISPs. This protocol and the necessary equipment enable data, voice, and other types of traffic to travel over a medium in a digital manner that was previously used only for analog voice transmission. Telephone companies went all digital many years ago, except for the local loops, which consist of the copper wires that connect houses and businesses to their carrier provider's central offices. These central offices contain the telephone company's switching equipment, and it is here that the analog-to-digital transformation takes place. However, the local loop is always analog, and is therefore slower. ISDN was developed to replace the aging telephone analog systems, but it has yet to catch on to the level that was expected.

ISDN uses the same wires and transmission media used by analog dial-up technologies, but it works in a digital fashion. If a computer uses a modem to communicate with an ISP, the modem converts the data from digital to analog to be transmitted over the phone line. If that same computer were configured and had the necessary equipment to utilize ISDN, it would not need to convert the data from digital to analog, but would keep it in a digital form. This, of course, means that the receiving end would also require the necessary equipment to receive and interpret this type of communication properly. Communicating in a purely digital form provides higher bit rates that can be sent more economically.

ISDN is a set of telecommunications services that can be used over public and private telecommunications networks. It provides a digital point-to-point circuit-switched medium and establishes a circuit between the two communicating devices. An ISDN connection can be used for anything that a modem can be used for, but it provides more functionality and higher bandwidth. This switched digital service can provide bandwidth on an as-needed basis and can be used for LAN-to-LAN on-demand connectivity, instead of using an expensive dedicated link.

As stated earlier, analog uses a full channel for communication, but ISDN can break up this channel into multiple channels to provide full-duplex communication and a higher level of control and error handling. ISDN provides two basic home and business services: Basic Rate Interface (BRI) and Primary Rate Interface (PRI). BRI has two B channels that enable data to be transferred and one D channel that provides for call setup, connection management, error control, caller ID, and more. The bandwidth available with BRI is 144 Kbps, whereas the top modems can provide only 56 Kbps.

The D channel provides for a quicker call setup and process of making a connection. An ISDN connection may require a setup connection time of only 2 to 5 seconds, whereas a modem may require a timeframe of 45 to 90 seconds. This D channel is an out-of-band communication link between the local loop equipment and the user's terminal. It is out of band because the control data is not mixed in with the user communication data. This makes it more difficult for a would-be defrauder to send bogus instructions back to the service provider's equipment in the hopes of causing a DoS, obtaining services not paid for, or conducting some other type of destructive behavior.

The BRI service is common for residential use and the PRI, which has 23 B channels and one D channel, is more commonly used in corporations. ISDN is not usually the primary telecommunications connection for companies, but it can be used as a backup in case the primary connection goes down. A company can also choose to implement dial-on-demand routing (DDR), which can work over ISDN. DDR allows a company to send WAN data over its existing telephone lines and use the public circuit-switched network as a temporary type of WAN link. It is usually implemented by companies that send out only a small amount of WAN traffic and is a much cheaper solution than a real WAN implementation. The connection activates when it is needed and then idles out.

## ISDN Examined

ISDN breaks the telephone line into different channels and transmits data in a digital form rather than the old analog form. Three ISDN implementations are in use:

- **BRI ISDN**   This implementation operates over existing copper lines at the local loop and provides digital voice and data channels. It uses two B channels and one D channel with a combined bandwidth of 144 Kbps and is used usually for home subscribers.

- **PRI ISDN**   This implementation has up to 23 B channels and 1 D channel, at 64 Kbps per channel. The total bandwidth is equivalent to a T1, which is 1.544 Mbps. This would be more suitable for a company that requires a higher amount of bandwidth.

- **Broadband ISDN (BISDN)**   This implementation can handle many different types of services at the same time and is mainly used within telecommunications carrier backbones. When BISDN is used within a backbone, ATM is used to encapsulate data at the data link layer into cells, which travel over a SONET network.

DDR is also implemented as a backup in case the primary WAN link goes down. It provides redundancy and ensures that a company will still be able to communicate if something happens to the primary WAN communication channel.

## DSL

*Digital Subscriber Line (DSL)* is another type of high-speed connection technology used to connect a home or business to the service provider's central office. It can provide 6 to 30 times higher bandwidth speeds than ISDN and analog technologies. It uses existing phone lines and provides a 24-hour connection to the Internet. This does indeed sound better than sliced bread, but only certain people can get this service because you have to be within a 2.5-mile radius of the DSL service provider's equipment. As the distance between a residence and the central office increases, the transmission rates for DSL decrease.

DSL is a broadband technology that can provide up to 52-Mbps transmission speed without replacing the carrier's copper wire. The end user and the carrier's equipment do need to be upgraded for DSL, though, and this is why many companies and residents cannot use this service at this time. The user and carrier must have DSL modems that use the same modulation techniques.

DSL provides faster transmission rates because it uses all of the available frequencies that are available on a voice-grade UTP line. When you call someone, your voice data travels down this UTP line and the service provider "cleans up" the transmission by removing the high and low frequencies. Humans do not use these frequencies when they talk, so if there is anything on these frequencies, it is considered line noise and thus removed. So in reality, the available bandwidth of the line that goes from your house to the telephone company's central office is artificially reduced. When DSL is used, this does not take place and therefore the high and low frequencies can be used for data transmission.

DSL offers several types of services. With *symmetric services,* traffic flows at the same speed upstream and downstream (to and from the Internet or destination). With *asymmetric services,* the downstream speed is much higher than the upstream speed. In most situations, an asymmetric connection is fine for residence users because they usually download items from the Web much more often than they upload data.

## Cable Modem

*We already have a cable running to your house, so just buy this extra service.*

The cable television companies have been delivering television services to homes for years, and then they started delivering data transmission services for users who have cable modems and want to connect to the Internet at high speeds.

*Cable modems* provide high-speed access, up to 50 Mbps, to the Internet through existing cable coaxial and fiber lines. The cable modem provides upstream and downstream conversions.

Not all cable companies provide Internet access as a service, mainly because they have not upgraded their infrastructure to move from a one-way network to a two-way network. Once this conversion takes place, data can come down from a central point

## xDSL

There are many different flavors of DSL, each with its own characteristics and specific uses.

- **Symmetrical DSL (SDSL)**   Data travels upstream and downstream at the same rate. Bandwidth can range between 192 Kbps–1.1 Mbps. Used mainly for business applications that require high speeds in both directions.

- **Asymmetrical DSL (ADSL)**   Data travels downstream faster than upstream. Upstream speeds are 128 Kbps–384 Kbps and downstream speeds can be as fast as 768 Kbps. Usually used by residential users.

- **ISDN DSL (IDSL)**   Provides DSL for customers who cannot get SDSL or ADSL because of their distance from the central office. It is capable of reaching customers who are up to 36,000 feet (almost 7 miles) from the provider's central office. IDSL operates at a symmetrical speed of 128 Kbps.

- **High-bit-rate DSL (HDSL)**   Provides T-1 (1.544 Mbps) speeds over regular copper phone wire without the use of repeaters. Requires two twisted pairs of wires, which many voice-grade UTP lines do not have.

(referred to as the head) to a residential home and back up to the head and onto the Internet.

Coaxial and fiber cables are used to deliver hundreds of television stations to users, and one or more of the channels on these lines are dedicated to carrying data. The bandwidth is shared between users in a local area; therefore, it will not always stay at a static rate. So, for example, if Mike attempts to download a program from the Internet at 5:30 P.M., he most likely will have a much slower connection than if he had attempted it at 10:00 A.M., because many people come home from work and hit the Internet at the same time. As more people access the Internet within his local area, Mike's Internet access performance drops.

## Always Connected

Unlike modem connections, DSL lines and cable modems are connected to the Internet all the time. No dial-up steps are required. This can cause a huge security issue because many hackers look for just these types of connections. Systems using these types of connections are always online and available for scanning, probing, hacking, and attacking. However, these systems are often used in DDoS attacks. Because the systems are on all the time, attackers plant Trojan horses that lie dormant until they get the command from the attacker to launch an attack against a victim. Many of the DDoS attacks use as their accomplices systems with DSL and cable modems, and usually the owner of the computer has no idea that their system is being used to attack another system.

Sharing the same media brings up a slew of security concerns, because users with network sniffers can easily view their neighbors' traffic and data as it travels to and from the Internet. Many cable companies are now encrypting the data that goes back and forth over shared lines through a type of data link encryption.

## Reference

- **CableModemInfo.com**  www.cablemodeminfo.com

## VPN

*Here's the secret handshake. Now you can use the secret tunnel.*

A *virtual private network (VPN)* is a secure, private connection through a public network or an otherwise unsecure environment, as shown in Figure 7-49. It is a *private* connection because the encryption and tunneling protocols are used to ensure the confidentiality and integrity of the data in transit. It is important to remember that VPN technology requires a tunnel to work and it assumes encryption. The protocols that can be used for VPNs are Point-to-Point Tunneling Protocol (PPTP), IPSec, and L2TP.

The sending and receiving ends must have the necessary hardware and software to set up an encrypted tunnel, which provides the private link. The tunneling encryption protocol that is used encrypts the data and protects it as it travels through the untrusted public network, usually the Internet.

Remote users, or road warriors, can use VPNs to connect to their company network to access their e-mail, network resources, and corporate assets. A remote user must have the necessary software loaded on his computer to use a VPN. The user first makes a PPP connection to an ISP, and the ISP makes a full connection for the user to the destination network. PPP encapsulates datagrams to be properly transmitted over a telecommunication link. Once this connection has been made, the user's software initiates a VPN connection with the destination network. Because data exchanged between the two entities will be encrypted, the two entities go through a handshaking phase to agree upon the type of encryption that will be used and the key that will be employed to encrypt their data. The ISP is involved with the creation of the PPP connection, which

Private link provided by VPN

Remote user                                                                          Server

**Figure 7-49**   A VPN provides a virtual dedicated link between two entities across a public network.

is a type of foundation for the VPN connection. Once the PPP connection is set up, the ISP is out of the picture and the VPN parameters are negotiated and decided upon by the user and the destination network. After this is complete, the user and network can then communicate securely through their newly created virtual connection.

VPN connections can be used not only by remote users to access a network but also to provide a connection between two routers (many times called a gateway-to-gateway connection) or two users. It is a flexible connection, and the only requirements are that each entity must have a connection, VPN software, the necessary protocols, and the same encryption mechanisms. Once the VPN connection is made, the user can access network resources in the same manner that he can access them via dial-up connections.

Up to this point, we have been discussing a VPN that exists over dial-up and Internet connections; but a VPN can also take place between firewalls that have VPN functionality. Within a network, the VPN device sits on the outer edge of the security domain. When a company implements a firewall that has VPN functionality embedded, the company can centralize administration for the VPN and firewall. In this type of configuration, packets that enter the network can come in encrypted through the VPN connection and must be decrypted to allow the firewall to inspect the packets and either allow or deny them. Because extra work is being done on the packets as they enter and leave a network, much more overhead is generated, which causes degradation in performance. However, today most of the processing that takes place is being moved to hardware and integrated circuits, which can work at much faster speeds than pure software.

## Tunneling Protocols

*How do we get our message through this sea of packets? Response: Create a tunnel.*

As previously mentioned, VPNs use tunneling protocols, but what the heck are they anyway? A *tunnel* is a virtual path across a network that delivers packets that are encapsulated and possibly encrypted. Encapsulation and encryption sound alike, but they describe two different reasons a tunnel would be used in the first place.

If one network uses NetBIOS Enhanced User Interface (NetBEUI) and needs to be connected to another network that also uses NetBEUI, but they are two states apart, what is the problem? NetBEUI is nonroutable. So for these two networks to communicate, the NetBEUI packets must be encapsulated within a routable protocol, such as IP. This type of encapsulation happens all the time on the Internet and between networks. When an Ethernet network is connected to an FDDI backbone, that FDDI network does not understand the Ethernet frame format; thus, the packets must be encapsulated within the FDDI protocol when they are sent over the FDDI network. If two networks use IPX and need to communicate across the Internet, these messages must also be encapsulated in a protocol that the Internet can understand, such as IP.

The second variation to a tunnel is one that uses encapsulation *and* encryption. The encapsulation reasons stay the same, and the encryption is used to protect the data's confidentiality and integrity as it travels through untrusted environments. These are both ways of tunneling through another network.

Tunneling is the main ingredient to a VPN because that is how the VPN creates its private connection. Three main tunneling protocols are used in VPN connections: PPTP, L2TP, and IPSec. (IPSec is described in depth in Chapter 8.)

## IPSec

IPSec is fully covered in Chapter 8, but let's take a quick look at some configuration possibilities for this protocol suite.

IPSec can be configured to provide *transport adjacency*, which just means that more than one security protocol (ESP and AH) is applied to a packet. IPSec can also be configured to provide *iterated tunneling*, in which an IPSec tunnel is tunneled through another IPSec tunnel. Iterated tunneling would be used if the traffic needed different levels of protection at different junctions of its path. For example, if the IPSec tunnel started from an internal host to an internal border router, this may not require encryption, so only the AH protocol would be used. But when that data travels from that border router throughout the Internet to another network, then the data requires more protection. So the first packets travel through a semisecure tunnel until they get ready to hit the Internet and then they go through a very secure second tunnel.

**PPP**  Before we dig too deeply into true tunneling protocols, let's take a look at an encapsulation protocol. Tunneling and encapsulation protocols sound very similar, because tunneling protocols use encapsulation. Encapsulation just means that an extra header, and possibly trailer, has been added to a frame. A tunneling protocol adds these headers and trailers so that the packets can be transmitted over a certain network type. So, if you needed to get packets using the network and transport protocols of IPX/SPX over the Internet, a gateway would add the necessary TCP/IP headers and trailers, which are required to be routable on the Internet. Once these packets get to their destination, these headers and trailers are removed and the packets are sent to their designated host.

*Point-to-Point Protocol (PPP)* is not really a tunneling protocol, but an encapsulation protocol. It does not need to wrap up current frames with special headers and trailers, which will be taken off at the destination. Instead it allows TCP/IP traffic to be transmitted over a medium that was developed for telephone voice data.

PPP is used to encapsulate messages and transmit them over a serial line. Therefore, it allows TCP/IP and other protocols to be carried across telecommunication lines. PPP is used to establish telecommunication connections between routers, user-to-router, and user-to-user. It is also used to establish an Internet connection between a computer and an Internet *point of presence* (PoP)—usually a bank of modems and access servers at an ISP location. The user dials into this PoP over a telecommunications line and communicates using PPP.

When you connect to the Internet, you may be using a serial asynchronous dial-up connection or a point-to-point connection, such as a T1 line. A T1 line is a *serial* connection, meaning one bit follows the one in front of it, compared to a *parallel* connection, where channels of bits travel simultaneously. This serial connection is the telephone company's line, and it knows nothing about networking protocols such as IP, IPX, AppleTalk, and so on, which is what our computers use to communicate. Therefore, this traffic needs to be encapsulated before it is put onto this serial link, which is what PPP does. PPP *encapsulates* the data coming from our computer or network, which means that it puts the data into the correct format to travel over the telecommunications link. PPP frames our data with start and stop bits so that the other end knows how to process the data. PPP allows us to set up and establish an Internet connection.

Once a link is established, the user must authenticate to a network authentication server at the ISP site. PPP can use Password Authentication Protocol (PAP), Challenge Handshake Authentication Protocol (CHAP), or Extensible Authentication Protocol (EAP) to accomplish this task. If the user is attempting to dial into her company's network, another step must take place: a protocol must deliver this PPP session to the actual corporate network. So what does this mean? The data that is encapsulated within PPP must now travel over the Internet, which does not understand PPP, but instead uses IP. So another protocol must encapsulate the PPP data in IP packets and tunnel it through the Internet to the corporate network, as shown in Figure 7-50. PPP encapsulates data to travel over a private network (between you and your ISP), and a tunneling protocol encapsulates the data to travel over a public network, such as the Internet.

Three of the main tunneling protocols used today for setting up a VPN are IPSec, PPTP, and L2TP. They reduce the cost of remote dial-up networking because the user can dial into a local ISP instead of dialing directly to the corporate network, which may accrue long-distance charges.

**Figure 7-50**   A VPN connection can be used to extend a PPP connection securely.

PPP has, for the most part, replaced *Serial Line Internet Protocol (SLIP)*, an older protocol that was used to encapsulate data to be sent over serial connection links. PPP has several capabilities that SLIP does not have:

- Implements header and data compression for efficiency and better use of bandwidth

- Has error correction

- Supports different authentication methods

- Can encapsulate protocols other than just IP

- Does not require both ends to have an IP address assigned before data transfer can occur

## PPTP

*The Internet does not understand my dial-up packets. Response: Wrap them up in PPTP.*

Why do we need tunneling protocols? Because some protocols cannot be properly routed over specific networks. We have been talking specifically about PPP frames, which are not routable over the Internet, but the Internet does not understand some other protocols that we use today, such as IPX, NetBEUI, and AppleTalk. Alone, these frames could not find their way to the ultimate destination they are seeking when crossing the Internet, so they need a hand; that is what the tunneling protocol does—similar to a ferry taking cars across a body of water. The car could not get to the other side by itself because it was not built to deal with water, but the ferry can move and navigate in the water, as the tunneling protocol can move in the IP-based Internet.

PPTP, a Microsoft protocol, allows remote users to set up a PPP connection to a local ISP and then create a secure VPN to their destination. PPTP has been the de facto industry-standard tunneling protocol for years, but the new de facto standard for VPNs is IPSec, which is covered in Chapter 8.

Although tunneling does not by default mean that the user's data is encrypted, in most implementations tunneling and encryption are both used. When using PPTP, the PPP payload is encrypted with Microsoft Point-to-Point Encryption (MPPE) using MS-CHAP or EAP-TLS. The keys used in encrypting this data are generated during the authentication process between the user and the authentication server.

Along with encryption, the frame has to be encapsulated as well. A series of encapsulations takes place in this technology. The user's data is encapsulated within PPP, and then this frame is encapsulated by PPTP with a Generic Routing Encapsulation (GRE) header and IP header, as shown in Figure 7-51. This encapsulation allows the resulting frame to be routable over public networks, such as the Internet.

One limitation of PPTP is that it can work only over IP networks, so other protocols must be used to move data over frame relay, X.25, and ATM links. Cisco started to develop a protocol, Layer 2 Forwarding (L2F), that would tunnel PPP traffic through these other types of networks, but it was asked by the IETF to combine its work with PPTP for the sake of interoperability. As a result, Cisco developed Layer 2 Tunneling Protocol (L2TP), which combines the best of PPTP and L2F.

**Figure 7-51**
PPTP encapsulates
a PPP frame.

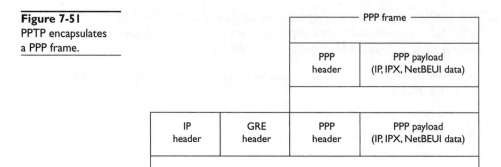

### L2TP

*L2TP was R2D2's little cousin. Response: You are* still *not funny.*

L2TP provides the functionality of PPTP, but it can work over networks other than just IP, and it provides a higher level of security when combined with IPSec. L2TP does not provide any encryption or authentication services, so it needs to be combined with IPSec if those services are required.

The processes that L2TP uses for encapsulation are similar to those used by PPTP. The PPP frame is encapsulated with L2TP.

When the destination system receives the L2TP frame, it processes the headers. Once it gets to the IPSec trailer, it verifies the integrity and authentication of the frame. Then it uses the information in the ESP header to decrypt the rest of the headers and data payload properly. (IPSec is covered in detail in Chapter 8.)

The following items outline the differences between PPTP and L2TP:

- PPTP can run only on top of IP networks. It is dependent on IP. L2TP, on the other hand, can run on top and tunnel through networks that use other protocols, such as frame relay, X.25, and ATM.

- PPTP is an encryption protocol and L2TP is not; thus, L2TP lacks the security to be called a *true* VPN solution. L2TP is often used in conjunction with IPSec to provide the necessary encryption.

- L2TP supports TACACS+ and RADIUS, and PPTP does not.

## Authentication Protocols

*Hey, how do I know you are who you say you are?*

**Password Authentication Protocol (PAP)** is used by remote users to authenticate over PPP lines. It provides identification and authentication of the user who is attempting to access a network from a remote system. This protocol requires a user to enter a password before being authenticated. The password and the username credentials are sent over the network to the authentication server after a connection has been established via PPP. The authentication server has a database of user credentials that are compared to the supplied credentials to authenticate users.

## Summary of Tunneling Protocols

**Point-to-Point Tunneling Protocol (PPTP):**

- Designed for client/server connectivity
- Sets up a single point-to-point connection between two computers
- Works at the data link layer
- Transmits over IP networks only

**Layer 2 Forwarding (L2F):**

- Created before L2TP by Cisco
- Merged with PPTP, which resulted in L2TP
- Provides mutual authentication
- No encryption

**Layer 2 Tunneling Protocol (L2TP):**

- Hybrid of L2F and PPTP
- Sets up a single point-to-point connection between two computers
- Works at the data link layer
- Transmits over multiple types of networks, not just IP
- Combined with IPSec for security

**IPSec:**

- Handles multiple connections at the same time
- Provides secure authentication and encryption
- Supports only IP networks
- Focuses on LAN-to-LAN communication rather than a dial-up protocol
- Works at the network layer, and provides security on top of IP
- Can work in *tunnel mode*, meaning the payload and the header are protected, or *transport mode*, meaning that only the payload is protected

Please review Chapter 8 for a full understanding of the IPSec protocol suite.

PAP is one of the least secure authentication methods, because the credentials are sent in cleartext, which renders them easy to capture by network sniffers. Although it is not recommended, some systems revert to PAP if they cannot agree on any other authentication protocol. During the handshake process of a connection, the two entities negotiate how authentication is going to take place, what connection parameters to use, the speed of data flow, and other factors. Both entities will try to negotiate and agree upon the most secure method of authentication; they may start with EAP, and if one computer does not have EAP capabilities, they will try to agree upon CHAP; if one of the computers does not have CHAP capabilities, they may be forced to use PAP. If this type of authentication is unacceptable, the administrator will configure the RAS to accept only CHAP authentication and higher, and PAP cannot be used at all.

*Challenge Handshake Authentication Protocol (CHAP)* addresses some of the vulnerabilities found in PAP. It uses a challenge/response mechanism to authenticate the user instead of sending a password. When a user wants to establish a PPP connection and both ends have agreed that CHAP will be used for authentication purposes, the user's computer sends the authentication server a logon request. The server sends the user a challenge, which is a random value. This challenge is encrypted with the use of a predefined password as an encryption key, and the encrypted challenge value is returned to the server. The authentication server also uses the predefined password as an encryption key and decrypts the challenge value, comparing it to the original value that was sent. If the two results are the same, the authentication server deduces that the user must have entered the correct password, and authentication is granted. The steps that take place in CHAP are depicted in Figure 7-52.

*Extensible Authentication Protocol (EAP)* is also supported by PPP. Actually, EAP is not a specific authentication mechanism as are PAP and CHAP; instead, it provides a framework to enable many types of authentication techniques to be used during PPP connections. As the name states, it extends the authentication possibilities from the norm (PAP and CHAP) to other methods such as one-time passwords, token cards, biometrics, Kerberos, and future mechanisms. So when a user dials into an authentication server and both have EAP capabilities, they can negotiate between a longer list of possible authentication methods.

## References

- *Linux PPP HOWTO,* Chapter 16, "If Your PPP Server Uses PAP," by Corwin-Light Williams and Joshua Drake (2000)   http://en.tldp.org/HOWTO/PPP-HOWTO/pap.html

- RFC 2284 – PPP Extensible Authentication Protocol (EAP)   www.faqs.org/rfcs/rfc2284.html

**Figure 7-52**
CHAP uses a
challenge/response
mechanism instead
of having the user
send the password
over the wire.

## PAP vs. CHAP

PAP characteristics:

- Sends credentials in cleartext during transmission
- Use has decreased because it does not provide a high level of security
- Supported by most networks and NASs

CHAP characteristics:

- Used the same way PAP is used but provides a higher degree of security
- Authenticates using a challenge/response method
- Used by remote users, routers, and NASs to provide authentication before providing connectivity

PAP is vulnerable to sniffing because it sends the password and data in plaintext, but it is also vulnerable to man-in-the-middle attacks. CHAP is not vulnerable to man-in-the-middle attacks because it continues this challenge/response activity throughout the connection to ensure that the authentication server is still communicating with a user who holds the necessary credentials.

## Remote Access Guidelines

Remote users should be identified and authenticated and their activities audited to ensure that no malicious activity is taking place and that no one is abusing access rights. All remote users should be justified in their right to access the network, and their access privileges should be reviewed on an annual basis. For example, if Brian worked in the software development group and required remote access to work from home, and then six months later he was moved into the logistics group, he might not require remote access any longer; thus, remote access should no longer be available to him.

Expected activity and behavior pertaining to remote access should be within the company's security policy or in an issue-specific policy that outlines who should do what and when. This policy should be presented and available to all users to help clear up confusion and enable the company to take steps if someone is abusing her use of remote access.

The access modems should be set to answer after the fourth ring. Wardialers are often configured to move to another phone number if the number they are dialing rings longer than two or three times, because connections that ring more than three times are usually telephone lines and not data lines. Configuring the modem to answer on the fourth ring or higher is done in the hopes that attackers will not be able to tell that the telephone line is actually being used for remote data access.

The remote access facilities should be consolidated when possible. This means that all access servers are housed in the same server room and administered by the same person or group. This helps to ensure consistency in how remote entry points are maintained and monitored, and helps to ensure that when changes take place, they happen to all entry points. This also facilitates centralized auditing and logging, and makes it more difficult for administrators to forget all the ways the company is allowing users to access the environment.

Strong two-factor user authentication should be used via RADIUS or TACACS+ servers, which are explained in Chapter 4. If the data that users and the company will be transmitting is confidential or sensitive, users should connect via a VPN. Various levels of security should be provided to various types of users entering the network to help ensure that each user has only the necessary access rights and permissions he needs.

Companies may restrict access based on the address of the source computer that is trying to gain access. If the address is unknown or not on the ACL, the connection should be denied. A firewall can also be implemented to ensure that remote users access only the services and ports the network administrator wants them to access.

Caller ID and callback settings, as well as two-factor authentication, can be configured on the RAS server. The *caller ID* functionality can view the source telephone number and decide whether or not to allow access based on a predefined list of approved phone numbers. For an attacker to get around this, she must call from a preauthorized telephone number or compromise the telephone company's central office equipment. The *callback* option requires the RAS to call the user requesting access in return. With callback configured, after a user authenticates to the RAS, the RAS drops the connection and calls the user back at a preconfigured telephone number. Callback does not protect against unauthorized access from an authorized location and can be bypassed by call forwarding.

Caller ID and callback options are great, but they are usually not practical because they require users to call in from a static phone number each time they access the network. Most users who are accessing the network remotely are doing so because they are on the road and moving from place to place.

## References

- Windows 2000 Technical Resources: How It Works—Remote Access www.microsoft.com/windows2000/techinfo/howitworks/communications/ remoteaccess
- "Evolution of the Network Router Market," by John Rendleman, *InformationWeek* (Aug. 19, 2002) www.informationweek.com/story/ IWK20020819S0002
- *The Evolution of the Remote Access Server (RAS) to a Universal Port-Enabled Platform*, Internet Engineering Consortium www.iec.org/online/tutorials/ ras_univ/

# Wireless Technologies

*Look, Ma, no wires!*

Wireless communications take place much more often than we think, and a wide range of broadband wireless data transmission technologies are used in various frequency ranges. Broadband wireless signals occupy frequency bands that may be shared with microwave, millimeter-wave, satellite, radar, and ham radio use, for example. We use these technologies for television transmissions, cellular phones, satellite transmissions, spying, surveillance, and garage door openers. This section focuses on how wireless technologies are used in LAN environments.

## Wireless Communications

When two people are talking, they are using wireless communication because their vocal cords are altering airwaves, which are signals that travel with no cables attached to another person. Wireless communication involves transmitting signals via radio waves through air and space, which also alters airwaves.

Signals are measured in *frequency* and *amplitudes*. The frequency of a signal dictates how much data can be carried and how far. The higher the frequency, the more data the signal can carry, but the higher the frequency, the more susceptible the signal is to atmospheric interference. A higher frequency can carry more data but over a shorter distance.

In a wired network, each computer and device has its own cable connecting it to the network in some fashion. In wireless technologies, each device must instead share the allotted radio frequency spectrum with all other wireless devices that need to communicate. This spectrum of frequencies is finite in nature, which means that it cannot grow if more and more devices need to use it. The same thing happens with Ethernet—all the computers on a segment share the same medium, and only one computer can send data at any given time, otherwise a collision can take place. Wired networks using Ethernet employ the CSMA/CD (collision detection) technology. Wireless technology is actually very similar to Ethernet but it uses CSMA/CA (collision avoidance). The wireless device sends out a broadcast indicating that it is going to transmit data. This is received by other devices on the shared medium, which causes them to hold off on transmitting information. It is all about trying to eliminate or reduce collisions. (The two versions of CSMA are explained earlier in this chapter in the section "CSMA.")

A number of technologies have been developed to allow wireless devices to access and share this limited amount of medium for communication purposes. We will look at two different types of spread spectrum techniques: frequency hopping and direct sequence. The goal of each of these wireless technologies is to split the available frequency into usable portions, since it is a limited resource, and to allow the devices to share them efficiently.

## Spread Spectrum

*Can I spread these signals with a butter knife? Response: Whatever.*

In wireless technologies, certain technologies and industries are allocated specific *spectrums,* or frequency ranges, to be used for transmissions. In the United States, the FCC decides upon this allotment of frequencies and enforces its own restrictions. *Spread spectrum* means that something is distributing individual signals across the allocated frequencies in some fashion. So when a spread spectrum technology is used, the sender spreads its data across the frequencies over which it has permission to communicate. This allows for more effective use of the available bandwidth, because the sending system can use more than one frequency at a time. Think of it in terms of serial versus parallel communication. In serial transmissions, all the bits have to be fed into one channel, one after the other. In parallel transmissions, the bits can take several channels to arrive at their destination. Parallel is a faster approach because more channels can be used at one time. This is similar to checkout lanes in a grocery store. We have all been in the situation where there was just one checkout lane open, which drastically slows down the amount of traffic (people and their food) that can get properly processed in a short period of time. Once the manager calls more checkers to the front to open their lanes, then parallel processing can be done and the grumbling stops. So spreading the signal allows the data to travel in a parallel fashion by allowing the sender and receiver to send data over more than one frequency.

We will look at two types of spread spectrum: frequency hopping spread spectrum (FHSS) and direct sequence spread spectrum (DSSS).

## References

- "802.11 and Spread Spectrum: A Close Look at the MAC and Physical Layers of Wireless WANs," by Anita Karve, *Network Magazine* (Dec. 1, 1997)   www.networkmagazine.com/article/NMG20000726S0001
- "Spread Spectrum Scene Primer," *Spread Spectrum Scene Online* www.sss-mag.com/primer.html
- Get IEEE 802 Program: IEEE 802.11 LAN/MAN Wireless LANS, IEEE Standards Association   http://standards.ieee.org/getieee802/802.11.html

**Frequency Hopping Spread Spectrum**   FHSS takes the total amount of bandwidth (spectrum) and splits it into smaller subchannels. The sender and receiver work at one of these channels for a specific amount of time and then move to another channel. The sender puts the first piece of data on one frequency, the second on a different frequency, and so on. The FHSS algorithm determines the individual frequencies that will be used and in what order, and this is referred to as the sender and receiver's hop sequence.

Interference is a large issue in wireless transmissions because it can corrupt signals as they travel. Interference can be caused by other devices working in the same frequency space. The devices' signals step on each other's toes and distort the data that is being sent. The FHSS approach to this is to hop between different frequencies so that if another device is operating at the same frequency, it will not be drastically affected. Consider another analogy: Suppose George and Marge have to work in the same room. They could get into each other's way and affect each other's work. But if they periodically change rooms, the probability of them interfering with each other is reduced.

A hopping approach also makes it much more difficult for eavesdroppers to listen in on and reconstruct the data being transmitted when used in technologies other than WLAN. FHSS has been used extensively in military wireless communications devices because the only way that the enemy could intercept and capture the transmission is by knowing the hopping sequence. But in today's WLAN devices, the hopping sequence is known and does not provide any security. The receiver has to know the sequences to be able to obtain the data.

So how does this FHSS stuff work? The sender and receiver hop from one frequency to another based on a predefined hop sequence. Several pairs of senders and receivers can move their data over the same set of frequencies because they are all using different hop sequences. Let's say you and I share a hop sequence of 1, 5, 3, 2, 4, and Nicole and Ed have a sequence of 4, 2, 5, 1, 3. I send my first message on frequency 1, and Nicole sends her first message on frequency 4 at the same time. My next piece of data is sent on frequency 5, the next on 3, and so on until each reaches its destination, which is your wireless device. So your device listens on frequency 1 for a half second, and then listens on frequency 5, and so on, until it receives all of the pieces of data that are on the line on those frequencies at that time. Ed's device is listening to the same frequencies but at different times and in a different order, so his device ignores my message because it is out of synch with his predefined sequence. Without knowing the right code, Ed treats my messages as background noise and does not process it.

**Direct Sequence Spread Spectrum**   DSSS takes a different approach by applying sub-bits to a message. The sub-bits are used by the sending system to generate a different format of the data before it is transmitted. The receiving end uses these sub-bits to reassemble the signal into the original data format. The sub-bits are called *chips* and the sequence of how the sub-bits are applied is referred to as the *chipping code.*

When the sender's data is combined with the chip, to anyone who does not know the chipping sequence, these signals appear as random noise; this is why the sequence is sometimes called a *pseudo-noise* sequence. Once the sender combines the data with the chipping sequence, the new form of the information is modulated with a radio carrier signal, and it is shifted to the necessary frequency and transmitted. What the heck does that mean? When using wireless transmissions, the data is actually moving over radio signals that work in specific frequencies. Any data that is to be moved in this fashion must have a carrier signal, and this carrier signal works in its own specific range, which is a *frequency.* So you can think of it this way: once the data is combined with the chipping code, it is put into a car (carrier signal), and the car travels down its specific road (frequency) to get to its destination.

The receiver basically reverses the process, first by demodulating the data from the carrier signal (removing it from the car). The receiver has to know the correct chipping sequence to change the received data into its original format. This means that the sender and receiver must be properly synchronized.

The sub-bits provide error-recovery instructions, just as parity does in RAID technologies. If a signal is corrupted using FHSS, it has to be re-sent, but by using DSSS, even if the message is somewhat distorted, the signal can still be regenerated because it can be rebuilt from the chipping code bits. The use of this code allows for prevention of interference, allows for tracking of multiple transmissions, and provides a level of security.

**FHSS vs. DSSS**   FHSS uses only a portion of the total bandwidth available at any one time, while the DSSS technology uses all of the available bandwidth continuously. DSSS provides more security because the signals are more difficult to detect from background noise without knowing the specific code. DSSS spreads the signals over a wider frequency band, whereas FHSS uses a narrow band carrier.

Since DSSS sends data across all frequencies at once, it has a higher data throughput than FHSS. The first WAN standard, 802.11, used FHSS, but as bandwidth requirements increased DSSS was implemented. By using FHSS, the 802.11 standard can provide a data throughput of only 1–2 Mbps. By using DSSS instead, 802.11b provides a data throughput of up to 11 Mbps.

## WLAN Components

A wireless LAN (WLAN) uses a transceiver, called an *access point (AP)*, which connects to an Ethernet cable, which is the link that wireless devices use to access resources on the wired network, as shown in Figure 7-53. When the AP is connected to the LAN Ethernet by a wired cable, it is the component that connects the wired and the wireless worlds. The APs are in fixed locations throughout a network and work as communication *beacons*. A wireless user has a device with a wireless NIC, which modulates her data onto radio frequency signals that are accepted and processed by the AP. The signals that are transmitted from the AP are received by the wireless NIC and converted into a digital format, which the device can understand.

When APs are used to connect wireless and wired networks, this is referred to as an *infrastructure WLAN*, which is used to extend an existing wired network. When there is just one AP and it is not connected to a wired network, it is considered to be in *stand-alone* mode and just acts as a wireless hub.

For a wireless device and AP to communicate, they must be configured to communicate over the same channel. A *channel* is a certain frequency within a given frequency

**Figure 7-53** A wireless device must authenticate with an access point.

band. The AP is configured to transmit over a specific channel, and the wireless device will "tune" itself to be able to communicate over this same frequency.

Any hosts that wish to participate within a particular WLAN must be configured with the proper *Service Set ID (SSID)*. Various hosts can be segmented into different WLANs by using different SSIDs. The reasons to segment a WLAN into portions are the same reasons wired systems are segmented on a network: the users require access to different resources, have different business functions, or have different levels of trust.

An *ad hoc WLAN* has no APs; the wireless devices communicate with each other through their wireless NICs instead of going through a centralized device. To construct an ad hoc network, wireless client software is installed on contributing hosts and configured for peer-to-peer operation mode. Then, the user clicks Network Neighborhood in a Windows platform, and the software searches for other hosts operating in this similar mode and shows them to the user.

**NOTE** When wireless devices work in infrastructure mode, the AP and wireless clients form a group referred to as a Basic Service Set (BSS). This group is assigned a name, which is the SSID value.

The SSID is usually required when a wireless device wants to authenticate to an AP. For the device to prove that it should be allowed to communicate with the wired network, it must first provide a valid SSID value. The SSID should not be seen as a reliable security mechanism because many APs broadcast their SSIDs, which can be easily sniffed and used by attackers.

The wireless device can authenticate to the AP in two main ways: *open system authentication (OSA)* and *shared key authentication (SKA)*. OSA does not require the wireless device to prove to the AP that it has a specific cryptographic key to allow for authentication purposes. In many cases, the wireless device needs to provide only the correct SSID value. In OSA implementations, all transactions are in cleartext because no encryption is involved. So an intruder can sniff the traffic, capture the necessary steps of authentication, and walk through the same steps to be authenticated and associated to an AP.

**NOTE** OSA just means that the device does not need to prove that it has a specific cryptographic key for authentication. Depending upon the product and the configuration, a network administrator can also limit access to specific MAC addresses. This would still be considered OSA.

When an AP is configured to use SKA, the AP sends a random value to the wireless device. The device encrypts this value with its cryptographic key and returns it. The AP decrypts and extracts the response, and if it is the same as the original value, the device is authenticated. In this approach, the wireless device is authenticated to the network by proving that it has the necessary encryption key. This method is based on the *Wired Equivalent Privacy (WEP)* protocol, which also enables data transfers to be encrypted.

WEP is usually disabled by default on the commonly purchased wireless AP devices. If a non-security educated individual or employee purchases one of these devices on his own, he may not be familiar with setting up the interoperating devices in a secure fashion. With WEP disabled, there is no privacy, and the AP is broadcasting its location and identity.

A long list of deficiencies in this protocol has been uncovered; the new solutions that are being developed to remedy these deficiencies are explained in the upcoming "802.11i" section.

## Wireless Standards

*We don't need no stinking standards! Response: Uh, yeah we do.*

Standards are developed so that many different vendors can create various products that will work together seamlessly. Standards are usually developed on a consensus basis among the different vendors in a specific industry. The Institute of Electrical and Electronics Engineers (IEEE) develops standards for a wide range of technologies— wireless being one of them.

The first WLAN standard, 802.11, was developed in 1997 and provided a 1–2 Mbps transfer rate. It worked in the 2.4-GHz frequency range. This fell into the available range that is unlicensed by the FCC, which means that companies and users do not need to pay to use this range.

The 802.11 standard outlines how wireless clients and APs communicate, lays out the specifications of their interfaces, dictates how signal transmission should take place, and describes how authentication, association, and security should be implemented.

Now just because life is unfair, a long list of standards actually fall under the 802.11 main standard. You may have seen this alphabet soup (802.11a, 802.11b, 802.11i, 802.11g, 802.11h, and so on) and not clearly understood the differences among them. IEEE created several task groups to work on specific areas within wireless communications. Each group had its own focus and was required to investigate and develop standards for its specific section. The letter suffixes indicate the order in which they were proposed and accepted.

## 802.11b

This standard was the first extension to the 802.11 WLAN standard and is the most common standard used today. (Although 802.11a was conceived and approved first, it was not released first because of the technical complexity that was involved with this proposal, and it required special approval from the FCC to be able to use the *orthogonal frequency division multiplexing [OFDM]* signaling technique.) 802.11b provides a transfer rate of up to 11 Mbps and works in the 2.4-GHz frequency range. It uses DSSS and is backward compatible with 802.11 implementations.

OFDM is a modulation scheme (FHSS and DSSS are two other examples of modulation schemes) that splits a signal over several narrowband channels. The channels are then modulated and sent over specific frequencies. By dividing the data across these different channels (spectrum), any interference from the environment will degrade only a small portion of the signal. This allows for greater throughput. Like FHSS and DSSS, OFDM is a physical layer specification. It can be used to transmit high-definition digital audio and video broadcasting, and WLAN traffic.

## 802.11a

This standard uses a different method of modulating data onto the necessary radio carrier signals. Whereas 802.11b uses DSSS, 802.11a uses OFDM and works in the 5-GHz frequency band. Because of these differences, 802.11a is not backward compatible with 802.11b or 802.11. Several vendors have developed products that can work with both 802.11a and 802.11b implementations; the devices must be properly configured or may be able to sense the technology already being used and configure themselves appropriately.

This technology offers advantages in two areas: speed and frequency. 802.11a provides up to 54 Mbps, and it does not work in the already very crowded 2.4-GHz spectrum. The 2.4-GHz frequency band is referred to as a "dirty" frequency because several devices already work there—microwaves, cordless phones, baby monitors, and so on. In many situations, this means that contention for access and use of this frequency can cause loss of data or inadequate service. But because 802.11a works at a higher frequency, it does not provide the same range as the 802.11b and 802.11g standards. The maximum speed for 802.11a is attained at short distances from the AP, up to 25 feet.

One downfall of using the 5-GHz frequency range is that other countries have not necessarily allocated this band for use of WLAN transmissions. So 802.11a products may work in the United States, but they may not necessarily work in other countries around the world.

## 802.11e

This working group has provided QoS and proper support of multimedia traffic. Multimedia and other types of time-sensitive applications have a lower tolerance for delays in data transmission. QoS provides the capability to prioritize traffic, and it affords guaranteed delivery. This specification and its capabilities may open the door to allow many different types of data to be transmitted over wireless connections.

## 802.11f

When a user moves around in a WLAN, her wireless device often needs to communicate with different APs. An AP can cover only a certain distance, and as the user moves out of the range of the first AP, another AP needs to pick up and maintain her signal to ensure that she does not lose network connectivity. This is referred to as *roaming*, and for this to happen seamlessly, the APs need to communicate with each other. If the second AP needs to take over this user's communication, it will need to be assured that this user has been properly authenticated and must know the necessary settings for this user's connection. This means the first AP would need to be able to convey this information to the second AP. The conveying of this information between the different APs during roaming is what 802.11f deals with. It outlines how this data can be properly shared.

## 802.11g

We are never happy with what we have; we always need more functions, more room, and more speed. The 802.11g standard provides for higher data transfer rates—up to 54 Mbps. This is basically a speed extension for current 802.11b products. If a product meets the specifications of 802.11b, its data transfer rates are up to 11 Mbps; and if a product is based on 802.11g, that new product can be backward compatible with older equipment but work at a much higher transfer rate.

So do we go with 802.11g or with 802.11a? They both provide higher bandwidth. 802.11g is backward compatible with 802.11b, so that is a good thing if you already have a current infrastructure. But 802.11g still works in the 2.4-GHz range, which is continually getting more crowded. 802.11a works in the 5-GHz band and may be a better bet if you use other devices in that frequency range. But working at higher frequency means that a device's signal cannot cover as wide of a range. Your decision will also come down to what standard wins out in the standards war. Most likely, one or the other standard will eventually be ignored by the market, so you will not have to worry about making this decision. Only time will tell which one will be the keeper.

## 802.11h

As stated earlier, 802.11a works in the 5-GHz range, which is not necessarily available in countries other than the United States for this type of data transmission. The 802.11h standard builds upon the 802.11a specification to meet the requirements of European wireless rules so that products working in this range can be properly implemented in European countries.

## 802.11i

A wide range of security flaws have been documented in 802.11, which has reduced the possible implementations of WLANs and has caused serious security breaches for those who chose to implement them anyway. Each of the mentioned WLAN standards is based on the same security model, so they have all inherited the same deficiencies.

### The New Wireless Standard

The first WLAN standard, IEEE 802.11, has a tremendous number of security flaws. These are found within the core standard itself, as well as in different implementations of this technology. To address these issues, a new IEEE Task Group has been developed to improve upon the standard and close the holes that the current wireless implementations are faced with. The deficiencies within the original 802.11 standard include no user authentication, no mutual authentication between the wireless device and AP, and a flawed encryption protocol. The encryption protocol allows for specific bits to be modified without the receiver recognizing it, and the different encryption components (key and initialization vectors) do not provide enough randomness to the encryption process. This lack of randomness allows for encrypted wireless traffic to be easily broken with free downloadable tools available on different web sites.

 **NOTE** Many of the cryptography topics in this section are clearly defined in Chapter 8. It may be beneficial to re-read this section after completing Chapter 8 if you are new to cryptography.

The use of Extensible Authentication Protocol (EAP) and 802.1X (introduced later in this section) to enforce user authentication and mutual authentication has been integrated into the new WLAN standard, 802.11i. To detect modifications of bits during transmission, Message Integrity Code (MIC) was also integrated. And the *Temporal Key Integrity Protocol (TKIP)* generates random values that are used in the encryption process, which makes it much harder for an attacker to break. To allow for an even higher level of encryption protection, the standard also includes the new Advanced Encryption Standard (AES) algorithm to be used in new WLAN implementations. This section looks at these different components and their relationships to one another.

**What Is Wrong with the Current Implementations?**   The types of attacks that can be carried out on the current wireless devices and networks are numerous and unnerving. Current implementations are vulnerable to this long laundry list of attacks if they use products that are based purely on the original 802.11 standard. Wireless traffic can be easily sniffed, data can be modified during transmission without the receiver being notified, rogue APs can be erected (that users can authenticate to and communicate with, not knowing it is a malicious entity), and encrypted wireless traffic can be decrypted quickly and easily. Unfortunately, these vulnerabilities usually provide doorways to the actual wired network where the more destructive attacks can begin.

Many vendors who produce WLAN products have developed their own security techniques and technologies to overcome the 802.11 security flaws and issues, but this usually amounts to just wrapping Band-Aids around the crux of the problem, which is a poorly constructed and implemented standard and technology. When vendors are forced to develop their own solutions, there are always many interoperability issues that customers have to deal with.

The 802.11i standard employs two different approaches that provide much more security and protection than the protocol used in the original 802.11 standard, WEP. This enhancement of security and protection is accomplished through specific protocols, technologies, and algorithms. The first protocol is TKIP, and it is backward compatible for the many WLAN products and networks currently implemented in networks everywhere. TKIP actually works with WEP by feeding it keying material, which is data to be used for generating new dynamic keys. WEP uses the RC4 encryption algorithm, and the current implementation of the algorithm provides very little protection. More complexity is added to the key generation process with the use of TKIP, which makes it much more difficult for attackers to uncover the encryption keys. The IEEE working group provided TKIP so that customers would only need to obtain firmware or software updates instead of purchasing new equipment for this type of protection.

802.11i has another capability of providing encryption protection with the use of the AES algorithm in counter mode with CBC-MAC (CCM), which is referred to as the *CCM Protocol (CCMP)*. AES is a much stronger algorithm than RC4 but requires more processing power. AES is not backward compatible with current WLAN products, so customers should implement this configuration only if they have not yet deployed a WLAN in their network.

 **NOTE**   Cipher Block Chaining (CBC) mode is explained in Chapter 8.

The algorithms, technologies, and protocols that make up the new wireless standard are complex. It is important to understand each component and how they all work together to provide a higher degree of confidence and protection for our future WLAN environments.

In the next section, we will look at the different encryption processes in the 802.11i standard (CCMP and TKIP), and the following sections will cover the other components that make up this standard that are not included in the original 802.11 standard.

**802.1X** The 802.11i standard can be understood as three main components in two specific layers. The lower layer contains the improved encryption algorithms (TKIP and CCMP). The layer that resides on top of it contains 802.1X. They work together to provide more layers of protection than the current 802.11 standard provides.

So what is 802.1X anyway? The *802.1X* standard is a port-based network access control that ensures that a user cannot make a full network connection until he is properly authenticated. This means that a user cannot access network resources and no traffic is allowed to pass, other than authentication traffic, from the wireless device to the network until the user is properly authenticated. An analogy is having a chain on your front door that enables you open the door slightly to identify a person who knocks before you allow him to enter your house.

By incorporating 802.1X, the new standard allows for the *user* to be authenticated, whereas using only WEP provides *system* authentication. User authentication provides a higher degree of confidence and protection than system authentication.

The 802.1X technology actually provides an authentication framework and a method of dynamically distributing encryption keys. The three main entities in this framework are the supplicant (wireless device), the authenticator (AP), and the authentication server (usually a RADIUS server). If the environment does not have an authentication server, the AP can fulfill the roles of authenticator and authentication server.

The AP usually does not have much intelligence and acts like a middleman by passing frames between the wireless device and the authentication server. This is usually a good approach, since this does not require a lot of processing overhead for the AP, and the AP can deal with controlling several connections at once instead of having to authenticate each and every user.

The AP controls all communication and allows the wireless device to communicate with the authentication server and wired network only when all authentication steps are completed successfully. This means that the wireless device cannot send or receive HTTP, DHCP, SMTP, or any other type of traffic until the user is properly authorized. WEP does not provide this type of strict access control; this is just one example of more security being provided by 802.11i.

Another disadvantage of the original 802.11 standard is that mutual authentication is not possible. When using WEP alone, the wireless device can authenticate to the AP, but the authentication server is not required to authenticate to the wireless device. This means that a rogue AP can be set up to capture users' credentials and traffic without the users being aware of this type of attack. 802.11i deals with this issue by using EAP. EAP allows for mutual authentication to take place between the authentication server and wireless device, and provides flexibility in that users can be authenticated by using passwords, tokens, one-time passwords, certificates, smart cards, or Kerberos. This allows wireless users to be authenticated using the current infrastructure's authentication technology that is already in place. The wireless device and authentication server that are 802.11i-compliant have different authentication modules that plug into 802.1X to allow for these different options. So, 802.1X provides the framework that allows for the different EAP modules to be added by a network administrator. The two entities (supplicant and authenticator) agree upon one of these authentication methods (EAP modules) during their initial handshaking process.

The 802.11i standard does not deal with the full protocol stack but addresses only what is taking place at the data link layer of the OSI model. Authentication protocols reside at a higher layer than this, so 802.11i does not specify specific authentication protocols. The use of EAP, however, allows for different protocols to be used by different vendors. For example, Cisco uses a purely password-based authentication framework called Lightweight Extensible Authentication Protocol (LEAP). Other vendors, including Microsoft, use EAP and Transport Layer Security (EAP-TLS), which carries out authentication through digital certificates. And yet another choice is Protective EAP (PEAP), where only the server uses a digital certificate.

If EAP-TLS is being used, the authentication server and wireless device exchange digital certificates for authentication purposes. If PEAP is being used instead, the user of the wireless device sends the server a password and the server authenticates to the wireless device with its digital certificate. In both cases, some type of public key infrastructure (PKI) needs to be in place. If a company does not have a PKI currently implemented, it can be an overwhelming and costly task to deploy a PKI just to secure wireless transmissions.

When using EAP-TLS, the steps the server takes to authenticate to the wireless device are basically the same as when an SSL connection is being set up between a web server and web browser. Once the wireless device receives and validates the server's digital certificate, it creates a master key, encrypts it with the server's public key, and sends it over to the authentication server. Now the wireless device and authentication server have a master key, which they use to generate individual symmetric session keys. Both entities use these session keys for encryption and decryption purposes, and it is the use of these keys that sets up a secure channel between the two devices.

Companies may choose to use PEAP instead of EAP-TLS because they don't want the hassle of installing and maintaining digital certificates on every wireless device. Before you purchase a WLAN product, you should understand the requirements and complications of each method to ensure that you know what you are getting yourself into and if it is the right fit for your environment.

As stated earlier, Cisco took a different approach to this authentication game. It implemented LEAP, which is based purely on passwords. This means that no PKI is required and the wireless device and server authenticate to each other by exchanging predetermined passwords.

A large concern with current WLANs using just WEP is that if individual wireless devices are stolen, they can easily be authenticated to the wired network. 802.11i has added steps to require the user to authenticate to the network instead of just requiring the wireless device to authenticate. By using EAP, the user needs to send some type of credential set that is tied to his identity. When using only WEP, the wireless device authenticates itself by proving that it has a symmetric key that was manually programmed into it. Since the user does not need to authenticate using WEP, a stolen wireless device can allow an attacker easy access to your precious network resources.

**Dynamic Keys and the Use of Initialization Vectors**   The three core deficiencies with WEP are the use of static encryption keys, the ineffective use of initialization vectors, and the lack of packet integrity assurance. The WEP protocol uses the RC4 algorithm, which is a stream symmetric cipher. Symmetric means that the sender and receiver must use the exact same key for encryption and decryption purposes. The 802.11 standard does not stipulate how to update these keys through an automated process, so in most environments, the RC4 symmetric keys are never changed out. And usually all of the wireless devices and the AP share the exact same key. This is like having everyone in your company use the exact same password. Not a good idea. So that is the first issue—static WEP encryption keys on all devices.

The next flaw is how initialization vectors (IVs) are used. An IV is a numeric seeding value that is used with the symmetric key and RC4 algorithm to provide more randomness to the encryption process. Randomness is extremely important in encryption because any patterns can give the bad guys insight into how the process works, which may allow them to uncover the encryption key that was used. The key and IV value are inserted into the RC4 algorithm to generate a key stream. The values (1s and 0s) of the key stream are XORed with the binary values of the individual packets. The result is ciphertext, or encrypted packets.

In most WEP implementations, the same IV values are used over and over again in this process, and since the same symmetric key (or shared secret) is usually used, there is no way to provide effective randomness in the key stream that is generated by the algorithm. The appearance of patterns allows attackers to reverse-engineer the process to uncover the original encryption key, which can then be used to decrypt future encrypted traffic.

So now we are onto the third mentioned weakness, which is the integrity assurance issue. WLAN products that use only the 802.11 standard introduce a vulnerability that is not always clearly understood. An attacker can actually change data within the wireless packets by flipping specific bits and altering the Integrity Check Value (ICV) so that the receiving end is oblivious to these changes. The ICV works like a CRC function; the sender calculates an ICV and inserts it into a frame's header. The receiver calculates his own ICV and compares it with the ICV that was sent with the frame. If the ICVs are the same, the receiver can be assured that the frame was not modified during transmission. If the ICVs are different, it indicates a modification did indeed take place and thus the receiver discards the frame. In WEP there are certain circumstances in which the receiver cannot detect whether an alteration to the frame has taken place, thus there is no true integrity assurance.

So the problems identified with the 802.11 standard include poor authentication, static WEP keys that can be easily obtained by attackers, IV values that are repetitive and do not provide the necessary degree of randomness, and a lack of data integrity. The use of the 802.1X technology in the new 802.11i standard provides access control by restricting network access until full authentication and authorization have been completed, and provides a robust authentication framework that allows for different EAP modules to be plugged in. These two technologies (802.1X and EAP) work together to enforce mutual authentication between the wireless device and authentication server. So what about the static keys, IV value, and integrity issues?

TKIP addresses the deficiencies of WEP pertaining to static WEP keys and inadequate use of IV values. Two very useful and powerful programs, AirSnort and WEP-Crack, can be used to easily crack WEP's encryption by taking advantage of these weaknesses and the ineffective use of the key scheduling algorithm within the WEP protocol. If a company is using products that implement only WEP encryption and is not using a third-party encryption solution (such as a VPN), these programs can break its encrypted traffic within minutes to hours. There is no "maybe" pertaining to breaking WEP's encryption; using these tools means it will be broken no matter if 40-bit or 128-bit keys are being used. This is one of the most serious and dangerous vulnerabilities pertaining to the original 802.11 standard.

The use of TKIP provides the ability to rotate encryption keys to help fight against these types of attacks. The protocol increases the length of the IV value and ensures that each and every frame has a different IV value. This IV value is combined with the transmitter's MAC address and the original WEP key, so that even if the WEP key is static, the resulting encryption key will be different for each and every frame. (WEP key + IV value + MAC address = new encryption key.) So what does that do for us? This brings more randomness to the encryption process, and it is randomness that is necessary to properly thwart cryptanalysis and attacks on cryptosystems. The changing IV values and resulting keys make the resulting key stream less predictable, which makes it much harder for the attacker to reverse-engineer the process and uncover the original key.

TKIP also deals with the integrity issues by using a MIC instead of an ICV function. If you are familiar with a message authentication code (MAC) function, this is the same thing. A symmetric key is used with a hashing function, which is similar to a CRC function but stronger. The use of MIC instead of ICV ensures that the receiver will be properly alerted if changes to the frame take place during transmission. The sender and receiver calculate their own separate MIC values. If the receiver generates a MIC value that is different than the one sent with the frame, the frame is seen as compromised and it is discarded.

---

 **NOTE**   These cryptography concepts and technologies are covered in Chapter 8.

---

**The Answer to All of Our Prayers?**   Up to now, if a company required more protection than what was provided in the original 802.11 standard, it had to place a firewall between the AP and the wired network. Also, the wireless devices could have VPN software installed to provide another, stronger layer of encryption. And as stated earlier, different vendors have come up with their own proprietary security solutions. But hopefully with 802.11i, continual Band-Aids will not need to be applied on top of this wireless technology. Instead, the security will be provided from the core of the technology itself.

So does the use of EAP, 802.1X, AES, and TKIP result in secure and highly trusted WLAN implementations? Maybe, but we need to understand what we are dealing with here. TKIP was created as a quick fix to WEP's overwhelming problems. It does not provide an overhaul for the wireless standard itself because WEP and TKIP are still based on the RC4 algorithm, which is not the best fit for this type of technology. The use of AES is closer to an actual overhaul, but it is not backward compatible with current 802.11 implementations. In addition, we should understand that using all of these new components and mixing them with the current 802.11 components will add more complexity and steps to the process. Security and complexity do not usually get along. The highest security is usually accomplished with simplistic and elegant solutions to ensure that all of the entry points are clearly understood and protected. These new technologies add more flexibility to how vendors can choose to authenticate users and authentication servers, but can also bring us interoperability issues because the vendors will not all choose the same methods. This means that if a company buys an AP from company A, then the wireless cards it buys from company B and C may not work seamlessly.

So does that mean that all of this work has been done for naught? No, 802.11i provides much more protection and security than WEP ever did. The working group has had very knowledgeable people involved and some very large and powerful companies aiding in the development of these new solutions. But the customers who purchase these new products need to understand what will be required of them *after* the purchase order is made out. For example, with the use of EAP-TLS, each wireless device needs its own digital certificate. Are your current wireless devices programmed to handle certificates? How will the certificates be properly deployed to all the wireless devices? How will the certificates be maintained? Will the devices and authentication server verify that certificates have not been revoked by periodically checking a certificate revocation list (CRL)? What if a rogue authentication server or AP was erected with a valid digital certificate? The wireless device would just verify this certificate and trust that this server is the entity it is supposed to be communicating with. And if the certificate authority is ever compromised, the whole EAP-TLS infrastructure is compromised, as with any PKI environment.

The original 802.11 standard has received so much bad press and attention that it is very likely that the new working group worked hard to ensure that all of the i's were dotted and all of the t's were crossed pertaining to this new release. But time will tell through rounds of testing and real-life implementations. This new and improved standard will get us much farther down the security road than we are now, but there are two other things to keep in mind concerning new products being developed and released. First, the vendors need to properly interpret and adhere to the standards to provide the level of assurance and security promised by the standard itself, and second, customers need to have awareness and intelligence about what they are purchasing and implementing into their environments. Many times products and technologies are installed without the company knowing exactly what this newcomer does and how to properly test and secure it. True security is based on education, knowledge, and experience. So the ultimate goals are to have a solid standard that is used to develop a secure product and to ensure that the customer is knowledgeable about this new product so that the overall level of protection is actually achieved. If one of these components does not meet its own individual goal, it can bring havoc to the overall efforts.

Wireless technologies are fascinating, and the capabilities that they provide for individuals and companies are extensive. But these technologies are at an immature state

## New Products

Today, new WLAN products are already being developed following the stipulations of this new wireless standard. Many products will straddle the fence by providing TKIP for backward compatibility with current WLAN implementations and AES for companies that are just now thinking about extending their current wired environments with a wireless component. Customers should review the Wi-Fi Alliance's certification findings before buying wireless products, since it has already started assessing systems against the 802.11i proposed standard.

of their evolution, and thus continual changes and new vulnerabilities may yet be introduced.

## 802.11j

Many countries have been developing their own wireless standards, which inevitably causes massive interoperability issues. This can be frustrating for the customer because he cannot use certain products, and it can be frustrating and expensive for vendors because they have a laundry list of specifications to meet if they want to sell their products in various countries. If vendors are unable to meet these specifications, whole customer bases are unavailable to them. The 802.11j task group has been working on bringing together many of the different standards and streamlining their development to allow for better interoperability across borders.

## 802.11n

The proposal for 802.11n by the World Wide Spectrum Efficiency (WWiSE) is an attempt to replace the current mix of various Wi-Fi technologies in 2006. 802.11n is designed to be much faster, with throughput expected to exceed 100 Mbps, and it works at the same frequency range of 802.11a (5 GHz). The intent is to maintain some backward compatibility with current Wi-Fi standards, while combining a mix of the current technologies. The proposals for this standard use a concept called multiple input, multiple output (MIMO) to increase the throughput. This will necessitate the use of two receive and two transmit antennas to broadcast in parallel using a 20-MHz channel.

Not enough different wireless standards for you? You say you want some more? Okay. here you go!

## 802.16

All the wireless standards covered so far are WLAN-oriented standards. 802.16 is a metropolitan area network (MAN) wireless standard, which allows for wireless traffic to cover a much wider geographical area. This technology is also referred to as *broadband* wireless access.

## 802.15

This standard deals with a much smaller geographical network, which is referred to as a *wireless personal area network (WPAN)*. This technology allows for connectivity to take place among local devices, such as a computer communicating with a PDA, a cellular phone communicating with a computer, or a headset communicating with another device. The goal here—as with all wireless technologies—is to allow for data transfer without all of those pesky cables.

## Bluetooth Wireless

The *Bluetooth wireless* technology is actually a portion of the 802.15 standard. It has a 1–3 Mbps transfer rate and works in a range of approximately ten meters. If you have a cell phone and a PDA that are both Bluetooth enabled, and both have calendar functionality, you could have them update each other without any need to connect them physically. If you added some information to your cell phone contacts list and task list, for example, you could just place the phone close to your PDA. The PDA would sense that the other device was nearby, and it would then attempt to set up a network connection with it. Once the connection is made, synchronization between the two devices would take place and the PDA would add the new contact and task list data. This sounds very much like a *Jetson's* scenario, but several types of devices already work this way. Bluetooth works in the frequency range of other 802.11 devices (2.4 GHz), and plans are currently underway to make various technologies interoperable.

There are real security risks when transferring unprotected data via Bluetooth in a public area, because any device within a certain range can capture this type of data transfer.

Another attack that Bluetooth is vulnerable to is referred to as *Bluejacking*. In this attack, someone sends an unsolicited message to a device that is Bluetooth enabled. Bluejackers look for a receiving device (phone, PDA, laptop) and then send a message to it. Often, the Bluejacker is trying to send someone else their business card, which will be added to the victim's contact list in their address book. The countermeasure is to put the Bluetooth-enabled device into nondiscoverable mode so that others cannot identify this device in the first place. If you receive some type of message this way, just look around you. Bluetooth only works within a ten-meter distance, so it is coming from someone close by.

 **NOTE** Some of these standards are still being developed, and not all of these standards and technologies will survive; it will take time to see which catch on and are accepted by vendors and customers alike. Wireless is still an immature technology that is currently undergoing painful growth spurts, and it is difficult to determine at this stage of the game the true future of each standard. But wireless has caught on like wildfire, and it will be interesting to watch it grow and consume the market.

## References

- **IEEE 802 Working Groups**   grouper.ieee.org/groups/802/dots.html
- **IEEE Wireless Standards Zone**   http://standards.ieee.org/wireless
- **"802.11 Alphabet Soup," by Jim Geier, Small Business Computing** (Aug. 6, 2002)   www.smallbusinesscomputing.com/buyersguide/article.php/1440011

- "Exploiting and Protecting 802.11b Wireless Networks," by Craig Ellison, ExtremeTech (Sept. 4, 2001)  www.extremetech.com/ article2/0,1558,11388,00.asp

- Official Bluetooth Special Interest Group (SIG) web site  www.bluetooth.com

## WAP

*There is a hole in this security. Response: Yep, we call it the gap in the WAP.*

**Wireless Application Protocol (WAP)** is not a standard per se. Instead, WAP is a de facto market and industry-driven protocol stack. What's the difference? When a governing body, such as IEEE, determines that there is a need for a new technology, it creates a working group to develop the corresponding standard. This standard works as a blueprint for all of the vendors that want to develop this type of technology. If no recognized standard is in place, organizations can come together and outline specifications for the new technology for all to follow.

WAP provides a common architecture for wireless devices to be able to communicate over the Internet. It enables wireless devices to send and receive data (in addition to voice data), meaning cell phones and PDAs can now connect to content providers on the Internet and find out stock quotes, get weather updates, access e-mail, and more. It also opened the door for new types of wireless devices to be created and sold.

Some of these wireless devices do not have the full resources that PCs and laptops have—they do not have the same amount of processing power, memory, storage space, and supporting circuitry. This means that these devices cannot use the same protocol stack (as in TCP/IP) used by these more powerful systems, and they cannot run the same type of applications. The WAP protocol stack was developed to be used with the limited resources and applications that have been created to work in this new environment.

WAP is a set of communications protocols used to standardize the way that wireless devices interface with each other and the Internet. The WAP model contains protocols that perform similar functionalities to those performed by protocols in the TCP/IP stack. Because wireless can be a web-based technology, WAP provides a way to present web pages. Personal computers and servers use HTML or XML to present web-based material and JavaScript to perform the processing in the background. WAP uses an XML-compliant Wireless Markup Language (WML) and WMLScript to perform these similar tasks. WAP has its own session and transport protocols and a transport layer security protocol called *Wireless Transport Layer Security (WTLS)*, which is similar to TLS and SSL. The wireless device has a WAP microbrowser that displays the web pages to the user.

The vision for developing this type of technology and these devices is to provide users with the functionality to check e-mail, voice messages, a calendar, and more from anywhere without needing physically to plug into any network. A user can watch the stock market on her PDA while riding a bus and hit a few buttons when she wants to sell her stocks because of a dip in the market. Users can also transfer funds from one bank account to another on their mobile phones, receive the daily news, and much more. The devices could be used to communicate with financial institutions or other organizations that provide information and wireless capabilities through the Internet.

Because these devices use a different set of protocols, a gateway is required to translate between WAP and the Internet's protocols and application types, as shown in Figure 7-54. Service providers can provide this gateway much as they can provide the service for users and companies to access the Internet today.

When data comes from the wireless mobile device, it can be encrypted with WTLS, which must be translated into TLS or SSL by the gateway. Because the wireless devices use the Internet for transmission, and the Internet does not understand WTLS, WTLS must be translated into a protocol the Internet does understand. This translation takes place at the service provider's gateway.

A security concern is that this data will be decrypted at the service provider's site and then encrypted with SSL or TLS. That means for a second or two, the data is not protected. This is referred to as the *gap in the WAP*, and it has caused a lot of concern for businesses and security professionals and is still one of the issues that needs to be dealt with.

WTLS works similarly to SSL/TLS, by encrypting data and allowing for authentication to take place between the communicating devices. WTLS has three classes that define how authentication takes place between a wireless device and a gateway server:

| Class 1 | Anonymous authentication | The wireless device and server do not authenticate to each other. |
|---------|--------------------------|-------------------------------------------------------------------|
| Class 2 | Server authentication | The server authenticates to the wireless device. |
| Class 3 | Two-way client and server authentication | The server and the wireless device authenticate to each other. |

In most cases, the gateway server dictates which type of authentication will be used, but the wireless device needs to be properly configured so that it can actually work in this type of implementation.

## i-Mode

WAP and *i-Mode* are the two main protocols used for wireless Internet transmissions used by cell phones and other PDA-like devices. WAP was developed by a consortium of companies with the goal of allowing people to carry out business-oriented activities. i-Mode was developed by a company in Japan (NTT DoCoMo) and is geared more toward providing an entertainment platform than toward providing functionality for business-oriented individuals.

**Figure 7-54**   A WAP gateway is required to translate WAP protocols to Internet protocols.

i-Mode works with a slimmed-down version of HTML, called Compact HTML (cHTML), and WAP uses Wireless Markup Language (WML), a markup language based on XML. Both i-Mode and WAP use an architecture consisting of a content server, gateway, and user terminal. The server can be a WAP or HTTP server and the gateway translates the protocols so that they can be understood and work over the Internet. The user terminal is a cell phone or mobile device that has a microbrowser, which interprets and presents the web content to the user.

i-Mode has exploded in popularity in Japan and is currently spreading throughout Asia and parts of Europe. WAP is currently in its second version and is used mainly in North America. They are both relatively new technologies that will continue to advance because we just love to be on the Internet anywhere we go!

## Mobile Phone Security

No matter what technology is being used on mobile phones and PDAs, the same types of security breaches seem to take place. Most corporations do not incorporate the use of these types of technologies into their security policies. This was alright when phones were just phones, but today they are small computers that can connect to computers and networks, and thus are new entry points for malicious activities. Since they are computers with operating systems, many employees save sensitive data on them, such as credentials, contacts, company files, and more, none of which is usually encrypted. And since many cell phones also have a camera functionality, organizations should be aware that this is a new way that sensitive data and activities can be captured and released to the world. Every organization should include this new technology and source of security breaches into their policies and security program.

Another common security issue with cell phones is that the cell phone must authenticate to a base station before it is allowed to make a call, but the base station is not required to authenticate to the cell phone. This has opened the door for attackers to set up rouge base stations. When a cell phone sends authentication data to this rouge base station, the attacker captures it and can now use it to authenticate and gain unauthorized access to the cellular network.

*Cell phone cloning* has been around for many years and this activity is not going to stop any time soon. A regular cell phone can be stolen and then reprogrammed with someone else's access credentials. This is a common activity used by organized crime rings and drug dealers who do not want their information readily available to law enforcement. Global System Mobile (GSM) phones use a Subscriber Identity Module (SIM) chip, which contains authentication data, phone numbers, saved messages, and more. Before a GSM phone can gain access to the cellular network, the SIM must be present in the phone. Attackers are cloning these SIM chips so that they can make fraudulent calls on the cell phone owner's account.

It is important to be aware that many cell phones move their data over the air waves and then the data is put on a wired network by the telephone company or service provider. So, a portion of the distance that the traffic must travel over is wireless but then the remaining distance may take place over a wired environment. Thus, if someone encrypts their data and sends it on their cell phone, typically it is encrypted only while it is traveling over the wireless portion of the network. Once it hits the wired portion of the network, it may no longer be encrypted. So encrypting data for transmission on a cell phone or PDA does not necessarily promise end-to-end encryption.

Unfortunately, these types of attacks on cell phones will never really stop. We will come up with more countermeasures and the bad guys will come up with new ways to exploit vulnerabilities that we did not think of. It is the same cat and mouse game that is carried out in the traditional network world. But the main issue pertaining to cell phone attacks is that they are not usually included in a corporation's security program or even recognized as a threat. This will change as more attacks take place through this new entry point and more viruses are written and spread through the interactions of cell phones and PDAs and the corporate network.

**NOTE** Universal Mobile Telecommunications System is a proposed new standard for third-generation mobile communications. The Internet Engineering Consortium provides a good introduction in *Universal Mobile Telecommunications System (UMTS) Protocols and Protocol Testing*, located at **www.iec.org/online/tutorials/umts/**.

Cell phone firewall products are available that can be implemented to protect against the following types of security issues:

- VoIP signaling and DoS attacks
- Toll fraud
- VoIP bandwidth abuses
- Virus infections
- Restricting file transfer
- Voicemail and PBX attacks
- Unauthorized employee connections
- Wardialing

Implementation of these types of firewalls is rare today, but will probably be more common as more companies experience these types of threats.

### References

- **WAP 2.0 Forum Releases**   www.wapforum.org/what/technical.htm
- **"WAP NG and iMode 2: Convergence Effects on Services," by Johan Hjelm et al. (INET 2001 conference)**   www.isoc.org/isoc/conferences/inet/01/CD_proceedings/6/INET-WAP.htm

### War Driving for WLANs

A common attack on wireless networks is *war driving,* which is when one or more people either walk or drive around with a wireless device equipped with the necessary equipment and software with the intent of identifying APs and breaking into them. Traditionally, this activity has taken place by using a laptop and driving in the proximity of buildings that have WLANs implemented, but today even PDAs can be used for this type of attack.

Kismet and NetStumbler are shareware programs that sniff (monitor) for APs. When one of these programs identifies an AP's signal, it logs the network name, SSID, MAC address of the AP, manufacturer of the AP, channel it was heard on, signal strength, signal-to-noise ratio, and whether WEP is enabled. Attackers drive around in their cars with a laptop running NetStumbler, actively looking for APs. They can usually find APs within a range of up to 350 feet, but with a more powerful antenna, the attacker can locate APs much farther away. NetStumbler broadcasts probes once each second, waiting for APs to respond. Airsnarf, AirSnort, and WEPCrack are utilities that can be used to break and capture the WEP encryption keys, if it is enabled.

 **NOTE** Inventive individuals have used Pringles cans and beverage cans as inexpensive antennas for war-driving endeavors. These antennas can focus on an AP from well over a mile away.

Some of the best practices pertaining to WLAN implementations are listed here:

- *Enable WEP.* Even though it can be broken into, it might deter casual attackers.

- *Change default SSID.* Each AP comes with a preconfigured default SSID value.

- *Disable "broadcast SSID" on the AP.* Most APs allow for this to be turned off.

- *Implement another layer of authentication (RADIUS, Kerberos).* Before the user can access the network, require him to authenticate.

- *Physically put AP at the center of the building.* The AP has a specific zone of coverage it can provide.

- *Logically put the AP in a DMZ with a firewall between the DMZ and internal network.* Allow the firewall to investigate the traffic before it gets to the wired network.

- *Use 104-bit WEP, not 40-bit.* This may, or may not, provide more protection depending upon the vendor's implementation.

- *Implement VPN for wireless devices to use.* This adds another layer of protection for data being transmitted.

- *Configure the AP to allow only known MAC addresses into the network.* Allow only known devices to authenticate. But remember that these MAC addresses are sent in cleartext, so an attacker could capture them and masquerade himself as an authenticated device.

- *Assign static IP addresses to wireless devices and disable DHCP.* If an attacker gains access and DHCP is enabled, you have just given the attacker a valid working IP address to use.

- *Carry out penetration tests on the WLAN.* Use the tools described in this section to identify APs and attempt to break the current encryption scheme being used.

- *Move to a product following the 802.11i standard.*

## Satellites

Today, satellites are used to provide wireless connectivity between different locations. For two different locations to communicate via satellite links, they must be within the satellite's line of sight and *footprint* (area covered by the satellite). The sender of information (ground station) modulates the data onto a radio signal that is transmitted to the satellite. A transponder on the satellite receives this signal, amplifies it, and relays it to the receiver. The receiver must have a type of antenna, one of those circular, dish-like things we see on top of buildings. The antenna contains one or more microwave receivers, depending upon how many satellites it is accepting data from.

Satellites provide broadband transmission that is commonly used for television channels and PC Internet access. If a user is receiving TV data, then the transmission is set up as a one-way network. If a user is using this connection for Internet connectivity, then the transmission is set up as a two-way network. The available bandwidth depends upon the antenna and terminal type and the service provided by the service provider. Time-sensitive applications can suffer from the delays that are experienced as the data goes to and from the satellite. These types of satellites are placed into a low Earth orbit, which means that there is not as much distance between the ground stations and the satellites as in other types of satellites. In turn, this means that smaller receivers can be used, which makes low Earth orbit satellites ideal for two-way paging, international cellular communication, TV stations, and Internet use.

 **NOTE**  As of this writing, there are around 12 million satellite subscribers in the United States and 30 million in Europe, mainly digital TV subscribers.

The size of the footprint depends upon the type of satellite that is being used. It can be as large as a country or only a few hundred feet in circumference. The footprint covers an area on the Earth for only a few hours or less, so the service provider usually has a large number of satellites dispatched to provide constant coverage at strategic areas.

## 3G Wireless Communication

The third generation in mobile telephony is the technology that often is referred to as *broadband wireless*. The first generation dealt with analog transmissions of voice-only data over circuit-switched networks. The second generation allows for digitally encoded voice and data to be transmitted between wireless devices, such as cell phones, and content providers. This generation provides a throughput of around 19.2 Kbps. Time Division Multiple Access (TDMA), Code Division Multiple Access (CDMA), Global System for Mobile Communications (GSM), and Personal Communications Services (PCS) all fall under the umbrella of 2G mobile telephony. This technology can transmit data over circuit-switched networks and supports data encryption, fax transmissions, and short message services (SMSs).

3G has taken a broader step by combining high-speed mobile access with IP-based services. Cell phones today can provide a web interface, e-mail terminal, CD player,

DVD player, gaming system, operating system, and applications—oh yeah, and a phone. This technology can provide 384 Kbps while moving and 2 Mbps while stationary.

A complete description of telephony and its various generations is beyond the scope of this book, but Table 7-12 provides a breakdown of their different characteristics.

## References

- **WarDriving.com**  www.wardriving.com
- **Wardrive.net wardriving tools, software, and utilities**  www.wardrive.net/wardriving/tools
- **"War Driving by the Bay," by Ken Poulsen, SecurityFocus (April 12, 2001)**  http://online.securityfocus.com/news/192
- **"War Driving," by Sandra Kay Miller,** *Information Security* (Nov. 2001) www.infosecuritymag.com/articles/november01/technology_wardriving.shtml
- **"Packet Leashes: A Defense Against Wormhole Attacks in Wireless Networks," by Yih-Chun Hu, Adrian Perrig, and David B. Johnson (IEEE Infocom 2003 conference)**  www.ieee-infocom.org/2003/papers/48_03.PDF

| | 1G | 2G | 3G | 4G |
|---|---|---|---|---|
| **Spectrum** | 900 MHz | 1800 MHz | 2 GHz | 40 GHz and 60 GHZ |
| **Multiplexing Type** | Analog FDMA | TDMA | CDMA | OFDM |
| **Voice Support** | Basic telephony | Caller ID and voicemail | Conference calls and low-quality video | Telepresence and high-definition video |
| **Messaging Features** | None | Text only | Graphics and formatted text | Full unified messaging |
| **Data Support** | None | Circuit switched (packet switched in 2.5G) | Packet switched | Native IPv6 |
| **Target Data Rate** | N/A | 14.4 Kbps (approx. 115 Kbps in 2.5G) | 2 Mbps (10 Mbps in 3.5G) | 100 Mbps |
| **Real Data Rate** | 2.4 Kbps | 9.6 Kbps (approx. 40 Kbps in 2.5G) | 64 Kbps | Unknown |
| **Interface with Other Devices** | Acoustic coupler | RS232 serial cable or IrDA | IEEE 802.11 or Bluetooth | Seamless connection via multiple methods |
| **Time Frame** | 1980–1994 | 1995–2001 | 2002–2005 | 2006–2010 |

**Table 7-12**  Various Generation Characteristics

> ## Mobile Technology Generations
> Like many technologies, the mobile communication technology has gone through several different generations.
> **First generation (1G):**
>
> - Analog services
> - Voice service only
>
> **Second generation (2G):**
>
> - Primarily voice, some low-speed data (circuit switched)
> - Phones were smaller in size
> - Added functionality of e-mail, paging, and caller ID
>
> **Generation 2½ (2.5G):**
>
> - Higher bandwidth than 2G
> - "Always on" technology for e-mail and pages
>
> **Third generation (3G):**
>
> - Integration of voice and data
> - Packet-switched technology, instead of circuit switched

# Rootkits

*Just leave your tools here. So when you want to come back and attack me again, it will be much easier.*

Many times, when a computer is successfully compromised, a hacker will attempt to elevate his privileges to obtain administrator or root user level. Working in the security context of these types of privileged users allows the attacker to carry out more dangerous activities. Once the level of access is achieved, the attacker can upload a bundle of tools, collectively called a *rootkit*. The first thing that is usually installed is a backdoor program, which allows the attacker to enter the system at any time without having to go through any authentication steps. (A backdoor is just a service that listens on a specific port.) The other tools in the rootkit may vary, but they usually comprise utilities that are used to cover the attacker's tracks. For example, every operating system has basic utilities that a root or administrator user can use to detect the presence of the rootkit, an installed sniffer, and the backdoor. The hacker replaces these default utilities with new utilities, which share the same name. They are referred to as "Trojaned programs" because they carry out the intended functionality but do some devious activity in the background. For example, on a Unix system the ps (process status) utility lists all the processes running on the system and their status. The `top` utility lists the processes, their status, and the amount of memory each process is using. Most rootkits have Trojaned programs that replace these utilities, because the root user could run `ps` or `top` and see that there is a backdoor service running, and thus detect the presence of an attack. But when this user runs one of these Trojaned programs, the program lists all other services except the backdoor process. Most rootkits also contain sniffers, so that the data can be captured and reviewed by the attacker. For a sniffer to work, the system's NIC must be put into promiscuous mode, which just means that it can "hear" all the traffic on the network link. The default `ipconfig` utility allows the root user to use a specific parameter to see whether or not the NIC is running in promiscuous mode. So, the rootkit also contains a Trojaned `ipconfig` program, which hides the fact that the NIC is in promiscuous mode.

 **NOTE** Ipconfig is a utility used in Windows environments to view network configurations. In Unix\Linux, this utility is called `ifconfig`.

Rootkits usually contain "log scrubbers" that remove traces of the attacker's activities from the system logs. They can also contain Trojaned programs that replace `find` and `ls` Unix utilities, so that when a user does a listing of what is in a specific directory, the rootkit will not be listed.

Some of the more powerful rootkits actually update the kernel of the system, instead of just replacing individual utilities. The kernel is the brain of the operating system, so modifying its code gives the attacker much more control over a system. It is also very difficult to detect kernel updates, compared to replaced utilities, because most host IDS products look at changes to file sizes and modification dates, which would apply to utilities and programs but not necessarily to the kernel of the operating system.

 **NOTE** Ironically, sometimes when an attacker compromises a system and installs a rootkit, he fortifies the system against other attackers. This means that when the attacker gets onto the system, he does all the things that the administrator should have done, such as disabling unnecessary services and user accounts, patching the system, etc. The attacker does this so that no other attacker can use this system or the installed rootkit.

The countermeasures to rootkits include properly hardening the system and running updated antivirus and antispyware software. Another protection mechanism is to use a host IDS (covered in Chapter 4), which looks for suspicious activities and keeps track of the integrity of the system. As stated earlier, however, the functionality of the HIDS usually cannot detect modifications to the kernel. Therefore, the best defense is to use a monolithic kernel rather than individual kernel modules. If you are familiar with working in Unix and Linux, you know that you can install the operating system within individual kernel modules or use one big kernel. A kernel rootkit loads itself as a kernel module. It cannot (or it is more difficult to) modify or affect the kernel if it is one unit. Any system that is providing some type of protection (proxy server, firewall, IDS) that is running on a Linux or Unix system should be installed with a monolithic kernel.

## Spyware and Adware

The terms spyware and adware vary in definition depending upon who you ask. In general terms, both are some type of software that is installed on a computer without the user knowing about it. The software usually collects some type of data that can be used by a vendor to better market its products to the user, or it may collect data for a hacker. *Adware* is usually the term used when companies want to track a user's buying and browsing habits through the use of cookies, so a merchant can know how to effectively market to this user. Some adware is software installed on your system that causes pop-up ads to appear continuously as you are surfing the Web. The software could be part of another software package you installed or a stealth installation could have taken place.

*Spyware* is usually considered more dangerous than adware because it may be written to capture keystrokes, capture system information, or install a backdoor on a system. Through the use of keyloggers, spyware can capture passwords, credit card information, or other sensitive data. The use of spyware is increasing the frequency of identify fraud, because hackers are gathering account numbers, social security numbers, PIN numbers, and more. Unfortunately, not all antivirus software can detect adware and spyware. Antivirus software looks for specific virus signatures and reproduction activities, but adware and spyware do not currently attempt to reproduce and spread themselves as viruses (as worms do), so they could be doing their devious work even after antivirus software has scanned your system and told you that everything is happy and healthy.

**NOTE**  Products have been developed to identify adware and spyware, and antivirus vendors are starting to incorporate this functionality into their products.

## Instant Messaging

*Instant messaging (IM)* allows people to communicate with one another through a type of real-time and personal chat room. It alerts individuals when someone who is on their "buddy list" has accessed the Internet, so that they can send text messages back and forth in real time. The technology also allows for files to be transferred from system to system. The technology is made up of clients and servers. The user installs an IM client (AOL, ICQ, Yahoo Messenger, etc.) and is assigned a unique identifier. This user gives out this unique identifier to people who she wants to communicate with via IM.

IM is an effective communication mechanism that is ever growing in popularity, but this technology has many security issues that need to be understood. The traffic is not encrypted, so confidential data could be captured. Also, because this provides a communication channel that allows for file transfer between systems, it can be used to spread viruses, worms, and Trojan horses. It has been reported that within the first six weeks of 2005, ten IM worms were spread across AOL, ICQ, and the MSN network. The following are a few of the IM worms that have been around since 2001 and are still circulating:

- W32.Choke
- W95.SoFunny.Worm@m
- W32.Goner.A@mm
- W32.Led@mm
- W32.Seesix.Worm

Because of the lack of strong authentication, accounts can be spoofed so that the receiver accepts information from a malicious user instead of the legitimate sender. There have also been numerous buffer overflow and malformed packet attacks that have been successful with different IM clients. These attacks are usually carried out with the goal of obtaining unauthorized access to the victim's system.

Many firewalls do not have the capability to scan for this type of traffic to uncover suspicious activity. Blocking specific ports on the firewalls is not usually effective because the IM traffic may be using common ports that need to be open (HTTP port 80 and FTP port 21). Many of the IM clients autoconfigure themselves to work on another port if their default port is unavailable and blocked by the firewall.

Even with all of these issues and potential vulnerabilities, many companies allow their employees to use this technology because it allows for quick and effective communication to take place. So, if you absolutely have to allow this technology in your environment, there are some things that you should do to help reduce your threat level. The following are best practices for protecting an environment from these types of security breaches:

- Establish a security policy specifying IM usage restrictions
- Implement an integrated antivirus/firewall product on all computers
- Configure firewalls to block IM traffic
- Upgrade IM software to more secure versions
- Implement corporate IM servers so that internal employees communicate within the organization's network only

Another alternative is to not allow employees to use this functionality and force them to communicate the old-fashioned way—through e-mail and by phone.

## References

- "Intro to Root-Kits," Lineman.net (April 9, 2004)   http://lineman.net/article127.html
- "Rootkit: Attacker Undercover Tools," by Saliman Manap, National ICT Security and Emergency Response Centre (NISER)   www.niser.org.my/resources/rootkit.pdf
- "Intro to Spyware," SpywareGuide   www.spywareguide.com/txt_intro.php

- "Symptoms of Spyware and Other Pests," *Intranet Journal*
  www.intranetjournal.com/spyware/symptoms.html

- "Instant Insecurity: Security Issues of Instant Messaging," by Neal Hindocha, SecurityFocus (Jan. 13, 2003)   www.securityfocus.com/infocus/1657

- "Securing Instant Messaging," *Symantec Advantage*, Issue 14 (Spring 2002)   www.symantec.com/symadvantage/014/instant.html

## Summary

This chapter touched on many of the different technologies within different types of networks, including how they work together to provide an environment in which users can communicate, share resources, and be productive. Each piece of networking is important to security, because almost any piece can introduce unwanted vulnerabilities and weaknesses into the infrastructure. It is important that you understand how the various devices, protocols, authentication mechanisms, and services work individually and how they interface and interact with other entities. This may appear to be an overwhelming task because of all the possible technologies involved. However, knowledge and hard work will keep you up to speed and hopefully in front of the hackers and attackers.

## Quick Tips

- Dual-homed firewalls can be compromised if the operating system does not have packet forwarding or routing disabled.

- A protocol is a set of rules that dictates how computers communicate over networks.

- The application layer, layer 7, has services and protocols required by the user's applications for networking functionality.

- The presentation layer, layer 6, formats data into a standardized format and deals with the syntax of the data, not the meaning.

- Routers work at the network layer, layer 3.

- The session layer, layer 5, sets up, maintains, and breaks down the dialog (session) between two applications. It controls the dialog organization and synchronization.

- The transport layer, layer 4, provides end-to-end transmissions.

- The network layer, layer 3, provides routing, addressing, and fragmentation of packets. This layer can determine alternative routes to avoid network congestion.

- The data link layer, layer 2, prepares data for the network medium by framing it. This is where the different LAN and WAN technologies live.

- The physical layer, layer 1, provides physical connections for transmission and performs electrical encoding of data. This layer transforms bits to electrical signals.

- TCP/IP is a suite of protocols that is a de facto standard for transmitting data across the Internet. TCP is a reliable, connection-oriented protocol, and IP is an unreliable connectionless protocol.

- Data is encapsulated as it travels down the OSI model on the source computer, and the process is reversed on the destination computer. During encapsulation, each layer adds its own information so that the corresponding layer on the destination computer knows how to process the data.

- The data link layer defines how the physical layer transmits the network layer packets. ARP and RARP are two protocols at this layer.

- Two main protocols at the transport layer are TCP and UDP.

- UDP is a connectionless protocol that does not send or receive acknowledgments when a datagram is received. It does not ensure that data arrives at its destination. It provides "best-effort" delivery.

- TCP is a connection-oriented protocol that sends and receives acknowledgments. It ensures that data arrives at its destination.

- ARP translates the IP address into a MAC address (physical Ethernet address), and RARP translates a MAC address into an IP address.

- ICMP works at the network layer and informs hosts, routers, and devices of network or computer problems. It is the major component of the ping utility.

- DNS resolves hostnames into IP addresses and has distributed databases all over the Internet to provide name resolution.

- Altering an ARP table so that an IP address is mapped to a different MAC address is called ARP poisoning and can redirect traffic to an attacker's computer or an unattended system.

- Packet filtering (screening routers) is accomplished by ACLs and is a first-generation firewall. Traffic can be filtered by addresses, ports, and protocol types.

- Tunneling protocols move frames from one network to another by placing them inside of routable encapsulated frames.

- Packet filtering provides application independence, high performance, and scalability, but it provides low security and no protection above the network layer.

- Firewalls that use proxies transfer an isolated copy of each approved packet from one network to another network.

- An application proxy requires a proxy for each approved service and can understand and make access decisions on the protocols used and the commands within those protocols.

- Circuit-level firewalls also use proxies but at a lower layer. Circuit-level firewalls do not look as deep within the packet as application proxies do.

- A proxy server is the middleman in communication. It does not allow anyone to connect directly to a protected host within the internal network. Proxy firewalls are second-generation firewalls.

- Application proxy firewalls provide good security and have full application layer awareness, but they have poor performance, limited application support, and poor scalability.

- Stateful inspection keeps track of each communication session and lets in only those packets that are responding to an internal host's request. It must maintain a state table that contains data about each connection. It is a third-generation firewall.

- VPN uses tunneling protocols and encryption to provide a secure network link between two networks or hosts. A private and secure connection can be made across an unsecure network.

- VPN can use PPTP, L2TP, or IPSec as a tunneling protocol.

- PPTP works at the data link layer. IPSec works at the network layer and can handle multiple tunnels at the same time.

- Dedicated links are usually the most expensive type of WAN connectivity method because the fee is based on the distance between the two destinations rather than on the amount of bandwidth used. T1 and T3 are examples of dedicated links.

- Frame relay and X.25 are packet-switched WAN technologies, which use virtual circuits instead of dedicated ones.

- An intranet is an internal network that uses web-based technology. An extranet is a private network that connects to an external network by using Internet protocols. An extranet is usually set up between partners, suppliers and vendors, and with customers.

- A hub (concentrator) in star topologies serves as the central meeting place for all cables from computers and devices.

- A bridge divides networks into more controllable segments to ensure more efficient use of bandwidth. Bridges work at the data link layer and understand MAC addresses, not IP addresses.

- A switch is a device with combined repeater and bridge technology. It works at the data link layer and understands MAC addresses.

- Routers link two or more network segments, where each segment can function as an independent network. A router works at the network layer, works with IP addresses, and has more network knowledge than bridges, switches, or repeaters.

- A bridge filters by MAC addresses and forwards broadcast traffic. A router filters by IP addresses and does not forward broadcast traffic.

- Layer 3 switching combines switching and routing technology.

- Attenuation is the loss of signal strength when a cable exceeds its maximum length.

- STP and UTP are twisted-pair cabling types that are the most popular, cheapest, and easiest to work with. However, they are the easiest to tap into, have crosstalk issues, and are vulnerable to electromagnetic interference (EMI).

- Coaxial cable is more expensive than UTP and STP, is more resistant to EMI, and can carry baseband and broadband technologies.

- Fiber-optic cabling carries data as light waves, is expensive, can transmit data at high speeds, is difficult to tap into, and is resistant to EMI. If security is extremely important, fiber cabling should be used.

- ATM transfers data in fixed cells, is a WAN technology, and transmits data at very high rates. It supports voice, data, and video applications.

- FDDI is a LAN and MAN technology, usually used for backbones, uses token-passing technology, and has redundant rings in case the primary ring goes down.

- Ethernet, 802.3, is the most commonly used LAN implementation today and can operate at 10 to 1000 Mbps.

- Token Ring, 802.5, is an older LAN implementation that uses a token-passing technology.

- Ethernet uses CSMA/CD, which means all computers compete for the shared network cable, listen to see when they can transmit data, and are susceptible to data collisions.

- Circuit-switching technologies set up a circuit that will be used during a data transmission session. Packet-switching technologies do not set up circuits— instead, packets can travel along many different routes to arrive at the same destination.

- A permanent virtual circuit (PVC) is programmed into WAN devices, whereas a switched virtual circuit (SVC) is temporary. SVCs are set up and then torn down quickly when they are no longer needed.

- CSU/DSU is used when a LAN device needs to communicate with WAN devices. It ensures that the necessary electrical signaling and format are used. It interfaces between a DTE and a DCE.

- ISDN has a BRI rate that uses two B channels and one D channel, and a PRI rate that uses up to 23 B channels. They support voice, data, and video.

- Frame relay is a WAN protocol that works at the data link layer and performs packet switching. It is an economical choice because the fee is based on bandwidth usage.

- PPP is an encapsulation protocol for telecommunication connections. It replaced SLIP and is ideal for connecting different types of devices over serial lines.

- DSL transmits high-speed bandwidth over existing phone lines.

- Remote access servers can be configured to call back remote users, but this can be compromised by enabling call forwarding.

- PAP sends credentials in cleartext, and CHAP authenticates using a challenge/response mechanism and therefore does not send passwords over the network.

- SOCKS is a proxy-based firewall solution. It is a circuit-based proxy firewall and does not use application-based proxies.

- IPSec tunnel mode protects payload and header information of a packet, and IPSec transport mode protects only the payload.
- A screened-host firewall lies between the perimeter router and the LAN.
- A screened subnet is a DMZ created by two physical firewalls.
- NAT is used when companies do not want systems to know internal hosts' addresses and enables companies to use private, nonroutable IP addresses.
- The 802.11 standard is a WLAN technology and has several variations—802.11a, 802.11b, 802.11f, 802.11g, and 802.11i.
- The 802.15 standard outlines wireless personal area network (WPAN) technologies, and 802.16 addresses wireless MAN technologies.
- WAP is a protocol stack used instead of TCP/IP on wireless devices.
- Environments can be segmented into different WLANs by using different SSIDs
- The 802.11b standard works in the 2.4-GHz range at 11 Mbps, and 802.11a works in the 5-GHz range at 54 Mbps.

## Questions

Please remember that these questions are formatted and asked in a certain way for a reason. You must remember that the CISSP exam is asking questions at a conceptual level. Questions may not always have the perfect answer, and the candidate is advised against always looking for the perfect answer. The candidate should look for the best answer in the list.

1. What does it mean if someone says that they were a victim of a Bluejacking attack?
   A. Unsolicited message was sent
   B. Cell phone was cloned
   C. IM channel introduced a worm
   D. Traffic was analyzed

2. How does TKIP provide more protection for WLAN environments?
   A. Uses the AES algorithm
   B. Decreases the IV size and uses the AES algorithm
   C. Adds more keying material
   D. Uses MAC and IP filtering

3. Which of the following is not a characteristic of the IEEE 802.11a standard?
   A. Works in the 5-GHz range
   B. Uses the OFMD spread spectrum technology
   C. Provides 52 Mbps in bandwidth
   D. Covers a smaller distance than 802.11b

4. What can be used to compromise and defeat callback security?
   A. Passive wiretapping

B. Call forwarding

C. Packet spoofing

D. Brute force attack

5. Which is not considered a firewall architecture used to protect networks?

A. Screened host

B. Screened subnet

C. NAT gateway

D. Two-tiered DMZ

6. Why are switched infrastructures safer environments than routed networks?

A. It is more difficult to sniff traffic since the computers have virtual private connections.

B. They are just as unsafe as nonswitched environments.

C. The data link encryption does not permit wiretapping.

D. Switches are more intelligent than bridges and implement security mechanisms.

7. What functionality hangs up on a remote caller and looks at a table of predefined valid phone numbers?

A. Caller ID

B. RAS

C. Callback

D. NOS

8. Which of the following protocols is considered connection oriented?

A. IP

B. ICMP

C. UDP

D. TCP

9. Which of the following best describes Ethernet transmissions over a LAN?

A. Traffic is sent to a gateway that sends it to the destination system.

B. Traffic is bursty in nature and broadcasts data to all hosts on the subnet.

C. Traffic streams and does not broadcast data.

D. Traffic is contained within collision domains but not broadcast domains.

10. Which of the following proxies cannot make access decisions on protocol commands?

A. Application

B. Packet filtering

C. Circuit

D. Stateful

11. A security concern that is prevalent in distributed environments and systems is _____.

    A. Knowing the proper proxy and default gateway

    B. Knowing whom to trust

    C. Knowing what authentication method is most appropriate

    D. Knowing how to resolve hostnames

12. Which protocol is commonly used to authenticate users on dial-up connections?

    A. PPTP

    B. IPSec

    C. CHAP

    D. L2F

13. Which of the following shows the sequence of layers as layer 2, 5, 7, 4, and 3?

    A. Data link, session, application, transport, and network

    B. Data link, transport, application, session, and network

    C. Network, session, application, network, and transport

    D. Network, transport, application, session, and presentation

14. What is another name for a VPN?

    A. Transport session

    B. Tunnel

    C. End-to-end connection

    D. Bandwidth

15. When security is a high priority, why is fiber cabling used?

    A. It has high data transfer rates and is less vulnerable to EMI.

    B. It multiplexes data, which can confuse attackers.

    C. It has a high degree of data detection and correction.

    D. Data interception is very difficult.

16. Why are mainframe environments considered more secure than LAN environments?

    A. They usually have fewer entry points.

    B. They have stronger authentication mechanisms.

    C. They have more auditing and encryption implemented.

    D. They are actually weaker than LANs.

17. What does it mean when computers communicate logically and physically with each other?

    A. They speak physically through headers and trailers and logically through physical connections.

B. They speak physically through PVCs and logically through SVCs.

C. They speak physically when connected to a backbone network and logically when they speak to each other within the same LAN.

D. They speak physically through electrons and network cables and logically through layers in the OSI model.

18. How does data encapsulation and the protocol stack work?

A. Each protocol or service at each layer in the OSI model multiplexes other packets to the data as it is passed down the protocol stack.

B. Each protocol or service at each layer in the OSI model adds its own information to the data as it is passed down the protocol stack.

C. The packet is encapsulated and grows as it hops from router to router.

D. The packet is encapsulated and grows when it is passed up the protocol stack.

19. Systems that are built on the OSI framework are considered open systems. What does this mean?

A. They do not have authentication mechanisms configured by default.

B. They have interoperability issues.

C. They are built with internationally accepted protocols and standards so that they can easily communicate with other systems.

D. They are built with international protocols and standards so that they can choose what types of systems they will communicate with.

20. Which of the following protocols work in the following layers: application, data link, network, and transport?

A. FTP, ARP, TCP, and UDP

B. FTP, ICMP, IP, and UDP

C. TFTP, ARP, IP, and UDP

D. TFTP, RARP, IP, and ICMP

21. What is the purpose of the presentation layer?

A. Addressing and routing

B. Data syntax and formatting

C. End-to-end connection

D. Framing

22. What is the purpose of the data link layer?

A. End-to-end connection

B. Dialog control

C. Framing

D. Data syntax

23. What takes place at the session layer?

    A. Dialog control

    B. Routing

    C. Packet sequencing

    D. Addressing

24. At what layer does a bridge work?

    A. Session

    B. Network

    C. Transport

    D. Data link

25. Which best describes the IP protocol?

    A. Connectionless protocol that deals with dialog establishment, maintenance, and destruction

    B. Connectionless protocol that deals with addressing and routing of packets

    C. Connection-oriented protocol that deals with addressing and routing of packets

    D. Connection-oriented protocol that deals with sequencing, error detection, and flow control

## Answers

1. **A.** Bluejacking occurs when someone sends an unsolicited message to a device that is Bluetooth enabled. Bluejackers look for a receiving device (phone, PDA, laptop) and then send a message to it. Often, the Bluejacker is trying to send someone else their business card, which will be added to the victim's contact list in their address book.

2. **C.** The TKIP protocol actually works with WEP by feeding it keying material, which is data to be used for generating random keystreams. TKIP increases the IV size, ensures that it is random for each packet, and adds the sender's MAC address to the keying material.

3. **C.** The IEEE standard 802.11a uses the OFDM spread spectrum technology, works in the 5-GHz frequency band, and provides bandwidth up to 54 Mbps.

4. **B.** A remote access server can be configured to drop a remote user's connection and call him back at a predefined number. If call forwarding is enabled, this security measure can be compromised.

5. **C.** The other answers describe basic firewall architectures, meaning where they can be placed within an environment. Network address translation (NAT) maps public addresses to private addresses and does not provide traffic monitoring

capabilities. Some firewalls provide NAT services, but the goals of the services are different.

6. **A.** Switched environments use switches to allow different network segments and/or systems to communicate. When this communication takes place, a virtual connection is set up between the communicating devices. Since it is a dedicated connection, broadcast and collision data is not available to other systems, as in an environment that uses purely bridges and routers.

7. **C.** The goal of a callback system is to provide another layer of authentication. For an attacker to compromise this setup successfully and obtain unauthorized access, she would need to be at the preconfigured phone number or reconfigure the telephone company's equipment to forward the call to her.

8. **D.** TCP is the only connection-oriented protocol listed. A connection-oriented protocol provides reliable connectivity and data transmission, while a connectionless protocol provides unreliable connections and does not promise or ensure data transmission.

9. **B.** Ethernet is a very "chatty" protocol because it allows all systems to hear each other's broadcasts, and the technology has many collisions because all systems have to share the same medium.

10. **C.** Application and circuit are the only types of proxy-based firewall solutions listed here; the others do not use proxies. Circuit-based proxy firewalls make decisions based on header information and not the protocol's command structure. Application-based proxies are the only ones that understand this level of granularity about the individual protocols.

11. **B.** Distributed environments bring about a lot more complexity and drastically increase the difficulty of access control. Since you now have many different applications, devices, services, and users, it is much more difficult to know which entities to trust and to what degree.

12. **C.** The other protocols listed are used for tunneling and/or VPN connectivity, not user authentication. CHAP uses the challenge-response method of authenticating a user.

13. **A.** The OSI model is made up of seven layers: application (layer 7), presentation (layer 6), session (layer 5), transport (layer 4), network (layer 3), data link (layer 2), and physical (layer 1).

14. **B.** A VPN sets up a private and secure tunnel by encapsulating and encrypting data. This allows data to be safely transmitted over untrusted networks.

15. **D.** It is difficult to tap into a fiber line, and fiber does not radiate signals as the other cable types do.

16. **A.** This is a relative and general statement. Mainframes are more closed systems and work in more closed environments when compared to the distributed environments we work in today. Mainframes usually have a smaller number of entry points, which are generally very controlled.

17. **D.** Systems, of course, communicate physically using network cables or airwaves. But they also communicate logically. An FTP protocol on one system "speaks" to the FTP protocol on another system and is not aware that many other protocols, devices, and cables are involved. Protocols, services, and applications communicate logically, and this communication is transmitted over physical means.

18. **B.** Data encapsulation means that a piece of data is put inside another type of data. This usually means that individual protocols apply their own instruction set in the form of headers and trailers. As a data package goes down the OSI layers, or protocol stack, of a system, each protocol that is involved adds its own instructions. This process is reversed at the destination.

19. **C.** An open system is a system that has been developed based on standardized protocols and interfaces. Following these standards allows the systems to interoperate more effectively with other systems that follow the same standards.

20. **C.** Different protocols have different functionalities. The OSI model is an attempt to describe conceptually where these different functionalities take place in a networking stack. The model attempts to draw boxes around reality to help people better understand the stack. Each layer has specific functionality and has several different protocols that can live at that layer that can carry out that specific functionality.

21. **B.** No protocols work at the presentation layer, but services that carry out data formatting, compression/decompression, and encryption/decryption processes do occur at that layer. Putting data into a standardized format allows for a large subset of applications to be able to understand and interpret it.

22. **C.** The data link layer, in most cases, is the only layer that understands the environment in which the system is working, whether it be Ethernet, Token Ring, wireless, or connection to a WAN link. This layer adds the necessary headers and trailers to the frame. Other systems on the same type of network using the same technology understand only the specific header and trailer format used in their data link technology.

23. **A.** The session layer is responsible for controlling how applications communicate, not how computers communicate. Not all applications use protocols that work at the session layer, so this layer is not always used in networking functions. A session layer protocol will set up the connection to the other application logically and control the dialog going back and forth. Session layer protocols allow applications to keep track of the dialog.

24. **D.** A bridge will read header information only in the data link layer and no higher because it makes forwarding and filtering decisions based on what is held within this header, which is the MAC address.

25. **B.** The IP protocol is connectionless and works at the network layer. It adds source and destination addresses to a packet as it goes through its data encapsulation process. IP can also make routing decisions based on the destination address.

# Cryptography

This chapter presents the following:

- History of cryptography
- Cryptography components and their relationships
- Government involvement in cryptography
- Symmetric and asymmetric key algorithms
- Public key infrastructure (PKI) concepts and mechanisms
- Hashing algorithms and uses
- Types of attacks on cryptosystems

*Cryptography* is a method of storing and transmitting data in a form that only those it is intended for can read and process. It is considered a science of protecting information by encoding it into an unreadable format. Cryptography is an effective way of protecting sensitive information as it is stored on media or transmitted through untrusted network communication paths.

One of the goals of cryptography, and the mechanisms that make it up, is to hide information from unauthorized individuals. However, with enough time, resources, and motivation, hackers can break most algorithms and reveal the encoded information. So a more realistic goal of cryptography is to make obtaining the information too work-intensive or time-consuming to be worthwhile to the attacker.

The first encryption methods date back to 4000 years ago and were considered more of an art. Encryption was later adapted as a tool to use in warfare, commerce, government, and other arenas in which secrets need to be safeguarded. With the relatively recent birth of the Internet, encryption has gained new prominence as a vital tool in everyday transactions. Throughout history, individuals and governments have worked to protect communication by encrypting it. As a result, the encryption algorithms and the devices that use them have increased in complexity, new methods and algorithms have been continually introduced, and encryption has become an integrated part of the computing world.

Cryptography has had an interesting history and has undergone many changes through the centuries. It seems that keeping secrets has been important throughout the ages of civilization. Keeping secrets gives individuals and groups the ability to hide their true intentions, gain a competitive edge, and reduce vulnerability, among other things.

The changes that cryptography has undergone closely follow advances in technology. The earliest cryptography methods involved a person carving messages into wood or stone, which was then delivered to the intended individual who had the necessary means to decipher the messages. This is a long way from how cryptography is used today. Now it is inserted into streams of binary code that pass over network wires, Internet communication paths, and airwaves.

# History of Cryptography

*Look, I scrambled up the message so no one can read it. Response: Yes, but now neither can we.*

Cryptography has roots that began around 2000 B.C. in Egypt, when hieroglyphics were used to decorate tombs to tell the life story of the deceased. The intention of the practice was not so much about hiding the messages themselves; rather, the hieroglyphics were intended to make the life story seem more noble, ceremonial, and majestic. An example of hieroglyphics is shown here:

Encryption methods evolved from being mainly for show into practical applications used to hide information from others.

A Hebrew cryptographic method required the alphabet to be flipped so that each letter in the original alphabet was mapped to a different letter in the flipped, or shifted, alphabet. The encryption method was called *atbash*, which was used to hide the true meaning of messages. An example of an encryption key used in the atbash encryption scheme is shown here:

```
ABCDEFGHIJKLMNOPQRSTUVWXYZ
ZYXWVUTSRQPONMLKJIHGFEDCBA
```

For example, the word "security" is encrypted into "hvxfirgb." What does "xrhhk" come out to be?

This is an example of a **substitution cipher**, because each character is replaced with another character. This type of substitution cipher is referred to as a **monoalphabetic substitution cipher** because it uses only one alphabet, whereas a **polyalphabetic substitution cipher** uses multiple alphabets.

**NOTE** Cipher is another term for algorithm.

This simplistic encryption method worked for its time and for particular cultures, but eventually more complex mechanisms were required.

Around 400 B.C., the Spartans used a system of encrypting information in which they would write a message on a sheet of papyrus (a type of paper) that was wrapped around a staff (a stick or wooden rod), which was then delivered and wrapped around a different staff by the recipient. The message was only readable if it was wrapped around the correct size staff, which would make the letters properly match up, as shown in Figure 8-1. This is referred to as the *scytale cipher*. When the papyrus was not wrapped around the staff, the writing appeared as just a bunch of random characters. The Spartan military had carriers run these pieces of papyrus to different groups of soldiers. The soldiers would then wrap the papyrus around a staff of the right diameter and length, and all the seemingly random letters would match up and form an understandable message. These could be used to instruct the soldiers on strategic moves and provide them with military directives.

Later, in Rome, Julius Caesar (100–44 B.C.) developed a simple method of shifting letters of the alphabet, similar to the atbash scheme. He simply shifted the alphabet by three positions. The following example shows a standard alphabet and a shifted alphabet. The alphabet serves as the algorithm, and the key is the number of locations that are shifted during the encryption and decryption process.

**Standard Alphabet:**
ABCDEFGHIJKLMNOPQRSTUVWXYZ

**Cryptographic Alphabet:**
DEFGHIJKLMNOPQRSTUVWXYZABC

As an example, suppose that we need to encrypt the message "Logical Security." We take the first letter of this message, *L*, and shift up three locations within the alphabet. The encrypted version of this first letter is *O*, so we write that down. The next letter to be encrypted is *O*, which matches *R* when we shift three spaces. We continue this process for the whole message. Once the message is encrypted, a carrier takes the encrypted version to the destination, where the process is reversed.

**Plaintext:**
LOGICAL SECURITY

**Ciphertext:**
ORJLFDO VHFXULWB

**Figure 8-1**
The scytale was used by the Spartans to decipher encrypted messages.

Today, this technique seems too simplistic to be effective, but in the time of Julius Caesar, not very many people could read in the first place, so it provided a high level of protection. The Caesar cipher is an example of a monoalphabetic cipher. Once more people could read and reverse-engineer this type of simplistic encryption process, the cryptographers of that day increased the complexity by creating polyalphabetic ciphers.

## Vigenere Cipher

In the 16th century in France, Blaise de Vigenere developed a polyalphabetic substitution cipher for Henry III. This was based on the Caesar cipher, but increased the difficulty of the encryption and decryption process.

As shown in Figure 8-2, we have a message that needs to be encrypted, which is SYSTEM SECURITY AND CONTROL. We have a key with the value of SECURITY. We also have a Vigenere table, or algorithm, which is really the Caesar cipher on steroids. Whereas the Caesar cipher used one shift alphabet (letters were shifted up three places), the Vigenere cipher has 27 shift alphabets and the letters are shifted up only one place.

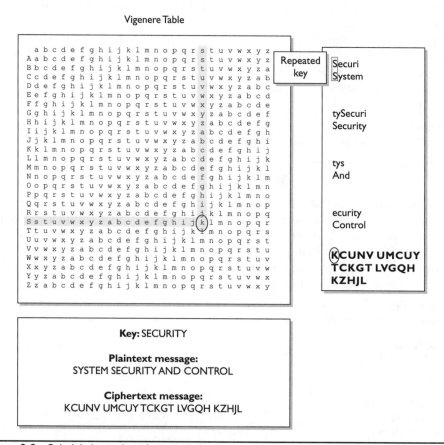

Figure 8-2   Polyalphabetic algorithms were developed to increase encryption complexity.

**NOTE** Plaintext is the readable version of a message. After an encryption process, the resulting text is referred to as ciphertext.

So, looking at the example in Figure 8-2, we take the first value of the key, *S*, and, starting with the first alphabet in our algorithm, trace over to the *S* column. Then we look at the first value of plaintext that needs to be encrypted, which is *S*, and go down to the *S* row. We follow the column and row and see that they intersect on the value *K*. That is the first encrypted value of our message, so we write down *K*. Then we go to the next value in our key, which is *E*, and the next value of plaintext, which is *Y*. We see that the *E* column and the *Y* row intersect at the cell with the value of *C*. This is our second encrypted value, so we write that down. We continue this process for the whole message (notice that the key repeats itself, since the message is longer than the key). The resulting ciphertext is the encrypted form that is sent to the destination. The destination must have the same algorithm (Vigenere table) and the same key (SECURITY) to properly reverse the process to obtain a meaningful message.

The evolution of cryptography continued as countries refined their practices using new methods, tools, and practices throughout the Middle Ages. By the late 1800s, cryptography was commonly used in the methods of communication between military factions.

During World War II, encryption devices were used for tactical communication, which drastically improved with the mechanical and electromechanical technology that provided the world with telegraphic and radio communication. The rotor cipher machine, which is a device that substitutes letters using different rotors within the machine, was a huge breakthrough in military cryptography that provided complexity that proved difficult to break. This work gave way to the most famous cipher machine in history to date: Germany's *Enigma* machine. The Enigma machine had separate rotors, a plugboard, and a reflecting rotor.

The originator of the message would configure the Enigma machine to its initial settings before starting the encryption process. The operator would type in the first letter of the message, and the machine would substitute the letter with a different letter and present it to the operator. This encryption was done by moving the rotors a predefined number of times. So, if the operator typed in a *T* as the first character, the Enigma machine might present an *M* as the substitution value. The operator would write down the letter *M* on his sheet. The operator would then advance the rotors and enter the next letter. Each time a new letter was to be encrypted, the operator would advance the rotors to a new setting. This process was followed until the whole message was encrypted. Then the encrypted text was transmitted over the airwaves, most likely to a German U-boat. The chosen substitution for each letter was dependent upon the rotor setting, so the crucial and secret part of this process (the key) was the initial setting and how the operators advanced the rotors when encrypting and decrypting a message. The operators at each end needed to know this sequence of increments to advance each rotor in order to enable the German military units to properly communicate.

Although the mechanisms of the Enigma were complicated for the time, a team of Polish cryptographers broke its code and gave Britain insight into Germany's attack plans and military movement. It is said that breaking this encryption mechanism shortened World War II by two years. After the war, details about the Enigma machine were published—one of the machines is exhibited at the Smithsonian Institute.

Cryptography has a deep, rich history. Mary, Queen of Scots, lost her life in the 16th century when an encrypted message she sent was intercepted. During the Revolutionary War, Benedict Arnold used a codebook cipher to exchange information on troop movement and strategic military advancements. Militaries have always played a leading role in using cryptography to encode information and to attempt to decrypt the enemy's encrypted information. William Frederick Friedman, who published *The Index of Coincidence and Its Applications in Cryptography* in 1920, is called the "Father of Modern Cryptography" and broke many messages that were intercepted during WWII. Encryption has been used by many governments and militaries and has contributed to great victory for some because it enabled them to execute covert maneuvers in secrecy. It has also contributed to great defeat for others, when their cryptosystems were discovered and deciphered.

When computers were invented, the possibilities for encryption methods and devices expanded exponentially and cryptography efforts increased dramatically. This era brought unprecedented opportunity for cryptographic designers to develop new encryption techniques. The most well-known and successful project was *Lucifer*, which was developed at IBM. Lucifer introduced complex mathematical equations and functions that were later adopted and modified by the U.S. National Security Agency (NSA) to establish the U.S. Data Encryption Standard (DES) in 1976, a federal government standard. DES has been used worldwide for financial and other transactions, and is imbedded into numerous commercial applications. DES has had a rich history in computer-oriented encryption and has been in use for over 25 years.

A majority of the protocols developed at the dawn of the computing age have been upgraded to include cryptography and to add necessary layers of protection. Encryption is used in hardware devices and in software to protect data, banking transactions, corporate extranet transmissions, e-mail messages, web transactions, wireless communications, storage of confidential information, faxes, and phone calls.

The code breakers and cryptanalysis efforts and the amazing number-crunching capabilities of the microprocessors hitting the market each year have quickened the evolution of cryptography. As the bad guys get smarter and more resourceful, the good guys must increase their efforts and strategy. *Cryptanalysis* is the science of studying and breaking the secrecy of encryption processes, compromising authentication schemes, and reverse-engineering protocols. Cryptanalysis is an important piece of cryptography and cryptology. When carried out by the "good guys," cryptanalysis is intended to identify flaws and weaknesses so that developers can go back to the drawing board and improve the components. It is also performed by curious and motivated hackers, to identify the same types of flaws, but with the goal of obtaining the encryption key for unauthorized access to confidential information.

**NOTE** Cryptanalysis is a very sophisticated science that encompasses a wide variety of tests and attacks. We will cover these types of attacks at the end of this chapter. Cryptology is the study of cryptanalysis and cryptography.

Different types of cryptography have been used throughout civilization, but today cryptography is deeply rooted in every part of our communications and computing world. Automated information systems and cryptography play a huge role in the effectiveness of militaries, functionality of governments, and economics of private businesses. As our dependency upon technology increases, so does our dependency upon cryptography, because secrets will always need to be kept.

## References

- "A Short History of Cryptography," by Shon Harris, *Information Security Magazine* (July 2001)    www.infosecuritymag.com/articles/july01/columns_logoff.shtml

- Chapter 2.1, "Security Strategies for E-Companies," by Fred Cohen    http://all.net/books/ip/Chap2-1.html

- "An Introduction to Cryptography"    http://home.earthlink.net/~mylnir/crypt.intro.html

- Trinity College Department of Computer Science Historical Cryptography web site    http://starbase.trincoll.edu/~crypto

- Open Directory Project Historical Cryptography links    http://dmoz.org/Science/Math/Applications/Communication_Theory/Cryptography/Historical

# Cryptography Definitions and Concepts

*Why can't I read this? Response: It is in ciphertext.*

Encryption is a method of transforming readable data, called *plaintext*, into a form that appears to be random and unreadable, which is called *ciphertext*. Plaintext is in a form that can be understood either by a person (a document) or by a computer (executable code). Once it is transformed into ciphertext, neither human nor machine can properly process it until it is decrypted. This enables the transmission of confidential information over insecure channels without unauthorized disclosure. When data is stored on a computer, it is usually protected by logical and physical access controls. When this same sensitive information is sent over a network, it can no longer take these controls for granted, and the information is in a much more vulnerable state.

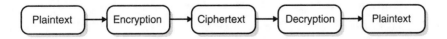

A system or product that provides encryption and decryption is referred to as a *cryptosystem* and can be created through hardware components or program code in an application. The cryptosystem uses an encryption algorithm, which determines how simple or complex the encryption process will be, keys, and the necessary software components and protocols. Most algorithms are complex mathematical formulas that are applied in a specific sequence to the plaintext. Most encryption methods use a secret value called a key (usually a long string of bits), which works with the algorithm to encrypt and decrypt the text.

The *algorithm*, the set of rules, dictates how enciphering and deciphering take place. Many of the mathematical algorithms used in computer systems today are publicly known and are not the secret part of the encryption process. If the internal mechanisms of the algorithm are not a secret, then something must be. The secret piece of using a well-known encryption algorithm is the key. A common analogy used to illustrate this point is the use of locks that you would purchase from your local hardware store. Let say that 20 people bought the same brand of lock. Just because these people share the same type and brand of lock does not mean that they can now unlock each other's doors and gain access to their private possessions. Instead, each lock comes with its own key, and that one key can only open that one specific lock.

In encryption, the *key* (cryptovariable) is a value that comprises a large sequence of random bits. Is it just any random number of bits crammed together? Not really. An algorithm contains a *keyspace*, which is a range of values that can be used to construct a key. When the algorithm needs to generate a new key, it uses random values from this keyspace. The larger the keyspace, the more available values that can be used to represent different keys—and the more random the keys are, the harder it is for intruders to figure them out. For example, if an algorithm allows a key length of 2 bits, the keyspace for that algorithm would be 4, which indicates the total number of different keys that would be possible. (Remember that we are working in binary and that $2^2$ equals 4.) That would not be a very large keyspace, and certainly it would not take an attacker very long to find the correct key that was used.

A large keyspace allows for more possible keys. (Today, we are commonly using key sizes of 128, 256, or 512 bits. So a key size of 512 bits would provide a $2^{512}$ keyspace.) The encryption algorithm should use the entire keyspace and choose the values to make up the keys as randomly as possible. If a smaller keyspace were used, there would be fewer values to choose from when generating a key, as shown in Figure 8-3. This would

## Cryptosystem

A cryptosystem encompasses all of the necessary components for encryption and decryption to take place. Pretty Good Privacy (PGP) is just one example of a cryptosystem. A cryptosystem is made up of at least the following:

- Software
- Protocols
- Algorithms
- Keys

**Figure 8-3**
Larger keyspaces allow for more possible key values.

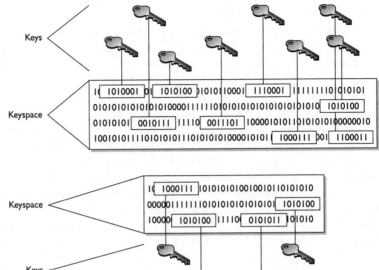

increase an attacker's chance of figuring out the key value and deciphering the protected information.

If an eavesdropper captures a message as it passes between two people, she can view the message, but it appears in its encrypted form and is therefore unusable. Even if this attacker knows the algorithm that the two people are using to encrypt and decrypt their information, without the key, this information remains useless to the eavesdropper, as shown in Figure 8-4.

**Figure 8-4**
Without the right key, the captured message is useless to an attacker.

## Kerckhoff's Principle

Auguste Kerckhoff published a paper in 1883 stating that the only secrecy involved with a cryptography system should be the key. He claimed that the algorithm should be publicly known. He asserted that if security were based on too many secrets, there would be more vulnerabilities to possibly exploit.

So, why do we care what some guy said over 120 years ago? Because this debate is still going on. Cryptographers in the private and academic sectors agree with Kerckhoff's principle, because making an algorithm publicly available means that many more people can view the source code, test it, and uncover any type of flaws or weaknesses. It is the attitude of "many heads are better than one." Once someone uncovers some type of flaw, the developer can fix the issue and provide society with a much stronger algorithm.

But, not everyone agrees with this philosophy. Governments around the world create their own algorithms that are not released to the public. Their stance is that if a smaller number of people know how the algorithm actually works, then a smaller number of people will know how to possibly break it. Cryptographers in the private sector do not agree with this practice and do not trust algorithms that they cannot examine.

It is basically the same as the open-source versus compiled software debate that is in full force today.

## Strength of the Cryptosystem

*You are the weakest link. Goodbye!*

The *strength* of an encryption method comes from the algorithm, secrecy of the key, length of the key, initialization vectors, and how they all work together within the cryptosystem. When strength is discussed in encryption, it refers to how hard it is to figure out the algorithm or key, whichever is not made public. Attempts to break a cryptosystem usually involve processing an amazing number of possible values in the hopes of finding the one value (key) that can be used to decrypt a specific message. The strength of an encryption method correlates to the amount of necessary processing power, resources, and time required to break the cryptosystem or figure out the value of the key. Breaking a cryptosystem can be accomplished by a brute force attack, which means trying every possible key value until the resulting plaintext is meaningful. Depending on the algorithm and length of the key, this can be an easy task or a task that is close to impossible. If a key can be broken with a Pentium II processor in three hours, the cipher is not strong at all. If the key can only be broken with the use of a thousand multiprocessing systems over 1.2 million years, then it is pretty darn strong.

 **NOTE** Initialization vectors are explained in the sidebar with the same name later in this chapter.

The goal when designing an encryption method is to make compromising it too expensive or too time-consuming. Another name for cryptography strength is *work factor*, which is an estimate of the effort and resources it would take an attacker to penetrate a cryptosystem.

How strong of a protection mechanism is required depends on the sensitivity of the data being protected. It is not necessary to encrypt information about a friend's Saturday barbeque with a top-secret encryption algorithm; conversely, it is not a good idea to send intercepted spy information using PGP. Each type of encryption mechanism has its place and purpose.

Even if the algorithm is very complex and thorough, other issues within encryption can weaken encryption methods. Because the key is usually the secret value needed to actually encrypt and decrypt messages, improper protection of the key can weaken the encryption. Even if a user employs an algorithm that has all the requirements for strong encryption, including a large keyspace and a large and random key value, if she shares her key with others, the strength of the algorithm becomes almost irrelevant.

Important elements of encryption are to use an algorithm without flaws, use a large key size, use all possible values within the keyspace, and protect the actual key. If one element is weak, it could be the link that dooms the whole process.

## Services of Cryptosystems

Cryptosystems can provide the following services:

- **Confidentiality**  Denies unauthorized parties access to information.
- **Authenticity**  Validates the source of the message, to ensure that the sender is properly identified.
- **Integrity**  Provides assurance that the message was not modified, accidentally or intentionally.
- **Nonrepudiation**  Establishes that a particular sender has sent the message so that they cannot deny having sent the message at a later date.

As an example of how these services work, suppose that your boss sends you a message telling you that you will be receiving a raise that doubles your salary. The message is encrypted, so you can be sure that it really came from your boss (authenticity), that someone did not alter it before it arrived at your computer (integrity), that no one else was able to read it as it traveled over the network (confidentiality), and that your boss cannot deny sending it later when he comes to his senses (nonrepudiation).

Different types of messages and transactions require higher or lower degrees of one or all of the services that encryption methods can supply. Military and intelligence agencies are very concerned about keeping information confidential, so they would choose encryption mechanisms that provide a high degree of secrecy. Financial institutions care about confidentiality, but care also about the integrity of the data being transmitted, so the encryption mechanism they would choose may differ from the military's encryption methods. If messages were accepted that had a misplaced decimal point or zero, the ramifications could be far reaching in the financial world. Legal agencies may care most about the authenticity of messages that they receive. If information that was received ever needed to be presented in a court of law, its authenticity would certainly be questioned; therefore, the encryption method used should ensure authenticity, which confirms who sent the information.

**NOTE** If David sends a message and then later claims that he did not send the message, this is an act of repudiation. When an encryption mechanism provides nonrepudiation, the sender cannot later deny that they sent the message (well, they can try to deny it, but the cryptosystem proves otherwise). It's a way of keeping the sender honest.

The types and uses of cryptography have increased over the years. At one time, cryptography was mainly used to keep secrets secret (confidentiality), but today we use cryptography to ensure the integrity of data, to authenticate messages, to confirm that a message was received, for access control, and much more. Throughout this chapter, we will cover the different types of cryptography that provide these different types of functionality, along with any related security issues.

## Cryptography Definitions

The following definitions are critical for your understanding of cryptography:

- **Access control** Restricting and controlling subject and object access attempts
- **Algorithm** Set of mathematical rules used in encryption and decryption
- **Cipher** Another name for algorithm
- **Cryptography** Science of secret writing that enables you to store and transmit data in a form that is available only to the intended individuals
- **Cryptosystem** Hardware or software implementation of cryptography that transforms a message to ciphertext and back to plaintext
- **Cryptanalysis** Practice of obtaining plaintext from ciphertext without a key, or of breaking the encryption
- **Cryptology** The study of both cryptography and cryptanalysis
- **Ciphertext** Data in encrypted or in an unreadable format
- **Data origin authentication** Proving the source of a message (system-based authentication)
- **Encipher** Act of transforming data into an unreadable format
- **Entity authentication** Proving the identity of the entity that sent a message
- **Decipher** Act of transforming data into a readable format
- **Key** Secret sequence of bits and instructions that governs the act of encryption and decryption
- **Key clustering** Instance when two different keys generate the same ciphertext from the same plaintext
- **Keyspace** A range of possible values used to construct keys
- **Plaintext** Data in readable format, also referred to as cleartext

- **Receipt**   Acknowledgement that a message has been received
- **Work factor**   Estimated time, effort, and resources necessary to break a cryptosystem

If some of these terms do not make sense now, just hold on. We will cover them all in the following sections.

## One-Time Pad

*I want to use my one-time pad three times. Response: Not a good idea.*

A **one-time pad** is a perfect encryption scheme because it is considered unbreakable if implemented properly. It was invented by Gilbert Vernam in 1917, so sometimes it is referred to as the Vernam cipher.

This cipher does not use shift alphabets, as do the Caesar and Vigenere ciphers discussed earlier, but instead uses a pad that is made up of random values, as shown in Figure 8-5. Our plaintext message that needs to be encrypted has been converted into bits, and our one-time pad is made up of random bits. This encryption process uses a binary mathematic function called exclusive-OR, usually abbreviated as XOR.

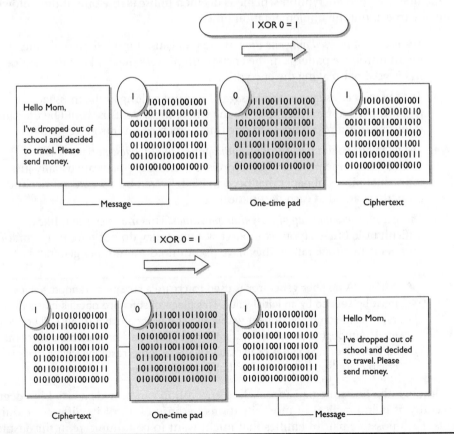

**Figure 8-5**   One-time pad

XOR is an operation that is applied to two bits and is a function commonly used in binary mathematics and encryption methods. When combining the bits, if both values are the same, the result is 0 (1 XOR 1 = 0). If the bits are different from each other, the result is 1 (1 XOR 0 = 1). For example:

| | |
|---|---|
| **Message stream** | 1001010111 |
| **Keystream** | 0011101010 |
| **Ciphertext stream** | 1010111101 |

So in our example, the first bit of the message is XORed to the first bit of the one-time pad, which results in the ciphertext value 1. The second bit of the message is XORed with the second bit of the pad, which results in the value 0. This process continues until the whole message is encrypted. The result is the encrypted message that is sent to the receiver.

In Figure 8-5, we also see that the receiver must have the same one-time pad to decrypt the message, by reversing the process. The receiver takes the first bit of the encrypted message and XORs it with the first bit of the pad. This results in the plaintext value. The receiver continues this process for the whole encrypted message, until the entire message is decrypted.

The one-time pad encryption scheme is deemed unbreakable only if the following things are true about the implementation process:

- *The pad must be used only one time.* If the pad is used more than one time, this might introduce patterns in the encryption process that will aid the evildoer in his goal of breaking the encryption.

- *The pad must be as long as the message.* If it is not as long as the message, the pad will need to be reused to cover the whole message. This would be the same thing as using a pad more than one time, which could introduce patterns.

- *The pad must be securely distributed and protected at its destination.* This is a very cumbersome process to accomplish, because the pads are usually just individual pieces of paper that need to be delivered by a secure courier and properly guarded at each destination.

- *The pad must be made up of truly random values.* This may not seem like a difficult task, but even our computer systems today do not have truly random number generators; rather, they have pseudorandom number generators.

 **NOTE** A number generator is used to create a stream of random values and must be seeded by an initial value. This piece of software obtains its seeding value from some component within the computer system (time, CPU cycles, etc.). Although a computer system is complex, it is a predictable environment, so if the seeding value is predictable in any way, the resulting values that are created are not truly random—but pseudorandom.

Although the one-time pad approach to encryption can provide a very high degree of security, it is impractical in most situations because of all of its different requirements. Each possible pair of entities that might want to communicate in this fashion

## One-Time Pad Requirements

For a one-time pad encryption scheme to be considered unbreakable, each pad in the scheme must meet the following requirements:

- Made up of truly random values
- Used only one time
- Securely distributed to destination
- Secured at sender's and receiver's sites
- At least as long as the message

must receive, in a secure fashion, a pad that is as long as or longer than the actual message. This type of key management can be overwhelming and may require more overhead than it is worth. The distribution of the pad can be challenging, and the sender and receiver must be perfectly synchronized so that each is using the same pad.

One-time pads have been used throughout history to protect different types of sensitive data. Today, they are still in place for many types of militaries as a backup encryption option if current encryption processes (that require computers and a power source) are unavailable for reasons of war or attacks.

## Running and Concealment Ciphers

*I have my decoder ring, spyglasses, and secret handshake. Now let me figure out how I will encrypt my messages.*

Two spy-novel-type ciphers are the running key cipher and the concealment cipher. The *running key cipher* could use a key that does not require an electronic algorithm and bit alterations, but cleverly steps in the physical world around you. For instance, the algorithm could be a set of books agreed upon by the sender and receiver. The key in this type of cipher could be a book page, line number, and column count. If I get a message from my super-secret spy buddy and the message reads "149l6c7.299l3c7.911l5c8," this could mean for me to look at the 1st book in our predetermined series of books, the 49th page, 6th line down the page, and the 7th column. So I write down the letter in that column, which is *m*. The second set of numbers starts with 2, so I go to the 2nd book, 99th page, 3rd line down, and then to the 7th column, which is *p*. The last letter I get from the 9th book, 11th page, 5th line, 8th column, which is *t*. So now I have come up with my important secret message, which is *mpt*. This means nothing to me, and I need to look for a new spy buddy. Running key ciphers can be used in different and more complex ways, but I think you get the point.

A *concealment cipher* is a message within a message. If my other super-secret spy buddy and I decide our key value is every third word, then when I get a message from him, I will pick out every third word and write it down. Suppose he sends me a message that reads, "The saying, 'The time is right' is not cow language, so is now a dead subject." Because my key is every third word, I come up with "The right cow is dead." This again means nothing to me, and I am now turning in my decoder ring.

No matter which of these two types of cipher is used, the roles of the algorithm and key are the same, even if they are not mathematical equations. In the running key cipher, the algorithm may be a predefined set of books. The key indicates the book, page, line, and word within that line. In substitution ciphers, the algorithm dictates that substitution will take place using a predefined alphabet or sequence of characters, and the key indicates that each character will be replaced with another character, as in the third character that follows it in that sequence of characters. In actual mathematical structures, the algorithm is a set of mathematical functions that will be performed on the message, and the key can indicate in which order these functions take place. So even if an attacker knows the algorithm, and we have to assume that he does, if he does not know the key, the message is still useless to him.

## Reference

- **Classical Cryptography**  www-math.cudenver.edu/~wcherowi/courses/ m5410/m5410cc.html

## Steganography

*Where's the top-secret message? Response: In this picture of my dogs.*

*Steganography* is a method of hiding data in another media type so that the very existence of the data is concealed. Steganography is mainly accomplished by hiding messages in graphic images. The least significant bit of each byte of the image can be replaced with bits of the secret message. This practice does not affect the graphic enough to be detected.

Steganography does not use algorithms or keys to encrypt information. This is a process to hide data within another object so that no one will detect its presence. A message can be hidden in a WAV file, in a graphic, or in unused spaces on a hard drive or sectors that are marked as unusable. Steganography can also be used to insert a digital watermark on digital images so that illegal copies of the images can be detected.

Secret message hidden in the picture. → Weapons are stockpiled in the hills.

## References

- Steganography and digital watermarking resource links, Johnson & Johnson Technology Consultants  www.jjtc.com/Steganography

- "Steganography Revealed," by Kristy Westphal, SecurityFocus (April 9, 2003)  www.securityfocus.com/infocus/1684

# Governments Involvement with Cryptography

*Big Brother is watching you! Um, I mean we are only watching the bad guys.*

In the United States, in the 1960s to 1980s, exportation of cryptographic mechanisms and equipment was very carefully regulated and monitored. The goal was to make obtaining and using encryption technology harder for terrorists and criminals. Harry Truman created the NSA in 1952, and its main mission was, and still is, to listen in on communications in the interest of national security for the United States. The NSA keeps an extremely low profile, and its activities are highly secret. The NSA also conducts research in cryptology to create secure algorithms and to break other cryptosystems to enable eavesdropping and spying.

The government attempted to restrict the use of public cryptography so that enemies of the United States could not employ encryption methods that were too strong for it to break. These steps caused tension and controversy between cryptography researchers, vendors, and the NSA pertaining to new cryptographic methods and the public use of them. The fear of those opposed to the restrictions was that if the government controlled all types of encryption and was allowed to listen in on private citizens' conversations, the obtained information would be misused in "Big Brotherly" ways. Also, if the government had the technology to listen in on everyone's conversations, the possibility existed that this technology would fall into the wrong hands, to be used for the wrong reasons.

## Wassenaar Arrangement

At one time a group existed whose duty was to control the export of specific types of weapons and cryptographic products to communist countries. This group came up with the Coordinating Committee on Multilateral Export Controls (COCOM). Because the threat of communism decreased over time, this group was disbanded. Then, in 1996, a group of 33 countries reached an agreement to control exportation of the same types of items to several countries deemed to be "terrorist states." These countries (Iran, Iraq, Libya, North Korea, Sudan, Cuba, and Syria) were identified as having connections with terrorist groups and activities. The group set up agreed upon guidelines regarding how to regulate exportation of certain types of weapons and technologies that contained cryptography functionality. In part, this group worked together to ensure that "dual-use" products (products that have both civilian and military application) that contain encryption capabilities were not made available to the "terrorist states." Because one of the main goals of every military is to be able to eavesdrop on its perceived enemies, the group of 33 countries was concerned that if terrorist states were able to obtain strong encryption methods, spying on them would be much harder to accomplish.

Just as the United States has the NSA, different countries have government agencies that are responsible for snooping on the communications of potential enemies, which involves using very powerful systems that can break a certain level of encryption. Since these countries know, for example, that they can break encryption methods that use symmetric keys of up to 56 bits, they will allow these types of products to be exported in an uncontrolled manner. Anything using a symmetric key over 56 bits needs to be controlled, because the governments are not sure that they can efficiently crack those codes.

The following outlines the characteristics of specific algorithm types that are considered too dangerous to fall into the hands of the enemy and thus are restricted:

- Symmetric algorithms with key sizes over 56 bits
- Asymmetric algorithms that carry out factorization of an integer with key sizes over 512 bits (such as RSA)
- Asymmetric algorithms that compute discrete logarithms in a field with key sizes over 512 bits (such as El Gamal)
- Asymmetric algorithms that compute discrete logarithms in a group (not in a field) with key sizes over 112 bits (such as ECC)

The Wassenaar Arrangement contains the agreed upon guidelines that this group of countries came up with, but the decision of whether or not to follow the guidelines has been left up to the individual countries. The United States has relaxed its export controls over the years and today exportation can take place to any country, other than the previously listed "terrorist states," after a technical review. If the product is an open-source product, then a technical review is not required, but it is illegal to provide this type of product directly to identified terrorist groups and countries. Also, a technical review is not necessary for exportation of cryptography to foreign subsidiaries of U.S. firms.

# Types of Ciphers

There are two basic types of symmetric encryption ciphers: substitution and transposition (permutation). The *substitution cipher* replaces bits, characters, or blocks of characters with different bits, characters, or blocks. The *transposition cipher* does not replace the original text with different text, but rather moves the original values around. It rearranges the bits, characters, or blocks of characters to hide the original meaning.

## Substitution Cipher

*Give me your A and I will change it out for an M. Now, no one can read your message. Response: That will fool them.*

A substitution cipher uses a key to dictate how the substitution should be carried out. In the *Caesar cipher*, each letter is replaced with the letter three places beyond it in the alphabet. The algorithm is the alphabet and the key is the instruction "shift up three."

As a simple example, if George uses the Caesar cipher with the English alphabet to encrypt the important message "meow," the encrypted message would be "phrz." Substitution is used in today's symmetric algorithms, but it is extremely complex compared to this example, which is only meant to show you the concept of how a substitution cipher works in its most simplistic form.

## Transposition Cipher

In a transposition cipher, the values are scrambled, or put into a different order. The key determines the positions that the values are moved to, as illustrated in Figure 8-6.

This is a simplistic example of a transposition cipher and only shows one way of performing transposition. When implemented with complex mathematical functions, transpositions can become quite sophisticated and difficult to break. Symmetric algorithms used today use both long sequences of complicated substitutions and transpositions on messages. The algorithm contains the possible ways that substitution and transposition processes *can* take place (represented in mathematical formulas). The key is used as the instructions for the algorithm, dictating exactly how these processes *will* happen and in what order. To understand the relationship between an algorithm and a key, let's look at Figure 8-7. Conceptually, an algorithm is made up of different boxes, each of which has a different set of mathematical formulas that dictates the substitution and transposition steps that will take place on the bits that enter the box. To encrypt our message, the bit values must go through these different boxes. If each of our messages goes through each of these different boxes in the same order with the same values, the evildoer will be able to easily reverse-engineer this process and uncover our plaintext message.

**Figure 8-6**
Transposition cipher

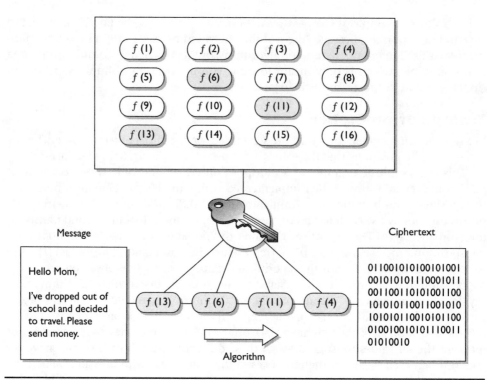

**Figure 8-7** Algorithm and key relationship

To foil the evildoer, we use a key, which is a set of values that indicates which box should be used, in what order, and with what values. So if message A is encrypted with key 1, the key will make the message go through boxes 1, 6, 4, and then 5. When we need to encrypt message B, we will use key 2, which will make the message go through boxes 8, 3, 2, and then 9. It is the key that adds the randomness and the secrecy to the encryption process.

Simple substitution and transposition ciphers are vulnerable to attacks that perform *frequency analysis*. In every language, some words and patterns are used more often than others. For instance, in the English language, the most commonly used letter is *E*. If Mike is carrying out frequency analysis on a message, he will look for the most frequently repeated pattern of 8 bits (which make up a character). So, if Mike sees that there are 12 patterns of 8 bits and he knows that *E* is the most commonly used letter in the language, he will replace these bits with this vowel. This allows him to gain a foothold on the process, which will allow him to reverse-engineer the rest of the message.

Today's symmetric algorithms use substitution and transposition methods in their encryption processes, but the mathematics that are used are (or should be) too complex to allow for simplistic frequency-analysis attacks to be successful.

# Methods of Encryption

Although there can be several pieces to an encryption process, the two main pieces are the algorithms and the keys. As stated earlier, algorithms used in computer systems are complex mathematical formulas that dictate the rules of how the plaintext will be turned into ciphertext. A key is a string of random bits that will be used by the algorithm to add to the randomness of the encryption process. For two entities to be able to communicate via encryption, they must use the same algorithm and, many times, the same key. In some encryption technologies, the receiver and the sender use the same key, and in other encryption technologies, they must use different but related keys for encryption and decryption purposes. The following sections explain the differences between these two types of encryption methods.

## Symmetric vs. Asymmetric Algorithms

Cryptography algorithms are either *symmetric algorithms*, which use symmetric keys (also called secret keys), or *asymmetric algorithms*, which use asymmetric keys (also called public and private keys). As if encryption were not complicated enough, the terms that are used to describe the key types only make it worse. Just pay close attention and you will get through this fine.

## Symmetric Cryptography

In a cryptosystem that uses symmetric cryptography, the sender and receiver use two instances of the same key for encryption and decryption, as shown in Figure 8-8. So the key has dual functionality, in that it can carry out both encryption and decryption processes. Symmetric keys are also called secret keys, because this type of encryption relies on each user to keep the key a secret and properly protected. If an intruder were to get this key, the intruder could decrypt any intercepted message encrypted with this key.

**Figure 8-8**
When using symmetric algorithms, the sender and receiver use the same key for encryption and decryption functions.

Symmetric encryption uses the same keys.

Encrypt message

Decrypt message

Message

Message

Each pair of users who want to exchange data using symmetric key encryption must have two instances of the same key. This means that if Dan and Iqqi want to communicate, both need to obtain a copy of the same key. If Dan also wants to communicate using symmetric encryption with Norm and Dave, he needs to have three separate keys, one for each friend. This might not sound like a big deal until Dan realizes that he may communicate with hundreds of people over a period of several months, and keeping track and using the correct key that corresponds to each specific receiver can become a daunting task. If ten people needed to communicate securely with each other using symmetric keys, then 45 keys would need to be kept track of. If 100 people were going to communicate, then 4950 keys would be involved. The equation that is used to calculate the number of symmetric keys needed is

$N(N - 1)/2$ = number of keys

The security of the symmetric encryption method is completely dependent on how well users protect the key. This should raise red flags for you if you have ever had to depend on a whole staff of people to keep a secret. If a key is compromised, then all messages encrypted with that key can be decrypted and read by an intruder. This is complicated further by how symmetric keys are actually shared and updated when necessary. If Dan wants to communicate with Norm for the first time, Dan has to figure out how to get the right key to Norm securely. It is not safe to just send it in an e-mail message, because the key is not protected and can be easily intercepted and used by attackers. Dan has to get the key to Norm through an *out-of-band method*. Dan can save the key on a floppy disk and walk over to Norm's desk, or have a secure courier deliver it to Norm. This is a huge hassle, and each method is very clumsy and insecure.

Because both users employ the same key to encrypt and decrypt messages, symmetric cryptosystems can provide confidentiality but they cannot provide authentication or nonrepudiation. There is no way to prove who actually sent a message if two people are using the same key.

If symmetric cryptosystems have so many problems and flaws, why use them at all? They are very fast and can be hard to break. Compared with asymmetric systems, symmetric algorithms scream in speed. They can encrypt and decrypt relatively quickly large amounts of data that would take an unacceptable amount of time to encrypt and decrypt with an asymmetric algorithm. It is also difficult to uncover data that is encrypted with a symmetric algorithm if a large key size is used. For many of our applications that require encryption, symmetric key cryptography is the only option.

The following list outlines the strengths and weakness of symmetric key systems:

- **Strengths**
  - Much faster than asymmetric systems.
  - Hard to break if using a large key size.
- **Weaknesses**
  - Requires a secure mechanism to deliver keys properly.

- Each pair of users needs a unique key, so as the number of individuals increases so does the number of keys, and key management can become overwhelming.

- Provides confidentiality but not authenticity or nonrepudiation.

The following are examples of symmetric algorithms, which will be explained later in the "Block and Stream Ciphers" section:

- Data Encryption Standard (DES)
- Triple-DES (3DES)
- Blowfish
- IDEA
- RC4, RC5, and RC6
- Advanced Encryption Standard (AES)

## References

- *Security in Open Systems,* **Node 208, "Symmetric Key Cryptography," by Paul Markovitz, NIST Special Publication 800-7 (July 1994)** http://csrc.nist.gov/publications/nistpubs/800-7/node208.html

- **Understanding the Public Key Cryptography** www.ibm.com/developerworks/ibm/library/it-sinn1

## Asymmetric Cryptography

*Some things you can tell the public, but some things you just want to keep private.*

In symmetric key cryptography, a single secret key is used between entities, whereas in public key systems, each entity has different keys, or *asymmetric keys*. The two different asymmetric keys are mathematically related. If a message is encrypted by one key, the other key is required in order to decrypt the message.

In a public key system, the pair of keys is made up of one public key and one private key. The *public key* can be known to everyone, and the *private key* must be known and used only by the owner. Many times, public keys are listed in directories and databases of e-mail addresses so that they are available to anyone who wants to use these keys to encrypt or decrypt data when communicating with a particular person. Figure 8-9 illustrates the use of the different keys.

The public and private keys of an asymmetric cryptosystem are mathematically related, but if someone gets another person's public key, she should not be able to figure out the corresponding private key. This means that if an evildoer gets a copy of Bob's public key, it does not mean that she can now use some mathematical magic and find out Bob's private key. But if someone got Bob's private key, then there is big trouble—no one other than the owner should have access to a private key.

**Figure 8-9**
Asymmetric
cryptosystem

Asymmetric systems use two different keys
for encryption and decryption purposes.

Public
key

Private
key

Encrypt
message

Decrypt message
with different key

Message

Message

If Bob encrypts data with his private key, the receiver must have a copy of Bob's public key to decrypt it. The receiver can decrypt Bob's message and decide to reply to Bob in an encrypted form. All she needs to do is encrypt her reply with Bob's public key, and then Bob can decrypt the message with his private key. It is not possible to encrypt and decrypt using the same key when using an asymmetric key encryption technology because, although mathematically related, the two keys are not the same key, as they are in symmetric cryptography. Bob can encrypt data with his private key, and the receiver can then decrypt it with Bob's public key. By decrypting the message with Bob's public key, the receiver can be sure that the message really came from Bob. A message can be decrypted with a public key only if the message was encrypted with the corresponding private key. This provides authentication, because Bob is the only one who is supposed to have his private key. If the receiver wants to make sure Bob is the only one that can read her reply, she will encrypt the response with his public key. Only Bob will be able to decrypt the message because he is the only one who has the necessary private key.

The receiver can also choose to encrypt data with her private key instead of using Bob's public key. Why would she do that? Authentication—she wants Bob to know that the message came from her and no one else. If she encrypted the data with Bob's public key, it does not provide authenticity because anyone can get Bob's public key. If she uses her private key to encrypt the data, then Bob can be sure that the message came from her and no one else. Symmetric keys do not provide authenticity because the same key is used on both ends. Using one of the secret keys does not ensure that the message originated from a specific entity.

If confidentiality is the most important security service to a sender, she would encrypt the file with the receiver's public key. This is called a *secure message format* because it can only be decrypted by the person who has the corresponding private key.

If authentication is the most important security service to the sender, then she would encrypt the data with her private key. This provides assurance to the receiver that the only person who could have encrypted the data is the individual who has possession of that private key. If the sender encrypted the data with the receiver's public key, authentication is not provided because this public key is available to anyone.

Encrypting data with the sender's private key is called an *open message format* because anyone with a copy of the corresponding public key can decrypt the message. Confidentiality is not ensured.

Each key type can be used to encrypt and decrypt, so do not get confused and think the public key is only for encryption and the private key is only for decryption. They both have the capability to encrypt and decrypt data. However, if data is encrypted with a private key, it cannot be decrypted with a private key. If data is encrypted with a private key, it must be decrypted with the corresponding public key.

An asymmetric algorithm works much more slowly than a symmetric algorithm, because symmetric algorithms carry out relatively simplistic mathematical functions on the bits during the encryption and decryption processes. They substitute and scramble (transposition) bits, which is not overly difficult or processor intensive. The reason that it is hard to break this type of encryption is that the symmetric algorithms carry out this type of functionality over and over again. So a set of bits will go through a long series of being substituted and scrambled.

Asymmetric algorithms are slower than symmetric algorithms because they use much more complex mathematics to carry out their functions, which requires more processing time. Although they are slower, asymmetric algorithms can provide authentication and nonrepudiation, depending on the type of algorithm being used. Asymmetric systems also provide for easier and more manageable key distribution than symmetric systems and do not have the scalability issues of symmetric systems. The reason for these differences is that, with asymmetric systems, you can send out your public key to all of the people you need to communicate with, instead of keeping track of a unique key for each one of them. The "Hybrid Encryption Methods" section shows how these two systems can be used together to get the best of both worlds.

**NOTE** "Public key cryptography" is "asymmetric cryptography." The terms can be used interchangeably.

The following outlines the strengths and weaknesses of asymmetric key algorithms:

- **Strengths**
  - Better key distribution than symmetric systems
  - Better scalability than symmetric systems
  - Can provide authentication and nonrepudiation
- **Weaknesses**
  - Works much more slowly than symmetric systems
  - Mathematically intensive tasks

The following are examples of asymmetric key algorithms:

- RSA
- Elliptic curve cryptosystem (ECC)

- Diffie-Hellman
- El Gamal
- Digital Signature Algorithm (DSA)
- Knapsack

These algorithms will be explained further in the "Types of Asymmetric Systems" section later in the chapter.

Table 8-1 summarizes the differences between symmetric and asymmetric algorithms.

 **NOTE**  Digital signatures will be discussed later in the section "Digital Signatures." (We like to keep it simple around here.)

## References

- *Security in Open Systems,* Node 210, "Asymmetric Key Cryptography," by Paul Markovitz, NIST Special Publication 800-7 (July 1994) http://csrc.nist.gov/publications/nistpubs/800-7/node210.html

- "Cryptography Defined/Brief History," by Sarah Simpson (Spring 1997)  www.eco.utexas.edu/~norman/BUS.FOR/course.mat/SSim/history.html

- "Asymmetric Cryptography," by Daniel Steffen (March 1997)  www.maths .mq.edu.au/~steffen/old/PCry/report/node8.html

- Frequently Asked Questions About Today's Cryptography, Version 4.1, Section 2.1.4.5, "What Is Output Feedback Mode?" by RSA Laboratories  www.rsasecurity.com/rsalabs/node.asp?id=2173

- "Report on the Symmetric Key Block Cipher Modes of Operation Workshop, October 20, 2001"  http://csrc.nist.gov/CryptoToolkit/modes/workshop1/workshop-report.pdf

| Attribute | Symmetric | Asymmetric |
|---|---|---|
| Keys | One key is shared between two or more entities. | One entity has a public key and the other entity has a private key. |
| Key exchange | Out-of-band through secure mechanisms. | Public key is made available to everyone and private key is kept secret to the owner. |
| Speed | Algorithm is less complex and faster. | Algorithm is more complex and slower. |
| Use | Bulk encryption, which means encrypting files and communication paths. | Key distribution and digital signatures. |
| Security service provided | Confidentiality. | Authentication and nonrepudiation. |

**Table 8-1**  Differences Between Symmetric and Asymmetric Systems

# Block and Stream Ciphers

*Which should I use, the stream or block cipher? Response: The stream cipher because it makes you look skinnier.*

The two main types of symmetric algorithms are block ciphers, which work on blocks of bits, and stream ciphers, which work on one bit at a time.

## Block Ciphers

When a *block cipher* is used for encryption and decryption purposes, the message is divided into blocks of bits. These blocks are then put through mathematical functions, one block at a time. Suppose that you need to encrypt a message that you are sending to your mother and you are using a block cipher that uses 64 bits. Your message of 640 bits is chopped up into 10 individual blocks of 64 bits. Each block is put through a succession of mathematical formulas, and what you end up with is 10 blocks of encrypted text. You send this encrypted message to your mother. She has to have the same block cipher and key, and those 10 ciphertext blocks go back through the algorithm in the reverse sequence and end up in your plaintext message.

A strong cipher contains the right level of two main attributes: confusion and diffusion. *Confusion* is commonly carried out through substitution, and *diffusion* is carried out by using transposition. For a cipher to be considered strong, it must contain both of these attributes, to ensure that reverse-engineering is basically impossible. The randomness of the key values and the complexity of the mathematical functions dictate the level of confusion and diffusion that is involved.

In algorithms, diffusion takes place as individual bits of a block are scrambled, or diffused throughout that block. Confusion is provided by carrying out complex substitution functions so that the bad guy cannot figure out how to substitute the right values and come up with the original plaintext. Suppose that I have 500 wooden blocks with individual letters written on them. I line them all up to spell out a paragraph (plaintext). Then I substitute 300 of them with another set of 300 blocks (confusion through substitution). Then I scramble all of these blocks up (diffusion through transposition) and leave them in a pile. For you to figure out my original message, you would have to substitute the correct blocks and then put them back in the right order. Good luck.

Confusion pertains to making the relationship between the key and resulting ciphertext as complex as possible so that the key cannot be uncovered from the ciphertext. Each ciphertext value should depend upon several parts of the key, but this mapping between the key values and the ciphertext values seems to be completely random to the observer.

Diffusion, on the other hand, means that a single plaintext bit has influence over several of the ciphertext bits. Changing a plaintext value should change many ciphertext values, not just one. In fact, in a strong block cipher, if one plaintext bit is changed, it will change every ciphertext bit with the probability of 50 percent. This means that if one plaintext bit changes, then about half of the ciphertext bits will change.

Block ciphers use diffusion and confusion in their methods. Figure 8-10 shows a conceptual example of a simplistic block cipher. It has four block inputs and each block is made up of 4 bits. The block algorithm has two layers of 4-bit substitution boxes called *S-boxes*. Each S-box contains a lookup table that is used by the algorithm as instructions on how the bits should be encrypted.

**Figure 8-10** A message is divided into blocks of bits, and substitution and transposition functions are performed on those blocks.

Figure 8-10 shows that the key dictates what S-boxes are to be used when scrambling the original message from readable plaintext to encrypted nonreadable ciphertext. Each S-box contains the different substitution and transposition methods that can be performed on each block. This example is simplistic—most block ciphers work with blocks of 32, 64, or 128 bits in size, and many more S-boxes are usually involved.

## Stream Ciphers

As stated earlier, a block cipher performs mathematical functions on blocks of bits. A stream cipher, on the other hand, does not divide a message into blocks; instead, a *stream cipher* treats the message as a stream of bits and performs mathematical functions on each bit individually.

When using a stream cipher, a plaintext bit will be transformed into a different ciphertext bit each time it is encrypted. Stream ciphers use *keystream generators*, which produces a stream of bits that is XORed with the plaintext bits to produce ciphertext, as shown in Figure 8-11.

**Figure 8-11**
With stream ciphers, the bits that are generated by the keystream generator are XORed with the bits of the plaintext message.

 **NOTE** This process is very similar to the one-time pad explained earlier. The individual bits in the one-time pad are used to encrypt the individual bits of the message through the XOR function, and in a stream algorithm the individual bits created by the keystream generator are used to encrypt the bits of the message through XOR also.

If the cryptosystem were only dependent upon the symmetric stream algorithm, an attacker could get a copy of the plaintext and the resulting ciphertext, XOR them together, and find the keystream to use in decrypting other messages. So the smart people decided to stick a key into the mix.

In block ciphers, it is the key that determines what functions are applied to the plaintext and in what order. The key provides the randomness of the encryption process. As stated earlier, most encryption algorithms are public, so people know how they work. The secret to the secret sauce is the key. In stream ciphers, the key also provides randomness, but to the stream of bits that are XORed to the plaintext. This concept is shown in Figure 8-12. As you can see in this graphic, both the sending and receiving ends must have the same key to generate the same keystream for proper encryption and decryption purposes.

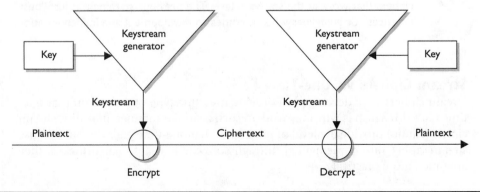

**Figure 8-12**   The sender and receiver must have the same key to generate the same keystream.

## Initialization Vectors

Initialization vectors (IVs) are random values that are used with algorithms to ensure that patterns are not created during the encryption process. They are used with keys and do not need to be encrypted when being sent to the destination. If IVs are not used, then two identical plaintext values that are encrypted with the same key will create the same ciphertext. Providing attackers with these types of patterns can make their job easier in breaking the encryption method and uncovering the key. For example, if we have the plaintext value of "See spot run" two times within our message, we need to make sure that even though there is a pattern in the plaintext message, a pattern in the resulting ciphertext will not be created. So the IV and key are both used by the algorithm to provide more randomness to the encryption process.

A strong and effective stream cipher contains the following characteristics:

- **Long periods of no repeating patterns within keystream values**   Bits that are generated by the keystream must be random.

- **Statistically unpredictable keystream**   The bits that are generated from the keystream generator cannot be predicted.

- **A keystream not linearly related to the key**   If someone figures out the keystream values, that does not mean that she now knows the key value.

- **Statistically unbiased keystream (as many 0s as 1s)**   There should be no dominance in the number of 0s or 1s in the keystream.

Stream ciphers require a lot of randomness and encrypt individual bits at a time. This requires more processing power than block ciphers require, which is why stream ciphers are better suited to be implemented at the hardware level. Because block ciphers do not require as much processing power, they can be easily implemented at the software level.

 **NOTE**   We do have block ciphers that work at the silicon level and stream ciphers that work at the software level. The previous statement is just "best practices" or guidelines when it comes to development and implementation.

## Stream Ciphers vs. One-Time Pads

Stream ciphers were developed to provide the same type of protection that one-time pads do, which is why they work in such a similar manner. In reality, stream ciphers cannot provide the level of protection that one-time pads do, but because stream ciphers are implemented through software and automated means, they are much more practical.

# Hybrid Encryption Methods

Up to this point, we have figured out that symmetric algorithms are fast but have some drawbacks (lack of scalability, difficult key management, and provide only confidentiality). Asymmetric algorithms do not have these drawbacks but are very slow. We just can't seem to win. So we turn to a hybrid system that uses symmetric and asymmetric encryption methods together.

## Asymmetric and Symmetric Algorithms Used Together

*Public key cryptography* uses two keys (public and private) generated by an asymmetric algorithm for protecting encryption keys and key distribution, and a secret key is generated by a symmetric algorithm and used for bulk encryption. Then there is a hybrid use of the two different algorithms: asymmetric and symmetric. Each algorithm has its pros and cons, so using them together can bring together the best of both worlds.

In the hybrid approach, the two technologies are used in a complementary manner, with each performing a different function. A symmetric algorithm creates keys that are used for encrypting bulk data, and an asymmetric algorithm creates keys that are used for automated key distribution.

When a symmetric key is used for bulk data encryption, this key is used to encrypt the message you want to send. When your friend gets the message you encrypted, you want him to be able to decrypt it, so you need to send him the necessary symmetric key to use to decrypt the message. You do not want this key to travel unprotected, because if the message were intercepted and the key were not protected, an evildoer could intercept the message that contains the necessary key to decrypt your message and read your information. If the symmetric key that is needed to decrypt your message is not protected, there is no use in encrypting the message in the first place. So we use an asymmetric algorithm to encrypt the symmetric key, as depicted in Figure 8-13. Why do we use the symmetric key on the message and the asymmetric key on the symmetric key? As stated earlier, the asymmetric algorithm takes longer because the math is more complex. Because your message is most likely going to be longer than the length of the key, we use the faster algorithm on the message (symmetric) and the slower algorithm on the key (asymmetric).

**Figure 8-13**
In a hybrid system, the asymmetric key is used to encrypt the symmetric key, and the symmetric key is used to encrypt the message.

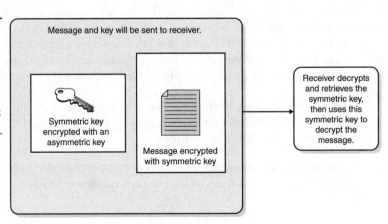

Message and key will be sent to receiver.

Symmetric key encrypted with an asymmetric key

Message encrypted with symmetric key

Receiver decrypts and retrieves the symmetric key, then uses this symmetric key to decrypt the message.

How does this actually work? Let's say Bill is sending Paul a message that Bill wants only Paul to be able to read. Bill encrypts his message with a secret key, so now Bill has ciphertext and a symmetric key. The key needs to be protected, so Bill encrypts the symmetric key with an asymmetric key. Remember that asymmetric algorithms use private and public keys, so Bill will encrypt the symmetric key with Paul's public key. Now Bill has ciphertext from the message and ciphertext from the symmetric key. Why did Bill encrypt the symmetric key with Paul's public key instead of his own private key? Because if Bill encrypted it with his own private key, then anyone with Bill's public key could decrypt it and retrieve the symmetric key. However, Bill does not want anyone who has his public key to read his message to Paul. Bill only wants Paul to be able to read it. So Bill encrypts the symmetric key with Paul's public key. If Paul has done a good job protecting his private key, he will be the only one who can read Bill's message.

Paul receives Bill's message and Paul uses his private key to decrypt the symmetric key. Paul then uses the symmetric key to decrypt the message. Paul then reads Bill's very important and confidential message that asks Paul how his day is.

Now when I say that Bill is using this key to encrypt and that Paul is using that key to decrypt, those two individuals do not necessarily need to find the key on their hard drive and know how to properly apply it. We have software to do this for us—thank goodness.

If this is your first time with these issues and you are struggling, don't worry. I remember when I first started with these concepts, and they turned my brain into a pretzel. Just remember the following points:

- An asymmetric algorithm performs encryption and decryption by using public and private keys that are related to each other mathematically.

- A symmetric algorithm performs encryption and decryption by using a symmetric key.
- A symmetric key is used to encrypt the actual message.
- Public keys are used to encrypt the symmetric key for secure key exchange.
- A secret key is synonymous to a symmetric key.
- An asymmetric key refers to a public or private key.

So, that is how a hybrid system works. The symmetric algorithm creates a secret key that will be used to encrypt the bulk, or the message, and the asymmetric key encrypts the secret key.

Now to ensure that some of these concepts are driven home, ask these questions of yourself without reading the answers provided:

1. If a symmetric key is encrypted with a receiver's public key, what security service(s) is provided?
2. If data is encrypted with the sender's private key, what security service(s) is provided?
3. If the sender encrypts data with the receiver's private key, what security services(s) is provided?
4. Why do we encrypt the message with the symmetric key?
5. Why don't we encrypt the symmetric key with another symmetric key?
6. What is the meaning of life?

**Answers:**

1. Confidentiality, because only the receiver's private key can be used to decrypt the symmetric key and only the receiver should have access to this private key.
2. Authenticity of the sender and nonrepudiation. If the receiver can decrypt the encrypted data with the sender's public key, then she knows that it was encrypted with the sender's private key.
3. None, because no one but the owner of the private key should have access to it. Trick question.
4. Because the asymmetric key is too slow.
5. We need to get the necessary symmetric key to the destination securely, which can only be carried out through asymmetric cryptography through the use of public and private keys.
6. 42

## Session Keys

*Hey, I have a disposable key! Response: Amazing. Now go away.*

A *session key* is a symmetric key that is used to encrypt messages between two users. A session key is no different from the symmetric key that was described in the previous section, but it is only good for one communication session between users.

If Tanya has a symmetric key that she uses to encrypt messages between Lance and herself all the time, then this symmetric key would not be regenerated or changed. They would use the same key every time they communicated using encryption. However, using the same key repeatedly increases the chances of the key being captured and the secure communication being compromised. If, on the other hand, a new symmetric key were generated each time Lance and Tanya wanted to communicate, as shown in Figure 8-14, it would be used only during their one dialog and then destroyed. If they wanted to communicate an hour later, a new session key would be created and shared.

A session key provides more protection than static symmetric keys because it is valid for only one session between two computers. If an attacker were able to capture the session key, she would have a very small window of time to use it to try to decrypt messages being passed back and forth.

In cryptography, almost all data encryption takes place through the use of session keys. When you write an e-mail and encrypt it before sending it over the wire, it is actually being encrypted with a session key. If you write another message to the same person one minute later, a brand new session key is created to encrypt that new message. So if an evildoer happens to figure out one session key, that does not mean that she has access to all other messages you write and send off.

When two computers want to communicate using encryption, they must first go through a handshaking process. The two computers agree on the encryption algorithms that will be used and exchange the session key that will be used for data encryption. In a sense, the two computers set up a virtual connection between each other and are said to be in session. When this session is done, each computer tears down any data struc-

1) Tanya sends Lance her public key.
2) Lance generates a random session key and encrypts it using Tanya's public key.
3) Lance sends the session key, encrypted with Tanya's public key, to Tanya.
4) Tanya decrypts Lance's message with her private key and now has a copy of the session key.
5) Tanya and Lance use this session key to encrypt and decrypt messages to each other.

**Figure 8-14** A session key is generated so that all messages can be encrypted during one particular session between users.

---

**Wireless Security Woes**

We covered the different 802.11 standards and the Wired Equivalent Privacy (WEP) protocol in Chapter 7. Among the long laundry list of security problems with WEP, not using unique session keys for data encryption is one of them. If only WEP is being use to encrypt wireless traffic, then in most implementations, just one static symmetric key is being used over and over again to encrypt the packets. This is one of the changes and advancements in the 802.11i standard, which makes sure that each packet is encrypted with a unique session key.

---

tures it built to enable this communication to take place, releases the resources, and destroys the session key. These things are taken care of by operating systems and applications in the background, so a user would not necessarily need to be worried about using the wrong type of key for the wrong reason. The software will handle this, but it is important for security professionals to understand the difference between the key types and the issues that surround them.

 **NOTE**   Private and symmetric keys should not be available in cleartext. This may seem obvious to you, but there have been several implementations over time that have allowed for this type of compromise to take place.

# Types of Symmetric Systems

There are several types of symmetric algorithms used today. They have different methods of providing encryption and decryption functionality. The one thing they all have in common is that they are symmetric algorithms, meaning the sender and receiver are using two instances of the same key.

In this section we will be walking through the following algorithms and their characteristics:

- Data Encryption Standard (DES)
- 3DES
- AES
- IDEA
- Blowfish
- RC4
- RC5

## Data Encryption Standard

*Data Encryption Standard (DES)* has had a long and rich history within the computer community. The National Institute of Standards and Technology (NIST) researched the need for the protection of sensitive but unclassified data during the 1960s and initiated a cryptography program in the early 1970s. NIST invited vendors to submit data encryption algorithms to be used as a cryptographic standard. IBM had already been developing encryption algorithms to protect financial transactions. In 1974, IBM's 128-bit algorithm, named *Lucifer*, was submitted and accepted. The NSA modified this algorithm to use a key size of 64 bits (8 bits used for parity, resulting in an effective key length of 56 bits) instead of the original 128 bits, and named it the *Data Encryption Algorithm (DEA)*. There was controversy about whether the NSA weakened Lucifer on purpose to enable it to decrypt messages not intended for it, but in the end the modified Lucifer became a national cryptographic standard in 1977 and an American National Standards Institute (ANSI) standard in 1978.

 **NOTE** DEA is the algorithm that fulfills DES, which is really just a standard. So DES is the standard and DEA is the algorithm, but in the industry we usually just refer to it as DES. The CISSP exam may refer to the algorithm by either name, so remember both.

DES has been implemented in a majority of commercial products using cryptography functionality and in the applications of almost all government agencies. It was tested and approved as one of the strongest and most efficient cryptographic algorithms available. The continued overwhelming support of the algorithm is what caused the most confusion when the NSA announced in 1986 that, as of January 1988, the agency would no longer endorse DES and that DES-based products would no longer fall under compliance with Federal Standard 1027. The NSA felt that because DES had been so popular for so long, it would surely be targeted for penetration and become useless as an official standard. Many researchers disagreed, but NSA wanted to move on to a newer, more secure, and less popular algorithm as the new standard.

NSA's decision to drop its support for DES caused major concern and negative feedback. At that time, it was shown that DES still provided the necessary level of protection; that projections estimated a computer would require thousands of years to crack DES; that DES was already embedded in thousands of products; and that there was no equivalent substitute. NSA reconsidered its decision and NIST ended up recertifying DES for another five years.

In 1998, the Electronic Frontier Foundation built a computer system for $250,000 that broke DES in three days using a brute force attack against the keyspace. It contained 1536 microprocessors running at 40 MHz, which performed 60 million test decryptions per second per chip. Although most people do not have these types of systems to conduct such attacks, as Moore's Law holds true and microprocessors increase in processing power, this type of attack will become more feasible for the average attacker. This brought about 3DES, which provides stronger protection, as discussed later in the chapter.

DES was later replaced by the Rijndael algorithm as the *Advanced Encryption Standard (AES)* by NIST. This means that Rijndael is the new approved method of encrypting sensitive but unclassified information for the U.S. government; it has been accepted by and is widely used in the public arena today.

# How Does DES Work?

*How does DES work again? Response: Voodoo magic and a dead chicken.*

DES is a symmetric block encryption algorithm. When 64-bit blocks of plaintext go in, 64-bit blocks of ciphertext come out. It is also a symmetric algorithm, meaning the same key is used for encryption and decryption. It uses a 64-bit key: 56 bits make up the true key, and 8 bits are used for parity.

When the DES algorithm is applied to data, it divides the message into blocks and operates on them one at a time. The blocks are put through 16 rounds of transposition and substitution functions. The order and type of transposition and substitution functions depend on the value of the key that is used with the algorithm. The result is 64-bit blocks of ciphertext.

# What Does It Mean When an Algorithm Is Broken?

*I dropped my algorithm. Response: Well, now it's broken.*

As described in an earlier section, DES was finally broken with a dedicated computer lovingly named the DES Cracker. But what does "broken" really mean?

In most instances, an algorithm is broken if someone is able to uncover a key that was used during an encryption process. So let's say that Kevin encrypted a message and sent it to Valerie. Marc captures this encrypted message and carries out a brute force attack on it, which means he tries to decrypt the message with different keys until he uncovers the right one. Once he identifies this key, the algorithm is considered broken. So does that mean that the algorithm is worthless? It depends upon who your enemies are.

If an algorithm is broken through a brute force attack, this just means that the attacker identified the one key that was used for one instance of encryption. But in proper implementations, we should be encrypting data with session keys, which are good only for that one session. So even if the attacker uncovers one session key, it may be useless to the attacker, in which case he now has to work to identify a new session key.

If your information is of sufficient value that enemies or thieves would exert a lot of resources to break the encryption (as may be the case for financial transactions or military secrets), then you would not use an algorithm that has been broken. If you are encrypting messages to your mother about a meatloaf recipe, you likely are not going to worry about whether the algorithm has been broken.

So breaking an algorithm can take place through brute force attacks or by identifying weaknesses in the algorithm itself. Brute force attacks have increased in potency because of the increased processing capacity of computers today. An algorithm that uses a 40-bit key has around 1 trillion possible key values. If a 56-bit key is used, then there are approximately 72 quadrillion different key values. This may seem like a lot, but relative to today's computing power, these key sizes do not provide much protection at all.

And as one final note, algorithms are built on current understanding of mathematics. As the human race advances in mathematics, the level of protection that today's algorithms provide may crumble.

# DES Modes

There are several modes of operation when using block ciphers. Each mode specifies how a block cipher will operate. One mode may work better in one type of environment for specific functionality, whereas another mode may work better in another environment with totally different requirements. It is important that vendors who employ DES (or any block cipher) understand the different modes and which one to use for which purpose.

DES has several distinct modes of operation that are used in different situations for different results; you just need to understand five of them:

- Electronic Code Book (ECB)
- Cipher Block Chaining (CBC)
- Cipher Feedback (CFB)
- Output Feedback (OFB)
- Counter Mode (CM)

**Electronic Code Book Mode**   ECB mode operates like a code book. A 64-bit data block is entered into the algorithm with a key, and a block of ciphertext is produced. For a given block of plaintext and a given key, the same block of ciphertext is always produced. Not all messages end up in neat and tidy 64-bit blocks, so ECB incorporates padding to address this problem. ECB is the easiest and fastest mode to use, but as we will see it has its dangers.

A key is basically instructions for the use of a code book that dictates how a block of text will be encrypted and decrypted. The code book provides the recipe of substitutions and permutations that will be performed on the block of plaintext. The security issue that comes up with using ECB mode is that each block will be encrypted with the exact same key, and thus the exact same code book. So, two bad things can happen here: an attacker could uncover the key and thus have the key to decrypt all the blocks of data, or an attacker could gather the ciphertext and plaintext of each block and build the code book that was used, without needing the key.

The crux of the problem is that there is not enough randomness to the process of encrypting the independent blocks, so if this mode is used to encrypt a large amount of data, it could be cracked more easily than the other modes that block ciphers can work in. So the next question to ask is, why even use this mode? This mode is the fastest and easiest, so we use it to encrypt small amounts of data, such as PINs, challenge-response values in authentication processes, and encrypting keys.

Because this mode works with blocks of data independently, data within a file does not have to be encrypted in a certain order. This is very helpful when using encryption in databases. A database has different pieces of data accessed in a random fashion. If it is encrypted in ECB mode, then any record or table can be added, encrypted, deleted, or decrypted independently of any other table or record. Other DES modes are dependent upon the text that was encrypted before them; this dependency makes it harder to encrypt and decrypt smaller amounts of text, because the previous encrypted text would need to be decrypted first. (Once we cover chaining in the next section, this dependency will make more sense.)

Because ECB mode does not use chaining, you should not use it to encrypt large amounts of data, because patterns would eventually show themselves.

**Cipher Block Chaining Mode**    In ECB mode, a block of plaintext and a key will always give the same ciphertext. This means that if the word "balloon" were encrypted and the resulting ciphertext were "hwicssn," each time it was encrypted using the same key, the same ciphertext would always be given. This can show evidence of a pattern, enabling an evildoer, with some effort, to discover the pattern and get a step closer to compromising the encryption process.

*Cipher Block Chaining (CBC)* does not reveal a pattern, because each block of text, the key, and the value based on the previous block are processed in the algorithm and applied to the next block of text, as shown in Figure 8-15. This results in more random ciphertext. Ciphertext is extracted and used from the previous block of text. This provides dependence between the blocks, in a sense chaining them together. This is where the name Cipher Block Chaining comes from, and it is this chaining effect that hides any patterns.

The results of one block are XORed with the next block before it is encrypted, meaning that each block is used to modify the following block. This chaining effect means that a particular ciphertext block is dependent upon all blocks before it, not just the previous block.

As an analogy, let's say that you have five buckets of marbles. Each bucket contains a specific color of marbles, red, blue, yellow, black, and green. The first bucket of red marbles (block of bits) you shake and tumble around (encrypt) to get them all mixed up. Then you take the second bucket of marbles, which are blue, and pour in the red marbles and go through the same exercise of shaking and tumbling them. You pour this bucket of marbles into your next bucket and shake them all up. This illustrates the incorporated randomness that is added when using chaining in a block encryption process.

When we encrypt our very first block using CBC, we do not have a previous block of ciphertext to "dump in" and use to add the necessary randomness to the encryption process. If we do not add a piece of randomness when encrypting this first block, then the bad guys could identify patterns, work backward, and uncover the key. So, we use an initialization vector (IVs were introduced previously in the "Initialization Vectors" sidebar). The 64-bit IV is XORed with the first block of plaintext and then it goes through its encryption process. The result of that (ciphertext) is XORed with the second block of plaintext, and then the second block is encrypted. This continues for

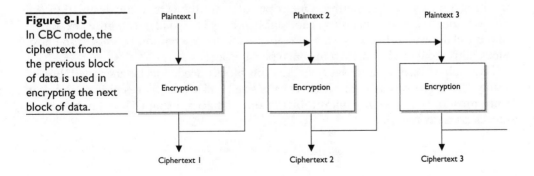

**Figure 8-15**
In CBC mode, the ciphertext from the previous block of data is used in encrypting the next block of data.

the whole message. It is the chaining that adds the necessary randomness that allows us to use CBC mode to encrypt large files. Neither the individual blocks nor the whole message will show patterns that will allow an attacker to reverse-engineer and uncover the key.

If we choose a different IV each time we encrypt a message, even if it is the same message, the ciphertext will always be unique. This means that if you send the same message out to 50 people and encrypt each one using a different IV, the ciphertext for each message will be different. Pretty nifty.

**Cipher Feedback Mode**   Sometimes block ciphers can emulate a stream cipher. Before we dig into how this would happen, let's first look at why.

If you are going to send an encrypted e-mail to your boss, your e-mail client will use a symmetric block cipher working in CBC mode. The e-mail client would not use ECB mode, because most messages are long enough to show patterns that can be used to reverse-engineer the process and uncover the encryption key. The CBC mode is great to use when you need to send large chunks of data at a time. But what if you are not sending large chunks of data at one time, but instead are sending a steady stream of data to a destination? If you are working on a terminal that communicates with a back-end terminal server, what is really going on is that each keystroke and mouse movement you make is sent to the backend server in chunks of 8 bits to be processed. So even though it seems as though the computer you are working on is carrying out your commands and doing the processing that you are requesting, it is not—this is happening on the server. Thus, if you need to encrypt the data that goes from your terminal to the terminal server, you could not use CBC mode because it only encrypts blocks of data 64 bits in size. You have blocks of 8 bits that you need to encrypt. What do you know, we have just the mode for this type of situation!

Figure 8-16 illustrates how CFB mode works, which is really a combination of a block cipher and a stream cipher. For the first block of 8 bits that needs to be encrypted, we do the same thing we did in CBC mode, which is to use an IV. Recall how stream ciphers work: The key and the IV are used by the algorithm to create a keystream, which is just a random set of bits. This set of bits is XORed to the block of plaintext, which results in the same size block of ciphertext. So the first block (8 bits) is XORed to the set of bits that is created through the keystream generator. Two things take place with this resulting 8-bit block of ciphertext. One copy goes over the wire to the destination (in our scenario, to the terminal server) and another copy is used to encrypt the next block of 8-bit plaintext. Adding this copy of ciphertext to the encryption process of the next block adds more randomness to the encryption process.

We walked through a scenario where 8-bit blocks needed to be encrypted, but in reality CFB mode can be used to encrypt any size blocks, even blocks of just 1 bit. But since most of our encoding maps 8 bits to one character, using CFB to encrypt 8-bit blocks is very common.

**Figure 8-16** Block cipher working in CFB mode

 **NOTE** When using CBC mode, it is a good idea to use a unique IV value per message, but it is not necessary since the message that is being encrypted is usually very large. When using CFB mode, we are encrypting a smaller amount of data, so it is imperative to use a new IV value to encrypt each new stream of data.

**Output Feedback Mode**   As you have read, you can use ECB mode for the process of encrypting small amounts of data, such as a key or PIN value. These components will be around 64 bits or more, so ECB mode works as a true block cipher. You can use CBC mode to encrypt larger amounts of data, in block sizes of 64 bits. In situations where you need to encrypt a smaller amount of data, you need the cipher to work like a stream cipher and encrypt individual bits of the blocks, as in CFB. In some cases, you still need to encrypt a small amount of data at a time (1–8 bits), but you need to ensure that possible errors do not affect your encryption and decryption processes.

If you look back at Figure 8-16, you see that the ciphertext from the previous block is used to encrypt the next block of plaintext. What if a bit in the first ciphertext gets corrupted? Then we have corrupted values going into the process of encrypting the next block of plaintext, and this problem just continues because of the use of chaining in this mode. Now look at Figure 8-17. It looks terribly similar to Figure 8-16, but notice

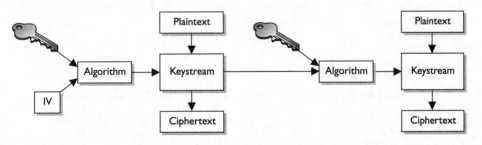

**Figure 8-17** Block cipher working in OFB mode

that the values that are used to encrypt the next block of plaintext are coming directly from the keystream, not from the resulting ciphertext. This is the difference between the two modes.

If you need to encrypt something that would be very sensitive to these types of errors, such as digitized video or digitized voice signals, you should not use CFB mode. You should use OFB mode, which reduces the chance that these types of bit corruptions can take place.

So OFB is a mode that a block cipher can work in when it needs to emulate a stream, because it encrypts small amounts of data at a time, but it has a smaller chance of creating and extending errors throughout the full encryption process.

To ensure that OFB and CFB are providing the most protection possible, the size of the ciphertext (in CFB) or keystream values (in OFB) needs to be the same size as the block of plaintext being encrypted. This means that if you are using CFB and are encrypting 8 bits at a time, the ciphertext that you bring forward from the previous encryption block needs to be 8 bits. Otherwise, you are repeating values over and over, which introduces patterns. (This is the same reason why a one-time pad should be used only one time and should be as long as the message itself.)

**Counter Mode**   Counter Mode (CM) is very similar to OFB mode, but instead of using a randomly unique IV value to generate the keystream values, this mode uses an IV counter that increments for each plaintext block that needs to be encrypted. The unique counter ensures that each block is XORed with a unique keystream value.

The other difference is that there is no chaining involved, which means that no ciphertext is brought forward to encrypt the next block. Since there is no chaining, the encryption of the individual blocks can happen in parallel, which increases the performance. The main reason that CM would be used instead of the other modes is performance.

This mode has been around for quite some time and is used in encrypting ATM cells for virtual circuits, in IPSec, and is now integrated in the new wireless security standard, 802.11i. A developer would choose to use this mode in these situations because individual ATM cells or packets going through an IPSec tunnel or over radio frequencies may not arrive at the destination in order. Since chaining is not involved, the destination can decrypt and begin processing the packets without having to wait for the full message to arrive and *then* decrypt all the data.

## References

- **"Cryptography," by Bill Unruh**   http://axion.physics.ubc.ca/crypt.html
- **Cryptography Research, Inc. home page**   www.cryptography.com

### Here We Are

If this is your first time trying to understand cryptography, you may be exasperated by now. Don't get too uptight. Many people are new to cryptography, because all of this magic just seems to work in the background without us having to understand it or mess with it. If you need more foundational understanding, check out the above references.

# Triple-DES

We went from DES to Triple-DES (3DES), so it might seem that we skipped Double-DES. We did. Double-DES has a key length of 112 bits, but there is a specific attack against Double-DES that reduces its work factor to about the same as DES. Thus, it is no more secure than DES. So we will move on to 3DES.

Many successful attacks against DES and the realization that the useful lifetime of DES was about up brought much support for 3DES. NIST knew that a new standard had to be created, which ended up being AES, but a quick fix was needed in the meantime to provide more protection for sensitive data. The result: 3DES.

3DES uses 48 rounds in its computation, which makes it highly resistant to differential cryptanalysis. However, because of the extra work that 3DES performs, there is a heavy performance hit. It can take up to three times longer than DES to perform encryption and decryption.

Although NIST has selected the Rijndael algorithm to replace DES as the AES, NIST and others expect 3DES to be around and used for quite some time.

3DES can work in different modes, and the mode that is chosen dictates the number of keys that are used and what functions are carried out:

- **DES-EEE3**   Uses three different keys for encryption, and the data is encrypted, encrypted, encrypted.

- **DES-EDE3**   Uses three different keys for encryption, and the data is encrypted, decrypted, and encrypted.

- **DES-EEE2**   The same as DES-EEE3 but uses only two keys, and the first and third encryption processes use the same key.

- **DES-EDE2**   The same as DES-EDE3 but uses only two keys, and the first and third encryption processes use the same key.

EDE may seem a little odd at first. How much protection could be provided by encrypting something, decrypting it, and encrypting it again? The decrypting portion here is decrypted with a different key. When data is encrypted with one symmetric key and decrypted with a different symmetric key, it is jumbled even more. So the data is not actually decrypted in the middle function; it is just run through a decryption process with a different key. Pretty tricky.

# Advanced Encryption Standard

After DES was used as an encryption standard for over 20 years and it was cracked in a relatively short time once the necessary technology was available, NIST decided a new standard, the Advanced Encryption Standard (AES), needed to be put into place. In January 1997, NIST announced its request for AES candidates and outlined the requirements in FIPS PUB 197. AES was to be a symmetric block cipher supporting key sizes of 128, 192, and 256 bits. The following five algorithms were the finalists:

- **MARS**   Developed by the IBM team that developed Lucifer

- **RC6**   Developed by RSA Laboratories

- **Serpent**   Developed by Ross Anderson, Eli Biham, and Lars Knudsen
- **Twofish**   Developed by Counterpane Systems
- **Rijndael**   Developed by Joan Daemen and Vincent Rijmen

Out of these contestants, Rijndael was chosen. The block sizes that Rijndael supports are 128, 192, and 256 bits. The number of rounds depends upon the size of the block and key length:

- If both key and block size is 128 bits, there are 10 rounds
- If both key and block size is 192 bits, there are 12 rounds
- If both key and block size is 256 bits, there are 14 rounds

Rijndael works well when implemented in software and hardware in a wide range of products and environments. It has low memory requirements and has been constructed to easily defend against timing attacks.

Rijndael was NIST's choice to replace DES. It is now the algorithm that is required to protect sensitive but unclassified U.S. government information.

**NOTE**   DEA is the algorithm that is used within DES, and Rijndael is the algorithm that is used in AES. In the industry, we refer to these as DES and AES instead of the actual algorithms.

## International Data Encryption Algorithm

*International Data Encryption Algorithm (IDEA)* is a block cipher and operates on 64-bit blocks of data. The 64-bit data block is divided into 16 smaller blocks, and each has eight rounds of mathematical functions performed on it. The key is 128 bits long and IDEA is faster than DES when implemented in software.

The IDEA algorithm offers different modes similar to the modes described in the DES section, but it is considered to be harder to break than DES because it has a longer key size. IDEA is used in the PGP and other encryption software implementations. It was thought to replace DES, but it is patented, meaning that licensing fees would have to be paid to use it.

As of this writing, there have been no successful practical attacks against this algorithm, although there have been numerous attempts.

## Blowfish

*One fish, two fish, red fish, blowfish. Response: Hmm, I thought it was blue fish.*

   *Blowfish* is a block cipher that works on 64-bit blocks of data. The key length can be up to 448 bits, and the data blocks go through 16 rounds of cryptographic functions. Bruce Schneier designed it.

# RC4

*RC4* is one of the most commonly implemented stream ciphers. It has a variable key size, is used in the SSL protocol, and was (improperly) implemented in the 802.11 WEP protocol standard. RC4 was developed in 1987 by Ron Rivest and was considered a trade secret of RSA Data Security, Inc. until someone posted the source code on a mailing list. Since the source code was released nefariously, the stolen algorithm is sometimes implemented and referred to as ArcFour or ARC4, because the title RC4 is trademarked.

The algorithm is very simple, fast, and efficient, which is why it became so popular.

# RC5

*RC5* is a block cipher that has a variety of parameters it can use for block size, key size, and the number of rounds used. It was created by Ron Rivest and analyzed by RSA Data Security, Inc. The block sizes used in this algorithm are usually 32, 64, or 128 bits, and the key size goes up to 2048 bits.

# RC6

*RC6* is a block cipher that was built upon RC5, so it has all the same attributes as RC5. The algorithm was developed mainly to be submitted as AES, but Rijndael was chosen instead. There were some modifications of the RC5 algorithm to increase the overall speed, the result of which is RC6.

---

### Cryptography Notation

In some resources, you may run across rc5-w/r/b or RC5-32/12/16. This is a type of shorthand that describes the configuration of the algorithm.

- w = Word size, in bits, which can be 16, 32, or 64 bits in length
- r = Number of rounds, which can be 0 to 255
- b = Number of bytes in the key, which can be 0 to 255

So RC5-32/12/16 would mean the following:

- 32-bit words, which means that it encrypts 64-bit data blocks
- Using 12 rounds
- 16-byte (128-bit) key

A developer configures these parameters (words, number of rounds, key size) for the algorithm for specific implementations. The existence of these parameters gives developers extensive flexibility.

---

# Types of Asymmetric Systems

As described earlier in the chapter, using purely symmetric key cryptography has three drawbacks, which affect the following:

- **Security services**   Purely symmetric key cryptography provides confidentiality only, not authentication or nonrepudiation.

- **Scalability**   As the number of people who need to communicate increases, so does the number of symmetric keys required, meaning more keys have to be managed.

- **Secure key distribution**   The symmetric key has to be delivered to its destination through a secure courier.

Despite these drawbacks, symmetric key cryptography was all that the computing society had available for encryption for quite some time. Symmetric and asymmetric cryptography did not arrive in this world on the same day or even in the same decade. We dealt with the issues surrounding symmetric cryptography for quite some time, waiting for someone smarter to come along and save us from some of this grief.

## Diffie-Hellman Algorithm

The first group to address the shortfalls of symmetric key cryptography decided to attack the issue of secure distribution of the symmetric key. Whitfield Diffie and Martin Hellman worked on this problem and ended up developing the first asymmetric key agreement algorithm, called, naturally, Diffie-Hellman.

To understand how Diffie-Hellman works, consider an example. Let's say that Tanya and Erika would like to communicate over an encrypted channel by using Diffie-Hellman. They would both generate a private and public key pair and exchange public keys. Tanya's software would take her private key (which is just a numeric value) and Erika's public key (another numeric value) and put them through the Diffie-Hellman algorithm. Erika's software would take her private key and Tanya's public key and insert them into the Diffie-Hellman algorithm on her computer. Through this process, Tanya and Erika derive the same shared value, which is used to create instances of symmetric keys.

So, Tanya and Erika exchanged information that did not need to be protected (their public keys) over an untrusted network, and in turn generated the exact same symmetric key on each system. They both can now use these symmetric keys to encrypt, transmit, and decrypt information as they communicate with each other.

 **NOTE**   The preceding example describes *key agreement*, which is different from *key exchange*, the functionality used by the other asymmetric algorithms that will be discussed in this chapter. With key exchange functionality, the sender encrypts the symmetric key with the receiver's public key before transmission.

The Diffie-Hellman algorithm enables two systems to receive a symmetric key securely without requiring a previous relationship or prior arrangements. The algorithm allows for key distribution, but does not provide encryption or digital signature func-

## Diffie-Hellman Mathematical Steps

1. Tanya chooses a large random integer (x) and sends it to Erika.

2. Erika also chooses a large random integer (y) and sends it to Tanya.

3. Tanya's software computes the following:

   $K = Y^x \bmod n$

4. Erika's software computes the following:

   $K = X^y \bmod n$

Erika's and Tanya's results are the same (K), which is the symmetric key that they can now use to encrypt data that they will send back and forth.

tionality. The algorithm is based on the difficulty of calculating discrete logarithms in a finite field.

## Man-in-the-Middle Attack

The Diffie-Hellman algorithm is vulnerable to a man-in-the-middle attack, because no authentication occurs before public keys are exchanged. In our example, when Tanya sends her public key to Erika, how does Erika really know that it is Tanya's public key? What if Lance spoofed his identity, told Erika he was Tanya, and sent over his key? Erika would accept this key, thinking that it came from Tanya. Let's walk through the steps of how this type of attack would take place, as illustrated in Figure 8-18:

1. Tanya sends her public key to Erika, but Lance grabs the key during transmission so that it never makes it to Erika.

2. Lance spoofs Tanya's identity and sends over his public key to Erika. Erika now thinks that she has Tanya's public key.

3. Erika sends her public key to Tanya, but Lance grabs the key during transmission so that it never makes it to Tanya.

4. Lance spoofs Erika's identity and sends over his public key to Tanya. Tanya now thinks that she has Erika's public key.

5. Tanya combines her private key and Lance's public key and creates symmetric key S1.

6. Lance combines his private key and Tanya's public key and creates symmetric key S1.

7. Erika combines her private key and Lance's public key and creates symmetric key S2.

8. Lance combines his private key and Erika's public key and creates symmetric key S2.

9. Now Tanya and Lance share a symmetric key (S1) and Erika and Lance share a different symmetric key (S2). Tanya and Erika think that they are sharing a key between themselves and do not realize that Lance is involved.

**Figure 8-18**
Man-in-the-middle
attack

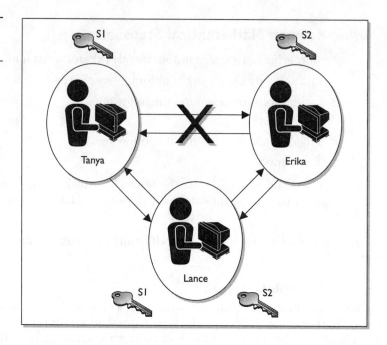

10. Tanya writes a message to Erika, uses her symmetric key (S1) to encrypt the message, and sends it.

11. Lance grabs the message and decrypts it with symmetric key S1, reads or modifies the message and re-encrypts it with symmetric key S2, and sends it to Erika.

12. Erika takes symmetric key S2 and uses it to decrypt and read the message.

The countermeasure to this type of attack is to have authentication take place before accepting someone's public key, which usually happens through the use of digital signatures and digital certificates.

 **NOTE** Although the Diffie-Hellman algorithm is vulnerable to a man-in-the-middle attack, this does not mean that this type of compromise can take place anywhere this algorithm is deployed. Most implementations include another piece of software or a protocol that compensates for this vulnerability. But some do not. As a security professional, you should understand these issues.

## RSA

*Give me an R, give me an S, give me an... How do you spell "RSA" again? Response: Sigh.*

*RSA*, named after its inventors Ron Rivest, Adi Shamir, and Leonard Adleman, is a public key algorithm that is the most popular when it comes to asymmetric algorithms. RSA is a worldwide de facto standard and can be used for digital signatures, key exchange, and encryption. It was developed in 1978 at MIT and provides authentication as well as key encryption.

## What Is the Difference Between Public Key Cryptography and Public Key Infrastructure?

*Public key cryptography* is the use of an asymmetric algorithm. Thus, the terms asymmetric algorithm and public key cryptography are interchangeable and mean the same thing. Examples of asymmetric algorithms are RSA, elliptic curve cryptosystem (ECC), Diffie-Hellman, El Gamal, LUC, and Knapsack. These algorithms are used to create public/private key pairs, perform key exchange or agreement, and generate and verify digital signatures.

**NOTE** Diffie-Hellman can only perform key agreement and cannot generate or verify digital signatures.

*Public key infrastructure (PKI)* is a different animal. It is not an algorithm, a protocol, or an application—it is an infrastructure that is based on public key cryptography. Let's look at why we even need PKIs today. When Erika needs to send Tanya a symmetric key securely, she needs to obtain Tanya's public key. Erika could get the key from a public repository that holds public keys for many individuals, but if Lance has switched out Tanya's public key and inserted his own, when Erika acquires a key that she thinks is Tanya's, she actually receives Lance's key and Erika has no idea.

Suppose that you ask me to send over my public key. When I send over a public key, how do you know that it is *my* public key? You do not know me and should not trust me. So if you need to know that I am who I claim to be and that the public key that I submit to you is actually mine, then you and I need to participate in a PKI. The reason that we have PKIs today is that people cannot trust each other directly and need to have a third party (certificate authority) vouch for each individual's identity and public key.

For example, if Erika and Tanya did not know each other, thus did not trust each other they would need a third party to implement some level of trust. Erika and Tanya know and trust Susan. Susan vouches for both Erika and Tanya and now they feel more comfortable dealing with each other. In PKI, this third party is referred to as the certificate authority. (We will dig much deeper into PKI in the "Public Key Infrastructure" section, later in the chapter.)

The security of this algorithm comes from the difficulty of factoring large numbers. The public and private keys are functions of a pair of large prime numbers, and the necessary activity required to decrypt a message from ciphertext to plaintext using a private key is comparable to factoring a product into two prime numbers.

**NOTE** A prime number is a positive whole number with no proper divisors, meaning the only numbers that can divide a prime number are 1 and the number itself.

One advantage of using RSA is that it can be used for encryption and digital signatures. Using its one-way function, RSA provides encryption and signature verification, and the inverse direction performs decryption and signature generation.

RSA has been implemented in applications; operating systems by Microsoft, Apple, Sun, and Novell; and at the hardware level in network interface cards, secure telephones, and smart cards. It can be used as a *key exchange protocol*, meaning that it is used to encrypt the symmetric key to get it securely to its destination. RSA has been most commonly used with the symmetric algorithm DES, which is quickly being replaced with AES. So, when RSA is used as a key exchange protocol, a cryptosystem generates a symmetric key using either the DES or AES algorithm. Then the system encrypts the symmetric key with the receiver's public key and sends it to the receiver. The symmetric key is protected because only the individual with the corresponding private key can decrypt and extract the symmetric key.

## Diving into Numbers

Cryptography is really all about using mathematics to scramble bits into an undecipherable form and then using the same mathematics in reverse to put the bits back into a form that can be understood by computers and people. RSA's mathematics are based on the difficulty of factoring a large integer into its two prime factors. Put on your nerdy hat with the propeller and let's look at how this algorithm works.

The algorithm creates a public key and a private key from a function of large prime numbers. When data is encrypted with a public key, only the corresponding private key can decrypt it. This act of decryption is basically the same as factoring the product of two prime numbers. So, let's say that I have a secret (encrypted message), and for you to be able to uncover the secret, you have to take a specific large number and factor it and come up with the two numbers I have written down on a piece of paper. This may sound simplistic, but the number you must properly factor can be $2^{300}$ in size. Not as easy as one may think.

The following sequence describes how the RSA algorithm comes up with the keys in the first place:

1. Choose two random large prime numbers, $p$ and $q$.

2. Generate the product of these numbers: $n = pq$.

3. Choose a random number to be the encryption key, $e$. Make sure that $e$ and $(p - 1)(q - 1)$ are relatively prime.

4. Compute the decryption key, $d$. This is $ed = 1 \bmod (p - 1)(q - 1)$ or $d = e^{-1} \bmod ((p - 1)(q - 1))$.

5. The public key = $(n, e)$.

6. The private key = $d$.

7. The original prime numbers $p$ and $q$ are discarded securely.

We now have our public and private keys, but how do they work together?

If you need to encrypt message $m$ with your public key $(e, n)$, the following formula is carried out:

$C = m^e \bmod n$

Then you need to decrypt the message with your private key (d), so the following formula is carried out:

$$M = c^d \bmod n$$

You may be thinking, "Well, I don't understand these formulas, but they look simple enough. Why wouldn't someone be able to break these small formulas and be able to uncover the encryption key?" Maybe someone will one day. As the human race advances in its understanding of mathematics and as processing power increases and cryptanalysis evolves, the RSA algorithm may be broken one day. If we figure out how to quickly and more easily factor large numbers into their original prime values, all of these cards fall down and this algorithm would no longer provide the security it does today. But we have not hit that bump in the road yet, so we are all happily using RSA in our computing activities.

## One-Way Function

A *one-way function* is a mathematical function that is easier to compute in one direction than in the opposite direction. An analogy of this is when you drop a glass on the floor. Although dropping a glass on the floor is easy, putting all the pieces back together again to reconstruct the original glass is next to impossible. This concept is similar to how a one-way function is used in cryptography, which is what the RSA algorithm, and all other asymmetric algorithms, is based upon.

The easy direction of computation in the one-way function that is used in the RSA algorithm is the process of multiplying two large prime numbers. Multiplying the two numbers to get the resulting product is much easier than factoring the product and recovering the two initial large prime numbers used to calculate the obtained product, which is the difficult direction. RSA is based on the difficulty of factoring large numbers that are the product of two large prime numbers. Attacks on these types of cryptosystems do not necessarily try every possible key value, but rather try to factor the large number, which will give the attacker the private key.

When a user encrypts a message with a public key, this message is encoded with a one-way function (breaking a glass). This function supplies a *trapdoor* (knowledge of how to put the glass back together), but the only way the trapdoor can be taken advantage of is if it is known about and the correct code is applied. The private key provides this service. The private key knows about the trapdoor, knows how to derive the original prime numbers, and has the necessary programming code to take advantage of this secret trapdoor to unlock the encoded message (reassembling the broken glass). Knowing about the trapdoor and having the correct functionality to take advantage of it are what make the private key private.

When a one-way function is carried out in the easy direction, encryption and digital signature verification functionality are available. When the one-way function is carried out in the hard direction, decryption and signature generation functionality are available. This means that only the public key can carry out encryption and signature verification and only the private key can carry out decryption and signature generation.

As explained earlier in this chapter, *work factor* is the amount of time and resources it would take for someone to break an encryption method. In asymmetric algorithms, the work factor relates to the difference in time and effort that carrying out a one-way function in the easy direction takes compared to carrying out a one-way function in the hard direction. In most cases, the larger the key size, the longer it would take for the bad guy to carry out the one-way function in the hard direction (decrypt a message).

The crux of this section is that all asymmetric algorithms provide security by using mathematical equations that are easy to perform in one direction and next to impossible to perform in the other direction. The "hard" direction is based on a "hard" mathematical problem. RSA's hard mathematical problem requires factoring large numbers into their original prime numbers. Diffie-Hellman and El Gamal are based on the difficulty of calculating logarithms in a finite field.

## El Gamal

*El Gamal* is a public key algorithm that can be used for digital signatures, encryption, and key exchange. It is based not on the difficulty of factoring large numbers but on calculating discrete logarithms in a finite field. El Gamal is actually an extension of the Diffie-Hellman algorithm.

Although El Gamal provides the same type of functionality as some of the other asymmetric algorithms, its main drawback is performance. When compared to other algorithms, this algorithm is usually the slowest.

## Elliptic Curve Cryptosystem

*Elliptic curves. That just sounds like fun.*

Elliptic curves are rich mathematical structures that have shown usefulness in many different types of applications. An *elliptic curve cryptosystem (ECC)* provides much of the same functionality that RSA provides: digital signatures, secure key distribution, and encryption. One differing factor is ECC's efficiency. ECC is more efficient that RSA and any other asymmetric algorithm.

Figure 8-19 is an example of an elliptic curve. In this field of mathematics, points on the curves comprise a structure called a group. These points are the values that are used in mathematical formulas for ECC's encryption and decryption processes. The algorithm computes discrete logarithms of elliptic curves, which is different from calculating discrete logarithms in a finite field (which is what Diffie-Hellman and El Gamal use).

Some devices have limited processing capacity, storage, power supply, and bandwidth, such as wireless devices and cellular telephones. With these types of devices, efficiency of resource use is very important. ECC provides encryption functionality, requiring a smaller percentage of the resources needed by RSA and other algorithms, so it is used in these types of devices.

In most cases, the longer the key, the more protection that is provided, but ECC can provide the same level of protection with a key size that is shorter than what RSA requires. Because longer keys require more resources to perform mathematical tasks, the smaller keys used in ECC require fewer resources of the device.

## LUC

This algorithm is based on "Lucas sequences" and implements a discrete logarithm in a finite field, but by using the Lucas sequences, computation may take place more quickly.

**Figure 8-19**
Elliptic curves

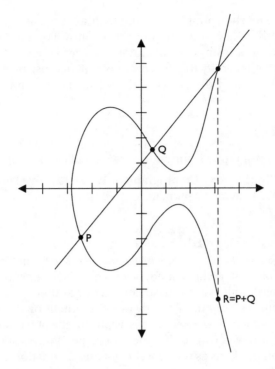

## Knapsack

There have been different versions of knapsack algorithms. The first one that was developed, Merkle-Hellman, could be used only for encryption, but it was later improved upon to provide digital signature capabilities. These types of algorithms are based on the "knapsack problem," a mathematical problem that poses the following question: If you have several different items, each having its own weight, is it possible to add these items to a knapsack so that the knapsack has a specific weight?

This algorithm was discovered to be insecure and is not currently used in cryptosystems.

## Zero Knowledge Proof

*This is how I feel after reading all of this cryptography stuff! Response: Just put your head between your knees and breath slowly.*

When military representatives are briefing the news media about some big world event, they have one goal in mind: to tell the story that the public is supposed to hear and nothing more. Do not provide extra information that someone could use to infer more information than they are supposed to know. The military has this goal because it knows that not just the good guys are watching CNN. This is an example of zero knowledge proof. You tell someone just the information that they need to know without "giving up the farm."

Zero knowledge proof is used in cryptography also. If I encrypt something with my private key, you can verify that my private key was used by decrypting the data with my public key. By encrypting something with my private key, I am proving to you that I have my private key—but I do not give or show you my private key. I do not "give up the farm" by disclosing my private key. In a zero knowledge proof, the verifier cannot prove to another entity that this proof is real, because he does not have the private key to prove it. So, only the owner of the private key can prove that he has possession of the key.

### References

- **Cryptography information** www.cs.berkeley.edu/~daw/crypto.html
- **"Elliptic Curve Cryptography FAQ v1.12," by George Barwood (Dec. 12, 1997)** www.cryptoman.com/elliptic.htm

# Message Integrity

*My message was altered, thus it has character flaws. Response: So do you.*

Parity bits and cyclic redundancy check (CRC) functions have been used in protocols to detect modifications in streams of bits as they are passed from one computer to another, but they can usually only detect unintentional modifications. Unintentional modifications can happen if there is a spike in the power supply, if there is interference or attenuation on a wire, or if some other type of physical condition occurs that causes the corruption of bits as they travel from one destination to another. Parity bits cannot identify whether a message was captured by an intruder, altered, and then sent on to the intended destination. The intruder can just recalculate a new parity value that includes his changes, and the receiver would never know the difference. For this type of protection, hash algorithms are required to successfully detect intentional and unintentional unauthorized modifications to data. We will now dive into hash algorithms and their characteristics.

## One-Way Hash

*Now, how many times does the one-way hash run again? Response: One, brainiac.*

A **one-way hash** is a function that takes a variable-length string, a message, and produces a fixed-length value called a hash value. For example, if Kevin wants to send a message to Maureen and wants to ensure that the message does not get altered in an unauthorized fashion while it is being transmitted, he would calculate a hash value for the message and append it to the message itself. When Maureen receives the message, she performs the same hashing function that Kevin used and compares her result with the hash value that was sent with the message. If the two values are the same, Maureen can be sure that the message was not altered during transmission. If the two values are different, Maureen knows that the message was altered, either intentionally or unintentionally, and she discards the message.

The hashing algorithm is not a secret—it is publicly known. The secrecy of the one-way hashing function is its "one-wayness." The function is run in only one direction, not the other direction. This is different from the one-way function used in public key cryptography, in which security is provided based on the fact that, without knowing a trapdoor, it is very hard to perform the one-way function backward on a message and come up with readable plaintext. However, one-way hash functions are never used in reverse; they create a hash value and call it a day. The receiver does not attempt to reverse the process at the other end, but instead runs the same hashing function one way and compares the two results.

The hashing one-way function takes place without the use of any keys. This means, for example, that if Cheryl writes a message, calculates a message digest, appends the digest to the message, and sends it on to Scott, Bruce can intercept this message, alter Cheryl's message, recalculate another message digest, append it to the message, and send it on to Scott. When Scott receives it, he verifies the message digest, but never knows that the message was actually altered by Bruce. Scott thinks that the message came straight from Cheryl and that it was never modified, because the two message digest values are the same. If Cheryl wanted more protection than this, she would need to use *message authentication code (MAC)*.

A MAC function is an authentication scheme that is derived by applying a secret key to a message in some form. This does not mean that the symmetric key is used to encrypt the message, though. There are two basic types of MACs that you need to be aware of: a hash MAC (HMAC) and a CBC-MAC.

## HMAC

In the previous example, if Cheryl were to use an HMAC function instead of just a plain hashing algorithm, a symmetric key would be concatenated with her message. The result of this process would be put through a hashing algorithm, and the result would be a MAC value. This MAC value is then appended to her message and sent to Scott. If Bruce were to intercept this message and modify it, he would not have the necessary

---

### Why Can't We Call an Apple an Apple?

The idea of a hashing function is simple. You run a message through a hashing algorithm, which in turn generates a hashing value. It must have been too simple, because someone threw in a lot of terms to make it more confusing:

- A hashing value can also be called a *message digest* or *fingerprint*.

- Hashing algorithms are also called *nonkeyed message digests*.

- Two types of message authentication code (MAC) exist: hashed MAC (HMAC) and CBC-MAC.

- MAC is also sometimes called *message integrity code (MIC)* or *modification detection code (MDC)*.

Good luck, and may the force be with you.

symmetric key to create the MAC value that Scott will attempt to generate. Figure 8-20 walks through these steps.

The top portion of Figure 8-20 shows the steps of a hashing process:

1. The sender puts the message through a hashing function.

2. A message digest value is generated.

3. The message digest is appended to the message.

4. The sender sends the message to the receiver.

5. The receiver puts the message through a hashing function.

6. The receiver generates her own message digest value.

7. The receiver compares the two message digest values. If they are the same, the message has not been altered.

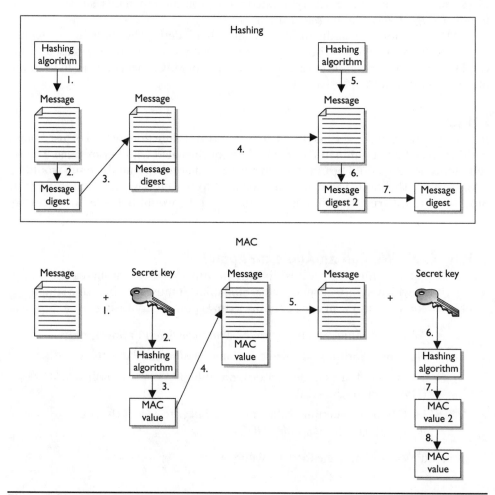

**Figure 8-20** Steps of using a hashing algorithm and HMAC function

The bottom half of Figure 8-20 shows the steps of an HMAC:

1. The sender concatenates a symmetric key with the message.

2. The result is put through a hashing algorithm.

3. A MAC value is generated.

4. The MAC value is appended to the message.

5. The sender sends the message to the receiver. (Just the message with the attached MAC value. The sender does not send the symmetric key with the message.)

6. The receiver concatenates a symmetric key with the message.

7. The receiver puts the results through a hashing algorithm and generates her own MAC value.

8. The receiver compares the two MAC values. If they are the same, the message has not been modified.

Now, when we say that the message is concatenated with a symmetric key, we don't mean that a symmetric key is used to encrypt the message. The message is not encrypted in a HMAC function, so there is no confidentiality being provided. Think about throwing a message in a bowl and then throwing a symmetric key in the same bowl. If you dump the contents of the bowl into a hashing algorithm, the result will be a MAC value.

This type of technology requires the sender and receiver to have the same symmetric key. The HMAC function does not involve getting the symmetric key to the destination securely; that would have to happen through one of the other technologies we have discussed already (Diffie-Hellman and key agreement, or RSA and key exchange).

## CBC-MAC

If a CBC-MAC is being used, the message is encrypted with a symmetric block cipher in CBC mode and the output of the final block of ciphertext is used as the MAC. The sender does not send the encrypted version of the message, but instead sends the plaintext version and the MAC attached to the message. The receiver receives the plaintext message and encrypts it with the same symmetric block cipher in CBC mode and calculates an independent MAC value. The receiver compares the new MAC value with the MAC value that was sent with the message. This method does not use a hashing algorithm, as does HMAC.

The use of the symmetric key ensures that the only person who can verify the integrity of the message is the person who has a copy of this key. No one else can verify the data's integrity, and if someone were to make a change to the data, he could not generate the MAC value (HMAC or CBC-MAC) the receiver would be looking for. Any modifications would be detected by the receiver.

Now the receiver knows that the message came from the system that has the other copy of the same symmetric key, so MAC provides a form of authentication. It provides *data origin authentication*, sometimes referred to as *system authentication*. This is different from user authentication, which would require the use of a private key. A private key is bound to an individual; a symmetric key is not. MAC authentication provides the weakest form of authentication because it is not bound to a user, just to a computer or device.

**NOTE**    The same key should not be used for authentication and encryption.

## Hashes, HMACs, and CBC-MACs—Oh My!

MACs and hashing processes can be confusing. The following table simplifies the differences between them:

| Function | Steps | Security Service Provided |
|---|---|---|
| Hash | 1. Sender puts a message through a hashing algorithm and generates a message digest (MD) value. 2. Sender sends message and MD value to receiver. 3. Receiver runs just the message through the same hashing algorithm and creates an independent MD value. 4. Receiver compares both MD values. If they are the same the message was not modified. | Integrity; not confidentiality or authentication Can detect only unintentional modifications |
| HMAC | 1. Sender concatenates a message and secret key and puts the result through a hashing algorithm. This creates a MAC value. 2. Sender appends the MAC value to the message and sends it to the receiver. 3. The receiver takes just the message and concatenates it with her own symmetric key. This results in an independent MAC value. 4. The receiver compares the two MAC values. If they are the same, the receiver knows that the message was not modified and knows from which system it came. | Integrity and data origin authentication; confidentiality is not provided |
| CBC-MAC | 1. Sender encrypts a message with a symmetric block algorithm in CBC mode. 2. The last block is used as the MAC. 3. The plaintext message and the appended MAC are sent to the receiver. 4. The receiver encrypts the message, creates a new MAC, and compares the two values. If they are the same, the receiver knows that the message was not modified and from which system it came. | Data origin authentication and integrity |

# Various Hashing Algorithms

As stated earlier, the goal of using a one-way hash function is to provide a fingerprint of the message. If two different messages produce the same hash value, then it would be easier for an attacker to break that security mechanism, because patterns would be revealed.

A strong one-hash function should not provide the same hash value for two or more different messages. If a hashing algorithm takes steps to ensure that it does not create the same hash value for two or more messages, it is said to be *collision free*.

Good cryptographic hash functions should have the following characteristics:

- The hash should be computed over the entire message.
- The hash should be a one-way function so that messages are not disclosed by their values.
- Given a message and its hash value, computing another message with the same hash value should be impossible.
- The function should be resistant to birthday attacks (explained in the upcoming section "Attack Against One-Way Hash Functions").

Table 8-2 and the following sections quickly describe some of the available hashing algorithms used in cryptography today.

## MD2

*MD2* is a one-way hash function designed by Ron Rivest that creates a 128-bit message digest value. It is not necessarily any weaker than the other algorithms in the "MD" family, but it is much slower.

## MD4

*MD4* is a one-way hash function designed by Ron Rivest. It also produces a 128-bit message digest value. It is used for high-speed computation in software implementations and is optimized for microprocessors.

| Algorithm | Description |
|---|---|
| Message Digest 2 (MD2) algorithm | One-way function. Produces a 128-bit hash value. Much slower than MD4 and MD5. |
| Message Digest 4 (MD4) algorithm | One-way function. Produces a 128-bit hash value. |
| Message Digest 5 (MD5) algorithm | One-way function. Produces a 128-bit hash value. More complex than MD4. |
| HAVAL | One-way function. Variable-length hash value. Modification of MD5 algorithm that provides more protection against attacks that affect MD5. |
| Secure Hash Algorithm (SHA) | One-way function. Produces a 160-bit hash value. Used with DSA. |
| SHA-1, SHA-256, SHA-384, SHA-512 | Updated version of SHA. SHA-1 produces a 160-bit hash value, SHA-256 creates a 256-bit value, and so on. |

**Table 8-2**   The Different Hashing Algorithms Available

## MD5

*MD5* was also created by Ron Rivest and is the newer version of MD4. It still produces a 128-bit hash, but the algorithm is more complex, which makes it harder to break. MD5 added a fourth round of operations to be performed during the hashing functions and makes several of its mathematical operations carry out more steps or more complexity to provide a higher level of security.

## SHA

*SHA* was designed by NIST and NSA to be used with the Digital Signature Standard (DSS). SHA was designed to be used in digital signatures and was developed when a more secure hashing algorithm was required for U.S. government applications.

SHA produces a 160-bit hash value, or message digest. This is then inputted into an asymmetric algorithm, which computes the signature for a message.

SHA is similar to MD4. It has some extra mathematical functions and produces a 160-bit hash instead of a 128-bit hash, which makes it more resistant to brute force attacks, including birthday attacks.

SHA was improved upon and renamed SHA-1. Recently, newer versions of this algorithm have been developed and released: SHA-256, SHA-384, and SHA-512.

## HAVAL

*HAVAL* is a variable-length one-way hash function and is a modification of MD5. It processes message blocks twice the size of those used in MD5; thus, it processes blocks of 1024 bits.

## References

- Counterpane Internet Security, Inc. home page   www.counterpane.com
- The Search Directory: Cryptography, 3DES, Hash algorithm, MD5, SHA-1 links   www.the-search-directory.com/cryptography
- RFC 1321 – The MD5 Message-Digest Algorithm   www.faqs.org/rfcs/rfc1321.html
- "Asymmetric Cryptography," sample chapter from *.NET Security and Cryptography,* by Peter Thorsteinson and G. Ganesh (Prentice Hall PTR, August 2003)   www.informit.com/articles/article.asp?p=102212&seqNum=3
- iNFOSYSSEC cryptography, encryption, and stenography links   www.infosyssec.net/infosyssec/cry2.htm

## Attack Against One-Way Hash Functions

A good hashing algorithm should not produce the same hash value for two different messages. If the algorithm does produce the same value for two distinctly different messages, this is called a *collision*. An attacker can attempt to force a collision, which is referred to as a *birthday attack*. This attack is based on the mathematical birthday paradox that exists in standard statistics. Now hold on to your hat while we go through this—it is a bit tricky:

> How many people must be in the same room for the chance to be greater than even that another person has the same birthday as you?

**Answer: 253**

> How many people must be in the same room for the chance to be greater than even that at least two people share the same birthday?

**Answer: 23**

This seems a bit backwards, but the difference is that in the first instance, you are looking for someone with a specific birthday date that matches yours. In the second instance, you are looking for any two people who share the same birthday. There is a higher probability of finding two people who share a birthday than of finding another person who shares your birthday. Or, stated another way, it is easier to find two matching values in a sea of values than to find a match for just one specific value.

Why do we care? The birthday paradox can apply to cryptography as well. Since any random set of 23 people most likely (at least a 50 percent chance) includes two people who share a birthday, by extension, if a hashing algorithm generates a message digest of 60 bits, then there is high likelihood that an adversary can find a collision using only $2^{30}$ inputs.

The main way that an attacker can find the corresponding hashing value that matches a specific message is through a brute force attack. If he finds a message with a specific hash value, it is equivalent to finding someone with a specific birthday. If he finds two messages with the same hash values, it is equivalent to finding two people with the same birthday.

The output of a hashing algorithm is $n$, and to find a message through a brute force attack that results in a specific hash value would require hashing $2^n$ random messages. To take this one step further, finding two messages that hash to the same value would require review of only $2^{n/2}$ messages.

## How Would a Birthday Attack Take Place?

Sue and Joe are going to get married, but before they do, they have a prenuptial contract drawn up that states if they get divorced, then Sue takes her original belongings and Joe takes his original belongings. To ensure that this contract is not modified, it is hashed and a message digest value is created.

One month after Sue and Joe get married, Sue carries out some devious activity behind Joe's back. She makes a copy of the message digest value without anyone knowing. Then she makes a new contract that states that if Joe and Sue get a divorce, Sue owns both her own original belongings and Joe's original belongings. Sue hashes this new contract and compares the new message digest value with the message digest value that correlates with the contract. They don't match. So Sue tweaks her contract ever so slightly and creates another message digest value and compares them. She continues to tweak her contract until she forces a collision, meaning that her contract creates the same message digest value as the original contract. Sue then changes out the original contract with her new contract and quickly divorces Joe. When Sue goes to collect Joe's belongings and he objects, she shows him that no modification could have taken place on the original document because it still hashes out to the same message digest. Sue then moves to an island.

Hash algorithms usually use message digest sizes (the value of $n$) that are large enough to make collisions difficult to accomplish, but they are still possible. An algorithm that has 160-bit output, like SHA-1, may require approximately $2^{80}$ computations to break. This means that there is a less than 1 in $2^{80}$ chance that someone could carry out a successful birthday attack.

The main point of discussing this paradox is to show how important longer hashing values truly are. A hashing algorithm that has a larger bit output is less vulnerable to brute force attacks such as a birthday attack. This is the primary reason why the new versions of SHA have such large message digest values.

## Reference

- *The PGP Attack FAQ*, Part 3, "The One-Way Hash"  www.stack.nl/~galactus/remailers/attack-3.html

## Digital Signatures

*To do a digital signature, do I sign my name on my monitor screen? Response: Sure.*

A digital signature is a hash value that has been encrypted with the sender's private key. The act of signing means encrypting the message's hash value with a private key, as shown in Figure 8-21.

From our earlier example in the "One-Way Hash" section, if Kevin wants to ensure that the message he sends to Maureen is not modified *and* he wants her to be sure that it came only from him, he can digitally sign the message. This means that a one-way hashing function would be run on the message, and then Kevin would encrypt that hash value with his private key.

When Maureen receives the message, she will perform the hashing function on the message and come up with her own hash value. Then she will decrypt the sent hash value (digital signature) with Kevin's public key. She then compares the two values, and if they are the same, she can be sure that the message was not altered during transmission. She is also sure that the message came from Kevin because the value was encrypted with his private key.

The hashing function ensures the integrity of the message, and the signing of the hash value provides authentication and nonrepudiation. The act of signing just means that the value was encrypted with a private key.

We need to be clear on all the available choices within cryptography, because different steps and algorithms provide different types of security services:

- A message can be encrypted, which provides confidentiality.
- A message can be hashed, which provides integrity.

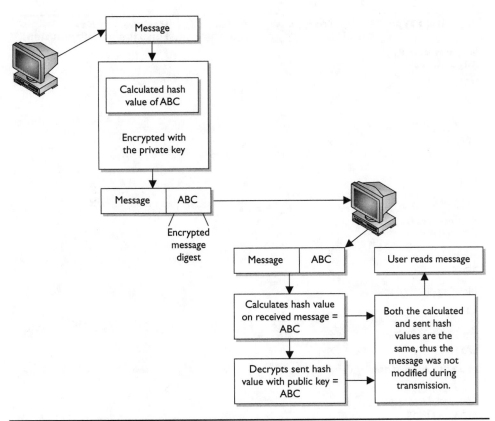

**Figure 8-21** Creating a digital signature for a message

- A message can be digitally signed, which provides authentication, nonrepudiation, and integrity.
- A message can be encrypted and digitally signed, which provides confidentiality, authentication, nonrepudiation, and integrity.

Some algorithms can only perform encryption, whereas others support digital signatures and encryption. When hashing is involved, a hashing algorithm is used, not an encryption algorithm.

It is important to understand that not all algorithms can necessarily provide all security services. Most of these algorithms are used in some type of combination to provide all the necessary security services required of an environment. Table 8-3 shows the services provided by the algorithms.

| Algorithm Type | Encryption | Digital Signature | Hashing Function | Key Distribution |
|---|---|---|---|---|
| **Asymmetric Key Algorithms** | | | | |
| RSA | X | X | | X |
| ECC | X | X | | X |
| Diffie-Hellman | | | | X |
| El Gamal | X | X | | X |
| DSA | | X | | |
| LUC | X | X | | X |
| Knapsack | X | X | | X |
| **Symmetric Key Algorithms** | | | | |
| DES | X | | | |
| 3DES | X | | | |
| Blowfish | X | | | |
| IDEA | X | | | |
| RC4 | X | | | |
| SAFER | X | | | |
| **Hashing Algorithms** | | | | |
| Ronald Rivest family of hashing functions: MD2, MD4, and MD5 | | | X | |
| SHA | | | X | |
| HAVAL (variable-length hash values using a one-way function design) | | | X | |

**Table 8-3** Various Functions of Different Algorithms

## Digital Signature Standard

Because digital signatures are so important to proving who sent what messages, the U.S. government decided to establish standards pertaining to their functions and acceptable use. In 1991, NIST proposed a federal standard called the *Digital Signature Standard (DSS)*. It was developed for federal departments and agencies, but most vendors designed their products to meet these specifications also. The federal government requires its departments to use DSA, RSA, or the elliptic curve digital signature algorithm (ECDSA) and SHA. SHA creates a 160-bit message digest output, which is then inputted into one of the three mentioned digital signature algorithms. SHA is used to ensure the integrity of the message, and the other algorithms are used to digitally sign the message. This is an example of how two different algorithms are combined to provide the right combination of security services.

RSA and DSA are the best known and most widely used digital signature algorithms. DSA was developed by the NSA. Unlike RSA, DSA can be used only for digital signatures, and DSA is slower than RSA in signature verification. RSA can be used for digital signatures, encryption, *and* secure distribution of symmetric keys.

# Public Key Infrastructure

*Let's put all of these cryptography pieces in a bowl and figure out how they all work together.*

*Public key infrastructure (PKI)* consists of programs, data formats, procedures, communication protocols, security policies, and public key cryptographic mechanisms working in a comprehensive manner to enable a wide range of dispersed people to communicate in a secure and predictable fashion. In other words, a PKI establishes a level of trust within an environment. PKI is an ISO authentication framework that uses public key cryptography and the X.509 standard. The framework was set up to enable authentication to happen across different networks and the Internet. Particular protocols and algorithms are not specified, which is why PKI is called a framework and not a specific technology.

PKI provides authentication, confidentiality, nonrepudiation, and integrity of the messages exchanged. PKI is a *hybrid* system of symmetric and asymmetric key algorithms and methods, which were discussed in earlier sections.

There is a difference between public key cryptography and PKI. Public key cryptography is another name for asymmetric algorithms. PKI is what its name states—it is an infrastructure. The infrastructure assumes that the receiver's identity can be positively ensured through certificates and that an asymmetric algorithm will automatically carry out the process of key exchange. The infrastructure therefore contains the pieces that will identify users, create and distribute certificates, maintain and revoke certificates, distribute and maintain encryption keys, and enable all technologies to communicate and work together for the purpose of encrypted communication and authentication.

Public key cryptography is one piece in PKI, but many other pieces make up this infrastructure. An analogy can be drawn with the e-mail protocol Simple Mail Transfer Protocol (SMTP). SMTP is the technology used to get e-mail messages from here to there, but many other things must be in place before this protocol can be productive. We need e-mail clients, e-mail servers, and e-mail messages, which together build a type of infrastructure—an e-mail infrastructure. PKI is made up of many different parts: certificate authorities, registration authorities, certificates, keys, and users. The following sections explain these parts and how they all work together.

Each person who wants to participate in a PKI requires a *digital certificate*, which is a credential that contains the public key for that individual along with other identifying information. The certificate is created and signed (digital signature) by a trusted third party, which is a *certificate authority (CA)*. When the CA signs the certificate, it binds the individual's identity to the public key, and the CA takes liability for the authenticity of that individual. It is this trusted third party (the CA) that allows people who have never met to authenticate to each other and communicate in a secure method. If Kevin has never met David, but would like to communicate securely with him, and they both trust the same CA, then Kevin could retrieve David's digital certificate and start the process.

## Certificate Authorities

*How do I know I can trust you? Response: The CA trusts me.*

A CA is a trusted organization (or server) that maintains and issues digital certificates. When a person requests a certificate, the registration authority (RA) verifies that individual's identity and passes the certificate request off to the CA. The CA constructs the certificate, signs it, sends it to the requester, and maintains the certificate over its lifetime. When another person wants to communicate with this person, the CA will basically vouch for that person's identity. When David receives a digital certificate from Kevin, David will go through steps to validate it. Basically, by providing David with his digital certificate, Kevin is stating, "I know you don't know or trust me, but here is this document that was created by someone you do know and trust. The document says that I am a good guy and you should trust me."

Once David validates the digital certificate, then he extracts Kevin's public key that is embedded within it. Now David knows that this public key is bound to Kevin. He also knows that if Kevin uses his private key to create a digital signature and David can properly decrypt it using this public key, then it did indeed come from Kevin.

Certificate
authority

Dave and Kevin trust each other indirectly.

Kevin trusts the CA                                    Dave trusts the CA

**NOTE**    Remember the man-in-the-middle attack covered earlier in the "Diffie-Hellman Algorithm" section? This attack is possible if two users are not working in a PKI environment and do not truly know the identity of the owners of the public keys.

The CA can be internal to an organization. Such a setup would enable the company to control the CA server, configure how authentication takes place, maintain the certificates, and recall certificates when necessary. Other CAs are organizations dedicated to this type of service, and other individuals and companies pay them to supply it. Some well-known CAs are Entrust and VeriSign. Many browsers have several well-known CAs configured by default.

**NOTE** More and more organizations are setting up their own internal PKIs. When these independent PKIs need to interconnect to allow for secure communication to take place (either between departments or different companies), there has to be a way for the two root CAs to trust each other. The two CAs do not have a CA above them that they can both trust, so they must carry out cross certification. A cross certification is the process undertaken by CAs to establish a trust relationship in which they rely upon each other's digital certificates and public keys as if they had issued them themselves. When this is set up, a CA for one company can validate digital certificates from the other company and vise versa.

The CA is responsible for creating and handing out certificates, maintaining them, and revoking them if necessary. Revocation is handled by the CA and the revoked certificate information is stored on a *certificate revocation list (CRL)*. This is a list of every certificate that has been revoked. This list is maintained and updated periodically. A certificate may be revoked because the key holder's private key was compromised or because the CA discovered that the certificate was issued to the wrong person. An analogy for the use of a CRL is how a driver's license is used by a police officer. If an officer pulls over Sean for speeding, the officer will ask to see Sean's license. The officer will then run a check on the license to find out if Sean is wanted for any other infractions of the law and to verify that the license has not expired. The same thing happens when a person compares a certificate to a CRL. If the certificate became invalid for some reason, the CRL is the mechanism for the CA to let others know this information.

**NOTE** CRLs are the thorn in the side of many PKI implementations. They are challenging for a long list of reasons. It is interesting to know that, by default, web browsers do not check a CRL to ensure that a certificate is not revoked. So when you are setting up an SSL connection to do e-commerce over the Internet, you could be relying on a certificate that has actually been revoked. Not good.

*Online Certificate Status Protocol (OCSP)* is being used more and more compared to the cumbersome CRL approach. When using just a CRL, the user's browser must either check a central CRL to find out if the certification has been revoked or continually push out CRL values to the clients to ensure that they have an updated CRL. If OCSP is implemented, it does this work automatically in the background. It carries out real-time validation of a certificate and reports back to the user whether the certificate is valid, invalid, or unknown. OCSP checks the CRL that is maintained by the CA. So the CRL is still being used, but now we have a protocol developed specifically to check the CRL during a certificate validation process.

## Certificates

One of the most important pieces of a PKI is its digital certificate. A *certificate* is the mechanism used to associate a public key with a collection of components in a manner that is sufficient to uniquely identify the claimed owner. The standard for how the CA creates the certificate is X.509, which dictates the different fields used in the certificate and the valid values that can populate those fields. We are currently at version 4 of this standard, which is often denoted as X.509v4. Many cryptographic protocols use this type of certificate, including SSL.

The certificate includes the serial number, version number, identity information, algorithm information, lifetime dates, and the signature of the issuing authority, as shown in Figure 8-22.

## Registration Authority

The *registration authority (RA)* performs the certification registration duties. The RA establishes and confirms the identity of an individual, initiates the certification process with a CA on behalf of an end user, and performs certificate life-cycle management functions. The RA cannot issue certificates, but can act as a broker between the user and the CA. When users need new certificates, they make requests to the RA, and the RA verifies all necessary identification information before allowing a request to go to the CA.

 **NOTE** A few years ago, VeriSign assigned some very powerful certificates to two individuals who claimed to work for Microsoft. They did not work for Microsoft and this opened the doors to a lot of potential security compromises.

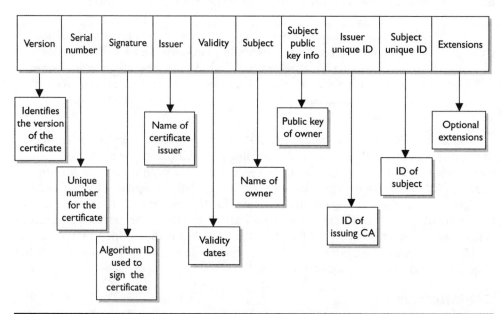

**Figure 8-22**   Each certificate has a structure with all the necessary identifying information in it.

## PKI Steps

Now that we know some of the main pieces of a PKI and how they actually work together, let's walk through an example. First, suppose that John needs to obtain a digital certificate for himself so that he can participate in a PKI. The following are the steps to do so:

1. John makes a request to the RA.

2. The RA requests certain identification information from John, such as a copy of his driver's license, his phone number, his address, and other identifying information.

3. Once the RA receives the required information from John and verifies it, the RA sends his certificate request to the CA.

4. The CA creates a certificate with John's public key and identity information embedded. (The private/public key pair is generated either by the CA or on John's machine, which depends on the systems' configurations. If it is created at the CA, his private key needs to be sent to him by secure means. In most cases, the user generates this pair and sends in his public key during the registration process.)

Now John is registered and can participate in a PKI. John and Diane decide that they want to communicate, so they take the following steps, shown in Figure 8-23:

1. John requests Diane's public key from a public directory.

2. The directory, sometimes called a repository, sends Diane's digital certificate.

3. John verifies the digital certificate and extracts her public key. John uses this public key to encrypt a session key that will be used to encrypt their messages. John sends the encrypted session key to Diane. John also sends his certificate, containing his public key, to Diane.

**Figure 8-23**
CA and user
relationships

Directory

CA

1. John requests
   Diane's public key.

2. Diane's public
   key is sent.

3. Session key is encrypted
   with Diane's public key.

4. Diane validates
   John's public key.

John

Diane

4. When Diane receives John's certificate, her browser looks to see if it trusts the CA that digitally signed this certificate. Diane's browser trusts this CA and, after she verifies the certificate, both John and Diane can communicate using encryption.

A PKI may be made up of the following entities and functions:

- CA
- RA
- Certificate repository
- Certificate revocation system
- Key backup and recovery system
- Automatic key update
- Management of key histories
- Timestamping
- Client-side software

PKI supplies the following security services:

- Confidentiality
- Access control
- Integrity
- Authentication
- Nonrepudiation

A PKI needs to keep a key history, which keeps track of all the old and current public keys that have been used by individual users. For example, if Kevin encrypted a symmetric key with David's old public key, there should be a way that David can still have access to this data. This can only happen if the CA keeps a proper history of David's old certificates and keys.

 **NOTE** Another important component that needs to be integrated into a PKI is a reliable time source that provides a way for secure timestamping. This comes into play when true nonrepudiation is required.

## References

- **Network World Cryptography page** www.nwfusion.com/research/crypto.html

- *Introduction to Public Key Technology and the Federal PKI Infrastructure,* **by D. Richard Kuhn et al., NIST Special Publication 800-32 (Feb. 26, 2001)** http://csrc.nist.gov/publications/nistpubs/800-32/sp800-32.pdf

- **The Open Group Secure Messaging Toolkit** www.opengroup.org/messaging/G260/pki_tutorial.htm

# Key Management

*I am the manager of all keys! Response: I am sorry.*

Cryptography can be used as a security mechanism to provide confidentiality, integrity, and authentication, but not if the keys are compromised in any way. The keys can be captured, modified, corrupted, or disclosed to unauthorized individuals. Cryptography is based on a trust model. Individuals must trust each other to protect their own keys, trust the administrator who is maintaining the keys, and trust a server that holds, maintains, and distributes the keys.

Many administrators know that key management causes one of the biggest headaches in cryptographic implementation. There is more to key maintenance than using them to encrypt messages. The keys have to be distributed securely to the right entities and updated continuously. The keys need to be protected as they are being transmitted and while they are being stored on each workstation and server. The keys need to be generated, destroyed, and recovered properly. Key management can be handled through manual or automatic processes.

The keys are stored before and after distribution. When a key is distributed to a user, it does not just hang out on the desktop; it needs a secure place within the file system to be stored and used in a controlled method. The key, the algorithm that will use the key, configurations, and parameters are stored in a module that also needs to be protected. If an attacker were able to obtain these components, she could masquerade as another user and decrypt, read, and reencrypt messages that were not intended for her.

Historically, physical cryptographic keys were kept in secured boxes and delivered by escorted couriers. The keys could be distributed to a main server, and then the local administration would distribute them, or the courier would visit each computer individually. Some implementations distributed a master key to a site, and then that key was used to generate unique secret keys to be used by individuals at that location. Today, most key distributions are handled by a protocol through automated means and not manually by an individual. A company must evaluate the overhead of key management, required security level, and cost-benefit issues to decide on how it will conduct key management, but overall, automation provides a more accurate and secure approach.

When using the Kerberos protocol (described in Chapter 4), a Key Distribution Center (KDC) is used to store, distribute, and maintain cryptographic session and secret keys. This method provides an automated method of key distribution. The computer that wants to access a service on another computer requests access via the KDC. The KDC then generates a session key to be used between the requesting computer and the computer providing the requested resource or service. The automation of this process reduces the possible errors that can happen through a manual process, but if the ticket granting service (TGS) portion of the KDC gets compromised in any way, then all the computers and their services are affected and possibly compromised.

In some instances, keys are still managed through manual means. Unfortunately, although many companies use cryptographic keys, they rarely if ever change them, either because of the hassle of key management or because the network administrator is already overtaxed with other tasks or does not realize the task actually needs to take place. The frequency of use of a cryptographic key has a direct correlation to how often the key should be changed. The more a key is used, the more likely it is to be captured and compromised. If a key is used infrequently, then this risk drops dramatically. The necessary level of security and the frequency of use can dictate the frequency of key updates. A mom-and-pop diner might only change its cryptography keys every month, whereas an information warfare military unit might change them every day or every week. The important thing is to change the keys using a secure method.

Key management is the most challenging part of cryptography and also the most crucial. It is one thing to develop a very complicated and complex algorithm and key method, but if the keys are not securely stored and transmitted, it does not really matter how strong the algorithm is.

## Key Management Principles

Keys should not be in cleartext outside the cryptography device. As stated previously, many cryptography algorithms are known publicly, which puts more stress on protecting the secrecy of the key. If attackers know how the actual algorithm works, then, in many cases, all they need to figure out is the key to compromise a system. This is why keys should not be available in cleartext; the key is what brings secrecy to encryption.

These steps, and all of key distribution and maintenance, should be automated and hidden from the user. These processes should be integrated into software or the operating system. It only adds complexity and opens the doors for more errors when processes are done manually and depend upon end users to perform certain functions.

Keys are at risk of being lost, destroyed, or corrupted. Backup copies should be available and easily accessible when required. If data is encrypted and then the user accidentally loses the necessary key to decrypt it, this information would be lost forever if there were not a backup key to save the day. The application being used for cryptography may have key recovery options, or it may require copies of the keys to be kept in a secure place.

Different scenarios highlight the need for key recovery or backup copies of keys. For example, if Bob has possession of all the critical bid calculations, stock value information, and corporate trend analysis needed for tomorrow's senior executive presentation, and Bob has an unfortunate confrontation with a bus, someone is going to need to access this data after the funeral. As another example, if an employee leaves the company and has encrypted important documents on her computer before departing, the company would probably want to have a way to still have access to that data. Similarly, if the vice president did not know that running a large magnet over the floppy disk that holds his private key was not a good idea, he would want his key replaced immediately instead of listening to a lecture about electromagnetic fields and how they rewrite sectors on media.

Of course, having more than one key increases the chance of disclosure, so a company needs to decide whether it wants to have key backups and, if so, what precautions to put into place to protect them properly. A company can choose to have multiparty control for emergency key recovery. This means that if a key needs to be recovered, more than one person is required to be involved with this process. The key recovery process could require two or more other individuals to present their private keys or authentication information. These individuals should not all be members of the IT department. There should be a member from management, an individual from security, and one individual from the IT department. All of these requirements reduce the potential for abuse and would require collusion for fraudulent activities to take place.

## Rules for Keys and Key Management

Key management is critical for proper protection. The following are responsibilities that fall under the key management umbrella:

- The key length should be long enough to provide the necessary level of protection.
- Keys should be stored and transmitted by secure means.
- Keys should be extremely random and the algorithm should use the full spectrum of the keyspace.
- The key's lifetime should correspond with the sensitivity of the data it is protecting. (Less secure data may allow for a longer key lifetime, whereas more sensitive data might require a shorter key lifetime.)
- The more the key is used, the shorter its lifetime should be.
- Keys should be backed up or escrowed in case of emergencies.
- Keys should be properly destroyed when their lifetime comes to an end.

## References

- **QuaMeta Compendium of Electronic Commerce Resources: Cryptography** www.quameta.com/security.htm
- **SSH Communications Security Support: Cryptography A–Z** www.ssh.fi/tech/crypto/intro.html

# Link Encryption vs. End-to-End Encryption

Encryption can be performed at different communication levels, each with different types of protection and implications. Two general modes of encryption implementation are link encryption and end-to-end encryption. *Link encryption* encrypts all the data along a specific communication path, as in a satellite link, T3 line, or telephone circuit. Not only is the user information encrypted, but the header, trailers, addresses, and routing data that are part of the packets are also encrypted. The only traffic that is not encrypted in this technology is the data link control messaging information, which includes instructions and parameters that the different link devices use to synchronize communication methods. Link encryption provides protection against packet sniffers and eavesdroppers. In *end-to-end encryption*, the headers, addresses, routing, and trailer information are not encrypted, enabling attackers to learn more about a captured packet and where it is headed.

### Encryption at Different Layers

In reality, encryption can happen at different layers of an operating system and network stack. The following are just a few examples:

- End-to-end encryption happens within the applications.
- SSL encryption takes place at the transport layer.
- IPSec encryption takes place at the network layer.
- PPTP encryption takes place at the data link layer.
- Link encryption takes place at the data link and physical layers.

Link encryption, which is sometimes called *online encryption,* is usually provided by service providers and is incorporated into network protocols. All of the information is encrypted, and the packets have to be decrypted at each hop so that the router, or other intermediate device, knows where to send the packet next. The router must decrypt the header portion of the packet, read the routing and address information within the header, and then re-encrypt it and send it on its way.

With end-to-end encryption, the packets do not need to be decrypted and then en-crypted again at each hop, because the headers and trailers are not encrypted. The de-vices in between the origin and destination just read the necessary routing information and pass the packets on their way.

End-to-end encryption is usually initiated by the user of the originating computer. It provides more flexibility for the user to be able to determine whether or not certain messages will get encrypted. It is called "end-to-end encryption" because the message stays encrypted from one end of its journey to the other. Link encryption has to decrypt the packets at every device between the two ends.

Link encryption occurs at the data link and physical layers, as depicted in Figure 8-24. Hardware encryption devices interface with the physical layer and encrypt all data that passes through them. Because no part of the data is available to an attacker, the attacker cannot learn basic information about how data flows through the environ-ment. This is referred to as *traffic-flow security.*

 **NOTE** A *hop* is a device that helps a packet reach its destination. It is usually a router that looks at the packet address to determine where the packet needs to go next. Packets usually go through many hops between the sending and receiving computers.

The following list outlines the advantages and disadvantages of end-to-end and link encryption methods.

Advantages of end-to-end encryption include the following:

- It provides more flexibility to the user in choosing what gets encrypted and how.
- Higher granularity of functionality is available because each application or user can choose specific configurations.

End-to-end encryption happens at higher
layers and does not encrypt headers and trailers.

| 1010 | Encrypted message | 1011 |

Encrypted message

Link encryption happens at lower layers
and encrypts headers and trailers
of the packet.

**Figure 8-24**   Link and end-to-end encryption happen at different OSI layers.

- Each hop computer on the network does not need to have a key to decrypt each packet.

Disadvantages of end-to-end encryption include the following:

- Headers, addresses, and routing information are not encrypted, and therefore not protected.

Advantages of link encryption include the following:

- All data is encrypted, including headers, addresses, and routing information.
- Users do not need to do anything to initiate it; it works at a lower layer in the OSI model.

Disadvantages of link encryption include the following:

- Key distribution and management is more complex because each hop device must receive a key, and when the keys change, each must be updated.
- Packets are decrypted at each hop; thus, there are more points of vulnerability.

## Reference

- *On Distributed Communications: IX Security, Secrecy, and Tamper-Free Considerations,* Section 3, "Some Fundamentals of Cryptography," by Paul Baran (Rand Corp., August 1964)   www.rand.org/publications/RM/ RM3765/RM3765.chapter3.html

> ## Hardware vs. Software Cryptography Systems
> Encryption can be done through software or hardware, and there are trade-offs with each. Generally, software is less expensive and provides a slower throughput than hardware mechanisms. Software cryptography methods can be more easily modified and disabled compared to hardware systems, but it depends on the application and the hardware product.
>
> If a company needs to perform high-end encryption functions at a higher speed, the company will most likely implement a hardware solution.

# E-Mail Standards

Like other types of technologies, cryptography has industry standards and de facto standards. Standards are necessary because they help to ensure interoperability among vendor products. Standards usually mean that a certain technology has been under heavy scrutiny and properly tested and accepted by many similar technology communities. A company still needs to decide on what type of standard to follow and what type of technology to implement.

A company needs to evaluate the functionality of the technology and perform a cost-benefit analysis on the competing products within the chosen standards. For a cryptography implementation, the company would need to decide on what needs to be protected by encryption, whether digital signatures are necessary, how key management should take place, what type of resources are available to implement and maintain the technology, and what the overall cost will amount to.

If a company only needs to encrypt some e-mail messages here and there, then PGP may be the best choice. If the company wants all data encrypted as it goes throughout the network and to sister companies, then a link encryption implementation may be the best choice. If a company wants to implement a single sign-on environment where users need to authenticate to use different services and functionality throughout the network, then implementing a PKI or Kerberos might serve it best. The network administrators should understand each type of technology and standard, to help make the most informed decision, and should research and test each competing product within the chosen technology before making the final purchase. Cryptography can be a complicated subject, including how to implement and maintain it. Doing homework versus buying into buzzwords and flashy products might help a company reduce its headaches down the road.

The following sections briefly describe some of the most popular e-mail standards in use.

## Multipurpose Internet Mail Extension

*Multipurpose Internet Mail Extension (MIME)* is a technical specification indicating how multimedia data and e-mail attachments are to be transferred. The Internet has mail standards that dictate how mail is to be formatted, encapsulated, transmitted, and opened. If a message or document contains a binary attachment, MIME dictates how that portion of the message should be handled.

When an attachment contains an audio clip, graphic, or some other type of multimedia component, the e-mail client will send the file with a header that describes the file type. For example, the header might indicate that the MIME type is Image and the subtype is jpeg. Although this will be in the header, many times systems also use the file's extension to identify the MIME type. So, in the preceding example, the file's name might be stuff.jpeg. The user's system will see the extension jpeg, or see the data in the header field, and look in its association list to see what program it needs to initialize to open this particular file. If the system has JPEG files associated with the Explorer application, then Explorer will open and present the picture to the user.

Sometimes systems either do not have an association for a specific file type or do not have the helper program necessary to review and use the contents of the file. When a file has an unassociated icon assigned to it, it might require the user to choose the Open With command and choose an application in the list to associate this file with that program. So when the user double-clicks on that file, the associated program will initialize and present the file. If the system does not have the necessary program, the web site might offer the necessary helper program, like Acrobat or an audio program that plays WAV files.

MIME is a specification that dictates how certain file types should be transmitted and handled. This specification has several types and subtypes, enables different computers to exchange data in varying formats, and provides a standardized way of presenting the data. So if Sean views a funny picture that is in GIF format, he can be sure that when he sends it to Debbie, it will look exactly the same.

## Secure MIME

*Secure MIME (S/MIME)* is a standard for encrypting and digitally signing electronic mail and for providing secure data transmissions. S/MIME extends the MIME standard by allowing for the encryption of e-mail and attachments. The encryption and hashing algorithms can be specified by the user of the mail package, instead of having it dictated to them.

S/MIME provides confidentiality through the user's encryption algorithm, integrity through the user's hashing algorithm, authentication through the use of X.509 public key certificates, and nonrepudiation through cryptographically signed message digests.

## Privacy-Enhanced Mail

*Privacy-Enhanced Mail (PEM)* is an Internet standard to provide secure e-mail over the Internet and for in-house communication infrastructures. The protocols within PEM provide authentication, message integrity, encryption, and key management. This standard was developed to provide compatibility with many types of key-management processes and symmetric and public key methods of encryption.

PEM is a series of message authentication and encryption technologies developed by several governing groups. PEM can use AES for encryption and RSA for sender authentication and key management. It also provides support for nonrepudiation. The following are specific components that can be used in PEM:

- Messages encrypted with AES in CBC mode
- Public key management, provided by using RSA
- X.509 standard, used for certification structure and format

PEM has not caught on to the extent that the developers had planned. The main issue is that PEM provides too much structure for different environments that require more flexibility in their secure communication infrastructure.

## Message Security Protocol

*The military has its own way to secure messages. Response: It has its own way of doing most things.*

The *Message Security Protocol (MSP)* is the military's PEM. Developed by the NSA, it is an X.400-compatible application-level protocol used to secure e-mail messages. MSP can be used to sign and encrypt messages and perform hashing functions. Like PEM, applications that incorporate MSP enable different algorithms and parameters to be used to provide greater flexibility.

## References

- **Encryption and Security Tutorial, by Peter Gutmann** www.cs.auckland .ac.nz/~pgut001/tutorial
- *Defective Sign & Encrypt in S/MIME, PKCS#7, MOSS, PEM, PGP, and XML,* **by Don Davis** http://world.std.com/~dtd/sign_encrypt/sign_encrypt7.html

## Pretty Good Privacy

*Pretty Good Privacy (PGP)* was designed by Phil Zimmerman as a freeware e-mail security program and was released in 1991. It was the first widespread public key encryption program. PGP is a complete cryptosystem that uses cryptographic protection to protect e-mail and files. It can use RSA public key encryption for key management and use IDEA symmetric cipher for bulk encryption of data, although the user has the option of picking different types of algorithms for these functions. PGP can provide confidentiality by using the IDEA encryption algorithm, integrity by using the MD5 hashing algorithm, authentication by using the public key certificates, and nonrepudiation by using cryptographically signed messages. PGP uses its own type of digital certificates rather than what is used in PKI, but they both have similar purposes.

The user's private key is generated and encrypted when the application asks the user to randomly type on her keyboard for a specific amount of time. Instead of using passwords, PGP uses passphrases. The passphrase is used to encrypt the user's private key that is stored on her hard drive.

PGP does not use a hierarchy of CAs, or any type of formal trust certificates, but instead relies on a "web of trust" in its key management approach. Each user generates and distributes his or her public key, and users sign each other's public keys, which creates a community of users who trust each other. This is different from the CA approach, where no one trusts each other; they only trust the CA. For example, if Mark and Joe want to communicate using PGP, Mark can give his public key to Joe. Joe signs Mark's key and keeps a copy for himself. Then Joe gives a copy of his public key to Mark so that they can start communicating securely. Later, Mark would like to communicate with Sally, but

Sally does not know Mark and does not know if she can trust him. Mark sends Sally his public key, which has been signed by Joe. Sally has Joe's public key, because they have communicated before, and she trusts Joe. Because Joe signed Mark's public key, Sally now also trusts Mark and sends her public key and begins communicating with him.

So, basically, PGP is a system of "I don't know you, but my buddy Joe says you are an alright guy, so I will trust you on behalf of Joe's word."

Each user keeps in a file, referred to as a *key ring*, a collection of public keys he has received from other users. Each key in that ring has a parameter that indicates the level of trust assigned to that user and the validity of that particular key. If Steve has known Liz for many years and trusts her, he might have a higher level of trust indicated on her stored public key than on Tom's, whom he does not trust much at all. There is also a field indicating who can sign other keys within Steve's realm of trust. If Steve receives a key from someone he doesn't know, like Kevin, and the key is signed by Liz, he can look at the field that pertains to whom he trusts to sign other people's keys. If the field indicates that Steve trusts Liz enough to sign another person's key, then Steve will accept Kevin's key and communicate with him because Liz is vouching for him. However, if Steve receives a key from Kevin and it is signed by untrustworthy Tom, then Steve might choose to not trust Kevin and not communicate with him.

These fields are available for updating and alteration. If one day Steve really gets to know Tom and finds out he is okay after all, he can modify these parameters within PGP and give Tom more trust when it comes to cryptography and secure communication.

Because the web of trust does not have a central leader, such as a CA, certain standardized functionality is harder to accomplish. If Steve were to lose his private key, he would need to notify everyone else trusting his public key that it should no longer be trusted. In a PKI, Steve would only need to notify the CA, and anyone attempting to verify the validity of Steve's public key would be told not to trust it upon looking at the most recently updated CRL. In the PGP world, this is not as centralized and organized. Steve can send out a key revocation certificate, but there is no guarantee that it will reach each user's key ring file.

PGP is a public domain software that uses public key cryptography. It has not been endorsed by the NSA, but because it is a great product and free for individuals to use, it has become somewhat of an encryption defacto standard on the Internet.

---

 **NOTE** PGP is considered a cryptosystem because it has all the necessary components: symmetric key algorithms, asymmetric key algorithms, message digest algorithms, keys, protocols, and the necessary software components.

## References

- **MIT Distribution Center for PGP**   http://web.mit.edu/network/pgp.html
- *Introduction to Cryptography,* **Chapter 1, "How PGP Works"**   www.pgpi.org/doc/pgpintro
- **The International PGP home page**   www.pgpi.org

# Internet Security

*Is the Internet tied up into a web? Response: Well, kind of.*

The Web is not the Internet. The Web runs on top of the Internet, in a sense. The Web is the collection of HTTP servers that hold and process web sites that we see. The Internet is the collection of physical devices and communication protocols used to transverse these web sites and interact with them. (These issues were touched upon in Chapter 2.) The web sites look the way they look because the creator used a language that dictates the look, feel, and functionality of the page. Web browsers enable users to read web pages by enabling them to request and accept web pages via HTTP, and the user's browser converts the language (HTML, DHTML, and XML) into a format that can be viewed on the monitor. The browser is the user's window to the World Wide Web.

Browsers can understand a variety of protocols and have the capability to process many types of commands, but they do not understand them all. For those protocols or commands that the user's browser does not know how to process, the user can download and install a viewer or plug-in, a modular component of code that integrates itself into the system or browser. This is a quick and easy way to expand the functionality of the browser. However, this has caused serious security compromises, because the payload of the module can easily carry viruses and malicious software that the users do not know about until it is already installed and has started to do damage.

## Start with the Basics

Why do we connect to the Internet? This is a basic question at first, but as we dive deeper into the question, the complexity creeps in. We connect to download MP3s, check e-mail, order security books, look at web sites, communicate with friends, and much more. But what are we really doing? We are using services provided by a computer's protocols and software. The services may be file transfer provided by FTP, remote connectivity provided by Telnet, Internet connectivity provided by HTTP, secure connections provided by SSL, and much, much more. Without these protocols, there would be no way to even connect to the Internet.

Management needs to decide what functionality employees should have pertaining to Internet use, and the administrator needs to implement these decisions by controlling services that can be used inside and outside the network. There are different ways to restrict services: allow certain services to only run on a particular system and restrict access to that system; employ a secure version of a service; filter the use of services; or block services altogether. These choices determine how secure the site will be and indicate what type of technology is needed to provide this type of protection.

Let's go through many of the technologies and protocols that make up the World Wide Web.

## HTTP

TCP/IP is the protocol suite of the Internet, and HTTP is the protocol of the Web. HTTP sits on top of TCP/IP. When a user clicks her mouse on a link within a web page, her browser uses HTTP to send a request to the web server hosting that web site. The web server finds the corresponding file to that link and sends it to the user via HTTP. So where is TCP/IP in all of this? The TCP protocol controls the handshaking and maintains the connection between the user and the server, and the IP protocol makes sure that the file is routed properly throughout the Internet to get from the web server to the user. So, the IP protocol finds the way to get from A to Z, TCP makes sure that the origin and destination are correct and that no packets are lost along the way, and, upon arrival at the destination, HTTP presents the payload, which is a web page.

HTTP is a stateless protocol, which means the client and web server make and break a connection for each operation. When a user requests to view a web page, that web server finds the requested web page, presents it to the user, and then terminates the connection. If the user requests a link within the newly received web page, a new connection has to be set up, the request goes to the web server, and the web server sends the requested item and breaks the connection. The web server never "remembers" the users that ask for different web pages, because otherwise the web server would use and commit a lot of resources.

## HTTP Secure

*HTTP Secure (HTTPS)* is HTTP running over SSL. (HTTP works at the application layer and SSL works at the transport layer.) *Secure Sockets Layer (SSL)* uses public key encryption and provides data encryption, server authentication, message integrity, and optional client authentication. When a client accesses a web site, that web site may have both secured and public portions. The secured portion would require the user to be authenticated in some fashion. When the client goes from a public page on the web site to a secured page, the web server will start the necessary tasks to invoke SSL and protect this type of communication.

The server sends a message back to the client, indicating that a secure session needs to be established, and the client in response sends its security parameters. The server compares those security parameters to its own until it finds a match. This is the handshaking phase. The server authenticates to the client by sending it a digital certificate, and if the client decides to trust the server, the process continues. The server can require the client to send over a digital certificate for mutual authentication, but that is rare.

The client generates a session key and encrypts it with the server's public key. This encrypted key is sent to the web server, and they both use this symmetric key to encrypt the data they send back and forth. This is how the secure channel is established.

SSL keeps the communication path open until one of the parties requests to end the session. The session is usually ended when the client sends the server a FIN packet, which is an indication to close out the channel.

SSL requires an SSL-enabled server and browser. SSL provides security for the connection but does not provide security for the data once it is received. This means that the data is encrypted while it is being transmitted, but not after it is received by a computer. So if a user sends bank account information to a financial institution via a connection protected by SSL, that communication path is protected, but the user must trust the financial institution that receives this information, because at this point, SSL's job is done.

The user can verify that a connection is secure by looking at the URL to see that it includes https://. The user can also check for a padlock or key icon, depending on the browser type, at the bottom corner of the browser window.

In the protocol stack, SSL lies beneath the application layer and above the network layer. This ensures that SSL is not limited to specific application protocols and can still use the communication transport standards of the Internet. Different books and technical resources place SSL at different layers of the OSI model, which may seem confusing at first. But the OSI model is a conceptual construct that attempts to describe the reality of networking. This is like trying to draw nice neat boxes around life; some things don't fit perfectly and hang over the sides. SSL is actually made up of two protocols: one works at the lower end of the session layer, and the other works at the top of the transport layer. This is why one resource will state that SSL works at the session layer and another resource puts it in the transport layer. For our purpose, which is to pass the CISSP exam, the SSL protocol works at the transport layer.

Although SSL is almost always used with HTTP, it can be used with other types of protocols. So if you see a common protocol that is followed by an *s*, that protocol is using SSL to encrypt its data.

## Secure HTTP

Their names are very similar, but there is a difference between *Secure HTTP (S-HTTP)* and HTTP Secure (HTTPS). S-HTTP is a technology that protects each message that is sent between two computers. HTTPS protects the communication channel between two computers, messages and all. HTTPS uses SSL and HTTP to provide a protected circuit between a client and server. So, S-HTTP is used if an individual message needs to be encrypted, but if all information that passes between two computers needs to be encrypted, then HTTPS is used, which is SSL over HTTP.

## References

- *Security Issues in WWW*   http://nsi.org/Library/Internet/security.htm
- **Keesook J. Han's security links page**   www.ece.umn.edu/users/kjhan/security
- **"SSL/TLS Strong Encryption: An Introduction," Apache Software Foundation, with permission from Frederick J. Hirsch**   http://httpd .apache.org/docs-2.0/ssl/ssl_intro.html

## Secure Electronic Transaction

*Secure Electronic Transaction (SET)* is a security technology proposed by Visa and MasterCard to allow for more secure credit card transaction possibilities than what is currently available. SET has been waiting in the wings for full implementation and acceptance as a standard for quite some time. Although SET provides an effective way of transmitting credit card information, businesses and users do not see it as efficient because it requires more parties to coordinate their efforts, more software installation and configuration for each entity involved, and more effort and cost than the widely used SSL method.

SET is a cryptographic protocol and infrastructure developed to send encrypted credit card numbers over the Internet. The following entities would be involved with a

SET transaction, which would require each of them to upgrade their software and possibly hardware:

- **Issuer (cardholder's bank)**  Financial institution that provides a credit card to individual

- **Cardholder**  Individual authorized to use a credit card

- **Merchant**  Entity providing goods

- **Acquirer (merchant's bank)**  Financial institution that processes payment cards

- **Payment gateway**  Processes merchant payment; may be acquirer

To use SET, a user must enter her credit card number into her electronic wallet software. This information is stored on the user's hard drive or on a smart card. The software then creates a public key and a private key used specifically for encrypting financial information before it is sent.

Let's say Tanya wants to use her electronic credit card to buy her mother a gift from a web site. When she finds the perfect gift and decides to purchase it, she sends her encrypted credit card information to the merchant's web server. The merchant does not decrypt the credit card information, but instead digitally signs it and sends it on to its processing bank. At the bank, the payment server decrypts the information, verifies that Tanya has the necessary funds, and transfers the funds from Tanya's account to the merchant's account. Then the payment server sends a message to the merchant telling it to finish the transaction, and a receipt is sent to Tanya and the merchant. At each step, an entity verifies a digital signature of the sender and digitally signs the information before it is sent to the next entity involved in the process. This would require all entities to have digital certificates and participate in a PKI.

This is basically a very secure way of doing business over the Internet, but today everyone seems to be happy enough with the security SSL provides. They do not feel motivated enough to move to a different and more encompassing technology. The lack of motivation comes from all of the changes that would need to take place to our current processes and the amount of money that these changes would require.

## Cookies

*Hey, I found a web site that is giving out free cookies! Response: Great, I will bring the milk!*

*Cookies* are text files that a browser maintains on a user's hard drive. There are different uses for cookies, but they can be used for demographic and advertising information. As a user travels from site to site on the Internet, the sites could be writing data to the cookies stored on the user's system. The sites can keep track of the user's browsing and spending habits and the user's specific customization for certain sites. For example, if Emily goes to mainly gardening sites on the Internet, those sites will most likely record this information and the types of items in which she shows most interest. Then, when Emily returns to one of the same or similar sites, it will retrieve her cookies, find that she has shown interest in gardening books in the past, and present her with its line of gardening books. This increases the likelihood of Emily purchasing a book of her liking. This is a way of zeroing in on the right marketing tactics for the right person.

The servers at the web site determine how cookies are actually used. When a user adds items to his shopping cart on a site, this data is usually added to a cookie. Then, when the user is ready to check out and pay for his items, all the data in this specific cookie is extracted and the totals are added.

As stated before, HTTP is a stateless protocol, meaning that a web server has no memory of any prior connections. This is one reason to use cookies. They retain the memory between HTTP connections by saving prior connection data to the client's computer.

For example, if you carry out your banking activities online, your bank's web server keeps track of your activities through the use of cookies. When you first go to its site and are looking at public information, such as branch locations, hours of operation, and CD rates, no confidential information is being transferred back and forth. Once you make a request to access your bank account, the web server sets up an SSL connection and requires you to send credentials. Once you send your credentials and are authenticated, the server generates a cookie with your authentication and account information in it. The server sends it to your browser, which either saves it to your hard drive or keeps it in memory.

 **NOTE** Some cookies are stored as text files on your hard drive. These files should not contain any sensitive information, such as account numbers and passwords. In most cases, cookies that contain sensitive information stay resident in memory and are not stored on the hard drive.

So, suppose you look at your checking account and do some work there and then request to view your savings account information. The web server sends a request to see if you have been properly authenticated for this activity by checking your cookie.

Most online banking software also periodically request your cookie, to ensure that no man-in-the-middle attacks are going on and that someone else has not hijacked the session.

It is also important to ensure that secure connections time out. This is why cookies have timestamps within them. If you have ever been working on a site that has an SSL connection set up for you and it required you to reauthenticate, the reason is that your session had been idle for a certain amount of time and, instead of leaving a secure connection open, the web server software closed it out.

A majority of the data within a cookie is meaningless to any entities other than the servers at specific sites, but some cookies can contain usernames and passwords for different accounts on the Internet. The cookies that contain sensitive information should be encrypted by the server at the site that distributes them, but this does not always happen, and a nosey attacker could find this data on the user's hard drive and attempt to use it for mischievous activity. Some people who live on the paranoid side of life do not allow cookies to be downloaded to their systems (controlled through browser security controls). Although this provides a high level of protection against different types of cookie abuse, it also reduces their functionality on the Internet. Some sites require cookies because there is specific data within the cookies that the site needs to perform correctly and to be able to provide the user with the services she requested.

**NOTE**   There are third-party products that can limit the type of cookies downloaded, hide the user's identities as he travels from one site to the next, and mask the user's e-mail addresses and the mail servers he uses if he is concerned about concealing his identity and his tracks.

## Secure Shell

*Secure Shell (SSH)* functions as a type of tunneling mechanism that provides terminal-like access to remote computers. SSH is a program and a protocol that can be used to log into another computer over a network. For example, the program can let Paul, who is on computer A, access computer B's files, run applications on computer B, and retrieve files from computer B without ever physically touching that computer. SSH provides authentication and secure transmission over vulnerable channels like the Internet.

SSH should be used instead of Telnet, FTP, rlogin, rexec, or rsh, which provide the same type of functionality that SSH provides but in a much less secure manner. SSH is a program and a set of protocols that work together to provide a secure tunnel between two computers. The two computers go through a handshaking process and exchange via Diffie-Hellman a session key that will be used during the session to encrypt and protect the data that is exchanged. The steps of an SSH connection are outlined in Figure 8-25.

Once the handshake takes place and a secure channel is established, the two computers have a pathway to exchange data with the assurance that the information will be encrypted and its integrity will be protected.

Secure channel

**Figure 8-25**
SSH is used for remote terminal-like functionality.

SSH steps to establish a secure connection

1. Client requests SSH connection
2. Handshake to find out protocol version
3. Algorithm negotiation and key exchange
4. Secure session setup
5. Client runs remote application

## References

- **SSH (Secure Shell) FAQ, by Thomas König**   www.uni-karlsruhe.de/~ig25/ ssh-faq

- **The Secure Shell Frequently Asked Questions, by Anne Carasik and Steve Acheson**   www.onsight.com/faq/ssh/ssh-faq.html

- *Unix System Administration*, **Chapter 29, "Secure Shell, SSH," by Frank G. Fiamingo**   wks.uts.ohio-state.edu/sysadm_course/html/sysadm-558.html

## Internet Security Protocol

*Hey, is there a really complex protocol to provide me network layer protection? Response: Yep, IPSec.*

The *Internet Protocol Security (IPSec)* protocol suite provides a method of setting up a secure channel for protected data exchange between two devices. The devices that share this secure channel can be two servers, two routers, a workstation and a server, or two gateways between different networks. IPSec is a widely accepted standard for providing network layer protection. It can be more flexible and less expensive than end-to-end and link encryption methods.

IPSec has strong encryption and authentication methods, and although it can be used to enable tunneled communication between two computers, it is usually used to establish virtual private networks (VPNs) among networks across the Internet.

IPSec is not a strict protocol that dictates the type of algorithm, keys, and authentication method to use; rather, it is an open, modular framework that provides a lot of flexibility for companies when they choose to use this type of technology. IPSec uses two basic security protocols: *Authentication Header (AH)* and *Encapsulating Security Payload (ESP)*. AH is the authenticating protocol, and ESP is an authenticating and encrypting protocol that uses cryptographic mechanisms to provide source authentication, confidentiality, and message integrity.

IPSec can work in one of two modes: *transport mode*, in which the payload of the message is protected, and *tunnel mode*, in which the payload and the routing and header information are protected. ESP in transport mode encrypts the actual message information so that it cannot be sniffed and uncovered by an unauthorized entity. Tunnel mode provides a higher level of protection by also protecting the header and trailer data that an attacker may find useful. Figure 8-26 shows the high-level view of the steps of setting up an IPSec connection.

Each device will have at least one *security association (SA)* for each VPN it uses. The SA, which is critical to the IPSec architecture, is a record of the configurations the device needs to support an IPSec connection. When two devices complete their handshaking process, which means that they have agreed upon a long list of parameters they will use to communicate, this data must be recorded and stored somewhere, which is in the SA. The SA can contain the authentication and encryption keys, the agreed-upon algorithms, key lifetime, and the source IP address. When a device receives a packet via the IPSec protocol, it is the SA that tells the device what to do with the packet. So if device B receives a packet from device C via IPSec, device B will look to the corresponding SA to tell it how to decrypt the packet, how to properly authenticate the source of the packet, which key to use, and how to reply to the message if necessary.

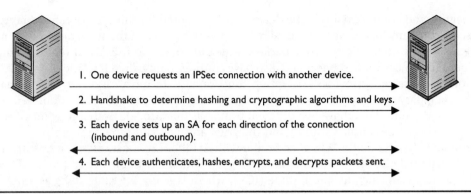

1. One device requests an IPSec connection with another device.

2. Handshake to determine hashing and cryptographic algorithms and keys.

3. Each device sets up an SA for each direction of the connection (inbound and outbound).

4. Each device authenticates, hashes, encrypts, and decrypts packets sent.

**Figure 8-26** Steps that two computers follow when using IPSec

SAs are directional, so a device will have one SA for outbound traffic and a different SA for inbound traffic for each individual communication channel. If a device is connecting to three devices, it will have at least six SAs, one for each inbound and outbound connection per remote device. So how can a device keep all of these SAs organized and ensure that the right SA is invoked for the right connection? With the mighty *security parameter index (SPI)*, that's how. Each device has an SPI that keeps track of the different SAs and tells the device which one is appropriate to invoke for the different packets it receives. The SPI value is in the header of an IPSec packet, and the device reads this value to tell it which SA to consult, as depicted in Figure 8-27.

IPSec can authenticate the sending devices of the packet by using MAC (covered in an earlier section, "One-Way Hash"). The ESP protocol can provide authentication,

**Figure 8-27** The SPI and SA help the system process IPSec packets.

integrity, and confidentiality if the devices are configured for this type of functionality. So if a company just needs to make sure it knows the source of the sender and needs to be assured of the integrity of the packets, it would choose to use AH. If the company would like to use these services and also have confidentiality, then it would use the ESP protocol because it provides encryption functionality. In most cases, the reason that ESP is employed is that the company needs to set up a secure VPN connection.

It may seem odd to have two different protocols that provide overlapping functionality. AH provides authentication and integrity, and ESP can provide those two functions *and* confidentiality. Why even bother with AH then? In most cases, the reason has to do with whether the environment is using network address translation (NAT). IPSec will generate an integrity check value (ICV), which is really the same thing as a MAC value, over a portion of the packet. Remember that the sender and receiver generate their own values. In IPSec, it is called an ICV value. The receiver compares her ICV value with the one that was sent by the sender. If the values match, the receiver can be assured that the packet has not been modified during transmission. If the values are different, the packet has been altered and the receiver discards the packet.

The AH protocol calculates this ICV over the data payload, transport, and network headers. If the packet then goes through a NAT device, the NAT device changes the IP address of the packet; that is its job. This means that a portion of the data (network header) that was included to calculate the ICV value has now changed, and the receiver will generate an ICV value that is different from the one that was sent with the packet, which means the packet will be discarded automatically.

The ESP protocol follows similar steps, except it does not include the network header portion when calculating its ICV value. When the NAT device changes the IP address, it will not affect the receiver's ICV value because it does not include the network header when calculating the ICV. The differences are shown in Figure 8-28.

Because IPSec is a framework, it does not dictate which hashing and encryption algorithms are to be used or how keys are to be exchanged between devices. Key management can be handled manually or automated by a key management protocol. The de facto standard for IPSec is to use Internet Key Exchange (IKE), which is a combination of the ISAKMP and OAKLEY protocols. The *Internet Security Association and Key Management Protocol (ISAKMP)* is a key exchange architecture that is independent of the type of keying mechanisms used. Basically, ISAKMP provides the framework of what can be negotiated to set up an IPSec connection (algorithms, protocols, modes, keys). The OAKLEY protocol is the one that carries out the negotiation process. You can think of ISAKMP as providing the playing field (the infrastructure) and OAKLEY as the guy running up and down the playing field (carrying out the steps of the negotiation).

 **NOTE** Simple Key management Protocol for IP (SKIP) is another key exchange protocol that provides basically the same functionality as IKE. It is important to know that all of these protocols work at the network layer.

IPSec is very complex with all of its components and possible configurations. This complexity is what provides for a great degree of flexibility, because a company has many different configuration choices to achieve just the right level of protection. If this

**Figure 8-28**
AH and ESP use different portions of the packet to calculate the ICVs.

is all new to you and still confusing, please review one or more of the following references to help fill in the gray areas.

## References

- "A Cryptographic Evaluation of IPSec," by N. Ferguson and Bruce Schneier   www.schneier.com/paper-ipsec.html
- "An Introduction to IP Security (IPSec) Encryption," Cisco Systems, Inc.   www.cisco.com/warp/public/105/IPSECpart1.html

# Attacks

Eavesdropping and sniffing data as it passes over a network are considered *passive attacks* because the attacker is not affecting the protocol, algorithm, key, message, or any parts of the encryption system. Passive attacks are hard to detect, so in most cases methods are put in place to try to prevent them rather than detect and stop them.

Altering messages, modifying system files, and masquerading as another individual are acts that are considered *active attacks* because the attacker is actually doing something instead of sitting back gathering data. Passive attacks are usually used to gain information prior to carrying out an active attack. The following sections address some active attacks that relate to cryptography.

## Ciphertext-Only Attack

In this type of attack, the attacker has the ciphertext of several messages. Each of the messages has been encrypted using the same encryption algorithm. The attacker's goal is to discover the key that was used in the encryption process. Once the attacker figures out the key, she can decrypt all other messages encrypted with the same key.

A ciphertext-only attack is the most common type of active attack because it is very easy to get ciphertext by sniffing someone's traffic, but it is the hardest attack to actually be successful at because the attacker has so little information about the encryption process.

## Known-Plaintext Attack

In this type of attack, the attacker has the plaintext and ciphertext of one or more messages. Again, the goal is to discover the key used to encrypt the messages so that other messages can be deciphered and read.

Messages usually start with the same type of beginning and close with the same type of ending. An attacker might know that each message that a general sends out to his commanders always starts with certain greetings and ends with specific salutations and the general's name and contact information. In this instance, the attacker has some of the plaintext (the data that is the same on each message) and can capture an encrypted message, and therefore capture the ciphertext. Once a few pieces of the puzzle are discovered, the rest is accomplished by reverse-engineering, frequency analysis, and brute force attempts. Known-plaintext attacks were used by the United States against the Germans and the Japanese during World War II.

## Chosen-Plaintext Attack

In this attack, the attacker has the plaintext and ciphertext, but the attacker can choose the plaintext that gets encrypted to see the corresponding ciphertext. This gives her more power and possibly a deeper understanding of the way that the encryption process works so that she can gather more information about the key that is being used. Once the key is discovered, other messages encrypted with that key can be decrypted.

How would this be carried out? I can e-mail a message to you that I think you not only will believe, but also will panic about, encrypt, and send to someone else. Suppose I send you an e-mail that states, "The meaning of life is 42." You may think you have received an important piece of information that should be concealed from others, everyone except your friend Bob, of course. So you encrypt my message and send it to Bob. Meanwhile I am sniffing your traffic and now have a copy of the plaintext of the message, because I wrote it, and a copy of the ciphertext.

## Chosen-Ciphertext Attack

In this attack, the attacker can choose the ciphertext to be decrypted and has access to the resulting decrypted plaintext. Again, the goal is to figure out the key. This would be a harder attack to carry out compared to the previously mentioned attacks, and the attacker may need to have control of the system that contains the cryptosystem.

## Public vs. Secret Algorithms

The public mainly uses algorithms that are known and understood versus the secret algorithms where the internal processes and functions are not released to the public. In general, cryptographers in the public sector feel as though the strongest and best-engineered algorithms are the ones that are released for peer review and public scrutiny, because a thousand brains are better than five, and many times some smarty-pants within the public population can find problems within an algorithm that the developers did not think of. This is why vendors and companies have competitions to see if anyone can break their code and encryption processes. If someone does break it, that means the developers must go back to the drawing board and strengthen this or that piece.

Not all algorithms are released to the public, such as the ones developed by the NSA. Because the sensitivity level of what the NSA encrypts is so important, it wants as much of the process to be secret as possible. The fact that the NSA does not release its algorithms for public examination and analysis does not mean that its algorithms are weak. Its algorithms are developed, reviewed, and tested by many of the top cryptographic smarty-pants and are of very high quality.

 **NOTE** All of these attacks have a derivative form, the names of which are the same except with the word "adaptive" in front of them: adaptive chosen-plaintext and adaptive chosen-ciphertext. What this means is that the attacker can carry out one of these attacks and, depending upon what she gleaned from that first attack, modify her next attack. This is the process of reverse-engineering or cryptanalysis attacks, using what you learned to improve your next attack.

## Differential Cryptanalysis

This type of attack also has the goal of uncovering the key that was used for encryption purposes. It was invented in 1990 as an attack against DES, and it turned out to be an effective and successful attack against DES and other block algorithms.

The attacker takes two messages of plaintext and follows the changes that take place to the blocks as they go through the different S-boxes. (Each message is being encrypted with the same key.) The differences that are identified in the resulting ciphertext values are used to map probability values to different possible key values. The attacker continues this process with several more sets of messages and reviews the common key probability values. One key will continue to show itself as the most probable key that was used in the encryption processes. Since the attacker chooses the different plaintext messages for this attack, it is considered to be a type of chosen-plaintext attack.

## Linear Cryptanalysis

This is another type of attack that carries out functions to identify the highest probability of a specific key that was used during the encryption process using a block algorithm. The attacker carries out a known-plaintext attack on several different messages encrypted with the same key. The more messages that the attacker can use and put through this type of attack the higher the confidence level in the probability of a specific key value.

The attacker evaluates the input and output values for each S-box. He evaluates the probability of input values ending up in a specific combination. Identifying specific output combinations allows him to assign probability values to different keys until one shows a continual pattern of having the highest probability.

## Side Channel Attacks

All of the attacks we have covered thus far have been based mainly on the mathematics of cryptography. Using plaintext and ciphertext involves high-powered mathematical tools that are needed to uncover the key used in the encryption process.

But what if we took a different approach? Let's say we see something that looks like a duck, walks like a duck, sounds like a duck, swims in water, and eats bugs and small fish. We could confidently conclude that this is a duck. Similarly, in cryptography, we can review facts and infer the value of an encryption key. For example, we could detect how much power consumption is used for encryption and decryption (the fluctuation of electronic voltage). We could also intercept the radiation emissions that are released and calculate how long the processes take. Looking around the cryptosystem, or its attributes and characteristics, is different from looking into the cryptosystem and trying to defeat it through mathematical computations.

If I want to figure out what you do for a living, but I don't want you to know I am doing this type of reconnaissance work, I won't ask you directly. Instead, I will find out when you go to work and come home, the types of clothing that you wear, the items that you carry, whom you talk to...or I can just follow you to work. These are examples of side channels.

So, in cryptography, gathering "outside" information with the goal of uncovering the encryption key is just another way of attacking a cryptosystem.

An attacker could measure power consumption, radiation emissions, and the time it takes for certain types of data processing. With this information, he can work backward by reverse-engineering the process to uncover an encryption key or sensitive data. A power attack reviews the amount of heat that is released; this type of attack has been successful in uncovering confidential information from smart cards. In 1995, RSA private keys were uncovered by measuring the relative time cryptographic operations took.

The idea is that, instead of attacking a device head on, just watch how it performs to figure out how it works. In biology, scientists can choose to carry out a noninvasive experiment, which will watch an organism eat, sleep, mate, and so on. This type of approach learns about the organism through understanding its behaviors instead of killing it and looking at it from the inside out.

## Replay Attack

A big concern in distributed environments is the *replay attack*, in which an attacker captures some type of data and resubmits it with the hopes of fooling the receiving device into thinking it is legitimate information. Many times, the data that is captured and resubmitted is authentication information, and the attacker is trying to authenticate herself as someone else to gain unauthorized access.

Timestamps and sequence numbers are two countermeasures to replay attacks. Packets can contain sequence numbers, so each machine will expect a specific number on each receiving packet. If a packet has a sequence number that has been previously used, this is an indication of a replay attack. Packets can also be timestamped. A threshold can be set on each computer to only accept packets within a certain timeframe. If a packet is received that is past this threshold, it can help identify a replay attack.

## References

- *Wikipedia* **entry for ciphertext-only attack**  www.answers.com/topic/ciphertext-only-attack
- **Frequently Asked Questions About Today's Cryptography, Version 4.1, Section 2.4.2, "What Are Some of the Basic Types of Cryptanalytic Attacks?" by RSA Laboratories**  www.rsasecurity.com/rsalabs/node.asp?id=2201
- **"Linear Cryptanalysis: A Literature Survey," by Terry Ritter**  www.ciphersbyritter.com/RES/LINANA.HTM
- **"Linear Cryptanalysis of Block Ciphers," by Edward Schaefer**  http://math.scu.edu/~eschaefe/linear.pdf
- **"Introduction to Side Channel Attacks," by Hagai Bar-El, Discretix Technologies Ltd.**  www.discretix.com/PDF/Introduction%20to%20Side%20Channel%20Attacks.pdf

## Summary

Cryptography has been used in one form or another for over 4000 years, and the attacks on cryptography have probably been in place for 3999 years and 364 days. As one group of people works to find new ways to hide and transmit secrets, another group of people is right on their heels finding holes in the newly developed ideas and products. This can be viewed as evil and destructive behavior, or as the thorn in the side of the computing world that pushes it to build better and more secure products and environments.

Cryptographic algorithms provide the underlying tools to most security protocols used in today's infrastructures. The algorithms work off of mathematical functions and provide various types of functionality and levels of security. A big leap was made when encryption went from purely symmetric key use to public key cryptography. This evolution provided users and maintainers much more freedom and flexibility when it came to communicating with a variety of users all over the world.

Encryption can be supplied at different layers of the OSI model by a range of applications, protocols, and mechanisms. Today, not much thought has to be given to cryptography and encryption because it is taken care of in the background by many operating systems, applications, and protocols. However, for administrators who maintain these environments, for security professionals who propose and implement security solutions, and for those interested in obtaining a CISSP certification, knowing the ins and outs of cryptography is essential.

# Quick Tips

- Cryptography is the science of protecting information by encoding it into an unreadable format.

- The most famous rotor encryption machine is the Enigma used by the Germans in WWII.

- A readable message is in a form called plaintext, and once it is encrypted, it is in a form called ciphertext.

- Cryptographic algorithms are the mathematical rules that dictate the functions of enciphering and deciphering.

- Cryptanalysis is the study of breaking cryptosystems.

- Nonrepudiation is a service that ensures that the sender cannot later falsely deny sending a message.

- Key clustering is an instance in which two different keys generate the same ciphertext from the same plaintext.

- The range of possible keys is referred to as the keyspace. A larger keyspace and the full use of the keyspace allow for more random keys to be created. This provides more protection.

- The two basic types of encryption mechanisms used in symmetric ciphers are substitution and transposition. Substitution ciphers change a character (or bit) out for another, and transposition ciphers scramble the characters (or bits).

- A polyalphabetic cipher uses more than one alphabet to defeat frequency analysis.

- Steganography is a method of hiding data within another media type, such as a graphic, WAV file, or document. This method is used to hide the existence of the data.

- A key is a random string of bits that is inserted into an encryption algorithm. The result determines what encryption functions will be carried out on a message and in what order.

- In symmetric key algorithms, the sender and receiver use the same key for encryption and decryption purposes.

- In asymmetric key algorithms, the sender and receiver use different keys for encryption and decryption purposes.

- Symmetric key processes provide barriers of secure key distribution and scalability. However, symmetric key algorithms perform much faster than asymmetric key algorithms.

- Symmetric key algorithms can provide confidentiality, but not authentication or nonrepudiation.

- Examples of symmetric key algorithms include DES, 3DES, Blowfish, IDEA, RC4, RC5, RC6, and AES.

- Asymmetric algorithms are used to encrypt keys, and symmetric algorithms are used to encrypt bulk data.

- If a user encrypts data with his private key, it can only be decrypted by his public key.

- Asymmetric key algorithms are much slower than symmetric key algorithms, but can provide authentication and nonrepudiation services.

- Examples of asymmetric key algorithms include RSA, ECC, Diffie-Hellman, El Gamal, Knapsack, and DSA.

- Two main types of symmetric algorithms are stream and block ciphers. Stream ciphers use a keystream generator and encrypt a message one bit at a time. A block cipher divides the message into groups of bits and encrypts them.

- Block ciphers are usually implemented in software, and stream ciphers are usually implemented in hardware.

- Many algorithms are publicly known, so the secret part of the process is the key. The key provides the necessary randomization to encryption.

- Data Encryption Standard (DES) is a block cipher that divides a message into 64-bit blocks and employs S-box-type functions on them.

- Because technology has allowed the DES keyspace to be successfully broken, Triple-DES (3DES) was developed to be used instead. 3DES uses 48 rounds of computation and up to three different keys.

- International Data Encryption Algorithm (IDEA) is a symmetric block cipher with a key of 128 bits.

- RSA is an asymmetric algorithm developed by Rivest, Shamir, and Adleman and is the de facto standard for digital signatures.

- Elliptic curve cryptosystems (ECCs) are used as asymmetric algorithms and can provide digital signature, secure key distribution, and encryption functionality. They use much less resources, which makes them better for wireless device and cell phone encryption use.

- When symmetric and asymmetric key algorithms are used together, this is called a hybrid system. The asymmetric algorithm encrypts the symmetric key, and the symmetric key encrypts the data.

- A session key is a symmetric key used by the sender and receiver of messages for encryption and decryption purposes. The session key is only good while that communication session is active and then it is destroyed.

- A public key infrastructure (PKI) is a framework of programs, procedures, communication protocols, and public key cryptography that enables a diverse group of individuals to communicate securely.

- A certificate authority (CA) is a trusted third party that generates and maintains user certificates, which hold their public keys.

- The CA uses a certification revocation list (CRL) to keep track of revoked certificates.

- A certificate is the mechanism the CA uses to associate a public key to a person's identity.

- A registration authority (RA) validates the user's identity and then sends the request for a certificate to the CA. The RA cannot generate certificates.

- A one-way function is a mathematical function that is easier to compute in one direction than in the opposite direction.

- RSA is based on a one-way function that factors large numbers into prime numbers. Only the private key knows how to use the trapdoor and decrypt messages that were encrypted with the corresponding public key.

- Hashing algorithms provide data integrity only.

- When a hash algorithm is applied to a message, it produces a message digest, and this value is signed with a private key to produce a digital signature.

- Some examples of hashing algorithms include SHA-1, MD2, MD4, MD5, and HAVAL.

- HAVAL produces a variable-length hash value, whereas the others produce a fixed-length value.

- SHA-1 produces a 160-bit hash value and is used in DSS.

- A birthday attack is an attack on hashing functions through brute force. The attacker tries to create two messages with the same hashing value.

- A one-time pad uses a pad with random values that are XORed against the message to produce ciphertext. The pad is at least as long as the message itself and is used once and then discarded.

- A digital signature is the result of a user signing a hash value with a private key. It provides authentication, data integrity, and nonrepudiation. The act of signing is the actual encryption of the value with the private key.

- Examples of algorithms used for digital signatures include RSA, El Gamal, ECDSA, and DSA.

- Key management is one of the most challenging pieces of cryptography. It pertains to creating, maintaining, distributing, and destroying cryptographic keys.

- The Diffie-Hellman protocol is a key agreement protocol and does not provide encryption for data and cannot be used in digital signatures.

- Link encryption encrypts the entire packet, including headers and trailers, and has to be decrypted at each hop. End-to-end encryption does not encrypt the headers and trailers, and therefore does not need to be decrypted at each hop.

- Privacy-Enhanced Mail (PEM) is an Internet standard that provides secure e-mail over the Internet by using encryption, digital signatures, and key management.

- Message Security Protocol (MSP) is the military's PEM.

- Pretty Good Privacy (PGP) is an e-mail security program that uses public key encryption. It uses a web of trust instead of the hierarchical structure used in PKI.

- S-HTTP provides protection for each message that is sent between two computers, but not the actual link. HTTPS protects the communication channel. HTTPS is HTTP that uses SSL for security purposes.

- Secure Electronic Transaction (SET) is a proposed electronic commerce technology that provides a safer method for customers and merchants to perform transactions over the Internet.

- In IPSec, AH provides integrity and authentication, and ESP provides those plus confidentiality.

- IPSec protocols can work in transport mode (data payload is protected) or tunnel mode (payload and headers are protected).

- IPSec uses IKE as its key exchange protocol. IKE is the de facto standard and is a combination of ISAKMP and OAKLEY.

- DEA is the algorithm that was used for the DES standard.

## Questions

Please remember that these questions are formatted and asked in a certain way for a reason. You must remember that the CISSP exam is asking questions at a conceptual level. Questions may not always have the perfect answer, and the candidate is advised against always looking for the perfect answer. The candidate should look for the best answer in the list.

1. What is the goal of cryptanalysis?

   A. To determine the strength of an algorithm

   B. To increase the substitution functions in a cryptographic algorithm

   C. To decrease the transposition functions in a cryptographic algorithm

   D. To determine the permutations used

2. The frequency of brute force attacks has increased because:

   A. The use of permutations and transpositions in algorithms has increased.

   B. As algorithms get stronger, they get less complex, and thus more susceptible to attacks.

   C. Processor speed and power has increased.

   D. Key length reduces over time.

3. Which of the following is not a property or characteristic of a one-way hash function?

   A. It converts a message of arbitrary length into a value of fixed length.

   B. Given the digest value, it should be computationally infeasible to find the corresponding message.

   C. It should be impossible or rare to derive the same digest from two different messages.

   D. It converts a message of fixed length to an arbitrary length value.

4. What would indicate that a message had been modified?

   A. The public key has been altered.

   B. The private key has been altered.

   C. The message digest has been altered.

   D. The message has been encrypted properly.

5. Which of the following is a U.S. federal government algorithm developed for creating secure message digests?

   A. Data Encryption Algorithm

   B. Digital Signature Standard

   C. Secure Hash Algorithm

   D. Data Signature Algorithm

6. Which of the following best describes the difference between HMAC and CBC-MAC?

   A. HMAC creates a message digest and is used for integrity; CBC-MAC is used to encrypt blocks of data for confidentiality.

   B. HMAC uses a symmetric key and a hashing algorithm; CBC-MAC uses the first block for the checksum.

   C. HMAC provides integrity and data origin authentication; CBC-MAC uses a block cipher for the process of creating a MAC.

   D. HMAC encrypts a message with a symmetric key and then puts the result through a hashing algorithm; CBC-MAC encrypts the whole message.

7. What is an advantage of RSA over the DSA?

   A. It can provide digital signature and encryption functionality.

   B. It uses fewer resources and encrypts faster because it uses symmetric keys.

   C. It is a block cipher rather than a stream cipher.

   D. It employs a one-time encryption pad.

8. Many countries restrict the use or exportation of cryptographic systems. What is the reason given when these types of restrictions are put into place?

   A. Without standards, there would be many interoperability issues when trying to employ different algorithms in different programs.

   B. The systems can be used by some countries against their local people.

   C. Criminals could use encryption to avoid detection and prosecution.

   D. Laws are way behind, so adding different types of encryption would confuse the laws more.

9. What is used to create a digital signature?

   A. The receiver's private key

    **B.** The sender's public key

    **C.** The sender's private key

    **D.** The receiver's public key

10. Which of the following best describes a digital signature?

    **A.** A method of transferring a handwritten signature to an electronic document

    **B.** A method to encrypt confidential information

    **C.** A method to provide an electronic signature and encryption

    **D.** A method to let the receiver of the message prove the source and integrity of a message

11. How many bits make up the effective length of the DES key?

    **A.** 56

    **B.** 64

    **C.** 32

    **D.** 16

12. Why would a certificate authority revoke a certificate?

    **A.** If the user's public key has become compromised

    **B.** If the user changed over to using the PEM model that uses a web of trust

    **C.** If the user's private key has become compromised

    **D.** If the user moved to a new location

13. What does DES stand for?

    **A.** Data Encryption System

    **B.** Data Encryption Standard

    **C.** Data Encoding Standard

    **D.** Data Encryption Signature

14. Which of the following best describes a certificate authority?

    **A.** An organization that issues private keys and the corresponding algorithms

    **B.** An organization that validates encryption processes

    **C.** An organization that verifies encryption keys

    **D.** An organization that issues certificates

15. What does DEA stand for?

    **A.** Data Encoding Algorithm

    **B.** Data Encoding Application

    **C.** Data Encryption Algorithm

    **D.** Digital Encryption Algorithm

16. Who was involved in developing the first public key algorithm?

    A. Adi Shamir

    B. Ross Anderson

    C. Bruce Schneier

    D. Martin Hellman

17. What process usually takes place after creating a DES session key?

    A. Key signing

    B. Key escrow

    C. Key clustering

    D. Key exchange

18. DES performs how many rounds of permutation and substitution?

    A. 16

    B. 32

    C. 64

    D. 56

19. Which of the following is a true statement pertaining to data encryption when it is used to protect data?

    A. It verifies the integrity and accuracy of the data.

    B. It requires careful key management.

    C. It does not require much system overhead in resources.

    D. It requires keys to be escrowed.

20. If different keys generate the same ciphertext for the same message, what is this called?

    A. Collision

    B. Secure hashing

    C. MAC

    D. Key clustering

21. What is the definition of an algorithm's work factor?

    A. Time it takes to encrypt and decrypt the same plaintext

    B. Time it takes to break the encryption

    C. Time it takes to implement 16 rounds of computation

    D. Time it takes to apply substitution functions

22. What is the primary purpose of using one-way hashing on user passwords?

    A. Minimizes the amount of primary and secondary storage needed to store passwords

B. Prevents anyone from reading passwords in plaintext

C. Avoids excessive processing required by an asymmetric algorithm

D. Prevents replay attacks

23. Which of the following is based on the fact that it is hard to factor large numbers into two original prime numbers?

A. ECC

B. RSA

C. DES

D. Diffie-Hellman

24. Which of the following describes the difference between the Data Encryption Standard and the Rivest-Shamir-Adleman algorithm?

A. DES is symmetric, while RSA is asymmetric.

B. DES is asymmetric, while RSA is symmetric.

C. They are hashing algorithms, but RSA produces a 160-bit hashing value.

D. DES creates public and private keys, while RSA encrypts messages.

25. Which of the following uses a symmetric key and a hashing algorithm?

A. HMAC

B. Triple-DES

C. ISAKMP-OAKLEY

D. RSA

## Answers

1. **A.** Cryptanalysis is the process of trying to reverse-engineer a cryptosystem with the possible goal of uncovering the key that was used. Once this key is uncovered, all other messages encrypted with this key can be accessed. Cryptanalysis is carried out by the white hats to test the strength of the algorithm.

2. **C.** A brute force attack is resource intensive. It guesses values until the correct one is obtained. As computers have more powerful processors added to them, attackers can carry out more powerful brute force attacks.

3. **D.** A hashing algorithm will take a string of variable length, the message can be of any size, and compute a fixed-length value. The fixed-length value is the message digest. The MD family creates the fixed-length value of 128 bits, and SHA creates one of 160 bits.

4. **C.** Hashing algorithms generate message digests to detect whether modification has taken place. The sender and receiver independently generate their own digests, and the receiver compares these values. If they differ, the receiver knows the message has been altered.

5. **C.** SHA was created to generate secure message digests. Digital Signature Standard (DSS) is the standard to create digital signatures, which dictates that SHA must be used. DSS also outlines the digital signature algorithms that can be used with SHA: RSA, DSA, ECDSA.

6. **C.** In an HMAC operation, a message is concatenated with a symmetric key and the result is put through a hashing algorithm. This provides integrity and system or data authentication. CBC-MAC uses a block cipher to create a MAC, which is the last block of ciphertext.

7. **A.** RSA can be used for data encryption, key exchange, and digital signatures. DSA can be used only for digital signatures.

8. **C.** The U.S. government has greatly reduced its restrictions on cryptography exportation, but there are still some restrictions in place. Products that use encryption cannot be sold to any country the United States has declared as terrorist in nature. The fear is that the enemies of the country would use encryption to hide their communication, and the government would be unable to break this encryption and spy on their data transfers.

9. **C.** A digital signature is a message digest that has been encrypted with the sender's private key. A sender, or anyone else, should never have access to the receiver's private key.

10. **D.** A digital signature provides authentication (knowing who really sent the message), integrity (because a hashing algorithm is involved), and nonrepudiation (sender cannot deny sending the message).

11. **A.** DES has a key size of 64 bits, but 8 bits are used for parity, so the true key size is 56 bits. Remember that DEA is the algorithm used for the DES standard, so DEA also has a true key size of 56 bits, because we are actually talking about the same algorithm here. DES is really the standard and DEA is the algorithm; we just call it DES in the industry because it is easier.

12. **C.** The reason that a certificate is revoked is to warn others who use that person's public key that they should no longer trust the public key because, for some reason, that public key is no longer bound to that particular individual's identity. This could be because an employee left the company, or changed his name and needed a new certificate, but most likely it is because the person's private key was compromised.

13. **B.** Data Encryption Standard was developed by NIST and NSA to be used to encrypt sensitive but unclassified government data.

14. **D.** A registration authority (RA) accepts a person's request for a certificate and verifies that person's identity. Then the RA sends this request to a certificate authority (CA), which generates and maintains the certificate. Some companies are in business solely for this purpose; Entrust and VeriSign are just two examples.

15. **C.** DEA is the algorithm that fulfilled the DES standard. So DEA has all of the attributes of DES: symmetric block cipher that uses 64-bit blocks, 16 rounds, and a 56-bit key.

16. **D.** The first released public key cryptography algorithm was developed by Whitfield Diffie and Martin Hellman.

17. **D.** After a session key has been created, it has to be exchanged securely. In most cryptosystems, an asymmetric key (the receiver's public key) is used to encrypt this session key, and it is sent to the receiver.

18. **A.** DES carries out 16 rounds of mathematical computation on each 64-bit block of data it is responsible for encrypting. A round is a set of mathematical formulas that is used for encryption and decryption processes.

19. **B.** Data encryption always requires careful key management. Most algorithms are so strong today that it is much easier to go after key management rather than launch a brute force attack. Hashing algorithms are used for data integrity, encryption does require a good amount of resources, and keys do not have to be escrowed for encryption.

20. **D.** Message A was encrypted with key A and the result is ciphertext Y. If that same message A were encrypted with key B, the result should not be ciphertext Y. The ciphertext should be different since a different key was used. But if the ciphertext is the same, this occurrence is referred to as key clustering.

21. **B.** The work factor of a cryptosystem is the amount of time and resources necessary to break the cryptosystem or its encryption process. The goal is to make the work factor so high that an attacker could not be successful at this type of attack.

22. **B.** Passwords are usually run through a one-way hashing algorithm so that the actual password is not transmitted across the network or stored on the authentication server in plaintext. This greatly reduces the risk of an attacker being able to obtain the actual password.

23. **B.** The RSA algorithm's security is based on the difficulty of factoring large numbers into their original prime numbers. This is a one-way function. It is easier to calculate the product than it is to identify the prime numbers that were used to generate that product.

24. **A.** DES is a symmetric algorithm. RSA is a public key algorithm. DES is used to encrypt data, and RSA is used to create public/private key pairs.

25. **A.** When an HMAC function is used, a symmetric key is combined with the message, and then that result is put though a hashing algorithm. The result is an HMAC value. HMAC provides data origin authentication and data integrity.

# Business Continuity Planning

This chapter presents the following:

- Project initiation steps
- Recovery and continuity planning requirements
- Business impact analysis
- Selecting, developing, and implementing disaster and continuity plans
- Backup and offsite facilities
- Types of drills and tests

We can't prepare for every possibility, as recent events have proved. The hurricanes that hit Florida in 2004 carried out extensive damage. Businesses were not merely affected—their buildings were destroyed and lives were lost. The catastrophic Indian Ocean tsunami that took place in December 2004 struck with complete surprise. California had power fluctuations because of the lack of power supplies in the summer of 2001, which several businesses were clearly not ready to deal with. The World Trade Center towers coming down after terrorists crashed planes into them affected many surrounding businesses, U.S. citizens, the government, and the world in a way that most people would have never dreamed. Every year, thousands of businesses are affected by floods, fires, tornadoes, terrorist attacks, and vandalism in one area or another. The companies that survive these traumas are the ones that thought ahead, planned for the worst, estimated the possible damages that could occur, and put the necessary controls in place to protect themselves. This is a very small percentage of businesses today. Most businesses affected by these events have to close their doors forever. The companies that have survived these negative eventualities had a measured, approved set of advance arrangements and procedures.

An organization is dependent upon resources, personnel, and tasks that are performed on a daily basis in order to stay healthy, happy, and profitable. Most organizations have tangible resources, intellectual property, employees, computers, communications links, facilities, and facility services. If any one of these is damaged or inaccessible for one reason or another, the company can be crippled. If more than one is damaged, the company may be in a darker situation. The longer these items are unusable, the longer it will probably take for an organization to get back on its feet. Some companies are never able to recover after certain disasters. However, the companies that thought ahead, planned for the possible disasters, and did not put all of their eggs in one basket have had a better chance of resuming business and staying in the market.

# Business Continuity and Disaster Recovery

*What do we do if everything blows up? And how can we still make our widgets?*

The goal of disaster recovery is to minimize the effects of a disaster and take the necessary steps to ensure that the resources, personnel, and business processes are able to resume operation in a timely manner. This is different from continuity planning, which deals with providing methods and procedures for dealing with longer-term outages and disasters. The goal of a disaster recovery plan is to deal with the disaster and its ramifications right after the disaster hits; the disaster recover plan is usually very information technology (IT) focused.

A disaster recovery plan is carried out when everything is still in emergency mode and everyone is scrambling to get all critical systems back online. A business continuity plan (BCP) takes a broader approach to the problem. This includes getting critical systems to another environment while repair of the original facilities is taking place, getting the right people to the right places, and performing business in a different mode until regular conditions are back in place. It also involves dealing with customers, partners, and shareholders through different channels until everything returns to normal. So, disaster recovery deals with, "Oh my goodness, the sky is falling," and continuity planning deals with, "Okay, the sky fell. Now, how do we stay in business until someone can put the sky back where it belongs?"

There is a continual theme throughout many of the chapters in this book: availability, integrity, and confidentiality. Because each chapter deals with a different topic, each looks at these three security characteristics in a slightly different way. In Chapter 4, for example, which discussed access control, availability meant that resources should be available to users and subjects in controlled and secure manners. The access control method should protect the integrity and/or confidentiality of a resource. In fact, the access control method must take many steps to ensure that the resource is kept confidential and that there is no possibility its contents can be altered while they are being accessed. In this chapter, integrity and confidentiality need to be considered not in everyday procedures, but in the procedures that will be taking place right after a disaster or disruption. It may not be appropriate to leave a server that holds confidential information in one building while everyone else moves to another building.

It is also important to note that a company may be much more vulnerable after a disaster hits, because the security services that are used to protect it may be unavailable or operating at a reduced capacity. Therefore, it is important that if the business has secret stuff, it stays secret and that the integrity of data and systems is ensured even when people and the company are in dire straits. Availability is one of the main themes behind business continuity planning in that it ensures that the resources required to keep the business going will continue to be available to the people and systems that rely upon them. This may mean that backups need to be done religiously and that redundancy needs to be factored into the architecture of the systems, networks, and operations. If communication lines are disabled or if a service is rendered unusable for any significant period of time, there must be a quick and tested way of establishing alternate communications and services.

When looking at business continuity planning, some companies focus mainly on backing up data and providing redundant hardware. Although these items are extremely important, they are just small pieces of the company's overall operations pie. Hardware and computers need people to configure and operate them, and data is usually not useful unless it is accessible by other systems and possibly outside entities. Thus, a larger picture of how the various processes within a business work together needs to be understood. Planning needs to include getting the right people to the right places, documenting the necessary configurations, establishing alternate communications channels (voice and data), providing power, and making sure all dependencies, including processes and applications, are properly understood and taken into account. For example, there may be no point in bringing a server back online if the DNS server is not working on the network.

It is also important to understand how automated tasks can be carried out manually, if necessary, and how business processes can be safely altered to keep the operation of the company going. This may be critical to ensuring that the company will survive the event with the least impact to its operations. Without this type of vision and planning, when a disaster hits, a company could have its backup data and redundant servers physically available at the alternate facility, but the people responsible for activating them may be standing around in a daze not knowing where to start or how to perform in such a different environment.

## Business Continuity Steps

Although there is not a specific scientific equation that must be followed to create continuity plans, there are best practices that have proven themselves over time. The National Institute of Standards and Technology (NIST) organization is responsible for developing these best practices and documenting them so that they are easily available to all. NIST outlines the following steps in its Special Publication 800-34, *Continuity Planning Guide for Information Technology Systems,* (**http://csrc.nist.gov/publications/nistpubs/800-34/sp800-34.pdf**):

1. *Develop the continuity planning policy statement.* Write a policy that provides the guidance necessary to develop a BCP and assigns authority to the necessary roles to carry out these tasks.

2. *Conduct the business impact analysis (BIA).* Identify critical functions and systems and allow the organization to prioritize them based on necessity. Identify vulnerabilities, threats, and calculate risks.

3. *Identify preventive controls.* Once threats are identified, identify and implement controls and countermeasures to reduce the organization's risk level in an economical manner.

4. *Develop recovery strategies.* Formulate methods to ensure that systems and critical functions can be brought online quickly.

5. *Develop the contingency plan.* Write procedures and guidelines for how the organization can still stay functional in a crippled state.

6. *Test the plan and conduct training and exercises.* Test the plan to identify deficiencies in the BCP and conduct training to properly prepare individuals on their expected tasks.

7. *Maintain plan.* Put in place steps to ensure that the BCP is a living document that is updated regularly.

## Understanding the Organization First

A company has no real hope of rebuilding itself and its processes after a disaster if it does not have a good understanding of how the company works in the first place. This might seem absurd at first. You might think, "Well, of course a company knows how it works." But you would be surprised at how truly difficult it is to fully understand an organization to the level of detail that is required to rebuild it if necessary. Each individual knows and understands their little world within the company, but hardly anyone at any company can fully explain how each and every business process takes place. It is out of the scope of this book to go into business processes and enterprise architecture, but you can review a mature and useful model at **www.intervista-institute.com/resources/zachman-poster.html**. This is one of the most comprehensive approaches to understanding a company's architecture and all the pieces and parts that make it up. This model breaks down the core portions of a corporate enterprise to illustrate the various requirements of every business process. It looks at the data, function, network, people, time, and motivation components of the enterprise's infrastructure and how they tie to the roles within the company. The beauty of this model is that it dissects business processes down to their atomic pieces and shows the necessary interdependencies that exist, which must be working correctly for effective and efficient processes to be carried out.

 **NOTE** This link points to a poster that illustrates the comprehensive model, which helps companies classify the various components of the enterprise. This site also contains other resources pertaining to this model.

It would be very beneficial for a BCP team to use this type of model to understand the core components of an organization, because the team's responsibility is to make sure that the organization can be rebuilt if needed.

**Figure 9-1** Process components of developing a business continuity plan

The necessary steps that are required to roll out a business continuity planning process are illustrated in Figure 9-1.

Although the NIST 800-34 document deals specifically with IT contingency plans, these steps are the same when creating enterprise-wide BCPs. This chapter steps you through these different phases and what you should do to build an effective and useful BCP.

## References

- **Business Continuity Planning Model,** *Disaster Recovery Journal* www.drj .com/new2dr/model/bcmodel.htm

- **iNFOSYSSEC Business Continuity and Disaster Recovery Planning resources page** www.infosyssec.net/infosyssec/buscon1.htm

## Make BCP Part of the Security Policy and Program

*Why would we need to combine business and security plans anyway? Response: They both protect the business, unenlightened one.*

As stated in Chapter 3, every company should have security policies, procedures, standards, and guidelines. Having these in place is part of a well managed environment, and thus brings forth operational and cost-savings benefits. Together, they provide the framework of a security program for an organization. As such, the program needs to be a living entity. As a company goes through changes, so should the program, thereby ensuring it stays current, usable, and effective.

Business continuity should be a part of the security program and business decisions, as opposed to being an entity that stands off in a corner by itself. When properly integrated with change management processes, it stands a much better chance of being continually updated and improved upon. Business continuity is a foundational piece of an effective security program and is critical to ensuring relevance in time of need.

A very important question to be asked when first developing a BCP is why it is being developed. This may seem silly and the answer may at first appear obvious, but it is not always so. One would think that the reason to have these plans is to deal with an unexpected disaster and to get people back to their tasks at hand as quickly and as safely as possible, but this is not always the full story. Why are most companies in business? To make money and be profitable. If these are usually the main goals of businesses, then any BCP needs to be developed to help achieve and, more importantly, maintain these goals. The main reason to develop these plans in the first place is to reduce the risk of financial loss by improving the company's ability to recover and restore operations. This encompasses the goals of mitigating the effects of the disaster.

Not all organizations are businesses that exist to make profits. Government agencies, military units, nonprofit organizations, and the like exist to provide some type of protection or service to a nation or society. While a company needs to create its BCP to ensure that revenue continues to come in so that it can stay in business, other types of organizations need to create their BCPs to make sure that they can still carry out their critical tasks. Although the focus and business drivers of the organizations and companies may differ, their BCPs often will have similar constructs—which is to get their critical processes up and running.

Protecting what is most important to a company is rather difficult if what is most important is not first identified. Senior management is usually involved with this step because it has a point of view that extends beyond each functional manager's focus area of responsibility. The company's business plan usually defines the company's critical mission and business function. The functions must have priorities set upon them to indicate which is most crucial to a company's survival.

For many companies, financial operations are most critical. As an example, an automotive company would be far more impacted if its credit and loan services were unavailable for a day or more than it would if, say, an assembly line went down for a day, since credit and loan services are where it generates the biggest revenues. For other organizations, customer services might in fact be most critical. For example, if a company makes heart pacemakers and its physician services department is unavailable at a time when an operating room surgeon needs to contact it because of a complication, the results could be disastrous for the patient. The surgeon and the company would likely be sued and the company would likely never be able to sell another pacemaker to that surgeon, her colleagues, or perhaps even the patient's HMO. It would be very difficult to rebuild a reputation and sales after something like that happened.

Advanced planning for emergencies covers issues that were thought of and foreseen. Many other problems may arise that are not covered in the plan; thus, flexibility in the plan is crucial. The plan is a systematic way of providing a checklist of actions that should take place right after a disaster. These actions have been thought through to help the people involved be more efficient and effective in dealing with traumatic situations.

The most critical part of establishing and maintaining a current continuity plan is management support. Management must be convinced of the necessity for such a plan. Therefore, a business case must be made to obtain this support. The business case may include current vulnerabilities, regulatory and legal obligations, the current status of recovery plans, and recommendations. Management is mostly concerned with cost/benefit issues, so preliminary numbers need to be gathered and potential losses estimated. The decision of how a company should plan to recover is purely a business decision and should always be treated as such.

## Project Initiation

Before everyone runs off in 2000 different directions at one time, let's understand what needs to be done in the project initiation phase. This is the phase in which the company really needs to figure what it is doing and why. So, after someone gets the donuts and coffee, it is time to get down to business.

Once management's support is solidified, a *business continuity coordinator* needs to be identified. This will be the leader for the BCP team and will oversee the development, implementation, and testing of the continuity and disaster recovery plans. It is best if this person has good social skills, is somewhat of a politician, and has a cape, because he will need to coordinate a lot of different departments and busy individuals with their own agendas. This person needs to have direct access to management and have the credibility and authority to carry out leadership tasks.

A leader needs a team, so a BCP committee needs to be put together. Management and the coordinator should work together to appoint specific, qualified people to be on this committee. The team must be comprised of people who are familiar with the different departments within the company, because each department is unique in its functionality and has distinctive risks and threats. The best plan is when all issues and threats are brought to the table and discussed. This cannot be done effectively with a few people who are familiar with only a couple of departments. Representatives from each department must be involved with not only the planning stages but also the testing and implementation stages.

The committee should be made up of representatives from *at least* the following departments:

- Business units
- Senior management
- IT department
- Security department
- Communications department
- Legal department

If the BCP coordinator is a good management leader, she will understand that it is best to make these team members feel a sense of ownership pertaining to their tasks and roles. The people who develop the BCP should also be the ones who execute it. If you knew that in a time of crisis you would be expected to carry out some critical tasks, you might pay more attention in the planning and testing phases.

The team must then work with the management staff to develop the ultimate goals of the plan, identify the critical parts of the business that must be dealt with first during a disaster, and ascertain the priorities of departments and tasks. Management needs to help direct the team on the scope of the project and the specific objectives. At first glance, it might seem as though the scope and objectives are quite clear—protect the company. But it is not that simplistic. Is the team supposed to develop a BCP for just one facility or for more than one facility? Is the plan supposed to cover just large potential threats (hurricanes, tornadoes, floods) or deal with smaller issues as well (loss of a communications line, power failure, Internet connection failure)? Should the plan address possible terrorist attacks and bomb threats? What is the threat profile of the company? If the scope of the project is not properly defined, how do you know when you are done?

 **NOTE**  Most companies outline the scope of their BCP to encompass only the larger threats; the smaller threats are then covered by independent departmental contingency plans.

At this phase, the team works with management to develop the *continuity planning policy statement*. This statement lays out the scope of the BCP project, the team member roles, and goals of the project. Basically, it is a document that outlines what needs to be accomplished after the team communicates with management and comes to agreement on the terms of the project. The document should be returned to management to make sure that there are no assumptions or omissions and that everyone is in agreement.

The BCP coordinator would then need to implement some good, old-fashioned project management skills. A project plan should be developed that has the following components:

- Objective-to-task mapping
- Resource-to-task mapping
- Milestones
- Budget estimates
- Success factors
- Deadlines

Once the project plan is completed, it should be presented to management for written approval before any further steps are taken. It is important that there are no assumptions in the plan and the coordinator obtains permission to use the necessary resources to move forward.

# Business Continuity Planning Requirements

A major requirement for anything that has such far-reaching ramifications as business continuity planning is management support. It is critical that management understands what the real threats are to the company, the consequences of those threats, and the potential loss values for each threat. Without this understanding, management may only give lip service to continuity planning, and in some cases, that is worse than not having any plans at all because of the false sense of security that it creates. Without management support, the necessary resources, funds, and time will not be devoted, which could result in bad plans that, again, may instill a false sense of security. Failure of these plans usually means a failure in management understanding, vision, and due-care responsibilities.

Executives may be held responsible and liable under various laws and regulations. They could be sued by stockholders and customers if they do not practice due diligence and due care and fulfill all of their responsibilities when it comes to disaster recovery and business continuity items. Organizations that work within specific industries have strict regulatory rules and laws that they have to abide by, and these should be researched and integrated into the plan from the beginning. For example, banking and investment organizations must ensure that even if a disaster occurs, their customers' confidential information will not be disclosed to unauthorized individuals or be altered or vulnerable in any way. Disaster recovery, continuity development, and planning work best in a top-down approach, not a bottom-up approach. This means that management, not the staff, should be driving the project.

Many companies are running so fast to try to keep up with a dynamic and changing business world that they may not see the immediate benefit of spending time and resources on disaster recovery issues. Those individuals who *do* see the value in these efforts may have a hard time convincing top management if management does not see a potential profit margin or increase in market share as a result. But if a disaster does hit and they did put in the effort to properly prepare, the result can literally be priceless. Today's business world requires two important characteristics: the drive to produce a great product or service and get it to the market, and the insight and wisdom to know that unexpected trouble can easily find its way to one's doorstep.

It is important that management set the overall goals of continuity planning, and it should help set the priorities of what should be dealt with first. Once management sets the goals, policies, and priorities, other staff members who are responsible for these plans can fill in the rest. However, management's support does not stop there. It needs to make sure that the plans and procedures developed are actually implemented. Management needs to make sure that the plans stay updated and represent the real priorities—not simply those perceived—of a company, which change over time.

## Business Impact Analysis

*How bad is it going to hurt and how long can we deal with this level of pain?*

Business continuity planning deals with uncertainty and chance. What is important to note here is that even though you cannot predict whether or when a disaster will happen, that doesn't mean you can't plan for it. Just because we are not planning for an earthquake to hit us tomorrow morning at 10 A.M. doesn't mean that we can't plan the activities required to successfully survive when an earthquake (or similar disaster) does hit. The point of making these plans is to try to think of all the possible disasters that could take place, estimate the potential damage and loss, categorize and prioritize the potential disasters, and develop viable alternatives in case those events do actually happen.

A *business impact analysis (BIA)* is considered a *functional analysis,* in which a team collects data through interviews and documentary sources; documents business functions, activities, and transactions; develops a hierarchy of business functions; and finally applies a classification scheme to indicate each individual function's criticality level. But how do we determine a classification scheme based on criticality levels? The BCP committee must identify the threats to the company and map them to the following characteristics:

- Maximum tolerable downtime
- Operational disruption and productivity
- Financial considerations
- Regulatory responsibilities
- Reputation

The committee will not truly understand all business processes, the steps that must take place, or the resources and supplies that these processes require. So the committee must gather this information from the people who do know, which are department managers and specific employees throughout the organization. The committee starts by identifying the people who will be part of the BIA data-gathering sessions. The committee needs to identify how it will collect the data from the selected employees, be it surveys, interviews, or workshops. Next, the team needs to collect the information by actually conducting surveys, interviews, and workshops. Data points obtained as part of the information gathering will be used later during analysis. It is important that the team members ask about how different tasks get accomplished within the organization, be it a process, transaction, or service, along with any relevant dependencies. Process flow diagrams should be built, which will be used throughout the BIA and plan development stages.

Upon completion of the data collection phase, the BCP committee needs to conduct an analysis to establish which processes, devices, or operational activities are critical. If a system stands on its own, doesn't affect other systems, and is of low criticality, then it can be classified as a tier two or three recovery step. This means that these resources will not be dealt with during the recovery stages until the most critical (tier one) resources are up and running. This analysis can be completed using standard risk assessment and analysis methodologies. (For a full examination of risk analysis, refer to Chapter 3.)

Threats can be manmade, natural, or technical. A manmade threat may be an arsonist, a terrorist, or a simple mistake that can have serious outcomes. Natural threats may be tornadoes, floods, hurricanes, or earthquakes. Technical threats may be data corruption, loss of power, device failure, or loss of a data communications line. It is important to identify all possible threats and estimate the probability of them happening. Some

## BIA Steps

The more detailed and granular steps of a BIA are outlined here:

1. Select individuals to interview for data gathering.
2. Create data-gathering techniques (surveys, questionnaires, qualitative and quantitative approaches).
3. Identify the company's critical business functions.
4. Identify the resources that these functions depend upon.
5. Calculate how long these functions can survive without these resources.
6. Identify vulnerabilities and threats to these functions.
7. Calculate risk for each different business function.
8. Document findings and report them to management.

We cover each of these steps in this chapter, but many times it is easier to comprehend the BIA process when it is clearly outlined in this fashion.

issues may not immediately come to mind when developing these plans, such as an employee strike, vandals, disgruntled employees, or hackers, but they do need to be identified. These issues are often best addressed in a group with scenario-based exercises. This ensures that if a threat becomes reality, the plan includes the ramifications on *all* business tasks, departments, and critical operations. The more issues that are thought of and planned for, the better prepared a company will be if and when these events take place.

The committee needs to step through scenarios that could produce the following results:

- Equipment malfunction or unavailable equipment
- Unavailable utilities (HVAC, power, communications lines)
- Facility becomes unavailable
- Critical personnel become unavailable
- Vendor and service providers become unavailable
- Software and/or data corruption

The next step in the risk analysis is to assign a value to the assets that could be affected by each threat. This helps to establish economic feasibility of the overall plan. As discussed in Chapter 3, assigning values to assets is not as straightforward as it seems. The value of an asset is not just the amount of money that was paid for it. The asset's role to the company has to be considered along with the labor hours that went into creating it, if it is a piece of software. The value amount could also encompass the liability issues that surround the asset if it were damaged or insecure in any manner. (Review Chapter 3 for an in-depth description and criteria for calculating asset value.)

Qualitative and quantitative impact information should be gathered and then properly analyzed and interpreted. The goal is to see exactly how a business will be affected by different threats. The effects can be economical, operational, or both. Upon completion of the data analysis, it should be reviewed with the most knowledgeable people within the company to ensure that the findings are appropriate and describe the real risks and impacts the organization faces. This will help flush out any additional data points not originally obtained and will give a fuller understanding of all the possible business impacts.

Loss criteria must be applied to the individual threats that were identified. The criteria may include the following:

- Loss in reputation and public confidence
- Loss of competitive advantages
- Increase in operational expenses
- Violations of contract agreements
- Violations of legal and regulatory requirements
- Delayed income costs
- Loss in revenue
- Loss in productivity

These costs can be direct or indirect and must be properly accounted for.

So if the BCP team is looking at the threat of a terrorist bombing, it is important to identify which business function most likely would be targeted, how all business functions could be affected, and how each bulleted item in the loss criteria would be directly or indirectly involved. The timeliness of the recovery can be critical for business processes and the company's survival. For example, it may be acceptable to have the customer support functionality out of commission for two days, whereas five days may leave the company in financial ruin.

After identifying the critical functions, it is necessary to find out exactly what is required for these individual business processes to take place. The resources that are required for the identified business processes are not necessarily just computer systems, but may include personnel, procedures, tasks, supplies, and vendor support. It needs to be understood that if one or more of these support mechanisms is not available, the critical function may be doomed. The team must determine what type of effect unavailable resources and systems will have on these critical functions.

The BIA identifies the company's critical systems that are needed for survival and estimates the outage time that can be tolerated by the company as a result of various unfortunate events. The outage time that can be endured by a company is referred to as the *maximum tolerable downtime (MTD)*.

Here are some MTD estimates that may be used within an organization:

- **Nonessential**   30 days
- **Normal**   7 days

- **Important**    72 hours
- **Urgent**    24 hours
- **Critical**    Minutes to hours

Each business function and asset should be placed in one of these categories, depending upon how long the company can survive without it. These estimates will help the company to determine what backup solutions are necessary to ensure the availability of these resources. For example, if being without a T1 communication line for three hours would cost the company $130,000, the T1 line would be considered critical and thus the company should put in a backup T1 line from a different carrier. If a server going down and being unavailable for ten days will only cost the company $250 in revenue, this would fall into the normal category and thus the company may not need to have a fully redundant server waiting to be swapped out. Instead, the company may choose to count on its vendor service level agreement (SLA), which, for example, may promise to have it back online in eight days.

The BCP team must try to think of all possible events that could take place that could turn out to be detrimental to a company. The BCP team also must understand that it will not contemplate all events, and thus protection may not be available for every scenario introduced. Being properly prepared specifically for a flood, earthquake, terrorist attack, or lightning strike is not as important as being properly prepared to respond if one of the following results becomes reality:

- Equipment malfunction or unavailable equipment
- Unavailable utilities (HVAC, power, communications lines)
- Facility becomes unavailable
- Critical personnel become unavailable
- Vendor and service providers become unavailable
- Software and/or data corruption

All of the previously mentioned disasters could cause these results, but so could a meteor strike, a tornado, or a wing falling off of a plane passing overhead. So the moral to the story is to be prepared for the loss of any or all business resources, instead of focusing on the events that could cause the loss.

 **NOTE**    A BIA is performed at the beginning of business continuity planning to identify the areas that would suffer the greatest financial or operational loss in the event of a disaster or disruption. It identifies the company's critical systems needed for survival and estimates the outage time that can be tolerated by the company as a result of a disaster or disruption.

## Interdependencies

*Operations depend on manufacturing, manufacturing depends on R&D, payroll depends on accounting, and they all depend on IT. Response: Hold on. I need to write this down.*

It is important to look at a company as a complex animal instead of a static two-dimensional entity. It comprises many types of equipment, people, tasks, departments, communications mechanisms, and interfaces to the outer world. The biggest challenge of true continuity planning is understanding all of these intricacies and their interrelationships. A team may develop plans to back up and restore data, implement redundant data processing equipment, educate employees on how to carry out automated tasks manually, and obtain redundant power supplies. But if all of these components don't know how to work together in a different environment to get the products out the door, it might all be a waste of time.

The following interrelation and interdependency tasks should be carried out by the BCP team and addressed in the resulting plan:

- Define essential business functions and supporting departments.
- Identify interdependencies between these functions and departments.
- Discover all possible disruptions that could affect the mechanisms necessary to allow these departments to function together.
- Identify and document potential threats that could disrupt interdepartmental communication.
- Gather quantitative and qualitative information pertaining to those threats.
- Provide alternative methods of restoring functionality and communication.
- Provide a brief statement of rationale for each threat and corresponding information.

The main goal of business continuity is to resume business as quickly as possible, spending the least amount of money. The overall business interruption and resumption plan should cover all organizational elements, identify critical services and functions, provide alternatives for emergency operations, and integrate each departmental plan. This can be accomplished by in-house appointed employees, outside consultants, or a combination of both. A combination can bring many benefits to the company, because

### Enterprise Wide

The agreed upon scope of the BCP will indicate if one or more facilities will be included in the plan. Most BCPs are developed to cover the enterprise as a whole, instead of dealing with only portions of the organization. In larger organizations, it can be helpful for each department to have its own specific contingency plan that will address its specific needs during recovery. These individual plans need to be compatible with the enterprise-wide BCP.

the consultants are experts in this field and know the necessary steps, questions to ask, issues to look out for, and general reasonable advice, whereas in-house employees know their company intimately and have a full understanding of how certain threats can affect operations. It is good to cover all the necessary ground, and many times a combination of consultants and employees provides just the right recipe.

Up until now, we have established management's responsibilities as the following:

- Committing fully to the BCP
- Setting policy and goals
- Making available the necessary funds and resources
- Taking responsibility for the outcome of the development of the BCP
- Appointing a team for the process

The BCP team's responsibilities are as follows:

- Identifying regulatory and legal requirements that must be met
- Identifying all possible vulnerabilities and threats
- Estimating the possibilities of these threats and the loss potential
- Performing a BIA
- Outlining which departments, systems, and processes must be up and running before any others
- Developing procedures and steps in resuming business after a disaster

There are several software tools available for developing a BCP that simplify the process. Automation of these procedures can quicken the pace of the project and allow easier gathering of the massive amount of information. Many of the necessary items are provided in the boilerplate templates.

This information, along with other data explained in previous sections, should be presented to senior management. Management usually wants information stated in monetary, quantitative terms, not in subjective, qualitative terms. It is one thing to know that if a tornado were to hit, the result would be *really bad*, but it is another thing to know that if a tornado were to hit and affect 65 percent of the facility, the company could be at risk of losing computing capabilities for up to 72 hours, power supply for up to 24 hours, and a full stop of operations for 76 hours, which would equate to a loss of $125,000 each day. Management has a much harder time dealing with *really bad* than with real numbers.

It is important to realize that up until now, the BCP team has not actually developed any of its BCP. It has been collecting data, carrying out analysis on this data, and presenting it to management. Management must review these findings and give the "okay" for the team to move forward and actually develop the plan. In our scenario, we will assume that management has given the thumbs up and the team will now move into the next stages.

## References

- *Business Continuity Planning & Disaster Recovery Planning Directory,* "Business Impact Analysis," Disaster Recovery World   www.disasterrecoveryworld.com/bia.htm
- **Business Continuity Institute (BCI)**   www.thebci.org
- **DRI International (DRII)**   www.drii.org

## Preventative Measures

*Let's just wait and see if a disaster hits. Response: How about we be more proactive?*

During the BIA, the BCP team identified the maximum tolerable downtime for the critical resources. This was done to understand the business impact that would be caused if the assets were unavailable for one reason or another. It only makes sense that the team would try to reduce this impact and mitigate these risks by implementing preventative measures. Not implementing preventative measures would be analogous to going to a doctor, being told to stop eating 300 candy bars a day, increase physical activities, and start taking blood pressure medicine, and then choosing not to follow any of these preventative measures. Why go to the doctor in the first place? The same concept holds true with companies. If a team has been developed to identify risks and has come up with solutions, but the company does not implement at least some of these solutions, why put this team together in the first place?

So, instead of just waiting for a disaster to hit to see how the company holds up, countermeasures should be integrated to better fortify the company from the impacts that were recognized. Appropriate and cost-effective, preventative methods and proactive measures are more preferable than reactionary methods. Which types of preventative mechanisms should be put in place depends upon the results of the BIA, but they may include some of the following components:

- Fortification of the facility in its construction materials
- Redundant servers and communications links
- Power lines coming in through different transformers
- Redundant vendor support
- Purchasing of insurance
- Purchasing of UPS and generators
- Data backup technologies
- Media protection safeguards
- Increased inventory of critical equipment
- Fire detection and suppression systems

**NOTE**   Many of these controls are discussed in this chapter, but others are covered in Chapter 6 and Chapter 12.

# Recovery Strategies

Up to this point, the BCP team has carried out the project initiation phase. In this phase, the team obtained management support, the necessary resources, laid out the scope of the project, and identified the BCP team. It has also completed the BIA phase. This means that the committee has carried out a risk assessment and analysis, which resulted in a report of the real risk level the company faces.

The BCP committee already had to figure out how the organization works as a whole in its BIA phase. It drilled down into the organization and identified the critical functions that absolutely have to be up and running for the company to continue to run. It identified the resources that these functions require and calculated MTD values for the individual resources and the functions themselves. So it may seem as though the BIA phase is already completed. But when the BCP committee carried out these tasks, it was in the "risk assessment" phase of the BCP process. Its goals were to figure out how bad the company could be hurt in different disaster scenarios.

In the recovery strategy stage, the team approaches this information from a different perspective. It now has to figure out what the company needs to do to actually recover the items that it has identified to be so important to the organization overall. The BIA provides the blueprint for the recovery strategies for all the components, because the business processes are totally dependent upon these other recovery strategies to take place properly.

At this point, the findings from the BIA have been reported to management and management has allocated the necessary resources to move into the next phases. The BCP committee now must discover the most cost-effective recovery mechanisms that need to be implemented to address the threats that were identified in the BIA stage. Remember that in the BIA phase, the team calculated the potential losses for each identified threat. (If the facility were unavailable, it would cost the organization $200,000 a day, if the Internet connection were to go down, it would cost the company $12,000 per hour, and so on.) The team will use these values in its cost-benefit analysis when reviewing and choosing the necessary recovery solutions that need to be put into place to mitigate the organization's risk level.

---

## What Is the Difference Between Preventative Measures and Recovery Strategies?

Preventative mechanisms are put into place to try to reduce the possibility of the company experiencing a disaster and, if a disaster does hit, to lessen the amount of damage that will take place. Although the company cannot stop a tornado from coming, it could choose to move its facility from tornado valley in Kansas. The company cannot stop a car from plowing into and taking out a transformer, but it can have a separate feed from a different transformer in case this happens.

Recovery strategies are processes on how to rescue the company after a disaster takes place. These processes will integrate mechanisms such as establishing alternate sites for facilities, implementing emergency response procedures, and possibly activating the preventative mechanisms that have already been implemented.

So what does the BCP team need to accomplish in the recovery strategy stage? The team needs to actually define the recovery strategies, which are a set of predefined activities that will be implemented and carried out in response to a disaster. Sounds simple enough, but in reality this phase requires just as much work as the BIA phase.

In the BIA, the team has calculated the necessary *recovery times* that must be met for the different critical business functions and the resources those functions rely upon. For example, let's say that the team has figured out it would cost the company $200,000 per day in lost revenue if its facility were destroyed and unusable. Now the team knows that the company *has* to be up and running within five to six hours or the company could be financially crippled. This would mean that the company needs to obtain a hot site or redundant facility that would allow it to be up and running in this amount of time.

The team has figured out these types of timelines for the individual business functions, operations, and resources. Now it has to identify the recovery mechanisms and strategies that must be implemented to make sure that everything is up and running within the timelines that it has calculated. The team needs to break down these recovery strategies into the following sections:

- Business process recovery
- Facility recovery
- Supply and technology recovery
- User environment recovery
- Data recovery

## Business Process Recovery

A business process is a set of interrelated steps linked through specific decision activities to accomplish a specific task. Business processes have starting and ending points and are repeatable. The processes should encapsulate the knowledge of services, resources, and operations provided by a company. For example, when a customer requests to buy a car via an organization's e-commerce site, a set of steps must be followed, such as these:

1. Validate that the car is available.
2. Validate where the car is located and how long it would take to ship it to the destination.
3. Provide the customer with the price and delivery date.
4. Accept the customer's credit card information.
5. Validate and process the credit card order.
6. Send a receipt and tracking number to the customer.
7. Send the order to the car inventory location.
8. Restock inventory.
9. Send the order to accounting.

The BCP team needs to understand these different steps of the company's most critical steps. The data is usually presented as a workflow document that contains the roles and resources that are needed for each process.

## Facility Recovery

*That mean storm hurt our office. Let's go find another one.*

There are three main categories of disruptions and they are usually classified as nondisasters, disasters, and catastrophes. A *nondisaster* is a disruption in service as a result of a device malfunction or failure. The solution could include hardware, software, or file restoration. A *disaster* is an event that causes the entire facility to be unusable for a day or longer. This usually requires the use of an alternate processing facility and restoration of software and data from offsite copies. The alternate site must be available to the company until its main facility is repaired and usable. A *catastrophe* is a major disruption that destroys the facility altogether. This requires both a short-term solution, which would be an offsite facility, and a long-term solution, which may require rebuilding the original facility.

Disasters and catastrophes are rare compared to nondisasters, thank goodness. Nondisasters can usually be taken care of by replacing a device or restoring files from onsite backups. The BCP team needs to think through onsite backup requirements and make well-informed decisions. The team needs to identify the critical equipment and estimate the mean time between failure (MTBF) and mean time to repair (MTTR) to provide the necessary statistics of when a device may be meeting its maker and a new device may be required.

 **NOTE** MTBF is the estimated lifetime of a piece of equipment. MTBF is calculated by the vendor of the equipment or a third party. The reason for using this value is to know approximately when a particular device will need to be replaced. MTTR is an estimate of how long it will take to fix a piece of equipment and get it back into production. These concepts are further explained in Chapter 6.

For larger disasters that affect the primary facility, an offsite backup facility must be accessible. Generally, contracts are established with third-party vendors to provide such services. The client pays a monthly fee to retain the right to use the facility in a time of need and then incurs a large activation fee when the facility actually has to be used. In addition, there would be a daily or hourly fee imposed for the duration of the stay. This is why subscription services for backup facilities should be considered a short-term solution and not a long-term solution.

It is important to note that most recovery site contracts do not promise to house the company in need at a specific location, but rather promise to provide what has been contracted for somewhere within the company's locale. On and subsequent to September 11, 2001, many organizations with Manhattan offices were surprised when they were redirected by their backup site vendor not to sites located in New Jersey, which were already full, but rather to sites located in Boston, Chicago, or Atlanta. This adds yet another level of complexity to the recovery process, specifically the logistics of transporting people and equipment to locations originally unplanned for.

Companies can choose from three main types of leased or rented offsite facilities:

- **Hot site**  A facility that is leased or rented and is fully configured and ready to operate within a few hours. The only missing resources from a hot site are usually the data, which will be retrieved from a backup site, and the people who will be processing the data. The equipment and system software must absolutely be compatible with the data being restored from the main site and must not cause any negative interoperability issues. These sites are a good choice for a company that needs to ensure that a site will be available for it as soon as possible.

  A hot site can support a short- or long-term outage. Most hot-site facilities support annual tests that can be done by the company to ensure the site is functioning in the necessary state. This is the most expensive of the three types of offsite facilities and can have problems if a company requires proprietary or unusual hardware or software.

 **NOTE**  The vendor of a hot site will provide the most commonly used hardware and software products to attract the largest customer base. This will most likely not include one specific customer's proprietary or unusual hardware or software products.

- **Warm site**  A leased or rented facility that is usually partially configured with some equipment, but not the actual computers. In other words, a warm site is usually a hot site without the expensive equipment. Staging a facility with duplicate hardware and computers configured for immediate operation is extremely expensive, so a warm site provides an alternate facility with some peripheral devices. This is the most widely used model. It is less expensive than a hot site and can be up and running within a reasonably acceptable time period. It may be a better choice for companies that depend upon proprietary and unusual hardware and software, because they will bring their own hardware and software with them to the site after the disaster hits. The odds of finding a remote site vendor that would have a Cray supercomputer that is readily available in a time of need are pretty slim. The drawback, however, is that the annual testing available with hot-site contracts is not usually available with warm-site contracts and thus a company cannot be certain that it will in fact be able to return to an operating state within hours.

- **Cold site**  A leased or rented facility that supplies the basic environment, electrical wiring, air conditioning, plumbing, and flooring, but none of the equipment or additional services. It may take weeks to get the site activated and ready for work. The cold site could have equipment racks and dark fiber (fiber that does not have the circuit engaged) and maybe even desks, but would require the receipt of equipment from the client, since it does not provide any. The cold site is the least expensive option but takes the most time and effort to actually get up and functioning right after a disaster. Cold sites are often used as backups for call centers, manufacturing plants, and other services that either can be moved lock, stock, and barrel in one shot or would require extensive retooling and building.

## Tertiary Sites

During the BIA phase, the team may recognize the danger of the primary backup facility not being available when needed, which could require a tertiary site. This is a secondary backup site, just in case the primary backup site is unavailable. The secondary backup site is sometimes referred to as a "backup to the backup." This is basically plan B if plan A does not work out.

**NOTE** It is important to understand that the different site types listed here are provided by service bureaus, meaning a company pays a monthly subscription fee to another company for this space and service. A hot site is a subscription service. A redundant site is a site owned and maintained by the company, meaning the company does not pay anyone else for the site. A redundant site might be "hot" in nature, meaning it is ready for production quickly, but the CISSP exam differentiates between a hot site (subscription service) and a redundant site (owned by the company).

Most companies use warm sites, which have some devices such as disk drives, tape drives, and controllers, but very little else. These companies usually cannot afford a hot site, and the extra downtime would not be considered detrimental. A warm site can provide a longer-term solution than a hot site. Companies that decide to go with a cold site must be able to be out of operation for a week or two. The cold site usually includes power, raised flooring, climate control, and wiring.

The following provides a quick overview of the differences between offsite facilities:

- **Hot Site Advantages**
  - Ready within hours for operation
  - Highly available
  - Usually used for short-term solutions, but available for longer stays
  - Annual testing available
- **Hot Site Disadvantages**
  - Very expensive
  - Limited on hardware and software choices
- **Warm and Cold Site Advantages**
  - Less expensive
  - Availability for longer timeframes because of the reduced costs
  - Practical for proprietary hardware or software use
- **Warm and Cold Site Disadvantages**
  - Not immediately available
  - Operational testing not usually available
  - Resources for operations not immediately available

Backup tapes or other media should be tested periodically on the equipment kept at the hot site to make sure the media is readable by those systems. If a warm site is used, the tapes should be brought to the *original* site and tested on those systems. The reason for the difference is that when a company uses a hot site, it depends on the systems located at the hot site; therefore, the media needs to be readable by those systems. If a company depends on a warm site, it will most likely bring its original equipment with it, so the media needs to be readable by the company's systems.

## Offsite Location

When choosing a backup facility, it should be far enough away from the original site so that one disaster does not take out both locations. In other words, it is not logical to have the backup site only a few miles away if the company is concerned about tornado damage, because the backup site could also be affected or destroyed. There is a rule of thumb that suggests that alternate facilities should be at a bare minimum at least 5 miles away from the primary site, while 15 miles is recommended for most low-to-medium critical environments, and 50–200 miles is recommended for critical operations to give maximum protection in cases of regional disasters.

## Reciprocal Agreements

*If my facility is destroyed, can I come over to yours? Response: Only if you bring hot cocoa and popcorn.*

Another approach to alternate offsite facilities is to establish a *reciprocal agreement*, also referred to as mutual aid, with another company. This means that company A agrees to allow company B to use its facilities if company B is hit by a disaster, and vice versa. This is a cheaper way to go than the other offsite choices, but it is not always the best choice. Most environments are maxed out pertaining to the use of facility space, resources, and computing capability. To allow another company to come in and work out of the same shop could prove to be detrimental to both companies. The stress of two companies working in the same environment could cause tremendous levels of tension. If it did work out, it would only provide a short-term solution. Configuration management could be a nightmare, and the mixing of operations could introduce many security issues.

If you allow another company to move into your facility and work from there, you may have a solid feeling about your friend, the CEO, but what about all of her employees whom you do not know? Now you have a new subset of people who may need to have privileged and direct access to your resources in the shared environment. This other company could be your competitor in the business world, so many of the employees may see you and your company more as a threat than one that is offering a helping hand in need. Close attention needs to be paid when assigning these other people access rights and permissions to your critical assets and resources, if they need access at all.

Reciprocal agreements have been known to work well in specific businesses, such as newspaper printing. These businesses require very specific technology and equipment that will not be available through any subscription service. These agreements follow a "you scratch my back and I'll scratch yours" mentality. For most other organizations, they are generally, at best, a secondary option for disaster protection. The other issue to consider is that these agreements are not enforceable. This means that although company A said company B could use its facility when needed, when the need arises, company A legally does not have to fulfill this promise. However, there are still many companies who do opt for this solution either because of the appeal of low cost or, as noted earlier, because it may be the only viable solution in some cases.

There are important issues that need to be addressed before a disaster hits if a company decides to participate in a reciprocal agreement with another company:

- How long will the facility be available to the company in need?
- How much assistance will the staff supply in integrating the two environments and ongoing support?
- How quickly can the company in need move into the facility?
- What are the issues pertaining to interoperability?
- How many of the resources will be available to the company in need?
- How will differences and conflicts be addressed?
- How does change control and configuration management take place?
- How often can drills and testing take place?
- How can critical assets of both companies be properly protected?

## Redundant Sites

*It's mine and mine alone. Response: Okay, keep it then.*

Some companies choose to have *redundant sites*, meaning one site is equipped and configured exactly like the primary site, which serves as a redundant environment. These sites are owned by the company and are mirrors of the original production environment. This is one of the most expensive backup facility options, because a full environment must be maintained even though it usually is not used for regular production activities until after a disaster takes place that triggers the relocation of services to the redundant site. But expensive is relative here. If the company would lose a million dollars if it were out of business for just a few hours, the loss potential would override the cost of this option. Many organizations are subjected to regulations that dictate that they must have redundant sites in place, so expense is not an issue in these situations.

Another type of facility-backup option is a *rolling hot site*, or mobile hot site, where the back of a large truck or a trailer is turned into a data processing or working area. The trailer has all of the necessary power, telecommunications, and systems to allow for processing to take place right away. The trailer can be brought to the company's parking lot or another location. Another, similar solution is a prefabricated building that can be easily and quickly put together. Military organizations and large insurance companies typically have rolling hot sites or trucks preloaded with equipment because they often need the flexibility to quickly relocate some or all of their processing facilities to different locations around the world depending on where the need arises.

Another option for organizations is to have *multiple processing centers*. An organization may have ten different facilities throughout the world, which may include products and technologies that would move all data processing from one facility to another in a matter of seconds when an interruption is detected. This technology can be implemented within the organization or from one facility to a third-party facility. There are service bureaus that provide this type of functionality to their customers. So if a company's data processing is interrupted, all or some of the processing can be moved to the service bureau's servers.

It is best if a company is aware of all available options for hardware and facility back-ups, to ensure that it makes the best decision for its specific business and critical needs.

## Supply and Technology Recovery

At this point the BCP team has mapped out the necessary business functions that need to be up and running and the specific backup facility option that is best for its organization. Now the team needs to dig down into the more granular items, such as backup solutions for the following:

- Network and computer equipment
- Voice and data communications resources
- Human resources
- Transportation of equipment and personnel
- Environment issues (HVAC)
- Data and personnel security issues
- Supplies (paper, forms, cabling, and so on)
- Documentation

The organization's current technical environment must be understood. This means the planners have to know the intimate details of the network, communications technologies, computers, network equipment, and software requirements that are necessary to get the critical functions up and running. What is surprising to some people is that many organizations do not *totally* understand how their network is configured and how it actually works, because the network was most likely established five to ten years ago and has kept growing like a teenage boy going through puberty. New devices are added, new computers are added, new software packages are added, VoIP may have been integrated, and the DMZ may have been split up into three DMZs, with an extranet for the company's partners. Maybe the company bought and merged with another company and network. Over ten years, a number of technology refreshes most likely have taken place and the individuals who are maintaining the environment now are not the same people who built it ten years ago. Many IT departments experience employee turnover every one to five years. And most organizational network schematics are notoriously out of date, because everyone is busy with their current tasks or will come up with new tasks just to get out of having to update the schematic.

So the BCP team has to make sure that if the networked environment is partially or totally destroyed, the recovery team has the knowledge and skill to properly rebuild it.

 **NOTE** Many organizations are moving to Voice over IP (VoIP), which means that if the network goes down, network and voice capability are unavailable. The team should address the possible need of redundant voice systems.

The BCP team needs to take into account several things that are commonly overlooked, such as hardware replacements, software products, documentation, environmental needs, and human resources.

## Hardware Backups

*I have an extra floppy, video card, and some gum. Response: I am sure that is all we will need.*

The team has identified the equipment that is required to keep the critical functions up and running. This may include servers, user workstations, routers, switches, tape backup devices, hubs, and more. The needed inventory may seem simplistic enough, until the team drills down into more detail. If the recovery team is planning to use images to rebuild newly purchased servers and workstations (because the original ones were destroyed), will the images work on the new computers? Using images instead of building systems from scratch can be a time-saving task, unless the team finds out that the replacement equipment is a newer version and thus the images cannot be used. The BCP team should plan for the recovery team to use the company's current images, but also have a manual process of how to build each critical system from scratch with the necessary configurations.

The BCP team also needs to identify how *long* it will take for new equipment to arrive. For example, if the organization has identified Gateway as its equipment replacement supplier, how long will it take this vendor to send 20 servers and 30 workstations to the offsite facility? After a disaster hits, the company could be in its offsite facility only to find that its equipment will take three weeks to be delivered. So, the SLA for the identified vendors needs to be investigated to make sure that the company is not further damaged by delays. Once the parameters of the SLA are understood, the team needs to make a decision between depending upon the vendor or purchasing redundant systems and storing them as backups in case the primary equipment is destroyed. As described earlier, when potential company risks are identified, it is better to take preventive steps to reduce the potential damage. After the calculation of the MTD values, the team will know how long the company can be without a specific device. This data should be used to make the decision regarding whether the company should depend on the vendor's SLA or make readily available a hot-swappable redundant system. If the company will lose $50,000 per hour if a particular server were to go down, then the team should elect to implement redundant systems and technology.

If an organization is using any legacy computers and hardware and a disaster hits tomorrow, where would it find replacements for this legacy equipment? The team should identify legacy devices and understand the risk that the organization is under if replacements are unavailable. This type of finding has caused many companies to move from legacy systems to commercial off the shelf (COTS) products to ensure that replacement is possible.

**NOTE** Different types of backup tape technologies can be used (digital linear tape, digital audio tape, advanced intelligent tape). The team needs to make sure it knows the type of technology that is used by the company and identify the necessary vendor in case the tape-reading device needs to be replaced.

## Software Backup

*I have a backup server and my backed-up data, but no operating system or applications. Response: Good luck.*

Most company's IT departments have their array of software disks and licensing information here or there—or possibly in one centralized location. If the facility were destroyed and the IT department's current environment had to be rebuilt, how would it gain access to these software packages? The BCP team should make sure to have an inventory of the necessary software that is required for mission-critical functions and have backup copies at an offsite facility. Hardware is usually not worth much to a company without the software required to run on it. The software that needs to be backed up can be in the form of applications, utilities, databases, and operating systems. The continuity plan must have provisions to back up and protect these items along with hardware and data.

The BCP team should make sure that there are at least two copies of the company's operating system software and critical applications. One copy should be stored onsite and the other copy should be stored at a secure offsite location. These copies should be tested periodically and re-created when new versions are rolled out.

It is common for organizations to work with software developers to create customized software programs. For example, in the banking world, individual financial institutions need software that will allow their bank tellers to interact with accounts, hold account information in databases and mainframes, provide online banking, carry out data replication, and perform a thousand other types of bank-like functionalities. This specialized type of software is developed and available through a handful of software vendors that specialize in this market. When bank A purchases this type of software for all of its branches, the software has to be specially customized for their environment and needs. Once this banking software is installed, the whole organization depends upon it for its minute-by-minute activities.

When bank A receives the specialized and customized banking software from the software vendor, bank A does not receive the source code. Instead, the software vendor provides bank A with a compiled version. Now, what if this software vendor goes out of business because of a disaster or bankruptcy? Bank A will require a new vendor to maintain and update this banking software; thus, the new vendor will need access to the source code.

The protection mechanism that bank A should implement is called *software escrow*. Software escrow means that a third party holds the source code, backups of the compiled code, manuals, and other supporting materials. A contract between the software vendor, customer, and third party outlines who can do what and when with the source code. This contract usually states that the customer can have access to the source code only if and when the vendor goes out of business, is unable to carry out stated responsibilities, or is in breach of the original contract. If any of these activities takes place, then the customer is protected because it can still gain access to the source code and other materials through the third-party escrow agent.

Many companies have been crippled by not implementing software escrow. Such a company would have paid a software vendor to develop specialized software, and when the software vendor went belly up, the customer did not have access to the code that its whole company ran on.

The BCP committee needs to identify this issue as a vulnerability during its analysis and implement a preventative countermeasure—software escrow.

## Documentation

*We came up with a great plan six months ago. Did anyone write it down?*

Documentation seems to be a dreaded task to most people, who will find many other tasks to take on to ensure that they are not the ones stuck with documenting processes and procedures. However, a company may do a great and responsible job of backing up hardware and software to an offsite facility, maintaining it, and keeping everything up to date and current, but without documentation, when a disaster hits, no one will know *how* to put Humpty-Dumpty back together again.

Restoration of files can be challenging, but restoring a whole environment that was swept away in a flood can be overwhelming, if not impossible. Procedures need to be documented because when they are actually needed, it will most likely be a chaotic and frantic atmosphere with a demanding time schedule. The documentation may need to include information on how to install images, configure operating systems and servers, and properly install utilities and proprietary software. Other documentation could include a calling tree, which outlines who should be contacted, in what order, and who is responsible for doing the calling. The documentation must also contain contact information for specific vendors, emergency agencies, offsite facilities, and any other entity that may need to be contacted in a time of need.

Most network environments evolve over time. Software has been installed on top of other software, configurations have been altered over the years to properly work in a unique environment, and service packs and patches have been installed to fix this problem or that issue. To expect one person or a group of people to go through all of these steps during a crisis and end up with an environment that looks and behaves exactly like the original environment and in which all components work together seamlessly may be a lofty dream.

---

### Plans

Once the business continuity and disaster recovery plans are completed, where do you think they should be stored? Should the company have only one copy and keep it safely in a file cabinet next to Bob so that he feels safe? Nope. There should be two or three copies of these plans. One copy may be at the primary location, but the other copies should be at other locations in case the primary facility is destroyed. Typically, a copy is stored at the BCP coordinator's home and a copy is stored at the offsite facility. This reduces the risk of not having access to the plans when needed.

These plans should not be stored in a file cabinet, but rather in a fire-resistant safe. When they are stored offsite, they need to be stored in a way that provides just as much protection as the primary site would provide.

So, the dreaded task of documentation may be the saving grace one day. It is an essential piece of business, and therefore an essential piece in disaster recovery and business continuity.

It is important to make one or more roles responsible for proper documentation. As with all the items that are being addressed in this chapter, saying "All documentation will be kept up to date and properly protected" is the easy part—saying and doing are two different things. Once the BCP team identifies tasks that must be done, the tasks must be assigned to individuals and those individuals have to be accountable. If these steps are not taken, the BCP team could have wasted a lot of time and resources defining these tasks and the company could be in grave danger if a disaster takes place.

 **NOTE**  An organization may need to solidify communications channels and relationships with government officials and emergency response groups. The goal of this activity is to solidify proper protocol in case of a city- or region-wide disaster. During the BIA phase, local authorities should be contacted so that the team understands the risks of its geographical location and how to access emergency zones. If the company has to initiate its BCP, many of these emergency response groups will need to be contacted during the recovery stage.

## Human Resources

*We have everything up and running now—where are all the people to run these systems?*

One of the resources that is commonly left out of the equation is people. A company may restore its networks and critical systems and get business functions up and running, only to realize that it doesn't know the answer to the question, "Who will take it from here?" Human resources is a critical component to any recovery and continuity process, and it needs to be fully thought out and integrated into the plan.

What happens if we have to move to an offsite facility that is 250 miles away? We cannot expect people to drive back and forth from home to work. Should we pay for temporary housing for the necessary employees? Do we have to pay their moving costs? Do we need to hire new employees in the area of the offsite facility? If so, what skill set do we need from them? The BCP team should go through a long succession of these types of questions.

If a large disaster takes place that affects not only the company's facility but also surrounding areas, including housing, do you think your employees will be more worried about your company or their families? Some companies assume that employees will be ready and available to help them get back into production, when in fact they may need to be at home because they have responsibilities to their families.

Regrettably, some employees may be killed in the disaster and the team may need to look at how it will be able to replace employees quickly through a temporary agency or a headhunter. This is extremely unfortunate, but it is part of reality. The team that identifies all threats and is responsible for identifying solutions needs to think about all of these issues and many more.

Organizations should already have *executive succession planning* in place. This means that if someone in a senior executive position retires, leaves the company, or is killed, the organization has predetermined steps to carry out to protect the company. The loss of a senior executive could tear a hole in the company's fabric, creating a leadership vacuum that must be filled quickly with the right individual. The line of succession plan defines who would step in and assume responsibility for this role. Many organizations have "deputy" roles. For example, an organization may have a deputy CIO, deputy CFO, and deputy CEO ready to take over the necessary tasks if the CIO, CFO, or CEO becomes unavailable.

Often, larger organizations also have a policy indicating that two or more of the senior staff cannot be exposed to a particular risk at the same time. For example, the CEO and president cannot travel on the same plane. If the plane went down and both individuals were killed, then the company could be in danger. This is why you don't see the President of the United States and the Vice President together too often. It is not because they don't like each other and thus keep their distance from each other. It is because there is a policy indicating that to protect the United States, its top leaders cannot be under the same risk at the same time.

## Reference

- *BCP IT Examination Handbook*, Federal Financial Institutions Examination Council (March 2003)   www.ffiec.gov/ffiecinfobase/booklets/bcp/bus_continuity_plan.pdf

## End-User Environment

*Do you think the users could just use an abacus for calculations and fire for light?*

Because the end users are usually the worker bees of a company, they must be provided a functioning environment as soon as possible after a disaster hits. This means that the BCP team needs to understand the current operational and technical functioning environment and examine critical pieces so that they can be replicated.

The first issue pertaining to users is how they will be notified of the disaster and who will tell them where to go and when. A tree structure of managers can be developed so that once a disaster hits, the person at the top of the tree calls two managers, and they in turn call three managers, and so on until all managers are notified. Each manager would be responsible for notifying the people he is responsible for until everyone is on the same page. Then, one or two people must be in charge of coordinating the issues pertaining to users. This could mean directing them to a new facility, making sure they have the necessary resources to complete their tasks, restoring data, and being a liaison between the different groups. The folks in charge of directing should be readily identifiable—by wearing an emergency hat and vest, for example—and should be located in areas where they can be seen by all. This will help ease confusion and reduce panic during difficult and strenuous times.

In most situations, after a disaster, only a skeleton crew is put back to work. The BCP committee identified the most critical functions of the company during the analysis stage, and the employees who carry out those functions must be put back to work first. So the recovery process for the user environment should be laid out in different stages. The first stage is to get the most critical departments back online, the next stage is to get the second most important back online, and so on.

The BCP team needs to identify user requirements, such as whether users can work on stand-alone PCs or need to be connected in a network to fulfill specific tasks. For example, in a financial institution, users who work on stand-alone PCs might be able to accomplish some small tasks like filling out account forms, word processing, and accounting tasks, but they would need to be connected to a host system to update customer profiles and to interact with the database.

The BCP team also needs to identify how current automated tasks can be carried out manually if that becomes necessary. If the network is going to be down for 12 hours, could the necessary tasks be carried out through traditional pen and paper methods? If the Internet connection is going to be down for five hours, could the necessary communications take place through phone calls? Instead of transmitting data through the internal mail system, could couriers be used to run information back and forth? Today, we are extremely dependent upon technology, but we often take for granted that it will always be there for us to use. It is up to the BCP team to realize that technology may be unavailable for a period of time and come up with solutions for those situations.

## Data Backup Alternatives

As we have covered so far, backup alternatives are needed for hardware, software, personnel, and offsite facilities. It is up to each company and its continuity team to decide if all of these components are necessary for its survival and the specifics for each type of backup that is needed.

Data has become one of the most critical assets to nearly all organizations. This data may include financial spreadsheets, blueprints on new products, customer information, product inventory, trade secrets, and more. In Chapter 3, we stepped through risk analysis procedures and data classification processes. The BCP team should not be responsible for setting up and maintaining the company's data classification procedures, but the team may recognize that the company is at risk because it does not have these procedures in place. This should be seen as a vulnerability that is reported to management. Management would need to establish another group of individuals who would identify the company's data, define a loss criterion, and establish the classification structure and processes.

The BCP team's responsibility is to provide solutions to protect this data and identify ways to restore it after a disaster. In this section, we look at different ways that data can be protected and restored when needed.

Data usually changes more often than hardware and software, so these backup procedures must happen on a continual basis. The data backup process must make sense and be reasonable and effective. If data in the files changes several times a day, backup procedures should happen a few times a day or nightly to ensure that all the changes are captured and kept. If data is changed once a month, backing up data every night is a waste of time and resources. Backing up a file and its corresponding changes is usually more desirable than having multiple copies of that one file. Online backup technologies usually have the changes to a file made to a transaction log, which is separate from the original file.

As covered in Chapter 12, the operations team is responsible for defining what data gets backed up and how often. These backups can be full, differential, or incremental backups and are usually used in some type of combination with each other. Most files are not altered every day, so, to save time and resources, it is best to devise a backup plan that does not continually back up data that has not been modified. So, how do we know what data has changed and needs to be backed up without having to look at every file's modification date? This is accomplished by an archive bit. Operating systems' file systems keep track of what files have been modified by setting an archive bit. If a file is modified or created, the file system sets the archive bit to 1. Backup software has been created to review this bit setting when making its determination on what gets backed up and what does not.

Figure 9-2 shows the Windows interpretation of the archive bit being set to 1, which is a check in the File Is Ready For Archiving box. This indicates that the file has been modified since the last backup.

The first step is to do a *full backup*, which is just what it sounds like—all data is backed up and saved to some type of storage media. During a full backup, the archive bit is clear, which means that it is set to 0. A company can choose to do full backups only, in which case the restoration process is just one step, but the backup and restore processes could take a long time.

Most companies choose to combine a full backup with a differential or incremental backup. A *differential process* backs up the files that have been modified since the *last full backup*. When the data needs to be restored, the full backup is laid down first and then the differential backup is put down on top of it. The differential process does not change the archive bit value.

An *incremental process* backs up all the files that have changed since the *last full or incremental backup* and sets the archive bit to 0. When the data needs to be restored, the full backup data is laid down and then each incremental backup is laid down on top of it in the proper order. If a company experienced a disaster and it used the incremental process, it would first need to restore the full backup on its hard drives and lay down every incremental backup that was carried out before the disaster took place. So, if the

**Figure 9-2**
Backup software may alter the archive bit.

full backup was done six months ago and the operations department carried out an incremental backup each month, the restoration team would restore the full backup and start with the older incremental backups and restore each one of them until they were all restored.

Which backup process is best? If a company wants the backup and restoration processes to be simplistic and straightforward, then it can carry out just full backups—but this may require a lot of hard drive space and time. Although using differential and incremental backup processes is more complex, it requires less resources and time. A differential backup takes more time in the backing up phase than an incremental backup, but it also takes less time to restore than an incremental backup, because carrying out restoration of a differential backup happens in two steps, whereas in an incremental backup every incremental backup has to be restored in the correct sequence.

Whatever the organization chooses, it is important to not mix differential and incremental backups. This overlap could cause files to be missed, since the incremental backup changes the archive bit and the differential backup does not.

Critical data should be backed up to both an onsite area *and* an offsite area. The onsite backup copies should be easily accessible in the case of nondisasters and should provide a quick restore process so that operations can return to normal. However, onsite backup copies are not enough to provide real protection. The data should also be held in an offsite facility in case of actual disasters or catastrophes. One choice that needs to be made is where the offsite location should be in reference to the main facility. The closer the offsite backup storage site is, the easier it is to access, but this can put the backup copies in danger if a large-scale disaster manages to take out the company's main facility and backup facility. It may be wiser to choose a backup facility farther away, which makes accessibility harder but reduces the risk. Some companies choose to have more than one backup facility: one that is close and one that is farther away.

The onsite backup information should be stored in a fire-resistant, heat-resistant, and waterproof safe. The procedures for backing up and restoring data should be easily accessible and comprehensible even to operators or administrators who are not intimately familiar with a specific system. In an emergency situation, the same guy who always does the backing up and restoring may not be around, or outsourced consultants may need to be temporarily hired in order to meet the restoration time constraints.

A backup strategy must take into account that failure can take place at any step of the process, so if there is a problem during the backup or restoration process that could corrupt the data, there should be a graceful way of backing out or reconstructing the data from the beginning.

## Can We Actually Restore the Data?

Backing up data is a wonderful thing in life, but making sure that it can be properly restored is even better. Many organizations have developed a false sense of security based on the fact that they have a very organized and effective process of backing up their data. That sense of security can disappear in seconds when a company realizes in a time of crises that its restore processes do not work. For example, one company had paid an offsite backup facility to use a courier to collect its weekly backup tapes and transport them to the offsite facility for safe keeping. What the company did not realize is that this courier used the subway and many times set the tapes on the ground while waiting for the subway train. A subway has many large engines that create their own magnetic field. This can have the same effect on media as large magnets, meaning that the data can be erased or corrupted. The company never tested its restore processes and eventually experienced a disaster. Much to its surprise, it found out that three years of data was corrupted and unusable.

There are many other stories and experiences like this. Don't let your organization end up as an anecdote in someone else's book because it failed to verify that its backups can be restored.

## Electronic Backup Solutions

Manually backing up systems and data can be time consuming, error prone, and costly. There are several technologies that serve as automated backup alternatives. Although these technologies are usually more expensive, they are quicker and more accurate, which may be necessary for online information that changes often.

Among the many technologies and ways to back up data electronically is disk-shadowing, or data-mirroring. A *disk-shadowing* process uses two physical disks, and the data is written to both at the same time for redundancy purposes. If one disk fails, the other is readily available.

 **NOTE**  *Disk duplexing* means that there is more than one disk controller. If one disk controller fails, the other is ready and available.

Disk shadowing is used to ensure availability of data and provide a fault-tolerant solution by duplicating hardware and maintaining more than one copy of the information. The data is dynamically created and maintained on two or more identical disks. If purely disk mirroring is used, then each disk would have a corresponding mirrored disk that contains the exact same information. If shadow sets are used, then the data can be stored as images on two or more disks.

Systems that need to interact with this data are connected to all the drives at the same time. All of these drives "look" like just one drive to the user. This provides transparency to the user so that when she needs to retrieve a file, she does not have to worry about which drive to go to for this process. When a user writes data to be stored on this media, the data is written to all disks in the shadow set.

Disk shadowing provides online backup storage, which can either reduce or replace the need for periodic offline manual backup operations. Another benefit to this solution is that it can boost read operation performance. Multiple paths are provided to duplicate data, and a shadow set can carry out multiple read requests in parallel.

Disk shadowing is commonly seen as an expensive solution, because two or more hard drives are used to hold the exact same data. If a company has data that will fill up 100 hard drives, it must purchase and maintain at least 200 hard drives. A company would choose this solution if fault tolerance were required.

If a disk drive fails, at least one shadow set is still available. A new disk can be assigned to this set through proper configurations, and the data can be copied from the shadow set. The copying can take place offline, but this means that the data is unavailable for a period of time. Most products that provide disk-shadowing functionality allow for online copying, where disks are hot swapped into the set and can carry out the necessary copy functions without having to bring the drives offline.

Electronic vaulting and remote journaling are other solutions that companies should be aware of. *Electronic vaulting* makes copies of files as they are modified and periodically transmits them to an offsite backup site. The transmission does not happen in real time, but is carried out in batches. So, a company can choose to have all files that have been changed sent to the backup facility every hour, day, week, or month. The information can be stored in an offsite facility and retrieved from that facility in a short period of time.

This form of backup takes place in many financial institutions, so when a bank teller accepts a deposit or withdrawal, the change to the customer's account is made locally to that branch's database and to the remote site that maintains the backup copies of all customer records.

Electronic vaulting is a method of transferring bulk information to offsite facilities for backup purposes. *Remote journaling* is another method of transmitting data offsite, but this usually only includes moving the journal or transaction logs to the offsite facility, not the actual files. These logs contain the deltas (changes) that have taken place to the individual files. If and when data is corrupted and needs to be restored, the bank can retrieve these logs, which are used to rebuild the lost data. Journaling is efficient for database recovery, where only the reapplication of a series of changes to individual records is required to resynchronize the database.

 **NOTE** Remote journaling takes place in real time and transmits only the file deltas. Electronic journaling takes place in batches and moves the entire file that has been updated.

It may be necessary to keep different versions of software and files, especially in a software development environment. The object and source code should be backed up along with libraries, patches, and fixes. The offsite facility should mirror the onsite facility, meaning that it does not make sense to keep all of this data at the onsite facility and only the source code at the offsite facility. Each site should have a full set of the most current and updated information and files.

Two other backup technologies are *hierarchical storage management (HSM)* and *storage area network (SAN)*. HSM provides continuous online backup functionality. It combines hard disk technology with the cheaper and slower optical or tape jukeboxes. The HSM system dynamically manages the storage and recovery of files, which are copied to storage media devices that vary in speed and cost. The faster media holds the data that is accessed more often, and the seldom-used files are stored on the slower devices, or *near-line* devices, as shown in Figure 9-3. The storage media could include optical disks, magnetic disks, and tapes. This functionality happens in the background without the knowledge of the user or any need for user intervention.

SAN is made up of several storage systems that are connected together to form a single backup network. A SAN is a networked infrastructure that allows several systems to be connected to any storage device. This is usually provided by using switches to create a switching fabric, as shown in Figure 9-4. The switching fabric enables several devices to

**Figure 9-3**
Hierarchical storage management system

communicate with back-end storage devices and provides redundancy and fault tolerance by not depending upon one specific line or connection. Private channels or storage controllers are implemented so that hosts can access the storage devices transparently.

The last software backup technology we will discuss is referred to as tape vaulting. Many businesses back up their data to tapes that are then manually transferred to an offsite facility by a courier or an employee. With automatic *tape vaulting*, the data is sent over a serial line to a backup tape system at the offsite facility. The company that maintains the offsite facility maintains the systems and changes out tapes when necessary. Data can be quickly backed up and retrieved when necessary. This technology reduces the manual steps in the traditional tape backup procedures.

## Choosing a Software Backup Facility
*I like this facility because it is pink.*

A company needs to address several issues and ask specific questions when it is deciding upon a storage facility for its backup materials. The following provides a list of

**Figure 9-4** Storage area network

just some of the issues that need to be thought through before committing to a specific vendor for this service:

- Can the media be accessed in the necessary timeframe?
- Is the facility closed on weekends and holidays, and does it only operate during specific hours of the day?
- Are the access control mechanisms tied to an alarm and/or the police station?
- Does the facility have the capability to protect the media from a variety of threats?
- What is the availability of a bonded transport service?
- Are there any geographical environmental hazards such as floods, earthquakes, tornadoes, and so on?
- Is there a fire detection and suppression system?
- Does the facility provide temperature and humidity monitoring and control?
- What type of physical, administrative, and logical access controls are used?

The questions and issues that need to be addressed will vary depending on the type of company, its needs, and the requirements of a backup facility.

## Insurance

*Can someone else just pay for this mess? Response: Sure, we just need a monthly fee.*

During the BIA, the team most likely uncovered several threats that the organization could not prevent. Taking on the full risk of these threats often is dangerous, which is why insurance exits. The decision of whether or not to obtain insurance for a particular threat, and how much coverage to obtain when choosing to insure, should be based on the probability of the threat becoming real and the loss potential, which was identified during the BIA. The BCP team should work with management to understand what the current coverage is, the various insurance options, and the limits of each option. The goal here is to make sure that the insurance coverage fills in the gap of what the current preventative countermeasures cannot protect against. We can eat healthy, work out, and take our vitamins—but these things cannot prevent death. We purchase life insurance so that after we die, our loved ones are taken care of. (Seems more appropriate to call this death insurance, but that would really hurt marketing efforts of insurance companies.)

Just as people are given different premiums on health and life insurance, companies are given different premiums on the type of insurance they purchase. Different types of insurance policies can be purchased by companies, cyberinsurance being one of them. *Cyberinsurance* is a new type of coverage that insures losses caused by denial-of-service attacks, malware damages, hackers, electronic theft, privacy-related lawsuits, and more. Where a person is asked how old he is, previous health issues, if he smokes, and so on to determine his health insurance premium, companies are asked questions about their security program, such as whether they have an IDS, antivirus software, firewalls, and other security measures.

A company could also choose to purchase a *business interruption insurance* policy. With this type of policy, if the company is out of business for a certain length of time, the insurance company will pay for specified expenses and lost earnings. Another policy that can be bought insures accounts receivable. If a company cannot collect on its accounts receivable for one reason or another, this type of coverage covers part or all of the losses and costs.

The company's insurance should be reviewed annually, because threat levels may change and the company may expand into new ventures that need to be properly covered. Purchasing insurance should not lull a company into a false sense of security, though. Insurance coverage has its limitations, and if the company does not practice due care, the insurance company may not be legally obligated to pay if a disaster hits. It is important to read and understand the fine print when it comes to insurance and make sure that you know what is expected of your company—not just what is expected from the insurance organization.

## Recovery and Restoration

*Now, who is going to fix everything? Response: We thought you were.*

The BCP coordinator needs to define several different teams that should be properly trained and available if a disaster hits. The types of teams that an organization needs depends upon the organization. The following are some examples of teams that a company may need to construct:

- Damage assessment team
- Legal team

- Media relations team
- Network recovery team
- Relocation team
- Restoration team
- Salvage team
- Security team
- Telecommunications team

The BCP coordinator should have an understanding of the needs of the company and the types of teams that need to be developed and trained. Employees should be assigned to the specific teams based on their knowledge and skill set. Each team needs to have a designated leader, who will direct the members and their activities. These team leaders will be responsible not only for ensuring that their team's objectives are met, but also for communicating with each other to make sure that each team is working in parallel phases.

The *restoration team* should be responsible for getting the alternate site into a working and functioning environment, and the *salvage team* should be responsible for starting the recovery of the original site. Both teams must know how to do many tasks, such as install operating systems, configure workstations and servers, string wire and cabling, set up the network and configure networking services, and install equipment and applications. Both teams must also know how to restore data from backup facilities, and how to do so in a secure manner that ensures that the system's and data's confidentiality, integrity, and availability are not compromised.

The BCP must outline the specific teams, their responsibilities, and notification procedures. The plan must indicate the methods that should be used to contact team leaders during business hours and after business hours.

A role, or a team, needs to be created to carry out a *damage assessment* once a disaster has taken place. The assessment procedures should be properly documented and include the following steps:

1. Determine the cause of the disaster.
2. Determine the potential for further damage.
3. Identify the affected business functions and areas.
4. Identify the level of functionality for the critical resources.
5. Identify the resources that must be replaced immediately.
6. Estimate how long it will take to bring critical functions back online.

After this information is collected and assessed, it will indicate what teams need to be called to action and whether the BCP actually needs to be activated. The BCP coordinator and team must develop an activation criterion. After the damage assessment, if one or more of the situations outlined in the criteria have taken place, then the team is moved into recovery mode.

Different organizations have different criteria, because the business drivers and critical functions will vary from organization to organization. The criteria may comprise some or all of the following elements:

- Danger to human life
- Danger to state or national security
- Damage to facility
- Damage to critical systems
- Estimated value of down time that will be experienced

Once the damage assessment is completed and the plan is activated, various teams must be deployed, which signals the company's entry into the recovery phase. Each team has its own tasks; for example, the restoration team prepares the offsite facility (if needed), the network team rebuilds the network and systems, and the relocation team starts organizing the staff to move into a new facility.

The recovery process needs to be as organized as possible to get the company up and running as soon as possible. This is much easier to state in a book than to carry out in reality. This is why written procedures are critical. During the BIA, the critical functions and their resources were identified. These are the things that the teams need to work together on getting up and running first. Templates should be developed during the plan development stage. These templates are used by the different teams to step them through the necessary phases and to document their findings. For example, if one step could not be completed until new systems were purchased, this should be indicated on the template. If a step is partially completed, this should be documented so that the team does not forget to go back and finish that step when the necessary part arrives. These templates keep the teams on task and also quickly tell the team leaders about the progress, obstacles, and potential recovery time.

 **NOTE**  Examples of possible templates can be found in NIST's *Contingency Planning Guide for Information Technology Systems*, available online at **http://csrc .nist.gov/publications/nistpubs/800-34/sp800-34.pdf**.

When it is time for the company to move back into its original site or a new site, the company is ready to enter into the *reconstitution phase*. A company is not out of an emergency state until it is back in operation at the original primary site or a new site that was constructed to replace the primary site, because the company is always vulnerable while operating in a backup facility. There are many logistical issues to consider when a company must return from the alternate site to the original site. The following are some of the issues that must be considered:

- Ensuring the safety of employees
- Ensuring an adequate environment is provided (power, facility infrastructure, water, HVAC)
- Ensuring that the necessary equipment and supplies are present and in working order

- Ensuring proper communications and connectivity methods are working
- Properly testing the new environment

Once the coordinator, management, and salvage team sign off on the readiness of the facility, then the salvage team should carry out the following steps:

1. Back up data from the alternate site and restore it within the new facility
2. Carefully terminate contingency operations
3. Securely transport equipment and personnel to the new facility

The least critical functions should be moved back first, so if there are issues in network configurations or connectivity, or important steps were not carried out, the critical operations of the company are not negatively affected. Why go through the trouble of moving the most critical systems and operations to a safe and stable site, only to return it to a main site that is untested? Let the less critical departments act as the canary. If they survive, then move over the more critical components of the company.

Up to now, the BCP team has covered the following steps:

1. Developed the continuity planning policy statement
   - Outlined the scope and goals of the BCP and roles of the BCP team

2. Performed the business impact analysis (BIA)
   - Identified critical business functions, their resources, and MTD values
   - Identified threats and calculated the impact of these threats
   - Identified solutions
   - Presented findings to management

3. Identified and implemented preventive controls
   - Put controls into place to reduce the company's identified risks
   - Bought more insurance, implemented facility structural reinforcements, rolled out backup solutions for data, installed redundant and fault-tolerant mechanisms, and so on

4. Developed recovery strategies
   - Implemented processes of getting the company up and running in the necessary time
   - Created the necessary teams, developed goals and procedures for each team, created notification steps and planned activation criteria, identified alternate backup solutions, and so on

So, the BCP team has worked long and hard and has all of the previous items figured out. Now it needs to put all of these solutions and steps in the plan itself, test the plan, train the people, and lay out strategies of how the plan is to be maintained and kept up to date. No rest for the weary…let's march on!

## References

- *Business Continuity Planning & Disaster Recovery Planning Directory*, **Disaster Recovery World**   www.disasterrecoveryworld.com
- *Business Continuity Directory*, **Business Continuity Planning Group** www.business-continuity-and-disaster-recovery-world.co.uk
- *Business Impact Analysis*, **Disaster Recovery Institute Canada**   www.dri.ca/ dric_pp3.html

## Developing Goals for the Plans

*My goals are to own a boat, retire at 55, and grow more hair. Response: Great, we will integrate this into our BCP.*

If you do not have established goals, then how do you know when you are done and whether your efforts were actually successful? Goals are established so that everyone knows the ultimate objectives. Establishing goals is important for any task, but especially for business continuity and recovery plans. The definition of the goals helps direct the proper allocation of resources and tasks, develops necessary strategies, and assists in economical justification of the plans and program overall. Once the goals are set, they provide a guide to the development of the actual plans themselves. Anyone who has been involved in large projects that entail many small, complex details knows that at times it is easy to get off track and not actually accomplish the major goals of the project. Goals are established to keep everyone on track and ensure that the efforts pay off in the end.

Great, we have established that goals are important. But the goal could be, "Keep the company in business if an earthquake hits." Good goal, but not overly useful without more clarity and direction. To be useful, a goal must contain certain key information, such as the following:

- **Responsibility**   Each individual involved with recovery and continuity should have their responsibilities spelled out in writing to ensure a clear understanding in a chaotic situation. Each task should be assigned to the individual most logically situated to handle it. These individuals must know what is expected of them, which is done through training, drills, communication, and documentation. So, for example, instead of just running out of the building screaming, an individual must know that he is responsible for shutting down the servers before he can run out of the building screaming.
- **Authority**   In times of crisis, it is important to know who is in charge. Teamwork is important in these situations, and almost every team does much better with an established and trusted leader. Such leaders must know that they are expected to step up to the plate in a time of crisis and understand what type of direction they should provide to the rest of the employees. Clear-cut authority will aid in reducing confusion and increasing cooperation.
- **Priorities**   It is extremely important to know what is critical versus what is merely nice to have. Different departments provide different functionality for an organization. The critical departments must be singled out from the departments that provide functionality that the company can live without

for a week or two. It is necessary to know which department must come online first, which second, and so on. That way, the efforts are made in the most useful, effective, and focused manner. Along with the priorities of departments, the priorities of systems, information, and programs must be established. It may be necessary to ensure that the database is up and running before working to bring the file server online. The general priorities must be set by the management with the help of the different departments and IT staff.

- **Implementation and testing**   It is great to write down very profound ideas and develop plans, but unless they are actually carried out and tested, they may not add up to a hill of beans. Once a continuity plan is developed, it actually has to be put into action. It needs to be documented and put in places that are easily accessible in times of crisis. The people who are assigned specific tasks need to be taught and informed how to fulfill those tasks, and dry runs need to be done to walk people through different situations. The drills should take place at least once a year, and the entire program should be continually updated and improved.

Studies have shown that 65 percent of businesses that lose computing capabilities for over one week are never able to recover, and subsequently go out of business. Not being able to bounce back quickly or effectively by setting up shop somewhere else can make a company lose business and, more importantly, its reputation. In such a competitive world, customers have a lot of options. If one company is not prepared to bounce back after a disruption or disaster, customers may go to another vendor and stay there.

## Implementing Strategies

Once the strategies have been decided upon, they need to be documented and put into place by the BCP team. This moves the efforts from a purely planning stage to an actual implementation and action phase.

As stated previously, copies of the plans need to be kept in one or more locations other than the primary site, so that if the primary site is destroyed or negatively affected, the continuity plan is still available to the teams. It is also critical that different formats of the plan be available to the team, including both electronic and paper versions. An electronic version of the plan is not very useful if you don't have any electricity to run a computer. In addition to having copies of the recovery documents located at their offices and homes, key individuals should also have easily accessible versions of critical procedures and call tree information. One simple way to accomplish this is to publish the call tree data on cards that can be affixed to personnel badges or kept in a wallet. In an emergency situation, valuable minutes are better spent responding to an incident than looking for a document or having to wait for a laptop to power up.

The plan should address in detail all of the topics that we have covered so far. The actual format of the plan will depend on the environment, goals of the plan, priorities, and identified threats. After each of those items is examined and documented, the topics of the plan can be divided into the necessary categories.

A commonly accepted structure for a BCP is illustrated in Figure 9-5. Each organization's BCP looks different, but these core topics should be covered in some fashion. We walked through these different components earlier in this chapter. The role of the

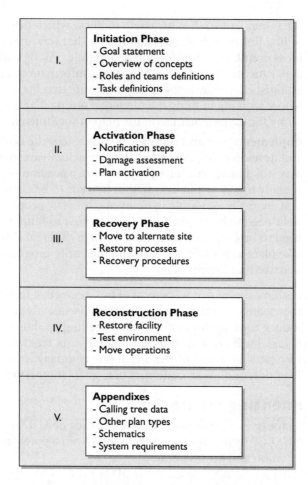

**Figure 9-5**
General structure of
a business continuity
plan

I. **Initiation Phase**
- Goal statement
- Overview of concepts
- Roles and teams definitions
- Task definitions

II. **Activation Phase**
- Notification steps
- Damage assessment
- Plan activation

III. **Recovery Phase**
- Move to alternate site
- Restore processes
- Recovery procedures

IV. **Reconstruction Phase**
- Restore facility
- Test environment
- Move operations

V. **Appendixes**
- Calling tree data
- Other plan types
- Schematics
- System requirements

plan is to provide preplanned and sequenced structure to these different processes. The plan also needs to integrate a degree of flexibility, because no one knows exactly what type of disaster will take place nor its effects. Although procedures need to be documented for the different phases of the plan, a balance between detail and flexibility needs to be achieved so that the company is not ready for only one type of disaster.

Some organizations develop individual plans for specific tasks and goals. These different plans are described in Table 9-1. It is up to management and the BCP team to determine the number and types of plans that should be developed and implemented.

The BCP team can choose to integrate many of these components into the BCP, if the company is small, or include these plans as appendices to the BCP. It is usually better to include these stand-alone plans as appendices so that each document is clear, concise, and useable.

## Testing and Revising the Plan

*We made a plan and tested it and it doesn't work. Response: Let's just go home then.*

The BCP should be tested regularly, because environments continually change. Interestingly, many organizations are moving away from the concept of "testing" because

| Plan Type | Description |
|---|---|
| Business resumption plan | Focuses on how to re-create the necessary business processes that need to be reestablished instead of focusing on IT components (i.e., process oriented instead of procedural oriented). |
| Continuity of operations plan (COOP) | Establishes senior management and a headquarters after a disaster. Outlines roles and authorities, orders of succession, and individual role tasks. |
| IT contingency plan | Plan for systems, networks, and major applications recovery procedures after disruptions. A contingency plan should be developed for each major system and application. |
| Crisis communications plan | Includes internal and external communications structure and roles. Identifies specific individuals who will communicate with external entities. Contains predeveloped statements that are to be released. |
| Cyber incident response plan | Focuses on malware, hackers, intrusions, attacks, and other security issues. Outlines procedures for incident response. |
| Disaster recovery plan | Focuses on how to recover various IT mechanisms after a disaster. Whereas a contingency plan is usually for nondisasters, a disaster recovery plan is for disasters that require IT processing to take place at another facility. |
| Occupant emergency plan | Establishes personnel safety and evacuation procedures. |

**Table 9-1**    Different Types of Recovery Plans

a test naturally leads to a pass or fail score, and in the end, that type of score is not very productive. Instead, many organizations are adopting the concept of exercises, which appear to be less stressful, better focused, and ultimately more productive. Each time the plan is exercised or tested, improvements and efficiencies are generally uncovered, yielding better and better results over time. The responsibility of establishing periodic exercises and the maintenance of the plan should be assigned to a specific person or persons who will have overall ownership responsibilities for the business continuity initiatives within the organization.

As noted earlier, the plan's maintenance should be incorporated into change management procedures so that any changes in the environment are reflected in the plan itself.

Tests and disaster recovery drills and exercises should be performed at least once a year. A company should have no real confidence in a developed plan until it has actually been tested. The tests and drills prepare personnel for what they may be faced with and provide a controlled environment to learn the tasks expected of them. These tests and drills also point out issues to the planning team and management that may not have been previously thought about and addressed as part of the planning process. The exercises, in the end, demonstrate whether a company can actually recover after a disaster.

The exercise should have a predetermined scenario that the company may indeed be faced with one day. Specific parameters and a scope of the exercise must be worked out before sounding the alarms. The team of testers must agree upon what exactly is getting tested and how to properly determine success or failure. The team must agree upon the timing and duration of the exercise, who will participate in the exercise, who will receive which assignments, and what steps should be taken. Also, the team needs to determine whether hardware, software, personnel, procedures, and communications lines are going to be tested, and whether it is some, all, or a subset combination. If the test will include moving some equipment to an alternate site, then transportation, extra equipment, and alternate site readiness must be addressed and assessed.

Most companies cannot afford for these exercises to interrupt production or productivity, so the exercises may need to take place in sections or at specific times, which will require logistical planning. Written exercise plans should be developed that will test for specific weaknesses in the overall disaster recovery plan. The first exercise should not include all employees, but rather a small group of people here and there until each learns his or her responsibilities. Then, larger drills can take place so that overall operations will not be negatively affected. The people carrying out these drills should expect problems and mistakes; this is why they are having the drills in the first place. A company would rather have employees make mistakes during a drill so that they can learn from them and perform their tasks more effectively during a real disaster.

**NOTE**   After a disaster, telephone service may not be available. For communications purposes, there should be alternatives in place, such as cell phones or ham radios.

There are a few different types of drills and tests that can take place, each with its own pros and cons. The following sections explain the different types of drills.

## Checklist Test
*Okay, did we forget anything?*

In this type of test, copies of the BCP are distributed to the different departments and functional areas for review. This is done so that each functional manager can review the plan and indicate if anything has been left out or if some approaches should be modified or deleted. This is a method that ensures that some things have not been taken for granted or omitted. Once the departments have reviewed their copies and made suggestions, the planning team then integrates those changes into the master plan.

## Structured Walk-Through Test
*Let's get in a room and talk about this.*

In this test, representatives from each department or functional area come together to go over the plan to ensure its accuracy. The group reviews the objectives of the plan, discusses the scope and assumptions of the plan, reviews the organization and reporting structure, and evaluates the testing, maintenance, and training requirements described. This gives the people who are responsible for making sure that a disaster recovery happens effectively and efficiently a chance to review what has been decided upon and what is expected of them.

The group walks through different scenarios of the plan from beginning to end to make sure nothing was left out. This also raises the awareness of the recovery procedures to team members.

## Simulation Test

*Everyone take your places. Okay, action!*

This type of test takes a lot more planning and people. In this situation, all employees who participate in operational and support functions, or their representatives, come together to practice executing the disaster recovery plan based on a specific scenario. The scenario is used to test the reaction of each operational and support representative. Again, this is done to ensure that specific steps were not left out and certain threats were not overlooked. It acts as a catalyst to raise the awareness of the people involved.

The drill includes only those materials that will be available in an actual disaster, to portray a more realistic environment. The simulation test continues up to the point of actual relocation to an offsite facility and actual shipment of replacement equipment.

## Parallel Test

*Let's do a little processing here and a little processing there.*

A parallel test is done to ensure that the specific systems can actually perform adequately at the alternate offsite facility. Some systems are moved to the alternate site and processing takes place. The results are compared with the regular processing that is done at the original site. This points out any necessary tweaking, reconfiguring, or steps that need to take place.

## Full-Interruption Test

*Shut down and move out!*

This type of test is the most intrusive to regular operations and business productivity. The original site is actually shut down and processing takes place at the alternate site. The recovery team fulfills its obligations in preparing the systems and environment for the alternate site. All processing is done only on devices at the alternate offsite facility.

This is a full-blown drill that takes a lot of planning and coordination, but it can reveal many holes in the plan that need to be fixed before an actual disaster hits. Full-interruption tests should be performed only after all other types of tests have been successful. They are the most risky and can impact the business in very serious and devastating ways if not managed properly; therefore, senior management approval needs to be obtained prior to performing full-interruption tests.

The type of organization and its goals will dictate what approach to the training exercise is most effective. Each organization may have a different approach and unique aspects. If detailed planning methods and processes are going to be taught, then specific training may be required, rather than general training that provides an overview. Higher-quality training will result in an increase of employee interest and commitment.

During and after each type of test, a record of the significant events should be documented and reported to management so that it is aware of all outcomes of the test.

## Other Types of Training

*I think I stopped breathing. Quick, blow into my mouth! Response: Leave me alone.*

Employees need to be trained on other issues besides disaster recovery, including first aid and CPR, how to properly use a fire extinguisher, evacuation routes and crowd control methods, emergency communications procedures, and how to properly shut down equipment in different types of disasters.

The more technical employees may need to know how to redistribute network resources and use different telecommunications lines if the main one goes down. A redundant power supply needs to be investigated, and the procedures for how to move critical systems from one power supply to the next should be understood and tested.

## Emergency Response

*You must save your fellow man before equipment. Response: But I love my computer more than anyone I know.*

Often, the initial response to an emergency affects the ultimate outcome. Emergency response procedures are the prepared actions that are developed to help people in a crisis situation better cope with the disruption. These procedures are the first line of defense when dealing with a crisis situation.

People who are up to date on their knowledge of disaster recovery will perform the best, which is why training and drills are very important. Emergencies are unpredictable, and no one knows when they will be called upon to perform.

Protection of life is of the utmost importance and should be dealt with first before looking to save material objects. Training and drills should show the people in charge how to evacuate personnel safely. All personnel should know their designated emergency exits and destinations. Emergency gathering spots should take into consideration the effects of seasonal weather. One person in each designated group is often responsible for making sure that all people are accounted for. One person in particular should be responsible for notifying the appropriate authorities: the police department, security guards, fire department, emergency rescue, and management. With proper training, employees will be better equipped to handle emergencies rather than just running to the exit.

If the situation is not life threatening, systems should be shut down in an orderly fashion, and critical data files or resources, along with critical personal items like purses and wallets, should be removed during evacuation. There is a reason for the order of activities. As with all processes, there are dependencies with everything we do. Deciding to skip steps or add steps could in fact cause more harm than good.

Once things have approached a reasonable plateau of activity, one or more people will most likely be required to interface with external entities, such as the press, customers, shareholders, and civic officials. One or more people should be prepped in their reaction and response to the recent disaster so that a uniform and reasonable response is given to explain the circumstances, how the company is dealing with the disaster, and what customers and others should now expect from the company. The company should quickly present this information instead of having others come to their own conclusions and start false rumors. At least one person should be available to the press to ensure that proper messages are being reported and sent out.

Another, unfortunate issue needs to be addressed prior to an emergency: potential looting, vandalism, and fraud opportunities from both a physical and logical perspective. After a company is hit with a large disturbance or disaster is usually when it is most vulnerable, and others may take advantage of this vulnerability. Careful thought and planning needs to take place so that these issues can be dealt with properly and the necessary and expected level of protection is provided at all times.

## Maintaining the Plan

*Wow, this plan was developed in 1958! Response: I am sure it is still fine. Not much has changed since then.*

Unfortunately, the various plans that have been covered in this chapter can become quickly out of date. An out of date BCP may provide a company with a false sense of security, which could be devastating if and when a disaster actually takes place.

The main reasons plans become outdated include the following:

- The business continuity process is not integrated into the change management process.
- Infrastructure and environment changes occur.
- Reorganization of the company, layoffs, or mergers occur.
- Changes in hardware, software, and applications occur.
- After the plan is constructed, people feel that their job is done.
- Personnel turns over.
- Large plans take a lot of work to maintain.
- Plans do not have a direct line to profitability.

Organizations can keep the plan updated by taking the following actions:

- Make business continuity a part of every business decision.
- Insert the maintenance responsibilities into job descriptions.
- Include maintenance in personnel evaluations.
- Perform internal audits that include disaster recovery and continuity documentation and procedures.
- Perform regular drills that use the plan.
- Integrate the BCP into the current change management process.

One of the simplest and most cost-effective and process-efficient ways to keep a plan up to date is to incorporate it within the change management process of the organization. When you think about it, it makes a lot of sense. Where do you document new applications, equipment, or services? Where do you document updates and patches? Your change management process should be updated to incorporate fields and triggers that alert the BCP team when a significant change will occur and should provide a means to update the recovery documentation. What's the point of removing the dust bunnies off a plan if it has your configurations from three years ago? There is nothing worse than that feeling at the pit of your stomach when you realize the one thing you thought was going to save you will in fact only serve to keep a fire stoked with combustion material.

## References

- **Business Continuity Planning Model,** *Disaster Recovery Journal* www.drj .com/new2dr/model/bcmodel.htm
- **Disaster Prevention and Recovery Program of the Virginia Community College System** www.so.cc.va.us/its/models/secpl.htm

# Summary

Although business continuity planning is usually given low priority in most organizations today, that does not mean that it is not important and crucial. Unfortunately, many companies have to experience the pain of a disaster to understand how it could have circumvented or mitigated the events that caused the pain to occur.

To develop and carry out business continuity efforts successfully, plenty of thought, planning, time, and effort must go into the different phases of this activity. The real threats must be identified and understood, reasonable countermeasures must be put into place, and detailed plans must be outlined for the unfortunate but anticipated day when they are needed.

# Quick Tips

- A business continuity plan (BCP) contains strategy documents that provide detailed procedures that ensure that critical business functions are maintained and help minimize losses of life, operations, and systems.

- A BCP provides procedures for emergency responses, extended backup operations, and post-disaster recovery.

- A BCP should reach enterprise-wide, with individual organizational units each having their own plans.

- A BCP needs to prioritize critical applications and provide a sequence for efficient recovery.

- A BCP requires senior executive management support for initiating the plan and final approval.

- BCPs can quickly become outdated due to personnel turnover, reorganizations, and undocumented changes.

- Executives may be held liable if proper BCPs are not developed and used.

- Threats can be natural, manmade, or technical.

- Continuity planning involves identifying critical resources, identifying potential threats and possible damages, and developing plans to respond to those threats.

- The steps of recovery planning include initiating the project, performing business impact analyses, developing a recovery strategy, developing a recovery plan, and implementing, testing, and maintaining the plan.

- The project initiation phase involves getting management support, developing the scope of the plan, and securing funding and resources.

- The business impact analysis is one of the most important first steps in the planning development. Qualitative and quantitative data needs to be gathered, analyzed, interpreted, and presented to management.

- Executive commitment and support are the most critical elements in developing the BCP.

- A business case must be presented to gain executive support. This is done by explaining regulatory and legal requirements, exposing vulnerabilities, and providing solutions.

- Plans should be prepared by the people who will actually carry them out.
- The planning group should comprise representatives from all departments or organizational units.
- The BCP team should identify the individuals who will interact with external entities such as the press, shareholders, customers, and civic officials. Response to the disaster should be given quickly and honestly, and should be consistent with any other employee response.
- Disaster recovery and continuity planning should be brought into normal business decision-making procedures.
- The loss criteria for disasters includes much more than direct dollar loss. It may include added operational costs, loss in reputation and public confidence, loss of competitive advantage, violation of regulatory or legal requirements, loss in productivity, delayed income, interest costs, and loss in revenue.
- A survey should be developed and given to the most knowledgeable people within the company to obtain the most realistic information pertaining to a company's risk and recovery procedures.
- The plan's scope can be determined by geographical, organizational, or functional means.
- Many things need to be understood pertaining to the working environment so that it can be replicated at an alternate site after a disaster.
- Subscription services can supply hot, warm, or cold sites.
- A reciprocal agreement is one in which a company promises another company that it can move in and share space if it experiences a disaster and vice versa. Reciprocal agreements are very tricky to implement and are unenforceable. However, they are cheap and sometimes the only choice.
- A hot site is fully configured with hardware, software, and environmental needs. It can usually be up and running in a matter of hours. It is the most expensive option, but some companies cannot be out of business longer than a day without detrimental results.
- A warm site does not have computers, but it does have some peripheral devices such as disk drives, controllers, and tape drives. This option is less expensive than a hot site but takes more effort and time to get operational.
- A cold site is just a building with power, raised floors, and utilities. There are no devices available. This is the cheapest of the three options but can take weeks to get up and operational.
- When returning to the original site, the least critical organizational units should go back first.
- An important part of the disaster recovery and continuity plan is to communicate its requirements and procedures to all employees.

- Testing, drills, and exercises demonstrate the actual ability to recover and can verify compatibility of backup facilities.

- Before tests are performed, there should be a clear indication of what is being tested, how success will be determined, and how mistakes should be expected and dealt with.

- A checklist test is one in which copies of the plan are handed out to each functional area to ensure that the plan properly deals with the area's needs and vulnerabilities.

- A structured walk-through test is one in which representatives from each functional area or department get together and walk through the plan from beginning to end.

- A simulation test is one in which a practice execution of the plan takes place. A specific scenario is established and the simulation continues up to the point of actual relocation to the alternate site.

- A parallel test is one in which some systems are actually run at the alternate site.

- A full-interruption test is one in which regular operations are stopped and processing is moved to the alternate site.

- Remote journaling involves transmitting the journal or transaction log offsite to a backup facility.

## Questions

Please remember that these questions are formatted and asked in a certain way for a reason. You must remember that the CISSP exam is asking questions at a conceptual level. Questions may not always have the perfect answer, and the candidate is advised against always looking for the perfect answer. The candidate should look for the best answer in the list.

1. What procedures should take place to restore a system and its data files after a system failure?

    A. Restore from storage media backup

    B. Perform a parallel test

    C. Implement recovery procedures

    D. Perform a walk-through test

2. What is one of the first steps in developing a business continuity plan?

    A. Identify backup solution

    B. Decide whether the company needs to perform a walk-through, parallel, or simulation test

    C. Perform a business impact analysis

    D. Develop a business resumption plan

3. How often should a business continuity plan be tested?

   A. At least every ten years

   B. Only when the infrastructure or environment changes

   C. At least every two years

   D. Whenever there are significant changes in the organization

4. During a test recovery procedure, one important step is to maintain records of important events that happen during the procedure. What other step is just as important?

   A. Schedule another test to address issues that took place during that procedure

   B. Make sure someone is prepared to talk to the media with the appropriate responses

   C. Report the events to management

   D. Identify essential business functions

5. Which of the following actions is least important when quantifying risks associated with a potential disaster?

   A. Gathering information from agencies that report the probability of certain natural disasters taking place in that area

   B. Identifying the company's key functions and business requirements

   C. Identifying critical systems that support the company's operations

   D. Estimating the potential loss and impact the company would face based on how long the outage lasted

6. The purpose of initiating emergency actions right after a disaster takes place is to prevent loss of life and injuries, and to _____.

   A. Secure the area to ensure that no looting or fraud takes place

   B. Mitigate further damage

   C. Protect evidence and clues

   D. Investigate the extent of the damages

7. Which of the following is the best way to ensure that the company's backup tapes can be restored and used at a warm site?

   A. Retrieve the tapes from the offsite facility and verify that the equipment at the original site can read them

   B. Ask the offsite vendor to test them and label the ones that were properly read

   C. Test them on the vendor's machine, which won't be used during an emergency

   D. Inventory each tape kept at the vendor's site twice a month

8. Which best describes a hot-site facility versus a warm- or cold-site facility?

   A. A site that has disk drives, controllers, and tape drives

   B. A site that has all necessary PCs, servers, and telecommunications

   C. A site that has wiring, central air, and raised flooring

   D. A mobile site that can be brought to the company's parking lot

9. Which is the best description of remote journaling?

   A. Backing up bulk data to an offsite facility

   B. Backing up transaction logs to an offsite facility

   C. Capturing and saving transactions to two mirrored servers in-house

   D. Capturing and saving transactions to different media types

10. Which of the following is something that should be required of an offsite backup facility that stores backed-up media for companies?

    A. The facility should be within 10 to 15 minutes of the original facility to ensure easy access.

    B. The facility should contain all necessary PCs and servers and should have raised flooring.

    C. The facility should be protected by an armed guard.

    D. The facility should protect against unauthorized access and entry.

11. Which item will a business impact analysis not identify?

    A. Whether the company is best suited for a parallel or full-interrupt test

    B. What areas would suffer the greatest operational and financial loss in the event of a particular disaster or disruption

    C. What systems are critical for the company and must be highly protected

    D. What amount of outage time a company can endure before it is permanently crippled

12. Which areas of a company are recovery plans recommended for?

    A. The most important operational and financial areas

    B. The areas that house the critical systems

    C. All areas

    D. The areas that the company cannot survive without

13. Who has the final approval of the business continuity plan?

    A. The planning committee

    B. Each representative of each department

    C. Management

    D. External authority

14. Which are the proper steps for developing a continuity plan?

    A. Project initiation, strategy development, business impact analysis, plan development, implementation, testing, and maintenance

    B. Strategy development, project initiation, business impact analysis, plan development, implementation, testing, and maintenance

    C. Implementation and testing, project initiation, strategy development, business impact analysis, and plan development

    D. Plan development, project initiation, strategy development, business impact analysis, implementation, testing, and maintenance

15. What is the most crucial piece of developing a business continuity plan?

    A. Business impact analysis

    B. Implementation, testing, and following through

    C. Participation from each and every department

    D. Management support

16. During development, testing, and maintenance of the continuity plan, a high degree of interaction and communications is crucial to the process. Why?

    A. This is a regulatory requirement of the process.

    B. The more people that talk about it and are involved, the more awareness will increase.

    C. This is not crucial to the plan and should not be interactive because it will most likely affect operations.

    D. Management will more likely support it.

17. To get proper management support and approval of the plan, a business case must be made. Which of the following is least important to this business case?

    A. Regulatory and legal requirements

    B. Company vulnerabilities to disasters and disruptions

    C. How other companies are dealing with these issues

    D. The impact the company can endure if a disaster hits

18. Which of the following describes a parallel test?

    A. It is performed to ensure that some systems will run at the alternate site.

    B. All departments receive a copy of the disaster recovery plan and walk through it.

    C. Representatives from each department come together and go through the test collectively.

    D. Normal operations are shut down.

19. Which of the following describes a structured walk-through test?

    A. It is performed to ensure that critical systems will run at the alternate site.

    B. All departments receive a copy of the disaster recovery plan and walk through it.

    C. Representatives from each department come together and go through the test collectively.

    D. Normal operations are shut down.

20. When is the emergency actually over for a company?

    A. When all people are safe and accounted for

    B. When all operations and people are moved back into the primary site

    C. When operations are safely moved to the offsite facility

    D. When a civil official declares that all is safe

21. Which of the following does not describe a reciprocal agreement?

    A. The agreement is enforceable.

    B. It is a cheap solution.

    C. It may be able to be implemented right after a disaster.

    D. It could overwhelm a current data processing site.

22. Which of the following describes a cold site?

    A. Fully equipped and operational in a few hours

    B. Partially equipped with data processing equipment

    C. Expensive and fully configured

    D. Provides environmental measures but no equipment

23. Which of the following best describes what a disaster recovery plan should contain?

    A. Hardware, software, people, emergency procedures, recovery procedures

    B. People, hardware, offsite facility

    C. Software, media interaction, people, hardware, management issues

    D. Hardware, emergency procedures, software, identified risk

24. Which of the following is not an advantage of a hot site?

    A. Offers many hardware and software choices

    B. Is readily available

    C. Can be up and running in hours

    D. Annual testing is available

25. Disaster recovery plans can stay updated by doing any of the following except:

    A. Make disaster recovery a part of every business decision

    B. Make sure it is part of employees' job descriptions

    C. Perform regular drills that use the plan

    D. Make copies of the plan and store them in an offsite facility

## Answers

1. **C.** In this and similar situations, recovery procedures should be followed, which most likely includes recovering data from the backup media. Recovery procedures could include proper steps of rebuilding a system from the beginning, applying the necessary patches and configurations, and ensuring that what needs to take place to ensure productivity is not affected. Some type of redundant system may need to be put into place.

2. **C.** A business impact analysis includes identifying critical systems and functions of a company and interviewing representatives from each department. Once management's support is solidified, a business impact analysis needs to be performed to identify the threats the company faces and the potential costs of these threats.

3. **D.** The plans should be tested if there have been substantial changes to the company or the environment. They should also be tested at least once a year.

4. **C.** When recovery procedures are carried out, the outcome of those procedures should be reported to the individuals who are responsible for this type of activity, which is usually some level of management. If the procedures worked properly, management should know it, and if problems were encountered, management should definitely be made aware of them. Members of management are the ones who are responsible overall for fixing the recovery system and will be the ones to delegate this work and provide the necessary funding and resources.

5. **A.** The question asked you about quantifying the risks, which means to calculate the potential business impact of specific natural disasters. The core components of a business impact analysis are

   • Identifying the company's key functions and business requirements

   • Identifying critical systems that support the company's operations

   • Estimating the potential loss and impact the company would face based on how long the outage lasted

   Gathering information from agencies that report the probability of certain natural disasters taking place in that area is an important piece in determining the probability of these threats, but it is considered least necessary when quantifying the potential damage that could be experienced.

6. **B.** The main goal of disaster recovery and business continuity plans is to mitigate all risks that could be experienced by a company. Emergency procedures first need to be carried out to protect human life and then other procedures need to be executed to reduce the damage from further threats.

7. **A.** A warm site is a facility that will not be fully equipped with the company's main systems. The goal of using a warm site is that, if a disaster takes place, the company will bring its systems with it to the warm site. If the company cannot bring the systems with it because they are damaged, the company

must purchase new systems that are exactly like the original systems. So, to properly test backups, the company needs to test them by recovering the data on its original systems at its main site.

8. **B.** A hot site is a facility that is fully equipped and properly configured so that it can be up and running within hours to get a company back into production. Answer B gives the best definition of a fully functionally environment.

9. **B.** Remote journaling is a technology used to transmit data to an offsite facility, but this usually only includes moving the journal or transaction logs to the offsite facility, not the actual files.

10. **D.** This question addresses a facility that is used to store backed-up data; it is not talking about an offsite facility used for disaster recovery purposes. The facility should not be only 10–15 minutes away because some types of disaster could destroy both the company's main facility and this facility if they are that close together, in which case the company would lose all of its information. The facility should have the same security standards as the company's security, including protection against unauthorized access.

11. **A.** All the other answers address the main components of a business impact analysis. Determining the best type of exercise or drill to carry out is not covered under this type of analysis.

12. **C.** It is best if every department within the company has its own contingency plan and procedures in place. These individual plans would "roll up" into the overall BCP enterprise plan.

13. **C.** Management really has the final approval over everything within a company, including these plans.

14. **A.** These steps outline the processes that should take place from beginning to end pertaining to these types of plans.

15. **D.** Management's support is the first thing to obtain before putting any real effort into developing these plans. Without management's support, the effort will not receive the necessary attention, resources, funds, or enforcement.

16. **B.** Communication not only spreads awareness of these plans and their contents, but also allows more people to discuss the possible threats and solutions, which may lead to ideas that the original team did not consider.

17. **C.** The other three answers are key components when building a business case. Although it is a good idea to investigate and learn about how other companies are dealing with similar issues, it is the least important of the four items listed.

18. **A.** In a parallel test, some systems are run at the alternate site and the results are compared with how processing takes place at the primary site. This is to ensure that the systems work in that area and productivity is not affected. This also extends the previous test and allows the team to walk through the steps of setting up and configuring systems at the offsite facility.

19. **C.** During a structured walk-through test, functional representatives review the plan to ensure its accuracy and that it correctly and accurately reflects the company's recovery strategy.

20. **B.** The emergency is not actually over until the company moves back into its primary site. The company is still vulnerable and at risk while it is operating in an altered or crippled state. This state of vulnerability is not over until the company is operating in the way it was prior to the disaster. Of course, this may mean that the primary site has to be totally rebuilt if it was destroyed.

21. **A.** A reciprocal agreement is not enforceable, meaning that the company that agreed to let the damaged company work out of its facility can decide not to allow this to take place. A reciprocal agreement is a better secondary backup option if the original plan falls through.

22. **D.** A cold site only provides environmental measures—wiring, air conditioning, raised floors—basically a shell of a building and no more.

23. **A.** The recovery plan should contain information about how to deal with people, hardware, software, emergency procedures, recovery procedures, facility issues, and supplies.

24. **A.** Because hot sites are fully equipped, they do not allow for different hardware and software choices. The subscription service offers basic software and hardware products and does not usually offer a wide range of proprietary items.

25. **D.** Storing the plan in an offsite facility is one sure way of ensuring the plan will become outdated. The plan should be part of normal business activities. A lot of time and resources go into creating disaster recovery plans, after which they are usually stored away and forgotten about. They need to be updated continuously as the environment changes to ensure that the company can properly react to any type of disaster or disruption.

# Regulations and Compliance

This chapter presents the following:

- Ethics, pertaining to information security professionals and best practices
- Computer crimes and computer laws
- Motives and profiles of attackers
- Computer crime investigation process and evidence collection
- Incident-handling procedures
- Various types of evidence
- Laws and acts put into effect to fight computer crime

Computer and associated information crimes are the natural response of criminals to society's increasing use of and dependence upon technology. However, crime has always taken place, with or without a computer. A computer is just another tool and, like other tools before it, it can be used for good or evil.

Fraud, theft, and embezzlement have always been part of life, but the computer age has brought new opportunities for thieves and crooks. A new degree of complexity has been added to accounting, record keeping, communications, and funds transfer. This degree of complexity brings along its own set of vulnerabilities, which many crooks are all too eager to take advantage of.

Companies are being blackmailed by cybercriminals who discover vulnerabilities in their networks. Company trade secrets and confidential information are being stolen when security breaches take place. Online banks are seeing a rise in fraud, and retailers' databases are being attacked and robbed of their credit card information. More and more companies are losing money in profits and productivity because of the rise in denial-of-service (DoS) attacks.

As e-commerce and online business become enmeshed in today's business world, these types of issues become more important and more dangerous. Hacking and attacks are continually on the rise, and companies are well aware of it. The legal system and law enforcement seem to be behind in their efforts to track down cybercriminals and successfully prosecute them. New technologies to fight many types of attacks are on the way, but a great need still exists for proper laws, policies, and methods of actually catching the perpetrators and making them pay for the damage they cause. This chapter looks at some of these issues.

# The Many Facets of Cyberlaw

Legal issues are very important to companies because a violation of legal commitments can be damaging to a company's bottom line and its reputation. A company has many ethical and legal responsibilities that it is liable for pertaining to computer fraud. The more knowledge one has about these responsibilities, the easier it is to stay within the proper boundaries.

These issues may fall under laws and regulations pertaining to incident handling, privacy protection, computer abuse, control of evidence, or the ethical conduct expected of companies, their management, and their employees. This is an interesting time for law and technology because technology is changing at an exponential rate. Legislators, judges, law enforcement, and lawyers are behind the eight ball because of their inability to keep up with technological changes in the computing world and the complexity of the issues involved. Law enforcement needs to know how to capture a cybercriminal, properly seize and control evidence, and hand that evidence over to the prosecutorial and defense teams. Both teams must understand what actually took place in a computer crime, how it was carried out, and what legal precedents to use to prove their points in court. Many times, judges and juries are confused by the technology, terms, and concepts used in these types of trials, and laws are not written fast enough to properly punish the guilty cybercriminals. Law enforcement, the court system, and the legal community are definitely experiencing growth pains as they are being pulled into the technology of the twenty-first century.

Many companies are doing business across state lines and in different countries. This brings even more challenges when it comes to who has to follow what laws. Different states can interpret the same law differently. One country may not consider a particular action against the law at all, whereas another country may determine that the same action demands five years in prison. One of the complexities in these issues is jurisdiction. If a cracker from another country steals a bunch of credit card numbers from a U.S. financial institution and he is caught, a U.S. court would want to prosecute him. His homeland may not see this issue as illegal at all or have laws restricting such activities. Although the attackers are not restricted or hampered by country borders, the laws are restricted to borders in many cases.

Despite all of this confusion, companies do have some clear-cut responsibilities pertaining to computer security issues and specifics on how companies are expected to prevent, detect, and report crimes.

# Ethics

*Just because something is not illegal does not make it right.*

Ethics are based on many different issues and foundations. They can be relative to different situations and interpreted differently from individual to individual. Therefore, they are often a topic of debate. However, some ethics are less controversial than others, and these types of ethics are easier to expect of all people.

(ISC)² requires all certified system security professionals to commit to fully supporting its Code of Ethics. If a CISSP intentionally or knowingly violates this Code of

Ethics, he or she may be subject to a peer review panel, who will decide whether the certification should be relinquished.

The full set of (ISC)² Code of Ethics for the CISSP is listed on the (ISC)² site at **www .isc2.org**. The following list is an overview, but each CISSP candidate should read the full version and understand the Code of Ethics before attempting this exam:

- Act honorably, honestly, justly, responsibly, and legally, and protect society.

- Work diligently, provide competent services, and advance the security profession.

- Encourage the growth of research—teach, mentor, and value the certification.

- Discourage unnecessary fear or doubt, and do not consent to bad practices.

- Discourage unsafe practices, and preserve and strengthen the integrity of public infrastructures.

- Observe and abide by all contracts, expressed or implied, and give prudent advice.

- Avoid any conflict of interest, respect the trust that others put in you, and take on only those jobs you are fully qualified to perform.

- Stay current on skills, and do not become involved with activities that could injure the reputation of other security professionals.

There is an interesting relationship between law and ethics. Most often, laws are based on ethics and are put in place to ensure that others act in an ethical way. However, laws do not apply to everything—that is when ethics should kick in. Some things may not be illegal, but that does not necessarily mean they are ethical.

Corporations should have a guide developed on computer and business ethics. This can be part of an employee handbook, used in orientation, posted, and made a part of training sessions.

There are common ethical fallacies that are used by many in the computing world to justify their unethical acts. They exist because people look at issues differently and interpret (or misinterpret) rules and laws that have been put into place. The following are examples of these ethical fallacies:

- Hackers only want to learn and improve their skills. Many of them are not making a profit off of their deeds; thus, their activities should not be seen as illegal or unethical.

- The First Amendment protects and provides the right of U.S. citizens to write viruses.

- Information should be shared freely and openly; thus, sharing confidential information and trade secrets should be legal and ethical.

- Hacking does not actually hurt anyone.

## Computer Ethics Institute

The Computer Ethics Institute is a nonprofit organization that works to help advance technology by ethical means.

The Computer Ethics Institute has developed its own Ten Commandments of Computer Ethics:

1. Thou shalt not use a computer to harm other people.
2. Thou shalt not interfere with other people's computer work.
3. Thou shalt not snoop around in other people's computer files.
4. Thou shalt not use a computer to steal.
5. Thou shalt not use a computer to bear false witness.
6. Thou shalt not copy or use proprietary software for which you have not paid.
7. Thou shalt not use other people's computer resources without authorization or proper compensation.
8. Thou shalt not appropriate other people's intellectual output.
9. Thou shalt think about the social consequences of the program you are writing or the system you are designing.
10. Thou shalt always use a computer in ways that ensure consideration and respect for your fellow humans.

## Internet Architecture Board

The Internet Architecture Board (IAB) is the coordinating committee for Internet design, engineering, and management. It is an independent committee of researchers and professionals with a technical interest in the health and evolution of the Internet. IAB has two principal subsidiary task forces: the Internet Engineering Task Force (IETF) and the Internet Research Task Force (IRFT). As such, they issue ethics-related statements concerning the use of the Internet.

IAB considers the Internet to be a resource that depends upon availability and accessibility to be useful to a wide range of people. It is mainly concerned with irresponsible acts on the Internet that could threaten its existence or negatively affect others. It sees the Internet as a great gift and works hard to protect it for all who depend upon it. IAB sees the use of the Internet as a privilege, which should be treated as such and used with respect.

IAB considers the following acts as unethical and unacceptable behavior:

- Purposely seeking to gain unauthorized access to Internet resources
- Disrupting the intended use of the Internet
- Wasting resources (people, capacity, and computers) through purposeful actions
- Destroying the integrity of computer-based information
- Compromising the privacy of others
- Conducting Internet-wide experiments in a negligent manner

IAB vows to work with federal agencies to take whatever actions are necessary to protect the Internet. This could be through new technologies, methods, or procedures that are intended to make the Internet more resistant to disruption. There is a balance between enhancing protection and reducing functionality. One of the Internet's main purposes is to enable information to flow freely and not be prohibited; thus, IAB must be logical and flexible in its approaches and the restrictions it attempts to implement. The Internet is everyone's tool, so everyone should work together to protect it.

## Generally Accepted Information Security Principles

The Generally Accepted Information Security Principles (GAISP) committee seeks to develop and maintain GAISP with guidance from security professionals, IT product developers, information owners, and other organizations that have extensive experience in defining and stating the principles of information security.

**NOTE**  Generally Accepted Information Security Principles (GAISP) was previously referred to as Generally Accepted System Security Principles (GASSP). Review the following site for more information: **www.issa.org/ gaisp/gaisp.html**.

The committee creates, maintains, and monitors the adherence to GAISP for information security on an international level. The following lists the committee's objectives:

- Identify and develop pervasive, broadly functional, and detailed GAISP and protection profiles in a comprehensive framework of emergent principles, standards, conventions, and mechanisms that will preserve the availability, confidentiality, and integrity of information.

- Be an authoritative source for opinions, practices, and principles for information owners, information security practitioners, information technology products, and information systems.

- Define, implement, and subsequently operate under the governing GAISP infrastructure.

- Define and establish linkage to the Common Criteria Project.

- Maintain close liaison and coordination with other international authoritative bodies that have developed related works, to establish and maintain GAISP based on these efforts.

- Define and establish liaison with bodies responsible for certifying professionals, to encourage convergence.

- Promote broad awareness of information security and GAISP.

- Address concerns of management, users, and other interested parties at all levels to gain the broadest acceptance.

It would be great if everyone played by all the rules that different organizations have laid out. However, we know that they do not; in fact, security would not be such an important subject in the computing world if everyone did play by the rules.

Many times, when figuring out a computer crime, or any type of crime, one has to understand why and how crimes are committed. To be a good detective, one would need to know how a criminal thinks, what motivates him to do the things he does, what his goals and demons are, and how these are reflected in the crimes he commits. This is how the detective gets inside the criminal's mind so that she can predict his next move as well as understand what circumstances and environments are more prone to fraud and illegal acts. This is true with cybercrime. To properly stop, reduce, or prohibit cybercrime, it is best to know why people do what they do in the first place.

## References

- (ISC)$^2$   www.isc2.org
- Internet Architecture Board   www.iab.org
- NIST Computer Security Bulletin, "Generally Accepted System Security Principles (GASSPs): Guidance on Securing Information Technology (IT) Systems" (Oct. 1996)   http://csrc.nist.gov/publications/nistbul/csl96-10.txt

## Motive, Opportunity, and Means

*MOM did it.*

To understand the "whys" in crime, it is necessary to understand the motive, opportunity, and means—or MOM.

*Motive* is the "who" and "why" of a crime. The motive may be induced by either internal or external conditions. A person may be driven by the excitement, challenge, and adrenaline of committing a crime, which would be an internal condition. Examples of external conditions might include financial trouble, a sick family member, or other dire straits. Understanding the motive for a crime is an important piece of figuring out who would engage in such an activity. For example, many hackers attack big-name sites because when the sites go down, it is splashed all over the news. However, once technology advances to the point where attacks cannot bring down these sites, or once these activities are no longer so highly publicized, the individuals will eventually stop initiating these types of attacks because their motive will have been diminished.

*Opportunity* is the "where" and "when" of a crime. Opportunities usually arise when certain vulnerabilities or weaknesses are present. If a company does not have a firewall, hackers and attackers have all types of opportunities within that network. If a company does not perform access control, auditing, and supervision, employees may have many opportunities to embezzle funds and defraud the company. Once a crime fighter finds out why a person would want to commit a crime (motive), she will look at what could allow the criminal to be successful (opportunity).

*Means* pertains to the capabilities a criminal would need to be successful. Suppose that a crime fighter was asked to investigate a complex embezzlement that took place within a financial institution. If the suspects were three people who knew how to use a mouse, keyboard, and a word processing application, but only one of them was a programmer and system analyst, the crime fighter would realize that this person may have the means to commit this crime much more successfully than the other two individuals.

# Hackers and Crackers

A majority of the hackers, sometimes called crackers, are usually curious and interested to see how far their skill will take them, or they are interested in seeing what type of destruction a new tool can cause. They see hacking as a type of intellectual game in which only the smartest people actually win. However, it is the definition of "winning" that can get disturbing. People who write viruses usually do so to see how far the virus can spread and how much damage one small program they wrote can cause. It usually is not an act of vengeance against a particular target, although that does happen.

Some hackers may get a thrill about being able to break into a corporation's network and snoop around. This was Kevin Mitnick's drive. He did not intend to hurt anyone or any company per se—he just wanted to see what he could get away with. It is the thrill of the challenge. (This does not mean that Kevin's actions were legal or right in any sense. He and other hackers who are out for a thrill ride break laws just as hackers who are driven to carry out specific crimes.) Other hackers like to see their acts in headlines and will work to bring down large web sites like Microsoft, Yahoo!, eBay, and MSN. This gives them self-satisfaction and bragging rights to other hackers.

There is another breed of hacker who is usually more serious in nature. These hackers know the extent of the damage they can cause and hack with malicious intent. They usually work in small groups and have goals of stealing funds, credit card information, confidential information, and military secrets. These groups are usually much more organized and driven than other types of hackers who are just curious, and therefore they are more dangerous. An example of this type of hacker is the group of Ukrainian hackers who stole credit card information from financial institutions in the United States, which affected several thousand people. This group then threatened that it would publish the credit cards on a public web site if it were not paid hundreds of thousands of dollars by the financial institutions. (This extortion case is discussed further in Chapter 2.) Similar to the bank robber who enters a bank through the front door with a gun, hackers enter the bank through telephone lines with a set of potentially dangerous tools. Why do people rob banks? Because that's where the money is.

Therefore, the people who want to be successful in fighting crime over computer wires and airwaves must understand the mentality of the enemy, just as the police officers on the street must understand the mentality of the traditional types of criminal.

## Operations Security

There are several categories of computer crimes that can be committed and different methods of committing those crimes. The following sections go over some of the types of computer fraud and abuses.

## Salami

*I will take a little bit of your salami, and another little bit of your salami, and a bit more of your salami, and no one will ever notice.*

A *salami* attack is one in which the attacker commits several small crimes with the hope that the overall larger crime will go unnoticed. Salami attacks usually take place in the accounting departments of companies, and the most common example of a salami attack involves subtracting a small amount of funds from many accounts with the hope that such an insignificant amount would be overlooked. For example, a bank employee may alter a banking software program to subtract 5 cents from each of the bank's customers' accounts once a month and move this amount to the employee's bank account. If this happened to all of the bank's 50,000 customer accounts, the intruder could make up to $30,000 a year.

---

### Script Kiddies

Script kiddies are hackers who do not necessarily have the skill to carry out specific attacks without the tools that are provided for them on the Internet and through friends. Since these people do not necessarily understand how the attacks are actually carried out, they most likely do not understand the extent of damage they can cause.

---

## Data Diddling

*Can I just diddle the data a little? Response: Nope, it's illegal.*

*Data diddling* refers to the alteration of existing data. Many times, this modification happens before the data is entered into an application or as soon as it completes processing and is outputted from an application. For instance, if a loan processor is entering information for a customer's loan of $100,000, but instead enters $150,000 and then moves the extra approved money somewhere else, this would be a case of data diddling. Another example is if a cashier enters an amount of $40 into the cash register, but really charges the customer $60 and keeps the extra $20.

There was an incident in 1997, in Maryland, where a Taco Bell employee was sentenced to ten years in jail because he reprogrammed the drive-up window cash register to ring up every $2.99 order as one penny. He collected the full amount from the customer, put the penny in the till, and pocketed the other $2.98. He made $3600 before his arrest.

There are many reasons to enter false information into a system or application, but the usual reason is to overstate revenue and assets and understate expenses and liabilities. Sometimes managers do this to deceive shareholders, creditors, superiors, and partners.

This type of crime is extremely common and one of the crimes easiest to prevent by using access and accounting controls, supervision, auditing, separation of duties, and authorization limits. This is just one example of how insiders can be more dangerous than outsiders.

## Excessive Privileges

Excessive privileges is a common security issue that is extremely hard to control in vast, complex environments. It occurs when a user has more computer rights, permissions, and privileges than what is required for the tasks she needs to fulfill. If a user only needs to be able to read and print materials on the file server, she should not be granted full control. A common example of this is when a manager in accounting is granted full control of all files on a specific server, including payroll information. When this person is moved from accounting to the research department, his rights should be revoked or at least reduced, but most companies do not have procedures in place to make sure this happens. (This is referred to as authorization creep.) Now he has full control over the account records and the research records, and thus has excessive privileges. If he ever becomes disgruntled with the company for one reason or another, the company could have much more damage to deal with than if it had properly restricted his access.

## Password Sniffing

*I think I smell a password!*

*Password sniffing* is just what it sounds like—sniffing network traffic with the hope of capturing passwords being sent between computers. Several tools are available on the Internet that provide this functionality. Capturing a password is tricky, because it is a piece of data that is usually only used when a user wants to authenticate into a domain or access a resource. Once the password is caught, deciphering it can also be tricky, because it is usually encrypted or only the hash value of the password is sent. Some systems and applications do send passwords over the network in cleartext, but a majority of them do not anymore. Instead, the user's workstation performs a one-way hashing function on the password and sends only the resulting value to the authenticating system or service. The authenticating system has a file containing all users' password hash values, not the passwords themselves, and when the authenticating system is asked to verify a user's password, it compares the hashing value sent to what it has in its file.

Many of the tools that are used to capture passwords also have the functionality of breaking the encryption of the password. They have several dictionaries of words that are commonly used as passwords, and these tools run all of these possibilities against the captured password until a match is found. This is called a *dictionary attack*.

## IP Spoofing

*I couldn't have carried out that attack. I have a different address! Response: I'm not convinced.*

Networks and the Internet use IP addresses like we use building numbers and street names to find our way from one place to another. Each computer is assigned an IP address so that packets know where they came from and where they are going. However, many attackers do not want anyone to know their real location, so they either manually change the IP address within a packet to show a different address or, more commonly, use a tool that is programmed to provide this functionality for them. This type of activity is referred to as *IP spoofing*. Almost all attacks that take place use spoofed IP addresses, which gives the victim little hope of finding the real system and individual who initiated the attack.

One reason that IP spoofing is so easily accomplished is that the protocol of the Internet, IP, was developed in a time when security was rarely considered. At that point in time, the developers were much more focused on functionality and probably could not imagine all the types of attacks that would be carried out using the protocols they developed.

IPv6 and IPv4 using IPSec, described in Chapter 8, can be used to help fight IP spoofing, but for this to be successful, everyone would need to use this technology. Change is hard to implement when it means that millions of people would need to modify the way they do things.

 **NOTE**  Spoofing can be considered a masquerading attack. Masquerading is the act of trying to pretend to be someone else.

## Denial of Service

*I'm going to keep bothering you until you do not have the time or energy to carry out your job.*

**Denial of service (DoS)** is a general term for many different types of attacks. However, each attack has one thing in common, which is the goal to deny others the service that the victim system usually provides.

Most DoS attacks occur over the Internet and are pointed at a company's web servers, routers, or firewalls. Each of these devices has a finite set of resources, and the attacks that are waged on them have the goal of using up these resources so that no resources are left. Once a system has no resources available, it cannot fulfill requests from legitimate systems. An analogy is a bank. If a bank's main purpose is to lend money, and a bank robber takes all the money, then when people request a loan from the bank, the bank no longer has the necessary resources to fulfill its main purpose. (Simplistic example, I know, but I think you get the point.)

Some attackers like to target well-known web sites like Yahoo!, Microsoft, eBay, and others, because when one of these sites is brought down, the event is on the news and in the headlines. This type of attention strokes certain attackers' egos. At the time of this writing, it is estimated that 4000 DoS attacks happen each and every week.

Several types of tools are available to perform DoS attacks, which makes DoS attacks extremely easy to carry out. Many systems are vulnerable to SYN attacks, Ping of Death attacks, fragment attacks, and DDoS attacks, because these attacks are mainly aimed at the use of the protocols within the TCP/IP stack, which almost all computers have to use. (These attacks are examined in Chapter 12.)

There are not many successful methods of fighting DoS attacks, because they come in so many different forms, originate from all over the Internet, and use fake or spoofed addresses. Only recently have service providers started looking at new technology and products that will help them stop DoS attack traffic so that it does not pass through their networks and onto their customers' networks.

## Dumpster Diving

*I went through your garbage and found your Social Security number, credit card number, network schematics, mother's maiden name, and that you wear funny underwear.*

*Dumpster diving* refers to the concept of rummaging through a company's or individual's garbage for discarded documents, information, and other precious items that could then be used in an attack against that person or company. The intruder would have to gain physical access to the premises, but the area where the garbage is kept is usually not highly guarded. Dumpster diving is unethical, but it's not illegal unless it's done by trespassing on someone else's property. (Laws may vary in different states.)

Industrial spies can raid corporate dumpsters to find proprietary and confidential information. Credit card thieves can go through dumpsters to retrieve credit card information from discarded receipts. Phreakers have been known to dumpster dive at telephone companies, hoping to find manuals on how the internals of the telephone systems work. (Phreakers are described a bit later in the "Well-Known Computer Crimes" section.)

## Emanations Capturing

*Do you think we should be worried about that white van in the parking lot with the huge antenna, large amount of power cords, and pizzas continually delivered to it? Response: Nope.*

Emanations, and the way that attackers eavesdrop on them, are addressed in Chapter 4 in the "Tempest" section. Basically, every electrical device emits electrical waves into the surrounding environment. These waves contain information, comparable to how wireless technologies work. These waves can be carried over a distance, depending on the strength of the signals and the material and objects in the surrounding area. Attackers have used devices to capture these waves and port them to their own computer systems so that they can access information not intended for them.

Attackers need to have specialized tools that tune into the frequency that these waves are carried over. They also have to be within close proximity to the building that is emitting the waves. Companies that have information of such sensitive nature that attackers would go through this much trouble usually have special computer systems with shielding that permit only a small amount of electrical signals to be emitted—one example is Tempest. The companies can also use material within the walls of the building to stop these types of electrical waves from passing through them.

These types of attacks are usually the stuff of spy novels, with three guys in a service van full of high-grade technological devices in the parking lot of a company. However, a recent development has caused this type of eavesdropping to happen without such spy-like activities: wireless networks. When a company installs a wireless network, certain configurations can be set to prevent outsiders from being able to eavesdrop on its employees' network traffic. Unfortunately, most companies do not employ these configurations for one reason or another. This enables anyone with a laptop and a wireless network interface card (NIC) to drive into a company's parking lot and eavesdrop on network traffic. (Wireless technology and its security ramifications are covered in Chapter 7.)

## Wiretapping

Most communications signals are vulnerable to some type of wiretapping or eaves-dropping. It can usually be done undetected and is referred to as a passive attack. Tools used to intercept communications include cellular scanners, radio receivers, micro-phone receivers, tape recorders, network sniffers, and telephone-tapping devices.

 **NOTE** A passive attack is non-intrusive, as in eavesdropping or wiretapping. An active attack is intrusive, as in DoS or penetration attacks.

It is illegal to intentionally eavesdrop on another person's conversation under many countries' existing wiretap laws. In many cases, this action is only acceptable if the person consents or there is a court order allowing law enforcement to perform these types of activities. Under the latter circumstances, the law enforcement officers must show probable cause to support their allegation that criminal activity is taking place and can only listen to relevant conversations. These regulations are in place to protect an individual's privacy expectations.

## Social Engineering

*Hi, I am someone else. Now, tell me all your secrets!*

*Social engineering* plays a very important role in many types of attacks. It is the art of tricking people into unknowingly supplying information and then maliciously using that information. For example, if a technical help-desk employee gets a frantic call from someone who claims to be the vice president of the company, saying he forgot his pass-word and needs it right now or heads are going to roll, the help-desk employee may quickly hand over this information. If the person calling was not the vice president, the employee was a victim of social engineering. If the person was the vice president, he should understand that he is not above the rules of security and should not put the employee in such a tough position.

Social engineering attacks may take many forms. For example, an employee may be called by someone who claims to be the network administrator and explains to the employee that, due to some technical difficulties pertaining to some accounts, she needs to change her current password to "password." If the employee believes this person and does what was asked of her, the attacker would now know that employee's password and could use it for malicious purposes. As another example, social engi-neering may take the form of an e-mail message with a source address of someone the victim knows. Social engineering may even involve someone showing up in person and spinning a tale in the hope of accessing information not intended for him. One example is a person who goes to an office in a uniform and says he is there to work on a broken device or network problem. If he convinces the person at the greeting desk, he can then go into the facility and attempt to sniff the network, break into computers and servers, or plant Trojan horses, viruses, or backdoors. The possibilities are over-whelming.

## References

- *Handbook of Information Security Management*, Domain 6, "Law, Investigation, and Ethics," Micki Krause and Harold F. Tipton, Editors (CRC Press LLC)   www.cccure.org/Documents/HISM/522-525.html

- "Computer Crime and Security," Virginia Tech Department of Computer Science, Professionalism in Computing Digital Library   http://courses.cs.vt .edu/~cs3604/lib/Crime/notes.html

- Social Engineering page, SANS InfoSec Reading Room   www.sans.org/rr/ whitepapers/engineering/

# Well-Known Computer Crimes

Most computer crimes do not hit the news and headlines because companies choose to keep them quiet. This is done mainly for two reasons: to avoid the embarrassment of everyone finding out their dirty laundry and the fact that they have vulnerabilities, and to avoid pointing out the vulnerabilities to other opportunistic hackers.

However, there are some computer crimes that have gone down in the history book of hacking, and this section takes a quick look at some of them.

The 2600 Group publishes the *2600: The Hacker Quarterly* magazine, which is full of ways to hack into computers and telephone systems. The name 2600 stands for the tone that phreakers used to send down a telephone line and get free long-distance service in return. This 2600 tone tricked the system at the other end into thinking that the person making the call was authorized to receive long-distance access, so it opened up a line and let the person make that type of call. The 2600 group is basically made up of *phreakers*, who are hackers specializing in telephone and Private Branch Exchange (PBX) fraud.

One of the earliest actual phreaking clubs called itself the *414 Club* because they all lived in that area code (Milwaukee). This group of teenage hackers was suspected of breaking into more than 60 businesses and government systems in the United States and Canada in the early 1980s. Today, a group of hackers breaking into 60 businesses would not cause the stir that it did in 1983. *Newsweek* magazine even ran a story on this group in the mid-1980s with a picture of one of the group members and his TRS-80 computer.

## The Cuckoo's Egg

*The Cuckoo's Egg* is a book describing how Clifford Stoll, an astronomy student at the University of California at Berkeley, was assigned to track down a 75-cent accounting error in the late 1980s. This small error started him on an investigation that led him to find that someone was on the school's network who was not supposed to be. He tracked this intruder, back in the days when no sophisticated software tools were available to do this, and found out that the intruder had been breaking into U.S. military systems and stealing sensitive information. He set up one of the first known honeypots and lured the hacker into one of the university's servers, by making it seem as though the server was holding confidential information. Cliff then worked with people and companies all over the United States and other countries to track this intruder while the connection was still active. This mainly had to be done by workers at the phone company. At the time, the ability to perform these types of tasks was far from as automated as it is today. After many attempts, he finally got the U.S. counterintelligence agents involved. It ended up being a small group of hackers in the former Soviet Union working for the KGB.

This is an amazing and true story of someone who stumbled onto an intruder, did not have any sophisticated tracking tools (because they did not exist yet), and was incredibly creative, intelligent, and motivated enough to solicit many people all over the world to help him.

### Kevin Mitnick

Kevin Mitnick is one of the most well-known hackers and at one time was one of the FBI's most wanted criminals. He was in jail for almost five years for wire fraud and illegally stealing files from Sun Microsystems, Nokia, Motorola, and others.

Mitnick violated his previous probation terms in 1992, three years before his arrest and five-year jail term, and went into hiding for two years. During that time, he stole corporate secrets, hacked into computers, broke into the national defense warning system, and scrambled telephone networks. He was finally caught, charged, and pled guilty to five felony charges.

The main reason that he is so popular is that he is a martyr to many hackers. He claims he did not do any damage and that he could have done massive damage if his intentions were malicious. Mitnick, like many others, views hacking as an intellectual challenge and said he did it mainly to learn how different systems worked and were integrated.

### Chaos Computer Club

This club is a group of German hackers committed to freedom of information across borders. It was formed in 1981 and has tested the security strength of many corporations' technologies and made demonstrations of the ones they found lacking. The club demonstrated how easy it is to clone information from European ATM cards and defraud financial institutions. It also demonstrated how a web-based Trojan horse could siphon money from a bank account. This ActiveX application scanned users' computers to see which had Quicken installed, and extracted bank account information from that program. The Trojan horse then made a bogus transaction to one of the hackers' own bank accounts.

### Cult of the Dead Cow

This is a group of hackers that has come up with many different hacking tools. The best-known tool that this group developed is Back Orifice, which was designed to remotely take over Windows 95 and Windows 98 systems. It can record keystrokes, record logins and passwords, take screenshots, delete files, and run programs.

## Phone Phreakers

*You're a phreak. Response: I know, now give me the phone.*

This is not a specific group, but a classification of hackers who specialize in telephone fraud. The first known case of toll fraud was committed in 1961 when the Bell Telephone Company uncovered a method, called **Blue Boxing**, that enabled people to make free long-distance phone calls. At that time, all long-distance trunks were sensitive to signals at the 2600-Hz frequency. The Blue Box device simulated this tone and other tones to trick telephone systems and gain free, unauthorized long-distance access.

Later came **Red Boxes**, which simulated the tones of coins being deposited into a pay phone. This enabled phreakers to also get free local and long-distance calls. Then came **Black Boxes**, which is a method to manipulate line voltage to enable people to call toll-free. As the telephone companies advanced their systems and went digital, most of the phreaker phone tricks were no longer effective.

**NOTE** Much of the "boxing" technology described here has been rendered useless because of the advances of switching technologies in the telecommunications industry. At one time the telecommunications networks were purely analog and the control information that was used to set up calls was in-band. Today those networks are digital and the control information is sent out-of-band, so phreakers cannot have as much fun and cause as much damage as they used to.

In 1972, a phreaker called Cap'n Crunch made it known that a toy whistle in Cap'n Crunch cereal could generate the 2600-Hz tone used to fool the telephone company systems and give anyone free long-distance phone calls.

Although these types of crimes are no longer effective, there is still a lot of fraud that takes place at PBXs. Today, phreakers still steal phone services from PBXs and other systems, and pass the long-distance charges to the owners of those systems. This crime is very hard to trace and is successful mainly because many large companies do not audit their phone bills.

As stated earlier, many attacks are carried out by curious semitalented, or very talented, individuals who want to see how far they can go. Although the individuals may not be out to cause massive damage or actually harm others directly, their efforts can cost companies thousands or millions of dollars. Therefore, companies and authorities take these acts very seriously.

Some attackers have specific goals in sight, instead of trying to bring down a system they come across here or there. One company can perform espionage on its competitors by breaking into networks and servers and stealing trade secrets and copyright information. Countries can also do this to other countries, which is referred to as *international economic espionage* or *information warfare*. (In Chapter 2, information warfare is described at some length.) Information warfare and international espionage will most likely only increase because society is becoming more and more dependent upon technology. Governments are looking at these issues much more seriously and are putting the funds and resources toward training their own soldiers to be able to participate in this type of warfare. You can be sure that many of these activities will not be in the news or headlines like we see when a Microsoft site is brought down. These activities are much more covert in nature.

## References

- **Open Directory Project Hacking Groups links**  http://dmoz.org/Computers/Hacking/Groups
- **"The Trials of Kevin Mitnick," by John Christensen, CNN Interactive (March 18, 1999)**  www3.cnn.com/specials/1999/mitnick.background
- *Computer underground Digest*  www.soci.niu.edu/~cudigest

# Identification, Protection, and Prosecution

Hacking, cracking, and attacking have only increased over the years and will not stop anytime soon. There are several issues that deal with why these activities have not been properly stopped or even curbed. These include proper identification of the attackers, the necessary level of protection for networks, and successful prosecution once an attacker is captured.

Most attackers are never caught because they spoof their addresses and use methods to cover their footsteps. Many attackers break into networks, take whatever resources they were after, and clean the logs that tracked their movements and activities. Because of this, many companies do not even know that they have been violated. Even if an attacker's activities trigger an intrusion detection system (IDS) alert, it does not usually find the true identity of the individual, though it does alert the company that a specific vulnerability was exploited.

Local law enforcement departments, the FBI, and the Secret Service are called upon to investigate a range of computer crimes. Although each of these entities works to train its people to identify and track computer criminals, collectively they are very far behind the times in their skills and tools, and are outnumbered by the number of hackers actively attacking networks. Because the attackers use tools that are automated, they can perform several serious attacks in a short timeframe. When law enforcement is called in, its efforts are usually purely manual—checking logs, interviewing people, scanning for vulnerabilities, and setting up traps in case the attacker comes back. Each agency can spare only a small number of people for computer crimes, and generally they are behind in their expertise compared to many hackers. Because of this, most attackers are never found, much less prosecuted.

As mentioned earlier, only a handful of laws deal specifically with computer crimes, making it more challenging to successfully prosecute the attackers who are caught. Many companies that are victims of an attack usually just want to ensure that the vulnerability the attacker exploited is patched and removed, instead of spending the time and money to go after and prosecute the attacker.

 **NOTE**  The author of the ILOVEYOU virus was caught, but could not be prosecuted because there was no specific law in the Philippines indicating that his actions were illegal. This virus cost companies billions of dollars, and the responsible person did not get fined a dollar or spend any time in jail.

These trends will most likely change, but changes will probably happen a lot slower than most would like. As companies lose more and more money to attacks, there will be more and more pressure on law enforcement agencies to stop this type of crime. Each agency will put more money and resources into this problem, and the courts will devise useful laws to hold individuals who are doing these acts accountable. Down the road, people will most likely think twice about letting loose a crippling e-mail virus after 20 other people have been jailed for the same actions.

 **NOTE** Portions of the U.S. Homeland Security Act are dedicated to computer crimes. This legislative trend is growing in most countries across the globe, which means that a lot more attention and funds are being put into place to improve the current ways of protecting against, investigating, and prosecuting computer criminals.

Another thing that is changing every day is how companies are protecting themselves from these attacks. Five to ten years ago, most companies had never heard of a firewall, but today it is a known essential. Five to ten years ago, someone would have a full-time position in computer security only if he worked for the government, but today most organizations are screaming for help when it comes to their network and information security. Security is not only part of the IT staff's vocabulary, it is also an issue that has forced itself into board meetings and shareholders' concerns. Some executives have lost their job because they did not make sure computer security was up to par within their respective organization. As attackers and hackers evolve in their skills and numbers, many business-oriented individuals who would rather deal with other issues are forced to make security a priority.

Because an attacker must have access to the systems that hold the wanted resources, it is usually easier for insiders than outsiders to access resources that companies fight to protect. In this sense, employees present a greater potential for computer crimes than outsiders trying to get in. Many statistics and security professionals have indeed indicated that employees cause more security breaches and computer fraud than outside attackers, but the media usually only touts stories about external hackers and crackers. Therefore, fighting off that group of people receives more attention and effort than fighting the threat of employees taking advantage of their position and access.

# Liability and Its Ramifications

As legislatures, courts, and law enforcement develop and refine their respective approaches to computer crimes, so too must corporations. Corporations should develop not only their preventive, detective, and corrective approaches, but also their liability and responsibility approaches. As these crimes increase in frequency and sophistication, so do their destruction and lasting effects. In most cases, the attackers are not caught, but there is plenty of blame to be passed around, so a corporation needs to take many steps to ensure that the blame and liability do not land clearly at its doorstep.

The same is true for other types of threats that corporations have to deal with today. If a company has a facility that burns to the ground, the arsonist is only one small piece of this tragedy. The company is responsible for providing fire detection and suppression systems, fire-resistant construction material in certain areas, alarms, exits, fire extinguishers, and backups of all the important information that could be affected by a fire. If a fire burns a company's building to the ground and consumes all the records (customer data, inventory records, and similar information that is necessary to rebuild the business), then the company did not exercise due care to ensure that it was protected from such loss (by backing up to an offsite location, for example). In this case, the employees, shareholders, customers, and everyone affected could successfully sue the company. However, if the company did everything expected of it in the previously listed respects, it could not be successfully sued for failure to practice due care (negligence).

In the context of security, *due care* means that a company did all that it could have reasonably done, under the circumstances, to prevent security breaches, and also took reasonable steps to ensure that if a security breach did take place, proper controls or countermeasures were in place to mitigate the damages. In short, due care means that a company practiced common sense and prudent management and acted responsibly. *Due diligence* means that the company properly investigated all of its possible weaknesses and vulnerabilities.

Before you can figure out how to properly protect yourself, you need to find out what it is that you are protecting yourself against. This is what due diligence is all about—researching and assessing the current level of vulnerabilities so that the true risk level is understood. Only after these steps and assessments take place can effective controls and safeguards be identified and implemented.

The same type of responsibility is starting to be expected of corporations pertaining to computer crime and resource protection. Information security is developed and implemented to protect an organization's valuable resources; thus, appropriate safeguards need to be in place to protect the company's mission by protecting its tangible and intangible resources, reputation, employees, customers, shareholders, and legal position. Security is a means to an end and not an end within itself. Security is not practiced just for the sake of doing it. Security should be practiced in a way to accomplish fully understood, planned, and attainable goals.

 **NOTE** In the United States, in 1997, the Federal Sentencing Guidelines were extended to cover computer crimes and specified that senior corporate officers could be personally responsible to pay up to $290 million in fines if their company did not comply with the laws set out for them.

Senior management has an obligation to protect the company from a long list of activities that can negatively affect it, including protection from malicious code, natural disasters, privacy violation, infraction of the law, and more.

Various laws dictate that management must follow the *prudent person rule*, which requires management members to perform duties that prudent and responsible people would exercise in similar circumstances. They are to perform these duties with diligence and care when carrying out their responsibilities.

The costs and benefits of security should be evaluated in monetary and nonmonetary terms to ensure that the cost of security does not outweigh the expected benefits. Security should be proportional to potential loss estimates pertaining to the severity, likelihood, and extent of potential damage.

Security mechanisms should be employed to reduce the frequency and severity of security-related losses. A sound security program is a smart business practice.

Senior management needs to decide upon the amount of risk it is willing to take pertaining to computer and information security, and implement security in an economical and responsible manner. (These issues are discussed in great detail in Chapter 3.) These risks do not always stop at the boundaries of the organization. Many companies have extranets set up with other companies, value-added networks (VANs), telecommunications lines, and more to enable them to work quickly and efficiently with other organizations. However, these relationships can get more complicated when it comes to liability and responsibilities.

When companies come together to work in an integrated manner, such as via extranets and VANs, special care must be taken to ensure that each party promises to provide the necessary level of protection, liability, and responsibility, which should be clearly defined in the contracts that each party signs. Auditing and testing should be performed to ensure that each party is indeed holding up its side of the bargain and that its technology integrates properly with all the other parties. Interoperability can become a large, frustrating, and expensive issue in these types of arrangements.

If one of the companies does not provide the necessary level of protection and its negligence affects a partner it is working with, the affected company can sue the upstream company. For example, let's say company A and company B have constructed an extranet. Company A does not put in controls to detect and deal with viruses. Company A gets infected with a destructive virus and it is spread to company B through the extranet. The virus corrupts critical data and causes massive disruption to company B's production. Company B can sue company A for being negligent. Both companies need to make sure that they are doing their part to ensure that their activities, or lack of them, will not negatively affect another company, which is referred to as *downstream liability*.

---

 **NOTE** *Responsibility* generally refers to the obligations and expected actions and behaviors of a particular party. An obligation may have a defined set of specific actions that are required or a more general and open approach, which enables the party to decide how it will fulfill the particular obligation. *Accountability* refers to the ability to hold a party responsible for certain actions or inaction.

---

Computer security usually has some interesting interdependencies with other factions of the company, such as management functions, legal issues, employee privacy, disaster recovery and business continuity plans, and daily operations. The company that clearly understands these types of issues and the interrelations between them can better plan, implement, and maintain its security program.

The following list describes some of the actions required of a corporation to ensure that is practicing due care:

- Establishing adequate physical and logical access controls
- Establishing adequate telecommunications security, which could require encryption
- Performing proper information, application, and hardware backups
- Maintaining disaster recovery and business continuity plans
- Performing periodic reviews, drills, tests, and improvement in disaster recovery and business continuity plans
- Informing employees properly of expected behavior and ramifications of not following expectations
- Developing a security policy, standards, procedures, and guidelines
- Performing security-awareness training
- Running updated antivirus software
- Performing penetration tests periodically from outside and inside the network
- Implementing dial-back or preset dialing features on remote access applications
- Abiding by and updating external service level agreements (SLAs)
- Ensuring that downstream security responsibilities are being met
- Implementing measures that ensure that software piracy is not taking place
- Ensuring that proper auditing and review of those audit logs are taking place
- Conducting background checks on potential employees

Each company has different requirements when it comes to this list of due care responsibilities. If these steps are not taken, the company may be charged with negligence if damage arises out of its failure to follow these steps. To prove negligence in court, the plaintiff must establish that the defendant had a *legally recognized obligation*, or duty, to protect the plaintiff from unreasonable risks, and that the defendant's failure to protect the plaintiff from an unreasonable risk (breach of duty) was the *proximate cause* of the plaintiff's damages.

The following are some example scenarios in which a company could be held liable for negligence in its actions and responsibilities.

## Personal Information

A company that holds medical information, Medical Information Inc., does not have strict procedures on how patient information is disseminated or shared.

A person pretends to be a physician and calls into Medical Information Inc. and requests medical information on the patient Don Hammy. The receptionist does not question the caller and explains that Don Hammy has a brain tumor. A week later, Don

Hammy does not receive the job he interviewed for and finds out that the employer called Medical Information Inc. for his medical information.

So what was improper about this activity and how would liability be determined? If and when this case went to court, the following items would be introduced and addressed:

- **Legally recognized obligation**
    - Medical Information Inc. does not have policies and procedures in place to protect patient information.
    - The employer does not have the right to make this kind of call and is not able to use medical information against potential employees.
- **Failure to conform to the required standard**
    - Sensitive information was released to an unauthorized person by a Medical Information Inc. employee.
    - The employer requested information it did not have a right to.
- **Proximate causation and resulting injury or damage**
    - The information leaked by Medical Information Inc. caused Don Hammy great embarrassment and prevented him from obtaining a specific job.
    - The employer made its decision based on information that it did not have a right to inquire about in the first place. The employer's illegal acquisition and review of Don's private medical information caused it to not hire him.

The outcome was a long legal battle, but Don Hammy ended up successfully suing both companies, recovered from his brain tumor, bought an island, and has never had to work again.

## Hacker Intrusion

A financial institution, Cheapo Inc., buys the necessary middleware to enable it to offer online bank account transactions for its customers. It does not add any of the necessary security safeguards required for this type of transaction to take place over the Internet.

Within the first two weeks, 22 customers have their checking and savings accounts hacked into, with a combined loss of $439,344.09.

What was improper about this activity and how would liability be determined? If and when this case went to court, the following items would be introduced and addressed:

- **Legally recognized obligation**
    - Cheapo Inc. did not implement a firewall or IDS, harden the database holding the customer account information, or use encryption for customer transactions.
    - Cheapo Inc. did not effectively protect its customers' assets.

- **Failure to conform to the required standard**
  - By not erecting the proper security policy and program and implementing the necessary security controls, Cheapo Inc. broke 12 federal regulations used to govern financial institutions.
- **Proximate causation and resulting injury or damage**
  - The financial institution's failure to practice due care and implement the basic requirements of online banking directly caused 22 clients to lose $439,344.09.

Eventually, a majority of the accounts were attacked and drained, a class action suit was brought against Cheapo Inc., a majority of the people got most of their money back, and the facility Cheapo Inc. was using as a financial institution is now used to sell tacos.

These scenarios are simplistic and described in a light-hearted manner, but failure to implement computer and information security properly can expose a company and its board of directors to litigation and legal punishment. Many times people cannot hide behind the corporation and are held accountable individually and personally. The board of directors can compromise its responsibilities to the stockholders, customers, and employees by not ensuring that due care is practiced and that the company was not being negligent in any way.

## Types of Laws

Like other areas of law, computer laws fall into the three main categories: civil, criminal, and administrative (regulatory).

*Civil law*, also called *tort*, deals with wrongs against individuals or companies that result in damages or loss. A civil lawsuit would result in financial restitution and/or community service instead of jail sentences. When someone sues another person in civil court, the jury decides upon liability instead of innocence or guilt. If the jury determines that the defendant is liable for the act, then the jury decides upon the punitive damages of the case.

*Criminal law* is used when an individual's conduct violates the government laws, which have been developed to protect the public. Jail sentences are commonly the punishment for criminal law cases, whereas in civil law cases the punishment is usually an amount of money that the guilty individual has to pay to the victim. For example, in the O.J. Simpson case, he was first tried and found not guilty in the criminal law case; then, he was found liable in the civil law case. This seeming contradiction can happen because the burden of proof is lower in civil cases than in criminal cases.

 **NOTE** Civil law generally is derived from common law (case law), cases are initiated by private parties, and the defendant is found "liable" or "not liable" for damages. Criminal law typically is statutory, cases are initiated by government prosecutors, and the defendant is found guilty or not guilty.

*Administrative/regulatory law* deals with regulatory standards that regulate performance and conduct. Government agencies create these standards, which are usually applied to companies and individuals within those companies. Some examples of administrative laws could be that every building used for business must have a fire detection and suppression system, must have easily seen exit signs, and cannot have blocked doors, in case of a fire. Companies that produce and package food and drug products are regulated by many standards so that the public is protected and aware of their actions. If a case was made that specific standards were not abided by, high officials in the companies could be held accountable, as in a company that makes tires that shred after a couple of years of use. The people who held high positions in this company were most likely aware of these conditions but chose to ignore them to keep profits up. Under administrative, criminal, and civil law, they may have to pay dearly for these decisions.

Not every country uses each category of these laws, and many countries interpret or use them differently for different reasons. This is one challenge of fighting cybercrime. If someone from Germany breaks into a financial institution in Russia, but each country has different laws with different meanings applied to this type of action, which law is used to punish the criminal? Is it the German version, because the criminal committed the crime from Germany, or is the Russian version used because the actual crime took place there? These issues and more are being debated, but clear-cut resolutions are much farther down the road.

## Legal Systems Used Throughout the World

Various countries work under different legal systems. The following lists the types of legal systems used today.

- **Civil Law System**
  - Uses prewritten rules and is not based on precedence
  - Is different than civil (tort) laws used in the U.S., which works under a common law system
  - Used in France, Germany, Quebec, South America
- **Common Law System**
  - Made up of criminal, civil (tort), and administrative laws
- **Customary Law System**
  - Addresses mainly personal conduct, and uses regional traditions and customs as the foundations of the laws
  - Is usually mixed with another type of listed legal system rather than being the sole legal system used in a region
- **Religious Law System**
  - Laws are derived from religious beliefs and address an individual's religious responsibilities
  - Commonly used in Muslim countries or regions
- **Mixed Law System**
  - Using two or more legal systems

## Intellectual Property Laws

Intellectual property laws are different from the three previously mentioned categories of law. Intellectual property laws do not necessarily look at who is right or wrong, but rather how a company can protect what it rightfully owns and what it can do if these laws are violated.

A major issue in many intellectual property cases is what the company did to protect the resources it claims have been violated in one fashion or another. A company must go through many steps to protect resources that it claims to be intellectual property and must show that it exercised due care in its efforts to protect those resources. If an employee sends a file to a friend and the company attempts to terminate the employee based on the activity of illegally sharing intellectual property, it must show the court and jury why this file is so important to the company, what type of damage could be or has been caused as a result of the file being shared, and, most importantly, what the company had done to protect that file. If the company did not secure the file and tell its employees that they were not allowed to copy and share that file, then the company will most likely lose the case. However, if the company went through many steps to protect that file, explained to its employees that it was wrong to copy and share the information within the file, and that the punishment could be termination, then the company could not be charged with falsely terminating an employee.

Intellectual property can be protected by several different laws, depending upon the type of resource it is.

### Trade Secret

Trade secret law protects certain types of information or resources from unauthorized use or disclosure. For a company to have its resource qualify as a trade secret, the resource must provide the company with some type of competitive value or advantage. A trade secret can be protected by law if developing it requires special skill, ingenuity, and/or expenditure of money and effort. This means that a company cannot say that the sky is blue and call it a trade secret.

A *trade secret* is something that is proprietary to a company and important for its survival and profitability. An example of a trade secret is the formula used for a soft drink, such as Coke or Pepsi. The resource that is claimed to be a trade secret must be confidential and protected with certain security precautions and actions. A trade secret could also be a new form of mathematics, source code of a program, a method of making the perfect jelly bean, or ingredients for a special, secret sauce.

Many companies require their employees to sign a nondisclosure agreement, confirming that they understand its contents and promise not to share the company's trade secrets with competitors. Companies require this both to inform the employees of the importance of keeping certain information secret and to deter them from sharing this information. Having them sign the nondisclosure agreement also gives the company the right to fire the employee or bring charges if the employee discloses a trade secret.

### Copyright

In the United States, copyright law protects the right of an author to control the public distribution, reproduction, display, and adaptation of his original work. The law covers many categories of work: pictorial, graphic, musical, dramatic, literary, pantomimes, motion picture, sculptural, sound recording, and architectural. Copyright law does not cover the specific resource, as does trade secret law. It protects the expression of the idea of the resource instead of the resource itself. A copyright law is usually used to protect an author's writings, an artist's drawings, a programmer's source code, or specific rhythms and structures of a musician's creation. Computer programs and manuals are just two examples of items protected under the Federal Copyright Act. The item is covered under copyright law once the program or manual has been written. Although including a warning and the copyright symbol (©) is not required, doing so is encouraged, so that others cannot claim innocence after copying another's work.

The protection does not extend to any method of operations, process, concept, or procedure, but it does protect against unauthorized copying and distribution of a work. It protects the form of expression rather than the subject matter. A patent deals more with the subject matter of an invention; copyright deals with how that invention is represented.

Computer programs can be protected under the copyright law as literary works. The law protects both the source and object code, which can be an operating system, application, or database. In some instances, the law can protect not only the code, but also the structure, sequence, and organization. The user interface is part of the definition of a software application structure; therefore, one vendor cannot copy the exact composition of another vendor's user interface.

## Trademark

*My trademark is my stupidity. Response: Good for you!*

A *trademark* is slightly different from a copyright in that it is used to protect a word, name, symbol, sound, shape, color, or combination of these. The reason a company would trademark one of these, or a combination, is that it represents their company to a group of people or to the world. Companies have marketing departments that work very hard in coming up with something new that will cause the company to be noticed and stand out in a crowd of competitors, and trademarking the result of this work is a way of properly protecting it and ensuring that others cannot copy and use it.

## Patent

*Patents* are given to individuals or companies to grant them legal ownership of, and enable them to exclude others from using or copying, the invention covered by the patent. The invention must be novel, useful, and not obvious—which means, for example, that a company could not patent air. Thank goodness. If a company figured out how to patent air, we would have to pay for each and every breath we took!

After the inventor completes an application for a patent and it is approved, the patent grants a limited property right to exclude others from making, using, or selling the invention for a specific period of time. For example, when a pharmaceutical company develops a specific drug and acquires a patent for it, that company is the only one that can manufacture and sell this drug until the stated year in the patent is up. After that, all companies are allowed to manufacture and sell this product, which is why the price of a drug drops substantially after its patent expires.

This also takes place with algorithms. If an inventor of an algorithm acquires a patent, she has full control over who can use it in their products. If the inventor lets a vendor incorporate the algorithm, then she will most likely get a fee and possibly a royalty fee on each instance of the product that is sold.

## Internal Protection of Intellectual Property

Ensuring that specific resources are protected by the previously mentioned laws is very important, but there are other measures that must be taken internally to make sure the resources that are confidential in nature are properly identified and protected.

The resources protected by one of the previously mentioned laws need to be identified and integrated into the company's data classification scheme. This should be directed by management and carried out by the IT staff. The identified resources should have the necessary level of access control protection, auditing enabled, and a proper storage environment. If it is deemed secret, then not everyone in the company should be able to access it. Once the individuals who are allowed to have access are identified, their level of access and interaction with the resource should be defined in a granular method. Attempts to access and manipulate the resource should be properly audited, and the resource should be stored on a protected server with the necessary security mechanisms.

Employees must be informed of the level of secrecy or confidentiality of the resource, and of their expected behavior pertaining to that resource.

If a company fails in one or all of these steps, it may not be covered by the laws described previously, because it may have failed to practice due care and properly protect the resource that it has claimed to be so important to the survival and competitiveness of the company.

## References

- **United States Copyright Office**   www.copyright.gov/
- **Electronic Frontier Foundation, Intellectual Property Online: Patent, Trademark, Copyright**   www.eff.org/IP/
- **Caltech Office of the Intellectual Property Counsel**   www.caltech.edu/ott/security/OIPC_Home.htm
- **Kansas State University Intellectual Property Information Center: Online Copyright Tutorials**   www.k-state.edu/academicservices/intprop/tutorial.htm

## Software Piracy

Software piracy occurs when the intellectual or creative work of an author is used or duplicated without permission or compensation to the author. It is an act of infringement on ownership rights, and if the pirate is caught, he could be sued civilly for damages, be criminally prosecuted, or both. Duplicate software is everywhere and software piracy is everywhere. Until now, efficient mechanisms have not been put into place to ensure that software cannot be copied and illegally used. Companies are testing out new features, and within time, illegally copying and using software will most likely not be as easy as it is now.

When a vendor develops an application, it usually licenses the program rather than sell it outright. The license agreement contains provisions relating to the use and security of the software and the corresponding manuals. If an individual or company fails to observe and abide by those requirements, the license may be terminated and, depending on the actions, criminal charges may be leveled. The risk to the vendor that develops and licenses the software is the loss of profits that it would have earned. Many companies and their employees do not abide by their software licenses and the employees use the company's software for their home use.

Some software vendors sell bulk licenses, which enable several users to use the product simultaneously. Some vendors incorporate a monitoring system that keeps track of the usability to ensure that the customer does not go over the license limit. The network administrator or security officer should be aware of all of these types of contractual commitments required by software companies. This person needs to be educated on the restrictions the company is under and make sure proper enforcement mechanisms are in place. If a company is found guilty of illegally copying software or using more copies than its license permits, the network administrator or security officer in charge of this task will be primarily responsible.

The Software Protection Association (SPA) has been formed by major companies to enforce proprietary rights of software. The association was formed to protect the founding companies' software developments, but it also helps others to ensure that their software is properly licensed. These are huge issues for companies that develop and produce software, because a majority of their revenue comes from licensing fees.

Other international groups have been formed to protect against software piracy, including the Federation Against Software Theft (FAST), headquartered in London, and the Business Software Alliance (BSA), based in Washington, D.C. They provide similar functionality as the SPA and make efforts to protect software around the world.

One of the offenses an individual or company can commit is to decompile vendor object code. This is usually done to figure out how the application works by obtaining the original source code, which is confidential, and perhaps to reverse-engineer it in the hope of understanding the intricate details of its functionality. Another purpose of reverse-engineering products is to detect security flaws within the code that can later be exploited. This is how some buffer overflow vulnerabilities are discovered.

Many times, an individual decompiles the object code into source code and either finds security holes to take advantage of or alters the source code to produce some type of functionality that the original vendor did not intend. In one example, an individual decompiled a program that displays e-books and publications. The vendor did not want anyone to be able to copy the e-publications its product displayed and thus inserted an encoder within the object code of its product that enforced this limitation. The individual decompiled the object code and figured out how to create a decoder that would overcome this restriction and enable users to make copies of the e-publications, which infringed upon those authors' and publishers' copyrights.

The individual was arrested and prosecuted under the new Digital Millennium Copyright Act (DMCA), which makes it illegal to create products that circumvent copyright protection mechanisms. As of this writing, this new act and how it will be enforced have caused many debates and controversy because of its possible negative effects on free speech and legitimate research.

Interestingly enough, many computer-oriented individuals protested this individual's arrest, which included several marches, and the company that was prosecuting (Adobe) quickly decided to drop all charges.

# Equipment and Software Disposal Issues

When equipment is discarded, sold, or moved to a different department or company, all previous information and files should be completely erased. Although this seems obvious, some not-so-obvious requirements may exist pertaining to the hardware and the software that is loaded on it. Depending on the vendor of the system, it may be illegal to sell a computer with an operating system without proper licensing, or it may be illegal to sell the system without an operating system at all.

In one example, a company wanted to sell 2000 of its older 486 and lower-end Pentium systems. The network administrator instructed the network engineers to format and fdisk each and every system. After this task was complete, the network administrator found out that its agreement with the vendor of the computers prohibited selling even one of those computers without a functioning operating system. Thus, the network administrator or security officer should investigate the proper procedures to protect the company pertaining to license and vendor agreements at each stage of a system's life cycle. In the preceding example, the network engineers had to go back and reinstall the necessary operating system on each of the 2000 computers.

 **NOTE** Most reporting of illegal use of software comes from disgruntled employees.

Trade secret, copyright, patent, and trademark laws differ from country to country. Any vendor that is interested in selling its product should be aware of these differences and should take the necessary steps to properly protect its product.

# Computer Crime Investigations

As mentioned earlier in the chapter, law enforcement has many challenges and barriers when it comes to fighting cybercrime. In most instances, a law enforcement agency has only a small force that is properly trained; the rules of jurisdiction can get fuzzy; and determining exactly what laws have been broken in this quickly evolving computing age can be overwhelming at best. Another issue that law enforcement has to deal with is properly gathering evidence from a computer or media, which is very different from collecting evidence from a regular crime scene. This section goes over some of these barriers and provides guidelines that have been developed to help with future investigations.

### Incident Response

Many computer crimes go unreported because the victim, in many cases, is not aware of the incident or wants to just patch the hole the hacker came in through and keep the details quiet to escape embarrassment or the risk of hurting its reputation. This makes it harder to know the real statistics of how many attacks happen each day, what degree of damage that is caused, and what types of attack and methods are being used.

This lack of reporting crimes does not make fighting this type of crime any easier. A law enforcement agent who investigates a computer crime has to deal with a shift from physical damage and thefts to an intangible electronic environment that requires a different type of skill to get around in, identify clues, and be able to obtain usable evidence. The ease of committing a cybercrime, the relative anonymity available to the attacker, and the difficulty in tracking down the attacker usually gives the criminal more advantages than the cybercop. The Internet and its interconnection of computers is making targets much more accessible than ever before, and the criminals have a much lower risk of getting caught.

Many of the existing theft, damage, and extortion laws are written to protect physical property, not necessarily the type of damage that can be done by bytes over a phone line or network wire.

When a company endures a computer crime, it should leave the environment and evidence unaltered and contact the authorities. Someone who is unfamiliar with the proper process of collecting data and evidence from a crime scene could destroy evidence. All hope of prosecuting and achieving a conviction would be lost. Companies should have procedures for many issues in computer security such as enforcement procedures, disaster recovery and continuity procedures, and backup procedures. It is best to also have a procedure for dealing with a cybercrime or incident. Most companies do not have a clue as to who to call or what to do right after they have been the victim of a cybercrime. This means the company should have an incident response policy and procedures set up just for this type of event before it actually takes place.

The incident response policy should indicate if systems can be taken offline to try to save evidence or if systems have to continue functioning with the risk of destroying evidence. Each system and functionality should have a priority assigned to it. For instance, if the file server is hit, it should be removed from the network, but not shut down. However, if the mail server is hit, it should not be removed from the network or shut down, because of the priority the company attributes to the mail server over the file server. Trade-offs and decisions will have to be made, but it is better to think through these issues before the situation occurs, because better logic is usually possible before a crisis, with less emotion and chaos.

If the company would like to handle these types of issues in-house, it should develop an *incident response team* to respond to major security incidents. The team should have someone from senior management, the network administrator, security officer, possibly a network engineer and/or programmer, and a liaison for public affairs. The purpose of having an incident response team is to ensure that there is a group of people who are properly skilled, who follow a standard set of procedures, and who are singled out and called upon when this type of event takes place.

---

 **NOTE** In reality, usually the technical team members are called to the scene to carry out their functions, and the other team members may be called to update them on the situation and possibly ask them for direction pertaining to specific issues of the situation.

---

The team should have proper reporting procedures established, have the ability to provide prompt reaction, have coordination with law enforcement, and be an important element of the overall security program.

The incident response team should have the following basic items:

- List of outside agencies and resources to contact or report to
- List of computer or forensics experts to contact
- Steps on how to search for evidence
- Steps on how to secure and preserve evidence
- List of items that should be included on the report
- Description of how the different systems should be treated in this type of situation (for example, removed from the Internet and the network and powered down)

When a suspected crime is reported, the incident response team should follow a set of predetermined steps to ensure both uniformity in approach and that no steps are skipped. First, the incident response team should investigate the report and determine that an actual crime has been committed. If the team determines that a crime has been carried out, senior management should be informed immediately. If the suspect is an employee, a human resources representative must be called right away. The sooner the documenting of events begins, the better; if someone is able to document the starting time of the crime along with the company employees and resources involved, it would provide a foundation. At this point, the company must decide if it wants to conduct its own forensics investigation or call in the big guns. If experts are going to be called in, the system that was attacked should be left alone, to try to preserve as much evidence of the attack as possible. If the company decides to conduct its own forensics investigation, it has to deal with many issues and address tricky elements.

## Computer Forensics and Proper Collection of Evidence

*I just spilled coffee on our only evidence. Response: Case closed. Let's all go home.*

The people conducting the forensics investigation must be properly skilled in this trade and know what to look out for. If someone reboots the attacked system or goes around looking at different files, it could corrupt viable evidence, change timestamps on key files, and erase footprints the criminal may have left. In most situations, it is best to remove the system from the network, dump the contents of the memory, power down the system, and make a sound image of the attacked system and perform forensic analysis on this copy. Working on the copy instead of the original drive will ensure that the evidence stays unharmed on the original system in case some steps in the investigation actually corrupt or destroy data. Dumping the memory contents to a file before doing any work on the system or powering it down is a crucial step, because of the information that could be stored there. This is another method of capturing fragile information.

The incident response team needs specialized forensics tools, an evidence collection notebook, containers, a camera, and evidence identification tags. The notebook should not be a spiral notebook, but a notebook that is bound in a way that one can tell if pages have been removed.

**NOTE** In most cases, an investigator's notebook cannot be used as evidence in court. It can only be used by the investigator to refresh his memory during a proceeding.

The next crucial piece is to keep a proper *chain of custody* of the evidence. Because evidence from these types of crimes can be very volatile and easily dismissed from court because of improper handling, it is important to follow very strict and organized procedures when collecting and tagging evidence.

When copies of data need to be made, this process must meet certain standards to ensure quality and reliability. Specialized software for this purpose can be used. The copies must be able to be independently verified and must be tamperproof.

Each piece of evidence should be marked in some way with the date, time, initials of the collector, and a case number if one has been assigned. Magnetic disk surfaces should not be marked on, and floppy disks should only be marked with a felt-tip pen. Reel-to-reel magnetic tape can be marked on the nonshiny side of the tape within the first 10 to 15 feet, also known as the *leader* part. The piece of evidence should then be sealed in a container, which should be marked with the same information. The container should be sealed with evidence tape and, if possible, the writing should be on the tape so that a broken seal can be detected.

**NOTE** The chain of custody of evidence dictates that all evidence be labeled with information indicating who secured and validated it.

Wires and cables should be labeled, and a photograph of the labeled system should be taken before it is actually disassembled. Media should be write-protected. Storage should be dust free, kept at room temperature without much humidity, and, of course, not close to any strong magnets or magnetic fields.

If possible, the crime scene should be photographed, including behind the computer if the crime involved some type of physical break in. Documents, papers, and devices should be handled with cloth gloves and placed into containers and sealed. All storage media should be contained, even if it has been erased, because data still may be obtainable.

Because this type of evidence can be easily erased or destroyed and is complex in nature, identification, recording, collection, preservation, transportation, and interpretation are all important. After everything is properly labeled, a chain of custody log should be made of each container and an overall log should be made capturing all events.

For a crime to be successfully prosecuted, solid evidence is required. Computer forensics is the art of retrieving this evidence and preserving it in the proper ways to make it admissible in court. Without proper computer forensics, hardly any computer crimes could ever be properly and successfully presented in court.

The most common reasons for improper evidence collection are no established incident response team, no established incident response procedures, poorly written policy, and a broken chain of custody.

**NOTE** A chain of custody is a history that shows how evidence was collected, analyzed, transported, and preserved in order to be presented as evidence in court. Because electronic evidence can be easily modified, a clearly defined chain of custody demonstrates that the evidence is trustworthy.

There are other issues to think through when a company is developing incident response procedures, such as how the incident will be explained to the press, customers, and shareholders. This could require the collaboration of the public relations department, management, human resources (if employees are involved), IT department, and the legal department. A cybercrime may have legal ramifications that are not immediately apparent and must be handled delicately. The company should decide how it will report the matter to outsiders, to ensure that the situation is not perceived in a totally different light.

## Incident Handling

In the previous sections, incident handling was addressed in an indirect manner. This section provides a clear definition of incident handling and its place within a company, which is important to understand.

There are many types of threats that a computer and network may face, each requiring a specialized way to properly recover. However, an incident response team should draft and enforce a basic outline of how *all* incidents are to be handled. This is a much better approach than the way that most companies deal with these threats, which is usually in an ad hoc, reactive, and confusing manner. A clearly defined incident-handling process is more cost effective, enables recovery to happen more quickly, and provides a uniform approach with certain expectation of its results.

Incident handling should be closely related to disaster recovery planning and should be part of the company's disaster recovery plan. Both are intended to react to some type of incident that requires a quick reaction so that the company can return to normal operations. Incident handling is a recovery plan that responds to malicious technical threats.

The primary goal of incident handling is to contain and repair any damage caused by an event and to prevent any further damage. It can also improve internal communications and a company's preparation for threats and disasters.

Without an effective incident-handling program, individuals who have the best intentions can sometimes make the situation worse by damaging evidence, damaging systems, or spreading malicious code. Many times, the attacker booby-traps the compromised system to erase specific critical files if a user does something as simple as list the files in a directory. A compromised system can no longer be trusted because the internal commands listed in the path could be altered to perform unexpected activities. The system could now have a backdoor for the attacker to enter when he wants, or could have Trojan horses silently waiting for a user to start snooping around only to destroy any and all evidence.

Incident handling should be closely linked to the company's security training and awareness program to ensure that these types of mishaps do not take place. The past issues that the incident recovery team encountered can be used in future training sessions to help others learn what the company is faced with.

Employees need to know how to report an incident to the incident-handling team. The process must be centralized, easy to accomplish (or the employees won't bother), convenient, and welcomed. Some employees feel reluctant to report incidents because they are afraid they will get pulled into something they do not want to be involved with or accused of something they did not do. There is nothing like trying to do the right thing and getting hit with a big stick. Employees should feel comfortable about the process, which means suggestions on improving the process should be looked at seriously.

A sound incident-handling program works with outside agencies and counterparts. The members of the team should be on the mailing list of the Computer Emergency Response Team (CERT) so that they can keep up to date about new issues and can spot malicious events, hopefully before they get out of hand. CERT is responsible for monitoring and advising users and companies about security preparation and security breaches on the Internet. The team tracks and reports security issues and develops recommendations with clearly written steps to be taken if faced with specific threats.

## References

- **CERT Coordination Center** www.cert.org
- **The University of Georgia Computer Security and Ethics** www.uga.edu/compsec
- **Bibliography of Computer Security Incident Handling Documents,** by Klaus-Peter Kossakowski, DFN-CERT (Germany) www.cert.dfn.de/eng/pre99papers/certbib.html
- **NIST Incident Handling Information** http://csrc.nist.gov/topics/inchand.html

## What Is Admissible in Court?

*He is guilty because I don't like him. Response: Um, I need more than that.*

Computer logs are important in many aspects of the IT world. They are usually used to troubleshoot an issue or to try to understand the events that took place at a specific moment in time. When computer logs are to be used as evidence in court, they must be collected in the regular course of business. Most of the time, computer-related documents are considered *hearsay*, meaning the evidence is secondhand evidence. Hearsay evidence is not normally admissible in court unless it has firsthand evidence that can be used to prove the evidence's accuracy, trustworthiness, and reliability, such as the testimony of a businessperson who generated the computer logs and collected them. This person must generate and collect logs as a normal part of his business and not just this one time for court. The value of evidence depends upon the genuineness and competence of the source.

It is important to show that the logs, and all evidence, have not been tampered with in any way, which is the reason for the chain of custody of evidence. There are several tools that run some type of checksum or hashing function on the logs, which will allow the team to be alerted if something has been modified.

When evidence is being collected, one issue that can come up is the user's expectation of privacy. If an employee is suspected of and charged with a computer crime, he might claim that his files on the computer he uses are personal and not available to law enforcement and the courts. This is why it is important for companies to conduct security-awareness training, have employees sign contracts pertaining to the acceptable use of the company's computers and equipment, and to have legal banners pop up on every employee's computer when they log on. These are key elements to establish that a user has no right to privacy when he is using company equipment. The following banner is suggested by CERT Advisory:

> This system is for the use of authorized users only. Individuals using this computer system without authority, or in excess of their authority, are subject to having all of their activities on this system monitored and recorded by system personnel.

> In the course of monitoring an individual improperly using this system, or in the course of system maintenance, the activities of authorized users may also be monitored.

> Anyone using this system expressly consents to such monitoring and is advised that if such monitoring reveals possible evidence of criminal activity, system personnel may provide the evidence of such monitoring to law enforcement officials.

This explicit warning strengthens a legal case that can be brought against an employee or intruder, because the continued use of the system after viewing this type of warning implies that the person acknowledges the security policy and gives permission to be monitored.

Evidence has its own life cycle, and it is important that the individuals involved with the investigation understand the phases of the life cycle and properly follow them.

The life cycle of evidence includes:

- Collection and identification
- Storage, preservation, and transportation
- Presentation in court
- Return to the victim or owner

There are several types of evidence that can be used in a trial: written, oral, computer generated, and visual or audio. Oral evidence is testimony of a witness. Visual or audio is usually a captured event during the crime or right after it.

Not all evidence is equal in the eyes of the law and some types of evidence have more clout, or weight, than other types. The following sections quickly describe the different ways evidence can be categorized and valued.

## Best Evidence

*Best evidence* is the primary evidence used in a trial because it provides the most reliability. An example of something that would be categorized as best evidence is an original signed contract. Oral evidence is not considered best evidence because there is no firsthand reliable proof that supports its validity, and it therefore does not have as good of a standing as legal documents. Oral evidence cannot be used to dispute a legal document, but it can be used to interpret the document.

## Secondary Evidence

*Secondary evidence* is not viewed as reliable and strong in proving innocence or guilt (or liability in civil cases) when compared to best evidence. Oral evidence, such as a witness's testimony, and copies of original documents are placed in the secondary evidence category.

## Direct Evidence

*Direct evidence* can prove a fact all by itself and does not need backup information to refer to. When using direct evidence, presumptions are not required. One example of direct evidence is the testimony of a witness who saw a crime take place. Although this oral evidence would be secondary in nature, meaning a case could not rest on just it alone, it is also direct evidence, meaning the lawyer does not necessarily need to provide other evidence to back it up. Direct evidence often is based on information gathered from a witness's five senses.

## Conclusive Evidence

*Conclusive evidence* is irrefutable and cannot be contradicted. Conclusive evidence is very strong all by itself and does not require corroboration.

## Circumstantial Evidence

*Circumstantial evidence* can prove an intermediate fact that can then be used to deduce or assume the existence of another fact. This type of fact is used so that the judge or jury will logically assume the existence of a primary fact. For example, if a suspect told a friend he was going to bring down eBay's web site, a case could not rest on that piece of evidence alone because it is circumstantial. However, this evidence can cause the jury to assume that because the suspect said he was going to do it, and hours later it happened, maybe he was the one who did the crime.

## Corroborative Evidence

*Corroborative evidence* is supporting evidence used to help prove an idea or point. It cannot stand on its own, but is used as a supplementary tool to help prove a primary piece of evidence.

## Opinion Evidence

When a witness testifies, the *opinion rule* dictates that she must testify to only the facts of the issue and not her opinion of the facts. This is slightly different from when an expert witness is used, because an expert is used primarily for his educated opinion. Most lawyers call in expert witnesses to testify and help the defending or prosecuting sides to better understand the subject matter so that they can help the judge and jury to better understand the matters of the case.

## Hearsay Evidence

*Hearsay evidence* pertains to oral or written evidence presented in court that is secondhand and that has no firsthand proof of accuracy or reliability. If a witness testifies about something he heard someone else say, it is too far removed from fact and has too many variables that can cloud the truth. If business documents were made during regular business routines, they may be admissible. However, if these records were made just to be presented in court, they could be categorized as hearsay evidence.

It is important that evidence be sufficient, reliable, and relevant to the case at hand. These characteristics of evidence provide a foundation for a case and help ensure that the evidence is legally permissible.

For the evidence to be *sufficient*, it must be persuasive enough to convince a reasonable person of the validity of the evidence. This means that the evidence cannot be subject to personal interpretation. Sufficient evidence also means that it cannot be easily doubted.

For evidence to be *reliable*, or competent, it must be consistent with fact. Evidence cannot be reliable if it is based on someone's opinion or copies of an original document, because there is too much room for error. Reliable evidence means that it is factual and not circumstantial.

For evidence to be *relevant*, it must have a reasonable and sensible relationship to the findings. If a judge rules that a person's past traffic tickets cannot be brought up in a murder trial, this means that the judge has ruled that the traffic tickets are not relevant to the case at hand. Thus, the prosecuting lawyer cannot even mention them in court.

If a piece of evidence is found to be sufficient, reliable, and relevant to the case, it must also be legally permissible, meaning that it was obtained in a legal way. The evidence must not have been obtained through an unlawful search and seizure, recorded illegally, or obtained through a coerced confession. All of these steps must be taken to ensure that the evidence will not be thrown out once it gets to court. (This section not only will help you on the CISSP exam, but will also come in handy the next time you watch *Law & Order*.)

## Surveillance, Search, and Seizure

There are two main types of surveillance when it comes to identifying computer crimes: physical surveillance and computer surveillance. Physical surveillance pertains to security cameras, security guards, and closed-circuit TV (CCTV), which may capture evidence. Physical surveillance can also be used by an undercover agent to learn about the suspect's spending activities, family and friends, and personal habits in the hope of gathering more clues for the case.

Computer surveillance pertains to auditing events, which passively monitors events by using network sniffers, keyboard monitors, wiretaps, and line monitoring. In most jurisdictions, active monitoring may require a search warrant. In most workplace environments, to legally monitor an individual, the person has to be warned ahead of time that her activities may be subject to this type of monitoring.

Search and seizure activities can get tricky depending on what is being searched for and where. For example, American citizens are protected by the Fourth Amendment against unlawful search and seizure, so law enforcement agencies must have probable cause and request a search warrant from a judge or court before conducting such a search. The actual search can only take place in the areas outlined by the warrant. The Fourth Amendment does not apply to actions by private citizens unless they are acting as police agents. So, for example, if Kristy's boss warned all employees that the management could remove files from their computers at any time, and her boss was not a police officer or acting as a police agent, she could not successfully claim that her Fourth Amendment rights were violated. Kristy's boss may have violated some specific privacy laws, but he did not violate Kristy's Fourth Amendment rights.

There are circumstances in which a law enforcement agent may seize evidence that is not included in the warrant, such as if the suspect tries to destroy the evidence. In other words, if there is an impending possibility that evidence might be destroyed, law enforcement may quickly seize the evidence to prevent its destruction. This is referred to as *exigent circumstances*, and a judge will later decide whether the seizure was proper and legal before allowing the evidence to be admitted. For example, if a police officer had a search warrant that allowed him to search a suspect's living room but no other rooms, and then he saw the suspect dumping cocaine down the toilet, the police officer could seize the cocaine even though it was in a room not covered under his search warrant.

After evidence is gathered, the chain of custody needs to be enacted and enforced to make sure the evidence's integrity is not compromised.

## Enticement and Entrapment

A thin line exists between enticement and entrapment when it comes to capturing a suspect's actions. Enticement is legal and ethical, whereas entrapment is neither legal nor ethical. In the world of computer crimes, a honeypot is always a good example to show the difference between enticement and entrapment. Companies put systems in their screened subnets that either emulate services that attackers usually like to take advantage of or actually have the services enabled. The hope is that if an attacker breaks into the company's network, she will go right to the honeypot instead of the systems that are actual production machines. The attacker will be enticed to go to the honeypot system because it has many open ports and services running and exhibits vulnerabilities that the attacker would want to exploit. The company can log the attacker's actions and later attempt to prosecute.

The action in the preceding example is legal unless the company crosses the line to entrapment. For example, suppose a web page has a link that indicates that if the attacker clicks it, she could then download thousands of MP3 files for free. However, when the attacker clicks on that link, she is taken to the honeypot system instead and the company records all of her actions and attempts to prosecute. Entrapment does not prove that the suspect had the intent to commit a crime; it only proves that she was successfully tricked.

## Interviewing and Interrogating

Once surveillance and search and seizure activities have been performed, it is very likely that suspects must be interviewed and interrogated. When this is needed, there should be one person in charge of the interview or interrogation, with one or two others present. The topics of discussion and questions should be prepared beforehand and asked in a systematic and calm fashion, because the purpose of an interrogation is to obtain evidence for a trial.

The employee interrogator should be in a position that is senior to the employee suspect. A vice president is not going to be very intimidated or willing to spill his guts to the mailroom clerk. The interrogation should be held in a private place, and the suspect should be relatively comfortable and at ease. If exhibits are going to be shown to the suspect, they should be shown one at a time, and otherwise kept in a folder. It is not necessary to read a person their rights before questioning unless law enforcement officers do the interview.

What the interrogators do not want to happen during an interrogation is to be deceived by the suspect, to relinquish important information pertaining to the investigation, or to have the suspect flee before a trial date is set.

# Import and Export Laws

As stated earlier, various countries have different laws pertaining to copyright, trade secrets, trademarks, and such. Countries also have different import and export restrictions.

The main technology that countries restrict in transborder commerce is encryption technology. Some countries restrict the type or strength of encryption that can be used between countries or that can be bought and sold between different countries. This is because governments want to be able to break the encryption and listen in on communications if they are suspected of being about illegal activities, terrorist communications, or other data that is important to protecting the nation.

 **NOTE** There are no current restrictions on domestic use in the United States pertaining to encryption products.

If a vendor wants to sell encryption technologies to another country or include encryption within its product, it must thoroughly research the restrictions of the source and destination countries and seek legal advice to ensure that no laws or regulations are being broken accidentally. In the United States, the Bureau of Export Administration (BXA), in the U.S. Department of Commerce, governs exportation of encryption mechanisms. In the past, exportation of these technologies has been extremely strict. In October 2000, the BXA published a rule creating a "free-trade zone" approved by the president and vice president, which enables U.S. exporters to export most encryption products to 15 European Union member states and 8 additional trading partners. This included PCs, laptops, handheld devices, wireless technologies, software, and network devices that use encryption technologies. This greatly reduced the process that vendors had to go through to get their products approved to be sold in other countries.

There are still strict exportation regulations on the countries considered terrorist-supporting states. For further information on these issues, refer to the references provided in the upcoming "References" section.

## Transborder Information Flow

Many companies communicate internationally every day through e-mail, telephone lines, satellites, fiber cables, and long-distance wireless transmission. It is important for a company to research the laws of different countries pertaining to information flow and privacy.

Data can route through many different countries before arriving at its destination. Network routing should be analyzed regularly to understand how data moves from one place to another. Some countries restrict the flow of personal information and financial data and deem it illegal to transmit this type of information. Wiretapping may be able to occur without any legal consequence. It all depends on the laws of the countries you are passing data through, and thus you should be aware of those laws.

The following are issues that have increased the need for more privacy laws and governance:

- **Data retrieval advances** Ways of collecting a vast amount of personal data and storing it in central repositories
- **Convergent technologies** Technical methods of gathering, analyzing, and distributing information
- **Globalization** Distributing information beyond national borders

If these technologies and methods are used to collect and store private data, the data must be properly secured and access must be drastically restricted.

### References

- **U.S. Department of Commerce Bureau of Industry and Security (BIS)** www.bxa.doc.gov
- **BIS Export Administration Regulations Marketplace FAQ** http://chaos .fedworld.gov/bxa/faq.html

# Privacy

There is a sense that privacy is becoming more threatened as the world relies more and more on technology. In response, countries have enacted privacy laws. For example, although the United States already had the Federal Privacy Act of 1974, it has enacted new laws, such as the Gramm-Leach-Bliley Act of 1999 and the Health Insurance Portability and Accountability Act (HIPAA), in response to an increased need to protect personal privacy information.

The Federal Privacy Act was put into place to protect the U.S. citizens' sensitive information that is collected by government agencies. It states that any data collected must be done in a fair and lawful manner. The data is to be used only for the purposes for which it was collected and held only for a reasonable amount of time. If an agency collects data on a person, that person has the right to receive a report outlining data collected about him if it is requested. Similar laws exist in many countries around the world.

Many of the privacy principles addressed in most countries' privacy laws state that the information must be accurate, kept up-to-date, and cannot be disclosed to a third party unless authorized by statute or consent of that individual. People also have the right to make a correction to their personal information. If data is to be transmitted to a location where the equivalent security protection cannot be ensured, then transmission is prohibited.

Within a corporation, there are several employee privacy issues that must be thought through and addressed if the company wants to be properly protected. An understanding that each state may have different privacy laws should prompt the company to investigate exactly what it can and cannot monitor before it does so.

If a company has learned that the state the facility is located in permits keyboard, e-mail, and surveillance monitoring, it must take the proper steps to ensure that the employees know that these types of monitoring may be put into place. This is the best way for a company to protect itself, make sure it has a legal leg to stand on if necessary, and not present the employees with any surprises.

The monitoring has to be work related, meaning that a manager may have the right to listen in on his employees' conversations with customers, but he does not have the right to listen in on personal conversations that are not work related. Monitoring also must happen in a consistent way, such that all employees are subjected to monitoring, instead of picking out one or two people.

If a company feels that it may be necessary to monitor e-mail messages and usage, this needs to be explained to the employees, first through a security policy and then through a constant reminder such as a computer banner or regular training. It is best to have an employee read a document describing what type of monitoring they could be subjected to, what is considered acceptable behavior, and what the consequences of not meeting those expectations are. The employees should sign this document, which can later be treated as a legally admissible document if necessary.

A company that wants to be able to monitor e-mail should address this point in its security policy. It should outline who can and cannot read employee messages, describe the circumstances under which e-mail monitoring may be acceptable, and specify where the e-mail can be accessed. Some companies indicate that they will only monitor e-mail that lives on the mail server, whereas other companies declare the right to read employee messages if they reside on the mail server or the employee's computer. A company must not promise privacy to employees that it does not then provide, because that could result in a lawsuit.

Although IT and security professionals have access to many parts of computer systems and the network, this does not mean it is ethical and right to overstep the bounds that could threaten a user's privacy. Only the tasks necessary to enforce the security policy should take place and nothing further that could compromise another's privacy.

## Prescreening Personnel

Chapter 3 described why it is important to properly screen individuals before hiring them into a corporation. These steps are necessary to help the company protect itself and to ensure that it is getting the type of employee that is required for the job. This chapter looks at some of the issues from the other side of the table, which deals with that individual's privacy rights.

There are limitations on the type and amount of information that an organization can obtain on a potential employee. The limitations and regulations for background checks vary from jurisdiction to jurisdiction, so the hiring manager needs to consult the legal department. Usually human resources has an outline for hiring managers to follow when it comes to interviews and background checks.

There are also potential problems when an employee leaves the company. If the employee is terminated, laid off, moves on to a competitor company, or has any unresolved issues with the company, that person may commit fraud, destroy property, or share confidential information. An exit interview should be performed that requires the employee to sign a document indicating he does not have any confidential papers and promises not to violate the trade secret and confidential information rules that he agreed to when he was hired.

# Laws, Directives, and Regulations

Regulation in computer and information security covers many areas for many different reasons. Some issues that require regulation are data privacy, computer misuse, software copyright, data protection, and controls on cryptography. These regulations can be implemented in various arenas, such as government and private sectors for reasons dealing with environmental protection, intellectual property, national security, personal privacy, public order, health and safety, and prevention of cruelty and corruption.

Security professionals have so much to keep up with these days, from understanding how the latest worm attacks work and how to properly protect against them, to how new versions of DoS attacks take place and what tools are used to accomplish them. Professionals also need to follow what new security products are released and how they compare to the existing products. This is followed up by keeping track of new technologies, service patches, hotfixes, encryption methods, access control mechanisms, telecommunications security issues, social engineering, and physical security. Laws and regulations are not usually at the top of security professionals' list of interests or things to know. However, they are important, especially if you are asked to be involved with identifying and investigating a computer crime or asked to provide your professional opinion or work as an expert witness. Laws and regulations can be another item on the large heap of information a security professional is expected to keep current on, but in many situations it is just as important as any other security issues.

**NOTE** In many countries, to deal more effectively with computer crime, legislative bodies have broadened the definition of property to include data.

Laws, regulations, and directives developed by governments or appointed agencies do not usually provide detailed instructions to follow to properly protect computers and company assets. Each environment is too diverse in topology, technology, infrastructure, requirements, functionality, and personnel. Because technology changes at such a fast pace, these laws and regulations could never successfully represent reality if they were too detailed. Instead, they specify requirements expected from different business types. They work as a framework of rules, and it is up to each company to fill in that framework but properly stay within its bounds.

**NOTE** Over time, the CISSP exam has become more global in nature and less U.S.-centric. Specific questions on U.S. laws have been taken out of the test recently, so you do not need to spend a lot of time learning them. Be familiar with why laws are developed and put in place and their overall goals, instead of memorizing specific laws and dates.

## Health Insurance Portability and Accountability Act

HIPAA, a relatively new U.S. federal regulation, has been mandated to provide national standards and procedures for the storage, use, and transmission of personal medical information and health care data. This regulation provides a framework and guidelines to ensure security, integrity, and privacy when handling confidential medical information. HIPAA outlines how security should be managed for any facility that creates, accesses, shares, or destroys medical information.

People's health records can be used and misused in different scenarios for many reasons. As health records migrate from a paper-based system to an electronic system, they become easier to maintain, access, and transfer, but they also become easier to manipulate and access in an unauthorized manner. Traditionally, health care facilities have lagged behind other businesses in their information and network security mechanisms, architecture, and security enforcement because there was no real business need to expend the energy and money to put these items in place. Now there is.

HIPAA mandates steep federal penalties for noncompliance. If medical information is used in a way that violates the privacy standards dictated by HIPAA, even by mistake, there are monetary penalties of $100 per violation, up to $25,000 per year, per standard. If protected health information is obtained or disclosed knowingly, the fines can be as much as $50,000 and one year in prison. If the information is obtained or disclosed under false pretenses, the cost can go up to $250,000 and ten years in prison if there is intent to sell or use the information for commercial advantage, personal gain, or malicious harm. This is serious business.

## Gramm-Leach-Bliley Act of 1999

This act requires financial institutions to develop privacy notices and give their customers the option to prohibit banks from sharing their information with nonaffiliated third parties. The act dictates that the board of directors is responsible for many of the security issues within a financial institution, that risk management must be implemented, that all employees need to be trained on information security issues, and that implemented security measures must be fully tested. It also requires these institutions to have a written security policy in place.

## Computer Fraud and Abuse Act

This act, written in 1986 and amended in 1996, is the primary U.S. federal antihacking statute. It prohibits seven forms of activity and makes them federal crimes:

- The knowing access of computers of the federal government to obtain classified information without authorization or access through the use of excess of authorization

- The intentional access of a computer to obtain information from a financial institution, the federal government, or any protected computer involved in interstate or foreign communications without authorization or through the use of excess of authorization

- The intentional and unauthorized access of computers of the federal government, or computers used by or for the government when the access affects the government's use of that computer

- The knowing access of a protected computer without authorization or in excess of authorization with the intent to defraud

- Knowingly causing the transmission of a program, information, code, or command and, as a result of such conduct, intentionally causing damage without authorization to a protected computer

- The knowing trafficking of computer passwords with the intent to defraud

- The transmission of communications containing threats to cause damage to a protected computer

These acts range from felonies to misdemeanors with corresponding small to large fines and jail sentences.

## Federal Privacy Act of 1974

In the mid-1960s, there was a proposal that the U.S. government would compile and collectively hold in a main federal data bank each individual's information pertaining to the Social Security Administration, Census Bureau, Internal Revenue Service, Bureau of Labor Statistics, and other limbs of the government. The committee that made this proposal saw this as an efficient way of gathering and centralizing data. Others saw it as a dangerous move against individual privacy. The federal data bank never came to pass because of strong opposition.

To keep the government in check on gathering information on U.S. citizens and other matters, a majority of its files are considered open to the public. Government files are open to the public unless there are specific issues enacted by legislature deeming specific files unavailable. This is what is explained in the Freedom of Information Act. This is different from what the Privacy Act outlines and protects. The Privacy Act applies to records and documents developed and maintained by specific branches of the federal government, such as executive departments, government corporations, independent regulatory agencies, and government-controlled corporations. It does not apply to congressional, judiciary, or territorial subdivisions.

An actual *record* is information about an individual's education, medical history, financial history, criminal history, employment, and other similar types of information. Agencies can maintain this type of information only if it is necessary and relevant to accomplishing the agency's purpose. The Privacy Act dictates that an agency cannot disclose this information without written permission from the individual. However, like most government acts, legislation, and creeds, there is a list of exceptions.

So what does all of this dry legal mumbo-jumbo mean? Basically, agencies can gather information about individuals, but it must be relevant and necessary for its approved cause. In addition, that agency cannot go around town sharing other people's private information. If it does, private citizens have the right to sue the agency to protect their privacy.

This leaks into the computer world because this information is usually held by one type of computer or another. If an agency's computer holds an individual's confidential information, it must provide the necessary security mechanisms to ensure that it cannot be compromised or copied in an unauthorized way.

## European Union Principles on Privacy

Compared to many other countries, European countries have strict laws pertaining to data that is considered private in nature. The *European Union Principles on Privacy* has six areas that address using and transmitting data considered sensitive in nature. All states in Europe must abide by these six principles to be in compliance. The following gives a quick overview of the different areas of privacy that are addressed under this law:

- *The reason for gathering of data must be specified at the time of collection.* This helps reduce the possible misuse of data and forces the individual to justify the reason for gathering the information.

- *Data cannot be used for other purposes.* The data can only be used for the original reason it was gathered.

- *Unnecessary data should not be collected.* Only information that is required to meet the stated purpose should be gathered and no more.

- *Data should only be kept for as long as it is needed to accomplish the stated task.* This helps to ensure that the data is current and prevents indefinite archiving of data.

- *Only the necessary individuals who are required to accomplish the stated task should be allowed access to the data.* This helps prevent the selling of private data to others.

- *Whoever is responsible for securely storing the data should not allow unintentional "leaking" of data.* This helps enforce strong security for those who are responsible for storing private information.

## Computer Security Act of 1987

This act requires U.S. federal agencies to identify computer systems that will contain sensitive information. The agency must develop a security policy and plan for each of these systems and conduct periodic training for individuals who operate, manage, or use these systems. Federal agency employees must be provided with security-awareness training and be informed of how the agency defines acceptable computer use and practices.

Because the U.S. federal government deals with a lot of important, confidential, and secret information, it wants to make sure that all individuals and systems within all federal government agencies meet a certain level of awareness and protection.

## Security and Freedom Through Encryption Act

This act was approved in 1997 and guarantees the right of all U.S. citizens and residents to be able to use and sell encryption products and technology. This act was developed to relax encryption export controls and to make it legal for people to own and use encryption software no matter what algorithm it employs or key length it uses. It also prohibits state and federal governments from requiring anyone to relinquish his encryption key so that these agencies can snoop on conversations or decrypt information. This means the government cannot require key escrow.

## Federal Sentencing Guidelines

In 1991, U.S. Federal Sentencing Guidelines were developed and passed down to provide judges with courses of action to take when overseeing white collar crimes that take place within organizations. These guidelines deal with antitrust, federal securities, mail and wire fraud, bribery, breach of contract, and money laundering.

These guidelines provide ways in which companies and law enforcement should prevent, detect, and report computer crimes. They outline the responsibilities of senior executives for the computer and information security decisions they make and for what actually takes place within their organizations, and set a maximum fine of $290 million dollars.

The actual punishments and fines could be reduced if the company in question exercised due diligence and showed steps of responsible behavior. The guidelines require companies to develop security policies, standards, and procedures, and to properly inform employees of these issues.

## Economic Espionage Act of 1996

Prior to 1996, industry and corporate espionage was taking place with no real guidelines for who could properly investigate the events. This act provides the necessary structure when dealing with these types of cases and further defines trade secrets to be technical, business, engineering, scientific, or financial. This means that an asset does not necessarily need to be tangible to be protected or to be stolen. This act enables the FBI to investigate industrial and corporate espionage cases.

# International Cooperation Efforts

Governments all over the world have realized that they must cooperate with each other if they hope to properly deal with computer crimes. This means different channels of communication had to be opened, agreements on the meaning and definitions of specific crimes had to be made, and barriers that usually stood in the way of effective investigative work that crossed geographical boundaries had to be lessened or erased. The following sections quickly describe some of the organizations that are involved with this type of work.

## Group of Eight

The G8 represents the world's leading industrialized countries. During a Paris meeting in May 2000, the members agreed to cooperate to fight cybercrime. This was prompted by the global concern over the growing threat of cybercrime, and the success of viruses like ILOVEYOU, which cost companies all over the world thousands to millions of dollars. G8 vowed to extend the powers of the European law enforcement agency, Europol, to fight illegal acts committed with technology. This was done so that countries would work together to develop similar laws and open doors to help each other enforce laws and regulations pertaining to computer and information crimes.

## Interpol

The international police organization, Interpol, collects and distributes information about cross-border crimes. It works to keep companies, law enforcement agencies, and governments informed about cybercrimes and who could be a target of malicious hackers.

## European Commission

In January 2000, the European Commission revealed its proposals on fighting cyber-crime. The Commission presented its paper to the Council of Ministers of the European Union and Parliament, which outlined a policy that describes the methods necessary to fight computer crimes without hindering e-commerce. The proposal suggests harmonizing the member states' laws to deal with criminal law on high-tech crimes, including hacking and DoS attacks.

## References

- **Interpol IT Security and Crime Prevention Methods** www.interpol.int/Public/TechnologyCrime/CrimePrev/ITSecurity.asp
- **"Interpol's Contribution to Combating Information Technology Crime"** www.interpol.com/Public/TechnologyCrime
- **Global Internet Policy Initiative (GIPI) Best Practices** www.internetpolicy.net/practices/

# Summary

Law, ethics, and investigations are very important parts of computer and information security. They are elements that do not usually come to mind when one speaks of information security, but they are a must if a society is serious about controlling this type of crime and punishing the guilty.

In many ways, the laws and courts are in their infancy stages when attempting to deal with computer crimes. They are faced with not having many precedents to fall back on when interpreting what is legal and illegal and what the proper punishments are for each type of computer crime. However, the legal system is quickly developing laws and providing ways to properly interpret these laws to help all arms of the law enforcement agencies and the victims. Over the last few years, hacking and attacking have been performed for fun, mainly by curious computer individuals, but as the punishments increase, the fun may quickly come to an end.

Security professionals should be aware of and well versed in computer security laws and regulations that apply in their environments. They should be able to properly inform their management and customers of expected responsibilities, as well as know what boundaries they are expected to work within themselves.

# Quick Tips

- Dumpster diving refers to going through someone's trash to find confidential or useful information. It is legal, unless it involves trespassing, but in all cases it is considered unethical.

- Wiretapping is a passive attack that eavesdrops on communications. It is only legal with prior consent or a warrant.

- Social engineering is the act of tricking or deceiving a person into giving confidential or sensitive information that could then be used against him or his company.

- Data diddling is the act of willfully modifying information, programs, or documentation in an effort to commit fraud or disrupt production.

- Excessive privileges means that an employee has more rights than necessary to complete her tasks.

- Criminal law deals with an individual's conduct that violates government laws that were developed to protect the public.

- Civil law deals with wrongs committed against individuals or companies that result in injury or damages. Civil law does not use prison time as a punishment, but usually requires financial restitution.

- Administrative, or regulatory, law covers standards of performance or conduct expected by government agencies from companies, industries, and certain officials.

- A patent grants ownership and enables that owner to legally enforce his rights to exclude others from using the invention covered by the patent.

- Copyright protects the expression of ideas rather than the ideas themselves.

- Trademarks protect words, names, product shape, symbol, color, or a combination of these used to identify products or a company. These items are used to distinguish products from the competitors' products.

- Trade secrets are deemed proprietary to a company and often include information that provides a competitive edge. The information is protected as long as the owner takes the necessary protective actions.

- Crime over the Internet has brought about jurisdiction problems for law enforcement and the courts.

- Privacy laws dictate that data collected by government agencies must be collected fairly and lawfully, must be used only for the purpose for which it was collected, must only be held for a reasonable amount of time, and must be accurate and timely.

- If companies are going to use any type of monitoring, they need to make sure it is legal in their business sector and must inform all employees that they may be subjected to monitoring.

- Employees need to be informed regarding what is expected behavior pertaining to the use of the company's computer systems, network, e-mail system, and phone system. They need to also know what the ramifications are for not meeting those expectations. These requirements are usually communicated through policies.

- Logon banners should be used to inform users of what could happen if they do not follow the rules pertaining to using company resources. This provides legal protection for the company.

- Countries differ in their view of the seriousness of computer crime and have different penalties for certain crimes. This makes enforcing laws much harder across country borders.

- The three main types of harm addressed in computer crime laws pertain to unauthorized intrusion, unauthorized alteration or destruction, and using malicious code.

- The Federal Sentencing Guidelines of the United States gives judges and courts procedures for how to prevent, detect, and report computer crimes, along with penalty ranges. These guidelines also make senior executives responsible for their company's actions.

- Law enforcement and the courts have a hard time with computer crimes because of the newness of the types of crimes, the complexity involved, jurisdictional issues, and evidence collection. New laws are being written to properly deal with cybercrime.

- If a company does not practice due care in its efforts to protect itself from computer crime, it can be found to be negligent and legally liable for damages.

- Elements of negligence include not fulfilling a legally recognized obligation, failure to conform to a standard of care that results in injury or damage, and proximate causation.

- Most computer crimes are not reported because the victims are not aware of the crime or are too embarrassed to let anyone else know.

- Theft is no longer restricted to physical constraints. Assets are now also viewed as intangible objects that can also be stolen or disclosed via technological means.

- The primary reason for the chain of custody of evidence is to ensure that it will be admissible in court by showing that it was properly controlled and handled before being presented in court.

- Companies should develop their own incident response team, which is made up of people from management, IT, legal, human resources, public relations, security, and other key areas of the organization.

- Hearsay evidence is secondhand and usually not admissible in court.

- To be admissible in court, business records have to be made and collected in the normal course of business, not specially generated for a case in court.

Business records can easily be hearsay if there is no firsthand proof of their accuracy and reliability.

- The life cycle of evidence includes identification and collection of the evidence, storage, preservation, transportation, presentation in court, and return back to the owner.

- Collection of computer evidence is a very complex and detail-oriented task. Only skilled people should attempt it; otherwise, evidence can be ruined forever.

- When looking for suspects, it is important to consider the motive, opportunity, and means (MOM).

- For evidence to be admissible in court, it needs to be relevant, sufficient, and reliable.

- Evidence must be legally permissible, meaning that it was seized legally and the chain of custody was not broken.

- All evidence should be marked and stored in a container, which also should be marked.

- In many jurisdictions, law enforcement agencies must obtain a warrant to search and seize an individual's property, as stated in the Fourth Amendment. Private citizens are not required to protect the Fourth Amendment rights of others unless acting as a police agent.

- Enticement is the act of luring an intruder and is legal. Entrapment induces a crime, tricks a person, and is illegal.

- The salami attack is executed by carrying out smaller crimes with the hope that the larger crime will not be noticed. The common salami attack is the act of skimming off a small amount of money.

- Phreakers are hackers who specialize in committing telephone fraud.

- After a computer system is seized, the investigators should make a bit mirror image copy of the storage media before doing anything else.

## Questions

Please remember that these questions are formatted and asked in a certain way for a reason. You must remember that the CISSP exam is asking questions at a conceptual level. Questions may not always have the perfect answer, and the candidate is advised against always looking for the perfect answer. The candidate should look for the best answer in the list.

1. Which of the following does the IAB consider unethical?

   A. Creating a computer virus

   B. Entering information into a web page

   C. Performing a penetration test on a host on the Internet

   D. Disrupting Internet communications

2. What is the study of computers and surrounding technologies and how they relate to crime?

   A. Computer forensics

   B. Computer vulnerability analysis

   C. Incident handling

   D. Computer information criteria

3. Which of the following does IAB consider unethical behavior?

   A. Internet users who conceal unauthorized accesses

   B. Internet users who waste computer resources

   C. Internet users who write viruses

   D. Internet users who monitor traffic

4. After a computer forensics investigator seizes a computer during a crime investigation, what is the next step?

   A. Label and put it into a container, and label the container

   B. Dust the evidence for fingerprints

   C. Make an image copy of the disks

   D. Lock the evidence in the safe

5. A CISSP candidate signs an ethics statement prior to taking the CISSP examination. Which of the following would be a violation of the (ISC)$^2$ Code of Ethics that could cause the candidate to lose his or her certification?

   A. E-mailing information or comments about the exam to other CISSP candidates

   B. Submitting comments on the questions of the exam to (ISC)$^2$

   C. Submitting comments to the board of directors regarding the test and content of the class

   D. Conducting a presentation about the CISSP certification and what the certification means

6. If your company gives you a new PC and you find residual information about confidential company issues, what should you do based on the (ISC)$^2$ Code of Ethics?

   A. Contact the owner of the file and inform him about it. Copy it to a disk, give it to him, and delete your copy.

   B. Delete the document because it was not meant for you.

   C. Inform management of your findings so that it can make sure this type of thing does not happen again.

   D. E-mail it to the author and to management so that everyone is aware of what is going on.

7. Why is it difficult to investigate computer crime and track down the criminal?

    A. Privacy laws are written to protect people from being investigated for these types of crimes.

    B. Special equipment and tools are necessary to detect these types of criminals.

    C. Criminals can spoof their address and hop from one network to the next.

    D. The police have no jurisdiction over the Internet.

8. Protecting evidence and providing accountability for who handled it at different steps during the investigation is referred to as what?

    A. Rule of best evidence

    B. Hearsay

    C. Evidence safety

    D. Chain of custody

9. If an investigator needs to communicate with another investigator but does not want the criminal to be able to eavesdrop on this conversation, what type of communication should be used?

    A. Digitally signed messages

    B. Out-of-band messages

    C. Forensics frequency

    D. Authentication and access control

10. Why is it challenging to collect and identify computer evidence to be used in a court of law?

    A. The evidence is mostly intangible.

    B. The evidence is mostly corrupted.

    C. The evidence is mostly encrypted.

    D. The evidence is mostly tangible.

11. The chain of custody of evidence describes who obtained the evidence and _____.

    A. Who secured it and stole it

    B. Who controlled it and broke it

    C. Who secured it and validated it

    D. Who controlled it and duplicated it

12. Before shutting down a system suspected of an attack, the investigator should do what?

    A. Remove and back up the hard drive

    B. Dump memory contents to disk

    C. Remove it from the network

    D. Save data in the spooler queue and temporary files

13. Why is computer-generated documentation usually considered unreliable evidence?

    A. It is primary evidence.

    B. It is too difficult to detect prior modifications.

    C. It is corroborative evidence.

    D. It is not covered under criminal law, but it is covered under civil law.

14. Which of the following is a necessary characteristic of evidence for it to be admissible?

    A. It must be real.

    B. It must be noteworthy.

    C. It must be reliable.

    D. It must be important.

15. In the United States, what agency usually works with the FBI when investigating computer crimes?

    A. (ISC)²

    B. Secret Service

    C. CIA

    D. State police

16. If a company deliberately planted a flaw in one of its systems in the hope of detecting an attempted penetration and exploitation of this flaw, what would this be called?

    A. Incident recovery response

    B. Entrapment

    C. Illegal

    D. Enticement

17. If an employee is suspected of wrongdoing in a computer crime, what department must be involved?

    A. Human resources

    B. Legal

    C. Audit

    D. Payroll

18. When would an investigator's notebook be admissible in court?

    A. When he uses it to refresh memory

    B. When he cannot be present for testimony

    C. When requested by the judge to learn the original issues of the investigations

    D. When no other physical evidence is available

19. Disks and other media that are copies of the original evidence are considered what?

    A. Primary evidence

    B. Reliable and sufficient evidence

    C. Hearsay evidence

    D. Conclusive evidence

20. If a company does not inform employees that they may be monitored and does not have a policy stating how monitoring should take place, what should a company do?

    A. Don't monitor employees in any fashion.

    B. Monitor during off-hours and slow times.

    C. Obtain a search warrant before monitoring an employee.

    D. Monitor anyway—they are covered by two laws allowing them to do this.

21. What is one reason why successfully prosecuting computer crimes is so challenging?

    A. There is no way to capture electrical data reliably.

    B. The evidence in computer cases does not follow best evidence directives.

    C. These crimes do not always fall into the traditional criminal activity categories.

    D. Wiretapping is hard to do legally.

22. When can executives be charged with negligence?

    A. If they do not follow the transborder laws

    B. If they do not properly report and prosecute attackers

    C. If they do not properly inform users that they may be monitored

    D. If they do not practice due care when protecting resources

23. To better deal with computer crime, several legislative bodies have taken what steps in their strategy?

    A. Expanded several privacy laws

    B. Broadened the definition of property to include data

    C. Required corporations to have computer crime insurance

    D. Redefined transborder issues

24. Many privacy laws dictate which of the following rules?

    A. Individuals have a right to remove any data they do not want others to know.

    B. Agencies do not need to ensure that the data is accurate.

    C. Agencies need to allow all government agencies access to the data.

    D. Agencies cannot use collected data for a purpose different from what it was collected for.

25. Which of the following is not true about dumpster diving?

  A. It is legal.

  B. It is illegal.

  C. It is a breach of physical security.

  D. It is gathering data from places people would not expect to be raided.

## Answers

1. **D.** The Internet Architecture Board (IAB) is a committee for Internet design, engineering, and management. It considers the use of the Internet to be a privilege that should be treated as such.

   The IAB considers the following acts unethical and unacceptable behavior:

   - Purposely seeking to gain unauthorized access to Internet resources
   - Disrupting the intended use of the Internet
   - Wasting resources (people, capacity, and computers) through purposeful actions
   - Destroying the integrity of computer-based information
   - Compromising the privacy of others
   - Involving negligence in the conduct of Internet-wide experiments

2. **A.** Computer forensics is a field that specializes in understanding and properly extracting evidence from computers and peripheral devices for the purpose of prosecution. Collecting this type of evidence requires a skill set and understanding of several relative laws.

3. **B.** This question is similar to question 1. The IAB has declared wasting computer resources through purposeful activities unethical because it sees these resources as assets that are to be available for the computing society.

4. **C.** There are several steps that need to be followed when gathering and extracting evidence from a scene. Once a computer has been confiscated, the first thing the computer forensics team should do is to make an image of the hard drive. The team will work from this image instead of the original hard drive so that it stays in a pristine state and the evidence on the drive is not accidentally corrupted or modified.

5. **A.** A CISSP candidate and a CISSP holder should never discuss with others what was on the exam. This degrades the usefulness of the exam to be used as a tool to test someone's true security knowledge. If this type of activity is uncovered, the person could be stripped of their CISSP certification.

6. **C.** When dealing with the possible compromise of confidential company information or intellectual property, management should be informed and be involved as soon as possible. Management members are the ones who

are ultimately responsible for this data and who understand the damage its leakage can cause. An employee should not attempt to address and deal with these issues on his own.

7. **C.** Spoofing one's identity and being able to traverse anonymously through different networks and the Internet increase the complexity and difficulty of tracking down criminals who carry out computer crimes. It is very easy to commit many damaging crimes from across the country or world, and this type of activity can be difficult for law enforcement to track down.

8. **D.** Properly following the chain of custody for evidence is crucial for it to be admissible in court. A chain of custody is a history that shows how evidence was collected, analyzed, transported, and preserved in order to establish that it is sufficiently trustworthy to be presented as evidence in court. Because electronic evidence can be easily modified, a clearly defined chain of custody demonstrates that the evidence is trustworthy.

9. **B.** Out-of-band communication means to communicate through some other type of communication channel. For example, if law enforcement agents are investigating a crime on a network, they should not share information through e-mail that passes along this network. The criminal may still have sniffers installed and thus be able to access this data.

10. **A.** The evidence in computer crimes usually comes straight from computers themselves. This means that the data is held as electronic voltages, which are represented as binary bits. Some data can be held on hard drives and peripheral devices, and some data may be held in the memory of the system itself. This type of evidence is intangible in that it is not made up of objects one can hold, see, and easily understand. Other types of crimes usually have evidence that is more tangible in nature, which is easier to handle and control.

11. **C.** The chain of custody outlines a process to ensure that under no circumstance was there a possibility for the evidence to be tampered with. If the chain of custody is broken, there is a high probability that the evidence will not be admissible in court. If it is admitted, it will not carry as much weight.

12. **B.** If the computer was actually attacked or involved in a computer crime, there is a good possibility that useful information could still reside in memory. Specific tools can be used to actually dump this information and save it for analysis before the power is removed.

13. **B.** It can be very difficult to determine if computer-generated material has been modified before it is presented in court. Since this type of evidence can be altered without being detected, the court cannot put a lot of weight on this evidence. Many times, computer-generated evidence is considered hearsay, in that there is no firsthand proof backing it up.

14. **C.** For evidence to be admissible, it must be sufficient, reliable, and relevant to the case. For evidence to be reliable, it must be consistent with fact and must not be based on opinion or be circumstantial.

15. **B.** The FBI and Secret Service are both responsible for investigating computer crimes. They have their own jurisdictions and rules outlining who investigates which types of crimes.

16. **D.** Companies need to be very careful about the items they use to entice intruders and attackers, because this may be seen as entrapment by the court. It is best to get the legal department involved before implementing these items. Putting a pseudo-flaw or honeypot in place is usually seen as the use of enticement tools.

17. **A.** It is imperative that the company gets human resources involved if an employee is considered a suspect in a computer crime. This department knows the laws and regulations pertaining to employee treatment and can work to protect the employee and the company at the same time.

18. **A.** Notes that are taken by an investigator will, in most cases, not be admissible in court as evidence. This is not seen as reliable information and can only be used by the investigator to help him remember activities during the investigation.

19. **C.** In most cases, computer-related evidence falls under the hearsay category, because it is seen as copies of the original data that is held in the computer itself and can be modified without any indication. Evidence is considered hearsay when there is no firsthand proof in place to validate it.

20. **A.** Before a company can monitor its employees, it is supposed to inform them that this type of activity can take place. If a company monitors an employee without telling him, this could be seen as an invasion of privacy. The employee had an expected level of privacy that was invaded. The company should implement monitoring capabilities into its security policy and employee security-awareness programs.

21. **C.** We have an infrastructure set up to investigate and prosecute crimes: law enforcement, laws, lawyers, courts, juries, judges, and so on. This infrastructure has a long history of prosecuting "traditional" crimes. Only in the last five years have computer crimes been prosecuted more regularly; thus, these types of crimes are not fully rooted in the legal system with all of the necessary and useful precedents.

22. **D.** Executives are held to a certain standard and are expected to act responsibly when running and protecting a company. These standards and expectations equate to the due care concept under the law. Due care means to carry out activities that a reasonable person would be expected to carry out in the same situation. If an executive acts irresponsibly in any way, she can be seen as not practicing due care and be held negligent.

23. **B.** Many times what is corrupted, compromised, or taken from a computer is data, so current laws have been updated to include the protection of intangible assets, as in data. Over the years, data and information have become many companies' most valuable asset, which must be protected by the laws.

24. **D.** The Federal Privacy Act of 1974 and European Union Principles on Privacy were created to protect citizens from government agencies using information that they collected improperly. These acts have many stipulations, including that the information can only be used for the reason for which it was collected.

25. **B.** Dumpster diving is the act of going through someone's trash with the hope of uncovering useful information. Dumpster diving is legal if it does not involve trespassing, but it is unethical.

# Applications Security

This chapter presents the following:

- Various types of software controls and implementation
- Database concepts and security issues
- Data warehousing and data mining
- Software life-cycle development processes
- Change control concepts
- Object-oriented programming components
- Expert systems and artificial intelligence

Applications and computer systems are usually developed for functionality first, not security first. To get the best of both worlds, security and functionality would have to be designed and developed at the same time. Security should be interwoven into the core of a product and provide protection at different layers; this is a better approach than trying to develop a front end or wrapper that may reduce the overall functionality and leave security holes when the product has to be integrated with other applications.

## Software's Importance

Application system controls come in various flavors with many different goals. They can control input, processing, number-crunching methods, interprocess communication, interfacing to the system and other programs, access, and output. They should be developed with the potential risks in mind, and many types of threat models and risk analyses should be invoked at different stages of development. The goal is to prevent security compromises and to reduce the vulnerabilities and the possibility of data corruption. The controls can be preventive, detective, or corrective. They can come in the form of administrative and physical controls, but are usually more technical in this context.

The specific application controls depend upon the application itself, its objectives, the security goals of the developers, and the environment the application will be placed in. If an application is purely proprietary and will run only in closed, trusted environments, fewer security controls may be needed than those required for applications that will connect businesses over the Internet and provide financial transactions. The trick is to understand the security needs of an application, implement the right controls and mechanisms, thoroughly test the mechanisms and how they integrate into the application, follow structured development methodologies, and provide secure and reliable distribution methods. This can be harder than it sounds.

# Device vs. Software Security

Today, many security efforts look to solve security problems through devices such as firewalls, intrusion detection systems (IDSs), sensors, and vulnerability scanners. This reliance on devices occurs because networks—and how they are thought of—work on a basic outside and inside notion. The bad people and potential threats are on the outside, and what needs to be protected is on the inside. This notion has worked, to an extent, because networks were closed environments, which usually meant controlled environments. However, our environments then incorporated electronic data interchange (EDI), remote dial-in capabilities, Internet sites, and virtual private networks (VPNs). Now environments are incorporating wireless communication, instant messaging, and business-to-business (B2B) capabilities, which add complexity to the concept of us and them and inside and outside.

The division between software security and device security deals with providing security at the beginning stages of software development versus providing devices (firewalls, routers, ACLs, IDS, bastion hosts) that protect the perimeters of networks. The perimeter devices try to prevent attackers from exploiting the security holes that reside in the software. Firewalls and IDSs are studied and talked about within circles of security much more than inadvertent flaws in design and poorly written software. In reality, the flaws within the software cause a majority of the vulnerabilities in the first place. Several reasons explain why perimeter devices are more often considered than software development for security:

- In the past, it was not crucial to implement security during the software development stages; thus, many programmers do not practice these procedures.
- Many security professionals are not software developers.
- Many software developers do not have security as a main focus.
- Software vendors are trying to rush their products to market with their eyes set on functionality, not security.
- The computing community is used to receiving software with bugs and applying patches.

Finger pointing and quick judgments are neither useful nor necessarily fair at this stage of our computing evolution. Twenty years ago, mainframes had tight security because only a handful of people knew how to run them, users worked on computers (dumb terminals) that could not introduce malicious code to the mainframe, and environments were closed. The core protocols and framework were developed at a time when threats and attacks were not prevalent. There was no need for such stringent security. Then computer and software evolution took off, and the possibilities splintered into a thousand different directions. The high demand for computer technology and different types of software increased the demand for programmers, system designers, administrators, and engineers. This demand brought in a wave of people who had little experience. The lack of experience, the high change rate of technology, and the race to market add problems to security that are not always clearly understood. Although it is easy to blame the big software vendors in the sky for producing flawed or buggy software, this is driven by customer demand. Understanding how security works within programs, how programs integrate into environments, and how compromises take place will cause consumers to demand more security-oriented software and better programming and development practices.

This chapter is an attempt to show how to address security at its source, which is at the software and development level. This requires a shift from *reactive* to *proactive* actions toward security problems to ensure that they do not happen in the first place, or at least happen to a smaller extent. Figure 11-1 illustrates our current way of dealing with security issues.

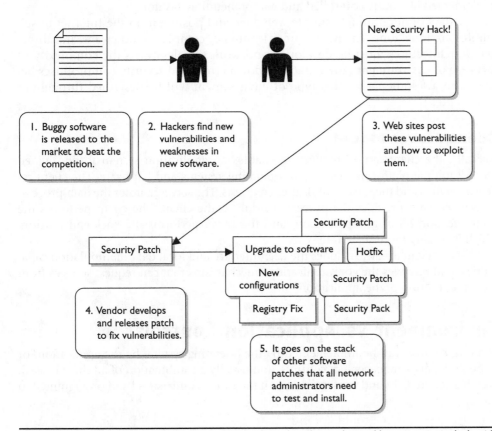

**Figure 11-1**    The usual trend of software being released to the market and how security is dealt with

# Different Environments Demand Different Security

Today, a network administrator is in an overwhelming position of having to integrate different applications and computer systems to keep up with her company's demand on expandable functionality and the new gee-whiz components that executives buy into and demand quick implementation of. This integration is further frustrated by the company's race to provide a well-known presence on the Internet by implementing web sites with the capabilities of taking online orders, storing credit card information, and setting up extranets with partners. This can quickly turn into a confusing ball of protocols, devices, interfaces, incompatibility issues, routing and switching techniques, telecommunications routines, and management procedures. It could make an administrator choose to buy some land in Montana and raise goats instead.

On top of this, security is expected, required, and depended upon. When security compromises creep in, the finger pointing starts, liability issues are tossed like hot potatoes, and people might even lose their jobs. An understanding of the environment, what is currently in it, and how it works is required so that the new technologies can be implemented in a more controlled and comprehendible fashion.

The days of developing a simple web page and posting it on the Internet to sell candles are long gone. Today, customer front-end, complex middleware, and three-tiered architectures must be developed and work seamlessly. As the complexity of this type of environment grows, tracking down errors and security compromises becomes an awesome task. (This type of environment will be described throughout this chapter.)

## Client/Server Model

Basically, the client/server architecture enables an application system to be divided across multiple platforms that vary in operating systems and hardware. The client requests services and the server fulfills these requests. The server handles the data-processing services and provides the processed result to the client. The client performs the front-end portion of an application, and the server performs the back-end portion, which is usually more labor intensive.

The front end usually includes the user interface and local data-manipulation capabilities, and provides the communications mechanisms that can request services from the server portion of the application.

# Environment vs. Application Controls

Software controls can be implemented by the operating system, by the application, or through database management controls, and usually a combination of all three is used. Each has its strengths and weaknesses, but if they are all understood and programmed to work in a concerted effort, then many different scenarios and types of compromises can be thwarted. One downside to relying mainly on operating system controls is that although they can control a subject's access to different objects and restrict the actions of that subject within the system, they do not necessarily restrict the subject's actions within an application. If an application has a security compromise that is created by the programming code, it is hard for the operating system to predict that this type of compromise could take place or to audit it once it does happen. A file system is a broad environment for many applications to work within. It is unfair to expect the operating system to understand all the nuances of different programs and their internal mechanisms.

On the other hand, application controls and database management controls are very specific to their needs and in the security compromises they understand. Although an application might be able to protect data by allowing only certain types of input and not allowing certain users to view data kept in sensitive database fields, it cannot prevent the user from deleting system files or inserting bogus data into the Address Resolution Protocol (ARP) table. Operating system and application controls have their place and limitations. The trick is to find out where one type of control stops so that the next type of control can be configured to kick into action.

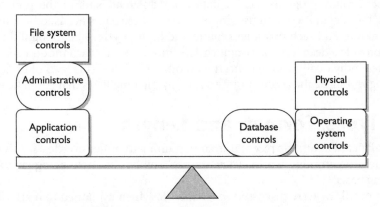

The different types of controls need to be understood and utilized to provide a balanced and useful security level.

Security has been mainly provided by environmental and perimeter devices rather than controls built into applications. The devices can cover a wide range of applications, can be controlled by a centralized management console, and are further away from application control. However, this approach does not always provide the necessary level of granularity, and it does not approach compromises that can take place because of problematic coding and programming routines. Firewalls and access control mechanisms can provide a level of protection by preventing attackers from exploiting buffer overflows, but the real protection happens at the core of the problem—proper software development and coding practices must be in place.

# Complexity of Functionality

Programming is a complex trade—the code itself, routine interaction, global and local variables, input received from other programs, output fed to different applications, attempts to envision future user inputs, calculations, and restrictions form a laundry list of possible negative security consequences. Many times, trying to account for all the what-ifs and programming on the side of caution can reduce the overall functionality of the application. As you limit the functionality and scope of an application, the market share and potential profitability of that program could be reduced. A balancing act always exists between functionality and security, and in the development world, functionality is usually deemed the most important.

So, programmers and application architects need to find a happy medium between the necessary functionality of the program, the security requirements, and the mechanisms that should be implemented to provide this security. This can add more complexity to an already complex task.

More than one road may lead to enlightenment, but as these roads increase in number, it is hard to know if a path will eventually lead you to bliss or to a fiery doom of unpleasantness. Many programs accept data from different parts of the program, other programs, the system itself, and user input. Each of these paths needs to be followed in a methodical way, and each possible scenario and input needs to be thought through and tested to provide a deep level of assurance. It is important that each module be capable of being tested individually and in concert with other modules. This level of understanding and testing will make the product more secure by catching flaws that could be exploited.

# Data Types, Format, and Length

We have all heard about the recent uproar pertaining to buffer overflows, as if they were new to the programming world. They are not new but are now being exploited on a reoccurring basis.

Buffer overflows were discussed in Chapter 5, which explained that attacks are carried out when the application does not check the length of input that is actually being accepted. Extra data could be executed in a privileged mode that would enable an attacker to take control of the system. If a programmer wrote a program that expected the input length to be 5KB, then this needs to be part of the code so that the right amount of buffer space is available to hold this data when it actually comes in. However, if that program does not make sure the 5KB is accepted, and only 5KB is accepted, an evildoer can input the first 5KB for the expected data to process, and then another 50KB containing malicious instructions that can also be processed by the CPU.

Length is not the only thing programmers need to be worried about when it comes to accepting input data. Data also needs to be in the right format and data type. If the program is expecting alpha ASCII characters, it should not accept hexadecimal or UNICODE values.

The accepted value also needs to be reasonable. This means that if an application asks Stacy to enter the amount she would like to transfer from her checking account to her savings account, she should not be able to enter "Bob." This means the data that is accepted by the program must be in the correct format (numbers versus alphabet characters), but parameters also need to be in place to watch for bogus entries so that errors can be stopped at their origin instead of being passed to calculations and logic procedures.

These examples are extremely simplistic compared with what programmers have to face in the real programming world. However, they are presented to show that software needs to be developed to accept the correct data types, format, and length of input data for security and functionality purposes.

# Implementation and Default Issues

*If I have not said "yes," then the answer is "no."*

As many people in the computer field know, out-of-the-box implementations are usually far from secure. Most security has to be configured and turned on after installation; not being aware of this can be dangerous for the inexperienced IT person. Windows NT has received its share of criticism for lack of security, but the platform can be secured in many ways. It just comes out of the box in an insecure state, because settings have to be configured to properly integrate into different environments, and this is a friendlier way of installing the product for users. For example, if Mike is installing a new software package that continually throws messages of "Access Denied" when he is attempting to configure it to interoperate with other applications and systems, his patience might wear thin, and he might decide to hate that vendor for years to come because of the stress and confusion inflicted upon him.

Yet again, we are at a hard place for developers and architects. When a security application or device is installed, it should default to "No Access." This means that when Laurel installs a packet-filter firewall, it should not allow any packets to pass into the network that were not specifically granted access. However, this requires Laurel to know how to configure the firewall for it to ever be useful. There is a fine balance between security, functionality, and user-friendliness. If an application is extremely user-friendly, it is probably not as secure. For an application to be user-friendly, it usually requires a lot of extra coding for potential user errors, dialog boxes, wizards, and step-by-step instructions. This extra coding can result in bloated code that can create unforeseeable compromises. So vendors have a hard time winning, but they usually keep making money as they keep trying.

## Implementation

Implementation errors and misconfigurations are common issues that cause a majority of the security issues in networked environments. Many people do not realize that various services are enabled when a system is installed. These services can provide evildoers with information that can be used during an attack. Many services provide an actual way into the environment itself. NetBIOS services can be enabled to permit sharing resources in Windows environments, and remote procedure call (RPC) services, which let remote users run command shells, and other programs can be enabled with no restrictions. Many systems have File Transfer Protocol (FTP), Telnet, and Internet Relay Chat (IRC) services enabled that are not being used and have no real safety measures in place. Some of these services are enabled by default, so when an administrator installs an operating system and does not check these services to properly restrict or disable them, they are available for attackers to uncover and use.

Because vendors have user-friendliness and user functionality in mind, the product will usually be installed with defaults that provide no or very low security protection. It would be very hard for vendors to know the security levels required in all the environments that the product will be installed in, so they usually do not attempt it. It is up to the person installing the product to learn how to properly configure the settings to achieve the necessary level of protection.

Another problem in implementation and security is the number of unpatched systems. Once security issues are identified, vendors develop patches to address and fix these security holes. However, they often do not get installed on the systems that are vulnerable. The reasons for this vary: an administrator may not keep up-to-date on the recent security vulnerabilities and patches, may not fully understand the importance of these patches, or may be afraid that the patches will cause other problems. All of these reasons are quite common, but they all have the same result—insecure systems. Many vulnerabilities that are exploited have had patches developed and released months or years ago.

It is unfortunate that adding security (or service) patches can adversely affect other mechanisms within the system. The patches should be tested for these types of activities before they are applied to production servers and workstations, to help prevent service disruptions that can affect network and employee productivity.

## Failure States

Many circumstances are unpredictable and are therefore hard to plan for. However, unpredictable situations can be planned for in a general sense, instead of trying to plan and code for every situation. If an application fails for any reason, it should return to a safe and more secure state. This could require the application to shut down or present the user with a logon screen to start the application from its initialization state. This is why some systems "blue-screen" and/or restart. When this occurs, something is going on within the system that is unrecognized or unsafe, so the system dumps its memory contents and starts all over.

Different system states were discussed in Chapter 5, which described how processes can be executed in a privileged or user state. If an application fails and is executing in a privileged state, these processes should be shut down properly and released to ensure that disrupting a system could not provide compromises that could be exploited. If a privileged process does not shut down properly and it stays active, an attacker can figure out how to access the system, using this process, in a privileged state. This means that the attacker could have administrative or root access to a system, which opens the door for more severe destruction.

## Database Management

Databases have a long history of storing important intellectual property and items that are considered valuable and proprietary to companies. Because of this, they usually live in an environment of mystery to all but the database and network administrators. The less anyone knows about the databases, the better. Users usually access databases indirectly through a client interface, and their actions are restricted to ensure the confidentiality and integrity of the data held within the database and the structure of the database itself.

**NOTE** A database management system (DBMS) is a suite of programs used to manage large sets of structured data with ad hoc query capabilities for many types of users. These can also control the security parameters of the database.

This norm is changing as companies run to connect their networks to the Internet, which usually includes indirect access to a back-end database. In the past, employees accessed customer information held in databases instead of customers accessing it themselves. Today, many companies allow their customers to access data in their databases through a browser. The browser makes a connection to the company's middleware, which then connects them to the back-end database. This adds levels of complexity, and the database will be accessed in new and unprecedented ways.

One example is in the banking world, where online banking is all the rage. Many financial institutions want to keep up with the times and add the services they think their customers will want. But online banking is not just another service like being able to order checks. Most banks work in closed (or semiclosed) environments, and opening their environments to the Internet is a huge undertaking. The perimeter network needs to be secured, middleware software has to be developed or purchased, and the database should be behind one, preferably two, firewalls. Many times, components in the business application tier are used to extract data from the databases and process the customer requests.

Access control can be restricted by only allowing roles to interact with the database. The database administrator can define specific roles that are allowed to access the database. Each role will have assigned rights and permissions, and customers and employees are then ported into these roles. Any user who is not within one of these roles is denied access. This means that if an attacker compromises the firewall and other perimeter network protection mechanisms and then is able to make requests to the database, if he is not in one of the predefined roles, the database is still safe. This process streamlines access control and ensures that no users or evildoers can access the database directly, but must access it indirectly through a role account. Figure 11-2 illustrates these concepts.

## Database Management Software

A *database* is a collection of data stored in a meaningful way that enables multiple users and applications to access, view, and modify data as needed. Databases are managed with software that provides these types of capabilities. It also enforces access control restrictions, provides data integrity and redundancy, and sets up different procedures for data manipulation. This software is referred to as a *database management system (DBMS)* and is usually controlled by a database administrator. Databases not only store data, but also process data and represent it in a more usable and logical form. DBMSs interface with programs, users, and data within the database. They help us store, organize, and retrieve information effectively and efficiently.

**Figure 11-2**   One type of database security is to employ roles.

A database is the mechanism that provides structure for data that is collected. The actual specifications of the structure may be different per database implementation, because different organizations or departments work with different types of data and need to perform diverse functions upon that information. There may be different workloads, relationships between the data, platforms, performance requirements, and security goals.

Because the needs and requirements for databases vary, different data models can be implemented that align with different business and organizational needs.

## Database Models

*Ohhh, that database model is very pretty, indeed. Response: You have problems.*

The database model defines the relationships between different data elements, dictates how data can be accessed, and defines acceptable operations, the type of integrity offered, and how the data is organized. A model provides a formal method of representing data in a conceptual form and provides the necessary means of manipulating the data held within the database. There are several types of data models for databases; we will only touch on a few of them.

A *relational data model* uses attributes (columns) and tuples (rows) to contain and organize information (see Figure 11-3). The relational model is the most widely used method of organizing databases today. It presents information in the form of tables. A relational database is composed of two-dimensional tables, and each table contains unique rows, columns, and cells (the intersection of a row and a column). A primary key is a field that links all the data within a record to a corresponding value. For example, in the table in Figure 11-3, the primary keys are Product G345 and Product G978. When an application or another record refers to this primary key, it is actually referring to all the data within this one row.

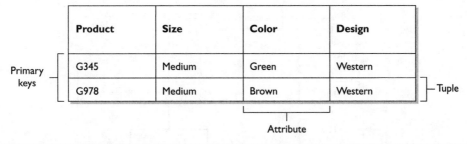

**Figure 11-3**  Relational databases hold data in table structures.

A *hierarchical data model* (see Figure 11-4) combines records and fields that are related in a logical tree structure. The structure and relationship between the data elements are different from those in a relational database.

The parents can have one child, many children, or no children. The tree structure contains branches, and each branch has a number of leaves, or data fields. These databases have well-defined, prespecified access paths, but they are not as flexible in relating information as a relational database. Hierarchical databases are useful for mapping one-to-many relationships. LDAP uses this model type.

A *distributed data model* has data stored in more than one database, but it is logically connected. Different databases may live at different places on a network or reside in totally different networks. Because they are logically connected, the users see the

## Database Jargon
The following are some key database terms:

- **Record**   Collection of related data items
- **File**   Collection of records of the same type
- **Database**   Cross-referenced collection of files
- **DBMS**   Manages and controls the database
- **Base relation**   A table stored in a database
- **Tuple**   A row in a two-dimensional database
- **Attribute**   A column in a two-dimensional database
- **Primary key**   Columns that make each row unique; every row of a table must include primary key
- **View**   Virtual relation defined by the database to keep subjects from viewing certain data
- **Foreign key**   Attribute of one table that is the primary key of another table
- **Cell**   Intersection of a row and column
- **Schema**   Holds data that describes a database
- **Data dictionary**   Central repository of data elements and their relationships

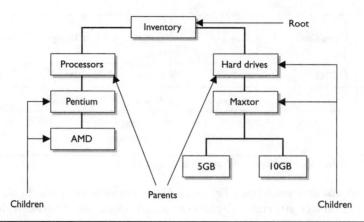

**Figure 11-4** Hierarchical databases use a tree structure and a parent/child relationship.

database as one full entity, instead of several entities. When users access data, they do not need to know which database they are accessing; one database may transfer a user to another database, which is transparent to the user.

This model enables different databases to be managed by different administrators, although one person or group must manage the entire logical database. This may be useful if each database contains information that is specialized, but the complexity of load balancing, fault tolerance, and shifting of users is quite high.

An *object-oriented database* is designed to handle a variety of data (images, audio, documents, video). The objects within the database contain information that is used to access the objects actually containing these different data types and defines their properties. An object-oriented database is more dynamic in nature than a relational database, because objects can be created when needed and the data *and* procedure go with the object when it is requested. In a relational database, an application uses its procedures to obtain data from the database. The database does not actually provide procedures, as object-oriented databases do. The object-oriented database has classes to define the attributes and procedures of its objects.

Object-oriented databases can be used to dynamically build different web pages for different users depending upon their requests and input to a particular web site. The objects are used to build the page, and the procedures within the objects dictate how the data within the objects will actually be used to perform their tasks.

## Database Interface Languages

Data is of no use if you can't get to it and do something with it. Applications need to be able to obtain and interact with the information stored in databases. They need some type of interface and communication mechanism. The following sections address some of these interface languages:

- **Open Database Connectivity (ODBC)**   An application programming interface (API) that allows an application to communicate with a database either locally or remotely. The application sends requests to the ODBC, which in turn translates them into database commands. ODBC tracks down the necessary database driver for the application.

- **Object Linking and Embedding Database (OLE DB)**   Separates data into components that run as middleware on a client or server. It provides a low-level interface to link information across different databases and provides access to data no matter where it is located or how it is formatted.

- **ActiveX Data Objects (ADO)**   An API that allows applications to access back-end database systems. It is a set of ODBC interfaces that exposes the functionality of a database through accessible objects. ADO uses the OLE DB interface to connect with the database and can be developed with many different scripting languages.

- **Java Database Connectivity (JDBC)**   An API that allows a Java application to communicate with a database. The application can connect through ODBC or directly to the database.

- **Extensible Markup Language (XML)**   A standard for structuring data so that it can be easily shared by applications using web technologies. It is a markup language that is self-defining and provides a lot of flexibility in how information within the database is presented. The web browser interprets the XML tags.

## Relational Database Components

Like all software, databases are built with programming languages. Most database languages include a *data definition language (DDL)*, which defines the schema; a *data manipulation language (DML)*, which examines and manipulates the data within the database; a *data control language (DCL)*, which defines the internal organization of the database; and an ad hoc *query language (QL)*, which enables users to make queries and access the data within the database.

Each type of database model may have many other differences, which vary from vendor to vendor. Most, however, contain the following basic core functionalities:

- **Data definition language (DDL)**   Defines the structure and schema of the database. The *structure* could mean the table size, key placement, views, and data element relationship. The *schema* describes the type of data that will be held and manipulated, and its properties. It defines the structure of the database, access operations, and integrity procedures.

- **Data manipulation language (DML)**   Contains all the commands that enable a user to view, manipulate, and use the database (`view`, `add`, `modify`, `sort`, and `delete` commands).

- **Query language (QL)**   Enables users to make requests of the database.

- **Report generator**   Produces printouts of data in a user-defined manner.

## Data Dictionary

*Will the data dictionary explain all the definitions of database jargon to me? Response: Wrong dictionary.*

A *data dictionary* is a central repository of data elements and their relationships. It stores critical information about data usage, data relationships, data sources, and data formats. It is a tool used to centrally manage parts of a database by controlling data

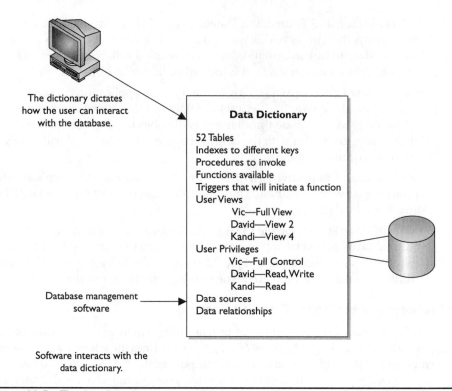

The dictionary dictates how the user can interact with the database.

**Data Dictionary**

52 Tables
Indexes to different keys
Procedures to invoke
Functions available
Triggers that will initiate a function
User Views
      Vic—Full View
      David—View 2
      Kandi—View 4
User Privileges
      Vic—Full Control
      David—Read, Write
      Kandi—Read
Data sources
Data relationships

Database management software

Software interacts with the data dictionary.

**Figure 11-5** The data dictionary is a centralized program that contains information about a database.

about the data (referred to as *metadata*) within the database. It provides a cross-reference between groups of data elements and the databases.

A data dictionary is a central collection of data element definitions, schema objects, and reference keys. The schema objects can contain tables, views, indexes, procedures, functions, and triggers. A data dictionary can contain the default values for columns, integrity information, the names of users, the privileges and roles for users, and auditing information.

The database management software creates and reads the data dictionary to ascertain that schema objects exist and checks to see if specific users have the process access rights to view them (see Figure 11-5). When users look at the database, they can be restricted by specific views. The different view settings for each user are held within the data dictionary. When new tables, new rows, or new schema are added, the data dictionary is updated to reflect this.

## Primary vs. Foreign Key

The primary key is an identifier of a row and it must be unique. Each row must have a primary key. When a user makes a request to view a record, the database tracks this record by its unique primary key. If the primary key were not unique, the database would not know which record to present to the user. In the following illustration, the primary keys for Table A are the dogs' names.

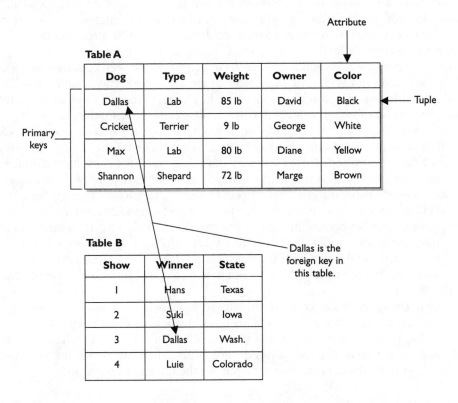

A primary key is different from a foreign key, although they are closely related. If an attribute in one table has a value matching the primary key in another table, this attribute is considered a foreign key. This foreign key is not necessarily the primary key in its current table; it only has to contain the same information that is held in another table's primary key. In the following illustration, a primary key for Table A is Dallas. Because Table B has an attribute that contains the same data as this primary key and there is a relationship set up between these two keys, it is referred to as a foreign key. This is another way for the database to track relationships between data that it houses.

## Integrity

*You just wrote over my table! Response: Well, my information is more important than yours.*

Like other resources within a network, a database can run into **concurrency** problems. Concurrency ensures that different subjects receive the most up-to-date information and that the database can properly handle various requests at the same time. As an example of a concurrency problem, suppose that a group uses one price sheet to know how many supplies to order for the next week and also to calculate the expected profit. If Dan and Elizabeth copy this price sheet from the file server to their workstations, they each have a copy of the original file. Suppose that Dan changes the stock level of computer books from 120 to 5, because they sold 115 in the last three days. He also uses the current prices listed in the price sheet to estimate his expected profits for the next week. Elizabeth reduces the price on several software packages and sees that the stock level of computer books is still over 100, so she chooses not to order any more for next week. Dan and Elizabeth do not communicate this different information to each other, but place it on this price sheet for everyone to view and use.

Dan copies his changes back to the file server, and then 30 seconds later Elizabeth copies her changes over Dan's changes. So, the file only reflects Elizabeth's changes. Because they did not synchronize their changes, they are both now using incorrect data. Dan's profit estimates are off because he does not know that Elizabeth reduced the prices, and next week Elizabeth will have no computer books because she did not know that the stock level had dropped to five.

The same thing happens in databases. If controls are not in place, two users can access and modify the same data at the same time, which can be detrimental to a dynamic environment. To ensure that concurrency problems do not exist, processes can **lock** tables within a database, make changes, and then release the software lock. The next process that accesses the table will then have the updated information. Locking ensures that two processes do not access the same table at the same time. Pages, tables, rows, and fields can be locked to ensure that updates to data happen one at a time, which enables each process and subject to work with correct and accurate information.

Database software performs three main types of integrity services: semantic, referential, and entity. A *semantic integrity* mechanism makes sure that structural and semantic rules are enforced. These rules pertain to data types, logical values, uniqueness constraints, and operations that could adversely affect the structure of the database. A database has *referential integrity* if all foreign keys reference existing primary keys. There should be a mechanism in place that ensures that no foreign key contains a reference to a primary key of a nonexisting record, or a null value. *Entity integrity* guarantees that the tuples are uniquely identified by primary key values. In the previous illustration, the primary keys are the names of the dogs. For the sake of entity integrity, every tuple must contain one primary key. If it does not have a primary key, it cannot be referenced by the database.

The database must not contain unmatched foreign key values. Every foreign key refers to an existing primary key. In the previous illustration, if the foreign key in Table B is Dallas, then the primary key that it is related to in Table A must have the same value, which is Dallas. If these values do not match, then their relationships can be broken, and again the database cannot reference the information properly.

Other configurable operations are available to help protect the integrity of the data within a database. These operations are rollbacks, commits, savepoints, and checkpoints.

The *rollback* is an operation that ends a current transaction and cancels the current changes to the database. These changes could have taken place with the data itself or with schema changes that were typed in. When a rollback operation is executed, the changes are cancelled, and the database returns to its previous state. A rollback can take place if the database has some type of unexpected glitch or if outside entities disrupt its processing sequence. Instead of transmitting and posting partial or corrupt information, the database will roll back to its original state and log these errors and actions so that they can be reviewed later.

The *commit* operation completes a transaction and executes all changes that were just made by the user. As its name indicates, once the commit command is executed, the changes are committed and reflected in the database. These changes can be made to data or schema information. By committing these changes, they are then available to all other applications and users. If a user attempts to commit a change and it cannot complete correctly, a rollback is performed. This ensures that partial changes do not take place and that data is not corrupted.

*Savepoints* are used to make sure that if a system failure occurs, or if an error is detected, the database can attempt to return to a point before the system crashed or hiccupped. For a conceptual example, say Dave typed, "Jeremiah was a bullfrog. He was <savepoint> a good friend of mine." (The system inserted a savepoint.) Then a freak storm came through and rebooted the system. When Dave got back into the database application, he might see "Jeremiah was a bullfrog. He was," but the rest was lost. Therefore, the savepoint saved some of his work. The databases and other applications will use this tool to attempt to restore the user's work and the state of the database after a glitch, but some glitches are just too large and invasive to overcome.

Savepoints are easy to implement within databases, but a balance has to be struck between too many and not enough savepoints. Having too many savepoints can degrade the performance of the database, whereas not having enough savepoints runs the risk of losing data and decreasing user productivity because the lost data would have to be reentered. Savepoints can be initiated by a time interval, a specific action by the user, or the number of transactions or changes made to the database. For example, a database can set a savepoint for every 15 minutes, every 20 transactions completed, each time a user gets to the end of a record, or every 12 changes made to the databases.

So a savepoint restores data by enabling the user to go back in time before the system crashed or hiccupped. This can reduce frustration and help us all live in harmony.

**NOTE** Checkpoints are very similar to savepoints. When the database software fills up a certain amount of memory, a checkpoint is initiated, which saves the data from the memory segment to a temporary file. If a glitch is experienced, the software will try to use this information to restore the user's working environment to its previous state.

## Reference

- **Security Issues in SQL**   www.mirrors.wiretapped.net/security/info/reference/ nist/special-publications/sp-800-8.txt

## Database Security Issues

*Oh, I know this and know that. Now I know the big secret! Response: Then I am changing the big secret—hold on.*

The two main database security issues this section addresses are aggregation and inference. *Aggregation* happens when a user does not have the clearance or permission to access specific information, but she does have the permission to access components of this information. She can then figure out the rest and obtain restricted information. She can learn of information from different sources and combine it to learn something that she does not have the clearance to know.

 **NOTE**   Aggregation is the act of combining information from separate sources. The combination of the information forms new information, which the subject does not have the necessary rights to access. The combined information has a sensitivity that is greater than that of the individual parts.

The following is a silly conceptual example. Let's say a database administrator does not want anyone in the Users group to be able to figure out a specific sentence, so he segregates the sentence into components and restricts the Users group from accessing it, as represented in Figure 11-6. However, Emily can access components A, C, and F. Because she is particularly bright, she figures out the sentence and now knows the restricted secret.

To prevent aggregation, the subject, and any application or process acting on the subject's behalf, needs to be prevented from gaining access to the whole collection, including the independent components. The objects can be placed into containers,

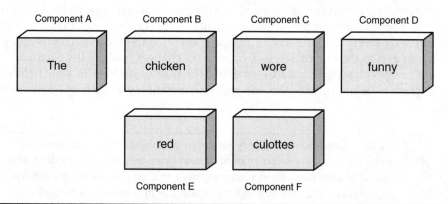

**Figure 11-6**   Because Emily has access to components A, C, and F, she can figure out the secret sentence through aggregation.

which are classified at a higher level to prevent access from subjects with lower-level permissions or clearances. A subject's queries can also be tracked, and context-dependent access control can be enforced. This would keep a history of the objects that a subject has accessed and restrict an access attempt if there is an indication that an aggregation attack is under way.

The other security issue is *inference*, which is similar to aggregation. The inference problem happens when a subject deduces, or figures out, the full story from the pieces he learned of through aggregation. This is seen when data at a lower security level indirectly portrays data at a higher level.

 **NOTE**  Inference is the ability to derive information that is not explicitly available.

For example, if a clerk were restricted from knowing the planned movements of troops based in a specific country, but did have access to food shipment requirements forms and tent allocation documents, he could figure out that the troops were moving to a specific place because that is where the food and tents are being shipped. The food shipment and tent allocation documents were classified as confidential, and the troop movement was classified as top secret. Because of the varying classifications, the clerk could access and ascertain top-secret information he was not supposed to know.

The trick is to prevent the subject, or any application or process acting on behalf of that subject, from indirectly gaining access to the inferable information. This problem is usually dealt with in the development of the database by implementing context-dependent access control rules. Such rules track the subject's query requests and restrict patterns that represent inference.

Database security takes a different approach than operating system security. In an operating system, the identity and authentication of the subject control access. This is done through access control lists (ACLs), capability tables, roles, and security labels. The operating system only makes decisions about whether a subject can access a file; it does not make this decision based on the contents of the file itself. If Mitch can access file A, it does not matter if that file contains information about a cookie recipe or secret information from the Cold War. On the other hand, database security does look at the contents of a file when it makes an access control decision, which is referred to as *content-dependent access control*. This type of access control increases processing overhead, but it provides higher granular control.

Common attempts to prevent inference attacks are cell suppression, partitioning the database, and noise and perturbation. *Cell suppression* is a technique used to hide or not show specific cells that contain information that could be used in inference attacks. *Partitioning* a database involves dividing the database into different parts, which makes it much harder for an unauthorized individual to find connecting pieces of data that can be brought together and other information that can be deduced or uncovered. *Noise and perturbation* is a technique of inserting bogus information in the hopes of misdirecting an attacker or confusing the matter enough that the actual attack will not be fruitful.

Often, security is not integrated into the planning and development of a database. Security is an afterthought and a trusted front end is developed to be used with the database instead. This approach is limited in the granularity of security and in the types of security functions that can take place.

A common theme in security is a balance between effective security and functionality. In many cases, the more you secure something, the less functionality you have. Although this could be the desired result, it is important to not impede user productivity when security is being introduced.

## Database Views

*Don't show your information to everybody, only a select few.*

Databases can permit one group, or a specific user, to see certain information while restricting another group from viewing it altogether. This functionality happens through the use of *database views*. If a database administrator wants to allow middle management members to see their departments' profits and expenses but not show them the whole company's profits, she can implement views. Senior management would be given all views, which contain all the departments' and the company's profit and expense values, whereas each individual manager would only be able to view his or her department values.

Like operating systems, databases can employ discretionary access control (DAC) and mandatory access control (MAC) (explained in Chapter 4). Views can be displayed according to group membership, user rights, or security labels. If a DAC system were being employed, then groups and users could be granted access through views based on their identity, authentication, and authorization. If a MAC system were in place, then groups and users would be granted access based on their security clearance and the data's classification level.

## Polyinstantiation

*Polyinstantiation. Response: Gesundheit.*

Sometimes a company does not want users at one level to access and modify data at a higher level. There are different ways of handling this type of situation. One approach denies access when a lower-level user attempts to access a higher-level object. However, this gives away information indirectly by telling the lower-level entity that something sensitive lives inside that object at that level.

Another way of dealing with this issue is *polyinstantiation*. This enables a relation to contain multiple tuples with the same primary keys, with each instance distinguished by a security level. When this information is inserted into a database, lower-level subjects need to be restricted from it. Instead of just restricting access, another set of data is created to fool the lower-level subjects into thinking that the information actually means something else. For example, if a naval base has a cargo shipment of weapons going from Delaware to the Ukraine via the *Oklahoma* ship, this type of information could be classified as top secret. Only the subjects with the security clearance of top secret and above should know this information, so a dummy file is created that states that the *Oklahoma* is carrying a shipment from Delaware to Africa containing food, and it is given a security clearance of unclassified, as shown in Table 11-1. It will be obvious

| Level | Ship | Cargo | Origin | Destination |
|-------|------|-------|--------|-------------|
| Top Secret | Oklahoma | Weapons | Delaware | Ukraine |
| Unclassified | Oklahoma | Food | Delaware | Africa |

**Table 11-1** Example of Polyinstantiation to Provide Illusion of a Cover Story to Subjects at Lower Security Level

that the *Oklahoma* is gone, but individuals at lower security levels will think that the ship is on its way to Africa, instead of to the Ukraine. This will also make sure that no one at a lower level will try to commit the *Oklahoma* for any other missions. The lower-level subjects know that the *Oklahoma* is not available, and they will use other ships for cargo shipments.

 **NOTE** Polyinstantiation is a process of interactively producing more detailed versions of objects by populating variables with different values or other variables. It is often used to prevent inference attacks.

In this example, polyinstantiation was used to create two versions of the same object so that the lower-level subjects will not know the true information, and it stops them from attempting to use or change that data in any way. It is a way of providing a cover story for the entities that do not have the necessary security level to know the truth. This is just one example of how polyinstantiation can be used. Polyinstantiation is not strictly related to security, although that is the most common use for it. Whenever a copy of an object is created and populated with different data, meaning two instances of the same object have different attributes, polyinstantiation is in place.

## Online Transaction Processing
*What if our databases get overwhelmed? Response: OLTP to the rescue!*

**Online transaction processing (OLTP)** is usually used when databases are clustered to provide fault tolerance and higher performance. OLTP provides mechanisms that watch for problems and deal with them appropriately when they do occur. For example, if a process stops functioning, the monitor mechanisms within OLTP can detect this and attempt to restart the process. If the process cannot be restarted, then the transaction that was taking place will be rolled back to ensure that no data is corrupted or that only part of a transaction happens. Any erroneous or invalid transactions that are detected should be written to a transaction log and to a report log to be reviewed at a later time.

OLTP will load balance incoming requests if necessary. This means that if requests to update databases increase, and the performance of one system decreases because of the large volume, OLTP can move some of these requests to other systems. This makes sure that all requests are handled and that the user, or whoever is making the requests, does not have to wait a long time for the transaction to complete.

When there is more than one database, it is important that they all contain the same information. Consider this scenario—Katie goes to the bank and withdraws $6500 from her $10,000 checking account. Database A receives the request and records a new checking account balance of $3500, but database B does not get updated; it still shows a balance of $10,000. Then, Katie makes a request to check the balance on her checking account, but that request gets sent to database B, which returns inaccurate information because the withdrawal transaction was never carried over to this database. OLTP will make sure that a transaction is not complete until *all databases receive and reflect this change*. This is a *two-phase commit* service.

OLTP records transactions as they occur (in real time), which usually updates more than one database in a distributed environment. This type of complexity can introduce many integrity threats, so the database software should implement the characteristics of what's known as the ACID test:

- **Atomicity**   Divides transactions into units of work and ensures that all modifications take effect or none takes effect. Either the changes are committed or the database is rolled back.

- **Consistency**   A transaction must follow the integrity policy developed for that particular database and ensure that all data is consistent in the different databases.

- **Isolation**   Transactions execute in isolation until completed, without interacting with other transactions. The results of the modification are not available until the transaction is completed.

- **Durability**   Once the transaction is verified as accurate on all systems, it is committed, and the databases cannot be rolled back.

 **TIP**   Atomicity is used so that if one step in the transaction fails, subsequent steps are not processed.

## Data Warehousing and Data Mining

*Data warehousing* combines data from multiple databases or data sources into a large database for the purpose of providing more extensive information retrieval and data analysis. Data from different databases is extracted and transferred to a central data storage device called a warehouse. This enables users to query one entity rather than accessing and querying different databases.

Data warehousing is not simply a process of mirroring data from different databases and presenting the data in one place. It is a method of selecting useful information that is then processed and presented in a more useful and understandable way. Related data is summarized and correlated before it is presented to the user. Instead of having every piece of data presented, the user is given data in a more abridged form that best fits her needs.

Although this provides easier access and control, because the data warehouse is in one place, it also requires more stringent security. If an intruder were to get into the data warehouse, he could access all of the company's information at once.

*Data mining* is the process of massaging the data held in the data warehouse into more useful information. Data-mining tools are used to find an association and correlation in data to produce *metadata*. Metadata can show previously unseen relationships between individual subsets of information. It can show abnormal patterns that were not previously apparent. A simplistic example in which data mining could be useful is in detecting insurance fraud. Suppose that the information, claims, and specific habits of millions of customers are kept in a database, or warehouse, and a mining tool is used to look for certain patterns in claims. It might find that each time John Smith moved, he had an insurance claim two to three months following the move. If he moved in 1967 and two months later had a suspicious fire, then moved in 1973 and had a motorcycle stolen three months after that, and then moved again in 1984 and had a burglar break-in two months afterward, a pattern arises. This might be hard for people to manually catch because he had different insurance agents over the years, the files were just updated and not reviewed, or the files were not kept in a centralized place for agents to review.

Data mining can look at complex data and simplify it by using fuzzy logic, a set theory, and expert systems to perform the mathematical functions and look for patterns in data that are not so apparent. (See Figure 11-7.) In many ways, the metadata is more valuable than the data it was derived from; thus, it must be highly protected. (Fuzzy logic and expert systems are discussed later in the chapter, in the "Artificial Neural Networks" section.)

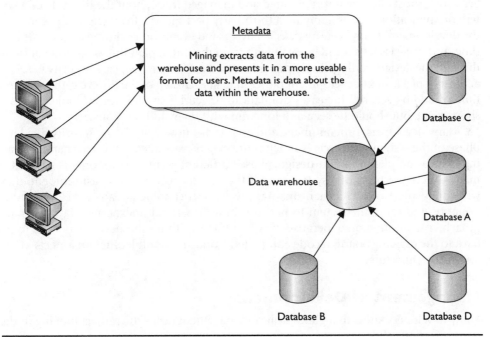

**Figure 11-7** Mining tools are used to identify patterns and relationships in data warehouses.

**NOTE** Data mining is the process of analyzing a database using tools that look for trends, correlations, relationships, and anomalies without having the knowledge of the meaning of the data. Metadata is the result of storing data within a database and mining the data with tools. Data goes into a database and metadata comes out of the database.

Data mining is also known as *knowledge discovery in database (KDD)*, and is a combination of techniques to identify valid and useful patterns. Different types of data can have various interrelationships, and the method used depends on the type of data and patterns that are sought. The following are three approaches used in KDD systems to uncover these patterns:

- **Classification**   Groups together data according to shared similarities.
- **Probabilistic**   Identifies data interdependencies and applies probabilities to their relationships.
- **Statistical**   Identifies relationships between data elements and uses rule discovery.

# System Development

Security is most effective if it is planned and managed throughout the life cycle of a system or application, versus applying a third-party package as a front end at the end after the development. Many security risks, analyses, and events occur during a product's lifetime, and these issues should be dealt with from the initial planning stage and continue through the design, coding, implementation, and operational stages. If security is added at the end of a project development rather than at each step of the life cycle, the cost and time of adding security increases dramatically. Security should not be looked at as a short sprint, but should be seen as a long run with many hills and obstacles.

Many developers, programmers, and architects know that adding security at a later phase of the system's life cycle is much more expensive and complicated than integrating it into the planning and design phase. Different security components can affect many different aspects of a system, and if they are thrown in at the last moment, they will surely affect other mechanisms negatively, restrict some already developed functionality, and cause the system to perform in unusual and unexpected ways. This approach costs more money because of the number of times the developers have to go back to the drawing board, recode completed work, and rethink different aspects of the system's architecture.

## Management of Development

Many developers know that good project management keeps the project moving in the right direction, allocates the necessary resources, provides the necessary information, and plans for the worst and hopes for the best. Project management is an important part of product development, and security management is an important part of project management.

A security plan should be drawn up at the beginning of a development project and integrated into the functional plan to ensure that security is not overlooked. The first plan is broad, covers a wide base, and refers to documented references for more detailed information. The references could include computer standards (RFCs, IEEE standards, and best practices), documents developed in previous projects, security policies, accreditation statements, incident-handling plans, and national or international guidelines (Orange Book, Red Book, and Common Criteria). This makes the plan easier to read and more usable.

The security plan should have a lifetime of its own. It will need to be added to, subtracted from, and explained in more detail as the project continues. It is important to keep it up-to-date for future reference. It is always easy to lose track of actions, activities, and decisions once a large and complex project gets underway.

The security plan and project management activities may likely be audited so that security-related decisions can be understood. When assurance in the system needs to be guaranteed, indicating that security was fully considered in each phase of the life cycle, the procedures, development, decisions, and activities that took place during the project will be reviewed. The documentation must accurately reflect how the system or product was built and how it operates once implemented into an environment.

## Life-Cycle Phases

*There is a time to live, a time to die, a time to love... Response: And a time to shut up.*

Several types of models are used for system and application development, which include varying life cycles. This section outlines the core components that are common to all of them. Each model basically accomplishes the same thing; the main difference is how the development and lifetime of a system is broken into sections.

A project may start with a good idea, only to have the programmers and engineers just wing it; or, the project may be carefully thought out and structured to follow the necessary life cycles, and the programmers and engineers may stick to the plan. The first option may seem more fun in the beginning, because the team can skip stuffy requirements, blow off documentation, and get the product out the door in a shorter time and under budget. However, the team that takes its time to think through all the scenarios of each phase of the life cycle would actually have more fun, because its product would be more sound and more trusted by the market, and the team would make more money in the long run and would not need to chaotically develop several service and security patches to fix problems missed the first time around.

The different models integrate the following phases in one fashion or another:

- Project initiation
- Functional design analysis and planning
- System design specifications
- Software development
- Installation/implementation
- Operational/maintenance
- Disposal

Security is not listed as an individual bullet point because it should be embedded throughout all phases. Addressing security issues after the product is released costs a lot more money than addressing it during the development of the product. Functionality is the main force driving product development, and several considerations need to take place within that realm, but this section addresses the *security* issues that need to be examined at each phase of the product's life cycle.

## Project Initiation
*So what are we building and why?*

This is the phase when everyone involved attempts to understand why the project is needed and what the scope of the project entails. Either a specific customer needs a new system or application or a demand for the product exists in the market. During this phase, the project management team examines the characteristics of the system and proposed functionality, brainstorming sessions take place, and obvious restrictions are reviewed.

A conceptual definition of the project needs to be initiated and developed to ensure that everyone is on the right page and that this is a proper product to develop that will be, hopefully, profitable. This phase could include evaluating products that are currently on the market and identifying any demands that are not being met by current vendors. It could also be a direct request for a specific product from a current or future customer.

In either case, because this is for a specific client or market, an initial study of the product needs to be started, and a high-level proposal should be drafted that outlines the necessary resources for the project and the predicted timeline of development. The estimated profit expected from the product also needs to be conducted. This information is submitted to senior management, who will determine whether the next phase should begin or further information is required.

In this phase, the user needs are identified and basic security objectives of the product are acknowledged. It must be determined if the product will be processing sensitive data, and if so, the levels of sensitivity involved should be defined. An initial risk analysis should be initiated that evaluates threats and vulnerabilities to estimate the cost/benefit ratios of the different security countermeasures. Issues pertaining to security integrity, confidentiality, and availability need to be addressed. The level of each security attribute should be focused upon so that a clear direction of security controls can begin to take shape.

A basic security framework is designed for the project to follow, and risk management processes are established. Risk management will continue throughout the lifetime of the project. Risk information may start to be gathered and evaluated in the project initiation phase, but it will become more granular in nature as the phases graduate into the functional design and design-specification phase.

## Risk Management
*Okay, question one. How badly can we screw up?*

One of the most important pieces of risk management is to know the right questions to ask. Risk management was discussed in Chapter 3, but that chapter dealt with identifying and mitigating risks that directly affect the business as a whole. Risk management must also be performed when developing and implementing software. Although the two functions are close in concepts, goals, and objectives, they have different specific tasks and focus.

Software development usually has a focus on rich functionality and getting it out the door and on the shelves for customers to buy as soon as possible. Most of the time security is not part of the process or quickly falls by the wayside when a deadline seems imminent. It is not just the programmer who should be thinking about coding in a secure manner, but the design of the product should have security integrated and layered throughout the project. Software engineers should address security threat scenarios and solutions during their tasks. It is not just one faction of a development team that might fall down when it comes to security. Security has never really been treated as an important function of the process—that is, until the product is bought by several customers who undergo attacks and compromises that tie directly to how the product was developed and programmed. Then security is quite a big deal, but it is too late to integrate security into the project; instead, a patch is developed and released.

The first step in risk management is to identify the threats and vulnerabilities and to calculate the level of risk involved. When all the risks are evaluated, management will decide upon the acceptable level of risk. Of course, it would be nice for management to not accept any risks and for the product to be designed and tested until it is foolproof; however, this would cause the product to be in development for a long time and to be too expensive to purchase. Compromises and intelligent business decisions need to be made to provide a balance between risks and economic feasibility.

## Risk Analysis

A risk analysis is performed to identify the relative risks and the potential consequences of what a customer can be faced with when using the particular product that is being developed. This process usually involves asking many, many questions to find out the laundry list of vulnerabilities and threats, the probability of these vulnerabilities being exploited, and the outcome if one of these threats actually becomes real and a compromise takes place. The questions vary from product to product—its intended purpose, the expected environment it will be implemented into, the personnel involved, and the types of businesses that would purchase and use this type of product. The following is a short list of the types of questions that should be asked during a software risk analysis:

- What is the possibility of buffer overflows, and how do we avoid them?
- Are threat agents outside and inside the environment? What are those threat agents?
- What type of businesses would depend on this product, and what type of business loss would it cause if the product were to go offline for a specific period?
- Are there covert channel issues that need to be dealt with?
- What type of fault tolerance is to be integrated into the product, and when would it be initiated?

- Is encryption needed? Which type? What strength?
- Are contingency plans needed for emergency issues?
- Would another party (ISP or hosting agency) be maintaining this product for the customer?
- Is mobile code necessary? How and why?
- Will this product be in an environment that is connected to the Internet? What effects could this have on the product?
- Does this product need to interface to vulnerable systems?
- How could this product be vulnerable to denial of service (DoS) attacks?
- How could this product be vulnerable to viruses?
- Are intrusion alert mechanisms necessary?
- Would there be motivation for insiders or outsiders to sabotage this product? How and why?
- Would competitor companies of the purchaser want to commit fraud via this product? How and why?
- What other systems would be affected if this product failed?

This is a short list, and each question can branch off into other questions to ensure that all possible threats and risks are identified and thought through.

Once all the risks are identified, the probability of them actually taking place needs to be quantified, and the consequences of these risks need to be properly evaluated to ensure that the right countermeasures are implemented within the development phase and the product itself. If a product will only be used to produce word documents, a lower level of security countermeasures and tests would be needed compared with a product that maintains credit card data.

Many of the same risk analysis steps outlined in Chapter 3 can be applied in the risk analysis that needs to be performed when developing a product. Once the threats are identified by the project team members, the probability of their occurrence is estimated, and their consequences are calculated, the risks can be listed in order of importance. If the possibility of a DoS taking place is high and could devastate a customer, then this is at the high end of importance. If the possibility of fraud is low, then this is pushed down the priority list. The most probable and potentially devastating risks are approached first, and the less likely and less damaging are dealt with after the more important risks.

These risks need to be addressed in the design and architecture of the product as well as in the functionality the product provides, the implementation procedures, and the required maintenance. A banking software product may need to be designed to have web server farms within a demilitarized zone (DMZ) of the branch, but have the components and databases behind another set of firewalls to provide another layer of protection. This means that the architecture of the product would include splitting it among different systems and developing communications methods between the different parts. If the product is going to provide secure e-mail functionality, then all the risks involved with just this service need to be analyzed and properly accounted for. Implementation procedures need to be thought through and addressed. How will the customer set up this product? What are the system and environment requirements? Does this product need to be supplied with a public key infrastructure (PKI)? The level of maintenance required after installation is important to many products. Will the vendor need to keep the customer abreast of certain security issues? Should any logging and auditing take place? The more these things are thought through in the beginning, the less scrambling that will be involved at the end of the process.

It is important to understand the difference between project risk analysis and security risk analysis. They often are confused or combined. The project team may do a risk analysis pertaining to the risk of the project failing. This is much different from the security risk analysis, which has different threats and issues. The two should be understood and used, but in a distinctively different manner.

## Functional Design Analysis and Planning

*I would like to design a boat to carry my yellow ducky. Response: You are in the wrong meeting.*

In this phase, a project plan is developed by the software architectures to define the security activities and to create security checkpoints to ensure that quality assurance for security controls takes place and that the configuration and change control process is identified. At this point in the project, resources are identified, test schedules start to form, and evaluation criteria are developed to be able to properly test the security controls. A formal functional baseline is formed, meaning the expectations of the product are outlined in a formal manner, usually through documentation. A test plan is developed, which will be updated through each phase to ensure that all issues are properly tested.

Security requirements can be derived from several different sources:

- Functional needs of the system or application

- National, international, or organizational standards and guidelines

- Export restrictions

- Sensitivity level of data being processed (militarily strategic data versus private-sector data)

- Relevant security policies

- Cost/benefit analysis results

- Required level of assurance to achieve the targeted security level rating

The initial risk assessment will most likely be updated throughout the project as more information is uncovered and learned. In some projects, more than one risk analysis needs to be performed at different stages of the life cycle. For example, if the project team knows that the product will need to identify and authenticate users in a domain setting that requires a medium level of security, it will perform an initial risk analysis. Later in the life cycle, if it is determined that this product should work with biometric devices and have the capability to integrate with systems that require high security levels, the project team will perform a whole new risk analysis, because new morsels have been added to the mix.

This phase addresses the functionality required of the product and is captured in a design document. If the product is being developed for a customer, the design document is used as a tool to explain to the customer what the developing team understands to be the requirements of the product. A design document is usually drawn up by analysts, with the guidance of engineers and architects, and presented to the customer. The customer can then decide if more functionality needs to be added or subtracted, after which the customer and development team can begin hammering out exactly what is expected from the product.

With regard to security issues, this is where high-level questions are asked. Examples of these questions include the following: Are authentication and authorization necessary? Is encryption needed? Will the product need to interface with other systems? Will the product be directly accessed via the Internet?

Many companies skip the functional design phase and jump right into developing specifications for the product. Or a design document is not shared with the customer. This can cause major delays and retooling efforts, because a broad vision of the product needs to be developed before looking strictly at the details. If the customer is not involved at this stage, the customer will most likely think that the developers are developing a product that accomplishes X, while the development team thinks that the customer wants Y. A lot of time can be wasted developing a product that is not what the customer actually wants, so clear direction and goals need to be drawn up before the beginning of coding. This is usually an important function of the project management team.

## System Design Specifications

Software requirements come from three models:

- **Informational model**  Dictates the type of information to be processed and how it will be processed
- **Functional model**  Outlines the tasks and functions that the application needs to carry out
- **Behavioral model**  Explains the states that the application will be in during and after specific transitions take place

For example, an antivirus software application may have an informational model that dictates what information is to be processed by the program, such as virus signatures, modified system files, checksums on critical files, and virus activity. It would also have a functional model that dictates that the application should be able to scan a hard drive, check e-mail for known virus signatures, monitor critical system files, and update itself. The behavioral model would indicate that when the system starts up, the antivirus software application will scan the hard drive. The computer coming online would be the event that changes the state of the application. If a virus were found, the application would change state and deal with the virus appropriately. The occurrence of the virus is the event that would change the state. Each state has to be accounted for to ensure that the product does not go into an insecure state and act in an unpredictable way.

The informational, functional, and behavioral model data goes into the software design as requirements. What comes out of the design is the data, architectural, and procedural design, as shown in Figure 11-8.

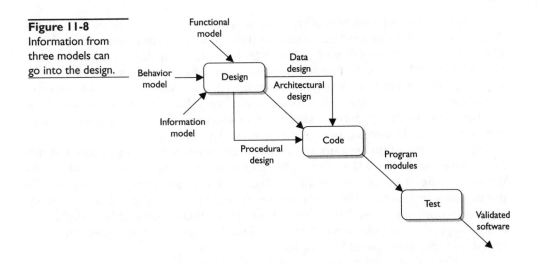

**Figure 11-8**
Information from three models can go into the design.

The architects and developers take the data design and the informational model data and transform it into the data structures that will be required to implement the software. The architectural design defines the relationships between the major structures and components of the application. The procedural design transforms structural components into descriptive procedures.

This is the point where access control mechanisms are chosen, subject rights and permissions are defined, the encryption method and algorithm are chosen, the handling of sensitive data is ironed out, the necessary objects and components are identified, the interprocessing communication is evaluated, the integrity mechanism is identified, and any other security specifications are appraised and solutions are determined.

The work breakdown structure (WBS) for future phases needs to be confirmed, which includes the development and implementation stages. This includes a timeline and detailed activities for testing, development, staging, integration testing, and product delivery.

The system design is a tool used to describe the user requirements and the internal behavior of a system. It then maps the two elements to show how the internal behavior actually accomplishes the user requirements.

This phase starts to look at more details of the product and the environment that it will be implemented within. The required functionality was determined in the last phase. This phase addresses what mechanisms are needed to provide this functionality and determines how it will be coded, tested, and implemented.

The modularity and reusability of the product, or the product components, need to be addressed. Code that provides security-critical functions should be simple in design, to catch errors in a less confusing fashion, and should be small enough to be fully tested in different situations. Components can be called and used by different parts of the product or by other applications. This attribute, reusability, can help streamline the product and provide for a more efficient and more structured coding environment.

The product could have portability issues that need to be dealt with and handled at the early stages of the product development. If the product needs to work on Unix and Windows systems, then different coding requirements are needed compared with a product that will be installed only on mainframes. Also, the environment that will implement this product needs to be considered. Will this product be used by individual users, or will all the users within the network access this product in one fashion or another? Whether the product is a single-user product or a multiuser product has large ramifications on the development of the necessary specifications.

The testability of the product and components needs to be thought about at this early phase instead of at later phases. Programmers can code in *hooks* that show the testers the state of the product at different stages of data processing. Just because the product appears to act correctly and produces the right results at the end of the processing phases does not mean that internal errors are not taking place. This is why testing should happen in modular ways, the flow of data through the product needs to be followed, and each step should be analyzed.

This phase should look closely at all the questions asked at the project initiation and ensure that specifications are developed for each issue addressed. For example, if authentication is required, this phase will lay out all the details necessary for this process to take place. If fraud is a large risk, then all the necessary countermeasures should be identified and how they integrate into the product should be shown. If covert channels are a risk, then these issues should be addressed, and pseudocode should be developed to show how covert channels will be reduced or eliminated.

If the product is being developed for a specific customer, the specifications of the product should be shared with the customer to again ensure that everyone is still on the same page and headed in the right direction. This is the stage to work out any confusion or misunderstanding before the actual coding begins.

The decisions made during the design phase are pivotal steps to the development phase. The design is the only way that the customer requirements are translated into software components; thus, software design serves as the foundation, and greatly affects software quality and maintenance. If good product design is not put into place in the beginning of the project, the following phases will be much more challenging.

## Software Development

*Code jockeys to your cubes and start punching those keys!*

This is the phase where the programmers and developers become deeply involved. They are usually involved up to this point for their direction and advice, but at this phase, it is basically put into their laps. Let the programming and testing begin!

This is the stage where the programmers should code in a way that does not permit software compromises. Among other issues to address, the programmers need to check input lengths so buffer overflows cannot take place, code to prevent the presence of covert channels, check for proper data types, make sure checkpoints cannot be bypassed by users, verify syntax, and perform checksums. Different attack scenarios should be played out to see how the code could be attacked or modified in an unauthorized fashion. Debugging and code reviews should be carried out by peer developers, and everything should be clearly documented.

## Verification vs. Validation

*Verification* determines if the product accurately represents and meets the specifications. A product can be developed that does not match the original specifications. This step ensures that the specifications are properly met.

*Validation* determines if the product provides the necessary solution for the intended real-world problem. In large projects, it is easy to lose sight of the overall goal. This exercise ensures that the main goal of the project is met.

Most programmers do not like to document and will find a way to get out of the task. Six to twelve months later, no one will remember specific issues that were addressed, how they were handled, or the solutions to problems that have already been encountered—or the programmer who knew all the details will have gone to work for a competitor or won the lottery and moved to an island. This is another cause of rework and wasted man-hours. Documentation is extremely important, for many different reasons, and can save a company a lot of money in the long run.

Formal and informal testing should begin as soon as possible. Unit testing can start very early in development. After a programmer develops a component, or unit of code, it is tested with several different input values and in many different situations. Unit testing usually continues throughout the development phase. A totally different group of people should carry out the formal testing. This is an example of *separation of duties*. A programmer should not develop, test, and release software. The more eyes that see the code and the more fingers that are punching keys, the greater the chance that bugs will be found before the product is released.

Of course, any software hooks inserted for testing or modification purposes need to be removed from the application prior to being released to production because these can easily provide attackers backdoors into the product.

There is no cookie-cutter recipe for security testing, because the applications and products can be so diverse in functionality and security objectives. It is important to map security risks to test cases and code. Linear thinking can be followed by identifying a risk, providing the necessary test scenario, performing the test, and reviewing the code for how it deals with such a risk, as illustrated in Figure 11-9. At this phase, tests are conducted in an actual network, which should mirror the production environment to ensure the code does not work only in the labs.

**Figure 11-9**
After risks are identified, test scenarios need to be developed and used to verify that those risks are addressed.

> ### Separation of Duties
> Different environmental types (development, testing, and production) should be properly separated, and functionality and operations should not overlap. Developers should not have access to code used in production. The code should be tested, submitted to the library, and then sent to the production environment.

Security attacks and penetrations usually take place during this phase to identify any missed vulnerabilities. Functionality, performance, and penetration resistance are evaluated. All the necessary functionality required of the product should be in a checklist to ensure that each function is accounted for.

Security tests should be run to test against the risks identified earlier within the project. Buffer overflows should be attempted, the product should be hacked and attacked, interfaces should be hit with unexpected inputs, DoS situations should be tested, unusual user activity should take place, and if a system crashes, the product should react by reverting back to a more secure state. The product should be tested in various environments with different applications, configurations, and hardware platforms. A product may respond fine when installed on a clean Windows 2000 installation on a stand-alone PC, but it may throw unexpected errors when installed on a laptop that is remotely connected to a network and has an SMS client installed.

At this stage, issues found in unit and formal testing are relayed to the development team in problem reports. The problems are fixed and retesting occurs. This is a continual process until everyone is satisfied that the product is ready for production. If there is a specific customer, the customer would run through a range of tests before formally accepting the product. Then the product is formally released to the market or customer.

 **NOTE** Sometimes developers enter lines of code in a product that will allow them to do a few keystrokes and get right into the application. This allows them to bypass any security and access controls so that they can quickly access the application's code. This is referred to as a "backdoor" or "maintenance hook" and should be removed before the code goes into production.

## Installation/Implementation

The implementation stage focuses on how to use and operate the developed system or application. At this phase, the customer has purchased the developed product and installed it into its environment. The product would then be configured for the right level of protection. Functionality and performance tests should be performed, and the results should be analyzed and compared with the company's security requirements.

The configurations should be documented by the vendor and supplied with product for the customer to use. User guides and operation and maintenance manuals are developed so that users know how to properly use the systems and the technical staff know how to properly configure the product if needed. Security activities need to be monitored to ensure that the system or application performs in the manner promised by the service level agreement.

Accreditation should occur between the implementation and the beginning of operational use of the system or application. This process follows the certification process, which formally or informally tests all the security features to determine if they accomplish the required security needs. Certification is the process of reviewing and evaluating security controls and functionality. It is usually a task assigned to an outside, independent reviewer. (Certification and accreditation were covered in detail in Chapter 5.)

The accreditation is the formal acceptance of the system by management and an explicit acceptance of risk. The accreditation looks at the whole system, not just at an application or a newly upgraded feature, because security is a service that takes place at different layers of the system and can be manifested in many ways. The accreditation process forces the management and technical staff to work together to ensure quality and a level of protection provided by purchased and implemented technologies. The technical staff understand operational and mechanical issues, and the management staff understand mission, financial, and liability issues. Together, they can cover a lot of ground during the certification accreditation processes.

Once management is sure of the security provided by the new system and understands and accepts the risk, it should issue a formal accreditation statement.

Auditing needs to be enabled and monitored, and contingency recovery plans and procedures should be developed and tested to make sure the system and product react as planned in the event of a system failure or emergency situation.

## Operational and Maintenance

*Okay, the thing is out there. Now someone has to take care of that thing.*

When you reach this phase, do not think that security is done and in control, and that all you have to do now is sit back and eat donuts. On the contrary, security is just as, or more, important during the operational phase than during earlier phases.

The initial part of this phase includes configuring the new system and inserting it properly into the network and environment. Many times, security controls are not enabled or properly configured for the environment, so even if they were correctly coded from the beginning, it does not really matter if they are not actually used or are used in an unintended way.

Operational assurance is carried out by continually conducting vulnerability tests, monitoring activities, and auditing events. It is through operational assurance activities that an administrator learns of new vulnerabilities or security compromises, so that the proper actions can take place.

If major changes happen to the system, product, or environment, a new risk analysis may need to be performed along with a new certification and accreditation process. These major changes could include adding new systems and/or new applications, relocating the facility, or changing data sensitivity or criticality.

## Disposal

*All good things must come to an end.*

When it is time for "out with the old and in with the new," certain steps may need to take place to make sure this transition happens in a secure manner. Depending on the sensitivity level of the data held on a system, various disposal activities may be necessary. Information may need to be archived, backed up to another system, discarded, or destroyed. If the data is sensitive and needs to be destroyed, it may need to be purged by overwriting, degaussing, or physically destroying the media. It depends on the data and the company's policy about destroying sensitive information.

If the product that is being replaced is just a word processor or an antivirus software package, this phase can be easily taken care of. But if the software is integrated into every part of the company's processing infrastructure, properly extracting it without affecting productivity and security can be an overwhelming task.

## Postmortem Review

It is important that the team gather after the completion of a project to exhale, talk about the overall project, and discuss things that should be improved for the next time. If this phase is taken seriously and handled properly, the company can save money and time on future projects, because the team can pass along lessons that it has learned so that mistakes will not be repeated and the process will be streamlined. All of these activities will help the next project run more smoothly with fewer mistakes and in less time.

This should be a structured event in which someone leads the meeting(s) and someone takes notes, but it should also be a relaxed atmosphere so that each team member feels comfortable in expressing opinions and ideas. The review must not become a finger-pointing session or a cesspool of complaining. It is a method of looking at the project from an objective view and identifying issues that could be improved upon the next time around.

Some companies do not see the value in this exercise and just race off to start the next project, which will most likely be cursed with the problems of the prior project.

---

### System Life-Cycle Phases

The following are the common phases of system and software development along with the core security tasks that take place at each phase.

- **Project initiation**
  - Conception of project definition
  - Proposal and initial study
  - Initial risk analysis
- **Functional design analysis and planning**
  - Requirements uncovered and defined
  - System environment specifications determined
  - Formal design created

- **System design specifications**
  - Functional design review
  - Functionality broken down
  - Detailed planning put into place
  - Code design
- **Software development**
  - Developing and programming software
- **Installation**
  - Product installation and implementation
  - Testing and auditing
- **Maintenance support**
  - Product changes, fixes, and minor modifications
- **Disposal**
  - Replace product with new product

Projects are learning processes, and business is about making the best product in the least amount of time for the least amount of money. It is beneficial for management to understand how the two go together and to make sure that a postmortem review is part of every project. The most successful businesses streamline the processes of projects and project management and hone them to become a repeatable procedure that produces the expected level of quality. These businesses continually take the time to look at how processes can be improved and built upon.

This chapter explains a life cycle containing seven phases. Other models may use different cycles and a different number of phases, but they accomplish the basic components shown in Figure 11-10.

## Software Development Methods

There are several different life-cycle models that outline the significant phases of software development. The following list provides a quick glimpse at some of these different models:

- **Waterfall** A classical method that uses discrete phases of development that require formal reviews and documentation before moving into the next phase of the project.
- **Spiral** A method that builds upon the waterfall method with an emphasis on risk analysis, prototypes, and simulations at different phases of the development cycle.
- **Joint Analysis Development (JAD)** A method that uses a team approach in application development in a workshop-oriented environment.

- **Rapid Application Development (RAD)** A method of determining user requirements and developing systems quickly to satisfy immediate needs.

- **Cleanroom** An approach that attempts to prevent errors or mistakes by following structured and formal methods of developing and testing. This approach is used for high-quality and critical applications that will be put through a strict certification process.

## References

- **Software Lifecycles, Prof. Steve Easterbrook, University of Toronto Department of Computer Science (2001)** www.cs.toronto.edu/~sme/CSC444F/slides/L04-Lifecycles.pdf

- **The Software Life Cycle** http://bmrc.berkeley.edu/courseware/cs169/spring01/lectures/lifecycle/lifecycle.pdf

## Change Control

*I am changing stuff left and right. Response: Was it approved and tested first?*

Changes during development or production can cause a lot of havoc if not done properly. There are several reasons for changes to take place. During the development

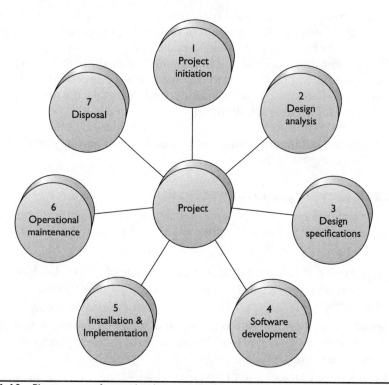

**Figure 11-10** Phases to a software development project

phases, a customer may alter requirements and ask that certain functionality be added, removed, or modified. In production, changes may need to happen because of other changes in the environment, new requirements of a product or system, or newly released patches or upgrades. These changes should be controlled to make sure they are approved, incorporated properly, and do not affect any original functionality in an adverse way. Configuration management is the process of controlling the life cycle of an application and documenting the necessary change control activities.

A process for dealing with changes needs to be in place at the beginning of a project so that everyone knows how changes are dealt with and what is expected of each entity when a change request is made. Some projects have been doomed from the start because proper change control was not put into place and enforced. Many times in development, the customer and vendor agree on the design of the product, the requirements, and the specifications. The customer is then required to sign a contract confirming that this is the agreement, and that if they want any further modifications, they will have to pay the vendor for that extra work. If this is not put into place, then the customer can continually request changes, which requires the development team to put in the extra hours to provide these changes, the result of which is that the vendor loses money and the product does not meet its completion deadline.

There are other reasons to have change control in place. These reasons deal with organization, standard procedures, and expected results. If a product is in the last phase of development and a change request comes in, the team should know how to deal with it. Usually, the team leader must tell the project manager how much extra time will be required to complete the project if this change is incorporated and what steps need to be taken to ensure that this change does not affect other components within the product. In addition, security cannot be compromised, and management must approve the change. If these processes are not controlled, one part of a development team could implement the change without another part of the team being aware of the change. This could break some of the other development team's software pieces. When the pieces of the product are integrated and it is found that some pieces are incompatible, some jobs may be in jeopardy, because management never approved the change in the first place.

The change must be approved, documented, and tested. Some tests may need to be rerun to ensure that the change does not affect the product's capabilities. When a programmer makes a change to source code, it should be done on the test version of the

## Official Definition of Configuration Management

*Configuration management* refers to the procedures that are used to carry out changes that affect the network, individual systems, or software:

- Identifying, controlling, accounting for, and auditing changes made to the baseline trusted computing base (TCB), which includes changes to hardware, software, and firmware.

- A system that controls changes and tests documentation through the operational life cycle of a system.

code. Under no conditions should a programmer change the code that is already in production. The changes to the code should be made, and then the new code should go to the librarian. Production code should come only from the librarian and not from a programmer or directly from a test environment.

Change control should be evaluated during system audits. It is possible to overlook a problem that a change has caused in testing, so the procedures for how change control is implemented and enforced should be examined during a system audit.

The following are some necessary steps for a change control process:

1. Make a formal request for a change.
2. Analyze the request.
    A. Develop the implementation strategy.
    B. Calculate the costs of this implementation.
    C. Review any security implications.
3. Record the change request.
4. Submit the change request for approval.
5. Develop the change.
    A. Recode segments of the product and add or subtract functionality.
    B. Link these changes in the code to the formal change control request.
    C. Submit software for testing and quality approval.
    D. Repeat until quality is adequate.
    E. Make version changes.
6. Report results to management.

The changes to systems may require another round of certification and accreditation. If the changes to a system are significant, then the functionality and level of protection may need to be reevaluated (certified), and management would have to approve the overall system, including the new changes (accreditation).

## Capability Maturity Model

The *Capability Maturity Model (CMM)* describes procedures, principles, and practices that underlie software development process maturity. This model was developed to help software vendors improve their development processes by providing an evolutionary path from an ad hoc, "fly by the seat of your pants" approach, to a more disciplined and repeatable approach that improves software quality, reduces the life cycle of development, provides better project management capabilities, allows for milestones to be created and met in a timely manner, and takes a more proactive approach than the less effective reactive approach.

This model provides policies, procedures, guidelines, and best practices to allow an organization to develop a standardized approach to software development that can be used across many different groups. The goal is to continue to review and improve upon the processes to optimize output, increase capabilities, and provide higher-quality software at a lower cost.

The model provides a layered framework that enables different organizations to implement continuous improvement. It is a tool for the software development company and a tool for those wanting to assess a vendor's development consistency and quality. For example, if the company StuffRUs wants a software development company, SoftwareRUs, to develop an application for it, it can choose to buy into the sales hype about how wonderful SoftwareRUs is, or it can ask for SoftwareRUs to be evaluated against the CMM model. Third-party companies evaluate software development companies to certify the organizations' product development processes. Many software companies have this evaluation done so that they can use this as a selling point to attract new customers.

Five maturity levels are used:

- **Initial**  Development process is ad hoc or even chaotic. The company does not use effective management procedures and plans. There is no assurance of consistency, and quality is unpredictable.

- **Repeatable**  A formal management structure, change control, and quality assurance are in place. The company can properly repeat processes throughout each project. The company does not have formal process models defined.

- **Defined**  Formal procedures are in place that outline and define processes that are carried out in each project. The organization has a way to allow for quantitative process improvement.

- **Managed**  The company has formal processes in place to collect and analyze qualitative data, and metrics are defined and fed into the process-improvement program.

- **Optimized**  The company has budgeted and integrated plans for continuous process improvement.

## Software Escrow

*Will someone keep a copy of my source code?*

If a company pays another company to develop software for it, it should have some type of *software escrow* in place for protection. In a software escrow, a third party keeps a copy of the source code, and possibly other materials, which it will release to the customer only if specific circumstances arise, mainly if the vendor who developed the code goes out of business or for some reason is not meeting its obligations and responsibilities. This procedure protects the customer, because the customer pays the vendor to develop software code for it, and if the vendor goes out of business, the customer otherwise would no longer have access to the actual code. This means that the customer code could never be updated or maintained properly.

A logical question would be, "Why doesn't the vendor just hand over the source code to the customer, since the customer paid for it to be developed in the first place?" It does not work that way. The code is the vendor's intellectual property. The vendor employs and pays people with the necessary skills to develop that code, and if the vendor were to just hand it over to the customer, it would be giving away its intellectual property, its secrets. The customer gets compiled code instead of source code. Compiled code is code that has been put through a compiler and is unreadable to humans. Most software profits are based on licensing, which outlines what customers can do with the compiled code.

# Application Development Methodology

Applications are written in programming code, which tells the operating system and processor what needs to happen to accomplish the user's requirements when operating a specific application. Programming languages have gone through several generations, each generation building on the next, providing richer functionality and giving the programmers more powerful tools as the languages evolve.

There are different types of languages: machine language, assembly language, and high-level languages. *Machine language* is in a form that the processor can understand and work with directly. *Assembly* and *high-level languages* cannot be understood directly by the processor and must be translated, which results in machine language. The process is typically done by a compiler, whose function is to turn human-understandable programming language into machine-understandable language, or object code.

When a customer purchases a program, it is in object code form. The program has already been compiled, and it is ready to be executed and set up on the system. The compiler will put it into a form that specific processors can understand. This is why a program that works on a computer with an Alpha processor may not work on a computer with a Pentium processor. The programs use different processors and require a different form of machine language.

If the program was actually sold in the form of original source code, it would have to be complied on the customer's computer; thus, the customer must have the correct complier. Also, original source code would enable competing vendors to view each other's original ideas and techniques. Source code is considered intellectual property by vendors who develop software, and thus should be highly protected.

Various programs are used to turn high-level programming code (or source code) into object or machine code. These programs are interpreters, compilers, and assemblers. They work as translators. *Interpreters* translate one command at a time during execution, and *compilers* translate large sections of code at a time. *Assemblers* translate assembly language into machine language. Most applications are compiled, whereas many scripting languages are interpreted.

## Object-Oriented Concepts

*Objects are so cute, and small, and modular. I will take one in each color!*

Software development used to be done by classic input-processing-output methods. This development used an information flow model from hierarchical information structures. Data was input into a program, and the program passed the data from the beginning to end, performed logical procedures, and returned a result.

---

### Compiled or Interpreted

Interpreted programs have instructions that are read and interpreted by a program one instruction at a time. This program, the interpreter, converts high-level instructions into machine-readable format in real time. Compiled programs are written in a high-level language and turned into machine-readable format by a program called a compiler.

---

*Object-oriented programming (OOP)* methods perform the same functionality but with different techniques that work in a more efficient manner. First, you need to understand the basic concepts of OOP.

OOP works with classes and objects. A real-world object, such as a table, is a member (or instance) of a larger class of objects called "furniture." The furniture class may have a set of attributes associated with it, and when an object is generated, it inherits these attributes. The attributes may be color, dimensions, weight, style, and cost. These attributes apply if a chair, table, or loveseat object is generated or instantiated. Because the table is a member of the class furniture, the table inherits all attributes defined for the class (see Figure 11-11).

Once the class is defined, the attributes can be reused for each new member, or instance, of the class that is created.

A *method* is the functionality or procedure that an object can carry out. An object may be constructed to accept data from a user and to reformat the request so that a back-end server can understand and process it. Another object may perform a method that extracts data from a database and populates a web page with this information. Or an object may carry out a withdrawal procedure to allow a user of an ATM to extract money from her account.

---

 **NOTE** In OOP, objects are unique instances of a data structure defined by the template provided by their corresponding classes.

---

**Figure 11-11**
In object-oriented inheritance, each object belongs to a class and takes on the attributes of that class.

The objects encapsulate the attribute values, which means that this information is packaged under one name and can be reused as one entity by other objects. Objects need to be able to communicate with each other, and this happens by using *messages*. If object A needs to tell object B that a user's checking account needs to be reduced by $40, it sends object B a message. The message is made up of the destination, the method that needs to be performed, and the corresponding arguments. Figure 11-12 shows this example.

An object can have a shared portion and a private portion. The shared portion is the interface that enables it to interact with other components. Messages enter through the interface to specify the requested operation, or method, to be performed. The private part of an object may be how it actually works and performs the requested operations. Other components need not know how each object works internally—only that it does the job requested of it. This is how *information hiding* is possible. The details of the processing are hidden from all other program elements outside the object. Objects communicate through well-defined interfaces; therefore, they do not need to know how each other works.

**NOTE** Data hiding is provided by encapsulation, which protects an object's private data from outside access. No object should be allowed to or have the need to access another object's internal data or processes.

Once the objects are defined, it might be necessary to develop a classification structure, which defines and names instances of objects. For example, if the main object is named Dog, then the three objects under and related to this object could be Labrador, Terrier, and Bulldog. This gives structure to the classification and defines the necessary relationships between the objects. Structure representation is a way of partitioning the requirements of the model.

These objects can grow to great numbers, so the complexity of understanding, tracking, and analyzing can get a bit overwhelming. Many times, the objects are shown in connection to a reference or pointer in documentation. Figure 11-13 shows how related objects are represented as a specific piece, or reference, in an ATM system. This enables analysts and developers to look at a higher level of operation and procedures without having to look at each individual object. This modularity provides for a more easily understood model.

*Abstraction* is the capability to suppress unnecessary details so that the important, inherent properties can be examined and reviewed. It enables the separation of conceptual aspects of a system. For example, if a software architect needed to understand how data flows through the program, she would want to understand the big pieces of the program and trace the steps that the data takes from first being input into the program all the way until it exits the program as output. It would be difficult to understand this concept if the small details of every piece of the program were presented. Instead,

**Figure 11-12**
Objects
communicate
via messages.

Object A

Message
(Object B, Withdrawal, 40.00)

Object B

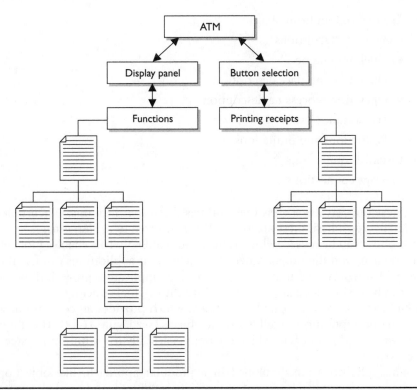

**Figure 11-13** Programs can get very complicated, with many different objects. They are usually represented by references, which point to several objects, to show the main functionality of the application itself.

through abstraction, all the details are suppressed so that she can understand a crucial part of the product.

Messaging can happen in several ways. Two objects can have a single connection (one to one), a multiple connection (one to many), and a mandatory connection or an optional connection. It is important to map these communication paths to identify if information can flow in a way that is not intended. This will help ensure that sensitive data cannot be passed to objects of a lower security level.

Each object should have specifications that it should adhere to. This discipline provides cleaner programming and reduces programming errors and omissions. The following list is an example of what should be developed for each object:

- Object name
- Attribute descriptions
  - Attribute name
  - Attribute content
  - Attribute data type
- External input to object

- External output from object
- Operation descriptions
  - Operation name
  - Operation interface description
  - Operation processing description
  - Performance issues
  - Restrictions and limitations
- Instance connections
- Message connections

The developer creates a class that outlines these specifications. When objects are instantiated, they inherit these attributes. This is referred to as *abstraction*.

Each object can be reused, which is the beauty of OOP. This enables more efficient use of resources and the programmer's time. Different applications can use the same objects, which reduces redundant work, and as an application grows in functionality, objects can be easily added and integrated into the original structure.

The objects can be catalogued in a library, which provides an economical way for more than one application to call upon the objects (see Figure 11-14). The library provides an index and pointers to where the objects actually live within the system or on another system.

When applications are developed in a modular approach, like object-oriented methods, components can be reused, complexity is reduced, and parallel development can be done. These characteristics allow for fewer mistakes, easier modification, resource efficiency, and more timely coding than the classic information flow models. OOP also provides functional independence, which means that each module addresses a specific subfunction of requirements and has an interface that is easily understood by other parts of the application.

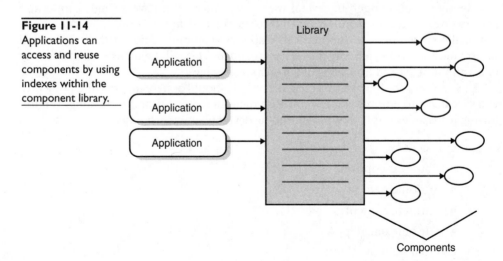

**Figure 11-14**
Applications can access and reuse components by using indexes within the component library.

An object is encapsulated, meaning that the data structure (the operation's functionality) and the acceptable ways of accessing it are grouped into one entity. Other objects, subjects, and applications can use this object and its functionality by accessing it through controlled and standardized interfaces and sending it messages (see Figure 11-15).

*Object-oriented design (OOD)* creates a representation of a real-world problem and maps it to a software solution. The result of an OOD is a design that modularizes data and procedures. The design interconnects data objects and processing operations. This programming approach is different from others because it allows for abstraction, modularity, and information hiding. Modularity is accomplished by using objects, applets, and agents.

**NOTE** Object-oriented design (OOD) is a design method in which a system is modeled as a collection of cooperating objects. Each individual object is treated as an instance of a class within a class hierarchy.

## Polymorphism

*Polymorphism is a funny name. Response: You are funny looking.*

Polymorphism adds another dimension to an object's behavior and aids in providing a better description for the object. *Polymorphism* means that an object's response to a message is determined by the class to which the object belongs. Different objects that

**Figure 11-15**
The different components of an object and the way that it works are hidden from other objects.

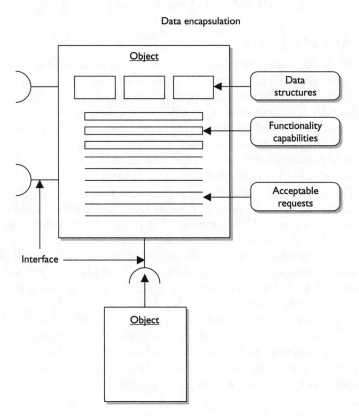

Data encapsulation

Object

Data structures

Functionality capabilities

Acceptable requests

Interface

Object

belong to different classes can be addressed in a uniform manner, but they exhibit different behaviors.

As a simplistic example of polymorphism, suppose that three different objects receive the input "Bob." Object A would process this input and produce the output "43-year-old white male." Object B would receive the input "Bob" and produce the output "Husband of Sally." Object C would produce the output of "Member of User group." Each object received the same input, but responded with a different output.

 **NOTE**  Polymorphism is when different objects respond to the same command, input, or message in different ways.

*Object-oriented analysis (OOA)* is the process of classifying objects that will be appropriate for a solution. A problem is analyzed to determine the classes of objects to be used in the application.

OOD enables an engineer or developer to indicate the objects that will derive from each class and how these objects will work together. So the problem needs to be analyzed by the developer, and a solution should be decided upon. Then the details of that solution are attacked and hammered out.

OOP is a class of programming languages and techniques that are based on the concepts of objects and a set of routines and methods, which operate on the data.

## Data Modeling

*Let's see. The data went thataway. Oh no, it went thataway. I lost the data.*

The previous paragraphs have provided a simple look at a **structured analysis approach**. A full structured analysis approach looks at all objects and subjects of an application and maps the interrelationships, communications paths, and inheritance properties. This is different from **data modeling**, which considers data independently of the way that the data is processed and of the components that process the data. A data model follows an input value from beginning to end and verifies that the output is correct. OOA is an example of a structured analysis approach. If an analyst is reviewing the OOA of an application, she will make sure that all relationships are set up correctly, that the inheritance flows in a predictable and usable manner, that the instances of objects are practical and provide the necessary functionality, and that the attributes of each class cover all the necessary values used by the application. When another analyst does a data model review of the same application, he will follow the data and the returned values after processing takes place. An application can have a perfect OOA structure, but when 1 + 1 is entered and it returns –3, something is wrong. This is what the data modeling looks at.

Another example of data modeling deals with databases. Data modeling can be used to provide insight into the data and the relationships that govern it. A data item in one file structure, or data store, might be a pointer to another file structure or to a different data store. These pointers must actually point to the right place. Data modeling would verify this, not OOA structure analysis.

## Software Architecture

Software architecture relates the components that make up a software solution to the parts of a real-world problem. Software architects view the application at a higher level than do the programmers, who are focused on data structures, coding rules, variables, and communication paths between objects. An architectural view looks at how the application actually meets and fulfills the requirements recognized and agreed upon in the design phase.

Software architecture involves the process of partitioning requirements into individual problems that can be solved by individual software solutions. This process is the transition phase between the software requirement analysis and the design of the actual components that make up the resulting application.

If the requirements are that the application will scan hard drives and e-mail messages for viruses, the software architecture will break these requirements into individual units that need to be achieved by functionality within that application. These units may include the following functionality:

- Virus signature storage

- An agent that compares software strings on hard drives to virus signatures

- A process of parsing an e-mail message before the user can view it

- Procedures necessary if data on a hard drive is compressed

- Actions taken if a virus is found

- Actions taken if an e-mail attachment is encrypted

This way of developing a product provides more control and modularity of issues and solutions. If a group of programmers is told to develop an antivirus software package, the group may sit there like deer caught in headlights. However, if one developer is told to write a piece of the program that holds and updates signature files, another developer is told to determine how data on the hard drive will be compared with the signatures within the signature files, and another developer is instructed to program a way to read compressed files, then the programmers will have set goals and start pounding at the keyboards.

Software architects need to provide this type of direction: a high-level view of the application's objectives and a vision of the overall goals of the project.

## Data Structures

A *data structure* is a representation of the logical relationship between elements of data. It dictates the degree of association between elements, methods of access, processing alternatives, and the organization of data elements.

The structure can be simple in nature, like the scalar item, which represents a single element that can be addressed by an identifier and accessed by a single address in storage. The scalar items can be grouped in arrays, which provide access by indexes. Other data structures include hierarchical structures by using multilinked lists that contain scalar items, vectors, and possibly arrays. The hierarchical structure provides categorization and association. If a user can make a request of an application to find all computer books written on security and that application returns a list, then this application is using a hierarchical data structure of some kind. Figure 11-16 shows simple and complex data structures.

## Cohesion and Coupling

*I am very needy and like to talk to others a lot. Response: Low cohesion and high coupling describes you best, then.*

A *cohesive* module can perform a single task with little or no help from other modules. A cohesive module does just one function, and it does it with little interaction from other modules. The more a module can do on its own, the better, because requiring a lot of interaction between modules makes it harder to modify one module down the road without affecting other modules. Similarly, the more interactions there are, the more complexity, which makes it harder to track down problems. The best programming uses the most cohesive modules possible, but because different modules need to pass data and communicate, they usually cannot be totally cohesive. Figure 11-17 shows a linear approach of looking at cohesion.

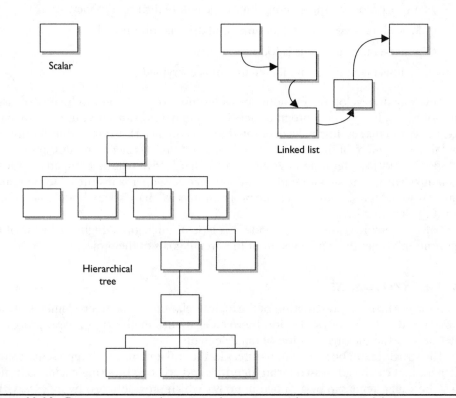

Scalar

Linked list

Hierarchical
tree

**Figure 11-16** Data structures can be very simple to very complex in nature and design.

"Dependant upon others"     "Very independent"

Cohesion spectrum

Low cohesion ◄─────────────────────────► High cohesion

**Figure 11-17** A cohesion spectrum shows the different levels of cohesion that a module can obtain.

*Coupling* is a measure of interconnection among modules in an application. The level of coupling involved between modules depends on the interface's complexity, the data being passed between modules, and the point of entry or reference made to the module itself. The lower the coupling, the better the software design, because it promotes module independence. The more independent a component is, the less complex the application is, and the easier it is to modify and troubleshoot.

An example of *low coupling* would be one module passing a variable value to another module. As an example of *high coupling*, module A would pass a value to module B, which would perform calculations on the data and pass it to module C, which in turn would perform a lookup in a database to make sure this value is within a range and then pass the resulting value back to module A.

**NOTE**  Modules should be self-contained and perform a single logical function, which is high cohesion. Modules should not drastically affect each other, which is low coupling.

## ORBs and CORBA

*Has anyone seen my ORB? I need to track down an object.*

The Object Management Architecture (OMA) provides standards to build a complete distributed environment. It contains two main parts: system-oriented components (*object request brokers [ORBs]* and object services) and application-oriented components (application objects and common facilities). The ORB manages all communications between components and enables them to interact in a heterogeneous and distributed environment, as shown in Figure 11-18. The ORB works independently of the platforms where the objects reside, which provides greater interoperability.

ORBs rely on object services to provide access control, track relocated objects, and create objects. The application objects and common facilities are farther from the system and closer to the end user. When they need services from the system, they invoke services from the ORB and object services.

*Common Object Request Broker Architecture (CORBA)* provides interoperability among the vast array of software, platforms, and hardware in environments today. CORBA enables applications to communicate with one another no matter where the applications are located or who developed them.

Figure 11-18
The ORB enables different components throughout a network to communicate and work with each other.

Components

Components

ORB

Components

Components

The Object Management Group (OMG) developed the CORBA model for the use of these different services in an environment. The model defines object semantics so that the external visible characteristics are standard and viewed the same by all other objects in the environment. This standardization enables many different developers to write hundreds or thousands of components that can interact with other components in an environment without having to know how the component actually works. The developers know how to communicate with the components because the interfaces are uniform and follow the rules of the model.

In the model, clients request services from objects. The client passes the object a message that contains the name of the object, the requested operation, and any necessary parameters.

ORB is the middleware that establishes the client/server relationship between objects. When a client needs to access an object on a server for that object to perform an operation or method, the ORB intercepts the request and is responsible for finding the object. Once the object is found, the ORB invokes a method (or operation), passes the parameters, and returns the result to the client. The client software does not need to know where the object resides nor go through the trouble of finding it. That is the ORB's job. The objects can be written in different languages and reside on different operating systems and platforms, but the client does not need to worry about any of this (see Figure 11-19).

When objects communicate with each other, they use *pipes*, which are intercomponent communications services. There are different types of pipes, such as remote procedure calls (RPCs) and ORBs. ORBs provide communications between distributed objects. If an object on a workstation needs to have an object on a server process data, it can make a request through the ORB, which will track down the needed object and facilitate the communication path between these two objects until the process is complete. This is the client/server communication pipe used in many networking environments.

ORBs are mechanisms that enable objects to communicate locally or remotely. They enable objects to make requests to objects and receive responses. This happens transparently to the client and provides a type of pipeline between all corresponding objects. CORBA specifies interface definitions and APIs that interface to the ORB. Using

The main reason this works is because standardized interfaces are used.

**Figure 11-19** CORBA provides standard interface definitions between OMG-compliant objects, which provides greater interoperability in heterogeneous environments.

CORBA enables an application to be usable with many different types of ORBs. It provides portability for applications and tackles many of the interoperability issues that many vendors and developers run into when their products are implemented into different environments.

## Computer-Aided Software Engineering

*Computer-aided software engineering (CASE)* tools are broad and far reaching in functionality and uses. "CASE tools" is a general term for many types of tools used by programmers, developers, project managers, and analysts that help them make program applications more quickly and with fewer errors in an automated fashion and run the project in a controlled and organized manner. Different tools provide managerial, administrative, and technical help in software projects. They provide several layers of organization that are not available when a developer is just programming by hand.

The first CASE tools were translators, compilers, assemblers, linkers, and loaders. However, as programming and projects became more complex, the need for more complex tools grew. The tools graduated into program editors, debuggers, code analyzers, and version-control mechanisms. The tools aid in keeping more detailed records of requirements, design, and implementation and in testing the program and project overall. A CASE tool is aimed at supporting one or more software engineering tasks and activities in the process of developing software. It applies engineering principles to the development and analysis of specifications using specific tools.

Many vendors can get their products to the market faster because they are "computer aided." The CASE tools enable software engineering to be done correctly and fast, relatively speaking.

When the automation covers the complete life cycle of a product, the tools are referred to as *integrated computer-aided software engineering (I-CASE) tools,* and if tools are used for one specific part of the life cycle, then the tools are referred to as *CASE tools.*

Many CASE tools utilize **rapid prototyping** technologies that enable applications to be developed faster with higher quality and lower cost. A prototype can be made so that testing can begin earlier in the development process. The more testing that is performed, the more errors that can be caught. Because it costs more to find and fix problems at the end of a project compared with the beginning of a project, prototyping can save a lot of time and money.

As previously stated, a wide range of tools falls into the category of CASE tools. The tools can provide and support the data flow, aid structured development, produce documentation, provide design method support, and generate application code for a specific goal within the project. They also help when a project is large, with many developers working on specific pieces of the product. It is easy to get disjointed when everyone has his own little piece he is responsible for, and when the different pieces come together, they may not integrate properly. The different tools can work together with a shared database and a conceptual notion, like a shared philosophy on architecture and common semantics about the objects and the tools that manipulate them.

## Prototyping

*I would like a prototype of a mini-me. Response: One of you is enough.*

Many times, it is necessary to build for the customer and the developers a model of the gathered requirements of a software product. This model, called a **prototype,** can show the customer where the development team is headed and its interpretation of the customer's stated requirements. This enables the customer to agree on the direction the team is headed and get an idea of what the product will look like, or enables the customer to make changes and further explain any requirements that were uncertain or confusing. The prototype also enables testing to begin earlier in the development process so that errors or problems can be uncovered and addressed.

Some projects are very large and may require the product to be partitioned so that each part has its own prototype to be reviewed and built upon. In either case, while partitioning or prototyping the full product, an analyst will develop an abbreviated representation of the requirements for the prototype. The software can be created using prototyping tools, which speed up the process. This enables the design to be translated into executable form.

Security testing can begin at an earlier stage if a prototype is developed. Penetration, vulnerability, and data format tests can be performed at each stage of development and with each prototype developed.

If a software prototype is impractical, paper prototypes can be developed where interaction, queries, displays, and logic are shown on paper for the customer to see and the developers to walk through. A series of storyboard sheets can be used to represent each screenshot and the actions that take place behind the screen.

## COM and DCOM

*Component Object Model (COM)* defines how components interact and provides an architecture for simple interprocess communication (IPC). *Distributed Component Object Model (DCOM)* supports the same model for component interaction, but supports distributed IPC. COM enables applications to use components on the same systems, and DCOM enables applications to access objects that reside in different parts of a network.

Without DCOM, programmers would have to write much more complicated code to find necessary objects, set up network sockets, and incorporate the services necessary to allow communication. DCOM takes care of these issues and more, and enables the programmer to focus on his tasks at hand. DCOM has a library that takes care of session handling, synchronization, buffering, fault identification and handling, and data format translation.

DCOM works as the middleware that enables distributed processing and provides developers with services that support process-to-process communications across networks (see Figure 11-20).

Other types of middleware provide similar functionality: ORB, message-oriented middleware (MOM), RPC, ODBC, and so on. DCOM provides ORB services, data connectivity services, distributed messaging services, and distributed transaction services layered over its RPC mechanism. DCOM integrates all of these functionalities into one technology that uses the same interface as COM (see Figure 11-21).

## Open Database Connectivity

*Open Database Connectivity (ODBC)* is a de facto standard that provides a standard SQL dialect that can be used to access many types of rational databases. ODBC is the middleman between applications and databases. An application makes a request to the ODBC driver manager, which decides which driver needs to be used for communications purposes. (The driver is a piece of software that provides communications between a system and a database. Different databases require different drivers.) The request is passed through the ODBC manager, through the driver, and to the database, as shown in Figure 11-22. The database answers the request, which goes back through the driver, through ODBC, and to the application.

**Figure 11-20**
Although DCOM provides communication mechanisms in a distributed environment, it still works off of the COM architecture.

It is the middleware portion of DCOM that allows different processes to communicate across a network.

**Figure 11-21**
DCOM provides several services over its RPC mechanism and a COM interface.

## Object Linking and Embedding

*Object linking and embedding (OLE)* provides a way for objects to be shared on a local personal computer and to use COM as their foundation. OLE enables objects to be embedded into documents, like graphics, pictures, and spreadsheets. In this book, there are many graphics placed throughout the text. The OLE technology puts the graphics into the text documents that make up this book.

OLE also allows for linking different objects and documents. For example, when Chrissy creates a document that contains a URL, that URL turns blue and is underlined, indicating that a user can just double-click it to be taken to the appropriate web site. This is an example of linking capabilities. If Chrissy adds a spreadsheet to her document, this is an example of embedding. If she needs to edit the spreadsheet, she can double-click the spreadsheet, and the operating system will open the correct environment (which might be Excel) to let her make her changes.

**Figure 11-22**
ODBC provides a standardized interface for many different applications to be able to communicate with many different types of databases.

> ## OLE
> The capability for one program to call another program is called *linking*. The capability to place a piece of data inside a foreign program or document is called *embedding*.

This technology was evolved to work on the World Wide Web and is called ActiveX. The components are like other components, but are meant to be portable. ActiveX components can run on any platform that supports DCOM (using the COM model) or that communicates using DCOM services.

## Dynamic Data Exchange

*Dynamic Data Exchange (DDE)* enables applications to share data by providing IPC. It is based on the client/server model and enables two programs to send commands to each other directly. DDE is a communications mechanism that enables direct conversation between two applications. The source of the data is called the *server*, and the receiver of the data is the *client*.

A spreadsheet can use a DDE link to another program that keeps track of stock prices. The spreadsheet can display the current trading information because updates are being received from the server via a DDE communication link.

## Distributed Computing Environment

*Distributed Computing Environment (DCE)* is a standard that was developed by the Open Software Foundation (OSF), also called Open Group. It is basically middleware that is available to many vendors to use within their products. This middleware has the capability to support many types of applications across an enterprise. DCE provides an RPC service, security service, directory service, time service, and distributed file support.

DCE is a set of management services with a communications layer based on RPC. It is a layer of software that sits on the top of the network layer and provides services to the applications above it. DCE and DCOM provide a lot of the same functionality. DCOM was developed by Microsoft and is more proprietary in nature.

DCE's time service provides host clock synchronization and enables applications to determine sequencing and schedule events based on this clock synchronization. This time synchronization is for applications. Users cannot access this functionality directly. The directory service enables users, servers, and resources to be contacted anywhere on the network. When the directory service is given the name, it returns the network address of the resource along with other necessary information. DCOM uses a *globally unique identifier (GUID)*, and DCE uses a *universal unique identifier (UUID)*. They are both used to uniquely identify users, resources, and components within an environment. DCE is illustrated in Figure 11-23.

The RCP function collects the arguments and commands from the sending program and prepares them for transmission over the network. RCP determines the network transport protocol that is to be used and finds the receiving host's address in the directory

**Figure 11-23** DCE provides many services wrapped into one technology.

service. The thread service provides real-time priority scheduling in a multithreading environment. The security services support authentication and authorization services. The distributed file service (DFS) provides a single integrated file system that all DCE users can use to share files. This is important because many environments have different operating systems that cannot understand other file systems. However, if DCE is being used, a DCE local file system exists alongside the native file system.

## Mobile Code

Code that can be transmitted across a network, to be executed by a system or device on the other end, is called *mobile code*. There are many legitimate reasons to allow mobile code; for example, web browser applets that may execute in the background to download additional content for the web page, such as music or a video image.

There is a demonstration application for Java, called HotJava, that is a complete web browser. This is used to demonstrate that the Java language can behave as a complete browser, with decent performance. This is an example of a legitimate use of mobile code.

The cautions arise when a web site downloads code intended to do malicious or compromising actions, especially when the recipient is unaware that the compromising activity is taking place. If a web site is compromised, it can be used as a platform from which to launch attacks against anyone visiting the site and just browsing. On a web browser, having security settings set to high, or disallowing various scripting or active web components, may be an appropriate countermeasure. Java and ActiveX are discussed later in this chapter.

## Enterprise JavaBeans

*Enterprise JavaBeans (EJB)* is a structural design for the development and implementation of distributed applications written in Java. EJB provides interfaces and methods to allow different applications to be able to communicate across a networked environment. By using the Internet Inter-ORB Protocol (IIOP), the client portion does not have to be a program written in Java, but can be any valid CORBA client.

---

**NOTE** A Java component is called a Java Bean.

## Expert Systems and Knowledge-Based Systems

*Hey, this computer is smarter than me! Response: No surprise there.*

*Expert systems*, also called *knowledge-based systems*, use artificial intelligence (AI) to solve problems.

AI software uses nonnumerical algorithms to solve complex problems, recognize hidden patterns, prove theorems, play games, mine data, and help in forecasting and diagnosing a range of issues. The type of computation done by AI software cannot be accomplished by straightforward analyses and regular programming logic techniques.

Expert systems emulate human logic to solve problems that would usually require human intelligence and intuition. These systems represent expert knowledge as data or rules within the software of a system, and this data and these rules are called upon when it is necessary to solve a problem. Knowledge-based systems collect data of human know-how and hold it in some type of database. These fragments of data are used to reason through a problem.

A regular program can deal with inputs and parameters only in the ways that it has been designed and programmed to. Although a regular program can calculate the mortgage payments of a house over 20 years at an 8 percent interest rate, it cannot necessarily forecast the placement of stars in 100 million years because of all the unknowns and possible variables that come into play. Although both programs—a regular program and an expert system—have a finite set of information available to them, the expert system will attempt to think like a person, reason through different scenarios, and provide an answer even without all the necessary data. Conventional programming deals with procedural manipulation of data, whereas humans attempt to solve complex problems using abstract and symbolic approaches.

A book may contain a lot of useful information, but a person has to read that book, interpret its meaning, and then attempt to use those interpretations within the real world. This is what an expert system attempts to do.

Professionals in the field of AI develop techniques that provide the modeling of information at higher levels of abstraction. The techniques are part of the languages and tools used, which enable programs to be developed that closely resemble human logic. The programs that can emulate human expertise in specific domains are called *expert systems*.

## Expert System

An expert system is a computer program containing a knowledge base and a set of algorithms and rules used to infer new facts from knowledge and incoming data.

*Rule-based programming* is a common way of developing expert systems. The rules are based on if-then logic units. The rules specify a set of actions to be performed for a given situation. This is one way that expert systems are used to find patterns, which is called *pattern matching*. A mechanism, called the *inference engine*, automatically matches facts against patterns and determines which rules are applicable. The actions of the corresponding rules are executed when the inference engine is instructed to begin execution.

Huh? Okay, let's say Dr. Gorenz is puzzled by a patient's symptoms and is unable to match the problems the patient is having to a specific ailment and find the right cure. So he uses an expert system to help him in his diagnosis. Dr. Gorenz can initiate the expert system, which will then take him through question-and-answer scenarios. The expert system will use the information gathered through this interaction, and it will go step by step through the facts, looking for patterns that can be tied to known diseases, ailments, and medical issues. Although Dr. Gorenz is very smart and one of the top doctors in his field, he cannot necessarily recall all possible diseases and ailments. The expert system can analyze this information because it is working off of a database that has been stuffed full of medical information that can fill up several libraries.

As the expert system goes through the medical information, it may see that the patient had a case of severe hives six months ago, had a case of ringing in the ears and blurred vision three months ago, and has a history of diabetes. The system will look at the patient's recent complaints of joint aches and tiredness. With each finding, the expert system digs deeper, looking for further information, and then uses all the information obtained and compares it with the knowledge base that is available to it. In the end, the expert system returns a diagnosis to Dr. Gorenz that says that the patient is suffering from a rare disease found only in Brazil that is caused by a specific mold that grows on bananas. Because the patient has diabetes, his sensitivity is much higher to this contaminant. The system spits out the necessary treatment. Then Dr. Gorenz marches back into the room where the patient is waiting and explains the problem and protects his reputation of being a really smart doctor.

The system not only uses a database of facts, but also collects a wealth of knowledge from experts in a specific field. This knowledge is captured by using interactive tools that have been engineered specifically to capture human knowledge. This knowledge base is then transferred to automated systems that help in human decisions by offering advice, free up experts from repetitive routine decisions, ensure that decisions are made in a consistent manner in a quicker fashion, and help a company retain its organization's expertise even as employees come and go.

An expert system usually consists of two parts: an inference engine and a knowledge base. The inference engine handles the user interface, external files, scheduling, and program-accessing capabilities. The knowledge base contains data pertaining to a specific problem or domain. Expert systems use the inference engine to decide how to execute a program or how the rules should be initiated and followed. The inference engine of a knowledge-based system provides the necessary rules for the system to take the original facts and combine them to form new facts.

The systems employ AI programming languages to allow for real-world decision making. The system is built by a knowledge system builder (programmer), a knowledge engineer (analyst), and subject matter expert(s), as shown in Figure 11-24. The system is built on facts, rules of thumb, and the expert's advice. The information gathered from the expert(s) during the development of the system is kept in a knowledge base and is used during the question-and-answer session with the end user. The system works as a consultant to the end user and can recommend several alternative solutions by considering competing hypotheses at the same time.

Expert systems are commonly used to automate a security log review for an IDS.

**NOTE**  Expert systems use automatic logical processing, inference engine processing, and general methods of searching for problem solutions.

## Artificial Neural Networks

An *artificial neural network (ANN)* is an electronic model based on the neural structure of the brain. Computers perform activities like computing large numbers, keeping large ledgers, and performing complex mathematical functions, but they cannot recognize patterns or learn from experience as the brain can. ANNs contain many units that stimulate neurons, each with a small amount of memory. The units work on data that is input through their many connections. Through training rules, the systems are able to learn from examples and have the capability to generalize.

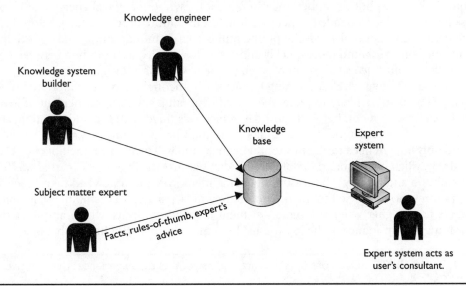

**Figure 11-24**  What goes into developing an expert system and how the system is used once developed.

The brain stores information in forms of patterns. People have the ability to recognize another person's face from several different angles. Each angle of that person's face is made up of a complex set of patterns. Even if only half the face is seen or the face is viewed in a shadow or dark lighting, the human brain can insert the missing pieces, and people can recognize their friends and acquaintances. A computer that uses conventional programming and logic would have to have each piece of the pattern and the full face in one particular angle to be able to match or recognize it.

The brain uses neurons to remember, think, apply previous experiences, perform logic, and recognize patterns. The capacity of the brain comes from the large number of neurons and the multiple connections between them. The power of the brain comes from genetic programming and learning.

ANNs try to replicate the basic functions of neurons and their circuitry to solve problems in a new way. They consist of many simple computational neural units connected to each other. An input value is presented to one, some, or all the units, which in turn perform functions on the data.

The brain has clusters of neurons that process in an interactive and dynamic way. Biologically, neurons have no restrictions of interconnections between themselves; therefore, a neuron can have thousands of connections. In addition, the neurons in the brain work in a three-dimensional world, whereas the electronic units in ANNs have a physical limitation on the possible number of connections and operate in a two-dimensional world.

Like the brain, the ANN's real power comes from its capability to learn. Within the brain, when something is learned and used often, the connection path to where that information is stored is strengthened to provide quicker access. This is why sometimes you know something but "can't put your finger on it." This means that there is not a pronounced pathway to the information that is stored somewhere in the brain. If a person is asked her phone number, she can rattle it off without any real energy. But if you ask her who her third-grade teacher was, it might take more time and energy. Both facts are held within her brain, but the phone number has a more pronounced connection path and comes to mind more quickly and easily. In an ANN, a connection between two units that is often activated might be strengthened, which is a form of learning.

It is known that when something happens to someone in a highly emotional state, that person is more likely to remember specifics about a situation or incident. If Joyce had a surprise party on her 35th birthday, which was filled with fun and emotion, she will most likely remember that birthday more than her 36th birthday, when her husband only bought her a card. But she and her husband will probably remember her 45th birthday, when her husband forgot her birthday, because the fight that occurred was full of emotion and activity. The reason that some memories are more vivid than others is that more emotion is tied to them, or more weight is assigned to them. In ANNs, some inputs have higher weights assigned to them than other inputs, which amplifies the meaning or importance of the inputs, just like emotion does with human beings.

**NOTE**   Decisions by ANNs are only as good as the experiences they are given.

Intuition is a hard quality to replicate in electrical circuits and logic gates. Fuzzy logic and other mathematical disciplines are used for intuition, forecasting, and intelligent guessing. These approaches work with types of probability within mathematics and memberships of different sets. One simple example of the use of fuzzy logic is a washing machine that has built-in intelligence. When a person puts a load of clothes in the washing machine and the tank fills with water, the machine that is using fuzzy logic sends a beam from one part of the tank to the other. Depending on how much light actually was received at the other end, it can determine how dirty the clothes are because of the density of the dirt in the water. Then there are other tests to see if the dirt is oily or dry and to check other relevant attributes. The washing machine takes in all this information and estimates the right temperature and the right amount of laundry soap to use. This provides a more efficient way of washing, by saving on water and soap and washing the clothes at the right temperature for the right amount of time. The washing machine does not necessarily know all the facts or know that the information that it gathered is 100 percent correct, but it can make guesses that will be pretty close to reality.

ANNs are programmed with the capability to decide and to learn to improve their functionality through massive trial-and-error decision making.

Fuzzy logic is necessary because a regular computer system does not see the world in shades of gray. It cannot differentiate between good, bad, few, and many. Fuzzy logic is an approach to enable the computer to use these vague values that mean something to humans but nothing to computers.

Stock market forecasting and insurance and financial risk assessments are examples of where fuzzy logic can be used and is most beneficial. They require a large number of variables and decision-making information from experts in those particular domains. The system can indicate which insurance or financial risks are good or bad without the user having to input a stack of conditions, if-then statements, and variable values.

Conventional systems see the world in black and white, and work in a sea of precision and decimal points. Fuzzy logic enables the computer to incorporate imprecision into the programming language, which opens up a whole new world for computing and attacking complex issues. Neural network researchers attempt to understand more of how the brain works and of nature's capabilities so that newly engineered ANN solutions can solve more complex problems than could be solved through traditional computing means.

## Object Code vs. Machine Code

When source code is processed by a compiler, the result is object code, which is written for a specific platform and processor. This object code is the executable form of an application that a user purchases from a vendor. When the object code runs, it must be converted into binary machine code, which is what the processor actually understands.

## Java

Java is an object-oriented, platform-independent programming language. It is used as a full-fledged programming language and is used to write complete programs and short programs, called *applets*, which run on a user's browser.

Other languages are compiled to object code, but each processor type understands a different object code. This is why a particular application may run on Windows but not run on Macintosh. An Intel processor does not necessarily understand machine code compiled for an Alpha processor and vice versa. Java is platform independent because it creates intermediate code, *bytecode*, which is not processor specific. The Java Virtual Machine (JVM) then converts the bytecode to the machine code that the processor on that particular system can understand (see Figure 11-25). Let's quickly walk through these steps:

1. A programmer creates a Java applet and runs it through a compiler.
2. The Java compiler converts the source code into bytecode (non–processor specific).
3. The user downloads the Java applet.
4. If the user's browser is Java-enabled and has a JVM installed, the browser knows what to do.
5. The JVM converts the bytecode into machine-level code (processor specific).
6. The applet runs.

### Java Security

Java applets use a security scheme that employs a *sandbox* to limit the applet's access to certain specific areas within the user's system and protects the system from malicious or poorly written applets. The applet is supposed to run only within the sandbox. The sandbox restricts the applet's environment by restricting access to a user's hard drives and system resources. If the applet does not go outside the sandbox, it is considered safe.

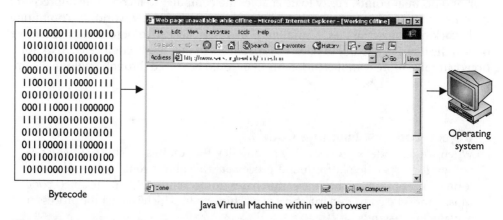

Bytecode

Java Virtual Machine within web browser

Operating system

**Figure 11-25** Java is platform independent because it is not compiled to processor-specific machine code. The JVM interprets bytecode to machine code for that specific computer system.

> **Browser Settings**
> Java applets and the actions that they perform can be prevented and controlled by specific browser settings. These settings do not affect full-fledged Java applications running outside of the browser.

However, as with many other things in the computing world, the bad guys have figured out how to escape their confines and restrictions. Programmers have figured out how to write applets that enable the code to access hard drives and resources that are supposed to be protected by the Java security scheme. This code can be malicious in nature and cause destruction and mayhem to the user and her system.

Java employs a sandbox in its security scheme, but if an applet can escape the confines of the sandbox, the system can be easily compromised.

There is a different type of Java applet, which is deemed *trusted* because it provides a digital signature. This type of applet has access to all system resources and is not confined to a sandbox. This type of applet is usually not a component on the Internet for users to download and install, but is developed by in-house programmers and distributed within an intranet to provide some type of business-oriented functionality. The browser checks the digital signature presented by the Java applet and makes a decision on whether it comes from a known, trusted source before allowing it to execute.

## ActiveX

ActiveX is a Microsoft technology that is used to write controls that Internet users can download to increase their functionality and Internet experience. Instead of trying to keep ActiveX components in a safe area for its computations and activities, this language practices security by informing the user where the program came from. The user can decide whether to trust this origin or not.

ActiveX technology provides security levels and authentication for users to be able to control the security of the ActiveX components they download. Unlike Java applets, ActiveX components are downloaded to a user's hard drive when he chooses to add the functionality that the component provides. This means that the ActiveX component has far greater access to the user's system.

The security level setting of the user's browser dictates if an ActiveX component is downloaded automatically or if the user is first prompted with a warning. The security level is configurable by the user via his browser controls. As the security level increases, so too does the browser's sensitivity level to signed and unsigned components and controls, and to the initialization of ActiveX scripts.

The main difference between Java and ActiveX security is that Java sets up a sandbox for the code to execute in, and this restricts the code's access to resources within the user's computer. ActiveX uses Authenticode technology, which relies on digital certificates and trusting certificate authorities. (Signing, digital certificates, and certificate authorities are explained in detail in Chapter 8.) Although both are good and interesting technologies, they have inherent flaws. Java has not been able to ensure that all code stays within the sandbox, which has caused several types of security compromises; these instances are examples of malware. (*Malware* is a general term for malicious code.) ActiveX doesn't necessarily provide security and presents annoying dialog boxes to users. The users do not necessarily know what they are viewing and can become confused and scared or continually click OK because they don't understand the risks involved.

## Malicious Software (Malware)

There are several types of malicious code: viruses, worms, Trojan horses, and logic bombs. They usually are dormant until activated by an event the user or system initiates. They can be spread through using e-mail, sharing media (floppy disks), sharing documents and programs, or downloading things from the Internet, or they can be purposely inserted by an attacker.

Adhering to the usual rule of not opening an e-mail attachment that comes from an unknown source is one of the best ways to combat malicious code. However, recent viruses and worms have infected personal e-mail address books, so this precaution is not a sure thing to protect systems from malicious code. If an address book is infected and used during an attack, the victim gets an e-mail message that seems to have come from a person he knows. Because he knows this person, he will proceed to open the e-mail message and double-click the attachment. Bam! His address book is now infected, and his system just spread the virus to all his friends and acquaintances.

Antivirus software should be installed to watch for known virus signatures, and host intrusion detection software can be used to watch for suspicious activity, file access, and changes to help detect evildoers and their malicious activity.

Malicious code can be detected through the following clues:

- File size increase
- Many unexpected disk accesses
- Change in update or modified timestamp
- Sudden decrease of hard drive space
- Unexpected and strange activity by applications

The following section quickly looks at a few types of malicious code.

**NOTE** A "pseudo-flaw" is code inserted into an application on purpose to trap potential intruders.

## Virus

A *virus* is a small application, or string of code, that infects applications. The main function of a virus is to reproduce, and it requires a host application to be able to do this. In other words, viruses cannot replicate on their own. A virus infects files by inserting or attaching a copy of itself to the file. The virus may also cause destruction by deleting system files, displaying graphics, reconfiguring systems, or overwhelming mail servers. Several viruses have been released that achieved self-perpetuation by mailing themselves to every entry in a victim's personal address book. The virus masqueraded as coming from a trusted source. The ILOVEYOU, Melissa, and Naked Wife viruses used the programs Outlook and Outlook Express as their host applications and were replicated when the victim chose to open the message.

Macros are programs written in Word Basic, Visual Basic, or VBScript and are usually used with Microsoft Office products. Macros automate tasks that users would otherwise have to carry out themselves. Users can define a series of activities and common tasks for the application to perform when a button is clicked, instead of doing each of those tasks individually. A *macro virus* is a virus written in one of these macro languages and is platform independent. They infect and replicate in templates and within documents. Macro viruses are common because they are extremely easy to write, and Office products are in wide use.

Some viruses infect the boot sector (*boot sector viruses*) of a computer and either move data within the boot sector or overwrite the sector with new information. Some boot sector viruses have part of their code in the boot sector, which can initiate the virus, and the rest of their code in sectors on the hard drive it has marked off as bad. Because the sectors are marked as bad, the operating system and applications will not attempt to use those sectors; thus, they will not get overwritten.

Other types of viruses append themselves to executables on the system and compress them by using the user's permissions (*compression viruses*). When the user chooses to use that executable, the system automatically decompresses it and the malicious code, which usually causes the malicious code to initialize and perform its dirty deeds.

A *stealth virus* hides the modifications that it has made to files or boot records. This can be accomplished by monitoring system functions used to read files or sectors and forging the results. This means that when applications or users attempt to read an infected file, or sector, the original, uninfected form will be presented instead of the actual infected form.

### What Is a Virus?

A virus is a program that searches out other programs and infects them by embedding a copy of itself. When the infected program executes, the embedded virus is executed, which propagates the infection.

> ## Macro Languages
> Macro languages enable users to edit, delete, and copy files. Because these languages are so easy to use, many more types of macro viruses are possible.

So a stealth virus is a virus that hides its tracks after infecting a system. Once infected, the virus can make modifications to make the computer appear the same as before. The virus can show the original file size of a file it infected instead of the new, larger size to try to trick the antivirus software into thinking that no changes have been made.

A *polymorphic virus* produces varied but operational copies of itself. This is done in the hopes of outwitting a virus scanner. Even if one or two copies are found and disabled, other copies may still remain active within the system.

The polymorphic virus can use different encryption schemes requiring different decryption routines. This would require an antivirus scan to exploit several scan strings, one for each possible decryption method, in order to identify all copies of this type of virus.

These viruses can also vary the sequence of their instructions by including *noise*, or bogus instructions, with other useful instructions. They can also use a mutation engine and a random-number generator to change the sequence of their instructions in the hopes of not being detected. A polymorphic virus has the capability to change its own code, enabling the virus to have hundreds or thousands of variants. These activities can cause the virus scanner to not properly recognize the virus and to leave it alone.

A *multipart virus* infects both the boot sector of a hard drive and executable files. The virus first becomes resident in memory and then infects the boot sector. Once it is in memory, it can infect the entire system.

A *self-garbling virus* attempts to hide from antivirus software by garbling its own code. As the virus spreads, it changes the way its code is formatted. A small portion of the virus code decodes the garbled code when activated.

*Meme viruses* are not actual computer viruses but types of e-mail messages that are continually forwarded around the Internet. They can be chain letters, e-mail hoax virus alerts, religious messages, or pyramid selling schemes. They are replicated by humans, not software, and can waste bandwidth and spread fear. There are several e-mails that are passed around describing dangerous viruses, even though the viruses are not real. People believe the e-mails and feel as though they are doing the right thing by passing them on and telling their friends about this supposedly dangerous malware, but really the people have been duped and are themselves spreading a meme virus.

 **NOTE** An EICAR test is done with antivirus software by introducing a benign virus to test the detection and reaction activities of the software. Antivirus software products have an EICAR.com file and a signature that matches this file. After software configurations are completed, then you put this file on the system to test the antivirus product's reactions to a virus.

## Worm

*Worms* are different from viruses in that they can reproduce on their own without a host application, and are self-contained programs. A worm can propagate itself by using e-mail, TCP/IP, and disk drives. The definitions of a worm and virus are continually merging, and the distinction is becoming more blurred. The ILOVEYOU program was a worm. When the user executed an e-mail attachment, several processes were spawned automatically. The worm was copied and sent to all addresses within the victim's address book. Some files on the hard drive were deleted and replaced. If these were opened, the worm self-propagation started again. ILOVEYOU acts as a virus by requiring the use of an e-mail client, like Outlook, and works as a worm by reproducing itself when the user opens infected files that reside on his hard drive.

## Logic Bomb

A *logic bomb* executes a program, or string of code, when a certain event happens or a date and time arrives. For example, if a user accesses her bank account software, a logic bomb may be initiated, and a program may be triggered to copy the user's account number and transaction codes. Another example is when a user accesses the Internet through his modem, as shown in Figure 11-26. This action can initiate a planted bomb that sends a message to an attacker over the Internet to let him know that the user is online and in position for an attack.

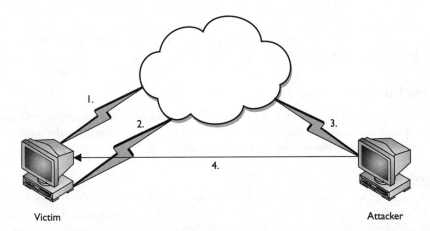

1. Victim connects to the Internet, which is the event that kicks off a logic bomb.
2. The logic bomb "calls" the attacker to indicate that the victim is on the Internet.
3. The attacker receives the message.
4. The attacker attacks the victim.

**Figure 11-26** A logic bomb is initiated by specific events.

## Trojan Horse

A *Trojan horse* is a program that is disguised as another program. For example, a Trojan horse can be named Notepad.exe and have the same icon as the regular Notepad program. However, when a user executes Notepad.exe, the program can delete system files. Trojan horses perform the useful functionality in addition to the malicious functionality in the background. So the Trojan horse named Notepad.exe may still run the Notepad program for the user but in the background manipulate files or cause some other malicious acts. A host-based IDS can be configured to watch certain files and detect when they grow in size, which is often a sign of a Trojan horse. If the original Notepad .exe was 50KB in size and then grew to 2MB, it may indicate that a Trojan horse has infected that program.

*Remote access Trojans* are malicious programs that run on systems and allow intruders to access the system remotely. They mimic the functionality of legitimate remote control programs used for remote administration, but they are used for sinister purposes instead of helpful activities. They are developed to allow for stealth installation and operation. They are usually hidden in some type of mobile code, such as in Java applets or ActiveX controls that are downloaded from web sites.

The Trojan can send an e-mail to the attacker to indicate that the system has been infected. The Trojan and attacker work in a client/server model. The remote access Trojan installed on the victim's system is the server portion, and the attacker has a client piece. The server portion of the Trojan listens on a specific port, which allows a remote backdoor into the victim's system. The fun never ends.

So a Trojan horse appears to serve one purpose, but in reality it performs different and often malicious tasks. This malware was named after the Trojan horse of Greek mythology that Greek soldiers used to sneak into the city of Troy. The horse looked like a gift, but it was filled with Greek soldiers ready for battle.

## Attacks

This section shows how software weaknesses and bugs are used to provide methods of bringing down systems and/or networks. The weaknesses can reside in the applications, the operating system, protocols, and the network stack.

## Denial of Service

The network stack is the portion of the operating system that enables devices to communicate over the network. This is where packets are built and sent over the wire and where packets are received and processed. Different operating systems and vendors interpret the Requests for Comments (RFCs) for networking protocols differently, which end up in slightly different network stacks. These differences can contain their own

---

### What Is a Trojan Horse?

A Trojan horse is a useful program that contains hidden code that exploits the authorization process to violate security.

flaws that can be taken advantage of to produce a *denial-of-service (DoS)* attack. These attacks are performed by sending malformed packets to a system that does not recognize the format and thus does not know how to properly process it. This can cause the system to crash or stop processing other packets (denial of service).

DoS attacks cost businesses millions of dollars each year because of system downtime, lost revenue and productivity, diminished reputation, and the man-hours involved in tracking down the problem and fixing it. DoS attacks can interrupt service or completely deny legitimate users access to needed system resources.

DoS attacks can consume a victim's bandwidth by flooding the network connection either from an attacker with more bandwidth than the victim or from several attackers working together to saturate the victim's network and bring it to its knees. If more than one attack is involved, each attacker amplifies the effects of the other attackers by combining their bandwidth capabilities and overwhelming the victim's network segment, as Figure 11-27 illustrates.

**Figure 11-27**
DoS attacks can be amplified by several attackers combining their bandwidth and attacking simultaneously.

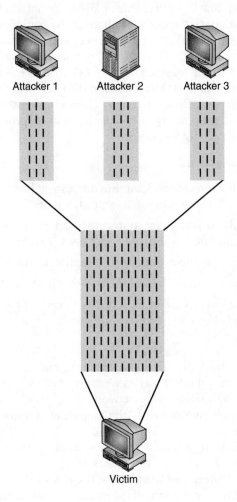

Another type of DoS attack uses up all of the victim's resources instead of consuming the network's bandwidth. The resources can be processes, file system quotas, memory allocation, and CPU utilization. The following sections discuss some of the possible DoS attacks available.

## Smurf

*Oh, a cute little blue attack.*

The Internet Control Message Protocol (ICMP) is the mini-messenger of IP and can be used to find out what systems are up and running (or alive) when being used within the ping utility. ICMP reports status reports and error messages. When a user pings another computer, the ping utility sends an ICMP ECHO REQUEST message, and if the system is up and running, it responds with an ECHO REPLY message. It basically says, "Hello, computer 10.10.10.1, are you up and running?" and that computer answers back, "Yep."

The *smurf* attack requires three players: the attacker, the victim, and the amplifying network. The attacker spoofs, or changes the source IP address in a packet header, to make an ICMP ECHO REQUEST packet seem as though it originated at the victim's system. This ICMP ECHO REQUEST message is broadcast to the amplifying network, which replies to the message in full force. The victim system and victim's network are overwhelmed. The ECHO functions of ICMP are there to determine if a computer is up and running and accepting requests. However, this attack takes advantage of the protocol's lack of certain safety measures built in to protect computers from being overwhelmed with ECHO messages.

### Countermeasures

- Disable direct broadcast functionality at border routers to make sure a certain network is not used as an amplifying site.
- Configure parameter routers to reject as incoming messages any packets that contain internal source IP addresses. These packets are spoofed.
- Allow only the necessary ICMP traffic into and out of an environment.
- Employ a network-based IDS to watch for suspicious activity.
- Some systems are more sensitive to certain types of DoS, and patches have already been released. The appropriate patches should be applied.

## Fraggle

*Fraggle* is an attack that is similar to smurf, but instead of using ICMP, it uses the User Datagram Protocol (UDP) as its weapon of choice. The attacker broadcasts a spoofed UDP packet to the amplifying network, which in turn replies to the victim's system. The larger the amplifying network, the larger the amount of traffic that is pointed at the victim's system.

Different ICMP and UDP packets should be restricted from entering a network, for many reasons. An attacker often uses these protocols to learn the topology of a network, locate routers, and learn about the types of systems within the network. Because we want to limit the amount of information available to attackers, the following restrictions should take place at the network's perimeter routers.

## Countermeasures

- Disable direct broadcast functionality at perimeter routers to make sure a certain network is not used as an amplifying site.

- Packets that contain internal source IP addresses should not be accepted by perimeter routers as incoming messages. These packets are spoofed.

- Allow only the necessary UDP packets into and out of the environment.

- Employ a network-based IDS to watch for suspicious activity.

- Some systems are more sensitive to certain types of DoS, and patches have already been released. The appropriate patches should be applied.

## SYN Flood

*Wanna talk? Wanna talk? Wanna talk? Wanna talk? Wanna talk? Wanna talk? Response: This is looking like a SYN attack.*

Because TCP is a connection-oriented protocol, it must set up a virtual connection between two computers. This virtual connection requires handshaking, and when using the TCP protocol, this requires a three-way process. If computer Blah would like to communicate with computer Yuck, Blah will send a synchronous (SYN) packet to a specific port on Yuck that is in a LISTEN state. If Yuck is up, running, and accepting calls, it will reply to Blah with an SYN/ACK acknowledgment message. After receiving that message, Blah will send an ACK message to Yuck, and the connection will be established.

Systems, and their network stack, are expected to only have to deal with a certain number of these types of connections, so they have allocated only a certain amount of resources necessary for these types of functions. A quick analogy is in order. If Katie is only expecting three to five friends to show up at her house for a get-together on Friday night, she will most likely only buy a couple of six packs of beer and munchies. When Friday night comes around and over 100 people show up, the party comes to a standstill when there is no more beer and only a bag of pretzels to go around. The same sort of thing is true within the network stack. Once 10 to 12 SYN requests are received, the system runs out of resources to process any more requests to set up communications paths.

Attackers can take advantage of this design flaw by continually sending the victim SYN messages with spoofed packets. The victim will commit the necessary resources to set up this communications socket, and it will send its SYN/ACK message waiting for the ACK message in return. However, the victim will never receive the ACK message, because the packet is spoofed, and the victim system sent the SYN/ACK message to a computer that does not exist. So the victim system receives an SYN message, and it dutifully commits the necessary resources to set up a connection with another computer. This connection is queued waiting for the ACK message, and the attacker sends another SYN message. The victim system does what it is supposed to and commits more resources, sends the SYN/ACK message, and queues this connection. This may only need to happen a dozen times before the victim system no longer has the necessary resources to open up another connection. This makes the victim computer unreachable from legitimate computers, denying other systems service from the victim computer.

The SYN message does not take a lot of bandwidth, and this type of attack can leave the victim computer in this state from about a minute and a half up to 23 minutes, depending on the TCP/IP stack. Because the SYN packet is spoofed, tracking down the evildoer is more difficult. Vendors have released patches that increase the connection queue and/or decrease the connection establishment timeout period, which enables the system to flush its connection queue.

### Countermeasures

- Decrease the connection-established timeout period. (This only lessens the effects of an SYN attack.)
- Increase the size of the connection queue in the IP stack.
- Install vendor-specific patches, where available, to deal with SYN attacks.
- Employ a network-based IDS to watch for this type of activity and alert the responsible parties when this type of attack is under way.
- Install a firewall to watch for these types of attacks and alert the administrator or cut off the connection.

## Teardrop

When packets travel through different networks, they may need to be fragmented and recombined depending on the network technology of each specific network. Each network technology has a maximum transmission unit (MTU), which indicates the largest packet size it can process. Some systems make sure that packets are not too large, but do not check to see if a packet is too small. The receiving system, the victim, would receive the fragments and attempt to recombine them, but these fragments have been made in such a way by an attacker that they cannot be properly reassembled. Many systems do not know how to deal with this situation. Attackers can take advantage of this design flaw and send very small packets that would cause a system to freeze or reboot.

### Countermeasures

- Install the necessary patch or upgrade the operating system.
- Disallow malformed fragments of packets to enter environment.
- Use a router that combines all fragments into a full packet prior to routing it to the destination system.

## Distributed Denial of Service

A *distributed denial-of-service (DDoS)* attack is a logical extension of the DoS attack that gets more computers involved in the act. DoS attacks overwhelm computers by one computer sending bad packets or continually requesting services until the system's resources are all tied up and cannot honor any further requests. The DDoS attack uses hundreds or thousands of computers to request services from a server or server farm until the system or web site is no longer functional.

The more recent victims of this type of attack have been Yahoo!, CNN.com, ZDNet, and E*Trade. These sites are developed to handle many hits to their sites and have the capability to process a large number of service requests each hour. However, a DDoS attack implements a volume of service requests that could overload any site. The attack can use other computers that knowingly participate, but most likely are unknowingly used as slaves in the process. The attacker creates master controllers that can in turn control slaves, or *zombie* machines. The master controllers are systems that an attacker has been able to achieve administrative rights to, so that programs can be loaded that will wait and listen for further instructions. The components of the third tier of computers are referred to as zombies because they do not necessarily know that they are involved in an attack. Scripts that have been put on their hard drives execute, and together all the zombies work in concert to overwhelm a victim. An example of a DDoS attack is shown in Figure 11-28.

## Countermeasures

- Use perimeter routers to restrict unnecessary ICMP and UDP traffic.
- Employ a network-based IDS to watch for this type of suspicious activity.
- Disable unused subsystems and services on computers.
- Rename the administrator account and implement strict password management so that systems cannot be used unknowingly.
- Configure parameter routers to reject as incoming messages any packets that contain internal source IP addresses. These packets are spoofed.

**Figure 11-28**
In a DDoS attack, the attacker uses masters to control the zombies to overwhelm the victim with requests.

## DNS DoS Attacks

Domain Name Service (DNS) servers are used to map hostnames to IP addresses. DNS is used on almost every network and all over the Internet. People understand hostnames (for example, **www.isc2.org**), and the network layer of the network stack understands IP addresses. So, when a user types in a URL, a DNS server transforms this address into the numerical equivalent that is understandable by computers and network devices. Once the system and network devices know the right IP address, they know how to route the packets properly and communicate with the destination computer. It is like stopping at a gas station for directions. If you tell the guy behind the counter that you are looking for the post office, he will tell you that the post office is on Main Street and proceed to tell you the streets and turns to get to this destination. Thank goodness for gas stations and DNS servers!

Each DNS server is responsible for certain hosts, which are collectively referred to as a *zone*. Each host has its own record within the DNS server that contains its IP addresses, and this is how the DNS translates the hostname to the IP address. If a record that indicates that **www.isc2.org** is mapped to 10.10.10.1 is replaced with a record that says that **www.isc2.org** is mapped to 10.10.10.2 instead, the real web site would not be able to receive hits. Users would not be able to get to this site, resulting in a DoS. This is how DNS DoS attacks can occur. If the actual DNS records are unattainable to the attacker to alter in this fashion, which they should be, the attacker can insert this data into the cache of the server instead of replacing the actual records, which is referred to as *cache poisoning*. DNS servers often cache previously resolved requests to make the next request for that hostname quicker. If the attacker replaces real data with bogus information in the server's cache, the DNS server and user would not necessarily know about this violation.

Because DNS servers are responsible only for a finite number of clients, many times one DNS server will have to ask another DNS server for help in finding out the requested information for the user. The DNS server can ask a root server for the address of the DNS server that is authoritative for the destination domain. This recursively resolves DNS names, and the original DNS server acts as a middleman by sending the user the address of the DNS server that is responsible for the host the user is asking about. An attacker can send a bogus response to the requesting DNS server, and the DNS server will in turn send this bogus information to the requesting user. This points the user to a different site from what was planned, resulting in a DoS because the user cannot get the service he requested.

### Countermeasures

- Ensure that DNS servers have public and internal records. The public records serve Internet requests and contain no sensitive information pertaining to the internal network. The internal records should be unreachable from the Internet and are used to resolve queries from internal users.

- Use a primary and secondary DNS server per zone so that DNS servers are redundant.

- Update the DNS BIND version, because different DNS BIND versions have different vulnerabilities.

- Employ secure DNS, which is explained in the next section.

## Secure DNS

DNS servers contain records that enable the mapping between hostnames and IP addresses, as stated earlier. Primary DNS servers make all the necessary changes to the records when host and/or IP addresses change, and these records are then distributed to the secondary DNS servers. If a secondary server received bogus records from an attacker instead of receiving legitimate records from the primary DNS server, the secondary server would not know the difference and would update its records accordingly. Then, when a user's computer contacted this secondary DNS server to translate hostnames to IP addresses, the records would contain incorrect information. Attacks like this have taken place mainly to embarrass businesses, by redirecting users to indecent sites or to competitors' sites. However, this also causes DoS because the users cannot get where they need to go.

When Security DNS (DNSSEC) is implemented, the secondary DNS servers must authenticate the systems that are updating their records. Integrity checks are also performed to ensure that records were not modified or corrupted during transmission. Secure DNS protects DNS servers from having their records updated by unauthorized sources.

## Timing Attacks

Attacks work because computers act in a predictable manner. Computers have to follow a sequence of steps, and when an attacker understands these steps and figures out how to take advantage of them, she can perform a type of timing attack. The following are three types of timing attacks you should be familiar with:

- **Between-the-lines entry attack**   The attacker taps into and uses an active communications line. The user may not be using the connection at that time, but it is still active, so the attacker jumps in and uses it.

- **NAK/ACK attack**   A NAK is a negative acknowledgement to tell a system that a certain piece of information was not received or that a certain message or parameter is unacceptable. Some systems do not deal with negative acknowledgements properly—they were only programmed to accept ACK packets, and attackers use this weakness to their advantage.

- **Line-disconnect attack**   An attacker may access and keep a communications session open after the user attempts to terminate it. In this case, the user drops off, thinking the connection is closed, but actually the attacker kept the connection active and is now using it.

# Summary

Although functionality is the first concern when developing software, adding security into the mix before the project starts and integrating it into every step of the development process would be highly beneficial. Although many companies do not view this as the most beneficial approach to software development, they are becoming convinced of it over time as more security patches and fixes have to be developed and released, and as their customers continually demand more secure products.

Software development is a complex task, especially as technology changes at the speed of light, environments evolve, and more expectations are placed upon vendors who wish to be the "king of the mountain" within the software market. This complexity also makes implementing effective security more challenging. For years, programmers and developers did not need to consider security issues within their code, but this trend is changing. Education, experience, awareness, enforcement, and the demands of the consumers are all necessary pieces to bring more secure practices and technologies to the program code we all use.

# Quick Tips

- Buffer overflows happen when an application does not check the length of data that is input.
- If an application fails for any reason, it should go directly to a secure state.
- A database management system (DBMS) is the software that controls the access restrictions, data integrity, redundancy, and the different types of manipulation available for a database.
- In relational database terminology, a database row is called a tuple.
- A database primary key is how a specific row is located from other parts of the database.
- A view is an access control mechanism used in databases to ensure that only authorized subjects can access sensitive information.
- A relational database uses two-dimensional tables with rows (tuples) and columns (attributes).
- A hierarchical database uses a tree-like structure to define relationships between data elements, using a parent/child relationship.
- A distributed database, or network database, has databases that are physically in different areas but logically connected to represent one main database.
- Most databases have a data definition language (DDL), a data manipulation language (DML), a query language (QL), and a report generator.
- A pseudo-flaw is code inserted into an application or system on purpose with the intention of trapping future intruders.

- A data dictionary is a central repository that describes the data elements within a database and their relationships. A data dictionary contains data about a database, which is called metadata.

- Database integrity is provided by concurrency mechanisms. One concurrency control is locking, which prevents users from accessing and modifying data that is being used by someone else.

- Entity integrity makes sure that a row, or tuple, is uniquely identified by a primary key, and referential integrity ensures that every foreign key refers to an existing primary key.

- A rollback cancels changes and returns the database to its previous state. This takes place if there was a problem during a transaction.

- A commit statement terminates a transaction and saves all changes to the database.

- A checkpoint is used if there is a system failure or problem during a transaction. The user is returned to the state of the last checkpoint.

- Aggregation can happen if a user does not have access to a group of elements, but has access to some of the individual elements within the group. Aggregation happens if the user combines the information of these individual elements and figures out the information of the group of data elements, which is at a higher sensitivity level.

- Inference is the capability to derive information that is not explicitly available.

- Common attempts to prevent inference attacks are partitioning the database, cell suppression, and adding noise to the database.

- Polyinstantiation is the process of allowing a table to have multiple rows with the same primary key. The different instances are distinguished by their security levels or classifications.

- Polymorphism is when different objects are given the same input and react differently.

- The two largest security problems associated with database security are inference and aggregation.

- Data warehousing combines data from multiple databases and data sources.

- Data mining is the process of massaging data held within a data warehouse to provide more useful information to users.

- Data-mining tools produce metadata, which can contain previously unseen relationships and patterns.

- Security should be addressed in each phase of system development. Security should not be addressed only at the end of development, because of the added cost, time, and effort and the lack of functionality.

- Systems and applications can use different models that use different life cycles, but all models contain project initiation, functional design analysis and planning, system design specifications, software development, installation, operations and maintenance, and disposal in some form or fashion.

- Risk management and assessments should start at the beginning of a project and continue throughout the lifetime of the product.

- If proper design for a product is not put into place in the beginning, more effort will have to take place in the implementation, testing, and maintenance phases.

- Separation of duties should be practiced in roles, environments, and functionality pertaining to development of a product.

- A programmer should not have direct access to code in production. This is an example of separation of duties.

- Certification deals with testing and assessing the security mechanism in a system, and accreditation pertains to management formally accepting the system and its security level.

- Media that contains sensitive information must be disposed of in a controlled and secure way. This may mean physical destruction of the media.

- Change control needs to be put in place at the beginning of a project and must be enforced through each phase.

- Changes must be authorized, tested, and recorded. The changes must not affect the security level of the system or its capability to enforce the security policy.

- High-level programming languages are translated into machine languages for the system and its processor to understand.

- Source code is translated into machine code, or object code, by compilers, assemblers, and interpreters.

- Object-oriented programming provides modularity, reusability, and more granular control within the programs themselves.

- Objects are members, or instances, of classes. The classes dictate the objects' data types, structure, and acceptable actions.

- Objects communicate with each other through messages.

- A method is functionality that an object can carry out.

- Data and operations internal to objects are hidden from other objects, which is referred to as data hiding. Each object encapsulates its data and processes.

- Objects can communicate properly because they use standard interfaces.

- Object-oriented design represents a real-world problem and modularizes the problem into cooperating objects that work together to solve the problem.

- If an object can perform a function without the help of others, it has high cohesion.

- If an object does not require much interaction with other modules, it has low coupling.

- The best programming design enables objects to be as independent and modular as possible; therefore, the higher the cohesion and the lower the coupling, the better.

- An object request broker (ORB) manages communications between objects and enables them to interact in a heterogeneous and distributed environment.

- Common Object Request Broker Architecture (CORBA) provides a standardized way for objects within different applications, platforms, and environments to communicate. It accomplishes this by providing standards for interfaces between objects.

- Component Object Model (COM) provides an architecture for components to interact on a local system. Distributed COM (DCOM) uses the same interfaces as COM, but enables components to interact over a distributed, or networked, environment.

- Open Database Connectivity (ODBC) enables several different applications to communicate with several different types of databases by calling the required driver and passing data through that driver.

- Object linking and embedding (OLE) enables a program to call another program (linking) and enables a piece of data to be inserted inside another program or document (embedding).

- Dynamic Data Exchange (DDE) enables applications to work in a client/server model by providing the interprocess communication (IPC) mechanism.

- Distributed Computing Environment (DCE) provides much of the same functionality as DCOM, which enables different objects to communicate in a networked environment.

- DCE uses universal unique identifiers (UUIDs) to keep track of different subjects, objects, and resources.

- An expert system uses a knowledge base full of facts, rules of thumb, and expert advice. It also has an inference machine that matches facts against patterns and determines which rules are to be applied.

- Expert systems are used to mimic human reasoning and replace human experts.

- Artificial neural networks (ANNs) attempt to mimic a brain by using units that react like neurons.

- ANNs can learn from experiences and can match patterns that regular programs and systems cannot.

- Java security employs a sandbox so that the applet is restricted from accessing the user's hard drive or system resources. Programmers have figured out how to write applets that escape the sandbox.

- ActiveX uses a security scheme that includes digital signatures. The browser security settings determine how ActiveX controls are dealt with.

- A virus is an application that requires a host application for replication.
- Macro viruses are common because the languages used to develop macros are easy to use and they infect Office products, which are everywhere.
- A boot sector virus overwrites data in the boot sector and can contain the rest of the virus in a sector it marked as "bad."
- A stealth virus hides its tracks and its actions.
- A polymorphic virus tries to escape detection by making copies of itself and modifying the code and attributes of those copies.
- Multipart viruses can have one part of the virus in the boot sector and another part of the virus on the hard drive.
- A self-garbling virus tries to escape detection by changing, or garbling, its own code.
- A worm does not require a host application to replicate.
- A logic bomb executes a program when a predefined event takes place, or a date and time are met.
- A Trojan horse is a program that performs useful functionality and malicious functionally without the user knowing it.
- Smurf and Fraggle are two examples of DoS attacks that take advantage of protocol flaws and use amplifying networks.
- Expert systems use inference engine processing, automatic logical processing, and general methods of searching for problem solutions.

## Questions

Please remember that these questions are formatted and asked in a certain way for a reason. You must remember that the CISSP exam is asking questions at a conceptual level. Questions may not always have the perfect answer, and the candidate is advised against always looking for the perfect answer. The candidate should look for the best answer in the list.

1. What is the final stage in the change control management process?
   A. Configure the hardware properly.
   B. Update documentation and manuals.
   C. Inform users of the change.
   D. Report the change to management.

2. Which best describes a logic bomb?
   A. Used to move assets from one computer to another
   B. Action triggered by a specified condition
   C. Self-replicating
   D. Performs a useful action and a malicious action

3. An application is downloaded from the Internet to perform disk cleanup and to delete unnecessary temporary files. The application is also recording network login data and sending it to another party. This application is best described as which of the following?

   A. Virus

   B. Trojan horse

   C. Worm

   D. Logic bomb

4. Why are macro viruses so prevalent?

   A. They replicate quickly.

   B. They infect every platform in production.

   C. The languages used to write macros are very easy to use.

   D. They are activated by events that happen commonly on each system.

5. Which action is not part of configuration management?

   A. Submitting a formal request

   B. Operating system configuration and settings

   C. Hardware configuration

   D. Application settings and configuration

6. Expert systems are used to automate security log review for what purpose?

   A. To develop user behavioral models

   B. To ensure best access methods

   C. To detect intrusion

   D. To provide statistics that will not be used for baselines

7. Which form of malware has a purpose of reproducing itself utilizing system resources?

   A. Worm

   B. Virus

   C. Trojan horse

   D. Multipart virus

8. Expert systems use each of the following items except for _____.

   A. Automatic logical processing

   B. General methods of searching for problem solutions

   C. Inference engine

   D. Cycle-based reasoning

9. Which of the following replicates itself by attaching to other programs?

   A. Worm

   B. Virus

   C. Trojan horse

   D. Malware

10. What is the importance of inference in an expert system?

    A. The knowledge base contains facts, but must also be able to combine facts to derive new information and solutions.

    B. The inference machine is important to fight against multipart viruses.

    C. The knowledge base must work in units to mimic neurons in the brain.

    D. The access must be controlled to prevent unauthorized access.

11. A system has been patched many times and has recently become infected with a dangerous virus. If antivirus software indicates that disinfecting a file may damage it, what is the correct action?

    A. Disinfect the file and contact the vendor.

    B. Back up the data and disinfect the file.

    C. Replace the file with the file saved the day before.

    D. Restore an uninfected version of the patched file from backup media.

12. Which of the following centrally controls the database and manages different aspects of the data?

    A. Data storage

    B. Database

    C. Data dictionary

    D. Access control

13. What is the purpose of polyinstantiation?

    A. To restrict lower-level subjects from accessing low-level information

    B. To make a copy of an object and modify the attributes of the second copy

    C. To create different objects that will react in different ways to the same input

    D. To create different objects that will take on inheritance attributes from their class

14. When a database detects an error, what enables it to start processing at a designated place?

    A. Checkpoint

    B. Data dictionary

    C. Metadata

    D. Data-mining tool

15. Database views provide what type of security control?

    A. Detective

    B. Corrective

    C. Preventive

    D. Administrative

16. If one department can view employees' work history and another group cannot view their work history, what is this an example of?

    A. Context-dependent access control

    B. Content-dependent access control

    C. Separation of duties

    D. Mandatory access control

17. Which of the following is used to deter database inference attacks?

    A. Partitioning, cell suppression, and noise and perturbation

    B. Controlling access to the data dictionary

    C. Partitioning, cell suppression, and small query sets

    D. Partitioning, noise and perturbation, and small query sets

18. What is a disadvantage of using content-dependent access control on databases?

    A. It can access other memory addresses.

    B. It can cause concurrency problems.

    C. It increases processing and resource overhead.

    D. It can cause deadlock situations.

19. If security was not part of the development of a database, how is it usually handled?

    A. Cell suppression

    B. Trusted back end

    C. Trusted front end

    D. Views

20. What is an advantage of content-dependent access control in databases?

    A. Processing overhead

    B. Ensures concurrency

    C. Disallows data locking

    D. Granular control

21. Which of the following is used in the Distributed Computing Environment technology?

    A. Globally unique identifier (GUID)

    B. Universal unique identifier (UUID)

    C. Universal global identifier (UGID)

    D. Global universal identifier (GUID)

22. When should security first be addressed in a project?

    A. During requirements development

    B. During integration testing

    C. During design specifications

    D. During implementation

23. Online application systems that detect an invalid transaction should do which of the following?

    A. Roll back and rewrite over original data.

    B. Terminate all transactions until properly addressed.

    C. Write a report to be reviewed.

    D. Checkpoint each data entry.

24. What is the final phase of the system development life cycle?

    A. Certification

    B. Unit testing

    C. Development

    D. Accreditation

25. Which of the following are rows and columns within relational databases?

    A. Rows and tuples

    B. Attributes and rows

    C. Keys and views

    D. Tuples and attributes

## Answers

1. **D.** A common CISSP theme is to report to management, get management's buy in, get management's approval, and so on. The change must first be approved by the project or program manager. Once the change is completed, it is reported to senior management, usually as a status report in a meeting or a report that addresses several things at one time, not necessarily just this one item.

2. **B.** A logic bomb is a program that has been coded to carry out some type of activity when a certain event takes place, or when a time and date are met. For example, an attacker may have a computer attack another computer on Michelangelo's birthday, the logic bomb may be set to execute in two weeks and three minutes, or it may initiate after a user strikes specific keys in a certain sequence.

3. **B.** A Trojan horse looks like an innocent and helpful program, but in the background it is carrying out some type of malicious activity unknown to the user. The Trojan horse could be corrupting files, sending the user's password to an attacker, or attacking another computer.

4. **C.** A macro language is written specifically to allow nonprogrammers to program macros. Macros are sequences of steps that can be executed with one keystroke, and they were developed to reduce the repetitive activities of users. The language is very simplistic, which is why macro viruses are so easy to write.

5. **A.** Submitting a formal request would fall under the change control umbrella. Most environments have a change control process that dictates how all changes will be handled, approved, and tested. Once the change is approved, there needs to be something in place to make sure the actual configurations that are implemented to carry out this change take place properly. This is the job of configuration management.

6. **C.** An IDS can be based on an expert system or have an expert system component. The job of the expert system is to identify patterns that would represent an intrusion or an attack that an IDS without this component may not pick up on. The expert system will look at a history of events and identify a pattern that would be otherwise very hard to uncover.

7. **A.** A worm does not need a host to replicate itself, but it does need an environment, which would be an operating system and its resources. A virus requires a host, which is usually a specific application.

8. **D.** An expert system attempts to reason like a person by using logic that works with the gray areas in life. It does this by using a knowledge base, automatic logical processing components, general methods of searching for solutions, and an inference engine. It carries out its logical processing with rule-based programming.

9. **B.** As stated in an earlier answer, a virus requires a host to replicate, which is usually a specific application.

10. **A.** The whole purpose of an expert system is to look at the data that it has to work with and what the user presents to it and to come up with new or different solutions. It basically performs data-mining activities, identifies patterns and relationships the user could not see, and provides solutions. This is the same reason you would go to a human expert. You would give her your information, and she would combine it with the information she knows and give you a solution or advice, which is not necessarily the same data you gave her.

11. **D.** Some files cannot be properly sanitized by the antivirus software without destroying them or affecting their functionality. So, the administrator must replace such a file with a known uninfected file. And the administrator needs to make sure he has the patched version of the file, or else he could be introducing other problems. Answer C is not the *best* answer because the administrator may not know that the file was clean yesterday, so just restoring yesterday's file may get him into the same boat.

12. **C.** A data dictionary holds the schema information about the database. This schema information is represented as metadata. When the database administrator modifies the database attributes, he is modifying the data dictionary because it is the central component that holds this type of information. When a user attempts to access the database, the data dictionary will be consulted to see if this activity is deemed appropriate.

13. **B.** Instantiation is what happens when an object is created from a class. Polyinstantiation is when more than one object is made, and the other copy is modified to have different attributes. This can be done for several reasons. The example that was given in the chapter was a way to use polyinstantiation for security purposes, to ensure that a lower-level subject could not access an object at a higher level.

14. **A.** Savepoints and checkpoints are similar in nature. A savepoint is used to periodically save the state of the application and the user's information. A checkpoint saves data held in memory to a temporary file. Both are used so that if the application endures a glitch, it has the necessary tools to bring the user back to his working environment without losing any data. You experience this with a word processor when it asks you if you want to review the recovered version of a file you were working on.

15. **C.** A database view is put into place to prevent certain users from viewing specific data. This is a preventive measure, because the administrator is preventing the users from seeing data that is not meant for them. This is one control to use to prevent inference attacks.

16. **B.** Content-dependent access control carries out its restrictions based upon the sensitivity of the data. Context-dependent control reviews the previous access requests and makes an access decision based on the previous activities.

17. **A.** Partitioning means to logically split the database into parts. Views then dictate what users can view specific parts. Cell suppression means that specific cells are not viewable by certain users. And noise and perturbation is when bogus information is inserted into the database to try to give potential attackers incorrect information.

18. **C.** Relative to other types of access control, content-dependent control requires a lot of overhead and processing, because it makes decisions based on the sensitivity of the data instead of purely on the identity of the requesting subject.

19. **C.** A trusted front end can be developed to implement more security that the database itself is lacking. It can require a more granular and stringent access control policy by requiring tighter identification and authorization pieces than those that are inherent in the database. Front ends can also be developed to provide more user friendliness and interoperability with other applications.

20. **D.** As stated in an earlier answer, content-dependent access control bases its access decision on the sensitivity of the data. This provides more granular control, which almost always means that more processing is required.

21. **B.** A universal unique identifier (UUID) is used by DCE, and a globally unique identifier (GUID) is used by DCOM. DCE and DCOM both need a naming structure to keep track of their individual components, which is what these different naming schemes provide.

22. **A.** The trick to this question, and any one like it, is that security should be implemented at the first possible phase of a project. Requirements are gathered and developed at the beginning of a project, which is project initiation. The other answers are steps that follow this phase, and security should be integrated right off the bat instead of in the middle or at the end.

23. **C.** This can seem like a tricky question. It is asking you if the system detected an invalid transaction, which is most likely a user error. This error should be logged so that it can be reviewed. After the review, the supervisor, or whoever makes this type of decision, will decide whether or not it was a mistake and investigate it as needed. If the system had a glitch, power fluctuation, hangup, or any other software- or hardware-related error, that would not be an invalid transaction, and in that case the system would carry out a rollback function.

24. **D.** Out of this list, the last phase is accreditation, which is where management formally approves of the product. The question could have had different answers. For example, if it had listed disposal, that would be the right answer because that would be the last phase listed.

25. **D.** In a relational database, a row is referred to as a tuple, and a column is referred to as an attribute.

# Operations Security

This chapter presents the following:

- Administrative management responsibilities
- Product evaluation and operational assurance
- Configuration management
- Trusted recovery states
- Redundancy and fault-tolerant systems
- E-mail security
- Threats to operations security

Operations security pertains to everything that takes place to keep a network, computer systems, applications, and environment up and running in a secure and protected manner. It consists of ensuring that people, applications, and servers have the proper access privileges to only the resources that they are entitled to and that oversight is implemented via monitoring, auditing, and reporting controls. Operations take place after the network is developed and implemented. This includes the continual maintenance of an environment and the activities that should take place on a day-to-day or week-to-week basis. These activities are routine in nature and enable the network and individual computer systems to continue to run correctly and securely.

Networks and computing environments are evolving entities; just because they are secure one week does not mean that they are still secure three weeks later. Many companies pay security consultants to come in and advise them on how to improve their infrastructure, policies, and procedures. A company can then spend thousands or even hundreds of thousands of dollars to implement the consultant's suggestions, install properly configured firewalls, intrusion detection systems (IDSs), and antivirus software, and patch management systems. However, if the IDS and antivirus software do not continually have updated signatures, if the systems are not continually patched, and if firewalls and devices are not tested for vulnerabilities, then the company can easily slip back into an insecure and dangerous place. This can happen if the company does not keep its operations security tasks up to date.

Most of the necessary operations security issues have been addressed in earlier chapters. They were integrated with related topics and not necessarily pointed out as actual operations security issues. So instead of repeating what has already been previously stated, this chapter reviews and points out the operations security topics that are important for organizations and CISSP candidates.

# Role of the Operations Department

*I am a very prudent man. Response: That is debatable.*

The continual effort to make sure that the correct policies, procedures, standards, and guidelines are in place and being followed is an important piece of the *due care* and *due diligence* efforts that companies need to perform. Due care and due diligence are comparable to the "prudent person" concept. A prudent person is seen as responsible, careful, cautious, and practical, and a company practicing due care and due diligence is seen in the same light. The right steps need to be taken to achieve the necessary level of security, while balancing ease of use, compliance with regulatory requirements, and cost constraints. It takes continued effort and discipline to retain the proper level of security. Operations security is all about ensuring that people, applications, equipment, and the overall environment are properly and adequately secured.

Although operations security is the practice of continual maintenance to keep an environment running at a necessary security level, liability and legal responsibilities also exist when performing these tasks. Companies, and senior executives at those companies, often have legal obligations to ensure that resources are protected, safety measures are in place, and security mechanisms are tested to guarantee that they are actually providing the necessary level of protection. If these operations security responsibilities are not fulfilled, the company may have more than antivirus signatures to be concerned about.

There are many threats that an organization needs to consider, including disclosure of confidential data, theft of assets, corruption of data, interruption of services, and destruction of the physical or logical envrionment. It is important to identify systems and operations that are sensitive, meaning they need to be protected from disclosure, and critical, meaning they must remain available at all times. (Refer to Chapter 10 to learn more about the legal, regulatory, and ethical responsibilities of companies when it comes to security.)

It is also important to note that while organizations have a significant portion of their operations activities tied to computing resources, they still rely on physical resources as well to make things work, including paper documents and data stored on microfilm, tapes, and other removable media. A large part of operations security includes ensuring that the physical and environmental concerns are adequately addressed, such as temperature and humidity controls, media reuse, disposal, and destruction of media containing sensitive information.

Overall, operations security is about configuration, performance, fault tolerance, security, and accounting and verification management to ensure that proper standards of operations and compliance requirements are met.

## Administrative Management

*I think our tasks should be separated, because I don't trust you. Response: Fine by me.*

Administrative management is a very important piece of operations security. One aspect of administrative management is dealing with personnel issues. This includes separation of duties and job rotation. The objective of *separation of duties* is to ensure that one person acting alone cannot compromise the company's security in any way.

High-risk activities should be broken up into different parts and distributed to different individuals or departments. That way, the company does not need to put a dangerously high level of trust in certain individuals. For fraud to take place, collusion would need to be committed, meaning more than one person would have to be involved in the fraudulent activity. Separation of duties, therefore, is a preventive measure that requires collusion to occur in order for someone to commit an act that is against policy.

Table 12-1 shows many of the common roles within organizations and their corresponding job definitions. Each role needs to have a completed and well defined job description. Security personnel should use these job descriptions when assigning access rights and permissions, to ensure that individuals have access only to the resources required to carry out their tasks.

Table 12-1 contains just a few roles with a few tasks per role. Organizations should create a *complete* list of roles used within their environment, with each role's associated tasks and responsibilities. This should then be used by data owners and security personnel when determining who should have access to specific resources and the type of access.

Separation of duties helps to prevent mistakes and to minimize conflicts of interest that can take place if one person is performing a task from beginning to end. For instance, a programmer should not be the only one to test her own code. Another person with a different job and agenda should perform functionality and integrity testing on the programmer's code, because the programmer may have a focused view of what the program is supposed to accomplish and thus may test only certain functions and input values, and only in certain environments.

| Organizational Role | Core Responsibilities |
|---|---|
| Control Group | Obtains and validates information obtained from analysts, administrators, and users and passes it on to various user groups. |
| Systems Analyst | Designs data flow of systems based on operational and user requirements. |
| Application Programmer | Develops and maintains production software. |
| Help Desk/Support | Resolves end user and system technical or operations problems. |
| IT Engineer | Performs the day-to-day operational duties on systems and applications. |
| Database Administrator | Creates new database tables and manages the database. |
| Network Administrator | Installs and maintains the LAN/WAN environment. |
| Security Administrator | Defines, configures, and maintains the security mechanisms protecting the organization. |
| Tape Librarian | Receives, records, releases, and protects system and application files backed up on media such as tapes or disks. |
| Quality Assurance | Can consist of both Quality Assurance (QA) and Quality Control (QC). QA ensures that activities meet the prescribed standards regarding supporting documentation and nomenclature. QC ensures that the activities, services, equipment, and personnel operate within the accepted standards. |

**Table 12-1** Roles and Associated Tasks

Another example of separation of duties is the difference between the functions of a computer user and the functions of a system administrator. There must be clear-cut lines drawn between system administrator duties and computer user duties. These will vary from environment to environment and will depend on the level of security required within the environment. System administrators usually have the responsibility of performing backups and recovery procedures, setting permissions, adding and removing users, and developing user profiles. The computer user, on the other hand, may be allowed to install software, set an initial password, alter desktop configurations, and modify certain system parameters. The user should not be able to modify her own security profile, add and remove users globally, or make critical access decisions pertaining to network resources. This would breach the concept of separation of duties.

*Job rotation* means that, over time, more than one person fulfills the tasks of one position within the company. This enables the company to have more than one person who understands the tasks and responsibilities of a specific job title, which provides backup and redundancy if a person leaves the company or is absent. Job rotation also helps identify fraudulent activities, and therefore can be considered a detective type of control. If Keith has performed David's position, Keith knows the regular tasks and routines that are to be completed to fulfill the responsibilities of that job. Thus, Keith is better able to identify if David does something out of the ordinary and suspicious. (Refer to Chapters 4 and 6 for further examples pertaining to job rotation.)

Least privilege and need to know are also administrative-type controls that should be implemented in an operations environment. *Least privilege* means that an individual should have just enough permissions and rights to fulfill his role in the company and no more. If an individual has excessive permissions and rights, it could open the door to abuse of access and put the company at more risk than is necessary. For example, if Dusty is a technical writer for a company, he does not necessarily need to have access to the company's source code. So, the mechanisms that control Dusty's access to resources should not let him access source code. This would properly fulfill operations security controls that are in place to protect resources.

Least privilege and need to know have a symbiotic relationship. Each user should have a need to know about the resources that he is allowed to access. If Mike does not have a need to know how much the company paid last year in taxes, then his system rights should not include access to these files, which would be an example of exercising

## Security and Network Personnel

The security administrator must not report to the network administrator, because their responsibilities have different focuses. The network administrator is under pressure to ensure high availability of the network and resources. High availability does not usually mean the most secure configurations—and in this we find the conflict. A security administrator's responsibility is to ensure a high level of protection, not high availability and "up time." The security administrator should be within a different chain of command from that of the network personnel, to ensure that security is not ignored or assigned a lower priority.

least privilege. The use of new identity management software that combines traditional directories, access control systems, and user provisioning within servers, applications, and systems is becoming the norm within organizations. This software provides the capabilities to ensure that only specific access privileges are granted to specific users and often includes advanced audit functions that can be used to verify compliance to legal and regulatory directives.

A user's access rights may be a combination of the least-privilege attribute, the user's security clearance, the user's need to know, the sensitivity level of the resource, and the mode in which the computer operates. A system can operate in different modes depending on the sensitivity of the data being processed, the clearance level of the users, and what those users are authorized to do. The mode of operation describes the conditions under which the system actually functions. These are clearly defined in Chapter 5.

*Mandatory vacations* are another type of administrative control, though the name may sound a bit odd at first. Chapter 3 touches on reasons to make sure that employees take their vacations; the reasons include being able to identify fraudulent activities and enabling job rotation to take place. If an accounting employee has been performing a salami attack by shaving off pennies from multiple accounts and putting the money into his own account, a company would have a better chance of figuring this out if that employee is required to take a vacation for a week or longer. When the employee is on vacation, another employee has to fill in. She might uncover questionable documents and clues of previous activities, or the company may see a change in certain patterns once the employee who is committing fraud is gone for a week or two.

It is best for auditing purposes if the employee takes two contiguous weeks off from work. The belief is that an organization can often do without the services of an employee for a week without requiring someone to take over their work. If this is also the case for a two-week absence, there may be other questions that should be discussed regarding that overall position. Again, the idea behind mandatory vacations is that, traditionally, those employees who have committed fraud are usually the ones who have resisted going on vacation because of their fear of being found out while away.

## Accountability

*You can't prove that I did it. Response: Ummm, yes we can.*

Users' access to resources must be limited and properly controlled to ensure that excessive privileges do not provide the opportunity to cause damage to a company and its resources. Users' access attempts and activities while using a resource need to be properly monitored, audited, and logged. The individual user ID needs to be included in the audit logs to enforce individual responsibility. Each user should understand his responsibility when using company resources and be accountable for his actions.

Capturing and monitoring audit logs helps to determine if a violation has actually occurred or if system and software reconfiguration is needed to better capture only the activities that fall outside of established boundaries. If user activities were not captured and reviewed, it would be very hard to determine if users have excessive privileges or if there has been unauthorized access.

Auditing needs to take place in a routine manner. Also, someone needs to review audit and log events; if no one looks at the output, there really is no reason to run audits. Audit and function logs often contain too much cryptic or mundane information to be interpreted manually. This is why products are available that parse logs for companies and report important findings. Logs should be monitored and reviewed, through either manual or automatic methods, to uncover suspicious activity and to identify an environment that is shifting away from its original baselines. This is how administrators can be warned of many problems before they become too big and out of control. (See Chapters 3, 6, and 10 for auditing, logging, and monitoring issues.)

When monitoring, administrators need to ask certain questions that pertain to the users, their actions, and the current level of security and access:

- *Are users accessing information and performing tasks that are not necessary for their job description?* The answer would indicate whether users' rights and permissions need to be reevaluated and possibly modified.

- *Are repetitive mistakes being made?* The answer would indicate whether users need to have further training.

- *Do too many users have rights and privileges to sensitive or restricted data or resources?* The answer would indicate whether access rights to the data and resources need to be reevaluated, whether the number of individuals accessing them needs to be reduced, and/or whether the extent of their access rights should be modified.

## Security Operations and Product Evaluation

When products are evaluated for the level of trust and assurance they provide, many times operational assurance and life-cycle assurance are part of the evaluation process. *Operational assurance* concentrates on the product's architecture, embedded features, and functionality that enable a customer to continually obtain the necessary level of protection when using the product. Examples of operational assurances examined in the evaluation process are access control mechanisms, the separation of privileged and user program code, auditing and monitoring capabilities, covert channel analysis, and trusted recovery when the product experiences unexpected circumstances.

*Life-cycle assurance* pertains to how the product was developed and maintained. Each stage of the product's life cycle has standards and expectations it must fulfill before it can be deemed a highly trusted product. Examples of life-cycle assurance standards are design specifications, clipping-level configurations, unit and integration testing, configuration management, and trusted distribution. Vendors that are looking to achieve one of the higher security ratings for its products will have each of these issues evaluated and tested.

The following sections address several of these types of operational assurance and life-cycle assurance issues not only as they pertain to evaluation, but also as they pertain to a company's responsibilities once the product is implemented. A product is just a tool for a company to use for functionality and security; it is up to the company to ensure that this functionality and security are continually available through responsible and proactive steps.

## Clipping Levels

*I am going to keep track of how many mistakes you make.*

Companies can set predefined thresholds for the number of certain types of errors that will be allowed before the activity is considered suspicious. The threshold is a baseline for violation activities that may be normal for a user to commit before alarms are raised. This baseline is referred to as a *clipping level*. Once this clipping level has been exceeded, further violations are recorded for review. Most of the time, IDS software is used to track these activities and behavior patterns, because it would be too overwhelming for an individual to continually monitor stacks of audit logs and properly identify certain activity patterns. Once the clipping level is exceeded, the IDS can e-mail a message to the network administrator, send a message to his pager, or just add this information to the logs, depending on how the IDS software is configured.

The goal of using clipping levels, auditing, and monitoring is to discover problems before major damage occurs and, at times, to be alerted if a possible attack is underway within the network.

 **NOTE** The security controls and mechanisms that are in place must have a degree of transparency. This enables the user to perform tasks and duties without having to go through extra steps because of the presence of the security controls. Transparency also does not let the user know too much about the controls, which helps prevent him from figuring out how to circumvent them. If the controls are too obvious, an attacker can figure out how to compromise them more easily.

## References

- NIST Security Configuration Checklists Program for IT Products
  http://csrc.nist.gov/checklists/

- *An Introduction to Computer Security: The NIST Handbook*   http://csrc.nist.gov/publications/nistpubs/800-12/

- "The Operations Security Connection," by Arion N. Pattakos, *PM*
  (Jan.-Feb. 1999)   www.au.af.mil/au/awc/awcgate/dau/pattakjf.pdf

## Configuration Management

*The only thing that is constant is change.*

Every company should have a policy indicating how changes take place within a facility, who can make the changes, how the changes are approved, and how the changes are documented and communicated to other employees. Without these policies in place, people can make changes that others do not know about and that have not been approved, which can result in a confusing mess at the lowest end of the impact scale, and a complete breakdown of operations at the high end. Heavily regulated industries such as finance, pharmaceuticals, and energy have very strict guidelines regarding what specifically can be done and at exactly what time and under which conditions. These guidelines are intended to avoid problems that could impact large segments of the population or downstream partners. Without strict controls and guidelines, vulnerabilities can be introduced into an environment. Tracking down and reversing the changes after everything is done can be a very complicated and potentially nearly impossible task.

The changes can happen to network configurations, system parameters, applications, and settings when adding new technologies, application configurations, or devices, or when modifying the facility's environmental systems. Change control is important not only for an environment, but also for a product during its development and life cycle. Changes must be effective and orderly, because time and money can be wasted by continually making changes that do not meet an ultimate goal.

**NOTE** Change control is the management of security features and the implementation of levels of assurance through the diligent control of all changes made to a system's hardware, software, and firmware configurations throughout the entire development and operational life cycle.

Some changes can cause a serious network disruption and affect systems' availability. This means that changes must be thought through, approved, and carried out in a structured fashion. Backup plans may be necessary in case the change causes unforeseen negative effects. For example, if a facility is changing its power source, there should be backup generators on hand in case the transition does not take place as smoothly as planned. Or if a server is going to be replaced with a different server type, interoperability issues could prevent users from accessing specific resources, so a backup or redundant server should be in place to ensure availability and continued productivity.

A well-structured change management process should be put into place to aid staff members through many different types of changes to the environment. This process should be laid out in the change control policy. Although the types of changes vary, a standard list of procedures can help keep the process under control and ensure that it is carried out in a predictable manner. The following steps are examples of the types of procedures that should be part of any change control policy:

1. **Request for a change to take place**   Requests should be presented to an individual or group that is responsible for approving changes and overseeing the activities of changes that take place within an environment.

2. **Approval of the change**   The individual requesting the change must justify the reasons and clearly show the benefits and possible pitfalls of the change. Sometimes the requester is asked to conduct more research and provide more information before the change is approved.

3. **Documentation of the change**   Once the change is approved, it should be entered into a change log. The log should be updated as the process continues toward completion.

4. **Tested and presented**   The change must be fully tested to uncover any unforeseen results. Depending on the severity of the change and the company's organization, the change and implementation may need to be presented to a change control committee. This helps show different sides to the purpose and outcome of the change and the possible ramifications.

5. **Implementation**    Once the change is fully tested and approved, a schedule should be developed that outlines the projected phases of the change being implemented and the necessary milestones. These steps should be fully documented and progress should be monitored.

6. **Report change to management**    A full report summarizing the change should be submitted to management. This report can be submitted on a periodic basis to keep management up to date and ensure continual support.

These steps, of course, usually apply to large changes that take place within a facility. These types of changes are usually expensive and can have lasting effects on a company. However, smaller changes should also go through some type of change control process. If a server needs to have a patch applied, it is not good practice to have an engineer just apply it without properly testing it on a nonproduction server, without having the approval of the IT department manager or network administrator, and without having backup and backout plans in place in case the patch causes some negative effect on the production server. Of course, these changes need to be documented.

It is also critical that the operations department create approved backout plans before implementing changes to systems or the network. It is very common for changes to cause problems that were not properly identified before the implementation process began. Many network engineers have experienced the headaches of applying poorly developed "fixes" or patches that end up breaking something else in the system. To ensure that productivity is not negatively affected by these issues, a backout plan needs to be developed. This plan describes how the team will restore the system to its original state, before the change was implemented.

**Change Control Documentation**    Failing to document changes to systems and networks is only asking for trouble, because no one will remember, for example, what was done to that one server in the DMZ six months ago or how the main router was fixed when it was acting up last year. Changes to software configurations and network devices take place pretty often in most environments; keeping all of these details properly organized is impossible, unless someone keeps a log of this type of activity.

Numerous changes can take place in a company, some of which are listed here:

- New computers installed
- New applications installed
- Different configurations implemented
- Patches and updates installed
- New technologies integrated
- Policies, procedures, and standards updated
- New regulations and requirements implemented
- Network or system problems identified and fixes implemented
- Different network configuration implemented
- New networking devices integrated into the network
- Company acquired by or merged with another company

The list could go on and on and could be general or detailed. Many companies have experienced some major problem that affects the network and employee productivity. The IT department may run around trying to figure out the issue and go through hours or days of trial-and-error exercises to find and apply the necessary fix. If no one properly documents the incident and what was done to fix the issue, the company may be doomed to repeat the same scramble six months to a year down the road.

## Media Controls

Media and devices that can be found in an operations environment require a variety of controls to ensure that they are properly preserved and that the integrity, confidentiality, and availability of the data that is held on them are not compromised.

The operational controls that pertain to these issues come in many flavors. The first are controls that prevent unauthorized access, which can be physical, administrative, and technical controls that are put into place. If the company's backup tapes are to be properly protected, they need to be stored in a place where only authorized people have access to them, which could be in a locked server room or an offsite facility. If the tapes need to be protected from environmental issues such as humidity, heat, cold, fire, and natural disasters, they should be kept in a fireproof safe in a regulated environment or in an offsite facility that controls the environment to be hospitable to data processing components. These issues are covered in detail in Chapter 6.

Companies may have a media library with a librarian in charge of protecting its resources. Users may be required to check out specific types of media and resources, instead of having the resources readily available for anyone to access them. If the library controls backed-up data, each tape should be labeled with the following information:

- The date of creation
- The individual who created the backup
- The retention period (how long the data needs to be maintained)
- The classification
- The volume name and version

Media should be clearly marked and logged, its integrity should be verified, and it should be properly erased of data when necessary. When media is cleared of its contents, it is said to be *sanitized*. There are several methods to sanitize media: overwriting (zeroization), degaussing, and destruction. As stated in earlier chapters, deleting files on a piece of media does not actually make the data disappear; it only deletes the pointers to where those files still live on the disk. This is how companies that specialize in restoration can recover the deleted files intact after they have been apparently destroyed.

---

 **NOTE**  A device that performs degaussing generates a coercive magnetic force that reduces the magnetic flux density of the storage media to zero. This magnetic force is what properly erases data from media.

*Data remanence* is the residual physical representation of information that was saved and then erased in some fashion. This remanence may be enough to enable the data to be reconstructed and restored to a readable form. This can pose a security threat to a company that thinks it has properly erased confidential data from its media.

If the media does not hold confidential or sensitive information, overwriting or deleting the files may be the appropriate step to take. If the data is sensitive, degaussing may be required. If the data is highly confidential or the media cannot be properly degaussed, the appropriate action would be to physically destroy it. (Refer to Chapters 3 and 4 for further discussion on these issues.)

## System Controls

System controls are also part of operations security. Within the operating system itself, certain controls must be in place to ensure that instructions are being executed in the correct security context. The system has mechanisms that restrict the execution of certain types of instructions so that they can take place only when the operating system is in a privileged or supervisor state. This protects the overall security and state of the system and helps to ensure that it runs in a stable and predictable manner.

Operational procedures need to be developed that indicate what constitutes the proper operation of a system or resource. This would include a system startup and shutdown sequence, error handling, and restoration from a known good source.

An operating system does not provide direct access to hardware by processes of lower privilege, which are usually processes used by user applications. If a program needs to send instructions to hardware devices, the request is passed off to a process of higher privilege. To execute privileged hardware instructions, a process must be running in a restrictive and protective state. This is an integral part of the operating system's architecture, and the determination of what processes can submit what type of instructions is made based on the operating system's control tables.

Many input/output (I/O) instructions are defined as privileged and can be executed only by the operating system kernel processes. When a user program needs to send I/O information, it must notify the system's core, privileged processes that work at the inner rings of the system. These processes (called system services) authorize either the user program processes to perform these actions and temporarily increase their privileged state or the system's processes are used to complete the request on behalf of the user program. (Review Chapter 5 for a more in-depth understanding of these types of system controls.)

## Trusted Recovery

*What if my application or system blows up? Response: It should do so securely.*

When an operating system or application crashes or freezes, it should not put the system in any type of insecure state. The usual reason for a system crash in the first place is that it encountered something that it perceived as insecure or did not understand and decided that it was safer to freeze, shut down, or reboot than to perform the current activity.

An operating system's response to a type of failure can be classified as one of the following:

- System reboot
- Emergency system restart
- System cold start

A *system reboot* takes place after the system shuts itself down in a controlled manner in response to a trusted computing base (TCB) failure. If the system finds inconsistent object data structures or if there is not enough space in some critical tables, a system reboot may take place. This releases resources and returns the system to a more stable and safer state.

An *emergency system restart* takes place after a system failure happens in an uncontrolled manner. This could be a TCB or media failure caused by lower-privileged user processes attempting to access memory segments that are restricted. The system sees this as an insecure activity that it cannot properly recover from without rebooting. The system goes into a maintenance mode and recovers from the actions taken. The system is brought back up in a consistent and stable state.

A *system cold start* takes place when an unexpected TCB or media failure happens and the regular recovery procedure cannot recover the system to a more consistent state. The system, TCB, and user objects may remain in an inconsistent state while the system attempts to recover itself, and intervention may be required by the user or administrator to restore the system.

It is important to ensure that the system does not enter an insecure state when it is affected by any of these types of problems, and that it shuts down and recovers properly to a secure and stable state. (Refer to Chapter 5 for more information on TCB components and activities.)

## References

- *Configuration Management Plans: The Beginning to Your CM Solution,* **by Nadine M. Bounds and Susan Dart, Software Engineering Institute, Carnegie Mellon University** www.sei.cmu.edu/legacy/scm/papers/ CM_Plans/CMPlans.MasterToC.html

- **Configuration Management Resources from the Georgia Institute of Technology** www.cc.gatech.edu/computing/classes/cs3302_98_spring/ handouts/cm-info.html

## Input and Output Controls

*Garbage in, garbage out.*

What is input into an application has a direct correlation to what that application outputs; thus, input needs to be monitored for errors and suspicious activity. If a checker at a grocery store continually puts in the amount of $1.20 for each prime rib steak that customers buy, the store could eventually lose a good amount of money. This activity could be done either by accident, which would require proper retraining, or on purpose, which would require disciplinary actions.

Because so many companies are extremely dependent upon computers and applications to process their data, input and output controls are very important. Chapter 10 addresses illegal activities that take place when users alter the data going into a program or the output generated by a program, usually for financial gain.

The applications themselves also need to be programmed to only accept certain types of values input into them and to do some type of logic checking about the received input values. If an application requests the user to input a mortgage value of a property and the user enters 25 cents, the application should ask the user for the value again so that wasted time and processing is not done on an erroneous input value. Also, if an application has a field that is used to hold monetary values only, a user should not be able to enter "bob" in the field without the application barking. These and many more input and output controls are discussed in Chapter 11.

All the controls mentioned in the previous sections must be in place and must continue to function in a predictable and secure fashion to ensure that the systems, the applications, and the environment as a whole continue to be operational.

# Network and Resource Availability

In the triangle of security services, *availability* is one of the foundational components, the other two being *confidentiality* and *integrity*. Network and resource availability often is not fully appreciated until it is gone. That is why administrators and engineers need to implement effective backup and redundant systems to make sure that when something happens (and something will happen), users' productivity will not be drastically affected.

The network needs to be properly maintained to make sure that the network and its resources will always be available when they're needed. For example, the cables need to be the correct type for the environment and technology used, and cable runs should not exceed the recommended lengths. Older cables should be replaced with newer ones, and period checks should be made for possible cable cuts and malfunctions.

A majority of networks use Ethernet technology, which is very resistant to failure. Token Ring was designed to be fault tolerant and does a good job when all the computers within this topology are configured and act correctly. If one network interface card (NIC) is working at a different speed than the others, the whole ring can be affected and traffic may be disrupted. Also, if two systems have the same MAC address, the whole network can be brought down. These issues need to be considered when maintaining an existing network. If an engineer is installing a NIC on a Token Ring network, she should ensure that it is set to work at the same speed as the others and that there is no possibility for duplicate MAC addresses.

## Single Points of Failure

*Don't put all your eggs in one basket or all your electrons in one device.*

A *single point of failure* poses a lot of potential risk to a network, because if the device fails, a segment or even the entire network is negatively affected. Devices that could represent single points of failure are firewalls, routers, network access servers, T1 lines, switches, bridges, hubs, and authentication servers—to name a few. The best defenses against being vulnerable to these single points of failure are proper maintenance, regular backups, and redundancy.

Multiple paths should exist between routers in case one router goes down, and dynamic routing protocols should be used so that each router will be informed when a change to the network takes place. For WAN connections, a failover option should be configured to enable an ISDN to be available if the WAN router fails.

An uninterruptible power supply (UPS) and redundant array of inexpensive disks (RAID) should be in place and properly configured. UPS is addressed in Chapter 6, so we will just touch upon it here and show how it relates to network availability.

The UPS should be able to provide a clean and steady power source to the crucial systems and resources on the network. RAID provides fault tolerance for hard drives and can improve system performance. Redundancy and speed are provided by breaking up the data and writing it across several disks so that different disk heads can work simultaneously to retrieve the requested information. Control data is also spread across each disk—this is called *parity*—so that if one disk fails, the other disks can work together and restore its data.

## RAID

*Everyone be calm—this is a raid. Response: Wrong raid.*

**Redundant array of inexpensive disks (RAID)** is a technology used for redundancy and performance improvement. It combines several physical disks and aggregates them into logical arrays. When data is saved, it is written across all drives. A RAID appears as a single drive to applications and other devices.

When data is written across all drives, the technique of *striping* is used. This activity divides and writes the data over several drives. The write performance is not affected, but the read performance is increased dramatically because more than one head is retrieving data at the same time. It might take the RAID system six seconds to write a block of data to the drives and only two seconds or less to read the same data from the disks.

Various levels of RAID dictate the type of activity that will take place within the RAID system. Some levels deal only with performance issues, while other levels deal with performance and fault tolerance. If fault tolerance is one of the services that a RAID level provides, parity is involved. If a drive fails, the parity is basically instructions that tell the RAID system how to rebuild the lost data on the new hard drive. Parity is used to rebuild a new drive so that all the information is restored. Most RAID systems have *hot-swapping* disks, which means they can replace drives while the system is running. When a drive is swapped out, or added, the parity data is used to rebuild the data on the new disk that was just added.

### Intrusion Prevention System

Several intrusion prevention system (IPS) products are considered "inline" devices, which means that traffic must be processed by and go through this device before being able to move on to its destination. The concern is that if this device goes down, then all traffic will be stopped—which is a denial of service. Different IPS vendors have approached this issue in various ways. (IPSs were discussed in Chapter 4.)

The most common RAID levels used today are levels 1, 3, and 5. Table 12-2 describes each of the possible RAID levels.

 **NOTE** RAID level 15 is actually a combination of levels 1 and 5, and RAID 10 is a combination of levels 1 and 0.

## References

- **The RAID Tutorial from the University of Massachusetts**   www.ecs.umass.edu/ece/koren/architecture/Raid/raidhome.html
- **"A Case for Redundant Arrays of Inexpensive Disks (RAID)," by David A. Patterson, Garth Gibson, and Randy H. Katz**   www-2.cs.cmu.edu/~garth/RAIDpaper/Patterson88.pdf

| RAID Level | Activity | Name |
|---|---|---|
| 0 | Data striped over several drives. No redundancy or parity is involved. If one volume fails, the entire volume is unusable. It is used for performance only. | Striping |
| 1 | Mirroring of drives. Data is written to two drives at once. If one drive fails, the other drive has the exact same data available. | Mirroring |
| 2 | Data striping over all drives at the bit level. Parity data is created with a hamming code, which identifies any errors. This level specifies that up to 39 disks can be used: 32 for storage and 7 for error recovery data. This is not used in production today. | Hamming code parity |
| 3 | Data striping over all drives and parity data held on one drive. If a drive fails, it can be reconstructed from parity drive. | Byte-level parity |
| 4 | Same as level 3, except parity is created at the block level instead of the byte level. | Block-level parity |
| 5 | Data is written in disk sector units to all drives. Parity is written to all drives also, which ensures that there is no single point of failure. | Interleave parity |
| 6 | Similar to level 5 but with added fault tolerance, which is a second set of parity data written to all drives. | Second parity data (or double parity) |
| 10 | Data is simultaneously mirrored and striped across several drives and can support multiple drive failures. | Striping and mirroring |

**Table 12-2**   Different RAID Levels

## Clustering

*Okay, everyone gather over here and perform the same tasks.*

*Clustering* is a fault-tolerant server technology that is similar to redundant servers, except each server takes part in processing services that are requested. A *server cluster* is a group of servers that are viewed logically as one server to users and can be managed as a single logical system. Clustering provides for availability and scalability. It groups physically different systems and combines them logically, which provides immunity to faults and improves performance. Clusters work as an intelligent unit to balance traffic, and users who access the cluster do not know that they may be accessing different systems at different times. To the users, all servers within the cluster are seen as one unit.

If one of the systems within the cluster fails, processing continues because the rest pick up the load, although degradation in performance could occur. This is more attractive, however, than having a secondary server that waits in the wings in case a primary server fails, because this secondary server may just sit idle for a long period of time, which is wasteful. When clustering is used, all systems are used to process requests and none sits in the background waiting for something to fail.

Clustering offers a lot more than just availability, however. It also provides load balancing (each system takes a part of the processing load), redundancy, and failover (other systems continue to work if one fails).

## Backups

Backing up software and having backup hardware devices are two large parts of network availability. (These issues are covered extensively in Chapters 6 and 9, so they are discussed only briefly here.) You need to be able to restore data if a hard drive fails, a disaster takes place, or some type of software corruption occurs.

A policy should be developed that indicates what gets backed up, how often it gets backed up, and how these processes should occur. If users have important information on their workstations, the operations department needs to develop a method that indicates that backups include certain directories on users' workstations or that users move their critical data to a server share at the end of each day to ensure that it gets backed up. Backups may occur once or twice a week, every day, or every three hours. It is up to the company to determine this routine. The more frequent the backups, the more staff time that will be dedicated to it, so there needs to be a balance between backup costs and the actual risk of potentially losing data.

A company may find that conducting automatic backups through specialized software is more economical and effective than spending IT work hours on the task. The integrity of these backups needs to be checked to ensure that they are happening as expected—rather than finding out right after two major servers blow up that the automatic backups were saving only temporary files. (Review Chapters 6 and 9 for more information on backup issues.)

# E-Mail Security

The Internet was first developed mainly for government agencies and universities to communicate and share information, but today businesses depend upon it for productivity and profitability. Millions of individuals depend upon it for their window to a larger world and as a quick and efficient communications tool.

E-mail has become an important and integrated part of people's lives. It is used to communicate with family and friends, business partners and customers, coworkers and management, and online merchants and government offices. Generally, the security, authenticity, and integrity of an e-mail message are not considered in day-to-day use. Users are more aware that attachments can carry viruses than of the fact that an e-mail can be easily spoofed and that its contents can be changed while in transmission.

It is very easy to *spoof* e-mail messages, which means to alter the name in the From field. All an attacker needs to do is modify information within the Preferences section of his mail client and restart the application. As an example of a spoofed e-mail message, an attacker could change the name in the From field to the name of the network administrator and send an e-mail message to the CEO's secretary, telling her that the IT department is having problems with some servers and needs her to change her network logon to "password." If she receives this e-mail and sees that the From field has the network administrator's name in it, she will probably fulfill this request without thinking twice.

This type of activity is rampant today, and has become more of a social-engineering tactic. Another variant is referred to as *phishing*. This is the act of sending spoofed messages that pretend to originate from a source the user trusts and has a business relation with, such as a bank. In this scheme, the user is asked to click a link contained within the e-mail that will supposedly take them to their account login page so that they can do account maintenance activities. The link takes the user to a web site that looks very similar to their bank's web site but is in fact owned by the attacker. The moment the user enters their credentials, the attacker has access to the users' account information on the real site.

The solution to this and similar types of attacks is to require proper authentication to ensure that the message actually came from the source indicated. Companies that regard security as one of their top priorities would implement an e-mail protection application that can digitally sign messages, like Pretty Good Privacy (PGP), or use a public key infrastructure (PKI). These companies may also consider using an encryption protocol to help fight network sniffing and unauthorized interception of messages.

An e-mail message that travels from Arizona to Maine has many hops in between the source and destination. There are several potential interception points that can allow an attacker to intercept, view, modify, or delete the message during its journey, as shown in Figure 12-1.

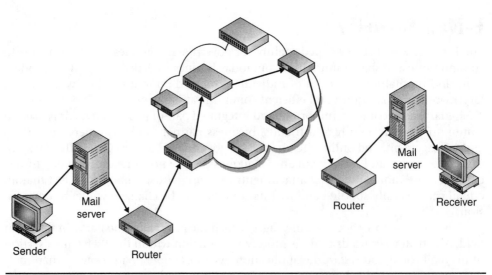

**Figure 12-1** There are several possible points where an e-mail message can be intercepted.

If a user is going to use a security scheme to protect his messages from eavesdropping, modification, and forgery, he and the recipient must use the same encryption scheme. If public key cryptography is going to be used, both users must have a way to exchange encryption keys. This is true for PGP, digital signatures, and products that follow the S/MIME standard, which are discussed in detail in Chapter 8. If an administrator, or security professional, wants to ensure that all messages are encrypted between two points and does not want to have to depend on the users to properly encrypt their messages, she can implement a VPN (also discussed in Chapter 8).

## How E-Mail Works

*I think e-mail is delivered by an e-mail fairy wearing a purple dress. Response: Exactly.*

A user has an e-mail client that is used to create, modify, address, send, receive, and forward messages. This e-mail client may provide other functionality, such as a personal address book and the ability to add attachments, set flags, recall messages, and store messages within different folders.

A user's e-mail message is of no use unless it can actually be sent somewhere. This is where *Simple Mail Transfer Protocol (SMTP)* comes in. SMTP works as a message transfer agent, as shown in Figure 12-2, and moves the message from the user's computer to the mail server when the user clicks the Send button. SMTP is also a message-exchange standard, and most people are used to seeing its familiar addressing scheme: *something@somewhere.com*.

Many times, a message needs to travel throughout the Internet and through different mail servers before it arrives at its destination mail server. SMTP is the protocol that carries this message, and it works on top of the Transmission Control Protocol (TCP). TCP is used as the transport protocol because it is a reliable protocol and provides se-

**Figure 12-2** SMTP works as a transfer agent for e-mail messages.

quencing and acknowledgments to ensure that the e-mail message arrived successfully at its destination.

The user's e-mail client must be SMTP compliant to be properly configured to use this protocol. The client provides an interface to the user so that she can create and modify messages as needed, and then the client passes the message off to SMTP. So, to use the analogy of sending a letter via the post office, the e-mail client is the typewriter that a person uses to write the message, SMTP is the mail courier who picks up the mail and delivers it to the post office, and the post office is the mail server. The mail server has the responsibility of understanding where the message is heading and properly routing the message to that destination.

The mail server is often referred to as an SMTP server. The most common SMTP server software within the Unix world is Sendmail, which is actually an e-mail server application. This means that Unix uses Sendmail software to store, maintain, and route e-mail messages. Within the Microsoft world, Microsoft Exchange is mostly used, and in Novell, GroupWise is the common SMTP server. SMTP works closely with two mail server protocols, POP and IMAP, which are explained in the following sections.

## POP

*Post Office Protocol (POP)* is an Internet mail server protocol that supports incoming and outgoing messages. A mail server that uses POP stores and forwards e-mail messages and works with SMTP to move messages between mail servers.

A smaller company may have one POP server that holds all employee mailboxes, whereas larger companies may have several POP servers, one for each department within the organization. There are also Internet POP servers that enable people all over the world to exchange messages. This system is useful because the messages are held on the mail server until users are ready to download their messages, instead of trying to push messages right to a person's computer, which may be down or offline.

The e-mail server can implement different authentication schemes to ensure that an individual is authorized to access a particular mailbox, but this is usually handled through usernames and passwords.

## IMAP

*Internet Message Access Protocol (IMAP)* is also an Internet protocol that enables users to access mail on a mail server. IMAP provides the same types of functionality as POP, but has more capabilities and functionality. If a user is using POP, when he accesses his mail server to see if he has received any new messages, all messages are automatically downloaded to his computer. Once the messages are downloaded from the POP server, they are usually deleted from that server, depending upon configuration. POP can cause frustration for mobile users because the messages are automatically pushed down to their computer or device and they may not have the necessary space to hold all the messages. This is especially true for mobile devices that can be used to access e-mail servers. This is also inconvenient for people checking their mail on other people's computers. If Christina checks her e-mail on Jessica's computer, all of Christina's new mail could be downloaded to Jessica's computer.

If a user uses IMAP instead of POP, she can download all the messages or leave them on the mail server within her remote message folder, referred to as a mailbox. The user can also manipulate the messages within this mailbox on the mail server as if the messages resided on her local computer. She can create or delete messages, search for specific messages, and set and clear flags. This gives the user much more freedom and keeps the messages in a central repository until the user specifically chooses to download all messages from the mail server.

IMAP is a store-and-forward mail server protocol that is considered POP's successor. IMAP also gives administrators more capabilities when it comes to administering and maintaining the users' messages.

## E-Mail Relaying

*Could you please pass on this irritating message that no one wants? Response: Sure.*

E-mail has changed drastically from the purely mainframe days. In those days, mail used simple Systems Network Architecture (SNA) protocols and ASCII format. Today, there are several types of mail systems that run on different operating systems and offer a wide range of functionality. Sometimes companies need to implement different types of mail servers and services within the same network, which can become a bit overwhelming and a challenge to secure.

Most companies have their public mail servers in their DMZ and may have one or more mail servers within their LAN. The mail servers in the DMZ are in this protected space because they are directly connected to the Internet. These servers should be tightly locked down and their relaying mechanisms should be correctly configured. Mail servers use a *relay agent* to send a message from one mail server to another. This relay agent needs to be properly configured so that a company's mail server is not used by another for spamming activity.

Spamming usually is illegal, so the people doing the spamming do not want the traffic to seem as though it originated from their equipment. They will find mail servers on the Internet, or within company DMZs, that have loosely configured relaying mechanisms and use these computers to send their spam. If relays are configured "wide open" on a mail server, the mail server can be used to receive *any* mail message and send it on to the intended recipients, as shown in Figure 12-3. This means that if a company does not properly configure its mail relaying, its server can be used to distribute advertisements for other companies, spam messages, and pornographic material. It is important that mail servers have proper antispam features enabled, which are actually antirelaying features. A company's mail server should only accept mail destined for its domain and should not forward messages to other mail servers and domains.

Many companies employ antivirus and content-filtering applications on their mail servers to try to stop the spread of malicious code and not allow unacceptable messages through the e-mail gateway. It is important to filter both incoming and outgoing messages. This helps to ensure that inside employees are not spreading viruses or sending out messages that are against company policy.

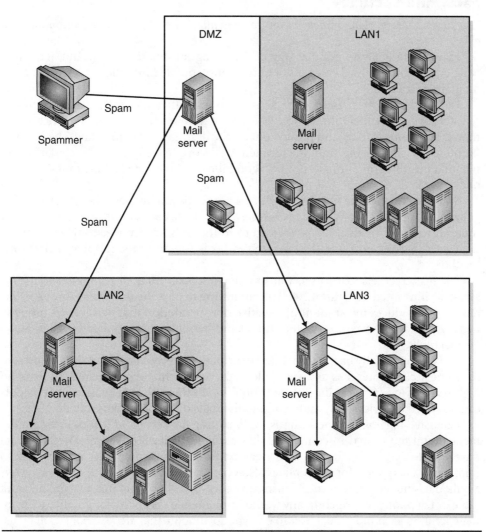

**Figure 12-3**  Mail servers can be used for spam if relay functionality is not properly configured.

## References

- "How E-Mail Works," by Marshall Brain, HowStuffWorks   http://computer.howstuffworks.com/email.htm
- IETF S/MIME Mail Security (smime) Charter   www.ietf.org/html.charters/smime-charter.html
- "IMAP: A New Internet Message Access Protocol," by Gordon Benett, *Intranet Journal*   http://idm.internet.com/foundation/imap4.shtml

## Facsimile Security

*Your covert strategic plans on how we are going to attack are sitting in a fax bin in the front office.*

Faxing data is a very popular way of delivering information today and, like other types of communications channels, it must be incorporated into the security policy and program of companies.

Fax machines can present some security issues if they are being used to transmit sensitive or confidential information. The information is scanned into the device, transmitted over a phone line, and printed out on the destination fax machine. The received fax often just sits in a bin until the recipient walks over to retrieve it. If it contains confidential information, it might not be a good idea to have it just lying around for anyone to see it.

Some companies use *fax servers*, which are systems that manage incoming and outgoing faxed documents. When a fax is received by the fax server, the fax server properly routes it to the individual it is addressed to so that it is kept in electronic form rather than actually printed. Typically, the received fax is routed to the recipient's electronic mailbox.

The fax server lets many users transmit documents from their computers to the fax server, as illustrated in Figure 12-4, without having to pass the document through a fax device. This reduces the amount of sensitive documentation that needs to be properly destroyed and can save money on printing and thermal paper required by stand-alone fax machines.

A fax server usually has the capability to print the received faxes, but this can present the same security breaches as a stand-alone fax device. In environments that demand high security levels, the print feature should be disabled so that sensitive documents can be stored and viewed by authorized individuals only and never printed.

Extensive logging and auditing is available for fax servers and should be implemented and monitored in companies that require this level of security. Because data travels to and from the fax server in cleartext form, some companies may choose to implement encryption for faxed materials. A company may implement a *fax encryptor*, a bulk data-link encryption mechanism that encrypts all fax data that hits the network cable or telephone wire. A company would implement a fax encryptor if it did not want to depend on each individual user to encrypt documents that are faxed; instead, by us-

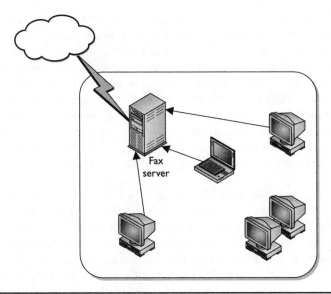

**Figure 12-4**   A fax server can be used instead of stand-alone fax devices.

ing a fax encryptor, the company is sure that all data leaving that system is properly encrypted.

## Hack and Attack Methods

Several types of attacks have been explained in the chapters throughout this book. This section brings together these attack methods, and others that have not been presented, to show how they are related, how they can be detected, and how they can be countered.

A majority of the tools used by hackers have dual capabilities in that they can be used for good or evil. An attacker could use tool ABC to find a vulnerability to exploit, and a security professional could use the same tool to identify a vulnerability so that she could fix it. When this tool is used by black hats (attackers), it is referred to as *hacking*. When a white hat (security professional) uses this tool, it is considered *ethical hacking* or *penetration testing*.

The tools used to perform attacks on networks and systems have, over time, become so sophisticated that they offer even a moderately skilled individual (sometimes called a *script kiddie*) the ability to perform very damaging attacks. The tools are simple to use and often come with a GUI that walks the person through the steps of resource identification, network mapping, and the actual attack. The person no longer needs to understand protocol stacks, know what protocols' fields are used by different systems, understand how operating systems process program and assembly code, or know how to write program code at all. The hacker just needs to insert an IP range within a GUI tool and click Go. There are now many different types of tools used by the attacker community, some of which are even capable of generating virus and worm autocode and building specific exploits for a given operating system, platform, or application release level.

Hacking tools are easily and widely available to anyone who wants them. At one time, these types of tools were available only to a small group of highly skilled people, but today hundreds of web sites are devoted to telling people how to perform exploits and providing the tools for a small fee or for free. The ease of use of these tools, the increased interest in hacking, and the deep dependence that companies and people have upon technology have provided the ingredients to a recipe that can cause continuous damage.

Any network administrator who maintains a firewall, or any person who runs a personal firewall on a computer, knows how active the Internet is with probes and port scanners. These front-end protection devices are continually getting hit with packets requesting information. Some probes look for specific types of computers, such as Unix systems, web servers, or databases, because the attacker has specific types of attacks she wants to carry out, and these attacks target specific types of operating systems or applications. These probes could also be looking to plant Trojan horses or viruses in computers in the hope of causing destruction or compromising the systems so that they can be used in future distributed denial-of-service (DDoS) attacks. These probes scan thousands of networks and computers with no one target in mind. They just look for any and all vulnerabilities, and the attacker does not necessarily care where the vulnerable system happens to be located.

Sometimes the attacker has a specific target in mind and thus does not send out a wide-sweeping probe. When an attacker identifies her target, she will do network mapping and port scanning. Network-mapping tools send out seemingly benign packets to many different systems on a network. These systems respond to the packets, and the mapping tool interrogates the returned packets to find out what systems are up and running, the types of operating systems that responded, and possibly their place within the network. This might seem like a lot of information from just some packets being sent out, but these tools are highly calibrated to extract as much data from the returned packet as possible. Different operating systems vary in their protocol stacks, meaning they use different fields within protocol frames or populate those fields differently than other operating systems. So if the tool sent a message to two computers running different operating systems, they may respond with two slightly different answers. They may both respond with the same basic answer using the same protocol, but because the two operating systems use varied protocol stacks, one computer may use a certain value within its response and the other system may use a different value within its response, as shown in Figure 12-5. When the tool receives these two slightly different responses, it can determine what type of operating system just replied. The tool and the attacker start to put together the topology of the victim's network.

The network-mapping tool may have a database that maps operating systems, applications, and versions to the type of responses and message fields they use. So if the networking tool received a reply from its ICMP ping sweep, which sends out ICMP packets to targets within a configured IP address range, and one reply has the

**Figure 12-5** A tool can be used to determine the type of operating system with which an attacker is communicating.

ICMP "Don't fragment" bit enabled, the tool may determine that the target is a Unix host. Or if the tool sent out a TCP SYN packet and the response received was an FIN/ACK, the tool may determine that the target is a Windows NT system. This activity is referred to as *operating system fingerprinting*.

It is important to the attacker to know what systems are alive on the network. When the tool first sends out packets, it is looking to see what computers respond, which indicates that they are powered on and alive. Normally, when a computer sends an SYN packet, it is requesting to set up a conversation channel with the destination computer, the first step in the TCP handshaking procedure. However, hacking tools that use the SYN packet have no intention of setting up a real conversation channel, but instead hope to trick the target system into replying. The normal response to an SYN packet is SYN/ACK, but the network administrator may have blocked this type of traffic at the firewall or router or disabled the port on the computer. The attacker may receive no response or receive a message saying "Port Unreachable." This response tells the network-mapping tool that the company's firewall allows this type of traffic to enter the network, but that specific port is closed on the target machine. These are all clues used by the attacker to learn more and more about an environment. This knowledge enables the attacker to figure out the most successful ways of attacking.

So, the first step for the attacker is to find out what systems are alive, attempt to find out what type of operating systems the targets are running, and start to build the network's topology. The next step for an attacker is to do *port scanning* on the target machines, which identifies open ports on a computer. Ports provide doors into the operating system for other computers, processes, protocols, and attackers. If an attacker can find out what ports are open, she can have a pretty good idea of what services are running on the systems. Knowing what services are available can further clarify the type of system the target is. For example, if a target computer responds to an SMTP packet sent to its port 25, the attacker could conclude that this computer may be an e-mail server. However, more work would need to be done to confirm this.

The attacker wants to know what operating systems, applications, and services are running so that she knows what types of attacks to run. If she finds a Unix server running Apache, she would run totally different types of attacks on it than she would run for a Windows 2000 server running IIS. Each operating system, application, and service has its own vulnerabilities, and properly identifying these enables the attacker to be more successful in her attack.

There are 65,535 TCP and 65,535 UDP ports on every computer system. The first 1024 are said to be well-known ports. This means that a specific port number under 1025 is usually mapped to a well-known and used protocol. For instance, port 80 is almost always mapped to the Hypertext Transfer Protocol (HTTP), port 21 is mapped to the File Transfer Protocol (FTP), and port 25 is mapped to SMTP. These ports can be reconfigured so that port 21 is mapped to HTTP, let's say, but that is very uncommon.

A port-scanning utility is used to find out what ports are open on a system so that the attacker knows what doors are available to her. This tool will send packets to each and every port on a system and listen for its response. If there is no response or a message indicating "Port Unreachable," this usually indicates that the port and its corresponding service is disabled. If a predictable response comes from the port, the attacker knows the port is open and available for attack.

A port needs to be open and available for functionality. For example, most networks require the use of SMTP, port 25, for e-mail activity. The administrator needs to put a barrier between the potential attackers and this vulnerable port and its service. Of course, the first step is to implement a perimeter network with firewalls, proxy servers, and routers that only permit acceptable connections to the internal hosts. However, if an administrator or security professional wanted to add another layer of protection, he could implement *TCP wrappers*. These software components (wrappers) monitor incoming network traffic and control what can and cannot access the services mapped to specific ports. When a request comes to a computer at a specific port, the target operating system will check to see if this port is enabled. If it is enabled and the operating system sees that the corresponding service is wrapped, it knows to look at an access control list, which spells out who can access this service. If the person or computer attempting to access this service is allowed within the access control list, the operating system allows the connection to be made. If this person or computer is not allowed, the packet is dropped or a message is sent back to the initiator of the request, indicating that the request is refused.

At this point, the attacker has an idea of what systems are alive, what ports are open, and what services are listening and available for attack. Although the search for exploitable vulnerabilities is becoming more focused, there is still an incredible number of possible vulnerabilities one network can have. Sometimes attackers specialize in a few specific attacks that they know well enough to carry out manually or have scripts that carry out specific attacks for them. But many attackers want a large range of possible attacks available to them, so they use *vulnerability scanning tools*.

Vulnerability scanning tools have a large database of vulnerabilities and the capability to exploit many of the vulnerabilities they identify. New vulnerabilities are found each week in operating systems, web servers, database software, and applications. It can be overwhelming to try to keep up to date on each of these and the proper steps to carry them out. The vulnerability scanners can do this for the security professional—and, unfortunately, for the attacker. These tools have an engine that can connect to the target machine and run through its database of vulnerabilities to see which apply to the target machine. Some tools can even go a step further and attempt the exploit to determine the actual degree of vulnerability.

As stated earlier, these tools are dual purpose in nature. Network administrators and security professionals should be using these types of tools on their environments to see what vulnerabilities are present and available to potential attackers. That way, when a vulnerability or weakness is uncovered, the security professional can fix it before an attacker finds it.

## Browsing

*I am looking for something, but I have no idea what it looks like.*

*Browsing* is a general technique used by intruders to obtain information that they are not authorized to access. This type of attack takes place when an attacker is looking for sensitive data but does not know the format the data is in (word processing document, spreadsheet, database, piece of paper). Browsing can be accomplished by looking through another person's files kept on a server or workstation, rummaging through garbage looking for information that was carelessly thrown away, or reviewing information that has been saved on floppy disks. A more advanced and sophisticated example of browsing is when an intruder accesses residual information on storage media. The original user may have deleted the files from a floppy disk, but, as stated earlier, this only removes the pointers to the files within the file system on that disk. The talented intruder can access this data (residual information) and access information that he is unauthorized to obtain.

Another type of browsing attack is called *shoulder surfing*, where an attacker looks over another's shoulder to see items on that person's monitor or what is being typed in at the keyboard.

## Sniffers

A *network sniffer* is a tool that monitors traffic as it traverses a network. Administrators and network engineers often use sniffers to diagnose network problems. Sniffers are also referred to as *network analyzers* or *protocol analyzers*. When used as a diagnostic tool, a sniffer enables the administrator to see what type of traffic is being generated, in the hope of getting closer to the root of the network problem. When a sniffer is used as a tool by an attacker, the sniffer can capture usernames, passwords, and confidential information as they travel over the network.

The sniffer tool is usually a piece of software that runs on a computer with its NIC in promiscuous mode. NICs usually only pay attention to traffic addressed to them, but if they are in promiscuous mode, they see all traffic that is going past them on the network wire. Once a computer has been compromised by an attacker, the attacker will often install a sniffer on that system to look for interesting traffic. Some sniffers only look for passwords that are being transmitted and ignore the rest.

Sniffers have been very successful because a majority of LANs use Ethernet, which is a broadcast technology. Because so much data is continually broadcasted, it is easily available for an attacker who has planted a sniffer on a network segment. However, sniffers are becoming less successful because of the move to switched environments. Switched environments separate network segments by broadcast and collision domains. If the attacker is not within the broadcast and collision domain of the environment she is interested in sniffing, she will not receive the information she is looking for, because a switch is usually configured so that the required source and destination ports on the switch carry the traffic, meaning the traffic is not blasted for everyone in the vicinity to hear. Switched traffic travels from point A to point B through the switch and does not spill over to every computer on the network, as it does in nonswitched networks. (Broadcast and collision domains are discussed in detail in Chapter 7.)

To combat sniffers within an environment, secure versions of services and protocols should be used whenever possible. Many services and protocols were developed to provide functionality, not security, but once it was figured out that security is also required in many environments, the protocols and services were improved upon to provide the same levels of functionality and security. Several protocols have a secure version. This means the regular protocol operates in a way that has vulnerabilities that can be exploited, and a more secure version has been developed to counter those vulnerabilities. One example is *Secure RPC (S-RPC)*, which uses Diffie-Hellman public key cryptography to determine the shared secret key for encryption with the DES algorithm. If S-RPC is used in an environment, a sniffer can capture this data, but not necessarily decrypt it.

Most protocols are vulnerable because they do not require strong authentication, if it is required at all. For example, the *r-utilities* used in Unix (rexec, rsh, rlogin, and rcp) are known to have several weaknesses. Authentication is usually provided through a .rhosts file that looks at IP addresses instead of individual usernames and passwords. These utilities should be replaced with one that requires stronger authentication, like Secure Shell (SSH).

## Session Hijacking

Many attackers spoof their addresses, meaning that the address within the frame that is used to commit the attack has an IP address that is not theirs. This makes it much harder to track down the attacker, which is the attacker's purpose for spoofing in the first place. This also enables an attacker to hijack sessions between two users without being noticed.

If an attacker wanted to take over a session between two computers, she would need to put herself in the middle of their conversation without being detected. Two tools used for this are Juggernaut and the HUNT Project (**http://lin.fsid.cvut.cz/~kra**). These tools enable the attacker to spy on the TCP connection and then hijack it if the attacker decides that is what she wants to do.

If Kristy and David were communicating over a TCP session and the attacker wanted to bump David off and trick Kristy into thinking she is still communicating with David, the attacker would use a tool to spoof her address to be the same as David's and temporarily take David off the network with a type of DoS attack. Once this is in place, when Kristy sends a message to David, it actually goes to the attacker, who can then respond to Kristy. Kristy thinks she is getting a reply from David. The attacker may also choose to leave David on the network and intercept each of the users' messages, read them, and repackage them with headers that indicate that no session hijacking took place, as shown in Figure 12-6.

If session hijacking is a concern on a network, the administrator can implement a protocol, such as IPSec or Kerberos, that requires mutual authentication between users or systems. Because the attacker will not have the necessary credentials to authenticate to a user, she cannot act as an imposter and hijack sessions.

## Loki

A common covert channel in use today is the Loki attack. This attack uses the ICMP protocol for communications purposes. This protocol was not developed to be used in this manner; it is only supposed to send status and error messages. But someone developed a tool (Loki) that allows an attacker to write data right behind the ICMP header. This allows the attacker to communicate with another system through a covert channel. It is usually very successful because most firewalls are configured to allow ICMP traffic in and out of their environments. This channel is covert because it uses something for communication purposes that was not developed for this type of communication functionality. More information on this type of attack can be found at **http://xforce.iss .net/xforce/xfdb/1452**.

## Password Cracking

Chapter 4 discussed access control and authentication methods in depth. Although there are various ways of authenticating a user, most of the time a static password is the method of choice for many companies. The main reason for this choice is that the computing society is used to using static passwords; this is how many systems and applications have their authentication processes coded, and it is an easier technique to maintain and cheaper than other options such as smart cards or biometrics.

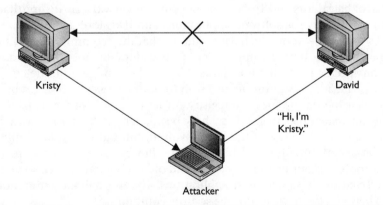

**Figure 12-6**   Session hijacking between Kristy and David

However, this static password method is easily cracked when a determined attacker has the right tools. John the Ripper is an example of a sniffer and password cracker that listens for authentication data being passed over network cables. Once the data is captured, the attacker can initiate a dictionary attack using the same tool to try to reveal the captured password. The powerful tools Crack and L0phtcrack are also used to perform dictionary and brute force attacks on the captured password or password file.

A strong password policy is a major countermeasure to password-cracking efforts. The policy should dictate that passwords must be at least eight characters, with upper- and lowercase letters and two special characters (*.,$@). If the passwords are long, contain special characters, and are hard to guess, it will take cracking tools much longer to uncover them. The longer this process takes, the higher the chance of the attacker moving on to an easier victim. Software applications and add-ons are available to ensure that the password that each user chooses meets the company's security policy.

## Backdoors

Chapter 5 discussed backdoors and some of the potential damage that can be caused by them. It also looked at how backdoors are inserted into the code so that a developer can access the software at a later time, bypassing the usual security authentication and authorization steps. Now we will look at how and why attackers install backdoors on victims' computers.

A *backdoor* is a program that is installed by an attacker to enable her to come back into the computer at a later date without having to supply login credentials or go through any type of authorization process. Access control is thwarted by the attacker because she can later gain access to the compromised computer. The backdoor program actually listens on specific ports for the attacker, and once the attacker accesses those ports, the backdoor program lets her come right in.

An attacker can compromise a computer and install the backdoor program or hide the code within a virus or Trojan horse that will install the backdoor when a predefined event takes place. Many times, these backdoors are installed so that the attacker can later control the computer remotely to perform the tasks she is interested in. The tools used for backdoor remote-control actions are Back Orifice, NetBus, and SubSeven. A comprehensive list of backdoors and Trojans can be found at **www.tlsecurity.org/tlfaq.htm**.

Today, many antivirus software applications and IDSs look for signatures of these tools and scan for the known behavior patterns that they commit. Using a host-based IDS can be one of the best attempts to detect a backdoor. Because the backdoor will be listening on specific ports, the host-based IDS can be configured to detect suspicious port activity. The administrator can also scan for known executables used by backdoor programs, view the startup files and registry entries for suspicious executables, and run checksums on system files to see if any have been altered. These activities are not usually done manually, because of the time involved, but rather are done automatically through the use of antivirus and IDS software. But because attackers are smart and tricky, new tools are continually developed and old tools are morphed so that they will not be detected by these detection applications. The inevitable cat-and-mouse game continues between the hackers and the security community.

The following list contains a brief description of a sampling of attack types you should be familiar with:

- **Denial-of-service (DoS) attack**   An attacker sends multiple service requests to the victim's computer until they eventually overwhelm the system, causing it to freeze, reboot, and ultimately not be able to carry out regular tasks.

- **Man-in-the-middle attack**   An intruder injects herself into an ongoing dialog between two computers so that she can intercept and read messages being passed back and forth. These attacks can be countered with digital signatures and mutual authentication techniques.

- **Mail bombing**   This is an attack used to overwhelm mail servers and clients with unrequested e-mails. Using e-mail filtering and properly configuring e-mail relay functionality on mail servers can be used to protect against this type of DoS attack.

- **Wardialing**   This is a brute force attack in which an attacker has a program that systematically dials a large bank of phone numbers with the goal of finding ones that belong to modems instead of telephones. These modems can provide easy access into an environment. The countermeasures are to not publicize these telephone numbers and to implement tight access control for modems and modem pools.

- **Ping of death**   This is a type of DoS attack in which oversized ICMP packets are sent to the victim. Systems that are vulnerable to this type of attack do not know how to handle ICMP packets over a specific size and may freeze or reboot. Countermeasures are to patch the systems and implement ingress filtering to detect these types of packets.

- **Fake login screens**   A fake login screen is created and installed on the victim's system. When the user attempts to log into the system, this fake screen is presented to the user, requesting that he enter his credentials. When he does so, the screen captures the credentials and exits, showing the user the actual login screen for his system. Usually the user just thinks he mistyped his password and attempts to authenticate again without knowing anything malicious just took place. A host-based IDS can be used to detect this type of activity.

- **Teardrop**   This attack sends malformed fragmented packets to a victim. The victim's system usually cannot reassemble the packets correctly and freezes as a result. Countermeasures to this attack are to patch the system and to use ingress filtering to detect these packet types.

- **Traffic analysis**   This is a method of uncovering information by watching traffic patterns on a network. For example, heavy traffic between the HR department and headquarters could indicate an upcoming layoff. Traffic padding can be used to counter this kind of attack, in which decoy traffic is sent out over the network to disguise patterns and make it more difficult to uncover patterns.

- **Slamming and cramming**   Slamming is when a user's service provider has been changed without that user's consent. Cramming is adding on charges that are bogus in nature that the user did not request. Properly monitoring charges on bills is really the only countermeasure to these types of attacks.

This section only talked about some of the possible attacks. One of the most beneficial things a company, network administrator, network engineer, or security professional can do is to develop some good habits that deal with the previously mentioned items. Although it is great that an administrator installs a security patch after he reads about a dangerous attack that has recently become popular, it is more important that he continue to stay on top of all potential threats and vulnerabilities, scan his network regularly, and remain aware of some symptomatic effects of particular attacks, viruses, Trojan horses, and backdoors. It can be a tall order to follow, but these good habits, once developed, will keep a network healthy and the administrator's life less chaotic. One of the best ways to ensure that you are properly protected is to investigate the matter yourself, instead of waiting for the hackers to find out for you. This is where penetration testing comes into play.

## Penetration Testing

*Excuse me. Could you please attack me? Response: I would love to!*

Penetration testing is the process of simulating attacks on a network and its systems at the request of the owner, senior management. Penetration testing uses a set of procedures and tools designed to test and possibly bypass security controls of a system. Its goal is to measure an organization's level of resistance to an attack and to uncover any weaknesses within the environment. Organizations need to determine the effectiveness of their security measures and not just trust the promises of the security vendors. Good computer security is based on reality, not on some lofty goals of how things are supposed to work.

A penetration test emulates the same methods that attackers would use. Attackers can be clever, creative, and resourceful in their techniques, so penetration attacks should align with the newest hacking techniques along with strong foundational testing methods. The test should look at each and every computer in the environment, as shown in Figure 12-7, because an attacker will not necessarily scan one or two computers only and call it a day.

The type of penetration test that should be used depends on the organization, its security objectives, and the management's goals. Some corporations perform periodic penetration tests on themselves using different types of tools or use scanning devices that continually examine the environment for new vulnerabilities in an automated fashion. Other corporations ask a third party to perform the vulnerability and penetration tests to provide a more objective view.

Penetration tests can evaluate web servers, DNS servers, router configurations, workstation vulnerabilities, access to sensitive information, remote dial-in access, open ports, and available services' properties that a real attacker might use to compromise the company's overall security. Some tests can be quite intrusive and disruptive. The timeframe for the tests should be agreed upon so that productivity is not affected and personnel can bring systems back online if necessary.

The result of a penetration test is a report given to management that describes the vulnerabilities that were identified and the severity of those vulnerabilities, along with suggestions on how to deal with them properly. From there, it is up to management to determine how the vulnerabilities are actually dealt with and what countermeasures are implemented.

**Figure 12-7** Penetration testing is used to prove that an attacker can actually compromise systems.

## Types of Tests

A vulnerability assessment identifies a wide range of vulnerabilities in the environment. This is commonly carried out through a scanning tool. By contrast, in a penetration test, the security professional exploits one or more vulnerabilities, to prove to the customer (or your boss) that a hacker can actually gain access to company resources.

It is critical that senior management be aware of the risks that may be involved in performing a penetration test before it gives authorization for one to be conducted. In rare instances, a system or application may be taken down inadvertently using the tools and techniques employed during the test. As expected, the goal of penetration testing is to identify vulnerabilities, estimate the true protection the security mechanisms within the environment are providing, and see how suspicious activity is reported—but accidents can and do happen.

Security professionals should obtain an authorization letter that includes the extent of the testing that is authorized. The letter or memo needs to be available to members of the team during the testing activity. This letter is commonly referred to as a "Get Out of Jail Free Card." Contact information for key personnel should also be available along with a call tree in the event that something does not go as planned and the recovery of a system needs to be initiated.

 **NOTE** A "Get Out of Jail Free Card" is a document that you can present to someone who thinks that you are up to something malicious, when in fact you are carrying out an approved test. There have been many situations in which an individual (or a team) was carrying out a penetration test and was approached by a security guard or someone who thought that this person was in the wrong place at the wrong time.

When performing a penetration test, the team goes through a five-step process:

1. **Discovery**   Footprinting and gathering information about the target

2. **Enumeration**   Performing port scans and resource identification methods

3. **Vulnerability mapping**   Identifying vulnerabilities in identified systems and resources

4. **Exploitation**   Attempting to gain unauthorized access by exploiting vulnerabilities

5. **Report to management**   Delivering to management documentation of test findings along with suggested countermeasures

The penetration testing team can have varying degrees of knowledge about the penetration target before the tests are actually carried out.

- **Zero knowledge**   Team does not have much knowledge of target and must start from ground zero

- **Partial knowledge**   Team has some information about target

- **Full knowledge**   Team has intimate knowledge of target

It is important that the team start off with only basic user-level access, to properly simulate different attacks. The team needs to utilize a variety of different tools and attack methods, and look at all possible vulnerabilities, because this is how actual attackers will function.

As noted earlier—and it cannot be over emphasized—it is extremely important that the team gets written permission from the right level of management before proceeding with any of these types of activities.

## References

- *NIST Security Self-Assessment Guide for Information Technology Systems,* by Marianne Swanson, NIST Special Publication 800-26 (Nov. 2001) http://csrc.nist.gov/publications/nistpubs/800-26/sp800-26.pdf

- Computer Security course, Module 16, "Vulnerability Analysis," Polytechnic University (Nov. 2003)   http://isis.poly.edu/courses/cs392/Lectures/ module_9.pdf

- Indiana University Advanced Networking Management Lab DDoS Resources   www.anml.iu.edu/ddos/tools.html

- "DDoS: A Look Back from 2003," presentation by Dave Dittrich, University of Washington   http://staff.washington.edu/dittrich/talks/I2-ddos.ppt

- "Password Cracking, Sniffing, and Man-in-the-Middle," Prof. Henry Owen, Georgia Tech University   http://users.ece.gatech.edu/~owen/Academic/ ECE4112/Fall2004/Lab2.ppt

## Operations Department

*I think this computer is possessed by the devil. Response: Call the operations guy.*

Operations security encompasses safeguards and countermeasures to protect resources, information, and the hardware on which the resources and information reside. The goal of operations security is to reduce the possibility of damage that could result from unauthorized access or disclosure by limiting the opportunities of misuse.

Some organizations may have an actual operations department that is responsible for activities and procedures that are required to keep the network running smoothly and to keep productivity at a certain level. Other organizations may have a few individuals who are responsible for these things, but no structured department dedicated just to operations. Either way, the people who hold these responsibilities are accountable for certain activities and procedures and must monitor and control specific issues.

Operations within a computing environment may pertain to software, personnel, and hardware, but an operations department often focuses on the hardware and software aspects. Management is responsible for employees' behavior and responsibilities. The people within the operations department are responsible for ensuring that systems are protected and continue to run in a predictable manner.

The operations department usually has the objectives of preventing reoccurring problems, reducing hardware failures to an acceptable level, and reducing the impact of hardware failure or disruption. This group should investigate any unusual or unexplained occurrences, unscheduled initial program loads, deviations from standards, or other odd or abnormal conditions that take place on the network.

## Unusual or Unexplained Occurrences

Networks, and the hardware and software within them, can be complex and dynamic. At times, conditions occur that are at first confusing and possibly unexplainable. It is up to the operations department to investigate these issues, diagnose the problem, and come up with a logical solution.

One example could be a network that has hosts that are continually kicked off the network for no apparent reason. The operations team should conduct controlled troubleshooting to make sure that it does not overlook any possible source for the disruption and that it investigates different types of problems. The team may look at connectivity issues between the hosts and the wiring closet, the hubs and switches that control their connectivity, and any possible cabling defects. The team should work methodically until it finds a specific problem.

## Deviations from Standards

In this instance, "standards" pertains to computing service levels and how they are measured. Each device can have certain standards applied to it: the hours of time to be online, the number of requests that can be processed within a defined period of time, bandwidth usage, performance counters, and more. These standards provide a baseline that is used to determine whether or not there is a problem with the device. For example, if a device usually accepts approximately 300 requests per minute, but suddenly it is only able to accept 3 per minute, the operations team would need to investigate the deviation from the standard that is usually provided by this device. The device may be failing or under a DoS attack.

Sometimes the standard needs to be recalibrated so that it portrays a realistic view of the service level it can provide. If a server was upgraded from a Pentium II to a Pentium III, the memory was quadrupled, the swap file was increased, and three extra hard drives were added, the service level of this server should be reevaluated.

## Unscheduled Initial Program Loads

*Initial program load (IPL)* is a mainframe term for loading the operating system's kernel into the computer's main memory. On a personal computer, booting into the operating system is the equivalent to IPLing. This activity takes place to prepare the computer for user operation.

The operations team needs to investigate computers that reboot for no reason, which could indicate that the operating system is experiencing major problems.

# Summary

Operations security involves keeping up with implemented solutions, keeping track of changes, properly maintaining systems, continually enforcing necessary standards, and following through with security practices and tasks. It does not do much good for a company to develop a strong password policy if, after a few months, enforcement gets lax and users can use whatever passwords they want. It is similar to working out and staying physically fit. Just because someone lifts weights and jogs for a week does not mean he can spend the rest of the year eating jelly donuts and expect to stay physically fit. Security requires discipline day in and day out, sticking to a regime, and practicing due care.

# Quick Tips

- Facilities that house systems that process sensitive information should have physical access controls to limit access to authorized personnel only.
- Data should be classified, and the necessary technical controls should be put into place to protect its integrity, confidentiality, and availability.
- Hacker tools are becoming increasingly more sophisticated while requiring increasingly less knowledge by the attacker about how they work.
- Quality assurance involves the verification that documentation and support requirements are met.
- Quality control ensures that an asset is operating within accepted standards.
- System and audit logs should be monitored and protected from unauthorized modification.
- Repetitive errors can indicate lack of training or issues resulting from a poorly designed system.
- Sensitive data should not be printed and left at stand-alone printers or fax devices.
- Users should have the necessary security level to access data and resources, but must also have a need to know.
- Identity management systems combine traditional directories, access control systems, and user provisioning under a single management umbrella.
- Clipping levels should be implemented to establish a baseline of user activity and acceptable errors.
- Separation of responsibilities and duties should be in place so that if fraud takes place, it requires collusion.
- Sensitive information should contain the correct markings and labels to indicate the corresponding sensitivity level.
- Contract and temporary staff members should have more restrictive controls put upon their accounts.
- Unauthorized access should be restricted to printed output storage areas.
- Access to resources should be limited to authorized personnel, applications, and services and should be audited for compliance to stated policies.
- Change control and configuration management should be put into place so that changes are approved, documented, tested, and properly implemented.
- Activities that involve change management include requesting a change, approving a change, documenting a change, testing a change, implementing a change, and reporting to management.
- Systems should not allow their bootup sequences to be altered in a way that could bypass operating system security mechanisms.
- Potential employees should have background investigations, references, experience, and education claims checked out.

- Proper fault-tolerant mechanisms should be put into place to counter equipment failure.

- Antivirus and IDS signatures should be updated on a continual basis.

- System, network, policy, and procedure changes should be documented and communicated.

- When media is reused, it should contain no residual data.

- Media holding sensitive data must be properly purged, which could be accomplished through zeroization, degaussing, or media destruction.

- Life-cycle assurance involves protecting a system from inception to development to operation to removal.

- The key aspects of operations security include resource protection, change control, hardware and software controls, trusted system recovery, separation of duties, and least privilege.

- Least privilege ensures that users, administrators, and others accessing a system have access only to the objects they absolutely require to complete their job.

- Vulnerability assessments should be done on a regular basis to identify new vulnerabilities.

- The operations department is responsible for any unusual or unexplained occurrences, unscheduled initial program loads, and deviations from standards.

- Standards need to be established that indicate the proper startup and shutdown sequence, error handling, and restoration procedures.

- A teardrop attack involves sending malformed fragmented packets to a vulnerable system.

- Improper mail relay configurations allow for mail servers to be used to forward spam messages.

- Phishing involves an attacker sending false messages to a victim in the hopes that the victim will provide personal information that can be used to steal their identity.

- A browsing attack occurs when an attacker looks for sensitive information without knowing what format it is in.

- A fax encryptor encrypts all fax data leaving a fax server.

- A system can fail in one of the following manners: system reboot, emergency system restart, and system cold start.

- The main goal of operations security is to protect resources.

- Operational threats include disclosure, theft, corruption, interruption, and destruction.

- Operations security involves balancing the necessary level of security with ease of use, compliance, and cost constraints.

# Questions

Please remember that these questions are formatted and asked in a certain way for a reason. You must remember that the CISSP exam is asking questions at a conceptual level. Questions may not always have the perfect answer, and the candidate is advised against always looking for the perfect answer. The candidate should look for the best answer in the list.

1. Which of the following best describes operations security?

    A. Continual vigilance about hacker activity and possible vulnerabilities

    B. Enforcing access control and physical security

    C. Taking steps to make sure an environment, and the things within it, stay at a certain level of protection

    D. Doing strategy planning to develop a secure environment and then implementing it properly

2. Which of the following describes why operations security is important?

    A. An environment continually changes and has the potential of lowering its level of protection.

    B. It helps an environment be functionally sound and productive.

    C. It ensures that there will be no unauthorized access to the facility or its resources.

    D. It continually raises a company's level of protection.

3. What is the difference between due care and due diligence?

    A. Due care is the continual effort of ensuring that the right thing takes place, and due diligence is the continual effort to stay compliant to regulations.

    B. Due care and due diligence are in contrast to the "prudent person" concept.

    C. They mean the same thing.

    D. Due diligence involves investigating the risks, and due care involves carrying out the necessary steps to mitigate these risks.

4. Why should employers make sure employees take their vacations?

    A. They have a legal obligation.

    B. It is part of due diligence.

    C. It is a way that fraud can be uncovered.

    D. To ensure that the employee does not get burnt out.

5. Which of the following best describes separation of duties and job rotation?

    A. Separation of duties ensures that more than one employee knows how to perform the tasks of a position, and job rotation ensures that one person cannot perform a high-risk task alone.

B. Separation of duties ensures that one person cannot perform a high-risk task alone, and job rotation can uncover fraud and ensure that more than one person knows the tasks of a position.

C. They are the same thing with different titles.

D. They are administrative controls that enforce access control and protect the company's resources.

6. If a programmer is restricted from updating and modifying production code, what is this an example of?

A. Rotation of duties

B. Due diligence

C. Separation of duties

D. Controlling input values

7. Why is it important to control and audit input and output values?

A. Incorrect values can cause mistakes in data processing and can be evidence of fraud.

B. Incorrect values can be the fault of the programmer and do not comply with the due care clause.

C. Incorrect values can be caused by brute force attacks.

D. Incorrect values are not security issues.

8. What is the difference between least privilege and need to know?

A. A user should have least privilege that restricts her need to know.

B. A user should have a security clearance to access resources, a need to know about those resources, and least privilege to give her full control of all resources.

C. A user should have a need to know to access particular resources, and least privilege should be implemented to ensure she only accesses the resources she has a need to know.

D. They are two terms for the same issue.

9. Which of the following would not require updated documentation?

A. Antivirus signature update

B. Reconfiguration of a server

C. Change in security policy

D. Installation of a patch to a production server

10. If sensitive data is stored on a CD-ROM and it is no longer needed, which would be the proper way of disposing of the data?

A. Degaussing

B. Erasing

    C. Purging

    D. Physical destruction

11. If SSL is being used to encrypt messages that are transmitted over the network, what is a major concern of the security professional?

    A. The network segments that have systems that use different versions of SSL.

    B. The user may have encrypted the message with an application layer product that is incompatible with SSL.

    C. Network tapping and wiretapping.

    D. The networks that the message will travel that the company does not control.

12. What is the purpose of SMTP?

    A. To enable users to decrypt mail messages from a server

    B. To enable users to view and modify mail messages from a server

    C. To transmit mail messages from the client to the mail server

    D. To encrypt mail messages before being transmitted

13. If a company has been contacted because its mail server has been used to spread spam, what is most likely the problem?

    A. The internal mail server has been compromised by an internal hacker.

    B. The mail server in the DMZ has private and public resource records.

    C. The mail server has e-mail relaying misconfigured.

    D. The mail server has SMTP enabled.

14. Which of the following is not a reason that fax servers are used in many companies?

    A. They save money by not needing individual fax devices and the constant use of fax paper.

    B. They provide a secure way of faxing instead of having faxed papers sitting in bins waiting to be picked up.

    C. Faxes can be routed to employees' electronic mailboxes.

    D. They increase the need for other communication security mechanisms.

15. If a company wants to protect fax data while it is in transmission, which of the following are valid mechanisms?

    A. PGP and MIME

    B. PEM and TSL

    C. Data link encryption or fax encryptor

    D. Data link encryption and MIME

16. What is the purpose of TCP wrappers?

    A. Monitor requests for certain ports and control access to sensitive files

    B. Monitor requests for certain services and control access to password files

    C. Monitor requests for certain services and control access to those services

    D. Monitor requests to system files and ensure they are not modified

17. How do network sniffers work?

    A. They probe systems on a network segment.

    B. They listen for ARP requests and ICMP packets.

    C. They require an extra NIC to be installed and configured.

    D. They put the NIC into promiscuous mode.

18. Which of the following is not an attack against operations?

    A. Brute force

    B. Denial of service

    C. Buffer overflow

    D. ICMP Sting

19. Why should user IDs be included in data captured by auditing procedures?

    A. Shows what files were attacked

    B. Establishes individual accountability

    C. Needed to detect a denial-of-service attack

    D. Activates corrective measures

20. Which of the following controls requires separate entities, operating together, to complete a task?

    A. Least privilege

    B. Data hiding

    C. Dual control

    D. Administrative

21. Which of the following would not be considered an operations media control task?

    A. Compressing and decompressing storage materials

    B. Erasing data when its retention period is over

    C. Storing backup information in a protected area

    D. Controlling access to media and logging activities

22. How are the use of clipping levels a way to track violations?

    A. They set a baseline for normal user errors, and any violations that exceed that threshold should be recorded and reviewed to understand why they are happening.

B. They enable the administrator to view all reduction levels that have been made to user codes, which have incurred violations.

C. They disallow the administrator to customize the audit trail to record only those violations that are deemed security related.

D. They enable the administrator to customize the audit trail to capture only access violations and denial-of-service attacks.

23. Tape library management is an example of operations security through which of the following?

A. Archival retention

B. Reviewing clipping levels

C. Resource protection

D. Change management

24. A device that generates coercive magnetic force for the purpose of reducing magnetic flux density to zero on media is called:

A. Magnetic saturation

B. Magnetic field

C. Physical destruction

D. Degausser

25. Which of the following controls might force a person in operations into collusion with personnel assigned organizationally within a different function for the sole purpose of gaining access to data he is not authorized to access?

A. Limiting the local access of operations personnel

B. Enforcing auditing

C. Enforcing job rotation

D. Limiting control of management personnel

## Answers

1. C. All of these are necessary security activities and procedures; they just don't all fall under the operations umbrella. Operations is about keeping production up and running in a healthy and secure manner. Operations is not usually the entity that carries out strategic planning; it works at an operational, day-to-day level, not at the higher strategic level.

2. A. This is the best answer because operations has the goal of keeping everything running smoothly each and every day. Operations implements new software and hardware and carries out the necessary security tasks passed down to it. As the environment changes and security is kept in the loop with these changes, there is a smaller likelihood of opening up vulnerabilities.

3. **D.** Due care and due diligence are legal terms that do not just pertain to security. Due diligence involves going through the necessary steps to know what a company's or individual's actual risks are, and due care involves carrying out responsible actions to reduce those risks. These concepts correspond with the "prudent person" concept.

4. **C.** Many times, employees who are carrying out fraudulent activities do not take the vacation they have earned because they do not want anyone to find out what they have been doing. Forcing employees to take vacations means that someone else has to do that person's job and possibly uncover any misdeeds.

5. **B.** Rotation of duties enables a company to have more than one person trained in a position and can uncover fraudulent activities. Separation of duties is put into place to ensure that one entity cannot carry out a critical task alone.

6. **C.** This is just one of several examples of separation of duties. A system must be set up for proper code maintenance to take place when necessary, instead of allowing a programmer to make changes arbitrarily. These types of changes should go through a change control process and should have more entities involved than just one programmer.

7. **A.** There should be controls in place to make sure that the data that is input into a system and the results that are generated are in the proper format and have expected values. Improper data being put into an application or system could cause bad output and security issues, such as buffer overflows.

8. **C.** Users should be able to access only the resources they need to fulfill the duties of their positions. They also should only have the level of permissions and rights for those resources that is required to carry out the exact operations they need for their jobs and no more. This second concept is more granular than the first, but they have a symbiotic relationship.

9. **A.** Documentation is very important for data processing and networked environments. This task often gets pushed to the back burner or is totally ignored. If things are not properly documented, employees will forget what actually took place with each device. If the environment needs to be rebuilt, for example, it may be done incorrectly if the procedure was poorly or improperly documented. When new changes need to be implemented, the current infrastructure may not be totally understood. Continually documenting when virus signatures are updated would be an overkill. The other answers contain events that certainly require documentation.

10. **D.** One cannot properly erase data that is held on a CD-ROM. If the data is sensitive and you need to ensure that no one has access to it, the media should be physically destroyed.

11. **D.** This is not a great question, but could be something that you run into on the exam. Let's look at the answers. Different SSL versions are usually not a concern, because the two communicating systems will negotiate and agree

upon the necessary version. There is no security violation issue here. SSL works at the transport layer; thus, it will not be affected by what the user does, as stated in answer B. SSL protects against network tapping and wiretapping. Answer D talks about the network segments the company does not own. This is the best answer out of the four, but a company would use SSL to protect data that is traversing through others' equipment. If the data is decrypted at a different network's gateway, the data will be unprotected.

12. **C.** Simple Mail Transfer Protocol (SMTP) is the protocol used to allow clients to send e-mail messages to each other. It allows different mail servers to exchange messages.

13. **C.** Spammers will identify the mail servers on the Internet that have relaying enabled and are "wide open," meaning the server will forward any e-mail messages it receives. These servers can be put on a black list, which means that other mail servers will not accept mail from them.

14. **D.** The other three answers provide reasons why fax servers would be used instead of individual fax machines: ease of use, provides more protection, and supplies may be cheaper.

15. **C.** This is the best answer for this question. The other components could provide different levels of protection, but a fax encryptor (which is a data link encryptor) provides a higher level of protection across the board because everything is encrypted. Even if a user does not choose to encrypt something, it will be encrypted anyway before it is sent out the fax server.

16. **C.** This is a technology that wraps the different services that are available on a system. What this means is that if a remote user makes a request to access a service, this product will intercept this request and determine whether this request is valid and legal before allowing the interaction to take place.

17. **D.** A sniffer is a device or software component that puts the NIC in promiscuous mode, meaning the NIC will pick up all frames it "sees" instead of just the frames addressed to that individual computer. The sniffer then shows the output to the user. It can have capture and filtering capabilities.

18. **D.** The first three choices are attacks that can directly affect security operations. There is no attack referred to as ICMP Sting.

19. **B.** For auditing purposes, the procedure should capture user ID, time of event, type of event, and source workstation. Capturing the user ID allows the company to hold individuals accountable for their actions.

20. **C.** Dual control requires two or more entities working together to complete a task. An example is key recovery. If a key needs to be recovered, and key recovery requires two or more people to authenticate to a system, the act of them coming together and carrying out these activities is known as dual control. This reduces the possibility of fraud.

21. **A.** The last three tasks fall under the job functions of an individual or department that is responsible for controlling access to media. Compressing and decompressing data does not.

22. **A.** Clipping levels are thresholds of acceptable user errors and suspicious activities. If the threshold is exceeded, it should be logged and the administrator should decide if malicious activities are taking place or if the user needs more training.

23. **C.** The reason to have tape library management is to have a centralized and standard way of protecting how media is stored, accessed, and destroyed.

24. **D.** A degausser is a device that generates a magnetic field (coercive magnetic force) that changes the orientation of the bits held on the media (reducing magnetic flux density to zero).

25. **A.** If the operations personnel is limited in what they can access, they would need to collude with someone who actually has access to the resource. This question is not very clear, but it is very close to the way many CISSP exam questions are formatted.

# About the CD-ROM

The CD-ROM that comes with *CISSP All-in-One Exam Guide* includes:

- **Live cryptography video training**  A QuickTime video/audio file with "live" video training on cryptography, presented by Shon Harris (see Figure A-1). This is a portion of a complete CISSP training product. (For more information on the complete product, please see the ad that follows the index of this book.) The QuickTime player must be installed on your computer to play this file. It is available from **www.apple.com**. See the following sections for more instructions.

- **Practice questions**  Total Seminars' Total Tester Software, with more than 850 practice questions covering all ten CISSP domains. This testing engine features Practice and Final modes of testing.

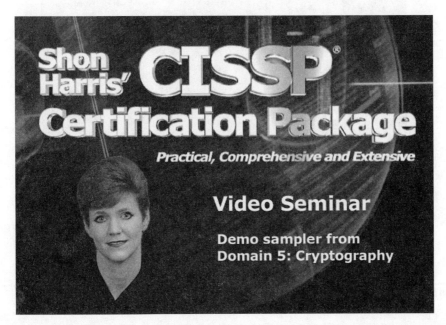

**Figure A-1**  CISSP CBT cryptography demo

The CD-ROM is set up with an autorun function. If your computer does not have autorun turned on, browse the CD-ROM and double-click the launcher.exe file to access the software menu page. From the software menu page, you can launch the installation wizard (to install the Total Tester) or run the video training QuickTime file.

# Running the QuickTime Cryptography Video Sample

Once you have started the launcher.exe file (either through autorun or by double-clicking the file on the CD-ROM), click the Play CISSP Video Training link to start the QuickTime file, a frame of which is shown in Figure A-2.

The following are the minimum system requirements for the cryptography video sample:

- Windows 98, 800 MHz Pentium II, 24X CD-ROM drive, 64MB RAM, 800×600 monitor, millions of colors, QuickTime 5, Microsoft Internet Explorer 5 or Netscape Navigator 4.5, and speakers or headphones

- Macintosh OS 9.2.1, 450 MHz G3, 24X CD-ROM drive, 64MB RAM, 800×600 monitor, millions of colors, QuickTime 5, Microsoft Internet Explorer 5 or Netscape Navigator 4.5, and speakers or headphones

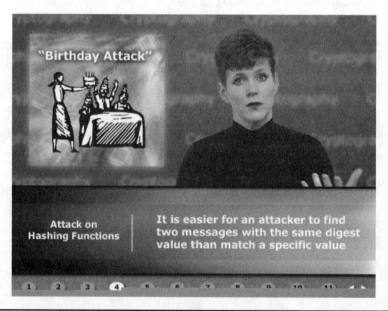

**Figure A-2**   CISSP computer-based training contains a full CISSP course

The following are the recommended system requirements for the cryptography video sample:

- Windows 2000, 2 GHz Pentium IV, 48X CD-ROM drive, 128MB RAM, 1024×768 monitor, millions of colors, QuickTime 6, Microsoft Internet Explorer 5.5 or Netscape Navigator 4.7, and speakers or headphones

- Macintosh OS 10.1, 800 MHz G4, 48X CD-ROM drive, 128MB RAM, 1024×768 monitor, millions of colors, QuickTime 6, Microsoft Internet Explorer 5.5 or Netscape Navigator 4.7, and speakers or headphones

## Troubleshooting

This software runs inside of your Internet browser. You must have its preferences set for correct playback of QuickTime movies to view the movie. The QuickTime installer (free download from **www.apple.com/quicktime**) may not change all of your file helpers properly.

After installing QuickTime, if movies take a very long time to load or don't load at all, verify that your browser associates the file type .mov with the QuickTime plug-in. To verify this, do the following:

- If using Internet Explorer for Windows, go to Tools | Internet Options | Advanced | Multimedia or Control Panels | QuickTime.

- If using Internet Explorer for Macintosh, go to Preferences | Receiving Files | Helpers.

# Installing Total Seminars' Test Software

Click the Install Test Software button on the wizard, and the installation will proceed automatically.

Once you've completed installation, you can open the test program by selecting Start | Programs | Total Seminars and then click on the CISSP tests. You can also start the program with the shortcut the installation places on your desktop.

## Navigation

The program enables you to test in each of the ten domains in either Practice or Final mode. An Adaptive mode exam, which uses a large pool of questions, is also included. Begin by selecting a testing mode and specific test from the menu bar.

## Practice Mode

In Practice mode, the test includes an assistance window. This gives you access to several features: Hint (helps you figure out the correct answer), Reference (where in the book to learn more), Check (is your selection correct?), and Explanation (a short note explaining the correct answer). This is a good way to study and review: Answer each question, check to see if you answered correctly, review the explanation, and refer to the book for more detailed coverage. At the end of the test, you are graded by topic and can review missed questions.

### Final Mode

Final mode enables you to test yourself without the ability to see the correct answers. This is a better way to see how well you understand the material. Upon completion, you receive a final grade by topic, and you can look over the questions you missed.

## Minimum System Requirements for Total Seminars' Software

The minimum system requirements for Total Seminars' software include:

- Pentium 200 MHz
- 4X or faster speed CD-ROM
- 16MB of RAM
- 30MB available hard disk space
- 800×600 resolution at 256 colors
- Windows 9x/2000/XP operating system

## Technical Support

For technical support of the Total Tester practice test application, please check **www .totalsem.com**. For other technical support issues, please go to **www.osborne.com** or e-mail **customer.service@mcgraw-hill.com**. For customers outside the 50 United States, e-mail **international_cs@mcgraw-hill.com**.

# Who's Who?

Acronyms for the names of companies and organizations are often used in literature without an explanation of who these organizations are and what their function in the world is. This section covers many of the organizations that have been discussed in this book.

## NSA

The *National Security Agency* is the agency officially responsible for security within the U.S. government. NSA was created in 1952 by President Harry Truman under the Department of Defense (DoD). Only recently has NSA been publicly discussed; for a majority of its life, most U.S. citizens were not aware of NSA's existence.

NSA deals with signal intelligence, meaning that it listens to foreign communications that are deemed important and pertinent to U.S. security. The agency has extremely sophisticated and complex hardware, devices, and software to capture signals, decrypt them, and decode their meaning. NSA also conducts in-depth research in cryptology to increase its ability to decrypt other encrypted communications and to develop secure algorithms to protect U.S. military and government communications mechanisms.

NSA is also usually in support of and a catalyst for restricting any type of encryption products that may be sold outside of the United States. NSA does not want potentially threatening countries to acquire encryption mechanisms that would make its job of cracking encryption any harder. So, many of the export laws that prohibit certain types of encryption software being sold outside of the United States have a direct correlation to NSA's directives and requirements.

James Bamford wrote two books about NSA: *The Puzzle Palace* (Penguin Books USA Inc., 1983) and *Body of Secrets* (Anchor Books, 2002).

### Reference

- **National Security Agency**   www.nsa.gov

# NIST

The *National Institute of Standards and Technology* is a division of the U.S. Department of Commerce. This organization was called the National Bureau of Standards (NBS) until 1988. It issues standards and guidelines to be adopted by U.S. computer system developers and vendors. NIST's core purpose is to promote open standards and interoperability with the hopes of spurring more developments within computer-based industries. The official standards that NIST produces and publishes are called Federal Information Processing Standards (FIPS).

In 1987, Congress passed the Computer Security Act, which authorized NIST to be responsible for defining standards to protect and ensure the security of information that is sensitive but unclassified within government agencies. NIST is responsible for providing guidelines on how to protect sensitive but unclassified information, and NSA is responsible for classified information.

NIST's Computer Systems Laboratory (CSL) is responsible for developing technical, management, physical, and administrative standards and guidelines for cost-effective security used to keep the government agencies' sensitive information protected. It is required to work with other government agencies, including NSA, to ensure the necessary level of protection for government agencies' computer systems and the programs, materials, testing, and reports pertaining to those systems. NSA is required to provide NIST with technical guidelines dealing with personal identification, telecommunications security, and trusted technologies.

NIST's CSL does the following:

- Develops computer security standards and works closely with accredited standards committees such as IEEE, ANSI, and ISO to develop and support these standards. The published standards are called FIPS PUBs. (The Rainbow Series, covered in Chapter 5, is an example.)

- Conducts research and publishes results on many security problems and solutions.

- Works with NSA to ensure that solutions meet DoD security standards for protecting classified and intelligence information.

- Develops test methods to properly test security mechanisms.

U.S. government agencies that employ cryptography must use software that follows NIST and FIPS standards. Many of the encryption standards mandated by NIST were developed by NSA. The public has been a bit suspicious of this relationship when it comes to developing and approving specific encryption algorithms, especially when they are not up for public review. The fear of the government inserting into algorithms backdoors that are unknown to the public raises many Big Brother issues and has caused outcries in the past.

## References

- **National Institute of Standards and Technology**   www.nist.gov
- **NIST Computer Security Special Publications**   http://csrc.nist.gov/publications/nistpubs/

# NCSC

The *National Computer Security Center* was established in 1981 within NSA to help support and drive NSA's DoD computer security responsibilities. NCSC's responsibility is to provide a centralized agency that deals with the evaluation process of computer security systems and products, provide technical support for government and industry groups doing computer security research and development, conduct and sponsor research in the computer and network security technology sector, develop and provide verification and analysis tools, provide computer security training, and disseminate information to other federal government agencies and to the computing industry.

The lines dividing NIST, NSA, and NCSC have not always been clear because they have overlapping responsibilities and, throughout their histories, their responsibilities and missions have expanded further into each other's territories. Basically, NSA protects classified military and intelligence information using computer security mechanisms and techniques, and NIST develops standards and computer security training programs. Evaluations of security systems were performed by NCSC through the Trusted Product Evaluation Program (TPEP), which is a part of NSA.

Vendors request that their products go through the TPEP for an evaluation targeting a particular level of assurance rating. These evaluations used the Trusted Computer System Evaluation Criteria (TCSEC) to assess the product and determine if it met the necessary requirements for the requested rating. The results are published in the Evaluated Products List (EPL) in Information Systems Security Products and Services Catalogs.

After the realization that TCSEC did not meet the requirements of all organizations and their security needs, the Common Criteria was developed and accepted. The TPEP was replaced by the Trusted Technology Assessment Program (TTAP), a program developed and supported by NSA and NIST that performs trusted product evaluations. The evaluations are based on the Common Criteria instead of the TCSEC.

# ISO

The *International Organization for Standardization*, known also as ISO, was established in 1947 and is an international organization made up of many national standards organizations. ISO's Open System Interconnection (OSI) model provides a conceptual model for explaining how data communications take place. The OSI model promotes open networking environments that enable multivendor computer systems that follow this model to communicate using internationally accepted protocols.

ISO is a worldwide federation with representatives from more than 100 countries. It is a nongovernmental organization with a mission to develop worldwide standards and promote international exchange of services and goods and to further develop cooperation of intellectual, technological, and scientific concepts between countries all around the world.

## Reference

- **International Organization for Standardization**   www.iso.ch

# ANSI

The *American National Standards Institute* is an organization that defines coding standards and signaling schemes in the United States and represents the United States in ISO and the International Telecommunication Union (ITU). The organization does not develop standards, but facilitates their development by bringing qualified groups together and providing them with guiding principles.

ANSI had a large part in the development of ISO and has an active role in governing it today. ANSI promotes and advocates U.S. policies internationally within different regional standards organizations. ANSI promotes U.S. standards by presenting them to international standards organizations. The organizations can choose to adopt the standards fully or extract specific parts of the standards to adopt for their regions.

Some of the well-known ANSI standards include C++, SQL, EDI, SONET, FDDI, and ANSI x9 security standards.

## Reference

- **American National Standards Institute**   www.ansi.org

# IEEE

The *Institute of Electrical and Electronic Engineers* is a nonprofit organization that develops standards, submits them for ANSI approval, and forwards drafts to ISO. This technical association is based in the United States and develops different types of standards, including security standards. IEEE is made up of a number of committees, or working groups, that work in specific technical areas like communications, nuclear engineering, aerospace electronics, telecommunications, security, and much more. IEEE's local area network/metropolitan area network (LAN/MAN) standards are known as the IEEE 802 standards. IEEE has a technical committee that works strictly with security and privacy issues.

## References

- **IEEE**   www.ieee.org
- **IEEE Catalog and Store**   http://shop.ieee.org
- **IEEE Computer Society's Technical Committee on Security and Privacy**   www.ieee-security.org

# A

**access** A subject's ability to view, modify, or communicate with an object. Access enables the flow of information between the subject and the object.

**access control** Mechanisms, controls, and methods of limiting access to resources to authorized subjects only.

**access control list (ACL)** A list of subjects that are authorized to access a particular object. Typically, the types of access are read, write, execute, append, modify, delete, and create.

**access control mechanism** Administrative, physical, or technical control that is designed to detect and prevent unauthorized access to a resource or environment.

**accountability** A security principle indicating that individuals must be identifiable and must be held responsible for their actions.

**accredited** A computer system or network that has received official authorization and approval to process sensitive data in a specific operational environment. There must be a security evaluation of the system's hardware, software, configurations, and controls by technical personnel.

**add-on security** Security protection mechanisms that are hardware or software retrofitted to a system to increase that system's protection level.

**administrative controls** Security mechanisms that are management's responsibility and referred to as "soft" controls. These controls include the development and publication of policies, standards, procedures, and guidelines, the screening of personnel, security awareness training, the monitoring of system activity, and change control procedures.

**AIC triad** The three security principles: availability, integrity, and confidentiality.

**annualized loss expectancy (ALE)** A dollar amount that estimates the loss potential from a risk in a span of a year.

single loss expectancy (SLE) × annualized rate of occurrence (ARO) = ALE

**annualized rate of occurrence (ARO)** The value that represents the estimated possibility of a specific threat taking place within a one-year timeframe.

**assurance**   A measurement of confidence in the level of protection that a specific security control delivers and the degree to which it enforces the security policy.

**attack**   An attempt to bypass security controls in a system with the mission of using that system or compromising it. An attack is usually accomplished by exploiting a current vulnerability.

**audit trail**   A chronological set of logs and records used to provide evidence of a system's performance or activity that took place on the system. These logs and records can be used to attempt to reconstruct past events and track the activities that took place and possibly detect and identify intruders.

**authenticate**   To verify the identity of a subject requesting the use of a system and/or access to network resources. The steps to giving a subject access to an object should be identification, authentication, and authorization.

**authorization**   Granting access to an object after the subject has been properly identified and authenticated.

**automated information system (AIS)**   A computer system that is used to process and transmit data. It is a collection of hardware, software, and firmware that works together to accept, compute, communicate, store, process, transmit, and control data-processing functions.

**availability**   The reliability and accessibility of data and resources to authorized individuals in a timely manner.

# B

**back up**   Copy and move data to a medium so that it may be restored if the original data is corrupted or destroyed. A full backup copies all the data from the system to the backup medium. An incremental backup copies only the files that have been modified since the previous backup. A differential backup backs up all files since the last full backup.

**backdoor**   An undocumented way of gaining access to a computer system. After a system is compromised, an attacker may load a program that listens on a port (backdoor) so that the attacker can enter the system at any time. A backdoor is also referred to as a trapdoor.

**baseline**   The minimum level of security necessary to support and enforce a security policy.

**Bell-LaPadula model**   The model uses a formal state transition model that describes its access controls and how they should perform. When the system must transition from one state to another, the security of the system should never be lowered or compromised. *See also* **multilevel security**, **simple security property**, and **star property (*-property)**.

**Biba model**  A formal state transition system of computer security policy that describes a set of access control rules designed to ensure data integrity.

**biometrics**  When used within computer security, used to identify individuals by physiological characteristics, such as a fingerprint, hand geometry, or pattern in the iris.

**browsing**  Searching through storage media looking for specific information without necessarily knowing what format the information is in. A browsing attack is one in which the attacker looks around a computer system either to see what looks interesting or to find specific information.

**brute force attack**  An attack that continually tries different inputs to achieve a predefined goal, which can be used to obtain credentials for unauthorized access.

## C

**callback**  A procedure for identifying a system that accessed an environment remotely. In a callback, the host system disconnects the caller and then dials the authorized telephone number of the remote terminal in order to reestablish the connection. Synonymous with dialback.

**capability**  A capability outlines the objects a subject can access and the operations the subject can carry out on the different objects. It indicates the access rights for a specific subject; many times, the capability is in the form of a ticket.

**certification**  The technical evaluation of the security components and their compliance for the purpose of accreditation. A certification process can use safeguard evaluation, risk analysis, verification, testing, and auditing techniques to assess the appropriateness of a specific system processing a certain level of information within a particular environment. The certification is the testing of the security component or system, and the accreditation is the approval from management of the security component or system.

**challenge-response method**  A method used to verify the identity of a subject by sending the subject an unpredictable or random value. If the subject responds with the expected value in return, the subject is authenticated.

**ciphertext**  Data that has been encrypted and is unreadable until it has been converted into plaintext.

**Clark-Wilson model**  An integrity model that addresses all three integrity goals: prevent unauthorized users from making modifications, prevent authorized users from making improper modifications, and maintain internal and external consistency through auditing.

**classification**  A systematic arrangement of objects into groups or categories according to a set of established criteria. Data and resources can be assigned a level of sensitivity as they are being created, amended, enhanced, stored, or transmitted. The classification level then determines the extent to which the resource needs to be controlled and secured, and is indicative of its value in terms of information assets.

**cleartext**   In data communications, cleartext is the form of a message or data which is transferred or stored without cryptographic protection.

**collusion**   Two or more people working together to carry out a fraudulent activity. More than one person would need to work together to cause some type of destruction or fraud; this drastically reduces its probability.

**communications security**   Controls in place to protect information as it is being transmitted, especially by telecommunications mechanisms.

**compartment**   A class of information that has need-to-know access controls beyond those normally provided for access to confidential, secret, or top-secret information. A compartment is the same thing as a category within a security label. Just because a subject has the proper classification, that does not mean it has a need to know. The category, or compartment, of the security label enforces the subject's need to know.

**compartmented mode workstation (CMW)**   A workstation that contains the necessary controls to be able to operate as a trusted computer. The system is trusted to keep data from different classification levels and categories in separate compartments and properly protected.

**compensating controls**   Controls that are alternative procedures designed to reduce the risk. They are used to "counterbalance" the effects of an internal control weakness.

**compromise**   A violation of the security policy of a system or an organization such that unauthorized disclosure or modification of sensitive information occurs.

**computer fraud**   Computer-related crimes involving deliberate misrepresentation, modification, or disclosure of data in order to compromise a system or obtain something of value.

**confidentiality**   A security principle that works to ensure that information is not disclosed to unauthorized subjects.

**configuration management**   The identification, control, accounting, and documentation of all changes that take place to system hardware, software, firmware, supporting documentation, and test results throughout the lifespan of the system.

**confinement**   Controlling information in a manner that prevents sensitive data from being leaked from a program to another program, subject, or object in an unauthorized manner.

**contingency plan**   A plan put in place before any potential emergencies, with the mission of dealing with possible future emergencies. It pertains to training personnel, performing backups, preparing critical facilities, and recovering from an emergency or disaster so that business operations can continue.

**control zone** The space within a facility that is used to protect sensitive processing equipment. Controls are in place to protect equipment from physical or technical unauthorized entry or compromise. The zone can also be used to prevent electrical waves carrying sensitive data from leaving the area.

**cost/benefit analysis** An assessment that is performed to ensure that the cost of a safeguard does not outweigh the benefit of the safeguard. Spending more to protect an asset than the asset is actually worth does not make good business sense. All possible safeguards must be evaluated to ensure that the most security-effective and cost-effective choice is made.

**countermeasure** A control, method, technique, or procedure that is put into place to prevent a threat agent from exploiting a vulnerability. A countermeasure is put into place to mitigate risk. Also called a **safeguard** or control.

**covert channel** A communications path that enables a process to transmit information in a way that violates the system's security policy.

**covert storage channel** A covert channel that involves writing to a storage location by one process and the direct or indirect reading of the storage location by another process. Covert storage channels typically involve a resource (for example, sectors on a disk) that is shared by two subjects at different security levels.

**covert timing channel** A covert channel in which one process modulates its system resource (for example, CPU cycles), which is interpreted by a second process as some type of communication.

**cryptanalysis** The practice of breaking cryptosystems and algorithms used in encryption and decryption processes.

**cryptography** The science of secret writing that enables storage and transmission of data in a form that is available only to the intended individuals.

**cryptology** The study of cryptography and cryptanalysis.

**cryptosystem** The hardware or software implementation of cryptography.

# D

**data classification** Assignments to data that indicate the level of availability, integrity, and confidentiality that is required for each type of information.

**data custodian** An individual who is responsible for the maintenance and protection of the data. This role is usually filled by the IT department (usually the network administrator). The duties include performing regular backups of the data, implementing security mechanisms, periodically validating the integrity of the data, restoring data from backup media, and fulfilling the requirements specified in the company's security policy, standards, and guidelines that pertain to information security and data protection.

**Data Encryption Standard (DES)**   Symmetric key encryption algorithm that was adopted by the government as a federal standard for protecting sensitive unclassified information. DES was later replaced with Advanced Encryption Standard (AES).

**data remanence**   A measure of the magnetic flux density remaining after removal of the applied magnetic force, which is used to erase data. Refers to any data remaining on magnetic storage media.

**database shadowing**   A mirroring technology used in databases, in which information is written to at least two hard drives for the purpose of redundancy.

**declassification**   An administrative decision or procedure to remove or reduce the security classification information.

**dedicated security mode**   The mode in which a system operates if all users have the clearance or authorization to access, and the need to know about, all data processed within the system. All users have been given formal access approval for all information on the system and have signed nondisclosure agreements pertaining to this information.

**degauss**   Process that demagnetizes magnetic media so that a very low residue of magnetic induction is left on the media. Used to effectively erase data from media.

**Delphi technique**   A group decision method used to ensure that each member of a group gives an honest and anonymous opinion pertaining to the company's risks.

**denial of service (DoS)**   Any action, or series of actions, that prevents a system, or its resources, from functioning in accordance with its intended purpose.

**dial-up**   The service whereby a computer terminal can use telephone lines, usually via a modem, to initiate and continue communication with another computer system.

**dictionary attack**   A form of attack in which an attacker uses a large set of likely combinations to guess a secret, usually a password.

**digital signature**   An electronic signature based upon cryptographic methods of originator authentication, computed by using a set of rules and a set of parameters such that the identity of the signer and the integrity of the data can be verified.

**disaster recovery plan**   A plan developed to help a company recover from a disaster. It provides procedures for emergency response, extended backup operations, and post-disaster recovery when an organization suffers a loss of computer processing capability or resources and physical facilities.

**discretionary access control (DAC)**   An access control model and policy that restricts access to objects based on the identity of the subjects and the groups to which those subjects belong. The data owner has the discretion of allowing or denying others access to the resources it owns.

**domain**   The set of objects that a subject is allowed to access. Within this domain, all subjects and objects share a common security policy, procedures, and rules, and they are managed by the same management system.

**due care**   Steps taken to show that a company has taken responsibility for the activities that occur within the corporation and has taken the necessary steps to help protect the company, its resources, and employees.

**due diligence**   The process of systematically evaluating information to identify vulnerabilities, threats, and issues relating to an organization's overall risk.

# E

**electronic vaulting**   The transfer of backup data to an offsite location. This process is primarily a batch process of transmitting data through communications lines to a server at an alternate location.

**emanations**   Electrical and electromagnetic signals emitted from electrical equipment that can transmit through the airwaves. These signals carry information that can be captured and deciphered, which can cause a security breach. These are also called emissions.

**encryption**   The transformation of plaintext into unreadable ciphertext.

**end-to-end encryption**   A technology that encrypts the data payload of a packet.

**Evaluated Products List (EPL)**   A list of products that have been evaluated and assigned an assurance rating. The products could be evaluated using several different criterion: TCSEC, ITSEC, or Common Criteria.

**exposure**   An instance of being exposed to losses from a threat. A weakness or vulnerability can cause an organization to be exposed to possible damages.

**exposure factor**   The percentage of loss a realized threat could have on a certain asset.

# F

**failover**   A backup operation that automatically switches to a standby system if the primary system fails or is taken offline. It is an important fault-tolerant function that provides system availability.

**fail-safe**   A functionality that ensures that when software or a system fails for any reason, it does not end up in a vulnerable state. After a failure, software might default to no access instead of allowing full control, which would be an example of a fail-safe measure.

**firmware**  Software instructions that have been written into read-only memory (ROM) or a programmable ROM (PROM) chip.

**formal security policy model**  A mathematical statement of a security policy. When an operating system is created, it can be built upon a predeveloped model that lays out how all activities will take place in each and every situation. This model can be expressed mathematically, which is then translated into a programming language.

**formal verification**  Validating and testing of highly trusted systems. The tests are designed to show design verification, consistency between the formal specifications and the formal security policy model, implementation verification, consistency between the formal specifications, and the actual implementation of the product.

# G

**gateway**  A system or device that connects two unlike environments or systems. The gateway is usually required to translate between different types of applications or protocols.

**guidelines**  Recommended actions and operational guides for users, IT staff, operations staff, and others when a specific standard does not apply.

# H

**handshaking procedure**  A dialog between two entities for the purpose of identifying and authenticating the entities to one another. The dialog can take place between two computers or two applications residing on different computers. It is an activity that usually takes place within a protocol.

**honeypot**  A computer set up as a sacrificial lamb on the network in the hope that attackers will attack this system instead of actual production systems.

# I

**identification**  A subject provides some type of data to an authentication service. Identification is the first step in the authentication process.

**information owner**  The person who has final corporate responsibility of data protection and would be the one held liable for any negligence when it comes to protecting the company's information assets. The person who holds this role—usually a senior executive within the management group of the company—is responsible for assigning a classification to the information and dictating how the information should be protected.

**integrity**  A security principle that makes sure that information and systems are not modified maliciously or accidentally.

**intrusion detection system (IDS)**   Software employed to monitor and detect possible attacks and behaviors that vary from the normal and expected activity. The IDS can be network based, which monitors network traffic, or host based, which monitors activities of a specific system and protects system files and control mechanisms.

**isolation**   The containment of processes in a system in such a way that they are separated from one another to ensure integrity and confidentiality.

# K

**kernel**   The core of an operating system, a kernel manages the machine's hardware resources (including the processor and the memory), and provides and controls the way any other software component accesses these resources.

**key**   A discreet data set that controls the operation of a cryptography algorithm. In encryption, a key specifies the particular transformation of plaintext into ciphertext, or vice versa during decryption. Keys are also used in other cryptographic algorithms, such as digital signature schemes and keyed-hash functions (also known as HMACs), which are often used for authentication and integrity.

**keystroke monitoring**   A type of auditing that can review or record keystrokes entered by a user during an active session.

# L

**lattice-based access control model**   A mathematical model that allows a system to easily represent the different security levels and control access attempts based on those levels. Every pair of elements has a highest lower bound and a lowest upper bound of access rights. The classes stemmed from military designations.

**least privilege**   The security principle that requires each subject to be granted the most restrictive set of privileges needed for the performance of authorized tasks. The application of this principle limits the damage that can result from accident, error, or unauthorized use.

**life-cycle assurance**   Confidence that a trusted system is designed, developed, and maintained with formal designs and controls. This includes design specification and verification, implementation, testing, configuration management, and distribution.

**link encryption**   A type of encryption technology that encrypts packets' headers, trailers, and the data payload. Each network communications node, or hop, must decrypt the packets to read its address and routing information and then re-encrypt the packets. This is different from **end-to-end encryption**.

**logic bomb**   A malicious program that is triggered by a specific event or condition.

**loss potential**   The potential losses that can be accrued if a threat agent actually exploits a vulnerability.

# M

**maintenance hook**   Instructions within a program's code that enable the developer or maintainer to enter the program without having to go through the usual access control and authentication processes. Maintenance hooks should be removed from the code before it is released to production; otherwise, they can cause serious security risks. Also called trapdoor or **backdoor**.

**malware**   Malicious software. Code written to perform activities that circumvent the security policy of a system. Examples are viruses, malicious applets, Trojan horses, logical bombs, and worms.

**mandatory access control (MAC)**   An access policy that restricts subjects' access to objects based on the security clearance of the subject and the classification of the object. The system enforces the security policy, and users cannot share their files with other users.

**masquerading**   Impersonating another user, usually with the intention of gaining unauthorized access to a system.

**message authentication code (MAC)**   In cryptography, a message authentication code (MAC) is a generated value used to authenticate a message. A MAC can be generated by HMAC or CBC-MAC methods. The MAC protects both a message's integrity (by ensuring that a different MAC will be produced if the message has changed) as well as its authenticity, because only someone who knows the secret key could have modified the message.

**multilevel security**   A class of systems containing information with different classifications. Access decisions are based on the subject's security clearances, need to know, and formal approval.

# N

**need to know**   A security principle stating that users should have access only to the information and resources necessary to complete their tasks that fulfill their roles within an organization. Need to know is commonly used in access control criterion by operating systems and applications.

**node**   A system that is connected to a network.

# O

**object**   A passive entity that contains or receives information. Access to an object potentially implies access to the information that it contains. Examples of objects include records, pages, memory segments, files, directories, directory trees, and programs.

**object reuse**   Reassigning to a subject media that previously contained information. Object reuse is a security concern because if insufficient measures were taken to erase the information on the media, the information may be disclosed to unauthorized personnel.

**one-time pad**   A method of encryption in which the plaintext is combined with a random "pad," which should be the same length as the plaintext. This encryption process uses a nonrepeating set of random bits that are combined bitwise (XOR) with the message to produce ciphertext. A one-time pad is a perfect encryption scheme, because it is unbreakable and each pad is used exactly once, but it is impractical because of all of the required overhead.

**operational assurance**   A level of confidence of a trusted system's architecture and implementation that enforces the system's security policy. This can include system architecture, covert channel analysis, system integrity, and trusted recovery.

**operational goals**   Daily goals to be accomplished to ensure the proper operation of an environment.

**operator**   An individual who supports the operations of computer systems—usually a mainframe. The individual may monitor the execution of the system, control the flow of jobs, and develop and schedule batch jobs.

**Orange Book**   The common name for the Trusted Computer Security Evaluation Criteria (TCSEC).

**overt channel**   A path within a computer system or network that is designed for the authorized transfer of data.

**P**

**password**   A sequence of characters used to prove one's identity. It is used during a logon process and should be highly protected.

**penetration**   A successful attempt at circumventing security controls and gaining access to a system.

**penetration testing**   Penetration testing is a method of evaluating the security of a computer system or network by simulating an attack that a malicious hacker would carry out. This is done so that vulnerabilities and weaknesses can be uncovered.

**permissions**   The type of authorized interactions that a subject can have with an object. Examples include read, write, execute, add, modify, and delete.

**personnel security**   The procedures that are established to ensure that all personnel who have access to sensitive information have the required authority as well as appropriate clearances. Procedures confirm a person's background and provide assurance of necessary trustworthiness.

**physical controls**   Controls that pertain to controlling individual access into the facility and different departments, locking systems and removing unnecessary floppy or

CD-ROM drives, protecting the perimeter of the facility, monitoring for intrusion, and checking environmental controls.

**physical security**   Controls and procedures put into place to prevent intruders from physically accessing a system or facility. The controls enforce access control and authorized access.

**piggyback**   Unauthorized access to a system by using another user's legitimate credentials.

**plaintext**   In cryptography, the original readable text before it is encrypted.

**playback attack**   Capturing data and resending the data at a later time in the hope of tricking the receiving system. This is usually carried out to obtain unauthorized access to specific resources.

**privacy**   A security principle that protects an individual's information and employs controls to ensure that this information is not disseminated or accessed in an unauthorized manner.

**procedure**   Detailed step-by-step instructions to achieve a certain task, which are used by users, IT staff, operations staff, security members, and others.

**protection ring**   An architecture that provides hierarchies of privileged operation modes of a system, which gives certain access rights to processes that are authorized to operate in that mode. Supports the integrity and confidentiality requirements of multitasking operating systems and enables the operating system to protect itself from user programs and rogue processes.

**protocol**   A set of rules and formats that enables the standardized exchange of information between different systems.

**pseudo-flaw**   An apparent loophole deliberately implanted in an operating system or program as a trap for intruders.

**public key encryption**   A type of encryption that uses two mathematically related keys to encrypt and decrypt messages. The private key is known only to the owner, and the public key is available to anyone.

**purge**   The removal of sensitive data from a system, storage device, or peripheral device with storage capacity at the end of a processing period. This action is performed in such a way that there is assurance proportional to the sensitivity of the data that the data cannot be reconstructed.

## Q

**qualitative risk analysis**   A risk analysis method that uses intuition and experience to judge an organization's exposure to risks. It uses scenarios and ratings systems. Compare to **quantitative risk analysis**.

**quantitative risk analysis**   A risk analysis method that attempts to use percentages in damage estimations and assigns real numbers to the costs of countermeasures for particular risks and the amount of damage that could result from the risk. Compare to **qualitative risk analysis**.

# R

**RADIUS (Remote Authentication Dial-in User Service)**   A security service that authenticates and authorizes dial-up users and is a centralized access control mechanism.

**read**   An operation that results in the flow of information from an object to a subject and does not give the subject the ability to modify the object or the data within the object.

**recovery planning**   The advance planning and preparations that are necessary to minimize loss and to ensure the availability of the critical information systems of an organization after a disruption in service or a disaster.

**reference monitor concept**   An access control concept that refers to an abstract machine that mediates all accesses to objects by subjects. The security kernel enforces the reference monitor concept.

**reliability**   The assurance of a given system, or individual component, performing its mission adequately for a specified period of time under the expected operating conditions.

**remote journaling**   A method of transmitting changes to data to an offsite facility. This takes place as parallel processing of transactions, meaning that changes to the data are saved locally and to an off-site facility. These activities take place in real time and provide redundancy and fault tolerance.

**repudiation**   When the sender of a message denies sending the message. The countermeasure to this is to implement digital signatures.

**residual risk**   The remaining risk after the security controls have been applied. The conceptual formulas that explain the difference between total and residual risk are

threats × vulnerability × asset value = total risk

(threats × vulnerability × asset value) × controls gap = residual risk

**risk**   The likelihood of a threat agent taking advantage of a vulnerability and the resulting business impact. A risk is the loss potential, or probability, that a threat will exploit a vulnerability.

**risk analysis**   A method of identifying risks and assessing the possible damage that could be caused in order to justify security safeguards.

**risk management**   The process of identifying, assessing, and reducing the risk to an acceptable level and implementing the right mechanisms to maintain that level of risk.

**role-based access control (RBAC)**   Type of model that provides access to resources based on the role the user holds within the company or the tasks that the user has been assigned.

# S

**safeguard**   A software configuration, hardware, or procedure that eliminates a vulnerability or reduces the risk of a threat agent from being able to exploit a vulnerability. Also called a **countermeasure** or control.

**secure configuration management**   Implementing the set of appropriate procedures to control the life cycle of an application, document the necessary change control activities, and ensure that the changes will not violate the security policy.

**security evaluation**   Assesses the degree of trust and assurance that can be placed in systems for the secure handling of sensitive information.

**security kernel**   The hardware, firmware, and software elements of a trusted computing base (TCB) that implement the reference monitor concept. The kernel must mediate all access between subjects and objects, be protected from modification, and be verifiable as correct.

**security label**   An identifier that represents the security level of an object.

**security perimeter**   An imaginary boundary between the components within the trusted computing base (TCB) and mechanisms that do not fall within the TCB. It is the distinction between trusted and untrusted processes.

**security policy**   Documentation that describes senior management's directives toward the role that security plays within the organization. It provides a framework within which an organization establishes needed levels of information security to achieve the desired confidentiality, availability, and integrity goals. A policy is a statement of information values, protection responsibilities, and organization commitment managing risks.

**security testing**   Testing all security mechanisms and features within a system to determine the level of protection they provide. Security testing can include penetration testing, formal design and implementation verification, and functional testing.

**sensitive information**   Information that would cause a negative effect on the company if it were lost or compromised.

**sensitivity label**   A piece of information that represents the security level of an object. Sensitivity labels are used by the TCB as the basis for mandatory access control (MAC) decisions.

**separation of duties**   A security principle that splits up a critical task among two or more individuals to ensure that one person cannot complete a risky task by himself.

**shoulder surfing**   When a person looks over another person's shoulder and watches keystrokes or watches data as it appears on the screen in order to uncover information in an unauthorized manner.

**simple security property**   A Bell-LaPadula security model rule that stipulates that a subject cannot read data at a higher security level.

**single loss expectancy (SLE)**   A dollar amount that is assigned to a single event that represents the company's potential loss amount if a specific threat were to take place.

asset value × exposure factor = SLE

**social engineering**   The act of tricking another person into providing confidential information by posing as an individual who is authorized to receive that information.

**spoofing**   Presenting false information, usually within packets, to trick other systems and hide the origin of the message. This is usually done by hackers so that their identity cannot be successfully uncovered.

**standards**   Rules indicating how hardware and software should be implemented, used, and maintained. Standards provide a means to ensure that specific technologies, applications, parameters, and procedures are carried out in a uniform way across the organization. They are compulsory.

**star property (\*-property)**   A Bell-LaPadula security model rule that stipulates that a subject cannot write data to an object at a lower security level.

**strategic goals**   Long-term goals that are broad, general statements of intent. Operational and tactical goals support strategic goals and all are a part of a planning horizon.

**subject**   An active entity, generally in the form of a person, process, or device, that causes information to flow among objects or that changes the system state.

**supervisor state**   One of several states in which an operating system may operate, and the only one in which privileged instructions may be executed by the CPU.

# T

**TACACS (Terminal Access Controller Access Control System)**   A client/server authentication protocol that provides the same type of functionality as RADIUS and is used as a central access control mechanism mainly for remote users.

**tactical goals**   Midterm goals to accomplish. These may be milestones to accomplish within a project or specific projects to accomplish in a year. Strategic, tactical, and operational goals make up a planning horizon.

**technical controls**   These controls, also called logical access control mechanisms, work in software to provide confidentiality, integrity, or availability protection. Some examples are passwords, identification and authentication methods, security devices, auditing, and the configuration of the network.

**Tempest**   The study and control of spurious electronic signals emitted by electrical equipment. Tempest equipment is implemented to prevent intruders from picking up information through the airwaves with listening devices.

**threat**   Any potential danger that a vulnerability will be exploited by a threat agent.

**top-down approach**   An approach in which the initiation, support, and direction for a project come from top management and work their way down through middle management and then to staff members.

**topology**   The physical construction of how nodes are connected to form a network.

**total risk**   When a safeguard is not implemented, an organization is faced with the total risk of that particular vulnerability.

**Trojan horse**   A computer program that has an apparently or actually useful function, but that also contains additional hidden malicious capabilities to exploit a vulnerability and/or provide unauthorized access into a system.

**trusted computer system**   A system that has the necessary controls to ensure that the security policy will not be compromised and that can process a range of sensitive or classified information simultaneously.

**trusted computing base (TCB)**   All of the protection mechanisms within a computer system (software, hardware, and firmware) that are responsible for enforcing a security policy.

**trusted path**   A mechanism within the system that enables the user to communicate directly with the TCB. This mechanism can be activated only by the user or the TCB and not by an untrusted mechanism or process.

**trusted recovery**   A set of procedures that restores a system and its data in a trusted manner after the system has been disrupted or a system failure has occurred.

# U

**user**   A person or process that is accessing a computer system.

**user ID**   A unique set of characters or code that is used to identify a specific user to a system.

## V

**validation**   The act of performing tests and evaluations to test a system's security level to see if it complies with security specifications and requirements.

**virus**   A small application, or string of code, that infects applications. The main function of a virus is to reproduce, and it requires a host application to do this. It can damage data directly or degrade system performance.

**vulnerability**   The absence or weakness of a safeguard that could be exploited.

## W

**wardialing**   An attack in which a long list of phone numbers is inserted into a wardialing program in the hope of finding a modem that can be exploited to gain unauthorized access.

**work factor**   The estimated time and effort required for an attacker to overcome a security control.

**worm**   An independent program that can reproduce by copying itself from one system to another. It may damage data directly or degrade system performance by tying up resources.

**write**   An operation that results in the flow of information from a subject to an object.

## References

- **Lynn Wheeler Security Glossary**   www.garlic.com/~lynn/secgloss.htm
- **NIST Consolidated Security Glossary**   http://csrc.nist.gov/posix/framework_wg/glossary.asc
- **Linux Security.com Security Dictionary**   www.linuxsecurity.com/content/view/117309/
- **Wikipedia, the Free Encyclopedia**   http://en.wikipedia.org/wiki/Security

# INDEX

*References to figures are in italics.*

*-integrity axiom, 282
*-property. *See* star property
10Base2, 448, 449
10Base5, 448
10Base-T, 448, 449
3G (third generation), 570–572
802.11a, 555
802.11b, 554
802.11e, 555
802.11f, 555
802.11g, 555–556
802.11h, 556
802.11i, 556
802.11j, 563
802.11n, 563
802.15, 563–564
802.16, 563
802.1X, 558–560

## A

absolute addresses, 249
abstraction, 242, 852, 854
access, 123
    defined, 953
access control administration, 171
    centralized, 172–179
    content-dependent, 170–171
    context-dependent, 171
    decentralized, 179–180

    Diameter, 176–179
    RADIUS, 173
    TACACS, 173–176
access control lists, 148, 170, 474
    defined, 953
access control matrix, 169
    access control lists, 170
    capability tables, 169–170
access control mechanism, defined, 953
access control methods, 180
    access control layers, 180–181
    administrative controls, 181–183
    auditing, 188
    cabling, 184–185
    computer controls, 184
    control zone, 187–188
    data backups, 184
    encryption and protocols, 187
    network access, 187
    network architecture, 185–187
    network segregation, 183
    perimeter security, 184
    personnel controls, 182
    physical controls, 183–185
    policy and procedures, 181–182
    security-awareness training, 182–183
    supervisory structure, 182
    system access, 185
    technical controls, 185–188
    testing, 183
    work area separation, 184

access control models, 161, 166
  discretionary access control, 162
  identity-based access control, 163
  mandatory access control, 163–164
  role-based access control, 165–166
access control monitoring, 200
  intrusion detection, 200–211
  intrusion prevention, 211–214
access control practices, 197
  control zone, 200
  emanation security, 199
  object reuse, 198
  Tempest, 199–200
  unauthorized disclosure of
    information, 198
  white noise, 200
access controls
  constrained user interfaces,
    168–169
  defined, 953
  logical, 127–128
  overview, 123–124
  rule-based access control, 167
access control techniques, 172
access control types, 188–193
access criteria, 146–147
accountability, 193–194, 903–904
  defined, 953
  keystroke monitoring, 195–196
  protecting audit data and log
    information, 196
  review of audit information,
    194–195
accreditation vs. certification, 314–317
accredited, defined, 953
ACLs. See access control lists
active monitors, 450
ActiveX, 873–874
add-on security, defined, 953
address buses, 233
Address Resolution Protocol. See ARP
administrative controls, 53
  defined, 953

administrative management,
  900–903
Advanced Encryption Standard (AES)
  algorithm, 93, 622, 629–630
adware, 574
AIC triad, 55–57
  defined, 953
Airsnarf, 569
AirSnort, 569
AIS. See automated information system
ALE. See annualized loss expectancy
algorithms, 594
American National Standards Institute.
  See ANSI
amplitude, 439, 549
analog signals, 440, 459
analog transmission, 439
annualized loss expectancy, 76
  defined, 953
annualized rate of occurrence, 77
  defined, 953
ANSI, 452, 952
application controls, 809–810
  vs. environment, 812–813
application development
  methodology, 850
  object-oriented concepts, 850–855
  polymorphism, 855–856
  See also software development
application layer, 420–421, 428
application owner, 101–102
application-level proxies, 488–489
application-specific integrated circuits
  (ASICs), 476
architecture
  CPUs, 229–235
  operating systems, 235–240,
    256–258
  security, 268
  software, 857
  system, 266–275
  two-tier, 35–37
arithmetic logic units (ALUs), 230

ARO. *See* annualized rate of occurrence
ARP, 463–464
        and RARP, 465
        table poisoning, 464
artificial neural networks (ANN),
        869–871
assemblers, 850
asset identification, 85
assurance, 300
        defined, 954
asymmetric mode, 235
Asymmetrical DSL (ADSL), 538
asynchronous communication, 441, 459
asynchronous token devices, 140
Asynchronous Transfer Mode (ATM),
        516–518, 526–527
attacking. *See* hacking
attacks
        active, 675
        chosen-ciphertext attack, 676
        chosen-plaintext attack, 676
        ciphertext-only attack, 676
        data diddling, 758
        defined, 954
        denial of service, 878–880
        distributed denial-of-service,
                882–883
        DNS DoS attacks, 884–885
        fraggle, 880–881
        known-plaintext attack, 676
        passive, 675
        replay attack, 678–679
        salami, 758
        secure DNS attacks, 885
        side-channel attacks, 678
        smurf, 880
        SYN floods, 881–882
        teardrop attack, 882
        timing, 885
        *See also* legal issues
attack-signature-detection tools, 195
attenuation, 447, 456, 457
audit logs, 196

audit trails, 194–195
        defined, 954
auditing, 188
        physical access, 402
audit-reduction tools, 195
authenticate, defined, 954
authentication, 126–128, 129
        data origin, 643
        Kerberos, 152–155
        strong, 129
authorization, 126–128, 146
        access criteria, 146–147
        creep, 148
        default to no access, 148
        defined, 954
automated information system,
        defined, 954
autonomous systems (ASs), 467
availability, 56, 125, 228, 911
        defined, 954
Available Bit Rate (ABR), 527


**B**

backdoors, 928
        defined, 954
back-off algorithm, 461
backups, 914
        alternatives, 721–723
        defined, 954
        differential, 722
        electronic backup solutions,
                724–726
        full, 722
        hardware, 716
        incremental, 722–723
        restoring data, 723–724
        software, 717–718, 726–727
Bamford, James, 949
bandwidth, 440
base registers, 243, *244*
baseband, 441–442, 459

baselines, 91–92
    defined, 954
Basic Security Theorem, 281
bastion hosts, 493–496
beaconing, 450
BEDO DRAM, 246
Bell-LaPadula model, 279–282, 283
    defined, 954
best-effort service, 527
BGP, 425, 469
Biba model, 282–283
    defined, 955
biometrics, 131–133
    crossover error rate (CER),
        131–132
    defined, 955
    facial scans, 135
    fingerprints, 133
    hand geometry, 134
    hand topography, 135
    iris scans, 134
    keyboard dynamics, 134
    palm scans, 133
    retina scans, 134
    signature dynamics, 134
    Type I error, 131, 132
    Type II error, 131, 132
    voice prints, 134–135
birthday attacks, 646–648
blocked state, 236
Blowfish, 630
Blue Boxing, 765
Bluejacking, 564
Bluetooth wireless technology, 564
*Body of Secrets*, 949
bollards, 391
Boot Protocol (BOOTP), 465
Border Gateway Protocol. *See* BGP
bounds checking, 322
Brewer and Nash model, 293–294
bridges, 471–472, 475
broadband, 441–442, 459
    wireless access, 563

broadcast storms, 471
broadcast transmission, 458, 459
browsing, 925
    defined, 955
brute force attacks, 136, 215–216
    defined, 955
buffer overflow, 321–325
burst EDO DRAM. *See* BEDO DRAM
bus topology, 444
business continuity plan, 693–697
    business impact analysis,
        699–703
    business process recovery,
        708–709
    data backup alternatives,
        721–723
    documentation, 718–719
    electronic backup solutions,
        724–726
    end-user environment, 720–721
    facility recovery, 709–713
    goals, 732–733
    human resources, 719–720
    implementing strategies,
        733–734
    insurance, 728
    interdependencies, 704–705
    maintaining the plan, 739–740
    maximum tolerable downtime
        (MTD), 702–703
    preventative measures, 706, 707
    project initiation, 697–698
    reciprocal agreements, 713–714
    recovery and restoration, 728–731
    recovery strategies, 707–708
    redundant sites, 714–715
    requirements, 699
    restoring data, 723–724
    software backups, 726–727
    supply and technology recovery,
        715–716
    testing and revising the plan,
        734–739

# C

cable modems, 537–539
cables, 453–454
    access control, 184–185
    attenuation, 456, 457
    coaxial, 454
    crosstalk, 457
    fiber-optic, 456
    fire rating, 457–458
    noise, 456–457
    twisted-pair, 454–456
cache memory, 247–248
callback, 548
    defined, 955
caller ID, 548
call-processing manager, 530
Canadian Information Processing
    Society (CIPS), 7
Canadian Trusted Computer Product
    Evaluation Criteria (CTCPEC), 45
capability, 169
    defined, 955
Capability Maturity Model (CMM),
    848–849
capability tables, 169–170
carriers, 461
carrier-sensing access methods, 462
cascading errors, 72
CBC-MAC, 643–644
CBK, domains on CISSP exam, 4–6
CCM Protocol (CCMP), 557
CDDI, 453
    See also FDDI
CD-ROM, 945–946
    installing and running Total Semi-
      nars' test software, 947–948
    running the QuickTime cryptography
      video sample, 946–947
    system requirements, 948
    technical support, 948
cell phone cloning, 567
cell suppression, 827

central processing units. See CPUs
certificate authorities (CAs), 651,
    652–653
certificates, 651, 653–654
certification
    vs. accreditation, 314–317
    defined, 955
Challenge Handshake Authentication
    Protocol (CHAP), 542, 546, 547
challenge-response method, defined, 955
change control analyst, 102
change control documentation,
    907–908
Channel Service Unit/Data Service Unit.
    See CSU/DSU
Chaos Computer Club, 764
Chinese Wall model, 293–294
chipping code, 551
chips, 551
CIA triad. See AIC triad
cipher locks, 384, 385
    See also locks
ciphertext, 593
    chosen-ciphertext attack, 676
    ciphertext-only attack, 676
    defined, 955
circuit switching, 521–523
circuit-level proxies, 488–490
CISSP certification
    history of, 7
    how to become a CISSP, 7–8
    reasons to become certified, 1–2
    recertification requirements, 8–9
    requirements, 2
CISSP exam, 2–6
    tips for taking, 9–11
Clark-Wilson model, 284–287
    defined, 955
classes, 438
classification, 94–95
    controls, 98–99
    defined, 955

private industry vs. military classifications, 95–98
procedures, 98
cleartext, defined, 956
client/server architecture, security, 812
clipping levels, 136–137, 905
clock speed, 234
closed circuit TVs (CCTVs), 394–397, 398
closed systems, 318
clustering, 914
CMW. See compartmented mode workstation
coaxial cable, 454
Code of Ethics, 752–753
cognitive passwords, 128, 138–139
cohesion, 858–859
collision, 461, 646
collision domains, 461–462
collusion, 341
    defined, 956
committed information rate (CIR), 523
Common Body of Knowledge. See CBK
Common Criteria, 45, 303, 312–314, 315
Common Object Request Broker Architecture (CORBA), 859–861
communications security, defined, 956
compartment, defined, 956
compartmented mode workstation, defined, 956
compartmented security mode, 297–298
compensating controls, defined, 956
compilers, 850
Component Object Model (COM), 863
compromise, defined, 956
computer controls, 184
computer crimes, 758–762
    admissibility of evidence, 783–786
    enticement and entrapment, 787
    forensics and evidence collection, 780–782

identification, protection, and prosecution, 766–767
incident handling, 782–783
incident response, 778–780
interviewing and interrogating, 787–788
liability, 767–772
motive, opportunity and means, 756–757
surveillance, search and seizure, 786–787
well-known, 763–766
    See also legal issues
Computer Ethics Institute, 754
Computer Fraud and Abuse Act, 792–793
computer fraud, defined, 956
computer rooms, 359–362
Computer Security Act, 794, 950
Computer Security Institute (CSI), 7
Computer Systems Laboratory (CSL), 950
computer-aided software engineering (CASE), 861–862
concentrators, 471
confidentiality, 57, 126, 228
    defined, 956
configuration management, 847, 905–908
    defined, 956
confinement, defined, 956
connectionless protocols, 432, 433
connection-oriented protocols, 432, 433
Constant Bit Rate (CBR), 527
constrained user interfaces, 168–169
content-dependent access control, 170–171, 827
contention, 461
context-dependent access control, 171
contingency plan, defined, 956
continuing professional education. See CPE
control units, 231

control zone, 187–188, 200
    defined, 957
controlling unauthorized downgrading
    of information, 281
cookies, 574, 669–671
cooperative multitasking, 236
Copper Distributed Data Interface.
    *See* CDDI
Corporate Information Security Officer
    (CISO), 62
Corporate Security Officer (CSO), 62
cost/benefit analysis, 82
    defined, 957
cost/benefit comparison, 68
countermeasures, 58–59
    defined, 957
    functionality and effectiveness
        of, 84–85
    selection of, 82–84
counter-synchronization, 140
coupling, 859
covert channels, 288–289
    defined, 957
covert storage channels, 289
    defined, 957
covert timing channels, 289
    defined, 957
CPE, credits, 8
CPUs, 229–235
    evolution of processors, 234
    modes, 253–256
    *See also* memory
crackers, 757
cracking. *See* hacking
cramming, 929
Crime Prevention Through Environmental
    Design (CPTED), 344–346
    activity support, 349
    *See also* physical security
Critical Infrastructure Assurance Office
    (CIAO), 28
crossover error rate (CER), 131–132

crosstalk, 457
cryptanalysis, 592–593
    defined, 957
    differential, 677
    linear, 677–678
cryptographic keys, 141–142
cryptography, 587–588
    Advanced Encryption Standard (AES)
        algorithm, 622, 629–630
    asymmetric, 609–612, 632–640
    block ciphers, 613–614
    Blowfish, 630
    Caesar cipher, 590, 604–605
    CBC-MAC, 643–644
    concealment ciphers, 601–602
    confusion, 613
    cryptosystems, 594, 596–598, 957
    Data Encryption Standard (DES),
        621–628
    defined, 957
    Diffie-Hellman algorithm,
        632–633
    diffusion, 613
    digital signatures, 648–649
    Digital Signature Standard,
        650–651
    El Gamal, 638
    elliptic curve cryptosystems,
        638, *639*
    Enigma machine, 591–592
    frequency analysis, 606
    governments and, 603–604
    hardware vs. software systems, 662
    hash MAC (HMAC), 641–643
    hashing algorithms, 640–648
    HAVAL, 646
    history of, 588–590
    International Data Encryption
        Algorithm (IDEA), 630
    Kerckhoff's principle, 596
    key management, 657–659
    keystream generators, 614

knapsack algorithms, 639
LUC, 638
Lucifer, 592, 622
man-in-the-middle attacks, 633–634
MD2, 645
MD4, 645
MD5, 646
message integrity, 640
NIST and FIPS standards, 950
notation, 631
one-time pad, 599–601, 616
one-way hash functions, 637–638,
    640–644, 646–648
out-of-band method, 608
public key, 617–619, 635
RC4, 631
RC5, 631
RC6, 631
RSA, 634–638
running key ciphers, 601–602
running the QuickTime cryptography
    video sample on CD-ROM,
    946–947
scytale cipher, 589
secure message format, 610
session keys, 619–621
SHA, 646
steganography, 602
stream ciphers, 614–616
substitution cipher, 588,
    604–605
symmetric, 607–609, 612,
    621–631
terminology and concepts,
    593–595, 598–599
transposition cipher, 605–606
Triple-DES, 629
Vigenere cipher, 590–593
Wassenaar Arrangement,
    603–604
zero knowledge proof, 639–640
*See also* encryption; public key
    infrastructure

cryptology, defined, 957
cryptosystems, 594
    defined, 957
    services of, 597–598
    strength of, 596–597
CSMA, 461
CSMA/CA, 461, 549
CSMA/CD, 461, 549
CSU/DSU, 520
*The Cuckoo's Egg*, 763–764
Cult of the Dead Cow, 764
cyberinsurance, 728
cyberlaw. *See* legal issues
cybersecurity czar, 45


**D**

DAC. *See* discretionary access control
data analyst, 102
data backups, 184
data buses, 233
data centers, 360–362
Data Circuit-Terminating Equipment
    (DCE), 524
data classification, defined, 957
data custodian, 100
    defined, 957
data diddling, 758
Data Encryption Standard, 621–623
    Cipher Block Chaining mode,
        625–626
    Cipher Feedback mode,
        626–627
    Counter mode, 628
    defined, 958
    Electronic Code Book mode, 624
    modes, 623–624
    Output Feedback mode,
        627–628
    Triple-DES, 629
Data Factory Object, 38
data hiding, 257, 260–261

data link layer, 426–428, 430
data mining, 831–832
data modeling, 856
data origin authentication, 643
data owner, 100
Data Processing Management Association (DPMA), 7
data remanence, 909
  defined, 958
data structures, 436–437, 857–858
Data Terminal Equipment (DTE), 520, 524
data warehousing, 830
data width, 234
database management, 816–817
  ActiveX Data Objects (ADO), 821
  aggregation, 826–827
  commit operations, 825
  content-dependent access control, 827
  data dictionary, 821–822
  data mining, 831–832
  data warehousing, 830
  database interface languages, 820–821
  database models, 818–820
  Extensible Markup Language (XML), 821
  inference, 827
  integrity, 824
  Java Database Connectivity (JDBC), 821
  Object Linking and Embedding Database (OLE DB), 821
  online transaction processing, 829–830
  Open Database Connectivity (ODBC), 820, 863
  polyinstantiation, 828–829
  primary vs. foreign keys, 822–823
  relational database components, 821
  rollbacks, 825
  roles, 37–38
  savepoints, 825
  security, 826–828
  shadowing, 958
  software, 817–818
  terminology, 819
  views, 168, 828
datagrams, 437
DDR SDRAM, 246
deadlocks, 240
declassification, defined, 958
dedicated links, 518
dedicated security mode, 297
  defined, 958
degauss, defined, 958
delayed loss, 72
Delphi technique, 79, 81
  defined, 958
demilitarized zones. See DMZs
denial of service, 56, 760, 878–880, 929
  defined, 958
  DoS attacks, 469–470
DES. See Data Encryption Standard
device security, vs. software security, 810–811
dialog management, 423
dial-on-demand routing (DDR), 536
dial-up, defined, 958
Diameter, 176–179
dictionary attacks, 136, 214–215, 759
  defined, 958
differential cryptanalysis, 677
differential power analysis, 144–145
differentiated service, 527
Diffie-Hellman algorithm, 632–633
digital signals, 440, 459
digital signatures, 648–649
  defined, 958
  Digital Signature Standard, 650–651
Digital Subscriber Line. See DSL
direct memory access. See DMA

direct sequence spread spectrum, 551
directory services, 160, 508–509
disaster recovery plan, 692–693
    business continuity plan, 693–697
    data backup alternatives, 721–723
    defined, 958
    documentation, 718–719
    electronic backup solutions,
      724–726
    end-user environment, 720–721
    facilities, 709–713
    goals, 732–733
    hardware backups, 716
    human resources, 719–720
    implementing strategies, 733–734
    insurance, 728
    maintaining the plan, 739–740
    recovery and restoration, 728–731
    restoring data, 723–724
    software backups, 717–718,
      726–727
    supply and technology recovery,
      715–716
    testing and revising the plan,
      734–739
    *See also* business continuity plan
discretionary access control, 162, 166
    defined, 958
disk duplexing, 724
disk shadowing, 724–725
distance-vector routing protocols, 468
Distributed Component Object Model
    (DCOM), 863
Distributed Computing Environment
    (DCE), 865–866
distributed denial-of-service attacks,
    882–883
DMA, I/O using, 265
DMZs, 33–34, 483
DNS, 502–503
    DoS attacks, 884–885
    poisoning, 505
    secure DNS attacks, 885

DNS servers
    Internet DNS and domains,
      503–505
    primary and secondary, 503
DNSSEC, 505
dogs, 401
Domain Name Service. *See* DNS
domains, 258–260
    in the CISSP CBK, 4–6
    defined, 959
    Internet DNS and, 503–505
DoS. *See* denial of service
double data rate SDRAM.
    *See* DDR SDRAM
downstream liability, 769
DRAM, 245
DSL, 537
    Asymmetrical DSL, 538
    High-bit-rate DSL, 538
    ISDN DSL, 538
    Symmetrical DSL, 538
DSSS vs. FHSS, 551–552
dual-homed firewalls, 493
due care, 54, 94, 768
    defined, 959
due diligence, 94, 768
    defined, 959
dumpster diving, 761
Dynamic Data Exchange (DDE), 865
dynamic link libraries (DLLs), 243
dynamic mapping, 511
dynamic packet filtering firewalls, 491
dynamic passwords, 139
dynamic RAM. *See* DRAM
dynamic routing protocols, 468

## E

Economic Espionage Act of 1996, 795
EDO DRAM, 246
EEPROM, 247
EF. *See* exposure factor

El Gamal, 638
electric power, 365
    blackouts, 368
    brownouts, 369
    definitions, 367
    interference, 366–368
    line conditioners, 369
    noise, 369
    power protection, 365–366
    preventive measures, 369–370
    surges, 368
    UPSs, 365–366
    voltage regulators, 369
electrically erasable programmable
   read-only memory. *See* EEPROM
electromagnetic analysis, 145
electronic access control tokens, 388
electronic mail gateways, 480
electronic monitoring, 136
electronic vaulting, 725
    defined, 959
elliptic curve cryptosystems, 638, *639*
e-mail security, 915–916
    e-mail relaying, 918–919
    how e-mail works, 916–917
    IMAP, 918
    POP, 917
e-mail standards, 662
    Message Security Protocol
      (MSP), 664
    MIME, 662–663
    Pretty Good Privacy (PGP),
      664–665
    Privacy-Enhanced Mail (PEM),
      663–664
    Secure MIME, 663
emanations
    capturing, 761
    defined, 959
    security, 199
emergency system restart, 910
employee controls, 106

encapsulation, 241, 418–419,
   436–437
encryption, 137–138, 187
    defined, 959
    at different layers, 660
    end-to-end encryption, 659–661
    fax encryptors, 920–921
    link encryption, 659–661
    methods of, 607–621
    Security and Freedom Through
      Encryption Act, 794
    trapdoors, 637
    *See also* cryptography
end-to-end encryption, 659–661
    defined, 959
Enterprise JavaBeans (EJBs), 867
environmental issues, 370–372
EPL. *See* Evaluated Products List
EPROM, 247
equipment disposal, 778
equipment rooms, 359–362
erasable and programmable read-only
   memory. *See* EPROM
Ethernet, 447–450, 451
ethical hacking, 921
ethics, 752–753
    Computer Ethics Institute, 754
European Commission, 796
European Union Principles on Privacy, 794
Evaluated Products List, 951
    defined, 959
Evaluation Assurance Level (EAL),
   312–313
excessive privileges, 759
exclusive-OR (XOR), 599–600, 615
execution domains, 259, 270
    switching, 271
expert systems, 867–869
exposure, 58
    defined, 959
exposure factor, 76
    defined, 959

extended data out DRAM. *See* EDO DRAM
Extensible Authentication Protocol (EAP),
    542, 546, 556–557
Exterior Gateway Protocol, 469
extranets, 513

# F

facial scans, 135
facilities, 351–353
    access control, 381–387
    cold sites, 710, 712
    construction, 353–356
    entry points, 356–359
    hot sites, 710, 712, 714
    internal compartments, 359
    locks, 382–387
    offsite locations, 713
    recovery planning, 709–713
    redundant sites, 714–715
    tertiary sites, 711
    warm sites, 710, 712
failover, defined, 959
fail-safe, 357
    defined, 959
fail-secure, 357
failure states, 816
fake login screens, 929
Faraday cage, 199
Fast Ethernet, 448–449
    *See also* Ethernet
fault generation, 144
fax security, 920–921
FCC. *See* Federal Communications
    Commission
FDDI, 427, 451
FDDI-2, 453
Federal Communications
    Commission, 416
Federal Information Processing
    Standards, 950
Federal Privacy Act of 1974, 793
Federal Sentencing Guidelines, 795

fencing, 389–391
FHSS vs. DSSS, 551–552
Fiber Distributed Data Interface.
    *See* FDDI
fiber-optic cable, 456
file access protection, 41
File Transfer Protocol. *See* FTP
fingerprints, 133, 641
    operating system fingerprinting, 923
FIPS. *See* Federal Information Processing
    Standards
fire
    detection, 373, 374–376
    fire resistant ratings, 374
    prevention, 373
    suppression, 373–374, 377–380
firewalls, 482–484, 492
    appliances, 493
    architecture, 493–496, 498
    bastion hosts, 493–496
    dual-homed, 493
    dynamic packet filtering, 491
    kernel proxy, 491–492
    multihomed, 488, 493–494
    packet filtering, 484–485
    proxy, 486–490
    recommendations for, 496–499
    screened hosts, 494
    screened subnets, 495–496
    stateful, 485–486
firmware, defined, 960
flash memory, 247
forking, 236
formal security policy model,
    defined, 960
formal verification, defined, 960
forwarding tables, 472–473
fractional T lines, 519
fraggle attacks, 880–881
frame relay, 523–524
    virtual circuits, 524–525
frames, 437
frequency, 439, 549, 551

frequency analysis, 606
frequency hopping spread spectrum,
    550–551
FTP, 421
full-duplex, 423, 435
fully mapped I/O, 265
functionality, complexity of, 814


# G

G8, 795
gap in the WAP, 566
garbage collectors, 252
gateways, 479–480
    defined, 960
general registers, 231–232
Generally Accepted Information Security
    Principles (GAISP), 755–756
Generic Routing Encapsulation
    (GRE), 543
Generic Security Services Application
    Programming Interface (GSS-API), 156
"Get Out of Jail Free Card", 932
GIF, 422
glass windows, 358
Graham-Denning model, 294–295
Gramm-Leach-Bliley Act of 1999, 792
Graphic Interchange Format. *See* GIF
Group of Eight. *See* G8
groups, 147
guaranteed service, 527
guards, 298, 400–401
guidelines, 92
    defined, 960


# H

H.323 gateways, 531–532
hacker intrusion, 771–772
hackers, 757
hacking, 29–30, 921–925
    browsing, 925
    denial of service, 929

evolution of, 22–24
fake login screens, 929
how companies are affected, 26–27
how nations are affected, 24–26
information warfare, 21–22
Loki attacks, 927
mail bombing, 929
man-in-the-middle attacks,
    633–634, 929
password cracking, 927–928
phisher scams, 24
ping of death, 929
session hijacking, 926–927
slamming and cramming, 929
sniffers, 925–926
teardrop attack, 929
traffic analysis, 929
U.S. government actions against,
    27–28
wardialing, 929
*See also* penetration testing; security;
    worms
half-duplex, 423
halon, 378
hand geometry, 134
hand topography, 135
handshaking procedure, 435, *437*
    defined, 960
hardware backups, 716
hardware segmentation, 244
hashing, 137–138
    algorithms, 640–648
HDLC, 528
Health Insurance Portability and
    Accountability Act, 792
hierarchical storage management
    (HSM), 725
High-bit-rate DSL (HDSL), 538
High-level Data Link Control. *See* HDLC
High-Speed Serial Interface. *See* HSSI
HMAC, 641–643
honeypots, 213, 499–500
    defined, 960

hops, 660
host-based IDS (HIDS), 201–202
HSSI, 529
HTTP, 421, 666–667
    HTTP Secure (HTTPS), 667–668
    Secure HTTP (S-HTTP), 668
hubs, 471
Hypertext Transfer Protocol. *See* HTTP

# I

ICANN, 502
ICMP, 425, 465–466
Idaho State University, 7
identification, 126–128, 129
    component requirements, 129
    defined, 960
identity management, 130–131
Identity Theft Resource Center, 24
identity-based access control, 163
IDS. *See* intrusion detection systems
IEEE, 952
IGMP, 425
IGP, 467
IGRP, 469
IIS, 38
illogical processing, 72
IM. *See* instant messaging
IMAP, 918
i-Mode, 566–567
inference attacks, 291
inference engines, 868
information classification, 94–95
    controls, 98–99
    private industry vs. military
        classifications, 95–98
    procedures, 98
information flow model, 287–290
information owner, 53–54
    defined, 960
information risk management (IRM),
    65–66
    policy, 66–67
    team, 67–68

Information Sharing and Analysis Centers
    (ISACs), 28
Information Systems Security Association
    (ISSA), 7
Information Technology Security Evalua-
    tion Criteria (ITSEC), 309–311
information warfare, 21–22, 765
initial program loads (IPLs),
    unscheduled, 934
initialization vectors, 560–561, 616
input/output controls, 910–911
input/output devices, 263
instant messaging, 574–575
Institute of Electrical and Electronic
    Engineers. *See* IEEE
insurance, 728
Integrated Services Digital Network.
    *See* ISDN
integrity, 56–57, 125, 228
    database, 824
    defined, 960
Integrity Check Value (ICV),
    560–561
Interior Gateway Protocol. *See* IGP
Interior Gateway Routing Protocol.
    *See* IGRP
International Data Encryption Algorithm
    (IDEA), 630
international economic espionage, 765
International Information Systems Security
    Certification Consortium. *See* (ISC)²
International Organization for
    Standardization. *See* ISO
International Telecommunication Union
    (ITU), 416–417, 952
Internet, 32–34
Internet Architecture Board (IAB),
    754–755
Internet Assigned Numbers Authority
    (IANA), 502
Internet Control Message Protocol.
    *See* ICMP
Internet Corporation for Assigned Names
    and Numbers. *See* ICANN

Internet Group Management Protocol. *See* IGMP

Internet Message Access Protocol. *See* IMAP

Internet Protocol. *See* IP

Internet security, 666
  cookies, 669–671
  HTTP, 666–667
  HTTP Secure (HTTPS), 667–668
  Internet Protocol Security (IPSec), 672–675
  Secure Electronic Transaction (SET), 668–669
  Secure HTTP (S-HTTP), 668
  Secure Shell (SSH), 671

Internet Security Association and Key Management Protocol (ISAKMP), 674

Internet service providers. *See* ISPs

Internetwork Packet Exchange. *See* IPX

internetworks, 446, 472

interoperability, 145

Interpol, 796

interpreters, 850

interrupt-drive I/O, 265

interrupts, 237, 264–265

intranets, 512–513

intrusion detection systems, 200–201, 397–400
  attack techniques, 203
  defined, 961
  host-based, 201–202
  knowledge- or signature-based, 202, 204
  model-based, 207–208
  network traffic, 211
  network-based, 201
  protocol anomaly-based, 204–205
  rule-based, 205–206
  sensors, 209–211
  state-based, 207
  statistical anomaly-based, 202–204
  traffic anomaly-based, 205
  types of, 208

intrusion prevention systems, 211–212, 912
  honeypots, 213
  network sniffers, 213–214

invocation property, 283

I/O using DMA, 265

IP, 432

IP addressing, 438

IP next generation (IPng). *See* IPv6

IP spoofing, 759–760

Ipconfig, 573

IPSec, 541, 672–675

IPv4, 438

IPv6, 438, 439

IPX, 479

iris scans, 134

(ISC)$^2$
  Code of Ethics, 7
  credential process, 3

ISDN, 427, 535–537
  BRI, 536
  Broadband (BISDN), 536
  PRI, 536

ISDN DSL (IDSL), 538

ISO, 416–417, 951
  ISO 17799, 63–64
  *See also* Common Criteria; OSI model

ISO Standard 7498, 418

ISO/IEC 14443, 145

isolation, defined, 961

ISPs, 502

iterated tunneling, 541


**J**

Java, 872
  sandbox, 872
  security, 872–873

Java Virtual Machine (JVM), 261–262

jittering, 530

job rotation, 902

Joint Photographic Experts Group.
    *See* JPEG
JPEG, 422

# K

Kerberos, 151–152
    authentication process,
        152–155
    Key Distribution Center
        (KDC), 152
    and password-guessing
        attacks, 155
    principals, 152
    realm, 152
    tickets, 152
    weaknesses, 155
    *See also* SESAME
kernel proxy firewalls, 491–492
kernels, 232
    defined, 961
key management, 657–659
key rings, 665
keyboard dynamics, 134
keys, defined, 961
keyspace, 594–595
keystroke monitoring, 195–196
    defined, 961
Kismet, 569
knapsack algorithms, 639
knowledge discovery in database
    (KDD), 832
knowledge-based IDS, 202
knowledge-based systems, 867–869

# L

L2TP, 427, 543, 544
LANs, 42
    media access technologies, 446–453,
        460–463
    protocols, 463–466, 516
    *See also* VLANs; WLANs

last mile, 440
latency, 462
lattice model, 291–293
lattice-based access control model,
    defined, 961
Layer 2 Forwarding (L2F), 427, 543
Layer 2 Tunneling Protocol. *See* L2TP
layer 3 and 4 switches, 477–478
layering, 260–261
LDAP, 509
leased lines, 518
least privilege, 148, 275, 902–903
    defined, 961
legal issues, 752, 774–776
    Computer Fraud and Abuse Act,
        792–793
    Computer Security Act of 1987, 794
    copyrights, 774–775
    Economic Espionage Act of
        1996, 795
    European Union Principles on
        Privacy, 794
    Federal Privacy Act of 1974, 793
    Federal Sentencing Guidelines, 795
    Gramm-Leach-Bliley Act of
        1999, 792
    Health Insurance Portability and
        Accountability Act, 792
    import and export laws, 788
    intellectual property laws, 774
    international cooperation,
        795–796
    legal systems throughout the
        world, 773
    patents, 775
    privacy, 789–791
    Security and Freedom Through
        Encryption Act, 794
    software piracy, 776–777
    trade secrets, 774
    trademarks, 775
    transborder information flow,
        788–789

types of laws, 772–773
    *See also* attacks; computer crimes
liability, 767–772
life-cycle assurance, 904
    defined, 961
lighting, 391–393
Lightweight Directory Access Protocol.
    *See* LDAP
limit registers, 243, *244*
Line Printer Daemon. *See* LPD
linear bus topology, 444
linear cryptanalysis, 677–678
Link Access Procedure-Balanced
    (LAPB), 528
Link Access Procedure (LAP), 528
link encryption, 659–661
    defined, 961
link-state routing protocols, 468
local bridges, 471
local loop, 440
locks, 382–387
log scrubbers, 573
logic bombs, 877
    defined, 961
logical access controls, 127–128
logical addresses, 249
logical controls, 53
Logical Link Control (LLC), 427
logical location, 147
logon attempts, limiting, 138
Loki attacks, 466, 927
loss potential, 72
    defined, 961
LPD, 421
LUC, 638

## M

MAC. *See* mandatory access control
mail bombing, 929
maintenance hooks, 318–319
    defined, 962
malware, 874
    defined, 962

logic bombs, 877
Trojan horses, 878
viruses, 875–876
worms, 877
mandatory access control, 163–164, 166
    defined, 962
    sensitivity labels, 164
man-in-the-middle attacks, 633–634, 929
MANs, 514–515
mapping
    memory, 248–251
    virtual, 242
masquerading, 464, 496–497
    defined, 962
maximum transmission units. *See* MTUs
MDACs. *See* Microsoft Data Access
    Components
Media Access Control (MAC), 427,
    463–464
media controls, 908–909
memory
    BEDO DRAM, 246
    cache, 247–248
    DDR SDRAM, 246
    DRAM, 245
    EDO DRAM, 246
    EEPROM, 247
    EPROM, 247
    flash memory, 247
    leaks, 251–252
    management, 242–244
    mapping, 248–251
    PROM, 246
    RAM, 244–246, 264
    ROM, 246–247
    SDRAM, 246
    SRAM, 245
    types of, 244–248
    virtual, 252–253
memory cards, 142–143
mesh topology, 445
message authentication code, defined, 962
message digests, 641
message integrity code (MIC), 641

Message Security Protocol (MSP), 664
messages, 437
metadata, 508
metadirectories, 508
metropolitan area networks. *See* MANs
microkernel, 258
microns, 234
microprobing, 145
Microsoft Data Access Components,
   38–40
Microsoft Internet Information Services.
   *See* IIS
Microsoft Point-to-Point Encryption, 543
MIME, 662–663
MIPS, 234
Mitnick, Kevin, 764
mobile code, 866
mobile IP, 177
mobile phone security, 567–568
model-based IDS, 207–208
modification detection code (MDC), 641
modulation, 439
Moore's Law, 266
MPPE. *See* Microsoft Point-to-Point
   Encryption
MTUs, 460
multicast transmission, 458–459
multihomed firewalls, 488, 493–494
multilayered switches, 476
multilevel security, 298
   defined, 962
multiplexing, 516
   orthogonal frequency division
     multiplexing (OFDM), 554
   statistical time-division
     multiplexing, 522
   time multiplexing, 241–242
   time-division multiplexing, 519
multiprocessing, 234–235, 239
multiprogramming, 235, 239
Multiprotocol Label Switching
   (MPLS), 477
multiservice access technologies, 529–531

Multistation Access Units (MAUs), 450
multitasking, 236, 239
multithreaded applications, 239
multithreading, 239

## N

naming distinctions, 242
NAS. *See* network access, servers
NAT, 439, 510–512
National Bureau of Standards (NBS).
   *See* NIST
National Centers of Excellence, 7
National Computer Security Center
   (NCSC), 301
National Infrastructure Protection Center
   (NIPC), 22, 28
National Institute of Standards and
   Technology. *See* NIST
National Science Foundation (NSF), 502
National Security Agency. *See* NSA
natural access control, 346–347
natural surveillance, 348
need to know, 148–149
   defined, 962
NetBIOS, 423
NetStumbler, 569
network access, 187
   servers, 480
network address translation. *See* NAT
network architecture, 185–187
   client/server, 258
Network File System. *See* NFS
Network Information System. *See* NIS
network layer, 425–426, 429
network operating systems. *See* NOSs
network segregation, 183
   and isolation, 500
network sniffers, 213–214
Network Solutions, Inc., 502
network topology, 443, 445–446
   bus, 444
   mesh, 445

ring, 443–444
star, 444
network-based IDS, 201
networking, 442
networking devices, 481
    bridges, 471–472, 475
    forwarding tables, 472–473
    gateways, 479–480
    layer 3 and 4 switches, 477–478
    repeaters, 470–471
    routers, 472, 473–475
    switches, 475–476
    VLANs, 477, 478–479
networking security, 415–417
NFS, 423
NICs, 449
NIS, 505–507
NIST, 621–622, 950
node, defined, 962
noise, 369, 456–457
    and perturbation, 827
    *See also* pseudo-noise; white noise
nonce, 140
nondisclosure agreements, 105–106
noninterference model, 290–291
nonkeyed message digests, 641
nonplenum cables, 458
NOSs, 501
NSA, 301, 592, 949

# O

object linking and embedding (OLE),
    864–865
object request brokers (ORBs), 859–861
object reuse, 198
    defined, 962–963
object-oriented design (OOD), 855
object-oriented programming (OOP), 851
objects, 123–124, 268
    defined, 962
Office of Homeland Security, 28
OLTP. *See* online transaction processing

one-time pad, 599–601, 616
    defined, 963
one-time passwords, 139, 141
one-way functions, 637–638
Online Certificate Status Protocol
    (OCSP), 653
online encryption, 660
online transaction processing, 829–830
Open Database Connectivity (ODBC), 863
open network architecture, 418
Open Shortest Path First. *See* OSPF
open system authentication (OSA), 553
Open System Interconnection model. *See*
    OSI model
open systems, 317, 420
operating system fingerprinting, 923
operating systems
    architecture, 235–240, 256–258, 259
    client/server architecture, 258
    layered, 256
    layering and data hiding, 260–261
    memory management, 242–244
    monolithic operating system
        architecture, 256
    process management, 235–238
    process scheduling, 240
    thread management, 238–239
    trusted recovery, 909–910
    virtual machines, 261–262
    *See also* NOSs
operational assurance, 904
    defined, 963
operational goals, 60
    defined, 963
operations department, 933
operations security, 900
    accountability, 903–904
    administrative management,
        900–903
    change control documentation,
        907–908
    clipping levels, 905
    configuration management, 905–908

input and output controls, 910–911
media controls, 908–909
system controls, 909
trusted recovery, 909–910
operator, defined, 963
Orange Book
defined, 963
*See also* Trusted Computer System
Evaluation Criteria (TCSEC)
organizations
ANSI, 952
IEEE, 952
ISO, 951
NCSC, 951
NIST, 950
NSA, 949
orthogonal frequency division
multiplexing (OFDM), 554
OSI model, 41, 417–420, 951
application layer, 420–421, 428
data link layer, 426–428, 430
functions and protocols, 428–430
how the layers work together,
430, *431*
network layer, 425–426, 429
OSI and TCP/IP networking
models, *418*
physical layer, 428, 430
presentation layer, 421–422, 429
session layer, 422–424, 429
transport layer, 424, 429
*See also* ISO
OSPF, 425, 468–469
overt channel, defined, 963

**P**

packet filtering
dynamic packet filtering
firewalls, 491
firewalls, 484–485
packet switching, 522–523
packets, 437

page frames, 252
paging, 252
palm scans, 133
partitioning, 827
passphrases, 142
Password Authentication Protocol (PAP),
542, 544–546, 547
passwords, 135
accessing the password files, 136
aging, 138
checkers, 137
cognitive, 128, 138–139
cracking, 927–928
defined, 963
dynamic, 139
hashing and encryption, 137–138
Kerberos and password-guessing
attacks, 155
limiting logon attempts, 138
management, 135–137
one-time, 139, 141
sniffing, 759
token devices, 140–141
virtual passwords, 142
patrol force, 400–401
pattern matching, 868
PBXs, 481–482
PDAs, security, 567–568
penetration, defined, 963
penetration testing, 921, 930–933
defined, 963
*See also* hacking
perimeter security, 184, 380–381
permanent virtual circuits, 525
permissions, defined, 963
personal information, 770–771
personnel controls, 182
personnel security, 104
defined, 963
dual control, 106
employee controls, 106
facility access control, 381–387
hiring practices, 105–106
mandatory vacation policy, 106, 903

nondisclosure agreements, 105–106
    personnel access controls, 387–388
    prescreening personnel, 790–791
    rotation of duties, 106
    split knowledge, 106
    structure, 104–105
    termination, 106–107
personnel, security and network, 902
phisher scams, 24
phishing attacks, 216, 915
phreakers, 482, 765
physical controls, 53
    defined, 963–964
physical layer, 428, 430
physical location, 147
physical security, 337–340
    auditing physical access, 402
    bollards, 391
    closed circuit TVs (CCTVs),
        394–397, *398*
    computer and equipment rooms,
        359–362
    construction, 353–356
    Crime Prevention Through Environ-
        mental Design (CPTED), 344–346
    defined, 964
    designing a program, 349–351
    dogs, 401
    doors, 357
    entry points, 356–359
    environmental issues, 370–372
    external boundary protection
        mechanisms, 388–397
    facility, 351–353
    fencing, 389–391
    fire prevention, detection and
        suppression, 373–380
    internal compartments, 359
    layered defense model, 339–340
    lighting, 391–393
    mantraps, 357
    natural access control, 346–347
    natural surveillance, 348
    patrol force and guards, 400–401

    personnel access controls, 387–388
    planning process, 340–344
    power issues, 365–370
    protecting assets, 362–364
    surveillance, 393
    territorial reinforcement,
        348–349
    ventilation, 373
    windows, 358–359
    *See also* intrusion detection systems
piggyback, 387
    defined, 964
ping of death, 929
PKI. *See* public key infrastructure
plaintext, 593
    chosen-plaintext attack, 676
    defined, 964
    known-plaintext attack, 676
planning horizon, 61
playback attack, defined, 964
plenum space, 377, 458
point of presence (PoP), 541
point-to-point links, 518
Point-to-Point Protocol. *See* PPP
polling, 462–463
polymorphism, 855–856
POP, 917
port address translation (PAT), 511
port scanning, 923
ports, well-known, 434–435
positive drains, 370
Post Office Protocol. *See* POP
PPP, 427, 541–543
PPTP, 543–544
preeemptive multitasking, 236
premapped I/O, 265
presentation layer, 421–422, 429
President's Commission on Critical Infra-
    structure Protection (PCCIP),
    27–28, 341
pressurized conduits, 458
Pretty Good Privacy (PGP), 664–665
privacy, 789–791
    defined, 964

European Union Principles on
    Privacy, 794
Federal Privacy Act of 1974, 793
Privacy-Enhanced Mail (PEM), 663–664
Private Branch Exchanges. *See* PBXs
private keys, 142, 609–611
privileged mode, 232
problem state, 232
procedure, defined, 964
procedures, 92–93
process activation, 270
process activity, 240–242
process isolation, 241
process owner, 102–103
process scheduling, 240
process tables, 237, 238
processes, 235
processors, evolution of, 234
product line manager, 103
program counter registers, 232
program status words (PSWs), 232, 233
programmable I/O, 265
programmable read-only memory.
    *See* PROM
programming languages, 850
project sizing, 68
PROM, 246
protection profiles, 313
protection rings, 253–256
    defined, 964
protocol anomaly-based IDS, 204–205
protocols, 187
    defined, 417, 964
prototyping, 862
proxy firewalls, 486–488
    application- and circuit-level,
    488–490
prudent person rule, 768
pseudo-flaw, defined, 964
pseudo-noise, 551
public algorithms, vs. secret
    algorithms, 677
public key encryption, defined, 964

public key infrastructure, 635, 651
    certificate authorities (CAs), 651,
    652–653
    certificate revocation list (CRL), 653
    digital certificates, 651, 653–654
    key management, 657–659
    Online Certificate Status Protocol
    (OCSP), 653
    registration authorities (RAs), 654
    steps, 655–656
public keys, 142, 609–611, 635
public-switched telephone network
    (PSTN), 529
purge, defined, 964
PVCs. *See* permanent virtual circuits


**Q**

qualitative risk analysis, 73–74, 78–81
    defined, 964
    vs. quantitative risk analysis, 81–82
Quality of Service (QoS), 526–527
quantitative risk analysis, 73–74
    defined, 965
    vs. qualitative risk analysis, 81–82


**R**

race condition, 127, 319
RADIUS, 173
    defined, 965
RAID, 912–913
Rainbow Series, 306–307
raking, 387
RAM, 244–246
    and video card, 264
random access memory. *See* RAM
RARP, 427, 465
RBAC. *See* role-based access control
RC4, 631
RC5, 631
RC6, 631

read, defined, 965
read-only memory. *See* ROM
ready state, 236
recertification requirements, 8–9
recovery planning, defined, 965
Red Book, 307–309
redirectors, 501
reference monitor concept, 272–274
    defined, 965
registration authorities (RAs), 654
relative addresses, 249
relay agents, 918
reliability, defined, 965
remote access, 534
    authentication protocols, 544–547
    cable modems, 537–539
    callback, 548
    caller ID, 548
    dial-on-demand routing (DDR), 536
    dial-up and Remote Access Service
        (RAS), 534–535
    DSL, 537
    guidelines, 547–548
    ISDN, 535–537
    tunneling protocols, 540–544, 545
    virtual private networks (VPNs),
        539–540
    *See also* wireless technologies
Remote Access Service (RAS), 534–535
Remote Authentication Dial-in User
    Service. *See* RADIUS
remote bridges, 471
remote journaling, 725
    defined, 965
remote procedure call (RPC), 423
repeaters, 470–471
replay attack, 678–679
repudiation, defined, 965
residual risk, 86
    defined, 965
    *See also* risk analysis
resource records, 503
retina scans, 134

Reverse Address Resolution Protocol.
    *See* RARP
ring topology, 443–444
RIP, 425, 468
risk, 58
    accepting, 77
    defined, 965
    handling, 86–87
risk analysis, 68–69, 345
    automated methods, 74, 75
    cascading errors, 72
    cost/benefit comparison, 68, 82
    costs that make up value, 70–71
    countermeasure selection, 82–84
    defined, 965
    delayed loss, 72
    functionality and effectiveness of
        countermeasures, 84–85
    handling risk, 86–87
    identifying threats, 71–73
    illogical processing, 72
    loss potential, 72
    project sizing, 68
    protection mechanisms, 82
    results of, 78
    steps of, 74–78, *86*
    team, 69–70
    total risk vs. residual risk, 86
    value of information and assets, 70
    *See also* qualitative risk analysis;
        quantitative risk analysis
risk management, 65–66
    defined, 966
    information risk management (IRM)
        policy, 66–67
    team, 67–68
Roaming Operations (ROAMOPS), 177
role-based access control, 165–166
    defined, 966
roles, 147
    and associated tasks, 901
ROM, 246–247
rootkits, 572–574

route flapping, 468
routers, 472, 473–475
Routing Information Protocol. *See* RIP
routing policies, 469
routing protocols, 467–470
RSA, 634–638
rule-based access control, 167
rule-based IDS, 205–206
rule-based programming, 868
running state, 236

## S

safeguards, 58
    characteristics to seek when
      obtaining, 84–85
    defined, 966
salami, 758
satellites, 570
Scalable Processor Architecture (SPARC),
    229–230
schemas, 508
screened hosts, 494
screened subnets, 495–496
script kiddies, 758, 921
scrubbing, 196
SDLC, 528
SDRAM, 246
secondary storage, 252
secret algorithms, vs. public
    algorithms, 677
secure configuration management,
    defined, 966
Secure Electronic Transaction (SET),
    668–669
Secure European System for Applications
    in a Multi-vendor Environment.
    *See* SESAME
Secure HTTP (S-HTTP), 668
Secure MIME, 663
Secure Remote Procedure Call. *See* S-RPC
Secure Shell (SSH), 671
Secure Sockets Layer. *See* SSL

SecureID, 139
security
    add-on security, 953
    an architectural view of, 41–44
    areas of, 20–21
    availability, 56, 125
    baselines, 91–92
    bottom-up approach, 52
    communications security, 956
    confidentiality, 57, 126
    countermeasures, 43–44
    cybersecurity czar, 45
    definitions, 57–59
    development of security as an issue,
      17–20, 29
    education, 46–47
    file access protection, 41
    guidelines, 92
    implementation, 93
    integrity, 56–57, 125
    layered approach, 40–41, 44–45
    mobile phones, 567–568
    multilevel security, 962
    order of concepts, 59
    perimeter security, 184, 380–402
    personnel security, 963
    politics and laws, 45–46
    principles of, 55–57, 124–126
    private industry vs. military require-
      ments, 64
    procedures, 92–93
    simple security rule, 279
    *See also* hacking; physical security
security administrator, 101
security analyst, 101
Security and Freedom Through Encryption
    Act, 794
security architecture, 268
    threats to, 318–325
security controls, services provided by,
    191–192
security domains, 157–159
security evaluation, 301–302
    defined, 966

Information Technology Security
Evaluation Criteria (ITSEC),
309–311
security kernel, 272–274
defined, 966
security labels, 163
defined, 966
security management, 30–32, 49–50
administrative controls, 53
application owner, 101–102
change control analyst, 102
Corporate Information Security
Officer (CISO), 62
Corporate Security Officer (CSO), 62
data analyst, 102
data custodian, 100
data owner, 100
example of, 54
information owner, 53–54
ISO 17799, 63–64
layers of responsibility, 99–105
organizational security model, 60–61
personnel security, 104
physical controls, 53
process owner, 102–103
product line manager, 103
program components, 61–64
responsibilities, 50–51
security administration, 52–55
security administrator, 101
security analyst, 101
solution provider, 103
state machine models, 277–279
supervisor, 102
system owner, 101
technical controls, 53
top-down approach, 51–52
user, 103
*See also* risk analysis
security models, 227–228, 275–276,
295–296
and architecture, 228–229
Bell-LaPadula model,
279–282, 283

Biba model, 282–283
Brewer and Nash model,
293–294
Clark-Wilson model, 284–287
formal models, 277
Graham-Denning model, 294–295
information flow model, 287–290
lattice model, 291–293
noninterference model, 290–291
and security policy, 276
threats to, 318–325
security modes of operation, 296, 299
compartmented security mode,
297–298
dedicated security mode, 297
multilevel security mode, 298
system high-security mode, 297
security parameter index (SPI), 673
security perimeter, 272
defined, 966
security policy, 88–89, *91*, 181–182,
227–228, 274–275
defined, 966
issue-specific, 89
organizational, 88–89
and security models, 276
system-specific, 89
types of policies, 90
*See also* business continuity plan
security testing, defined, 966
security zones, 347
security-awareness training, 107,
182–183
evaluating the program, 109
specialized training, 109
types of, 107–109
segments, 437
sensitive information, defined, 966
sensitivity labels, 163, 164
defined, 966
sensors, 209–211
separation of duties, 286, 841, 842,
900–901
defined, 967

Sequenced Packet Exchange. *See* SPX
Serial Line Internet Protocol. *See* SLIP
service bureaus, 513
SESAME, 156
    *See also* Kerberos
session hijacking, 926–927
session layer, 422–424, 429
shared key authentication (SKA), 553
shielded twisted pair (STP), 454
shoulder surfing, 57
    defined, 967
side-channel attacks, 144, 678
signature dynamics, 134
signature-based IDS, 202, 204
simple integrity axiom, 282
Simple Mail Transfer Protocol.
    *See* SMTP
simple security property, defined, 967
simplex, 423
single loss expectancy, 76
    defined, 967
single points of failure, 911–912
single sign-on, 149–151
SITT. *See* Spectrum, Information
    Technologies and Telecommunications
slamming, 929
SLE. *See* single loss expectancy
sleep, 237
SLIP, 427, 543
smart cards, 142, 143–144
    attacks, 144–145
smart locks, 385
    *See also* locks
SMDS, 528
SMTP, 421, 916–917
smurf attacks, 880
sniffers, 213–214, 925–926
social engineering, 57, 136, 762
    defined, 967
sockets, 433
SOCKS, 489–490
soft tokens, 141
software architecture, 857
software attacks, 145

software backups, 717–718, 726–727
software development, 840–842
    Capability Maturity Model (CMM),
        848–849
    change control documentation,
        846–848
    methods of, 845–846
    *See also* application development;
        malware
software disposal, 778
software escrow, 717–718, 849–850
software piracy, 776–777
software security
    complexity of functionality, 814
    data types, format and length,
        814–815
    vs. device security, 810–811
    failure states, 816
    implementation and default issues,
        815–816
solution provider, 103
SONET, 514–515, 518
source routing, 473, 498–499
Spanning Tree Algorithm (STA),
    472–473
Special Interest Group for Computer
    Security (SIG-CS), 7
special registers, 232
Spectrum, Information Technologies and
    Telecommunications, 416
spoofing, 496–497, 759–760, 915
    defined, 967
    at logon, 216–217
spread spectrum, 549–550
    direct sequence spread spectrum, 551
    frequency hopping spread spectrum,
        550–551
SPX, 424
spyware, 574
SQL, 423
SRAM, 245
S-RPC, 507, 926
SSL, 425
SSO. *See* single sign-on

stack pointers, 232
stacks, 232
standards, 90
    defined, 967
    deviation from, 934
star property, 280
    defined, 967
star topology, 444
state transitions, 277
state-based IDS, 207
stateful firewalls, 485–486
static electricity, preventing, 372
static mapping, 511
static RAM. *See* SRAM
static routing protocols, 468
statistical anomaly-based IDS, 202–204
statistical time-division multiplexing, 522
steganography, 602
storage, 262–263
    secondary, 252
storage area network (SAN), 725–726
strategic goals, 61
    defined, 967
strong authentication, 129
strong star property rule, 280
Structured Query Language. *See* SQL
subjects, 123, 268
    defined, 967
subnets, 438
subsystems, 258, *259*
supervisor, 102
supervisor mode, 232
supervisor state, defined, 967
surveillance, 348, 393
SVCs. *See* switched virtual circuits
swap space, 252
Switched Multimegabit Data Service.
    *See* SMDS
switched virtual circuits, 525
switches, 475–476
    layer 3 and 4 switches,
        477–478
switching, 520–523
symmetric mode, 234–235

Symmetrical DSL (SDSL), 538
SYN floods, 881–882
SYN/ACK packets, 435
synchronous communication, 441, 459
Synchronous Data Link Control.
    *See* SDLC
Synchronous Digital Hierarchy
    (SDH), 518
synchronous DRAM. *See* SDRAM
Synchronous Optical Networks.
    *See* SONET
synchronous token devices, 140
system access, 185
system architecture, 266–275
system authentication, 643
system cold start, 910
system controls, 909
system development, 832–833
    design specifications, 838–840
    disposal, 844
    functional design analysis and
        planning, 837–838
    installation/implementation,
        842–843
    operational assurance and mainte-
        nance, 843
    postmortem review, 844
    project initiation, 834
    risk analysis, 835–837
    risk management, 834–835
    software development, 840–842
system high-security mode, 297
system owner, 101
system reboot, 910


**T**

table poisoning, 464
TACACS, 173–176
    defined, 967
tactical goals, 61
    defined, 967
Tagged Image File Format. *See* TIFF

tape vaulting, 726
T-carriers, 519–520
TCB. *See* trusted computing base
TCP, 424, *425*, 432–435
    handshake, 435, *437*
    wrappers, 924
TCP/IP, 417, 431–432
    OSI and TCP/IP networking
        models, *418*
TDM. *See* time-division multiplexing
teardrop attack, 882, 929
technical controls, 53, 185–188
    defined, 968
telecommunications, 415–417
    defined, 416
    evolution, 516–518
Telnet, 421
Tempest, 199–200
    defined, 968
Temporal Key Integrity Protocol (TKIP),
    557, 561
Terminal Access Controller Access Control
    System. *See* TACACS
testing, 183
TFTP, 421
The Naked Wife worm, 22
*The Puzzle Palace*, 949
ThickNet, 448
thin clients, 160–161
ThinNet, 448
thread management, 238–239
threads, 239
threats, 58
    defined, 968
    identifying, 71–73
thunking, 261
TIFF, 422
time multiplexing, 241–242
time of day, 147
Time to Live (TTL), 438
time-division multiplexing, 519
time-of-check/time-of-use (TOC/TOU)
    attack, 319–321

token devices, 140–141
Token Ring networks, 450–451
token-passing technology,
    450, 460, 462
tokens, 460
    soft tokens, 141
top-down approach, 51–52
    defined, 968
topology, 443
    bus, 444
    defined, 968
    mesh, 445
    ring, 443–444
    star, 444
total risk, 86
    defined, 968
    *See also* risk analysis
Total Seminars' test software
    Final mode, 948
    installing, 947
    navigation, 947
    Practice mode, 947–948
    system requirements, 948
    technical support, 948
tracing software, 363–364
traffic analysis, 929
traffic anomaly-based IDS, 205
traffic flow security, 660
tranquility principle, 281
transaction-type restrictions, 147
translation bridges, 471
transmission
    methods, 458–459
    terminology, 459
    types of, 439–442
Transmission Control Protocol.
    *See* TCP
Transmission Control Protocol/Internet
    Protocol. *See* TCP/IP
transparent bridging, 472
transport adjacency, 541
transport layer, 424, 429
trapdoors, 637
tree topology, 444

Triple-DES, 629

Trivial File Transfer Protocol. *See* TFTP

Trojan horses, 878

    defined, 968

Trojaned programs, 572–573

troubleshooting, running the QuickTime cryptography video sample on CD-ROM, 947

trusted computer system, defined, 968

Trusted Computer System Evaluation Criteria (TCSEC), 45, 300–301, 302–307, 951

trusted computing base, 268, 269–272, 300–301

    defined, 968

Trusted Network Interpretation (TNI), 307–309

trusted paths, 269

    defined, 968

Trusted Product Evaluation Program (TPEP), 951

trusted recovery, 909–910

    defined, 968

trusted shells, 269

tunneling protocols, 540–544, 545

twisted-pair cable, 454–456

two-tier architecture, 35–37

Type of Service (ToS), 438


**U**

UDP, 424

    and TCP, 432–435, 436

uncertainty, 78

unicast transmission, 458, 459

uniform resource locators. *See* URLs

Universal Mobile Telecommunications System, 568

unshielded twisted pair (UTP), 454–456

Unspecified Bit Rate (UBR), 527

unusual or unexplained occurrences, 934

UPSs, 365–366

URLs, 502

user, 103

    defined, 968

User Datagram Protocol. *See* UDP

user ID, defined, 968

user mode, 232


**V**

validation, 841

    defined, 969

value-added networks (VANs), 513

Variable Bit Rate (VBR), 527

variance-detection tools, 195

ventilation, 373

verification, 841

virtual circuits, 524–525

virtual LANs. *See* VLANs

virtual machines, 261–262

virtual mapping, 242

virtual memory, 252–253

virtual passwords, 142

virtual private networks (VPNs), 539–540

    tunneling protocols, 540–544

virus, defined, 969

viruses, 875–876

VLANs, 477, 478–479

voice and media gateways, 480

voice gateway, 530

Voice over ATM (VoATM), 531

Voice over Frame Relay (VoFR), 531

Voice over IP (VoIP), 529

voice prints, 134–135

voicemail system, 530

vulnerabilities, 58

    analysis, 85

    defined, 969

    scanning tools, 924–925


**W**

WANs, 42, 446, 515

    Asynchronous Transfer Mode (ATM), 526–527

CSU/DSU, 520
frame relay, 523–525
H.323 gateways, 531–532
HDLC, 528
HSSI, 529
multiservice access technologies,
    529–531
protocols, 516
SDLC, 528
SMDS, 528
switching, 520–523
technologies, 533
X.25, 525
war driving, 568–569
wardialing, 534–535, 929
    defined, 969
watchdog, 175
water sprinklers, 379–380
The Web, 32–34
web sites hacked, 23–24
well-formed transactions, 286
well-known ports, 434–435
WEPCrack, 569
white noise, 200
wide area networks. *See* WANs
Wired Equivalent Privacy (WEP),
    553–554, 621
    problems with, 560–561
Wireless Application Protocol (WAP),
    565–566
wireless LANs. *See* WLANs
wireless standards, 554, 561–563
    802.11a, 555
    802.11b, 554
    802.11e, 555
    802.11f, 555
    802.11g, 555–556
    802.11h, 556
    802.11i, 556
    802.11j, 563
    802.11n, 563
    802.15, 563–564
    802.16, 563

802.1X, 558–560
i-Mode, 566–567
Integrity Check Value (ICV),
    560–561
new wireless standard, 556–557
orthogonal frequency division
    multiplexing (OFDM), 554
problems with current
    implementations, 557–558
problems with WEP, 560–561
Temporal Key Integrity Protocol
    (TKIP), 557, 561
Wireless Application Protocol
    (WAP), 565–566
wireless technologies, 548–549
    3G (third generation), 570–572
    Bluetooth, 564
    direct sequence spread
        spectrum, 551
    FHSS vs. DSSS, 551–552
    frequency hopping spread
        spectrum, 550–551
    satellites, 570
    spread spectrum, 549–550
    *See also* remote access; WLANs
Wireless Transport Layer Security
    (WTLS), 565
wiretapping, 762
WLANs
    access points (APs), 552
    ad hoc, 553
    best practices, 569
    channels, 552–553
    infrastructure WLANs, 552
    open system authentication
        (OSA), 553
    Service Set ID (SSID), 553
    shared key authentication
        (SKA), 553
    standalone mode, 552
    war driving, 568–569
    Wired Equivalent Privacy (WEP),
        553–554

work area separation, 184
work factor, defined, 969
wormhole attacks, 470
worms, 877
    defined, 969
    The Naked Wife, 22
    *See also* hacking
write, defined, 969
write-once media, 196

## X

X.25, 525
xDSL, 538
XOR, 599–600, 615

## Z

zero knowledge proof, 639–640
zombies, 497, 883
zone transfers, 503